CRIMINAL INVESTIGATION

10TH EDITION

CRIMINAL INVESTIGATION

10TH EDITION

CHARLES R. SWANSON

University of Georgia (Emeritus)

President, Swanson and Bracken

NEIL C. CHAMELIN

Assistant State Attorney, Leon County, Florida

LEONARD TERRITO

Saint Leo University

ROBERT W. TAYLOR

University of North Texas

Mc Graw Hill **Higher Education**

Boston   Burr Ridge, IL   Dubuque, IA   New York   San Francisco   St. Louis
Bangkok   Bogotá   Caracas   Kuala Lumpur   Lisbon   London   Madrid   Mexico City
Milan   Montreal   New Delhi   Santiago   Seoul   Singapore   Sydney   Taipei   Toronto

CRIMINAL INVESTIGATION

Published by McGraw-Hill, a business unit of The McGraw-Hill Companies, Inc., 1221 Avenue of the Americas, New York, NY 10020. Copyright © 2009 by The McGraw-Hill Companies, Inc. All rights reserved. No part of this publication may be reproduced or distributed in any form or by any means, or stored in a database or retrieval system, without the prior written consent of The McGraw-Hill Companies, Inc., including, but not limited to, any network or other electronic storage or transmission, or broadcast for distance learning.

Some ancillaries, including electronic and print components, may not be available to customers outside the United States.

1 2 3 4 5 6 7 8 9 0 DOW/DOW 0 9 8

ISBN: 978-0-07-340153-9
MHID: 0-07-340153-6

Vice president and editor-in-chief: *Michael Ryan*
Publisher: *Frank Mortimer*
Sponsoring editor: *Katie Stevens*
Director of development: *Rhona Robbin*
Development editor: *Craig Leonard*
Editorial assistant: *Teresa Treacy*
Marketing manager: *Leslie Oberhuber*
Senior production editor: *Mel Valentín*
Production assistant: *Rachel J. Castillo*

Manuscript editor: *Stacey Sawyer*
Art director: *Jeanne M. Schreiber*
Lead designer: *Cassandra Chu*
Cover designer: *Adrian Morgan*
Interior designer: *Brian Salisbury*
Art editor: *Emma Ghiselli*
Photo research manager: *Brian Pecko*
Media project manager: *Thomas Brierly*
Senior production supervisor: *Tandra Jorgensen*

The text was set in 10/12 Palatino by Aptara-India, and printed on acid-free 45# New Era Matte by R. R. Donnelley & Sons.

Cover image: • Crime scene photographer/bullets on the ground. © AP/Wide World Photos; DNA configurations on computer screen, Ryan McVay/Getty Images; Test tubes, Glowimages; Single bullet, © James Ferrie/iStockphoto; Skeleton, © Stefan Klein/iStockphoto

Because this page cannot legibly accommodate all acknowledgements for copyrighted material, credits appear at the end of the book, and constitute an extension of this copyright page.

Library of Congress Cataloging-in-Publication Data

Criminal investigation / Charles Swanson . . . [et al.]. — 10th ed.
    p. cm.
    Includes index.
    ISBN-13: 978-0-07-340153-9 (alk. paper)
    ISBN-10: 0-07-340153-6 (alk. paper)
    1. Criminal investigation. 2. Criminal investigation—United States.

I. Swanson, Charles R., 1942-
HV8073.S84 2009
363.25—dc22

                  2008008590

From Charles R. Swanson: For my mystery writing novelist wife, Paige Cummings, who inspires me, our granddaughter Keira Pless, a pistol although she is only 18 months old, our children with spouses—Traci and Mark, Kellie and Steve, Maggie and Steve, Cole and Kelley, and our two bachelor sons, Colin and Ben. Finally, this is for the women and men out there 24/7 doing a hard job incredibly well.

From Neil C. Chamelin: For my wife, Vicki, and our children, Chris and Todd; my daughter-in-law Heidi; my granddaughters, Tally and her little sister Casey; and a soon-to-be-born granddaughter whose name is held secret by her parents until she is born.

From Leonard Territo: For Elena, the kindest and sweetest woman I have ever known, and our children, Lorraine, Kseniya, and Ilia, and my grandchildren, Matthew and Branden.

From Robert W. Taylor: For my beautiful wife, Mary, for her enduring love and support.

Charles R. "Mike" Swanson is the managing partner of Swanson and Bracken, a firm specializing in police promotional testing. He has extensive experience in designing promotional systems and tests for state, county, and municipal public safety agencies, including the Kentucky State Police including the Kentucky State Police, the Georgia Bureau of Investigation, the Alabama State Troopers and the Georgia State Patrol. He has conducted over 60 job-analysis studies and written more than 125 promotional tests. He has designed and implemented at least 75 assessment centers, as well as written their exercises. Mike has trained assessors from 18 different states and has testified in federal court as an expert witness on police promotional matters.

Mike enlisted in the Marine Corps when he was 17 years old and then joined the Tampa Police Department, working as a uniformed officer in the highest crime areas of the city before being promoted to detective. Subsequently, he worked as the senior police planner, and later as the acting deputy director, of the Council on Law Enforcement in the Office of the Florida Governor. While working in Florida, Mike earned his bachelor's and master's degrees in criminology from Florida State University. Then, after a teaching stint at East Carolina University, Mike accepted a faculty position at the University of Georgia's Institute of Government, where he received a Ph.D. with an emphasis on public administration and rose through the administrative ranks, retiring as the interim director in late 2001.

In addition to this book, Mike has coauthored four others, including *Police Administration: Structures, Processes, and Behavior*, and has authored or coauthored a number of monographs, articles, and conference papers pertaining to policing. In 2003, he received the O. W. Wilson Award for Outstanding Police Scholarship. He has received multiple awards from the governors of three states and from the Georgia Association of Chiefs of Police, who recognized his contributions to their association by making him the first Honorary Chief of Police. He is currently working on a novel, tentatively titled *The Shield*, which is the first in a series set in the Tama Police Department.

Neil C. Chamelin is an assistant state attorney in Leon County, Florida. He previously served as a hearing officer in the Florida Division of Motor Vehicles; director of Criminal Justice Programs for Troy State University—European Region; director of the Florida Police Standards and Training Commission; division director, Standards and Training Division, Florida Department of Law Enforcement; administrator of the Police Science Division, Institute of Government, at the University of Georgia;

and director of the Florida Institute for Law Enforcement. He has also served as a police officer in Sarasota, Florida. Chamelin is author of *Criminal Law for Police Officers* and coauthor of *Introduction to Criminal Justice* and *Police Personnel Selection Process*.

Leonard Territo is presently a Visiting Distinguished Professor in the Department of Criminal Justice at Saint Leo University, Saint Leo, Florida, and Professor Emeritus in the Department of Criminology at the University of South Florida, Tampa, Florida. He was previously the Chief Deputy (Undersheriff) of the Leon County Sheriff's Office in Tallahassee, Florida. He also served for nine years with the Tampa Police Department as patrol officer, motorcycle officer, and homicide detective. He is a former chairperson of the Department of Police Administration and director of the Florida Institute for Law Enforcement at St. Petersburg Junior College (Now St. Petersburg College), St. Petersburg, Florida.

In addition to writing nearly 50 articles, book chapters, and technical reports, he has authored or coauthored nine books, including *Police Administration*, which is in its seventh edition; *Crime and Justice in America*, which is in its sixth edition; *Police Civil Liability; College Crime Prevention and Personal Safety Awareness; Stress and Police Personnel; Stress Management in Law Enforcement* which is in its second edition; *The Police Personnel Selection Process*; and *Hospital and College Security Liability*. His books have been used in more than a thousand colleges and universities in all 50 states, and his writings have been used and referenced by both academic and police departments in 16 countries, including Australia, Barbados, Belarus Canada, China, Chile, Czechoslovakia, England, France, Germany, Israel, the Netherlands, Poland, Saudi Arabia, South Korea, and Spain.

His teaching awards include being selected from among 200 criminal justice educators from the state of Florida as the Outstanding Criminal Justice Educator of the Year, and the Outstanding Teacher of the Year by the College of Social and Behavioral Sciences at the University of South Florida. He has been given awards by both the Florida Police Chiefs Association and the Tampa Police Academy for his years of teaching and meritorious service and has been selected for inclusion in *Who's Who in American Law Enforcement*. He's been also given an award for Distinguished Scholarly Publications at Saint Leo University, Saint Leo, Florida. He is also a qualified police procedures expert in Alaska, Arizona, District of Columbia, Florida, Georgia, Illinois, Iowa, Kansas, Kentucky, Louisiana, Michigan, New Jersey, Ohio, Oregon, Pennsylvania, Tennessee, Virginia, Washington, and Wisconsin.

Robert W. Taylor is currently professor and chair of the Department of Criminal Justice at the University of North Texas in Denton, Texas. For the past 25 years, Bob has studied police responses to terrorism. He has traveled extensively throughout the Middle East and Far East Asia. He currently serves as a consultant to numerous federal, state, and local agencies on intelligence analysis, human trafficking, terrorism, and Middle Eastern groups. Since September 11, 2001, Bob has been a consultant to the U.S. Department of Justice working with the Institute for Intergovernmental Research. He acts as a lead instructor in the State and Local Anti-Terrorism Training (SLATT) program, which is responsible for training law enforcement and other related criminal justice professionals (specifically the FBI Joint Terrorism Task Forces—JTTF, the Organized Crime Drug Enforcement Task Forces—OCDETF, and the DEA High Intensity Drug-Trafficking Area Strike Forces—HIDTA) on Middle Eastern groups and other terrorism issues. Bob focuses on the nexus between human trafficking, drug trafficking, and the financing of terrorist incidents internationally and domestically. He was recently awarded the University of North Texas, Regent's Lecture Award for 2003, for his work on the Middle East.

Bob also has written extensively in the area of law enforcement management and policy, community policing, and police responses to crime. He served as a sworn police officer in Portland, Oregon, for six years, three of which were as a major crimes detective. Aside from this work, Bob has coauthored three additional books: *Juvenile Justice: Policies, Programs, and Practices; Police Administration: Structures, Processes, and Behavior;* and *Digital Crime and Digital Terrorism.*

BRIEF CONTENTS

CONTENTS

As with the previous editions, the first purpose of this book is to provide a useful tool for those on law enforcement's front lines. Thus, *Criminal Investigation* is once again filled with practical "how to" information, case studies, and color photographs that illustrate important points and checklists that can be adapted to the needs of local agencies.

We have scrutinized all aspects of the book to keep what is deemed worthy by others. At the same time, we break new ground by introducing cutting edge topics, such as the investigation of staged crimes, remote sensing techniques, fusion centers, marijuana grow houses, handling of cold case backlogs, and dealing with deaf victims of sexual assaults. Many portions of chapters have been totally rewritten, such those on as crime scene sketching and forensic mapping, along with the usual updating of citations and tables. (These and other changes are identified in a later portion of this front matter to the tenth edition.)

Criminal Investigation continues to differ from other texts, and the differences are again reflected throughout this edition.

First, criminal investigation generally has been conceived of, and touted as, an art. This approach depreciates the precision required to conduct inquiries; it denies the existence of, and adherence to, rigorous methods; and it associates criminal investigation with unneeded mysticism. Criminal Investigation is in large part a science. The fact that criminals are not always apprehended does not make it less so. The rational scientific method is, of necessity, supplemented by initiative and occasional fortuitous circumstances, but it is the application of the method rather than shrewd hunches that most frequently produces results. The most successful investigators are those who know how to apply the rational scientific method; therefore, it is this method that we consistently use in *Criminal Investigation.*

A second major difference between this text and others arises from our belief that writing about techniques takes on more substance if one understands something of the nature of the event being investigated. Thus, we have discussed typologies—including offenses, offenders, and victims—in depth, so that our readers not only take away a more comprehensive understanding of criminal investigation than they would from another textbook but also have substantial information to use later as a reference.

Third, because crime-prevention technology has been a significant milestone for both the police and the public, we have inserted short sections on prevention in chapters where appropriate. The complexity of crime prevention dictates that it is a specialization within police departments. Yet, at the scene of a crime, the investigator may be in a unique position to make a few helpful, if rudimentary, suggestions to a victim on how to avoid further loss. *Criminal Investigation*'s crime prevention sections give investigators the tools to accomplish this task.

Finally, most investigative books tend to blur the distinction between the roles of uniformed officers and detectives; we draw this line distinctly. Although everyone may not agree with our dichotomizing, the uniformed officer's role must be recognized for the contribution it makes to the ultimate success of an investigation.

THE TENTH EDITION

Criminal investigation is always evolving owing to scientific, legal, and social developments, as well as to changes in the behavior of criminals. Although many investigative techniques are fundamental and remain basically the same over time, significant changes also occur on a continuing basis. In addition to having updated photographs, tables, figures, and citations, this edition reflects both the ongoing and the changing dimensions of criminal investigation by including the following text updates and revisions:

- **Chapter 1, "The Evolution of Criminal Investigation and Criminalistics,"** a historically oriented chapter, has undergone a more modest revision than have other chapters. However, the chapter does feature an updated section on institutional initiatives in investigation and criminalistics. Although some historical images (such as the one showing Allan Pinkerton with President Lincoln) of necessity remain as black and white, many color photographs have been added.

- **Chapter 2, "Legal Aspects of Investigation,"** is a new chapter that addresses topics uniformed officers and investigators encounter on a daily basis. It includes rewritten and updated materials on the laws of arrest largely taken from Chapter 21 in the previous editions, and it includes materials on the Exclusionary Rule and the law of search and seizure.

- **Chapter 3, "Investigators, the Investigative Process, and the Crime Scene,"** includes crime scene sketching and forensic mapping, entirely new to the tenth edition. A major section on staged crimes was added. Although people stage scenes to deflect suspicion of themselves, some such scenes are "forged" to save a family from embarrassment, for example, to make a suicide look like a murder. The chapter continues to emphasize its strong crime scene and preliminary investigation focus.

- **Chapter 4, "Physical Evidence,"** has been carefully updated with new material on the collection and the analysis of soil evidence. There is also new content on glass fracture matches and the types, features, and characteristics of such fractures. A new section on using florescent light to locate lip print evidence was also written.

- **Chapter 5, "Interviewing and Interrogation,"** has been reorganized and consolidated to provide a better flow of materials. Material has been updated, and several sections containing esoteric topics have been deleted.

- **Chapter 6, "Field Notes and Reporting,"** includes a rewrite of introductory materials on incident reports and emphasizes the importance of reporting an event in logical order and including all details. The term *primary questions* has been replaced by the term *interrogatory questions* to clarify the distinction with basic specific questions.

- **Chapter 7, "The Follow-Up Investigation and Investigative,"** contains two new major sections, remote sensing and fusion centers. Remote sensing is the collection and analysis of data on areas, objects, or events without being in contact with them. At the low technology end, this capability is illustrated by the use of cadaver dogs; at the high end, by ground-penetrating radar.

  Fusion centers (FCs) are more than computer networks or intelligence networks in that they support the implementation of prevention, response, and consequence management programs.

  The essence of FCs is the constant merging, analysis, and dissemination of information from many different sources to be used tactically and strategically for homeland security and crime-fighting purposes.

- **Chapter 8, "The Crime Lab,"** focuses on the new technology available in crime labs to scientifically analyze evidence discovered and collected at crime scenes. In particular, there is expanded treatment of DNA analysis and DNA banking with respect to using familial DNA to solve crimes.

- **Chapter 9, "Injury and Death Investigations,"** includes many new photographs and graphics to illustrate content. Ways to handle backlogs of cold case investigations have been added, such as the use of private labs and criminal justice university students.

- **Chapter 10, "Sex-Related Offenses,"** includes a new module on interviewing deaf victims of sexual assault. Although such incidents do not happen with great frequency, investigators need to be aware of the unique aspects of interviewing these victims. An entirely new section, including photographs, was written on homosexual homicide investigation.

- **Chapter 11, "Crimes against Children,"** was rewritten to include updating the sections on Sudden Infant Death Syndrome (SIDS); Internet crimes against children and Internet predators; child molestation; human trafficking and sex tourism; and the Amber Alert System. Also updated is the material on school shootings, including information and lessons learned from the Virginia Tech shootings in 2007.

- **Chapter 12, "Robbery,"** now addresses the use of surveillance cameras as a method of preventing and investigating robberies, along with a number of associated new photographs. An entirely new section on Bank Robberies and Bank Robbery Prevention has been added to this chapter.

- **Chapter 13, "Burglary,"** The references and data in this chapter have been updated. Portions of this chapter were rewriten to achieve additional clarity.

- **Chapter 14, "Larceny and White-Collar Crime"** places greater emphasis on larceny investigation without sacrificing the treatment of white-collar crime. The entire beginning of the chapter was rewritten to accomplish this. Shoplifting was substantially revised to accommodate the distinction between small-scale, but costly, shoplifting versus organized retail theft (ORT) accomplished by full-time rings of professionals.

- **Chapter 15, "Vehicle Thefts and Related Offenses,"** contains new material on the cloning of vehicles and has updated chapter materials.

- **Chapter 16, "Computer Crime,"** has been updated and expanded to include new material on computer manipulation crimes, common Internet scams, denial of service attacks, cyberstalking (on MySpace and YouTube), computer component theft, and virus hoaxes.

- **Chapter 17, "Agricultural, Wildlife, and Environmental Crimes,"** was rewritten in many areas to simplify the presentation of material, along with the usual updating of case studies, photographs and content. The section on "Livestock Identification" was totally rewritten.

- **Chapter 18, "Arson and Explosives,"** includes a rewritten section on collecting evidence at bomb scenes, as well as numerous new photographs and an entirely new section on bomb threat standoffs. The discussion on reading bombers' signatures is entirely new.

- **Chapter 19, "Recognition, Control, and Investigation of Drug Abuse,"** includes a new section on marijuana grow houses, along with coverage of heroin cheese and Strawberry "Quick" meth.

- **Chapter 20, "Terrorism,"** reflects the nature of terrorism, which is always changing and adapting. Thus, the chapter is always a "work in progress."

  The investigation of terrorism continues to involve agencies at every level of government and of every size. There is new material on international groups such as al-Qaeda, Jemaah Islamiya, Hizbollah, HAMAS, and Hizb ut Tahrir (HuT), as well as expanded material on terrorist money laundering and a checklist on investigating hawalas. We also include information on the impact of recent domestic cases involving the conviction of ELF leaders and ecoterrorism threats, as well as emerging threats along the U.S.-Mexico border with respect to illegal immigration. Finally, there is a discussion on private-public partnerships and intelligence-based software designed to prevent terrorist events in the United States.

- **Chapter 21, "The Trial Process and the Investigator as a Witness,"** describes pretrial and trial procedures and offers a detailed discussion on the law enforcement investigator's role in court. Discussion of the pretrial process has been expanded to cover jury selection and the effects of a recent U.S. Supreme Court decision on exceptions to the hearsay rule.

LEARNING AIDS

Working together, the authors and the editors have developed a format for the text that supports the goal of a readable, practical, user-friendly book. In addition to the changes already mentioned, we have added a host of new photographs, figures, and tables to reinforce and expand the text coverage. A visual presentation of the book's many lists—which are so critical in a text that teaches professionals and future professionals "how to" investigate crime—makes this material easy to digest. The learning aids in the edition go beyond these visual elements, however:

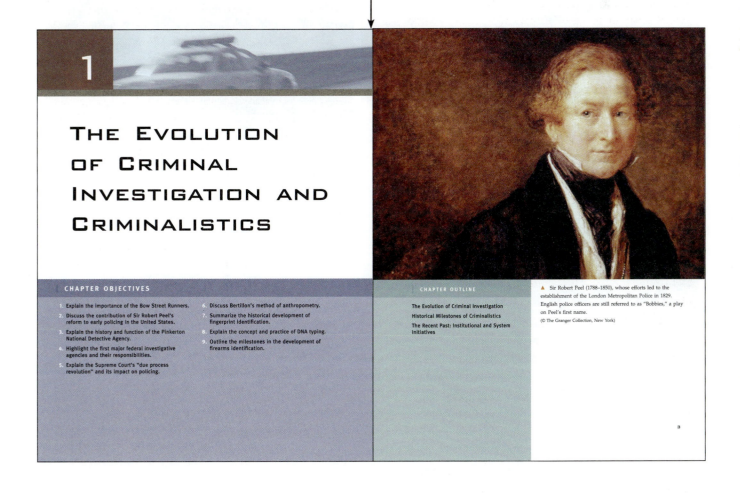

1

THE EVOLUTION OF CRIMINAL INVESTIGATION AND CRIMINALISTICS

CHAPTER OBJECTIVES

1. Explain the importance of the Bow Street Runners.
2. Discuss the contribution of Sir Robert Peel's reform to early policing in the United States.
3. Explain the history and function of the Pinkerton National Detective Agency.
4. Highlight the first major federal investigative agencies and their responsibilities.
5. Explain the Supreme Court's "due process revolution" and its impact on policing.
6. Discuss Bertillon's method of anthropometry.
7. Summarize the historical development of fingerprint identification.
8. Explain the concept and practice of DNA typing.
9. Outline the milestones in the development of firearms identification.

CHAPTER OUTLINE

The Evolution of Criminal Investigation
Historical Milestones of Criminalistics
The Recent Past: Institutional and System Initiatives

▲ Sir Robert Peel (1788–1850), whose efforts led to the establishment of the London Metropolitan Police in 1829. English police officers are still referred to as "Bobbies," a play on Peel's first name.
(© The Granger Collection, New York)

3

- **Chapter-opening photographs, outlines, and learning objectives** draw readers in and serve as a road map to the chapter.

- **Chapter-opening overviews** provide readers with a snapshot of the entire chapter and are excellent review tools for readers who are preparing for exams.

- **Detailed captions accompany photographs,** clarifying precisely what readers should be looking for and learning when examining each piece of art.

- **End-of-chapter review sections featuring key-term lists, review questions, and Internet activities** make preparing for exams easier than ever.

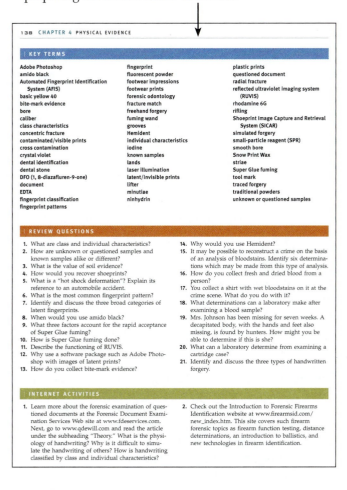

As mentioned, we have retained our plentiful, widely acclaimed "cases" within every chapter, ensuring that the tenth edition is not only the most current, definitive text on criminal investigation but also the most practical and relevant. And with the enhancements we have made to the learning aids, *Criminal Investigation* is, simply put, the most mastery-oriented text available for the course.

SUPPLEMENTS

As a full-service publisher of quality educational products, McGraw-Hill does much more than just sell textbooks. The company creates and publishes an extensive array of print, video, and digital supplements for students and instructors. This edition of *Criminal Investigation* is accompanied by a comprehensive supplements package.

For the Student

Online Learning Center Website: This unique, book-specific website features interactive cases that not only are fun to explore but also are terrific learning tools. The website also includes self-grading quizzes and other exercises to

assist students in mastering the concepts in the book. Visit it at www.mhhe.com/swanson10.

For the Instructor

- *Instructor's Manual and Testbank:* Includes detailed chapter outlines, key terms, overviews, lecture notes, transparency masters, and a complete testbank.

- *Computerized Testbank:* This easy-to-use computerized testing program is for both Windows and Macintosh computers.

- *PowerPoint Slides:* Complete chapter-by-chapter slide shows feature text, art, and tables.

- *Online Learning Center Website:* Password-protected access is provided for important instructor support materials and additional resources.

- *Course Management Systems:* Whether you use WebCT, Blackboard, e-College, or another course management system, McGraw-Hill will provide you with a cartridge that enables you either to conduct your course entirely online or to supplement your lectures with online material. And if your school does not yet have one of these course management systems, we can provide you with PageOut, an easy-to-use tool that allows you to create your own course web page and access all material on the Online Learning Center.

- *Primis Online:* A unique database publishing system that allows instructors to create a customized text from material in this text or elsewhere and deliver that text to students electronically as an e-book or in print format via the bookstore.

- *Videotapes:* A wide variety of videotapes from the *Films for the Humanities and Social Sciences* series is available to adopters of the text.

All the preceding supplements are provided *free of charge* to students and instructors. Orders of new (versus used) textbooks help us defray the cost of developing such supplements, which is substantial. Please contact your local McGraw-Hill representative for more information on any of the preceding supplements.

ACKNOWLEDGMENTS

Without the kindness of many people throughout the country—literally from Alaska to Maine—this book could not have been written. We are grateful for the support of our colleagues around the country who have contributed case histories, reviewed portions of the manuscript within their areas of expertise, written sections for inclusion in the book, contributed photographs, forms, and other illustrations, or otherwise gone out of their way to be helpful. Our continuing concern in writing these acknowledgments is that, inadvertently, we may have omitted someone. If this is so, let us know so that we may correct this oversight, and also please accept our apologies. Our acknowledgments include persons who have contributed to this edition and those who helped with earlier editions. Some of the people identified have retired or taken on new responsibilities since assisting us, but, unless otherwise requested, we include their organizational affiliation and status at the time of the original contribution, since we feel that the agencies then employing them are also deserving of continued recognition.

Colleagues who have contributed photographs, forms, and other illustrations are identified beginning on page xxviii; thank you one and all. We would also like to thank another group of individuals who helped out in a variety of ways. Ross Gardner reviewed the new section of forensic mapping and made helpful suggestions, as did Captain John P. Slater (retired), Training Director, National Institute for Truth Verification with respect to the CVSA II System. Special Agent, Joe Navarro, FBI (retired) was kind enough to provide us with a comprehensive discussion on interviewing terrorists and how the techniques employed in such interviews are radically different from those used in interviewing traditional criminals. Chief Jack Lumpkin and Sgt. David Leedahl, Athens Clarke County (Georgia) Police Department; Chief Dwayne Orrick, Cordele (Georgia) Police Department; Chief Rick Boren, Lt. Ronnie Griffin, and Sgt. Doug Shafer, Columbus (Georgia) Police Department; Major Tolbert and Lt. Zapal, Savannah Police Department; Bob Hopkins, Hillsborough County, Florida, Sheriff's Office gave us information to strengthen the section on follow-up investigations; Commander Michael Frazier, Phoenix, Arizona, Police Department, was helpful with information on arson and explosives, as were Chief Richard Pennington and Officer R. Bonelli from the New Orleans Police Department; Chief Lee Donahue and Major William Gulledge, Honolulu, Hawaii, Police Department; Kenneth V. Lanning, Supervising Special Agent of the Federal Bureau of Investigation and the National Center for Missing and Exploited Children allowed us to reprint in Chapter 11 ("Crimes against Children") from his previously published material on the topics of child molestation and child pornography. Major Andy Garrison and Frank Broadrick, Northeast Georgia Police Academy, reviewed the chapter on report writing and made good suggestions for its revision. Steven Gottlieb, executive director of the Alpha Group Center for Crime and Intelligence Analyst Training, allowed us to adopt portions of his textbook to explain the critical role of crime analysis in law enforcement investigations. Ron French of the Ecorse, Michigan, Fire Department provided updated commentary on where and how fires start, as well as on fire setting and related mechanisms. Leigh Herbst from the University of Nebraska helped with the new chapter-opening and -closing material.

Chief Robert Davis, Lt. Rick Martinez, and Police Artist Gil Zamora, San Jose California Police Department, provided photographs for the robbery chapter. Lt. Anthony Traina, Paterson (NJ) Police Department, provided information and a photograph on using street surveillance cameras to prevent street robberies. Sharon Osterman graciously and cheerfully typed major portions of this edition; her constructive criticism and editing greatly improved the final product.

Gene Lazarus, Florida State Fire College, Ocala, and Steve Mraz, formerly with the Pinellas County, Florida, Fire Academy, reviewed and contributed to the arson chapter. Bob Quinn, Tom Costigan, Mike Rendina, Jim Wilder, and Richard Frank, presently or formerly with the Drug Enforcement Administration; Tom Matthews, Temple Terrace, Florida, Police Department, and Mike Sciales, formerly with the Hillsborough County, Florida, Sheriff's Office, reviewed and contributed to the chapter on drug abuse. Richard Souviron, Chief Forensic Odontologist, Dade County Florida, Medical Examiners Office, was an early major contributor of material dealing with bite marks and dental evidence. Dr. Wally Graves, Medical Examiner for Lee, Henry, and Glades Counties, Florida, provided information on dental evidence. John Valor, forensic artist and photographer, provided illustrations for the dental section. Dick Williams of the FBI Crime

Laboratory read the questioned-documents section and made a number of suggestions to clarify and strengthen it. Don Hampton of the Springfield, Missouri, Police Department did the same for parts of the crime scene chapter. We benefited also from the reviews and research materials provided by Jim Halligan, formerly with the Florida Department of Law Enforcement and then a professor at Florida State University's School of Criminology. He was a superb teacher and a real friend.

Special thanks to Lt. Greg Terp, commander of the Miami-Dade Auto Theft Task Force, and to some special people with the National Insurance Crime Bureau—Special Agent Lawrence "Dave" Dempsey; Regional Manager Ron Poindexter; Vice-President and General Counsel Robert H. "Bob" Mason; and Member Relations Manager Ed Sparkman.

Thanks to professor Gail Anderson of Simon Frazer University in Burnaby, B.C., Canada, for providing us with updated information on forensic entomology. Robert Aristarco, Assistant Vice President for Corporate Communications, American Re-Insurance Company in Princeton, New Jersey, allowed us to reprint material on arson investigation published by his company. Linda Brown and Robyn Royall of Help A Child, Inc. and SAVE (Sexual Assault Victim Examination Program) in Pinellas Park, Florida, provided us with all the material they use to collect the physical evidence of sexual assault cases. Dave Crosbie of the Burnsville Minnesota Fire Department provided us with photos for the "Arson and Explosives" chapter. Michael Dorn of Dorn's, Inc. provided us with current information on crimes in schools. Dr. Thomas B. Kelley of Florida State University in Panama City (Department of Criminology and Criminal Justice) provided us with both narrative information on underwater crime scene investigation and photographs. Debbie Lewis, Records Custodian, William A. Pellan, Director of Forensic Investigations in Pasco and Pinellas Counties, Largo, Florida, and John R. Thogmartin, M.D. provided numerous photographs for Chapter 9 ("Injury and Death Investigations") and Chapter 10 ("Sex-Related Offenses"). Sergeant Jim Markey of the Sex Crimes Unit of the Phoenix, Arizona, Police Department supplied us with information on how to reopen cold case sex crimes; he also provided us with a photograph. Robert Parker, Director, and Major Raul M. Ubieta, Miami-Dade (Florida) Police Department, supplied us with their agency's Robbery Standard Operating Procedure along with model form letters sent to robbery victims. Greg C. Pauley of the Temple Terrace, Florida, Police Department provided us with a computer-generated composite image as well as a police mug shot of a robbery suspect at the time he was arrested. Lieutenant Ted Snodgrass of the Las Vegas, Nevada, Metropolitan Police Department Robbery Section supplied us with considerable information about his agency's "Team Approach" in dealing with robbery cases. Detective David Spraggs of the Boulder, Colorado, Police Department provided us with material used in the discussion of opening a cold case homicide investigation, along with several photographs. Laurie A. Ward, Crime Scene Administrator, Laura Sheffield, Forensic Artist, and Sheriff Grady C. Judd, Jr., all of the Polk County Sheriff's Department Office in Barstow, Florida, provided us with information on the use of forensic artists to re-create images of a robbery suspect along with a picture of the suspect at the time he was arrested. Sergeant Scott Whittington of the Colorado Springs, Colorado, Police Department supplied us with a video photo of a robbery in progress. Maryellin Territo and Sal Territo devoted long hours to researching sources for the most current information relating to all facets of criminal investigation.

A special thank you is extended to Mr. Ed Hueske for his invaluable help and assistance on the Physical Evidence and Crime Laboratory chapters. His forensics expertise was instrumental in helping acquire photographs and addressing new techniques in the area. Also, a very special thanks to Ms. Jennifer Davis for her hard work, research, and assistance in developing the book. She was an important coauthor on the "Crimes against Children" chapter. Chief Jimmy Perdue, North Richland Hills, Texas Police Department; Chief Richard Wiles, Deputy Chief Dianna Kirk, and Mr. Stuart Ed, El Paso, Texas Police Department; Chief Robert Lehner and Deputy Chief Chuck Tilby, Eugene, Oregon Police Department; and Chief David Kunkle, Dallas Police Department, provided opportunities within their departments for acquiring photographs and learning new techniques in the investigative process. Dr. Kall Loper has coauthored the "Computer Crime" chapter in previous editions, and some of his work was continued in this edition. Dr. David Carter, Dr. Richard Holden, Dr. Jonathon White, and Mr. Doug Bodrero, Institute for Intergovernmental Relations (Tallahassee, Florida), offered important information on terrorism and intelligence gathering analysis that highlighted the Terrorism Chapter.

We would also like to thank Professor Barry Glover and Ashlee Castle of the Department of Criminal Justice, Saint Leo University, Saint Leo, Florida for providing us with the material in Chapter 9, Injury and Death Investigation, on the discussion of the Utilization of Criminal Justice College Students to Evaluate Cold Cases.

This tenth edition of the book benefited from a counsel of reviewers. Thanks to:

James M. Adcock, University of New Haven;
William J. Vizzard, California State University, Sacramento;
Anthony C. Trevelino, Camden County College;
Norman J. Raasch, Lakeland Community College;
Dennis M. Payne, Michigan State University;
Richard H. DeLung, Wayland Baptist University;
Craig Hemmens, Boise State University;
C. Wayne Johnston, Arkansas State University;
Richard J. Mangan, Florida Atlantic University;
Michael J. McCrystle, California State University, Sacramento;

Daniel K. Maxwell, University of New Haven;
Steven Brandl, University of Wisconsin, Milwaukee;
Joseph Morris, Northwestern State University;
Tere Chipman, Fayetteville Technical College;
Stephan D. Kaftan, Hawkeye Community College;
Alexandro del Carmen, University of Texas, Arlington;
Michael Grimes, Miami Dade Community College; and
Roger L. Pennel, Central Missouri State University

Finally, a few words about the hard-working people at
McGraw-Hill who helped make this a better book: We
would like to thank our editors Katie Stevens and Craig
Leonard; project manager Mel Valentin, who kept this
project moving forward and on time; designer Cassandra
Chu; photo research manager Brian Pecko, who found us
photos and obtained permission to use them in a timely
manner; marketing manager Joyce Chiu; copyeditor
Stacey Sawyer; and everyone else from the McGraw-Hill
production staff in San Francisco who worked on this
edition of the text.

Charles R. "Mike" Swanson
Neil C. Chamelin
Leonard Territo
Robert W. Taylor

We are grateful to our colleagues from around the country who have been kind enough to contribute photographs, forms, and other figures to the text. The inclusion of such material helps ensure the relevancy and usefulness of the text for all readers in all states. For this, we are indebted to the following individuals, departments, and agencies:

Alaska
State of Alaska Scientific Crime Detection Laboratory

Arizona
Phoenix, Arizona, Police Department

California
California Bureau of Livestock Identification
Kern County, California, Sheriff's Department
Los Angeles County Sheriff's Department
Riverside County, California, Sheriff's Department
San Bernardino County, California, Sheriff's Department
San Diego County Sheriff's Department
San Jose Police Department
Santa Ana, California, Police Department
Santa Barbara County, California, Sheriff's Department

Colorado
Westminster, Colorado, Police Department

Delaware
Delaware State Police

Florida
Big Bend Bomb Disposal Team, Tallahassee, Florida
Dade County Medical Examiner Department, Miami, Florida
Florida Department of Law Enforcement
Leon County Sheriff's Department, Tallahassee, Florida
Miami-Dade Police Department
Pinellas County, Florida, Public Health Unit, Sexual Assault Victim Examination Program
Pinellas County, Florida, Sheriff's Office
Polk County Sheriff's Office
Port Orange, Florida, Police Department
Saint
St. Petersburg, Florida, Police Department
Tallahassee Regional Crime Laboratory, Florida Department of Law Enforcement
Tampa, Florida Fire Department
Tampa, Florida Police Department

Georgia
Athens-Clarke County, Georgia, Police Department
Atlanta Police Department
Cordele, (Georgia), Police Department
Columbus, (Georgia), Police Department
Georgia Bureau of Investigation
Savannah Police Department

Idaho
Idaho Bureau of Investigation

Illinois
Chicago Crime Laboratory
Chicago Police Department
Cook County, Illinois, Sheriff's Department
Illinois Environmental Protection Agency
Illinois State Police

Indiana
Indiana State Police

Iowa
Iowa Criminalistic Laboratory, Department of Public Safety
State Historical Society of Iowa

Kansas
Wichita, Kansas, Police Department

Kentucky
Kentucky State Police

Maine
Lewiston, Maine, Police Department

Maryland
The SANS Institute

Massachusetts
Massachusetts Environmental Police
National Fire Protection Association

Michigan
Ecorse, Michigan, Fire Department
Sterling Heights, Michigan, Police Department

Minnesota
Minneapolis, Minnesota, Police Department
Minnesota Department of Health

Mississippi
Yoknapatawpha County, Mississippi, Sheriff's Department

Missouri
Regional Criminalistics Laboratory, Metropolitan Kansas City, Missouri
Springfield, Missouri, Police Department
St. Louis County, Missouri, Police Department
St. Louis Police Department

New Jersey
New Jersey State Police
Paterson Police Department

New York
Nassau County, New York, Police Department
New York City Police Department

North Carolina
North Carolina Bureau of Investigation
SIRCHIE Fingerprint Laboratories, Inc.

Ohio
Geauga County, Ohio, Sheriff's Department

Pennsylvania
Pennsylvania State Police
Philadelphia Police Department

South Carolina
Georgetown, South Carolina,
    Police Department

Tennessee
Nashville Police Department
Tennessee Bureau of Investigation

Texas
Austin, Texas, Police Department
Dallas Police Department
Forensic Training and Consulting, LLC
Texas Department of Public Safety (Garland
    Crime Lab)
Texas Parks & Wildlife

Utah
Utah Department of Public Safety, Bureau of
    Forensic Sciences

Virginia
Alexandria, Virginia, Police Department
Fairfax County, Virginia, Police Department

Washington
Clark County Sheriff's Office,
    Vancouver, Washington

Washington, D.C.
Police Executive Research Forum

Wisconsin
Madison Police Department
Milwaukee County Department of Social Service
Wisconsin State Police

Wyoming
Lincoln County, Wyoming, Sheriff's Office
Wyoming Game and Fish Department
Wyoming State Archives and
    Historical Department

National & Federal Agencies
Bureau of Justice Statistics, U.S.
    Department of Justice
Centers for Disease Control
Chester A. Higgins, Jr., and the U.S. Department of
    Justice, Office of Justice Programs
Drug Enforcement Administration
Environmental Protection Agency
Federal Bureau of Investigation
Federal Emergency Management Agency
Immigration and Naturalization Service, Forensic
    Document Laboratory
National Automobile Theft Bureau
National Center for Missing and
    Exploited Children
National Drug Intelligence Center
National Institute of Justice
National Insurance Crime Bureau
National Park Service
Office of Justice Programs, National Institute of
    Justice
Pinkerton's Archives
U.S. Customs Service
U.S. Department of Justice
U.S. Department of the Treasury, Bureau of Alcohol,
    Tobacco, and Firearms
U.S. Forest Service
U.S. Public Health Service
U.S. Secret Service

International Agencies
London Metropolitan Police
Royal Canadian Mounted Police
Turkish National Police

1

THE EVOLUTION OF CRIMINAL INVESTIGATION AND CRIMINALISTICS

CHAPTER OBJECTIVES

1. Explain the importance of the Bow Street Runners.

2. Discuss the contribution of Sir Robert Peel's reform to early policing in the United States.

3. Explain the history and function of the Pinkerton National Detective Agency.

4. Highlight the first major federal investigative agencies and their responsibilities.

5. Explain the Supreme Court's "due process revolution" and its impact on policing.

6. Discuss Bertillon's method of anthropometry.

7. Summarize the historical development of fingerprint identification.

8. Explain the concept and practice of DNA typing.

9. Outline the milestones in the development of firearms identification.

▲ Sir Robert Peel (1788–1850), whose efforts led to the establishment of the London Metropolitan Police in 1829. English police officers are still referred to as "Bobbies," a play on Peel's first name.

(© The Granger Collection, New York)

Over a number of centuries, many people from different countries have made contributions to the fields of criminal investigation and forensic science. To recognize all of them is well beyond the scope of this chapter. Thus, without discounting anyone's work, it is necessary to draw some boundaries. For present purposes, the roots of criminal investigation can be traced back to England in the eighteenth century, a period marked by numerous social, political, and economic changes. These changes were catalysts in the creation of the first modern detective force, the Bow Street Runners. In addition, London was the home of the first police reformer, Robert Peel. Both of these factors contributed to the subsequent development of police organizations and criminal investigation in the United States.

Within the criminal investigation process, investigators frequently use various scientific methods found in criminalistics to help identify suspects, gather evidence, and collect information—all of which is done in the effort to convict criminal offenders. Criminalistics draws from diverse disciplines, such as geology, physics, chemistry, biology, and mathematics, to study physical evidence related to crime. If it is suspected that a person has died from poisoning, for example, a toxicologist, who specializes in identifying and recognizing poisons and their physiological effects on humans and animals, can assist in the investigation. Experts in other areas, such as botany, forensic pathology, entomology, and archaeology, may also provide helpful information to criminal investigators.

This chapter presents a brief history of criminalistics and criminal investigation and highlights major developments in the field. In addition, it discusses the creation and use of personal identification systems, such as anthropometry, fingerprint identification, and DNA typing, and provides an overview on the use of firearms identification in criminal investigation. Writing about these separate but intertwined topics is a difficult task. Many volumes have been written about them, but the space that can be devoted to them here is limited. Sufficient broad perspectives and supporting details, however, are included in this chapter to enable readers intrigued by these subjects to independently pursue their interest armed with a working knowledge of the basics.

THE EVOLUTION OF CRIMINAL INVESTIGATION

The evolution of criminal investigation began in eighteenth-century England, when massive changes were occurring. To fully appreciate the development of criminal investigation, you must first understand the social, economic, political, and legal contexts in which it evolved. Thus, this section provides this background and offers a brief history of criminal investigation from its early days in England to more recent times in the United States.

The Impact of the Agricultural and Industrial Revolutions

During the eighteenth century, two events—an agricultural revolution and an industrial revolution—began a process of change that profoundly affected how police services were delivered and investigations conducted. Improved agricultural methods, such as the introduction in 1730 of Charles Townshend's crop rotation system and Jethro Tull's four-bladed plow, gave England increased agricultural productivity in the first half of the eighteenth century.[1] Improvements in agriculture were essential preconditions to the Industrial Revolution in the second half of the eighteenth century, because they freed people from farm work for city jobs. As the population of England's cities grew, slums also grew, crime increased, and disorders became more frequent. Consequently, public demands for government to control crime grew louder.

The Fieldings: Crime Information and the Bow Street Runners

In 1748, **Henry Fielding** became chief magistrate of Bow Street and set out to improve the administration of justice. In 1750, he established a small group of volunteer, non-uniformed home owners to "take thieves." Known as the **"Bow Street Runners,"** these Londoners hurried to the scenes of reported crimes and began investigations, thus becoming the first modern detective force. By 1752, Fielding began publishing *The Covent Garden Journal* as a means of circulating the descriptions of wanted persons. Upon his death in 1754, Henry Fielding was succeeded by his blind half-brother, **John Fielding,** who carried on Henry's ideas for another 25 years.[2] Under John Fielding, Bow Street became a clearinghouse for information on crime, and by 1785 at least four of the Bow Street Runners were no longer volunteers but paid government detectives.[3]

The Metropolitan Police Act of 1829

In 1816, 1818, and again in 1822, England's Parliament rejected proposals for a centralized professional police force for London. Highly different political philosophies were at odds. One group argued that such a force was a direct threat to personal liberty. The other group—composed of reformers such as Jeremy Bentham and Patrick Colquhoun—argued that the absence, rather than the presence, of social control was the greater danger to personal liberty. Finally, in 1829, due in large measure to the efforts of **Sir Robert Peel,** Parliament passed the **Metropolitan Police Act,** which created a metropolitan police force for London. Police headquarters became known as **"Scotland Yard,"** because the building formerly had housed Scottish royalty. Police constables were referred to as **"Bobbies,"** a play on Peel's first name, Robert. Peel selected Charles Rowan and Richard Mayne as police commissioners, responsible for the development of this new force, and important new principles governing police work were stated:

1. The police must be stable, efficient, and organized along military lines.
2. The police must be under government control.
3. The absence of crime best proves the efficiency of police.
4. The distribution of crime news is essential.
5. The development of police strength both over time and by area is essential.
6. No quality is more indispensable to a police officer than a perfect command of temper; a quiet, determined manner has more effect than violent action.
7. Good appearance commands respect.
8. The securing and training of the proper people is at the root of efficiency.
9. Public security demands that every police officer be given a number.
10. Police headquarters should be centrally located and easily accessible to the people.
11. Police should be hired on a probationary basis.
12. Police records are necessary to the correct distribution of police strength.[4]

Because French citizens had experienced oppression under centralized police, the British public was suspicious of, and at times even hostile to, the new force. In response to the high standards set for the police force, there were 5,000 dismissals and 6,000 forced resignations from the force during the first three years of operations.[5] This record was a clear indication to the public that police administrators were requiring that officers maintain high standards of conduct. Within a few years, the London Metropolitan Police had won a reputation for fairness, and it became the international model of professional policing. Despite the growing popularity of the uniformed Bobbies, however, there was fear that the use of **"police spies"**—detectives in plain clothes—would reduce civil liberties.

In the years immediately following 1829, some Metropolitan Police constables were temporarily relieved from patrolling in uniform to investigate crimes on their beats.[6] As the distinction between the use of uniformed constables to prevent crime and the use of plainclothes detectives for investigation and surveillance became clear, the public became uneasy. Illustratively, in 1833, a **Sergeant Popay** was dismissed following a parliamentary investigation that revealed that he had infiltrated a radical group, acquired a leadership position, and argued for the use of violence. In 1842, a regular detective branch was opened at Scotland Yard, superseding the Bow Street forces.[7] (See Figure 1-1.) Initially, the detective force was limited to no more than 16 investigators, and its operations were restricted because of distrust of "clandestine methods."[8]

American Initiatives

The success of Peel's reform in England did not go unnoticed in the United States. **Stephen Girard** bequeathed $33,190 to Philadelphia to develop a competent police force. In 1833, Philadelphia passed an ordinance creating America's first paid, daylight police force. Although the

▲ **FIGURE 1-1** **New Scotland Yard**

In 1890, the Metropolitan Police left their original quarters and were housed in New Scotland Yard, pictured above. Subsequently, in 1967, the Metropolitan Police moved again, to their present facilities, which are also referred to as New Scotland Yard.

ordinance was repealed just three years later, the concept of a paid police force would reappear as American cities staggered under the burdens of tremendous population growth, poverty, and massive crime. In 1836, New York City rejected the notion of a police force organized along the lines advocated by Peel. The committee studying the idea concluded it was better in emergencies to rely on citizens than "despotic governments."[9]

Thus, before mid-century, few American cities had police service, and what existed was inadequate. Many cities had paid police service only at night or treated day and night police services as entirely separate organizations. Finally, in 1844, the New York state legislature created the first unified police force in the country, although New York City did not actually implement the measure until a year later. Other cities rapidly followed New York's lead: Chicago in 1851, New Orleans and Cincinnati in 1852, and Baltimore and Newark in 1857. By 1880, vir-

tually every major American city had a police force based on England's Peelian reforms of 1829 and pioneered in this country by New York City.

If one of the problems of the London Metropolitan Police had been getting the public to accept some constables' working out of uniform as detectives, in the United States the problem was getting the police to wear uniforms in the first place. American officers believed that a uniform made them easy targets for public harassment and made them look like servants. Only after the Civil War did the wearing of a uniform—invariably Union blue—become widely accepted by American police officers.

Pinkerton's National Detective Agency

American cities needed reliable detectives for several reasons. First, graft and corruption were common among America's big-city police officers. Second, police jurisdiction was limited. Third, there was little communication of information among departments in different cities. Thus, offenders often fled from one jurisdiction to another with impunity.

In 1846, seeing the need for reliable investigators, two former St. Louis police officers formed the first recorded private detective agency.[10] But the major private detective agency of the nineteenth century was formed by **Allan Pinkerton** (1819–1884). (See Figure 1-2.) In 1849, Chicago's Mayor Boone appointed Pinkerton as the city's first detective. Pinkerton enjoyed great success, but he resigned because of political interference and took a job as a special U.S. mail agent to solve a series of post office thefts and robberies in the Chicago area.[11] In 1850, after succeeding in this job, Pinkerton formed a private detective agency with attorney Edward Rucker.[12] Pinkerton's trademark was an open eye above the slogan "We never sleep."[13] The trademark gave rise to the use of the term "private eye" in reference to any private investigator.[14] The Pinkertons enjoyed such enormous success in the United States and throughout the world that some people thought "Pinkerton" was a nickname for any American government detective.[15]

The list of achievements by Pinkerton is impressive. Pinkerton reportedly discovered and foiled an assassination attempt on President-elect Lincoln in Baltimore.[16] At the outbreak of the Civil War in 1861, Pinkerton organized a Secret Service Division within the army (not to be confused with the U.S. Secret Service) and worked closely with General McClellan.[17] He infiltrated Confederate lines in disguise on several occasions and usually functioned as a military analyst.[18]

Following the Civil War, the Pinkertons were primarily engaged in two broad areas: (1) controlling a discontented working class, which was pushing for better wages and working conditions, and (2) pursuing bank and railroad robbers.[19] Unrestricted by jurisdictional limits, Pinkerton agents roamed far and wide pursuing lawbreakers. In a violent time, they sometimes used harsh and unwise methods. For instance, suspecting that they had found

▲ **FIGURE 1-2 Pinkerton at work**
Allan Pinkerton, President Lincoln, and General McClellan at Antietam, Maryland, about October 3, 1862. Born in Scotland, Allan Pinkerton was the son of a police sergeant. He found employment as a barrel maker and advanced to supervisor. At the same time, this red-headed, strong-willed man advocated more voice in government for ordinary people, a position that resulted in him becoming a wanted man. Narrowly avoiding arrest on his wedding day, Pinkerton and his wife fled to America, surviving a shipwreck while enroute. He started a successful barrel making company. While owner of that business, his initiative led to the arrest of counterfeiters. This gave him an appetite for police work, his father's profession, and changed his life and American policing forever.
(Courtesy Pinkerton's Archives)

No _P.N.D.A. - 1597_.
Name _Geo Cassidy alias Butch Cassidy al_
Alias _Ingersfield. right name Rob. Parker_
Age _32_ Height _5 ft 9_ Weight _165_
Complexion _Light_ Hair _Flaxen_
Eyes _Blue_ Beard_____ Teeth_____
Nationality _American_
Marks and Scars _2 cut scars. buck head_
Small red scar under left eye.
eyes deep set. Small brown
mole calf of leg.
Arrested _for Grd. Lar. Fremont Co. Wyo._
Remarks _July-15-94. Pardoned Jan 19-_
by Gov. Richards
Home is in Circle Valley. Utah
Sandy beard & Mustache if any.

▲ **FIGURE 1-3 Butch Cassidy's Pinkerton record**
Note the "P.N.D.A." initials on the first line, which stand for Pinkerton National Detective Agency. Pinkerton agents were highly successful in combating the bank and train robbers of the Old West, such as the Hole in the Wall gang, so named because of the small opening through rocky walls that led to the valley in Johnson County, Wyoming, used as their hideout. As many as 40 bandits may have lived there in six cabins. Butch Cassidy and the Sun Dance Kid were both members of the Hole in the Wall gang at various times.
(Courtesy Wyoming State Archives and Historical Department)

the hideout of Jesse James's gang, Pinkerton agents lobbed in a 32-pound bomb, killing a boy and injuring a woman.[20]

Pinkerton understood the importance of information, records, and publicity and made good use of all of them. For example, in 1868, Pinkerton agent Dick Winscott took on the Reno gang. Winscott located Fred and John Reno and, after a drinking bout, persuaded them to let him photograph them.[21] He sent the photographs to Pinkerton files, and within a year the Reno gang was smashed.[22] Pinkerton also collected photographs of jewel thieves and other types of criminals and photographed horses to prevent illegal substitutions before races.[23] The Pinkertons also pushed Butch Cassidy (Robert Parker) and the Sun Dance Kid (Harry Longabaugh) into leaving the United States for South America, where they were reportedly killed by Bolivian soldiers at San Vincente in 1909. (See Figure 1-3.) Because of their better-known antilabor activities, the Pinkertons' other work often is overlooked. But they were the only consistently competent detectives available in this country for over 50 years[24] and provided a good model for government detectives.

The Emergence of Municipal Detectives

As early as 1845, New York City had 800 plainclothes officers,[25] although not until 1857 were the police authorized to designate 20 patrol officers as detectives.[26] In November 1857, the New York City Police Department set up a **rogues' gallery** (see Figure 1-4)—photographs of known offenders arranged by criminal specialty and height—and by June 1858, it had over 700 photographs for detectives to study so that they might recognize criminals on the street.[27]

Photographs from rogues' galleries of that era reveal that some offenders grimaced, puffed their cheeks, rolled their eyes, and otherwise tried to distort their appearance to lessen the chance of later recognition.

To assist detectives, in 1884, Chicago established this country's first municipal Criminal Identification Bureau.[28] The Atlanta Police Department's Detective Bureau was organized in 1885 with a staff of one captain, one sergeant, and eight detectives.[29] In 1886, Thomas Byrnes, the dynamic chief detective of New York City, published *Professional Criminals in America,* which included pictures, descriptions, and the methods of all criminals known to him.[30] Byrnes thereby contributed to information sharing among police departments. To supplement the rogues' gallery, Byrnes instituted the **Mulberry Street Morning Parade.** At 9 o'clock every morning, all criminals arrested in the past 24 hours were marched before his detectives, who were expected to make notes and to recognize the criminals later.[31]

State and Federal Developments

From its earliest days, the federal government employed investigators to detect revenue violations, but their responsibilities were narrow and their numbers few.[32]

In 1865, Congress created the U.S. Secret Service to combat counterfeiting. In 1903—two years after President McKinley was assassinated by Leon Czolgosz in Buffalo—the previously informal arrangement of guarding the president was made a permanent Secret Service responsibility.[33]

In 1905, the California Bureau of Criminal Identification was set up to share information about criminal activity, and Pennsylvania governor Samuel Pennypacker signed legislation creating a state police force. Widely regarded then by labor as "strikebusters on management's side," the Pennsylvania State Police nevertheless was the prototype for modern state police organizations. (See Figure 1-5.) New York and Michigan in 1917 and Delaware in 1919 adopted the state police concept. Since then, state police forces have assumed the function of providing local police with help in investigations.

After Prohibition was adopted nationally in 1920, the Bureau of Internal Revenue was responsible for its enforcement. Eventually the ranks of the bureau's agents swelled to a massive 4,000.[34] Because the Bureau of Internal Revenue was lodged in the Department of the Treasury, these federal agents were referred to as **T-men.**

In 1908, U.S. Attorney General Charles Bonaparte created the embryo of what was later to become the Federal

▲ **FIGURE 1-5   The Pennsylvania State Police**
Troop D, Pennsylvania State Police, Punxsutawney, Pennsylvania, 1906. Note that both plainclothes and uniformed personnel are represented. (Courtesy Pennsylvania State Police)

Bureau of Investigation (FBI) when he ordered that investigations were to be handled by a special group. In 1924, J. Edgar Hoover (1895–1972) assumed leadership of the Bureau of Investigation; 11 years later Congress passed a measure giving the FBI its present designation.

When Prohibition was repealed by the Eighteenth Amendment to the U.S. Constitution in 1933, many former bootleggers and other criminals turned to bank robbery and kidnapping.[35] During the Depression, some people saw John Dillinger, "Pretty Boy" Floyd, Bonnie and Clyde, and Ma Barker and her boys as "plain folks" and did not grieve over a bank robbery or the "snatching" of a millionaire.[36] (See Figures 1-6 and 1-7.) Given the restricted roles of other federal investigative agencies, it became the FBI's role to deal with these criminals.

Under Hoover, who understood the importance and uses of information, records, and publicity as well as Allan Pinkerton had, the FBI became known for investigative efficiency.

In 1932, the FBI established a crime laboratory and made its services available free to state and local police. (See Figure 1-8.) In 1935, it started the **National Academy,** a training course for state and local police. In 1967, the **National Crime Information Center (NCIC)** was made operational by the FBI, providing data on wanted persons and property stolen from all 50 states. Altogether,

◄**FIGURE 1-6   Bonnie Parker**
Texas-born Bonnie Parker (1910–1934) was part of the murderous Barrow gang, which robbed and murdered its way across Oklahoma, Missouri, Texas, and New Mexico. In 1930, she smuggled a gun into the Waco (Texas) County Jail, helping Clyde Barrow and a companion to escape. From 1932 until 1934, Bonnie and Clyde left a deadly trail before they were stopped. (Courtesy Federal Bureau of Investigation)

▲ FIGURE 1-7   Clyde Barrow
Clyde Barrow (1909–1934) was captured after his escape from the Waco County Jail and served two years in prison. Upon his release, he and Bonnie began their rampage. Outside of Black Lake, Louisiana, they were killed by law enforcement officers who had persistently been pursuing them. (Courtesy Federal Bureau of Investigations)

by 1930 a separate Narcotics Bureau was established in the Treasury Department. In 1949, a federal commission noted that federal narcotics enforcement was fragmented among several agencies, resulting in duplication of effort and other ills. In 1968, some consolidation of effort was achieved with the creation of the Bureau of Narcotics and Dangerous Drugs in the Department of Justice, and in 1973, with the creation of its successor, the **Drug Enforcement Administration (DEA).** Today, the DEA devotes many of its resources to fighting international drug traffic. Like the FBI, the DEA trains state and local police in investigative work. The training focuses on recognition of illegal drugs, control of drug purchases, surveillance methods, and handling of informants.

The Police and the U.S. Supreme Court

As the highest court in this country, the Supreme Court is both obligated and well positioned to review cases and to make decisions that often have considerable impact. From 1961 to 1966, a period known as the "due process revolution," the Supreme Court became unusually active in hearing cases involving the rights of criminal suspects and defendants. Its decisions focused on the two vital areas of search and seizure and the right to legal representation. Among those cases was *Miranda* v. *Arizona* (1966), which established the well-known "Miranda rights."

Miranda and other decisions infuriated the police, who felt that the Supreme Court had "tied their hands" and "prevented them from doing their jobs." Crime was surging, and politicians running for public office played to public fears by running on "law-and-order" platforms. Chief Justice Earl Warren was often blamed for the "sorry state of affairs" and soon "Impeach Warren" billboards dotted the landscape. In fact, the Supreme Court was simply doing its job.

these developments gave the FBI considerable influence over law enforcement throughout the country. Although some people argue that such federal influence is undesirable, others point out that Hoover and the FBI strengthened police practices in this country, from keeping crime statistics to improving investigation.

The Hague Conference in 1914 called for international action against illicit drugs. Subsequently, Congress passed the Harrison Act, making the distribution of nonmedical drugs a federal crime. Enforcement responsibility was initially given to the Internal Revenue Service, although

◀ FIGURE 1-8
FBI crime laboratory
In 2003, the FBI occupied its 463,000 square foot state-of-the-art crime laboratory, which cost $130 million.
(© AP/Wide World Photos)

So what did the due process revolution and subsequent Supreme Court decisions really change? Questionable and improper police procedures and tactics were greatly reduced. In turn, this created the need to develop new procedures and tactics and to make sure that officers were well trained in their uses. There has been an ongoing cycle of decisions and adaptation to them by the police since the due process revolution. To no small extent, this cycle has hastened the continuing professionalization of the police while also asserting the principle that the action of police officers anywhere may be subject to close scrutiny by the Supreme Court.

HISTORICAL MILESTONES OF CRIMINALISTICS

The origins of criminalistics are largely European. **Criminalistics** draws from diverse disciplines, such as geology, physics, chemistry, biology, and mathematics, to study physical evidence related to crime. The first major book describing the application of scientific disciplines to criminal investigation was written in 1893 by **Hans Gross,** a public prosecutor and later a judge from Graz, Austria.[37] Translated into English in 1906 under the title *Criminal Investigation,* it remains highly respected today as the seminal work in the field. The Frenchman Edmond Locard established the first forensic laboratory in Lyon in 1910. All crime scenes are searched on the basis of Locard's exchange principle, which asserts that when perpetrators come into contact with the scene, they will leave something of themselves and take away something from the scene. Stated somewhat differently, Locard's exchange principle advocates that there is something to be found.

Criminalistics, like other scientific disciplines, enjoys periods of stability, but on the whole it is dynamic and in constant progress. To illustrate this principle of dynamic change, the histories of two commonly used services—personal identification and firearms identification—are traced in this section.

Personal Identification

There are three major scientific systems for personal identification of criminals in wide use: anthropometry, dactylography, and deoxyribonucleic acid (DNA) typing. (See Figure 1-9.) The first was relatively short lived. The second, dactylography, or fingerprint identification, remains in use today throughout the world. The third, DNA typing, is a contemporary development. Other biometric-based methods of identifying criminals which are in limited use or on the near horizon are hand geometry, retinal/iris scans (see Figure 1-10), ear matching,

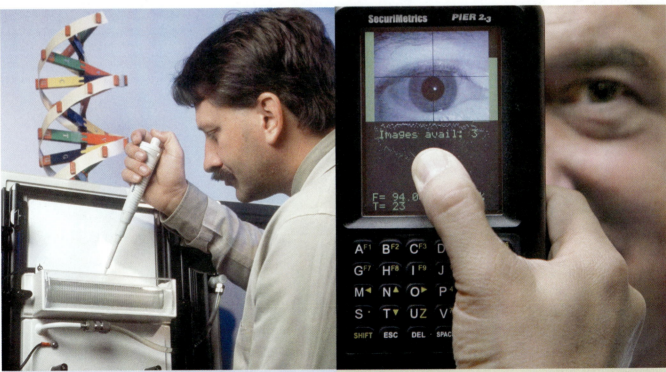

▲ **FIGURE 1-9   DNA typing**
Crime laboratory scientist conducting DNA testing; note the very rudimentary model of DNA at the left side of the picture.
(© Rob Crandall/The Image Works)

▲ **FIGURE 1-10   Iris scans**
Biometrics is the identification of a person through the analysis of a physical feature. One very accurate biometric method is through iris scans. (Courtesy of SecuriMetrics. © Ian Waldie/Getty Images)

facial recognition software, voice identification, and vein patterns.

Anthropometry

Anthropometry was developed by **Alphonse Bertillon** (1853–1914), who is rightly regarded as the father of criminal identification. (See Figure 1-11.) The first method of criminal identification that was thought to be reliable, **anthropometry** "was based on the fact that every human being differs from every other one in the exact measurements of their body, and that the sum of these measurements yields a characteristic formula for each individual."[38] Figure 1-12 depicts a New York City police detective taking one type of measurement used in the "Bertillon system."

There was little in Alphonse Bertillon's early life to suggest that he would later make significant contributions. He was the grandson of a well-known naturalist and mathematician and the son of a distinguished French physician and statistician, who was also the vice

president of the Anthropological Society of Paris.[39] Despite the advantages Bertillon had, he failed in a number of jobs. He was, therefore, able to obtain only a minor position in 1879, filing cards on criminals for the Paris police, because of his father's good connections.[40] The cards described criminals so vaguely that they might have fit almost anyone: "stature: average . . . face: ordinary."[41]

Bertillon asked himself why so much time, money, and human energy were wasted on a useless system of identifying criminals.[42] He became a source of jokes and popular amusement as he began comparing photographs of criminals and taking measurements of those who had been arrested.[43] Bertillon concluded that if 11 physical measurements of a person were taken, the chances of finding another person with the same 11 measurements were 4,191,304 to 1.[44] His report outlining his criminal identification system was not warmly received. After reading it, the chief said "your report sounds like a joke."[45]

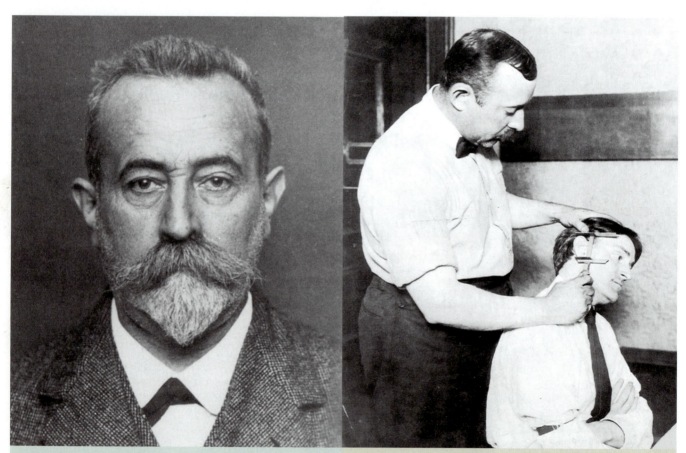

▲ **FIGURE 1-11** **Bertillon**
Alphonse Bertillon (1853–1914), the father of personal identification. In 1882, he began using his system on those incarcerated in Paris's Palais de Justice. **(Courtesy Jacques Genthial)**

▲ **FIGURE 1-12** **Taking a Bertillon measurement**
A New York City Police detective taking a Bertillon measurement of the right ear, one of the 11 measurements which made up anthropometry. This photograph was taken around 1896. Note in this photo and the one that immediately follows that the right ear is consistently part of the measurements made.
(Courtesy Library of Congress)

▲ FIGURE 1-13 Early identification card
A Bertillon-style identification card, combining both personal measurements and photographs, prepared on February 28, 1917, by the Chicago Police Department. (Courtesy Chicago Police Department)

Yet in 1883, the "joke" received worldwide attention, because within 90 days of its implementation on an experimental basis, Bertillon correctly made his first criminal identification. Soon, almost all European countries adopted Bertillon's system of anthropometry. In 1888, Bertillon's fertile mind produced yet another innovation, the *portrait parlé* or "speaking picture," which combines full-face and profile photographs of each criminal with his or her exact body measurements and other descriptive data onto a single card. (See Figure 1-13.)

One of Bertillon's students was Edmond Locard, identified earlier in this chapter as the developer of the exchange principle. Locard is also known is the father of poreoscopy, the study of pores and for advocating that if there were 12 points of agreement between two compared fingerprints the identity was certain.

After the turn of the century, many countries abandoned anthropometry and adopted the simpler and more reliable system of fingerprints instead. Bertillon himself was not insensitive to the potential of fingerprints. In 1902, he solved the murder of Joseph Riebel when he discovered the prints of Henri Scheffer on the pane of a glass cupboard.[46] Yet Bertillon's rigid personality would not allow him to acknowledge the clear superiority of dactylography to anthropometry. Even so, Bertillon's place in history is secure as the father of criminal identification.

Dactylography

Early Discoveries. Although in 1900 England became the first country to use **dactylography** as a system of criminal identification, fingerprints have a long, legal and scientific history. In a legal context, in the first century, the Roman lawyer Quintilianus introduced a bloody fingerprint in a murder trial, successfully defending a child against the charge of murdering his father.[47] Fingerprints also were used on contracts during China's T'ang Dynasty in the eighth century as well as on official papers in fourteenth-century Persia and seventeenth-century England.[48]

In a scientific context, in 1684 in England, Dr. Nehemiah Grew first called attention to the system of pores and ridges in the hands and feet.[49] Just two years later, Marcello Malpighi made similar observations.[50] In 1823, John Perkinje, a professor at the University of Breslau, named nine standard types of fingerprint patterns and outlined a broad method of classification.[51] Despite these early stirrings, dactylography as a system of criminal identification took nearly another 75 years to emerge.

The Herschel-Faulds Controversy. Beginning in 1858, William Herschel, a British official in India, requested the palm prints and fingerprints of those with whom he did business, thinking that it might awe people into keeping agreements.[52] Over the next 20 years, Herschel noted from his records that the patterns of the lines on the fingerprints never changed for an individual; a person might grow and undergo other physical changes, yet the fingerprints remained the same. Excited by the prospects of applying this knowledge to the identification of criminals, Herschel wrote in 1877 to the inspector general of the prisons of Bengal. The reply made it clear that the inspector general was not interested. Discouraged, Herschel made no further efforts to pursue his discovery. Meanwhile, Henry Faulds, a Scottish physician teaching physiology in Tsukiji Hospital in Tokyo, had been interested in fingerprints for several years before 1880. When a thief left a sooty print on a whitewashed wall, Faulds was able to tell that the person in police custody was not the thief[53] and to match another suspect's fingerprints with those on the wall.[54] Faulds reported his findings in the journal *Nature* in 1880. Herschel read the account and published a reply, claiming credit for the discovery over 20 years before. A controversy broke out that was never resolved to anyone's satisfaction. Because there was also no official interest in using fingerprints, both Herschel and Faulds were even further frustrated.

Galton's and Vucetich's Systems. In 1888, **Sir Francis Galton** (1822–1911), a cousin of Charles Darwin, turned his attention to criminal identification.[55] When the thorough Galton contacted the editor of *Nature* for both Herschel's and Faulds's addresses, he was by chance sent only Herschel's. Contacted by Galton, Herschel unselfishly turned over all of his files in the hopes that this revived interest would lead to practical uses of finger-prints.[56] In 1892, Galton published the first definitive book on dactylography, *Finger Prints.* It presented statistical proof of the uniqueness of fingerprints and outlined many principles of identification by fingerprints.[57] In Argentina, in 1894, **Juan Vucetich** (1858–1925) published *Dactiloscopia Comparada,* outlining his method of fingerprint classification. In 1892, a disciple of Vucetich's, an Inspector Alvarez, obtained South America's first criminal conviction based on fingerprints by using Vucetich's system to convict a woman of beating her two children to death.[58]

The Henry System. The final breakthrough for the finger-print method of personal identification was made by Edward Henry. At the age of 23 he went to India, and by 1891 had become the inspector general of police of Nepal, the same province in which Herschel had worked some 15 years earlier.[59] Subject to many of the same influences as Herschel, but apparently working independently, Henry developed an interest in fingerprints[60] and instituted Bertillon's system with the addition of fingerprints to the cards. In 1893, Henry obtained a copy of Galton's book and began working on a simple, reliable method of classification. The governor general of India received a report from Henry in 1897 recommending that anthropometry be dropped in favor of Henry's fingerprint classification system. It was adopted throughout British India just six months later.[61] In 1900, **Henry's system** was adopted in England. The next year, Henry enjoyed two personal triumphs, the publication of his *Classification and Use of Finger Prints* and his appointment as assistant police commissioner of London,[62] rising to the post of commissioner two years later.

Faurot and "James Jones". In 1904, New York City Detective Sergeant Joseph Faurot was sent to England to study fingerprints, becoming the first foreigner trained in the use of the Henry classification system. Upon Faurot's return, the new police commissioner told him to forget about such "scientific notions" and transferred him to walking a beat.[63] In 1906, Faurot arrested a man dressed in formal evening wear, but not wearing shoes, as the man crept out of a suite in the Waldorf-Astoria Hotel.[64] Claiming to be a respectable citizen named "James Jones," the man demanded to see the British consul and threatened Faurot with nasty consequences.[65] Faurot sent the man's fingerprints to Scotland Yard[66] and got back a reply that "James Jones" was actually Daniel Nolan, who had 12 prior convictions of hotel thefts and who was wanted for burglarizing a home in England. Confronted with this evidence, Nolan confessed to several thefts in the Waldorf-Astoria and received a sentence of seven years.[67] Newspaper stories about the case advanced the use of fingerprints in this country.

The West Case. Despite the fame achieved by Faurot, the most important incident to advance the use of fingerprints in this country was the **West case.** (See Figure 1-14.) In

	William West	Will West
	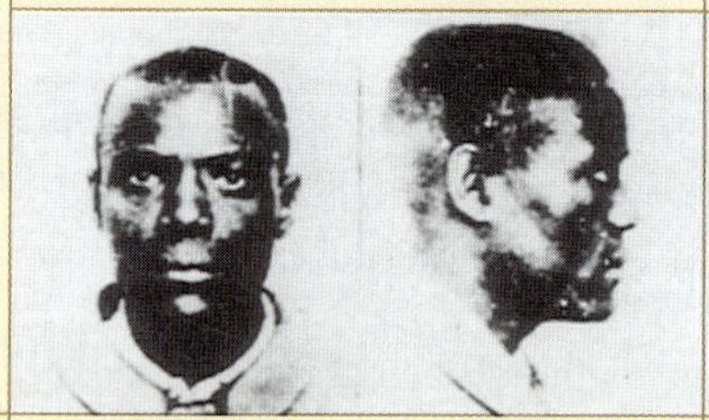	
Bertillon:		
Measurements (in centimeters)		
Height	177.5	178.5
Outstretched arms	188.0	187.0
Trunk	91.3	91.2
Head length	19.8	19.7
Head width	15.9	15.8
Cheek width	14.8	14.8
Right ear	6.5	6.6
Left foot	27.5	28.2
Left middle finger	12.2	12.3
Left little finger	9.6	9.7
Left forearm	50.3	50.2

▲ **FIGURE 1-14 The two Wests**
William West had been in Leavenworth Prison since 1901; Will West arrived two years later. Given their similar appearances and nearly identical anthropometry measurements, it is easy to understand the confusion created upon Will West's arrival.
(Courtesy Federal Bureau of Investigation)

1903, Will West arrived at the U.S. penitentiary at Leavenworth, Kansas. While West was being processed in through identification, a staff member said that there was already a photograph and Bertillon measurements for him on file. But a comparison of fingerprints showed that despite identical appearances and nearly identical Bertillon measurements, the identification card on file belonged to a William West, who had been in Leavenworth since 1901. The incident accelerated the recognition that fingerprints were superior to anthropometry as a system of identification.

Rivalry of Vucetich's and Henry's Systems

Vucetich's book on fingerprint classification was published in 1894, seven years before Henry's, but Henry's system has become much more widely used. To this day, however, some experts prefer Vucetich's system.[68] The rivalry between partisans of the two classification systems deserves attention.

In 1911, the provincial government of Buenos Aires passed a law requiring fingerprint registration for all adults subject to military service and eligible to vote.[69] By 1913, Vucetich had completed the task and decided to travel. In his travels, he was showered with decorations for his classification system. But when he visited Bertillon to pay his respects to the father of criminal identification,[70] Bertillon kept Vucetich waiting and finally opened the door just long enough to yell, "Sir, you have done me great harm," before slamming it shut again.[71] They were never to meet again. Upon his return to Argentina, Vucetich was to face further humiliation. When Buenos Aires planned an expansion of fingerprint registration, there were strong protests. In 1917, the Argentine government canceled registrations, seized Vucetich's records, and forbade him to continue his work.[72] In 1925, much as Bertillon had in 1914, Vucetich died a disappointed man. Although Vucetich's system is in use in South America today, Vucetich did not live long enough to see the vindication of his life's work.

In contrast, Henry became the head of what was then the world's most prestigious police organization and enjoyed the support of his government. These advantages, coupled with Vucetich's loss of support in his own country, meant that the Henry classification would become adopted virtually throughout the world.

DNA Typing

DNA as "Blueprint"

Although **deoxyribonucleic acid (DNA)** was discovered in 1868, scientists were slow to understand its role in heredity.[73] During the early 1950s, James Watson and Francis Crick deduced the structure of DNA, ushering in a new era in the study of genetics.[74] Such developments were seemingly of peripheral interest to forensic scientists until 1985, when research into the structure of the human gene by Alec Jeffreys and his colleagues at Leicester

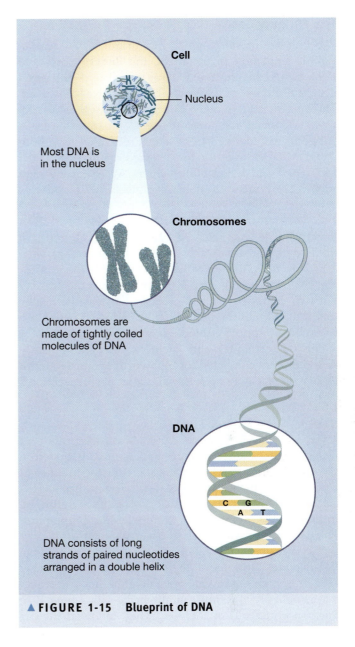

Cell

Nucleus

Most DNA is in the nucleus

Chromosomes

Chromosomes are made of tightly coiled molecules of DNA

DNA

C G A T

DNA consists of long strands of paired nucleotides arranged in a double helix

▲ **FIGURE 1-15**   **Blueprint of DNA**

University, England, led to the discovery that portions of the DNA structure of certain genes can be as unique to individuals as are fingerprints.[75] In fact, according to Jeffreys, the chance of two persons having identical DNA patterns is between 30 billion and 100 billion to 1.[76]

In all life forms—with the exception of a few viruses—the basis for variation lies in genetic material called DNA.[77] This DNA is a chemical "blueprint" that determines everything from hair color to susceptibility to diseases.[78] (See Figure 1-15.) In every cell of the same human that contains DNA, this blueprint is identical, whether the material is blood, tissue, spermatozoa, bone marrow, tooth pulp, saliva, or a hair root cell.[79] Thus, with the exception of identical twins, every person has distinctive DNA. Initially, the process of isolating and reading this genetic material was referred to as "DNA fingerprinting," but currently the term DNA typing is used to describe this practice.

The Enderby Cases

The first use of DNA typing in a criminal case was in 1987 in England,[80] in regard to the **Enderby cases.** In 1983, Lynda Mann, age 15, was raped and murdered near the village of Enderby. This case was unsolved. Three years later, another 15-year-old, Dawn Ashworth, was a victim in a similar offense. Comparing the DNA "fingerprints" derived from semen recovered from both victims' bodies, investigators realized that the same man had raped and killed both women. A 17-year-old man was initially arrested and a sample of his blood was subjected to DNA typing. This man's innocence, however, was clearly established by the lack of a DNA match, and he was released. Subsequently, all males in the Enderby area between 13 and 30 years of age were asked by the police to voluntarily provide blood samples for DNA typing. Of 5,500 men living in the area, all but two complied with the request. A man then came forward and told the police that he had used false identification to supply a blood sample in the name of a friend. This friend, Colin Pitchfork, was subsequently arrested and convicted of Ashworth's murder, with DNA evidence playing a crucial role in the prosecution's case.

The Orlando Cases

During 1986, a series of rapes and assaults occurred in Orlando, Florida, which set the stage for the first use of DNA typing in the United States.[81] The crimes shared a common pattern: the attacks occurred after midnight, in the victims' homes, by a knife-wielding perpetrator. The perpetrator was quick to cover the eyes of the victims with a sheet or blanket, so none of them could give detailed descriptions of their assailant. During early 1987, investigators staking out a neighborhood in which it was believed the rapist might strike saw a blue 1979 Ford speeding out of the area. They followed the car for a short distance before it crashed into a utility pole while making a turn. The suspect, Tommie Lee Andrews, lived just 3 miles from the home of the first victim, who identified him at a photographic lineup the next morning. The prosecutor's case was certainly not ironclad. The identification rested on the victim's having seen the defendant for 6 seconds in a well-lit bathroom nearly a year before the photo lineup. Standard forensic tests comparing characteristics of the suspect's blood with characteristics derived from the semen found on the victim suggested that only Andrews could have committed the offense; but 30% of the male population of the United States shared these same characteristics. In short, there was enough evidence to prosecute, but a conviction was by no means a certainty. However, upon learning about the Enderby cases, the prosecutor secured DNA processing of the evidence and Andrews was convicted.

DNA Analysis

In 1988, the FBI became the first public-sector crime laboratory in the United States to accept cases for DNA analysis.[82] Since that time, there has been a substantial increase in the number of crime laboratories providing this type of service. Private firms also offer DNA typing, including Cellmark Diagnostics in Germantown, Maryland.

While DNA analysis of blood and other evidence from humans in criminal investigation cases is widely understood and used, there was no application of "genetic fingerprinting" to plant evidence in criminal cases until the 1992 **palo verde seedpod case** in Phoenix, Arizona.[83] Joggers found the body of a female who had been strangled. At the scene, investigators found a beeper, which led them to a suspect. The suspect admitted that (1) he had been with the victim the evening she disappeared, (2) the victim had been in his vehicle, (3) he and the victim had had sex, and (4) he and the victim had struggled. However, the suspect also maintained that the victim had run off with his beeper when he refused to help her to get drugs and that he had not been anywhere near the place the body was found in 15 years. Investigators had found two seedpods from a palo verde tree in the bed of the suspect's truck. A University of Arizona plant geneticist was asked to determine if the seedpods came from a palo verde tree at the scene. The Maricopa County Sheriff's Office collected a total of 41 samples of palo verde seedpods from the crime scene and the surrounding region. The geneticist was able to exactly match the seedpods from the bed of the suspect's truck with those seized from the crime scene as part of the sample of 41 seedpods. Additionally, none of the 41 seedpods exactly matched another. This evidence was admitted at the trial. The defense attacked the evidence, properly arguing that the findings from a study based on 41 trees had substantial limitations and did not establish conclusively that the suspect could have gotten the seedpods only at the crime scene. However, along with other evidence, the testimony given by the geneticist had sufficient weight for the jury to convict the suspect.

Firearms Identification

Personal identification grew as several rival systems, with one of them finally predominating. In contrast, firearms identification moved forward in a series of successive steps. In the United States, the frequency of shootings has made firearms identification extremely important.[84] As a specialty within criminalistics, firearms identification extends far beyond the comparison of two fired bullets. It includes identification of types of ammunition, knowledge of the design and functioning of firearms, restoration of obliterated serial numbers on weapons, and estimation of the distance between a gun's muzzle and a victim[85] when the weapon was fired.

In 1835, **Henry Goddard,** one of the last of the Bow Street Runners, made the first successful attempt to identify a murderer from a bullet recovered from the body of a victim.[86] Goddard noticed that the bullet had a distinctive blemish on it, a slight gouge. At the home of one suspect, Goddard seized a bullet mold with a defect whose location corresponded exactly to the gouge on the bullet. When confronted with this evidence, the owner of the mold confessed to the crime.[87]

Professor Lacassagne removed a bullet in 1889 from a corpse in France. Upon examining it closely, he found seven grooves made as the bullet passed through the barrel of a gun.[88] Shown the guns of a number of suspects, Lacassagne identified the one that could have left seven grooves. On the basis of this evidence, a man was convicted of the murder.[89] However, any number of guns manufactured at that time could have produced seven grooves. There is no way of knowing whether the right person was found guilty.[90]

In 1898, a German chemist named Paul Jeserich was given a bullet taken from the body of a man murdered near Berlin. After firing a test bullet from the defendant's revolver, Jeserich took microphotographs of the fatal and test bullets and, on the basis of the agreement between both their respective normalities and abnormalities, testified that the defendant's revolver fired the fatal bullet, contributing materially to the conviction obtained.[91] Unknowingly at the doorstep of scientific greatness, Jeserich did not pursue this discovery any further, choosing instead to return to his other interests.

Gradually, attention began to shift from just bullets to other aspects of firearms. In 1913, Professor Balthazard published perhaps the single most important article on firearms identification. In it, he noted that the firing pin, breechblock, extractor, and ejector all leave marks on cartridges and that these vary among different types of weapons. With World War I looming, Balthazard's article was not widely read for some years.

Calvin Goddard (1858–1946), a U.S. physician who had served in the army during World War I, is the person considered most responsible for raising firearms identification to a science and for perfecting the bullet-comparison microscope. To no small degree, Goddard's accomplishments were contributed to heavily by three other Americans—Charles Waite, John Fisher, and Phillip Gravelle—working as a team on firearms identification. In 1925, Goddard joined Waite's team and upon Waite's death a year later, Goddard became its undisputed driving force and leader.[92] Like many pioneers, Waite's contributions are often overlooked. He had been interested in firearms since 1917, and from 1920 on he visited firearms manufacturers to get data on

those manufactured since 1850. Because of Waite, the first significant cataloged firearms collection in this country was assembled. Nonetheless, ultimately it was Goddard who raised firearms identification to the status of a science.

Other Contributors

There are many other contributors to the evolution of investigation and criminalistics. For example, in 1910 **Albert Osborn** (1858–1946) wrote *Questioned Documents*, which is still regarded as a definitive work. From at least 1911 onward, **Edmond Locard** (1877–1966) maintained a central interest in locating microscope evidence; all crime scenes processed today are based on the presumed validity of Locard's principle: There is something to be found. **Leone Lattes** (1887–1954) developed a procedure in 1915 that permits blood typing from a dried bloodstain, a key event in forensic serology. Although more an administrator and innovator than a criminalist, **August Vollmer** (1876–1955), through his support, helped **John Larson** produce the first workable polygraph in 1921. Vollmer established America's first full forensic laboratory in Los Angeles in 1923.

In 1935, **Harry Soderman** and **John O'Connell** coauthored *Modern Criminal Investigation*, the standard work for the field for decades until the publication of *Crime Investigation* by **Paul Kirk** in 1953. A biochemist, educator, and criminalist, Kirk helped develop the careers of many criminalists.

THE RECENT PAST: INSTITUTIONAL AND SYSTEM INITIATIVES

As shown in this chapter, individuals and teams working together have historically provided the scientific breakthroughs that have fueled the development of new forensic capabilities. For example, over the past two decades there has been a number of discoveries in the area of DNA profiling, and they have led to quicker procedures with excellent reliability. While individual and team-driven scientific breakthroughs will continue to foster progress, another important factor has been initiatives at the institutional and system levels. Characteristically, these initiatives are put forth by agencies blending old and new technologies and by agencies creating and managing new databases. Table 1-1 summarizes some of these initiatives.

In subsequent chapters some of the developments noted in Table 1-1 will be treated in greater detail or mentioned in the context of certain types of cases.

Table 1-1	Major Institutional and System Initiatives, 1997–2006

YEAR	INNOVATION	COMMENTS
1997	National Drug Pointer Index (NDPIX)	Run by the DEA, which uses the National Law Enforcement Telecommunications System (NLETS) as its communication spine. Participating local, state, and federal agencies submit active case data and get back "pointer" information so agencies know of common targets, can share information, and reduce risks to undercover operatives.
1998	Combined DNA Index System (CODIS)	Evolved from a 1990 pilot project and fully implemented in 1998. Today, all states participate. CODIS combines computer and DNA technology into a tool to combat violent crime. Its major databases include the Offender Index (profiles of convicted violent offenders contributed by the states) and Forensic Index (DNA evidence collected at the crime scene). CODIS includes the National DNA Index System (NDIS), the State DNA Information System (SDIS), and the Local DNA Information System (LDIS). CODIS software can link crimes in the Forensic Index, thereby identifying a predatory violent offender whose existence may not have been known previously. When such profiles are run against the Offender Index, the identity of the offender can be established.
1998	National Integrated Ballistic Information Network (NIBIN)	Through its NIBIN network, ATF distributes the Integrated Ballistic Identification System (IBIS) to local and state agencies. IBIS is used in imaging and comparing evidence from guns which were used to commit crimes. If the computer identifies matches, then a firearms examiner makes a comparison to confirm or disprove the IBIS match.
1998	National Infrastructure Protection Center (NIPC)	Established within the FBI with support from other agencies and the private sector, and then transferred in 2003 to the U.S. Department of Homeland Security, NIPC is designed for threat assessment, warning, investigation, and response to threats or attacks against energy and water systems, banking, finance, and government computer operations.
1998	Child Abduction and Serial Murder Investigative Resources (CASMIRC)	Lodged within the FBI, CASMIRC provides investigative support, training, assistance, and coordination to federal, state, and local agencies in matters involving child abductions and disappearances, child violence, and serial homicides.
1999	Safe School Initiative (SSI)	Study conducted by the Secret Service, which was completed in 2002. It was conducted in partnership with in partnership with U.S. Department of Education. Applies the Secret Service's threat assessment technology to help prevent school-based violence. Study found violence rarely spontaneous and that some children knew something of investigative significance prior to the violent incident.
1999	2000 National Crime Information Center (NCIC)	A major overhaul of the NCIC system, which became operational in 1967. For example, the Automated FingerPrint Identification System (AFIS) evolved into the Integrated Automated Fingerprint Identification System (IAFIS). IAFIS can provide electronic identification of persons, as well as their Criminal History Record Information (CHRI). The response to agencies' electronically submitted fingerprints can be made within two hours. This means that accurate information can be provided to agencies while a person is still in police custody.
2000	Internet Fraud Complaint Center (IFCC)	Joint FBI and National White Collar Crime Center (NW3C) venture to address Internet fraud. NW3C was created in 2000 by Congress as a nonprofit entity without investigative powers. Its mission is to support law enforcement agencies with an interest in this type of investigation.
2002	New Crime Lab	The Washington State Patrol's new crime lab opened in December 2002, but without sufficient staff, owing to state budget cuts.
2003	New Crime Labs: ATF, FBI, Minnesota Bureau of Criminal Identification	The new state-of-the-art Alcohol, Tobacco, and Firearms (ATF) crime lab in Arfimendale, Maryland replaces a cramped and obsolete facility and provides enhanced and expanded capabilities. The FBI's new $130 million lab is located on the grounds of the Quantico Marine Base. It occupies three adjoining five-story buildings and replaces an outdated facility. Minnesota's Bureau of Criminal Identification has a new 224,000-square-foot lab, which cost $83 million and will provide enhanced and expanded services.

CONTINUED

Table 1-1	CONTINUED

YEAR	INNOVATION	COMMENTS
2004	i2 Visual Notebook	i2 has been a leading provider of investigative software for some 15 years. In 2004, it launched Visual Notebook, powerful new visualization software that enables investigators to streamline the crime-solving process by graphically visualizing data from disparate cases.
2005	MRIs and Lie Detection	Based on preliminary findings, researchers have discovered that functional magnetic resonance imaging (fMRI) provides accurate identification about who is lying on the basis of increased brain activity in five critical brain areas. Stated more directly, when someone is lying the brain has to work harder and, therefore, produces higher levels of activity in the five areas.
2007	New Crime Lab for Phoenix, Arizona	This new 104,000 square foot facility is a major asset for investigators. It is staffed with 140 to 150 professionals and operates on a 24-hour basis.
2007	83 New Public Surveillance Cameras in Pittsburgh	Previously, 911 dispatchers could view about 150 cameras; with the addition of 83 cameras and other capabilities, streaming video can be provided in real time to any city networked computer, including those in police cars. All cameras are focused in public areas where there is no legal expectation of privacy.
2007	New DNA Laboratory in New York City	City officials opened a new $290 million, 75,000 square foot facility dedicated to the analysis of DNA evidence. Organizationally, The Forensic Biology Laboratory is part of the Office of the Chief Medical Examiner. With increased emphasis on collecting DNA evidence, analysis of it is expected to increase from 3,000 to 20,000 cases annually.
2008	Santa Clara (California) Crime Laboratory	The completion of the county's new 90,072 square foot laboratory—an investment of $71 million—is scheduled for 2008 with an anticipated initial staffing of 58.
2008	Interest in Biometrics Remains High	In part because of the need to combat terrorism and identify theft, interest in biometrics remains high. Although there are somewhat different definitions of biometrics, the essence of it is the automated identification, authentication, or verification of an individual based on a physical or behavioral characteristic. Illustrations include facial characteristics; hand geometry, or the length and shape of the hand and fingers; patterns of veins on the back of the hand and wrist; the characteristics of the iris—the colored ring surrounding a pupil—and the retina—the blood vessels at the rear of the eye and patterns associated with computer keystrokes.

KEY TERMS

anthropometry
Bertillon, Alphonse
bobbies
Bow Street Runners
criminalistics
dactylography
deoxyribonucleic acid (DNA)
Drug Enforcement Administration (DEA)
Enderby cases
Fielding, Henry
Fielding, John
Galton, Francis
Girard, Stephen

Goddard, Calvin
Goddard, Henry
Gross, Hans
Henry system
Kirk, Paul
Larson, John
Lattes, Leone
Locard, Edmond
Metropolitan Police Act (1829)
Mulberry Street Morning Parade
National Academy
National Crime Information Center (NCIC)
O'Connell, John

Osborn, Albert
palo verde seedpod case
Peel, Robert
Pinkerton, Allan
"police spies"
Popay, Sergeant
rogues' gallery
Scotland Yard
Soderman, Harry
T-men
Vollmer, August
Vucetich, Juan
West case

REVIEW QUESTIONS

1. Who were the Bow Street Runners, and of what historical importance are they?
2. Why did the British public object to the use of detectives after enactment of the Metropolitan Police Act of 1829?
3. Why did the profession of detective in this country basically evolve in the private sector?
4. What assessment can be made of the work of Pinkerton and his National Detective Agency?
5. What is a rogues' gallery?
6. What parallels can be drawn between Allan Pinkerton and J. Edgar Hoover?
7. What is anthropometry, and why was it abandoned in favor of dactylography?
8. What are the milestones in the development of dactylography?
9. Why does the Henry classification system enjoy greater use than Vucetich's system?
10. What are the different human sources of DNA material identified in this chapter?
11. Of what significance is the palo verde case?
12. What are the milestones in the development of firearms identification?

INTERNET ACTIVITIES

1. Research your local, county, and state police agencies. Do these agencies have a criminal investigation unit? Is there more than one unit that specializes in particular types of crimes (burglary, robbery, homicide, and so on)? How many investigators are assigned to such units? Do officers have to meet a certain criteria to be assigned to these units? Is there any history on the creation of these units?
2. Find out more about DNA forensics by logging onto the U.S. Department of Energy's Human Genome Program Web site at http://genomics.energy.gov/. Under the heading "Ethical, Legal and Social Issues," click "Forensics." Is DNA an effective identifier? What are some interesting uses of DNA forensics? What are the ethical, legal, and social issues associated with DNA data banking?
3. There are six biometric-based methods of individual identification that are in limited use or on the near horizon. How do these methods work, and what use is being made of them?

NOTES

1. Material on the evolution of criminal investigation is drawn, in part, from Thomas R. Phelps, Charles R. Swanson, Jr., and Kenneth Evans, *Introduction to Criminal Justice* (New York: Random House, 1979), pp. 42–55.
2. T. A. Critchley, *A History of Police in England and Wales,* 2nd ed. (Montclair, NJ: Patterson Smith, 1972), p. 34.
3. Ibid.
4. A. C. Germann, Frank D. Day, and Robert J. Gallati, *Introduction to Law Enforcement and Criminal Justice* (Springfield, IL: Charles C. Thomas, 1970), pp. 54–55.
5. Melville Lee, *A History of Police in England* (Montclair, NJ: Patterson Smith reprint, 1971), p. 240.
6. Thomas A. Reppetto, *The Blue Parade* (New York: Free Press, 1978), p. 26.
7. Ibid., pp. 26–28.
8. Ibid., p. 29.
9. James F. Richardson, *The New York Police* (New York: Oxford, 1970), p. 37.
10. James D. Horan, *The Pinkertons* (New York: Bonanza Books, 1967), p. 25.
11. Ibid., p. 23.
12. Ibid., p. 25.
13. Jurgen Thorwald, *The Marks of Cain* (London: Thames and Hudson, 1965), p. 129.
14. Reppetto, *The Blue Parade,* p. 258.
15. Thorwald, *The Marks of Cain,* p. 129.
16. Reppetto, *The Blue Parade,* p. 257. There seems to be some dispute over whether there was ever any real threat and, if so, whether Pinkerton or the New York City Police actually discovered it.
17. Ibid., pp. 257–258.
18. Ibid., p. 258. Reppetto asserts that as a military analyst Pinkerton was a failure. His overestimates of enemy strength may have made General McClellan too cautious, resulting in McClellan's dismissal by President Lincoln.
19. Ibid.
20. William J. Bopp and Donald Shultz, *Principles of American Law Enforcement and Criminal Justice* (Springfield, IL: Charles C. Thomas, 1972), pp. 70–71.
21. Thorwald, *The Marks of Cain,* p. 131.
22. Reppetto, *The Blue Parade,* p. 259, notes that in two separate instances a total of eight Reno gang members arrested by the Pinkertons were subsequently lynched. In the first instance, three gang members reportedly were taken from Pinkerton custody.
23. Thorwald, *The Marks of Cain,* p. 131.
24. Ibid., p. 263.
25. Clive Emsley, *Policing and Its Context 1750–1870* (New York: Schocken Books, 1983), p. 106.

26. Augustine E. Costello, *Our Police Protectors* (Montclair, NJ: Patterson Smith, 1972 reprint of an 1885 edition), p. 402.
27. Richardson, *The New York Police*, p. 122.
28. Bopp and Shultz, *Principles of American Law Enforcement and Criminal Justice*, p. 66.
29. William J. Mathias and Stuart Anderson, *Horse to Helicopter* (Atlanta: Community Life Publications, Georgia State University, 1973), p. 22.
30. Thorwald, *The Marks of Cain*, p. 136.
31. Ibid.
32. Reppetto, *The Blue Parade*, p. 263.
33. Ibid., p. 267.
34. Ibid., p. 278.
35. Ibid., p. 282.
36. Ibid., p. 283.
37. Richard Saferstein, *Criminalistics* (Englewood Cliffs, NJ: Prentice Hall, 1977), p. 5.
38. Jurgen Thorwald, *Crime and Science* (New York: Harcourt, Brace & World, 1967), p. 4.
39. Thorwald, *The Century of the Detective*, p. 6.
40. Ibid.
41. Ibid., p. 7.
42. Ibid., p. 9.
43. Ibid.
44. Ibid., p. 10.
45. Ibid., p. 12.
46. Ibid., pp. 83–84.
47. Anthony L. Califana and Jerome S. Levkov, *Criminalistics for the Law Enforcement Officer* (New York: McGraw-Hill, 1978), p. 20.
48. Ibid.; also see Frederick R. Cherrill, *The Finger Print System at Scotland Yard* (London: Her Majesty's Stationery Office, 1954), p. 3.
49. Cherrill, *The Finger Print System at Scotland Yard*, p. 2.
50. Califana and Levkov, *Criminalistics for the Law Enforcement Officer*, p. 20.
51. Cherrill, *The Finger Print System at Scotland Yard*, p. 4.
52. Thorwald, *The Century of the Detective*, pp. 14–16.
53. Ibid., p. 18.
54. Ibid.
55. Ibid., p. 32.
56. Ibid., p. 33.
57. Saferstein, *Criminalistics*, p. 4.
58. Thorwald, *The Marks of Cain*, p. 81.
59. Thorwald, *The Century of the Detective*, p. 58.
60. Ibid.
61. Ibid., p. 60.
62. Ibid., p. 62.
63. Thorwald, *The Marks of Cain*, p. 138.
64. Ibid.
65. Ibid.
66. Ibid., p. 139.
67. Ibid.
68. Saferstein, *Criminalistics*, p. 281.
69. Thorwald, *The Century of the Detective*, p. 88.
70. Ibid.
71. Ibid., p. 87.
72. Ibid., p. 88.
73. Richard Saferstein, *Criminalistics: An Introduction to Forensic Science*, 5th ed. (Englewood Cliffs, NJ: Prentice Hall, 1995), p. 384.
74. Tod W. Burke and Walter F. Row, "DNA Analysis: The Challenge for Police," *The Police Chief*, Oct. 1989, p. 92.
75. Saferstein, *Criminalistics*, 5th ed., p. 383.
76. "British Police Use Genetic Technique in Murder Arrest," *The Atlanta Constitution*, Sept. 22, 1987, p. A3.
77. David Bigbee et al., "Implementation of DNA Analysis in American Crime Laboratories," *The Police Chief*, Oct. 1989, p. 86.
78. Saferstein, *Criminalistics*, 5th ed., p. 384.
79. Bigbee et al., "Implementation of DNA Analysis," p. 86.
80. The account of the role of DNA in solving the Mann-Ashworth murders is drawn, in part, from Clare M. Tande, "DNA Typing: A New Investigatory Tool," *Duke Law Journal*, April 1989, p. 474.
81. This information is from Ricki Lewis, "DNA Fingerprints: Witness for the Prosecution," *Discover*, June 1988, pp. 44, 46.
82. Bigbee et al., "Implementation of DNA Analysis," p. 88.
83. This account is drawn from several sources: Jim Erickson, "Tree Genes: UA Professor's DNA Work Helps Convict Killer," *The Arizona Daily Star*, May 28, 1993, Metro/Region Section, p. 1; and Tim Henderson, "Report on Analysis of Palo Verde Samples," University of Arizona, April 14, 1993.
84. Saferstein, *Criminalistics*, 5th ed., p. 438.
85. Ibid., p. 30.
86. Thorwald, *The Marks of Cain*, p. 161.
87. Ibid.
88. Thorwald, *The Century of the Detective*, pp. 418–419.
89. Ibid., p. 419.
90. Thorwald, *The Marks of Cain*, p. 164.
91. Ibid.
92. Thorwald, *The Century of the Detective*, p. 434.

LEGAL ASPECTS OF INVESTIGATION

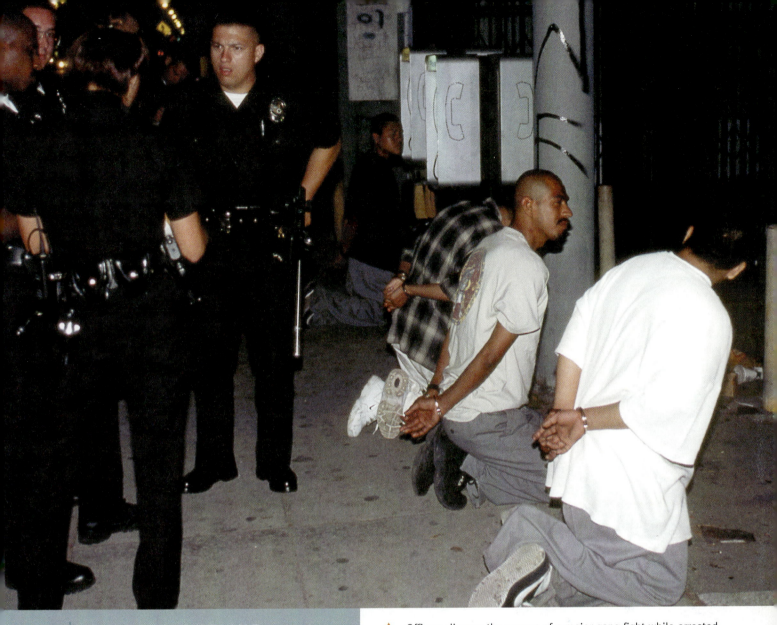

▲   Officers discuss the causes of a major gang fight while arrested gang members await transport to jail or youth centers. The suspects' handcuffed, kneeling, and facing away position enhances officer safety.

(© Michael Newman/PhotoEdit)

All law enforcement officers, uniformed and plainclothes, conduct investigations. That is a statement of fact. There are, of course, differing concentrations of the investigative process and varying responsibilities among different units and different people.

Every law enforcement officer must have a working knowledge of the criminal laws that he or she is charged with enforcing. The greater the knowledge, the better overall job one can do as an investigator. This will become apparent throughout the remainder of this text. It will be reinforced over and over because the criminal law is the foundation upon which every investigation is built.

Criminal law is divided into two major components that are interrelated yet serve different functions. The **substantive criminal law** deals with those elements that describe and define a crime. When an investigator has the needed proof to satisfy the particular elements of an offense, it can then be said that the crime did occur.

The other component of criminal law is **procedural criminal law.** It is not enough to know whether a crime has been committed. The investigator must understand what and how things need to be done with the people involved in an investigation, be it a victim, a witness, an informant, or a suspect. Thus, the procedural part of criminal law defines what can and cannot be done with, or to, people. The procedural law changes much more rapidly than does the substantive criminal law. Procedural law deals with processes of arrest, search and seizure, interrogations, confessions, admissibility of evidence, and testifying in court. Some of these topics will be discussed in other portions of this book because they are relevant to specific subject matter covered. Legal matters dealing with interrogations and confessions are dealt with in the chapter on interviews and interrogation. Rules regarding admissibility of evidence and testifying in court round out the book because these are important subjects to understand when an investigation is completed and the case is submitted for prosecution. This chapter concerns itself with the concepts of arrest and search and seizure. Knowing the current case law on these topics is not enough. The student must also understand the historical constitutional principles that got us to where we were, where we are today, and perhaps, where we are going tomorrow.

THE BILL OF RIGHTS AND THE STATES

An examination of constitutional history reveals that the powers yielded by the states were specifically granted for the purpose of establishing a national government. However, final ratification of the new constitution was delayed because some states wanted guarantees that individual liberties would be safeguarded from potential oppression by the newly formed government. This desire was based on the experiences of the colonists who supported the Declaration of Independence and fought the revolutionary war that won independence and created the United States of America, all of which occurred because the King of England was oppressing the colonies.

Congress of the United States
begun and held at the City of New-York, on
Wednesday the fourth of March, one thousand seven hundred and eighty nine

FIGURE 2-1 The Bill of Rights The Bill of Rights restricts actions only by the federal government.
(© The Granger Collection, New York)

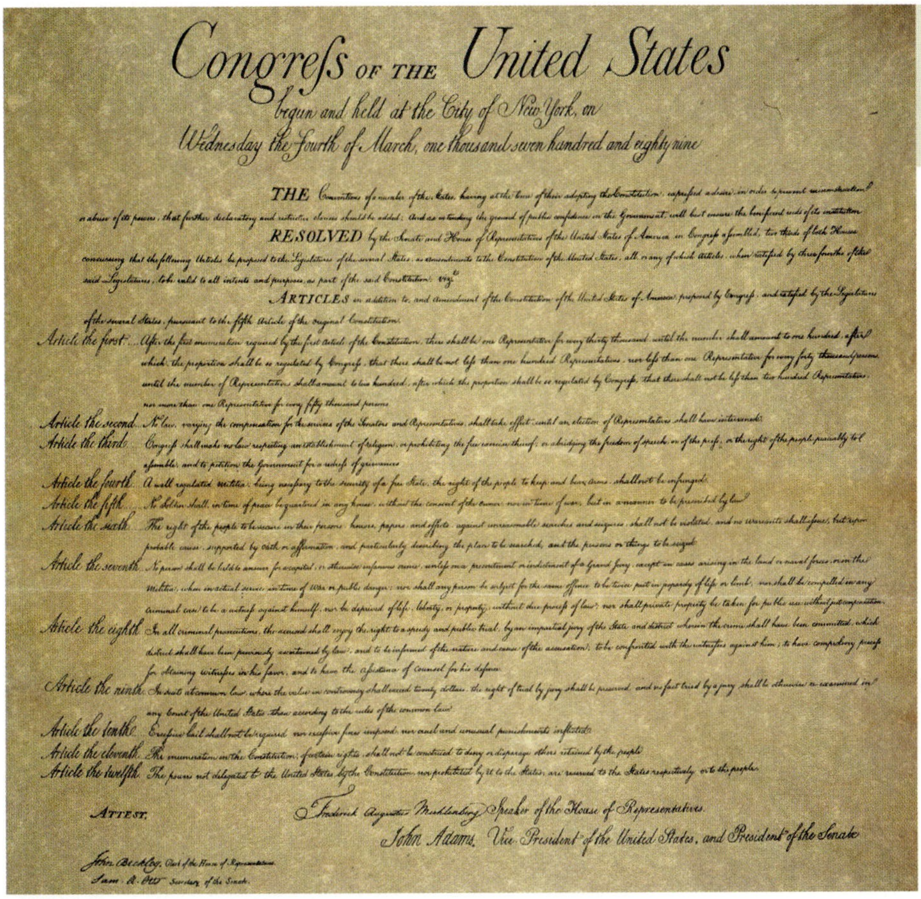

The guarantees came in the form of the first ten amendments to the Constitution known as the Bill of Rights. (See Figure 2-1.)

The Bill of Rights, however, restricts actions only by the federal government. It does not apply to, nor guarantee, the same protections from state governments. In addition, the Bill of Rights does not protect people from abuses by others who are not government officials or working on behalf of government officials. Thus, a private citizen could conduct an unreasonable search and seizure, then turn the results over to a government agency for use in court. Despite the fact that the seizing person may be criminally or civilly liable, the evidence seized could be used in court.[1]

The liberties protected by the specific clauses of the Bill of Rights are not exhaustive. One clause of the Fifth Amendment has been interpreted to leave the door open for additional protections. The **due process clause** provides, " . . . nor [shall any person] be deprived of life, liberty or property without due process of law." **Due process** is one of those concepts that has long been the subject of judicial controversy and has no universally accepted definition. The American concept of "fairness" is probably the closest one could get to an acceptable definition, in layman terms, without burdening the effort with reams of judicial history and philosophy. Thus the Supreme Court has the latitude to interpret the Constitution in any manner it deems to be fair and just under the American judicial system.[2]

During this time period and until the last part of the nineteenth century, the federal courts could insure fairness only in federal criminal proceedings.

Evolution of the Fourteenth Amendment

The Civil War was over. Slavery had been abolished. The Thirteenth, Fourteenth, and Fifteenth Amendments were all designed to guarantee the freedoms and equal protection of the laws for all citizens, especially the former slaves.

Interpretations given portions of the Fourteenth Amendment provide the foundation for much of modern criminal procedure in the United States today. The relevant portions of the Fourteenth Amendment read:

> No state shall make or enforce any law which shall abridge the privileges and immunities of citizens of the United States; nor shall any state deprive any person of life, liberty, or property, without due process of law; nor deny any person within its jurisdiction the equal protection of the laws.

The first three words of this quote provide the cornerstone to the foundation. Until this amendment was ratified in 1868, the people of the United States had never before granted the federal government the power to tell the states what they could or could not do. This section contains the Fourteenth Amendment's due process clause. This shift in power and authority was enhanced by another part of the Fourteenth Amendment. The first clause of Section 1 of the amendment reads:

> All persons born or naturalized in the United States, and subject to the jurisdiction thereof, are citizens of the United States and the state wherein they reside.

This wording creates what is commonly referred to as "dual citizenship" and gives the federal government the power to tell the states they cannot abuse the freedoms of those people—us; all of us.[3]

A few years after ratification of the Fourteenth Amendment, the United States Supreme Court was asked to determine the meaning of that amendment's due process clause. In the 1884 case of *Hurtado* v. *California*,[4] the defendant urged the Supreme Court to declare that the due process clause of the Fourteenth Amendment incorporated all the guarantees of the first eight amendments to the Bill of Rights. Hurtado was charged with a capital offense in the state court upon an Information filed by the District Attorney. He was convicted and sentenced to hang. The Fifth Amendment expressly requires that capital cases must be based on an indictment or presentment by a grand jury, but because Hurtado was being tried in a state court on a state charge, the Fifth Amendment was not applicable, as it would have been if he were being tried for a federal offense in federal court. He urged the high court to provide him the same guarantees in state court. This attempt to require carte blanche application of the first eight amendments to the states through the due process clause of the Fourteenth Amendment was rejected by a majority of the Court in this case and in many cases that followed. This attempted process became known as the "shorthand doctrine." The Supreme Court in rejecting the "shorthand doctrine" said that if the people and the states had intended for the Fourteenth Amendment to encompass the rights protected in the Bill of Rights and make them mandatorily applicable to the states, this would have been specified in the wording of the Fourteenth Amendment.[5]

Instead of adopting the "shorthand doctrine," the Supreme Court has reviewed cases on a case-by-case basis, determining whether the particular issue of the case calling into question a clause of the Bill of Rights should be made mandatorily applicable to the states through the due process clause of the Fourteenth Amendment. Although the Supreme Court rejected the quick way, the truth is, today, it doesn't matter anymore, because virtually everything in the first eight amendments has been ruled to apply to the states through the

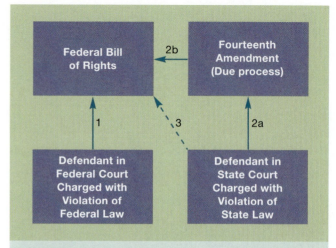

▲ **FIGURE 2-2   Federal and State constitutional relationships in criminal cases**
This chart represents the legal procedure a defendant would follow to claim a violation of constitutional rights in a criminal case. Line 1 represents a defendant claiming his rights in federal court directly from the Bill of Rights. Lines 2a and 2b are the correct procedure followed by an accused in a state court. Line 3 would be an incorrect attempt by a defendant to claim violation of constitutional rights directly from the protections guaranteed in the Bill of Rights.
(Source: Neil C. Chamelin, Vernon B. Fox, and Paul M. Whisenand, Introduction to Criminal Justice, 2nd Edition, Copyright 1979, reprinted with permission of Pearson Education, Inc., Upper Saddle River, NJ)

due process clause of the Fourteenth Amendment. It is still important to understand the relationship between the federal government and the states with respect to the Fifth and Fourteenth Amendments to the Constitution of the United States of America.[6] This relationship is diagramed in Figure 2-2.

Let's now look at some of these processes as they have evolved.

The Fourth Amendment

In part, the Fourth Amendment reads:

> The Right of the people to be secure in their persons, houses, papers, and effects, against unreasonable searches and seizures, shall not be violated, and no warrants shall issue, but upon probable cause, supported by oath or affirmation, and particularly describing the place to be searched, and the persons or things to be seized.

It is a common misconception that search and seizure is the sole topic covered by the Fourth Amendment. However, the authority for the laws of arrest is also derived from this amendment, as is seen in the last clause that provides, *and the persons . . . to be seized.*[7]

By strict construction of the Fourth Amendment, the only time an arrest can be made or a search and seizure be conducted is under the authority of a warrant. As will be seen in the following paragraphs, the courts have not been that stringent in their interpretation of this amendment.

ARREST

There are a number of definitions of the term **arrest.** They range from "any interference with a person which, if not privileged, would constitute false imprisonment," to "interfering with the freedom of a person who is suspected of criminal conduct to the extent of taking him to the police station for some purpose," to "the taking of custody upon sufficient and proper evidence for the purpose of prosecution."[8] Each of these definitions is valid and depends on context. For example, what may appear to be a simple street stop or field interrogation may, in fact, constitute an arrest according to the first definition. Taking a person to the police station or sheriff's department for interrogation may fit the second definition. When an investigator intends to incarcerate and charge a person with a crime, the third definition applies.

Ingredients of Arrest

There are three essential ingredients of an arrest:

1. Intention
2. Authority
3. Custody

The officer must have the intention of taking the suspect into custody. This factor distinguishes an arrest from a lesser form of detention, but actual or expressed intention is not always the controlling factor. The intention may be inferred by a court if its estimate of all the conduct and circumstances indicates that an arrest occurred, despite any contrary intent on the part of the law enforcement officer.

The officer must have real or assumed legal authority for taking the person into custody. The officer must have the actual authority to make a legal arrest or at least believe this to be the case. For example, an investigator may make an arrest under a defective warrant but not know about the defect. The third ingredient is that the person arrested must come within the custody and control of the law. This element can be satisfied either by physical restraint or by the arrestee's voluntary submission to the custody and control of the arresting officer.

Arrest Distinguished from Detention

Detention is a temporary and limited interference with the freedom of a person for investigative purposes. Some-times called investigative detention, it is also commonly referred to by law enforcement as a "street stop" or "field interrogation." In this instance, police are justified in employing **"stop and frisk"** measures—patting down the outer clothing—if they suspect that the person being questioned may be armed and their safety is in jeopardy.[9] This issue of "stop and frisk" is covered later near the end of the search and seizure section of this chapter.

There is a fine line between detention and arrest. Because an officer does interfere with the freedom of the individual stopped, even for only a few minutes, some theorists view any such action as constituting arrest. Most people and most courts recognize the validity of street stops and uphold them as not being arrests if conducted properly.

A valid detention must be brief and made for good reason. The officer must limit questioning and investigation and must then either release the subject or decide to arrest. Detention for an undue length of time could be construed as an arrest if later challenged in court.

Arrest Distinguished from Charging

As noted earlier, one definition of arrest is to interfere with the freedom of a person suspected of involvement in a crime to the extent that the person is taken to the police station. But investigators do not always intend to prosecute or have the ability to prosecute at that time. Formally **charging** a suspect with a crime does not automatically flow from an arrest. Charging follows a decision to prosecute. This decision may be made by the police, by the prosecutor, or by both. But they may also decide not to bring charges. For example, the evidence that justified the arrest may not be sufficient to warrant formal charges, because the prosecutor believes he or she cannot prove the case beyond, and to the exclusion of, every reasonable doubt. Perhaps additional information may come to light after the arrest that points to the accused's innocence. Maybe an arrest was unlawful or evidence was obtained in violation of constitutional standards.

Arrest Procedures

The laws of most jurisdictions permit an arrest in at least three and sometimes four types of situations:

1. When a warrant has been issued.
2. When a crime is committed in the presence of an arresting officer.
3. When an officer has probable cause to believe that the suspect being arrested has committed a felony.
4. In statutorily created instances.

The Arrest Warrant

The most preferred method of effecting an arrest is under the authority of a warrant. In fact, if one were to read the constitutional requirements in their strictest sense, arrests can be justified only if made with a warrant. Of course, the courts have chosen to be more liberal in their interpretation so that warrantless arrests can be made in certain situations. But there are sound reasons for both the warrant requirements and the exceptions created by judicial case law, and, in some instances, by legislation. In the U.S. constitutional system, the functions of government—executive, legislative, and judicial—are each the responsibility of a separate branch. The police function is an executive one, whereas the judicial responsibility obviously belongs to the courts. Although the mechanism of arrest is an executive function, it is subject to judicial scrutiny and review. This position is supported by the very wording of the Fourth Amendment to the U.S. Constitution:

> . . . and no warrant shall issue, but upon probable cause, supported by oath or affirmation, and particularly describing the . . . person . . . to be seized.

The two major benefits derived from securing prior judicial approval for arrests through the warrant process are that the approval relieves law enforcement of the burden of proving the legality of the arrest—so that officers need not fear charges of false arrest, malicious prosecution, or other civil suits—and it provides for an independent evaluation of the evidence.

Even the most objective, well-trained, and well-intentioned investigators sometimes become so involved in a case that their involvement may affect their ability to evaluate the case's merits objectively. Presenting the case before a qualified judge has the benefits of allowing an independent third party, with no emotional involvement in the investigation and with the knowledge of legal standards that must be met, to assist the investigator in determining whether those standards have been achieved. It is also logical to assume that the validity of an arrest made after this review and the issuance of a warrant is more likely to be upheld if later challenged in court than an arrest based solely on an officer's own determination of the sufficiency of the evidence. The wise law enforcement officer recognizes the value of obtaining a warrant whenever practical. The word "practical" has significance with regard to the propriety of securing an arrest warrant. The law recognizes that the innumerable situations encountered by law enforcement officers in daily activities and the variety of conditions inherent in the nature of the law enforcement function make it impossible and unrealistic to expect an officer to obtain a warrant in every situation before effecting an arrest—hence, the exceptions to the warrant requirement.

The procedure required for obtaining a warrant is often time-consuming and inconvenient. Frequently, the process in major felony cases requires that the investigator seek out the prosecutor; present the facts, which will be reduced to paper in affidavit form for a probable cause determination; find a judge who is authorized to issue warrants; present the case again for a determination of the sufficiency of the grounds for arrest; and then wait for the warrant to be typed up and signed. In many cases, the procedure can take several hours, even during the normal workday. On weekends and late at night, it may take even longer, as the prosecutor, judge, or both are located or roused from bed. As a consequence, officers sometimes tend to take the easy way out by making a warrantless arrest, hoping they are right and believing they have sufficient grounds to act. By conducting themselves in this manner, they neglect the basic rule of thumb—get a warrant—and its underlying rationale. But the warrantless arrest is not always a shortcut. As clear as the law may appear to be on the need for warrants, each case must rest on its own facts. There are relatively few cases in which it is obvious that an arrest can be made without a warrant. Similarly, the clear-cut instances for which a warrant is absolutely needed are relatively few. The majority of cases fall within that vast plane requiring evaluation of the merits of each case. An arrest without a warrant, however, does not save time. In reality, the time an officer spends on justifying this decision in motion hearings demanded by the defense attorney will equal or exceed the time it would have taken to get a warrant in the first place. The potential consequence is that the case may be dismissed for want of a valid arrest or that important evidence, seized as a result of the arrest, may be suppressed.

The investigator is not relieved of all responsibility for the legality of the arrest simply because a warrant was obtained. The investigator must be aware of what constitutes a valid warrant to ensure that the one he or she possesses permits a legal arrest.

An **arrest warrant** is a judicial order commanding the person to whom it is issued or some other person to arrest a particular individual and to bring that person promptly before a court to answer a criminal charge. The arrest warrant generally must be written. By legislation, some jurisdictions allow for verbal authorization supported by written authorization in warrant form that is issued later. (See Figures 2-3 and 2-4.)

In most cases, particularly major felonies, the warrant must be issued by a judge who personally reviews the facts to determine the existence of reasonable grounds as required by the Constitution. The warrant must be supported by an **affidavit**—a written statement of the information known to the officer that serves as the basis for the issuance of the warrant. In major cases, the requirements vary on whether the warrant must be issued in the county in which the offense occurred, but once issued, major case warrants can be served anywhere in the state.

The contents of a warrant are fairly standard and incorporate constitutional as well as statutory requirements. Most modern warrants, samples of which appear

▲ **FIGURE 2-3** **Review of affidavit for arrest warrant**
Photo 1 Investigator and judge review the paperwork prepared by the investigator in support of seeking the arrest warrant. (© Mike Karlsson/Arresting Images)

▲ **FIGURE 2-4** **Swearing or affirming to contents of affidavit for arrest warrant**
Photo 2 When the judge is satisfied that the arrest warrant affidavit is in order, and probable cause to arrest exists, he places the investigator under oath and the affidavit becomes a sworn document. (© Mike Karlsson/Arresting Images)

in Figures 2-5, 2-6, and 2-7, simply require that blanks be filled in.

The form and contents usually include:

1. The authority under which the warrant is issued (the name of the state).
2. The person who is to execute the warrant (generally addressed to any peace officer of the state).
3. The identity of the person to be arrested.
4. The designation of the offense.
5. The date, time, and place of the occurrence.
6. The name of the victim.
7. A description of the offense and how it occurred.

Blank warrants are not constitutionally valid. Before a warrant can be issued, the identity of the perpetrator must be known. The mere fact that a crime has been committed by someone unknown will not support a warrant's issuance. The Constitution requires that the warrant contain a particular description of the suspect. This description must be specific enough to permit an officer not acquainted with the case to identify the person to be arrested with reasonable certainty. Aliases may be used. If the suspect's name is not known, "John Doe" may be used provided there are other methods of describing the person to be arrested, such as place of residence, occupation, and a physical description.

A reprint of an Associated Press story appeared on the web on August 8, 2004, reporting that in Boston, prosecutors found a way to prevent the 15-year statute of limitations from destroying the possibility of bringing rapists to trial. In cases that have DNA evidence, prosecutors are obtaining indictments against "John Does" based on their DNA profiles. Massachusetts followed the lead of Wisconsin that started doing this in 1999. New York has also begun using the process. In a Wisconsin appellate case challenging the constitutionality of the statute claiming that the indictment does not specifically name the defendant, the court said that DNA evidence was the best method of identification available.

Crime Committed in Presence

Any offense committed in the presence of an officer, whether felony or misdemeanor, can be the basis of an arrest without a warrant. The in-presence requirement is usually thought of in the narrow context of sight. However, to satisfy the legal requirements, perception of some or all of the elements of an offense as they occur, through

FIGURE 2-5 Front of arrest warrant
(Source: Courtesy Geauga County, Ohio, Sheriff's Department)

National Graphics Corp., Cols., O.
Form No. M66-12

THE STATE OF OHIO

______________ Municipal Court

______________ County, Ohio
(City) (Name of County)

____
vs
____
Name
____
Address

No. ______________

WARRANT ON COMPLAINT
(Rule 4)

FORM VII

TO ______________
(officer authorized to execute a warrant)

A complaint, a copy of which is attached hereto, has been filed in this court charging
____
(describe the offense and state the numerical designation of the applicable statute or ordinance)
____
____

You are ordered to arrest ______________ (defendant) and bring (him)(her) before this court without unnecessary delay.

You (may) (may not) issue summons in lieu of arrest under Rule 4(A)(2) or issue summons after arrest under Rule 4(F) because ______________
(state specific reasons if issuance of summons restricted)
____

Special instructions to executing officer:

____
Judge—Officer designated by Judge(s)
Clerk—Deputy Clerk—Municipal Court

SUMMONS ENDORSEMENT
Use only in appropriate case

This warrant was executed / by arrest and / by issuing the following summons:

TO ______________
(defendant)

You are hereby summoned and ordered to appear at ______________ o'clock ____ .M.,
______________ (day), ______________ (month) (date), 19____, at the above captioned Court.
If you fail to appear at the time and place stated above you may be arrested.

____
Issuing Officer, Title
See Rule 4(A)(2) Rule 4(F) and Return Forms

NOTICE TO DEFENDANT: For information regarding your duty to appear call ______________
(fill in telephone number(s))

The address of the Court is: ______________

the use of any or all of the five senses—sight, hearing, taste, touch, or smell—can justify a warrantless arrest.

Probable Cause

The third major category in which a lawful arrest is generally permitted involves offenses not committed in the officer's presence and for which a warrant has not been issued. The law allows an officer to make warrantless arrests in felony cases provided reasonable grounds or probable cause exists to make the arrest. (See Figure 2-8.) (As previously noted, probable cause also must be shown in an affidavit to support the issuance of a warrant.)

RECEIPT OF WARRANT BY EXECUTING AUTHORITY

First Receipt

Received this warrant on _____, 19____,

at_____o'clock____m.

_____
Officer

By_____
Title

Subsequent Receipt

Received this (alias) (warrant) on _____,

19____, at_____o'clock____m.

_____
Officer

By_____
Title

****

RETURN OF EXECUTED WARRANT

Fees

Mileage $_____

_____

_____

_____

Total $_____

1. Execution By Arrest

I received this warrant on _____, 19_____, at

_____o'clock _____m. On _____, 19_____, I

arrested_____and gave / him/her / a copy of this warrant with

complaint attached and brought / him/her / to_____
state the place

_____
Arresting Officer, Title

Fees

Mileage $_____

_____

_____

_____

Total $_____

2. Execution By Issuance Of Summons Under Rule 4(A)(2) By Executing Officer

I received this warrant on _____, 19_____, at

_____o'clock _____m. On _____, 19_____, I

executed this warrant by issuing_____a summons by / personal

service / residence service / which ordered him/her to appear at_____
time

_____at the captioned Court. The sum-
day   date   room

mons was endorsed upon the warrant and accompanied by a copy of the complaint.

_____
Issuing Officer, Title

Fees

Mileage $_____

_____

_____

_____

Total $_____

3. Execution By Arrest And Issuance Of Summons Under Rule 4(F) By Arresting Officer

I received this warrant on _____, 19_____, at

_____o'clock _____m. On _____, 19_____, I

arrested_____and after arrest I issued him/her a summons by

personal service which ordered him/her to appear at captioned Court at_____
time

_____. The sum-
day, date, room

mons was endorsed upon the warrant and accompanied by a copy of the complaint.

_____
Arresting-Issuing Officer, Title

4. Execution By Arrest And Issuance Of Summons Under Rule 4(F) By Superior Of Arresting Officer

On _____, 19_____, _____was arrested by_____
name of arresting officer

and I issued_____a summons by personal service which ordered / him/her / to appear at

_____
time, day, date, room

at the captioned Court. The summons was endorsed upon the warrant and accompanied by a copy of the complaint.

_____
Issuing Officer, Title

****

RETURN OF UNEXECUTED WARRANT

Fees

Mileage $_____

_____

_____

_____

Total $_____

I received this warrant on _____, 19_____, at

_____o'clock _____m. On _____, 19_____, I

attempted to execute this warrant but was unable to do so because_____

_____
state specific reason or reasons and

_____
additional information regarding defendant's whereabouts

_____
Executing Officer, Title

****

RETURN OF UNEXECUTED WARRANT

Fees

Mileage $_____

_____

_____

_____

Total $_____

I received this warrant on _____, 19_____, at

_____o'clock _____m. On _____, 19_____, I

attempted to execute this warrant but was unable to do so because_____

_____
state specific reason or reasons and

_____
additional information regarding defendant's whereabouts

_____
Executing Officer, Title

◀ **FIGURE 2-6 Return of executed warrant**

(Source: Courtesy Geauga County, Ohio, Sheriff's Department)

Probable cause is a difficult term to define because in no two instances are circumstances identical. One acceptable definition of **probable cause** is that it is more than suspicion but less than actual knowledge. It is suspicion plus facts and circumstances that would lead a reasonable person exercising ordinary caution to believe that a crime has been, is being, or is about to be committed (see Figure 2-9).

Probable cause may be based on a number of sources of information, not all of which have to be the kind of evidence admissible at trial. However, if prosecution is an aim of the arrest, there must also be sufficient evidence to take the case to court. In addition, the probable cause must exist at the time the arrest is made and may not be developed by subsequently acquired evidence.

FIGURE 2-7 Application for complaint
(Source: Courtesy Boston Police Department)

APPLICATION FOR COMPLAINT NUMBER

Trial Court of Massachusetts
Boston Municipal Court Department

☐ ARREST ☐ HEARING ☐ SUMMONS ☐ WARRANT

The within named complainant requests that a complaint issue against the within named defendant, charging said defendant with the offense(s) listed below.

Boston Municipal Court
Criminal Division, Room 411 —
Fourth Floor, New Court House
Boston, MA 02108

DATE OF APPLICATION	DATE OF OFFENSE	PLACE OF OFFENSE

NAME, ADDRESS AND ZIP CODE OF COMPLAINANT

NAME, ADDRESS AND ZIP CODE OF DEFENDANT

NO.	OFFENSE	G.L. Ch. and Sec.
1.		
2.		
3.		
4.		

IF ADDITIONAL OFFENSES CHECK HERE. ☐ AND ATTACH.

DEFENDANT IDENTIFICATION INFORMATION — Complete data below if known.

C.C. #	DATE OF BIRTH	SEX	RACE	HEIGHT	WEIGHT	EYES	HAIR	SOCIAL SECURITY NUMBER

COURT USE ONLY ⟶ A hearing upon this complaint application will be held at the Boston Municipal Court, Rm. 411 on DATE OF HEARING AT TIME OF HEARING ⟵ COURT USE ONLY

CASE PARTICULARS — BE SPECIFIC

NO.	NAME OF VICTIM Owner of property, person assaulted, etc.	DESCRIPTION OF PROPERTY Goods stolen, what destroyed, etc.	VALUE OF PROPERTY Over or under $100.	TYPE OF CONTROLLED SUBSTANCE OR WEAPON Marijuana, gun, etc.
1				
2				
3				
4				

OTHER REMARKS:

X ____________________
SIGNATURE OF COMPLAINANT

IF PROCESS IS ORDERED, THIS APPLICATION MUST BE PRESENTED AT ONCE TO PLEADING CLERK AT ROOM 411

NAMES OF WITNESSES	Recog. to S.C.	Give place of business or employment, if in Boston, otherwise, residence	ST. NO.

COMPLAINANT'S COPY

State if defendant is arrested ____________ Date of Arrest ____________

BMC-CR-2 (5/85) **FOR ADDITIONAL REMARKS OR WITNESSES-USE REVERSE OF ORIGINAL AND CHECK HERE ☐**

Mere suspicion is not enough to justify an arrest; there must be supporting facts and circumstances. Certain factors may help to decide the existence of probable cause. The most common is the personal knowledge of the officer/investigator. Information obtained from informants also may be of value, although that information may not be admissible at a subsequent hearing or trial. The investigator must be able to establish the reliability of the information and the informant by indicating the length of time the investigator has known or dealt with the informant, the general character and reputation of the informant, the number of tips received from the informant in the past, the accuracy of previous information, whether the informant is paid for the information, and the informant's motives for volunteering the information. One of the current common instances is the use of confidential informants to make drug buys.

Other sources of probable cause include information from a police department or from other law enforcement agencies, such as notice of outstanding warrants, the past criminal record of the suspect, physical evidence found at the scene of the crime, other evidence detected in the follow-up investigation, crime laboratory analyses, and reports of victims and eyewitnesses.

There is a third exception to the warrant requirement for a valid arrest. By legislation, states allow officers to make arrests in nonfelony cases even though the offense is not committed in the officer's presence. Examples include domestic violence situations, violations of injunctions against domestic violence, and cases of battery.[10]

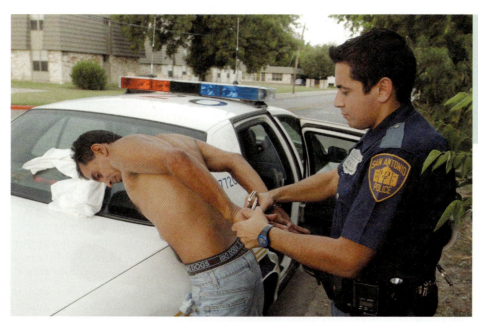

◄ FIGURE 2-8   Placing felon under arrest
A San Antonio, Texas, police officer arrests a person he has probable cause to believe just committed a felony battery. (© Bob Daemmrich/ PhotoEdit)

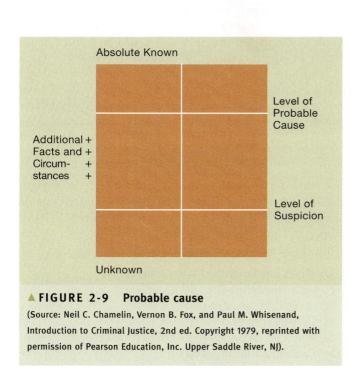

▲ FIGURE 2-9   Probable cause

(Source: Neil C. Chamelin, Vernon B. Fox, and Paul M. Whisenand, Introduction to Criminal Justice, 2nd ed. Copyright 1979, reprinted with permission of Pearson Education, Inc. Upper Saddle River, NJ).

SEARCH AND SEIZURE

The evolution of the law of **search and seizure** illustrates the relationship described earlier between federal and state court systems and between the Bill of Rights and its application to the states through the due process clause of the Fourteenth Amendment.[11]

Under early English common law, an illegal search and seizure that produced incriminating evidence was allowed, and the evidence obtained was admissible in court. Surprisingly, federal law enforcement officers in the United States were permitted to follow the same rule until 1914. Up to that time, the search and seizure practices of federal officials had not been scrutinized in light of the wording of the Fourth Amendment. In 1914, the case of Weeks v. United States[12] was decided by the United States Supreme Court. Weeks was charged by federal agents with using the mails for transporting materials that represented chances in a lottery. After his arrest for this federal offense, Weeks's room was searched twice without the authority of a valid search warrant. But Weeks had been arrested at his place of employment, not his home. During the **search,** the agents found and seized various incriminating papers and articles. This evidence was admitted at his trial for the federal violation, and Weeks was convicted. On appeal to the United States Supreme Court, the Court established what became known as the "Federal Exclusionary Rule." The Court ruled that any evidence unreasonably obtained by federal law enforcement officers could no longer be admissible in federal prosecutions. The Court made it quite clear that, because this was a federal case, the decision was applicable only to federal law enforcement officers and federal courts and was in no way applicable to the states. But this decision, as do many Supreme Court decisions, left a number of unanswered questions. Out of one question arose the "Silver Platter Doctrine." The Weeks decision prohibited federal officers from illegally seizing evidence but it did not prevent law enforcement officers of the states from illegally seizing the evidence and handing it over to federal agents on a "silver platter" for use in federal courts. This method of circumventing the Federal Exclusionary Rule remained unchallenged until 1960. In that year, the Supreme Court prohibited the introduction in federal courts of all illegally seized evidence obtained by state officers in violation of the Fourth Amendment.[13]

After the *Weeks* decision, very few states adopted their own exclusionary rule applicable within their own state. It was not until 1949 that a serious attempt was made to seek mandatory application of the exclusionary rule to the states through the due process clause of the Fourteenth Amendment. In *Wolf* v. *Colorado*,[14] the defendant was charged with abortion. Based on suspicion of similar prior offenses, officers searched Wolf's office, arrested him, and seized certain documents that were later admitted into trial. Wolf appealed his conviction contending that the unreasonable search and seizure was a denial of due process under the Fourteenth Amendment, as it would be under the Fourth Amendment had he been in federal court. The Supreme Court held that unreasonable searches and seizures by state officials in state cases did not constitute a denial of Fourteenth Amendment due process but added that the Court did have the authority to rule otherwise if the Justices so desired. The interesting point in this case seemed to be that the Court was giving the states fair warning that they disapproved of unreasonable searches and seizures by state authorities and that sooner or later they would rule in favor of incorporating the Fourth Amendment protection in the due process clause of the Fourteenth Amendment. Many states took the hint.

By 1961, only 18 states had not adopted an exclusionary rule. In that year, the warning that the Supreme Court had given 12 years earlier in the *Wolf* case came to pass. In May 1957, three Cleveland police officers arrived at Dolree Mapp's residence in that city with information that a person who was wanted for questioning in a recent bombing was hiding out in her home and that there was a large amount of gambling paraphernalia being hidden in the home. The officers knocked on the door and demanded entrance, but Ms. Mapp, after telephoning her attorney, refused to admit them without a search warrant. The officers advised their headquarters of the situation and undertook a surveillance of the house. Some three hours later, the officers, with reinforcements, again sought entrance. When Ms. Mapp did not come to the door immediately, one of the doors was forcibly opened and the officers gained entry. Ms. Mapp demanded to see the search warrant. One of the officers held up a paper that he claimed was the search warrant. She grabbed the paper and stuffed it down the front of her dress. A struggle ensued in which the officers recovered the piece of paper and handcuffed Ms. Mapp for her "belligerency" in resisting the attempt to recover the "warrant." A subsequent widespread search of the entire premises disclosed obscene materials. Ms. Mapps was convicted for possession of these materials. No search warrant was ever produced at the trial.

Following Ms. Mapp's conviction and the denial of her appeals in the state courts, her case was appealed to the United States Supreme Court. *Mapp* v. *Ohio*,[15] decided in 1961, established the rule that any evidence unreasonably searched and seized would no longer be admissible in any court—state or federal. The Exclusionary Rule was now applicable in all courts at all levels.

Among the many unanswered questions created by the *Mapp* decision, the crucial question revolved around the definition of the word **unreasonable.** It did not take the state courts long to find the loophole. In order to avoid applying the decision in the *Mapp* case to instances arising in state courts, state officials merely called previously unreasonable searches and seizures reasonable searches. Because no standards had been set for determining what constitutes a reasonable or unreasonable search, many of the state courts felt free to make their own determination on this issue. In effect, *Mapp* had little impact on these states. However, within two years of the *Mapp* decision, the Supreme Court had the opportunity to rule on this matter. The Court held in *Ker* v. *California*[16] that the state court judges were still free to determine the reasonableness of searches but that in making those determinations they would now be guided by the same standards as had been followed in the federal courts, which were established in the line of cases decided since the *Weeks* case in 1914. In essence, the Court said that states would be held to federal standards in search and seizure matters.

The long line of cases evolving since *Mapp* and *Ker* have essentially revolved around the single issue of what constitutes a reasonable search in instances where law enforcement officers act with or without a warrant.

Legal Searches and Seizures

As is true for arrests, the Fourth Amendment also recognizes searches and seizures only by government agents under the authority of a warrant. The United States Supreme Court recognizes judicially created exceptions. Thus, legal searches and seizures can be made:

1. When a warrant has been issued.
2. With consent.
3. Incident to an arrest.
4. Of a motor vehicle.
5. When an emergency (exigent circumstances) exists.
6. To conduct an inventory.

There are two additional areas that are closely related but can't truly be called searches and seizures—plain view seizures and stop and frisk encounters. These will also be covered.

Search with a Warrant

A **search warrant** is a written order, in the name of the state, signed by a judicial officer, exercising proper authority, and directing a law enforcement officer to search for certain specific property and bring it before the court. To be valid, the warrant must be signed by one who is authorized to sign. Normally, this is a judicial officer. In rare instances, state law may allow a prosecutor or law

Approved, SCAO

Original affidavit - Issuing court
1st copy - Prosecutor

AFFIDAVIT FOR SEARCH WARRANT

Please type or press hard   *See other side for instructions*   Police Agency Report Numer: _____

_____ , affiant(s), state that:

1. The person, place, or thing to be searched is described as and is located at:

2. The PROPERTY to be searched for and seized, if found, is specifically described as:

3. The FACTS establishing probable cause or the grounds for search are:

This affidavit consists of _____ pages.

Affiant

Subscribed and sworn to before me on _____
                                         Date

_____ Court

Review on _____
              Date

by _____
      Prosecuting official

_____
Judge/Magistrate

MC 231 (6/04) **AFFIDAVIT FOR SEARCH WARRANT**

enforcement officer to sign the warrant to expedite the process but only after the facts and circumstances have been reviewed over the telephone by a judicial officer, being later subject to that judicial officer's signature. In no case is a prosecutor or law enforcement officer permitted to sign a warrant without that judicial review. The independent impartial review is what provides the warrant with validity.

A warrant to search must be based upon probable cause. In this instance, probable cause can best be defined as facts and circumstances that would lead a reasonable person to believe that the place to be searched and the things to be seized are to be found. The probable cause is established by a written affidavit prepared by the law enforcement officer/investigator, stating all those known facts and circumstances. (See Figure 2-10.) As is true for

an arrest warrant, probable cause may be established by any number of sources, including information supplied by informants. In drug cases, probable cause is often established by confidential informants who make repeated drug buys from a specific house or store. The affidavit is then presented to the judicial officer, who independently evaluates it and, if she or he finds it sufficient, issues the warrant. As is pretty evident from the process described so far, probable cause must be established before the warrant is issued. Anything found as a result of the service of the warrant cannot be used to establish the probable cause.

The search warrant must particularly describe the place to be searched. (See Figure 2-11.) Although the Constitution does not define "particularly," the description must be sufficient to distinguish the place from all others.

► **FIGURE 2-11   Search warrant**

Original warrant - Return to issuing court
1st copy - Prosecutor
2nd copy - Serve
3rd copy - Issuing judge

Approved, SCAO

SEARCH WARRANT

TO THE SHERIFF OR ANY PEACE OFFICER:

Police Agency
Report Numer: _____

_____ , has sworn to the affidavit regarding the following:

1. The person, place, or thing to be searched is described as and is located at:

2. The PROPERTY to be searched for and seized, if found, is specifically described as:

IN THE NAME OF THE PEOPLE OF THE STATE OF MICHIGAN: I have found that probable cause exists and you are commanded to make the search and seize the described property. Leave a copy of this warrant and a tabulation (a written inventory) of all property taken with the person from whom the property was taken or at the premises. You are further commanded to promptly return this warrant and tabulation to the court.

Issued: _____   _____
        Date   Judge/Magistrate   Bar no.

RETURN AND TABULATION

Search was made _____ and the following property was seized:
                Date

☐ Continued on reverse side

_____
Officer

Copy of warrant and tabulation served on: _____
                                          Name

Tabulation filed: _____
                 Date
MC 231 (6/04) **AFFIDAVIT AND SEARCH WARRANT**

Normally, one might think of a building on a piece of property as a place to be searched. Using the legal description is not necessary but, on the other hand, a street address may not be sufficient. There are many appellate cases involving invalid warrants because the address failed to distinguish between two identical numbers on houses on "Main Street" because one was on "North Main" and the other on "South Main." In addition, numbers may be missing from the house or mailbox causing problems. What happens when a warrant is issued for "999 Main Street" but the numbers have come loose and flipped over at "666 Main Street" and now read "999"? Have investigators ever served a warrant at the wrong location? The appellate cases are full of examples. The warrant should contain information such as the color of the house, the type of floorplan (i.e., ranch style home); apartment on the third floor, east side of a brownstone tenement; cream colored, vinyl siding, one story house with green trim, green shutters, an American flag on a pole in the front yard, and so forth.

The phrase "particularly describe" also applies to the things to be seized. This governs the extent of the search. For example, if the affidavit and warrant are for the search and seizure of drugs in a house, the search can be pretty extensive. Thus, it would be permitted to search closets, under beds, in dresser drawers, in medicine cabinets, and in kitchen cupboards—and anything found, even evidence of other crimes, may be properly seized and considered admissible. For example, the search turns up a firearm; but the occupant of the house, being a previously convicted felon, is not allowed to possess firearms. The discovery of the weapon could be the legal basis for adding a charge of illegal possession of a firearm. But if the warrant is based on the belief that the house contains stolen tires, the places that can legally be searched in that same house are significantly reduced. A search of dresser drawers, kitchen cupboards, and medicine cabinets would be improper, and, if the firearm in the previous example is found under the pillow on the bed occupied by the suspect, its seizure would be improper unless the investigator could convince the court, during a hearing on a motion to suppress the seizure of the firearm, that the investigator reasonably believed there might have been a stolen tire under the pillow.

In another example, a law enforcement officer went outside the scope of his authority to search when, with consent, while searching for a stolen boat motor and a shotgun, picked up and opened a tackle box that contained drugs and drug paraphernalia. This served as the basis for charging. The court stated there was no reasonable belief the boat motor or shotgun was in the tackle box.[17]

Normally, investigators should include in their affidavits in support of a search warrant the justification for searching persons found at the place where the warrant is to be executed and the search conducted. In the absence of such authority in the warrant, persons found on the scene may not be searched unless they are first lawfully arrested.

Once issued, a warrant must be executed within whatever time limits the law of the state requires; time of day/night limits are applicable. In some instances, the warrant may specify that it may be served at nighttime if the probable cause supporting the warrant can justify that the specific criminal activity only occurs at night. Until recently, state laws required officers/investigators executing warrants to knock, announce their purpose and the fact that they were in possession of a warrant, and giving the occupants a reasonable time to answer and open the door. (See Figure 2-12.) In 2006, the Supreme Court ruled in *Hudson* v. *Michigan*[18] that violation of the knock and announce requirement for the service of a search warrant will no longer result in the suppression of evidence found during execution of the search warrant. The Court said the social cost of applying the exclusionary rule to knock and announce violations was considerable.

During the search, particularly if several investigators are involved, one investigator should be designated the property custodian. A detailed record must be kept of each piece of evidence, with a specific description, where it was found, and by whom. This list then becomes part of the return on the warrant that must be brought back and presented to the judge for review. It, of course, also becomes part of the case file. (See Figure 2-13.)

In 2005 in *Muehler* v. *Mena*,[19] the Supreme Court held that officers executing a search warrant of a house seeking

▲ FIGURE 2-12   **Preparing to serve a search warrant**
An investigator and a uniformed officer, each positioned to react if trouble should occur, are the advance party for the service of a search warrant. Other investigators wait to see if anyone inside opens the door. (© Tony Savino/The Image Works)

weapons and evidence of gang membership in the wake of a drive-by shooting acted reasonably by detaining the occupants of the house in handcuffs during the search, especially since there were only two officers to watch over four people.

Search with Consent

One of the most common situations arising today is when a uniformed officer, in encountering a citizen during a traffic stop or other routine activity, asks the person if they have any weapons or drugs on their person or in their vehicle. Sometimes the person says yes, and that might lead to an immediate arrest. Often, the person says no, and the officer may then ask if he/she can search the person and/or the vehicle. If the person gives affirmative consent, the search may be conducted. If the person denies consent, which he/she has the right to do, no search may be made unless there is probable cause to conduct a search under one of the other exceptions to the warrant requirement. A refusal to allow a search, standing

▶ **FIGURE 2-13 Investigators conducting a search**
Investigators conduct an office search. Note that while one of the investigators searches, another records the location where each piece of evidence was found, and a third officer packages and marks each piece of evidence. All these steps are important in maintaining and protecting the chain of custody. (© Mike Karlsson/Arresting Images)

alone, does not constitute probable cause to justify any further action.

The crux of a consent search is that the consent must be voluntarily given. It can't be based on intimidation or threats of any kind.

A person may give consent to the search of his/her home, but in the case where there are roommates living in the same house or apartment and each has his or her own bedroom, an occupant may give consent to the search only of his or her private room and any area shared in common by the roommates, such as the kitchen or living room.

Once consent is given for search of a home, car, office, or any other place, it may be withdrawn at any time by the person who had the authority and gave the consent. When consent is withdrawn, the search must stop. Any incriminating evidence found after consent is withdrawn is illegally seized and is not admissible.

Search Incident to Arrest

The courts have regularly recognized the right of law enforcement officers to search people who have been arrested without a warrant. Such searches are justified for officer safety and to preserve evidence.[20] In 1969, the United States Supreme Court limited the scope of a search when it ruled in *Chimel* v. *California*[21] that a warrantless search of the defendant's entire house, following his lawful arrest in the house on a burglary charge, was unreasonable. This case set the benchmark for searches incident to a valid arrest by holding that such searches may be made of the person arrested and the area under his/her immediate control from which he or she might obtain a weapon or destroy evidence. Initially, searches were reasonable only if conducted in conformity with

Chimel. Over the years, case law has expanded the allowable area of search following a legal arrest, particularly as applied to automobile searches, but as to searches of an arrestee's home, *Chimel* is still followed closely. In *Maryland* v. *Buie*,[22] a 1990 case, the Supreme Court reported that:

> Two men committed an armed robbery. The police obtained warrants for their arrest. Buie was one of the people to be arrested. The officers went to Buie's home to arrest him. When they entered, they found Buie coming from the basement. That is where he was arrested. One of the officers went into the basement, allegedly on a protective sweep, to make sure no one else was down there. While in the basement he saw "in plain view" a red running suit that matched the description of clothing that witnesses said one of the robbers was wearing. The officer seized the suit and it was used in evidence to help convict Buie.

The Supreme Court said that:

> . . . as an incident to the arrest of the accused, the officers could, as a precautionary measure and without a search warrant, probable cause, or reasonable suspicion, look in closets and other spaces immediately adjoining the place of arrest from which an attack could be immediately launched . . .[23]

As to conducting protective sweeps, the Supreme Court went on to say:

> . . . beyond that, the Fourth Amendment permits a warrantless protective sweep in conjunction with an in-home arrest—extending only to a cursory inspection

of those spaces where a person may be found, lasting no longer than is necessary to dispel the reasonable suspicion of danger, and in any event no longer than it takes to complete the arrest and depart the premises—when the searching officer possesses a reasonable belief based on specific and articulable facts which, taken with the rational inferences from those facts, would warrant a reasonably prudent officer in believing that the area to be swept harbors an individual posing a danger to those on the arrest scene.[24]

The Court made it clear that the officers had the right, pursuant to the arrest warrant, to search anywhere in the house, even the basement, until they found Buie.[25]

Search of a Motor Vehicle

The search of a motor vehicle, sometimes referred to as the automobile exception to the requirement that a search be conducted with a warrant, really involves two distinct legal issues under modern law. The first can be traced back to a 1925 Supreme Court case. In *Carroll* v. *United States*,[26] the Court created the "moveable vehicle" rule. The Court held that if there was sufficient probable cause to get a warrant, but, because the vehicle was moveable, it might be gone if time were taken to get a warrant, a warrantless search was justified. In this case, the vehicle was moving and contained bootleg whiskey during Prohibition. The search of the entire vehicle, including the trunk was justified in this case.

In *Chambers* v. *Maroney*[27] a service station was robbed by two armed men. About the time of the robbery, two teenagers saw a blue station wagon circling the block around the service station and later sped off with four men. The service station attendant described one of the robbers as wearing a green sweater and the other wearing a trench coat. Some time after, a vehicle fitting the description, carrying four men, one of whom was wearing a green sweater, was stopped. A trench coat was seen in the car. The occupants were arrested, and the car was searched without a warrant. The money, guns, and other evidence of the robbery were found. The Supreme Court approved of the search under the motor vehicle exception. The motor vehicle exception is still very viable.

In *Maryland* v. *Dyson*,[28] the Supreme Court continued to follow the ruling in *Carroll*. But it is not necessary that the vehicle actually be moving to justify such a warrantless search. Early on, the Supreme Court held that where a car was legally parked, agents did not have to speculate as to when the owner would return and whether there was time to obtain a search warrant.[29]

The second issue involves the search of a vehicle incident to a lawful arrest. Keeping in mind the foundation principle of the *Chimel* case, that a search may be made of the area under the arrestee's immediate control, the Supreme Court ruled in the 1981 case of *New York* v. *Belton*[30] that when a police officer makes a lawful custodial arrest of the occupant of an automobile, the officer may search the vehicle's passenger compartment as a contemporaneous incident of arrest. The right to search includes any open or closed containers found in the passenger compartment. It does not include the trunk.

On May 24, 2004, the Supreme Court decided *Thornton v. United States*.[31] In 2001, Officer Nichols was driving behind Thornton's Lincoln town car. He ran the town car's license plate. The response from DMV reported that the tag belonged on a 1982 Chevrolet. Before Nichols had a chance to pull the car over, Thornton drove into a parking lot, parked, and got out of his car. Officer Nichols saw Thornton leave his vehicle as he pulled in behind him. The officer parked, got out of his car, and accosted Thornton. He asked Thornton for his driver's license and told Thornton that the license plate did not match the vehicle to which it was properly assigned. Nichols then asked Thornton if he could pat him down. Thornton agreed. Nichols felt a bulge in Thornton's left front pocket and again asked him if he had any illegal narcotics on him. This time Thornton said that he did and pulled out two bags, one containing marijuana and the other crack cocaine. The officer handcuffed Thornton, informed him that he was under arrest, and put him in the back seat of the patrol car. Officer Nichols then searched the vehicle and found a 9-mm handgun under the driver's seat. Thornton was charged with federal firearms and drug offenses. He was convicted. His case was affirmed on appeal by the district court of appeals and then was appealed to the Supreme Court.

In brief, the Supreme Court said that the right to search the passenger compartment of a car still exists even if the officer does not make contact until the person arrested has left the vehicle. (See Figure 2-14.) The issue in this case asked the question on the reasonableness of the search whether the defendant was inside or outside the vehicle when first contacted and subsequently arrested. The opinion points out that the length of time the person had been out of the car and how far away from the vehicle the person was may all come into play in determining reasonableness of a search. Interestingly, in this case, the defendant had already been secured and was in the back seat of the patrol car when this search took place. This, of course, was pointed out by the dissenting Justices, who said there was no longer any chance to obtain a weapon or destroy evidence and the officer should have obtained a warrant before searching.

▶ **FIGURE 2-14** **Officer and investigator searching the passenger compartment of a motor vehicle** Uniformed officers search a vehicle in a warehouse district after making a major bust of cocaine traffickers. (© James Shaffer/PhotoEdit)

A vehicle search is not reasonable if conducted pursuant to stopping a vehicle for a traffic violation and writing a citation. A citation is not an arrest and no right to search arises.

Emergency (Exigent Circumstances)

The **exigent circumstances** exception recognizes that a warrantless entry by law enforcement officials may be legal when there is a compelling need for official action and no time to get a warrant. The exception covers several common situations including: danger of flight or escape, loss or destruction of evidence, risk of harm to the public or police, mobility of a vehicle (discussed earlier), and hot pursuit.[32] In *Warden* v. *Hayden*,[33] two taxi drivers reported seeing an armed robber run into a residence. Police arrived within minutes, entered the house without a warrant, found the defendant in an upstairs bedroom where he was arrested, and then conducted a search. They found and seized a shotgun and a pistol in the adjoining bathroom flush tank. They also seized a jacket and pants that were of the type witnesses said the robber was wearing. Hayden was convicted, and when the case reached the Supreme Court, it held the search and seizure was legal. The Court said that speed was essential to find out if other people were in the house who might be in danger and to protect the officers themselves by insuring they had possession of all weapons that could be used against them or to effect an escape. In all cases of exigent circumstances, there must be an emergency that justifies the warrantless search.

Officers responded to a residence after receiving two 911 calls saying that there was loud arguing and numerous

shots had been fired. Upon arrival, a husband and wife were on the porch of their mobile home. Officers, while behind their vehicle doors and with weapons drawn, ordered the people off the porch and told them to lie down with their palms facing up. After finally getting compliance and securing the pair along with a neighbor who appeared from the side of the house, officers entered the house to see if anyone was inside and hurt. In the process, when stepping on the porch, they found a shotgun leaning against the side of the mobile home about 3 feet from where the defendant had been standing and a number of expended shells on the porch and ground nearby. These were seized. The defendant was convicted of possession of a firearm by a convicted felon. He challenged the officers' actions of stepping on the porch as an illegal search.

When the case finally reached the Supreme Court, the search and seizure was upheld under exigent circumstances. The Court reasoned that there certainly was a reasonable belief by the officers that there might be injured people inside the home based on the multiple calls that shots had been fired. This emergency justified the warrantless entry and the seizure of the weapon that formed the basis of the charge.[34]

In 2006, in *Brigham City* v. *Stuart*,[35] the Supreme Court held that law enforcement officers may enter a home without a warrant where there is an objectively reasonable basis to believe that an occupant is seriously injured or imminently threatened with serious injury.

Speaking of balancing, consider the following situation: Police officers were called to accompany the defendant's wife to the couples' mobile home to remove some of her belongings. When she left the mobile home, she told the police chief, who happened to be one of

the officers on the scene, that her husband had "dope" inside and they may want to search. The chief knocked on the door, and when the husband answered and came outside, he told him what his wife said. The chief asked for the consent to search. Consent was refused by the husband. The chief sent one of his officers to get a search warrant. The husband/defendant was not allowed to go back in the house except to get a cigarette or make a phone call while being carefully watched by the chief. An officer returned within two hours with a search warrant, the execution of which turned up a small amount of marijuana and paraphernalia. The evidence was suppressed at every level of appellate court until it got to the high court.

The Supreme Court said there was probable cause to believe contraband was in the residence; that if left alone, there was good reason to believe the defendant would destroy the evidence; that law enforcement made reasonable efforts to balance the needs of law enforcement against the Fourth Amendment privacy guarantee; and that the restraint was limited to two hours. For these reasons, the Court said the demands of the Fourth Amendment were satisfied.[36]

Conducting an Inventory

Law enforcement agencies have not only the right but also the obligation to inventory property taken from a person arrested. This includes property taken from the person and from their presence, such as a motor vehicle. The inventory is done for the purpose of protecting the property of the person arrested and documenting what was found with a receipt given to the person arrested. In this manner, law enforcement can prevent accusations of stealing an offender's money or property. Similarly,

law enforcement should inventory a vehicle that was impounded pursuant to an arrest. This includes the contents of the trunk. (See Figure 2-15.) If contraband or evidence of a crime are found by virtue of a valid inventory search, the results are admissible. To justify admissibility of the fruits of an inventory search, the agency must have a standing policy that specifies the inventory in all cases. If such a policy does not exist, but this particular vehicle was inventoried, it will be ruled a pretext for a warrantless search and will be deemed unreasonable.

Plain View Seizures

If an investigator/officer is lawfully in a place and sees contraband or evidence in plain view, the investigator may seize the evidence, and it will be admissible. For example, investigators were called to a hotel room door because the occupant wanted to turn himself in on an outstanding warrant. When the defendant opened the door, officers could see crack cocaine lying on the counter inside the room. Their entry and seizure was lawful. Investigators are not required to turn their backs on a crime being committed in their presence. It is critical that the officer has a lawful right to be where she/he can see the evidence in plain view. An investigator on the street outside a house, who looks in a window and sees contraband can legally seize it, but if that same investigator is standing on a box, peering inside a window overlooking the backyard, without justification, he/she cannot expect any subsequent seizure to be upheld.

Consider this example: The men's restroom in a local club, frequented by young adults, is known for drug use. Users go in the stalls, lock the doors, and ingest cocaine.

▶ **FIGURE 2-16** **Officer frisking a suspicious person**

An officer conducts a "stop and frisk" of the outer clothing of a man to determine if he is armed, as authorized by *Terry* v. *Ohio*. This individual was driving on a back road near the Mexican border, acting very nervous, continually looking out the side window toward a distant point, and frequently checking his rearview mirror. (© Bob Daemmrich/The Image Works)

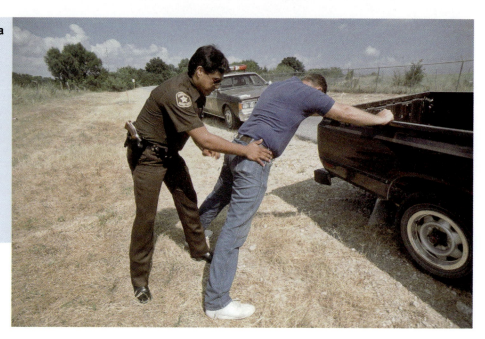

Off-duty, uniformed officers check out the whole club, including the men's room. Underneath the stall door they see an individual's feet turned sideways to the toilet. It's pretty obvious that the person is not using the toilet for its intended purpose. The officer looks through a crack between the stall door and the frame and sees the individual snorting cocaine. The officer tells the man to open the door, then arrests him for possession of cocaine. Whether this is a plain view seizure depends on two things. First, is a person in a public bathroom stall entitled to an expectation of privacy? Second, was the officer in a place where he had a lawful right to be when he viewed the offense? The answer to the first question is yes. A person does have a right to expect privacy in a bathroom stall. That's why there are stalls with doors on them. It doesn't matter that it was a restroom used by the public. The answer to the second question is a little trickier. If the opening between the door and the frame was small and, in order for the officer to see what was going on, he had to get right up to the door and peek in through the small space, this will likely be found to be an unwarranted invasion of privacy and in violation of the Fourth Amendment. However, if the space was large enough that anyone walking by might see what the accused was doing from a couple of feet away from the stall, there is no reasonable expectation of privacy, and a subsequent seizure would be reasonable.

Stop and Frisk

Earlier in this chapter, the stop and frisk topic was mentioned to distinguish arrest from detention. There is, of course, a search and seizure aspect to this concept. In *Terry* v. *Ohio*[37] (Figure 2-16), Cleveland Police Officer McFadden observed three men walking back and forth in front of a jewelry store. Believing the men were casing the store for commission of a crime, he approached them. The defendant, one of the three, was acting strangely and the officer, concerned for his own safety, patted down the defendant's outer clothing for weapons. The officer removed a pistol from the defendant's overcoat pocket. Over the defendant's objection, the weapon was introduced in evidence. The appellate process took the case to the Supreme Court. The defendant's challenge was that the officer conducted an unreasonable search because he did not first arrest Terry and there was no probable cause or exigent circumstances justifying a search. The Court ruled that under circumstances where a person is acting suspiciously and the officer is concerned about his own safety when approaching such an individual, the officer may pat down the outer clothing to determine if the person has a weapon even though there was no arrest. If a weapon is found, it may be seized, and, if its possession is a violation of the law, it is admissible in a subsequent proceeding. The Court said that officer safety in a detention situation justifies the frisk. The Court held that an officer cannot frisk for illegal drugs but only for weapons. If, however, the officer feels something that she/he believes might be a weapon but turns out to be contraband, it is admissible. However, if it is readily apparent that the item is not a weapon, its seizure is unreasonable. To illustrate, in the case of *Minnesota* v. *Dickerson*,[38] officers stopped the defendant whose actions were evasive when approached by police just after he left a building known for cocaine traffic. One officer conducted a pat down and found no weapon, but he did feel a lump in the defendant's jacket pocket. After feeling it and examining it with his fingers, the officer believed it to be crack cocaine. He reached into the pocket and withdrew a bag containing cocaine. The Supreme Court held that even

◄ **FIGURE 2-17 Investigator checking identification**
An investigator checks the identification of a young person in an abandoned house. Originally thought to be burglary suspects, these youths, it was discovered, were looking for a place to smoke marijuana. (© Kwame Zikomo/SuperStock)

though the detention and frisk were lawful under the *Terry* doctrine, it was obvious to the officer that the lump in the pocket was not a weapon. Therefore, the seizure of the cocaine was based on an unlawful search and should not have been admitted into evidence.

In an interesting collateral issue to a *Terry* stop, the Supreme Court, in 2004, upheld a conviction under a Nevada statute that requires a person to identify himself, when so requested, during a *Terry* stop. When the defendant refused to identify himself after 11 requests by the officer, he was arrested and charged with violating the statute.[39] In addition to Nevada, the following states have **stop and identify** statutes: Alabama, Arkansas, Colorado, Delaware, Florida, Georgia, Illinois, Kansas, Louisiana, Missouri, Nebraska, New Hampshire, New Mexico, New York, North Dakota, Rhode Island, Utah, Vermont, and Wisconsin.[40] (See Figure 2-17.)

Fruits of the Poisonous Tree

A final point is necessary to fully comprehend the consequences of an unreasonable search and seizure. The **fruits of the poisonous tree doctrine** provides that evidence obtained from an unreasonable search and seizure cannot be used as the basis for learning about or collecting new admissible evidence not known about before. Not only is the evidence obtained from the unreasonable search and seizure inadmissible, any evidence resulting from the unreasonably seized evidence is also tainted and is not admissible as fruits of the poisonous tree. This doctrine resulted from a 1963 decision of the high court in which a confession was obtained from the defendant after evidence was produced that had been obtained unreasonably.[41]

KEY TERMS

affidavit	due process clause	search and seizure
arrest	exigent circumstances	search warrant
arrest warrant	fruits of the poisonous tree doctrine	stop and frisk
charging	procedural criminal law	stop and identify
detention	probable cause	substantive criminal law
due process	search	unreasonable

REVIEW QUESTIONS

1. Define *arrest*.
2. Distinguish arrest from detention.
3. Distinguish arrest from charging.

4. What are the benefits to a police officer and the case if an arrest is made under the authority of a warrant?

5. Is a "John Doe" arrest warrant valid under any circumstances? Explain.
6. Define and describe *probable cause*.
7. During an ongoing criminal investigation, what factors must the criminal investigator consider in deciding whether to make an arrest and when to make it?
8. Explain how the laws of arrest and search and seizure flow from the Bill of Rights.
9. Distinguish the effects of the Fifth and Fourteenth Amendments on defendants in criminal cases.
10. List the requirements of a valid arrest warrant.
11. What is the Exclusionary Rule, and how did it evolve?
12. Describe the "Silver Platter" Doctrine. Is it still followed? Why or why not?
13. Under what circumstances may a search be conducted without a search warrant?

14. For what reasons do the courts allow searches incident to a lawful arrest?
15. What limitations have judicial cases placed on the search of a motor vehicle incident to a lawful arrest?
16. Give five examples justifying a search under exigent circumstances.
17. How does a law enforcement agency's policy affect the lawfulness of an inventory search of a motor vehicle?
18. What is meant by a plain view seizure, and what are the requirements for conducting such a seizure by a law enforcement officer?
19. What are the limitations on a law enforcement officer conducting a stop and frisk?
20. Explain the "fruits of the poisonous tree" doctrine.

INTERNET ACTIVITIES

1. Locate the requirements in two states for the legal issuance of a search warrant. These requirements can be found as a list or on a blank search warrant form. How alike or unalike are the two? What explanation do you have for your conclusion?
2. In this country and abroad, newspaper stories about defendants alleging unlawful arrest by police are not uncommon. Take three such stories from

this country and three from foreign countries and compare the fact situations for the arrest. Are there common denominators? For example, in some countries people are arrested because their speaking or writings are critical of a totalitarian government or "strong man" regime or they advocate for greater civil rights for citizens.

NOTES

1. Neil C. Chamelin, Vernon B. Fox, and Paul M. Whisenand, *Introduction to Criminal Justice*, 2nd ed. (Upper Saddle River, NJ: Prentice Hall, 1979), p. 236.
2. Ibid.
3. Ibid., pp. 236–237.
4. 110 U.S. 516 (1884).
5. Ibid., pp. 237–238.
6. Ibid., p. 238.
7. Ibid., p. 242.
8. Wayne LaFave, *Arrest: The Decision to Take a Suspect into Custody* (Boston: Little, Brown, 1965), pp. 3–4.
9. *Terry* v. *Ohio*, 392 U.S. 1 (1968).
10. See, for example, Section 901.15, Florida statutes, for these and other circumstances when arrest by an officer without a warrant is lawful.
11. The majority of this section is taken verbatim from Neil C. Chamelin, Vernon B. Fox, and Paul M. Whisenand, *Introduction to Criminal Justice*, 2nd ed. (Upper Saddle River, NJ: Prentice Hall, 1979), pp: 244–246.

12. 232 U.S. 383 (1914).
13. *Elkins* v. *United States*, 364 U.S. 206 (1960).
14. 338 U.S. 25 (1949).
15. 367 U.S. 643 (1961).
16. 374 U.S. 10 (1963).
17. *Jones* v. *State*, 895 So.2d 1246
18. *Hudson* v. *Michigan*, 126 S.Ct.2159 (2006).
19. *Muehler* v. *Mena*, 544 U.S. 93, 125 S.Ct. 1465 (2005).
20. *United States* v. *Robinson*, 414 U.S. 218 (1973).
21. 395 U.S. 752 (1969).
22. 494 U.S. 325 (1990).
23. *Maryland* v. *Buie*, 108 L.Ed.2d 276 (1990).
24. Ibid., p. 277.
25. Ibid., p. 283.
26. 267 U.S. 132 (1925).
27. *Chambers* v. *Maroney*, 399 U.S. 42 (1970).
28. 527 U.S. 465 (1999).
29. *Husty* v. *United States*, 282 U.S. 694 (1931).
30. 453 U.S. 454 (1981).
31. 75CrL 177 (U.S. 2004).

32. *United States* v. *Halloway,* 290 F.3d 1331 (C.A. 11 (Ala.) (2002). See also *Johnson* v. *United States,* 333 U.S. 10, 14–15 (1948), listing situations falling within exigent circumstances exception.
33. 387 U.S. 294 (1967).
34. *United States* v. *Holloway,* 290 F.3d 1331 (C.A 11 (Ala.) (2002).
35. *Brigham City* v. *Stuart,* 126 S.Ct. 1943 (2006).
36. *Illinois* v. *McArthur,* 531 U.S. 326 (2001).
37. 392 U.S. 1 (1968).
38. 508 U.S. 366 (1993).
39. *Hiibel* v. *Sixth Judicial Circuit Court of Nevada,* 124 S.Ct. 2451 (2004).
40. Ibid., pp. 2457–2458.
41. *Wong Sun* v. *United States,* 371 U.S. 471 (1963).

3

INVESTIGATORS, THE INVESTIGATIVE PROCESS, AND THE CRIME SCENE

▲ Police Officers in Silver Springs, Maryland using the line method of crime scene searching in an attempt to locate evidence at the Home Depot. It was at this location that the D.C. sniper murdered Linda Franklin, who was employed as an FBI analyst. Her selection as a victim was random and not related to her profession.

(© AP/Wide World Photos)

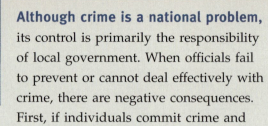

Although crime is a national problem, its control is primarily the responsibility of local government. When officials fail to prevent or cannot deal effectively with crime, there are negative consequences. First, if individuals commit crime and escape prosecution, future illegal acts are encouraged. Second, a continuing crime rate requires that resources, which could be devoted to other social problems, be diverted to crime control, resulting in further entrenchment of such ills as poverty, substandard housing, and inadequate medical care. Third, as crime increases, our system of government faces the real possibility of a crisis of confidence in its ability to maintain public welfare. Finally, crime tears the fabric of social relations and living patterns. People become fearful of strangers and of being on the streets after dark, homes become fortresses, and families move to new locations in search of a secure life. A terrible reality is that until significant inroads are made in controlling crime, the overall quality of life is lower than it could be.

While good investigative work will not significantly reduce crime by itself, the investigation of any crime places important responsibilities on the investigator. First, successful investigators must possess essential qualities such as good communication skills, strong ethics, initiative, resourcefulness, and compassion. Second, investigators must ensure that crimes are investigated effectively and thoroughly. This responsibility includes not only complete preliminary and follow-up investigations but also understanding the importance of physical evidence in a criminal investigation. The contributions of physical evidence to an investigation are diminished primarily by the inability, unwillingness, or failure to locate, properly collect, mark, and preserve the evidence, and by the drawing of improper conclusions from its analysis.

Investigators must also recognize that searching the crime scene for physical evidence is not limited to the location at which the offense was committed; it involves a wider area, including the perpetrator's lines of approach and flight. Thus, a crime scene search must include the specific setting of the crime and its general environs. Finally, there may be situations in which even the most organized and well-planned crime scene investigation experiences obstacles. Investigators must always be cautious and aware of potential problems at a crime scene and address these issues appropriately.

TYPES OF OFFENSES

A **crime** is the commission (doing) of any act that is prohibited or the omission (failing to do) of any act that is required by the penal code of an organized political state. There can be no crime unless there is advance notice that the conduct is prohibited or required.

Legislatures enact criminal laws that distinguish between felonies and misdemeanors. In most states, a **felony** is an act punishable by imprisonment for a term of one or more years, or by death. Generally, violations of the criminal code that are not felonies are designated as **misdemeanors,** lesser offenses that may be punishable by a fine, ordinarily not to exceed $500, and/or imprisonment for no more than a year. Some states have a third crime category called **violation** (e.g., criminal littering), which is punishable only by a fine, usually no more than $250.

THE INVESTIGATOR AND THE IMPORTANCE OF INVESTIGATION

An **investigator** is someone who gathers, documents, and evaluates evidence and information. This is accomplished through the process of *investigation.* The investigative process has the following objectives:

1. To establish that a crime was actually committed.
2. To identify and apprehend the suspect(s).
3. To recover stolen property.
4. To assist in the prosecution of the person(s) charged with the crime.

The investigator must have special knowledge and skills to achieve these objectives. The most important skill is the ability to converse equally well with a wide range of people, from corporate officers to prostitutes. This is essential because much of what we learn during an investigation comes from people. The competent investigator is aware of the difference between knowing things and doing things. Such an investigator will therefore consistently translate his or her special knowledge into actual investigative behaviors.

The investigation of any crime places significant responsibilities on the investigator. These responsibilities are particularly heavy during an arrest for a violent felony, since the investigator may have to use deadly force: investigators cannot legally use such force prematurely, but from a tactical standpoint they cannot be even a split second too late in responding to deadly force directed at them. When a person is arrested, whether for a felony or a misdemeanor, the arrest is often publicized, and the person, even if not convicted, incurs economic and/or social costs. The more heinous the charge, the greater these costs will be. If a criminal charge is sustained, the person may suffer any of the penalties authorized for conviction of a felony, misdemeanor, or violation, which run from a fine to execution. This means that investigators must evaluate information accurately and use sound judgment in making investigative decisions. Other qualities are also required, as discussed next.

Essential Qualities of the Investigator

Some investigators have a reputation of being lucky, and good fortune sometimes does play a role in solving a case. Most often, however, the "lucky" investigator is someone with strong professional training and solid experience who, by carefully completing every appropriate step in an investigation, leaves nothing to chance. By doing so, he or she forfeits no opportunity to develop evidence. In addition, successful investigators:

1. Invariably have a strong degree of self-discipline. It is not the presence or absence of a supervisor that causes them to get things done.
2. Use legally approved methods and are highly ethical.
3. Have the ability to win the confidence of people with whom they interact.
4. Do not act out of malice or bias.
5. Include in their case documentation all evidence that may point to the innocence of the suspect, no matter how unsavory his or her character.

6. Know that investigation is a systematic method of inquiry that is more science than art.
7. Realize that successful investigations are not always produced by rote application of the appropriate steps and therefore supplement the investigative procedures with their own initiative and resourcefulness.
8. Have wide-ranging contacts across many occupations.
9. Are not reluctant to contact experts from many different fields to help move the investigation forward.
10. Use both **inductive** and **deductive reasoning.** Inductive reasoning moves from the specific details to a general view. It uses the factual situation of a case to form a unifying and logically consistent explanation of the crime. In contrast, deductive reasoning creates a hypothesis about the crime. The explanation is tested against the factual situation. If the fit is not good, the hypothesis is reformulated and tested again. The process is repeated until everything "fits together."
11. Know that inductive and deductive reasoning can be distorted—by untenable inferences, logical fallacies, the failure to consider all alternatives, and bias—and self-monitor themselves to ensure effective use of these reasoning processes.
12. Learn something from every person with whom they come into contact, knowing that the wider their understanding of different lifestyles, occupations, vocabularies, views, and other factors, the more effective they will be.
13. Have the empathy, sensitivity, and compassion to do their job without causing unnecessary anguish (e.g., when interviewing a rape suspect).
14. Avoid becoming calloused and cynical from their constant contact with criminals, keeping in mind that the criminal element does not represent everyone. The failure to keep this distinction in mind can be the precursor of unethical behavior.

Organization of the Investigative Process

The major events in the investigation of crime are depicted in Figure 3-1. A discussion of these and their subelements provide an overview of the investigative process and introduce concepts covered in greater detail in subsequent chapters.

Once a criminal offense has been committed, three immediate outcomes are possible. It may go undetected, as in the case of a carefully planned and conducted murder by organized-crime figures, in which the body is disposed of in such a way that it will remain undiscovered. If a violation is detected, it may not be reported, such as when a proprietor finds that his or her business premises have been burglarized but does not contact the police because the loss is minor or because the insurance coverage would be adversely affected. Finally, the crime may come to the attention of the police through their observation, a complaint by the victim or witnesses, or a tip.

▶ FIGURE 3-1   Major events in
the investigation of a crime

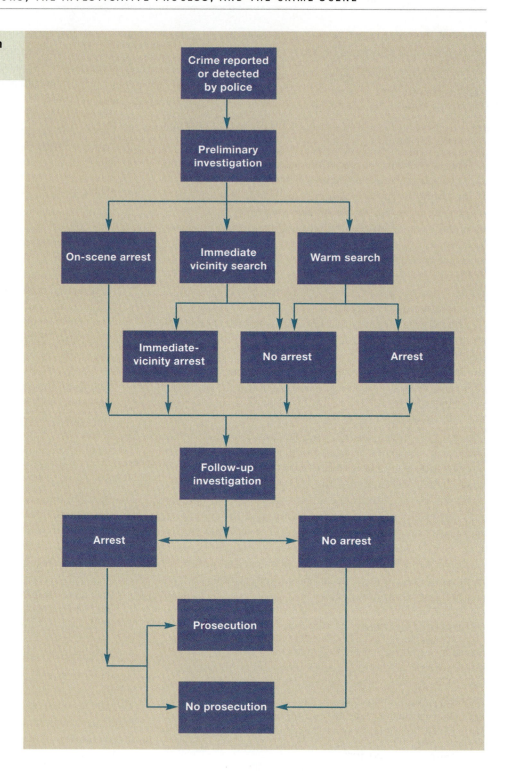

Regardless of the outcome, a crime has occurred in each of the three preceding instances. However, only in the last case, when it is both detected and reported, is the offense of concern to the investigator, because only at that time does it become subject to formal processing.

The Preliminary Investigation

The actions taken by the first officer to arrive at the scene of a crime after its detection and reporting are collectively termed the **preliminary investigation.** Normally the preliminary investigation is conducted by a uniformed officer from the Patrol Division and consists of the steps explained as follows.

1. Receipt of Information, Initial Response, and Officer Safety Procedures

 a. *Note all dispatch information:* time, date, type of call, location, names of parties involved, their descriptions, past history of incidents at the location, and, if known, whether any weapons are involved in this call.[1] Continue taking **field notes** throughout your preliminary investigation. In those notes, record the condition and placement of victims and things at the scene. Often the type of call to which you are dispatched is actually what happened at the scene. However, people who call 911 may be excited, confused, or not have enough or correct information. In turn, dispatchers may have a hard time hearing or understanding callers or fail to get sufficient information. Finally, what is going on at the scene at the time of the call may have violently escalated:

A solo unit was dispatched to a domestic disturbance in progress. The caller reported that it involved a man and a woman arguing on the small porch of a home. A solo backup was also dispatched. When the first unit arrived, the officer saw the man stab the woman. When the second unit arrived, less than 20 seconds later, the man had already stabbed the first officer and was attempting to stab him again.

b. *Be alert for people and cars leaving the crime scene or its immediate proximity and note their numbers and descriptions.* Information about the factors needed for full descriptions are identified in Section 4, which follows, in the context of issuing a BOLO (be-on-the-lookout) for persons and vehicles identified by victim or witness interviews as being involved in a crime to which a patrol officer is the first responder. Do not deviate from going to the call to which you are assigned, except for the most compelling reasons, e.g., being fired on or discovering a violent crime in progress.

c. *Approach the scene cautiously,* scan the entire area thoroughly, assess the scene, and be aware of people and vehicles in the vicinity that may be related to the call. Prioritize what needs to be prioritized. Wait for or request backup as needed.

d. *In assessing the scene, use all your senses:* look, listen, smell. Be alert for:

1. *The possibility that violence is still ongoing.*
2. *Dangers from "ordinary" people* (e.g., in one bank robbery, a backup gunman was dressed as a nun and shot a policeman in the back after the officer ran past the "nun" to the scene of the robbery).
3. *Dangers from special hazards* (e.g., natural gas or gasoline leaks; bomb threats, exploded bombs where there is structural damage to buildings and the possibility of one or more other bombs yet to explode, downed power lines, and adiological/chemical/radiological threats). You must

inform other responders about dangers and request specialized help and equipment (e.g., hazmat, and canine teams, the bomb squad, fire department, and EMTs) as the situation dictates. Maintain a safe distance from special hazards, and put on protective gear as needed. Do not just rush in to help; you cannot warn other responders if you are dead or incapacitated.

e. *Determine whether a tactical situation exists,* such as a barricaded subject with a gun or a robber who took a hostage because police arrived before he/she could flee the scene. Get help from other officers or specialized units as needed.

f. *Remain alert and attentive.* Assume that the crime is in progress until you can safely conclude—not assume—that it is over and the suspects are no longer on the scene.

g. *Make sure that you follow departmental contact protocols* for notifying supervisors immediately in special situations (e.g., the need for crime scene processing).

h. *Treat the location as a crime scene until you conclude otherwise.* Sometimes this is not an easy determination, as demonstrated by the photo "The Scene of a False Murder/Robbery Report" (Figure 3-2) and the following case history.

For over a year, a woman was tormented by a person dubbed the "Poet" because he sent threatening mail in verse form to her, as well as committing other acts. Among the acts reported to the police were having her telephone line cut, chunks of concrete thrown at her home, and being abducted and stabbed. When the woman was discovered mailing a "Poet" letter to herself at the post office, along with her normal bills, the truth came out. A psychologist speculated that the "Poet" incidents were motivated by the prior victimization of the woman, at that time age 16, when she was drugged, assaulted, and branded on both thighs by an assailant.[2]

i. *If suspect is still at the scene, arrest him/her,* conduct a search of his/her person, seize weapons, drugs, fruits of the crime, and other evidence. (See Figure 3-3.) Legal rules apply as to just how far you may search a person beyond his or her actual person (e.g., the immediate area, other rooms, and any vehicle involved). Make sure you know and follow such rules. If you intend to interrogate suspects, make sure they are given their Miranda warnings and document this action. In some situations (e.g., a growing hostile crowd), you may need to have suspects removed immediately from the scene.

▶ **FIGURE 3-2** **The scene of the false report of a murder/robbery** Mortally wounded wife and wounded husband, who used his car phone to describe the incident as a robbery, being helped by emergency personnel. Subsequent investigation revealed that the husband had shot his wife and then himself to make it appear they had both been shot by a third party. (Photograph ©1989 by Evan Richman/ The Boston Herald)

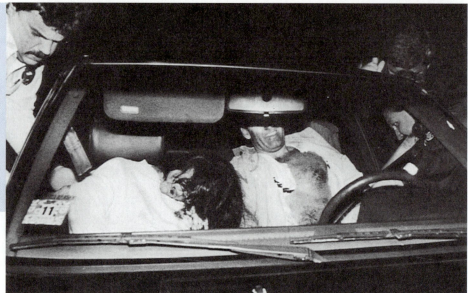

▶ **FIGURE 3-3** The investigator in the right foreground is handing a weapon discovered on the subject he is searching to the investigator at his immediate left. Notice that he carefully keeps his finger outside the trigger guard. However, the proper action to take is to have the partially visible covering investigator at the left side of the picture approach the investigator who found the weapon, who would hand it directly back to him. The action depicted distracts both investigators and keeps an unsecured weapon near the suspects, making the situation more dangerous. (© Mike Karlsson/On Scene Photography)

j. *An officer's field notes should also include information about a variety of scene conditions* initially observed that may prove to be significant later. Illustrations include what doors or windows were open or unlocked, what light switches were on, the condition of appliances (on-off, warm-cold, open-shut), and the general condition of the scene (e.g., clothes and items thrown about and temperature). If the victim has a motor vehicle, is the engine cold, warm, or hot?

2. Emergency Care

a. If there are no satisfactory options to causing or allowing the contamination or destruction of evidence, remember that *saving the victim's life has a higher value than preserving physical evidence.*

b. *Assess level of injuries to the victim and request any needed medical assistance,* which is usually provided by emergency medical technicians (EMTs). You may need to provide first aid to the victim until EMTs arrive.

c. *Point out potential evidence to medical personnel,* and ask them to have no contact with it or to have minimum contact with it. Instruct emergency personnel to preserve all clothing and personal effects; do not allow them to cut clothing through or along bullet holes or knife openings. Document all movement of people and items (e.g., furniture and blankets, weapons) by medical personnel.

Also make note of things EMTs may have added to or left at the scene, such as hypodermic needles and bandage wrappings, as well as personal items, such as jackets. Restrict the movement of the EMTs to areas at the scene where they are actually needed.

d. *Obtain as much information as possible from the victim before he/she is moved to the hospital by EMTs.*

e. *Do not allow EMTs to clean the scene*, because they may eradicate trace or larger types of evidence.

f. *Get the names of attending medical personnel, as well as their locator information,* including their employer and their telephone and pager numbers. Find out to which hospital the victim will be taken and send an officer, whenever possible, with the victim to get additional information.

g. *If there is a chance that the victim may die, attempt to get a dying declaration.* Also document other statements, comments, and spontaneous exclamations by victims, suspects, EMTs, and witnesses.

3. Secure and Control Persons at the Scene

a. *As rapidly as possible, identify the boundaries of the crime scene and secure it.* (See Figures 3-4 and 3-5.) This may mean checking an open field or all the

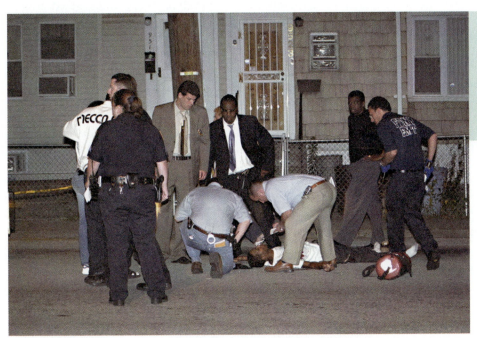

◀ **FIGURE 3-4   Crime scene interview**
Detectives question a shooting victim as EMTs prepare to transport him. Note the yellow crime-scene barrier tape in the left rear of the photo. (© Seth Gottfried/On Scene Photography)

◀ **FIGURE 3-5   Buffer zone**
Yellow police barrier tape marked "Police Line Do Not Cross" is widely used to create a buffer zone so that those with no official role do not enter the crime scene. Police do not rely solely on such tape to protect the scene and station officers at strategic points to intercept people who disregard the warning on the barrier tape. (© AP/Wide World Photos)

rooms in a structure. This is done for reasons of your safety, in case suspects may still be at the scene, caught there by your rapid arrival, or there may be multiple scenes. A classic example of multiple scenes occurred in 1966 in a Chicago townhouse, where Richard Speck killed eight student nurses in different rooms. Checking for multiple scenes may also identify other victims who are still alive and require medical attention. On rare occasions, such victims or witnesses may have hidden themselves in closets or elsewhere, fearing the return of their assailant (as did a ninth nurse).

b. *In defining the scene, officers must make sure that they also identify possible or actual lines of approach to, and flight from, the scene and protect them also.* These lines may contain shoe or tire impressions or residues, weapons, discarded fruits of the crime on which fingerprints may have been left, or other things which may provide investigative leads.

c. *Maintaining **crime scene control** is a crucial element in the preliminary investigation.* To the extent possible while meeting emergency care and other responsibilities, prevent individuals at the scene from committing any acts of theft, altering/destroying evidence, or attacking others. Identify all individuals at the scene, such as suspects, victims, bystanders, family, and friends. Crime scene control is also covered in different contexts (e.g., dealing with the news media) in subsequent portions of this chapter.

d. *Separate any potential combatants to avoid violence; separate persons arrested* so they cannot "get their story together"; and *ask witnesses not to discuss among themselves whatever they may know.* Exclude all nonessential personnel from the scene. Officers should be compassionate when dealing with the victim's family members and friends.

e. Set up a physical barrier to protect the scene. Use yellow crime scene tape, for example, or employ natural barriers such as doors, walls, gated areas, additional personnel, or official vehicles.

f. Maintain a crime scene entry log of persons coming to and leaving the scene. (See Figure 3-6.)

4. Issue a Be-on-the-Lookout

a. *If the suspect is not arrested at the scene, conduct interviews and issue a **be-on-the-lookout** (BOLO)* notice, which is broadcast to other officers. The

▶ **FIGURE 3-6 Crime scene entry log sheet**

CRIME SCENE ENTRY LOG SHEET

ALL PERSONS ENTERING THE CRIME SCENE MUST SIGN THIS SHEET

AGENCY: _____   INCIDENT #: _____

SCENE LOCATION: _____

NOTE: Officers assigned to maintain scene security must also log in and out on this sheet and should state their reason as "Log Officers."

NAME & TITLE	INITIALS	AGENCY	IN DATE / TIME	OUT DATE / TIME	REASON FOR ENTERING
			/	/	
			/	/	
			/	/	
			/	/	
			/	/	
			/	/	
			/	/	
			/	/	
			/	/	
			/	/	
			/	/	
			/	/	
			/	/	
			/	/	
			/	/	
			/	/	

BOLO is crucially important, because without its information other officers could be caught in the situation of approaching someone whom they think is a minor traffic violator when they have actually stumbled on a violent criminal fleeing the scene.

b. *Whenever possible, a BOLO should include* the following points: number of suspects, age, race, sex, height, weight, build, coloration, names and/or nicknames, clothing, scars, marks, tattoos, jewelry worn, deformities (e.g., missing finger), and accent, as well as whether the suspects were unarmed or armed, numbers and descriptions of weapons, the method and direction of flight, and a full description of their vehicle, including year, make, model, color, stickers, damage, things hanging from the mirror, and loud mufflers. The importance of details in BOLO is demonstrated by the following case:

A convenience store was hit by an armed robber. The first responding officer determined that a toy gun may have been used and that the suspect's vehicle had a white "hard hat" on the rear shelf. This information was included, along with a description of the suspect and his vehicle. Another officer found a vehicle matching the suspect's behind a tavern. A toy gun box was found on the rear floorboard, and a white hard hat was on the rear shelf. The bartender said a man matching the suspect's description had entered the tavern, called a taxi, had a quick drink, and left in the taxi when it arrived. The cab company reported that the fare was taken to the airport. There it was learned that he had boarded a flight to another city, where he was arrested when he got off of the plane.

5. Evidence Procedures Generally

Evidence procedures are also covered in a subsequent portion of this chapter and are discussed in great detail in Chapter 4, "Physical Evidence." The principle used in presenting the information on evidence is to move from the general to the more specific.

a. In smaller departments that do not have specialists, roughly those with 20 or fewer sworn personnel, the responding officer must recognize and identify physical evidence, document its location through sketching and photographs, collect it and mark it, package it (Figure 3-7), and take it to the station for storage in the evidence room, where a written receipt for it will be given to the officer. This receipt is then attached to the incident/offense report, which the officer subsequently writes. When serious crimes are committed in smaller jurisdictions, assistance with the crime scene may be available through mutual aid agreements with larger agencies or from the state investigative agency.

b. At all stages of handling the evidence, the chain of custody or control of it must be established. The **chain of custody** is the witnessed, unbroken, written chronological history of who had the evidence when. It also accounts for any changes in the evidence, noting, for example, if any portion was used for laboratory analysis.

c. In larger agencies that have sworn and/or civilian crime scene technicians, these specialists will process the crime scene. More detailed information about this subject is presented later in this chapter.

d. One or more plainclothes investigators may also come to the scene, depending on the severity of the crime. If they do, the first responding officer has the following crime scene turnover

◀**FIGURE 3-7 Crime scene investigators handling physical evidence**
A crime scene investigator examines blood-stained clothes before placing them in an evidence bag. Note that the investigators are going to place the clothes in a paper evidence bag, which is the appropriate action when seizing blood soaked clothing; each article should be placed in a separate bag to avoid cross-contamination. Chapter 4, "Physical Evidence" has additional information on identifying and collecting such evidence. (© Seth Gottfried/On Scene Photography)

responsibilities: (1) briefing the personnel taking charge, (2) assisting in controlling the scene, (3) turning over responsibility for starting another crime scene entry log, and (4) remaining at the scene until relieved.

6. The Incident/Offense Report

The officer assigned to the call must prepare an **incident/offense report** on his or her part in the investigation. After the initiating officer's supervisor reviews and approves the report, a copy of it is sent to the unit of the police department responsible for the follow-up investigation. Additional information on this subject is presented in Chapter 6, "Field Notes and Reporting."

The Follow-Up Investigation

The **follow-up investigation** is the effort expended by the police in gathering information during the period between the initiation of the original report and the time the case is ready for prosecution or closed.

Upon receipt of a major-case offense report, a supervisor in the investigative unit assigns it to a particular individual who will be responsible for the latent or follow-up work. Although the follow-up investigation will vary depending on the circumstances, the investigator conducting it engages in most of the following activities:

1. Read the offense report and become thoroughly conversant with it. Liaison with the originating officer to resolve any matters that are unclear. If other officers were at the scene, read any supplemental reports they wrote and contact them to see if they have anything to add.
2. View scene photographs.
3. Examine the physical evidence and review lab results as examinations are completed.
4. Contact victims and witnesses for interviews.
5. Have victim and witnesses study mug books and arrange the preparation of a drawing/likeness of the suspect. Release drawing and other information about the crime as needed to solicit the help of the public. Carefully consider any information before it is released to the press to prevent endangering people or hindering the investigation.
6. Make sure reconstruction of the crime is done on an ongoing basis as more information is added. This requires the investigator to periodically go back and review how they think the crime was committed.
7. Disseminate information about the crime and suspects—if any—throughout the agency.
8. If the suspect is involved in crimes in other jurisdictions, make the necessary notifications.
9. Read previous related reports and make an assessment if a method of operation—a modus operandi—can be identified.

10. Use the department's internal files such as crime analysis and intelligence bulletins. Review field interview records (to see if possible suspects were in the area around the time of the crime) and pawn shop files (to see if any items stolen have been pawned). In burglaries, items are often pawned or sold at flea markets or on eBay. In auto theft cases, valuable items may have been in the car at the time it was stolen and then pawned or sold.
11. Obtain information on known suspects from external sources, including the National Crime Information Center (NCIC). Check probation and parole, utilities, driver's licenses, and vehicle registrations.
12. Identify and interview known associates of the suspects.
13. Investigate the criminal histories of victims to search for motives.
14. If there is an arrested suspect, conduct a custodial interrogation to obtain a documented confession, identify any codefendants, and evaluate the suitability of the suspect as a confidential informant.
15. Talk to informants as needed.
16. Conduct and document a neighborhood canvass to see if area residents, business owners, or others saw anything material to the investigation. If the crime was committed near a public transit system, visit the system at the same time and on the same day of the week as the time and day of the crime.
17. Use specialized investigative procedures if appropriate (e.g., physical, technical, and electronic surveillance, polygraph examinations, and line-ups).
18. Prepare necessary affidavits, apply for, and execute search and arrest warrants as needed. Return to court regarding search and arrest warrants documenting what action was taken and the results.
19. Identify, locate, and apprehend the suspect, if not in custody.
20. Recover stolen property.
21. Determine if the suspect's auto or other property is subject to seizure under state laws. If so, seize and initiate condemnation procedures.
22. File supplemental reports on the progress of the investigation as required by departmental policy (e.g., note case progress and the release of any property to the victim or his/her family).
23. Keep all records well organized.
24. Keep victim/victim's family informed on any changes in the status of the case.
25. Meet with the prosecuting attorney.[3]

These steps may vary in terms of the sequence in which they are done, and some may be conducted simultaneously by different investigators assigned to the case. The remaining sections of this chapter address the crime scene and its handling. Bear in mind that even as the crime scene processing is going on, some elements of the follow-up investigation, such as the neighborhood canvass, will have already started. A fuller discussion of the follow-up investigation can be found in Chapter 7.

A final note is required with respect to various perceptions of what constitutes a successful investigation. The public thinks success is when the perpetrator is arrested and convicted. However, police consider success in two additional ways:

1. When a case is classified as **"exceptionally cleared,"** meaning the police can demonstrate who committed the crime, but for any of several reasons cannot pursue the case further. Examples of this are when the suspect is dead, witnesses refuse to testify, and another jurisdiction refuses to extradite. Two common reasons for one state declining to extradite a suspect to a second state are he/she will be tried on more serious charges in state one or is already incarcerated there on serious charges.

2. When an investigation is classified as **"cleared by arrest,"** meaning that the perpetrator has been arrested and there is sufficient evidence to file criminal charges against him/her. Note that this definition of success does not require a conviction.

Table 3-1 shows that many types of crimes committed do not result in arrest and conviction. This is frustrating to investigators who want to take violent, predatory, and other offenders off the street. In these situations, police have to accept the fact that some crimes are simply not going to be solved due to insufficient evidence or legal restrictions. In such situations, investigators have to accept the fact they have done their best, pursued all lines of inquiry, and go on to the next case. If they slip into cynicism, they only hurt themselves and over a period of years may become vulnerable to engaging in unethical evidence gathering, such as planting evidence, or commit perjury.

TABLE 3-1	Crimes Cleared by Arrest or Exceptional Means
OFFENSE	**MANSLAUGHTER % CLEARED**
Murder/non-negligent	60.7
Aggravated assault	54.0
Forcible rape	40.9
Robbery	25.2
Larceny-theft	17.4
Motor vehicle theft	12.6
Burglary	12.6
Arson	18.0

(Source: Federal Bureau of Investigation, Crime in the United States—2006 (Washington, D.C.: Government Printing Office, October 2007), Table 25, www.fbi.gov/ucr/06cius/data/Table_25.html.

TYPES OF CRIME SCENES

The fundamental assumption on which crime scene searches rest is Locard's principle: There is something to be found. We think of a crime scene as one particular place. Although this is often true, consider the 1988 terrorist bombing of Pan Am Flight 103 over Lockerbie, Scotland. Among the dead were 259 people on the plane and 11 people on the ground. Evidence from the explosion rained down over 800 square miles. In one of the greatest investigations ever, evidence was collected that led to the identification, arrest, and conviction of the bomber, who was a former Libyan intelligence officer.

Crime scenes vary in regard to the amount of physical evidence that is ordinarily expected to be recovered; a murder scene will yield more than a yard from which a lawn mower was stolen. At the most basic level, a **crime scene** is the location where the offense was committed. As discussed earlier, the search of the crime scene for physical evidence must include a wider area, such as the perpetrator's lines of approach to, and flight from, the scene.

The basic definition of a crime scene works well for many crimes, such as a burglary or a robbery at a liquor store. But where was the crime scene for Pan Am Flight 103? On a much smaller geographic scale, consider the example of a victim who is abducted from a mall parking lot, raped by one accomplice while the other one drives the van from one county to another. Later, the victim is taken to a secluded area, removed from the van, further abused, executed, and her body is dumped into a ravine in yet another jurisdiction. Clearly, we need additional ways to think about what a crime scene is, as noted in the following list.

1. Criminal incidents may have more than one crime scene. The **primary scene** is the location where the initial offense was committed; the locations of all subsequent connected events are **secondary scenes.**[4] Illustrating this statement is a Utah case in which a husband shot his wife while she was sleeping. He disposed of the body in a trash bin, and it ended up in a landfill. After 33 days of picking through 4,600 tons of compacted garbage up to 20 feet deep, investigators located the body. (See Figure 3-8.)

2. On the basis of size, there are macroscopic and microscopic scenes.[5] A **macroscopic scene** is the "large view." It includes such things as the relevant location(s), the victim's and the suspect's bodies, cars, and buildings. The **microscopic scene** consists of the specific objects and pieces of evidence that are associated with the commission of the crime, including knives, bite marks, hairs and fibers, shoe and tire impressions, cigar butts, blood, and so on.[6]

3. Other useful ways of thinking about crime scenes are based on the type of crime (larceny versus aggravated assault), the location (indoors or outdoors), the condition of the scene (organized or disorganized), and the type of criminal action (active or

► **FIGURE 3-8   Crime scene investigation**
Officers from the Salt Lake City Police Department search for the body of murder victim Lori Hacking, which was finally found three months after her death. Her husband subsequently pleaded guilty in the case. (© George Frey/Getty Images)

passive). Some further breakdown of these types may also be useful, such as if outside, whether the body is on the surface, buried, or underwater.[7]

The usefulness of having several frames of reference for crime scenes is that they can help organize your thinking about how to approach and process a crime scene. If there are multiple crime scene locations, the primary and secondary scenes may be located in different legal jurisdictions, a situation requiring a high level of cooperation and informational exchange between agencies. In cases where a serial offender is active and working across several jurisdictions, the case may be assigned to a standing interagency investigative task force, or a special one may be created. In such situations, it is important that departmental jealousies, the issue of who is going to get credit for solving the case, and other factors do not impede the success of the operation.

ORGANIZATION OF THE CRIME SCENE INVESTIGATION

Crime scene investigation is purposeful behavior and is intended to accomplish the following objectives:

1. Reconstruct what happened.
2. Determine the sequence of events.
3. Find out what the suspect did or didn't do.
4. Establish the modus operandi, the method of operation, used by the suspect.
5. Determine what property was stolen and what articles were left by the suspect.
6. Reveal the motive. For example, if the crime appears to be a home invasion that resulted in a murder, why wasn't the victim's cash and jewelry taken? Did the perpetrator panic and flee the scene before taking them, or is something else at work, such as a love triangle?
7. Locate and interview witnesses.

8. Document and recover physical evidence.[8]
9. Provide investigative leads.

To achieve these objectives, the work at the crime scene is divided into three major functions: overall coordination of the scene, technical services, and investigative services.

Overall Coordination

Depending on the nature of the crime, the resources needed at the scene, and other variables, crime scene coordination may be provided by the investigator in charge as he/she moves from one point to another, a mobile incident command van, or a temporary "headquarters." (See Figure 3-9.)

The senior investigator at the scene is ultimately responsible for what is done at the scene and what types of additional resources are requested. For example, in some situations, it may be necessary to get a search warrant. If there is a dead body, the medical examiner or the coroner must be called to the scene; generally this official has jurisdiction over a dead body, and it should not be searched or removed from the scene without his or her prior consent.[9] The overall coordinator will make sure that all the members of the crime scene team are briefed simultaneously by the first officer on the scene so that everyone hears and knows the same thing. This person is also responsible for ensuring that there is a continuous flow of information between members of the team when, for example, a piece of evidence is recovered. Other duties include making his or her own evaluation of potential safety issues, reviewing the actions of the person who conducted the preliminary investigation, allocating resources among the primary and any secondary scenes, establishing a secure area for the temporary storage of evidence, and establishing a command post and media function if the situation warrants them. The senior investigator also does a walkthrough of the scene with those responsible for technical services to make sure there is a common understanding of how the scene will be approached and processed.[10]

Figure 3-10 summarizes the types of equipment that crime scene vans may carry. Some jurisdictions also make use of a mobile crime laboratory in which technicians can carry out limited scientific tests. (See Figure 3-11.) The technical services function is concerned with the actual processing of the scene for physical evidence. This includes establishing a point for trash generated by processing the scene, including biohazard bags for the collection of disposable evidence equipment and personal protection equipment, and carrying out the identification, documentation, collection, marking, packaging, and transmission of physical evidence to the evidence room or the crime laboratory. Technicians process the scene on the basis of priorities established by the situation. For example, if there are both indoor and outdoor scenes, inclement weather may require that the outdoor scene be protected by tarps or tents and processed first. The presence of crowds or a hostile environment, which may be stimulated by such events as a shooting by a police officer, may also affect the sequencing of processing.[11]

Technical Services

This function is the responsibility of the ranking representative of the department's central crime laboratory or its crime scene processing unit, along with any subordinate specialists who are assigned to the scene. They may arrive to process the scene carrying one or more crime scene investigation kits or may have all the additional resources of a crime scene van.

Investigative Services

Investigative services include interviewing witnesses, conducting and documenting the neighborhood canvass

▶ FIGURE 3-11   Police department mobile crime scene unit The inside of a crime scene van; note the portable Kawasaki generator on the left and the light on the right. The balance of the van is filled with various types of equipment needed at crime scenes, such as gunshot residue, blood, fingerprint, and other collection kits. Many departments buy prepared evidence kits; others assemble kits to better meet their specific needs and capabilities. (Courtesy Chief Joeseph Lumpkin and Sgt. David Leedahl, Athens-Clarke County [Georgia] Police Department)

(discussed earlier) and a field interrogation of the suspect if he or she is in custody, and carrying out and recording the results of a vehicle information canvass. Occasionally a suspect may not have time to get to his or her car before the police arrive, so the suspect simply walks away, intending to return later. Checking the registrations of the cars identified in the vehicle canvass may also reveal additional witnesses and possible suspects.

TYPES OF EVIDENCE

There are three broad categories of evidence in which investigators have a particular interest: corpus delicti, associative, and tracing. The task of developing such evidence is spread across the three main crime scene functions, but the data from the different types of evidence are combined to create a larger and more unified picture of the crime. This picture helps determine, to a large extent, how the follow-up investigation will be conducted.

Corpus Delicti Evidence

Each criminal offense contains a distinct set of elements whose commission or omission must be demonstrated to have occurred in order to prove a case; **corpus delicti evidence** substantiates these elements. Thus, at each crime scene the investigator must keep in mind the unique requirements of proof for the case and attempt to locate related evidence.

Associative Evidence

Associative evidence is bidirectional in that it connects the perpetrator to the scene or victim, or connects the scene or victim to the suspect. A case history illustrates this:

A silent burglar alarm was triggered at a bar in a high-crime area. Officers responding to the scene found a point of forced entry at a rear window of the building. An individual was detected hiding in a small shed attached to the building. His statement was that when walking up the alley, he suddenly saw police cars, panicked, and hid in the shed. The search of this person following his arrest revealed the presence of valuables and materials taken from the burglarized premises, connecting the suspect with the scene.

Tracing Evidence

The identification and location of the suspect are the goals of **tracing evidence;** corpus delicti and associative evidence may also serve these purposes.

A 20-year-old female was at a laundromat washing her clothes. A male loitered nearby, observing her. When the woman was alone, he walked rapidly to the laundromat and entered the men's room. A few minutes later, with his pants and underwear around his ankles, he approached the woman, shook his genitals at her, pulled up his clothing, and ran off. The officer who responded to the call found a man's wallet on the floor of the men's rest room. A records check on the identification contained in it revealed that the owner of the wallet had a history of sex offenses and lived in the neighborhood of the laundromat. When the victim identified the suspect from a series of photographs, a warrant for the suspect's arrest was obtained.

Supplies for Scene Security

- Crime scene barrier tape ("Police Line, Do Not Cross"—available in several languages)
- Crime scene flags (marked "Sheriff," "Police," or "Evidence")
- Tents, rain-repellent tarps
- Sawhorses
- Spray paints (various colors)
- Marked police vehicles
- Cord, rope
- Flares, chem-lites, high-intensity lighting on poles
- Preprinted signs and poles (e.g., "Command Post," "Media Relations")
- Traffic cones

Telecommunications

- Fax machine
- Cell phones, pagers
- Portable copier/printer
- Laptop with modem
- Videoconferencing capability
- Departmental handheld radios
- Palm Pilots

Miscellaneous

- Consent search forms
- First-aid kit
- Reflective vests
- Audio recorder
- Handheld global positioning system (GPS)
- Magnetic compass
- Portable generator
- Refrigeration/cooling capability
- Flashlights, spare batteries
- Business cards
- Chalk (various colors)
- Hard-metal scribes
- Thermometers
- Logbooks
- Metal detector
- Telephone directories, phone numbers of special and/or important contacts
- Extension cords, adapters
- Area map
- Small mirrors for viewing hard-to-see places
- Ladders for reaching difficult-to-check places (e.g., rooftop) for evidence
- Magnifying glasses
- Disinfectants, "waterless" handwipes with germicide
- Privacy screen

◀ **FIGURE 3-12   Crime scene investigation equipment list**

◀ **Privacy screen**
Orange-colored crime scene privacy screen that can be arranged to shield a body at a crime scene from public view. The privacy screen can also be used to protect a crime scene from wind while it is being processed. (Courtesy Lynn Peavey Company)

▶ **FIGURE 3-12 Crime scene investigation equipment list (continued)**

Equipment for Crime Scene Documentation

Photography

- Video recorder
- Digital camera
- 35-mm camera
- Tripods
- 1:1 or close-up camera
- Tripods
- Stepladder for "shooting" the scene from different perspectives
- Scales, rulers
- Color and black-and-white film, videotapes, batteries (ample supply of each)
- Lens filters
- Remote flash units
- Auxiliary lighting
- Small tent-style plastic "signs" for showing the location of evidence (may be numbers, letters, or arrows)
- Photo evidence ruler tape, 30-foot rolls (sticks to surface and shows distances between evidence items), flexible vinyl scale and magnetized scale to place on metal objects
- Photographic ruler American Board of Forensic Odontology (ABFO) scale

▶ **Photographic ruler**

American Board of Forensic Odontology (ABFJO) Scale.

(Courtesy Lynn Peavey Company)

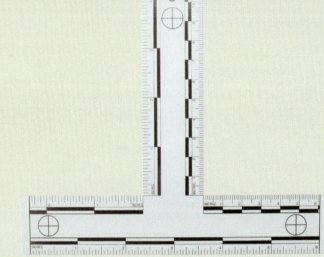

Sketching Equipment

- Retractable tape measures, lengths of 6 to 100 feet (several, e.g., steel and fiberglass)
- Walking wheels with visible readers for establishing longer distances (e.g., up to 1,000 feet)
- Sonic, laser and/or infrared measuring devices
- Paper, pencils, and pens
- Sketching templates (e.g., crime scene, traffic, curves, home furnishings, architect's, human figures, office plan)
- Chem-lites (previously listed) can not only be used to mark scene boundaries, but also to drop by evidence so it can be found in low light
- Surveyor's transit or similar device
- Total station for automated crime scene measurements and sketching
- Magnetic compass

▶ **Sketching templates**

Two types of templates used in sketching crime scenes: the Human Figure Template (left) and the Crime Scene Template (right). (Courtesy Lynn Peavey Company)

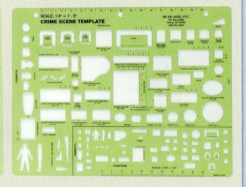

- colored markers
- Large clipboards or lap-size drawing board
- Straight-edge ruler, clear, 12 inches
- T-square, clear plastic triangles (e.g., 30/60 and 45 degrees)
- Protractor and magnetic compass
- Laser or sonic measuring "meter/tape"
- Laptop computer, crime scene sketching software

Equipment and Materials for Processing Crime Scenes

General Collection Equipment
- Tweezers, forceps
- Common hand tools (saws, drills, screwdrivers, chisels, etc.)
- Assorted yard tools (rakes, trowels, buckets, shovels, etc.)
- Nets for flying insects
- Framed screen sifters/sieves
- Tongue depressors
- Knives
- Disposable scalpels/scrapers
- Scissors

Special Evidence Collection Kits
- Latent fingerprint
- Imprint and impression
- Trace evidence with evidence vacuum
- Blood
- Excavation
- Sexual assault (separate ones for victim and suspect)
- Gunshot residue
- Casting (e.g., silicon, dental stone, and Snow Impression Wax)
- Forensic light sources, goggles
- Ultraviolet light source
- Presumptive/field drug testing
- Laser trajectory
- Blood splatter
- Entomology/insect collection

Evidence Packaging Materials
- Evidence tags, general identification labels
- Assorted Kraft/manila paper evidence bags and envelopes
- Special sticky labels (e.g., "Biohazard," "Latent Print Evidence")
- Evidence collection boxes (in which to mount guns, small tools, etc.)
- Clear tubes for syringes and small knives
- Evidence sealing tape, 1/2 inch to 3 inches wide (often marked "Evidence," "Security Seal, No Tampering," or similar wording)
- "Peel and seal" integrity evidence bags
- Pillboxes, jars, cans, tubes
- Sterile swabs, swab boxes
- Latent-fingerprint lifters (assorted)
- Butcher paper
- Blood tubes with and without preservatives
- Ziplock bags (assorted sizes)
- Evidence control/chain-of-custody labels
- Document sleeves

Source: Content drawn from Henry C. Lee, Timothy M. Palmbach, and Marilyn T. Miller, *Crime Scene Handbook* (San Diego: Academic Press, 2001), pp. 321–324; Technical Working Group on Crime Scene Investigation, *Crime Scene Investigation* (Washington, D.C.: U.S. Department of Justice, 2000), pp. 33–36; and National Institute of Justice, *Crime Scene Investigation: A Reference for Law Enforcement* (Washington, D.C.: NIJ, June 2004), pp. 55–57. Additional content was supplied by the authors.

◄ **FIGURE 3-12   Crime scene investigation equipment list (continued)**

TYPICAL CRIME SCENE PROBLEMS

Although the procedures to be followed at a crime scene investigation may be neatly delineated in theory, any number of conditions may render their accomplishment a good bit less orderly than the ideal. In a perfect world, every crime scene would be fastidiously processed. In reality, the scenes of misdemeanor offenses receive, at best, a cursory examination, and even the thoroughness with which felony crime scenes are processed is frequently affected by the severity of the offense. A crime scene processing unit cannot be called out to process every crime scene. To victims, the crime committed against them is important regardless of the severity. To investigators, that crime may be important or "just another report to fill out." Regardless of the situation, officers must convey a genuine interest in the complainant's situation.

At the scenes of violent crimes, especially those that are interracial, emotions may run high. Even a small crowd may add considerable confusion to the process of ascertaining what has happened and along what lines the investigation should proceed. In such situations, it is not unusual for witnesses to be lost, for their versions and perceptions of what occurred to be altered by contamination through contact with the crowd, or even for so-called witnesses to be added. In this last circumstance, a bystander may hear actual witnesses talking and suddenly believe they personally know something they should tell the police.

Police officers and supervisors occasionally make investigations more difficult when they drop by to see if they "can be of help," when in reality they are simply curious. Too many people at the scene can lead to confusion of assignments or the accidental alteration or destruction of evidence.

RULES FOR THE CRIME SCENE INVESTIGATOR

Regardless of the type of crime involved, five fundamental rules must be observed.

Maintain Control

Although mentioned previously in this chapter, the issue of control is so important that it warrants further elaboration. Without control, a life might be lost, evidence destroyed, assignments overlooked, or the investigation conducted in a generally slovenly manner. At the scene of sensational crimes, whether bank robberies and criminal homicides or those involving well-known figures, members of the news media typically arrive shortly after the investigation begins and immediately attempt to quickly obtain information and/or videotape investigators, witnesses, or bystanders in order to meet their deadlines. Unless properly handled, this situation has the potential to create both confusion and complicate the investigative process.

The person in charge of the crime scene should cooperate with the press, but the scope of cooperation is limited by the need to avoid interference with the investigation, to protect the legal rights of a suspect, avoid placing a witness in danger, and other factors. All investigators should have a thorough knowledge of their agency's media relations policy.

Although some states have enacted "shield laws" so that news media personnel are not required to divulge their sources, as a general matter reporters have no legal rights beyond those granted each citizen. Although news officials may be permitted to enter a crime scene, they do so at their own risk; if their presence in any way jeopardizes police operations, it should not be allowed. The arrest of a news media worker at a crime scene should be made only on the most serious provocation and with full awareness of the adverse publicity that is certain to follow for the police department.

News media personnel may photograph or report anything that they observe while legally at a crime scene or covering any other incident involving the police. If in this process they obtain information that could endanger people or adversely affect the investigative process, both they and their supervisors should be notified of the possible consequences.

When suspects have been interviewed but not arrested, their identities should not be disclosed. It is appropriate for the crime scene coordinator to generally describe to reporters the physical evidence found at the scene, proceeds of the crime, weapons, and the issuance and service of search warrants. However, detailed descriptions of evidence, proceeds, or weapons should not be disclosed, nor should information pertaining to how physical evidence, proceeds of the crime, or weapons were located.

In some investigations it is appropriate to withhold certain details about the crime scene, such as how a victim was mutilated, messages left at the scene by the perpetrator, particular types of evidence seized, or the exact words spoken to a rape victim. Such information could be vital in solving the case, evaluating informants' tips, or determining the authenticity of statements or confessions made by subsequently identified suspects. If a suspect has been identified and an identity established or a likeness generated by an artist's sketch or by facial composite software (see Chapter 12, "Robbery"), it may be advantageous to widely publicize this information if it is not likely to hinder apprehension of the suspect.

Relevant information can be supplied in **media statements** if it cannot be characterized as being prejudicial to a fair trial for the defendant (Figure 3-13). Among the actions and statements that are permissible and

◄**FIGURE 3-13 Investigations and the media**
Chief Charles Moose addresses the news media during the Washington, D.C. sniper investigation. A common police-news media question is whether the media help or hinder investigations. In the sniper case, this question was resurrected. The news media scrambled to get more information by interviewing many people as leads became known. Although new information was made available to the police by the media, at the same time some observers, including Chief Moose, believed that the investigation was hampered by the media making too much information available. (© AP/Wide World Photos)

impermissible under the policies of many departments are the following:

1. If a suspect is not in custody, investigators may:
   a. Release the type of call received and the time of dispatch.
   b. Disclose known facts and circumstances related to the commission of the crime to the extent it will not hinder or prejudice investigation and prosecution.
   c. Give a general description of the suspect(s).
   d. State the age, race, sex, and occupation of the suspect(s).
   e. Provide the name(s) of the suspect(s).
   f. Release the number, sex, and age of the victim(s) unless a juvenile is involved.
   g. Give general information about injuries.
   h. Release the identities of deceased victims if the families have been previously notified.
   i. Provide the identities of the investigators assigned if this does not place them at risk or hinder the investigation.
   j. If a victim has been transported to a hospital, refuse to release the name of that facility to the news media.[12]
   k. At this or any other stage, refuse to release information or reports that reveal information about confidential informants, or other information, such as medical conditions, which is privileged.
2. If a suspect is in custody, investigators should not do the following for the media:
   a. Require the suspect to pose for photographers.
   b. Give detailed descriptions of suspects or evidence that may jeopardize the successful conclusion of an investigation or prosecution.
   c. Reenact the crime.
   d. Provide the suspect's prior criminal record of arrests or other criminal charges which did not result in a final conviction.
   e. Disclose that the suspect told where weapons, proceeds of the crime, or other materials were located.
   f. Use derogatory terms to refer to the suspect, such as "depraved character," "real no-good," "sexual monster," and other terms.
   h. Reveal that the suspect declined to take certain types of tests or that the suspect did take certain tests (e.g., a blood alcohol test to determine the degree, if any, to which the suspect was under the influence of drugs or alcohol).
   i. Tell the results of any tests to which the suspect submitted.
   j. Make statements as to the guilt or innocence of a suspect.
   k. Release the identities of prospective witnesses or comment on the nature of their anticipated testimony or credibility.
   l. Release information about the existence or content of any confession, admission, or statement given by suspects in custody.
   m. Make statements of a purely speculative nature about any aspect of the case.
3. If a suspect is arrested, it is permissible in most states to release the following types of information about him/her:
   a. The defendant's name, age, sex, residence, employment, marital status, and similar background information, unless the defendant is a juvenile.
   b. The nature of the crime for which the arrest was made and the identity of the complainant

(as long as disclosing this information does not create a danger for the complainant and is not seriously embarrassing to him or her—as can be the case for victims of sexual offenses—or does not run counter to other reasons of good judgment or applicable laws).

c. The identities of any other agencies participating in the investigation, and/or making the arrest, as well as those of the individual officers involved.

d. The circumstances surrounding the arrest, such as the time and place, the extent of any pursuit, amount of resistance, possession and use of weapons, injuries to an officer (notification of the family should precede disclosing an individual officer's identity), and a general description of items seized at the time of arrest.

Conceptualize Events

In one case, an argument broke out inside a night club and then continued outside, where a 24-year-old man who was not involved was shot five times and killed. Other shots were also fired. By conceptualizing how the crime was committed, Washington State Police officers knew that the outside of the bar, called Bar Code, might contain places where bullet evidence could be recovered. (See Figure 3-14.)

Even experienced investigators may not take the time to conceptualize how a crime was committed. Or they develop a premature concept of how the crime was committed. This often results in available evidence not being recovered. In processing the crime scene, it is necessary to keep both known facts and inferences in mind. This facilitates the reconstruction of the offense and identification of the perpetrator's method of operation, suggests the possible existence of certain types of physical evidence, and assists in establishing appropriate lines of inquiry.

Multiple female murder victims were found strangled and stabbed in an apartment. The lead investigator studied the crime scene very carefully. One of the victims was lying near the doorway to one of the bedrooms with a pillow under her head. The investigator concluded that the perpetrator may have touched the very lowest portion of the door to steady himself as he stood up after killing that victim. The crime scene technician processed that portion of the door and located the only fingerprint of the suspect found at the crime scene. The suspect was identified by this print and subsequently convicted of the murders.

Without the investigator's thoughtful examination of the crime and reconstruction of how the perpetrator may have acted, that lower portion of the door would not have been dusted for fingerprints because it would have been illogical to expect to find a fingerprint there. Consequently, the most important piece of evidence would never have been located.

Assumptions that are made must be checked for accuracy as quickly as possible. The failure to do so may result in an offender's escaping prosecution and in embarrassment for the investigator and the department. It may

► **FIGURE 3-14   Investigators searching for bullet holes**
Investigators from the Washington State Police Crime Laboratory search for bullet holes in the front of the Bar Code, a local club. Note WSP officers in the "bucket," which can be moved to search higher spots. (Courtesy The Olympian.com. Photo by Ron Soliman)

also produce confusion in, or misdirect, the investigation. For example, a woman in a large city was murdered in her apartment. The investigators assumed that the woman's husband had thoroughly searched the apartment for their missing infant child when he first arrived and found his wife's body. Thus, they further assumed that the baby had been kidnapped. Some four days later the baby's body was found by the grandmother in the apartment under a sofa cushion.[13]

Human behavior is rich in its variety; in reconstructing the crime, investigators must be alert to the danger of imparting their own probable motives or actions to the perpetrator unless there are solid grounds for so doing. Alternatively stated, this proposition dictates that simply because, under the same or a similar set of circumstances, we would not have acted in a particular fashion does not preclude the possibility that the perpetrator may have acted in that way. Two cases illustrate the importance of this point: In Woodbridge, New Jersey, a series of burglaries was solved when it was established that two inmates had been breaking out of a correctional facility to commit the offenses, and then returning nightly to the facility.[14] In Palm Beach, Florida, a guard at a bank was surprised one night by an intruder who took $50,000 in gold coins. Unable to find a point of entry, investigators were puzzled until they received an anonymous tip that the intruder had shipped himself into the bank in a crate and broken out of it after the regular employees had gone home.[15]

Large physical evidence, such as a handgun used in a criminal homicide, is often easily found at the crime scene and requires little in the way of conceptualization. However, there is the possibility that much smaller types of evidence are also present; these will be located only if the investigator is able to conceptualize events:

A university student claimed that several hours previously her date had raped her at his apartment. This had been their second date. In addition to being able to identify her assailant, the victim gave the investigator a Polaroid photograph taken of the two of them earlier in the evening. In examining the photograph, the investigator noticed that the victim was wearing a sorority pin in the photograph, but the victim's pin was now missing. Believing that the pin could have been lost at the crime scene, the investigator went to the suspect's apartment. The suspect's version of events was that he told the victim he no longer wanted to date her and she swore to get even for "being dumped." The suspect also said that the woman had never been in his apartment and consented to a search. The investigator found the missing sorority pin in the perpetrator's bedroom, and the suspect subsequently gave her a confession.

It does not take a great deal of conceptualization to recognize larger items of evidence at a crime scene. Where this ability pays substantial dividends is in locating **trace evidence,** which is present in extremely small or limited amounts. Such evidence may be, but is not exclusively, microscopic in size.

Often this trace evidence is located using **alternative light systems (ALSs).** (See Figure 3-15.) Illustrations include portable lasers, such as the Polilight, BlueMaxx, and Luma-Lite, and handheld ultraviolet (UV) lighting. As illumination from ALSs sweep over a crime scene, the various colored lights cause many types of evidence to

◄**FIGURE 3-15 Forensic light**
Forensic light illuminating latent finger fingerprints. Chapter 4, "Physical Evidence," contains a major section on fingerprint evidence. Such illumination helps to find fingerprints that might otherwise be overlooked. (Courtesy Chief Joeseph Lumpkin and Sgt. David Leedahl, Athens-Clarke County [Georgia] Police Department)

fluoresce. Trace evidence that reacts to such illumination includes fingerprints, bodily fluids, hairs, fibers, drugs, glass and metal fragments, bite marks, bruises, human bone fragments, and gunshot residues. The following case illustrates the value of ALSs:

A small leaf was found on the windowsill where a burglar entered the building. The burglar had worked barefoot, and investigators located a portion of his footprint on the leaf using a Luma-Lite. Confronted with this and other evidence, the suspect pled guilty.[16]

Portable **trace evidence vacuums** are also quite useful in locating very small items of evidence. To prevent the accidental contamination of the evidence, the nozzle and the evidence filter unit (which sits on top of the vacuum's nozzle) is packaged and sealed at the factory's "clean room." At the crime scene, as each different area is vacuumed, the nozzle and the filter are detached and sealed as evidence. These systems are particularly effective in gathering hairs, fibers, and certain types of drug evidence, such as cocaine. Thus, trace-evidence vacuum systems can often be effectively used in assault, rape, and some drug cases. If clothing is seized as evidence and fiber, hair, or other evidence from the suspect or victim may be on it, crime laboratories generally prefer that the clothing not be vacuumed at the scene but instead be sent to the laboratory for processing to prevent the possibility that other valuable evidence may be lost during the vacuuming.

Proceed with Caution

Many crime scenes provide an immediate focus; in criminal homicide, for example, there is a tendency to move directly to the body. Such action, when the person is obviously deceased, has a number of disadvantages. In approaching the point of focus, small but extremely important evidence may be altered or destroyed, the area to be searched may be too rapidly defined, and other areas that might be fruitfully explored are overlooked or given only a cursory examination.

Apply Inclusiveness

The rule of inclusiveness dictates that every available piece of evidence be obtained and, where there is a question as to whether a particular item constitutes evidence, be defined as such. The rationale is that mistakes made in excluding potential evidence often cannot be rectified. One cannot always return to the crime scene and recover evidence. The rule of inclusiveness also requires that standard samples and elimination prints always be obtained when appropriate. If, for example, a burglary has been committed and a safe inside the building successfully attacked, exposing the insulation of the safe, then standard samples of the insulation should be obtained. This will ensure that if at some future time a suspect is identified, comparisons can be made between the standard sample of safe insulation and any traces of safe insulation that might be recovered from the soles of the suspect's shoes or his or her car floor mat.

Elimination prints are useful in determining whether a latent fingerprint found at a crime scene belongs to the suspect. In the case of a residential burglary, for example, if a latent print was discovered inside the house on the window ledge where the perpetrator entered, the residents of the household should be fingerprinted and a comparison made between the latent fingerprint and those of the residents. If the latent fingerprint does not belong to any of the residents, there is a good possibility that it belongs to the perpetrator. In some instances, the fingerprint might belong to someone having authorized access to the dwelling. In cases where this is found to be true, however, the possibility cannot be overlooked that the person with authorized access may be the perpetrator. An example of this is the case of a licensed real estate dealer operating in the Washington, D.C., area who may have entered more than 100 homes that were being offered for sale, stealing furs, tape recorders, silverware, and other valuables worth between $200,000 and $300,000.[17]

Maintain Documentation

Documentation of the crime scene is a constant activity, starting with the rough, shorthand record created by field notes. Other types of documentation that need to be maintained include:

1. The **crime scene entry log sheet,** which was shown in Figure 3-6.
2. The **administrative log,** which is the responsibility of the crime scene coordinator and details such things as who is assigned to what function at the crime scene and the sequence of events at the scene, including its release.
3. **Assignment sheets,** which are completed by each individual who is given specific work to do and which document the results—both positive and negative.
4. The incidence/offense report, which is the responsibility of the first officer on the scene.
5. **Photographic logs,** detailing who took which shots, from where, when, and under what circumstances (e.g., type of lighting). Typical photo logs are video, digital, conventional 35 millimeter, Polaroid, and aerial. (See Figure 3-16.)
6. The rough sketch of the crime scene; the data used to prepare the finished or final diagram, which may be drawn by hand or by computer.

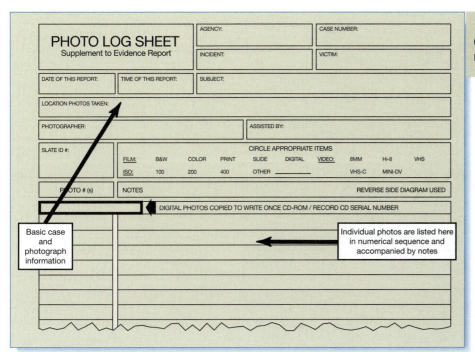

◀**FIGURE 3-16a** **Photo Log Sheet**
(Courtesy Imprimus Forensic Services, © 2000,
by permission)

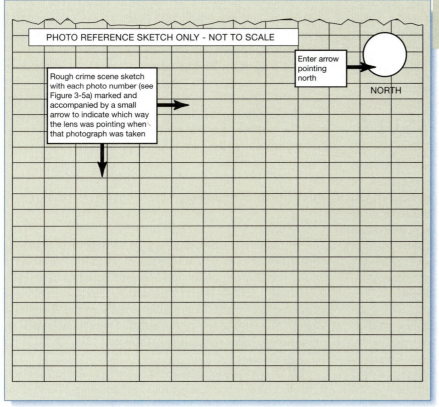

◀**FIGURE 3-16b** **Photo Log Sheet**
(continued)

7. The **evidence recovery log,** which lists each item of evidence; the names of the collector and witness; the location, date, and time of the collection; and documentation such as photos or diagrams (see Figure 3-17).

8. Emergency medical personnel documents.

9. The **lifted-prints log,** which contains the same type of basic information as the evidence recovery log.

10. If applicable, the consent search form or search warrant.

▶ **FIGURE 3-17 Evidence recovery log**
(Courtesy Imprimus Forensic Services, © 2000, by permission)

Incident #		Offense:		Victim:		Location:				

Item No.	Description	Collector	Witness	Location	Time/Date Collected	Photos		Diagramed	
						Y	N	Y	N
1									
2									
3									
4									
5									
6									
15									

Recorded by:
Name: _____
ID No.: _____
Unit: _____

Date: _____
Start Time: _____
End Time: _____

Recorded by:
Name: _____
ID No.: _____
Unit: _____

Page____of____Pages

In lesser offenses, a single officer may be the only representative of the police department at the scene. Thus, everything that is learned will be a result of his or her investigation. In such cases, the only documentation that may exist is the officer's field notes and the incident/offense report.

CRIME SCENE SAFETY ISSUES

There are numerous threats to investigators' health and safety. For example, at outdoor scenes people may be stung by insects (which could produce anaphylactic shock, a life-threatening allergic reaction), get West Nile Virus from a mosquito bite, lyme disease from ticks, scabies from mites, be bitten by animals, or get a severe skin reaction from poison ivy, oak, or sumac.[18] Investigators are at risk from inhaling vapors, fumes, mists, dust, and other contaminants and they may be affected when their skin comes into direct contact with, or absorbs, contaminants; such incidents may cause breathing difficulty, tremors, nausea, blurred vision, shock, or even total collapse and death. Irreversible vision problems may also occur, particularly if investigators don't wear appropriate goggles (those labeled with the American National Standards Institute's ANSI mark) when using alternative lights systems. Certain chemicals, such as those found in clandestine drug labs, may be flammable. Portable X-ray machines are used for various purposes at the crime scene, including examining packages. Radiation exposure is a low risk if proper precautions are used, like proper training, limiting the number of people in the area where the X-ray machine is operated, and using a shield to protect the operator.[19]

More often, however, investigators are at risk of exposure to infectious pathogens (disease-causing agents), such as HIV, hepatitis B, hepatitis C, and tuberculosis. After the September 11, 2001, attacks on the Twin Towers in New York City, biological terrorism came to the fore when anthrax was sent through the mail to elected officials and other persons. Beyond biological warfare are chemical, radiological, and nuclear threats. The following sections discuss the self-protection measures officers at crime scenes should take with respect to the more usual infectious diseases.

Infectious Diseases

HIV/AIDS

The **human immunodeficiency virus (HIV)** is a bloodborne pathogen that is also present in many other body fluids. If HIV progresses into acquired immunodeficiency syndrome (AIDS), the body's natural defenses against many types of diseases are substantially reduced, leaving victims vulnerable to "opportunistic infections," such as pneumonia, from which they ultimately die. There is no HIV/AIDS vaccine.

HIV is not spread from casual contact. You cannot get it from toilet seats, telephones, swimming pools, door knobs, a drinking fountain, or air.[20] There is no present evidence that HIV is spread through sweat, tears, saliva, or urine.[21] However, the presence of blood is not always obvious in such materials, nor may blood be immediately apparent on clothing, guns, knives, cars, drugs, and hypodermic needles; therefore, consistent caution is always warranted. It should be noted that HIV (and hepatitis B and C) can also be spread through shared razors, toothbrushes, and other personal care items. Biting insects, such as mosquitoes, do not transmit HIV.[22]

HIV/AIDS and Investigators The approximate risk of HIV infection after an accidental needle stick is less than 1%.[23] Given the frequency with which investigators deal with special populations, such as intravenous drug users (IDUs), homosexuals, and prostitutes, the risk for them may be somewhat greater because of repeated exposure. The greatest danger to officers arises when they are making arrests, seizing drug-related evidence, and processing crime scenes and accidents where blood and other bodily fluids are exposed.

At crime, accident, and other scenes with a potential or known HIV risk, investigators should be knowledgeable about and employ self-protection techniques, including the following:

1. Be cautious when conducting all types of searches; never put your hands anywhere you cannot see. Instead, use a mirror, or probe with a flashlight, wooden dowel, or metal rod.
2. The most important protective barrier against HIV infection is intact skin. Even the slightest opening in the skin can be a portal through which HIV enters the body. Protect skin wounds, abrasions, and openings with 360-degree fluid-proof bandages.
3. About 20% of AIDS patients develop raised, purplish-colored lesions (Kaposi's Sarcoma), which may be present anywhere on the body. (See Figure 3-18.) Most commonly these are seen on the head, neck, and oral cavity. Some of these are "weeping lesions" that let out an HIV-carrying fluid. You should be

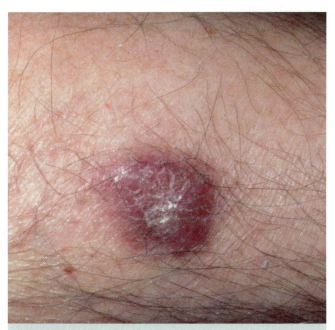

▲ **FIGURE 3-18**
An AIDS purple-colored lesion (© SPL/Photo Researchers, Inc.)

particularly careful around such lesions. Another condition (pseudo–Kaposi's sarcoma, or acroangiodermatitus) has a similar appearance but is not HIV related.

4. If you are bitten by a suspect, seek medical assistance and have an assessment made. Do not place your mouth to the bite area. There are only a few, rare reports of transmission of the HIV virus by biting. Other types of infections may result from biting.[24]
5. Bites, needle sticks, cuts, or similar incidents involving broken or punctured skin, however slight, should be washed immediately with soap in warm water for at least 30 seconds and treated medically.[25] Use soap from a dispenser, not a shared bar. Some agencies recommend the use of germicidal wipes approved by the Environmental Protection Agency (EPA). There is no evidence that squeezing or "milking" wounds reduces the risk of HIV.
6. If splashed in the eyes or on mucous membranes (e.g., inside the nose), flush the area for 15 minutes using water, sterile water, or a saline solution.
7. Do not attempt to recap hypodermic needles seized as evidence, and use care when seizing any other sharp items (e.g., knives, razor blades, broken glass, scissors, and metal pieces) at crime scenes. When handling sharp objects, use disposable tongs or forceps and place the objects in appropriate rigid, puncture-resistant containers.
8. There is a direct correlation between the type of gloves one wears and the tactile sensitivity they provide.[26] Although "double gloving" reduces the sense of touch somewhat, it does offer an additional level of protection. Remove any rings that could tear a glove. Wear latex gloves when contact with blood, body fluids, body parts, weeping lesions, body membranes, or nonintact skin of others is possible. Do not touch or handle petroleum products when wearing latex gloves; such products "eat" or degrade them. Wear vinyl gloves instead.[27] Use nitrile gloves if you are latex-sensitive.
9. The use of gloves may reduce the amount of blood transferred by an accidental needle stick by 50%.[28] Cut-resistant glove liners further reduce the chance of accidental needle sticks and other wounds. Because some new gloves may have leaks, supplies should be periodically evaluated and only the appropriate quality should be purchased for use.
10. Check your gloves frequently for wear and tear; replace them often. When you replace gloves, wash your hands and use a germicidal wipe on them.
11. Maintain a high sense of personal awareness at potential HIV scenes. When you are wearing gloves, do not handle personal items (such as your pen or clipboard), and do not put your hands in your pockets, touch your face, or scratch your head. If you do touch personal items or body areas, they should be disinfected. (See Figure 3-19.)

▶ **FIGURE 3-19   HIV infection control procedures**

- Wipe exposed areas with Environmental Protection Agency (EPA)-approved germicide, such as 70% isopropyl alcohol. Allow the area to which it is applied to air-dry naturally, and then immediately report the exposure as provided for by departmental guidelines. Make sure that a written report is generated.

- Use a 1:10 mixture of EPA-registered bleach and water. This requires, if a cup is used as the measuring size, 1 cup of bleach to 10 cups of water. If using a prepared bleach/water mixture, do not use one that is 24 hours old or older, because the bleach will lose some of its potency. Mixtures made "now" are best; significant contacts with blood require 20 minutes of contact with the mix and equipment—, e.g., car seats, batons, and handcuffs.

- Some police department policies require that wool uniforms that become contaminated be placed in biohazard bags and destroyed. Others recommend that contaminated uniforms that can be laundered be washed in water with a temperature of 140–165 degrees. Using bleach on white items or nonchlorine bleach for colored items adds another measure of safety.

Source: Colleen Wade, (ed.), *Handbook of Forensic Sciences* (Washington, D.C.: Federal Bureau of Investigation, 2003), p. 137. Also refer to the El Paso County Sheriff's Office, Policy 706, January 1, 2004. Additions and modifications have been made by the authors.

12. Always carry a flashlight, even during daylight hours, so that you can search dark areas more safely.
13. Do not eat, drink, smoke, handle contacts, or apply lip balm or cosmetics at HIV-risk crime scenes.
14. Wear a mask and a face shield or similar protective gear when scraping dried blood.
15. In addition to gloves, other **personal protection equipment (PPE)** may be necessary at high-risk scenes with exposed blood and splatters. Examples of such equipment are listed in Figure 3-20.
16. If you must give cardiopulmonary resuscitation (CPR), use protective eyewear and a CPR device with a one-way valve to prevent blood or other bodily fluids from entering your mouth. A resuscitation bag is an attractive alternative because it eliminates direct contact between the person giving the CPR and the person receiving it.
17. Contaminated evidence should be collected, marked, and packaged as appropriate for the particular type of evidence. If the evidence might be contaminated, mark it prominently as such or apply a "Biological Hazard" sticker.
18. All disposable worn PPE should be placed in a biohazard waste bag when you have completed your work at the crime scene. Many departments use specially colored bags, such as red or orange, for this purpose. When removing PPE, do so in a manner that does not contaminate your clothing. Wash your hands immediately afterward.
19. Know and follow your department's procedures for disinfecting uniforms and equipment. If you have

▼ **FIGURE 3-20   Crime scene personal protection equipment (PPE)**

- Gloves: cotton, latex (natural rubber), nitrile, polyvinyl chloride (PVC), and neoprene. Each of these has different characteristics and limitations; more detailed information on this can be obtained by referring to the FBI's Forensic Science Handbook, which is available on the Internet.

- Cut-resistant glove liners.

- Protective or impermeable "booties" or shoe covers, disposable gowns, coveralls or jumpsuits, aprons, hoods, chin-length face shields, eyewear with side shields.

- Masks: infiltration masks for protection from highly contagious people and situations; nuisance odor masks for reduction of unpleasant odors; and half-mask particulate respirators for protection from fumes, particulate/dust, and airborne pathogens.

- Self-contained breathing apparatus (SCBA).

- EPA-registered bleach, germicidal disinfectants, and wipes.

- First-aid kit.

- Biohazard bags.

- Insect repellant.

Source: Content drawn from Henry C. Lee, Timothy M. Palmbach, and Marilyn T. Miller, *Crime Scene Handbook* (San Diego: Academic Press, 2001), pp. 321–324, and Technical Working Group on Crime Scene Investigation, *Crime Scene Investigation* (Washington, DC: U.S. Department of Justice, 2000), pp. 33–36; additional content supplied by the authors.

not worn protective "booties," make sure you disinfect your shoes as you leave the crime scene; then wash your hands.

20. Report all exposures immediately to a supervisor.

21. Make sure you understand your state's confidentiality laws that pertain to disclosing information about HIV to others, including the news media.

Hepatitis B and C

Hepatitis B (HBV) is the most common serious disease in the world and is the leading cause of liver cancer.[29] It also results in cirrhosis (scarring) of the liver and liver failure. Its symptoms include fever, fatigue, muscle or joint pain, loss of appetite, jaundice (yellow eyes and skin), nausea, and vomiting.[30] Officers are likely to contract HBV in the same way that they would HIV: through exposure to blood and bodily fluids. However, HBV is much more potent than HIV, so officers are more likely to contract it in the absence of precautions. Since 1982, there has been a safe and effective HBV vaccine.

Spread by contact with the blood of an infected person, **hepatitis C (HCV)** is emerging as a major health concern. Unless effective new therapies are developed, deaths due to HCV will double or even triple over the next 15 to 20 years simply because 80% of those infected have no signs or symptoms and therefore may have been infected for a long time without knowing it.[31] The symptoms include jaundice, dark urine, fatigue, abdominal pain, nausea, and loss of appetite.[32] There is no vaccine for this disease. Neither HBV nor HCV is spread by casual contact such as hugging.

Tuberculosis

Tuberculosis (TB) is a chronic bacterial infection that is spread by air. Accountable for more deaths worldwide than any other infectious disease, it usually infects the lungs, although other organs may be involved.[33] One third of the world's population is infected with TB, although most will never develop active TB. The mortality rate for treated cases is about 10%.[34] The relatively recent dramatic rise in drug-resistant strains of TB is of concern to public health officials.[35]

When a person with active TB coughs into the air, infectious droplets are released; repeated exposure to them can cause the disease. People who eat healthy diets and lead healthy lifestyles are less at risk than others when such exposure occurs. Conversely, the homeless, alcoholics, drug addicts, and people in poor health are at greater risk.

A vaccine (BCG) is given to infants in some parts of the world where the disease is common; the effectiveness of BCG in adults varies widely, and in the United States its general use is not recommended.[36] Several drug therapies are available for people who have a high risk of developing active TB, that is, those who are in close contact with persons who are infected with TB or have active TB.[37]

The Americans with Disabilities Act

Investigators who contract the infectious diseases discussed previously may be covered by the federal **Americans with Disabilities Act (ADA).** Under this act, it is illegal to discriminate against an otherwise qualified employee in regard to employment actions—such as assignments and promotions—solely because the employee is thought to have, or actually has, a covered disability. Employers may be required to make "reasonable accommodations" for such employees. Reasonable accommodations include redesigning jobs, offering parttime hours, and modifying equipment and facilities. The legal provisions of ADA are broad and cover more than just infectious diseases; additional information is readily obtainable in personnel offices, from police unions, and on the Internet.

As a final note, some police agencies have taken the view that if an officer cannot fully perform all the functions required of a certified peace officer, she or he may be separated from the service or placed on involuntary medical retirement, depending on the situation. Other police departments have chosen to inventory their positions each year in order to determine how many of them could, with reasonable accommodations, be staffed by persons covered by ADA.

THE CRIME SCENE SEARCH

The purpose of the crime scene search is to obtain physical evidence useful in establishing the fact that an offense has been committed, identify the method of operation employed by the perpetrator, reduce the number of suspects, and identify the perpetrator.

Four major considerations dominate the crime scene search. Each is discussed next.

Boundary Determination

In terms of the boundary of the crime scene, it is useful to think of an inner perimeter and an outer perimeter. The inner perimeter delineated the area where the specific items of evidence are known to be, along with the lines of entry into, and exit from, the scene. The outer perimeter is set farther back than the inner perimeter and helps establish control of, and entry into, the scene.

The crime scene coordinator is responsible for deciding the positions of the inner and outer perimeters, which are determined by the locations of the primary and any secondary crime scenes—such as the perpetrator's lines of approach to and from the scene. Along these lines, the perpetrator may have accidentally left or dropped valuable evidence, such as items taken from the scene, the perpetrator's wallet or distinctive jewelry, matches from an establishment he or she works at or frequents, a water bottle the perpetrator drank from while waiting for the victim, and the butt from a cigarette he or she smoked.

Saliva traces from the bottle and the butt could yield key DNA evidence.

For an indoor crime scene, the physical limitations of the building can help determine where the inner and outer boundaries should be. More problematic is determining the boundaries for an outdoor crime scene. When a person is found shot to death in a large field, for instance, how narrow or broad should the perimeters be? As a general rule, in such situations, it is better to establish the perimeters more broadly. Although doing so may result in some "wasted" resources, items of evidence are occasionally found.

Choice of Search Pattern

There are five basic **crime scene search patterns** from which the crime scene coordinator may choose. The spiral, depicted in Figure 3-21(a) is usually employed in outdoor scenes and is normally executed by a single person. The searcher walks in slightly decreasing, less-than-concentric circles from the outermost boundary determination toward a central point. This pattern should not be operated in the reverse—beginning at some central point and working toward the perimeter of the crime scene in increasing, less-than-concentric circles—as there is a real danger that some evidence may be inadvertently destroyed while walking to the central point to initiate the search. Use of the strip/line search, shown in Figure 3-21(b), involves the demarcation of a series of lanes down which one or more persons proceed. On reaching the starting point, the searchers proceed down their respective lanes, reverse their direction, and continue in this fashion until the area has been thoroughly examined. If multiple searchers are being used, then whenever physical evidence is encountered, all searchers should stop until it is properly handled and they have received information with respect to its nature. The search is then resumed in the fashion described previously. A variation of the strip search is the grid, depicted in Figure 3-21(c). After completing the strip pattern, the searchers double back perpendicularly across the area being examined. Although more time-consuming than the strip search, the grid offers the advantage of being more methodical and thorough; examined from two different viewpoints, an area is more likely to yield evidence that might otherwise have been overlooked.

Figure 3-21(d) shows the zone/quadrant search pattern, which requires that an area be divided into four large quadrants, each of which is then examined using any of the methods already described. If the area to be searched is particularly large, each of the quadrants can be subdivided into four smaller quadrants. The pie/wheel search, shown in Figure 3-21(e), entails dividing the area into a number of pie-shaped sections, usually six. These are then searched, usually through a variation of the strip method.

In actual practice, both the spiral and the pie search patterns are rarely employed. When the area to be

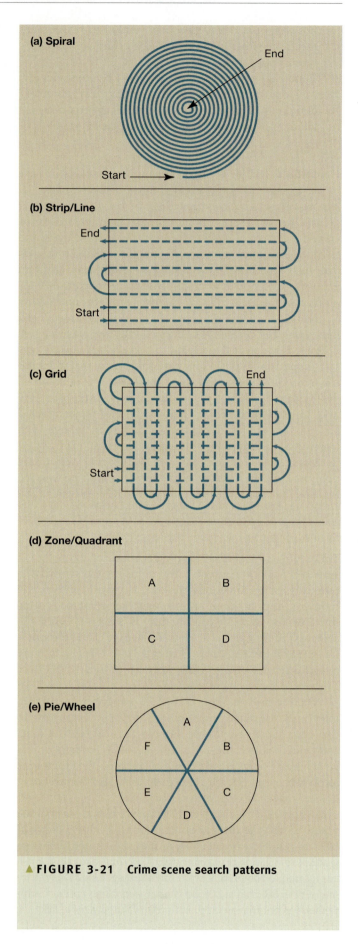

▲ **FIGURE 3-21   Crime scene search patterns**

◄ FIGURE 3-22   Police diver finds evidence
Police scuba diver with pistol used in murder case that was recovered from a lake. It is kept in the same type of water in which it was found until it arrives at the crime laboratory to be properly processed, preventing the accidental destruction or contamination of the evidence. (© AP/Wide World Photos)

searched is not excessively large, the strip or grid pattern is normally used. When the crime scene is of significant size, the zone search pattern is normally employed.

Instruction of Personnel

Although instruction of personnel was mentioned earlier in the chapter, its importance requires some further elaboration. Even when the same type of criminal offense has been committed, the variation among crime scenes may be enormous. (See Figure 3-22.) These variations are due to such factors as the physical settings, the manner and means that the perpetrators used to execute the offenses, and the lengths to which they may have gone to eliminate or destroy evidence. Thus, it is of paramount importance that the crime scene coordinator call together all the individuals who will be, in various capacities, processing the scene and share with them all the available information concerning the case. Doing so serves to minimize the possibility of excluding any available evidence. On receipt of this information, the members of the crime scene processing team may then begin their work.

Coordination

As discussed earlier, one of the most important responsibilities of the person in charge of the crime scene is integrating the efforts of those assigned to the technical and investigative service functions, along with ensuring the timely flow of pertinent information. For example, if a suspect is in custody and the interrogation yields information concerning the weapon or tool that may have been used, or where it may be located, then the crime scene coordinator should rapidly relay this information to those involved in technical services at the scene so that they will be alert to specific possibilities for the recovery

of physical evidence. Conversely, as significant physical evidence is recovered, the information should be conveyed to the crime scene coordinator, who can then transmit it to the investigators so they can move toward apprehending a suspect or be assisted in the interrogation of a possible perpetrator already in custody.

SUSPENDED SEARCHES, DEBRIEFING, AND RELEASE OF THE SCENE

The amount of time required to process a crime scene varies considerably, depending on such factors as the extent and nature of the area to be examined, the complexity of the case, the abundance or scarcity of physical evidence, and available personnel. Once it has been established that a crime has been committed, under no circumstances should the search be terminated until all possible fruitful avenues for developing physical evidence have been thoroughly explored. Occasionally, it may be necessary to suspend an operation temporarily. In one of the most common situations, a priority crime with evidence subject to decay requires the temporary diversion of personnel from a scene where delayed processing will not result in any loss of physical evidence. If it becomes necessary to stop the examination of a scene for a time, that scene should be secured in such a fashion that there is no possibility of contamination, alteration, or accidental destruction of any evidence that may exist.

Immediately before the **crime scene release,** the coordinator calls all team members together. In addition to ensuring that assignments were properly executed, the coordinator checks to make sure that all equipment brought to the scene has been retrieved and that all trash generated in processing the scene has been removed. Because each participant shares information during the debriefing, additional opportunities to develop evidence may be identified allowing all parties to leave the scene with a common understanding of the crime and of what the next steps are going to be. When the scene is finally released, the name of the party to whom it is released and his or her locator information should be noted in the administrative log.

Generally, you get only one chance to process a crime scene; any mistakes made may not be rectifiable. Once a scene is released, the person to whom it is released will often clean it up. Additionally, if the person is living there, the countless small things he or she does each day will alter and contaminate the scene so that returning to it for further processing is not a viable option. Therefore, the decision to release a scene must be well thought out. An absolute must is to photograph the scene again just before it is turned over to the responsible party. These photos will counter claims that the police "tore my sister's house apart when they were there."

UNDERWATER CRIME INVESTIGATION

For several decades, many police departments have maintained units designated as the dive recovery or scuba team, or some similarly titled unit.[38] Members of such units may be community volunteers, officers assigned full-time to the unit, or officers who have other full-time duties but come together periodically to train and maintain their capabilities or enhance them. The last-mentioned model is most common. The actual duties performed by underwater recovery teams (URTs) vary based on the needs of a jurisdiction, the available equipment, and the capabilities of personnel.

Historically, these entities have been responsible for finding underwater evidence, such as weapons, safes, and vehicles, and locating and extracting the bodies of victims of crimes or those who have accidentally drowned. More recently, such units have been used to help provide VIP protection and to conduct security sweeps of high-risk targets.

Members of these units face considerable dangers in some dives due to the cold, a lack of visibility, currents, and underwater debris and obstructions, along with other hazards. The use of a scanning sonar by dive teams has been an important development in being able to see the environment before a dive is made and in planning a dive which exposes divers to the least amount of risk possible.

Recognizing the importance of being able to conduct dive investigations, Florida State University was the first institution of higher learning to offer formal education in this field. (See Figure 3-23.) Offered by the School of Criminology and Criminal Justice, the five-course sequence in Underwater Crime Scene Investigation (UCSI) is taught at FSU's Panama City campus.

▶ **FIGURE 3-23 FSU students being trained**
Essentially, Florida is a peninsula surrounded by water and with an abundant number of lakes and rivers. Crimes are committed on such bodies of water and criminals also attempt to hide evidence of their crimes there also. Recognizing this, Florida State University established the first baccalaureate level program in Underwater Crime Scene Investigation (UCSI), which also offers various types of UCSI training and advanced certifications. FSU students participating in the UCSI program gather at the stern of a boat in preparation for a dive. (Courtesy Tom Kelley and Michael Zinszer, Underwater Crime Scene Investigation, Florida State University)

COLLECTION AND CARE OF EVIDENCE

The location of physical evidence during the crime scene search merely marks the first step in its long journey toward presentation in court. To satisfy legal requirements related to its introduction in a judicial proceeding, investigators must be able to:

1. Identify each item of evidence they collected or handled.
2. Describe the location and condition of the evidence at the time it was collected.
3. State who had contact with or handled the evidence.
4. State when, or during what time periods, the evidence was handled.
5. Declare under what circumstances, and why, the evidence was handled.
6. Explain what changes, if any, were made to the evidence.[39]

Chapter 4, "Physical Evidence," deals with various types of evidence and the specific ways to properly collect and package it. In general, investigators have many different options when it comes to packaging evidence. Among them are paper bags, paper cartons, Kraft envelopes, tamper-evident evidence sealing tape, seamless all-metal cans, cardboard tubes, pillboxes, document sleeves, and clear evidence pouches, which may be heat-sealed or be closed using a pouch's adhesive strips. Many of these items have preprinted forms incorporated into them. This eliminates having to attach forms, which can become separated and lost. The essence of packaging any evidence is to do it in a way that will make any tampering with it clearly evident. For example, if evidence is placed in a Kraft envelope, the envelope should be sealed with tamper-evident evidence tape. As a further measure, when the officer signs her or his initials or signature, the writing can start on the envelope, cross the tape, and go back onto the envelope.

Some evidence may be so large that packaging it is not reasonable; in such cases, attaching an evidence tag to the item is an approved way of identifying it. The information on an evidence tag is fundamentally the same as that required on printed forms incorporated into the packaging, and all entries should be made in permanent ink. They include the following:

1. Collecting officer's full name.
2. Collecting officer's identification number (e.g., badge or serial number).
3. Street address of, or other applicable information about, the place where the evidence was seized.
4. Exact location from which the evidence was collected (e.g., from the rearview mirror).
5. Time and date that the evidence was seized.
6. Content description, including size, condition, and/or amount.
7. Other related information, including case control number, type of offense, and witnesses to the collection.
8. Collecting officer's signature.[40]

The entries made on evidence forms and tags, along with strong evidence room procedures (such as the use of bar codes to track evidence handling) help in the introduction of evidence in a courtroom.

VISUAL DOCUMENTATION OF THE CRIME SCENE

Occasionally, the value of an otherwise excellent investigation is reduced by improper or inadequate visual documentation of the scene. People process information differently, so the more ways a crime scene is properly documented, the greater the likelihood that other people will accurately understand the scene and what happened there. This section examines three major methods of documenting crime scenes: videotaping, photographing, and sketching. In general, the methods should be used in the order presented here, with documentation moving from the general to the more specific.

Videotaping

Using a video camera, or **videotaping,** to document the crime scene offers several advantages. Such cameras are relatively inexpensive, they incorporate audio, their use can be quickly learned, the motion of videotapes holds the attention of viewers, and the images collected can be played back immediately. On the downside, neither the resolutions nor the color accuracy can compete with those in 35-millimeter photography, and tapes may be damaged by electromagnetic waves. Videotaped images are not an acceptable alternative to high-resolution still photographs. Listed next are guidelines for the use of crime scene videotaping:

1. Keep the camera's heads and lens clean to produce sharper images.
2. The use of appropriate lighting speeds up the focusing of the camera, thereby producing true colors and higher resolution. Battery-operated lights should be used to avoid dragging electrical cords through the scene.
3. Most crime scenes can be documented on a 30-minute tape, although longer-time tapes should be immediately available for more complicated situations.
4. Once you begin, keep the camera running; gaps in the tape may be hard to explain satisfactorily to jurors.
5. The use of a tripod with the camera will produce smoother, less jerky images.
6. Use the camera's title generator for future reference.

7. Begin with a short narrative of the situation, including the case number, the type of offense, the location, and other pertinent information. Plan your shots so that you can tell the viewer where you took them and what he or she will be seeing.

8. Department policies vary on whether there should be continuous narration as the entire scene is video-taped. On the plus side, it can provide viewers with additional understanding. However, if extraneous and nonobjective comments are made, portions or all of the tape may be ruled inadmissible.

9. The most common mistake in videotaping is going too fast; the speed you think is right is probably 50% too fast. Take your time and use the camera's capabilities for wide-area pans, close-ups, and very tight shots of the evidence.

When the videotaping of the scene is completed, the tape is evidence and needs to be packaged and marked in the same manner as other types of evidence. Tapes should be stored in an area free from dust and machinery that generates magnetic fields. If the tape is going to be viewed more than once or twice, a copy should be made to avoid the possibility of degrading the tape through repeated showings.

Photographing

In addition to videotaping, **photographing** is an important means of documenting major crime scenes. (See Figure 3-24.) It offers the benefits of various types of cameras and techniques. Aerial photography is effective in showing the point of interest and its position relative to other evidence in a broad area. Infrared aerial photographs are particularly useful when the need to show contrasting terrain features exists.

Digital cameras store images in a numeric format. High-end digital cameras, which are for professional use, offer features such as interchangeable lenses that make them more expensive, but they are a better option than the low-end ones intended for the consumer market.[41] The advantages of a digital camera are that the images can be immediately viewed, can be printed onsite, and be quickly transmitted and disseminated.[42] Among the disadvantages are that the stored images are subject to electromagnetic degrading, the storage media can be obtained only at special stores, and, because the technology continues to evolve rapidly, accessing older archived images may not be possible with newer equipment.[43]

Conventional silver-based film used in a 35-millimeter camera is still the primary means of capturing crime scene images. Such cameras offer high resolutions, the best color range, and the most durable storage medium, and they can be used with a variety of films.[44] These advantages are countered by the need for a processing and printing facility, the longer processing time required, and the inability to immediately evaluate the image.[45]

Polaroid cameras are easy to use and provide photographs very quickly. However, enlargements and duplicates of the photographs may take some time to get. Among their other uses, Polaroids can be useful in orienting the crime scene team, and pictures of suspects just arrested at the scene can be taken and used in the neighborhood canvass.

The guidelines listed next are general ones, appropriate for photographing almost any scene:[46]

- Photograph the crime scene as soon as possible.
- Prepare a photographic log that records all photographs and a description and location of evidence.
- Establish a progression of overall, medium, and close-up views of the crime scene.

▶ FIGURE 3-24
Police officer photographing the body of a 29-year-old mother of six who was found murdered in a parking lot. The words on the yellow crime scene tape are hard to read because they are printed on the opposite side, but they can be plainly seen by people approaching the crime scene. (Courtesy *Lexington* [KY] *Herald-Leader.* Photo by Pablo Alcala)

- Photograph from eye level to represent the normal view.
- Photograph the most fragile areas of the crime scene first.
- Photograph all stages of the crime scene investigation, including discoveries.
- Photograph the condition of evidence before recovery.
- Photograph the evidence in detail and include a scale, the photographer's name, and the date.
- Take all photographs intended for examination purposes with a scale. When a scale is used, first take a photograph without the scale.
- Photograph the interior crime scene in an overlapping series using a normal lens, if possible. Overall photographs may be taken using a wide-angle lens.
- Photograph the exterior crime scene, establishing the location of the scene by a series of overall photographs including a landmark. Photographs should have 360 degrees of coverage. Consider using aerial photography, when possible.
- Photograph entrances and exits from the inside and the outside.
- Photograph important evidence twice.
  —A medium-distance shot that shows the evidence and its position to other evidence.
  —A close-up shot that includes a scale and fills the frame.
- Before entering the scene, acquire, if possible, prior photographs, blueprints, or maps of the scene.

Crime Scene Sketching and Forensic Mapping

A **crime scene sketch** is a basic diagram of the scene showing important points, such as the locations where various pieces of physical evidence were located. Often, the sketch is not drawn to scale. Sketches made by hand in the field are called **"rough sketches"** as opposed to the more polished **"smooth or finished" sketches** typically drawn in the office. Finished sketches may also be drawn by hand, although it is often done using specialized computer software. Although there is a learning curve with any software, once the package is mastered computer generated sketches produce substantial reductions in the time required to make them—perhaps 75%–versus traditional sketching methods.

Forensic mapping is the process of taking and recording the precise measurements of items of evidence to be drawn or "fixed" on the sketch.[47] In theory, a crime scene sketch and associated mapping data should allow someone to return to the crime scene and place an item of evidence in exactly the same place as it was recovered. As a practical matter, the sketch allows the positioning of the evidence back into its original location with a reasonable degree of accuracy because there is some variation in the precision of sketching methods. The process of mapping the scene inherently intrudes into the scene because the investigator must move through and around the scene taking and recording measurements.[48] This requires a degree of caution in order to prevent the accidental moving, alteration, or destruction of physical evidence, all of which have the potential to confuse or misdirect the investigation.

It is critical that the entries on the sketch be as accurate as possible. Errors noted call into question not only the accuracy of the sketch but the investigation as a whole. For example, distances should not be paced off and then recorded as so many feet and inches. Distances may be measured using rulers or tape measures, as well as by using more sophisticated methods, such as lasers devices. Sketching and mapping methods are covered in the sections that follow.

Sketching Views

Regardless of the method, sketches typically employ one of four different views: (1) **overhead or bird's-eye view** (Figure 3-25), which is the most common; (2) the **elevation**

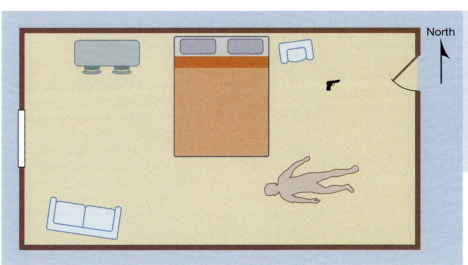

North

◄ **FIGURE 3-25 Overhead or bird's-eye view of a crime scene**
No measurements are included in this sketch because it is intended merely to portray the overhead or bird's-eye view. Occasionally it is also called a floor-plan sketch. As a convention, North is usually oriented toward the top of the sketch.

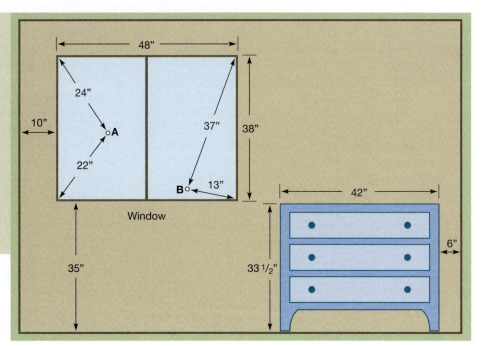

► **FIGURE 3-26 North wall elevation view of the crime scene** In common language, *elevation* refers to the height of something above a reference point. In this view, the reference point is the floor. An elevation view represents the front, side, or rear of a building. It is an excellent tool to record evidence on vertical surfaces. This view shows the North interior wall using the following legend: A: Apparent bullet hole in glass window. B: Apparent bullet hole in glass window.

view (Figure 3-26), which shows heights; (3) the **cross-projection view** (Figure 3-27), which "lays" the walls to a room down so objects of interest in the wall can be mapped; and (4) less commonly, **a three-dimensional (3D) view** of the scene (Figure 3-28), which can be created using sophisticated software to form virtual views of the scene.[49]

In Chapter 4, "Physical Evidence," information is available on how to determine if the shots were fired from inside or outside of the building; that is a determination beyond the purpose of an elevation view.

Forensic Mapping Methods

This section summarizes major mapping methods, including: (1) rectangular coordinates, (2) triangulation, (3) baseline coordinates, (4) polar coordinates, (5) grid system, and (6) total station. (Refer back to Figure 3-3 for a list of equipment used for these processes.) The choice of mapping methods can be influenced by a variety of factors, including the nature and the amount of evidence, the overall size of the crime scene, the number of personnel available, the number, size and types of line-of-sight-obstructions, and weather conditions.[50] It is not necessary to map everything that you can see; it is important to show the location of the items of physical evidence items and any decedent(s). Typically, each crime scene sketch employs only one of these mapping methods; the choice begins with the seriousness of the crime. More severe crimes dictate the use of more precise mapping methods.[51]

Rectangular Coordinates This method is the best to use with scenes having clear and specific boundaries, such

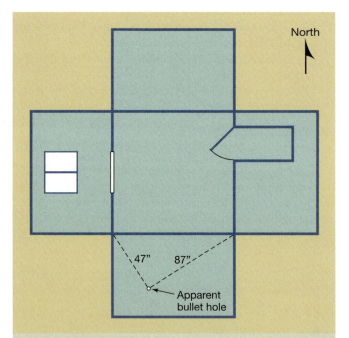

▲ **FIGURE 3-27 Cross-projection view of a crime scene** The cross-projection, or "exploded" view, "lays" the walls down flat, as though the room had been unfolded like a box. The purpose of doing this is to be able to show points of interest in the wall, which can also be done with an elevation sketch. The advantage of using the cross-projection method is that when there are multiple points of interest in several different walls, they can be displayed simultaneously in one sketch, as opposed to having to make and refer to multiple elevation sketches.

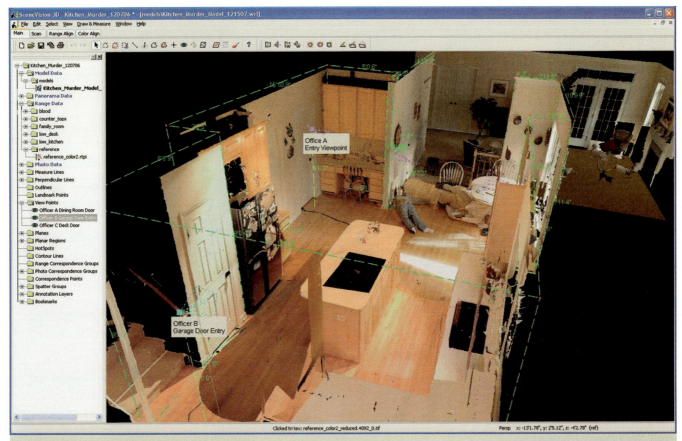

▲ **FIGURE 3-28   3D view of crime scene**
Using photographic and computer technologies, investigators can produce three-dimensional views of the evidence at a crime scene, which are more concrete images than those contained in ordinary sketches. Elaborate "immersive" 360-degree views can also be created so that observers feel as though they are actually walking through the crime scene. This technology is also useful in crime scene reconstruction, discussed later in this chapter. **(Courtesy of Doug Schiff, 3rd Tech, Durham, North Carolina)**

as interior walls, because **rectangular coordinates** can be measured fast and accurately, especially if one is using a sonic, laser, or infrared (IR) measuring device.[52] The crime scene investigator (CSI) usually takes two measurements at right angles from the center mass of the evidence to the two nearest walls. (See Figure 3-29.) It has one deficiency: Although evidence can be fixed at a particular location, the orientation of the evidence can be changed simply by rotating it on the axis where the two measurements intersect. In the case of Figure 3-29, this means the knife's tip could point in 360 different degrees.[53] This deficiency can be overcome by taking and recording additional measurements or, as is the more usual case, by using a different sketching technique, such as triangulation.

Triangulation The **triangulation** method is useful both for interior scenes in buildings, as well as for outdoor scenes, where measurements must spring from distinct,

"permanent" features or landmarks, such as the corner of a home, telephone, mailbox and lighting poles, fences, stop sign posts, the intersections of paved driveways and roads, and other similar features. **Regular evidence** is an item that does not change its shape when moved, such as a gun, knife, or chair; regular evidence is fixed using four measurements from different features or landmarks (see Figure 3-30); **irregular evidence,** such as articles of clothing, is fixed using two measurements.[54] Each pair of measurements, anchored by a reference point (RP), forms two sides of the triangle. In Figure 3-30, two measurements from separate points to the top of the foremost portion of the handgun and two similar measurements to the heel of the grip fix the location of the handgun with precision.[55] At the aftermath of the 1992 Ruby Ridge shootout, the FBI was criticized for not using triangulation to memorialize the location of physical evidence, a remark that failed to take into account the limitations of using it when the terrain is very uneven.

▶ **FIGURE 3-29   Rectangular coordinates**

In this example, the legend block is blank, because the two items of evidence were drawn in the sketch. If numbers or letters had been used to indicate the locations of the evidence, then the legend would read: 1, pool of blood, and 2, knife with blood on blade. Some investigators prefer to use letters rather than numbers to indicate the location of evidence, because letters are more easily differentiated from the measurements that appear in the sketch.

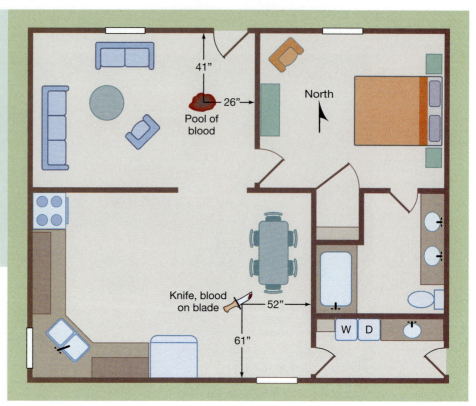

▶ **FIGURE 3-30   Triangulation**

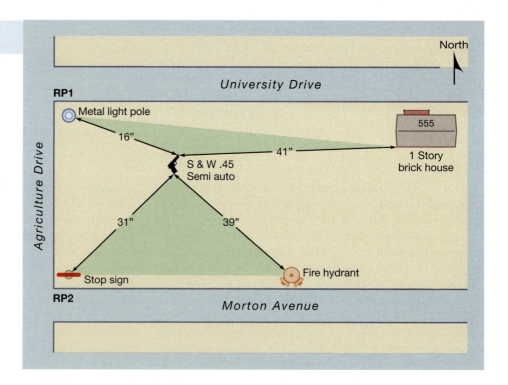

Baseline Coordinates "The baseline method of fixing evidence is very similar to the rectangular coordinates process."[56] **Baseline coordinates** can be used both inside and outside. Figure 3-31 depicts its use in an interior location. Establishing a straight baseline in a room is straightforward; once it exists, the distance on a right angle (90 degrees) between the center mass of the evidence and where it intersects with the baseline is recorded. The distance from this intersection along the baseline to a fixed point is also recorded. If greater precision in fixing

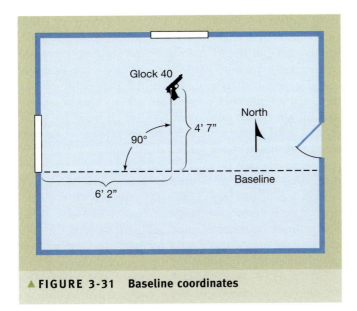

FIGURE 3-31   Baseline coordinates

the location of the Glock 40 in Figure 3-31 was desired, several 90-degree measurements from distinct parts of the Glock back to the baseline and then, respectively, along the baseline to the West wall could be made. Without those additional measurements, the orientation of the Glock could be rotated in the same manner described earlier regarding the use of the rectangular coordinates method. When this method is used outside, the baseline may be established by running a string or nonstretching tape measure between distinct features or landmarks. Some agencies do not use baseline coordinates when the distance from the physical evidence back to the baseline is more than 30 feet, because as the distance to be measured increases, so does the potential

for error.[57] However, this error potential may be greater with handheld tape measures than with lasers and other very accurate measuring devices. Therefore, it should be considered a rule of thumb rather than an iron-clad requirement.

Polar Coordinates   When you are mapping outdoor scenes at which evidence is scattered over a fairly large open area, the **polar coordinate** method is an effective tool; it is not useful at scenes where the line of sight is limited.[58] For example, when human remains in an open field are spread out owing to predation by animals, polar-coordinates are useful in fixing them. At its simplest, the polar-coordinates method requires measuring the straight line distance from a known reference point along a direction (angle) to the physical evidence to be fixed, as shown in Figure 3-32.[59]

The starting or **datum point** for polar coordinates may be established using a number of methods, including the baseline or triangulation, or in the absence of other possibilities, a global positioning system (GPS) can establish the datum point at which a metal rod may be driven into the ground as it can subsequently be located using a metal detector.[60] The distance from the datum point to the physical evidence may be measured using steel or fiberglass tapes, which are not subject to stretching or shrinkage, while the angle may be set by a handheld compass or protractor. Because of its greater accuracy, a surveyor's transit or similar device, which can also establish the elevation of evidence if this is important, is preferred to a handheld compass. In Figure 3-32, triangulation is used to establish the datum point from which the angles and distances to the evidence is determined.

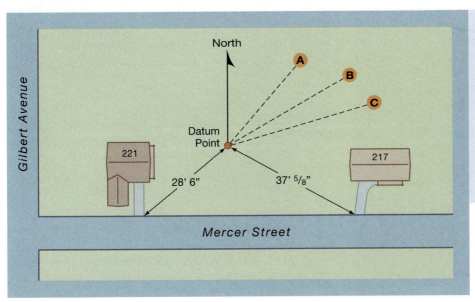

◄ **FIGURE 3-32   Polar coordinates**
The datum, or starting point, is established by triangulation using the points at which two paved driveways intersect with Mercer Street to form the base of the triangle. In this example, no elevation measurements were taken. Elevation is measured as the difference between the elevation of the datum point and each item of evidence.

Grid Systems A **grid system** is an excellent tool to use when there is a large outdoor scene with no significant features or landmarks.[61] For many years archaeologists have used grid systems to record where artifacts are found at a site; during the mid-1980s, there was a noticeable transfer of this technology as archaeologists instructed investigators on using the grid system and other techniques to process buried body scenes.[62] Both archaeologists and crime scene investigators typically lay out grids with sides of 3 meters or 10 feet, although they may be of any dimensions so long as they are of uniform size; grids as large as 30 feet to a side have been used. When dealing with buried bodies or human remains scattered in a relatively compact area, a grid system of smaller dimensions may be useful.[63] The boundary of each grid is fixed by a metal or wooden stakes; smaller sized grids may be connected using twine, although this may be impractical with large grids. If several search teams are working, each should be responsible for certain grids and as they find physical evidence, information about it should be immediately communicated to all other search teams. Laying out the grids and marking the boundaries of each is time consuming, but essential;[64] evidence may be fixed within the grids by employing whatever method is most useful (See Figure 3-33); this is an exception to the earlier guideline that typically each crime scene sketch uses only one mapping method; another exception is the use of triangulation to establish the datum point for the polar coordinates method.

Total Station A **total station** is a measuring device that can be used at both indoor and outdoor scenes; initially, totally stations found their way into law enforcement in the early to mid-1990s for use in traffic accident investigation and reconstruction. It functions much like the polar coordinates using a surveyor's transit, except that the process is automated. Although there are some robotic total stations that can be operated by one person, most, like a surveyor's transit, require at least two people to operate them. The following elements make up a total station: (1) a tripod; (2) a theodolite, which sits on top of the tripod; and (3) a pole with multiple prisms or reflectors on it. (See Figures 3-34 and 3-35.) The primary operator is responsible for looking through an eyepiece on the theodolite, focusing and aiming it at the prism pole, which a second person is holding at the point at which the physical evidence is located. The theodolite's electronic distance meter (EDM) emits an infrared laser beam that strikes the prisms and returns back to the theodolite's memory, where horizontal angles, vertical angles, and distances are all automatically calculated and recorded. Both transits and total stations can be used in establishing grid systems. The data captured by total stations has applications beyond forensic mapping. The data can be used with a variety of software packages that allow 3D views of the scene to be created and the development of animations of possible perpetrator and victim actions at a crime scene, the latter being particularly helpful in crime scene

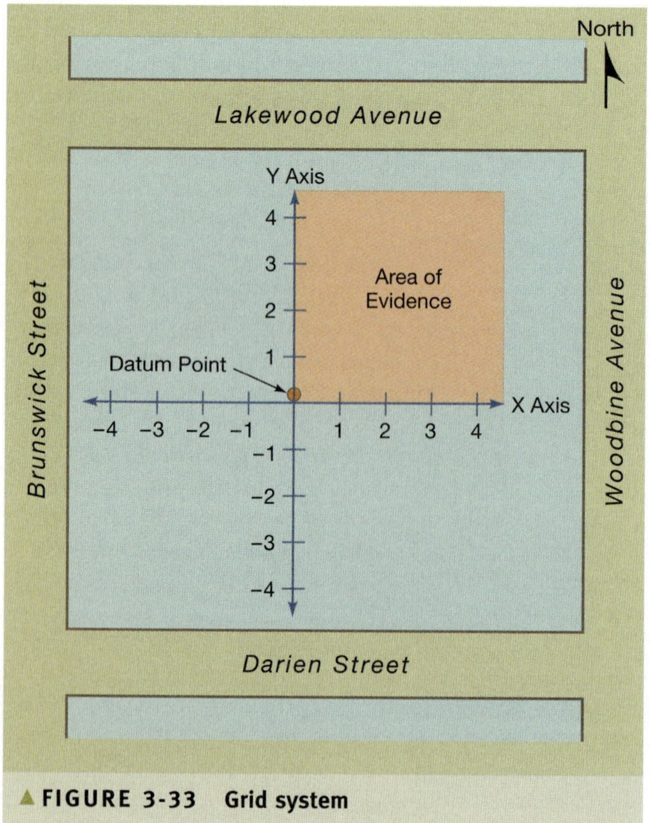

▲ FIGURE 3-33   Grid system

▲ FIGURE 3-34   Total station (theodolite)
(Photos by Donald Schmalzbauer, Forensic Photographer, Forensic Reconstruction Services LLC of St. Paul-Minneapolis, Minnesota.)

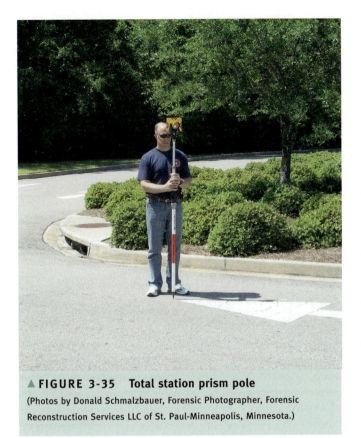

▲ **FIGURE 3-35   Total station prism pole**
(Photos by Donald Schmalzbauer, Forensic Photographer, Forensic Reconstruction Services LLC of St. Paul-Minneapolis, Minnesota.)

reconstruction, discussed later in this chapter. High capability total stations capture data so well that images produced from it are near-photographic in quality, even to the point of distinguishing between different textures; at the high end, it is also possible when preparing the crime scene sketch to simply click on two points and the distance between them is automatically entered into the sketch.[65]

SUBMISSION OF EVIDENCE TO THE LABORATORY GENERALLY

Evidence submitted to a crime laboratory is most often transmitted by courier, air express, or registered mail. In the ideal situation, the investigator most knowledgeable about the case takes it to the laboratory, where he or she can discuss the case with appropriate examiners. Given the caseloads all crime laboratories have, this situation is the exception. In general, the method of transmitting evidence is determined by the nature of the evidence and the urgency of getting an analyst's conclusions. Federal and state agency rules specify how some special classes of evidence must be sent. Examples of these classes are chemicals, blasting caps, flammable materials, and biological and chemical agents. With these materials, the safest procedure is to contact the laboratory to which the evidence is being sent to give lab personnel advance notice

and to get their guidance on how to properly package and send the evidence.

Submission of Evidence to the FBI Laboratory

The FBI accepts only evidence for analysis that is related to a violent crime from state and local law enforcement agencies. An exception may be made for property crimes in which there was an intent to harm or actual personal injury occurred. Examples of property crimes that are not routinely accepted for examination include burglaries, minor theft or fraud under $100,000, arson cases, and explosive incidents involving unoccupied residential and commercial buildings, auto thefts (except those involving rings), and hit-and-run automobile accidents not involving personal injury. When submitting evidence to the FBI laboratory, you must use the following guidelines.[66]

Requesting Evidence Examinations

All requests for evidence examinations should be in writing, on agency letterhead, and addressed to the FBI Laboratory Evidence Control Unit, unless otherwise indicated in the Examinations section. The **letter of transmittal** must contain the following information:

- The submitting contact person's name, agency, address, and telephone number.
- Previous case identification numbers, evidence submissions, and communications relating to the case.
- Description of the nature and the basic facts concerning the case as they pertain to evidence examinations.
- The name(s) and descriptive data about the individual(s) involved (subject, suspect, victim, or a combination of those categories) and the agency-assigned case identification number.
- A list of the evidence being submitted herewith (enclosed) or under separate cover. "Herewith" is limited to small items of evidence that are not endangered by transmitting in an envelope. Write on the envelope before placing evidence inside to avoid damaging or altering the evidence. The written communication should state: *Submitted herewith are the following items of evidence.* Separate cover is used to ship numerous or bulky items of evidence or both. Include a copy of the communication requesting the examinations. The written communication should state: *Submitted under separate cover by (list the method of shipment) are the following items of evidence.*
- What type(s) of examination is requested.
- Where the evidence should be returned and where the laboratory report should be sent.
- A statement if the evidence was examined by another expert in the same field, if there is local

controversy, or if other law enforcement agencies have an interest in the case.

- The reason(s) for an expeditious examination. Do not routinely request an expeditious examination.
- Submit separate communications for multiple cases.

Packaging and Shipping Evidence

- Before packaging and shipping evidence, call the pertinent unit for specific instructions.
- Take precautions to preserve the evidence.
- Wrap and seal each item of evidence separately to avoid contamination.
- Place the evidence in a clean, dry, and previously unused inner container.
- Seal the inner container with tamper-evident or filament tape.
- Affix "Evidence" and "Biohazard" labels, if appropriate, on the inner container. If any of the evidence needs to be examined for latent prints, affix a "Latent" label on the inner container.
- Affix the evidence examination request and all case information between the inner and outer containers.
- Place the sealed inner container in a clean, dry, and previously unused outer container with clean packing materials. Do not use loose Styrofoam.
- Completely seal the outer container so that any tampering would be evident.
- All *shipments of suspected or confirmed hazardous materials* must comply with U.S. Department of Transportation and International Air Transport Association regulations. Title 49 of the Code of Federal Regulations (CFR) lists specific requirements that must be observed when preparing hazardous materials for shipment by air, land, or sea. In addition, the International Air Transport Association annually publishes *Dangerous Goods Regulations* detailing how to prepare and package shipments for air transportation. Title 49 CFR 172.101 provides a Hazardous Materials Table that identifies items considered to be hazardous for the purpose of transportation. Title 49 CFR 172.101 also addresses special provisions for certain materials, hazardous materials communications, emergency response information, and training requirements for shippers. *A trained and qualified evidence technician must assist with the typing, labeling, packaging, and shipping of all hazardous materials.*
- U.S. Department of Transportation regulations and the following guidelines must be followed when *shipping live ammunition:*
  —Package and ship ammunition separately from firearm(s).
  —The outside of the container must be labeled "ORM-D, Cartridges, Small Arms."

  —The Declaration of Dangerous Goods must include the number of packages and the gross weight of the completed packages in grams.
- Unless otherwise indicated in the Examinations section, address the outer container as follows: Federal Bureau of Investigation Laboratory Division, Attention: Evidence Control Unit, 2501 Investigation Parkway, Quantico, VA 22135.
- Ship evidence by U.S. Postal Service Registered Mail, United Parcel Service, or Federal Express. Record the method of shipment and the tracking number(s) on the chain-of-custody form.

CRIME SCENE RECONSTRUCTION AND STAGED CRIMES

Reconstruction is "the process of utilizing information derived from physical evidence at the scene, from analyses of physical evidence (*in the laboratory*) and from inferences drawn from such analyses to test various theories of the occurrence of prior events."[67] Reconstruction is particularly valuable in cases for which eyewitness evidence is absent or unreliable. It is also a key tool in identifying staged crime scenes and determining the extent to which the statement of witnesses is consistent or inconsistent with the physical evidence.

There are six stages of crime scene reconstruction:[68]

- Recognition of evidence
- Appropriate documentation
- Proper collection
- Laboratory examination
- Analysis
- Synthesis

Crime scene reconstruction begins with the recognition, documentation, and collection of physical evidence. There can be no forensic analysis until the potentially useful items of physical evidence are separated from those items at the scene that have no evidential value. Thus, it is crucial that the team processing the crime scene know and act on the sure knowledge that, in addition to its ordinary importance as evidence, each item is part of the foundation on which the reconstruction effort rests.

Chapter 4 contains detailed information about how to properly collect different types of evidence. The work of the laboratory can be enhanced by a steady stream of communication among those working the scene, investigators assigned to the case, laboratory examiners, and the reconstruction or analyst team. Based on the totality of information available, a reconstruction of an event consistent with the evidence is synthesized or developed.

Types of Reconstruction

There are three major types or categories of reconstruction:

1. *Accident or transportation-oriented reconstruction.*
   This type of reconstruction involves trucks, motor-cycles, automobiles, trains, airplanes, and boats. Within policing, traffic accident reconstruction is a highly specialized field involving advanced training and techniques. A specialized team from the National Traffic Safety Board (NTSB) investigates and reconstructs airline accidents. A major part of these investigations involves reassembly of parts of the aircraft, as well as consideration of variables such as pilot error, weather, flight information, equipment failure, and metal fatigue. In 2007, the two most highly publicized NTSB investigations involved the crash of two news helicopters covering a police pursuit in Phoenix and the collapse of a bridge in Minneapolis.

▲ **FIGURE 3-36**   **After mid-air collision two helicopters plunge to the ground**
Two helicopters fall from the sky after colliding in mid-air as they videotaped a police pursuit (La Voz Arizona/Arthur Alexander)

2. *Specific crime reconstruction,* such as those involving homicide cases, sexual assault and/or rape, arson scene reconstruction, computer crime, and white-collar crime.[69] Reconstruction of sexual assault crimes is useful in determining whether the act was consensual or forced. Useful evidence may be gathered at the scene of the assault, from the medical examination of the victim, and the victim's and suspect's clothing.

3. *Shooting reconstruction.* Like all other types of reconstruction, each and every item of physical evidence, whether it is a fired bullet, a shot-pellet pattern, a bloodstain pattern, a firearm or any similar item, lends itself to the scientific method. For each item, the relevant question(s) must first be formulated, observations made, a hypothesis formulated, and tests conducted. If a man relates that he walked into the bedroom and saw his wife place a revolver to her temple and shoot herself with a revolver, among the first relevant questions are, what was the wife's position when she did this, was she right- or left-handed, where was the husband when this happened, where was the revolver found, and are the wound characteristics consistent with the actions described by the husband? Ultimately, the various pieces of the "puzzle" are put together into a coherent sequence that constitutes the theory of the shooting.[70]

Staged Crime Scenes and Reconstruction

Staged crime scenes are not new. In the Bible, Joseph's brothers sold him into slavery and then dipped his robe in the blood of a goat they had killed to convince their father that Joseph had been devoured by a wild animal.[71] There are no official statistics on how often investigators encounter **staged crime** scenes, but there is some limited evidence that about 3% of all cases may involve some element of staging.[72] One panel of experienced investigators concluded that the most common staged nonfatal crime was the false allegation of a sexual crime, followed by murder staged as a "burglary gone bad" or a robbery.[73] In part, the absence of statistics is due to the fact that when confronted with a staged crime scene, the police have simply unfounded the original report of a crime, reclassified it, or charged the person reporting it with filing a false report. In recent years, a few agencies have filed civil suits against the person falsely reporting a crime or staging a crime scene in order to recover costs of wasted investigative efforts.

The essence of staging a crime scene is to misdirect investigators, usually away from the actual perpetrator, although in some instances it may be done for other reasons, such as protecting a victim or family from social or religious embarrassment—for example, by attempting to make a suicide or accidental autoerotic death look like a murder (see Chapter 10, "Sex-Related Offenses").[74] A person who lies and totally fabricates a story about having been the victim of crime is essentially staging or "putting on" a crime. Earlier in this chapter a case was summarized that involved a woman who reported being tormented by the "poet;" she represents a "victim" who staged a crime by both lying about multiple crimes against herself and creating physical evidence to support her complaints. In addition to other charges that may apply to situations involving staged scenes, many states have specific state statutes dealing with fabricating false evidence and concealing, altering, or destroying evidence.

Some staged crimes are so clumsy that no elaborate reconstruction is needed. For example, a husband has a drug habit. To hide the fact that he has been selling his wife's jewelry for drugs, he breaks the window leading from the carport into the house and makes it looks like someone searched or "tossed" the house looking for valuables. However, all the broken glass is on the carport—there is none on the inside of the house—meaning that the window was broken from the inside, not the outside. However, with so many real crime investigation shows on television, people are learning more about police and laboratory capabilities and are becoming more sophisticated in staging scenes.

Staging investigations are confronted by two unusual factors: (1) what was the real act or crime that necessitated staging the scene, and (2) what was the motive for staging the scene, the determination of which usually leads to the perpetrator.[75] Often, the driving motive for the original crime is financial gain, revenge, or the desire to be rid of people or circumstances that are barriers to a seemingly more attractive future. The staging motive is often one of self-preservation, to get away with the crime, or the previously mentioned avoidance of embarrassment or shame.[76]

Because the possibility of a staged crime scene may not have been considered initially, the best tool for identifying one is to always be thorough in all aspects of the original investigation. That documentation remains available and unchanging, needing only additional consideration and analysis.[77] Often, the first inklings of something being wrong come from noticing that those who would seemingly be most affected by the crime, such as the murder of a spouse, display unusual behavior. Even allowing for the complexity of human behavior, when a surviving spouse treats the murder as an inconvenience, is only minimally distressed, or is even oddly undisturbed by it, investigators should be alerted. Stated somewhat differently, when there is an observable lack of congruence between the surviving spouse's affect and the murder, the cautious investigator wants to understand the reason for the gap.

Even when surviving spouses do not verbally express feelings of loss and despair to a significant degree, there are usually still nonverbal signs of distress, e.g., facial expressions, clutching their stomach, reaching for something to steady themselves or a chair to lower themselves into, moving their hands in circular motions as though they are trying to grasp the situation, and a mouth moving without the utterance of words suggest an inability to comprehend the loss. In other situations, slight inconsistencies between the statements of witnesses and the evidence at the scene are noted and lead

to more extensive investigation or the laboratory examination of physical evidence, revealing that the crime could not have happened as initially reported. Some staged crimes may be so successful that some time may go by before the documentation of the investigation is reexamined. For example, a new widow who comes into a considerable amount of inheritance from the deceased is suddenly out partying continuously, immediately having an intense emotional relationship with someone, cutting off contacts with the family's former friends and relatives, and rumors are surfacing about her previously having affairs; all these factors should invite cold case scrutiny.

Staged crime investigations profit from a five-step logical process:[78]

1. Conduct a comprehensive and thorough review of the documented scene, which may be very time-consuming in violent crimes because of the abundance of evidence.
2. Carefully consider the victim's character, lifestyle, personal and professional associates, drug and alcohol use, normal hangouts, daily schedule and routines, physical condition, occupation, prior complaints to the police, and recent conversations with neighbors and friends. Is this information consistent with the scene and any behavior imputed to the victim; do any inconsistencies emerge that are significant?
3. Identify and document in detail all possible indicators of staging.
4. Identify and document possible motives for the original act and for the staging. The person staging the scene is not someone who happened by and gratuitously changed things; it is almost always someone who knew the victim and had some association or relationship.[79]
5. Determine who benefits from the original act and the staging. Even in death cases the deceased may benefit. To illustrate, a suicide successfully staged as a murder means the insurance policy will be paid and the family financially protected and the deceased spared a long, painful, and expensive period of disability before finally dying. A variation of this is when a suicide is staged as a mishap, such as the "accidental discharge" of a firearm while handling or cleaning it, while crossing a barbwire fence in a field with it, or while climbing up to or down from a hunting stand in a tree with the gun.

The Use of Pattern Evidence in Reconstruction

Although some actions at a crime scene may produce previously unseen results, many actions can be expected to routinely produce familiar patterns with regularity. This regularity in physical evidence is called **pattern evidence.**

Pattern evidence is particularly useful in crime scene reconstructions efforts because it can identify actions that are consistent or inconsistent with the statements provided by witnesses, thereby identifying those who seek to mislead the investigation.

Generally, pattern evidence is created by the contact of two surfaces (persons, vehicles, or objects) that results in the formation of compressions, imprints, or markings. In some cases, the contact may be a transfer of material from one surface to another resulting in pattern evidence in the form of a stain or a deposit. Pattern evidence also results from the fracture, breaking, or cutting of an object. Illustrations include bloodstain, glass fracture, burns, tire and skid mark patterns, projectile trajectory patterns, and injury wound patterns. (See Figure 3-37.)

Animation and 3-D Modeling in Crime Scene Reconstruction

The use of computer animation and three-dimensional modeling deduced from photographs of a crime scene have become new tools for investigators developing a reconstruction (see Figure 3-38). Using powerful animation and modeling software programs, these new tools are designed to help in understanding complex crime scenes. The 3-D technology is ideally suited to reconstruct buildings or houses allowing a "walkthrough" of the recreated structures. The viewing perspective can then be placed anywhere in the 3-D scene—whether moving down the hall of a house during a burglary, showing the relevant locations of tables and chairs during a domestic fight, or following the flow of an accelerant from one room to another as in an arson investigation.

The capability of reconstructing a building or a crime scene on a computer also allows a specific aspect to become more visible. It is possible to remove or make any part of the building or crime scene transparent in order to show a particular view more clearly. For instance, a shooting reconstructionist can use "still" photographs from a computer-generated reconstruction to illustrate the trajectories of bullets. "Stills" are single frames taken from the computer animation of the scene. Continuing with this example, a crime scene can be reconstructed placing the victim and the alleged assailant in their exact positions at the time of the shooting. Using computer animation to track and illustrate the trajectory backward from the victim's bullet entry wound to the barrel of the gun being held by the suspect, the exact position of the two in the room can be determined with a visual line showing the trajectory of the bullet. Although these software tools are limited to the factual knowledge and physical evidence derived from the crime scene, they are particularly important in illustrating to court judges and juries relative distances, time changes, physical relationships, and bullet trajectories.

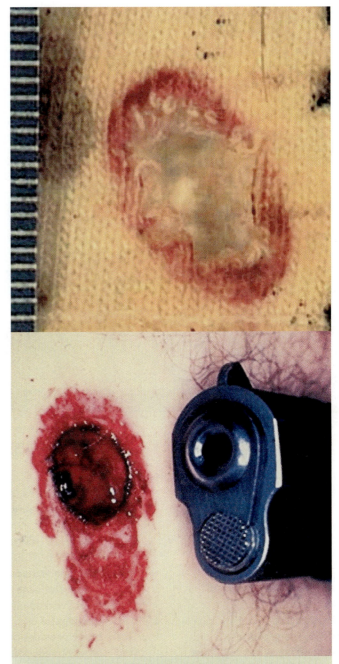

▲ **FIGURE 3-37 Specific crime scene reconstruction** An identification or the victim's wound with the suspect weapon is an important element in the reconstruction of a shooting incident. In this case, the suspect stated that he shot the victim from across the room in self-defense. However, the imprint of the pistol's nose and barrel clearly revealed that the shot was fired with the weapon having direct contact with the victim. This is an interesting case because the imprint was left on the skin, even though the shot was fired through the victim's sweater. (Courtesy Forensic Training and Consulting, LLC)

▶ **FIGURE 3-38   Animation**
Computer animation and 3-D modeling help illustrate relationships between people and inanimate objects, such as furniture. They also provide excellent trajectory and ballistic information from the crime scene. (Courtesy Mr. Ed Hueske, Forensic Training and Consulting, LLC, The Colony, Texas)

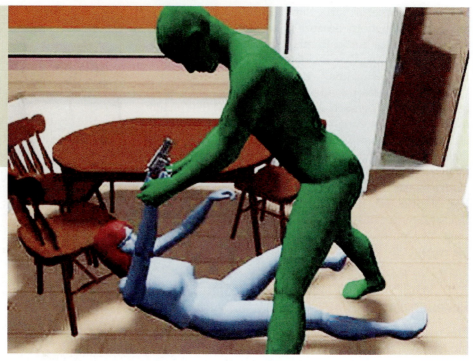

KEY TERMS

3D View
administrative log
alternative light systems (ALSs)
Americans with Disabilities Act (ADA)
assignment sheet
associative evidence
baseline coordinates
be-on-the-lookout (BOLO)
chain of custody
cleared by arrest
corpus delicti evidence
crime
crime scene
crime scene control
crime scene entry log sheet
crime scene release
crime scene search patterns
crime scene sketch
cross-projection view
datum point
deductive reasoning
elevation view

evidence recovery log
exceptionally cleared
felony
field notes
follow-up investigation
forensic mapping
grid system
hepatitis B (HBV)
hepatitis C (HCV)
human immunodeficiency virus (HIV)
incident/offense report
inductive reasoning
investigator
irregular evidence
letter of transmittal
lifted-prints log
macroscopic scene
media statement
microscopic scene
misdemeanor
overhead view
pattern evidence

personal protection equipment (PPE)
photographic log
photographing
polar coordinates
preliminary investigation
primary scene
reconstruction
rectangular coordinates
regular evidence
rough sketch
secondary scenes
smooth or finished sketch
staged crime
total station
trace evidence
trace evidence vacuums
tracing evidence
triangulation
tuberculosis (TB)
videotaping
violation

REVIEW QUESTIONS

1. What are the objectives of the investigative process? 29
2. How would you describe the "lucky" investigator? 49
3. Contrast inductive and deductive reasoning. A 9
4. What are the preliminary and follow-up investigations? 50 / 56

5. Name the major steps in the preliminary investigation. 50 - 56
6. How is a crime scene entry log properly used?
7. What is scene turnover?
8. What is scene release?

9. Define *primary scene* and *secondary scene*. 57
10. What are macroscopic and microscopic scenes? 57
11. Identify and explain the major crime scene functions. 58 - 59
12. State and explain three broad categories of evidence 60 in which investigators have a particular interest.
13. What are the rules for crime scene investigators, 62 and what do they mean?
14. State at least 12 measures police officers at crime 70 scenes can take to protect themselves against health risks from blood-borne pathogens, such as HIV/AIDS.
15. Identify and discuss three means by which a crime scene can be visually documented. 77

16. Draw a rough crime scene sketch of the room in which you live, assuming that there are two shell casings on the floor, one bullet hole in the west wall, and one in the north wall.
17. What kind of information should be included in a letter of transmittal accompanying evidence being 85 sent to the crime laboratory?
18. Identify and briefly discuss the various types of 79 / 80 views and forensic mapping techniques.
19. State why people stage crimes, and explain how to investigate crimes that appear staged. 84
20. What is crime scene reconstruction? 86

INTERNET ACTIVITIES

1. The Crime Scene Investigation website at www. crime-scene-investigator.net has many helpful articles on crime scene investigation and evidence collection. Go to this website and click "Crime Scene Response Guidelines." Read the article "Personnel Duties and Responsibilities," which discusses the different roles investigators have at a crime scene.
2. Learn more about the importance of understanding a crime scene and documenting crime scene evidence by reading the article "Crime Scene Interpretation" at www.feinc.net/cs-int.htm.

NOTES

1. Portions of the information on the preliminary investigation are drawn from several sources, including Technical Working Group on Crime Scene Investigation, *Crime Scene Investigation: A Guide for Law Enforcement* (Washington, D.C.: U.S. Department of Justice, January 2000), pp. 11–17, National Institute of Justice, *Crime Scene Investigation: A Reference for Law Enforcement Training* (Washington, D.C.: National Institute of Justice, June 2004), pp. 7–51, and the authors' own experiences.
2. "Mysterious Poet Assailant Proves to Victimize Herself," *Atlanta Journal and Constitution*, Oct. 3, 1981, p. A3.
3. Information in this section is derived from the authors' experiences, as well as Savannah-Chatham Metropolitan Police Department, Standard Operating Procedure (SOP) 2-01, "Criminal Investigations," April 4, 2004 and Springfield (Missouri) Police Department, SOP 402.8, "Follow-up Investigations," Dec. 1, 2002.
4. Henry C. Lee, Timothy Palbach, and Marilyn T. Miller, *Crime Scene Handbook* (San Diego, CA: Academic Press, 2001), pp. 2–3.
5. Ibid., p. 4.
6. Ibid.
7. Ibid., pp. 4–5, from which the content of this point is summarized.
8. Barry A. J. Fisher, *Techniques of Crime Scene Investigation,* 6th ed. (Boca Raton, FL: CRC Press, 2000), p. 46, with some restatement.
9. Ibid., p. 32.
10. Some of the points in this paragraph are restatements from *Crime Scene Investigation,* pp. 19–23.
11. Ibid.
12. Information in the three sections on releasing information to the news media has been drawn from various policies SOPs. For example, see Kansas City (Missouri) Police Department, Procedural Instruction 02-5, "Media Contacts and Interactions," February 15, 2002 and Madison (Wisconsin) Police Department, Policy Manual, 3-600, "News Media Relations," 2003.
13. Bill Berkeley, "Wrong Assumptions Ruined Probe," *Atlanta Journal and Constitution,* Feb. 17, 1982, pp. A1, A13.
14. "But Some Have Ins and Outs," *St. Petersburg* (Florida) *Times,* Feb. 24, 1979, p. A1.
15. "Man Accused of Shipping Self to Bank," *Atlanta Journal and Constitution,* May 10, 1979, p. A18.
16. John Lester, "Forensic Expert Uses Tiny Clues to Solve Crimes," *Tampa Tribune,* Sept. 9, 1992, pp. 1–2.
17. "Real Estate Agent Pleads Guilty to 5 'Lock Box' Thefts," *Washington Post,* Sept. 12, 1978, p. B5.
18. Fisher, *Techniques of Crime Investigation,* pp. 67–68.
19. Colleen Wade, editor, *Handbook of Forensic Services* (Washington, DC: Federal Bureau of Investigation, 2003), pp. 136–143.
20. Minnesota Department of Health, "Facts on AIDS: A Law Enforcement Guide," p. 2, July 15, 2004.
21. Centers for Disease Control, Division of HIV/AIDS Prevention, "HIV and Its Transmission," Aug. 17, 2004.

22. Centers for Disease Control, "HIV and Its Transmission" (Washington, DC: Oct. 21, 2001), p. 4.

23. Centers for Disease Control, Division of HIV/AIDS Prevention, "Are Health Workers at Risk of Getting HIV on the Job?" p. 1, Dec. 15, 2003.

24. Centers for Disease Control, Division of HIV/AIDS Prevention, "Can I Get HIV from a Bite?" p. 1, Dec. 15, 2003.

25. South Dakota Risk Management Bulletin, Issue #45, "State Employee Blood-Borne Pathogens Procedures," Sept. 26, 2002.

26. National Institute for Occupational Safety and Health and the Centers for Disease Control, "Guidelines for Prevention of Transmission of HIV Virus and Hepatitus B Virus to Health-Care and Public Safety Workers: A Response to P.L. 100–607, the Health Omnibus Programs Extension Act of 1988" (Washington, D.C., June 23, 1989), p. 9.

27. Ibid., p. 13.

28. S. T. Mast, G. D. Woolwine, and J. L. Gerberding, "Efficacy of Gloves in Reducing Blood Volumes Transferred during Simulated Needle Stick," *Journal of Infectious Diseases*, 1993, Vol. 168, No. 6, pp. 1589–1592.

29. Hepatitis B Foundation, "About Hepatitis B," www. hepb.org, 2003, p. 1.

30. Hepatitis B Foundation, "Symptoms," www.hepb.org, 2003, p. 1.

31. Centers for Disease Control, National Center for Infectious Diseases, "Viral Hepatitis C Fact Sheet," www.cdc.gov/ncidod/disease/hepatitis/c, Oct. 15, 2004, p. 1.

32. Ibid., p. 1.

33. National Institute of Allergy and Infectious Diseases, "Fact Sheet: Tuberculosis," www.hiaid.nih.gov/factsheets/tb.htm, Jan. 13, 2001, p. 1.

34. Ibid., p. 7.

35. Ibid., p. 1.

36. Ibid., p. 10.

37. Ibid., p. 7.

38. For example, see Savannah-Chatham Metropolitan Police Department, SOP 1-54, "Underwater Search and Recovery," Aug. 13, 2004.

39. California Commission on Peace Officer Standards and Training, "Basic Course Workbook Series: Learning Domain 30, Preliminary Investigation," Version 2 (Sacramento, CA: 2001), p. 2–14, with some additions.

40. Ibid., pp. 2–12, with minor restatement.

41. National Forensic Science and Technology Center, Scientific Working Group on Imaging Technologies, "Draft Guidelines for Field Application of Imaging Technology," Version 2.2, June 7, 2001, p. 4.

42. Ibid.

43. Ibid.

44. Ibid., p. 2.

45. Ibid., p. 3.

46. This section is taken from Colleen Wade, ed., *Handbook of Forensic Services* (Washington, D.C.: Federal Bureau of Investigation, 2003), pp. 162–163.

47. Ross M. Gardner, Practical Crime Scene Processing (Boca Raton, Florida: CRC Press, 2005), p. 163. This is an excellent work and should be in the library of any serious professional because of the numerous "hands on" details it provides.

48. Ibid., p. 171.

49. These four views are identified in Ibid., pp. 166-169. Although they have been well documented for years, Gardner does a crisp job of delineating between views and methods of fixing.

50. Tacoma Police Department, Forensic Services Policy and Procedures Manual, "Crime Scene Diagramming," May 11, 2004, p. 3.

51. Gardner, September 1, 2007 e-mail and attachment to Charles Swanson, handwritten note on manuscript he reviewed.

52. Gardner, Practical Crime Scene Processing, p. 171.

53. Ibid., 172.

54. Ibid., pp. 173–174.

55. Ibid., pp. 174–175.

56. Ibid., p. 178.

57. Forensic Services Policy and Procedures Manual, p. 4.

58. Gardner, Practical Crime Scene Processing, p. 178.

59. Mike Byrd, "Unearthing New Technology in Crime Scene Responses with Forensic Mapping," (www. Crime-Scene-Investigation.net//Forensic Mapping. HTML), undated, p.4.

60. Gardner, Practical Crime Scene Processing, pp. 181–183.

61. Ibid., p. 188.

62. Kent J. Buehler, "The Role of Archaeological Techniques in Forensic Settings" (Norman: University of Oklahoma, College of Arts and Sciences, *Oklahoma Archaeological Survey Newsletter*), Vol. 23, No. 1, July 2003, p. 1.

63. Gardner, Practical Crime Scene Processing, p. 188.

64. Ibid., p. 190.

65. Ross Gardner, August 25, 2007 e-mail to C. R. Swanson.

66. This section is taken from Wade, ed., *Handbook of Forensic Services*, pp. 7–11.

67. W. P. Bell, "A Proposed Definition of Homicide Reconstruction," *California Department of Justice Firearm/Toolmark Training Bulletin*, represented AFTE Journal, 23 (2), April 1991, pp. 740–744.

68. Although a variety of authors discuss different concepts within the crime scene reconstruction process, these six are most often agreed on as the basic stages in the process. See Henry Lee, *Crime Scene Handbook* (New York: Prometheus Books, 2001); Thomas Bevel, "Crime Scene Reconstruction," *Journal of Forensic Identification*, 41 (4), 1991, pp. 248–244; Frank Horvath and William Messig, "The Criminal Investigation Process and the Role of Forensic Evidence," *Journal of Forensic Science*, 41 (6), 1996, pp. 663–339; and Edward Hueske, *Practical Analysis & Reconstruction of Shooting Incidents* (Boca Raton, FL: CRC Press, 2005).

69. Robert Ogle, *Crime Scene Investigation and Reconstruction* (Upper Saddle River, NJ: Prentice Hall, 2003).

70. Edward Hueske, *Practical Analysis & Reconstruction of Shooting Incidents* (Boca Raton, FL: CRC Press, 2005).

71. Robert R. Hazelwood and Michael R. Napier, *International Journal of Offender Therapy and Comparative Criminology*, 2004, 48: p. P. 744. On this topic also see, Brent E. Turvey, "Staged Crime Scenes: A Preliminary Study of 25 Cases," *Journal of Behavioral Profiling*, December 2000, Vol. 1, No. 3, pp. 1–9.
72. Hazelwood and Napier, p. 746.
73. Ibid., p. 755.
74. Ibid., p. 754–755. On this point, also see J. E. Douglas and C. M. Munn, *Crime Classification Manual* (New York: Lexington Books, 1992), p. 251.
75. Hazelwood and Napier, pp. 746–747.
76. Ibid., pp. 747–751.
77. Ibid., p. 756.
78. Ibid., p. 756, from which these five points are taken with change and additional comment.
79. Ibid., p. 757.

4

PHYSICAL EVIDENCE

▲   Weapons are often found at the scene of a crime. Here, a large "bolo" type knife is found at the exit of the front door leading to the living room where a young woman was murdered in a domestic quarrel. As depicted in the photograph, this is the eighth piece of physical evidence found at the scene, and a rigid ruler is included to give an indication of size and proportionality. Note the faint blood spatter on the door frame revealing that the suspect exited the house and apparently dropped the knife after committing the crime. (Courtesy Dallas, Texas Police Department)

A common theme in all criminal investigations, and one of the most important throughout this text, is the collection of physical evidence. The topic of physical evidence is addressed in several chapters of this book; however, this chapter specifically focuses on the techniques used to identify, collect, package, and store particular types of physical evidence for subsequent examination.

Several types of physical evidence are covered in this chapter: soil and pollen, footwear and tire prints, paint, glass, lamp filaments, fibers, hair, lip prints, and tool marks. Details on collection and packaging techniques are provided for fingerprints, dental evidence, bloodstains, firearm evidence, and questioned documents. In addition, several software programs and investigative tools for each type of evidence is discussed. The importance of consulting specialized forensic and medical experts is emphasized throughout the chapter.

Thorough crime scene processing is vitally important to the effective prosecution of a case. In particular, rapid technological advances (such as those involving DNA evidence) have greatly expanded the amount of information that can be obtained from the analysis of physical evidence from a crime scene. To take advantage of these new opportunities, the crime scene investigator must follow sound evidence processing practices. The National Institute of Justice has developed a step-by-step protocol guiding investigators in the objective recognition, documentation, collection, preservation, and transmittal of physical evidence.[1] This protocol provides a basis for training in the area of crime scene processing and involves five key areas:

1. Initial response to the crime scene and prioritization of efforts.
2. Preliminary documentation and evaluation of the scene.
3. Processing the crime scene.
4. Completing and recording the crime scene.
5. Using crime scene equipment.

Each of these areas are further broken into steps having specific performance objectives for the investigator. These include checking for potential officer safety and hazardous substances, limiting scene access, ensuring contamination control, properly documenting and preserving evidence, and debriefing the crime scene team. The establishment of a routine and disciplined protocol helps to ensure the proper collection of evidence and avoids the embarrassment of careless crime scene processing that often jeopardizes a case.

CLASS VERSUS INDIVIDUAL CHARACTERISTICS

To fully appreciate the potential value of physical evidence, the investigator must understand the difference between class and individual characteristics. Characteristics of physical evidence that are common to a group of objects or persons are termed **class characteristics.** Regardless of how thoroughly examined, such evidence can be placed only into a broad category; an individual identification cannot be made because there is a possibility of more than one source for the evidence.[2] (See Figure 4-1.) Examples of this type of evidence include glass fragments too small to be matched to broken edges, and tool marks or shoeprints in instances where microscopic or accidental markings are insufficient for positive individual identification. Evidence with individual characteristics can be identified, with a high degree of probability, as originating with a particular person or source.[3] The ability to establish individuality distinguishes this type of physical evidence from that possessing only class characteristics. Some examples of evidence with individual characteristics are fingerprints, palm prints, and footprints.

Conceptually, the distinction between class and individual characteristics is clear. But as a practical matter, the crime scene technician or investigator often may not be able to make this differentiation and must rely on the results yielded by crime laboratory examination. For example, a shoeprint collected at one scene may yield only class characteristics: left by a man's shoe of a particular brand from the right foot on both the face of the victim and just outside the crime scene. However, Figure 4-1 illustrates a situation in which shoeprints yielded not only class characteristics but also individual ones, not to mention the cross contamination of blood evidence from the victim also found on the shoe. Thus, although the investigator must recognize that physical evidence that

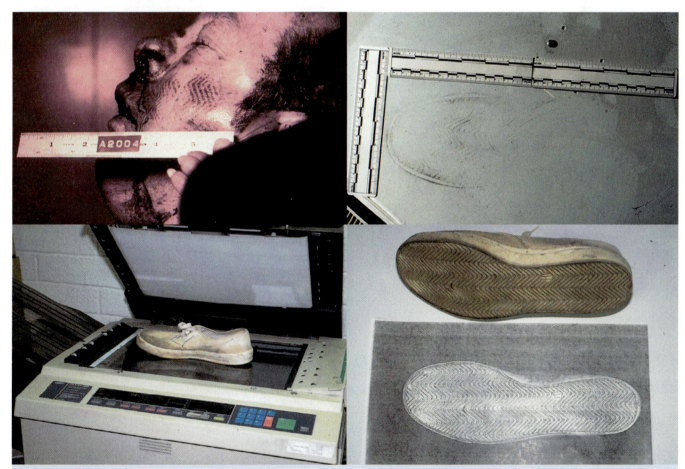

▲ **FIGURE 4-1 Class versus individual characterstics**
(*Upper left*) An impression of a shoeprint is observed on the face of a murder victim. (*Upper right*) A similar shoeprint is found on the hood of a car located just outside the apartment window of the crime scene, representing class characteristics. (*Lower left*) After officers arrest a person trying to run away from the scene as they arrive, they later make a photocopy of the suspect's right shoe at the police department. (*Lower right*) The photocopy of the shoeprint provides the basis for a positive identification of the two prints found at the murder scene. (**Courtesy Detroit, Michigan State Police**)

allows for individualization is of more value, he or she should not dismiss evidence that appears to offer only class characteristics, because it may show individual characteristics through laboratory examination. Furthermore, a preponderance of class-characteristic evidence tying a suspect (or other items in the suspect's possession) to the scene strengthens the case for prosecution. Note also that occasionally class-characteristic evidence may be of such an unusual nature that it has much greater value than that ordinarily associated with evidence of this type. In an Alaska case, a suspect was apprehended in the general area where a burglary had been committed; the pry bar found in his possession contained white stucco, which was of considerable importance, since the building burglarized was the only white stucco building in that town.[4] Finally, class-characteristic evidence can be useful in excluding suspects in a crime, resulting in a more effective use of investigative effort.

Comparison Samples

Much of the work of forensic science involves comparing various types of samples. Special terms are used to refer to these samples, and you must know what they mean so you can communicate with the laboratory and understand lab reports. At the most general level, comparison samples may be from **unknown or questioned sources** or from **known sources;** each of these two main categories has three subcategories.

Unknown or Questioned Samples

1. *Recovered crime scene sample whose source is in question:* This evidence may have been left, for example, by either victims or suspects. (It leads to questions such as, Did the suspect leave the fingerprint recovered at the point of entry for the burglary?)
2. *Questioned evidence that may have been transferred to an offender during the commission of a crime and been taken away by him or her:* When compared with the evidence from a known source, this evidence can be used to link the suspect to a person, vehicle, tool, or weapon. (For example, do any of the hairs combed from the suspect's hair match those of the victim?)
3. *Evidence from an unknown or questioned source that can be used to link multiple offenses:* This material might link crimes that were committed by the same person, tool, or weapon. (Illustratively, were the bullets recovered from the victims' bodies in three separate murders fired by the pistol the suspect was carrying when he was arrested?)[5]

Known Samples

1. *Standard or reference sample:* This is material from a known or verifiable source. It is compared to similar material from an unknown source to determine whether an association or linkage exists between a crime scene, a victim, and the offender. (For example, a sample of blood is taken under medical conditions from the suspect so that it can be compared with blood on the victim's shirt.)
2. *Control or blank sample:* This is material from a known source that was uncontaminated by the crime (e.g., carpet fibers taken from the far corner of a room in which a body was found). It is used to make sure that the material on which evidence was deposited (e.g., carpet fibers, under the body, on which there is blood) does not interfere with laboratory testing.
3. *Elimination sample:* This type of sample is taken from a source known to have had lawful access to the crime scene (such as a police officer, medical technician, or occupant). It is compared with unknown samples of the same type from the scene so that matches can be eliminated, thereby highlighting nonmatches. (An example is elimination prints. If latent fingerprints recovered at a crime scene do not match the fingerprints of those who have lawful access to the area, they immediately become of investigative interest in terms of determining whose prints they are.[6]

SOIL AND POLLEN

Soil is the natural accumulation of earth materials, such as weathering rocks, minerals, and decomposing plants, along with pollen; soil may also contain human-made materials, including pieces of brick, concrete, glass, and paint.[7] How soil develops depends on many factors, such as the basic materials, climate, and time.[8] By comparing color, texture, and composition, soil examinations can determine whether soils share a common origin.[9] Although soil is class-characteristic evidence, its analysis can help focus investigations and discredit alibis:

A man was arrested and charged with the beating of a young girl. The scene of the crime was a construction site adjacent to a newly poured concrete wall. The soil was sand, which had been transported to the scene for construction purposes. As such, it had received additional mixing during the moving and construction process and was quite distinctive. The glove of the suspect contained sand that was similar to that found at the scene and significantly different in composition and particle size from that in the area of the suspect's home. This was important because the suspect claimed that the soil on the gloves came from his garden.[10]

An elderly woman was robbed and murdered in a Washington, D.C., park, and her body was found under a park bench. Within a short time, a suspect was apprehended as a result of a description given by a witness who had seen the person leaving the park on the night of the murder. It was obvious that the suspect had been involved in a struggle and had soil adhering to his clothing and inside his trouser cuffs. He claimed to have been in a fight in another part of the city and gave the location of the fight. Study of the soil near the park bench and of that collected from the scene of the alleged fight revealed that the soil from the suspect's clothing was similar to soil near the park bench but did not compare favorably with samples from the area of the described fight. These comparisons strongly suggested that the suspect had been in contact with the ground in that area and cast strong doubt on his statement that he had not been in the park for years. Furthermore, the lack of similarity between the clothing soil samples and those from the area in which he claimed to have been fighting questioned the validity of his alibi.[11]

The pollen in soil or on plants and grass can also be very significant in determining whether or not a suspect was at the scene:

In a case of alleged sexual assault, the pollen content of samples from a grassy crime scene were compared to pollen recovered from the suspect's clothes and shoes. A very strong correlation with the variety of pollens present on the suspect's clothing and the sample collected at the scene very strongly supported the conclusion that the suspect was at the scene.[12]

Pollen come in a variety of shapes and sizes. To be useful, analysis must not only present correlation from the crime scene to the suspect (as in the preceding case) but also identify type and variety. The California Criminalist Institute, a unit of the California Department of Justice, maintains a database of 140 pollen images generated on a digital scanning electron microscope for identification purposes.[13] Interestingly, the CCI maintains this database on the Internet and continues to systematically add to images as new samples are collected.

Although soil and pollen are class-characteristic evidence, their specificity can approach the level of individual characterization:

In a rape case, the knees of the suspect's trousers contained encrusted soil samples; the sample from the right knee was different from that collected from the left. In examining the crime scene, investigators found two impressions in the soil corresponding to a right and a left knee; samples taken from these two impressions were different. The soil sample from the left-knee impression compared with that removed from the left trouser knee of the suspect, as did the right-knee impression and the right trouser knee soils. The significant difference in soil type between the two knee impressions and their consistency with samples obtained from the suspect's trousers strongly indicated his presence at the scene.[14]

Locating and Handling Soil Evidence

Soil evidence may be important when the suspect drives or walks on unpaved areas, since it is picked up by tire treads or the bottom of shoes and the cuffs of pants. It may also be recovered in a number of other places, such as on the floorboard of the subject's car or on articles in the trunk of the vehicle, including shovels and blankets. If there was a struggle with the victim, the suspect may also have soil on his or her body and clothing. If this soil is different from that in the area where the body was found, this may suggest that the victim was killed elsewhere. In hit-and-run accidents, soil samples may be encountered, for example, on the clothing of victims and on the road. In one unusual case, a solid soil sample in the rough shape of a triangle with 3-inch sides was found and later matched to a space on the underside of the suspect's vehicle.

The guidelines shown next should be followed in handling soil evidence:

1. Soil conditions at the scene can change, so gather the soil as quickly as sound action permits.
2. Collect soil not only from the crime scene but also from the logical points of access to, and escape from, the scene. Place the samples in clean plastic vials and labeled with the date, time, name of the crime scene technician, and the case number, if known.
3. Collect soil samples where there are noticeable changes in composition, color, and texture.
4. Collect soil samples from a depth that is consistent with the depth at which the questioned soil may have originated. In most cases, samples should be composed of about a tablespoon of material taken no more than ½ inch from the surface.
5. When possible, collect soil samples from alibi areas, such as the worksite, yard, or garden of the suspect.

6. Make a detailed drawing or map documenting where and at what depth you collected the soil samples.

7. Do not remove soil adhering to shoes, clothing, and tools. Do not process tools for latent prints at this time. Air-dry the soiled garments and package them separately in paper bags. Avoid jostling and transport to the crime lab for analysis and further processing.

8. Carefully remove soil adhering to vehicles. Air dry the soil and also package it separately in paper bags.

9. Submit unknown or questioned soil and known samples in separate leak-proof containers such as film canisters or plastic pill bottles. Avoid the use of paper envelopes or glass containers. If there are lumps in the soil, pack it in a way that keeps them intact.[15]

10. In packaging soil or other types of evidence, take care to avoid **cross contamination** of the samples.

11. Soil samples made by footwear should be photographed to scale before being recovered. If the soil is located near a footwear print or impression, document the location of the sample after photographing the print or impression to scale.

12. At indoor crime scenes, special vacuums may be used to collect microscopic soil samples from carpets and floors that may have been introduced by the suspect(s). Collect and document each procedure, before transporting the contents to the crime lab.[16]

The guidelines for collecting pollen evidence are consistent with those for soil evidence. It may be necessary to take grass or other clippings from different heights.

FOOTWEAR, FEET, AND TIRES: PRINTS AND IMPRESSIONS

Prints from footwear (shoes, boots, etc.), feet, and tires are common types of evidence, as are foot and tire impressions. Footwear prints, footprints, and tire prints (hereafter referred to inclusively as **footwear prints**) are formed when the soles are contaminated with foreign matter such as blood or dust and leave a print on a firm base, such as a floor, a chair, paper, or cloth.[17] Such prints are called *residue prints*. In contrast, footwear, foot, and tire impressions (hereafter, collectively, **footwear impressions**) occur when the footwear treads in some moldable material, such as earth, clay, and snow.[18] (See Figure 4-2.)

Preserving Footwear Prints

Footwear prints may or may not be readily visible. If they are not immediately apparent, turn off the lights and search for prints using a flashlight held close to, but obliquely from, the surface you are examining. When you find prints:

1. Take general crime scene photos showing the location of the footwear prints.
2. Take photos from directly overhead using lighting and a tripod. Include a linear scale next to, and on the same plane as, the footwear prints. Place a label in the area being photographed to correlate photos with crime scene and photo log records.[19]

There are several methods by which footwear prints can be recovered. The best approach is to send the original evidence to the lab. It should be taped in a rigid container so that there is no opportunity for accidental erasure of the footwear print; do not wrap it in plastic, because this can cause a partial erasure of the image. Footwear prints may be collected by using a transparent adhesive **lifter,** which measures roughly 6 feet by 15 feet, and then mounting the lifter on an appropriately colored card. Similarly,

▲ **FIGURE 4-2   Tire print on fabric**
Tire prints from the striking car were found across the shirt of a hit-and-run victim. Later, police located the vehicle that they believed was involved in the crime. A comparison of the tire marks on the victim's shirt along with other physical evidence recovered at the scene established that the vehicle was involved in the crime. However, the police still needed to put the car's owner behind the wheel at the time of the hit-and-run. The police confronted the suspect with the evidence, which destroyed his claim that the car was in his driveway all night. Ultimately, the man confessed. **(Courtesy Seattle, Washington State Police)**

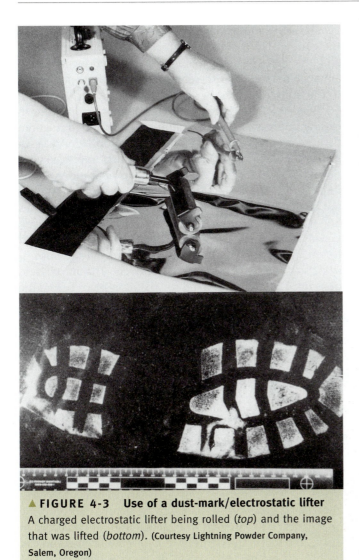

▲ FIGURE 4-3   Use of a dust-mark/electrostatic lifter
A charged electrostatic lifter being rolled (*top*) and the image
that was lifted (*bottom*). (Courtesy Lightning Powder Company,
Salem, Oregon)

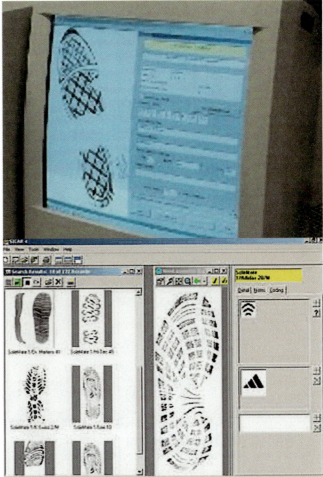

▲ FIGURE 4-4   Shoeprint image capture and retrieval
In the top photograph, a scanned image of a shoeprint
recovered at a crime scene is entered into the computer. In
the bottom photograph, known samples from various
manufacturers (e.g., Nike, New Balance, Converse), as well as
other suspect shoes in the database are compared with the
suspect print. Examinations of this type may establish the
manufacturer and model of a shoe, tie shoes seized from
the suspect to shoeprints recovered at the scene, or link
several cases together where the suspect is still at large.
(Courtesy North Carolina State Bureau of Investigation, Crime Laboratory
Division)

an appropriately colored and sized rubber-gelatin lifter
can be employed. Coated with a thin film of very sensitive
gelatin, the lifter is carefully placed over the print and
then removed. Transparent, black, and white lifters are
available. Transparent and white lifters can be used for
dark prints; a black lifter should be used for light prints.

Dust prints can also be lifted through the use of an
electrostatic device. (See Figure 4-3.) These devices use
static electricity to attract the dust particles of the print
onto a dark-colored lift film. The special film is taped
over the dust print, an electrical probe is touched to the
film to charge it with electricity, and a roller is then used
on the top surface of the film to ensure maximum contact
between the film and the dust print. The resulting image
must be photographed as soon as possible since it is in
dust and therefore not permanent.

Comparing Shoeprint Evidence

The **Shoeprint Image Capture and Retrieval System
(SICAR)** is a software package that classifies, archives,

and identifies shoeprints. (See Figure 4-4). It allows the
operator to create a coded description of a shoeprint,
which can then be compared against a database of known
shoeprints by make and model. SICAR can also do a
search against an operator-created database of suspects'
shoeprints in other cases. Final identification of matches
is always confirmed by an individual examiner.

Preserving Footwear Impressions

As in the case with footwear prints, the location of footwear impressions should be photographed as part of the

▲ FIGURE 4-5 Footwear impression photography
Here a crime scene technician is recording the location of
a shoe impression in dirt. The shoeprint runs left to right,
roughly between the two front legs of the tripod. The small
slip of white paper is just "north" of the impression and has
the necessary case identification information on it. The most
important of a series of photographs will be shot from directly
above the impression using a tripod and will include a ruler
alongside the impression. (Courtesy Nassau County, New York, Police
Department)

general scene and then with a scale. Note that in Figure 4-5,
the camera is on a tripod directly over the impression,
and the flash is being held at a low oblique angle to
enhance the detail in the shot, with the photo scale next
to the impression.

Plaster of Paris is no longer recommended for use in
casting impressions. **Dental stone** is the preferred medium
because of its greater strength, quicker setting time, ease of
use, and because it provides more detailed impressions.

The first step in casting is the preparation of the
impression. The rule is that the impression itself should
not be disturbed. Thus, if twigs, leaves, or other materials
are stuck *in* the impression, they should remain there.
Loose water lying in the impression should be allowed
to remain there. Only loose material lying *on* the impression, such as leaves, should be moved. The impression
does not need to be sprayed to "fix" it in place before the
casting begins. There is no need to use a casting form
around the impression unless it is on a hill or on uneven
ground.[20]

About 2 pounds of dental stone and 12 ounces of water
are needed to cast a shoe impression. (See Figure 4-6.) To
facilitate the casting process, 2-pound bags of dental
stone can be premeasured into 8- by 12-inch Ziplock bags.
Initially, 9 to 10 ounces of water should be added to the
Ziplock bag and the mixture massaged thoroughly
through the closed bag for 3 to 5 minutes.[21] Several
ounces of water may be added to adjust the mixture until
it has the consistency of pancake batter.[22] The dental
stone is then poured alongside the impression and
allowed to flow into it, or it can be gently laid onto the
impression. To prevent the accidental destruction of
detail, the fall of the dental stone into the impression can
be broken by using a spoon or tongue depressor. The
impression should be filled until the dental stone overflows from the impression.

Dental stone sets fairly rapidly. In warm weather, it
can be moved in 20 to 30 minutes, but a longer time

**▶ FIGURE 4-6 Footwear
impressions**
Many crime scene investigators view
impression evidence as second only
to fingerprints when considering the
relative value of physical evidence. In
this picture, shoeprints are found in
the mud near a burglary; a cast is
made from the shoeprint, and a
comparison matches the suspect's
shoe. (Courtesy SIRCHIE Fingerprint
Laboratories, Inc.)

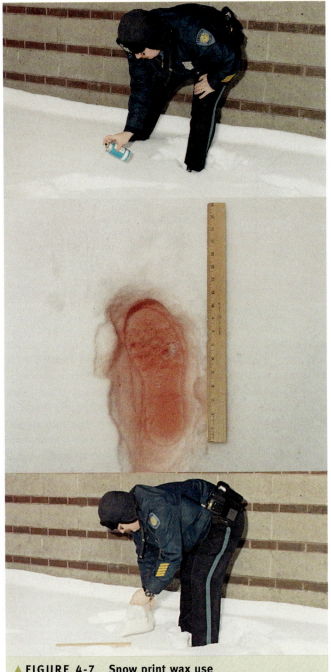

▲ FIGURE 4-7   Snow print wax use
Having already photographed the shoe impression in the snow, the officer sprays red-colored Snow Print Wax on the impression (*top*); the impression is rephotographed (*middle*); and the dental-stone mix is poured from a plastic pouch onto the impression (*bottom*). (Courtesy Lewiston, Maine, Police Department)

should be allowed when the weather is colder. When the cast is firm, but still soft, basic identifying information should be scratched on its back. Moving the cast requires that it be packed carefully, but without the use of plastic materials. The laboratory examiner will clean the cast and examine it in the laboratory after it has dried for at least 48 hours.

If there is standing water in the impression, the following procedure should be used: (1) Build a retaining wall around the impression so that a cast 2-inches deep can be made; (2) sift dental stone that has not been mixed with water directly into the impression to a depth of about 1 inch; (3) add enough mixed dental stone to form a second 1-inch layer; and (4) allow the cast to set in place for at least 1 hour.[23]

Soil evidence should be collected from the bottom of the impression after the cast is removed. The crime scene technician or other person casting the footwear impression should enter her or his initials, the date, and other relevant details on the bottom of the cast before it dries.[24] For submission to the laboratory, wrap the cast in clean paper, bubble wrap, or paper bags.[25]

Preserving Shoe Impressions in Snow

Dental stone is also the preferred material for casting impressions in snow, replacing the more difficult and time-consuming process of using sulfur, which has to be heated. Impressions in snow should first be photographed in the manner previously described. A red-colored product called **Snow Print Wax** is sprayed on the impression at a 30- to 45-degree angle until the highlights are lightly tinted. (See Figure 4-7.) A dark-colored spray paint will also serve the same purpose. In either case, the spray can must be held 30 to 40 inches away so that the force of the aerosol does not disturb the details of the impression. The impression is then rephotographed. The casting process is continued, with the impression being sprayed with enough Snow Print Wax to form a layer of wax, followed by the dental-stone casting process. Because some heat is generated when dental stone is mixed, use snow or cold water instead of warm water to form a consistency somewhat thinner than pancake batter. A box should be placed over the cast for at least 1 hour as it dries.

PAINT

During many investigations, there is the possibility of encountering paint that has been transferred accidentally or deliberately from one object to another.[26] The paint is transferred as fresh smears, dried chips, or "chalking" from old, dry paint. Cases in which such transfers occur include burglaries and hit-and-run accidents.[27] In these offenses, the paint may be found on tools in the suspect's possession or on clothing. In hit-and-run cases, the make and model of the involved vehicle might be identified by comparing paint evidence to FBI reference files on original-manufacturer finishes.

Usually, paint is class-characteristic evidence, although in some cases it reaches the level of individual evidence. If the chips are large enough, it may be possible to make a physical match between a questioned and a known

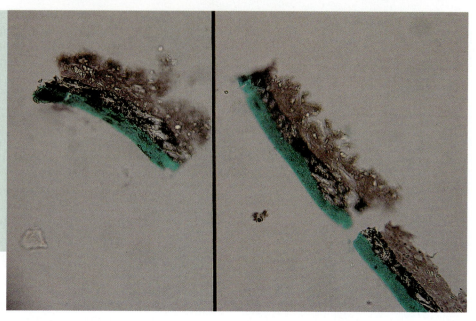

► **FIGURE 4-8 Paint chip comparison**
The photograph on the left is a known sample of paint found at the point-of-entry in a burglary. The photograph on the right is of a paint chip found in the suspect's pant cuff. Note the layers of paint from basecoat to primer to final enamel. In this case, the paint chips were a physical match, placing the suspect at the crime scene and providing the impetus to secure a confession. (Courtesy Texas Department of Public Safety)

source. (See Figure 4-8.) An example is matching recovered paint chips to a particular location, such as the point of entry in a burglary.

Paint is examined in several ways in the laboratory. Factors of importance in its identification are shade, composition, number of coats and their characteristics, texture, and weathering.[28]

In no case should paint chips or particles be collected with transparent tape or mounted on a card using this material, because doing so makes separation in the laboratory difficult to do without damage. Similarly, small particles should not be placed in cotton because it is difficult to separate them.[29] Paint evidence should not be placed in envelopes, because the chips may slip out or be broken; small plastic bags should be avoided, because they have a static electric charge that makes it extremely difficult to remove the chips in the crime laboratory.[30] Clear plastic containers are ideal because the paint evidence can be seen. Where it is particularly difficult to gather paint samples, a small portion of the surface to which the paint has adhered should be cut or chipped off.

GLASS

Glass is important as physical evidence because of the frequency with which it is encountered. Although it is ordinarily class-characteristic evidence, glass has high evidentiary value because of its variations in density, refractive index, and light-dispersion characteristics. Additionally, if the fragments are sufficiently large to allow for a **fracture match,** glass may assume individuality. (See Figure 4-9.) A fracture match can only be made in the crime laboratory. It consists of two or more objects either through physical, optical or photographic means which permit one to conclude that the objects were either

one entity, or were held or bonded together in a unique manner. Legendary forensic scientist Paul Leland Kirk indicated that no two broken edges will match perfectly over an extended length of measurement. If an edge matches that extends over a reasonable length (such as ¼ inch or more), it is virtual proof that the questioned fragment was broken from the exact spot in the original or is part of the original.[31] Glass fractures can be classified by the uniqueness of the occurrence as differentiated by the following types of fractures or characteristics:

- *Concentric cracks:* Fractures that form an approximately circular or oval pattern around the point of impact.
- *Cone or crater (Hertzian cone):* Fractures that are funnel shaped or cause deep bevels in damage caused by a high-velocity impact.
- *Hackle:* Line or crack surface fractures that run parallel to the direction of the crack.
- *Radial cracks:* Fractures that extend from the point of impact.
- *Ream:* Imperfections within a sample of nonhomogeneous layers of flat glass.
- *Wallner lines:* Rib-shaped marks with a wavelike pattern on glass fracture edges that are almost always concave in the direction from which the crack occurred.[32]

Thus, glass fracture patterns are unique and can assume individuality, and fracture features may reflect the nature of the glass and cause of the breaking force. The sequencing of events or fractures may also be possible if the samples are not contaminated.

Glass is a common form of evidence, particularly at the scenes of burglaries where a window has been the point of entry. When a suspect is apprehended soon after the commission of an offense, his or her clothing should

◄ FIGURE 4-9 Glass fracture match of a rear tail light and assembly
Pieces 1 through 4 were recovered at the scene of a hit-and-run automobile accident. The remaining pieces of the rear tail light and plastic assembly surrounding the glass lens were found still intact on the suspect's vehicle, parked in his garage several hours after the incident. Note how perfectly pieces 3 and 4 fit into the remaining pieces of the tail light. (Courtesy Mr. Ed Hueske and Ms. Sherry Bethune, Forensic Training and Consulting, LLC, 2007)

be carefully examined for minute traces of glass evidence.[33] Although they may be so small that they permit only the conclusion that they are consistent with samples obtained at the scene, this conclusion can strengthen the case for the prosecution. At other times, the clothing of a burglary suspect may contain pieces of glass large enough to make fracture matches. A case history illustrates this possibility:

Walking a beat in a downtown business section in the late evening hours, a uniformed officer heard an alarm go off and saw an individual round the corner and run toward him at full speed. On seeing the officer, the individual started to double back the other way and then stopped. As the officer approached, the man started to flee, but he stopped when commanded to do so. The man then told the officer that he had observed two people standing in front of a jewelry store window take a brick from a shopping bag and throw it through the window. The person said that, on seeing this, he became frightened and ran. Subsequent investigation revealed that the person who had rounded the corner was in fact the perpetrator of the offense and that he had fled before obtaining any material from the display window, because a lookout had seen a police car responding to a call in an adjacent block and had given warning. Processing of the perpetrator's clothing revealed pieces of glass in the cuff of his pants sufficiently large to make fracture matches with glass at the scene.

It is essential that the crime scene technician and investigator understand the ways in which glass reacts to force. Often this knowledge is critical in determining whether a crime has been committed and in establishing the credibility of statements given by parties at the scene. A case history illustrates this:

Police were called to a residence where the occupant alleged that while standing in his living room he was suddenly fired on by someone standing outside the window. The occupant further related that he immediately fell to the floor and crawled to a desk in which a handgun was kept and after a short period of time stood up, when second and third shots were fired from outside the building. The complainant stated he could clearly see the person and, in turn, fired one shot. The perpetrator identified by the complainant lived a short distance away and was at home when contacted by the police. The alleged suspect maintained that he was walking by the home of the complainant, with whom there had been a history of ill feelings, and was suddenly fired on three times, but he admitted firing one shot in return.

Figure 4-10 illustrates the four bullet holes found in the window by the police. When a glass window is broken by a shot, both **radial** and **concentric fracture** lines may develop. Radial fractures move away from the point of impact; concentric fracture lines more or less circle the

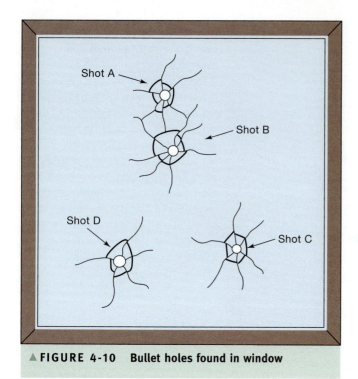

▲ FIGURE 4-10 Bullet holes found in window

same point. From Figure 4-10 we know that shot B came before shot A, because the radial and concentric fracture lines of shot B stop those of shot A. From examination, we know nothing of the relationship of holes C and D. However, as suggested in Figure 4-11, it is possible to determine the direction from which a bullet penetrated glass: on the side opposite the surface of initial impact, there will be a characteristic cone-shaped area. In the case being illustrated, shots A, B, and D all contained a cone-shaped characteristic on the inside of the window, indicating that these three shots had been fired from the outside.

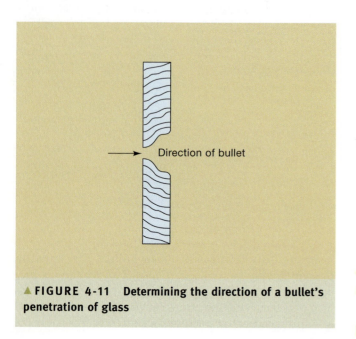

▲ FIGURE 4-11 Determining the direction of a bullet's penetration of glass

Shot C had the cone-shaped area on the outside, revealing that it had been fired from inside the house. Thus the physical evidence substantiated the complainant's statement.

Before any glass or window pane is moved at all, it should be photographed in detail to reflect the exact nature of the existent glass fractures. Moving the evidence may cause fracture extensions that could confuse or reverse the findings of the investigator and laboratory examiner. This same principle applies to fractures of automobile glass when a vehicle is pulled to the side of the road by a wrecker operator. Such examples underscore the importance of the investigator's paying particular attention to what has occurred between the time of the crime and the time that he or she arrives at the scene. In this light, a key question that the investigator must attempt to answer with all types of evidence is whether the characteristics could have been caused by someone other than the suspect, such as a witness, the victim, emergency medical personnel, or another officer.[34]

Handling Glass Evidence

Tape should not be used to collect glass evidence since any processing for latent prints is ordinarily done in the laboratory.[35] Glass should be packed in a rigid, leakproof container such as a film canister or a plastic pill bottle; paper and glass containers should not be used.[36] Samples gathered from different sides of a window or windshield should be marked as such and packaged separately.[37] If a vehicle is involved, use a vacuum to collect the glass from each area of the vehicle; evidence collected from different areas should be packaged separately.[38] If glass evidence is involved with suspects and/or victims, their hair, skin, and wounds must be inspected for particles; if their clothing is wet, allow it to dry and package it separately to avoid cross contamination.[39]

If the laboratory is to make a fracture match, the glass should be marked appropriately (e.g., "top, inside, left").[40] Do not place any objects in holes in the glass; if large pieces of glass are involved, pack them securely between pieces of plywood or sturdy cardboard.[41]

Lamp Filament Analysis

An important question often associated with motor vehicle accidents and hit-and-run cases involves whether or not the lights of a suspect vehicle were actually on, or energized. (See Figure 4-12.) This is particularly important when the suspect vehicle has been crashed or wrecked. Advances in lamp filament technology now allow the investigator to determine this question. A cold filament that receives a strong shock will break (often shatter into small pieces) without stretching. This is referred to as a *brittle break* or *cold shock deformation*. If the outer glass envelope was also broken, the cold metal will

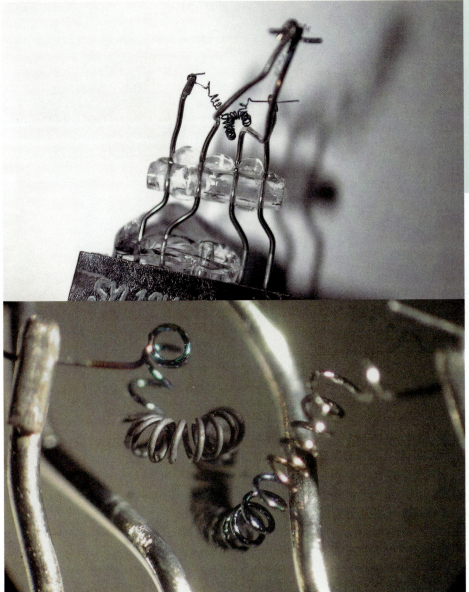

◀ **FIGURE 4-12** **Light filament analysis**
Close-up photography of a light element associated with a vehicle in a hit-and-run accident reveals that the filament is indeed intact. The vehicle's lights were on, negating the suspect's statement that the victim's vehicle was dark and parked alongside the roadway. (Courtesy Texas Department of Public Safety)

not oxidize. When a hot filament receives the same shock, it will stretch and deform. The spacing of the coils will become irregular (some coil spacing increased, others compressed) and the filament will be bent out of shape. This is referred to as a *hot shock deformation*. As the hot metal is drawn out to a narrow point, its temperature increases and the tungsten may melt, leaving a sphere of metal on one end after the filament burns through. In addition, exposure to air will cause extensive oxidation of the tungsten. If, as in the case of a motor vehicle accident, the glass lens (or outer glass envelope) around the filament breaks, there are usually small glass particles fused to the filament because of the extreme heat.[42] In such a case, with a hot impact deformation where glass particles are observed fused to the filament, a conclusive statement that the light was energized (or on) at the time of impact can be made.

FIBERS, CLOTH FRAGMENTS, AND IMPRESSIONS

Fibers are of greater value as evidence than are rootless hairs because they incorporate such variables as material type, number of fibers per strand, number of strands, thickness of fibers and strands, amount and direction of twists, dye content, type of weave, and the possible presence of foreign matter embedded in them. When something composed of fibers, such as clothing, comes into contact with other clothing or objects, there is the opportunity for the exchange or transfer of fibers. Fibers may also be located on the body of the victim or the suspect, serving to connect one to the other. (See Figure 4-13.)

Cloth fragments may be found at the scene of violent crimes or along the perpetrator's point of approach to, or

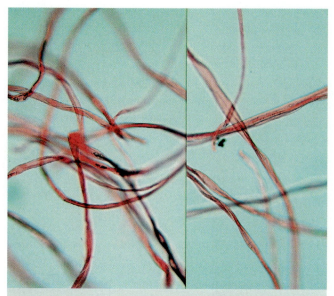

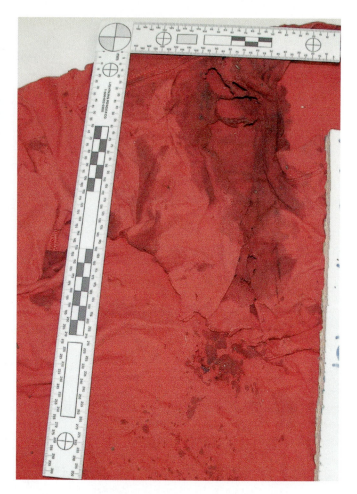

▲ **FIGURE 4-13** **Comparison of cotton fibers**
Photomicrographic comparison of cotton fibers from the victim's red shirt (*right*) versus fibers recovered from the trousers of the suspect who stabbed him (*above*), resulting in a finding that the two fibers matched in all characteristics. (Courtesy Chicago Police Department)

exit from, a crime scene. (See Figure 4-14.) They may be found on such diverse points as a chain fence, the splintered edge of a wooden building, or protruding nails. In hit-and-run offenses, cloth fragments may be found in the grille or undercarriage of the striking vehicle. Cloth impressions are found infrequently in investigations, usually on wet paint or some surface of a vehicle involved in striking a pedestrian.

Both fibers and cloth fragments should be packaged in a pillbox or in folded paper that is taped shut. Only on rare occasions will it be possible to obtain a cast of a cloth impression. This effort, however, should invariably be preceded by the taking of several photographs; at least

▶ **FIGURE 4-14** **Fabric match**
Physical matching (sometimes called *physical* fit or *jigsaw* fit) is powerful and incontrovertible evidence. Shown here is a fragment from a victim's clothing found in the grille of the suspect's vehicle involved in a hit-and-run case. The fabric fragment fitted the victim's raincoat and conclusively established the contact between the suspect's vehicle and the victim. (© The McGraw-Hill Companies, photographer Keith Eng)

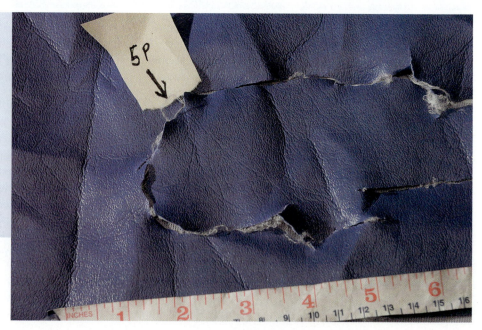

one of these photos should show a scale to allow for comparisons at some future date.

STRING, CORD, AND ROPE

String, cord, and rope evidence is usually found in robbery, criminal homicide, rape, and abduction cases.[43] Less frequently it is found in accidental hangings by children and accidental sexual asphyxiations. Cord and rope have essentially the same characteristics as string, and all have some characteristics of fibers. Known samples of these types of evidence can be compared to crime scene evidence on the basis of composition, diameter, color, and construction; if a tracer is present, it is possible to identify the manufacturer. In instances where the victim was tied, it may be possible to match the ends of rope, cord, twine, and tape with the rest of the roll in the suspect's possession. (See Figure 4-15.) When rope evidence is removed from a victim or from anyplace, knots should never be severed. Instead, a place away from the knot should be cut and a piece of twine used to loop the two ends together. A tag should be attached to indicate that the investigator has cut the rope. Ordinarily, because of its resilient nature, the packaging of this type of evidence poses no particular problem when standard procedures are followed.

FINGERPRINTS

Several different parts of the body—such as palms, fingers, toes, and the soles of the feet—have friction ridges that can form a "fingerprint." All such prints are collected, preserved, and identified in the same way. Moreover, it may not be immediately apparent which part of a body made the print. As used here, "fingerprint"

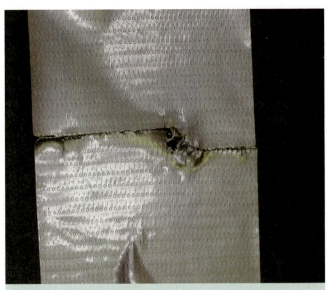

▲ **FIGURE 4-15 Tape match**
In a particularly violent rape, the suspect used gray duct tape to tie the victim's hands and cover her mouth. The victim was left for dead, but she managed to crawl out of an open window and seek help. The top portion of the photograph is the filament tape recovered from the victim's face covering her mouth. The bottom part of the photograph is the end of the tape roll found in the suspect's pocket. By showing that these two ends of the duct tape match, a physical match is established. **(Courtesy Portland, Oregon Police Bureau)**

includes all prints made by friction ridges.[44] Basically, a **fingerprint** is a replica of the friction ridges that touched the surface on which the print was found. These ridge characteristics are also called **minutiae.**

Fingerprints of offenders are found on a wide variety of surfaces and in various states. (See Figure 4-16.) In all

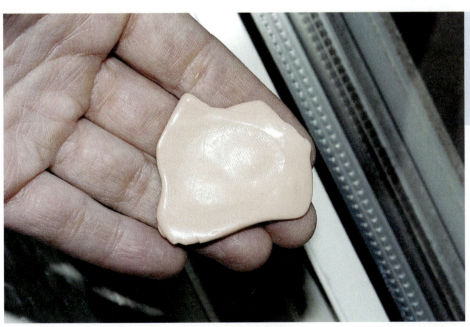

◀ **FIGURE 4-16 Plastic print**
A suspect left this print in a child's "silly putty" while keeping his victim's at bay during a home invasion robbery. **(© The McGraw-Hill Companies, Inc./Jill Braaten)**

cases, however, the prints are fragile and susceptible to destruction by any careless act. They are also in many instances difficult to locate.

With just a few exceptions—that is, some persons who are physically impaired—everyone has fingerprints. This universal characteristic is a prime factor in establishing a standard of identification. Since a print of one finger has never been known to duplicate exactly another fingerprint—even of the same person or an identical twin[45]—it is possible to identify an individual with just one impression. The relative ease with which a set of inked fingerprints can be taken as a means of identification is a further reason for using this standard. Despite such factors as aging and environmental influences, a person's fingerprints do not change. This unaltering pattern is a permanent record of the individual throughout life.

Although there are several different filing systems for fingerprints, each is based on classification of common characteristics. The **fingerprint classification** system works to categorize a set of fingerprints readily as well as to provide quick access to a set of prints with a given characteristic.

There are three broad categories of latent fingerprints:

1. **Plastic prints** are created when fingers touch material such as a newly painted surface, the gum on envelopes and stamps, oil films, explosives, thick layers of dust, edible fats, putty, and adhesive tape.
2. **Contaminated/visible prints** result after fingers, contaminated with foreign matter such as soot, oils, face powder, ink, and some types of safe insulation, touch a clean surface. The most common type of contaminated print results when a finger is pressed into a thin layer of dust before touching a smooth surface. Fingerprints that result from blood contamination are sometimes less distinct than those that result from other types of contamination.
3. **Latent/invisible prints** are associated with the small amounts of body perspiration and oil that are normally found on the friction ridges. A latent fingerprint is created when the friction ridges deposit these materials on a surface. While latent prints are easily developed on smooth, nonabsorbent surfaces, under favorable conditions they may also be developed on rough surfaces, such as starched shirts. Latent fingerprints are typically invisible to the unassisted eye. "Developing" a latent fingerprint refers to the process of making it visible.[46]

Note that the term *latent prints* can be used in two different ways: (1) to refer to all three categories of prints previously identified, in the sense that they have been found at the scene of the crime or on items of investigative interest, and (2) to refer specifically to latent/invisible prints. Ordinarily, the context in which the term is used helps in understanding which meaning is intended.

Basis of Identification of Fingerprints

The ridge detail of fingerprints—including ends of ridges, their separations, and their relationship to each other—constitutes the basis for identification of fingerprints. There are as many as 150 ridge characteristics in an averaged-sized fingerprint.[47] The major **fingerprint patterns** are shown in Figure 4-17. About 65% of the population have loops, roughly 30% have whorls, and the remaining 5% have arches.[48] Points are identical characteristics that are found in fingerprints from known and questioned sources. Positive identification cannot be made when an unexplained difference appears, regardless of the points of similarity.

There is no standard requirement of print size for positive identification. It is necessary only that the partial print be large enough to contain the necessary points of individuality. This number may be found in an area as small as the flat end of a pencil. Thus, the rule whenever an investigator develops a partial latent print that appears to have only a few ridges is that it should be submitted to the laboratory.

Some persons erroneously believe that the points used for identification of the fingerprint occur only in the pattern area of the finger. In fact, all the different types occur outside the pattern area on the finger as well as on the first and second joints of the finger and the entire palm of the hand. They are also present on the toes and the entire sole of the foot; they may be found in any area where friction ridges occur.

Conditions Affecting the Quality of Latent Fingerprints

The quality of latent fingerprints is affected by a number of conditions, including the following:

1. *The surface on which the print is deposited:* Plastic prints can last for years if undisturbed. Latent prints on smooth surfaces, such as porcelain and glass, can be developed after a similar period; those left on porous material such as paper vary more in how long they can survive. Latent prints on documents can fade or deteriorate beyond the point of being useful if they are subject to high humidity or if they become wet. Otherwise, latent prints on paper are fairly stable and can be developed even years after they were made.
2. *The nature of the material contaminating the fingerprint:* Latent fingerprints resulting from contamination by soot, safe insulation, and face powder are quickly destroyed; those made with blood, ink, or oil can last longer periods of time under favorable conditions.[49]
3. *Any physical or occupational defects of the person making the print.*
4. *How the object on which the prints appear was handled:* The distance between friction ridges is very small, and if the finger moves even slightly, that ridge detail can be lost.

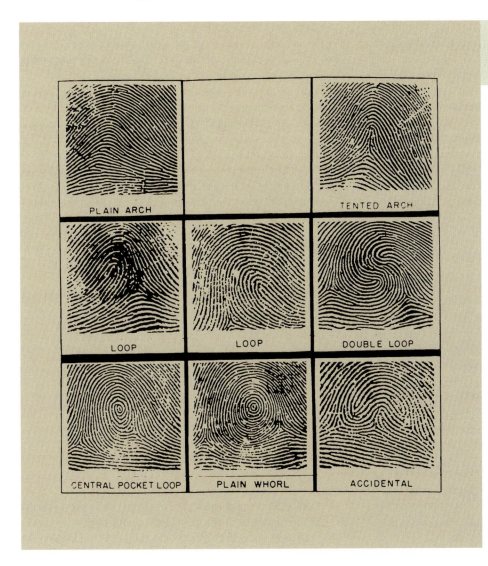

◀ **FIGURE 4-17 Major fingerprint patterns**
(Courtesy Wichita, Kansas, Police Department)

5. *The amount of the contamination:* When the finger leaving the print is very contaminated, both the ridge surfaces and their "valleys" get filled up, resulting in a smeared appearance with little value as evidence.

Locating Latent Fingerprints

Latent prints are such valuable evidence that extraordinary efforts should be made to recover them. The investigator must adopt a positive attitude about this, regardless of apparent problems or past failures.

It is imperative that the investigator thoroughly search all surface areas in and around the crime scene that might retain prints. Shining a flashlight at an oblique angle to the surface being examined is often helpful in this search. The fact that an individual may have worn gloves in no way lessens the need for a complete search. On occasion, gloves themselves leave impressions as individualized as fingerprints. Moreover, although unusual, it may be possible to develop a latent fingerprint on the inside of a glove recovered at a crime scene.[50] Particular attention

should be paid to less obvious places, such as the undersides of toilet seats, toilet handles, tabletops, and dresser drawers; the surfaces of dinner plates and filing cabinets; the backs of rearview mirrors; and the trunk lids of automobiles. Frequently handled objects, such as doorknobs and telephones, ordinarily do not yield good prints. But because they are likely to have been touched, they should always be processed.

It is never safe to assume that the offender took precautions against leaving prints or destroyed those left. The commission of a criminal offense involves stress, and the offender may have made a mistake. If gloves were worn, for example, the suspect may have removed them for some operation.

It helps to attempt to view the scene as the criminal did. Such conditions as time of day, weather, and physical layout may suggest that certain surfaces should be more closely examined. In conducting the examination for latent prints in a burglary case, for example, the investigators should begin at the point of entry. For other crimes, such as the issuance of worthless checks, the point of entry often takes on less importance. Ordinarily, however, whatever the crime and its attending circumstances, reconstruction by the investigator gives direction to the search.

A person who is familiar with the environment, such as the owner of the building or the occupant of an apartment, may give valuable aid in obtaining latent prints. The person should be allowed to observe the scene so that he or she can indicate any items out of place or brought to the scene by the suspect.

The development of latent fingerprints often involves the use of lasers, alternative light, ultraviolet light, powders, and chemicals that can be irritating or toxic. Therefore, appropriate safety precautions should be taken.

Methods of Developing Latent Fingerprints

Plastic and contaminated prints may require little or no development. However, there are numerous ways to develop latent prints. Five methods that investigators should be familiar with are (1) use of traditional powders, (2) use of fluorescent powders, (3) application of chemicals, (4) cyanoacrylate or superglue fuming, and (5) visualization under laser, alternative light, and ultraviolet illumination. The most common method of developing latent/invisible prints is through the use of traditional powders. (See Figure 4-18.)

Traditional Powders

Commercially prepared **traditional powders** come in a number of colors, including black, white, silver, red, and gray. To provide a good contrast between the print and the background on which it has been made, darker powders are used to locate latent/invisible prints on lighter-colored surfaces, and lighter ones are used on darker backgrounds. There are also dual-use powders, which appear black when dusted on a light-colored surface and silver when applied to a dark one. The tip of the brush is gently placed into the wide-mouthed powder container and then lightly tapped to allow excess powder to drop away. Caution must be used when applying the powder to a latent print. Too much powder creates a print in which the details are difficult to identify. This is why powder is never sprinkled directly on the surface to be dusted. The entire area to be dusted should be covered with smooth, light brush strokes until the ridge detail begins to show. Then, the brush strokes should follow the contours of the ridges until the latent/invisible print is fully visible. Even if the first attempt to develop a print is not successful, a second one may be.

The choices of brushes include squirrel hair, the Zephyr—a fiberglass brush—and feather dusters. There are also applicators that use special magnetic powders. These powders commonly come in black, gray, and white. There are also dual-use magnetic powders. When the magnetic applicator is dipped into the iron powder particles—which are covered with a color pigment—streamers of powder are created that develop a latent print when brought into contact with the surface being examined; the excess powder is then removed from the print by a magnet.[51]

Fluorescent Powders

Low concentrations of some naturally occurring substances will cause a latent print to fluoresce, or glow,

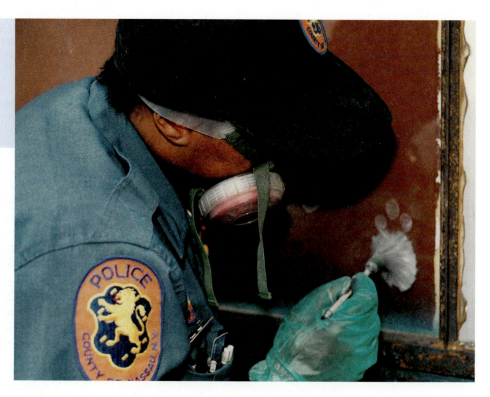

▶ **FIGURE 4-18 Locating prints**
A crime scene technician uses protective equipment while dusting for fingerprints. Several developed prints can be seen in the area the technician is dusting. (Courtesy Nassau County, New York, Police Department)

under laser, alternative light, or ultraviolet (UV) illumination. However, the intensity of the glow varies considerably, perhaps owing to the accidental acquisition of fluorescent materials from the environment.[52] To compensate for the typically low level of naturally occurring fluorescence, investigators can dust the area to be examined with a special **fluorescent powder,** which chemically enhances the print when viewed under laser, alternative light, or UV illumination. Fluorescent powders are also available in several colors for use with a magnetic applicator. (See Figure 4-19.)

Chemicals

A variety of chemicals are used to develop and enhance latent prints. These chemicals are applied by spraying or brushing the surface being examined, by fuming, or by dipping the object on which there may be prints in a solution.[53] Because chemicals may interfere with processes like blood typing, a forensic serologist should be consulted before using them.[54] Some of these chemicals will

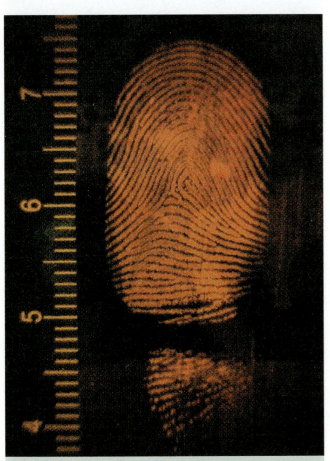

▲ **FIGURE 4-19   Fluorescent fingerprint**
Items of forensic interest such as body fluids, certain drugs, arson accelerants, and chemically treated latent fingerprints exhibit a phenomenon known as florescence. Here, a treated latent print is located and photographed at the scene of a murder. (Courtesy SIRCHIE Fingerprint Laboratories, Inc.)

develop prints that are immediately visible, whereas others—such as DFO, rhodamine 6G, and basic yellow 40—fluoresce under an alternative light source. Among chemicals in use are the following:

- **Amido black:** Amido black is a dye sensitive to properties in blood and may be used with contaminated/visible prints involving blood. It has the capability to turn blood proteins to a blue-black color. As in the case of any procedure aimed at developing prints, a photographic record of the print should be made both before and after treatment.

- **Crystal violet:** Crystal violet is used to develop latent prints on the adhesive side of almost any kind of tape. It may also be useful on plastic surfaces. Crystal violet is mixed with water, and the tape is soaked in the solution. The tape is then rinsed with tap water; any latent print that appears is dyed a purple color. The results produced by crystal violet can be enhanced by viewing the treated area under laser illumination.

- **Iodine:** One of the oldest and most proven methods of developing latent prints on both porous—particularly paper—and nonporous surfaces is iodine fuming. If use of ninhydrin is required, the iodine fuming should be done first.

- **Ninhydrin:** This chemical is also used to develop latent prints on paper and cardboard, producing purplish prints. It should not be used with money, because it turns the entire bill purple.[55] Ninhydrin may be applied by fuming, dipping, or spraying. (See Figure 4-20.)

- **DFO (1, 8-diazafluren-9-one):** While it functions similarly to ninhydrin, DFO is about three times more effective than ninhydrin in developing latent prints on paper. These red prints may be immediately visible to the naked eye. DFO prints fluoresce under almost all laser and alternative light sources. Both DFO and ninhydrin may be used on paper, but DFO must be used first to get any fluorescence.

- **Small-particle reagent (SPR):** SPR is used for developing latent prints that have been immersed in water, such as when a perpetrator has attempted to dispose of a firearm used in a crime by throwing it into a river or lake. It is also used to develop prints on dew- or rain-soaked cars; on surfaces covered with a residue, such as salt from being on or near the ocean; and on waxed materials, plastics, tile, and glass. Developed prints appear dark gray on a light surface and light gray on a dark surface. Although SPR can be sprayed on an object, immersion of the object for about 30 seconds in an SPR solution produces better results.

- **Rhodamine 6G:** This is an excellent fluorescent chemical dye to use on metal, glass, leather, plastic, wood, and many other types of nonabsorbent

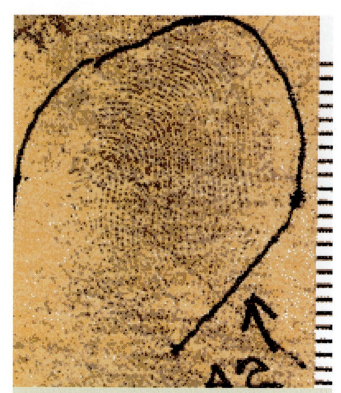

▲ FIGURE 4-20   Ninhydrin developed print
Using ninhydrin is an excellent technique to develop latent prints on paper. In this case, a thumb print is raised on an envelope containing an extortion note. **(Courtesy Wisconsin Department of Justice, Law Enforcement Services Division)**

surfaces. Rhodamine 6G may enhance latent prints already developed and also reveal others.

- **Basic yellow 40:** After superglue fuming, basic yellow 40 can be effectively used on surfaces such as cans, leathers, and plastics. The article is soaked in the basic-yellow-40 solution for about 1 minute; it will then fluoresce well under alternative lighting.

Cyanoacrylate (CA) or Super Glue Fuming

Super Glue fuming was developed in 1978 and its use quickly spread. The three factors associated with its rapid acceptance were ease of use, remarkable results, and low cost. The mechanics of Super Glue fuming are fairly straightforward. Cyanoacrylate (CA) is heated in a high-humidity chamber. As the fumes condense, they develop white-colored latent prints in 5 to 15 minutes. The developed prints may be further enhanced with powders or soaked in chemicals that fluoresce under alternative light sources.

In the "early days," 10-gallon fish tanks were used as fuming chambers and ordinary Super Glue was heated. While this procedure for fuming is still effective, it carries with it the risk of developing a toxic fume, hydrogen cyanide, which is caused by overheating of the cyanoacrylate or its vapors. This risk is pronounced at 200°F.

Today, there is a vast array of fuming options. Large programmable fuming chambers are available for use in the laboratory; these units, which may be 6 feet wide, 5 feet deep, and 7 feet high, can process large objects such as doors and long guns or process dozens of objects simultaneously. At the other end of the spectrum, investigators may employ a handheld superglue **fuming wand,** which was developed through the collaboration of the Alaska State Troopers and 3M. Additional options for cyanoacrylate fuming include compact, portable systems weighing about 30 pounds that can fume entire rooms and the interior and exterior of vehicles. (See Figure 4-21.)

Visualization under Laser, Alternative Light, and Ultraviolet Illumination

The use of alternative light sources—such as the Poli-light, BlueMaxx, Omnichrome, and Luma-Lite—and UV

▲ FIGURE 4-21   Portable Super Glue fuming chamber
This portable Super Glue unit is being used to process a weapon and liquor bottles at the scene of a murder-robbery in New York City. Note that the chamber can be used in the field or in the laboratory. (© Seth Gottfried/On Scene Photos)

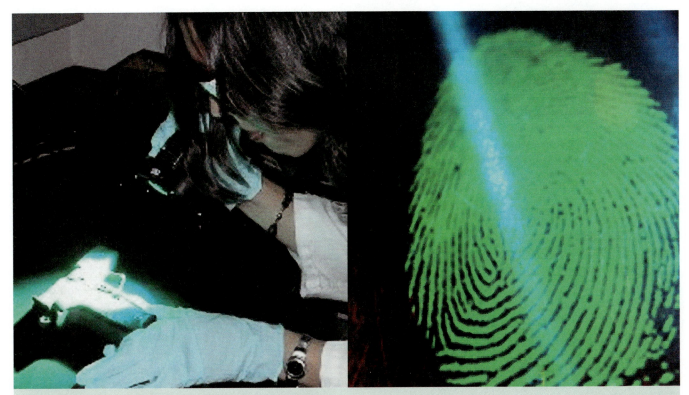

▲ **FIGURE 4-22 Reflected ultraviolet imaging system**
A technician uses the RUVIS SceneScope to capture a latent print on the surface of a Colt 45 semi-automatic pistol after the image was subjected to fluorescent powder. Note the fluorescent image has superior background rejection. **(Courtesy HORIBA Jobin Yvon S.A.S., North Carolina Bureau of Investigation, State Crime Lab, Latent Evidence Section, and the State of Utah Crime Lab)**

illumination was covered in Chapter 3. Therefore, the discussion here deals with using laser illumination and the reflected ultraviolet imaging system to detect latent fingerprints.

Laser Illumination Early work on the forensic use of lasers dates from 1976 and is based on the efforts of the Ontario Provincial Police Department and the Xerox Research Center in Toronto.[56] When excited by **laser illumination,** latent fingerprints fluoresce or glow a vivid yellow-orange when viewed through a special lens. Without such illumination, the prints might not be found. Fingerprints detected in this manner can be photographed. After latent fingerprints are located by lasers, other means of developing them, such as conventional powders and chemicals or dyes, can be used.

Lasers can be used on porous and nonporous surfaces with great effectiveness. Among these surfaces are Styrofoam cups, cloth, and documents nearly 30 years old. However, if latent fingerprints are located on surfaces that also fluoresce when excited by the laser, the print image will not stand out sharply from the background on which it rests. This difficulty can be overcome by developing the fingerprints in a manner (e.g., with chemicals or dyes) that causes them to stand out much more distinctly from their background.

Reflected Ultraviolet Imaging System The term **reflected ultraviolet imaging system (RUVIS)** is the generic name for a class of lighting and imaging systems that have been increasingly used in the past several years. (See Figure 4-22.) An example of this type of equipment is SPEX Forensic's SceneScope. Whereas conventional ultraviolet (UV) lighting causes many types of evidence to fluoresce, RUVIS operates on a different principle. When the UV light strikes an undetected fingerprint on most nonporous surfaces, it is "bounced" back to the RUVIS and the image is highly intensified. Prints located in this manner can then be developed and photographed. When no prints are initially found, Super Glue fuming can be used and the scene reexamined using RUVIS. The complete SceneScope system enables the technician to have hands-free operation, and prints can be videotaped or photographed using other capabilities of the system.

Marking and Identifying Print Lifts

When a latent print has been developed, lifted, and placed on a card, it is necessary that the card be properly identified. Information recorded on the card should include the date, type of case, case number, address of the crime scene, name of the officer who made the lift, exact place of the lift, and type of object from which the print was lifted. Regardless of how well the latent print was developed and lifted, if the card is not properly marked with all the data required or if the fingerprint specialist is not furnished with the information required, the entire process may be wasted effort. In describing the exact place that the lift was made, it is sometimes helpful to draw a simple sketch of the object. The sketch should be made on the fingerprint card that is sent to the laboratory. The inclusion of corresponding numbers on both the lift and the sketch establishes the location of the latent print.

Developing Latent Fingerprints on Bodies

For the most part, the history of trying to locate and develop latent fingerprints on the bodies of deceased victims is one of failure. There have been occasional success stories but no methods that regularly produced results. Once in a while, the application of powder directly on the deceased's skin developed usable prints.

However, glue fuming of the deceased's body, followed by the application of magnetic powders, is a recommended approach to developing latent prints on the bodies of deceased victims.[57] If possible, a body at the crime scene should be processed immediately after the medical examiner has completed the initial examination and released the body. At a minimum, the body should be fumed at the scene to preserve the prints and to prevent their obliteration when the body is moved. Ideally, bodies should not be refrigerated before they are fumed. Condensation from refrigeration can wash away prints and interfere with the proper functioning of glue fuming and the application of magnetic powder. Refrigerated bodies should not be processed until all moisture has evaporated naturally, which can take several minutes. A trial application should be done on an area of the body where latent prints are least likely to be found to ensure that the moisture isn't reacting to the glue and washing possible prints away, and that the powder can be used without its caking and destroying the prints. Skin that is warm or near normal body temperature should be gluefumed for 5 to 10 seconds. Colder skin should be fumed for not more than 15 seconds.

Collecting and Preserving Latent Prints

Occasionally items such as beer cans or glasses that have condensation on them need to be processed for prints. Heat lamps or any other source of artificial heat should not be used to dry the object quickly. Such objects should be allowed to air-dry naturally. Similarly, articles that have been frozen and need to be processed for prints must be allowed to thaw and dry naturally.

Once a print is found—regardless of whether it is plastic, contaminated/visible, or a latent print that has been developed with powders—it should be photographed immediately with a rigid scale in view. The ruler allows

a one-to-one, or actual-size, picture of the print to be made. This provides a permanent record of the print in the event that collecting the print, attempting to further develop and enhance it, or transporting it results in its accidental alteration or destruction. Many law enforcement agencies are using digital cameras to record important crime scene evidence such as latent fingerprints. This type of camera digitizes the image, which can then be put into a computer and enhanced through software such as **Adobe Photoshop.** In years past, every aspect of fingerprint examination was labor-intensive. However, computerized **Automated Fingerprint Identification Systems (AFISs;** see Chapter 8 for more information on this subject) have speeded up the process of fingerprint identification and comparison enormously. An AFIS can supply a list of potential matches for the submitted latent print(s) from the records on file. At that point, however, an experienced examiner then personally makes the comparison to see if there is indeed a match.

Whenever possible, a plastic print should be taken to the laboratory on the object on which it was found. If this is not practical, the photographic record of it may be supplemented by a cast of the print made of a material such as silicone.

Most latent prints are lifted with a clear strip of tape or clear flap lifter after they have been developed with powders. One end of the clear tape is placed on the surface just before the latent print appears. Pressure is then applied to progressively lay the tape over the print, taking care not to leave air bubbles. If air bubbles are accidentally created, the tape should be carefully smoothed over to eliminate them. The tape may be left on the object if the object is to be submitted to the laboratory. Alternatively, the pattern of the print is lifted by pulling up the tape, starting at one end and moving progressively to the other end. Now the powder that shows the print pattern is stuck to the sticky side of the tape. This tape is then laid back down on an appropriately colored backing card. For example, assume that a latent print is developed with dark powder on a clear window. The clear tape used to lift it would then be placed on a white card for maximum contrast. Occasionally, prints are found on uneven or curved surfaces, such as light bulbs, clothes hangers, and doorknobs. In these cases, a rubber-gelatin lifter, described earlier in this chapter, can be used to lift the print. Such prints can first be photographed with a Rotorgraph, a device invented in 1992 by Turner Pippin of the State of Alaska Crime Laboratory. The Rotorgraph makes it possible to accurately take photographs of developed latent prints on rounded surfaces.

DENTAL EVIDENCE

Forensic odontology is a specialty that relates dental evidence to investigation.[58] The dental apparatus, including teeth, prosthetic appliances, and morphological (shape

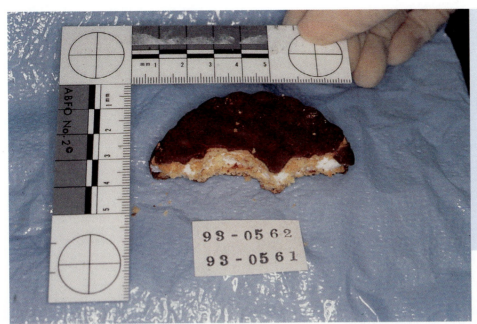

◀ **FIGURE 4-23** **Bite mark in food**
A partially eaten "Moon Pie" bitten by one of the suspects in a double homicide. From the bite marks it can be determined that the individual making them had two non-equally protruding upper front teeth. Such information can play an important role in determining probable cause for arrest and/or search warrants.
(Courtesy Dr. Richard R. Souviron, DDS, ABFO, Chief Forensic Odontologist, Dade County

and form) peculiarities, is of primary importance in the identification of mutilated, decomposed, or otherwise visually unrecognizable human remains. Teeth themselves leave patterns in the skin, and analysis of bite marks has played a major role in many criminal cases. Teeth marks left in food, pencils, Styrofoam cups, and other objects at crime scenes can be analyzed for the bite record; in addition, they can be the source of saliva samples for comparison of blood-type groups. Analysis of a bite mark in and of itself can be of great value in helping investigators eliminate suspects as well as identify a suspect. (See Figure 4-23.)

History

The teeth and facial bones are a major means of identifying skeletal remains and have been used by anthropologists for many years. It is interesting to speculate that the first forensic dentist in the United States may have been Paul Revere. In 1775, he constructed a silver bridge for his friend General Joseph Warren, who was later killed by the British during the Battle of Bunker Hill. Warren was buried in a mass grave, and Revere later identified his remains by the bridgework he had constructed for Warren—the earliest-known dental identification in the United States.

Nearly 100 years after Revere's identification, the body of President Lincoln's assassin, John Wilkes Booth, was identified by a gold "plug tooth" on the right side of his jaw. Probably the most publicized bite-mark case involved Ted Bundy, who allegedly committed homicides in Washington, California, Utah, Colorado, and Florida. He was arrested for murdering several women in a sorority house in 1978. At trial, the positive relationship between bite-mark evidence obtained from one of the victims and the teeth of the accused contributed to his successful prosecution. The Bundy trial represented one of the first cases using bite-mark analysis; today, the use of bite-mark evidence is quite common in violent crime prosecution. The governing body of experts specializing in forensic dentistry and odontology is the ABFO (American Board of Forensic Odontology) established in 1976 under the auspices of the National Institute of Justice. The ABFO not only maintains lists of individuals board certified in this area but also compiles information and guidelines relating to the collection, preservation, and analysis of bite-mark evidence.[59]

Dental Identification

Dental records include, but are not limited to, dental X-rays, dentagrams, dental charts, prosthetic molds, and dental casts. In **dental identification,** the forensic dentist compares antemortem (before death) records with postmortem (after death) findings to determine if there is a positive match. (See Figure 4-24.) No set number of points is required for a positive match. Sometimes one unique feature of the teeth can be enough for a positive identification. This usually includes some type of human-made anomaly, such as a root canal, a post, a crown, pins in the tooth, or a unique cavity or crown preparation form.

Like human fingerprints, human dentitions (teeth) are unique. The average adult has 32 teeth. Tooth form and arrangement, missing teeth, and mechanical alterations from dental fillings or accidents produce hundreds of thousands of possible combinations. It is important that the crime scene search not overlook dental evidence that appears to be useless. A single tooth with unusual anatomy may provide a basis for identification of the individual. On the basis of skull and jaw formations, a forensic dentist may be able to give investigators valuable opinions and information as to the victim's age, race, sex,

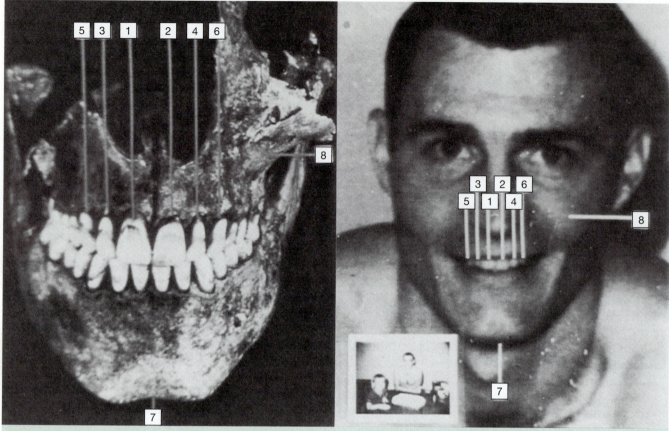

▲ **FIGURE 4-24   Dental comparison**
The left photo shows upper and lower jaws of an unknown white male. Some bone loss (pyorrhea) and tobacco staining are evident. There were no fillings, decay, or missing teeth and no evidence of any dental treatment. The right photo is an enhancement and enlargement of a photo of the victim at his son's birthday party. His kidnappers/killers were sentenced to life terms. (Courtesy Dr. Richard R. Souviron, D.D.S., ABFO, Chief Forensic Odontologist, Dade County Medical Examiner's Department, Miami, Florida)

and, possibly, unusual habits. A forensic dentist can state with reasonable certainty the approximate age within six months of an individual through age 13. From age 14 through 25, a one-year plus-or-minus estimate is possible. After age 25, sophisticated tests can be performed to approximate age.

Certain groups—Asians and Indians—have deep grooves in the inner aspect of the upper front teeth. These are referred to as shovel-shaped incisors. Functioning third molars (wisdom teeth) are common among blacks but are found in less than 20% of whites, who are likely to have had their wisdom teeth extracted to prevent crowding of their remaining teeth. Crowding of the teeth is common among whites but not among blacks or Native-Americans. The absence of certain teeth may help identify age and race. For example, the first premolars, like the wisdom teeth, are usually extracted for orthodontic reasons (crowding) among whites. Anterior wear suggests habits such as pipe smoking or nail biting. Fractured upper incisors are very useful not only in visual identification and photographic comparisons but also in bite-mark analysis. The jaws can show evidence of previous

injuries as well as past or present disease. In discussing these and other aspects of the case with a forensic dentist, investigators must be sure that they understand any distinctions made between scientific fact and investigative opinion.

Dental records are hard to obtain, and searches for them are not always productive because (1) many individuals under the age of 30 have had no dental decay and (2) individuals with decayed or missing teeth may never have sought treatment. In either case, there are no records of antemortem dental restorations that can be compared with the postmortem dental features of a victim. For these reasons, "smiling-photograph" comparisons have become important in making dental identifications. The technique is quick and cost effective but depends on having a reasonably good photograph of the front teeth. Several such photographs showing the front teeth will enhance the weight of the evidence. However, comparison with dental records such as X rays and dentagrams is far more accurate.

The use of teeth for identification purpose is not new. The practice can be traced back to 66 C.E. Rome during the reign of Nero. As the story goes, Nero's mother Agrippina ordered soldiers to kill a woman named Lollia Paulina and to bring back the woman's head as proof that the deed had been completed. When the soldiers presented Agrippina with the mutilated head she was unable to positively identify her lifeless adversary and decided to inspect the victim's mouth knowing that Lollia Paulina had a discolored front tooth. On observing the discolored tooth in the appropriate place within the victim's mouth, Agrippina made a positive identification. In more recent times, forensic odontology has been used to identify the bodies of infamous criminals, terrorists and political leaders. For instance, the examination of teeth helped identify Benito Mussolini, Adolf Hitler, and Eva Braun at the end of World War II, and the bodies of al-Qaeda terrorists Abu Musab al-Zarqawi and Mohammed Atef in the Middle East. Odontological examination has also been instrumental in identifying the bodies of victims of mass disasters such as the horrible events of September 11, 2001 and Hurricane Katrina in 2005, and the I-35W bridge collapse in Minneapolis, Minnesota in 2007. (See Figure 4-25.)

Bite-Mark Evidence

Investigators must be particularly alert to the possibility that **bite-mark evidence** exists whenever they are working violent-crime and child-abuse cases. The location of the bite mark on a person can provide investigators with important clues. Female victims are most often bitten on the breast, buttocks, and legs during a sexual assault, whereas male victims are more likely to be bitten on the arms and shoulders. Bite marks on the arms and hands are usually defensive wounds caused when a person holds up their arms to ward off an attacker. A recent study estimated that in 99% of all violent rapes, victims are bitten at least once by their attacker.[60] (See Figure 4-26.)

Bite-marks often provide sites for DNA collection from saliva. For this reason, the very first step in preserving

▲ **FIGURE 4-25 Identification of victims at disasters**
Cars and trucks lie in the wreckage of the I-35W bridge that spanned the Mississippi River in Minneapolis, Minnesota (August 1, 2007). Forensic odontology has been an invaluable tool in identifying the victims of disasters. (© AP/Wide World Photos)

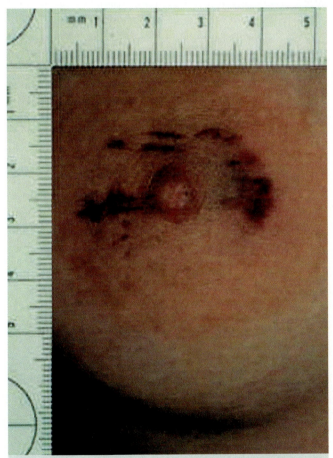

▲ **FIGURE 4-26 Bite mark on breast and nipple**
Bite marks are often found on victims of sexual abuse, rape, and violence. It is not uncommon that the suspect bites the victim as part of the sexual sadist ritual. Here, a bite mark is reflected on the breast and nipple of a sexual assault victim. First swab the area for traces of the suspect's saliva, which may yield DNA evidence. Photograph the bite mark and follow other guidelines set forth by the ABFO relating to bite mark evidence collection and preservation. (Courtesy Forensic Dentistry Online)

bite-mark evidence is to swab the area for saliva. Using cotton swab applicators dipped in distilled water and gently wiping the bite area can accomplish this task. The swabs should be sealed in a paper bag and transported to a qualified DNA laboratory for analysis with a potentially known suspect sample. Obviously, certain circumstances may preclude the collection of this evidence. If the region had been washed prior to the opportunity to swab, this procedure would not be possible. If swabbing the area would damage or alter the pattern, it should either not be done or accomplished only after all other preservation methods have been employed.[61]

All suspected or actual bites should be photographed using both black-and-white and color film if feasible. A color scale should always be included in color photographs, because it will be of use in determining the approximate time the victim was bitten. A ruler should be placed next to the bite area. When photographing the bite mark, a camera angle of 90 degrees is best for a flat surface, since camera tilt can cause significant distortion of the bite mark (e.g., a 40-degree angle will cause a 25% distortion). Accurate photographs can be crucial to cases involving bite mark evidence. (See Figure 4-27.) This documentation helps the forensic dentist make an exact replica of the bite, which can later be compared with that of a suspect. The ideal ruler to use is the ABFO (American Board of Forensic Odontology) scale, which corrects for curvature of the skin surface. The first set of photographs should be taken before the wound is cleaned. Qualified medical personnel should then swab the bites and save each swab for laboratory analysis of any saliva or blood. Each time a new bite area is swabbed, a new swab should

be used. As with other types of evidence, swabs should be packaged individually to avoid cross-contamination. After this procedure is complete, a second set of photographs should be taken. If feasible, follow-up photographs should be taken in 12 to 24 hours. Photographs of bites on live victims may actually be clearer when photographed several days later, as blood seeping into the wound will have lessened. If the victim is dead, embalming will bleach out the color of the wound and make photographs of it less instructive. Bite marks should also be documented by lifting them like latent prints and by making a cast of them using some suitable material, such as silicone.

Advances such as scanning and computer-enhanced digitization can allow for more accurate bite mark comparisons. Transparent overlays and computer bite analysis software can now permit investigators to line-up bite mark evidence with suspect impressions and detect any comparisons or inconsistencies between the two. Ultraviolet light can also be a significant help in detecting bite mark evidence invisible to the naked eye. In some cases, the tissue damage from a bite can last up to nine months, even after bite marks and bruises have faded. Ultraviolet light reveals this tissue damage, and allows the original bite marks to be observed and photographed for comparison.[62]

The records needed from the suspect for comparison are photographs and impressions of the teeth, wax bite records, X-rays, and saliva and blood samples. All may be obtained quickly and with little or no discomfort to the suspect. Duplicates of everything should be taken to safeguard against loss or breakage. A suspect may voluntarily bite into a Styrofoam cup or into a block of beeswax.

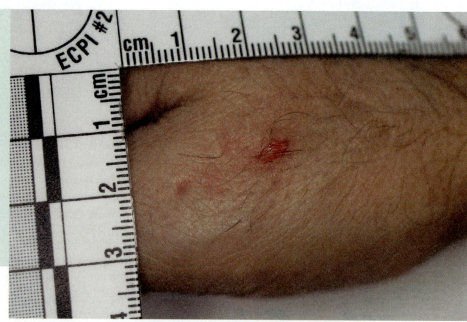

▶ **FIGURE 4-27   Hand abrasion by teeth**

An abrasion on the suspect's forethumb area from striking the victim in the mouth. Apparently, the suspect tried to place his hand around the victim's mouth from behind, striking the victim in the mouth and causing the abrasion. The victim then attempted to bite the suspect, but he pulled away before significant tissue damage could occur. Note the indentations (bite marks) around the abrasion. (Courtesy Los Angeles Police Department)

From this "impression," a duplicate or cast can quickly be made of the biting, or incisal, edges of the suspect's teeth. This can be extremely helpful in eliminating multiple suspects. However, care should be taken that a suspect is not forced to bite into an object but does so with his or her full consent. It is best that the forensic dentist making the comparisons get the evidence from the victim and the records from the suspect. Teeth can be altered, broken off, or removed by a suspect. If a suspect does this before dental impressions are taken, the bitemark comparison becomes more difficult or even impossible to make. Therefore, bite-mark evidence should not be publicized.

If the suspect does not give informed consent, the courts provide two methods of obtaining these records from the suspect—a court order or a search warrant. A court order is often used, but it has the disadvantage of informing the suspect, and in some cases his or her attorney, of the pending examination and permits sufficient time for the teeth to be altered. Thus, a search warrant is a safer method if the alteration of teeth is a distinct possibility. In this way, the suspect is prevented from knowing of the impending examination ahead of time. The dentist taking these records must have a signed copy of the court order or search warrant before he or she examines the suspect. Proceeding on any other basis will jeopardize the admissibility of any evidence obtained. The presence of the prosecutor or his or her representative is desirable but is not a requirement.

HAIR

An initial step in the forensic examination of hair is to determine whether or not it is of human origin. Human hair has unique characteristics, and ordinarily this determination is not difficult unless the hair has been subject to gross destruction. When the hair is not human, it is possible to establish the species involved, such as dog, cat, or horse.[63]

Human hair evidence is most frequently found in violent crimes. If the hair root is attached, it may be possible to establish individuality. Even when there are no roots attached to the hair, precluding a DNA identification,[64] there are a number of useful conclusions that can be established:

1. The area of the body from which the hair came, as well as the race of the donor.[65]
2. The manner in which the hair was removed, such as having been cut or forcibly pulled out.
3. Differentiations between hair samples, based on shampoo residues.[66]
4. Whether the hair has been bleached or dyed.[67]
5. What contaminants are in the hair, such as gunshot residues,[68] blood, semen, soil, paint, pet hair, or fibers.

6. Whether the hair has been subject to force, such as burning or blunt-instrument trauma.
7. What drugs, if any, were ingested, as well as how long ago they were taken.[69]
8. Whether the person is a smoker or nonsmoker.[70]

Although distinctions between the hair of infants and adults can be made, examiners cannot conclusively determine the age of a hair donor. Even when the condition of hair evidence is not sufficiently good to permit all these determinations to be made, the remaining conclusions that can be reached may be of considerable assistance in eliminating suspects or focusing the investigation. Additionally, these conclusions may have more than their ordinary value when combined with other evidence, or they may be useful in destroying an alibi. To illustrate, a rape suspect maintained that he had never had contact with the victim, and his mother stated that he was watching television with her when the crime occurred. An eyewitness maintained that she had seen the victim and the suspect in the parking lot of a mall. The suspect maintained that the eyewitness was mistaken. However, the suspect confessed when confronted with the fact that hairs consistent with the victim's were found in his car, as well as fibers consistent with the victim's sweater and skirt.

Hair recovered at the scene of the crime should be carefully gathered, using a pair of tweezers. Samples recovered at different locations, as in the case of other types of evidence, should be individually packaged. Hair evidence may be placed in a pillbox that is fully sealed with tape or placed in a folded piece of paper that is also fully taped shut. Some laboratories, such as the FBI's, request that hair evidence not be packaged in an envelope. In all cases, the container used should be marked with the appropriate identifying information.

Because most examinations of hair are comparative in nature, a collection of standards from both the victim and the suspect, where the latter is known, is critical. (See Figure 4-28.) The collection of hair standards is a function for medical personnel. When hair standards are collected from a deceased victim, representative samples should be obtained from throughout the body areas that are pertinent to the investigation; ordinarily, the collection of approximately 30 to 40 hairs from each area is sufficient, taking care to package the samples from each body area separately. If hair surrounds wounds on the body of a victim, special notation should be made of this point on the container in which the hair is placed.

In collecting hair samples, combing is used to gather hair left on the victim by the suspect or on the suspect by the victim.[71] For comparison purposes, standard hair samples must be plucked from the individual to ensure that the hair was indeed attached to that person. If this proves to be too painful, then the hair needed may be cut, but the person doing the cutting must be able to

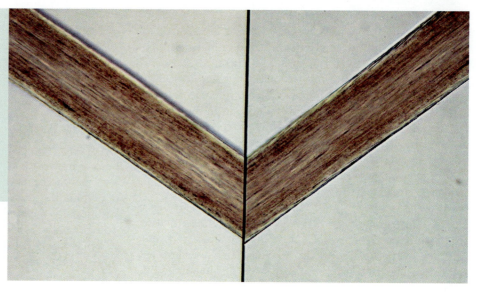

▶ **FIGURE 4-28 Hair analysis** Photomicrograph of hair found inside a rape suspect's vehicle (*left*) is matched with a sample of hair from the victim (*right*). Note the darker shading of brown near the outside of each strand as a result of color added to the victim's hair. These types of peculiarities provide direct physical matches between hair fibers. (Courtesy Texas Department of Public Safety)

substantiate that the hair was attached to the person. The hair should be cut as close to the skin as possible. Approximately 25 hairs from each area of concern are sufficient for a standard hair sample from a living donor.

The investigator should be present at the time the hair samples are obtained by medical personnel. If the latter are unfamiliar with investigative procedures, they might fail to clean the tweezers, comb, or scissors after each area is sampled, thereby introducing contamination.

BLOOD

An adult's body contains, on average, about 5 to 6 quarts of blood, and even small cuts can produce a lot of blood. At crime scenes, blood may be encountered in amounts ranging from small drops to large pools, in states ranging from fresh to dried, and in almost any place, including on floors, walls, ceilings, clothes, weapons, the suspect's and victim's bodies, and the exterior and interior of vehicles.

Because of the frequency with which blood is encountered and the fact that DNA analysis can provide individual identification (see Table 4-1), officers need to be alert to locating and protecting this type of evidence. Moreover, they should wear appropriate PPE and take the other kinds of protective measures discussed in Chapter 3.

The Appearance of Bloodstains

If blood at the crime scene is fresh and relatively uncontaminated, identifying it as blood is not difficult. If it is in some other condition, identifying blood merely by "eyeballing it" becomes increasingly difficult. Blood may appear as a rust-colored stain or have gray, black, green, or blue tints. It may also be mixed with earth, grease, paint, or other substances, making it difficult to see. One way of locating blood evidence is to do a preliminary or presumptive field test using, for example, Hemident (see Figure 4-29), which does not interfere with subsequent serology tests. **Hemident,** depending on which chemical reagent is used, may produce a vivid pink or blue-green color and reacts both to human and animal blood. As is the case with all presumptive tests, the quick results gained through testing in the field must be confirmed by more elaborate procedures in the laboratory to have legal significance.

The drying time of blood depends on a number of factors, including whether it is on a porous or nonporous surface, its size and thickness, and the presence or absence of a fan or breeze. Higher temperatures hasten the drying time of blood, while increased humidity decreases it. Drying first appears at the edges of a bloodstain and works toward its center. A dried bloodstain will begin to pucker and crack from the edges inward upon further drying. Thus, it is difficult to accurately estimate the age of bloodstains.

Using Bloodstains to Reconstruct the Crime

Bloodstains (known as blood spatter) may take many forms at a crime scene. These forms are not random but are produced by such factors as the type, location, and number of wounds inflicted; the type of weapon involved; movements by the victim while trying to escape, defend himself or herself, or attack the offender; changes in the location of the victim's body owing to its being moved by the offender or someone; and continuing postmortem violence to the body by the offender, suggesting that the killer was in a state of rage and possibly knew the victim.

| TABLE 4-1 | Sources of DNA Evidence |

EVIDENCE	POSSIBLE LOCATION OF DNA ON THE EVIDENCE	SOURCE OF DNA
Baseball bat or similar weapon	Handle, end	Sweat, skin, blood, tissue
Hat, bandanna, or mask	Inside	Sweat, hair, dandruff
Eyeglasses	Nose or ear pieces, lens	Sweat, skin
Facial tissue or cotton swab	Surface area	Mucus, blood, sweat, semen, earwax
Dirty laundry	Surface area	Blood, sweat, semen, vomit
Toothpick	Tips	Saliva
Used cigarette	Cigarette butt	Saliva
Stamp or envelope	Licked area	Saliva
Tape or ligature	Inside or outside surface	Skin, sweat
Bottle, can, or glass	Sides, mouthpiece	Saliva, sweat
Used condom	Inside or outside surface	Semen, vaginal or rectal cells
Blanket, pillow, or sheet	Surface area	Sweat, hair, semen, urine, saliva, dandruff
"Through and through" bullet	Outside surface	Blood, tissue
Bite mark	Person's skin or clothing	Saliva
Fingernail or partial fingernail	Scrapings	Blood, sweat, tissue

(Source: "What Every Law Enforcement Officer Should Know about DNA Evidence." National Commission on the Future of DNA Evidence [Washington, D.C.: National Institute of Justice, 1999], pp. 3–4.)

1. Wear protective gloves. Rub the stain with a clean cotton swab.

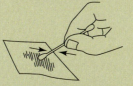

2. Insert the swab into the test unit and break off the excess handle.

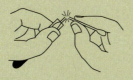

3. Put the cap back on the tube and break the bottom ampoule.

4. Tap the tube to make sure the swab is wet. Wait about 20 to 30 seconds.

5. Break the top ampoule in the lid.

6. Observe the color change on the point where the swab has the suspect stain.

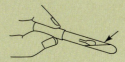

▲ FIGURE 4-29 Hemident

The use of Hemident in a presumptive or preliminary field test for blood. (Courtesy Lightning Powder Company, Salem, Oregon)

By studying bloodstain and spatter evidence, the investigator can learn significant facts that facilitate reconstruction of the crime. These facts include:

1. Direction in which blood droplets were traveling when they were deposited on the surface (see Figure 4-30).

2. Distance from the source of the blood to the surface on which the droplets were found (see Figure 4-31). An important fact to note concerning blood spatter is that blood droplets cannot exceed 4 feet in horizontal travel from a stationary point (e.g., blood spatter from a direct gunshot wound). Thus, the blood droplets in Figure 4-31 reflect vertical fall.[72]

▶**FIGURE 4-30** **Directionality of blood droplet**
To visualize or demonstrate directionality in a droplet, the analyst simply draws a line down the long axis of the stain, splitting it into two equal parts. This line is oriented to the scallops, spines, or satellite stains. (Source: Tom Bevel and Ross M. Gardner, *Bloodstain Pattern Analysis: With an Introduction to Crime Scene Reconstruction,* 2nd ed. (Boca Raton, FL: CRC Press, 2002), p. 146. Used by permission.)

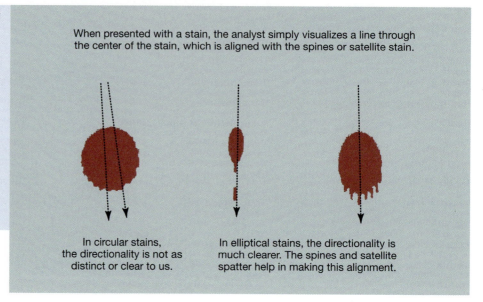

When presented with a stain, the analyst simply visualizes a line through the center of the stain, which is aligned with the spines or satellite stain.

In circular stains, the directionality is not as distinct or clear to us.

In elliptical stains, the directionality is much clearer. The spines and satellite spatter help in making this alignment.

▶**FIGURE 4-31** **Distance between bloodstain and source**
Increasing diameter of bloodstains as a function of increasing distance fallen by single drops of blood from fingertips onto smooth cardboard (Source: Stuart H. James and William G. Eckert, *Interpretation of Bloodstain Evidence at Crime Scenes,* 2nd ed. (Boca Raton, FL: CRC Press, 1998), p. 21. Used by permission.)

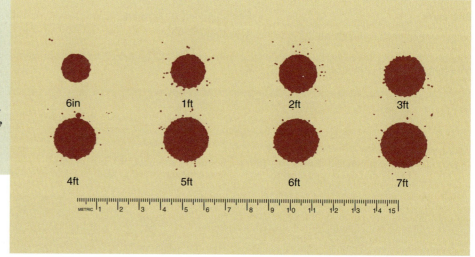

3. Angle at which the droplets impacted (see Figure 4-32).
4. Direction and relative speed of blood trails.
5. Nature of the object used as a weapon.
6. Number of blows struck.
7. Relative locations of other persons, surfaces, and objects having droplets on them.
8. Sequence of events, if multiple events are involved.
9. Interpretation of blood-contact or blood-transfer patterns.
10. Estimation of the elapsed time for the event and the volume of bloodshed.[73]

Locating Blood Evidence

The places at which the investigator will find blood stains are virtually unlimited. For example, if a criminal homicide occurred indoors, blood might be found not only on the floor but perhaps on the walls or even the ceiling. Ordinarily when perpetrators of violent crimes get blood on their bodies or clothing, they will attempt to rid themselves of it immediately. In some instances, they may be so repelled by the sight of blood on their hands that they will impulsively wipe it on a piece of furniture, such as a stuffed chair; if the fabric is multicolored or sufficiently dark, the stain may escape detection by the unobservant investigator. They may also attempt to clean bloodied hands before leaving the scene by using such surfaces as the reverse side of a small throw rug or the undersides of cushions on a couch. Occasionally, in a criminal homicide that occurs indoors, the perpetrator will remove the body to an outdoor area to avoid discovery and then will return to the scene and attempt to eliminate all traces of the crime. Typically, this involves washing hands and scrubbing or mopping the floor on which the body had lain. A case illustrates these types of behaviors and the actions required by the investigator:

◄ FIGURE 4-32   Impact angle and stain shape
The range of droplet shapes that result from the varying impact angles. The more elliptical the stain, the more acute the angle of impact. Round stains indicate the impact angle was closer to 90 degrees. (Source: Tom Bevel and Ross M. Gardner, *Bloodstain Pattern Analysis: With an Introduction to Crime Scene Reconstruction*, 2nd ed. (Boca Raton, FL: CRC Press, 2002), Color Figure 2. Used by permission.)

An aggravated assault occurred between two friends who mutually agreed to misrepresent the crime and claim the cutting was an accident. When the victim appeared at the local hospital for treatment, the police were summoned owing to the nature of the wounds and their locations, which suggested to the doctor that they were not accidentally inflicted. Subsequent examination of the scene revealed blood traces under the faucet handles in the kitchen, where the perpetrator had turned on the water to wash his hands, and in the trap of the sink; and although the perpetrator had washed portions of his shirt on which the victim's blood had fallen, he had done so in hot water, which merely set the stain, making it fairly readily observable to the naked eye. Additionally, although the floor at the scene had been mopped, traces of the same-type blood as the victim's were also recovered. The location of the blood evidence was particularly pertinent, because the people involved alleged that the accident had happened outside the house while they were barbecuing and that they had gone directly to the hospital.

The investigator must also be alert to the fact that even if there are no apparent bloodstains, laboratory examinations may be able to detect their existence. For example, blood from a victim may be on the perpetrator's clothes. A suspect may initially attempt to wipe the blood away with a washcloth and then later wash both it and his or her clothes. The retention of bloodstains on cloth after washing is variable; it is dependent on several factors, such as the type of fiber and the conditions under which the cloth was washed.[74]

At bloody scenes it is not uncommon for the suspect to have left a shoeprint on some hard, smooth surface. In turn, it is likely that some of the blood may be found in the cracks and crevices of the suspect's shoe soles. This is important evidence because it can tie the suspect to the scene with great certainty, particularly if DNA evidence from the blood can positively link the suspect to the scene.

Very fine drops of blood can be located by viewing the surfaces concerned at an oblique angle close to the plane of the surfaces. If the light is not strong or if the scene is dark, viewing the surfaces will be enhanced by shining a flashlight beam at the same oblique angle.

Handling Blood Evidence

Before handling any blood evidence, investigators must document its location and physical state (e.g., fresh) by some combination of notes, diagrams, videotapes, and photographs. Other details may be pertinent to record as well, such as the temperature, humidity, or existence of multiple severe wounds but little blood. The last condition suggests that the person was killed somewhere else or that an attempt was made to clean the victim and/or scene, an action possibly indicating that the perpetrator had an attachment to the victim.

Blood Samples from a Known Source

Only qualified medical personnel should collect blood samples from a person. The following guidelines apply:

1. Draw two 5-milliliter samples of blood in purple-stoppered tubes, the insides of which are coated with **EDTA,** a preservative used to prevent coagulation.
2. If drug or alcohol testing is to be done, collect a 10-milliliter sample in a grey-stoppered tube, which has a sodium fluoride/potassium oxalate preservative.
3. Identify each tube with the date, time, collector's name, case number, subject's name, location at which drawn, and evidence number.
4. Do not freeze blood samples. Refrigerate them, and use cold packs, not dry ice, to pack them for shipment to the laboratory.
5. Pack the blood tubes in special bubble packs, or wrap them in the same type of material.
6. After sealing the outer container or box, label it "Keep in a Cool Dry Place," "Refrigerate on Arrival," and "Biohazard."
7. Submit the samples to the laboratory as soon as possible.[75]

Fresh or Dried Blood on a Person

If there is fresh blood, absorb it on a clean cotton cloth or swab. If the blood is clotting or has dried, use distilled water to moisten a cotton cloth or swab and then absorb the blood with the moist surface. Leave a portion of the cloth or swab unstained as a control or blank sample. Let the cloth or swab air-dry naturally. Do not place it in direct sunlight or next to a heat source, and do not use a hair dryer on it. These actions could cause the evidence to begin decomposing, thus reducing or eliminating its evidentiary value. Wrap the evidence in clean, dry paper, or place it in an envelope with sealed corners; plastic or airtight containers should not be used.

Fresh Blood on Surfaces or in Snow or Water

The procedure for collecting fresh blood from most surfaces is the same as that previously described for blood on a person. However, when blood is in a filled bathtub or some other body of water or when it is on snow, a different approach is required. For blood in water, draw the sample from the thickest concentrations of blood whenever possible. When gathering blood from snow, eliminate as much snow as possible from the sample. Freeze it in a clean, airtight container, and submit the sample to the laboratory as rapidly as possible.

Fresh or Dried Bloodstains on Garments and Objects

Allow fresh bloodstains on garments to air-dry naturally; then fold the clothing with the crusts intact. Do not fold clothing in a way that creases bloodstains, since the creases may cause them to become dislodged. As you fold the clothing, place clean paper between each layer. Usually, bloodstained garments are found at the crime scene or retrieved from a hospital's emergency room.

Fresh bloodstains on a small movable item, such as a weapon, lamp, or door, should also be allowed to air-dry naturally. The item is then submitted to the laboratory for processing; pack the item in clean paper in such a way that the paper does not rub against the bloodstains, since rubbing could alter or eradicate the bloodstain pattern. When bloodstains are on a large immovable object, they can be collected, if fresh, by using the cotton cloth or swab technique or by cutting a large sample from a dried stain. If there are multiple stains on the object, use a new cloth or swab each time you switch from one stain to another; likewise, thoroughly clean the scalpel, razor blade, or knife you are using to cut dried samples when you switch from one collection area to another. In some cases, it may be necessary to cut a section out of the immovable object and transport it to the laboratory; do not forget the need for a control or blank sample.

Other Considerations in Handling Blood Evidence

During warm weather, especially during daylight hours, blood evidence should not be locked in car interiors or trunks, because heat could rapidly degrade the evidence. If dried-blood evidence is not submitted to the laboratory within 24 hours, the garments, objects, and/or samples taken should be refrigerated.

Laboratory Determinations

Under ordinary conditions, laboratory examination of blood evidence can determine the following about the source of the blood:

1. The species (human, dog, horse, etc.).
2. The sex.
3. The blood type and the DNA profile.
4. Whether drugs or alcohol have been used by the source of the blood.
5. The presence of certain types of illnesses (e.g., venereal disease).
6. The presence of carbon monoxide.
7. Whether the source was a smoker.

The importance of such determinations was highlighted when labor leader Jimmy Hoffa disappeared. It was thought that a person close to him may have betrayed him because of bloodstains found in that person's car. However, laboratory examination confirmed the person's statement that the bloodstains were from fish he was taking home.

LIP COSMETICS AND LIP PRINTS

Lip cosmetics include products such as lipsticks, glosses, balms, liners, and lipstick sealants. Many lipsticks will fluoresce under forensic lighting, making it possible to detect trace amounts. Laboratories can differentiate between types of lipstick; in one forensic study, 117 common types of lipstick from 15 different manufacturers were all separately identified.[76] When a case involves a custom lip gloss, such evidence may achieve even greater significance.

In a missing-person case, there may come a point at which it is important to have a DNA profile of the person. Excellent sources of DNA in such cases are lip cosmetics; examination of these personal effects may prove DNA in nearly 80% of the cases.[77] Lipstick evidence is occasionally encountered in a variety of offenses, but it is often not appreciated for the contributions it can make to an investigation, particularly its potential to connect the offender with the scene and/or victim and to help evaluate a suspect's alibi. For example, lipstick may be transferred from the victim to her assailant's clothing during rape. If a suspect is stopped in the general area shortly thereafter with lipstick on the collar or shoulder of his shirt, he may claim that it is that of his girlfriend. Comparisons of the victim's lipstick, the lipstick on the suspect's clothing, and the lipstick of the girlfriend could reveal that only the victim's lipstick and that on the suspect's clothing are consistent. Other types of crimes in which lipstick may be encountered as evidence include ritualistic slayings, armed robberies, and other crimes of violence. Even in property offenses, where there has been no victim-suspect contact, obscene messages may be left, with lipstick used to write on mirrors, walls, or other places.

Lipstick evidence should be photographed before disturbing it. When it is on clothing, the entire garment should be submitted to the laboratory, and care should be taken to pack it in such a fashion that the affected area is well protected. Where there are sufficient quantities on other surfaces, a sample should be collected with a clean razor blade or similar instrument and placed in a clean pillbox. Lipstick evidence encountered at several different locations of a crime scene should be collected and packaged separately. Dry cotton should not be used to protect lipstick evidence because it creates problems in handling the evidence in the laboratory. Nor should lipstick evidence be allowed to sit in the sun or remain in the trunk of a car, where it may be subject to extreme heat. In all cases, a generous sample of the victim's or other donor's lipstick should also be obtained.

The study of latent lip prints, or 'kiss marks' from protective lipstick (including long-lasting or permanent lipstick) that does not leave a visible print began in 1950 and has recently been the subject of serious debate as a means to prove identification.[78] The wrinkles and cracks of the lips have the same individual characteristics as do fingerprints. In other words, lip prints are unique to the individual and the groove patterns of the lips can be an important means of personal identification.[79] Lip prints are found under many of the same circumstances as lipstick evidence. Every individual has unique lip prints that do not change with age. As with fingerprints, technicians can lift these prints from objects at the crime scene, such as a glass, and compare them with the suspect's lip pattern. Lip prints are also found elsewhere, such as on the starched collar of a shirt.[80]

Visible lip prints at a crime scene should be photographed and recorded, and lifted with tape similar to a fingerprint as discussed above. Since the lip print may well have associated DNA from skin cells on the lips, the print should be sent to the lab for immediate processing. Invisible prints may also be present at a crime scene since essential oils that populate the fingers are also present on the lips. Luminescence is especially useful using a variety of florescent reagents, such as Nile Red, Red O, and Sudan Black, for revealing latent lip prints. In fact, Nile Red is being studied as a potential developer for latent lip prints at very old (over 1 year) crime scenes.[81]

While lip print identification has been utilized in court in isolated cases more research needs to be conducted in this field with regard to confirmation of uniqueness, the collection and interpretation of lip print evidence, and the development of lip print databases.[82]

FIREARMS

Firearm evidence is commonly encountered in murder, aggravated-assault, robbery, rape, drug, kidnapping, and suicide cases. Such evidence includes single- and double-action revolvers, semiautomatic handguns, rifles, scopes, shotguns, rim- and center-fire ammunition, bullets, shot pellets and slugs, shell cases, gunshot residues, clips and magazines, firing-pin impressions, and extractor and ejector marks. Moreover, there may be blood, tissue, and/or fingerprints on firearm evidence, making it even more important to a case. Police officers must acquire a broad, working knowledge of firearm evidence for three primary reasons: (1) the frequency with which they will encounter it, (2) the value of such knowledge in a combat situation, and (3) the personal safety of other personnel when an officer is handling firearms at a crime scene. Never assume that a firearm is unloaded, no matter who brings or hands it to you; that assumption could get you or someone else killed.

It was late on the evening watch in a detective division and three investigators were sitting around talking. Two other investigators brought a man in who was not handcuffed and told him to sit down in front of a desk. One of them laid a revolver on the desk and said, "We're charging this guy with murder; watch him until we get back." Ten minutes later, the suspect stood up, picked up the revolver, and killed himself in front of the three investigators.

The laboratory examination of firearm evidence may be able to provide answers to the questions discussed next.

Was this Bullet Fired from this Weapon? Shotguns are **smooth-bore** weapons, but pistols and rifles have **rifling.** The **caliber** is the diameter of a bullet, whereas the **bore** (see Figure 4-33) is the diameter of the barrel's interior between its opposing high sides, or **lands.** The low sides of the barrel's interior are called **grooves.** When a cartridge is fired, its bullet portion separates and passes through the barrel. Because the bullet's caliber is somewhat larger than the bore, the rifling grips the bullet, causing it to rotate, usually in a right-hand direction. The rotation increases the range and accuracy of the bullet. (See Figure 4-34.)

This rotation also creates striations on the bullet. These distinctive scratches can be compared to those on bullets fired through the weapon in question (see Figure 4-35). Identification, however, is affected by the condition of the gun and that of the bullet or fragments. Although it is ideal

▲ **FIGURE 4-34 Barrel rifling**
Cross-section photograph of the barrel of a 9-mm pistol with traditional rifling. Note how the lands and grooves "twist" to the right, spinning the bullet as it is propelled through the barrel of the weapon. Rifling allows the bullet to be much more aerodynamic, improving the accuracy and stability of the bullet in flight. **(Courtesy Forensic Training and Consulting, LLC)**

to have the firearm, bullets themselves can yield important data. By matching striations on bullets recovered at different crime scenes, investigators can tie together information from several cases; the combined data may produce new leads and result in the clearance of the case.

In some cases, the striations on a bullet recovered from a decomposed body may have been negatively affected by the interaction between the bullet material and the body tissue.[83] Conversely, an older revolver whose cylinders do not properly align may sheer off a portion of the bullet when fired, creating distinctive markings. Other aspects of how individual-class firearm evidence is produced are discussed later in this section.

What Else Can Be Learned from the Bullet? A fired bullet yields evidence of the class characteristics of the weapon that fired it with respect to the number of lands and grooves as well as their height, depth, and width. The class characteristics of a firearm are the design specifications to which it was manufactured; weapons of a given make and model will have the same class characteristics. The **individual characteristics** of the bore are found in the striae along the fired bullet. Examination of a fired bullet will suggest the type of weapon from which it was fired, whether the bullet is a hard-nose or soft-nose projectile,

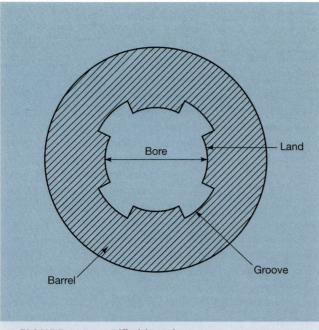

▲ **FIGURE 4-33 Rifled barrel**
Important features of a rifled firearm's barrel

◀ **FIGURE 4-35 Bullet comparison**
A drug user murdered his supplier in order to "cancel" his debt and obtain additional drugs. This is a photomicrograph of the bullet recovered from the body (*left*) compared to a bullet fired from the murder gun (*right*) after the revolver was recovered from a river by police divers. (Courtesy Royal Canadian Mounted Police)

and the pitch and direction of twist within the barrel. Additionally, if the fired bullet is recovered in sufficient size, it may be possible, through weighing and measurement, to determine its caliber. Since bullets are often recovered as fragments, the caliber may only be implied; for instance, the weight may rule out smaller calibers. Although it is possible to determine the caliber of the bullet, some caution must be taken with respect to determining the bore of the weapon from which it was fired, since a smaller-caliber bullet can be fired through a larger-bore weapon.

Fired bullets ordinarily experience some damage on impact. In some cases, one can see fabric impressions on the bullet's nose that were made as the bullet passed through the victim's outer garment. (See Figure 4-36.)

▲ **FIGURE 4-36 Fabric traces in spent bullet**
In some cases, the fabric of the garment being worn by the victim can actually be found attached to the bullet. In this unique homicide, the fibers from the sweater of the victim (*left*) are actually found inside the flattened "mushroom" of the bullet (*right*) recovered from the body. (Courtesy Forensic Training and Consulting, LLC)

Additionally, there may be minute traces of blood, tissue, bone, fabric, or other such materials. Great care must be taken by the investigator not to destroy or in any way alter such evidence. When the fired bullet is to be recovered from the victim, the investigator should alert the attending medical personnel, if there is any doubt about their familiarity with proper handling procedure, as to the irreparable damage that can be wrought by the careless application of forceps or other such instruments in removing the bullet.

Note that it is ordinarily not possible to make a positive identification as to whether pellets were fired from a particular shotgun. However, in extraordinarily rare circumstances involving smooth-bore firearms, it may be possible to make an individual identification on the basis of gross defects in the barrel.[84]

What Determinations Can Be Made from Cartridge Cases? In contrast to a bullet, which is typically acted on only by the barrel, a cartridge case is subject to a number of different forces that make marks on it, any of which can produce individual-class evidence. Such marks include:

1. Marks made on the cartridge case as it is loaded into the chamber for firing, which may be caused by the magazine or by the slide action of the firearm.
2. A pin impression made on the base of the cartridge case, which is caused by the firing of the weapon. (See Figure 4-37.)
3. Striations made when expanding gases force the cartridge case against the chamber wall and marks left by the same gases when they force the cartridge case back against the breach face of the weapon. (See Figure 4-38.)
4. Extractor marks made when the case is pulled out of the chamber and ejector marks made when the case is "kicked out," both of which are associated with semiautomatic and automatic weapons.

What Miscellaneous Determinations Can Be Made by Examination of Firearms Evidence? If a firearm is received at a crime laboratory, its general mechanical condition can be assessed, and the findings can lend credence to or discredit claims that the shooting was accidental. For example, if the trigger pull on a weapon is of the "hair" nature, requiring only the slightest pressure to pull it, this would indicate that an accidental shooting was possible. Laboratory examination might reveal that a firearm is constructed—or malfunctioning—in such a way that it could discharge if dropped on its hammer, thereby giving more credibility to a claim that a shooting was accidental. Furthermore, even though invisible to the naked eye, obliterated serial numbers can sometimes be restored by the laboratory, thus providing an additional investigative lead. Proximity of the gun to the victim at the time of discharge may be established by an examination of pow-

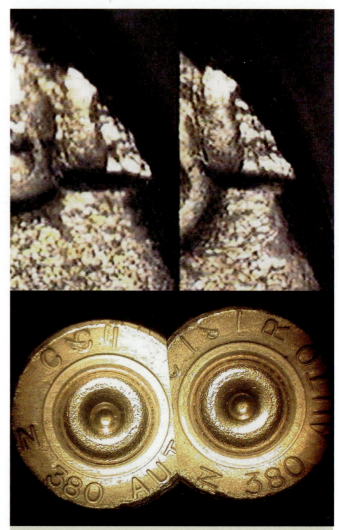

▲ **FIGURE 4-37   Firing pin impressions**
(*Top*) Photomicrograph showing comparison of questioned and known firing-pin impressions of .22-caliber rim-fire cartridge cases. (*Bottom*) Photomicrograph showing comparison of questioned and known firing-pin impressions on .380-caliber center-fire cartridge cases. Note the significant differences between a rim-fire and a center-fire cartridge: on the center-fire cartridge, the pin must strike the center of the primer to ignite the powder; however, on the rim-fire cartridge, contact may be anywhere around the face of the cartridge. **(Courtesy Forensic Training and Consulting, LLC)**

der residues on the victim's clothing or skin. A shot from 6 inches with black powder produces burning on the surface; a distinctive powder deposit is created at a range of 12 inches; and dispersed grains of powder may be found even when the weapon was fired at a distance of up to 3 feet.[85] The absence or presence of powder residues might be an important factor in assessing whether a shooting was a criminal homicide or a suicide.[86] Additionally, even if there is no apparent presence of powder residues, the victim's clothing should be processed by the laboratory.

▲ **FIGURE 4-38   Breach-face markings**
Photomicrograph of the breach-face markings on two Speer 9-mm cartridge cases that were recovered at different locations at the scene of a murder. The victim was scheduled to testify in the trial of a drug dealer the next day. The murder is unsolved and under active investigation. **(Courtesy Tennessee Bureau of Investigation)**

Finally, by assessing the amount of dust or other debris inside the barrel of a seized weapon, the expert can estimate how recently the weapon was fired. This can also be done, more accurately, through laboratory tests.[87]

Collecting Firearm Evidence

A cardinal rule in handling weapons at the scene of a crime is that they should never be picked up or moved until they have been photographed and measurements made for the crime scene sketch. As in the case of many rules for criminal investigations, there are several exceptions. First, if the weapon is found outdoors and there is any likelihood that inclement weather may destroy the possibility of obtaining latent fingerprints, it should be immediately removed to a protected area. Second, at the scenes of aggravated assaults and murders, feelings run high and there is a danger that an emotionally charged person may suddenly attempt to pick up the weapon and shoot another party. Third, there may be some compelling safety need, such as uncocking the weapon. Ordinarily,

however, the first handling of a weapon should be to process it for fingerprints. The investigator must pick up a firearm with great care, despite familiarity with weapons, because many weapons have individual peculiarities that may produce an accidental discharge through careless or indiscriminate handling.

In no case should a pencil or similar object be placed into the barrel of the gun to pick it up; this can dislodge evidence that may be in the barrel, such as tissue, blood, hair, or other trace evidence, and it can contaminate the barrel, thereby confusing the laboratory examiner. The proper method of packaging a handgun—once unloaded—is to suspend it in a small box by a ring that passes through the trigger guard. As bullets, cartridge cases, and related firearm evidence are gathered, they should be packaged separately. The practice of putting a handgun in a coat or pants pocket until transferred to an evidence envelope at some later time should be strictly avoided.

Marking Firearm Evidence

For identification purposes, the FBI does not recommend marking directly on cartridges, shell cases, bullets and fragments, shotgun shells and cases, firearms, magazines, clips, and related materials. Such marking runs the risk of disturbing latent fingerprints, bloodstains, or other evidence. Smaller types of firearm evidence should be surrounded in tissue paper and placed in a suitable rigid container to which an evidence sticker with the appropriate case information is attached. Larger items, such as handguns and long guns, should have a completed evidence tag affixed to them. For obvious reasons, loaded weapons should not be sent to the laboratory.

In all cases involving firearms, the number of shells or rounds remaining in a weapon should be noted, as should any misfeeds or other blockages to the proper functioning of the gun. Additionally, with revolvers there is the possibility of a mixture of unfired bullets, cartridge cases of fired rounds, and empty chambers. The numbers and locations of all these should be noted. The proper procedure is to designate the chamber aligned with the barrel as "1" and to continue numbering the chambers in a clockwise manner until all of them are accounted for. Afterward, each round should be placed in a rigid container.

TOOL MARKS

For forensic purposes, a **tool mark** is any impression, cut, gouge, or abrasion made when a tool comes into contact with another object.[88] Most often, tool marks are found at the scenes of burglaries because the perpetrators have forced their way into a building and then forced open such things as locked filing cabinets and safes. To illustrate, a pry bar may be used to force a door open, leaving an indented impression of the tool action on the doorframe. In the process, the pry bar may also scrape across the door,

▲ **FIGURE 4-39 Screwdriver marks**
The photomicrograph on the left depicts microscopic striae on the head of a woodscrew by a burglar attacking a door. The right side is a known or test impression made by the laboratory examiner using the screwdriver seized in the suspect's custody. Note that black and white photography is often used to highlight the straie.

its hinges, its screws, its edge, or the doorframe, cutting tiny furrows called **striae**.[89] (See Figure 4-39.) Because different types of tools are used in burglaries, other marks of investigative interest may be produced, such as the action of pliers or channel locks on a doorknob. As burglars force their way into buildings and their contents, they may

break tools. When a broken tool part is recovered at the scene of a burglary, one might be able to align it with a broken tool in the perpetrator's possession; the alignment is called a *fracture match*. (See Figure 4-40.)

The examination of a tool mark may yield a great deal of useful information, such as the type and size of the tool and the action employed when the instrument was operated. For example, a clear impression may suggest the use of a hammer or punch, whereas scrape marks may indicate the use of a flat-bladed tool such as a crowbar or screwdriver. A shearing instrument—whose blades pass one another, as with scissors and tin snips—may be suggested, or a pinching-type tool—whose blades butt against each other, as with wire cutters—may seem to have been used.

Additionally, by examining the manner in which the tool was employed, one can often make a fairly reliable determination with respect to the skill of the perpetrator. Perhaps most important in the examination of a tool mark is whether it offers sufficient characteristics to allow for individual identification should a tool be located in a suspect's possession.

In instances where a tool is found in a suspect's possession, the examination of it may yield foreign deposits, such as paint or metal, that may have either class or individual characteristics. The comparison of the tool with the tool mark may establish whether they have consistent class characteristics and, if sufficient microscopic marks are present, whether there are enough individual characteristics to say with certainty that this particular tool made this particular mark.

In most cases, tool marks are left at the scenes of burglaries and other property crimes where the suspect(s) tried to gain entry into a building. However, in rare circumstances, tool marks left on hard bone and skull

▶ **FIGURE 4-40 Fracture-match tool**
While trying to pry open a window during an attempted burglary-rape, the suspect broke the kitchen knife he was using as a tool, leaving the end of the knife embedded in the window sill. The suspect was later found walking in a nearby park with the broken knife and handle in his pocket. A fracture match of the knife tip was made with the remainder of the knife handle. (Courtesy Albuquerque Police Department)

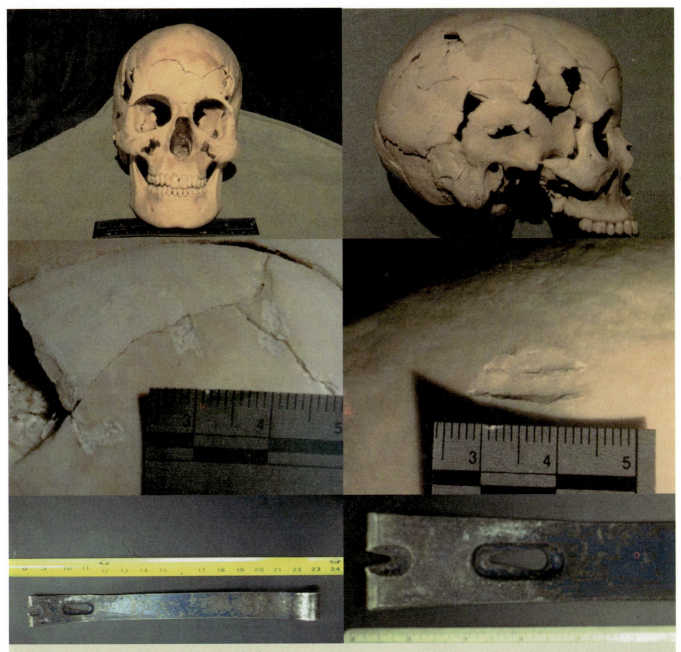

▲ FIGURE 4-41   Tool marks on human skull
A murder case in Arizona represents a unique tool match with wounds to the skull of the victim. The severely fractured skull and body of a young female victim were found in a freezer, presumably left there by the killer some two years before. Several tools were also found in the suspect's garage. By reconstructing the skull and carefully noting the unique types of wounds and marks, investigators determined that a pry bar was the murder weapon. Confirming the tool mark comparison and match were microscopic pieces of bone found on the prongs of the bar. (Courtesy Forensic Training and Consulting, LLC)

surfaces may also be used to tie the suspect to the victim. (See Figure 4-41.)

In collecting evidence of tool marks, make every effort to obtain and submit the actual area for direct comparison. When this is not possible, a cast should be made. There are several good choices for casting tool marks, including Mikrosil. Tool marks should be photographed to establish their locations; however, the images have no

forensic identification value. In no event should the investigator place a tool against a tool mark for size evaluation; doing so could lead to accidental cross contamination or result in the accidental destruction of evidence. When a tool is to be submitted to the crime laboratory for examination, the actual tool should be submitted; the making of test impressions or cuts is a function of qualified technicians in the laboratory. The importance of this last point is illustrated by the fact that under test conditions in the laboratory examiners found that when there was more than a 15-degree difference between the vertical angle at which a screwdriver was actually used and the comparison mark made in the laboratory, an improper finding of no identity from the same tool could result.[90]

QUESTIONED DOCUMENTS

There are numerous illustrations of **questioned documents:** Pensioners sued a corporation, alleging that $21 million was missing owing to forged signatures;[91] a check made payable to the "IRS" can be altered to "MRS" followed by a name for whom the forger has false identification;[92] six "newly discovered" piano sonatas by the famous composer Haydn turned out to be complete forgeries;[93] and counterfeiters have made bogus items such as automobile inspection stickers, coupons, ski-lift tickets, driver's licenses, gift certificates, baseball cards, and car and real estate titles (see Figures 4-42; 4-43, and 4-44).[94]

Loosely defined, a **document** is anything on which a mark is made for the purpose of transmitting a message. A disputed or questioned document is one whose source or authenticity is in doubt.[95] Examples of questions that document examiners may help answer are these: Is this the deceased's handwriting on the suicide note? Did the suspect handwrite or print this holdup note or harassing letter? Is the signature on this collector's item, credit application, jail release order, or other document genuine? Was the typewriter seized from the suspect's apartment used to prepare this letter?

Because of the important contributions that can be made, investigators must have a basic familiarity with the different types of document examination.

Document Examination

Handwriting and Handprinting Examinations

Because handwriting identification is based on the characteristics found in a person's normal writing, writers of a document can often be positively and reliably identified.[96] However, it is not always possible to reach a definite conclusion. Some of the reasons for inconclusive results are a limited amount of the writing in question and/or an inadequate sample from a known source, disguised handwriting, and insufficient identifying characteristics. There are three types of forgery:

1. A **traced forgery** is created by tracing over a genuine signature. A forgery of this type can be tied to the original, or master, signature if the original signature can be located.
2. A **simulated forgery** is produced by a writer who learns to mimic a genuine signature. It may or may not be possible to identify the forger, depending on the extent to which the suspect's normal handwriting characteristics remain in the signature.
3. A **freehand forgery** is written in the forger's normal handwriting, with no attempt to mimic the style of the genuine signature.

In addition, it is possible under certain conditions for offenders to lift an actual signature made with certain types of erasable pens for about 1 hour after the signature was

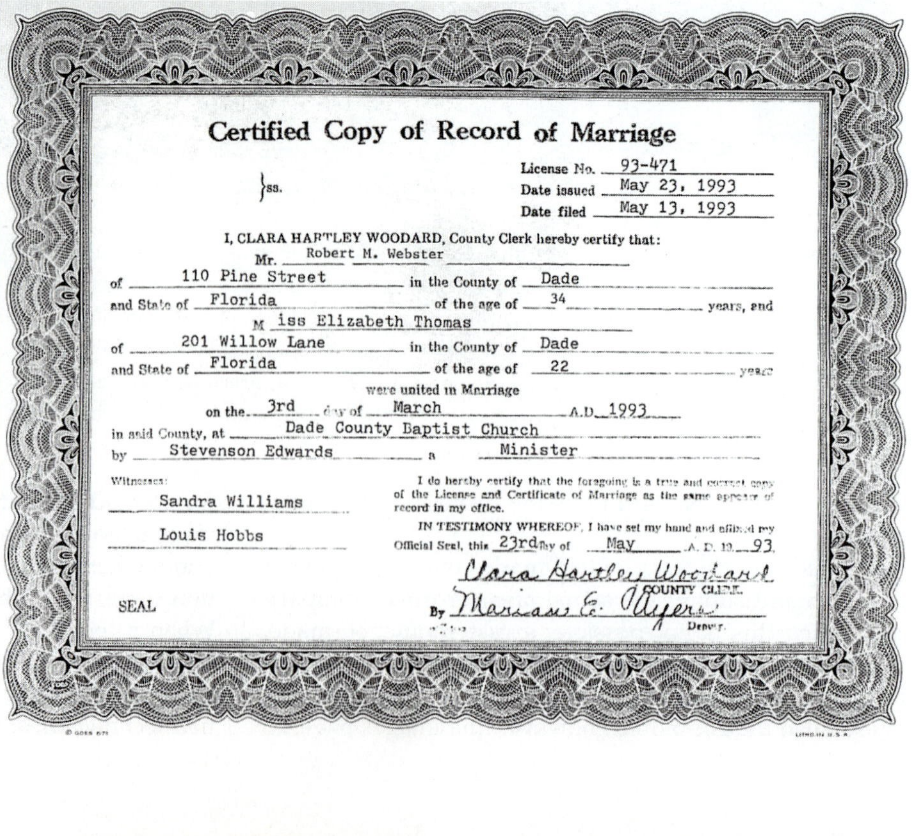
Certified Copy of Record of Marriage

ss.

License No. 93-471
Date issued May 23, 1993
Date filed May 13, 1993

I, CLARA HARTLEY WOODARD, County Clerk hereby certify that:
Mr. Robert M. Webster
of 110 Pine Street in the County of Dade
and State of Florida of the age of 34 years, and
M iss Elizabeth Thomas
of 201 Willow Lane in the County of Dade
and State of Florida of the age of 22 years
were united in Marriage
on the 3rd day of March A.D 1993
in said County, at Dade County Baptist Church
by Stevenson Edwards a Minister

Witnesses:
Sandra Williams
Louis Hobbs

I do hereby certify that the foregoing is a true and correct copy of the License and Certificate of Marriage as the same appear of record in my office.

IN TESTIMONY WHEREOF, I have set my hand and affixed my Official Seal, this 23rd day of May A. D. 19 93.

Clara Hartley Woodard
COUNTY CLERK
By Marian E. Ayers
Deputy.

SEAL

▶ FIGURE 4-42 A counterfeit marriage license
Note the differences between the "M" in "Robert M. Webster" and the "M" in "May," "March," and "Minister." Also, note the differences between the "3" and "4" in Webster's age and the same numbers elsewhere in the document. The differences in the type fonts as well as the gaps in the lines under the changed letters, left by whiting out the original entry, indicate a counterfeit document. (Courtesy Immigration and Naturalization Service, Forensic Document Laboratory)

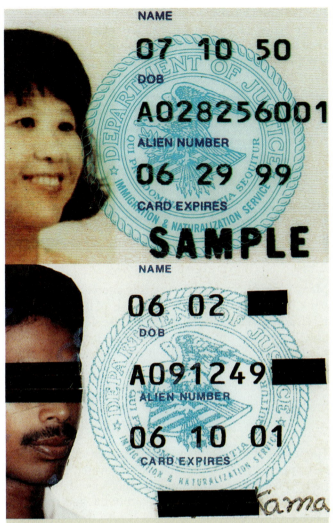

▲ FIGURE 4-43   Genuine alien registration card (*top*) and a counterfeit one (*bottom*)
A comparison of these two photographs illustrates a basic principle: In general, the difference between a genuine and a counterfeit document is found in the quality of the printing, especially in the area with the most fine detail. In this figure, that area is the INS seal. (Courtesy Immigrations and Customs Enforcement, Forensic Documents Laboratory)

▲ FIGURE 4-44   Counterfeit Social Security card
Note the lack of sharpness in areas of fine detail (particularly around the embossed red eagle) in this counterfeit Social Security card. (Courtesy Immigrations and Customs Enforcement, Forensic Documents Laboratory)

affixed to the paper. The lift is done using Scotch frosted tape; the tape is then laid back down on the signature block of a contract or other document and photocopied. The signature on the actual document remains intact, and the signature on the forged document looks right. This procedure can be detected by document examiners.

In obtaining a handwriting sample from a known source, such as a suspect, the following guidelines should be followed:

1. Provide the person with the same type of paper and writing instrument as were used in the questioned document.
2. Direct the person to use the same writing style—cursive or printed—as was used in the questioned document, to write the same words, and to execute the same signature.
3. Remove each page of writing from the person's sight as soon as it is completed.
4. Provide no instructions as to format, spelling, or punctuation.
5. If the writing in question is short—such as a forged check—have the person repeat it 10 to 20 times; for longer documents—such as death threats—dictate the entire text word for word and get at least three full copies.
6. In forgery cases, get at least 10 samples of the victim's signature.
7. If the person does not appear to be writing normally, have him or her speed up, slow down, or alter the slant of the writing. Another technique is to have the person provide some writing with the other hand.
8. Obtain samples of nondictated writing from employment records or correspondence.
9. At the end of the session have the writer and a witness initial and date each page.

Photocopier Examinations

Two documents can be photocopied and then spliced together to create a totally new and illegitimate, but legal-looking, document. This method can be detected by the appearance of faint lines where the documents were joined, as well as by slight variations in font size, typeface, and line spacing. It is possible to link a photocopied document with the machine that produced it if the document whose source is questioned and the samples taken from the machine are made relatively contemporaneously.[97] The following actions are recommended for collecting samples: (1) Make 10 copies of a paper with some writing or typewriting on it; (2) with the cover up and no documents on the glass, make 10 "copies"; and

(3) with no paper on the glass, and the cover down, make another 10 "copies." For laboratory purposes, record the machine's make, model, serial number, and features. When a questioned photocopy is examined, it may be possible to determine the brand or manufacturer of the photocopier. Among the conditions that can help link a copy to a machine are striations on the glass, distinctive indentation marks on the paper from passing over rollers, and "trash marks"—the spots that can appear on a copied document.[98]

Paper Examinations

This type of examination can yield several different results. It is possible to positively match the torn edges of paper.[99] For example, if a single paper match is found at a crime scene, it can be tied to the stub from which it originated in the matchbook recovered from a suspect. If there is a watermark on paper, the manufacturer can be determined; in addition, some watermarks include information indicating the date the paper was made. Paper can also be examined for indented writing impressions. It is important to realize that indentations not visible to the eye can be made readable by qualified examiners. Investigators should not attempt to develop any page that may have indented writing on it. The paper should not be folded or handled, and caution must be exercised so that additional indentations are not accidentally created by writing on a page that is on top of the evidence.

Age of Documents

The age of a document is often difficult to establish. It may, however, be possible to determine the earliest date at which a document could have been prepared through examination of watermarks, indented writing, printing, and typewriting.[100] Chemical analysis of the writing ink used may yield some useful information, since inks vary by manufacturer and even production lots.[101] A genuine document could not have been prepared any earlier than the date on which the ink was available. Examiners may also conclude that documents were treated in some manner, such as baking, to make them look older than they actually are.[102] The trash marks produced on copied documents may also be useful in determining the age of a document. By examining months or even years of documents copied and on file in a business, examiners may be able to conclude that a questioned document was produced during a certain time frame on the basis of the similarity between its trash marks and the trash marks of file documents.

Burned or Charred Paper

Illegal gambling operations, like other businesses, must maintain records. To prevent these records from falling into the hands of investigators, they may be chemically treated so that they will burn instantly when touched with a lighted cigarette or match in the event of a raid.

Burned and charred documents are also encountered in other types of investigations. For example, a person who has committed a simulated forgery on a check may have attempted to burn the pages on which he or she practiced mimicking the genuine signature in order to destroy evidence related to the crime. Also, a kidnapper may have prepared several drafts of a written ransom demand and tried to destroy unused versions of the note by burning them. Entries on such burned and charred evidence may be revealed when examined. The handling of this type of evidence should be kept to an absolute minimum to avoid its crumbling. It is desirable to ship burned and charred evidence to the laboratory in the container in which it was burned, such as an ashtray.[103]

Altered or Obliterated Writing

Many types of documents are easily altered. For example, bank deposit slips commonly have a line "less cash received." A dishonest teller could raise the figure in this line, pocket the difference, and still be in balance. Ways to obliterate an entry include the use of crayons, correction fluid, ink, and mechanical or chemical erasures. All these are detectable under laboratory examination by such means as alternative light sources. (See Figure 4-45.)

Writing Instruments

The ink used to write a message involved in a crime can be compared with the ink in a pen recovered from a suspect. This type of examination cannot identify a specific pen but can determine whether or not the inks are of the same formulation.

Mechanical-Impression Examination

A questioned document that is produced by mechanical impression can be compared with genuine printed documents to determine if it is counterfeit.[104] Two or more printed documents can be associated with the same printing source. It is possible to match a printed document with the source printing paraphernalia, such as negatives and plates. The examination of a checkwriter impression can determine the brand of the checkwriter that produced it, and this type of impression can then be matched with the individual checkwriter that produced it. If it is not possible to send a checkwriter to the laboratory for examination, make at least five copies of the questioned numbers and submit these instead. Both rubber stamps and embossers or seal impressions can be matched with the instruments that produced them. When seized as evidence, an embosser, seal, or rubber stamp should be sent to the laboratory for testing without cleaning or altering it in any way.

Typewriting

The first commercially successful typewriter was made by Remington in 1873, and there has been a slow but

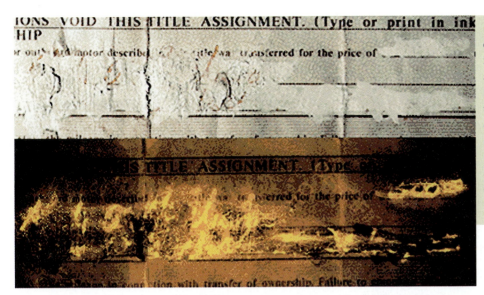

steady improvement in that technology since then. Despite the availability of personal computers, many agencies and people prefer, or have a need for, a typewriter. The possible brands or manufacturers may be determined from a typewritten document. It is also possible to identify the individual typewriter that produced a questioned document. The following are guidelines investigators should follow in collecting this type of evidence:

1. The ribbon should be removed and submitted to the laboratory, because the text of the material in question may be on it; the correction tape should also be included.
2. All samples of printing should be prepared with a fresh ribbon.
3. The entire text of the questioned document should be reproduced unless it is unusually long, in which case a representative sample will be sufficient.
4. After the ribbon is removed or the machine is placed in the stencil position, samples of each character should be obtained by typing through carbon paper onto a piece of white bond paper.
5. It is usually not necessary to submit the machine to the laboratory, although the document examiner may subsequently request it if comparisons of the questioned and known documents reveal questions about matters such as alignment, which can be satisfactorily determined only by examining the machine itself.
6. The dates of the machine's last cleaning, maintenance, and repair must be determined, because these procedures could affect the examiner's conclusion. Whenever possible, the machine should be maintained in its current condition until the document examiner submits his or her findings since the machine may have to be sent to the laboratory.

7. All specimens obtained by the investigator should include the machine's make, model, and serial number in addition to the investigator's usual identifying marks.[105]

Computer Printers and Fax Machines

Instead of printing an image in one stroke, a dot-matrix printer produces an image formed by many individual dots created by pins. The fewer pins in a printer, the easier the dots are to see. Some dot-matrix machines have an option for using a colored ribbon. Ink-jet printers fire droplets of ink at a page to make the dots that form the characters. Laser printers produce dots by shining light against a spinning mirror that flashes light to a rotating drum. The printer toner adheres electrostatically to the charged areas of the drum and is then fused to the paper, creating the characters. Color lasers are also available. The market for wax-jets is declining, with fewer units shipped each year. Thermal dye printers produce outstanding colors by holding a ribbon against the paper and applying heat, which transfers the dyes in the ribbon to a paper with polyester coating. Although there is still a market for stand-alone fax machines, faxing is increasingly being bundled with printing, duplicating, and scanning capabilities in multifunction printers for personal computers.

Technological changes in printers are racing ahead, and some manufacturers closely guard information about their printers because it is proprietary. Moreover, great precision is required for manufacturing printers, and this fact reduces variances that would be helpful with the identification process. Thus, printer identification is a difficult task. Although it may be possible to identify the make and model of a printer and to identify a page as having come from a specific printer, most often this cannot be done. Identifying faxes from multifunction printers is fraught with similar difficulties.

KEY TERMS

Adobe Photoshop
amido black
Automated Fingerprint Identification
  System (AFIS)
basic yellow 40
bite-mark evidence
bore
caliber
class characteristics
concentric fracture
contaminated/visible prints
cross contamination
crystal violet
dental identification
dental stone
DFO (1, 8-diazafluren-9-one)
document
EDTA
fingerprint classification
fingerprint patterns

fingerprint
fluorescent powder
footwear impressions
footwear prints
forensic odontology
fracture match
freehand forgery
fuming wand
grooves
Hemident
individual characteristics
iodine
known samples
lands
laser illumination
latent/invisible prints
lifter
minutiae
ninhydrin

plastic prints
questioned document
radial fracture
reflected ultraviolet imaging system
  (RUVIS)
rhodamine 6G
rifling
Shoeprint Image Capture and Retrieval
  System (SICAR)
simulated forgery
small-particle reagent (SPR)
smooth bore
Snow Print Wax
striae
Super Glue fuming
tool mark
traced forgery
traditional powders
unknown or questioned samples

REVIEW QUESTIONS

1. What are class and individual characteristics?
2. How are unknown or questioned samples and known samples alike or different?
3. What is the value of soil evidence?
4. How would you recover shoeprints?
5. What is a "hot shock deformation"? Explain its reference to an automobile accident.
6. What is the most common fingerprint pattern?
7. Identify and discuss the three broad categories of latent fingerprints.
8. When would you use amido black?
9. What three factors account for the rapid acceptance of Super Glue fuming?
10. How is Super Glue fuming done?
11. Describe the functioning of RUVIS.
12. Why use a software package such as Adobe Photoshop with images of latent prints?
13. How do you collect bite-mark evidence?

14. Why would you use Hemident?
15. It may be possible to reconstruct a crime on the basis of an analysis of bloodstains. Identify six determinations which may be made from this type of analysis.
16. How do you collect fresh and dried blood from a person?
17. You collect a shirt with wet bloodstains on it at the crime scene. What do you do with it?
18. What determinations can a laboratory make after examining a blood sample?
19. Mrs. Johnson has been missing for seven weeks. A decapitated body, with the hands and feet also missing, is found by hunters. How might you be able to determine if this is she?
20. What can a laboratory determine from examining a cartridge case?
21. Identify and discuss the three types of handwritten forgery.

INTERNET ACTIVITIES

1. Learn more about the forensic examination of questioned documents at the Forensic Document Examination Services Web site at www.fdeservices.com. Next, go to www.qdewill.com and read the article under the subheading "Theory." What is the physiology of handwriting? Why is it difficult to simulate the handwriting of others? How is handwriting classified by class and individual characteristics?

2. Check out the Introduction to Forensic Firearms Identification website at www.firearmsid.com/new_index.htm. This site covers such firearm forensic topics as firearm function testing, distance determinations, an introduction to ballistics, and new technologies in firearm identification.

NOTES

1. National Institute of Justice, *Crime Scene Investigation: A Reference for Law Enforcement Training*, NCJ 200160 (Washington, DC: Government Printing Office, June 2004).
2. Richard Saferstein, *Criminalistics*, 7th ed. (Upper Saddle River, NJ: Prentice Hall, 2001), p. 65.
3. Ibid., p. 64.
4. Federal Bureau of Investigation, *Handbook of Forensic Science* (Washington, D.C.: Government Printing Office, 1978), p. 2.
5. Technical Working Group on Crime Scene Investigation, *Crime Scene Investigation: A Reference for Law Enforcement* (Washington, D.C.: U.S. Department of Justice, June 2004).
6. Ibid.
7. Colleen Wade, ed., *Handbook of Forensic Services* (Washington, D.C.: Federal Bureau of Investigation, 1999), p. 92.
8. Ibid.
9. Ibid.
10. Raymond Murray and John Tedrow, *Forensic Geology* (New Brunswick, NJ: Rutgers University Press, 1975), pp. 17–19.
11. Ibid., p. 23.
12. M. Horrocks and K. J. Walsh, "Pollen on Grass Clippings: Putting the Suspect at the Scene," *Journal of Forensic Sciences*, 2001, Vol. 46, No. 4, pp. 947–949.
13. See www.cci.ca.gov/Reference/Pollen/pollen.htm.
14. Murray and Tedrow, *Forensic Geology*, p. 25.
15. Wade, *Handbook of Forensic Services*, pp. 92–93.
16. K. Steck-Flynn, "Analysis and Collection of Soil Samples," See www.crimeandclues.com/soil_analysis.htm (August, 2007).
17. Barry A. J. Fisher, *Techniques of Crime Scene Investigation*, 6th ed. (Boca Raton, FL: CRC Press, 2000), p. 251.
18. Ibid.
19. Wade, *Handbook of Forensic Services*, pp. 85–86.
20. Fisher, *Techniques of Crime Scene Investigation*, p. 254.
21. Wade, *Handbook of Forensic Services*, p. 87.
22. Ibid.
23. Fisher, *Techniques of Crime Scene Investigation*, p. 254.
24. Wade, *Handbook of Forensic Services*, p. 91.
25. Ibid.
26. Mike Byrd, *Crime Scene Evidence: A Guide to the Recovery and Collection of Physical Evidence* (Temecula, CA: Staggs Publishing, 2001), p. 70.
27. Ibid.
28. Fisher, *Techniques of Crime Scene Investigation*, p. 171.
29. Wade, *Handbook of Forensic Services*, p. 60.
30. Fisher, *Techniques of Crime Scene Investigation*, p. 173.
31. Paul Leland Kirk, *Crime Investigation: Physical Evidence and the Crime Laboratory* (1953).
32. Federal Bureau of Investigation, Scientific Working Group on Materials Analysis and Testing, "Glass Fractures," *Forensic Sciences Communications*, Volume 7, Number 1, July 2005.
33. R. Koons and J. Buscaglia, "The Forensic Significance of Glass Composition and Refractive Index Measurements," *Journal of Forensic Sciences*, 1999, Vol. 44, No. 3, pp. 496–503.
34. F. Brewster, J. Thorpe, G. Gettinby, and B. Caddy, "The Retention of Glass Particles in Woven Fabrics," *Journal of Forensic Sciences*, 1985, Vol. 30, No. 3, pp. 798–805.
35. Zug Standing Bear, "Glass Examinations in Old and New Reflections," paper presented at the 1983 meeting of the American Academy of Forensic Sciences. Occasionally, a defect in the glass itself may create unusual characteristics; see B. Burnette, "A Shot through the Window," *Journal of Forensic Sciences*, 2001, Vol. 46, No. 2, pp. 379–385.
36. Wade, *Handbook of Forensic Services*, p. 49.
37. Ibid.
38. Ibid.
39. Ibid.
40. Ibid.
41. Ibid.
42. State of Wisconsin, Department of Justice, Forensic Lab Trace Evidence Unit. See www.doj.state.wi.us/dles/crimelabs/trace.asp.
43. For information on the laboratory approach to comparing such evidence, see K. Wiggins, "Recognition, Identification, and Comparison of Rope and Twine," *Science and Justice*, 1995, Vol. 35, No. 1, pp. 53–58.
44. Fisher, *Techniques of Crime Scene Investigation*, p. 100. For detailed technical information on the subject of developing latent prints, refer to T. A. Trozzi, R. L. Schwartz, and M. L. Hollars, *Processing Guide for Developing Latent Prints* (Washington, D.C.: Federal Bureau of Investigation, 2000), p. 70.
45. Although the fingerprints of twins may have a high degree of similarity, variations still occur that permit their differentiation. See C. H. Lin, J. H. Liu, J. W. Osterburg, and J. D. Nicol, "Fingerprint Comparison I: Similarity of Fingerprints," *Journal of Forensic Sciences*, 1982, Vol. 27, No. 2, pp. 290–304.
46. Fisher, *Techniques of Crime Scene Investigation*, pp. 103–104.
47. Saferstein, *Criminalistics*, p. 397.
48. Ibid., p. 401.
49. Ibid., p. 117.
50. A. J. Brooks, "The Search for Latent Prints When an Offender Wears Gloves," *Fingerprint and Identification Magazine*, 1972, Vol. 53, No. 12, pp. 3–7, 15–16.
51. Fisher, *Techniques of Crime Scene Investigation*, pp. 105–106.
52. J. E. Watkin and A. H. Misner, "Fluorescence and Crime Scenes in the 90s," *RCMP Gazette*, 1990, Vol. 52, No. 9, p. 1.
53. James Osterburg and Richard H. Ward, *Criminal Investigation* (Cincinnati, OH: Anderson Publishing, 1992), p. 109. For general information on the subject, see S. Clark, "Chemical Detection of Latent Fingerprints," *Journal of Chemical Education*, July 1993, Vol. 70, No. 7, pp. 593–595.
54. Richard Saferstein, *Criminalistics*, 4th ed. (Englewood Cliffs, NJ: Prentice Hall, 1990), p. 378.

55. Osterberg and Ward, *Criminal Investigation,* p. 110.

56. E. Roland Menzel, "Applications of Laser Technology in Latent Print Enhancement," in Henry C. Lee and R. E. Gaensslen, *Advances in Fingerprint Technology* (Boca Raton, FL: CRC Press, 1994), p. 136.

57. This section is drawn from Ivan Ross Futrell, "Hidden Evidence: Latent Prints on Human Skin," *FBI Law Enforcement Bulletin,* April 1996, pp. 21–24.

58. The author of this section on dental evidence is Dr. Richard R. Souviron, Chief Forensic Odontologist, Dade County Medical Examiner Department, One Bob Hope Road, Miami, FL 33136-1133 (305-545-2400). His private practice number is 305-445-4956. Dr. Souviron graciously submitted more material than could be used in this book. His portion of the manuscript was, therefore, subject to editing. Any editing that may have unintentionally changed the meaning intended by him is the responsibility of the present authors.

59. See www.AFBO.com.

60. See Shannon Rasp, "Taking a Bite out of Crime: Forensic Dentistry," *Health Leader,* University of Texas at Houston Medical Center, November 4, 2005, as observed at www.healthleader.uthouston .edu/archive/Oral_Health/2005/forensicdentistry-1031.html; C. Michael Bowers, *Forensic Dentistry*: A Field Investigator's Handbook (New York: Elsevier Publishing, 2004); and Robert B. J. Dovion, *Bitemark Evidence* (Boca Raton, FL: CRC Press, 2004).

61. American Board of Forensic Odontology, *Bitemark Guidelines and Standards,* "Methods to Preserve Bitemark Evidence," pp. 1–2.

62. For more information regarding standard operating protocols in the computer analysis of dental evidence, refer to R. J. Johnson and C. M. Bowers, *Digital Analysis of Bite Mark Evidence* (Indianapolis, IA: Forensic Imaging Institute, 2000).

63. Wade, *Handbook of Forensic Services,* p. 49.

64. C. A. Linch, S. Smith, and J. A. Prahlow, "Evaluation of Human Hair Root for DNA Typing Subsequent to Microscopic Comparison," *Journal of Forensic Sciences,* Vol. 43, No. 2, pp. 305–314.

65. Henry C. Lee, Timothy Palmbach, and Marilyn T. Miller, *Crime Scene Handbook* (San Diego: Academic Press, 2001), p. 151.

66. J. Andrasko and B. Stocklassa, "Shampoo Residue Profiles in Human Head Hair," *Journal of Forensic Sciences,* May 1990, Vol. 35, No. 3, pp. 569–579.

67. N. Tanada, S. Kashimura, M. Kageura, and K. Hara, "Practical GC/MS Analysis of Oxidation Dye Components in Hair Fiber As a Forensic Investigative Procedure," *Journal of Forensic Sciences,* 1999, Vol. 44, No. 2, pp. 292–296.

68. S. Kage, K. Kudo, A. Kaizoji, J. Ryumoto, H. Ikeda, and N. Ikeda, "A Simple Method for Detection of Gunshot Residue Particles from Hands, Hair, Face, and Clothing Using Scanning Electron Microscopy/Wave Length Dispersive X Ray," *Journal of Forensic Sciences,* 2001, Vol. 46, No. 4, pp. 830–834.

69. This determination is possible across a range of drugs. For example, see C. Moore, D. Deitermann, D. Lewis, B. Feeley, and R. Niedbala, "The Detection of Cocaine in Hair Specimens Using Micro-Plate Immunoassay," *Journal of Forensic Sciences,* 1999, Vol. 44, No. 3, pp. 609–612.

70. P. Kintz, B. Ludes, and P. Mangin, "Evaluation of Nicotine and Cotinine in Human Hair," *Journal of Forensic Sciences,* 1992, Vol. 37, No. 1, pp. 72–76.

71. D. Exline, F. P. Smith, and S. Drexler, "The Frequency of Pubic Hair Transfer during Sexual Intercourse," *Journal of Forensic Sciences,* 1998, Vol. 43, No. 3, pp. 505–508. This study concluded that pubic-hair transfers occur 17.3% of the time. However, it was based on a relatively small sample of consenting heterosexual couples and may not be representative of forcible rapes.

72. Edward Hueske, *Practical Analysis & Reconstruction of Shooting Incidents* (Boca Raton, FL: CRC Press, forthcoming 2005).

73. Lee, Palmbach, and Miller, *Crime Scene Handbook,* p. 282.

74. M. Cox, "Effect of Fabric Washing on the Presumptive Identification of Bloodstains," *Journal of Forensic Sciences,* November 1990, Vol. 35, No. 6, pp. 1335–1341.

75. Wade, *Handbook of Forensic Services,* pp. 26–30, with additional commentary by the authors.

76. J. Andrasko, "Forensic Analysis of Lipsticks," *Forensic Science International,* 1981, Vol. 17, No. 3, pp. 235–251.

77. L. G. Webb, S. E. Egan, and G. R. Turbett, "Recovery of DNA for Forensic Analysis from Lip Cosmetics," *Journal of Forensic Sciences,* 2001, Vol. 46, No. 6, pp. 1474–1479.

78. J. Ball, "The Current Status of Lip Prints and Their Use for Identification," *Journal of Forensic Odontonostomatology,* 43:2 (December 2002).

79. R. W. Burns, "A Kiss for the Prosecution," *Identification News,* July 2001.

80. Mary Lee Schnuth, "Focus on Forensics: Lip Prints," *FBI Law Enforcement Bulletin,* November 1992, Vol. 61, No. 11, pp. 18–19.

81. A. Castello, M. Alvarez-Segui, and F. Verdu, "Luminous Lip-Prints as Criminal Evidence, *Forensic Science International,* Issue 2-3, December 2005. See www.sciencedirect.com/science/journal/03790738.

82. J. Ball, "The Current Status of Lip Prints and Their Use for Identification," *Journal of Forensic Odontonostomatology,* 43:2 (December 2002).

83. O. C. Smith, L. Jantz, H. E. Berryman, and S. A. Symes, "Effects of Human Decomposition on Striations," *Journal of Forensic Sciences,* 1993, Vol. 38, No. 3, pp. 593–598.

84. See R. Thomas, "Contribution to the Identification of Smooth Bore Firearms," *International Criminal Police Review,* 1974, Vol. 28, No. 280, pp. 190–193.

85. Saferstein, *Criminalistics,* pp. 432–433.

86. There are some unique exceptions to determining proximity by gunpowder residues. At one time, a compressed-air explosive-propellant .22 caliber was commercially available and used caseless ammunition; since no nitrates were present in the discharge residues, this method was voided. See H. L. MacDonell and V. J. Fusco, "An Unusual Firearm Suicide Case," *Canadian Society of Forensic Science Journal,* 1975, Vol. 8, No. 2, pp. 53–55.

87. J. Andrasko and S. Stahling, "Time Since Discharge of Rifles," *Journal of Forensic Sciences*, Vol. 45, No. 6, pp. 1250–1255.

88. Saferstein, *Criminalistics*, p. 441.

89. Ibid.

90. H. S. Maheshwari, "Influence of Vertical Angle of a Tool on Its Tool Mark," *Forensic Science International*, 1981, Vol. 18, No. 1, pp. 5–12.

91. Michael Davis, "Pensioners Suing Texas Gas Claim Signatures Faked," *Houston Post*, May 8, 1994, p. D1.

92. "Tax Report: Warning," *The Wall Street Journal*, May 25, 1994, p. A1. Reprinted by permission of Dow Jones, Inc., via Copyright Clearance Center, Inc. 1994 Dow Jones and Company, Inc. All rights reserved worldwide.

93. Michael Beckerman, "All Right, So Maybe Haydn Didn't Write Them. So What?" *The New York Times*, May 15, 1994, p. 33.

94. See Ethan Michaeli, "Cops Put End to Fake ID Operation," *Chicago Defender*, January 28, 1993, p. 3; "Business Bulletin: Cunning Copiers," *The Wall Street Journal*, Dec. 31, 1992, p. A1; Alexandra Peers, "Your Money Matters: Forgeries Are Coming to Bat More Often As Sports Memorabilia Prices Hit Homer," *The Wall Street Journal*, Aug. 14, 1992, p. C1; Beth Potter, "2 Brothers Arrested in Lift-Ticket Forgeries," *Denver Post*, Feb. 20, 1992, p. B1; Michael A. Smith, "Bogus Auto Inspection Stickers Increase," *Houston Post*, Jan. 3, 1992, p. A14; Peter Mantius, "High-Tech Forgeries Easy, Hard to Detect," *Atlanta Journal and Constitution*, Nov. 26, 1993, p. D8.

95. Saferstein, *Criminalistics*, p. 453.

96. Wade, *Handbook of Forensic Services*, pp. 69–75, is the source of information in this section.

97. Ibid., p. 73.

98. F. J. Gerhart, "Identification of Photocopiers from Fusing Roller Defects," *Journal of Forensic Sciences*, January 1992, Vol. 37, No. 1, pp. 130–139.

99. Wade, *Handbook of Forensic Services*, p. 74.

100. Ibid.

101. A. Lofgren and J. Andrasko, "HPLC Analysis of Printing Inks," *Journal of Forensic Sciences*, May 1993, Vol. 38, No. 5, pp. 1151–1160.

102. L. F. Stewart, "Artificial Aging of Documents," *Journal of Forensic Sciences*, February 1982, Vol. 27, No. 2, pp. 450–453.

103. Wade, *Handbook of Forensic Services*, p. 74.

104. Ibid., pp. 74–75.

105. Federal Bureau of Investigation, *Handbook of Forensic Science* (Washington, D.C.: Government Printing Office, 1992), pp. 76–77.

5

INTERVIEWING AND INTERROGATION

▲ Officers interview suspects arrested for possession of cocaine outside a house where a search warrant has been served. Interview questions focus on suspects' knowledge of the drug-related activities occurring inside the house.
(© A. Ramey/PhotoEdit)

From the first contact with a potential witness to a homicide: "Listen, you guys, I didn't see nothing. I don't want to get involved. My life's a mess right now and I don't need this. I only seen that guy that got shot around maybe two, three times. I stay to myself. I don't bother nobody. Leave me alone. I got nothin' to say."

From a suspect in another homicide case at the beginning of an interrogation: "You guys have to be kidding. Why would I want to kill her? Do you know how much I loved her? Why the hell should I talk to you when you're accusing me of killing her? Huh? Why?"

In fact, both people in these examples have something important to say but, for several reasons, do not want to acknowledge what he or she knows at the outset of the interview or interrogation. The job of the investigator is to get all the information about the cases from each of these individuals. This chapter deals with the basics of how to accomplish that goal.

The business of the police is people. While police rely on people to report and help solve crimes, every facet of police work is concerned with the problems of people. The job of the criminal investigator is no exception. People and the information they supply help accomplish investigative tasks; collecting information is the key investigative task of police work. Roughly 90% of an investigator's activity involves gathering, sorting, compiling, and evaluating information. The investigator cannot function without information, and information cannot be obtained without help from people. In short, people are the most valuable resource in any criminal investigation.

In every criminal investigation process, interviewing and interrogation are the most important means of obtaining needed information about a crime. Both require a combination of artistry and skill that must be cultivated and practiced. As can be seen from the preceding examples, not all people who possess information needed by the investigator are willing to share it. This is true in both interviews and interrogations. Witnesses may have various motivations and perceptions that can influence their responses during an interview. The motivations and perceptions may be based on either conscious choices or subconscious stimuli. In addition, gaining information from specific demographic groups such as the elderly and children requires unique skills on the part of the investigator. Situational characteristics such as the time and place of the interview or interrogation may also create challenges to eliciting information about a particular case. Each of these conditions must be effectively addressed in both interview and interrogation settings. The successful interviewer or interrogator must fully understand the techniques of interviewing and interrogation and be able to evaluate the psychological reasons why people are willing or reluctant to impart information.

The interviewer or interrogator must recognize his or her own capabilities and limitations. Personality and the manner in which interpersonal communications are handled can greatly influence the quality and quantity of information obtained. He or she must be able to convey various emotions at appropriate times but must always remain objective and keep an open mind. Above all, the successful interviewer or interrogator must have an insatiable curiosity.

OBJECTIVES OF INTERVIEWING AND INTERROGATION

Interviews are conducted in criminal cases for the purpose of gathering information from people who have, or may have, knowledge needed in the investigation. The information may come from a victim or from a person who has no other relationship to the criminal activity other than being where he or she was. But interviewing is not a haphazard process consisting of a list of questions. It is a planned conversation with a specific goal.

The job of the investigator-interviewer is to extract from the witness information actually perceived through one or more of the witness's five senses—sight, hearing, smell, taste, and touch. In any given case, any or all of a witness's senses may be involved. For example, in a case involving a drug-related killing, a witness may see the perpetrator pull the trigger, hear the victim scream, smell the pungent odor of marijuana burning, taste the white powdery substance later identified as heroin, and touch the victim to feel for a pulse.

Because witnesses report perceptions based on their own interests, priorities, and biases, extracting information from witnesses is not as easy as it may first appear. Investigators must always be sensitive to any and all psychological influences and motivations affecting witness perceptions, the specifics of which are discussed in the next section.

At the outset of the interview, the person to be interviewed must satisfy three requirements of being a witness: presence, consciousness, and attentiveness to what was happening.[1] Presence and consciousness are relatively easy to establish in the interview process; attentiveness is more difficult. Yet all three elements are important to establishing the accuracy of a witness's perception.

Interrogation is designed to match acquired information to a particular suspect to secure a confession. While interviewing is primarily for the purpose of gaining information, interrogation is the process of testing that information and its application to a particular suspect.

There are four commonly recognized objectives in the interrogation process:

1. To obtain valuable facts.
2. To eliminate the innocent.
3. To identify the guilty.
4. To obtain a confession.

As the investigator moves from the preliminary task of gathering valuable facts to the concluding task of obtaining a **confession,** there is an increase in the difficulty of acquiring information. That difficulty, however, is rewarded by an increase in the value of the information. Figure 5-1 illustrates these relationships. In attempting to obtain a confession from a suspect, the interrogator also gains information about the facts and circumstances surrounding the commission of an offense. In seeking such information, the investigator must be concerned with asking the basic questions that apply to all aspects of the investigative process: Who? What? Where? When? How? and Why?

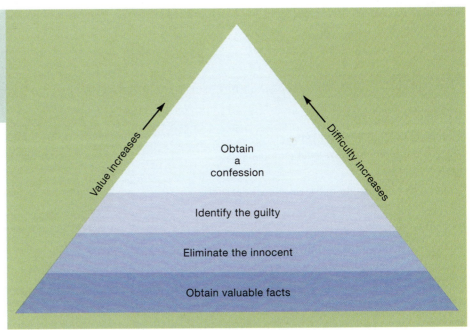

► **FIGURE 5-1**
Objectives of interrogation
(Source: John Fay, unpublished notebook, American Society for Industrial Security, Workshop in Criminal Interrogation [Jacksonville, FL: ASIS, 1981], p. A2-1)

Value increases

Difficulty increases

Obtain a confession

Identify the guilty

Eliminate the innocent

Obtain valuable facts

INTERVIEWS AND INTERROGATIONS: SIMILARITIES AND DIFFERENCES

As in interviewing, the success of an interrogation depends on a number of personal characteristics and commitments of the investigator. Planning for and controlling the events surrounding both interviews and interrogations are important but are generally viewed as more critical to the success of an interrogation. Establishing rapport, asking good questions, listening carefully, and keeping proper documentation are elements common to both forms of obtaining information. Table 5-1 illustrates the similarities between interviews and interrogations.

Besides the difference in purpose between interviewing and interrogation, many other distinctions exist. Of paramount importance are the myriad legal requirements that pertain to interrogations but are absent in interviews. Because of the criticality of confessions and their use in obtaining convictions, it is not surprising that numerous legal guidelines and standards apply in interrogations that would not be needed in interviewing witnesses or victims. Of course, it is more likely that a hostile and adversarial relationship will exist between an interrogator and a suspect than between an interviewer and a victim or witness. The differences between interviews and interrogations are noted in Table 5-2.

QUALIFICATIONS OF INTERVIEWERS AND INTERROGATORS

The effective interviewer or interrogator must be knowledgeable in the art and science of criminal investigation and know how to use psychology, salesmanship, and

TABLE 5-1	Similarities between Interviews and Interrogations
INTERVIEWS	**INTERROGATIONS**
Planning important	Planning critical
Controlling surroundings important	Controlling surroundings critical
Privacy or semiprivacy desirable	Absolute privacy essential
Establishing rapport important	Establishing rapport important
Asking good questions important	Asking good questions important
Careful listening	Careful listening
Proper documentation	Proper documentation

TABLE 5-2	Differences between Interviews and Interrogations
INTERVIEWS	**INTERROGATIONS**
Purpose is to obtain information	Purpose is to test information already obtained
Minimal or no preinterview legal requirements; no rights warning	Extensive preinterrogation legal requirements; rights warning required
Cooperative relationship between interviewer and subject likely	Adversarial or hostile relationship between interrogator and suspect likely
No guilt or guilt uncertain	Guilt suggested or likely
Moderate planning or preparation	Extensive planning and preparation
Private or semiprivate environment desirable	Absolute privacy essential

(Source: John Fay, unpublished notebook, American Society for Industrial Security, Workshop in Criminal Interrogation [Jacksonville, FL: ASIS, 1981], p. A1-1)

dramatics. Persuasiveness and perseverance are essential to success. The interviewer or interrogator must make himself or herself easy to talk to. By the appropriate use of vocal inflection, modulation, and emphasis, even the *Miranda* warnings can be presented to a suspect in a manner that does not cause the suspect to immediately assume a defensive posture. The words can be spoken without creating an adversarial atmosphere. The interviewer or interrogator must have a flexible personality and must be able to convey empathy, sympathy, anger, fear, and joy at appropriate times, but he or she must always remain objective. The interviewer or interrogator must keep an open mind and be receptive to all information, regardless of its nature.

A positive, firm approach, an ability to inspire confidence, and knowledge of a broad range of topics of general interest all help establish dominance or control in an interview: Behavior—not words—that shows confidence, determines dominance.[2]

In an interrogation, the investigator must carefully evaluate each development during the interrogation while studiously avoiding the pitfall of underestimating the capabilities of the subject being interrogated. Screaming or shouting, belittling the subject or the information, sneering, and other such unplanned and uncontrolled reactions most often adversely affect the interrogation. The investigator must at all times maintain control of the interrogation without being openly domineering, by being a good active listener, by being serious, patient, and, most importantly, by being persistent and persuasive.[3] An ability to categorize the psychological and emotional traits being manifested by the suspect helps the investigator react in a manner that increases the possibility of conducting a successful interrogation, for it is the job of the interrogator to make it easy for a suspect to confess.

TIME, PLACE, AND SETTING OF INTERVIEWING AND INTERROGATION

Law enforcement officers conduct interviews in a number of situations. The most common is the on-the-scene interview. Whether it is a routine traffic accident investigation or a major felony case, officers who respond to the scene should, at the earliest possible moment, seek out and identify individuals who may have knowledge of the event and whose information may contribute to the investigation. Such individuals, of course, include victims and other participants as well as uninvolved witnesses. Once witnesses have been identified, they should be separated from one another and, as much as possible, isolated from other people who may be loitering in the area. (See Figure 5-2.) This prevents the witnesses from seeing or hearing irrelevant matters that may taint their actual

▲ **FIGURE 5-2   Police interview witnesses separately**
A domestic violence complaint called to 911 by a neighbor who heard these people screaming at each other and what sounded like heavy objects being thrown around, hitting walls and the floor, brought these officers to the scene. It turned out to be an argument, but neither party committed a domestic assault or battery. (© Bob Daemmrich/The Image Works)

knowledge. All witnesses should be interviewed as soon as practical, while their memory is still fresh, but this rule must be applied with discretion to take into account all circumstances.

Although convenience of the witness is important to a successful interview, the interviewer need not relinquish the psychological advantage in selecting the time and place of the interview. It is not a good practice, for example, to rouse a witness from bed in the middle of the night. However, there are certain psychological advantages to questioning a witness at a law enforcement agency rather than in the witness's own home or office. A witness may feel in a better position to control the interview in familiar surroundings. The investigator cannot let this happen; he or she must be fair but always be in command of the situation.

After taking into account the factors of immediacy, privacy, convenience, and control, and weighing the importance of each in the context of the total circumstances, the investigator may decide to interview witnesses at their homes or places of business. As a matter of courtesy, the investigator should attempt to make an

◄FIGURE 5-3
Interviewing a witness
This lady saw a purse snatching incident occur on a main street in this city about an hour before this photo was taken. She is with one of the investigating officers explaining what she witnessed, describing the man who grabbed the other lady's purse and ran, and giving a statement.
(© Mike Karlsson/Arresting Images)

appointment to ensure convenience, particularly for professional and businesspeople. Others, such as salespeople, office workers, and laborers, may be interviewed during working hours with approval of their supervisors.

Privacy is of the utmost importance in conducting interviews (Figure 5-3). Distractions tend to have an adverse effect on the interview and its results. The interviewer should insist on as much privacy as possible, but the circumstances of on-the-scene interviews often have to be recognized as a fact of life for the investigator, who can be expected to perform only to the best of his or her ability in the given case. Similarly, investigators are often called on to canvass neighborhoods and interview residents. In these instances, investigators often are in no position to influence the conditions under which the interview takes place. Noisy children, blaring television sets, nosy neighbors, and similar factors must be accepted.

The physical and emotional states of the witnesses are important in conducting or in determining whether to conduct an interview. Cold, sleepy, hungry, or physically uncomfortable people generally prove to be unsatisfactory witnesses.[4] Similarly, persons suffering noticeable emotional problems can give, at the most, highly questionable information. Most investigators can recognize this state and wisely prefer to wait until the witness becomes lucid before conducting the interview.

Reinterviewing witnesses should be avoided if the reinterview is likely to produce nothing beyond the information given in the initial statement. Reinterviewing tends to become less and less convenient for witnesses, even though they may be friendly and cooperative. There may also be a tendency for reinterviewed witnesses to feel that the investigator does not know his or her job or was not prepared during the initial interview. To avoid this problem, the investigator should first tell the witness that the purpose of the interview is not to rehash old information and should then explain what new information is being sought. The investigator should ask for the information in a manner that does not elicit a repetition of the previous interview. But investigators should not hesitate to conduct follow-up interviews when necessary, whether because there was lack of skill in obtaining an initial statement, new information has developed, or the time or setting of the initial interview did not elicit the full attention of the witness.

Unlike the interview, which may take place in any number of different locations and at various times—which may or may not be advantageous to the investigator—interrogation is a controlled process, controlled by the interrogator. The interrogator is in command of the setting and governs the number and kinds of interruptions. The most critical factor in controlling the interrogation is to ensure privacy and to guarantee that any distractions, planned or otherwise, are controlled by the interrogator. Privacy may be used as a psychological tool; the suspect may feel more willing to unload the burden of guilt in front of only one person.

The traditional interrogation room should be sparsely furnished, usually with only two chairs. There should be no physical barriers, such as tables or desks, between the investigator and the suspect. From the officer's standpoint, such barriers may create an unwanted feeling of psychological well-being on the part of the suspect.

If there is a table or desk in the room, the chairs should be corner to corner rather than on opposite sides. This arrangement permits the interrogator to move both chairs away from the table and eliminate the barrier (Figure 5-4).[5]

▲ **FIGURE 5-4   Interrogation room**
Note that the table is round and the chairs can be moved around so that the table does not separate the interrogator from the suspect. Some experts believe this is important and "knee to knee" is the correct method for conducting an interrogation. (© Mike Karlsson/Arresting Images)

Proximity in an interrogation can also be important. For years, experts have favored the "knee-to-knee" approach in interrogation: subject and interrogator are close enough to touch without being too close and without having any object such as a chair or desk between them. "It seems, for example, that around 27 inches is the limit of proximity for white American middle-class males . . . If you move closer, people become uncomfortable . . . further away than 27 inches, you can't read a person's face well."[6]

The two-way mirror, although still a useful tool for allowing others to observe the interrogation, is widely known and may cause some subjects to refuse to cooperate in the interrogation. If a two-way mirror is to be used, it should be small and unobstrusive. As a standard practice, the interrogation room should be equipped with a video or audio system that includes a recording device, unless prohibited by state law.

Although the traditional interrogation room just described is designed to ensure control and domination over the interrogation because of its privacy, security, and aura of authority, this approach does not impress the habitual or experienced offender, who understands the rules and standards of conduct of the classical interrogation room. If the offender is skilled and intelligent, he or she not only can cope with the psychological

influences such a setting is designed to foster but perhaps also can become the dominant force, or at least be on the same psychological level as the interrogator. When this occurs, the skills of the interrogator become even more important.

PREPARATION FOR THE INTERVIEW OR INTERROGATION

The success of the interviewer or interrogator and of the interview or interrogation will often be determined by the time and dedication committed to preparing for the conversation. The interviewer must become familiar with the facts of the case under investigation and with the victim. To carry out the four objectives listed earlier, the interrogator must learn as much as possible about the offense, the victim(s), and the suspect through the process of collecting, assessing, and analyzing data and theorizing about the motivations and thought processes of the suspect. This begins the formulation of a profile that will then dictate the initial approach the interrogator will take upon first contacting the suspect.

The Witness

If the interview is to be conducted with a **witness** other than the victim, the interviewer should find out as much about the witness as possible before the interview. This includes learning about the witness's motivations and perceptions and any barriers that might exist.

The Offense

It is necessary that the interviewer know specifically what crime or crimes were allegedly committed. This knowledge includes a working familiarity with the elements of each offense and some understanding of the kind of information necessary to prove each. Accurate information on the date, time, place, and method of the crime—including tools used, points of entry and exit, method of travel to and from the scene, complete description of any property involved, weapons used, modus operandi, and physical evidence recovered—is essential. The interviewer should also obtain a full description of the crime scene and the surrounding area. In addition, any and all possible motives should be identified.

The Victim

If the **victim** is a person, the interviewer should learn as much as possible about his or her background, the nature of the injury or loss, attitudes toward the investigation, and any other useful information, such as the existence of insurance in a property crime case. If the victim is an

▲ **FIGURE 5-5   Investigator preparing for interview/ interrogation**

This investigator is reviewing her notes one last time to insure she has all available information on and statements of witnesses, information and statements of the victim, lab reports, investigative materials and a knowledge of the elements of the offense, and as much information as is available about the probable suspect before beginning her interviews or interrogation. (© Spencer Grant/PhotoEdit)

understanding the interaction of all these variables can the interrogator effectively evaluate the interrogation process as it will be initiated and as it will be modified during the interrogation.[8] To begin the preparation, the interrogator should review the offense report, statement of witnesses, laboratory reports, all file information pertaining to the suspect, and other related data. It is also essential that the interrogator know all the elements of the offense involved. Failure to possess this information may preclude obtaining a complete confession, which, by definition, must contain admissions by the suspect to the commission of each and every element of the crime.

The investigation should reveal as much personal background information on the suspect as can be obtained. This should include aliases, Social Security number, date and place of birth, education, marital status, employment history, financial history and current circumstances, prior offenses, past and present physical and mental health, any drug or alcohol abuse or addiction, relationship to the victim or crime scene, possible motive, biases and prejudices, home environment, sexual interests (if relevant), and hobbies. Additionally, the investigation and preparation for an interrogation should determine whether the suspect had the capability and opportunity to commit the offense and should confirm or disprove an alibi.

The interrogator should also obtain as much information as possible from other people involved to determine the suspect's attitude. This will enable the interrogator to anticipate levels of hostility or cooperativeness during the interrogation. Figure 5-6 can serve as a review and checklist for the investigator's planning and interrogation.

WITNESSES: MOTIVATIONS, PERCEPTIONS, AND BARRIERS

There are many types of witnesses, and each has different motivations and perceptions that influence his or her responses during an interview. The motivations and perceptions may be based on either conscious choices or subconscious stimuli. The interviewer must learn to recognize, overcome, and compensate for these factors.

There is no way to categorize all personalities, attitudes, and other character traits. The variables are too numerous and individualized; the combinations are as complex as the human mind. Nevertheless, there are some basic groupings that can be mentioned:

- Some witnesses may be honest and cooperative and desire to impart information in their possession to the investigator. Despite these admirable qualities, however, the information may still be affected by other factors that influence all witnesses, such as age, physical characteristics, and emotions. It may be wise in most circumstances to

organization or a business, a determination of any practices that would make the organization a criminal target could be extremely valuable. In addition, the interviewer should determine whether the business is insured against losses, if relevant.

The Suspect

The interrogator must evaluate himself or herself and the circumstances surrounding the conduct of the interrogation and must begin to evaluate the **suspect.** An effective interrogator understands that a successful interrogation cannot be organized and compartmentalized into a neat, orderly, step-by-step package. Rather, it is a combination of personality, behavior, and interpersonal communication skills between the interrogator and suspect. It is made up of verbal processes and the way they are communicated, nonverbal actions including body language, and personality characteristics that together might be characterized as a psychological fingerprint.[7] Only by

	Do You Have These Facts Regarding the Crime?	Check Here
1	The legal description of the offense	
2	The value and nature of loss	
3	Time, date, and place of occurrence	
4	Description of crime scene and surrounding area	
5	Physical evidence collected	
6	Weather conditions at time of offense	
7	Specific entry/exit points of perpetrator	
8	Approach and departure routes of perpetrator	
9	Methods of travel to and from scene	
10	The modus operandi of the perpetrator	
11	The tools or weapons used	
12	Names of persons having knowledge	
13	Possible motive	
14	Details from other case files that a. point to particular suspects	
	b. show matching modi operandi	
	c. suggest a pattern of criminality	

◄ FIGURE 5-6
Preinterrogation checklist
(Source: John Fay, Unpublished notebook, American Society for Industrial Security, Workshop in Criminal Interrogations [Jacksonville, FL: ASIS, 1981], p. A4-1)

interview this type of witness first to obtain basic information that can then be compared with later-acquired stories.

- Some witnesses may desire not to give any information in an interview regardless of what they know. Some of these witnesses simply may not want to get involved, others may fear any contact with a law enforcement agency, some may not understand the significance of information they have, and others may not want to do anything that would aide law enforcement.
- Some witnesses may be reluctant to cooperate or be suspicious of the motives of the interviewer until a rapport is established and the investigator can assure the witness of his or her good intentions.

Because some witnesses may be deceitful and provide incorrect information, it is a basic principle that an investigator should never take a witness's explanation totally at face value but, rather, should obtain supporting information or evidence.

There may be other barriers that must be overcome in order to successfully interview someone who has knowledge of the circumstances under which a crime was committed. Language barriers, which may not initially be recognized as significant, may prevent the interviewer from obtaining any useful information; however, some people may be so talkative and provide so much information that their motives should be questioned, along with the information they provide. A potential witness who may be under the influence of alcohol or drugs may or may not have information that could be used at trial, but the condition of the witness is a major factor to be considered in assessing the value of any information obtained.

Juveniles

In evaluating information provided by juveniles, investigators need to give consideration not only to chronological age but also to the level of schooling, verbal ability, and recall ability (Figure 5-7). Weaknesses in these areas may cause accounts of an event to be rambling and disjointed, accompanied by a poor distinction between relevant and irrelevant data, and by a limited ability to comprehend abstract concepts. A child may be able to focus only on one thought at a time and cannot combine thoughts into an integrated whole. Some children may have short attention spans, occasional problems in differentiating between what was seen and what was heard, and difficulty distinguishing between fact and fantasy.

◄ **FIGURE 5-7**

Investigator interviewing young people on street
Within the past 45 minutes, a convenience store was robbed two blocks from where this interview is taking place. The officer is attempting to find out if these two young men saw or heard anything that might help the investigation. They were not able to be of assistance. (© Mark Richards/ PhotoEdit)

Recall ability improves with age and maturity but develops differently for males and females. For example, males can recall the make and model of an automobile more accurately, while females can generally recall colors and clothing more accurately. (For a more detailed discussion of interviewing children, see Chapter 11, "Crimes against Children.")

The emotional characteristics exhibited by children are another factor that can affect the content and quality of information gleaned. Some children are expressive; they are outgoing and verbal. Other children are controlled and are timid and nonverbal. Expressive children often speak with ease on a range of topics and may, at times, be too talkative. Controlled children are generally quiet and do not show their feelings. They frequently avoid eye contact and keep their heads or bodies turned away from interviewers.[9]

Particular caution must be exercised in interviewing juveniles. In many jurisdictions, parents must be notified of the purpose of the interview and the nature of the information sought from the juvenile. In other jurisdictions, notification may be recommended but not required. In some instances, the presence of the parent during the interview is required or possibly desirable. Even when their presence is required, parents should not be allowed to distract or in any way influence the juvenile's responses. In addition, local law should be consulted.

Persons with Physical Infirmities

Interviewing an older person or any person with physical infirmities may also present a unique set of challenges. The interviewer must have knowledge of and appreciation for the physical changes that may occur with aging and be able to effectively respond to those changes when conducting an interview.[10]

Visual Infirmities

Changes in vision that are related to aging vary widely from person to person. These changes are not strictly dependent on chronological age or general health. The eye is so constructed that excellent vision without glasses is sometimes maintained even in extreme old age. However, this is an exception. About three-fourths of all older women and over half of all older men experience moderate to severe changes in visual functions. Those 65 or older account for half of all legally blind persons in the United States. The simple statistical probabilities are that an older person will have vision difficulties of one kind or another.

The investigator should ascertain if the witness had his or her glasses on, or contact lenses in, if the witness claims to have seen something, and determine, by asking, the degree of visual impairment. For example, the witness should be asked what the prescription is for their glasses or contacts.

Hearing Loss

Hearing loss resulting in a distortion of sounds generally is caused by changes in the inner ear. A person who suffers from a hearing loss must take advantage of every opportunity to use other skills in communicating, such as speech reading. Speech reading, often thought of as "lip reading," is the process of visually receiving cues from all lip movements, facial expressions, body posture, gestures, and the environment. Speech reading is a skill everyone has to a certain degree. It is only when hearing becomes impaired that this skill becomes important.

Interviewers will be able to communicate most effectively and patiently with hearing-impaired people by following these suggestions: (1) gain the person's attention; (2) speak to the person from 3–6 feet distance; (3) speak clearly and remind the person of the topic if necessary and rephrase questions if not understood; (4) control external noises as much as possible, and get the interviewee to talk, encourage participation.

Because a witness's information also must be evaluated in light of its potential value in court, the interviewer must evaluate the witness's competency and credibility.

Competency of a Witness

The term **competency** refers to a witness's personal qualifications for testifying in court. Competency must be established before a witness is permitted to give any testimony. The witness's personal qualification depends on circumstances that affect his or her legal ability to function as a sworn witness in court. Competency has nothing to do with the believability of a witness's information.

Among the factors an investigator must evaluate in determining the competency of a witness are age, level of intelligence, mental state, relationship to individuals involved in the case, and background characteristics that might preclude the testimony of the witness from being heard in court. For example, in many jurisdictions, a young child cannot be a witness unless it can be shown that the child knows the difference between truth and imagination and understands the importance of being honest. Similarly, any person whose intelligence or mental state prevents him or her from understanding the obligation of telling the truth is not permitted to testify, regardless of the information he or she may possess.

Relationships among individuals involved in a case may also affect a witness's competency. Husbands and wives need not testify against each other, nor may attorneys testify against clients, doctors against patients, or ministers against penitents. Privileges vary by state. Background characteristics also may preclude a witness's testimony from being accepted in court. For example, some state laws forbid a convicted perjurer from testifying.

Possibilities such as those described in the preceding paragraphs mean that the investigator must learn as much as possible about the witness before and during the interview.

Credibility

Credibility is that quality of a witness that renders his or her testimony worthy of belief. Credibility in this sense is the same as weight or believability. The credibility of a witness is established in terms of presence, consciousness, and attentiveness. During the interviewing process, the investigator must examine each of these requirements carefully and in detail. Among the questions to which the interviewer must receive satisfactory answers in evaluating the credibility of a witness are these:

- Was the witness conscious at the time of the event?
- Was the witness under the influence of alcohol or drugs?
- How did the witness happen to be in a position of seeing, hearing, or otherwise perceiving the crime?
- Where was the witness coming from or going to?
- What was the witness doing at the exact moment that the crime occurred?
- What else was going on at the time that might have distracted the witness's attention?

The investigator should also evaluate the witness and the information supplied to ascertain how believable the witness will be at a trial. To do this, the investigator must ascertain the following factors:

- Does the witness have any particular bias, prejudice, or personal interest in the case?
- Does the witness have any physical or mental impairments that may affect his or her ability to observe, recollect, or recount the events? (Does the witness normally wear glasses? Was the witness wearing them at the time? Does the witness have a hearing problem?)
- What physical conditions, such as weather, lighting, and visibility, existed at the crime scene?
- What is the witness's reputation for being a truthful person?

The effective interviewer cannot accept any witness's account at face value. The interviewer must question and requestion, check and recheck. The investigator must recognize and gauge the effects that physical and emotional characteristics, external influences, and attitudinal and behavioral factors have on the witness's perception and on the reliability of the information possessed. (These concepts are treated in more detail in Chapter 21, "The Trial Process and the Investigator as a Witness.")

WHY PEOPLE CONFESS

It is human nature to talk. Most people cannot keep a secret. It has been estimated that 80% of all people will confess to a crime. There are two basic categories of people who tend to confess to crimes: (1) guilty parties who psychologically need to "get it off their chest," and (2) persons who are not guilty but who act under some urge to confess. It is to protect the latter category of people that some procedural safeguards are provided. For example, a conviction cannot be based solely on a confession. There must be some other independent corroborating evidence to support the conviction.

The psychological and physiological pressures that build in a person who has committed a crime or who suffers from feelings of guilt concerning any other type of conduct are best alleviated by communicating. Talking is the best means of communicating. Therefore, in spite of having been advised of certain protections guaranteed by the Constitution, some people feel a need to confess. Even most confirmed criminals suffer from the same pangs of conscience as first-time offenders. However, fear of the potential punishments that await them contributes to their silence. Those who confess rarely regret it, for doing so gives them peace of mind. It permits them to look at themselves and life differently and to live with themselves. Most guilty individuals who confess are, from the outset, looking for the proper opening during an interrogation to communicate their guilt to the interrogator. The good interrogator will seek out and be able to recognize individuals who desire to confess and will approach the interrogation in such a way as to provide the accused with the proper opening and reason for the relief of the psychological and physiological pressures that have built up.[11] If it is human nature to talk and if people cannot generally keep secrets, then the job of the interrogator is to make it easy for a suspect to confess.

THE RELIABILITY OF EYEWITNESS IDENTIFICATION

Eyewitness identification and other information provided by eyewitnesses to a criminal event are relied on heavily by both law enforcement and courts in the investigative and adjudication stages of our system of justice,[12] yet research indicates that eyewitness testimony may be unreliable.[13] Eyewitness identification and description is regarded as the most unreliable form of evidence and causes more miscarriages of justice than any other method of proof.[14] Research and courtroom experience provide ample evidence that an eyewitness to a crime is being asked to be something and do something that a normal human being was not created to be or do. Human perception is sloppy and uneven.[15] Existing research does not permit precise conclusions about the overall accuracy of the eyewitness identifications that are a common feature of criminal prosecutions, but research does lead us to conclude that identification errors are not infrequent.[16] Such errors are borne out by case studies in which the use of DNA evidence exonerated people who had been convicted on the basis of eyewitness identification.[17]

Many factors influence an individual's ability to accurately recognize and identify persons, and all of them depend on the circumstances under which the information is initially perceived and encoded, stored, and retrieved.[18] Eyewitness identifications take place in a social context[19] in which the witness's own personality and characteristics, along with those of the target observed, are as critical as factors relating to the situation or environment in which the action takes place.

Thus, human perception and memory are selective and constructive functions, not exact copiers of the event perceived—constructive in that gaps will be filled to produce a logical and complete sequence of events. A person is motivated by a desire to be accurate as she or he imposes meaning on the overabundance of information that impinges on her or his senses, but also by a desire to live up to the expectations of other people and to stay in their good graces. The eye, the ear, and other sense organs are, therefore, social organs as well as physical ones.[20]

Agreeing with this theory of eyewitness perception, one observer notes:

Studies of memory for sentences and pictures indicate that when we experience an event, we do not simply file a memory, and then on some later occasion retrieve it and read off what we've stored. Rather, at the time of recall or recognition we reconstruct the event, using information from many sources. These include both the original perception of the event and inferences drawn later, after the fact. Over a period of time, information from these sources may integrate, so that a witness becomes unable to say how he knows a specific detail. He has only a single unified memory.[21]

The gender, age, expectations, intelligence, race, and facial recognition skills of the witness are factors that individually may or may not influence the eyewitness identification process but collectively or in combination with other variables are likely to have a bearing.[22] Facial attractiveness and distinctiveness, disguises, facial transformations, and the gender and race of the target (the person identified) are factors likely to influence identification.[23] Situational factors include such things as the presence of a weapon, exposure duration, and significance of the event in relation to all surrounding circumstances.[24]

Experts distinguish a number of factors that limit a person's ability to give a complete account of events or to identify people accurately. The following are among those factors:

- *The significance or insignificance of the event:* When an insignificant event occurs in the presence of an individual, it does not generally motivate the individual to bring fully into play the selective process of attention.
- *The length of the period of observation:* If ample opportunity is not provided for observation, the capability of the memory to record that which is perceived is decreased.
- *Lack of ideal conditions:* In situations where ideal conditions for observation are absent, the ability of the witness to perceive details is significantly

decreased. Distance, poor lighting, fast movement, or the presence of a crowd may significantly interfere with the efficient working of the attention process.

- *Psychological factors internal to the witness:* A witness under stress at the time of observation may find this to be a major source of unreliability in his or her observations.
- *The physical condition of the witness.*
- *Expectancy:* Research has shown that memory recall and judgment are often based on what psychologists term expectancy. This concept means that an individual perceives things in the manner in which he or she expects them to appear. For example, a right-handed eyewitness to a homicide might, in answer to a question and without positive knowledge, state that the assailant held the gun in his right hand, whereas a left-handed person might say the opposite. Biases or prejudices are also illustrated by the expectancy theory, as is the classic problem associated with stereotyping.[25]

An eyewitness's conduct can be influenced by expectations and inferences, which in turn can be influenced by the verbal and nonverbal behavior of investigators, the structure of the identification process, and the environment in which the identification takes place.[26] Much research has been conducted on lineups, showups, and photographic identifications, with a vast array of results indicating that such processes, by their nature, are suggestive, irrespective of whether law enforcement intended them to be so or not.[27] For example, taking a victim or witness from one place to another to observe a person who has been arrested may be suggestive enough to produce a false identification. The fact that a law enforcement agency spend time putting together a photographic lineup may suggest that they have identified a perpetrator whose picture will be among those presented, regardless of whether such suggestiveness is intended by law enforcement or not. Law enforcement may not even have a suspect.[28]

In addition, there can be significant error even when two or more eyewitnesses provide similar descriptions:

One might expect that two eyewitnesses—or 10 or 100—who agree are better than one. Similarity of judgment is a two-edged sword, however; people can agree in error as easily as in truth. A large body of research results demonstrates that an observer can be persuaded to conform to the majority opinion even when the majority is completely wrong.[29]

In one test, people were asked to describe a mock crime they had viewed earlier. They first gave individual responses then met as a group. The group descriptions were more complete and in greater detail than those reported by individual subjects, but the group descriptions also gave rise to significantly more errors as well as an assortment of incorrect and stereotyped details.[30]

In summary, the problems associated with eyewitness identification can result in errors. Mistaken identifications of people, things, places, times, events, and other facts can result in miscarriages of justice. In some instances, these errors can be corrected.

Addressing the problem of eyewitness fallibility, in 1999 the National Institute of Justice issued procedures to be followed by law enforcement personnel in the effort to ensure the highest level of integrity in the eyewitness identification process. Although the institute recognizes that accuracy cannot be guaranteed, its guidelines are designed to eliminate even inadvertent suggestibility from the eyewitness identification techniques employed by law enforcers. They cover a broad range of situations, including receiving a 911 call; initially arriving at the scene; conducting a follow-up investigation; reviewing mug-shot books; developing composite drawings (by an artist or with a kit or a computer imaging system); returning a suspect to a scene for a showup; and conducting photographic and live lineups.[31]

The guidelines also briefly address some areas for future consideration. For example, scientific research indicates that identification procedures such as lineups and photo arrays produce more reliable evidence when the individual lineup members or photographs are shown to the witness one at a time rather than simultaneously. (Thus, in the case illustrated in Figure 5-8, would identification have been more accurate if the photographs of all three men could have been shown to the individual victims sequentially? Even if the photos had been shown simultaneously, the results would have been interesting.[32]) Four years after publishing the guidelines, the National Institute of Justice published a *Trainer's Manual*, including a CD, to aid in explaining the processes and procedures called for in the original guidelines.[33]

Another area for future study involves unintentional cues. Psychology researchers point out that an investigator might provide an unintentional cue through body language, tone of voice, or other actions that would be suggestive to a witness. They believe that this could be avoided if lineups, showups, photo arrays, and the like were conducted under "blind" conditions—that is, if the identification procedure was conducted by someone who did not know who the suspect was and therefore could not do or say anything that would promote suggestibility.[34]

The Legal Perspective of Eyewitness Identification

Because eyewitness identification is so critical in obtaining a conviction in a criminal case and because of the

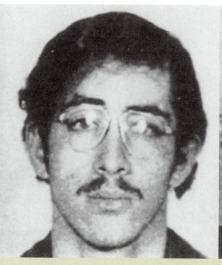

▲ **FIGURE 5-8 Look-alikes**

Mistaken identifications led to the arrests of two innocent men: Lawrence Berson (*left*) for several rapes and George Morales (*right*) for a robbery. Both men were picked out of police lineups by victims of the crimes. Berson was cleared when Richard Carbone (*center*) was arrested and implicated in the rapes. Carbone was convicted. He later confessed to the robbery, clearing Morales.

(Source: *Scientific American*, 1974, Vol. 231, No. 6. Reprinted by permission.)

problems associated with potential unreliability, there is no absence of judicial pronouncements on this issue. The problems were addressed by the U.S. Supreme Court in the 1960s and 1970s. In *Stoval* v. *Denno* (1967), the Court said that the police must follow recommended procedures to guarantee impartiality before, during, and after a lineup.[35]

In the 1972 case of *Neil* v. *Biggers,* the Supreme Court listed five factors to be used in determining the reliability of eyewitness identification, particularly in situations in which identification is delayed rather than made immediately at the crime scene:

- Opportunity of the witness to view the act at the time of the crime.
- Degree of attention paid by the witness.
- Accuracy of the witness's prior description of the criminal.
- Level of certainty of identification demonstrated by the witness at the confrontation.
- Length of time between the crime and the confrontation.[36]

Manson v. *Brathwaite,* decided in 1977, dealt with the corrupting effect of a suggestive eyewitness identification procedure.[37] The case produced the **Biggers-Brathwaite Factors Test,** which balances the five factors of *Biggers* with the "corrupting" effect of any suggestive procedures. As a result, if a law enforcement officer or an investigator accidentally does something that jeopardizes the fairness or impartiality of a procedure, the identification can still be used in court if the reliability of the eyewitness identification is strong.[38]

INTERVIEWING AND INTERROGATION PROCESSES

Regardless of the time, place, or setting of the interview, or ultimately the type of witness or victim interviewed, there exists some standardization in technique. "An interview . . . has a beginning, a middle—its main segment—and an end."[39] The beginning is the warm-up period, the time when the interviewer must establish rapport. The main segment is devoted to acquiring the desired information. The end occurs when the investigator has accomplished certain goals and shows appreciation to the witness.

The warm-up period allows the interviewer to provide identification, state the purpose of the interview, and put the witness at ease with small talk. Matters of common interest may be discussed, such as children, sports, military service, or membership in civic organizations. Friendly conversation can convey interest in the witness, get the witness talking, and provide the interviewer with an opportunity to evaluate the witness as well as to reduce anxiety on the part of the person being interviewed. The length of the warm-up period depends on a number of variables, including the attitude of the witness, the level of cooperation, and the degree to which the witness can be motivated to provide useful information. The warm-up is time well spent if it helps to ensure a successful interview.

When leading into the main body of the interview, the interviewer should take care not to lead the witness by asking questions that imply the answer.

Questions should always be phrased positively so that the response is also positive. Questions such as "You don't really believe that, do you?" imply that anything other than a negative answer will be unacceptable. "Do you believe that?" allows the witness more freedom to respond.

Studies substantiate that the exact manner in which interview questions are asked is critical to the response. The choice of a single word and its use in a sentence can dramatically affect the nature of a response. In laboratory studies in which subjects were shown a film of a traffic accident, portions of the study group were later asked if they had seen *the* broken headlight, while others were asked if they had seen *a* broken headlight. The group presented with the question containing "the" said yes significantly more often than did the group presented with the question using "a." These results were consistent whether witnesses had or had not seen a broken headlight. The significance of this illustration is that use of "the" by the questioner implies the existence of a broken headlight, causing the witness to assume its existence and potentially influence their answer.

Further studies attempted to determine if word substitutions could affect quantitative judgments as well as a simple yes or no answer. Seven films of traffic accidents were shown to a group of subjects. Later, they were all asked *substantially* the same question: "About how fast were the cars going when they hit each other?" The only difference was in the verb used in the question. When various subjects were asked the question, the words "smashed," "collided," "bumped," or "contacted" were substituted for "hit." Although any of the words could be used properly in the question, each tends to imply a difference in speed and force of impact. Results showed that estimates of the speed of vehicles involved tended to increase as a more forceful verb was used in the question.[40]

To avoid such problems, interviewers should use "open-ended" questions, asking witnesses to relate in their own words the events of which they have knowledge. Witnesses should be allowed to continue this narrative uninterrupted, unless the amount of superfluous or irrelevant material becomes excessive. Interviewers must remain attentive to what is and is not said and must prepare questions that separate facts from inferences and implications. To keep the witness talking, the investigator can ask, "What happened next?"

For the investigator to picture the occurrence with the same clarity and in the same order as the witness, questions should be asked in systematic and chronological order. They should be stated simply and clearly so that the witness understands them. Short, concise questions should be asked one at a time. Long or complex questions tend to produce disorganized and confused answers.

The interviewer should always permit a witness to save face if errors in the witness's statement become apparent. Provided the interviewer is satisfied that the mistake is an honest one and not the result of deliberate misrepresentations, he or she should attempt to assist the witness in clarifying the statement without seeming judgmental.

It is always advisable for the interviewer to verify the information presented by the witness. To do this, the interviewer should simply rephrase what he or she thinks was said and ask the witness to verify its accuracy. Although this is often not done, it can overcome a major stumbling block to proceeding with an effective investigation and a successful prosecution. Verifying what was heard can cause the witness to recall additional information that was not told during the basic part of the interview.[41]

Occasionally, the interviewer misses or fails to ask questions on some points simply because there was a lack of information that would have caused a question to be asked. Therefore, it is advisable for the interviewer to ask a final "catch-all" question, such as "Is there anything I have not asked that you think I should have asked?" This way, if there were any gaps in the questioning, the witness has the opportunity to provide the missing information to the investigator. This method ensures that if a relevant issue crops up later, the investigator will not have to ask, "Why didn't you tell me this during the interview," only to have the witness reply, "You didn't ask."[42]

When satisfied that all relevant information has been obtained, the interviewer should terminate the interview with a thank-you and a short statement of appreciation for the witness's time and efforts in cooperating with law enforcement in the investigation.

Effective interrogators, like interviewers, must be skilled in psychology, persuasiveness, and acting. Good interrogators must also be good seducers; they must be able to make others do what they want them to do. They must be capable of giving the appearance of empathy, sympathy, and objectivity when those characteristics are most appropriate to accomplishing their objectives. A successful interrogation requires that the investigator sell himself or herself to the subject as a concerned and helpful person.

Just as in interviewing, it is important in interrogating to establish a rapport with the person to be questioned. **Rapport** can be established by showing a sincere interest in the person and his or her personal problems. Complimenting the suspect on some outstanding trait or characteristic often gets the suspect talking. Small talk usually accomplishes the same result. Once the conversation has started, the objective is to keep the suspect talking—about anything.

It is essential that the interrogator be in complete command of the interrogation and that this be made absolutely clear to the suspect at the outset. The interrogator must project competence and self-confidence in making a first impression on the suspect. As an example, if the interrogator perceives that the suspect considers himself or herself superior to the interrogator, the suspect may be addressed by last name only, instructed to sit, instructed not to smoke, and manipulated in other ways.

At this stage, it is important for the interrogator, using personal observations and known facts about the suspect, to evaluate the suspect. The interrogator must consider the suspect's mental capacity, as well as his or her cultural and ethnic background. Often, behavioral signals have cultural roots. What might appear to be a sign of deception may, in fact, be quite the opposite. For example, it is not uncommon for Hispanic males to look down when in the presence of a person of authority, rather than looking directly at that person. Drugs or alcohol can also cause a suspect to produce a deceptive reaction, such as delaying in answering a question.[43]

INTERVIEWING AND INTERROGATION TECHNIQUES AND LEGAL REQUIREMENTS

Before examining some of the current theories and approaches to interviewing and interrogating, we must discuss the legal framework within which interrogations must be conducted.

Preinterrogation Legal Requirements

The legal issue became of critical concern during the 1960s. As a result, the Supreme Court handed down a landmark decision that has dramatically affected the conditions under which interrogations take place. The issue revolved around the Fifth Amendment protection against self-incrimination and the Sixth Amendment guarantee of the right to counsel, both as made applicable to the states through the due process clause of the Fourteenth Amendment. (See Chapter 2, "Legal Aspects of Investigation.")

Miranda v. Arizona

In *Miranda* **v.** *Arizona*[44] the Supreme Court, in a five-to-four decision, spelled out the requirements and procedures to be followed by officers when conducting an in-custody interrogation of a suspect.

In March 1963, Ernest Miranda was arrested for kidnapping and rape. After being identified by the victim, he was questioned by police for several hours and signed a confession that included a statement indicating that the confession was given voluntarily. The confession was admitted into evidence over the objections of Miranda's defense counsel, and the jury found him guilty. The Supreme Court of Arizona affirmed the conviction and held that Miranda's constitutional rights had not been violated in obtaining the conviction because following

the ruling from *Escobedo* v. *Illinois*[45] the year before, in which Escobedo's confession was ruled to have been improperly admitted because he asked to see his lawyer but was denied that right, Miranda had not specifically requested counsel. The U.S. Supreme Court, in reversing the decision, attempted to clarify its intent in the *Escobedo* case by spelling out specific guidelines to be followed by police before they interrogate persons in custody and attempt to use their statements as evidence. In clarifying the requirements of *Escobedo,* the Court felt compelled to include the Fifth Amendment requirements against self-incrimination in the decision. The guidelines require that after a person is taken into custody for an offense and before any questioning by law enforcement officers, if there is any intent to use a suspect's statements in court, the person must first be advised of certain rights. (See Figure 5-9.) These rights include:

1. The right to remain silent.
2. The right to be told that anything said can and will be used in court.
3. The right to consult with an attorney before answering any questions and the right to have an attorney present during interrogation.
4. The right to counsel. If the suspect cannot afford an attorney, the court will appoint one.[46]

Suspect's Response: Waiver and Alternatives

It is common practice for the officer to ask the suspect if he or she understands the rights as they have been explained. If the answer is yes, then the officer may ask if the subject wants to talk with the officer. At this point, four alternatives are open to the suspect:

1. *The suspect may choose to remain silent,* not wanting even to respond to the officer's question. The courts have held that choosing to remain silent does not imply consent to be interrogated and no questions should be asked.
2. *The suspect may request counsel.* At that point, the investigator must not undertake any questioning of the suspect, for anything said will not be admissible in court. In *Edwards* v. *Arizona* in 1981, the Supreme Court held that no police-initiated interrogation may lawfully take place once the suspect has invoked the right to counsel unless, and until, an attorney has been provided, or unless the defendant voluntarily begins to talk with the officers.[47] In *Minnick* v. *Mississippi* in 1990, the Supreme Court held that once counsel is requested, interrogation must cease; officials may not reinitiate interrogation without counsel being present, whether or not the accused has consulted with his or her attorney. The requirement that counsel be made available to the accused refers not to the opportunity to consult with a lawyer outside the interrogation room but to the right to have the attorney present during

THE EXPLANATION OF THE ADMONITION AND USE OR WAIVER OF YOUR RIGHTS	LA EXPLICACION DEL AVISO Y EL USO O NO DE TUS DERECHOS
1) You have the right to remain silent—you do not have to talk.	1) Tienes el derecho de quedar en silencio—no tienes que hablar.
2) What you say can be used, and shall be used against you in a court of law.	2) Lo que digas se puede usar y se usará en contra de ti en la corte de ley.
3) You have the right to talk with an attorney before you talk with us, and you have the right to have the attorney present during the time we are talking to you.	3) Tienes el derecho de hablar con un abogado antes de hablar con nosotros, y tienes el derecho de tener el abogado presente durante el tiempo que nosotros estamos hablando contigo.
4) If you do not have the funds to employ an attorney, one shall be appointed to represent you free of charge.	4) Si no tienes el dinero para emplear un abogado, uno sere fijado para que te represente, sin pagar.
5) Do you understand these rights as I have explained them to you, yes or no?	5) ¿Comprendes estos derechos como te los expliqué, si o no?
6) Do you want to talk to us about your case now, yes or no?	6) ¿Quieres hablar con nosotros de tu caso ahora, si o no?
7) Do you want an attorney present during the time we are talking to you, yes or no?	7) ¿Quieres un abogado presente durante el tiempo que estamos hablando contigo, si o no?

◄ FIGURE 5-9
Warning-rights card in English and Spanish
(Courtesy Los Angeles County Sheriff's Department)

custodial interrogation. This rule is necessary to remove suspects from the coercive pressure of officials who may try to persuade them to waive their rights. The rule also provides a clear and unequivocal guideline to the law enforcement profession.[48]

3. *The suspect may waive his or her rights and agree to talk with law enforcement without the benefit of counsel.* The waiver of rights is a sensitive topic for law enforcement, as it is the responsibility of law enforcement and the prosecutor to prove in court that the waiver was validly obtained. A valid waiver must be voluntarily, knowingly, and intelligently given by the suspect. The burden is on the prosecution to prove that the suspect was properly advised of his or her rights, that those rights were understood, and that the suspect voluntarily, knowingly, and intelligently waived those rights before the court will allow the introduction of any incriminating testimony in the form of a confession. The waiver cannot be presumed or inferred. It must be successfully proved by the prosecution. Therefore, it is preferable for the investigator who secures a waiver of rights from a suspect to attempt to get the waiver in writing with sufficient witnesses to substantiate its voluntariness. Figure 5-10 is a sample waiver form. A suspect who has waived his or her rights is free to withdraw that waiver at any time. If this occurs during questioning, the investigator is under a legal obligation to cease the interrogation at that point and either comply with the suspect's request for representation or simply cease the interrogation if the suspect refuses to talk.

4. *The suspect may indicate a desire not to talk with the investigators.* At this point, law enforcement has no choice other than to refrain from attempting to interrogate the suspect concerning the events of the crime for which he or she has been arrested. In this event, the case must be based on independent evidence, which may or may not be sufficient to warrant prosecution. The U.S. Supreme Court's emphatic position on terminating interrogation once a suspect has invoked the right to remain silent was announced in 1975 in the case of *Michigan* v. *Mosley.*[49]

Since the responsibility is on the prosecution, supported by evidence provided by the investigators, to substantiate the voluntariness of the waiver and the propriety of the warnings given to the suspect, many law enforcement agencies provide printed cards with the exact wording of the required warnings. They further recommend or require that when warnings are given they be read verbatim from the printed card. In this manner, the officer, when testifying in court, can positively state the exact words used in advising the suspect of his or her constitutional rights. Such a procedure avoids any confrontation with the defense as to the exact wording and contents of the *Miranda* requirements. But in 1989 in *Duckworth* v. *Eagen,* the Supreme Court held that it was not necessary that the warnings be given in the exact form described in the *Miranda* decision, provided that the warnings as a whole fully informed the suspect of his or her rights.[50]

A person being subjected to in-custody interrogation often chooses not to answer any questions posed by law enforcement—or at least not until an attorney is present. When counsel is made available to the suspect before or during interrogation, it is almost universal practice for the attorney to advise the client not to say anything to the police. Therefore, the effect of the *Miranda* decision has been to reduce significantly the number of valid interrogations by law enforcement agencies in this country

YOUR RIGHTS

Date_____

Time_____

WARNING

Before we ask you any questions, you must understand your rights.

You have the right to remain silent.

Anything you say can and will be used against you in court.

You have the right to talk to a lawyer for advice before we ask you any question and to have him with you during questioning.

If you cannot afford a lawyer, one will be appointed for you.

Geauga County has a Public Defender. Before answering any questions, you have a right to talk with the Public Defender.

If you decide to answer questions now, without a lawyer present, you will still have the right to stop answering at any time. You also have the right to stop answering at any time until you talk to a lawyer.

Do you understand these rights? _____

Signed: _____

Witnesses:

_____

_____

WAIVER OF RIGHTS

I have read this statement of my rights and I understand what my rights are. I am willing to make a statement and answer questions. I do not want a lawyer at this time. I understand and know what I am doing. No promises or threats have been made to me and no pressure or coercion of any kind has been used against me.

Signed: _____

Witnesses:

_____

_____

Date: _____

Time: _____

◄ FIGURE 5-10
Rights waiver form
(Courtesy Geauga County, Ohio, Sheriff's Department)

today. For the most part, however, confessions obtained in compliance with prescribed rules are of better quality and are more likely to be admissible in court.

It must be impressed on investigators that the failure to properly advise a suspect of the rights required by *Miranda* does not invalidate an otherwise valid arrest, nor does it necessarily mean that a case cannot be successfully prosecuted. Even in light of the line of court decisions indicating that *Miranda* warnings may not be required in all interrogation situations, good practice or departmental policy may require that all suspects in custody be advised of their rights.

In-Custody Interrogation

For investigators to understand the proper application of the *Miranda* requirements, it is essential that they under-

stand the meaning of **in-custody interrogation**. The *Miranda* case involved simultaneous custody and interrogation. Subsequent police actions revealed that all cases were not so nicely defined and that the meanings of "in custody" and "interrogation" required clarification. Although it may be difficult to separate the custody from the interrogation in certain factual situations, the two concepts must be considered separately. The cases cited in the following paragraphs should be examined from the standpoint of the subheading under which each is included.

Custody

Custody occurs when a person is deprived of his or her freedom in any significant way or is not free to leave the presence of law enforcement. Analyses of case decisions show that there is not yet a universally accepted definition of custody. Rather, case-by-case analysis is used to determine the applicability of the *Miranda* requirements.

In a 1977 case, the Court again emphasized that something more than suspicion or focus of an investigation is necessary before *Miranda* applies. In *Oregon* v. *Mathiason,* the defendant was asked to come to the state patrol office to be interviewed about a burglary. Mathiason was told that he was not under arrest but was informed that the police believed he had participated in the burglary. No *Miranda* warnings were given. He confessed, was convicted, and appealed. The Oregon Supreme Court reversed the conviction, finding that the defendant was interviewed in a "coercive environment" and that *Miranda* applied.[51] The U.S. Supreme Court disagreed with the state court, pointing out that the defendant had not been formally arrested and his freedom of locomotion had not been restrained in any significant way and that, without the presence of either of these factors, *Miranda* does not apply. The Court said:

> **Any interview** of one suspected of a crime by a police officer will have coercive aspects to it simply by virtue of the fact that the police officer is part of a law enforcement system which may ultimately cause the suspect to be charged with a crime. But police officers are not required to administer Miranda warnings to everyone whom they question. Nor is the requirement of warnings to be imposed simply because the questioning takes place in the station house, or because the questioned person is one whom the police suspect. Miranda warnings are required only where there has been such a restriction on a person's freedom as to render him "in custody." It was that sort of coercive environment to which Miranda by its terms was made applicable, and to which it is limited.[52]

In 1983, the Supreme Court again addressed the *Miranda* custody issue. In *California* v. *Beheler,* the defendant and several others had attempted to steal a quantity of hashish from the victim, who was selling the drug in the parking lot of a liquor store. While resisting the robbery, the victim was killed by one of the perpetrators. Shortly afterward, Beheler called the police and told them who had killed the victim. Later the same day, Beheler voluntarily agreed to accompany police to the police station and was specifically told he was not under arrest. During the 30-minute interview, he told police what had happened. He was not advised of his rights under the *Miranda* decision. After the interview, Beheler was permitted to return home. Five days later he was arrested for aiding and abetting first-degree murder. He was advised of his rights, which he waived, and confessed. Both confessions were used against him in his conviction. The California Court of Appeals reversed the decision,

▲ **FIGURE 5-11   Uniformed officer with handcuffed prisoner**
In deciding when Miranda warnings are required, there is no universally accepted definition of "custody." In this, photograph, it is clear that this suspect IS in custody between the officer leading him by the arm and the handcuffs; there is no doubt that the suspect is not free to leave. (© Cleve Bryant/ PhotoEdit)

holding that the first interview was "in custody" because it took place in the station, Beheler was a suspect at the time, and the interview was designed to elicit incriminating information.[53] (See Figure 5-11.)

The U.S. Supreme Court reversed the California appellate court decision and, following its previous holding in *Oregon* v. *Mathiason,* held that in determining whether custody exists for purposes of *Miranda,* the inquiry is simply whether there is a formal arrest or restraint on freedom of movement as usually associated with a formal arrest. Finding that no such restraint existed in this case, the Court added that the amount of information possessed by the police concerning the person to be questioned and the length of time between the commission of the crime and the time of questioning are not relevant to the issue of whether custody exists for purposes of applying *Miranda.*[54]

All interviews do not have to take place in a police station to have a coercive effect. In *Orozco* v. *Texas,* the Court held inadmissible a confession given after the defendant was questioned in his bed in the middle of the night by four police officers. The Court concluded in this 1969 case that the defendant had been deprived of his freedom in a significant way.[55]

Similarly, the defendant in *United States* v. *Lee* was questioned by two federal agents in a government car parked in front of his home. The questioning concerned the death of Lee's wife. Lee agreed to answer questions and was told he was free at any time to terminate the interview and leave. The conversation lasted between an hour and an hour-and-a-half, during which time the agents advised Lee of the incriminating evidence they possessed. Lee finally confessed to killing his wife but was not arrested until the next day when he voluntarily appeared at the police station for further questioning. At no time was he advised of his rights. Using a test called the **totality of the circumstances,** a federal appeals court in 1982 upheld the trial court's decision to exclude the statements on the basis that Lee was in custody and was not free to decline the interview under the circumstances, even though he had not been formally arrested.[56]

Other courts using the totality-of-circumstances test have come to conclusions different from those in the Lee case, but perhaps because of different factual conditions. In *United States* v. *Dockery*, a 24-year-old bank employee was questioned by FBI agents concerning the theft of bank funds. She was questioned for just over 15 minutes in a small vacant room in the bank. Dockery was told at the outset that she did not have to answer any questions, that she was not under arrest, that she was not going to be arrested, and that she was free to leave at any time. Dockery denied any involvement in the thefts. After the interview ended, Dockery was asked to wait outside the interview room. A few minutes later, she asked to see the agents, who again advised her that she did not have to talk to them and that she was free to leave whenever she desired. Shortly thereafter, Dockery gave a signed statement implicating herself in the thefts. In 1984, the federal appellate court reviewing the conviction ruled that Dockery was not in custody during the interviews and therefore that her confession was properly admitted at her trial.[57]

A 1984 decision of the Supreme Court for the first time recognized a "public safety" exception to *Miranda*. The facts in the case of *New York* v. *Quarles* involved an officer who entered a supermarket looking for an alleged rapist who was supposedly armed. The officer spotted the suspect, Quarles, who, on seeing the officer, ran toward the rear of the store with the officer in pursuit. The officer lost sight of Quarles for a few seconds. On regaining sight of the suspect, the officer ordered him to stop. While frisking Quarles, the officer discovered an empty shoulder holster. After handcuffing him, the officer asked Quarles where the gun was. Quarles nodded in the direction of some empty cartons and stated, "The gun is over there."

After retrieving the gun, the officer formally placed Quarles under arrest and advised him of his rights. Quarles waived his rights and, in answer to questions, admitted ownership of the gun and stated where he had obtained it. In the prosecution for the criminal possession of the weapon, the trial court suppressed all the statements about the location or ownership of the gun and suppressed evidence of the gun on the grounds that the officer had failed to initially advise the suspect of his constitutional rights and that the information acquired after the arrest and subsequent *Miranda* warnings was tainted by the first omission.

In reversing the decision, the Supreme Court agreed that Quarles was subjected to custodial interrogation without proper advisement and waiver of his rights. However, the Court ruled that the statements concerning the location of the gun and the gun itself were admissible under a public safety exception to the *Miranda* rule. The Court said that the need for answers to questions in a situation posing a threat to the public safety outweighs the need for protecting the subject's Fifth Amendment privilege against self-incrimination. The Court conceded that this exception lessened the clarity of the *Miranda* rule but held that it also would keep police officers from the untenable position of having to consider, often in a matter of seconds, whether it best serves society for them to ask questions without providing the *Miranda* warnings and chance having the evidence excluded or to give the warnings and chance not getting the evidence at all.

The Court further indicated it had confidence that law enforcement officials could easily determine the applicability of the public safety exception, but it cautioned that the burden is on the police later to articulate the specific facts and circumstances justifying the need for questioning, without the warnings, in order to protect themselves, other officers, or the public. Furthermore, because this is a very narrow exception to the *Miranda* rule, once the reason for the public safety exception ends, any further questioning should be preceded by the warnings and waiver.[58]

The question of whether *Miranda* applies to misdemeanor arrests was the subject of controversy for many years. In 1984, the Supreme Court settled this issue. The Court ruled in *Berkemer* v. *McCarty* that *Miranda* applies to the interrogation of an arrested person regardless of whether the offense is a felony or a misdemeanor. The justices found that to make a distinction would cause confusion because many times it is not certain whether the person taken into custody is to be charged with a felony or a misdemeanor.[59]

A 10-year-old girl disappeared from a playground in California in 1982. Early the next morning, about 10 miles away, a witness observed a large man emerge from a turquoise American sedan and throw something into a nearby flood-control channel. The witness called the police, who later discovered the girl's body in the channel. There was evidence that the girl had been raped and asphyxiated by a blunt-force trauma to the head. An investigator learned that the girl had talked to two ice-cream-truck drivers in the hours before her disappearance. One of the drivers was the defendant. The investigator's suspicions focused on the other driver. However, at 11 P.M. one evening, four uniformed officers arrived at the defendant's mobile home and asked him if he would accompany them to the police station to answer some questions. He agreed and rode in the front seat of the police car. At the police station, the investigator questioned him about his whereabouts on the evening the girl had been abducted. Nothing was out of the ordinary until the defendant mentioned that he had left his mobile home about midnight in his housemate's turquoise American-made car. This aroused the investigator's suspicion. He terminated the interview, and another officer advised the defendant of his *Miranda* rights. The defendant refused to make any further statements, requested an attorney, and was taken into custody. He was subsequently convicted of first-degree murder and other crimes.

The California Supreme Court affirmed the conviction. The case was heard by the U.S. Supreme Court to determine whether the defendant was in custody at the time he made the statements. The Court said that in deciding whether the defendant was in custody, the totality of the circumstances is relevant and no one factor alone disposes of the question. The Court went on to say that the most important considerations include where the interview took place, whether the investigation had focused on the subject, whether the objective bases for making an arrest were present, and the length of questioning. The Court, in reversing the decision, said the California Supreme Court was wrong in considering whether the investigation had focused on the subject to determine the custody issue, primarily because the officers never communicated their feelings so that the defendant was made aware that he was now a suspect in the case. Because the officers did not manifest this view, it could have no bearing on the question of whether the suspect was in custody at the time. The state subsequently acknowledged that the officer's subjective, undisclosed suspicions had no bearing on the question of whether the defendant was in custody for the purposes of *Miranda* during the questioning that occurred in the police station. The state, however, argued that the objective facts and records supported a finding that the defendant was not in custody until the arrest. The defendant, on the other hand, asserted that the objective circumstances showed that he was in custody during the entire time he was questioned.[60]

The cases cited clearly show that the statement offered in the beginning of this section is still correct. There is no universally accepted definition of custody, and with as much direction as the courts are trying to provide, many decisions are still subject to case-by-case scrutiny.

Interrogation

Interrogation includes any express questioning or any verbal or nonverbal behavior by a law enforcement officer that is designed to elicit an incriminating statement or response from the suspect of a crime. For many years following the *Miranda* ruling, there was considerable confusion over what constituted questioning or interrogation. For example, in a 1977 case the Supreme Court found that an impermissible interrogation occurred when an investigator delivered what has been called the "Christian burial speech" to a man suspected of murdering a young girl. While the suspect was being transported between cities, the investigator told the suspect to think about how the weather was turning cold and snow was likely. He pointed out how difficult it would be to find the body later. The investigator went on to say that the girl's parents were entitled to have a Christian burial for the little girl, who had been taken from them on Christmas Eve and murdered. Subsequent to this little speech, the suspect led the investigators to the spot where he had disposed of the body. The Supreme Court held this to be an interrogation within the scope of *Miranda,* even though direct questions had not been asked of the suspect.[61]

The Supreme Court faced the question of what constitutes interrogation for the first time in the 1980 case of *Rhode Island* v. *Innis.* In that instance a robbery suspect was arrested after the victim had identified him from photographs. The prisoner was advised several times of his constitutional rights and was being transported by three officers who had been specifically ordered not to question the suspect. During the trip, two of the officers were having a conversation about the case, and one commented how terrible it would be if some unsuspecting child found the missing shotgun (used in the robbery) and got hurt. The conversation was not directed at the suspect, nor did the officers expect a response from the suspect. However, the suspect interrupted the conversation and, after again being advised of his rights, led the officers to the shotgun. The Supreme Court stated the rule regarding interrogation as follows:

> We conclude that *Miranda* safeguards come into play whenever a person in custody is subjected to either express questioning or its functional equivalent. That is to say, the term "interrogation" under *Miranda* refers not only to express questioning, but also to any words or actions on the part of the police (other than those normally attendant to arrest and custody) that the police should know are reasonably likely to elicit an incriminating response from the suspect. The latter portion of this definition focuses primarily upon the perceptions of the suspect, rather than the intent of the police. This focus reflects the fact that the *Miranda* safeguards were designed to vest a suspect in custody with an added measure of protection against coercive police practices, without regard to objective proof of the underlying intent of the police.[62]

Interrogation, as defined by *Innis,* was found by one federal circuit to have been conducted when officers questioned the defendant about a homicide and showed him physical evidence linking him to the crime.[63] By applying this rule to the facts of the case, the Court held that the conversation between the officers did not amount to an interrogation and was properly admissible. Consequently, the current rules appear to be that if a suspect is in custody or otherwise deprived of freedom in a significant way, and if the suspect is to be asked pertinent questions, or if an officer uses words or acts in such a way that the officer knows would be reasonably likely to elicit incriminating responses from the suspect, the warnings must be given.[64] It is also fairly clear that volunteered statements, such as those given when a person walks into a police station and confesses to a crime, and general on-the-scene questioning by an investigator—such as "What happened?"—do not fall within the scope of *Miranda* requirements.[65]

The Court's position in the *Innis* case was again supported seven years later in *Arizona* v. *Mauro,* in which the police allowed the defendant's wife to talk with him after he had invoked his right to counsel. The conversation was conducted in the presence of a police officer, who was there for security purposes only, and it was also openly recorded. The officer asked no questions. Incriminating statements made by the defendant were held to be properly admissible.[66]

As a general rule, *Miranda* warnings need not precede routine booking questions that are asked in order to obtain personal-history data necessary to complete the booking process. As long as the questions are for that purpose and not a pretext to obtain incriminating information, *Miranda* warnings need not be given.[67]

As noted earlier, there are a number of theories and approaches describing the best techniques to use in conducting interviews. Every year someone develops a new approach that works for them. Creating an approach is an individual choice, based upon the investigator's research, practice, and experience. Similarly, identical techniques do not work for all interrogations. Approaches and questions differ with the type of suspect being questioned. Questioning a suspect whose guilt is certain requires a different approach from that used in questioning a suspect whose guilt is uncertain. Similarly, different approaches are used to interrogate unemotional and emotional suspects. Just as we saw in interviewing, there are many philosophies and approaches to conducting interrogations. In fact, some of the same concepts, like kinesics and evaluating body language, apply to both interviewing and interrogation. All these techniques assume either a logical approach or an emotional approach. The **logical approach** is based on common sense and sound reasoning. It tends to work better with males with past criminal records, educated people, and mature adults. The **emotional approach** appeals to the suspect's sense of honor, morals, righteousness, fair play, justice, family pride, religion, decency, and restitution. This approach tends to work better with women and first-time offenders.

When a suspect's guilt is certain, the interrogator should display confidence in this fact, perhaps by asking the suspect *why* rather than *if* he or she committed the crime, by pointing out the futility of telling lies, and by asking the suspect, "Aren't you sorry to have become involved in this mess?" Warning the suspect to tell the truth and pointing out some of the circumstantial evidence of guilt are also techniques to be used when guilt is certain. Calling attention to psychological and/or physiological symptoms of guilt can also work.

A sympathetic approach that gives the suspect a way out of a predicament can often be successful, and because the suspect is offered the opportunity to save face, confessions are sometimes forthcoming. Three mechanisms—rationalization, projection, and minimization, collectively called RPM—may be used (Figure 5-12). Rationalization offers the suspect a plausible way to explain his or her actions in a positive light. Projection excuses an act by placing the blame on someone or something else. Minimizing the offense or the suspect's role in its commission may provide psychological satisfaction that might

▲ **FIGURE 5-12 Investigators interrogating suspect**
This interrogation is taking place in an office rather than in a traditional sparsely furnished interrogation room. But, there is no table or desk separating the investigator and the suspect. They are essentially "knee to knee." You can see the smile on the investigator's face. He is using the RPM technique—rationalization, projection, and minimization—on this suspect in an attempt to obtain a confession.
(© Joel Gordon)

cause the suspect to acknowledge participation in the crime.[68]

When a suspect's guilt is uncertain, the interrogator should begin with an indirect approach, assuming that the interrogator already possesses all the necessary facts. By using all physical evidence, photographs, and sketches and challenging all lies, the interrogator may make this method extremely productive.

With the emotional suspect, the interrogator may call attention to physiological and psychological symptoms indicating guilt while pointing to the futility of resistance and appealing to the suspect's pride.

The "Mutt-and-Jeff," or good-guy/bad-guy, approach to interrogation works in some cases. One partner plays the bad guy, who rejects and refuses to believe all explanations put forth by the suspect. When that partner finally leaves the room, the good guy makes an emotional appeal and offers friendly assistance so that the suspect will not have to be confronted again by the bad guy.

Playing one person against the other sometimes works when there are at least two suspects, both of whom swear they are telling the truth during separate interrogations. The interrogator asks the first suspect to write on a piece of paper, "I swear I am telling the truth," and sign it. The interrogator then shows the paper to the second suspect, telling this suspect that the first suspect just told the whole story, but that before the interrogator totally accepts the story, he or she would like to hear the true story from this suspect.

Thus, trickery and deceit are often used in interrogation. The U.S. Supreme Court has not disapproved of these methods as long as they are not forcefully used to encourage an innocent person to incriminate himself or herself.

Guilty suspects often go through a progression of negative responses that include anger, then depression, followed by denial, bargaining, and finally, acceptance.[69] When a suspect whose guilt is certain enters a state of denial, the interrogator must go on the attack. This is an appropriate time to affirmatively accuse the suspect of the commission of the crime and to begin letting the suspect know that there already exists an assumption that he or she committed the crime and that it is time to move on to other issues.

When a suspect enters the state of bargaining, this indicates that the suspect accepts the reality of his or her involvement, but only to a limited extent. Normally, the suspect will still want to share responsibility. This is a good time to use techniques that will make it easier for the suspect to live with his or her involvement without expecting the suspect to accept full responsibility.

When the state of acceptance is reached, it is a positive state in which a confession is most likely to occur.[70]

It is highly advisable to keep current on all the recommended systems and techniques for interviewing and interrogating. A detailed discussion is, of course, beyond the scope of this book, but, in the following paragraphs, we will touch on a few.

The Cognitive Interview Technique

The **cognitive interview technique** was developed in the hope of improving the completeness and accuracy of eyewitness accounts.

The cognitive interview technique is deceptively simple. At first glance, it does not appear to be unique or particularly useful. However, the four general methods for jogging memory, used along with several specific techniques, become a very powerful and effective means of obtaining a complete and accurate picture of the events recalled.[71] The four techniques used to elicit information are explained to the witness beforehand and are designed to allow them to approach memory recall and retrieval from several different avenues.

The first step is to ask the witness to reconstruct the general circumstances surrounding the incident. The witness is asked to think about and recall what the surrounding environment looked like at the scene: rooms, arrangement of furniture, lighting, the presence of vehicles, weather conditions, smells, nearby objects or people, and any other details. In addition, the witness is asked how he or she was feeling at the time and what his or her reaction was to the incident. The purpose of this line of inquiry is to return the witness deeply into the scene.

Second, the investigator asks the witness to report everything remembered about the incident and all surrounding circumstances. The investigator explains that some people hold back information they don't think is relevant or important. The witness is asked not to edit any information or make any determination as to the importance of the material. In addition to the possibility that a tidbit of information may be of extreme importance, the mere act of relaying all information may cause the witness to remember something that had been forgotten.

An example of how obtaining all the details can work occurred when federal drug agents were debriefing an informant about what he had seen at a remote airstrip in Central America that had been used by drug smugglers. The informant recalled that there were mango trees around the airstrip and that he had eaten one of the mangoes. The answers given by the informant when he was asked to relive the experience of eating the mango and describe the taste, the smell, and the reactions of his other senses elicited some other memories of important details that enabled the drug agents to identify and locate the airstrip.[72]

Step three is to have the witness recall the events in a different order. For example, the witness may be asked to begin with the thing that most impressed him or her and work backward and forward from that point. Too often a witness asked to begin at the beginning will fill in gaps and tell a "complete" and logical story that makes sense but that may not be entirely accurate. Starting at a different point forces the witness to recall only events that actually occurred.

The fourth step is to have the witness change perspectives. The witness is asked to look at the incident from a different point of view or to put himself or herself in the position of some other person who was present and describe the incident from that other person's point of view.

Several other specific techniques may be used by an investigator to help strengthen the ability of the witness to retrieve stored memory. For example, in an attempt to obtain a physical description, the investigator may ask if the suspect reminded the witness of anyone. If so, who? Or why? Did anything about the person's appearance or clothing bring back any memories? How about names? Go through the alphabet to try to recall the first letter of a name. Did the person's voice remind the witness of anyone else's voice? Were any unusual words used? Any accent?

Many parts of the cognitive interview technique have been used for years. The parts are old, but using them together in a systematic method seems to be proving successful. Investigators can be trained in the technique easily, and, from the studies and experiments conducted thus far, it appears to be efficient and effective as a workable memory enhancement technique.[73]

Neuro-Linguistic Programming

Neuro-linguistic programming (NLP) embraces three simple concepts. First, behavior originates from neurological processes involving the five senses—seeing, hearing, smelling, tasting, and feeling. It is through these senses that we experience life. Then we communicate our life experiences through language, the linguistic element. Programming refers to how we organize our ideas and actions to produce results.[74] An interviewer or interrogator who understands these concepts and can get in sync with the witness or suspect by mirroring, or matching, mannerisms, actions, and words can make communication barriers disappear, foster trust, and create the flow of desired information. To achieve these results, the investigator should **mirror** the interviewee's kinesics, language, and paralanguage.

The term **kinesics** refers to body language, including gestures, posture, and movement of hands, feet, arms, and legs. The investigator must be cautious that the mirroring of behavior does not appear to be mimicry. The matching must be done subtly; otherwise, the interviewee might be offended, and the entire effort will be counterproductive.

Language used to relate experiences may take any of three forms: visual, auditory, or kinesthetic (feeling). Generally, one of these will be a person's dominant method of communicating. The dominant form appears readily in an interview setting. A person who answers a question with "It looks good to me" is predominantly visual; thus,

he or she might respond better to a question phrased in visual terms, such as "Picture this, John was sitting . . ." In contrast, someone who is auditory may say, "Sounds good to me"; in this case, the question might be worded "If you heard that John . . ." A feeling or kinesthetic person might say, "How do you think I feel?" The investigator might phrase the question, "How would you feel if what happened to John . . .?"[75]

A person's dominant mode can often be determined by watching his or her eyes. Generally speaking, left-brained individuals—about 90% of the population—display the following eye movements when searching their memories: Visually oriented people look up and to the left at a 45-degree angle; people with an auditory dominant mode look directly left; and "feeling" people look down and to the right at a 45-degree angle. People in the other 10% of the population are right-brained and will display a mirror image of their left-brained counterparts.[76] (See Figure 5-13.)

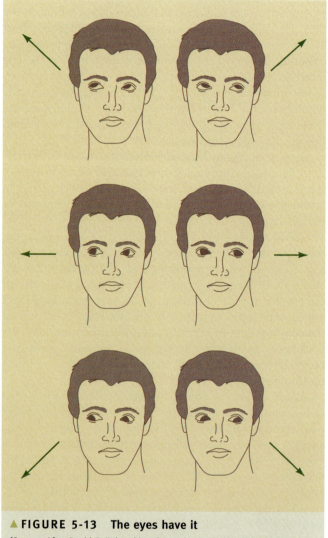

▲ **FIGURE 5-13** **The eyes have it**

(Source: After David E. Zulawski and Douglas E. Wicklander, *Practical Aspects of Interview and Interrogation* [New York: Elsevier, 1992], p. 154)

Paralanguage

Paralanguage involves how a person says something, along with the rate of speaking and the volume, pitch, tone, and tempo of the voice. Matching those characteristics can help build trust and can cause the interviewee to bond with the interviewer. This fosters communication and that flow will often provide the investigator with needed information.[77]

Verbal Signals

Verbal signals are generally easier for a deceptive subject to control than nonverbal signals. Verbal signals may take the form of changes in voice quality as well as specific statements. Stuttering or slurring words may be an indication of deception, as may a change in the speed of talking. Rapid speech may indicate nervousness, while abnormally slow speech may suggest careful planning of each word to avoid incriminating statements. An unusually high pitch or cracking of the voice may indicate deception.

Religious statements such as "Honest to God" and qualified answers beginning with such phrases as "to be perfectly honest" are potential indicators of deception and should be pursued by the attentive interrogator.

Kinesics: Nonverbal Signals: Body Language

Kinesics relates to the concept of body language. In the neuro-linguistic programming technique, kinesics is used to describe one of the three methods of communicating, through feeling as a dominant mode. But kinesics is really an approach of its own. It takes into account bodily responses to stress; the analysis of verbal communication, including the content, volume, pitch, and rate of speech; and body movements that involve the head, eyes, arms, legs, and the subject's posture when sitting. All these factors are used to evaluate a witness being questioned or a suspect being interrogated. As an example, most people have heard that if someone being interviewed has his/her arms crossed, this represents a defensive posture that must be overcome by the skilled interviewer in order to learn what information the interviewee possesses. Kinesics, however, looks for groups of various types of behavior to give the trained interviewer a better evaluation of the person being interviewed.[78]

There are generally far more nonverbal signals and behaviors than verbal. The primary reason for this is that suspects are generally not as able to control **body language** as they are to conceal verbal signals. Individually, a nonverbal signal is not as significant as a verbal signal. However, when body-language signals appear in clusters, they are generally much larger and much more symptomatic of deception. Body language is best considered as a means of confirming the symptoms and information generated from questions and answers in an interrogation. Thus, deception is generally taking place when the verbal cues are inconsistent with the nonverbal cues.[79] The body of a person who is being deceptive—lying—may experience certain physiological and psychological changes. The changes occur because of an inherent fear of detection. In many cases, the deceptive person's fears tend to intensify when questions focus on those investigative details posing the greatest threat to the suspect's personal welfare. Thus, the body language indicating deception tends to become more pronounced the closer the interrogator's questions come to incriminating the suspect. Often the deceptive person who attempts to disguise body language and to create an impression of nonconcern produces the opposite result. When this occurs, the body language is accentuated and more easily interpreted as signs of deception. Although not all persons who act deceptively are in fact deceptive, body language can supplement common sense, experience, and hunches for the investigator who wants and needs to distinguish truth from deception.

Among the more common symptoms that may appear as a result of pressure produced by lying are an increase in sweating; changes of color in the skin; a dry mouth, shown when the subject frequently swallows, wets the lips, or constantly indicates thirst; an increase in the pulse rate; an observable change in the breathing rate; a significant increase in the eye-blink rate; and eyes open wider than normal.[80] A good investigator is constantly alert for the manifestation of such symptoms and is able to use them to their advantage. Such manifestations should be pointed out to the suspect as indications of lying.

The deceptive individual often slouches rather than sitting upright, sits rigidly instead of relaxed, does not face the interrogator but looks to the side, sits with arms or legs crossed, and shifts sitting positions often and in a very jerky manner. Gestures indicating tension include wringing the hands, popping knuckles, chewing nails, picking lint from clothes, and clearing the throat, to name but a few. Facial expressions can display fear, anger, confusion, pleasure, and myriad other emotions.[81] (See Figure 5-14.)

Detecting deception, obviously, is not a science; hence, the phrase "may indicate deception" is frequently used. Behavioral actions and reactions must be interpreted in the social and psychological context of a specific situation, which can at times be misleading to even the most skillful interrogator.[82]

Three emotions closely related to the act of deception are worthy of explanation. The first emotion is the fear of being caught lying. The extent of the fear—mild, moderate, heavy—of course, influences the suspect's reaction. A number of determinants influence the extent of apprehension, including the suspect's belief (or knowledge) about the skill of the interrogator in detecting deception. The greater the interrogator's skills are, or are believed to be, the greater the apprehension on the part of the suspect. In actuality, the interrogator must be able to distinguish between the guilty person's fear of getting caught and the innocent person's fear of not being believed.

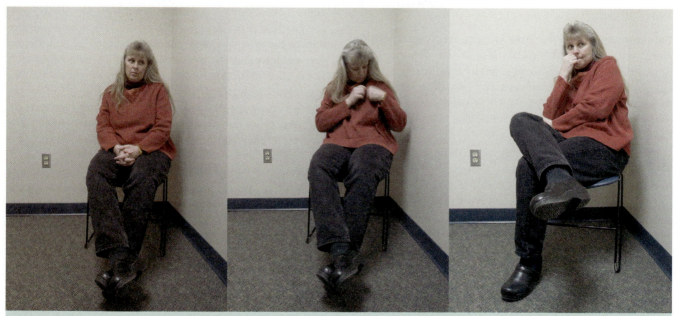

▲ **FIGURE 5-14** **Person in straight back chair exhibiting different types of behavior**
These behaviors—crossing the legs as in the photo on the far left, picking lint from clothing, and crossing leg and biting nails as depicted in the photo on the far right—are possible indicators of deception that would be readily observable to and interpreted by a trained interrogator. (© Mike Karlsson/Arresting Images)

Other determinants controlling the degree of apprehension include the level of experiences and successes the suspect has had in deceiving people in the past, the level of fear about the punishment for being detected, and the "acting ability" of the suspect (is he or she a good or bad liar?).[83]

The second emotion caused by deception is guilt about lying, as distinguished from any feelings about the content of the lie. The greater the guilt about lying, the greater will be the emotional reaction irrespective of the existence or degree of guilt about the criminal act itself.[84]

The third emotion, about which there is not much research, is the positive feeling that can accompany lying. Some subjects experience excitement at the challenge of being deceptive or at successfully deceiving the interrogator, especially if the interrogator has a reputation for being hard to deceive.[85]

Software Practice: Interviewing and Interrogation

Since 1998, the FBI has been using a software program that enables students to practice interviewing and interrogation techniques with a computerized subject that simulates a human personality. The "interviewee personality" emulates the many different types of individuals that investigators encounter in interview and interrogation situations. The user-friendly, self-paced learning package is interesting enough to make students want to use but is designed so that students cannot "beat the system" by learning a pattern of questions to ask.[86]

The subject character, Mike, has a "brain" designed with both logical and emotional components. The computer randomly selects fluctuations of Mike's emotional state so that his mood and his answers change each time the user conducts an interview or interrogation. Thus, the student-user never knows how Mike will respond from one interview to the next.[87]

A manual is provided with the CD software. Users review a case study and then select a category of questions from choices covering different parts of Mike's life, such as his personal habits, work relationships, or possible involvement in the crime. The user conducts the interview by selecting questions from a long list of possibilities. As Mike responds (or does not respond), the computer provides new questions and eliminates those that are no longer relevant. Mike's emotional responses also include body language that affects the line of questioning the user might take. At any time during the interview, the user can replay and review the interview. When the user decides to end the interview, he or she must determine whether Mike was truthful or deceptive. At the conclusion, the user is given a score. The program can be used repeatedly for practice purposes; as the user becomes more proficient, he or she can progress through four levels of increasing difficulty.[88]

At the FBI Academy, the software appears to be improving the interviewing and interrogating skills of those who are using it. The FBI provides the software free to state and local law enforcement agencies.[89]

Composing and Asking Questions

Often, an interrogator bombards a suspect with a series of questions, hoping to get satisfactory answers. The interrogator believes that he or she has conducted an interrogation when, in fact, all the interrogator did was try to cross-examine the suspect, which rarely produces a confession. As has been pointed out, a guilty person needs to have an acceptable reason to tell the truth. This does not mean that the interrogator should be noncommittal or anything but firm. It is suggested that at the outset of an interrogation, the interrogator should tell the suspect the exact purpose of the interrogation. Doing so may require initially coming out and accusing the suspect of committing the crime. If the interrogator is confident that the suspect is the offender, showing confidence in that position often weakens any defenses that the suspect may try to raise and puts the interrogation on a firm footing of understanding in regard to what is to be accomplished. For example, the interrogator might say, "I know that you have committed this offense, but we need to get beyond that and start talking about why you committed the offense," or "I know there are two sides to every story, and the purpose of this discussion is to find out your version of the truth so that we can get this truth working *for* you rather than *against* you."[90]

There are certain basic rules an interrogator should keep in mind when composing and asking questions. Questions should not be complex, because they will be difficult to understand; they should be short, direct, and confined to one topic. They must be clear and easily understood. Only words that the suspect can understand should be used. Questions should avoid legal terms—larceny, homicide—and, unless intended, accusatory questions should be avoided. Leading questions (those asked in a manner that suggests the answer desired, e.g., "You don't mean to tell me that you're actually denying pulling the trigger?") should be avoided unless necessary to facilitate the questioning process. Adherence to these basic rules ensures that both interrogator and suspect understand what each is talking about. As in most processes in criminal investigation, interrogation questions should initially focus on a wide base of general information and then narrow the focus continually to more specific issues.

Even while asking questions, the interviewer must continue the evaluation process. This includes the ability to recognize and cope with deception. The ability to effectively deal with deception is critical to the successful outcome of an interrogation. The basic premise is that an interrogator should never allow a suspect to lie and get away with it. If the lie is not detected, the suspect will be in control of the interrogation. This is an intolerable situation for the interrogator.

Recognizing and Coping with Deception

Deception is not always easy to detect, but, in general, there are both verbal and nonverbal cues that can be examined to determine whether a suspect is telling the truth or is being deceptive. In addition, statements can be written or recorded and analyzed to aid in this determination. Human behavior is diverse, and therefore there is no single nonverbal symptom or verbal cue that proves a person is being truthful or deceptive. To believe otherwise is foolish.[91]

To be effective in detecting when a suspect is being deceptive, the investigator who is thoroughly prepared should have some idea of the suspect's personality type. All the factors that are learned about the case and the suspect go into forming some opinion on how to approach the interrogation. In modern terms, this might be a type of "profiling." The interrogator alters and modifies the approaches and techniques used as the interrogation progresses and as he or she learns more about what is being said, how it is being said, and whether or not there are detectable signs of deception.

Neuro-linguistic programming, discussed earlier, can help the investigator not only in establishing rapport but also in detecting deception. Through the use of NLP, the interrogator can learn the suspect's dominant paralanguage pattern; identify his or her dominant visual, auditory, and kinesthetic speech patterns; and learn whether the suspect is left-brained or right-brained. By gaining these insights during the warm-up phase of an interrogation, the investigator will be in a better position to recognize deception.

Statement Analysis

A story told by a suspect while being interrogated is more than just facts. How the person says something may reveal far more than what is said. If possible, an experienced interrogator will attempt to have the suspect's statement reduced to a verbatim transcript, which will give the interrogator the opportunity to examine the statement thoroughly. This process is known as **statement analysis.** This transcript often provides additional insights into what the suspect intended to convey. For example, honest persons rarely talk about themselves in the third person, but dishonest persons often do so.

Pronoun usage offers a great opportunity for gaining insight into the suspect's thinking. The absence of the word "I" in the later portion of a statement, when questions are more specific about the suspect's involvement in the offense, suggest that the suspect is unwilling to acknowledge involvement. Refusal to use that personal pronoun shows an extremely impersonal approach to the topic about which questions are being asked. However, if the word "I" changes to "we" during the interrogation, the switch often suggests an attempt by the suspect to dilute his or her own responsibility and to imply the involvement of others—in other words, trying to spread the blame.

Verb tense can also be important. Normally, when an individual recalls a past event, he or she describes it in the past tense. That is because, when remembering, the mind sees what has occurred. However, if there is no memory, because the event never occurred, the mind must create the occurrence as it goes along. Hence, a suspect who is being deceptive may often use descriptive terms in the present tense. When this occurs, there is most likely some deception.

Balance is also a common element of speech. A story usually consists of an introduction, a body, and a closing. A deceptive person will sometimes spend just a short time talking about the important issues concerning the offense and spend a great deal of time describing extraneous information or trivia.[92]

Polygraph

The first workable **polygraph** is attributed to John Larson (1892–1983) in 1921. Its use spread relatively quickly in policing circles, and since then it has been improved upon a number of times, such as adding the use of computer scoring. (See Figure 5-15.) The primary purpose of a polygraph examination is to determine if victims, suspects, and informants are being truthful or untruthful about what they say. The polygraph is an adjunct to, but never a substitute for, other methods of investigation. Other common objectives for polygraph examinations are determining the reliability of informants, eliminating suspects, and narrowing the scope of an investigation. Research on the accuracy of the polygraph varies, roughly from 64% (laboratory studies) to 98% ("real world" use). Such differences may in part be attributable to laboratory protocols in which one group is told to lie about a mock crime scene or other event and the other group tells the truth. When people are not in real jeopardy for lying they may not have the same physiological responses as those who are lying to avoid criminal culpability for a felony.

Polygraphs record indicators of a person's cardiovascular pattern and fluctuations, respiratory patterns and fluctuations, and changes in skin resistance or sweat on their fingertips. The three most common findings by an examiner are no deception indicated, deception indicated, and inconclusive.

A supervisor's approval is required before an investigator can have a person examined by a polygraphist. The investigator is obliged to work with the examiner in a number of ways, such as:[93]

1. Providing the examiner with the information obtained in the investigation which supports and justifies the use of the polygraph.
2. Giving the polygraphist copies of incident, supplemental, and other relevant documents.
3. Calling attention to evidence which the subject does not yet know the police have.
4. Making available background information on the subject, including criminal history and possible motives.
5. Advising of statements made by the subject to victims and witnesses, as well as alibis provided.
6. Giving news articles and other general information about the case.
7. Helping the examiner arrange for a sign-language interpreter or translator as may be necessary.
8. Not trying to plan the procedures to be used, which is the purview of the examiner.
9. Not interrogating the suspect just before the examination.
10. Ensuring that persons authorized to be with the subject are present (e.g., attorneys, parents, or legal guardians).
11. Promptly advising the examiner if the subject is going to be late or has cancelled.

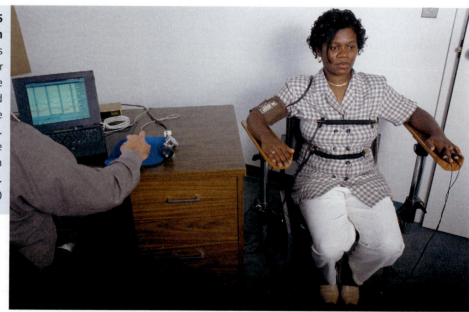

▶ **FIGURE 5-15**
Polygraph examination
Note that a blood pressure cuff is attached to the subject's right upper arm; two pneumograph tubes are stretched across the chest and abdomen; and metal plates are attached to the index and ring fingers. Readings from these sources are displayed on the examiner's screen at the left side of this photograph.
(Courtesy of the author)

Voice Stress Analysis

Computer Voice Stress Analysis (CVSA) was originally developed in 1988 by the National Institute for Truth Verification (NITV) and grew out of the Vietnam-era Psychological Stress Evaluator (PSE), which was used to differentiate between suspected Viet Cong and civilians. Around 1,600 police departments use the CVSA. The CVSA is small, easily portable, and, unlike the polygraph, does not require any attachments to the subject.

Basically, the CVSA notes microvariations in the audible and nonaudible portions of speech. Like the polygraph, reports of its accuracy varied. Illustratively, one laboratory study found it was not significantly better than random chance, while NITV cited a number of studies showing much higher rates. Here, too, the earlier comments about the absence or presence of real jeopardy affecting the studies' outcomes apply.

The NITV spent many years and invested tremendous resources to develop an automated system to accurately quantify CVSA patterns with the goal of removing any subjectivity in evaluating CVSA charts. A new scoring algorithm has been developed and field tested in state and local law enforcement agencies across the country. The charts under this new CVSA II, which was released in January 2007, reflect whether deception is or is not indicated. Field evaluations are showing a 96% accuracy rate for the new system with a false positive rate of less than 1%.[94]

Interviewing Terrorists

The traditional method of conducting interviews to elicit an admission or a confession of a terrorist is much different and much more complex than the interview of a traditional criminal. In fact, many of the traditional techniques which we have been taught for over 40 years

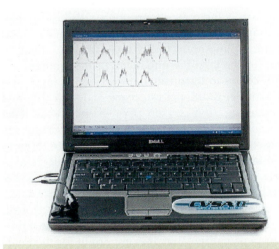

▲ Newly developed and released second generation computerized voice stress analysis system (CVSA II) displayed on a laptop computer. (Courtesy National Institute for Truth Verification).

for interviewing criminals actually do not work well when interviewing terrorists.[95]

Experience in investigating both domestic and foreign terrorists (e.g., KKK, Weather Underground, Baader Meinhoff Gang, Red Brigade, FALN, Macheteros, Abu Nidal, Palestinian Islamic Jihad, Al-Qaeda, et al.) has taught us that traditional interviewing techniques, which focus mainly on obtaining information that has had a probative value (seeks to prove the elements of the crime), simply fails in the complex arena of terrorism.

Unlike a criminal, the terrorist harbors two powerful features that the criminal simply does not posses: an *unyielding ideology* and *passionate hatred*.[96] The unyielding ideology of Theodore "Ted" Kaczynski, Timothy McVeigh, Ramzay Yousef, and Usama bin Laden is so inflexible and rigid as to drive their behavior with conviction and without remorse. For them violence is the "magical" solution to their ideology. Whether their ideology is against technology (Kaczynski), the militarization of U.S. law enforcement (McVeigh), or Western hegemony in the Middle East (Bin Laden), violence in the form of terror to exact "compliance from a populace," is the solution.[97]

The other unique feature of terrorists is their passionate hatred. This is a hatred that is so potent and compelling it propels them to action and to violence even where innocent victims are involved. Passionate hatred festers within the individual, nurturing rationalization, and driving a wedge between moral civility and the profligacy of terror.

Criminals, however, are not like this. Bank robbers may want to get rich quick but they do not harbor an overarching ideology that is unbending and unyielding, nor do they have a passionate hatred. For a criminal, violence is incidental for a terrorist, violence is required. Criminals may be upset at getting caught, but they do not harbor passionate hatred, that is reserved for the terrorist.

Because terrorists harbor these sentiments and beliefs, right from the start, they are more difficult to obtain information from than the average criminal. Their beliefs and hatred are so profound and pervasive that they act as a barrier or veneer resistant to traditional interview techniques.

First of all, to a terrorist, the law enforcement officer is the enemy. They represent, in most cases, all that the terrorist hates with a passion and wants to destroy. That alone is a disquieting barrier. To get the terrorist to cooperate the interrogator must get past their antipathy toward them as well as their rigidity and resolve for the cause to which they have dedicated themselves. This is no easy task. Additionally, the interviewer has to deal with a multitude of subtle pathologies that seem to afflict terrorists almost universally.[98]

We find many terrorists have features of or are fully paranoid.[99] Whether caused by the lives they live, the nature of their plans, or the ill they intend, terrorists tend to be paranoid. And within terrorist cells, paranoia is incubated. So by the time these individuals are intercepted or arrested, the features of paranoia are present.

They are suspicious, hypervigilant, distrustful, and reluctant to talk or communicate. And this in turn makes for a very difficult interview.

As Eric Hoffer revealed in *The True Believer*, every mass movement attracts a criminal element we now refer to as antisocials or psychopaths.[100,101] These individuals present a different problem in that they are self-centered, narcissistic, and have no remorse. These individuals will not hesitate to kill civilians or behead Westerners without the slightest regard or concern (e.g., Abu Musab al-Zarqawi).[102] These individuals find refuge within terrorist organizations, and although they may conveniently follow a cause, in the end their loyalty is to themselves and not some higher cause.

The majority of terrorist leaders are pathologically narcissistic (e.g., Saddam Hussein, Ramsay Yousef). If they are apprehended, chances are they will talk, but the interviewer has to deal first and foremost with their ideology and their overvaluation of themselves and devaluation of the rest of us.[103]

As can be seen, the interviewer is up against a wall of psychological baggage that must be overcome. The criminal may realize he is breaking the law; but for a terrorist, his actions are nothing more than "politics by other means."[104] Terrorists see laws as either part of the problem or an inconvenience without legitimacy; violence is the only legitimate or viable means to an end. The concept of criminality, with its reliance on guilt and duty to society, simply does not resonate with the terrorist.

There is also what is termed "dissonant priorities" between the priorities of law enforcement (e.g., preventing further attacks, public safety, identification of others, etc.) and those of the terrorist or enemy. One seeks to serve the public while the other seeks to serve a cause. For a police officer, getting to the facts and obtaining a confession are paramount.[105] For the terrorist, continuing to resist and to fight for his cause are paramount. This "dissonance of priorities," as has been experienced within the intelligence community, has derailed many interviews. Through habit, the officer immediately wants the facts; the terrorist or enemy combatant, not having yet been denuded of his powerful ideology, sees the interview as a continuation of the struggle, and so he will resist.

The interviewer is up against the personal and group mythologies of the terrorist with all the encumbering beliefs by which they see and sense the world.[106] They do not see the world as the interviewer sees it. For them perception, however wrong, is their reality. There is also a historical animus that exists (e.g., Jihadists against the hegemonic Christian West, Puerto Rican *Independentistas* against the United States, etc.) between them and us as well as the historical "wound collecting" that terrorists are famous for.[107] These all manifest in the terrorist interview, even the domestic terrorism interview (e.g., Timothy McVeigh).

It is very important to understand that many of today's terrorists come to us from cultures that are shame-based versus guilt-based, as we are in the West.[108] Where most interviews in the United States focus on confession to unburden guilt, most of the Eastern World does not subscribe to guilt but rather to shame. In these cultures, shame has a higher significance (this is why some Japanese politicians commit ritual suicide when they shame themselves). Public perception is very important, and it does not necessarily mirror traditional Western or American values. Where we deplore suicide bombers, in the occupied territories of Palestine, they are revered as *istishaddi* (martyrs) by the Palestinians.[109]

Another factor to consider is that of nonlinear cultures that think in clusters rather than linearly, as we do.[110,111] Nonlinear cultures tend to think more abstractly, and events can be married together during discourse. Also, how things are said are more important than how accurately they are portrayed, a factor that has led many investigators astray or caused them to label such information a fabrication or lie.

If an interview is being conducted with a Middle-East subject, the interviewer's badge alone does not carry any weight as it would in the West. First of all, in the Middle East, many police and law enforcement organizations are corrupt and terribly abusive, so there is little respect for what terrorists perceive as oppressors. The interviewer's status, hierarchy, age, knowledge, and pedigree are most important. Such subjects will talk to the interviewer, not because of his authority but because he is deemed worthy of their time and attention. Youth, irreverence, and ignorance are not appreciated by this type of subject.

So how should a terrorist or an enemy be interviewed? First and foremost, the interviewer must, at all times, treat the subject with dignity and respect.[112] One experienced interviewer reports he never had anyone confess who later said, "I chose to confess because you treated me with disrespect and were abusive."[113] On the contrary, what every successful terrorist interviewer has said is that you have to treat the subject with dignity and respect. It is imperative to establish a working rapport, but also the interviewer must be prepared, educated, and knowledgeable. Terrorism is the only offense for which history, religion, geography, anthropology, psychology, politics, and forensics are all important to the investigation. This process is not for the lazy, the impatient, or the ignorant.

When it comes to terrorists, the interviewer must stop thinking about a traditional interview and start thinking about "recruiting" this person psychologically, as if he were an informant. Think of the process as recruiting a human asset; a source that will eventually have to go to jail. The interviewer wants to obtain all the information the subject has, not just that which will get him prosecuted. Unlike a criminal interview, in the terrorism interview the interviewer wants information that is of lead, probative, historical, intelligence, prophylactic (force protection), or personality value. It is important for the interviewer to know what the subject has read as well as where he has traveled and what he believes.

A terrorist who tells the interviewer he follows religiously the writings of Sayyid Qutb, provides the sources of his belief system and why he hates the interviewer and the West in general.[114] This is not the kind of information obtained in criminal interviews. What the subject believes, who he follows, and what his spiritual lineage is may very well tell the interviewer about his life choices, his family, and so on. The interviewer finds no such beliefs among criminals.

To effectively interview terrorists, the interviewer must be willing to listen more than talk. In fact, in the experience of knowledgeable interviewers, the one key to success is to let the terrorist vent. Get him to tell the interviewer what he hate and fears, how much he despises the interviewer and his world. As the terrorist begins to expend himself, the interviewer must not let his passion die out but rather fuel the fire of his beliefs and allow him to rant about his hatred. This is exactly the opposite of what is usually taught in standard American interview and interrogation courses and textbooks. However, this is what must be done in these situations.

When the subject's ranting starts to die, the interrogator must fuel it again. The interviewer should not interrupt with questions or try to solve the case at this point. The details will eventually come out. The interviewer must first and foremost get the subject to vent all that passion and hatred that he has stored up. It is the same passion and animosity that drove his behavior. Let him vent until he finally exhausts himself; then he will begin to "talk."

What happens next is almost magical. He will self-exhaust, and the interviewer will be the primary beneficiary. Mentally exhausted and wasted, having purged his animus toward the interviewer, he becomes pliant and talkative. Whether it takes seven hours or two days, those who have been interviewed this way have eventually talked.

At this stage, subjects will begin to answer questions about themselves, where they have been, how they developed their philosophies, and what led them into terror. Eventually the interviewer will get everything needed to implicate the people in the offense from their own words and from the forensic investigation that corroborates what they say.

One practical caveat: if the subject is a foreigner, the interviewer will have to work with an interpreter. It is very important that the interpreter be trained before the interview is conducted. The interviewer must never assume that the translator will be competent or accurate. The interviewer must be certain the translator speaks the same dialect. For example, it must not be assumed that an Arab speaker from Morocco will be able to convey all the nuances of conversation to an Arab speaker from Yemen. The translator should have minimum eye contact with the interviewee (sit behind the subject), and the investigator must speak directly not indirectly through the translator. For example, the interviewer should not tell the translator, "Tell them I'm with [a specific law enforcement agency—e.g., FBI, CIA, local police department, military intelligence, etc.]." The interviewer should say this directly to the individual while making eye con-

tact and simply have the translator translate the information. For example, "I am here to ask you questions . . ." not, "Tell him I am here to ask him some questions."

By now it is obvious that there is a different art and science to the terrorist interview. The truth is that those few who have conducted successful terrorism or enemy interviews succeed because they are smart, patient, agile, tolerant, and gifted in their ability to conduct interviews. Just as it takes special qualities to conduct a child abuse interview, ingenuity, resolve, and erudition are required to do terrorism and enemy interviews.

The failings observed in conducting interviews in Afghanistan, Iraq, and elsewhere have been a result of asking unskilled and poorly trained individuals to do something they have not been trained to do.[115] In most cases, they meant well, but they had never been trained to do a terrorist interview, only a criminal interview. However, the terrorist interview is something unique for which the interviewer must train and prepare. Education is the first big step in that direction.

THE IMPORTANCE OF LISTENING

There never was and never will be a completely successful interview or interrogation if the investigator *hears* but does not *listen*. Hearing without listening, without concentrating, without comprehending that which is being communicated by the other party provides little useful information.

Being a good listener is not easy. To be effective, one must be an active listener, too. It has been estimated that 65% of communication is nonverbal. Active listening requires that listeners be conscious of their own body movements, eye contact, hand gestures, facial expressions, head nodding, and tones of voice. All these nonverbal forms of communication must convey interest in a witness or suspect and in what he or she is saying. Even a slight movement, such as leaning toward the person while listening, conveys interest and enthusiasm. Discouraging nonverbal messages may adversely affect an interview and cause an otherwise cooperative person to become evasive or defensive. In such an instance, a witness might wonder, "Why should I try to help if this investigator isn't interested enough to care what I'm saying?"

Another tactic in good listening is to repeat or paraphrase witnesses' or suspects' stories. This tactic, known as *verification*, provides the opportunity to check the stories and ensure the quality of communication in the interview.

Active listening is of utmost importance in an interrogation. In addition to being attuned to the body language of the suspect, the interrogator must listen to the verbal component of a communication in a two-dimensional manner. On the one hand, the content, per se, is an important outcome of the interrogation. On the other hand, and equally important, is the necessity of understanding the intention and meaning of what is being said. To effectively listen to and evaluate the communication in these two dimensions, it is necessary for the interrogator to follow the basic rule of being a good active listener: Be quiet!

DOCUMENTING THE INTERVIEW AND INTERROGATION

Handwritten notes made by the investigator during and immediately following an interview generally serve as sufficient documentation. (See Chapter 6, "Field Notes and Reporting.")

Note-taking during an interview raises two primary concerns for the interviewer. First, it may occasionally be distracting or suspicious to a witness; witnesses may be reluctant to give information knowing that it is being documented. Consequently, the investigator should tell witnesses that notes will prevent the need for subsequent interviews owing to lapses of the investigator's memory. This explanation usually reduces the reluctance of the witness. Second, the interviewer should avoid becoming preoccupied with taking notes, for this creates the appearance of inattentiveness. As important as notes may be, the interviewer should treat them as less important than conversation with the witness. Note-taking during the interview should be kept to a minimum, recording only salient details. As soon as possible after the interview, the investigator should complete the notes, before memory wanes.

In many instances, it is desirable for witnesses to write or sign statements concerning the events of which they have knowledge. In many jurisdictions, law enforcement officers are authorized to administer oaths so that such statements are sworn to or affirmed. The theory is that a victim or witness would be less inclined to fabricate a story that sounds good, only to later recant the version when it comes time to make prosecution decisions. Sometimes the theory doesn't work well in practice.

The best form of documentation is electronic sound recording or a sound-and-visual recording of the interview. Visual recordings are generally not practical when the interview is held anywhere other than at a law enforcement agency, where equipment can be permanently situated. Cassette tape recorders, however, are inexpensive, portable, and helpful in the majority of cases. The recorded interview has many significant advantages: All information is recorded in the witness's own words, details are not left to be recalled by human memory, concerns about detracting from the interview by note taking are absent, interviewers may listen to the verbatim conversations over and over at a later time to be sure that they have understood completely and accurately what was said, and the taped interview might avoid unnecessary reinterviews. The advantages and disadvantages of each type of documentation are shown in Table 5-3.

At the conclusion of an interview, investigators should review and evaluate their performance. The checklist in Table 5-4 can serve as a good review and basis for self-evaluation. Such a self-critique can serve as an excellent learning tool for improving one's ability as an interviewer.

| TABLE 5-3 | **Comparison of Types of Interview Documentation** |

TYPE	ADVANTAGES	DISADVANTAGES
Memory	Quick and easy	Limited absorption and recall
		Most information lost shortly afterward
Note-taking by interviewer	Sufficient in most cases	May distract or offend witness
	Captures salient details	May preoccupy interviewer, creating appearance of inattentiveness
	Prevents need for reinterviewing	May cause interviewer to miss nonverbal messages
Handwritten or signed statements by witness	Useful if witness cannot testify	Request may be offensive to witness
	Can be used to impeach if witness changes story in court	Not necessary in routine cases
Electronic sound or sound-and-visual recordings	Relatively inexpensive	Not necessary except in the most important cases
	Some equipment portable	Generally not practical
	All information recorded in witnesses' own words	
	Does not rely on inaccuracies of memory or another's notes	
	Does not distract	
	Prevents unnecessary reinterviews	

| TABLE 5-4 | Post-Interview Self-Evaluation Checklist |

With this Witness, Did I:

1. Conduct the interview as quickly, privately, yet conveniently as possible?

2. Establish a good rapport with the witness?

3. Listen?

4. Ask good questions?

5. Control the interview?

6. Establish the witness's presence, consciousness, and attentiveness?

7. Determine any factors that now would affect the witness's competency in court?

8. Evaluate the witness's potential credibility in court?

9. Use the right approach in seeking information?

10. Get complete and accurate information?

11. Document the interview well?

Experience is the best teacher only if you learn from your mistakes.[116]

Documenting an interrogation consists of three main phases: note-taking, recording, and obtaining written statements. All three of these phases are geared to accomplishing two basic functions: retaining information for the benefit of the interrogator and the continued investigation, and securing a written statement or confession from the accused for later use as evidence in court.

The methods of keeping notes of interrogations is the same as described above for interviews. Electronic recording of an interrogation is the best means of documentation. Audio, video, or a combination of both may be used, but case law and local requirements should be checked.

Law enforcement use of electronic audio-video technology to document interrogations became widespread in the 1990s. During that period, the Christopher Commission recommended video technology to the Los Angeles Police Department as a means of reducing police brutality and protecting officers from unfair accusations of using excessive force. One year later, the Kolts Commission criticized the Los Angeles County Sheriff's Department for failing to taperecord statements by witnesses and officers involved in police shootings. A citizen's videotape of Rodney King's beating illustrates the power video technology can have on judges and juries.[117]

Several states require electronic recording in all or in some crime specific cases. In 1980, the Alaskan Supreme Court ruled that law enforcement must electronically record interrogations when feasible, especially when conducted in a law enforcement agency. Alaska thus became the first state to mandate electronic recording.[118] Fourteen years later, the Minnesota Supreme Court ruled essentially

the same as Alaska had done.[119] In 2004, the Massachusetts Supreme Court ruled that failure to electronically record any interrogation could raise doubts about the voluntariness of *Miranda* waivers and, as was noted in the other decisions mentioned, can raise issues about the integrity of the investigative interrogator.[120]

Electronically recording interrogations offers many advantages, one of the primary being that it no longer is so expensive as to be beyond the means of even small law enforcement agencies. Electronic recording forces investigators to better prepare for conducting interrogations; clarify whether an interrogator missed something that requires further questioning; give prosecutors a better understanding of cases, thereby fostering better charging decisions, plea-bargaining options, and case preparation; minimize challenges by defense attorneys about the accuracy of the electronic recordings and the completeness of written confessions; reduce doubts about the voluntariness of confessions; and jog investigators' memories when they are testifying. In addition, tapes can be reviewed and used as training aids for interrogators and other investigators.[121]

Nearly all agencies electronically record openly, rather than covertly, and tell suspects that they are being taped. Often, the camera and microphone are visible during the session. There seems to be no significant difference between the number of confessions from videotaped suspects and that from nonvideotaped suspects. Some offenders may be less likely to incriminate themselves on tape, but others take advantage of the opportunity to either put on a show or "get if off their chest." As noted earlier, state and local law should be consulted in regard to electronically recording interrogations and the subsequent admissibility of electronically recorded confessions in court. Federal constitutional law is not be a bar, since a suspect would be hard-pressed to prove that he or she had a "reasonable expectation of privacy" in an interrogation room in a law enforcement agency after having been advised of his or her *Miranda* rights.[122]

Audio documentation is the second-best method for recording. Its introduction in court necessitates establishing the identity of the people involved in the interrogation and what each had to say. One disadvantage arises if the subject does not know that the interrogation is being recorded. The individual is likely to point out things or make statements that an interrogator can see but no one else will be able to identify from the audio recording. For example, the suspect may hold up a knife and say, "I held it like this." The interrogator knows what is meant, but to a third party listening to the recording later, the words may be meaningless.

Documenting information incriminating the accused may take a number of forms. All of them are generally admissible, but the weight they carry with the jury is likely to vary. The most convincing means that can be used is an audiovisual electronic recording of a confession or admission given by a suspect during an interrogation. After the use of such recordings, the next-best form

TABLE 5-5	Comparison of Types of Confession Documentation (in Descending Order of Believability to Juries)	
TYPE	**ADVANTAGES**	**DISADVANTAGES**
1. ElectronicVideo-audiotape		
2. or movie	May be required by legislative or judicial directive Shows all, including fairness, procedures, and treatment Easy to do Can be relatively inexpensive	May face legal constraints Quality equipment may be costly
3. Audio recording	Can hear conversations Can infer fairness	Some words or descriptions may be meaningless without pictorial support Necessitates identifying people and things involved
4. Statement written and signed in suspect's own handwriting	Can be identified as coming directly from suspect	Can't see demeanor or hear voice inflections Suspect may not agree to procedure
5. Typed statement signed by suspect	Signature indicates knowledge of and agreement with contents of statement	Less convincing than methods described above
6. Typed unsigned statement acknowledged by suspect	Contents of confession or admission are present Acknowledgment helps show voluntariness	Reduced believability of voluntariness and accuracy of contents
7. Testimony of someone who heard confession or admission given	Contents admissible	Carries little weight with juries

is a signed statement written in the first person by the suspect in his or her handwriting. Frequently, however, it is not possible to convince a suspect to prepare such a statement. Or perhaps the suspect cannot write.

Other forms in which statements may be admitted into evidence, listed in descending order of the credibility that they are likely to have with a jury, are a typed or hand-written statement by someone else that is signed in the accused's own hand; a typed or otherwise prepared state-ment that the accused does not sign but that is acknowl-edged in front of witnesses; and the oral testimony of a person who was present and overheard the subject give a confession or admission. In the last case, even though admissible, the testimony is likely to carry little weight with the jury. Table 5-5 lists the types of documentation in descending order of preference and the advantages and disadvantages of each.

Harold Johnson is on trial for burglary of a dwelling, five counts of grand theft of a firearm, possession of a firearm by a convicted felon, and three additional counts of grand theft of property other than firearms. In the pros-ecution's case, an investigator testifies that the investiga-tion narrowed down to an individual who happened to be in jail in another county on an unrelated charge. The inves-tigator interviewed the individual who admitted to him that he had a bad "crack" habit and that he committed the

burglary, stole the firearms and other property, and traded it all on the street for cocaine. On cross-examination, the investigator told the defense attorney that during his eight years on the force he had many occasions to interrogate suspects in crimes and that often these interrogations occurred outside his own agency. He was then asked if he recorded the interrogation and "confession" of his client. The investigator said no. The attorney asked if his agencies had portable cassette tape recorders that could be taken out of the building. The investigator acknowledged that it did. In response to the next question, the investigator said he knew that he and his partner were going to this other jail for the specific purpose of questioning the suspect and did not take a tape recorder with them. When pressed, he said he never takes a recorder with him. His explanation was that he just didn't do it. That was not the way he operated. The defense attorney then made his point by asking, "So you want the jury just to take your word that my client confessed because that's the way you prefer to conduct your interviews rather than recording them so the jury could hear what my client actually said?" Then the investigator's partner testified that he was in the room but he wasn't really paying much attention. He was doing some paperwork on another case while this interrogation was taking place. Largely because of this line of questioning, the jury acquitted the defendant of all charges.

The Written Statement

The form and content of a written statement should include a heading, which incorporates the data identifying the circumstances under which the statement was taken, the body of the statement, and a verification. The statement should open with an indication of the time and place where it was taken, and an identification of the person giving the statement that includes their name, address, and age. The heading must also include a definite statement to the effect that the subject is giving the statement freely and voluntarily after having been appropriately advised of his or her constitutional rights.

The body of the statement, which acknowledges the subject's involvement in the crime under investigation, should, if possible, be phrased in the first person, allowing the suspect to include his or her own ideas in a free-flowing manner. However, if this is not possible or practical, then the question-and-answer format is permissible. The terminology used should include the words, grammar, idioms, and style of the person making the statement. The body of the statement should be arranged so that its content follows the chronological order of the subject's involvement in the case under investigation.

At the end, the statement should indicate that the suspect has read the statement or has had it read to him or her, that its contents and implications are understood, and that the suspect attests to its accuracy.

Other suggestions for the interrogator to keep in mind include:

- Each page of the statement should be numbered consecutively with an indication that it is _____ page of _____ pages. If the pages get separated, they can later be easily restored to order.
- The interrogator should ensure that each page is initialed by the subject. If the subject is unwilling to sign, the statement should be acknowledged by him or her. If the subject cannot write, another identifying mark may be used.
- On occasion an interrogator may encounter someone who says, "I'll tell you what I've done, but I'm not writing anything and I'm not signing anything." In such circumstances, the interrogator can explain that the suspect confessed and that the interrogator or some other person who heard the confession can go into court and testify about it. By preparing or signing a statement, the suspect protects himself or herself against the interrogator's testifying to something more damaging by changing the story in court (another good reason for electronic recording.)
- If the suspect cannot read, the statement must be read to him or her, and the interrogator must ensure that the suspect understands its contents before the suspect is allowed to attest to its accuracy.
- All errors in the statement should be corrected on the final copy and initialed by the suspect. The

interrogator may accommodate the suspect by allowing small errors if this will help obtain the suspect's initials on each page of the statement.

- The interrogator should make sure that the suspect understands all the words used in the statement. If some words are confusing, their meanings should be explained to the suspect and the suspect should be required to explain them back in front of witnesses in order to confirm this understanding.
- During the process of drafting and attesting to a statement derived through interrogation, there should be at least one additional witness who can testify to the authenticity of the statement and the circumstances under which it was obtained. After the suspect signs the statement in ink, the witnesses should sign their names, addresses, and positions.[123]

ADMISSIBILITY OF CONFESSIONS AND ADMISSIONS

Prior to 1936, the only test for the validity and admissibility of a confession or **admission** was its voluntariness. However, the determination as to whether it was given voluntarily by the suspect was subject to very loose interpretation. There were no rules restricting the method by which law enforcement obtained "voluntary" statements. Physical violence, psychological coercion, empty promises, and meaningless guarantees of rewards were not considered objectionable procedures.

The Free-and-Voluntary Rule

The first notable incidence of Supreme Court intervention into interrogation practices came about in *Brown* v. *Mississippi*.[124] In this 1936 case, the Supreme Court held that under no circumstances could a confession be considered freely and voluntarily given when it was obtained as a result of physical brutality and violence inflicted by law enforcement officials on the accused. The reaction to this decision by law enforcement was not unexpected. Many threw up their hands and claimed that they could no longer function effectively because "handcuffs had been put on the police." However, as was true with many other decisions placing procedural restrictions on law enforcement agencies, the police found that they were able to compensate by conducting thorough criminal investigations.

Subsequent to the *Brown* decision, the Supreme Court, in a succession of cases, has continued to reinforce its position that any kind of coercion, whether physical or psychological, would be grounds for making a confession inadmissible as being in violation of the **free-and-voluntary rule.** This includes such conduct as threatening bodily harm to the suspect or members of the suspect's family,[125] using psychological coercion,[126] engaging in trickery or deceit, or holding a suspect incommunicado. Investigators are also cautioned about making promises to the suspect that cannot be kept. All these practices were condemned in *Miranda* v. *Arizona*.[127] Despite the appearance that *Miranda* has eliminated all coercive techniques previously used in interrogations, this is not actually the case. What *Miranda* seeks is to abolish techniques that would prompt *untrue* incriminatory statements by a suspect. Thus, unlike physical coercion, psychological coercion, threats, duress, and some promises, the use of trickery, fraud, falsehood, or similar techniques are not absolutely forbidden. If such methods are not likely to cause an individual to make self-incriminating statements or to admit to falsehoods in order to avoid threatened harm, confessions or admissions so obtained are admissible.[128]

THE DELAY-IN-ARRAIGNMENT RULE

In 1943, the Supreme Court delivered another decision concerning the admissibility of confessions. Even though the free-and-voluntary rule was in effect in both the federal and state courts, another series of statutes seemed to have gone unheeded. Every state and the federal government had legal provisions requiring that after arrest a person must be taken before a committing magistrate "without unnecessary delay." Before 1943, if there was an unnecessary delay in producing the accused before a committing magistrate, the delay was merely one of a number of factors that the courts were required to take into consideration in determining whether the confession was freely and voluntarily given.

The facts of *McNabb* v. *United States*[129] reveal that McNabb and several members of his family were involved in bootlegging. They were arrested after the murder of federal officers who were investigating their operation in Tennessee. McNabb was held incommunicado for several days before he was taken before a committing magistrate. He subsequently confessed, and the confession was admitted into evidence at his trial. He was convicted, but on appeal to the Supreme Court the conviction was reversed. The Court held that the failure of federal officers to take the prisoner before a committing officer without unnecessary delay automatically rendered his confession inadmissible. The significance of this case is that for the first time the Court indicated that failure to comply with this procedural requirement would render a confession inadmissible regardless of whether it was obtained freely and voluntarily. Thus, instead of examining the facts of the case to determine the voluntariness of the confession, the Court ruled, as a matter of law, that the procedural violation also rendered the confession inadmissible. The holding in the *McNabb* case was emphatically reaffirmed in 1957 by the Supreme Court in *Mallory* v. *United States*.[130]

As the mandate of the Supreme Court in the *McNabb* and *Mallory* cases had applicability only to federal prosecutions, the states were free to interpret their own statutes on unnecessary delay as they saw fit. Few chose to follow the *McNabb-Mallory* **delay-in-arraignment rule.** The majority have continued to require that there must be a connection between the failure of law enforcement to produce the accused before a committing magistrate without unnecessary delay and the securing of a confession.

| KEY TERMS

admission	eyewitness identification	paralanguage
Biggers-Brathwaite Factors Test	free-and-voluntary rule	polygraph
body language	in-custody interrogation	proximity
cognitive interview technique	interrogation	rapport
competency (of a witness)	interviewing	statement analysis
computer voice stress analysis (CVSA)	kinesics	suspect
confession	logical approach	totality of the circumstances
credibility (of a witness)	*Miranda* v. *Arizona*	victim
delay-in-arraignment rule	mirror	witness
emotional approach	neuro-linguistic programming (NLP)	

| REVIEW QUESTIONS

1. What is the importance of information to the criminal investigator? How is information obtained? 144

2. How do the purposes of interviewing and interrogation differ? 145

3. What are the qualities of an effective interviewer or interrogator? 147

4. How does an investigator prepare for an interview or interrogation? Are there differences? 149-150

5. What factors motivate witnesses to give or withhold information? 150

6. What special concerns must an interviewer be aware of when interviewing a person with a hearing impairment? 152

7. What criteria affect the competency of a witness? 153
8. In evaluating the credibility of a witness, with what factors must the investigator be concerned? 153
9. Despite the amount of reliance placed on information supplied by eyewitnesses, how reliable is it? Why? 152
10. What role can computerized voice stress analysis (CVSA) play in a criminal investigation?
11. If the setting for an interview is not ideal, what conditions should be established for conducting the interview?
12. Describe the steps in the interview process.
13. What is neuro-linguistic programming?
14. Describe the cognitive interview technique.
15. What requirements are imposed on law enforcement personnel by *Miranda* v. *Arizona*?
16. Why do some people confess?
17. What is the significance of understanding the meaning of "in-custody interrogation"?
18. How does an interrogator evaluate and thus control a suspect?
19. Describe the conditions under which an interrogation should take place.
20. Of what significance is the interrogator's ability to compose proper questions?
21. Why is an understanding of behavioral and psychological principles important for a successful interrogation?
22. How can statement analysis be of use to an interrogator?
23. Why is listening so important in interviews and interrogations?
24. How can the investigator best document an interview? An interrogation?
25. Why is it important to number the pages in a statement?
26. What is the evidentiary test for admissibility of confessions and admissions?

INTERNET ACTIVITIES

Much debate surrounds the fairness and effectiveness of eyewitness identification in police lineups. Go to www.eyewitness.utep.edu/consult05.html and read the summary of the whitepaper regarding evaluating lineup fairness. What two aspects of lineup fairness should investigators consider? How similar to one another should the members of the lineup be?

NOTES

1. Marshall Houts, *From Evidence to Proof* (Springfield, IL: Charles C. Thomas, 1956), pp. 10–11.
2. John E. Hess, *Interviewing and Interrogation for Law Enforcement* (Cincinnati: Anderson, 1997), p. 33.
3. John E. Hess, *Interviewing and Interrogation for Law Enforcement* (Cincinnati: Anderson, 1997), pp. 81–84; Charles L. Yeshke, *The Art of Investigative Interviewing* (Boston: Butterworth-Heinesmann, 1997), pp. 56–68.
4. Paul B. Weston and Kenneth M. Wells, *Criminal Investigation: Basic Perspectives* (Englewood Cliffs, NJ: Prentice Hall, 1970), p. 151.
5. John E. Hess, *Interviewing and Interrogation for Law Enforcement* (Cincinnati: Anderson, 1997), p. 84.
6. William Hart, "The Subtle Art of Persuasion," *Police Magazine*, January 1981, p. 10.
7. Stan B. Walters, *Principles of Kinesic Interview and Interrogation*, 2nd ed. (New York: CRC Press, 2003), p. 2.
8. Yeschke, *The Art of Investigative Interviewing*, pp. 25–40, 113–134.
9. David Gullo, "Child Abuse: Interviewing Possible Victims," *FBI Law Enforcement Bulletin*, Jan. 1994, p. 20.
10. New York City Police Department, *Student's Guide—Social Science 1998*, pp. 4–7. This discussion of the process of aging was provided by the New York City Police Department.
11. Fred E. Inbau and John E. Reid, *Criminal Interrogation and Confessions* (Baltimore: Williams & Wilkins, 1962), p. 1.
12. Brian L. Cutler and Steven D. Penrod, *Mistaken Identification: The Eyewitness, Psychology, and the Law* (New York: Cambridge University Press, 1995) p. 6.
13. Ibid. p. 7.
14. Robert L. Donigan, Edward C. Fisher, et al., *The Evidence Handbook*, 4th ed. (Evanston, IL: Traffic Institute, Northwestern University, 1980), p. 205.
15. Robert Buckhout, "Eyewitness Testimony," *Scientific American*, Dec. 1974, Vol. 231, No. 6, p. 23. Also see Elizabeth F. Loftus, Edith L. Greene, and James M. Doyle, "The Psychology of Eyewitness Testimony," in *Psychological Methods in Criminal Investigation and Evidence*, David C. Raskin, ed. (New York: Springer, 1989), pp. 3–45; Hunter A. McAllister, Robert H. I. Dale, and Cynthia E. Hunt, "Effects of Lineup Modality on Witness Creditability," *Journal of Social Psychology*, June 1993, Vol. 133, No. 3, p. 365.
16. Cutler and Penrod, *Mistaken Identification*, p. 112.
17. Janet Reno, "Message from the Attorney General," Introduction at the National Institute of Justice, Office of Justice Programs, *Eyewitness Evidence: A Guide for Law Enforcement* (Washington, DC: U.S. Department of Justice, Oct. 1999), p. iii.
18. Siegfried Ludwig Sporer, Roy S. Malpass, and Guenter Koehnken, *Psychological Issues in Eyewitness Identification* (Mahwah, NJ: Lawrence Erlbaum, 1996), p. 23.
19. Cutler and Penrod, *Mistaken Identification*, p. 113.
20. Buckhout, "Eyewitness Testimony," p. 24. See also, Steven Wallace, "The Puzzle of Memory: Reflections

on the Divergence of Truth and Accuracy," The Florida Bar Journal, October 2005, pp. 24–28.

21. Elizabeth Loftus, "Incredible Eyewitness," *Psychology Today,* Dec. 1974, Vol. 8, No. 7, p. 118.

22. Sporer, Malpass, and Koehnken, *Psychological Issues,* pp. 26–29.

23. Ibid. pp. 34–35.

24. Ibid. pp. 36–39.

25. Buckhout, "Eyewitness Testimony," pp. 24–26.

26. Cutler and Penrod, *Mistaken Identification,* p. 113.

27. Ibid., p. 135. See also Gary L. Wells, et al., "Eyewitness Identification Procedures for Lineups and Photospreads," www.unl.edu/ap-ls/whiteeye.html.

28. Cutler and Penrod, *Mistaken Identification,* p. 113.

29. Buckhout, "Eyewitness Testimony," p. 28.

30. Ibid.

31. Technical Working Group for Eyewitness Evidence, Office of Justice Programs, National Institute of Justice, *Eyewitness Evidence: A Guide for Law Enforcement* (Washington, D.C.: U.S. Department of Justice, Oct. 1999).

32. Ibid.

33. National Institute of Justice, "Eyewitness Evidence: A Trainer's Manual for Law Enforcement," (Washington, D.C.: Office of Justice Programs, National Institute of Justice, U.S. Department of Justice, Sept. 2003).

34. Technical Working Group, *Eyewitness Evidence: A Guide for Law Enforcement.*

35. 388 U.S. 293, 87 S.Ct. 1967, 18 L.Ed.2d 1199 (1967).

36. 409 U.S. 188, 93 S.Ct. 375, 34 L.Ed.2d 401 (1972).

37. 432 U.S. 98, 97 S.Ct. 2243, 53 L.Ed.2d 140 (1977).

38. Author unknown, "Identification, Bail, Asset Forfeiture, and Other Pretrial Procedures." http://faculty.ncwc.edu/toconner/325/32lect06.htm.

39. Charles C. Vanderbosch, *Criminal Investigation* (Washington, D.C.: International Association of Chiefs of Police, 1968), p. 196.

40. Loftus, "Incredible Eyewitness," p. 119. See also Vincent Sandoval, "Strategies to Avoid Interview Contamination," *FBI Law Enforcement Bulletin,* U.S. Department of Justice, Oct. 2003, pp. 1–12.

41. Hess, *Interviewing and Interrogation,* pp. 24–25. See also Andre B. Simmons and Brian P. Boetig, "The Structured Investigative Interview", *FBI Law Enforcement Bulletin,* June 2007, pp. 9–20.

42. Ibid., p. 25.

43. John Fay, unpublished notebook from a Workshop in Criminal Interrogation, Nov. 17–18, 1981, sponsored by the Jacksonville, Florida Chapter, American Society for Industrial Security, pp. A5-1–A5-2.

44. *Miranda v. Arizona,* 384 U.S. 436 (1966).

45. *Escobedo v. Illinois,* 378 U.S. 478 (1964).

46. 384 U.S. 436 (1966).

47. 451 U.S. 477, 101 S.Ct. 1880 (1981).

48. 498 U.S. 146 (1990).

49. 423 U.S. 96, 96 S.Ct. 321 (1975).

50. 492 U.S. 195, 109 S.Ct. 2875 (1989).

51. 429 U.S. 492 (1977).

52. 429 U.S. 492, 495 (1977).

53. 463 U.S. 1121 (1983).

54. 103 S.Ct. 3517 (1983).

55. 89 S.Ct. 1095 (1969).

56. 699 F.2d. 466 (9th Cir. 1982).

57. 736 F.2d. 1232 (8th Cir. 1984).

58. 104 S.Ct. 2626, 81 L. Ed. 550 (1984).

59. 82 L. Ed. 317 (1984).

60. *Stansbury v. California,* 511 U.S. 318 (1994).

61. 430 U.S. 387 (1977).

62. 446 U.S. 291, 100 S.Ct. 1682 (1980).

63. *Pope v. Zenon,* 69 F.3d 1018 (9th Cir. 1995).

64. John C. Klotter and Jacqueline R. Kanovitz, *Constitutional Law,* 4th ed. (Cincinnati: Anderson Publishing, 1981), p. 343.

65. Robert L. Donigan, Edward C. Fisher, David H. Hugel, Robert H. Reeder, and Richard N. Williams, *The Evidence Handbook,* 4th ed. (Evanston, IL: Traffic Institute, Northwestern University, 1980), p. 44.

66. 107 S.Ct. 1931 (1987).

67. *United States v. Clark,* 982 F.2d 965, at 968 (6th Cir. 1993).

68. Michael R. Napier and Susan H. Adams, "Magic Words to Obtain Confessions," *FBI Law Enforcement Bulletin,* Oct. 1998, pp. 11–15.

69. Yeschke, *The Art of Investigative Interviewing,* pp. 13–14.

70. Walters, *Principles of Kinesic Interview and Interrogation,* pp. 174.

71. Irwin W. Fisk, "Hypnotic Transition," *Police,* June 1990, p. 94; Geiselman and Fisher, "Interviewing Victims and Witnesses," p. 2.

72. R. Edward Geiselman and Ronald P. Fisher, "Interviewing Victims and Witnesses of Crime," National Institute of Justice, *Research in Brief,* Dec. 1985, p. 2.

73. Ibid., p. 3. For an exhaustive treatment of the cognitive interview technique and experiments that have been conducted, see R. Edward Geiselman and Ronald P. Fisher, "The Cognitive Interview Technique for Victims and Witnesses of Crime," David C. Raskin (ed.), *Psychological Methods in Criminal Investigation and Evidence* (New York: Springer Publishing, 1989), pp. 191–215.

74. Sandoval and Adams, "Subtle Skills for Building Rapport," p. 2.

75. Ibid. p. 3.

76. Law Enforcement Communications Unit, *Interviewing and Interrogation,* pp. 16–17.

77. Sandoval and Adams, "Subtle Skills for Building Rapport," pp. 4–5.

78. Stan B. Walters, *Principles of Kinetic Interview and Interrogation,* pp. 199–205.

79. Walters, *Principles of Kinesic Interview and Interrogation,* p. 73.

80. Charles G. Brougham, "Nonverbal Communication: Can What They Don't Say Give Them Away?" *FBI Law Enforcement Bulletin,* July 1992, pp. 15–18.

81. See Daniel Goleman, "People Who Read People," *Psychology Today,* July 1979. See also Daniel Goleman, "The 7000 Faces of Dr. Ekman," *Psychology Today,* Feb. 1981, p. 43; John Leo, "The Fine Art of Catching Liars," *Time,* April 22, 1985, p. 59.

82. Eckman and O'Sullivan, "Hazards in Detecting Deceit," p. 297. See also Mark L. Knapp and Judith

A. Hall, *Nonverbal Communication in Human Behavior*, 5th ed. (Belmont, CA: Wadsworth-Thomson Learning, Inc., 2002).

83. Ibid. pp. 302–306.
84. Ibid. pp. 306–310.
85. Ibid., pp. 310–312.
86. Owen Einspahr, "The Interview Challenge: Mike Simmen versus the FBI," *FBI Law Enforcement Bulletin*, April 2000, p. 17.
87. Ibid.
88. Ibid. pp. 17–20.
89. Ibid. p. 16
90. Hess, *Interviewing and Interrogation*, pp. 66–69. See also Brian P. Boetig, "Reducing a Guilty Suspect's Resistance to Confessing", *FBI Law Enforcement Bulletin*, August 2005, pp. 13–20.
91. Walters, *Principles of Kinesic Interview and Interrogation*, p. 11. See also Sharon S. Smith and Roger W. Shuy, "Forensic Psycholinguistics: Using Language Analysis for Identifying and Assessing Offenders," *FBI Law Enforcement Bulletin*, U.S. Department of Justice, April 2002, pp. 16–21, and, Joe Navarro, "A Four-Domain Model for Detecting Deception: An Alternative Paradigm for Interviewing," *FBI Law Enforcement Bulletin*, U.S. Department of Justice, June 2003, pp. 19–24.
92. Hess, *Interviewing and Interrogation*, pp. 59–64. See also Susan H. Adams, "Statement Analysis: What Do Suspects' Words Really Reveal?" *FBI Law Enforcement Bulletin*, U.S. Department of Justice, Oct. 1996, pp. 12–20.
93. These points are found on the Internet site for the American Association of Police Polygraphists, p. 2, January 21, 2005; see www.policepolygraph.org/standards.htm.
94. Based on information supplied by Captain John P. Slater (Ret.), Law Enforcement Training Coordinator, National Institute for Truth Verification, 2007.
95. This entire discussion on interviewing terrorists was provided by Joe Navarro (2008) MA. Retired, etc. Joe Navarro may be contacted at: Jnforensics@aol.com. This material is copyrighted and cannot be reprinted without the expressed permission of Joe Navarro.
96. Joe Narvarro. 2005. *Hunting Terrorists: A Look at the Psychology of Terror* (Springfield, IL: Charles C. Thomas Publishers), pp. 25–55.
97. Ibid. p. 10.
98. Ibid. pp. 37–41.
99. Ibid. pp. 47–50.
100. Eric Hoffer. 1951. *The True Believer* (New York: Harper and Row), p. 54.
101. Robert D. Hare. 1993. *Without Conscience: The Disturbing World of the Psychopaths among Us* (New York: Pocket Books), pp. 88–92.
102. Op cit., Navarro, 2005, p. 69.
103. Ibid. pp. 38–42.
104. Ibid. p. 9

105. Gisli H. Gudjonsson. 2006. "The Psychology of Interrogations and Confessions," in Ed. Tom Williamson, *Investigative Interviewing: Rights, Research, Regulation* (Devon, UK: Willian Publishing), pp. 123–125.
106. Daniel C. Maguire and A. Nicholas Fargnoli. 1991. *On Moral Grounds: The Art and Science of Ethics* (New York: Cross Roads Publishing), pp. 164–166.
107. Op cit., Navarro, 2005, pp. 50–54.
108. Raphael Patai. 2002. *The Arab Mind* (New York: Hatherleigh Press), p. 113.
109. Mark Juergensmeyer, 2000. *Terror in the Mind of God: The Global Rise of Religious Violence.* (Berkeley and Los Angeles: University of California Press), pp. 71–73.
110. Margaret K. Nydell. 1987. *Understanding Arabs* (Yarmouth, Maine: Intercultural Press, Inc.), pp. 122–123.
111. Op cit., Patai, 2002, pp. 43–77.
112. Joe Navarro. 2002. "Interacting with Arabs and Muslims," *FBI Law Enforcement Bulletin* (September): 20–23.
113. Op cit., Navarro, 2008.
114. Sayyid Qutb. 1953. *Social Justice in Islam* (New York: Islamic Publications International).
115. David Rose. 2006. "American Interrogation Methods in the War on Terror," in Ed. Tom Williamson, *Investigative Interviewing: Rights, Research, Regulation* (Devon, UK: Willian Publishing): pp. 42–62.
116. Hess, *Interviewing and Interrogation*, p. 26.
117. William A. Geller, "Videotaping Interrogations and Confessions," *Research in Brief*, Office of Justice Programs, National Institute of Justice (Washington, D.C.: U.S. Department of Justice March 1993), p. 1.
118. *Mallott v. State*, 608 P.2d 737 (Alaska 1980), *S.B. v. State*, 614 P.2d 786 (Alaska 1980), and *Stephan v. State*, 711 P.2d 1156 (Alaska 1985). See also Brian P Boetig, David M. Vinson, and Brad R. Weidel, "Revealing Incommunicado: Electronic Recording of Police Interrogations," *FBI Law Enforcement Bulletin*, Volume 75, Number 12, December 2006, pp. 1–8.
119. *State v. Scales*, 518 N.W.2d 587 (Minn. 1994).
120. *Commonwealth v. DiGiambattista*, 442 Mass. 423 (2004).
121. William A. Geller, "Videotaping Interrogations and Confessions," *Research in Brief*, pp.5–7.
122. Ibid. p. 4.
123. See Timothy T. Burke, "Documenting and Reporting a Confession: A Guide for Law Enforcement," *FBI Law Enforcement Bulletin*, Feb. 2001, Vol. 70, No. 2, pp. 17–21.
124. 297 U.S. 278 (1936).
125. *Payne v. Arkansas*, 356 U.S. 560 (1958).
126. *Miranda v. Arizona*, 384 U.S. 436 (1966).
127. Ibid.
128. Donigan et al., *The Evidence Handbook*, pp. 47–48. See also *Frazier v. Cupp*, 394 U.S. 731 (1969); *Oregon v. Mathiason*, 429 U.S. 492 (1977).
129. 318 U.S. 332 (1943).
130. 354 U.S. 449 (1957).

6

FIELD NOTES AND REPORTING

CHAPTER OBJECTIVES

1. Understand the importance of field notes.

2. List the six interrogatory investigative questions.

3. Understand formats for basic incident reports.

4. Discuss aids to information gathering.

5. Summarize the report approval and disposition processes.

6. List elements common to incident reports.

7. Explain techniques involved in writing effective reports.

▲ Deputy sheriff checking the identity of a person at an automotive service center. If the interview begins to yield useful information, the deputy will begin taking field notes.
(© Joel Gordon)

Taking field notes and writing reports is considered a necessary evil by most law enforcement officers and investigators. These tasks are not the most exciting or pleasurable parts of the profession. Yet, it cannot be overemphasized how important it is to perform these duties at the highest levels of accuracy and completeness. Field notes play a significant role in every criminal investigation. They provide a short written record of events, times, places, suspects, witnesses, and other information, and are used as the basis for preparing incident/offense reports. The importance of taking effective and complete notes in every investigation, regardless of the offense, should not be underestimated. Because field notes are more reliable than a person's memory, they can be used as a source of specific facts and details that otherwise might be forgotten. Detailed field notes also reduce the need to recontact victims and witnesses regarding information that was overlooked or questions that were not asked in the initial contact. Finally, it is not uncommon for officers to testify in court several months or years later regarding a particular investigation. Comprehensive field notes not only can help refresh the investigator's memory but also can strengthen his or her court testimony.

This chapter examines several aspects of the field-note-taking and report-writing processes. After discussing field notes and the basic and primary questions that need to be asked in an investigation, it addresses the importance of completing well-prepared incident/offense reports. Incident-report formats vary among law enforcement agencies. Despite the variation, however, there are common elements that should be included in all reports.

It is considered a standard practice that investigators should gain as much information as possible when arriving at the crime scene. Even facts and details that seem unnecessary at first may later prove to be highly valuable to the investigation. But this practice must be tempered with the following caution: it is critical that determinations be made as early as possible in the investigative process of what the case is about and what potential criminal charges may be filed. It is then important to know what information the prosecutor will need to file formal charges, what are the elements of the offense, and, importantly, what does the prosecutor need to prove a case. Armed with this information, the first responders and follow-up investigators can pursue the investigation and focus on the investigation so as to be able to separate the important from the "nice to have" or superfluous information. Such an approach is appreciated by prosecutors.

Aids to information gathering are also discussed in this chapter. Investigators will often interview witnesses and victims who may be unable to provide or articulate important details. Visual and descriptive aids such as suspect description forms and photographs of weapons can improve the information-gathering process. After presenting a brief overview on the growing use of mobile data terminals and other computerized tools that facilitate the report-writing process, the chapter concludes with a discussion on writing effective reports.

FIELD NOTES

Field notes are the shorthand written record made by a police officer from the time she or he arrives at the scene until the assignment is completed. The factors discussed next explain the importance of field notes.[1] (See Figure 6-1.)

Field notes are more reliable than an officer's memory. It is probably easy to remember what you had for breakfast this morning, but what about your lunch five months ago?[2] Often an officer responds to several calls before he or she has time to write an incident/offense report on an earlier call. Even during that short period of time, some important details can be forgotten. The only way to prevent the possibility of lost information is to prepare thorough field notes.

Field notes are the primary information source for preparing the incident/offense report. Because the first-responding officer is usually the person who writes any incident report required by the situation, field notes are important because they contain the information that forms the content of the incident report. Moreover, other officers who also responded may have taken actions or seen and heard things that are of investigative significance and for which there needs to be an investigative record. They will rely on their own field notes to write reports that supplement the incident report. Well-taken, detailed field notes are the wellspring for good incident reports.

Detailed field notes may reduce the need to recontact the parties involved. Once in a while, victims and witnesses get annoyed and even angry when they are recontacted by an officer who obviously didn't take good field notes when he or she talked to them earlier and therefore cannot complete the incident report without additional information. Comments such as "Weren't you listening to me?" or "You couldn't be very interested in my case or you would have asked about this when you talked to me the first time" can be avoided by thorough note taking. The follow-up investigator faces the possibility of similar comments when recontacting victims and witnesses: "Didn't you talk to the officer who took the report?" "With you guys, it looks like the left hand doesn't know what the right one is doing." Although follow-up investigators may be required by departmental policy to make such contacts, sometimes they may have to do so because of shortcomings in the incident report. (For more on this point, see Chapter 7, "The Follow-Up Investigation and Investigative Resources.")

Field notes can be used to defend the integrity of the incident/offense report. When an officer is testifying in a case for which he or she wrote the incident report, the officer can refer to field notes for assistance in recollecting the events. Most often, cases come to trial months after the incident report is written, so it would be rare for a testifying officer to remember everything about the event and all its details. In court, field notes are an indication of an officer's thoroughness as an investigator. Moreover, if at trial an officer is asked what sources of information were relied on in preparing the incident report, the notes add to the credibility of the report.

◄FIGURE 6-1 Homicide investigators sharing information from their field notes
These investigators have just finished interviewing neighbor residence in an apartment building where a homicide occurred. The investigators are discussing the information gleaned from their interviews. One investigator is conferring on a cell phone with a third colleague in an effort to join the pieces of the event into a whole story.
(© James D. DeCamp/Columbus Dispatch)

Guidelines for Note Taking

There are six main guidelines for taking notes:

1. Listen attentively, without interrupting the person who is speaking.
2. Intervene if the speaker is losing focus; bring the person back to the topic as gently as possible.
3. Review all specifics in your notes with the person providing the information.
4. Allow time for the person to consider the information you have stated and to verify it, correct it, or add information.
5. Add and/or correct information as needed.
6. Verify all changes in your notes with the speaker.[3]

Note-Taking Equipment

Officers typically use small loose-leaf and spiral-bound notebooks for their field notes. Through experience they learn which sizes and types best suit the way they work.[4] Most officers use a ballpoint pen to write their notes. If you are going to write on the front and back of pages, do not use a heavy ink, as it "bleeds" through to the other side of a page and you will not be able to use that side for note taking. Number the pages separately for each case, and use some kind of case identifier, such as the case number, on each page so that the pages can be put back in place if they are accidentally separated.

Officers should place a departmental business card, or duplicate its information, on the inside of the notebook used for field notes.

Entries in the notebook should be made on a chronological basis. If you are using a loose-leaf notebook, remove the pages when they are filled, place them in a sealed envelope with the covered time period noted on the outside, and insert new blank pages. If you are using a spiral-bound notebook, place the entire notebook in a sealed envelope and start with a new one. Too often, first-responding officers and investigators think it is all right to discard their field notes after they prepare the incident report. This is not a good idea. Frequently, in a later court proceeding, the officer/investigator will be asked to explain where or from whom he got the information contained in the incident report. If all the information and its sources are not contained in the incident report, referring to field notes made at the time of the investigation can often provide a reliable answer to the questions asked.

THE SIX INTERROGATORY AND BASIC INVESTIGATIVE QUESTIONS

To gather needed information, first-responding officers and follow-up investigators should phrase all questions beginning with the six interrogatories—who, what, where, when, how, and why. Although no single set of questions can meet the investigative needs in all types of crime, following this format should provide the needed information for the officer/investigator to understand the chronological order of events as they occurred and to enable the preparation of a well written and thorough incident report. Here are some examples of typical questions:

1. **Who**
   - was the victim?
   - discovered the crime?
   - reported the crime?
   - took the victim to his or her present location?
   - does the suspect associate with?
   - was last seen with the victim?
   - last saw the victim?
   - may be with the suspect when he or she is arrested?
   - are the witnesses connected with or related to?
   - had a motive and the means of committing the crime?
   - completed the crime scene entry and other logs?
   - processed the scene?
   - took what evidence where?
   - else may have heard, smelled, touched, or seen anything of investigative value?

2. **What**
   - crime was committed?
   - actions did the suspect take?
   - methods did the suspect use?
   - do witnesses know about the crime?
   - evidence is there?
   - tools or weapons were used?
   - actions did you take?
   - further action is needed?
   - much information may victims and witnesses be withholding?
   - much does the victim claim was stolen?
   - well does the victim's account of the event match that of any witnesses, the appearance of the scene, and the physical evidence?
   - much information (and evidence of what types) do you need to clear the crime?
   - is the suspect described by the victim and witnesses?
   - closely do the descriptions of victims and witnesses match and diverge?
   - knowledge, skills, or strength was needed?
   - other units or agencies are involved or need to be notified?

3. **Where**
   - was the crime discovered?
   - was the crime committed?
   - were any tools, evidence, or recovered property found?
   - was the victim when the crime was committed?
   - is the victim now?

- were the witnesses?
- did the suspect go?
- does the suspect frequent, live, and work?
- is the suspect now?
- was the suspect arrested?
- was the evidence marked?
- is the evidence stored?
- might other witnesses be located?

4. **When**
   - were you dispatched, and when did you arrive?
   - was the crime discovered?
   - was the crime committed?
   - was the victim last seen?
   - did help arrive, and what type was it?
   - was the suspect arrested?
   - did the suspect decide to commit the crime?

5. **How**
   - was the crime committed?
   - did the suspect get to and from the scene?
   - did the suspect get the information needed to commit the crime?
   - were tools and weapons obtained?
   - was the arrest made?
   - much injury was done to the victim?
   - much damage was there to any premises involved?
   - much money was taken, and what type of valuables?
   - difficult was it to carry off the property that was stolen?

6. **Why**
   - was the crime committed?
   - were particular tools or weapons used?
   - was the crime reported?
   - was there a delay in reporting the crime?
   - were the victim or witnesses reluctant to talk?
   - were the victim or witnesses so quick to identify the suspect?
   - am I uncomfortable with the victim's account and description of the suspect?

INCIDENT REPORTS

Despite the fact that **incident reports** are a crucial source of investigative information, writing them is often not a popular duty. One of the authors says that report writing "is not the favorite indoor sport of law enforcement officers." The significance of this jest has serious implications. An incident report, like an investigative report must tell a story. It must be written in such a manner that someone reading that report can understand what happened and can know the answers to the questions who, what, where, when, how, and why. Along with his or her memory, an officer/investigator must use the field notes taken to tell the story of the events. There are two indispensable elements of reports: (1) accuracy and (2) clear communication of the meaning that the writer intended.

More than a few excellent investigations have been wasted by an officer's failure to fully document what was done and not done. The case history that follows indicates the importance of recording all aspects of an investigation:

A burglary in progress was reported at a one-story doctor's office. As two officers moved to cover the building, a suspect was seen leaping from an office window carrying a small flight bag. The suspect ran from the scene, followed by one of the officers. He attempted to scale a fence. In the ensuing struggle, the suspect fell on the far side of the fence, breaking his arm. During treatment at a hospital, the suspect told the officer, in front of medical personnel, that he was going to claim his arm had been broken during questioning. He further indicated this would be an attempt to discredit the police, as he had only recently been released from the state prison and feared that such an immediate second violation would cause the court to invoke a stringent sentence upon conviction. Because many arrested people state that they are going to claim the police violated their civil rights, the officer regarded it as little more than a commonplace occurrence. Even though they did not relate directly to the investigation, the suspect's remarks and the identity of the persons witnessing them were included in the report as a matter of thoroughness. Subsequently, when the FBI investigated the matter of a possible violation of the suspect's rights, the allegation was easily refuted by corroborating statements from the medical personnel identified in the police officer's report.

A well-prepared incident report based on a thorough investigation of an offense can promote the rapid apprehension of the suspect, thus preventing further crimes and making the recovery of property more likely. The report also serves as the official memory of the department so that anyone who needs access to the file after the reporting officer or investigator is no longer available, can make sense of the report and the event.

Incident reports serve important operational and administrative purposes. When their data are combined, useful crime analysis reports can be produced, personnel assignments in the department can be properly aligned with the actual workloads, and geographic information system (GIS) data can produce informative maps showing, for example, where robberies with certain types of characteristics are being committed.

Supervisory Review

By reviewing the reports written by subordinates, supervisors get a current picture of the quality of their officers' investigative efforts and report-writing skills. On the basis of such information, supervisors can give constructive feedback to subordinates, as well as make appropriate performance evaluations. To carry out this responsibility at the highest level, supervisors must carefully read their subordinate's reports for content, not just style and spelling. Supervisors must take the time to understand the investigatory process involved in the particular incident and make sure that the reports accurately address what is needed for a prosecutor to file charges and prove a case. With this knowledge, constructive feedback to subordinates has meaning.

Formats for Incident Reports

While the exact layout for incident reports varies from one jurisdiction to another, they all have a "face" with blank spaces that must be filled in by the officer conducting the preliminary investigation. He or she enters basic case information in the blanks, such as information about the type of crime committed; the complainant, victim, witnesses, and offenders; and other details. Figure 6-2 is a basic incident report.

Almost always, there is more information to document than can fit on the face of an incident report. The additional information is entered in **narrative style** (Figure 6-3). There are a number of ways to organize the incident report to tell the story, but the narrative report generally makes the most sense if written in a chronological format beginning with the earliest thing that happened and progressing to the most recent fact or happening. The hardest part of writing a narrative is making sure that all the necessary information, including the smallest details, are transposed from the officer's/investigator's head and notes and recorded on paper. Doing a good job of report writing takes time, takes concentration, takes desire, and takes commitment. This sounds great on paper but the realities of law enforcement often mean that an officer or investigator has calls backed up or a heavy caseload and the object is to write the shortest, most direct report possible. The belief is that very few cases ever go to trial, so officers believe the saved time and effort writing short, direct reports is worth the risk. As the authors continue to point out in this chapter, the reality is that no one can predict which cases may later develop into something significant where the quality of a report is critical. The account is written in the blank space on the reverse of the report's face or on a page referred to as "continuation," "investigative narrative," or "supplemental" (see Figure 6-3, a case that started as a missing-person report and turned into a criminal homicide investigation). Furthermore, even cases that are plea bargained require certain information to pass muster with the local prosecutor's office. It is of utmost importance that first-responding officers and follow-up investigators learn the minimum amount of information required by the prosecutor to enable her or him to do the basic filing of formal charges. It

cannot be overly emphasized that complaints by law enforcement officers that prosecutors don't do a very good job are too often based on ineffective reports submitted by officers.

The incident report must also contain as much detail about the suspect as is known, including descriptive data, clothing, hair, complexion, language or accent information, and weapons displayed. All information from witnesses or other people interviewed, including details of the information provided, along with name and contact information needed by follow-up investigators and prosecutors, must be obtained. The report must include a listing of all evidence seized or found, with details about where it was found, by whom, who has control of it, how it was marked and recorded, and any other information necessary to protect the chain of custody.

NIBRS-Compliant Incident Reports

For more than a decade, a voluntary program has been moving law enforcement agencies away from the basic incident-report format and toward a detailed format that documents much more data about an offense. This program, the **National Incident-Based Reporting System (NIBRS),** was created as part of the **Uniform Crime Reports** and is administered by the FBI It is in use in over 4,000 small and medium-size local law enforcement agencies throughout the country, as well as a growing number of jurisdictions with populations in excess of 250,000. A large number of departments are working toward becoming NIBRS-compliant.

National crime reporting in this country dates back roughly 70 years, to the time when the FBI began collecting and publishing annual "counts" of offenses in its **Uniform Crime Reports (UCRs).** Over the past 25 years, the desire for detailed, descriptive data about criminal offenses for crime analysis and other uses has necessitated a shift in incident-report formats. With this shift, which is still in progress, police agencies have started accumulating data about the relationship between victims and offenders, the role of drugs and alcohol in offending, and other factors. The availability of NIBRS data means that law enforcement officials can more effectively allocate their resources to combat crime. Figure 6-4 reveals the level of detail in an NIBRS-compliant report, the last page of which is a continuation sheet for the chronological narrative. As computer technology continues to evolve, more and more of these reports are completed electronically (see Computer Generated Reports section below).

Aids to Information Gathering for Incident Reports

Whenever there are witnesses to a crime, even the most conscientious investigator may fail to elicit all information available. Certain aids, however, can be of critical

CRN 01-____-____-_____

Athens-Clarke County Police
INCIDENT REPORT

Press Hard - Multiple Copies   Press Hard - Multiple Copies

Page 1 of ____
ORI - GA0290100
Revised 0900

| From Date | From Time | To Date | To Time | ☐ Complainant ☐ Victim No. ___ ☐ Witness No. ___ | Premise Type | Case Status |

☐ Desires Personal Information Not Be Released

Department Title Most Serious Criminal / Traffic / Ordinance Offense. See Table.

Zone   ☐ Downtown ☐ AHA

Incident Location - Common Name   Address: No., Dir., St., Suffix, Apt.

☐ Athens
☐ Winterville
☐ Bogart

Premise Type
☐ 1. Highway
☐ 2. Serv. Station
☐ 3. Conv. Store
☐ 4. Bank
☐ 5. Commercial
☐ 6. Residence
☐ 7. School/Campus
☐ 8. All Other

Case Status
☐ Active
☐ Inactive
☐ Arrest -Adult
☐ Arrest-Juv.
☐ Ex. Cleared
☐ Unfounded
Status Date

☐ Alcohol Related **Type Of Drug(s)** ☐ Amphetamine ☐ Barbiturate ☐ Cocaine ☐ Hallucinogen
☐ Drug Related ☐ Heroin ☐ Marijuana ☐ Opium ☐ Methamphetamine ☐ Synthetic Narcotic
☐ Unknown ☐ Unknown ☐ Form: _____

Solvability Factors:
☐ M.O. Present ☐ Physical Evidence
☐ Property Traceable ☐ Witness

Suspect Can Be: ☐ Named   ☐ ID
☐ Located ☐ Described ☐ Vehicle ID

Complainant Information ☐ Juvenile ☐ Victim

Last   First
Middle   Suffix
Address: No., Dir., St., Suffix, Apt
City, State   ☐ Athens, GA Zip Code
Phone: Home   Work
Race   ☐ M ☐ F DOB

Victim Information ☐ Juvenile ☐ State Of GA ☐ A.C.C.

Last
First
Middle   Suffix
Address: No., Dir., St., Suffix, Apt
City, State   ☐ Athens, GA Zip Code
Home   Work   Cell/Pager
Race   ☐ M ☐ F DOB
Alias/Street Name
Employer   Occupation
☐ County Resident ☐ Student School
☐ Can ID Suspect ☐ Will File Charges ☐ Medical Treatment
Hospital
Type / Extent Of Injury: ☐ Fatal Injury ☐ Broken Bones
☐ Gun/Knife ☐ Superficial Injury ☐ Sexual Abuse ☐ Other
☐ Property Damage/Loss ☐ Mental Abuse ☐ Threats

Witness 1 Information ☐ Juvenile

Last, First, Middle, Suffix
Address: No., Dir., St., Suffix, Apt
City, State   ☐ Athens, GA Zip Code
Phone: Home   Work
Race   ☐ M ☐ F DOB

Witness 2 Information ☐ Juvenile

Last, First, Middle, Suffix
Address: No., Dir., St., Suffix, Apt
City, State   ☐ Athens, GA Zip Code
Phone: Home   Work
Race   ☐ M ☐ F DOB

Reporting Officer

Offender 1 Information ☐ Juvenile

Last
First
Middle   Suffix
Address: No., Dir., St., Suffix, Apt
City, State   ☐ Athens, GA Zip Code
Home   Work   Cell/Pager
Race   ☐ M ☐ F DOB
Alias/Street Name
Employer   Occupation
☐ County Resident ☐ Student School
OLN   State
Height   Weight   **Stranger To Stranger?**
                ☐ Yes ☐ No
Eye Color: ☐ Black ☐ Brown ☐ Blue ☐ Green
☐ Hazel ☐ Gray ☐ Other____
Hair Color: ☐ Blonde ☐ Brown ☐ Black ☐ Red
☐ Gray ☐ Salt&Pepper ☐ Other____
Offender's Vehicle Description   ☐ Vehicle Searched
Tag   Year   State
Veh. Year   Make
Model   Style
Color-Top   Color-Bottom

☐ **Incident Recorded**   ☐ Hand cuffed
Tape No.   ☐ D. L.   ☐ B. B.

Burglary Factors For Incident/Offense No.____
Forced Entry? ☐ Kicked ☐ Heavy Object
☐ Yes ☐ No ☐ Pushed ☐ Lock Tamper
☐ Unknown ☐ Pry Tool ☐ Cutting Tool
Point Of Entry? ☐ Front ☐ Rear
☐ Door ☐ Window ☐ Side
☐ Roof ☐ Wall ☐ Basement
☐ Attic ☐ Other ☐ Unk ☐ Move A/C
Point Of Exit? ☐ Same As Entry
☐ Other____
Structure Was: ☐ Occupied ☐ Unoccupied

Attached Documents:
☐ **Incident/Offense Continuation**
☐ **Persons Form**   ☐ **Juvenile Complaint**
☐ **Domestic Violence** ☐ **Property / Vehicle**
☐ **GCIC** ☐ **ABR**   ☐ **Victim Notification**

Emp. No.   Report Date   Approving Supervisor   Emp. No.

Incident /Offense 1 Code Section
☐ Attempted ☐ Committed
Title
Assault Factors   **Weapon Type**
☐ Assault ☐ Theft ☐ DV   ☐ Gun ☐ Other
☐ Sexual ☐ Mental Subject ☐ Knife/Cutting Tool
☐ Hate Crime ☐ Unknown   ☐ Hands/Fists/Etc.
Weapon Description
Offense Status ☐ Active   ☐ Inactive
☐ Unfounded   ☐ Arrest   ☐ Ex. Cleared
Involved Suspect No.(s)____ Victim No. (s)____
Murder Circumstance

Incident /Offense 2 Code Section
☐ Attempted ☐ Committed
Title
Assault Factors   **Weapon Type**
☐ Assault ☐ Theft ☐ DV   ☐ Gun ☐ Other
☐ Sexual ☐ Mental Subject ☐ Knife/Cutting Tool
☐ Hate Crime ☐ Unknown   ☐ Hands/Fists/Etc.
Weapon Description
Offense Status ☐ Active   ☐ Inactive
☐ Unfounded   ☐ Arrest   ☐ Ex. Cleared
Involved Suspect No.(s)____ Victim No. (s)____
Murder Circumstance

Incident /Offense 3 Code Section
☐ Attempted ☐ Committed
Title
Assault Factors   **Weapon Type**
☐ Assault ☐ Theft ☐ DV   ☐ Gun ☐ Other
☐ Sexual ☐ Mental Subject ☐ Knife/Cutting Tool
☐ Hate Crime ☐ Unknown   ☐ Hands/Fists/Etc.
Weapon Description
Offense Status ☐ Active   ☐ Inactive
☐ Unfounded   ☐ Arrest   ☐ Ex. Cleared
Involved Suspect No.(s)____ Victim No. (s)____
Murder Circumstance

Incident /Offense 4 Code Section
☐ Attempted ☐ Committed
Title
Assault Factors   **Weapon Type**
☐ Assault ☐ Theft ☐ DV   ☐ Gun ☐ Other
☐ Sexual ☐ Mental Subject ☐ Knife/Cutting Tool
☐ Hate Crime ☐ Unknown   ☐ Hands/Fists/Etc.
Weapon Description
Offense Status ☐ Active   ☐ Inactive
☐ Unfounded   ☐ Arrest   ☐ Ex. Cleared
Involved Suspect No.(s)____ Victim No. (s)____
Murder Circumstance

▲ **FIGURE 6-2   Basic incident report**

(Source: Courtesy Athens-Clarke County, Georgia, Police Department)

Incident #   2002710051   Report Date: Wednesday, September 27, 2000
THERESA ANDREWS 23 YOA...5·7 BROWNISH RED HAIR 9 MONTHS PREGNANT.
COP ENTRY SENT OUT AT 16:51. 17:19 TELETYPE OHALLTERM SENT OUT. RIVERS WAS
CALLED AT 17:57

We received a call to go to 207 W. Riddle Ave. reference a missing person. Circumstances as stated by dispatch was that a female adult was missing from the home. It was reported that the husband came home from work, found the door open, his wife's belongings such as purse, keys, and cell phone at the residence. It was also reported that a person was to take a test ride in a vehicle for sale this morning.

Based on information given by dispatch I asked Detective Francis to accompany myself and Ptl. Wilmington to the residence. Upon arrival we were met by Mr . Andrews who was in the front lawn talking on a cell phone. He appeared to be upset but not frantic.

Upon speaking to him he stated that his wife paged him at work around 9:00 am this morning and told him that a lady was coming by to take a look and test drive their jeep that was for sale. The Pr stated that they have the jeep listed in trading times and were trying to sell the car. He stated that he tried to call back around noon or so and could not get an answer. He stated that he told her not to go with anyone, just get their driver's license and let them take a drive. Pr stated that upon arriving home he found the front door wide open. He stated that his wife's purse, house keys, and cell phone were in the house but she was gone as was the jeep.

The Pr described his wife as being 8 1/2 months pregnant and not feeling well. He stated that she has to be helped in and out of bed and that she had not been feeling well. Pr stated he had checked the hospital and was trying to phone the doctor to see if something had happened with the baby. The jeep was described as all black 1999 with soft top and Ohio Reg. CAB4351 and is a Wrangler type.

Ptl. Wilmington, Det. Francis and myself checked the interior of the house as well as the yard and garage area. No one was located. The house appeared to be very tidy with no signs of foul play or struggle. I instructed dispatch to place a COPS teletype, administrative teletype, and radio broadcast with the information. I also advised dispatch to enter Mrs. Andrews as missing as well as the vehicle.

▲ **FIGURE 6-3   Portion of an investigative narrative**

importance in preventing this. One tool, shown in Figure 6-5, is a **suspect description form** for collecting personal-description information about the suspect.

One of the most frustrating experiences for investigators occurs when trying to obtain a description of a firearm, as the victim or witnesses are often injured, unfamiliar with firearms, or visibly shaken by their experience. One helpful device in such situations is photographs of some commonly encountered firearms, as shown in Figure 6-6 (a similar sheet is available for long guns). Very frequently, by viewing these, even emotionally upset victims or witnesses can make an identification or at least give a good description of the weapon.

Computer-Generated Reports

Since the 1980s, many law enforcement vehicles have been equipped with **mobile data terminals (MDTs)** (Figures 6-7 and 6-8). Although the terminals initially had limited capabilities and occasional reliability problems,

MDTs have reduced demands on the overcrowded voice channels and enhanced officer safety. Technological advances continue to create new options and possibilities for the use of wireless systems in law enforcement vehicles. Depending on the system and software used, current MDTs can do the following:

1. Provide consistently secure communications between 911 and law enforcement units, and among law enforcement units.
2. Allow officers to directly check important databases (rather than going through a dispatcher and waiting for a reply). They can access the National Crime Information Center (NCIC), as well as state and local systems. Officers can also receive information about newly wanted persons, including a facial composite likeness or mug shot. Outstanding warrants, court orders, stolen property inquiries, criminal and driving records, mug-shot files, crime analysis reports, and GIS maps of crimes

STERLING HEIGHTS POLICE DEPARTMENT

ADMINISTRATION

| OFFICER / #: | DATE: | TIME(S) OF INCIDENT: / | DATE(S) OF INCIDENT: / | INCIDENT #: |

| LOCATION OF INCIDENT: (Address or Block No.) | ARRIVAL TIME AND DATE: | AREA/SECTION | RELATED INCIDENT #: |

| REPORTEE: (Last, First, Middle) | DOB | PHONE (Home): ( ) |

| ADDRESS: (Street, City, State, Zip) | PHONE (Business): ( ) |

OFFENSE

OFFENSE:
1. 2. 3.

OFFENSE STATUS: (Check only one per offense)
1.A ☐ ATTEMPTED 2.A ☐ ATTEMPTED 3.A ☐ ATTEMPTED
C ☐ COMPLETED C ☐ COMPLETED C ☐ COMPLETED

Assist Agency

SUSPECT(S) USED: (Check as many as apply)
A ☐ ALCOHOL D ☐ DRUGS
C ☐ COMPUTER EQUIP. N ☐ NOT APPLICABLE

(For Burglary Only)
NUMBER OF PREMISES ENTERED: _____
METHOD OF ENTRY:
F ☐ FORCEABLE N ☐ NO FORCE

LOCATION OF OFFENSE: (Check Only One) (Enter Code Number for Offense #2 _____ #3 _____)

01 ☐ AIR/BUS/TRAIN TERMINAL
02 ☐ BANK/SAVINGS & LOAN
03 ☐ BAR/NIGHT CLUB
04 ☐ CHURCH/SYNAGOGUE/TEMPLE
05 ☐ COMMERCIAL/OFFICE BUILDING
06 ☐ CONSTRUCTION SITE
07 ☐ CONVENIENCE STORE
08 ☐ DEPARTMENT/DISCOUNT STORE
09 ☐ DRUG STORE/DR'S OFFICE/HOSPITAL
10 ☐ FIELD/WOODS

11 ☐ GOVERNMENT/PUBLIC BUILDINGS
12 ☐ GROCERY/SUPERMARKET
13 ☐ HIGHWAY/ROAD/ALLEY
14 ☐ HOTEL/MOTEL/ETC.
15 ☐ JAIL/PRISON
16 ☐ LAKE/WATER
17 ☐ LIQUOR STORE
18 ☐ PARKING LOT/GARAGE
19 ☐ RENTAL/STORAGE FACILITY
20 ☐ RESIDENCE/HOME

21 ☐ RESTAURANT
23 ☐ SERVICE/GAS STATION
24 ☐ SPECIALTY STORE (TV, FUR, ETC.)
31 ☐ SCHOOL
32 ☐ COLLEGE
33 ☐ REST AREA/ROADSIDE PARK
34 ☐ SCALE
88 ☐ OTHER
99 ☐ UNKNOWN

TYPE CRIMINAL ACTIVITY: (Check Up To Three)
B ☐ BUYING/RECEIVING
C ☐ CULTIVATING/MANUFACTURING/PUBLISHING
D ☐ DISTRIBUTING/SELLING
E ☐ EXPLOITING CHILDREN
O ☐ OPERATING/PROMOTING/ASSISTING
P ☐ POSSESSING/CONCEALING
T ☐ TRANSPORTING/TRANSMITTING/IMPORTING
U ☐ USING/CONSUMING

TYPE WEAPON/ FORCE INVOLVED: (Check Up To Three) (Enter A in Box if Automatic)
11 ☐ FIREARM (type not stated)
12 ☐ HANDGUN
13 ☐ RIFLE
14 ☐ SHOTGUN
15 ☐ OTHER FIREARM
20 ☐ KNIFE/CUTTING INSTRUMENT
30 ☐ BLUNT OBJECT
35 ☐ MOTOR VEHICLE
40 ☐ PERSONAL WEAPONS
50 ☐ POISON
60 ☐ EXPLOSIVES
65 ☐ FIRE/INCENDIARY
70 ☐ NARCOTICS/DRUGS
85 ☐ ASPHYXIATION
88 ☐ OTHER
99 ☐ UNKNOWN
00 ☐ NONE

ARRESTEE / SUSPECT

☐ ARRESTEE ☐ SUSPECT SUSPECT CONNECTED TO OFFENSE NUMBER: 1.☐ 2.☐ 3.☐

#1: (Last, First, Middle) | ADDRESS: (Street, City, State, Zip)

DOB:
M ☐ MALE W ☐ WHITE A ☐ ASIAN
F ☐ FEMALE B ☐ BLACK U ☐ UNKNOWN
U ☐ UNKNOWN I ☐ INDIAN

PHONE (Home): | PHONE (Business):

ARRESTEE WAS ARMED WITH: (Check Up To Two) (Enter A in Box if Automatic)
01 ☐ UNARMED 14 ☐ SHOTGUN
11 ☐ FIREARM, (type not stated) 15 ☐ OTHER FIREARM
12 ☐ HANDGUN 20 ☐ LETHAL CUTTING INSTRUMENT (e.g. Switchblade, Knife, etc.)
13 ☐ RIFLE 30 ☐ CLUB/BLACKJACK/BRASS KNUCKLES

TYPE OF ARREST:
O ☐ ON-VIEW
S ☐ SUMMONED/CITED
T ☐ TAKEN INTO CUSTODY

ARREST CHARGE:

| HEIGHT: | WEIGHT: | EYES: | HAIR: |

☐ ARRESTEE ☐ SUSPECT SUSPECT CONNECTED TO OFFENSE NUMBER: 1.☐ 2.☐ 3.☐

#2: (Last, First, Middle) | ADDRESS: (Street, City, State, Zip)

DOB:
M ☐ MALE W ☐ WHITE A ☐ ASIAN
F ☐ FEMALE B ☐ BLACK U ☐ UNKNOWN
U ☐ UNKNOWN I ☐ INDIAN

PHONE (Home): | PHONE (Business):

ARRESTEE WAS ARMED WITH: (Check Up To Two) (Enter A in Box if Automatic)
01 ☐ UNARMED 14 ☐ SHOTGUN
11 ☐ FIREARM, (type not stated) 15 ☐ OTHER FIREARM
12 ☐ HANDGUN 20 ☐ LETHAL CUTTING INSTRUMENT (e.g. Switchblade, Knife, etc.)
13 ☐ RIFLE 30 ☐ CLUB/BLACKJACK/BRASS KNUCKLES

TYPE OF ARREST:
O ☐ ON-VIEW
S ☐ SUMMONED/CITED
T ☐ TAKEN INTO CUSTODY

ARREST CHARGE:

| HEIGHT: | WEIGHT: | EYES: | HAIR: |

☐ ARRESTEE ☐ SUSPECT SUSPECT CONNECTED TO OFFENSE NUMBER: 1.☐ 2.☐ 3.☐

#3: (Last, First, Middle) | ADDRESS: (Street, City, State, Zip)

DOB:
M ☐ MALE W ☐ WHITE A ☐ ASIAN
F ☐ FEMALE B ☐ BLACK U ☐ UNKNOWN
U ☐ UNKNOWN I ☐ INDIAN

PHONE (Home): | PHONE (Business):

ARRESTEE WAS ARMED WITH: (Check Up To Two) (Enter A in Box if Automatic)
01 ☐ UNARMED 14 ☐ SHOTGUN
11 ☐ FIREARM, (type not stated) 15 ☐ OTHER FIREARM
12 ☐ HANDGUN 20 ☐ LETHAL CUTTING INSTRUMENT (e.g. Switchblade, Knife, etc.)
13 ☐ RIFLE 30 ☐ CLUB/BLACKJACK/BRASS KNUCKLES

TYPE OF ARREST:
O ☐ ON-VIEW
S ☐ SUMMONED/CITED
T ☐ TAKEN INTO CUSTODY

ARREST CHARGE:

| HEIGHT: | WEIGHT: | EYES: | HAIR: |

VEH.

| IMPOUND Y OR NO | MAKE | MODEL | YEAR | COLOR | V.I.N. | LIC. ST. | LIC. YR. | LICENSE NO. |

▲ **FIGURE 6-4 NIBRS-compliant incident report**

(Source: Courtesy Sterling Heights, Michigan, Police Department)

STERLING HEIGHTS POLICE DEPARTMENT

ADMINISTRATION

OFFICER / #:	DATE:	TIME(S) OF INCIDENT: /	DATE(S) OF INCIDENT: /	INCIDENT #:

LOCATION OF INCIDENT: (Address or Block No.) | ARRIVAL TIME AND DATE: | AREA/SECTION | RELATED INCIDENT #:

REPORTEE: (Last, First, Middle) | DOB | PHONE (Home): ( )

ADDRESS: (Street, City, State, Zip) | PHONE (Business): ( )

OFFENSE

OFFENSE:
1.　　　　　　　　　2.　　　　　　　　　3.

OFFENSE STATUS: (Check only one per offense)
1.A ☐ ATTEMPTED　2.A ☐ ATTEMPTED　3.A ☐ ATTEMPTED
　C ☐ COMPLETED　　C ☐ COMPLETED　　C ☐ COMPLETED
Assist Agency

SUSPECT(S) USED: (Check as many as apply)
A ☐ ALCOHOL　　　　　D ☐ DRUGS
C ☐ COMPUTER EQUIP.　N ☐ NOT APPLICABLE

(For Burglary Only)
NUMBER OF PREMISES ENTERED: _____
METHOD OF ENTRY:
F ☐ FORCEABLE　N ☐ NO FORCE

LOCATION OF OFFENSE: (Check Only One) (Enter Code Number for Offense #2 _____ #3 _____)

01 ☐ AIR/BUS/TRAIN TERMINAL
02 ☐ BANK/SAVINGS & LOAN
03 ☐ BAR/NIGHT CLUB
04 ☐ CHURCH/SYNAGOGUE/TEMPLE
05 ☐ COMMERCIAL/OFFICE BUILDING
06 ☐ CONSTRUCTION SITE
07 ☐ CONVENIENCE STORE
08 ☐ DEPARTMENT/DISCOUNT STORE
09 ☐ DRUG STORE/DR'S OFFICE/HOSPITAL
10 ☐ FIELD/WOODS

11 ☐ GOVERNMENT/PUBLIC BUILDINGS
12 ☐ GROCERY/SUPERMARKET
13 ☐ HIGHWAY/ROAD/ALLEY
14 ☐ HOTEL/MOTEL/ETC.
15 ☐ JAIL/PRISON
16 ☐ LAKE/WATER
17 ☐ LIQUOR STORE
18 ☐ PARKING LOT/GARAGE
19 ☐ RENTAL/STORAGE FACILITY
20 ☐ RESIDENCE/HOME

21 ☐ RESTAURANT
23 ☐ SERVICE/GAS STATION
24 ☐ SPECIALTY STORE (TV, FUR, ETC.)
31 ☐ SCHOOL
32 ☐ COLLEGE
33 ☐ REST AREA/ROADSIDE PARK
34 ☐ SCALE
88 ☐ OTHER
99 ☐ UNKNOWN

TYPE CRIMINAL ACTIVITY:
(Check Up To Three)
B ☐ BUYING/RECEIVING
C ☐ CULTIVATING/MANUFACTURING/ PUBLISHING
D ☐ DISTRIBUTING/SELLING
E ☐ EXPLOITING CHILDREN
O ☐ OPERATING/PROMOTING/ ASSISTING
P ☐ POSSESSING/CONCEALING
T ☐ TRANSPORTING/TRANSMITTING/ IMPORTING
U ☐ USING/CONSUMING

TYPE WEAPON/ FORCE INVOLVED:
(Check Up To Three)
(Enter A in Box if Automatic)
11 ☐ FIREARM (type not stated)
12 ☐ HANDGUN
13 ☐ RIFLE
14 ☐ SHOTGUN
15 ☐ OTHER FIREARM
20 ☐ KNIFE/CUTTING INSTRUMENT
30 ☐ BLUNT OBJECT
35 ☐ MOTOR VEHICLE
40 ☐ PERSONAL WEAPONS
50 ☐ POISON
60 ☐ EXPLOSIVES
65 ☐ FIRE/INCENDIARY
70 ☐ NARCOTICS/DRUGS
85 ☐ ASPHYXIATION
88 ☐ OTHER
99 ☐ UNKNOWN
00 ☐ NONE

ARRESTEE / SUSPECT

☐ ARRESTEE　☐ SUSPECT　SUSPECT CONNECTED TO OFFENSE NUMBER:　1. ☐　2. ☐　3. ☐

#1: (Last, First, Middle) | ADDRESS: (Street, City, State, Zip)

DOB:
M ☐ MALE　W ☐ WHITE　A ☐ ASIAN
F ☐ FEMALE　B ☐ BLACK　U ☐ UNKNOWN
U ☐ UNKNOWN　I ☐ INDIAN
PHONE (Home): | PHONE (Business):

ARRESTEE WAS ARMED WITH: (Check Up To Two) (Enter A in Box if Automatic)
01 ☐ UNARMED
11 ☐ FIREARM, (type not stated)
12 ☐ HANDGUN
13 ☐ RIFLE
14 ☐ SHOTGUN
15 ☐ OTHER FIREARM
20 ☐ LETHAL CUTTING INSTRUMENT (e.g. Switchblade, Knife, etc.)
30 ☐ CLUB/BLACKJACK/BRASS KNUCKLES

TYPE OF ARREST:
O ☐ ON-VIEW
S ☐ SUMMONED/CITED
T ☐ TAKEN INTO CUSTODY

ARREST CHARGE:

HEIGHT: __'__	WEIGHT:	EYES:	HAIR:

☐ ARRESTEE　☐ SUSPECT　SUSPECT CONNECTED TO OFFENSE NUMBER:　1. ☐　2. ☐　3. ☐

#2: (Last, First, Middle) | ADDRESS: (Street, City, State, Zip)

DOB:
M ☐ MALE　W ☐ WHITE　A ☐ ASIAN
F ☐ FEMALE　B ☐ BLACK　U ☐ UNKNOWN
U ☐ UNKNOWN　I ☐ INDIAN
PHONE (Home): | PHONE (Business):

ARRESTEE WAS ARMED WITH: (Check Up To Two) (Enter A in Box if Automatic)
01 ☐ UNARMED
11 ☐ FIREARM, (type not stated)
12 ☐ HANDGUN
13 ☐ RIFLE
14 ☐ SHOTGUN
15 ☐ OTHER FIREARM
20 ☐ LETHAL CUTTING INSTRUMENT (e.g. Switchblade, Knife, etc.)
30 ☐ CLUB/BLACKJACK/BRASS KNUCKLES

TYPE OF ARREST:
O ☐ ON-VIEW
S ☐ SUMMONED/CITED
T ☐ TAKEN INTO CUSTODY

ARREST CHARGE:

HEIGHT: __'__	WEIGHT:	EYES:	HAIR:

☐ ARRESTEE　☐ SUSPECT　SUSPECT CONNECTED TO OFFENSE NUMBER:　1. ☐　2. ☐　3. ☐

#3: (Last, First, Middle) | ADDRESS: (Street, City, State, Zip)

DOB:
M ☐ MALE　W ☐ WHITE　A ☐ ASIAN
F ☐ FEMALE　B ☐ BLACK　U ☐ UNKNOWN
U ☐ UNKNOWN　I ☐ INDIAN
PHONE (Home): | PHONE (Business):

ARRESTEE WAS ARMED WITH: (Check Up To Two) (Enter A in Box if Automatic)
01 ☐ UNARMED
11 ☐ FIREARM, (type not stated)
12 ☐ HANDGUN
13 ☐ RIFLE
14 ☐ SHOTGUN
15 ☐ OTHER FIREARM
20 ☐ LETHAL CUTTING INSTRUMENT (e.g. Switchblade, Knife, etc.)
30 ☐ CLUB/BLACKJACK/BRASS KNUCKLES

TYPE OF ARREST:
O ☐ ON-VIEW
S ☐ SUMMONED/CITED
T ☐ TAKEN INTO CUSTODY

ARREST CHARGE:

HEIGHT: __'__	WEIGHT:	EYES:	HAIR:

VEH.

IMPOUND Y OR NO	MAKE	MODEL	YEAR	COLOR	V.I.N.	LIC. ST.	LIC. YR.	LICENSE NO.

▲ Figure 6-4　**NIBRS-compliant incident report (*continued*)**
(Source: Courtesy Sterling Heights, Michigan, Police Department)

STERLING HEIGHTS POLICE DEPT.

INCIDENT NO.

▲ **Figure 6-4   NIBRS-compliant incident report (*concluded*)**
(Source: Courtesy Sterling Heights, Michigan, Police Department)

and other incidents may all be directly available to the officer.

3. Enable officers in the field to write incident reports electronically, with full access to spelling- and grammar-checking tools. In modest systems, the reports are saved to a disk, from which they are printed at the station. After supervisory review and approval, the reports go to the records unit. In advanced systems, reports are sent wirelessly to the supervisor. If the supervisor declines a report, it is sent back, with comments, to the officer, who resubmits it after addressing the comments. Once a report is approved, the supervisor sends it from his or her MDT to the records unit.

In addition to using MDTs, some agencies are using **personal digital assistants (PDAs)** (Figure 6-9). These small, handheld units are particularly useful in traffic enforcement.

The PDA prints a hard copy of the citation for the violator and sends a digital copy to the station.

Agencies using wireless technologies have experienced significant productivity gains as the systems reduce the amount of time officers must spend on paperwork. In general, the time gained per officer ranges from 2.5 to 4 hours per day.

Handwritten Reports

Despite the widespread use of MDTs, many officers still write all their reports by hand because their jurisdictions cannot afford MDT technology, have not made its acquisition a priority item in their budgets, or feel that the technology's cost outweighs its benefits. In actuality, when the formats of handwritten and MDT-generated reports are compared, the differences can be so slight that it is difficult to distinguish between the two.

Handwriting reports is slower, and officers do not have the advantages provided by spelling and grammar checkers. Moreover, if officers make mistakes, sometimes the only solution is to rewrite the page up to the point of the error and then continue with the correct information. While officers writing incident reports electronically also make mistakes, recovery is much easier because it is a simple matter to insert additional words, sentences, and paragraphs.

The approval process for handwritten incident reports is much like that described for MDT-generated reports. Several times during the shift, the officer's supervisor will call to meet with him or her to review any completed incident reports. If a report is accepted, the supervisor makes a disposition, signs the report, and takes it to the station for processing by the records unit. The original incident report is kept in records, and copies are made and distributed as required by the supervisor's disposition. For example, if the case is referred for follow-up investigation, a copy is sent to the appropriate supervisor, who reviews the report and then assigns the case on the basis of workloads, the level of skill required, and the amount of "heat" and media attention the crime may create.

Supervisory Disposition of Incident Reports

After approving an incident report, the supervisor must make a **disposition** of it. As depicted in Figure 6-10, any of the following dispositions may be made:

1. The case may be retained for further investigation by uniformed officers.
2. It may be unfounded (i.e., the complaint is false).

IN CASE OF CRIME

Try to remain calm and aware of everything around you. Observe the suspect as closely as possible.
Try not to focus on any weapon. Call police only when it is safe to do so, identify your situation, location, name,
phone number and wait for them to arrive. Utilize this sheet to record the incident as best you can.

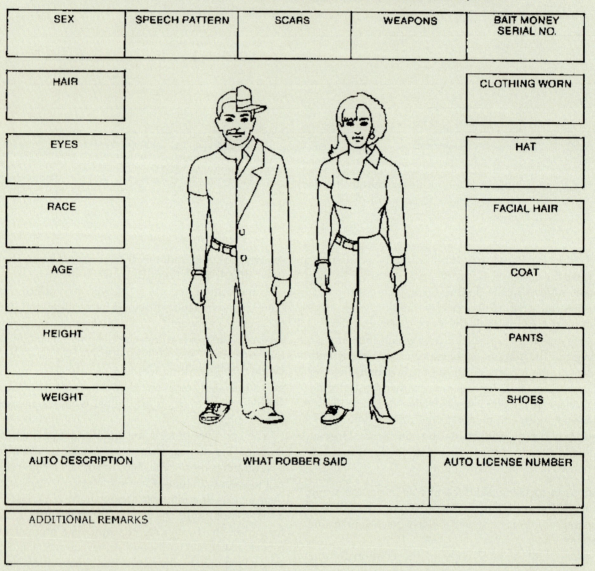

| SEX | SPEECH PATTERN | SCARS | WEAPONS | BAIT MONEY SERIAL NO. |

HAIR

EYES

RACE

AGE

HEIGHT

WEIGHT

CLOTHING WORN

HAT

FACIAL HAIR

COAT

PANTS

SHOES

| AUTO DESCRIPTION | WHAT ROBBER SAID | AUTO LICENSE NUMBER |

ADDITIONAL REMARKS

This form is designed to assist you in remembering the appearance of a suspect. Complete it as soon as possible after the incident. Start at the suspect's head and use the diagram to guide you. Use the reverse of worksheet if additional space is needed. Complete it alone. Do not discuss what you remember with others. The idea is to record what you remember, not to form an agreement with other witnesses.

suspectws.pdf

Philadelphia Police Department
One Franklin Square
Philadelphia, PA 19106

▲ Figure 6-5   Suspect description form

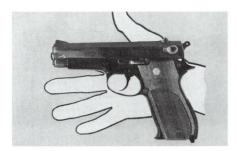

9-mm Smith & Wesson Semiautomatic

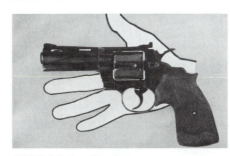

.22 RG-10 Revolver

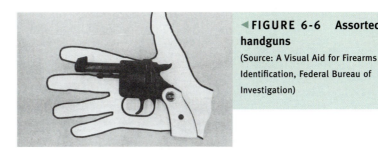

◄ FIGURE 6-6 Assorted handguns

(Source: A Visual Aid for Firearms Identification, Federal Bureau of Investigation)

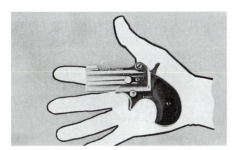

.357 Herter's Derringer

.357 Colt Python Revolver

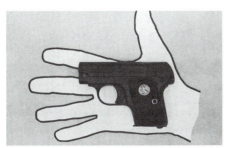

.25 Colt Semiautomatic

.45 U.S. Semiautomatic

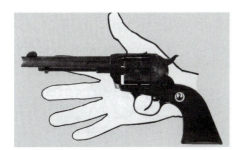

.22 Ruger Revolver

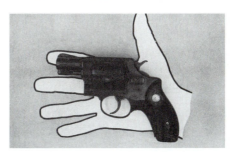

.38 Smith & Wesson Chief's Special Revolver

3. The case may be inactivated due to a lack of leads.
4. It may be referred to plainclothes investigators.
5. The case may be completed and closed.

To some extent, a department's situation and policies affect the supervisor's decision about which dispositions to use. If the Uniform Division is seriously understaffed and officers have been reduced to being "report takers" because they do not have time to conduct thorough preliminary investigations, rarely will a case be retained for further investigation. By policy or the strong will of the investigations commander, the authority to unfound a case may be reserved for an investigation supervisor. In addition, because copies of incident reports may be routinely routed to an investigations supervisor, a uniformed supervisor

who has inactivated cases only to have an investigations supervisor reactivate them may be slow about doing anything other than referring them to the investigations division, especially if the reactivations have at least occasionally resulted in the cases being successfully cleared.

Common Elements of Incident Reports

Incident-report contents vary, ranging from the essential data in a basic incident report to the more extensive information in an NIBRS-compliant report. However, certain elements are common to most reports. The importance of obtaining as much detailed and complete information as possible for inclusion in the incident report cannot be over emphasized. Each of these is discussed next.

Name

The full names of complainants, witnesses, and other parties must always be obtained. In recording proper names, the first time an individual is referred to in a report the sequence of names should be last, first, middle. When a person mentioned in the report is commonly known to acquaintances by some name other than the proper name or an apparent derivation, the nickname should also be provided.

Race or Ethnicity and Sex

Race or ethnic extraction should never be documented in such a manner as to cast aspersion on a person. Ordinarily race is indicated by use of one of the following abbreviations: W (White), B (Black), H (Hispanic), A (Asian or Pacific Islander), I (American Indian or Native Alaskan), and U (Unknown).[5] Sex is always designated by F for female and M for male. The proper sequence is race/sex—for example, W/F.

Age

On entries requiring only a person's age, it should be indicated as of the last birthday. However, the first reference to the individual in the narrative portion of the

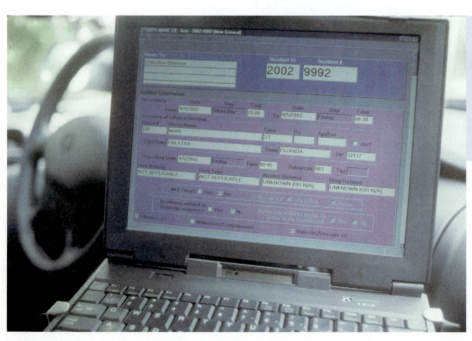

report should give the exact date of birth, if known. For certain parties, such as an unidentified deceased person or a suspect whose identity has not been established, age may be approximated or given in a narrow span of years—for example, "approximately 32 years" or "approximately 31–33 years."

Physical and E-Mail Addresses

This information is particularly important because it helps investigators find people for additional interviews or related procedures. Each residence and business address should show the street number and, when applicable, the apartment, suite, or room number. If this information is not immediately ascertainable, the general location should be described in sufficient detail to make its whereabouts known. When military personnel are involved, the location information should include serial numbers, unit designations, and ship or installation, if applicable. If a person is only visiting a location, both temporary and permanent addresses should be obtained. E-mail addresses have become so prevalent that they should be included in the report.

Telephone, Cell-Phone, and Pager Numbers

The telephone numbers of an individual should always be obtained, including area code, residence number, business number, and any extension number. Additionally, officers should inquire about and record any cell-phone or pager numbers.

Personal Description

A model form for recording personal descriptions of suspects was shown in Figure 6-5. Minimally, the following points should be included: sex, race, age, complexion, hair and eye color, physical defects, scars, marks, tattoos, build, and the nature and color of clothing worn.

Property Description

Elements useful in describing property are make, model, serial number, color, and type of material from which constructed. Other types of information may also be pertinent. Using the case of a stolen car as an example, the presence of stickers, cracked windows, articles hanging from the mirror, or loud engine noise would be additional information useful in locating the vehicle, and, of course, make, model year, color, vehicle identification number, and license plate state and number.

Occupation

The occupation of a person may be of some importance to an investigation. In the case of a suspect, it may establish familiarity with the use of certain types of equipment or procedures associated with a particular function, such as banking. It may also lend further credibility to the statement of a witness:

A man exited from a restaurant as two suspects ran about 15 feet from the bank they had just robbed, entered a vehicle, and rapidly drove around the corner. Despite being presented with only a brief view of the car, the witness was able to give the police a fairly detailed description of it. At the trial, the defense was unsuccessful in casting doubt on the accuracy of the description, as the witness operated an automobile repair service.

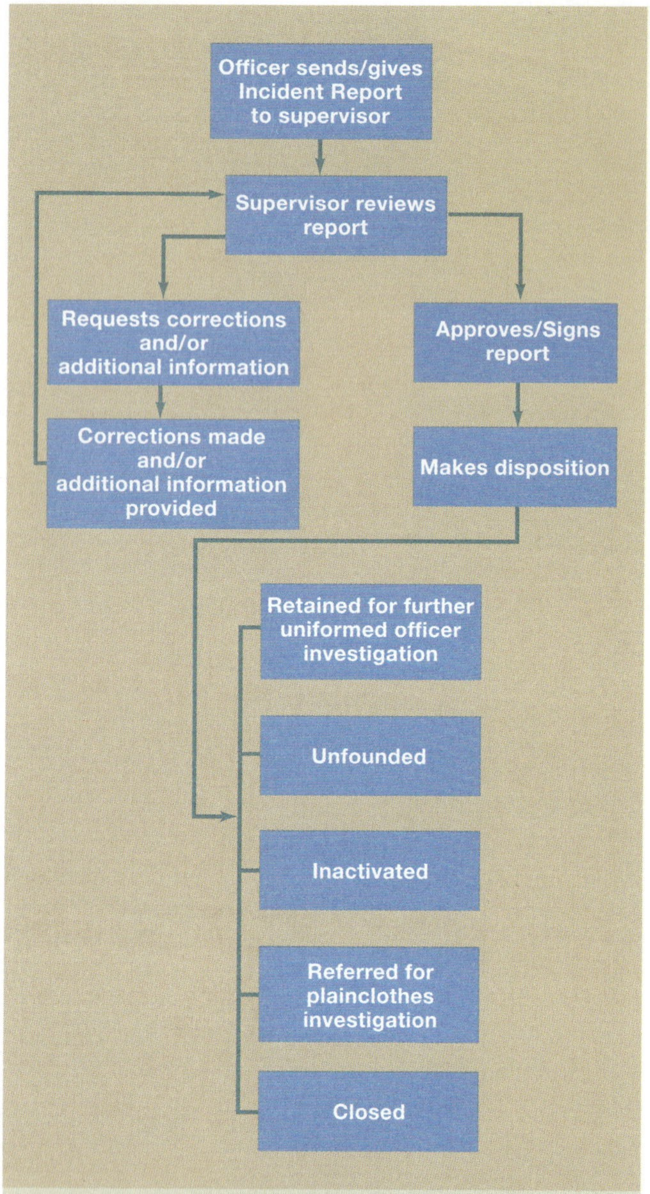

▲ **Figure 6-10   Report approval and disposition process**

replacement cost should be used. On goods stolen from retail establishments, the merchant's wholesale cost, which constitutes the actual dollar loss, is the proper value to use. The value placed on nonnegotiable instruments such as traveler's checks or money orders should be the cost of replacing them; negotiable instruments, including bonds payable to the bearer, are valued at the market price at the time of the theft.

When the stolen property is subject to appreciation from the time of its acquisition by the owner—for example, limited-edition prints—the current fair market value is to be indicated.

The value of recovered stolen property ordinarily equals the valuation placed on it at the time of theft unless damaged, in which case it is to be established by the fair market value. In cases where the value of the stolen article is not readily ascertainable, the conservative estimate of the owner may be used.

Date

Many dates are used in a report, but officers/investigators must know what dates are most critical. Often, important dates needed by prosecutors to file formal charges are hard to find or are missing from reports. For example: it is more critical to know what date a motor vehicle was stolen rather than recovered. It is important to know what date a bad check was presented for payment or to be cashed (uttered) rather than the date it was returned from the bank and reported to law enforcement. In any investigation, learn which dates are most important to include in the report.

Time

For all official business, excluding general public and related information, most police agencies use the military system, or 24-hour clock, of hundred hours. Time runs from 0001 hours (12:01 A.M.) through 2400 hours (12 A.M.).

Occupation is also useful in suggesting times when a person might be successfully and conveniently contacted by the investigator. An unemployed individual's ordinary line of work is to be given along with the notation "currently unemployed." College students or homemakers should be so designated. If the individual is employed, the occupation given in a report should be as specific as possible—for example, "brick mason" as opposed to "manual laborer."

Value

The value of property stolen may determine whether the offense is a felony or misdemeanor. For articles subject to depreciation, the fair market value should be used, unless the property is new or almost new, in which case the

WRITING EFFECTIVE REPORTS

If incident reports are going to serve the many uses to which they can be put, they must meet certain standards. Among the standards most usually cited are proper classification; complete, accurate, concise, objective, and fair information; and timely submission.[6] Keep the following guidelines in mind when you are preparing incident and investigative reports:

1. *Fill in all the blanks* on the incident report unless the information is not available or it is withheld, in which case this should be explained in the report. As discussed earlier, it is easier to get the necessary information at the scene than to try to recontact complainants and witnesses.

2. *Write the report in the first person,* using "I arrived at the scene at 1645 hours" as opposed to "Officer Morales arrived at the scene at 1645 hours." The reader of the report knows that Officer Morales wrote the report, and the officer's constant reference to himself or herself in the third person (Officer Morales) is awkward. Although some departments require the use of the third person in reports, the trend in report writing is to move away from it.

3. *Avoid unnecessary technical or legalistic jargon* such as "hereinafter," "point of fact," or "thereof," because you may convey a meaning that you do not intend or do not fully understand. Such jargon is a means by which your credibility can be attacked. Avoid writing statements of your own whose meaning you cannot fully explain. Certainly, if a suspect tells you, "I was abducted by aliens who implanted a control box in my head and they sent me commands to rob the pharmacy," you must faithfully record the statement even if you can't explain it—but the words are not your own.

4. *Write short sentences,* because they are less likely to be confusing to (or misunderstood by) readers, such as the prosecutor. A concise, "punchy" presentation of the facts makes it easier for the reader to "find the beef."

5. *Use short paragraphs* for the same reasons as those for writing short sentences.

6. *Support any conclusions you express with details,* because others who read the report, such as the prosecutor, need to know what facts shaped your thinking. Also, when a trial begins weeks, months, or even years later, you will have forgotten many facts. If you included them in the report, you will be able to refresh your recollection and provide convincing testimony.

7. *Don't repeat facts more than once,* unless doing so is required by your department's reporting format or policies. Duplication of entries wastes your time, and it creates the possibility that when you are distracted, tired, or in a hurry, your entries may conflict in some way with one another, calling your credibility into question.

8. *Check your spelling.* People who don't know you will form opinions of your capabilities on the basis of the reports you write and they read. Also, you are representing your department, so its reputation is on the line because defense attorneys, judges, members of the news media, juries drawn from the community, and prosecutors read police reports. Misspelled words can change the meaning of a sentence or cause the meaning to be lost. Spell-checker software is an aid to accuracy, but it does not catch words that are spelled correctly but used inappropriately (e.g., "E. Wazolewski took a write turn").

9. *Edit what you write.* Don't miss an opportunity to catch and correct your errors. Many people do this best when they read slowly and out loud, but you may find a system that works better for you. Taking the time to edit your report is more important than the system you use. If you are using a computer, editing is far easier than writing several successive handwritten drafts of a report. Moreover, the software includes a spell checker, thesaurus, and grammar checker.[7]

Not infrequently a new investigator will, if only at the subconscious level, attempt to impress those who will be reading the incident report by writing in an elaborate manner in order to display mastery of the English language. However, persons reading the report will learn much, or perhaps all, they will ever know about the investigation from what has been written. Therefore, it is essential to write in a clear and uncluttered style; the report must be written not only so that it can be understood but, more importantly, so that it cannot be misunderstood.

The report must be completely accurate. No detail should be added or deleted; the potential or actual consequences of such deviations, however innocent the motivation, are considerable. For example, at the scene of an armed robbery, a young investigator was conducting interviews necessary to prepare the original report. One of the questions he asked the victim was "Have you ever seen the perpetrator before this happened?" The response was "Yes, he works on the loading platform of the grocery on Sixth Avenue." Out of a desire to provide as much detail as possible, the investigator supplemented this statement with information from the telephone directory, writing a portion of the interview in the following manner:

The victim told the undersigned officer that the suspect works at Blake's Grocery Wholesale, located at 1425 Sixth Avenue, telephone number (813) 223-3291.

Later, the following exchange took place between the officer and the defense attorney in court:

Q Defense Attorney: *Officer, do you recognize this report?*
A Officer: *Yes, I do.*

Q Defense Attorney: *Did you prepare it?*
A Officer: *Yes, sir, I did.*

Q Defense Attorney: *Would it be fair to say that it represents your investigation?*
A Officer: *That is correct, sir.*

Q Defense Attorney: *Then, having conducted the investigation and having prepared the report, your testimony would be that it accurately and completely portrays your actions and what you learned?*

A Officer: *Yes, sir.*

Q Defense Attorney: *Would you read from page 2 of this report?*

A Officer: *"The victim told the undersigned officer that the suspect works at Blake's Grocery Wholesale, located at 1425 Sixth Avenue, telephone number (813) 223-3291."*

Q Defense Attorney: *Officer, the complainant in this case has already testified to the effect that she did not, in fact, tell you this. Why are you prejudiced toward the defendant in this case, and what else have you added to the report or subtracted from it in order to strengthen the state's case?*

Thus, a seemingly innocuous addition to a report reduced the credibility of the entire investigation. Clear communication and accuracy are the mainstays of effective reports. The absence of one diminishes the other.

THE FOLLOW-UP INVESTIGATION AND SUPPLEMENTAL REPORTS

Periodically during the follow-up investigation, supplemental reports must be initiated. Ordinarily, supplemental, or follow-up, reports should be written no less frequently than every 10 days, and the continuance of a particular investigation beyond 28 days should require supervisory approval to ensure proper use of an investigator's time. The purpose of writing follow-up reports is to keep the file current as new or corrected information is gathered. Additionally, specific acts or accomplishments might require individual supplemental reports, such as the activation or cancellation of a pickup order or BOLO, the issuance of a search warrant, the arrest of a suspect, the complainant's discovery that additional property was stolen that was not noticed as missing at the time the incident report was made, the recovery of all or part of the property taken, or a change in the title of the offense owing to improper classification on the original report—for example, a strong-arm robbery reclassified as a purse snatch.

Other circumstances under which supplemental reports are required include (1) when the offense is unfounded, (2) when it is exceptionally cleared, meaning that the police know who the perpetrator is but are unable to pursue the case further owing to circumstances beyond their control, such as the death of the only witness, and (3) when the case is inactivated. If the supervisor reviewing the incident report inactivates it because of to insufficient leads to warrant follow-up investigation, then a supplemental report is not required. However, if some follow-up work is done, no promising leads are developed, and the case is then inactivated, the person assigned responsibility for it must complete a supplemental report to substantiate the basis for inactivation.

As a general concluding note, case files inactivated may in later months or years receive further investigative work that is productive. Therefore, it is of considerable importance that at each stage of report writing care is exercised in presenting all available information.

KEY TERMS

disposition (of incident report)
field notes
incident reports
mobile data terminal (MDT)

narrative style
National Incident-Based Reporting System (NIBRS)
personal digital assistant (PDA)

suspect description form
Uniform Crime Reports (UCRs)

REVIEW QUESTIONS

1. Identify and briefly discuss four reasons why field notes are important.
2. What are the six interrogatory investigative questions?
3. Briefly discuss the operational and administrative uses of incident reports.
4. How would you characterize the difference between basic incident reports and those that are NIBRS compliant? (Check the Internet for additional information on how these reports differ.)
5. How are MDTs and PDAs being used in law enforcement?
6. After a uniformed supervisor accepts a report, he or she must make a disposition of it. What are five dispositions that might be made?

INTERNET ACTIVITIES

1. Learn more about NIBRS at www.search.org/nibrs. Find out if your state has recently received any NIBRS grants. Read the brief report entitled, "Effects of NIBRS on Crime Statistics." How do NIBRS statistics differ from UCR data? What impact does NIBRS have on crime statistics? What factors need to be considered when comparing summary UCR statistics and NIBRS data?

2. Log onto your local, county, or state law enforcement agency website and find out if the agency uses mobile data terminals. If it does, in what capacity are they used? Are all patrol vehicles equipped with MDTs? Does the site provide any information on other data technology used by officers (PDAs, etc.)? If so, what?

NOTES

1. California Commission on Peace Officer Standards and Training, Basic Course Workbook Series, *Investigative Report Writing* (Sacramento: Office of State Publishing, 1999), p. 2–1, with some additions to, and restatement of, the discussion of these points by the authors.
2. Michael Biggs, *Just the Facts: Investigative Report Writing* (Upper Saddle River, NJ: Prentice Hall, 2001), p. 16. Like citation 1, this is an excellent source of information on field notes and report writing.
3. California Commission, *Investigative Report Writing,* pp. 2–12, is the source of several of these points.
4. Biggs, *Just the Facts,* pp. 16–19, with some restatement by the authors.
5. U.S. Equal Employment Opportunity Commission, Standard Form 100, Rev. 3-97, "Employer Information Report EEO-1, 100–118," Instruction Book, www.eeoc. gov/stats/jobpat/e-1instruct.html, Nov. 14, 2001.
6. Allen Z. Gammage, *Basic Report Writing* (Springfield, IL: Charles C. Thomas, 1966), pp. 13–14. These points remain valid even today; for example, see California Commission, *Investigative Report Writing,* pp. 4–21.
7. These points are drawn from Paul L. Godwin, "Painless Report Writing," *Law and Order,* Feb. 1993, pp. 38–40, with some additions by the authors.

7

THE FOLLOW-UP INVESTIGATION AND INVESTIGATIVE RESOURCES

CHAPTER OBJECTIVES

1. Summarize the process and solvability factors used to determine whether a follow-up investigation is warranted.

2. Elaborate on the follow-up investigation process.

3. Explain the use of neighborhood and vehicle canvasses.

4. Discuss how databases are used in the follow-up.

5. Describe the use of live and photo lineups.

6. Understand the purposes and planning for physical surveillance.

7. Explain the handling and relationship with informants.

8. Summarize the use of facial recognition software.

9. Discuss the fusion center concept.

10. Explain the role of intelligence units and types of intelligence.

11. Describe the intelligence/analytical cycle.

12. Understand crime analysis and its techniques.

13. Explain time-event charting, link analysis, and telephone record analysis.

14. Discuss criminal and geographic profiling.

15. Identify financial difficulty indicators.

16. Discuss the use of the Internet in follow-up investigations.

17. Define remote sensing and explain methods associated with it.

▲ Two investigators reviewing the contents of an incident report with a patrol sergeant. Note that they are using good technique. One investigator focuses on the questions while the other takes notes.

(Courtesy Chief Jack Lumpkin and Sgt. David Leedahl, Athens Clarke County [Georgia] Police Department)

There are certain types of crimes that inherently are going to receive a follow-up investigation, such as murder and rape. In other instances, the information contained in the incident report will be evaluated for the presence of solvability factors. If there are insufficient solvability factors, the case is inactivated and receives no further attention until new information surfaces, whereas a case which has a sufficient number of such factors will be worked by investigators.

This chapter contains a major section on "The Follow-up Investigation Process," which largely identifies various types of sources of information and their importance, including such topics as the incident and supplemental reports, working leads, neighborhood and vehicle canvasses, reinterviewing victims and witnesses, jail booking reports, and the use of databases. Guidelines for conducting lineups are also covered in this section because their use is part of the basic skills needed by investigators.

Special investigative techniques and resources are also used in support of follow-up investigations as may be warranted by the applicable facts. The investigator may personally use some of these, while many will be performed by specialized units and personnel in support of the follow-up. Complete investigators must have a basic understanding of these techniques and resources and make use of them within the framework of their department's policies and procedures. Special investigative techniques and resources covered include planning and executing surveillance operations, the "dos and don'ts" of working informants, planning and executing surveillance operations, facial recognition software capabilities, fusion centers, intelligence units and the types of files they maintain, products provided by intelligence units, methods of crime analysis, time-event charting, link analysis, telephone record analysis, criminal and geographic profiling, financial analysis, remote sensing capabilities, the National Center for the Analysis of Violent Crime, the Combined DNA Index System, and the use of the Internet as an investigative tool.

THE DECISION TO INITIATE A FOLLOW-UP INVESTIGATION

In Chapter 3, "follow-up" investigation was defined and explained. This chapter provides additional information about follow-up investigations and identifies and explains some of the resources and techniques available to support such investigations. Other investigative resources and techniques are identified in subsequent crime-specific chapters.

Departmental policies vary as to how the decision to inactive a case or refer it for follow-up investigation is made. In some agencies this decision is made by a Patrol Division Supervisor. In others, all or many types of incident reports are forwarded to the Detective Division, where a supervisor screens them by hand or by entering information into case management software that determines the presence or absence of **solvability factors.** This determination may be done by judgment or by applying mathematical weights to the presence or absence of certain factors in the incident report, including:

- Is the suspect named?
- Can the suspect be identified?
- Is there a detailed description of the suspect?
- Is there significant physical evidence?
- Are other suspects named, identified, or described in detail?
- If a vehicle is involved, is there a license number or detailed description?
- Does the crime fit an established modus operandi or method of operation?
- Were deadly weapons displayed or used?
- To what extent was the victim physically harmed?

- What similarity is there to recently reported crimes?
- Will the victim be able to identify the suspect?
- Was traceable property taken?
- Are there witnesses?
- Does the nature of the crime (e.g., theft of explosives) necessitate a follow-up?
- Can a composite sketch of the suspect(s) be prepared?

Some case management software can provide both a mathematical score that determines whether there should be a follow-up and the number of investigative days to be allocated initially to the case if one is to be conducted. To help investigators keep their focus, many departments use a follow-up investigation checklist (Figure 7-1). It is described as a "universal" follow-up investigation checklist, meaning that it is not a crime-specific checklist (e.g., burglary or robbery).

Activity	Activity Description	Date Completed	Notes
1.	Autopsy/Crime Lab Reports		
2.	Bank Records Reviewed		
3.	Crime Vict. Notif. Record		
4.	Criminal Case Report Form		
5.	Department of Corrections		
6.	Department of Revenue Inq.		
7.	Identification Unit Rpts.		
8.	Intelligence Reporting		
9.	Interview Informants		
10.	Mandatory: Notify Victim		
11.	Medical Records		
12.	NCIC Criminal History		
13.	Neighborhood Canvass		
14.	Pawn Shop Records Check		
15.	Photographic Lineup		
16.	Phys. Evid./Property Disp.		
17.	Polygraph Examination		
18.	Search Warrant App./Exec.		
19.	Search Warrant Return		
20.	S.P.D. Records Check		
21.	State Fingerprint Record		
22.	State Probation & Parole		
23.	Stolen Property Files		
24.	Surveillance Conducted		
25.	Suspect Miranda/Interview		
26.	Suspect: P/C Item/Arrest		
27.	Witnesses Interviewed		
28.	Other:		
29.	Other:		
30.	Other:		
31.	Other:		

◄ **FIGURE 7-1 Universal follow-up investigation checklist** (Courtesy of Chief Lynn Rowe and Lt. Rick Headlee, Springfield [Missouri] Police Department)

THE FOLLOW-UP INVESTIGATION PROCESS

The manner in which a follow-up investigation is conducted varies by the type of crime, the existence of physical evidence, the condition of the victim, whether a suspect is already in custody, and other related variables. Moreover, new information, such as identifying a second suspect late in the follow-up investigation, may cause an earlier step (e.g., checking databases) to be repeated. The basics of the follow-up investigation were introduced and discussed in Chapter 3; this chapter provides greater detail. You will note that some steps of the follow-up are not discussed in this chapter because they have been amply covered elsewhere—the topics of search and arrest warrants were dealt with in Chapter 2, "Legal Aspects of Investigation," and Chapter 5 addressed interviews and interrogation. Thus the sections that follow identify and discuss major follow-up activities. To refresh readers' recall of certain points, some sections in this chapter briefly recapitulate information covered in Chapter 3, "Investigators, the Investigative Process, and the Crime Scene" and Chapter 6, "Field Notes and Reporting."

Incident and Supplemental Reports and Evidence Receipts

The preliminary investigation report, also called an incident report (Chapter 6), may answer many concerns of the follow-up investigator assigned to the case, such as how, when, and where the crime was committed, is the suspect described, known to the victim or witnesses, or in custody. If in custody, where is the suspect lodged (e.g., jail or hospital), has a suspect composite sketch been prepared and distributed, how many other suspects are involved, what are their descriptions, what are the identities and statements of witnesses, was a vehicle involved (if so, what's its description), what words were spoken by the suspect, what was the nature and value of the property stolen, what degree of violence (if any) was used, was a weapon employed, what's the medical condition of the victim, and what evidence was seized.

Supplemental reports are just what the name suggests: they provide information that adds to or supplements that contained in the incident report. For instance, a man displaying a gun attempts to rob a liquor store; however, rather than being intimidated, the owner pulls his own gun and shoots him. The suspect drops his gun and staggers from the store clutching his wound. Moments later, he collapses in a nearby alley, where he is taken into custody by an arriving police unit. The incident report would cover what happened in the store, including seizing the suspect's gun. Also included in the report are the details of affecting the arrest in the alley. The gun would be transported to the evidence/property control room, often by the officer who writes the incident report, and a detailed receipt would be given to this officer by the evidence custodian/officer, which is then appended to the incident report. Because a police officer should be in the ambulance transporting the suspect to the hospital, that officer would write a supplemental report. Thus, the assigned follow-up investigator may have information at hand to act on, but the amount of information can vary considerably.

Examine Physical Evidence

Early in the investigation, the physical evidence should be viewed (Figure 7-2) because it may soon be forwarded to the crime laboratory for analysis. Actually seeing the evidence adds a level of specific understanding about each item of evidence as to its appearance, color, weight, damage done to it in the commission of the crime, modifications to

◄ **FIGURE 7-2 Investigator examining evidence in the property room**

(Courtesy of Chief Jack Lumpkin, Athens Clarke County [Georgia] Police Department)

INVESTIGATION SUPERVISOR'S
LEAD ASSIGNMENT SHEET

Incident#:

Check When Lead Is Cleared

LEADS	DATE REC'D	DATE ASSIGNED	INVESTIGATOR	TASK / COMMENTS	X	Add'l LEAD #

◄ FIGURE 7-3   Lead-assignment sheet
(Source: Imprimus Forensic Services, LLC, copyright 2001. This form may be reproduced for law enforcement purposes only.)

weapons, and other matters. These observations may help the investigator make connections when he sees or hears a comment at a later stage in the follow-up.

Leads

Some leads turn out to be "good," whereas others are simply "dry holes" and an unproductive use of time. The truth is that both kinds chew up resources and must be followed up because often we can't accurately tell one from the other:

A burglary victim called an investigator to explain that she thought the offenders were two employees of a firm that the apartment complex had hired to do some work in her apartment. The described suspects, names unknown, had been given a key to her apartment in order to perform the necessary work. The burglary had been committed eight days later, and there had been no forced entry. The apartment manager, when contacted by the investigator, denied that the suspects would have committed the burglary but provided the name of the firm that employed them. The owner of the firm testified to the suspects' good employment records and reliability. A message was left for the suspects to contact the investigator. The suspects called back about a half-hour later and gave the investigator their full names, dates of birth, and past criminal histories and described the work done on the victim's apartment. The investigator used this information to check his own department's records and also requested a record check on the suspects from a neighboring jurisdiction. The investigator concluded after following up these leads that the suspects were not likely to have been the offenders and closed the investigation.

The fact that an incident report specifically names a suspect does not mean the person actually committed the offense or knows anything substantive about it. Victims

may report their suspicions as "fact" or attempt to cause problems for someone whom they do not like or have had difficulty with in the past.

Major cases, such as the murder of a community leader or a robbery with a large "score," typically require the combined efforts of a number of investigators, who report to the supervisor responsible for the case. A key responsibility of the case supervisor is coordination of information, especially with respect to making sure that leads are prioritized and worked and that the results are disseminated to all team members. One way this can be done, by hand or on a computer, is by using a lead-assignment sheet log (see Figure 7-3).

Neighborhood and Vehicle Canvasses

A fundamental aspect of most investigations is the **neighborhood canvass** of residents, merchants, and others who may have been in the immediate vicinity of a crime and have useful information (see Figure 7-4). It is estimated that a systematic neighborhood canvass soon after the commission of an offense results in information of investigative value in approximately 20% of all cases. The extent of the canvass depends on variables such as the type of offense, time of day, and characteristics of the crime scene. The timing of a neighborhood canvass is an important consideration. People not only move randomly through areas but also ebb and flow on a variety of schedules. To mistime a neighborhood canvass by 30 minutes, for example, may mean eliminating the possibility of locating persons who regularly catch a bus at a particular time and who, on the day of an offense, might have seen something of considerable investigative value.

Before a neighborhood canvass, investigators should be given all information relating to the offense, including a full description of the suspect, whether they are known or believed to be armed, any injuries sustained by the suspect, and the type of property taken. The possession of these facts is absolutely essential for two major reasons. First, investigators can then question witnesses intelligently, increasing the probability that all available information will be elicited. Second, the investigator is protected from unknowingly encountering the suspect and thus being placed in jeopardy.

BUILDING / NEIGHBORHOOD CANVASS

AGENCY: _____

INCIDENT#: _____

INSTRUCTIONS: Document whether or not all occupants of the residence were interviewed. Document locations where no persons were contacted. If available, list pager and / or cellphone numbers in the remarks column. Use the back side of this sheet for notes.

MULTIPLE UNIT OCCUPANCY: Address _____

Number of Units _____

(List only unit numbers below)

ADDRESS (indicate residence, business, etc.)	PERSON CONTACTED	DOB	HOME TX#	WORK TX#	REMARKS (pager / cell phone)
# OF OCC.					☐ FOLLOW-UP RQ'D ☐ NOTES ON BACK
# OF OCC.					☐ FOLLOW-UP RQ'D ☐ NOTES ON BACK
# OF OCC.					☐ FOLLOW-UP RQ'D ☐ NOTES ON BACK
# OF OCC.					☐ FOLLOW-UP RQ'D ☐ NOTES ON BACK
# OF OCC.					☐ FOLLOW-UP RQ'D ☐ NOTES ON BACK
# OF OCC.					☐ FOLLOW-UP RQ'D ☐ NOTES ON BACK
# OF OCC.					☐ FOLLOW-UP RQ'D ☐ NOTES ON BACK
# OF OCC.					☐ FOLLOW-UP RQ'D ☐ NOTES ON BACK
# OF OCC.					☐ FOLLOW-UP RQ'D ☐ NOTES ON BACK
# OF OCC.					☐ FOLLOW-UP RQ'D ☐ NOTES ON BACK
# OF OCC.					☐ FOLLOW-UP RQ'D ☐ NOTES ON BACK
# OF OCC.					☐ FOLLOW-UP RQ'D ☐ NOTES ON BACK
# OF OCC.					☐ FOLLOW-UP RQ'D ☐ NOTES ON BACK
# OF OCC.					☐ FOLLOW-UP RQ'D ☐ NOTES ON BACK
# OF OCC.					☐ FOLLOW-UP RQ'D ☐ NOTES ON BACK
# OF OCC.					☐ FOLLOW-UP RQ'D ☐ NOTES ON BACK
# OF OCC.					☐ FOLLOW-UP RQ'D ☐ NOTES ON BACK

CANVASSING OFFICER (Print): _____

INITIALS: _____ DATE: _____ START TIME _____ TIME END: _____

▲ FIGURE 7-4 Building/neighborhood canvass
(Courtesy of Imprimus Forensic Services, LLC)

Interviews should be conducted first at businesses or dwellings with a clear view of the crime scene and at the suspect's avenues of approach and flight. When there are substantial numbers of locations involved, several teams of officers canvassing simultaneously are helpful. If merchants or residents are not on site during the canvass, a later contact is necessary. Even when persons interviewed do not provide any useful information, investigators must record the fact that no information was obtained in order to eliminate the possibility of duplicating effort later on. Another reason for recording that no positive information has been provided is shown in the following case study:

On a Sunday morning, a residential burglary resulted in the theft of $3,800 in rare coins. The uniformed officer making the original investigation received permission to conduct the neighborhood canvass. Usually the follow-up investigator did the canvass, but the uniformed officer had extra time that day. The victim's home was situated on a cul-de-sac along with four other homes with some view of the victimized premises. There were no homes to the rear of the victim's residence. After interviewing residents of the four neighboring homes, including a teenage boy, the uniformed officer recorded the identities and statements of those with whom he had talked in his report. All indicated they had seen nothing. Because of the value of the property taken, the case was referred for follow-up investigation.

The investigator assigned to the case recently had been transferred from the Youth Services Bureau to the Burglary Bureau and recognized the name of the youth identified in the interview section of the uniformed officer's report as an individual with an extensive juvenile record for breaking and entering. Investigation revealed that the youth had committed the offense, and all coins taken were recovered.

Although luck played some part, the neighborhood canvass and adherence to sound reporting procedures not only avoided duplication of effort but also cleared the case so quickly that the perpetrator had no opportunity to dispose of the stolen property.

Like the neighborhood canvass, the **vehicle canvass** should be conducted as soon as there is sufficient information to do so. As Figure 7-5 shows, the address or location of each vehicle must be recorded, as well as its description and plate or tag number. Anything unusual about a vehicle should be noted, such as bullet holes; blood; odd appearance of the interior; recent damage; noteworthy stickers; unusual articles; items hanging from the rearview mirror, whether the car is hot, warm, cold, muddy, or clean. For vehicles that seem to be possibly related to the case, the types and condition of the tires should also be noted. If a suspect feels that an investigation is tightening around him or her and there is a possibility of tying tire marks to the scene, the suspect may buy new tires. If so, the vehicle canvass notes will reveal this change, and it may be possible to locate the old tires at the dealership where the new tires were bought.

The level of detail recorded for each vehicle varies according to the judgment of the investigator making the vehicle canvass. However, if any error is to be made on the amount of information, it is always better, without being wasteful of resources, to have too much detail than not enough.

NCIC and Public Databases

There is no shortage of databases, including national, regional, state, substate regional, and local. The ones mentioned here are illustrative rather than exhaustive. Criminal history records and intelligence files should be checked for suspects, complainants, and witnesses for a variety of reasons, including determining the possibility that a crime was staged to make an insurance claim, making a preliminary assessment of the witness's credibility in court, and assessing the possibility that the "witness" is offering bogus information to misdirect investigators. In a case involving the abduction of two girls on a rural road, a person known to the police brought much appreciated coffee and sandwiches to the mobile command center several times. Finally, someone decided that giving him access to the command center was not wise, and as an afterthought they ran a records check on him. A prior record for child molestation existed, and the man confessed to the abductions. He also related that he used what he heard in the command center to keep ahead of the investigation and also fabricated a story about seeing a car with an out-of-state tag cruising the road the day of the abductions.

Pawn shop databases should be queried to determine if stolen property has been hocked or sold. Firearms seized from the suspect should be checked to determine what their history is and if the weapons were stolen in a previous crime. Parole records should be examined for the possibility that someone recently released from prison could be involved. For a fee, credit reporting agencies such as Equifax, TransUnion, and Experian can be accessed to provide significant information about people of interest, including their financial status, that may help identify potential investigative targets in white-collar crime and fraud cases. Other sites that can provide information about persons of interest are People Finder, Yahoo People Search, Lycos People Search, AnyWho, and BigFoot. The types of information vary somewhat from one site to another but include current and past addresses, possible relatives, birth dates, current telephone numbers, marriage and divorce information, litigation history, and e-mail address.

Information about corporations can be obtained from each state's Secretary of State's Office. If a company uses a registered agent, some corporate information, such as

VEHICLE INFORMATION CANVASS

AGENCY: _____

INCIDENT#: _____

INSTRUCTIONS: Document all vehicles in the area you have been assigned. Include vehicles parked in the streets, driveways, alleyways and yards. Under "Remarks" list anything unusual noted about the vehicle (manner of parking, warm engine, fresh damage, etc.)

For vehicles without license plates, enter the VIN in the "Remarks" column.

ADDRESS (indicate alley, driveway, street, etc.)	MAKE	MODEL	COLOR	PLATE	REMARKS (VIN)

CANVASSING OFFICER (Print): _____ INITIALS: _____ DATE: _____ START TIME _____ TIME END: _____

▲ **FIGURE 7-5** Vehicle information canvass
(Courtesy of Imprimus Forensic Services, LLC)

officers, may not be available online, although some useful information about the corporation can be gleaned as a starting point. Dunn & Bradstreet can provide a Business Background Report, which provides summary coverage about the operations, history, and background of a company and its senior management; its Credit eValuator summarizes a business's credit worthiness and payment history.

Although many federal agencies maintain databases to serve their own agents, as well as state and local law enforcement officers, the FBI's **National Crime Information Center (NCIC)** provides access to the singlemost comprehensive set of databases (Figure 7-6). Implemented in 1967, NCIC has provided the information critical to solving high-profile cases, including the 1968 murder of Dr. Martin Luther King, which led to the arrest of James Earl Ray. NCIC was also instrumental in the arrest of Timothy McVeigh on the same day as the 1995 Oklahoma City bombing. In mid-1999, NCIC 2000 went online with its most recent major revision.

The NCIC database consists of the 18 files broken down into two categories: 1) stolen property and 2) persons as summarized below. Figure 7-6 shows some of the additional NCIC capabilities.

Stolen Property Files

1. **Articles,** generally stolen articles to be entered into NCIC must have a value of $500 or more and have a unique manufacturer's assigned serial number or one applied by the owner. Office equipment,

---

Additional NCIC 2000 Services

Enhanced name search (searches all derivatives of names, such as Jeff, Geoff, Jeffrey)

Search of right-index-finger prints

Mug shots

Other identifying images (such as scars, tattoos, and images of vehicles—e.g., Ford Mustang)

Convicted Sexual Offender Registry

Convicted Persons on Supervised Release Database

Persons Incarcerated in Federal Prisons

User manuals available online

Information linking (all information related to a case will be returned on a single inquiry; e.g., if guns are in a stolen vehicle, a query on the vehicle will return information on the stolen guns as well)

Improved data quality

Online ad-hoc searches to support criminal investigations

Maintains five days of system inquiries to allow agencies to be notified if they are looking for information on the same individual or stolen property

▲ **FIGURE 7-6 NCIC 2000 databases**
(Source: http://www.fbi.gov/hc/cjisd/NCJC.htm, February 27, 2008)

television sets and bicycles may be entered regardless of value. If the aggregate value of property stolen in a single instance exceeds $5,000, any uniquely numbered item may be entered. Uniquely numbered items not meeting the threshold value may be entered if the circumstances indicate the probability of it being moved interstate or the seriousness of the crime dictates an entry should be made to potentially assist the investigation. Items stolen abroad may be entered by the Customs Service if there is a high likelihood of it being transported to this country. Stolen or lost credit and ATM cards are not entered into NCIC.

2. **Boats,** in addition to thefts directly from owners, this file also covers thefts from loans, leases and rental arrangements.

3. **Firearms,** a substantial category ranging from antique guns to silencers, grenades, mines, missiles, rockets and disguised guns (e.g. in a walking cane, pen or belt buckle). BB and paint ball guns are entered in the Articles File.

4. **Stolen License Plates,** standard passenger automobile plates and special plates for which there is a theft report can be entered. In states where two plates (front and rear) are issued, either both must be stolen or the owner must agree not to use the remaining plate.

5. **Securities,** including stolen embezzled, counterfeited or used for ransom.

6. **Stolen Vehicles,** snowmobiles are part of this file, as well as vehicles wanted in conjunction with felonies or serious misdemeanors.

7. **Vehicle/Boat Parts,** a part is any serially-numbered component stolen from a vehicle or boat. Other items which may be entered into the V/B File include vehicle identification numbers (VINs) and certificates of origin/certificates of title. Satellite/FM/CB radios and musical entertainment players are entered in the Article File.

Persons Files

8. **Convicted Sexual Offender Registry,** contains records of individuals who are convicted sexual offenders or sexual predators.

9. **Foreign Fugitive,** If a country has an extradition treaty/convention with the United States and has issued an arrest warrant for an act which if committed in this country would be a felony, the data can be entered in NCIC.

10. **Identity Theft,** criteria for entry in this file are that someone is using a means of identification for another person, such identity is used without the victim's permission, the identity is intended or is being used to commit unlawful activity and the victim must sign a consent form prior to NCIC entering the data.

11. **Immigration Violator,** data in this file is the responsibility of the U.S. Department of Homeland Security and includes deported felons, those for whom an administrative warrant of removal exists and they remain illegally in this country and persons failing to comply with national security registration requirements.

12. **Missing Person,** examples of categories include, the disabled, disaster victims and adults or juveniles who appear to be involuntary missing (abducted) or for whom there is a reasonable concern for their safety. Children abductions entered into the system should include Amber Alert (AA) tags.

13. **Protective Orders,** A Protective order (PO) may be temporary or final and is issued by a civil or criminal court to prevent harassing, threatening or violent acts against a person by another or regulates communication, proximity or contact with the protected person.

14. **Supervised Release,** includes information on persons on probation or parole who must be meet certain restrictions, e.g., be drug free.

15. **Unidentified Person,** including deceased persons and recovered portions of dismembered bodies, remains from disasters and living persons unable to identify themselves, such as infants and amnesia or Alzheimer's victims.

16. **Persons Identified by the U.S. Secret Service** as posing a potential threat to the President or other protectees.

17. **Violent Gang and Terrorist Organization Members,** a two part file: Group Reference Capability (GRC) with information on gang and terrorist organizations and Group Member Capability (GMC) covering individuals.

18. **Wanted Persons,** includes individuals for whom a federal warrant, a felony warrant or serious misdemeanor warrant is outstanding, included are juveniles who will be tried as adults.

The broad usefulness of NCIC can be seen in the following examples:

- An officer notices a man, with a small child in the front passenger's seat, driving his car too rapidly and weaving through traffic, causing other drivers to slam on their brakes. The officer stops the vehicle and checks on the driver through NCIC 2000. It is learned from the Convicted Sexual Offender Registry and the Convicted Persons on Supervised Release Database that the subject is a registered sexual offender who should not be with a young child, is on parole in another state, and should not have left it.[1]

- Investigators working the fugitive detail get a tip that a person wanted on a rape warrant is in the Blue Light Lounge. This turns out not to be true, but as soon as they enter the bar, they notice a man nervously glancing over his shoulder at them as he makes a beeline to the rest room. When he does not come back, they locate him in the stall of the ladies room and ask him why he is so nervous. He gives them several different stories and names, but he has no identification. After using the single-print scanner in their unmarked vehicle, the investigators electronically send his print to NCIC 2000. In minutes they learn the identity of the subject, as well as the fact that he is wanted for a double homicide two states away.

- A patrolling officer sees a pickup pulling a sailboat. The brake lights for the trailer are either not working or not hooked up. The officer stops the truck with the intent of getting this potentially dangerous deficiency corrected. The driver nervously hands over his license when requested to do so. The officer notices a second driver's license on the dashboard of the pickup. Both photographs match the driver, but there are different names and birth dates on them. An NCIC 2000 check reveals that both names are aliases used by a man with a criminal history who is wanted in connection with a series of boat thefts. In his patrol car, the officer receives a mug shot, the suspect's real name, and a photograph of his tattoo, as well as photographs of, and other data on, the stolen boats, one of which is attached to the suspect's truck.

Victim and Witness Contacts

Victims or their families should be contacted very early in the process. They often have questions about the status of the case, their rights, whether they need protection, how a case gets processed through the criminal justice system, if they are eligible for victim's compensation for medical expenses or funerals, and if disabled by the crime, is there living assistance available to them. The investigator can answer some of these questions and then make sure the victims get linked to victim assistance entities, which may be state agencies. Some religious denominations also provide victims assistance on an ad-hoc or other basis.

Recontacting victims and witnesses serves to confirm information in the incident or supplemental reports and to develop further information. Unfortunately, such contacts are sometimes met with questions such as "I already told the other cops everything I know. Why aren't you out looking for the guy that did this instead of bothering me with the same questions? Don't you cops talk to each other?" Experienced investigators let such frustrated comments politely roll off of their backs. "Look, I'm only try to help you," has the potential to produce a downward spiral. It is better to "join" the victim or witness by using statements such as "I want to arrest the person that did this to you. In my experience sometimes victims or witnesses think of something else that is important, and rather than burden you with trying to find me, I thought it would be courteous for me to come to you."

Jail Booking Report

The **jail booking report** is created when a subject is in-processed at a jail. This jail may be part of the investigator's agency, or it may be operated by another entity, such as the sheriff. The booking report is often computer generated and may have an incident report integrated into it, as well as a color photo; fingerprints; the subject's health and medications; his mental state (e.g., drunk or verbally or physically combative); medical treatment received while in custody; a full description of the subject, including scars, marks, and tattoos; criminal history; employment and home addresses; aliases used; and an inventory of the personal effects seized by jailers during the in-processing. In particular, the personal effects may provide useful information. Among personal possession items often found are matchbooks, Zig Zag paper, condoms, business cards for the subject (and from his associates or people he recently met), foreign currency, identity and credit cards in several different names, scraps of paper with telephone numbers on them, and various types of lists. Such items may suggest places the subject habituates or recently visited, possible personal habits and associates, identify countries recently visited, or connect him to other crimes. In one case, an investigator went to the jail to interview a subject arrested for stabbing a man in a bar. Among the subject's personal possessions was a real estate card from a woman murdered several days previously. Although the man initially denied knowing the woman or being in the area where she was killed, he finally admitted to the crime after being confronted with the real estate card.

Field Interview Information Reports

A **field interview/information report (FIR)** is shown in Figure 7-7. Such reports are filled out when patrolling officers identify persons or vehicles that are suspicious to them but are not connected with any particular offense. These cards can establish whether a suspect was in the immediate area of a crime, how he or she was dressed at the time, what vehicle the suspect had access to, and who else was in the vehicle. On rare occasions, FIR cards have proved to be a suspect's best alibi witness.

Impounded Vehicle Inventory Report

If a suspect is arrested while driving a vehicle, the vehicle is inventoried and towed to an impoundment lot. Articles that appear on the inventory list may or may not have a relationship to the case. Moreover, the impounding officer may not recognize their significance, as can be the case with common tools that have been modified for use in burglaries. Thus, the impounding report should be carefully read. Under most circumstances, a follow-up investigator cannot search a car after it has been impounded without a search warrant issued on a showing of probable cause.

Traffic Citations

As with FIR cards, traffic citations can link suspects to the vehicles they register and drive, as well as those to which they may have access. Access to the vehicles of others usually denotes a special relationship and may help identify girlfriends or boyfriends, criminal associates, relatives, or operators of particular kinds of businesses, such as used-car and scrap-metal firms. Traffic citations can also pinpoint where the operator was at a particular date and time. Occasionally, FIR cards are also written during traffic stops, so these two sources of information are immediately associated.

GUIDELINES FOR CONDUCTING PHOTO AND LIVE LINEUPS

Juries attach great significance to lineup identification of suspects by witnesses. Yet every investigator and anyone who reads the newspaper knows that such identifications have led to miscarriages of justice. Because of the importance and perils of lineup identifications, investigators must carefully observe appropriate guidelines. Sometimes, as the following case history shows, this requires some effort:

A cab driver reported to the police that he had been robbed by one of his passengers. The cab driver made the report immediately after the suspect had fled on foot with the money. The driver reported that the suspect was a black male, approximately 25 years old, 6 feet 6 inches tall, 285 pounds, armed with a large chrome-plated semiautomatic pistol. The man was wearing an orange shirt, blue jeans, and a cowboy hat. Exactly $52 in cash had been taken. Approximately 1 hour after the crime was reported, the suspect was observed in the vicinity of the robbery by the same two officers who had taken the original report. The suspect was arrested by the police officers. A search produced a chrome-plated .45-caliber semiautomatic pistol and $52.12.

In their effort to conduct a lineup, the officers realized that they could not possibly find five people who approximated the suspect in size, race, age, attire, and so forth. The officers decided to use a photo lineup instead of a live lineup. They had a black-and-white photo taken of the suspect, minus the cowboy hat, and incorporated it into a packet of five other photos of similar black males. The cab driver was able to positively identify the photo of the suspect, who subsequently confessed to the crime.

FRONT

SPRINGFIELD POLICE DEPARTMENT FIELD INFORMATION

Data: _____ Time: _____   FIR #: _____

Stopped/Seen at: _____ Beat: _____

Subject #1:

Name: _____ Address: _____

Sex: ____ Race: ____ Age: ____ DOB: ____ Hgt: ____ Wgt: ____ Hair: ____ Eyes: ____

Tattoos/Misc Description: _____

Subject #2:

Name: _____ Address: _____

Sex: ____ Race: ____ Age: ____ DOB: ____ Hgt: ____ Wgt: ____ Hair: ____ Eyes: ____

Tattoos/Misc Description: _____

Subject #3:

Name: _____ Address: _____

Sex: ____ Race: ____ Age: ____ DOB: ____ Hgt: ____ Wgt: ____ Hair: ____ Eyes: ____

Tattoos/Misc Description: _____

BACK

Vehicle Color (top/bottom): _____ Year: _____

Make: _____ Model: _____ Style: _____

License Number _____ License Year: _____ State: _____

Misc. Description: _____

Reason for stop: _____

List Suspicious Activity/Admitted or Known Criminal History/Gang Activity:

_____

_____

_____

_____

_____

_____

_____

Officer/ DSN: _____ Supervisor: _____
                    Signature   Initial

◀ FIGURE 7-7   Field interview/ information report (FIR) card (Courtesy of Springfield, Missouri, Police Department)

Lineups may be conducted in a variety of ways, such as by showing witnesses individual photos sequentially or having them view all photos simultaneously. Likewise, participants in live lineups may appear sequentially or may all appear simultaneously. The trend in recent years has been to use photo lineups rather than live lineups owing to the problems inherent in the latter, but if a department does use live lineups, the following guidelines, procedures, and forms will work, although they are not a substitute for local legal advice.[2]

Following these guidelines enhances the possibility of a successful prosecution; conversely, shortcomings could cause lineup identification evidence to be ruled as inadmissible.

Conducting the Identification Procedure

The purpose of the identification procedure is to conduct the lineup in a consistent manner in order to ensure accuracy, reliability, fairness, and objectivity in the witness's identification. To do so, the person administering the process:

1. Must receive confirmation from the witness that he or she understands the process.
2. Must avoid doing or saying anything that might influence the witness.
3. Must not say anything about the witness's selection before obtaining the witness's statement of certainty.

4. Should encourage the witness to carefully consider his or her comments before responding to media contacts for the witness's own safety and to avoid the possibility that spontaneous or poorly thought out statements will impede the prosecution.

General Guidelines for Photo and Live Lineups

1. Care must be taken to ensure that the suspect does not unduly stand out, but complete uniformity of features is not required.
2. Whenever possible, the primary investigator should not be the person conducting the lineup, since he or she might give inadvertent verbal or body-language cues.
3. Witnesses should be instructed before the lineup that the suspect may not be in the lineup and that they should not feel compelled to make an identification.

Procedures for Photo Lineups

1. Include only one suspect in each identification procedure.
2. Select "fillers" (nonsuspects) who generally match the witness's description of the perpetrator. If the witness has provided a limited or "inadequate" description or if the description of the perpetrator differs significantly from the appearance of the suspect, fillers should resemble the suspect in significant features.
3. If multiple photos of the suspect are available, use the one made closest to the time that the crime was committed.
4. Lineups should include a minimum of five fillers.
5. If there are multiple witnesses, consider placing the suspect in a different position each time a lineup is shown to a witness.
6. If a new suspect is developed, avoid using fillers who were used in a previous lineup for the same witness.
7. Make sure that no writing or information about the suspect's previous criminal history can be seen by the witness.
8. Before the witness views the lineup, check again to make sure that the suspect does not unduly stand out.
9. Record the presentation order of the lineup and handle the original photographs as evidence.
10. Write a supplemental report that chronologically describes what happened; include the identification of all lineup participants, the names of all persons at the lineup, and the date and time it was conducted.

Procedures for Live Lineups

1. Apply the procedures listed earlier, which are not photo-lineup specific.

2. Use a minimum of four fillers or nonsuspects.
3. Document the lineup by photo or video, and handle this record as evidence.

Recording Identification Results

Some information about documenting lineup procedures was discussed earlier in this section. In addition, the following steps should be taken:

1. Check to make sure that all signatures needed on the various forms are complete.
2. Collect the information needed for completing standard forms before conducting the lineup.
3. If another witness will have contact with any photographs or forms, make sure that the previous witness has not put any marks or comments on them.
4. Include in the supplemental report a record of both identification and nonidentification results, as well as any statements about how sure or unsure the witnesses are.

Automated Photo Lineups

Photo lineups that are automated by computer must comply with the guidelines presented throughout this section. Once the witness's description has been entered, the computer searches the database of suspects and persons to locate those with similar features, scars, birthmarks, tattoos, ages, weights, and other characteristics. When the selection of the lineup is complete, it can be displayed in color or black and white on the screen for the witness to view or can be printed on paper for the witness. Automated lineup systems automatically generate much of the information needed for record keeping.

SPECIAL TECHNIQUES AND RESOURCES

Surveillance

While some think of **surveillance** as "following," it actually means the continued observance of people, places, and things to obtain information of investigative significance. Most frequently surveillance is covert, although there may be occasions when it is made obvious in an attempt to spook subjects into making mistakes. Surveillance is often broken into two types: physical and technical. Physical surveillance is personally done by one or more members of a surveillance team. Technical surveillance involves the use of various advanced technologies including automatic vehicle tracking, pinhole cameras, acoustic, ultrasonic, thermal image scanning, parabolic microphones, radio frequency (RF) bugs, and wiretaps. The balance of this section is devoted to physical surveillance.

Purposes of Surveillance

Physical surveillance is carried out by people; it may be stationary/fixed/static or "rolling." At its simplest, it is done on foot, but it can also use cars, motorcycles, fixed-wing and rotary aircraft, boats, and rental apartments and offices. The purposes of surveillance include:

1. Establishing the existence of a crime.
2. Obtaining probable cause for a search warrant application.
3. Apprehending suspects as they commit a crime.
4. Identifying the associates of criminals and the places they frequent.
5. Determining the reliability of informants.
6. Providing protection for undercover officers and informants.
7. Locating people, places, and things.
8. Gathering intelligence about targets and premises prior to serving a warrant.
9. Gathering intelligence on the activities of illegal groups and gangs.
10. Preventing a crime by signaling police awareness of specific subjects.

Planning and Preparing for Surveillance Operations

Departmental policies, including the applicable legal guidelines, drive how the surveillance is conducted. In smaller agencies, investigators may have to do their own surveillance; in larger ones, there will be a unit with a title such as technical services to whom the work is "farmed out" or assigned.

Planning the intelligence means making sure that the appropriate equipment is available (see Figure 7-8) and safety and security measures are reviewed (see Figure 7-9). Many investigators have been assaulted, wounded, and killed during operations, so risks must be assessed and the need for vigilance by all team members must be stressed. Additionally, all members of the team should be carefully briefed on such factors as:[3]

1. The facts in the case.
2. Surveillance objectives.
3. Warnings about the subject, including any known drug use and possession of weapons.
4. The subject's previous experience with surveillance, whether he/she might be surveillance conscious, and if surveillance countermeasures may be used against the team.

Surveillance Kit Checklist

- Department two-way radio.
- Handheld portable radio with harness and fully charged spare battery.
- Mobile phone.
- Still camera with telephoto lens, adequate supply of film or other removable medium, and spare battery.
- Video camera with supply of tapes and extra battery.
- Stabilizing device, such as a portable tripod.
- Binoculars and portable infrared or thermal-imaging devices.
- Detailed road maps for the area.
- Compass or Global Positioning System receiver.
- Flashlight with extra batteries.
- Change of clothing with props, such as hats, to alter appearance, and other personal items, including toiletries.
- Food and water in a cooler.
- Cash, including coins to use at toll lanes requiring exact change, and toll passes.
- Extra set of car keys.
- Towels and glass cleaner.
- Equipment gear bag to hold preceding items.

◄ **FIGURE 7-8 Surveillance kit checklist**
(Source: John T. Nason, "Conducting Surveillance Operations," FBI Law Enforcement Bulletin, Vol. 73, No. 5, May 2004, p. 3)

Safety and Security Measures

- During a mobile surveillance, do not take unnecessary risks to keep up with a subject speeding, running red lights, or otherwise driving recklessly.
- While stationary, keep the vehicle windows closed and the doors locked.
- Regularly scan rear view mirrors to observe anyone or any activity to the rear.
- Alert other team members to any suspicious or unusual persons or activity in the area.
- In high-crime areas and in hours of darkness, remain in a heightened state of alert.
- Position vehicle to enable a rapid response to assist others if needed.
- Ensure vehicle has emergency equipment lights, siren, and first-aid kit.
- Keep identification, weapon, and ballistic vest accessible.
- Know and use challenge, password, and other appropriate safety measures to prevent friendly fire situation from developing.
- When leaving a vehicle to go on foot surveillance, fully secure the vehicle and equipment inside.

◄ **FIGURE 7-9 Surveillance safety and security checklist**
(Source: John T. Nason, "Conducting Surveillance Operations," FBI Law Enforcement Bulletin, Vol. 73, No. 5, May 2004, p. 6)

5. Personal data about the subject, with photo, criminal history, associates, the vehicles of the subject and associates, locations the subject is known to visit, and whether the subject possesses unusual skills or abilities, such as being a martial arts practitioner or weightlifter.
6. Communication protocols for the team and their roles (e.g., photographer), and the keeper of the chronological surveillance log.
7. Prior to the surveillance, which investigator should be sent into the area to assess conditions and to identify the "eye" or central observation point.

Termination of Surveillance Operations

There must be a periodic evaluation of whether a surveillance should be continued or terminated that includes the following considerations:

1. Have other cases arisen in which the use of surveillance is a better allocation of resources?
2. Is the operation providing important ongoing intelligence and evidence?
3. Does the continuation of the surveillance outweigh the increased risk of detection?
4. Can other investigative techniques or technical surveillance do the job at least as effectively?
5. Are there indicators that suggest threats to the team's safety?

Informants

Informants are people who provide information of investigative significance to investigators. They may expect to be paid, to receive consideration on charges pending against them or family members, or they may do it for some similar reasons. They may also be designated as confidential informants; some departments have adopted the term "cooperating individual" for them. Police policies generally identify activities that investigators should refrain from with informants. This includes socializing with them, becoming romantically involved, paying an informant without a witness, entering into a business relationship with them, accepting gifts, gratuities, or money from them, and loaning them money or accepting a loan from them.

An informant file, to which there is restricted access, consists of a recent photo of the informant, a complete informant sheet providing detailed information about him/her, copies of warrants and NCIC, and other checks, including a criminal history, copies of cases in which the informant is a defendant, and debriefing reports after each time he or she is, which may be both of investigative and intelligence importance.

Policies also restrict who may be used as informants and determine whose use requires special approval. Typically, restrictions apply to persons under 18 years of age, those who have been previously used and were not reliable, former drug-dependent individuals, and those on federal or state probation or parole, which may require the approval of a judicial official.

As a practical matter, some officers run their own low-level informants, paying them out of pocket for their information or otherwise helping them. On the one hand, this is practical and works, but it violates policy. On the other hand, an officer could be lured into a trap when the informant is squeezed by a criminal. If the officer is killed, the department has to work the case in ignorance of the existence of the informant.

Relying too often on informants results in the possibility of the investigator unintentionally "burning" the informant, against whom criminals may retaliate. Such incidents make other sources dry up and make it harder to recruit top-flight informants for a period. Thus, informants should be treated as a resource and used as sparingly as possible, which also helps avoid the informant "playing" the investigator.

Facial Recognition Software

Facial recognition software began being deployed during the 1990s and has continued to be refined and updated. Such programs compare video and photographs with known subjects to make identifications for such purposes as identifying suspects, as well as wanted and missing persons. This capability can be deployed at airports and other public transportation centers, sporting events, nightclubs, and other places. One test was conducted at the 2001 Super Bowl in Tampa, where 19 people wanted on warrants were identified soon after they walked past video cameras.

Facial recognition software, such as FACEngine and Identix, operates by measuring the relationship between more than 80 points on an unknown person's face and comparing the results with a computer database. In terms of present investigative practices in the field, a camera is attached to a handheld computer, and when a subject's photo is taken, the comparison is made. As databases continue to grow, people who provide false identification or refuse to give the police their name can be identified. In a growing number of states, such as Colorado, Rhode Island, Oklahoma, Delaware, and North Carolina, applicants for driver's licenses are processed using this technology to fight identity theft and to prevent people who have suspended driver's licenses from getting a license in another name. It is also being used in homeland security efforts, such as at border-crossing stations. The claimed error rate for facial recognition software is 3% however, additional studies of this technology are still needed.

FUSION CENTERS, INTELLIGENCE UNITS, AND ANALYTICAL TECHNOLOGIES

Fusion Centers

Following 9/11, it was widely concluded that if the isolated parcels of information known about the terrorists

▲ FIGURE 7-10   Fusion center
(Courtesy Office of the Governor of Kentucky, Kentucky Office of Homeland Security)

and their activities before the attacks had been pooled and analyzed, then the attacks may have been disrupted, mitigated, or prevented. As part of the overall response, **fusion centers** (FCs), staffed by multiple federal, state, and local agencies, the private sector, and in some instances tribal personnel, have been created across the nation. (See Figures 7-10, 7-11, and 7-12.) Fusion is defined as turning information and intelligence into actionable knowledge; it is the fundamental process by which homeland security and crime-related information and intelligence are shared.[4] The importance of this is illustrated by local officers in Maryland who stopped a car in 2004 after they saw a woman videotaping the structure of the Chesapeake Bay Bridge; after running her name through the National Crime Information Center and a Terrorist Screening Center, they learned she was wanted in Chicago in connection with an investigation of Hamas.[5]

Fusion centers are more than intelligence centers or computer networks in that the fusion process supports the implementation of prevention, response, and consequence management programs (Figure 7-13).[6] The essence of FCs is the constant merging, analysis, and dissemination of information and data from many disparate sources, including hospitals and the epidemiological monitoring capabilities of the Centers for Disease Control; this information is used both tactically and strategically for homeland security and crime-fighting purposes.

There is some consistency, such as the use of the same lexicons, and also some variety in how fusion centers are organized and where they are placed organizationally, e.g., within a state's department of homeland security versus within a state police agency. The services and products of FCs include target identification, visual investigative, financial, association, link, critical infrastructure, telephone-toll, case pattern and network analysis, event charting, threat assessments, and intelligence reports and briefings.[7] FCs have resulted in a convergence of crime analysis and intelligence to produce real-time, immediately actionable information. The concentration of information has alarmed some civil libertarians concerned about abuses, and at the state level there is some sentiment that the federal government's intelligence contributions need to be more timely and substantial. It is predictable that issues will arise in an effort of such magnitude, and all such issues deserve the serious consideration they merit. It is also clear that if the fusion center concept continues to be carefully implemented, it will be a major enhancement to our national security and crime-reduction capabilities.

Criminal Intelligence Units

Police departments are making greater use of intelligence-led policing, which can be used in conjunction with other philosophies, such as community policing.[8] Intelligence-led policing fundamentally means that police resources are directed toward problems identified or confirmed by intelligence analysis. The use of intelligence-led policing requires changing the mission and capabilities of traditional intelligence units, such as adding full-time trained analysts or creating separate analytical units.

The analysis needs of police agencies are so vast that even with a central analytical unit, analysis is ongoing throughout operational units, albeit without the sophistication of trained and experienced analysts using various software packages.

Intelligence Files

Intelligence consists of pieces of raw information that when collected, evaluated, collated, and analyzed form meaningful and useful judgments that are both timely and accurate.[9] Two ways of thinking about intelligence files are as categories of intelligence and as specific types of files.

In terms of categories of intelligence, there are at least four different types:

- **Indicative intelligence,** which focuses on emerging and new criminal developments. It may include

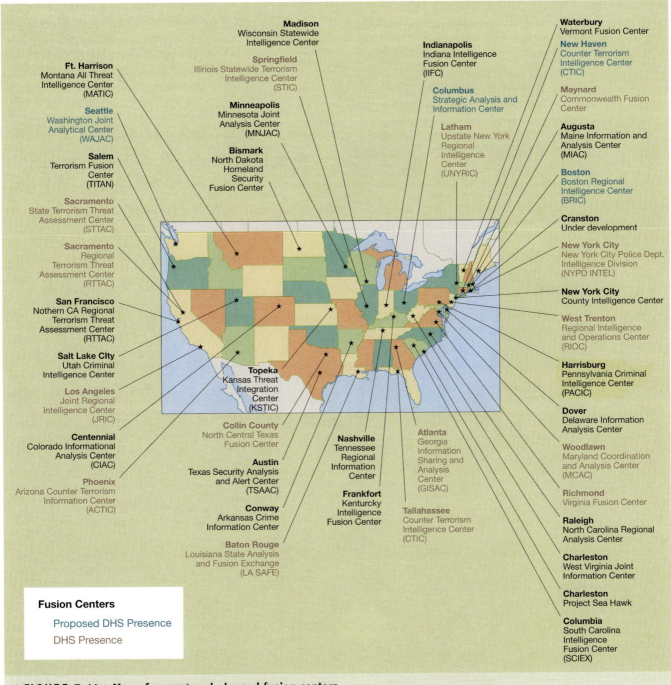

Ft. Harrison
Montana All Threat
Intelligence Center
(MATIC)

Seattle
Washington Joint
Analytical Center
(WAJAC)

Salem
Terrorism Fusion
Center
(TITAN)

Sacramento
State Terrorism Threat
Assessment Center
(STTAC)

Sacramento
Regional
Terrorism Threat
Assessment Center
(RTTAC)

San Francisco
Nothern CA Regional
Terrorism Threat
Assessment Center
(RTTAC)

Salt Lake City
Utah Criminal
Intelligence Center

Los Angeles
Joint Regional
Intelligence Center
(JRIC)

Centennial
Colorado Informational
Analysis Center
(CIAC)

Phoenix
Arizona Counter Terrorism
Information Center
(ACTIC)

Madison
Wisconsin Statewide
Intelligence Center

Springfield
Illinois Statewide Terrorism
Intelligence Center
(STIC)

Minneapolis
Minnesota Joint
Analysis Center
(MNJAC)

Bismark
North Dakota
Homeland
Security
Fusion Center

Topeka
Kansas Threat
Integration
Center
(KSTIC)

Collin County
North Central Texas
Fusion Center

Austin
Texas Security Analysis
and Alert Center
(TSAAC)

Conway
Arkansas Crime
Information Center

Baton Rouge
Louisiana State Analysis
and Fusion Exchange
(LA SAFE)

Indianapolis
Indiana Intelligence
Fusion Center
(IIFC)

Columbus
Strategic Analysis and
Information Center

Latham
Upstate New York
Regional
Intelligence
Center
(UNYRIC)

Nashville
Tennessee
Regional
Information
Center

Frankfort
Kenturcky
Intelligence
Fusion Center

Atlanta
Georgia
Information
Sharing and
Analysis
Center
(GISAC)

Tallahassee
Counter Terrorism
Intelligence Center
(CTIC)

Waterbury
Vermont Fusion Center

New Haven
Counter Terrorism
Intelligence Center
(CTIC)

Maynard
Commonwealth Fusion
Center

Augusta
Maine Information and
Analysis Center
(MIAC)

Boston
Boston Regional
Intelligence Center
(BRIC)

Cranston
Under development

New York City
New York City Police Dept.
Intelligence Division
(NYPD INTEL)

New York City
County Intelligence Center

West Trenton
Regional Intelligence
and Operations Center
(RIOC)

Harrisburg
Pennsylvania Criminal
Intelligence Center
(PACIC)

Dover
Delaware Information
Analysis Center

Woodlawn
Maryland Coordination
and Analysis Center
(MCAC)

Richmond
Virginia Fusion Center

Raleigh
North Carolina Regional
Analysis Center

Charleston
West Virginia Joint
Information Center

Charleston
Project Sea Hawk

Columbia
South Carolina
Intelligence
Fusion Center
(SCIEX)

Fusion Centers

Proposed DHS Presence

DHS Presence

▲ **FIGURE 7-11** **Map of current and planned fusion centers**

(Source: Todd Masse, Siobhan O'Neil, and John Rollins, *Fusion Centers: Issues and Options for Congress* [Washington, D.C.: Congressional Research Service, July 6, 2007], p. CRS-93)

both fragmentary and impossible-to-immediately-substantiate information, as well as hard facts. Examples of this type of information are plans to manufacture a new and more potent illicit drug, reports of an unnamed criminal ring that is seeking inside information on armored-car schedules, and anonymous reports that a mysterious group is accumulating explosives.

- **Tactical intelligence,** which implies immediate action and can lead to arrests and the collection of additional information. Tactical intelligence is illustrated by information derived from electronic or physical surveillance, as well as that provided by confidential informants. It may also be generated from the analytical and investigative tools discussed later in this chapter.

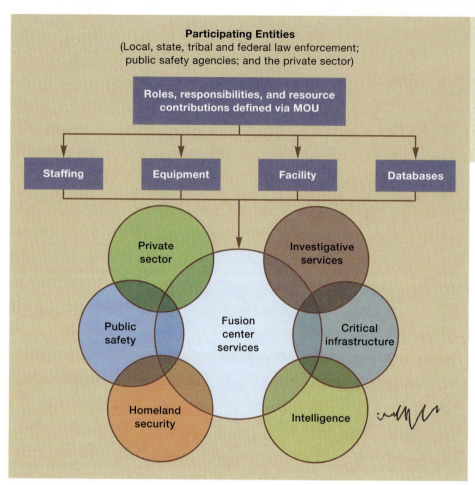

Participating Entities
(Local, state, tribal and federal law enforcement; public safety agencies; and the private sector)

◄ **FIGURE 7-12   Fusion center components**
A "MOU" is a memorandum of understanding. (Source: Department of Justice, Department of Homeland Security and Global Justice Information Sharing Initiative, *Fusion Center Guidelines* [Washington, D.C.: July 2005] p. 16)

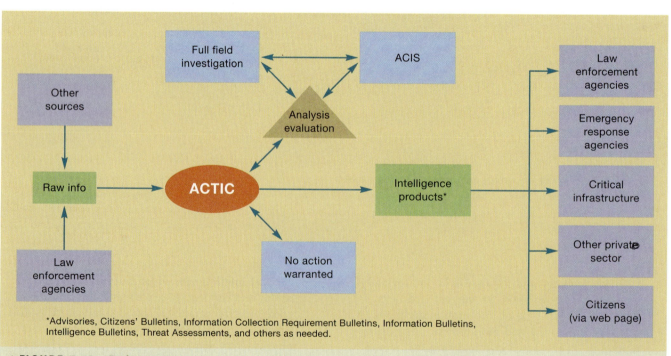

*Advisories, Citizens' Bulletins, Information Collection Requirement Bulletins, Information Bulletins, Intelligence Bulletins, Threat Assessments, and others as needed.

▲ **FIGURE 7-13   Fusion center**
Information flow for the Arizona Counter Terrorism Information Center (ACTIC). "ACIS" is the Arizona Criminal Investigation System.

- **Strategic intelligence,** which is gathered and analyzed over time and usually confirms new or newly discovered patterns of criminal activity. Some strategic intelligence accumulates from indicative and tactical intelligence. For instance, there may be rumors on the street of a new major fencing operation (indicative intelligence), and a burglary suspect may subsequently be arrested who trades information about the fence for favorable sentencing (tactical information). The resultant investigation produces strategic intelligence, which may then lead to an arrest of the fence and those with whom the fence does business.
- **Evidential intelligence,** which consists of factual, precise information that can be presented in court. Its use is determined by the needs of the investigative unit, not the intelligence unit. Evidential intelligence can be used in preparing tactical and strategic assessments, as well as in deciding which investigative techniques can best be employed.[10]

The specific types of intelligence files maintained by an agency are largely determined by the agency's mission and resources. In turn, this determination affects the nature of the information available to the investigator. Among the common types of files in intelligence units are modus operandi (MO) files, moniker or nickname files, threat-assessment files, and violator file summaries (target-identification files). The last type of file is a summary of all available data on a suspected or known violator. If the resources of the agency allow such files to be current, an investigator can learn a great deal about a suspect fairly quickly, because these files include the following data:

- Name
- Physical description
- Date of birth
- Place of birth
- AKA ("also known as") names
- Social Security number
- FBI number
- Vehicles registered to
- Telephone number
- Real estate owned
- Associates
- History
- Methods of operation
- Geographic area
- Interested agencies
- Supporting documentation
- Driver's license number
- State Bureau of Criminal Identification number
- Miscellaneous criminal number
- Last known address
- Employer or business
- Utilities paid

- Photographs
- Criminal activity involved in
- Violence potential and patterns
- Other interested agencies[11]

THE INTELLIGENCE/ ANALYTICAL CYCLE

The **intelligence/analytical cycle** is driven by the needs of the client or end-user, who, for purposes of illustration, may be the commander of a task force working a serial-murder case or the supervisor of an investigation unit trying to find a pattern in a string of violent convenience-store robberies (see Figure 7-14). It is the end-user who specifies the types of information he or she wants, and it is the responsibility of the intelligence unit to make sure that the end-user understands both the possibilities and the limitations of the intelligence process and its techniques. As depicted in Figure 7-14, the backbone of the intelligence/analytical cycle is a continuous six-step process,[12] which is discussed next.

1. Planning and Direction

The intelligence/analytical process must be managed throughout, from identifying the focus of the intelligence effort to delivering the finished product to the police unit requesting it.[13] Planning and direction is the beginning of the intelligence cycle, because it involves identifying a focus and specific data collection procedures, as well as processing, analysis, and dissemination requirements. As a practical matter, finished intelligence often creates new questions during the reevaluation stage, which starts the process all over again.

2. Collection

Collection is the gathering and managing of raw data, which is then analyzed to produce the finished product.[14] To be effective, collection must be planned, focused, and directed. There are many sources of information, including law enforcement and open-source records. Included in agency-generated sources are incident and supplemental investigations; field interview cards; traffic citations; undercover and informant records; criminal and driving histories; neighborhood- and vehicle-canvass results; photographic files; facial composites of suspects; previously prepared analytical reports; and files on known and active offenders. Similar types of data are accessible from other departments and available regionally and nationally through various types of databases, including that of the National Crime Information Center. Such sources are considered to be *restricted,* since they are generally not for use outside law enforcement.

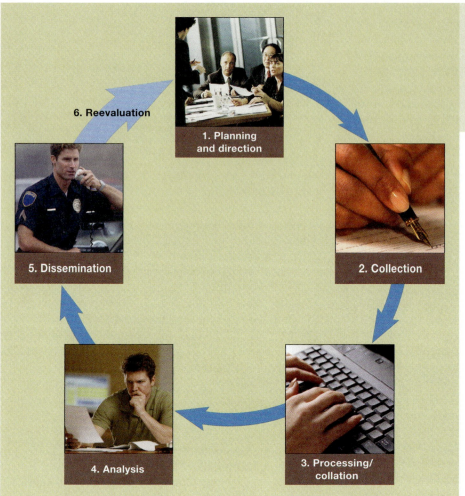

◄**FIGURE 7-14** **The intelligence cycle**
(Source: U.S. Department of Justice, Department of Homeland Security, and The Global Justice Information Sharing Initiative, *Fusion Center Guidelines* [Washington, D.C.: July 2005], p. 26)

Another broad category of information sources is called *open sources*, which means anyone can access them, either for free or for a fee. Included in this category are public records such as births, deaths, divorces, credit histories, news media reports, many periodicals and books, government reports, and annual corporate filings that state where a business is located and who occupies which leadership positions in it. The value of open-source information is indicated by the fact that the FBI made a budget request of $4.5 million for it in one year.[15]

Accessing some sources of information, such as bank, hotel, taxicab, e-mail, travel agency, public utility, and student records, may require some type of legal process.

3. Processing

In processing, raw information from all sources is converted into a form that can be used by analysts.[16] This is accomplished by information management, which is the indexing, sorting, and organizing of raw data into files for rapid retrieval. It includes entering the data into a computer, checking the entries for accuracy, and collating paper files. One of the key considerations in processing is ensuring that the data-processing methods fit the analytical techniques that will be used.

4. Analysis and Production

In the analysis and production step, the data that have been processed are translated into a finished intelligence product.[17] This includes integrating, collating, evaluating, and analyzing all the data, some of which may be fragmented and contradictory. Through analysis of the data, the value of intelligence work increases. Analysts, who are subject-matter specialists (e.g., organized crime, gangs, or terrorists), carefully scrutinize the data for timeliness, reliability, validity, and relevance. The role of the analyst is to combine the data and his or her analysis and judgment into a finished intelligence product that informs the end-user of the analyst's assessment of events and the implications of that assessment (see Figure 7-15). Methods of analysis are discussed later in this chapter.

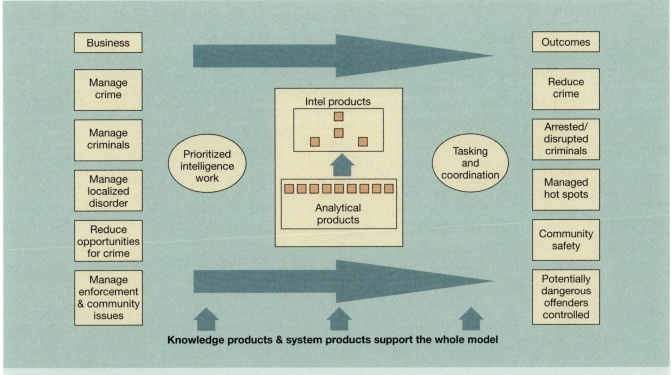

▲ **FIGURE 7-15   The product model**

(Source: Marilyn B. Peterson, Bob Morehouse, and Richard Wright, eds., *Intelligence 2000: Revising the Basic Elements* [New Jersey: International Association of Law Enforcement Analysts, 2000], p. 20)

5. Dissemination

The fifth element in the cycle is the dissemination of the finished intelligence report to the end-user who requested it.[18] The end-user can then make decisions or take actions on the basis of the intelligence provided.

6. Reevalauation

It is crucial that the end-user provide feedback about the value of the intelligence so that there can be an ongoing cycle of improvement. Moreover, the finished intelligence report itself, the decisions made, and the actions taken all have the potential to create new questions that lead back to the first element, planning and direction, thus beginning a new intelligence/analytical cycle.

ANALYTICAL AND INVESTIGATIVE TOOLS

To some extent, distinctions among crime, intelligence, and investigative analyses are artificial for three reasons: (1) all three share some common analytical techniques; (2) "intelligence" is simply information that has been processed; and (3) by concentrating on their differences, their commonalities are obscured.[19] Therefore, this section deals with a number of analytical techniques employed in police departments without pigeonholing them into one analysis type or another.

Crime Analysis

Crime analysis is the process of using systematic analytical methods to acquire timely and pertinent information on crime patterns and trend correlations.[20] There are a number of crime analysis software packages that can generate investigative leads from databases, such as the Automated Tactical Analysis of Crime (ATAC) and COPLINK. Crime analysis has also profited from the application of **geographic information systems (GIS)** to plot and to analyze crime on maps.

Googlemaps are being used by police agencies and citizen "watchdog" groups to make information about crime to the community, such as plotting where sexual predators are living. Some mapping systems allow you to drag a computer cursor along a street route, and the numbers and types of crimes, usually for only the previous 90 days, appear. Although not strictly a crime analysis technique, **COMPSTAT,** shortened from "computer statistics," is an accountability system pioneered during 1994 in the New York City Police Department, which

TABLE 7-1	Types of Crime Analysis
TYPE	**DESCRIPTION**
Tactical	Deals with recent offenses (e.g., immediate, to hours, days, or weeks) for the purpose of responding quickly to specific crimes; it provides uniformed officers and investigators with timely information (e.g., investigative leads) to guide their actions and apprehend offenders. Attempts to forecast where the next specific (e.g., burglary) crime will occur.
Strategic	Focuses on solving ongoing crime problems (months, quarters, or years) by matching police resources with crime, demands for service, and other variables.
Administrative	For police administrators, elected and appointed city and county officials, and others: analyzes crime, demographic, economic, geographic, and other factors on a long-range basis (quarterly, semi-annually, or even multiyear) with respect to how they interact with one another. The information may be used in annual reports, policy-making grant applications, and for other related purposes.

(Source: Synthesized from Crime Analysis Unit, "Types of Crime Analysis," Bernalillo County, New Mexico, Sheriff's Office, September 10, 2007, www.bernco.gov, and Crime Analyst, "Three Types of Crime Analysis," North Miami Police Department, September 10, 2007, www.northmiamipolice.com)

makes police managers accountable for controlling crime conditions in their precincts through regular meetings with their superiors. Widely adopted nationally since its inception, COMPSTAT is supported by a variety of crime analysis data and mapping information.

The three general types of crime analysis are summarized in Table 7-1. Discussed next are some of the specific elements analysts focus on to link crimes:[21]

- *Trends:* **Trends** are general tendencies in the occurrence of crime across large geographic areas over extended periods of time. They arise when areas become, for any number of reasons, more conducive or less conducive to a particular crime or crimes. Trends can be associated with shifts in demography; for example, as a neighborhood ages, its residents are seen as soft targets for muggings and home-invasion robberies. Trends can also stem from the creation of new targets; for instance, the presence of a new shopping mall increases the opportunities for shoplifting and thefts from, and of, vehicles. Although the same locations or victims may be repeatedly selected in a trend, there are usually multiple perpetrators.
- *Patterns:* In a **pattern,** the same crime is committed repeatedly over a short period of time, sometimes, but not always, by the same offender. For example, outside a five-star restaurant, female patrons who are leaving have their purses snatched; or, as students return to campus in the fall, the number of laptop thefts from dormitories rises.
- *Series:* In a **series,** the same type of crime is committed over a short period of time, probably by the same offender. For instance, in an affluent, gated residential community of 73 houses, six burglaries occur in nine days; two days later, a rape-burglary occurs when the victim enters her home while the perpetrator is still inside; and three days after that,

there is an aggravated assault-burglary when the victim awakes and discovers the offender leaving with his valuable coin collection.
- *Sprees:* In a **spree,** the same type of offense is committed at almost the same time by the same offender(s). An example is the vandalizing of cars by a group of kids who spray-paint license plates while walking through a neighborhood.
- *Hot spots:* A **hot spot** is a location where various crimes are committed on a regular basis, usually by different perpetrators. An example is a bar where underage drinkers are served, there are numerous fights, user-level drug sales take place, prostitution flourishes, and patrons are occasionally mugged, robbed, or carjacked in the parking lot (see Figure 7-16).
- *Crimogens:* A **crimogen** is either an individually known offender who is responsible for a large number of crimes or one victim who reports a large number of crimes. Examples include a career criminal and a convenience-store operator who reports gas drive-offs, shoplifting, robberies, assaults, and even thefts of entire ATM machines.

Crime Bulletins

One method by which crime analysts can disseminate information is through the publication of a series of **crime bulletins.** The frequency and extent of such bulletins are a function of how much time and other resources the analyst can devote to them. The most common crime bulletin is simply known as the "Daily Bulletin," and it is a chronological listing of reported crimes. Other bulletins are more specialized; for example:

1. Person crimes
2. Property crimes
3. Arrest information
4. Warrant and fugitive information (see Figure 7-17)

◀ **FIGURE 7-16 Hot blocks**
One way to see areas of interest larger than a "hot spot" is to highlight hot blocks, or areas where many incidents cluster. In this GIS map, auto thefts or recoveries occurred in tight groups. In the map, red spots indicate clusters of car thefts, and blue clusters represent recoveries.

◀ **FIGURE 7-17 A "wanted poster"**
(Courtesy FBI)

WANTED
BY THE FBI

UNLAWFUL FLIGHT TO AVOID PROSECUTION – ILLEGAL WIRE TAP
LORRIE JOHN TRITES

Aliases: L. John Trites, John Trites, John Morgan, "Buddy"

DESCRIPTION

Date of Birth Used:	November 19, 1961	**Hair:**	Brown
Place of Birth:	New Mexico	**Eyes:**	Brown
Height:	6'7"	**Sex:**	Male
Weight:	250 to 290 pounds	**Race:**	White
NCIC:	W150879142	**Nationality:**	American
Occupation:	Former swimming coach		
Scars and Marks:	None known		
Remarks:	Trites has ties to New Mexico, New Hampshire, New Jersey, Connecticut, Massachusetts, Florida, Canada, Trinidad, and the Bahamas. He may have facial hair. Trites is an avid swimmer and may be involved in some way with the swimming community.		

5. Probation and parole information
6. Most active criminals
7. Most wanted persons
8. Stolen autos
9. Crime series and trends
10. Suspicious activity
11. Field interviews
12. Sex offenders[22]

Crime bulletins containing sensitive information may be printed or available to members of the police department through the intranet. Bulletins of general interest to a community are increasingly appearing on the Internet.

Time-Event Charting

One of the most useful and quickly learned techniques for analyzing crime is creating a **time-event chart (TEC),** which displays events in chronological order. A simple time-event chart is shown in Figure 7-18; it depicts the major events involving an offender paroled from the state

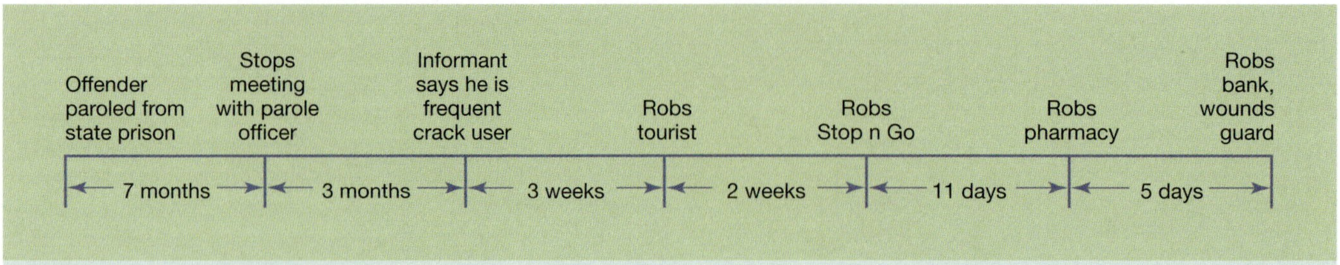

▲ **FIGURE 7-18** **Time-event chart**

prison. For seven months, he made his regularly scheduled meetings with his parole officer. Three months later, an informant described him as a frequent crack user. Three weeks after that, the parolee robbed a tourist. Over the next 30 days, he committed three more robberies, each time progressing upward to a more lucrative target. The choice of a pharmacy as a target gave him both money and drugs, which are the same as money on the streets. If he is selling drugs, informants may know of it. The interval between robberies is growing shorter, and the parolee has become violent. It is possible that he is pulling jobs while high, so the potential for further violence is great.

Link Analysis

Follow-up investigations often result in the accumulation of significant amounts of data. As a result, financial transactions, relationships, the importance of places, events, telephone calls, and other data can be obscured and their importance overlooked, resulting in an unnecessarily protracted or unsuccessful investigation. Link analysis, which can be combined with temporal analysis, can visually help to make sense out of the data. The leader in this market is i2, whose Analyst's Notebook analytical software for investigators is used by the FBI and numerous other enforcement agencies. Examples of link analyses are included in several crime-specific chapters.

Telephone Record Analysis

The most requested type of intelligence/analytical product is telephone toll, or record, analysis.[23] "**Telephone record analysis** is the compilation and review of telephone company, long-distance service, and/or dialed-number recorder information to show the strength and patterns of relationships between the subscriber and the numbers called."[24] It is particularly useful in conspiracy, drug, and organized-crime investigations, although it is routinely applied in many other types of investigations. Telephone record analysis consists of the following steps:

1. Collect the data to be analyzed from the targeted subscriber, including local and long-distance calls on home, business, car, and cell telephones, collect calls, and third-party calls (i.e., credit card or other calls billed to the subscriber in which the subscriber

is neither the number called to nor the number called from). With the approval of a court, a pen register/dialed-number recorder (DNR) can be used to gather additional information, such as the date a call is made, the time the call is made, the number called, and the duration of the call. For local calls, this information is usually not available from service providers, but cellular and digital companies make a record of such calls. Obtaining the records, however, requires a subpoena or some other type of legal sanction, and this increases the danger that the subscriber will learn of the investigative interest in him or her.

2. Determine the scope of the calls, including the dates they were made, the number of calls, and the dates between which the calls were made.
3. Establish the frequency of calls by date, day of week, and time made.
4. Count the frequency of calls to each number.
5. Add up the total amount of time spent on calls to each number.
6. Develop a primary listing of calls on the basis of the frequency determined in steps 3 and 4.
7. Analyze frequently called numbers for patterns (e.g., to particular countries). A number called at regular intervals and times may suggest that a subordinate is reporting to a superior or that illegal commodities, such as drugs, are being ordered from a supplier.
8. Prepare a report on the findings, including any recommendations for further investigative efforts.[25]

Assume that a known and reliable confidential informant tells the investigator that someone known to her only as "Crazy Joe" is putting together "a big drug deal." In the nickname files, there are records on 11 Crazy Joes. Eight of them are currently in prison, two of them are small-time felons, and the last one, Joseph "Crazy Joe" Barnes, has one conviction for drug trafficking. Subsequently, the informant picks Crazy Joe out of a photo lineup. An investigation is launched that includes getting the telephone records for the residence of Joseph Barnes, also known as (AKA) Crazy Joe.

Figure 7-19 is a link record for Crazy Joe's home telephone, 520-318-4475. It reveals that a total of 19 calls were

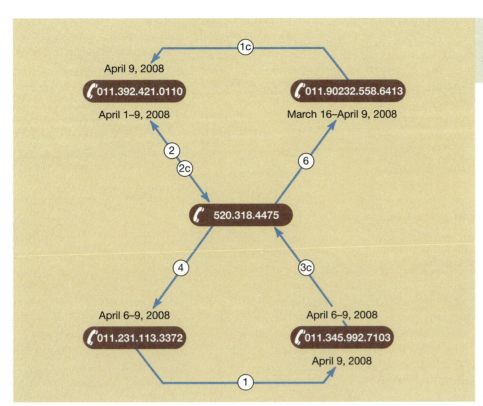

TABLE 7-2	Telephone Record Matrix for "Crazy Joe's" Home Telephone

	CALLS FROM:*				
CALLS TO:	**BARNES**	**MYSTIC**	**CASTLE**	**STANIC**	**FUENTES**
520-318-4475	0	0	2 c	0	3 c
Joseph Barnes residence, Tucson, Arizona					
011-90232-558-6413	6	0	0	0	0
Mystic Imports and Exports, Izmir, Turkey					
011-392-421-0110	2	1 c	0	0	0
Castle Virgin Oil Distributors, Milan, Italy					
011-231-113-3372	4	0	0	0	0
Stanic Charter, Bogota, Colombia					
011-345-992-7103	0	0	0	1	0
John Fuentes residence, Cayman Islands					
Total	12	1 c	2 c	1	3 c

*c [H11005] collect

made between March 16 and April 9, 2008. Of these, 17 were from 520-318-4475 or were made to that number by collect calls, establishing it as the central node. The 011 prefix identifies all 19 calls as being placed internationally. One interpretation of the pattern is that it indicates a period of negotiation between the central node and 011-90232-558-6413. The deal, which may be about a commodity exchange, appears to have been finalized on April 9, 2008. With minimal additional effort, the data shown in Table 7-2 are produced, providing numerous other leads to be investigated.

Criminal Profiling

"The process of inferring distinctive personality characteristics of individuals responsible for committing crimes has commonly been referred to as criminal **profiling**."[26] It is also known as behavioral, crime scene, criminal-personality, offender, and psychological profiling.[27] "There is currently a general lack of uniformity or agreement on the application of these terms to any one profiling method."[28] In general, profilers should, at a minimum, be well educated in logic and argument, sociology, psychology, criminalistics, and medico-legal death investigation.[29]

Criticisms of Profiling

Despite its successes, profiling as a field is not without its criticisms. Included in these criticisms are claims of using untrained or inadequately trained profilers, promising too much and delivering too little, relying on inadequate or dated databases, overstating the meaning of physical evidence, and engaging in racial profiling. Such criticism should be taken as a natural component of a discipline that is evolving as an important means for learning and making improvements. Any criticism should be evaluated with respect to the model to which it refers, the time period in which it was made, who the profiler was and his or her stage of development, and any possible motivations of the critic.

The Mad Bomber

Roughly speaking, criminal profiling has a history of about 50 years, with its most important milestones coming in the past quarter-century. Noteworthy among early events is the work of New York City criminal psychiatrist James Brussels on the "Mad Bomber" case. Between 1940 and 1956, with a "patriotic pause" during the years of World War II, the Mad Bomber left over 30 bombs in phone booths, public libraries, movie theaters, and other places.[30] Alarmed at the serious injuries created by a 1956 theater bombing, the police turned in desperation to Dr. Brussels for help. After reviewing all available information, including the Mad Bomber's letters to the newspapers, police, cinemas, and an electric company, Brussels produced the following profile:

> The mad bomber is male, middle-aged, meticulous, largely self-educated, Slavic, Roman Catholic, had an Oedipal Complex and lived in Connecticut . . . he worked for Consolidated Edison or one of its subsidiaries . . . The police would have to publicize the profile if the Mad Bomber was to be drawn out. When apprehended he will be wearing a buttoned double-breasted suit.[31]

The more publicity the Mad Bomber got, the more antagonized and arrogant he became. He eventually gave himself away through a published letter in which he

revealed details about his grievance against his former employer, Consolidated Edison.[32] When George P. Metesky was arrested in Waterbury, Connecticut, in 1957, he was wearing a buttoned double-breasted suit, and the other details in Brussels's profile were also eerily accurate.

Methods of Profiling

Because it was regarded as unconventional and its documented successes were isolated events, profiling did not make much progress for roughly 20 years after the apprehension of the Mad Bomber. However, during the 1970s, events began to unfold that led to the development of three approaches to criminal profiling: the organized/disorganized-offender model, investigative psychology, and behavioral evidence analysis.[33]

The Organized/Disorganized-Offender Model. The **organized/disorganized-offender model** was developed by the FBI. The bureau's initial efforts in profiling rest on the work of Agents Howard Teten and Pat Mullany, who in the late 1970s and early 1980s developed an applied criminology course that was taught throughout the country to state and local police officers.[34] The goal of the course was to promote a better understanding of criminal behavior in order to identify, arrest, and convict offenders.

After Teten left the Behavioral Science Unit (BSU), John Douglass and Robert Ressler were assigned to it in 1979. Over the next four years, these two agents and others undertook a large study that involved visiting prisons, interviewing offenders about their backgrounds and their crimes, and studying court records, including psychiatric reports. The data they collected and the conclusions they reached formed the basis of the organized/disorganized-offender model, a profiling method that is still used in many jurisdictions.[35] The organized/disorganized-offender dichotomy (see Table 7-3) has a strong crime scene focus (see Table 7-4). The model includes the six stages discussed next:

- *Stage 1: Collecting inputs:* Inputs are essential for accurate profiling.[36] The required information includes incident and supplemental reports, as well as detailed information about the crime scene, with any factors that may be relevant, such as weather conditions. Complete background data on the victim should cover domestic setting, employment, reputation, criminal history, habits, hobbies, physical condition, social conduct, and family relationships.[37] Complete forensic information is likewise needed, including the autopsy report (with toxicology and serology results), photographs of the wounds and the cleansed wounds,[38] and the medical examiner's conclusions and impressions about time of death, sequence of wounds, cause of death, and weapon used.[39]

TABLE 7-3   Profile Characteristics of Organized and Disorganized Murderers

ORGANIZED	DISORGANIZED
Average or above-average IQ	Below-average IQ
Socially adept	Socially inadequate, often never married, fearful of people, may have developed well-defined delusional system
Skilled-occupation employment history, but uneven work history, sometimes has jobs below abilities	Poor work history
Sexually competent	Sexually incompetent, may never have achieved sexual intimacy
High birth order in family, often first son	Low birth order in family
Father's work generally stable	Father's work history unstable
Parental discipline perceived by offender as inconsistent	Harsh parental discipline
May feel angry or depressed at time of crime, but reports himself as calm during it	Recurring obsessional and/or primitive thoughts, at time of crime is confused and distressed, acts impulsively under stress
May use alcohol prior to crime	Limited use of alcohol
Precipitating situational stress, e.g., financial, marital, relationships with females, and employment problems	Minimal situational stress
Usually living with partner	Lives alone or with parental figure
Likely to have car in good condition	Usually finds victims in his geographic area, lives in close proximity to scene
Follows crime in newspapers, clippings about crimes committed often found at offender's home, may take souvenirs from victim or scene	Little interest in news media

(Source: Robert Ressler, Ann W. Burgess, and John E. Douglas, *Sexual Homicides: Patterns and Motives* [New York: Free Press, 1992], pp. 121–122, 130)

- *Stage 2: Using decision process models:* This is the process of organizing and arranging the inputs into meaningful patterns.[40] It entails consideration of seven factors: homicide type and style, primary purpose of the murder (e.g., criminal enterprise or sexual?), victim risk (such as slight physical stature), offender risk (e.g., was the victim seized from a crowded street at midday or plucked from a bar's nearly empty parking lot at 4 A.M.?), potential for escalation of violence, time factors (e.g., how long did it take to kill the victim), and location (where the victim was first approached and similar data).[41]
- *Stage 3: Making the crime assessment:* This is the reconstruction of the sequence of events and of the behavior of both the victim and the offender.
- *Stage 4: Developing the criminal profile:* This process addresses the type of person who committed the crime and his or her behavioral organization in relation to the crime. Among the factors considered are background information, physical characteristics, habits, beliefs, values, preoffense behavior leading to the crime, and postoffense behavior.[42] Recommendations may be made with respect to investigating, identifying, interrogating, and apprehending the offender.[43]

- *Stage 5: Adjusting the profile:* While the investigation continues, the profiler makes adjustments in the profile if fresh information warrants them. He or she is available on an as-needed basis to discuss the case with persons assigned to it.[44]
- *Stage 6: Reviewing and following up:* After the apprehension, the profiler conducts a review to determine the amount of agreement between the outcome and the profile; various stages of the profiling process are examined. At an appropriate time, the profiler should interview the offender in detail to check the validity of the profiling process.[45]

Mixed Organized-Disorganized Homicides. While many offenders fit neatly into the organized or disorganized pattern, some of them reflect aspects of both patterns. A number of factors can lead to a mixed organized-disorganized crime: multiple offenders with different behaviors may be involved; a planned crime may deteriorate as unanticipated events unfold, such as being unable to control the victim; or the original motive may have been solely rape, but the victim's resistance (which sometimes leads to escape) or the offender's changed emotional state may lead to murder. Youthful offenders or the offender's use of drugs and alcohol can also lead to a mixed scene.[46]

| TABLE 7-4 | Crime Scene Differences between Organized and Disorganized Sexual Homicides

ORGANIZED	DISORGANIZED
1. Offense planned; semblance of order before, during, and after the crime suggests aim of avoiding detection	Spontaneous offense, appears to be no plan to avoid detection
2. Victim frequently a targeted stranger in a location staked out by offender, to some extent victim is a target of opportunity; serial victims may share common characteristics, and offender may spend considerable time waiting for "right" victim	May know victim or select randomly, often familiar with location of crime
3. Personalizes victim	Depersonalizes victim; specific areas of the body may be selected for extreme violence; overkill or excessive force to face is often attempt to dehumanize victim
4. Offender may strike up conversation with victim as attempt to gain her confidence in order to capture victim without resorting to physical force	Minimal conversation aside from orders and directions
5. Scene reflects overall control	Scene random and sloppy, in great disarray
6. Demands submissive and compliant victim; may require certain reactions, e.g., fear and passivity during sexual activity	Sudden, overpowering violence to victim; offender uses a surprise blitz-style attack
7. Restraints used, e.g., ropes, chains, handcuffs, chemicals, belts, gags, blindfolds	Minimal use of restraints; victim killed quickly to avoid victim's getting the upper hand
8. Aggressive acts prior to death, weapon displayed, victim's life threatened	Any sexually sadistic acts follow death, e.g., mutilation of face, breasts, and genitals
9. Body hidden	Body left in view, often left in position killed
10. Weapons and evidence absent	Evidence and weapons often present, normally much physical evidence available
11. Transports victim or body, often using his or her vehicle	Body left at death scene

(Source: Robert Ressler, Ann W. Burgess, and John E. Douglas, *Sexual Homicide: Patterns and Motives* [New York: Free Press, 1992], pp. 121–124, 131)

Investigative Psychology. Although more than a few psychologists and psychiatrists are involved in profiling, **investigative psychology** is associated with the work of Englishman David Canter, an environmental psychologist, who was asked by New Scotland Yard in 1985 to integrate investigative and psychological concepts.[47] The model he developed rests on five factors:[48]

1. *Interpersonal coherence* assumes that offenders will deal with their victims in a manner similar to the way they treat people in their day-to-day lives. Victims may represent significant people from the offender's noncrime life. For example, many of serial killer Ted Bundy's victims resembled his ex-girlfriend. Variations in criminal activity may relate to changes in how the offender treats people generally.

2. The *significance of time and place* may provide analysts with clues about the offender's mobility and even his or her residence. Because the offender picks the time and place of the attack, these factors may also be clues about his or her work, off time, and perhaps even employer.

3. *Criminal characteristics* are used by researchers and analysts to place offenders into broad categories, from which subcategories can be selected or developed. This information can then be passed along to investigators.

4. The *criminal-career* assessment determines whether the offender may have engaged in criminal activity before and, if so, what type of activity it most likely was.

5. *Forensic awareness* draws in part on item 4 of this list. It is an assessment of the scene and evidence to determine if the offender has any special knowledge of evidence-gathering procedures used by the police. Positive indications—or indications that the suspect has knowledge of evidence-gathering procedures—include such measures as the offender's wearing gloves and removing items contaminated with his or her body fluids.

| TABLE 7-5 | Behavioral Evidence Analysis: Fundamental Assumptions |

1. No offender acts without motivation, though sometimes only he or she knows what that motivation is.

2. Every offense should be investigated as its own unique motivational and behavioral event.

3. Different offenders exhibit the same or similar behavior for completely different reasons.

4. Given the nature of human behavior, human interaction, and environmental influences, no two cases are ever completely alike.

5. Human behavior develops uniquely over time in response to environmental and biological factors.

6. Criminal MO behavior can evolve over time and over the commission of multiple offenses.

7. A single offender is capable of multiple motives over the commission of multiple offenses or even during the commission of a single offense.

8. Statistical generalizations and theorizing, while sometimes initially helpful, can mislead an investigation if they cause us to think we have all the answers in a case or cause us not to collect evidence that does not fit those answers.

(Source: Brent Turvey, *Criminal Profiling: An Introduction to Behavioral Evidence Analysis* [London: Academic Press, 1999], p. 30)

Behavioral Evidence Analysis. A leading proponent of **behavioral evidence analysis (BEA)** is Brent Turvey, a private profiler and forensic scientist.[49] A deductive criminal-profiling method, BEA is based on the assumptions listed in Table 7-5. In operation, BEA is a four-step process that involves the following:[50]

1. *Equivocal forensic analysis:* "Equivocal" is a term applied to something that can be interpreted in more than one way or to an interpretation that can be questioned.[51] Thus, equivocal forensic analysis is a physical-evidence review that questions all assumptions and conclusions.[52] The "inputs" that are reviewed include all documents and reports; crime scene videos, photographs, sketches, and access logs; neighborhood and vehicle canvasses; the medical examiner's or coroner's report and autopsy videos and photographs; and written and taped statements from witnesses and victims.[53] A central aspect of this analysis is establishing what behaviors occurred on the part of the offender and the victim, such as the type of resistance used by the victim.[54]

2. *Victimology:* Victimology is the thorough study and analysis of the victim's characteristics.[55] Establishing this information can be useful in making inferences about the offender's behavior, modus operandi, and signature behaviors, as well as the victim's lifestyle.[56] Signature behaviors are actions that are not necessary to commit the crime but are taken by the offender to satisfy his or her psychological or emotional need.[57] Examples are placing a pillowcase over a deceased victim's face, positioning the body in a particular way, or urinating on the floor. Not all crime scenes include signatures.

3. *Crime scene characteristics:* These characteristics may include, among many other things, methods of approach, of attack, and of controlling the victim; location, nature, type, and sequence of sexual acts; materials used; verbal statements; and precautionary acts taken by the offender,[58] such as cutting telephone lines, bringing duct tape to bind the victim, wearing a mask, taking the victim's clothing, or setting a fire to destroy evidence. The crime scene characteristics are derived from the equivocal forensic analysis and victimology. Because identifying them depends on evidence, not all crime scene characteristics can be determined all the time.[59]

4. *Offender characteristics:* The first three steps are, for the most part, based on the scientific tenets of crime scene reconstruction and established forensic sciences. However, while relying on their inputs, the fourth step is more artful and therefore a matter of expertise rather than science.[60] Offender characteristics fall into two categories: "hard" and "soft." Examples of hard characteristics are age, sex, DNA and blood, secretor status, fingerprints, race (which may be a soft characteristic in some instances), and marital, medical, military, and incarceration histories, as well as property and vehicle ownership.[61] Hard characteristics are verifiable. Soft characteristics are demonstrated or suggested by the physical or behavioral evidence or by the victim's and witnesses' statements; they are potentially alterable, are affected by time, and/or are subject to interpretation.[62] The following are some of the many types of soft characteristics: offender's relationship history, grooming habits, physical characteristics (including dress), hobbies, criminal versatility, glibness or superficial charm, skill levels, aggressiveness, motive or fantasy, and impulsivity.[63]

The final report covers all the major elements previously related, as well as numerous subcategories that are not appropriate to detail in a general investigative text. It must be crafted with integrity, be devoid of bias, exaggeration, and preconceived ideas, recognize everyone's contributions, and be consistent with the evidence in the case.[64]

Geographic Profiling

Geographic information system (GIS) software provides the capability to superimpose different types of data onto a map. For example, by entering the pertinent data into a GIS, analysts can see where traffic citations are being issued versus where traffic accidents are happening. If these data points do not correspond, the reasonable conclusion is that the traffic enforcement effort is not properly focused and that officers are writing citations where it is easy to do so. Maps generated by GIS are very potent ways to present data visually because what is being shown is usually immediately understood.

The growth of GIS applications in police departments has spawned a specialized field, geographic information analysis (GIA). One of its techniques is **geographic profiling** or **geoprofiling (GP)**, the "father" of which is Dr. Kim Rossmo, formerly an inspector with the Vancouver, Canada, Police Department. He developed the concept of criminal geographic targeting (CGT) while working on his doctorate.[65] Not the least bit coincidentally, Rossmo headed the first geoprofiling unit, which was in the Vancouver Police Department.

Geoprofiling is an investigative strategy that uses the locations of a series of crimes to determine the most probable area of the offender's residence. It is usually used in cases of serial murder, rape, arson, and robbery, although it can also be used in investigating single crimes such as auto theft, burglary, and bombing, which typically involve primary and secondary scenes.[66] The distinctive feature of GP is determining where the offender lives, as opposed to where the next crime will take place. Using complex mathematical formulas, GP software processes the data inputted and then presents the results in the form of two- or three-dimensional surface maps called "jeopardies," one of which shows the probable location of the offender's residence (see geoprofiling probability map, Figure 7-20).[67] Geographic profiling typically involves the following steps:

1. A thorough perusal of the case file, including investigative reports, witness statements, autopsy reports, and the criminal profile, if available.
2. A detailed examination of the crime scene and area profiles.
3. Interviews with lead investigators and crime analysts.
4. Visits to each crime scene, if possible.
5. A review of the relevant neighborhoods and their characteristics (e.g., from where was the victim abducted and where was she or he left).
6. A study of street, land-use, and transit maps.
7. Analysis.
8. Report preparation.[68]

The information gathered by GP analysts is used to answer a series of questions, such as the following: Why did the offender pick victims from a particular neighborhood? Why did he dump the victim where he did? What route must he have used, and when did he use it? Is the route generally available to other people? Why was this route attractive to him? Are there escape routes? Are there geographic patterns? Was the area to which the victim was taken appropriate for predatory activities? Was the victim attacked in the same place the offender encountered her? If there was a vehicle involved, was it dumped?[69]

A key component of geoprofiling is the concept of a mental map: "This is a cognitive map of one's surroundings which is developed through experiences, travel routes, reference points, and centers of activity; it also includes the places where we feel safe and what we take for granted. These concepts also hold true for offenders."[70]

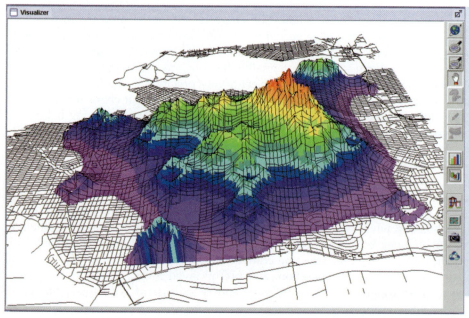

◄ **FIGURE 7-20** **Geoprofiling probability map**
The application of geographic information system (GIS) technology to mapping known crimes is becoming increasingly common. A geoprofiling probability map uses this type of technology from a different way; based on inputs about the crimes and other information pertaining to the cases the model predicts where the offender lives. The reddish-tipped peaks denote the area in which the offender is most likely to live.
(Courtesy of Philip MacLaren, Environmental Criminology Research Inc., Vancouver, B.C., Canada)

If offenders are geographically stable, they tend to stay in a certain area or region. Transient offenders, such as serial killer Ted Bundy, travel more widely; in Bundy's career he committed murders in 10 states from the Pacific Northwest to Florida.[71] Whether offenders are stable or transient depends on their experience with travel, their means for getting from one place to another, their sense of personal security, and their predatory motivations.[72] An offender's mental map may be dependent on his or her geographic style because the type of approach made toward a victim is related to a killer's "home base."[73] In GP terms, predatory criminals can be classified according to how they acquire victims:

- *Hunters,* who search for victims, often using their own residences as home base.
- *Poachers,* who travel away from home, including to other cities, to hunt.
- *Trollers,* who, while engaged in other activities, have opportunistic encounters with their victims.
- *Trappers,* whose strategy is to draw the victims to them.[74]

Predatory offenders attack their victims in different ways. Raptors attack their victims when they encounter them; stalkers follow and then attack those they prey on; and ambushers entice their victims to places they control and in which they feel comfortable, such as the offender's home, and then spring their attacks.[75]

GP does not solve crimes; it prioritizes suspects and their likely addresses, thereby allowing investigators to focus their resources and strategies (e.g., saturation patrol, surveillance, and neighborhood canvasses) where they have the highest probability of being successful. The following case illustrates the value of geoprofiling:

Ontario, Canada, Provincial Police (OPP) were investigating a series of over 80 burglaries in a cottage community near Midland. Using geoprofiling, police were able to focus their investigative effort on a small geographic area. Subsequently, an offender was arrested, 50 burglaries were solved, and stolen property was recovered. GP had indicated that the most likely place the offender lived was a particular area less than 100 meters by 100 meters. As it turned out, the person who was arrested lived in that small area.[76]

Financial Analysis

Financial investigations can be relatively modest, for crimes such as a credit card fraud involving two transactions and a total of $50, or very complex, as in the case of money-laundering schemes involving multiple corporate shells and banks in a dozen countries throughout the world. Fortunately, state and federal investigative agencies can assist with the more complicated cases. The Federal Law Enforcement Training Centers (FLETCs), state police academies, and other providers offer excellent instruction in financial investigations.

Nonspecialists in this area should be alert for the possibility of a financial motive, particularly in murder and arson cases. Among the indicators of financial difficulty are the following ones.[77]

Business Indicators of Financial Difficulty

- Decreasing revenue.
- Increasing production costs (e.g., labor and material).
- Increased competition; better products available.
- Costly rental and lease agreements.
- Failure to record depreciations.
- Numerous product defects, spoilage.
- Double payment of bills.
- Numerous bank accounts.
- Low or overdrawn bank balances.
- Increased borrowing.
- Large or frequent cash transactions.
- Bounced checks.
- Overinsured or hypothetical assets.
- Liens on assets.
- Credit limits imposed by suppliers or lenders; credit refused.
- Numerous overdue accounts.
- Delinquent loan payments.
- Frequent COD purchases.
- Inability to pay current utility bills.
- Delinquent or tardy tax accounts.
- Litigation against business and/or owners.
- Inventory reduced before fire.
- Overstocked because of overproduction or low demand for products.
- Duplicate sales receipts.
- Slow-moving items; obsolete inventory.
- Two sets of books maintained.
- Loans to or from corporate officers and employees.
- Bankruptcy proceedings.
- Losses in prior years.
- Duplicate insurance claims.
- Alleged renovations.
- Frequent change of ownership before fire.
- Bills paid by cashier's checks, certified checks, or money orders.
- Use of photocopies of records instead of original sources.

Personal Indicators of Financial Difficulty

- Bounced checks.
- Costly rental and lease agreements.
- Inability to pay current bills (e.g., utilities).
- Lenders impose or refuse loans or credit.
- Payment of bills by cashier's checks, certified checks, or money orders.

There are also personal life situations that may suggest financial difficulty. Such situations include marital discord; loss of overtime or job; substance, child, or spouse abuse; a recent divorce; and inability or refusal to make child support and/or alimony payments.

Financial Crimes Enforcement Network

The **Financial Crimes Enforcement Network (FinCen),** located within the U.S. Department of the Treasury, is one of the primary agencies responsible for preventing and detecting money laundering by arms dealers, terrorists, drug dealers, criminal enterprises, and others. It serves as a link among law enforcement, financial institutions, and regulatory agencies. Annually, in addition to its own investigative efforts, FinCen serves 165 different law enforcement agencies by providing approximately 6,500 analytical reports involving nearly 33,000 subjects. The value of FinCen for state and local law enforcement is the agency's expertise and its access to highly specialized databases, trained analysts using advanced technology, and worldwide sources of information.[78]

Remote Sensing

Remote sensing is the process of collecting and analyzing information about areas, objects or events without being in contact with the object.[79] Remote sensing capabilities have been accorded additional emphasis in the wake of the 9/11 attacks in terms of identifying and investigating terrorism threats, as well as screening cargo entering the country through our ports, along our railway systems, on our highways and through our airports. Gamma-ray technology is one of the widely deployed technologies used for these purposes and can provide non-intrusive radiological-like images of the contents of containers and pallets (Figure 7-21). Acoustic sensors are being employed to detect small boats in shallow waters, a boost both to national security and the monitoring of "go-fast" boats used to retrieve drugs dropped at sea by aircraft smuggling them from abroad. This section illustrates several different remote sensing processes used by law enforcement agencies in this country.

The processes employed are diverse. They can be as basic as the use of canines to detect contraband (Figure 7-22) or cadaver dogs to locate human remains in lakes and buried beneath the ground surface. More advanced methods include the use of high technology geophysical methods such as ground penetrating radar (GPR) and magnetometers. Wall-penetrating radar provides 3D color images, including static objects and moving people, from a distance through walls as thick as 8 inches of concrete. This capability can substantially reduce the danger to officers making high-risk entries into buildings to free hostages or apprehend violent offenders. Booby traps can be identified, the number and locations of suspects determined, and other important tactical information provided. The mini-buster contraband detector is a handheld apparatus that can identify variations in the density of objects being non-intrusively scanned, such as a building's walls and floors, as well as vehicle dashboards and doors. Such variations allow hidden compartments and contraband to be identified. One agency used the mini-buster to locate 600 pounds of marijuana in a truck's tires (Figure 7-23).

Aerial surveillance was the first type of remote sensing; during the U.S. Civil War (1861–1865), officers were sent aloft in balloons to observe the disposition of enemy forces and report on what they saw and some

◀ **FIGURE 7-22 Canine officer**
A U.S. Customs and Border Protection (CBP) canine officer checks a passenger's luggage after arrival into the U.S. (Photo by Gerald Nino/US Customs and Border Protection)

photographs were taken and used by commanders.[80] Today, remote aerial/visual sensing is conducted by manned space craft, satellites, rotary and fixed-wing aircraft, unmanned aerial vehicles (UAVs), and public surveillance cameras, including those with facial recognition software.

Aerial surveillance platforms may be equipped with not only visual recording and transmitting capabilities but other sensor packages as well. Many police aircraft are equipped with Forward Looking Infrared Radar (FLIR), which is a significant asset in tracking fugitives on foot at night through their heat signatures. Aerial remote sensing can be used by law enforcement personnel to detect illicit drug crops and clandestine labs and monitor airstrips, provide over-the-horizon (OTH) intelligence about drug smuggling boats and planes, quickly identify incipient forest fires, rescue lost hikers and mountain climbers, find airplane crash sites, locate fugitives and abducted persons, recover automobiles and other evidence from water systems, identify possible clandestine graves, as well as to provide investigative leads, the identification of suspects, and proof that the elements of a crime were committed.

◀ **FIGURE 7-23 Gamma rays**
Officer using gamma-ray based density meter to check tires for contraband. (© Bobbie DeHerrera/Getty Images)

Locating clandestine gravesites for a lone person or even several persons is most often a difficult task; such places may be only accidentally discovered or can be identified only by a confidential informant.[81] Even with some preliminary understanding of the general area in which to look, such variables as the depth at which the body is buried, climate, density of vegetation, continuous variations in the terrain, and the age of the case may hinder progress. Initially, a clandestine gravesite may stand out owing to a small cleared area of disturbed surface soil and uprooted vegetation that is turning brown. If the body is not buried sufficiently deep, evidence of animal predation may be present, with remains scattered on the surface. As time passes, the topsoil may slope or collapse somewhat back into the grave, and surface cracks may appear over it. Depending on the area, vegetation may return to the gravesite in about a year and may be more lush than the area immediately surrounding the grave. Some chemical alteration of the site also occurs as the body decomposes; notably, the gravesite will be richer in phosphorous and magnesium than contiguous areas. Potential burial sites can be worked from the surface to a depth of several feet using metal detectors to search for such items such as shell cases, projectiles, belt buckles, jewelry, buttons, and zippers. Advanced metal detectors with screens can show the depth of an item and estimate the probability that it is one type of artifact or another. Even in the absence of a "hit" from a metal detector, likely sites can be physically probed using 3/8-inch " metal rods with "T" handles; a "feel" for the area should be obtained by trial probes away from the suspected burial site so in actual use the value of physical evidence is not accidentally diminished or eliminated.[82]

Given the seriousness of murder and the difficulties associated with locating clandestine graves, the interest in applying remote sensing technologies is predictable. Archaeologists have been using some geophysical methods for nearly 60 years. However, their success with this technology has to some degree is driven by the fact they are interested in human habitation locations where there is more abundant evidence than that provided by a single grave. Forensic successes with geophysical equipment tend to be publicized, whereas failures receive less attention. The body of research literature on forensic remote sensing is more than sparse, but not yet robust; much of what is written comes from case studies of successful investigations.[83] Thus, it is easy to conclude that geophysical remote sensing is "the best thing since sliced bread." Part of the difficulty is that we are still adapting technology intended for one use to our forensic requirements. Geophysical equipment can identify anomalies in the ground, but determining whether they are tree roots or buried bodies requires some "shovel and pick" work. However, with these limitations noted, the use of geophysical equipment may be the only way to successfully conclude some investigations.

The most common types of geophysical equipment used to search for clandestine graves is ground penetrating radar (GPR), which was used as early as 1929 to measure the depth of glaciars.[84] GPR works by emitting high-frequency energy pulses that have a short duration; they travel through the ground and return back to the GPR allowing the substrata to be mapped. Interpretation of the results is best left to highly experienced forensically operators, such as those associated with NecroSearch International. GPR's success is indirect in that it identifies anomalies, which could be a buried body, rocks, or tree roots.[85] The source of the anomaly must then be verified by other means, such as finding physical evidence at the possible gravesite or digging an exploratory trench.[86] An advantage of GPR and other geophysical methods is that they do not destroy any physical evidence which may be present; a disadvantage is that it performs better on more level surfaces. Illustrations of the potential contributions of GPR include the successful location of a long-forgotten 102-year-old time capsule in the wall of the Williamsburg branch of the Brooklyn (NY) Public library and detecting a murder victim's body under the concrete pad of a swimming pool.

NATIONAL CENTER FOR THE ANALYSIS OF VIOLENT CRIME

Operated by the FBI, the **National Center for the Analysis of Violent Crime (NCAVC)** is organized into three components, discussed next.

The Behavioral Analysis Unit (BAU) provides behavior-based investigative and operational support for complex and time-sensitive cases typically involving threats and acts of violence. Its program areas include crimes against children, crimes against adults, communicated threats, corruption, bombing, and arson. The unit provides criminal-profiling services to federal, state, and local agencies if, after it screens a case, the offense and available data appear to be amenable to this technique. Figure 7-24 is a release from NCAVC that provides a linguistic and behavioral assessment of the person responsible for mailing anthrax letters to Tom Brokaw, the *New York Post*, and Senator Daschle.

The Child Abduction and Serial Murder Investigative Resources Center (CASMIRC) was mandated by Congress in 1998. As its name indicates, this unit focuses on children and provides agencies with advanced capabilities and expertise in dealing with abductions, mysterious disappearances, child homicides, and serial murders. The **Violent Criminal Apprehension Program (ViCAP)**

November 9, 2001
Amerithrax Press Briefing

Linguistic/Behavioral Analysis of Anthrax Letters
Critical Incident Response Group
National Center for the Analysis of Violent Crime

Today the FBI is releasing linguistic and behavioral assessments of the person responsible for mailing anthrax-laden letters on September 18 and October 9, 2001. We ask the American public to study these assessments and reflect on whether someone of their acquaintance might fit the profile. The safety of the American people is at stake. If you have credible information that might help identify this person, please contact the FBI immediately at 1-800-CRIMETV (274-6388), at www.ifccfbi.gov, or by calling your local FBI field office.

EVIDENCE DESCRIPTION

Letter 1

One page, hand-printed letter

Transmittal envelope, also similarly hand printed

Addressed to "NBC TV–Tom Brokaw"–No return address

Postmarked Trenton, NJ 09/18/2001 (Tues.)

Letter 2

One page, hand-printed letter

Transmittal envelope, also similarly hand printed

Addressed to "NY Post"_No return address

Postmarked Trenton, NJ 09/18/2001 (Tues.)

Letter 3

One page, hand-printed letter

Transmittal envelope, also similarly hand printed

Addressed to "Senator Daschle–509 Hart Senate Office Building"

Return address–"4th Grade, Greendale School Franklin Park, NJ"

Return address zip code – "08852"

Postmarked Trenton, NJ 10/09/2001 (Tues.)

LINGUISTIC ASSESSMENT

It is highly probable, bordering on certainty, that all three letters were authored by the same person. Letters 1 and 2 are identical copies. Letter 3, however, contains a somewhat different message than the other letters. The Anthrax utilized in Letter 3 was much more refined, more potent, and more easily disbursed than Letters 1 and 2.

In the past, the public has helped the FBI solve high profile investigations that involved writings by coming forward to identify the author, either by how he wrote or by what he wrote. We are asking for the public's help here again in the same way.

While the text in these letters is limited, there are certain distinctive characteristics in the author's writing style. These same characteristics may be evident in other letters, greeting cards, or envelopes this person has written. We hope someone has received correspondence from this person and will recognize some of these characteristics.

The characteristics include:

1. The author uses dashes ("-") in the writing of the date "09-11-01." Many people use the slash ("/") to separate the day/month/year.

2. In writing the number one, the author chooses to use a formalized, more detailed version. He writes it as "1" instead of the simple vertical line.

3. The author uses the words "can not," when many people prefer to spell it as one word, "cannot."

▲ **FIGURE 7-24   NCAVC release**

4. The author writes in all upper case block-style letters. However, the first letter of the first word of each sentence is written in slightly larger upper case lettering. Also, the first letter of all proper nouns (like names) is slightly larger. The is apparently the author's way of indicating a word should be capitalized in upper case letters. For whatever reason, he may not be comfortable or practiced in writing in lower case lettering.

5. The names and address on each envelope are noticeably tilted on a downward slant from left to right. This may be a characteristic seen on other envelopes he has sent.

6. The envelopes are of the pre-stamped variety, the stamps denoting 34 cents, which are normally available directly from the post office. They are not the traditional business size envelopes, but the smaller size measuring approximately 6¼ x 3 ½.

BEHAVIORAL ASSESSMENT

Based on the selection of Anthrax as the "weapon" of choice by this individual, the offender:

- Is likely an adult male.

- If employed, is likely to be in a position requiring little contact with the public, or other employees. He may work in a laboratory. He is apparently comfortable working with an extremely hazardous material. He probably has a scientific background to some extent, or at least a strong interest in science.

- Has likely taken appropriate protective steps to ensure his own safety, which may include the use of an Anthrax vaccination or antibiotics.

- Has access to a source of Anthrax and possesses knowledge and expertise to refine it.

- Possesses or has access to some laboratory equipment; i.e., microscope, glassware, centrifuge, etc.

- Has exhibited an organized, rational thought process in furtherance of his criminal behavior.

- Has a familiarity, direct or indirect with the Trenton, NJ, metropolitan area; however, this does not necessarily mean he currently lives in the Trenton, NJ, area He is comfortable traveling in and around this locale.

- Did not select victims randomly. He made an effort to identify the correct address, including zip code, of each victim and use sufficient postage to ensure proper delivery of the letters. The offender deliberately "selected" NBC News, the New York Post, and the office of Senator Tom Daschle as the targeted victims (and possibly AMI in Florida). These targets are probably very important to the offender. They may have been the focus of previous expressions of contempt which may have been communicated to others, or observed by others.

- Is a non-confrontational person, at least in his public life. He lacks the personal skills necessary to confront others. He chooses to confront his problems "long distance" and not face-to-face. He may hold grudges for a long time, vowing that he will get even with "them" one day. There are probably other, earlier examples of this type of behavior. While these earlier incidents were not actual Anthrax mailings, he may have chosen to anonymously harass other individuals or entities that he perceived as having wronged him. He may also have chosen to utilize the mail on those occasions.

- Prefers being by himself more often than not. If he is involved in a personal relationship it will likely be of a self-serving nature.

Pre-Offense Behavior

Following the events of September 11, 2001, this person may have become mission-oriented in this desire to undertake these Anthrax mailings. He may have become more secretive and exhibited an unusual pattern of activity. Additionally, he may have displayed a passive disinterest in the events which otherwise captivated the Nation. He also may have started taking antibiotics unexpectedly.

Post-Offense Behavior

He may have exhibited significant behavioral changes at various critical periods of time throughout the course of the Anthrax mailings and related media coverage. These may include the following;

1. Altered physical appearance.
2. Pronounced anxiety.
3. Atypical media interest.
4. Noticeable mood swings.
5. More withdrawn.
6. Unusual level of preoccupation.
7. Unusual absenteeism.
8. Altered sleeping and/or eating habits.

These post-offense behaviors would have been most noticeable during critical times, including but not limited to: the mailing of the letters (09/18/01 and 10/09/01), the death of the first Anthrax victim, media reports of each anthrax incident, and especially the deaths and illnesses of non-targeted victims.

▲ **FIGURE 7-24** NCAVC release *concluded*

facilitates cooperation, coordination, and communication among enforcement agencies in support of their efforts to investigate, identify, track, apprehend, and prosecute violent serial offenders.[87]

COMBINED DNA INDEX SYSTEM

It was immediately apparent that without DNA databases, a counterpart to fingerprint files, the full potential of DNA evidence in investigations would not be realized. States began enacting DNA database laws that mandated the collection of DNA samples from certain categories of

Endangered Runaway

SKY CREEK

DOB: Feb 20, 1990   **Age Now:** 15
Missing: Aug 19, 2004   **Sex:** Female
Height: 5'4" (163 cm)   **Weight:** 115 lbs (52 kg)
Eyes: Blue   **Hair:** Brown
Race: White

Missing From:
FORT WAYNE
IN
United States

Sky may be in the company of an adult male. They may still be in the local area or they may have traveled to New York.

ANYONE HAVING INFORMATION SHOULD CONTACT
National Center for Missing & Exploited Children
1-800-843-5678 (1-800-THE-LOST)

Fort Wayne Police Department (Indiana) 1-260-427-1222

In 1995, an unidentified woman's body was found on an off-ramp along an interstate highway in Iowa. After identifying the victim and considering the location where the body was found, the police investigation focused on the possibility that the offender was a truck driver. Biological evidence from the scene was sent to the FBI for DNA analysis. Five years after the offender's DNA profile was developed, it was uploaded to CODIS, where a match was made with a man incarcerated for a sexual offense in Florida. It was also learned that he had a commercial driver's license, validating the police belief that the offender was a truck driver.[88]

offenders, such as those convicted of murder, rape, and child abuse. By 1998, the FBI's **Combined DNA Index System (CODIS)** was fully operational, electronically linking local, state, and federal DNA files. This cooperative effort of the three levels of government is consistently providing results:

THE INTERNET

The Internet has transformed how people communicate and how often they communicate. All types of organizations have been quick to use the power and versatility of the Net, from the American Red Cross to pornographers. The possibilities of the Internet have not escaped the police, who have been quick to use it for investigative, administrative, and public information purposes. For investigative purposes, the police use the Internet in many ways, such as:

1. Appealing to the public for information about specific crimes, often through "crime-stopper" programs.

2. Requesting information about missing children and adults.

3. Posting federal, state, and local most-wanted lists. These lists may be limited to the "top 10," or there may be separate most-wanted lists, such as a list for the most-wanted violent felons or terrorists.

4. Publicizing individuals who are wanted as fugitives, as well as fugitives who have been located.

5. Alerting the public about jail and prison escapees and requesting information if they are sighted.

6. Requesting information about the identities of unknown subjects ("unsubs").

7. Showing photographs of recovered stolen property so that the owners can identify and claim it.

8. Providing beatwide and citywide crime-mapping capabilities so that investigators can approach their work with better information.

9. Conducting various types of electronic covert investigations.

Item 9 is well illustrated by an operation undertaken by the Lake County Sheriff's Office in Illinois. Members of the office's Child Exploitation Unit go online posing as youngsters in their early to mid-teens in order to apprehend child pornographers and pedophiles.[81] The investigators visit chat rooms that have sexually suggestive names, where they have been "hit on" as quickly as 5 seconds to 6 months after they began electronically talking to someone. This type of Internet investigation is a delicate dance in which the investigators must get sexual predators to make revealing remarks about themselves—without giving them any hint that they are actually talking to police officers. If a suspect asks for a photograph of the "boy" or "girl," he is talking to, a high school photograph of the investigator working the case is sent. The police can arrest an individual once he or she agrees to meet with the "boy" or "girl," because this shows that the person has the intent to commit a crime. The investigators call these predators "travelers" because they come from neighboring cities and states to meet their victims.

Law Enforcement Online (LEO) is a secure intranet system created and maintained by the FBI as a tool for communicating, obtaining mission-critical information, providing or participating in online educational programs, and participating in professional-interest or topically focused dialogs. Access to LEO is free to qualified enforcement officers. Through LEO's e-mail service, users can stay in contact with colleagues, make contact with experts, share information about unique MOs, request help with unsolved crimes, conduct research, participate in special-interest groups (LEOSIGs), and use the links to numerous websites, including those of the International Association of Auto Theft Investigators, Asset Forfeiture Program, NCAVC, National Drug Intelligence Center, and FBI Bomb Center.[89]

KEY TERMS

behavioral evidence analysis (BEA)
Combined DNA Index System (CODIS)
COMPSTAT
crime analysis
crime bulletin
crimogen
evidential intelligence
facial recognition software
field interview/information report (FIR)
Financial Crimes Enforcement
    Network (FinCen)
fusion centers
geographic information systems (GIS)
geographic profiling (geoprofiling) (GP)
hot spot/hot block

indicative intelligence
informant
intelligence/analytical cycle
investigative psychology
jail booking report
Law Enforcement Online (LEO)
lineup
National Center for the Analysis of
    Violent Crime (NCAVC)
National Crime Information
    Center (NCIC)
neighborhood canvass
organized/disorganized-offender
    model
pattern

profiling
series
solvability factors
spree
strategic intelligence
surveillance
tactical intelligence
telephone record analysis
time-event chart (TEC)
trends
vehicle canvass
Violent Criminal Apprehension
    Program (ViCAP)

REVIEW QUESTIONS

1. Incident reports are screened to determine the presence or absence of solvability factors. Identify at least six of these factors.

2. In follow-up investigations, there are leads which are "good" and those which are unproductive. What do both of these leads have in common?

3. What are neighborhood and vehicle canvasses? Why are investigators briefed before they begin these two types of canvasses?

4. Why are criminal history and other types of checks run on victims, witnesses, and suspects?

5. What is the purpose of checking the booking reports of jailed suspects?

6. Name seven things which should be in a surveillance kit.

7. Identify three reasons why there must be periodic evaluations about whether to continue or terminate a surveillance operation.

8. Police policies identify activities which investigators should do and not with their informants. What are four of these things?

9. What is a fusion center?

10. Briefly discuss the steps in the intelligence/analytical cycle.

11. Define *crime analysis*.

12. What are sprees, hot spots, and crimogens?

13. What is a time-event chart?

14. Why are computerized link analyses particularly valuable?

15. What are three approaches to criminal profiling?

16. What is the distinctive feature of geographical profiling?

17. Identify five indicators of personal financial difficulty.

18. State five ways that the Internet can be helpful to investigations.

19. Define remote sensing and give at least three illustrations of how it can be used in investigations.

INTERNET ACTIVITIES

1. Many police departments are accredited by the Commission on Accreditation for Law Enforcement Agencies (CALEA). Of this number, some agencies have their policies and procedures available on their Internet site. On some of these sites you can review a department's approach to handling informants; on other sites, the information is not available for review. How do you explain these differences?

2. Review the organizational charts for at least five departments that indicate where their intelligence unit is placed and to whom it reports. What similarities and differences do you see?

3. Arguably, the three most significant developments in policing in the past 50 years have been the advent of DNA evidence, community-oriented policing, and fusion centers. Visit www.fas.org/irp/agency/ise/guidelines.pdf and study the "Fusion Center Guidelines" issued by the U.S. Departments of Justice and Homeland Security and the Global Justice Information Sharing Initiative (July 2005). How does this change the policing and national security landscapes?

NOTES

1. Stephanie L. Bitt, "NCIC 2000," *FBI Law Enforcement Bulletin,* July 2000, Vol. 69, No. 7, p. 14.
2. These guidelines are drawn, with restatement, from John J. Farmer, Jr., "Attorney General Guidelines for Preparing and Conducting Photo and Live Identification Procedures," April 18, 2001, pp. 1–7.
3. This section is drawn, with modification, from John T. Nason, "Conducting Surveillance Operations," *FBI Law Enforcement Bulletin,* Vol. 73, No. 5, May 2004, pp. 1–6.
4. Department of Justice, Department of Homeland Security and the Department of Justice, Fusion Center Guidelines (Washington, D.C., July 2005), p. 2.
5. John S. Pistole, Deputy Director, FBI, in a speech before the National Fusion Center Conference, March 7, 2007., Destin, Florida.
6. Fusion Center Guidelines, ibid., p. 2.
7. Ibid., p. 69.
8. International Association of Law Enforcement Intelligence Analysts, *Starting an Analytical Unit for Intelligence Led Policing* (Lawrenceville, NJ: IALEIA, July 2001), p. 1.
9. Marilyn B. Peterson, Bob Morehouse, and Richard Wright, *Intelligence 2000* (Law Enforcement Intelligence Unit and International Association of Law Enforcement Intelligence Analysts, 2000), p. 7.
10. Chandler, Arizona, Police Department, General Order D-23, "Criminal Intelligence," Aug. 7, 2001, pp. 2–3.
11. California Department of Justice, *The Bureau of Investigation Intelligence Operations Manual* (Sacramento, CA: Division of Law Enforcement, 1993), pp. 14–16.
12. There is nothing magical about six steps. Some authorities say there are four steps and others as many as seven. Virtually all models agree on the sequence of steps.
13. This paragraph is drawn, with restatement, from Russell M. Porter, "The Intelligence Production Cycle."
14. Iowa Department of Public Safety, www.state.ia.us/government/dps/intellcycle.htm, Nov. 19, 2001, pp. 2, 6.
15. Louis Freeh (director of the FBI), "President's Fiscal Year Budget 2000," statement made before the House Committee on Appropriations, Subcommittee on the Departments of Commerce, Justice, and State, the Judiciary, and Related Agencies, May 17, 1999, p. 4.
16. Porter, "The Intelligence Production Cycle," p. 3.
17. Ibid.
18. Ibid.
19. These points came up during a November 21, 2001, telephone conversation with Marilyn Peterson, a widely recognized expert and author in the field of intelligence matters. She is director of training for the International Association of Law Enforcement Intelligence Analysts (IALEIA), which was founded in 1981.
20. Steven Gottlieb, Sheldon Arenberg, and Raj Singh, *Crime Analysis from First Report* (Montclair, CA: Alpha Publishing, 1994), pp. 13–24. (To obtain information about the purchase of this excellent book, contact Mr. Gottlieb, P.O. Box 8, Montclair, CA 91763 or telephone 909-989-4366.) Also see Victor Goldsmith, ed., *Analyzing Crime Patterns: Frontiers of Practice* (Thousand Oaks, CA: Sage, 2000), and Karim H. Vellani and Joel Nahoun, *Applied Crime Analysis* (Boston: Butterworth-Heinemann, 2001).
21. Massachusetts Association of Crime Analysts, "Crime Analysis," www.macrimeanalysts.com/aboutca.html, Oct. 18, 2001.
22. Susan Wernicke, "What Is a Crime Bulletin?" International Association of Crime Analysts, www.iaca.net/resources/articles/bulletins.html, Nov. 19, 2001.
23. Marilyn B. Peterson, "Telephone Record Analysis," in Paul B. Andrews and Marilyn B. Peterson, eds., *Criminal Intelligence Analysis* (Loomis, CA: Palmer Enterprises, 1990), p. 200.
24. Ibid.
25. Ibid., pp. 200–201.
26. Brent Turvey, *Criminal Profiling: An Introduction to Behavioral Evidence Analysis* (San Diego: Academic Press, 1999), p. 1. A second edition of this book is in progress.

27. Ibid.

28. Ibid.

29. Ibid., p. xxvii.

30. "New York's Mad Bomber," njnj.essortment.com/ madbomber_rwid.htm, Dec. 3, 2001, p. 1.

31. Ibid., pp. 1–2.

32. Ibid., pp. 2–3.

33. In a series of excellent articles, Wayne Petherick identifies and critiques various aspects of criminal profiling. See Wayne Petherick, "Criminal Profiling: Fact, Fiction, Fantasy, and Fallacy," www.crimelibrary.com/serial4/criminalprofiling/index.html, Dec. 4, 2001. The authors have adopted his structure of organized/disorganized offenders, investigative psychology, and behavioral evidence analysis. Wayne Petherick teaches at Bond University, Australia, and is an affiliate member of the Academy of Behavioral Profiling.

34. Petherick, "Criminal Profiling: How It Got Started and How It Is Used," www.crimelibrary.com/criminology/ criminalprofiling2/3.htm, Dec. 7, 2001, p. 1.

35. Ibid.

36. Robert K. Ressler, Ann W. Burgess, and John E. Douglas, *Sexual Homicides: Patterns and Motives* (New York: Free Press, 1992), p. 136.

37. Ibid.

38. Ibid.

39. Ibid.

40. Ibid., p. 138.

41. Ibid., pp. 138–142.

42. Ibid., p. 145.

43. Ibid.

44. Ibid.

45. Ibid., pp. 145–146.

46. John E. Douglas, Ann W. Burgess, and Robert K. Ressler, *Crime Classification Manual* (San Francisco: Jossey-Bass, 1992), pp. 133–134.

47. Petherick, "Criminal Profiling: How It Got Started," Dec. 4, 2001, p. 1.

48. Ibid., pp. 1–2.

49. Brent Turvey can be contacted at the Academy of Behavioral Profiling, BTurvey@profiling.org. The academy publishes the Internet-only *Journal of Behavioral Profiling*, which is accessible on a subscription basis.

50. Ibid., pp. 28–31.

51. Ibid., p. 57.

52. Ibid.

53. Ibid., pp. 63–64, with additions by the authors.

54. Ibid., p. 29.

55. Ibid.

56. Ibid.

57. Ibid., p. 69.

58. Ibid., p. 29.

59. Ibid.

60. Ibid., p. 31.

61. Ibid., p. 184.

62. Ibid., p. 185.

63. Ibid.

64. Daniel B. Kennedy, "Ethical Guidelines for Professional Conduct," Academy of Behavioral Profiling, www.profiling.org/abp_conduct.html, Aug. 21, 2001.

65. For more detailed information, see Kim Rossmo, *Geographic Profiling* (Boca Raton, FL: CRC Press, 2000).

66. Environmental Criminology Research, "What Is Geographic Profiling?" www.ecricanada.com/geopro/ index/html, Nov. 21, 2001, p. 1.

67. Environmental Criminology Research, Inc., "What Is Regel?" www.ecricanada.com/rigel/index.html/, Nov. 21, 2001, p. 1.

68. Environmental Criminology Research, Inc., "Requesting a Geographical Profile," www.ecricanada.com/ geopro/ref_request.html, Nov. 21, 2001, p. 1.

69. Katherine Ramsland, "Geographic Profiling: The Components of a Geographical Profile," www.crimelibrary.com/forensics/geog/4.html, 2000, p. 1.

70. Ibid., p. 2.

71. Ibid.

72. Ibid.

73. Ibid.

74. Ibid.

75. Ibid.

76. Environmental Criminology Research, Inc., "Case Studies," www.ecricanada.com/geopro/cs.html, Nov. 21, 2001, p. 1.

77. Douglas, Burgess, and Ressler, *Crime Classification Manual*, pp. 327–328. For detailed information about sources of information in financial investigations, see Bureau of Alcohol, Tobacco, and Firearms, Audit Services Division, "Financial Investigation Sources of Information," interfire.org/res_file/Fin-Srcs.htm.

78. Financial Crimes Enforcement Network, "Law Enforcement/Direct Case Support," www.ustreas.gov/ fincen/le_directcasesupp.html, Dec. 7, 2001, p. 1.

79. Robert Sanderson, Introduction to Remote Sensing, New Mexico Space Grant Consortium, New Mexico State University, undated.

80. The first balloonist photograph is credited to a Frenchman in 1858, Felix Tournachon; the oldest surviving photograph from a balloon was by James Wallace Black, who took an aerial shot of Boston in 1860.

81. Serious homicide investigators and trainers should read Kathryn Joy Powell, The Detection of Buried Human Skeletal Remains in the Australian Environment, a thesis submitted for the Doctor of Philosophy degree in the Department of Anatomical Sciences, University of Adelaide, April 2006. It has a superb summary of the research literature pertaining to buried body detection.

82. On this point see Hayden B. Baldwin and Cheryl Puskarich May, The Recovery of Human Remains— Back to Basics, Criminal Justice Institute, University of Arkansas System, pp. 6–1, www.cji.net/CJI/ CenterInfo/fscec/Recovery.htm.

83. On this point see Sabrina C. Buck, "Searching for Graves Using Geophysical Technology: Filed Tests with Ground Penetrating Radar, Magnetometry and Electrical Resistivity," *Journal of Forensic Science*, January 2003, Vol. 48.

84. For a broad and historical look at forensic geoscience, see Alastair Ruffell and Jennifer McKinley, "Forensic Geoscience: Applications of Geology, Geomorphology and Geophysics to Criminal Investigation,"

Earth-Science Reviews, Vol. 69, No. 3-4, March 2005, pp. 235–247.

85. See Gerald F. Schroedl, "What is RSS? *Geoarchaeology*, Vol. 21, No. 6, July 2006, pp. 641–642.

86. Kathryn Powell, "Detecting Buried Human Remains Using Near-Surface Geophysical Instruments," *Exploration Geophysics*, 2004, Vol. 35, p. 89.

87. www.fbi.gov/hq/codis/stories.htm, Nov. 23, 2001, p. 1.

88. Russell Lissau, "Police Hook Pedophiles on Web in Five Seconds," cnn.com/2000/local/westcentral/07/24/ahd.police.web/, July 24, 2000, pp. 1–4.

89. "Law Enforcement Online (LEO) Promotes Law Enforcement Information Sharing," *FBI Law Enforcement Bulletin*, August 2000, Vol. 69, No. 8, p. 21.

THE CRIME LABORATORY

CHAPTER OBJECTIVES

1. Define and distinguish forensic science and criminalistics.

2. Understand the importance of an investigator's understanding of crime laboratory capabilities.

3. Describe the three measures of effectiveness of crime laboratories.

4. Distinguish the Frye test from the Daubert test regarding the admissibility of scientific evidence.

5. Explain the role and importance of DNA analysis in criminal investigation, and identify the latest technologies in DNA evidence investigation and data banking.

6. Highlight the process of fingerprint identification and comparison.

7. Describe AFIS, IAFIS, and NIBIN.

8. Discuss some of the problems currently associated with police crime laboratories.

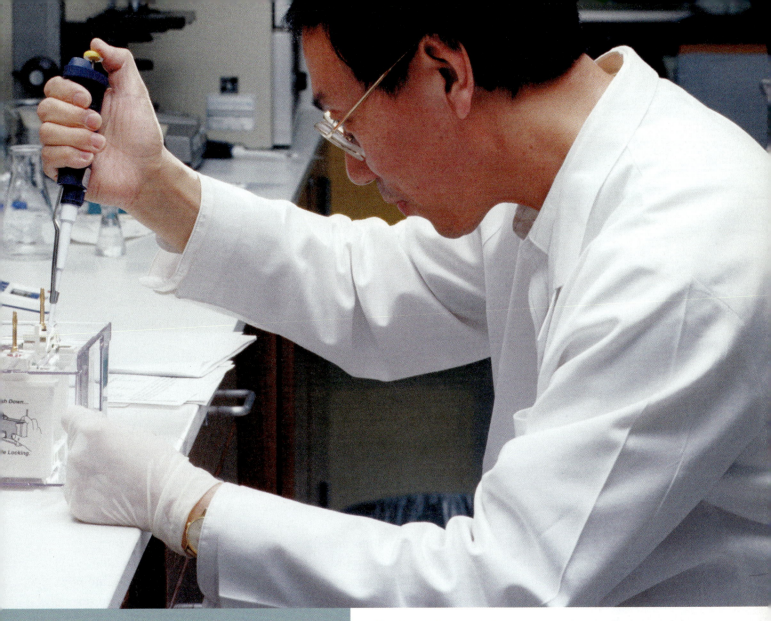

▲ The FBI crime laboratory is recognized as one of the most comprehensive and prestigious crime labs in the world. Since its inception in 1932, the FBI crime lab has provided valuable services for law enforcement agencies at the state, county, and municipal level.

(© PhotoDisc Collection/Getty Images)

A crime laboratory is a scientific organization with a dedicated mission of aiding the process of criminal justice. It provides this aid by answering, or helping to answer, the vital questions of whether a crime was committed, how and when it was committed, who committed it, and who could not have committed it. The criminal laboratory seeks answers to questions such as these through scientific analysis of material collected primarily from the scenes of crimes or from suspects.[1] Although there are hundreds of federal, state, and local crime laboratories throughout the country, the range of services and personnel expertise within the laboratories varies among the organizations.

To understand the role of crime laboratories, one must understand their relationship to the scientific community and to the functions of the criminal justice system. There are two distinct activities involved in laboratory work. One is the gathering of evidence at the scene of a crime, which is done by evidence technicians or investigators. The second function is the scientific analysis of evidence, which occurs in the laboratory. The effectiveness of the second activity often depends on the efficiency with which the first operation is performed.

An important issue addressed in this chapter is an investigator's expectations regarding the function and responsibilities of a crime laboratory. While the laboratory is one of the most valuable tools for a criminal investigator, he or she must be aware of its capabilities and limitations. It is not uncommon, for example, for an investigator to send evidence to a laboratory and delay the investigation until the laboratory results are received. Crime laboratories are not intended to replace field investigations. In addition, investigators are often not familiar with the types of evidence that are subject to laboratory analysis. Even the most minute and seemingly insignificant pieces of evidence may be subject to laboratory examination. If investigators are not aware of a laboratory's capabilities, critical pieces of evidence can go uncollected, unprocessed, and unused in substantiating guilt or innocence. Because the analysis of evidence is no better than the samples submitted, investigators themselves play an important role in the success of scientific analysis.

The terms "forensic science" and "criminalistics" are often used interchangeably. **Forensic science** is that part of science applied to answering legal questions. It is the examination, evaluation, and explanation of physical evidence in law. Forensic science encompasses pathology, toxicology, physical anthropology, odontology (dental structure, development, and diseases), psychiatry, questioned documents, firearms, tool-mark comparison, and serology, among other fields. Recent technological advances have added molecular biology and genetics to this list.

One of the branches of forensic science, **criminalistics**, deals with the study of physical evidence related to a crime. From such a study, a crime may be reconstructed. Criminalistics is interdisciplinary, drawing on mathematics, physics, chemistry, biology, anthropology, and many other scientific endeavors. The late Paul L. Kirk, a leader in the criminalistics movement in the United States, once remarked: "Criminalistics is an occupation that has all of the responsibilities of medicine, the intricacy of the law, and the universality of science."[2]

CRIME LABORATORIES

There are more than 350 federal, state, and local **crime laboratories** in this country. The oldest crime laboratory in the United States was established in 1923. Fifty-five percent of the labs were established between 1968 and 1978, just after Supreme Court decisions limited police interrogations and while funds were available from the now defunct Law Enforcement Assistance Administration. Seventy-nine percent of the laboratories are within public safety and law enforcement agencies; the remainder is distributed in medical examiners' offices, prosecutors' offices, scientific and health agencies, and other private and public institutions.[3]

Most crime laboratories have developed in response to a particular need in a community or region. The areas of scientific concentration in particular laboratories are based on those needs and also on the interests and skills of the people available. Not all crime laboratories have the same capabilities. Some can do much more than others. Laboratories also tend to emphasize and build up expertise in particular areas. The manner of collection of some types of physical evidence varies according to the type of test procedures the laboratory applies. Therefore, police investigators must familiarize themselves with the capabilities of the crime laboratories supporting their jurisdictions, as well as with the requirements of the national forensic science laboratories.[4]

As can be expected, almost all laboratories originated or were expanded to examine drugs (and, more recently, DNA), but the percentage of crime laboratories with the capability to examine other categories of physical evidence varies from 5% to 81%. In an effort to overcome some of the problems caused by varying specializations and concerns, and because of the absence of agreement on what should be the purpose, function, and services of crime laboratories, the **American Society of Crime Laboratory Directors (ASCLD)** was formed (Figure 8-1). This organization is a nonprofit professional society of more than 400 crime laboratory directors, managers, and supervisors from the United States and 17 other countries who have backgrounds as biologists, chemists, document examiners, physicists, toxicologists, and law enforcement officers. The ASCLD is devoted to the improvement of crime laboratory operations through sound management practices. Its purpose is to foster common professional interests, management practices, information, and communication among its members and to promote, encourage, and maintain the highest standards of practice for crime laboratories. To carry out its purpose, ASCLD has established two additional entities.[5]

ASCLD/LAB, the crime laboratory accreditation program, is a voluntary program in which any crime laboratory may participate to demonstrate that its management, operations, personnel, procedures, instruments, physical plant, security, and personnel safety procedures meet certain standards. At the federal level, the ATF laboratory system was the first to be accredited, and, the FBI laboratory, perhaps the most comprehensive crime laboratory in the world, received its accreditation a few years ago. This is not to imply that a laboratory is inadequate or untrustworthy if it chooses not to undertake this voluntary accreditation process.[6] Accreditation can be very time-consuming and expensive.

The National Forensic Science Technology Center (NFSTC) was established by ASCLD in 1995 and began operating in 1996. Its two primary functions are to help crime laboratories prepare for accreditation, especially laboratories whose primary focus is on DNA analysis, and to offer continuing education programs for crime laboratory personnel, including the support of college and university degree programs.[7]

The Morgue

One type of crime lab often forgotten is the morgue. A **morgue** is not just a place that houses the bodies of deceased persons; it is critical on the forensic scene as the place where cause of death is determined. Experienced forensic pathologists conduct autopsies and analyze body fluids, tissues, and organs to produce information useful in an investigation when cause of death is questionable or when death has been caused by something other than a known disease.

Digital Crime Labs

As our society has become increasingly reliant on computers and the exchange of digital information, police have addressed the collection of the digital evidence through specialized crime laboratories staffed with highly trained technicians. While many of the digital crime labs, servicing

▶ **FIGURE 8-1   ASCLD**
The ASCLD organization is dedicated to providing excellence in forensic science analysis through leadership in the management of crime laboratories. See www.ascld.org. (Courtesy American Society of Crime Laboratory Directors)

AMERICAN SOCIETY OF CRIME LABORATORY DIRECTORS

"Excellence Through Leadership in Forensic Science Management"

the needs of local law enforcement have been federally operated by the FBI or the U.S. Secret Service, today most large police agencies also have digital forensics laboratories to help recover deleted or damage files, restore hard drives, and collect digital information from almost any type of electronic device (e.g., personal computers, laptops, cell phones, MP3 devices, iPods, digital cameras and camcorders, and PDAs (personal digital assistants). There are also 14 FBI-operated Regional Computer Forensic Labs (RCFL) throughout the United States that attempt to combine federal and local law enforcement efforts in a more efficient and uniform manner in finding, extracting, and storing digital evidence and presenting it in court.[8]

There are three primary purposes for digital crime labs:

1. Examine and collect relevant digital evidence that may exist on personal computers in support of a crime. This activity is often associated with organized crime investigations involving vice, gambling, and drug trafficking. For instance, some of the most notorious vice cases involving U.S. Congressmen have developed from examining seized computers in the brothels of high paid madams. In a similar manner, narcotics officers have long used digital crime labs to discover patterns of contacts in large racketeering cases derived from e-mails sent from one courier to the next, supported by illegal payments and purchases involving off-shore accounts. More recently, police investigators have started seizing personal computers at the scenes of more traditional crimes. The following case study provides an insight into this methodology:

In the early morning hours of a cool October morning, police officers were called to the scene of what appeared to be the tragic suicide of a locally known jazz singer. Her lifeless body found in bed, along with a host of Vodka bottles and a prescription for a strong sleeping medicine. The scene was reminiscent of well-known actresses and musicians, hooked in the downward spiral of drug addiction that has taken lives over the years. During the investigation, detectives spoke with relatives and friends of the victim and found that she had recently broken up with her possessive boyfriend and manager and had started dating another person. She had fired her boyfriend-manger and was looking forward to starting a new life in Las Vegas at one of the major hotels on "the Strip." Further, there was information indicating that she had stopped drinking and was attending AA on a regular basis. In addition, her sponsor stated that the victim reported to her that she was receiving threatening e-mails from her old boyfriend and was "really scared of him." The old boyfriend had no alibi for the evening of the suicide,

and a nearby neighbor identified his car parked in front of the victim's house the night of the incident. Suspicion grew when the boyfriend denied being near the victim's house. An interview with the housekeeper revealed that the boyfriend had been observed at his computer looking at websites involving the interaction of drugs with alcohol. He had also been talking to friends about his past relationship with the victim and had said that he was "not going to let her go!" During one episode, he stated to a friend that he was "going to kill the bitch." Further investigation revealed that the drugs at the scene were the product of a fraudulent prescription and that the victim had not purchased them from the local pharmacy. In fact, the pharmacist identified the old boyfriend as being the person who purchased the prescription for the victim the night of the incident. The victim's computer was seized, and technicians in the digital crime lab discovered over 90 vicious e-mails sent to the victim from the boyfriend in a short three-day period. A search warrant was developed for the suspect's house focusing on securing digital evidence from his computer in support of the crime. His computer substantiated the e-mails as well as a long history of visiting websites involving suicide and murder through the use of drugs and alcohol. In his Word library, investigators found a "checklist" that the suspect followed on the night of the murder: "pick up prescription at the pharmacy, pick up Vodka and 7 Up at the liquor store, go over to the victim's house, apologize and talk about a new gig for the future, mix prescription with 7 Up and give to the victim, pour Vodka and drugs down her when she is semi-unconscious, wipe off fingerprints, toss bottles around, and leave early in the morning." Confronted with the evidence, the suspect confessed to the murder.

2. Digital crime labs are also instrumental in securing evidence that directly involve computer crimes such as money laundering, possessing child pornography, embezzlement, fraud, and identity theft. In these cases, the computer and other devices become instruments of the crime, and police technicians and investigators work closely to analyze digital information as evidence of crime. (See Figure 8-2.) (For more information relating to the computer as an instrument of the crime, refer to Chapter 16: Computer Crime.)

3. Police crime labs have also been instrumental in preventing and investigating terrorist attacks in the United States. In fact, the USA PATRIOT Act (2001) was instrumental in developing federal and local efforts in establishing digital crime labs to investigate suspected terrorist activities on our homeland. The threat of terrorist attacks on the Internet aimed at destroying the critical infrastructure of our country poses a significant risk. Digital crime labs are often

▲ **FIGURE 8-2   Digital crime lab**
A computer hard drive can provide vital evidence in some criminal cases. Computer crime technicians analyze digital evidence that may support everything from a murder case to a terrorist attack. (© Kim Kulish/Corbis)

involved in potential or real "cyber terrorism" attacks that include everything from defacing governmental websites and spreading malicious viruses to thwarting attempts to take over air traffic control systems and damage major energy and telecommunication systems. (Again, refer to Chapter 16 for a more detailed description of crimes involving computers.)

Expectations

It is not unusual to find situations in which investigators not acquainted with the services of the crime laboratory expect too much from scientific analysis. Some expect the crime laboratory to be able to provide a solution in every criminal case. When investigators do not receive answers to the questions they pose through the submission of physical evidence, they are not only disappointed but more than occasionally also reluctant to use the technical assistance of the laboratory again.

To some extent, investigators must be selective in collecting and preserving evidence that they believe can be profitably submitted for scientific analysis to a crime laboratory. Always keep in mind that the laboratory was never intended to replace a complete field investigation. The function of the laboratory is to support the investigator and the primary line units of the police agency. The laboratory is sometimes capable of lightening the burden of the investigator, but it can never completely assume that burden. Too often, personnel collect evidence at the scene, send it to the laboratory, and then allow the investigation to stall until the laboratory report is received, expecting the laboratory to come up with some magical solution. This is an unrealistic expectation and largely results because the investigator does not understand what is and is not evidence subject to laboratory examination.

The analysis of evidence can be no better than the samples submitted. The investigator therefore has a vital role to play in the success of laboratory examinations. James Osterburg, another criminalistics leader, summarizes why there is underutilization or total neglect of crime laboratories. What he said in 1968 is still largely true:

1. Lack of knowledge about how the laboratory can aid the criminal investigator.
2. Unfamiliarity with the more esoteric varieties of clue material, resulting in evidence not being preserved for examination.
3. Failure to collect physical evidence. This may be caused by a fear of cross-examination on some technical, legal, or scientific requirement that may be overlooked. It may be due to inadequate training or experience or to the overcautiousness of field investigators and the fear of destroying evidence.
4. Overrepresentation of laboratory capabilities.
5. Inconvenience to the investigator when there is no local laboratory available or backlogs are so great as to prohibit timely reports of laboratory results.[9]

This list is accurate and complete. The second and fourth points are especially important. If investigators do not know how the most minute or insignificant looking item can be processed at a properly equipped laboratory, critical pieces of material go uncollected, unprocessed, and unused in substantiating guilt or innocence. In addition, if the capabilities of a crime laboratory are overrepresented so that investigators, uniformed officers, prosecutors, and judges all believe it can produce results that it, in fact, cannot produce, these people eventually will underuse the laboratory. Too often scientists fail to keep justice personnel informed of the state of the art in forensic work.[10]

The laboratory can be an extremely valuable investigative tool if the field investigator uses it intelligently and understands its capabilities and limitations. The investigator must also assume responsibility for providing the laboratory with evidence that is properly collected, marked, and preserved so that laboratory analysis, to the effective limits of present technology, can be successful.[11]

MEASURES OF CRIME LABORATORY EFFECTIVENESS

The effectiveness of crime laboratory services can be measured in terms of three criteria: quality, proximity, and timeliness.[12]

Quality

Quality is judged largely on the technical capabilities of the laboratory and the abilities of the personnel who staff the laboratory.

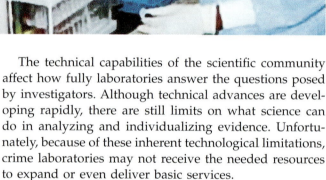

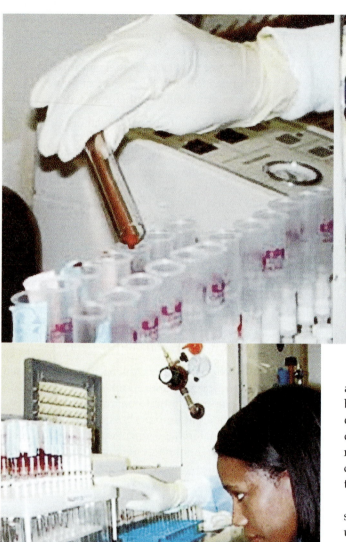

▲ FIGURE 8-3 Laboratory personnel at work
Modern police crime labs are typically equipped to scientifically examine a wide range of evidence submitted by investigators. The scientists working in these labs usually have college degrees in chemistry, biology, or the physical sciences and are often called on to testify in criminal trials regarding the evidence they examined. Here, a lab scientist separates biological evidence for comparative purposes.

(Courtesy Georgia Bureau of Investigation, Toxicology Section)

The technical capabilities of the scientific community affect how fully laboratories answer the questions posed by investigators. Although technical advances are developing rapidly, there are still limits on what science can do in analyzing and individualizing evidence. Unfortunately, because of these inherent technological limitations, crime laboratories may not receive the needed resources to expand or even deliver basic services.

Budget considerations largely determine the level of services that a crime laboratory can deliver. A lack of understanding of the extent to which efficient crime laboratory programs can contribute to the effectiveness of a law enforcement agency has led many administrators to channel financial resources into more traditional kinds of law enforcement operations.

"The most important resource in any crime laboratory is the scientific staff. Without an adequately trained, competent staff, the best organized and equipped laboratory will not be efficient."[13] Historically, there has been a shortage of qualified personnel with scientific backgrounds interested in working in a criminalistics laboratory. Many who are qualified shun police laboratory work, particularly on a local level, because private industry can offer much more attractive salaries.[14]

Proximity

It is understood, if not accepted, that most law enforcement agencies cannot afford to staff and maintain a crime laboratory. (See Figure 8-3.) In light of this fact, however, police agencies that desire and will use the facilities of a crime laboratory should not be denied the opportunity to have such services at their disposal. Experience indicates that police investigators rarely seek laboratory assistance when the facility is inconvenient. There are areas where the technician or investigator must travel an unreasonable distance to obtain laboratory services. Studies have shown that evidence submission decreased sharply as the distance from the crime scene to the laboratory increased.[15] The solution to this dilemma lies in adequate planning on the state level to provide needed laboratory services.

Studies have indicated that a unified state system can best serve the needs of the law enforcement community by providing a parent, or core, laboratory on the state level capable of delivering most laboratory services and strategically located regional laboratories that respond to immediate, less sophisticated analytical needs and funnel evidence when more sophisticated analysis is required. Texas, for example, has its headquarters laboratory located under the auspices of the Texas Department of Public Safety in Austin, with field laboratories in Dallas, Tyler, Houston, Corpus Christi, Midland, El Paso, Lubbock, and Waco. The division of Consolidated Laboratory Services in Richmond, Virginia, serves as a parent laboratory with regional facilities located in Norfolk, Roanoke, and Fairfax. Other states adopting the regionalized concept include Alabama, California, Florida, Georgia, and Illinois. Figure 8-4 shows the location of Florida's regional crime laboratories and state-subsidized local laboratories joined into a regional network.

Several studies have addressed the issue of proximity of crime labs. One recommended that a regional crime laboratory should be established to serve each population group of 500,000 to 1,000,000 in an area where at least 5,000 Part I crimes are committed each year. (Part I crimes are serious offenses categorized by the FBI's *Uniform*

Crime Reports into the following eight categories: murder, forcible rape, robbery, aggravated assault, burglary, larceny, arson, and auto theft.) Another study recommended that regional laboratories be located within a 20-mile radius of 90% of the law enforcement agencies' sworn personnel who would use the facilities. A third recommendation is that a regional laboratory be located within 50 miles of any agency that it routinely serves.[16] Local laboratories, such as those serving large cities or counties, continue to provide the level of services within their capabilities and also serve as regional laboratories for surrounding agencies.

Even in law enforcement agencies that have a crime laboratory, the organization of the lab and its placement within the organizational structure may reveal much about the importance the criminalistics function carries within the agency, which in turn affects budget considerations and the quality of services provided. It is highly unlikely that an administrator who has fought for and was instrumental in establishing a crime lab would give it anything other than high priority and provide for adequate funding. But what about the next administrator? Or the one after that? Priorities in a law enforcement agency, just as in any other organization, can and do change.

If the crime lab or forensic science program has any importance to the chief executive, that function will not be buried within the organization; rather, it will be accessible to the operation functions and "within sight" of the administration in case assistance is needed. The committed chief executive will ensure that the supervisory chain of command understands and appreciates the scientific roles and responsibilities of the laboratory. In fact, it is in

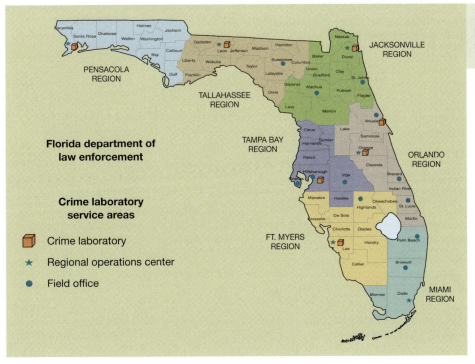

◀ **FIGURE 8-4**
Location of crime laboratories in Florida

the agency's and the laboratory's best interests for the entire supervising and command staff of the laboratory to be scientists who happen to have supervisory or command capabilities. In this manner, when resource allocation and criticality-of-function issues arise in the agency, the people representing the laboratory are knowledgeable about the scientific mission.

Timeliness

Timeliness, also extremely important to the investigator, is the third measure of effectiveness of a crime laboratory. A major portion of the caseload of most laboratories today results from investigators' requests for analysis of suspected or known samples of narcotics or dangerous drugs[17] and DNA evidence. Regarding narcotics and dangerous drugs, even in areas where officers carry and are trained to use presumptive test kits that are available on the commercial market, the results of laboratory analysis provide conclusive evidence necessary to the success of cases. Unlike the case with many other articles or items submitted to a laboratory for examination, which only corroborate evidence possessed by the investigator, the analysis of suspected narcotics or dangerous drugs can be the key to a successful prosecution. Their identification can significantly affect early stages of the judicial proceedings, such as the probablecause hearing; and very often this is an essential piece of corpus delicti evidence. Hence, it is necessary that the results of laboratory examinations be made available to the investigator as quickly as possible. Such a prompt turnaround requires an appropriate allocation of money and personnel to the process by those who control the purse strings and make the decisions.

Timeliness is occasionally affected by the length of the examination or the processing time necessary for accurate and reliable test results. Early DNA analysis, for example, took weeks before conclusions could be properly drawn. This lack of timeliness, in large measure, caused further research that has resulted in faster, easier, and more reliable DNA testing methods.

Admissibility of Examination Results

In 1923, a federal court rendered a decision in the case of *Frye v. United States* that ruled inadmissible the results of a "deception test," an early version of the polygraph. The decision established a standard which provided that, for the results of a scientific technique to be admissible, the technique must be sufficiently established to have gained general acceptance in its particular field.[18]

Half a century later, the federal **rules of evidence** were adopted, which provide that if scientific, technical, or other specialized knowledge will help the trier of fact understand the evidence or determine a fact in issue, such evidence is admissible. The federal rules of evidence do not apply to the states, and several circuits continued to follow *Frye* rather than the federal rules. In 1993, the U.S.

Supreme Court decided the case of ***Daubert v. Merrell Dow Pharmaceuticals, Inc.*** In that case, the Court said that the "general-acceptance" test of *Frye* is not part of the federal rules and, in fact, was superceded by the rules' adoption. The Court went on to say that the trial judge must make a preliminary assessment of whether the testimony of an expert provides an underlying reasoning or methodology that is scientifically valid and can properly be applied to the facts of the case. Many considerations will bear on the inquiry, including whether the theory or technique in question can be (and has been) tested, whether it has been subjected to peer review and publication, its known or potential error rate, the existence and maintenance of standards controlling its operation, and whether it has attracted widespread acceptance within a relevant scientific community. The Court went on to say that the inquiry is a flexible one and that its focus must be solely on principles and methodology, not on conclusions that they generate.[19]

Although *Daubert* applies only to cases in federal courts, a number of states have adopted the *Daubert* standard. Consequently, the application of *Daubert,* and its aftermath, has presented a challenge to crime laboratories to ensure that the standards imposed by the Court are followed in forensic examinations so that expert testimony and the results of examinations by crime laboratory personnel will be admissible, in both state and federal courts. In the most recent test of the *Daubert* standard, the 3rd Circuit Court of Appeals held in *United States* v. *Mitchell* that testimony be rigorously tested and excluded if compliance with requirements for ensuring accuracy in its application cannot be demonstrated.[20] (This case is discussed again later in this chapter.)

TECHNOLOGIES

The speed at which technological advances with forensic applications are developing, expanding, and evolving makes their description immediately obsolete. Computerization has increased speed and reliability of many of the processes formerly manually performed (Figure 8-5). Computer software is available to identify and track serial killers; produce aging progression, facial imaging, and other data to aid in the search for missing children; analyze hair to improve the detection of drug abuse, particularly after a long period of time has elapsed since the use of specified drugs; highlight fingerprints with laser technology that were previously unrecognizable or undetectable on smooth surfaces; and digitally enhance photographs.

The critical role that investigative and forensic sciences play in the U.S. justice system, as well as the attorney general's interest in the rightful conviction of criminals and the exoneration of innocent persons, prompted a significant investment in improving efforts in these areas. This has been accomplished through management efforts

▲ **FIGURE 8-5   Computer technology and forensic science**
New technologies that combine computer software with sophisticated scientific equipment have become powerful tools for analyzing evidence. (Courtesy Texas Department of Public Safety, Garland Regional Crime Lab)

of the Investigative and Forensic Sciences Division of the National Institute of Justice (NIJ) within the Office of Justice Programs (OJB) in the U.S. Department of Justice. The work has been coordinated with other bureaus in OJB and with the Federal Bureau of Investigation, the Drug Enforcement Agency, the Bureau of Alcohol, Tobacco, and Firearms, the U.S. Secret Service, and the Departments of Defense, Commerce, and Energy.[21]

The National Institute of Justice has demonstrated the use of teleforensic technology as a means for communicating knowledge from forensic scientists in a crime laboratory to investigators at a crime scene. This joint project with NASA and the New York State Police has explored the use of NASA space technology and other remote sensing technologies for remote crime scene imaging. The institute is developing a robot that can identify explosives and drugs and can be used to collect evidence at a crime scene. It is also developing a fluorescent imaging tool that will enable investigators to identify fingerprints or biological evidence under natural lighting conditions.[22] Private companies are developing numerous state-of-the-art tools to aid crime scene investigators and crime laboratories, including strong laser-directed light sources that will enhance the investigator's ability to detect and identify evidence.

Among the other forensic science projects in which the NIJ is involved is research to validate a procedure for determining the postmortem interval (the time between death and discovery of a body) by means of entomology; the development and validation of a ballistics-matching technology that uses three-dimensional images of bullets and cartridge cases; and a project with the Royal Canadian Mounted Police that will create a comprehensive

firearms identification system database to be made available to law enforcement agencies on CD-ROM. In addition, the institute is funding development of a computer-assisted procedure for handwriting analysis and comparison and is supporting a project for developing and validating a linguistic method of distinguishing authors of electronically created documents.[23]

The NIJ is heavily involved in many projects that aim to establish standards and protocols for DNA analysis, develop newer, faster, and more accurate DNA testing methods, and ensure that only accurate results are used as evidence in criminal trials.

DNA Analysis

Advances in technology have helped DNA testing to become an established part of criminal justice procedure. Despite early controversies and challenges by defense attorneys, the admissibility of DNA test results in the courtroom has become routine. In 1997, crime laboratories in the United States received DNA samples from about 21,000 known- or unknown-subject cases.[24] In a 1996 survey, almost half of the more than 2,300 prosecuting officers who participated indicated that they had used DNA evidence either in plea bargaining or in the trial of felony cases. It was primarily used in cases involving sex offenses, followed by a lesser number of murder and manslaughter cases and aggravated-assault cases.[25]

Questions about the validity and reliability of forensic DNA test methods have been addressed, and for the most part validity and reliability are established. As a result of DNA testing, traditional blood testing and saliva testing have been rendered obsolete, because DNA is found in these substances and, in fact, is found in all body tissues and fluids.

Deoxyribonucleic acid (DNA) consists of molecules that carry the body's genetic information and establish each person as separate and distinct. Until recently, DNA was found primarily within the nuclei of cells in the chromosomes. DNA can now be extracted and processed from blood, tissue, spermatozoa, bone marrow, hair roots, saliva, skin cells, urine, feces, and a host of other biological specimens, all of which may be found at crime scenes. DNA has been recovered from fingerprints, cigarette butts, drinking cups, and hatbands and other articles of clothing (e.g., Monica Lewinsky's dress).

DNA is generally found in cells that have a nucleus, hence the name **nuclear DNA.** However, some biological cells do not have nuclei such as those forming fingernails, hair shafts, and teeth. What those cells do have is a more primitive form of genetic coding called **mitochondrial DNA (mtDNA),** found in the mitochondria, which are in the body of the cell. When a sperm and an egg join at conception, the new individual gets half of his or her nuclear genetic information from each parent. Conversely, mitochondrial DNA is inherited only from the mother. At conception, all of the new person's mitochondria come from the mother. Since mitochondrial DNA is passed directly through maternal relatives, it serves as a perfect identity marker for those relatives.[26] Indeed, the mitochondrial-DNA sequencing technique was originally developed by anthropologists to help trace human ancestors.

Identifying and Collecting DNA at a Crime Scene

DNA evidence may be found and collected from virtually everywhere at a crime scene, and only a few cells can be sufficient to obtain useful DNA information. DNA does more than just identify the source of the sample; it can place a specific person at a crime scene, refute a claim of self-defense, disprove a claimed alibi, and put a weapon in a suspect's hand. Consequently, the more an investigator knows about how DNA can be used, the more powerful a tool it becomes.[27]

Because samples of DNA are easily contaminated, extreme care should be taken while collecting samples. Several precautions are offered to maintain the integrity of the sample and the analysis:

- As discussed in Chapter 4, collecting biological DNA evidence in the field requires special considerations. The standard recommendation for collecting biological evidence is not to remove the stain from an object, but rather to collect the object with the stain, provided that the stain can be adequately protected from contamination. If the entire object cannot be collected, then the next best way to gather such evidence is to remove the stain by cutting it out (e.g., from a piece of carpet or clothing). On occasions when it is impossible to collect a stain by cutting it from the object, the two preferred methods of collection are (1) to use a dampened cotton swab (with distilled water) to collect the stain or (2) to use a clean instrument such as a razor blade to scrape the stain into a clean paper bindle. In both cases, the samples should be placed in a clean paper bag and allowed to air dry.[28]
- Wear gloves and change them often.
- If the sample is not completely air-dried, it can be dried in the laboratory using a drying hood. Make sure the evidence is properly marked and the table below the drying hood is clean from contamination.
- Use disposable instruments, or clean instruments thoroughly before and after handling each sample.
- Use enough sample to optimize the chance of getting a clear result; however, consideration must be given to leaving a sufficient amount of sample so that a second test can be conducted by the defense. Avoid touching any area where it is believed DNA may exist.
- Avoid touching areas where the sample may exist or be placed. Avoid talking, sneezing, or coughing over evidence. Use physical face barrier protections

whenever possible. Avoid touching your face, nose, and mouth when handling evidence and conducting analysis.
- Return evidence to new paper bags or envelopes. Label and store in the evidence room. Do not use plastic bags, and do not use staples to seal bags or envelopes.[29]
- For long-term storage, keep biological evidence in the freezer.[30]

Successes

Even though DNA may be collected from a crime scene, it may not be submitted to a laboratory for a variety of reasons. Something may prevent further investigation on the case, or the DNA may not be needed to resolve the case. Over the past five years, the number of cases submitted to DNA crime laboratories has escalated. In 2007, DNA crime laboratories received over 100,000 subject cases, an increase from almost 21,000 cases in 1999. Cases with identified suspects accounted for almost three-quarters of the total. At the beginning of 2007, DNA crime laboratories had backlogs totaling nearly 40,000 subject cases. The dramatic increase forced nearly half (45%) of the crime labs to contract with a private DNA testing facility.[31] However, there have been some successes in both identifying offenders and clearing those who had been suspects. For instance, a woman informed the FBI that she had overheard a man talking on a pay phone. The man said that he had killed a woman and buried her in the woods of a local park reserve. The local police were notified, and they located the badly decomposed skeletal remains of a person but could not find the victim's teeth. Since the medical examiner could not visually identify the person or use dental records for identification, she sent the remains to the FBI laboratory, where examiners removed DNA from the victim's bones and performed mitochondrial-DNA analysis. The results were compared to the DNA of missing persons in a national database. Law enforcement authorities were able to identify the victim and later convicted her killer—the man on the pay phone.[32] Another example involved a threatening letter that was sent to a newspaper editor. The FBI swabbed the envelope flap and recovered some saliva cells, which were then typed using a DNA marker. The result was compared to a known suspect and was found to match.[33]

DNA can be extracted and analyzed from specimens that may be years or even decades old. In a case involving Kirk Bloodworth, who was found guilty of sexually assaulting and murdering a young girl, the verdict was based on an anonymous tip, identification from a police artist's sketch, eyewitness statements, and other evidence. He was later retried and again found guilty. But in 1993, more than eight years after his arrest, prosecutors compared DNA evidence from the victim's clothing to Bloodworth's DNA and found that the two did not match. He was subsequently released and then pardoned.[34]

DNA Technologies

In 1985, Alec Jeffreys and his colleagues in England first used DNA in a criminal case. Shortly thereafter, DNA evidence began making appearances in trials in the United States. Initially, DNA analysis required a fairly large sample, and the manual processing technique, called Restriction Fragment Length Polymorphism (RFLP), took up to 14 weeks, on average, to produce results. The RFLP system is slow but produces good results. Technological advancements have led to a polymerase chain reaction (PCR), which takes small samples of DNA and reproduces as many copies as are needed for adequate analysis. Short tandem repeats (STRs), which are even smaller pieces of the DNA helix (ladder), can be reproduced using PCR to generate multiple copies in an instrument called a *thermocycle*. With the PCR-STR process, it takes about 24 hours to extract DNA from an evidentiary sample and only 2 to 3 hours to type the DNA using automation. It works well on degraded samples and on analysis of old cases.[35]

Contamination

Just as contamination is an issue in the collection and packaging of evidence containing DNA, it is a very big issue in the handling of DNA during extraction and examination. It is also an issue that can affect the admissibility of, and credibility given to, DNA evidence in court. Coughing or sneezing while handling DNA evidence can cause contamination.

Population-Genetics Statistics

The effectiveness of DNA evidence in court depends on the ability of a witness to explain the probability that no other person, except an identical twin, has the same DNA type as that discovered on a crime scene sample that identically matches the DNA type of the defendant. Thus, the question is this: Is it possible to individualize the identity of a person on the basis of an analysis of his or her DNA? The answer is yes and maybe. Although there are a number of ways geneticists can calculate the probability that no other person has the same genetic chart or "footprint" as the defendant, the question often arises as to what database of individuals is being used to calculate the probability. (See Figure 8-6.) For example, if a Hispanic person is the defendant, would the probability that there would be another person with the same DNA sequence be any greater if the database used to compare DNA consisted of only Hispanics? Is this the fair way to determine probability? This is a simplified example of some of the issues being examined. In the end, the statistical probability derived by any method of calculation is an estimate.

Data Banking and CODIS

Today, all U.S. jurisdictions have legislation requiring the data banking of DNA evidence of convicted offenders. In some jurisdictions, DNA can be collected only from offenders convicted of sex-related crimes and homicides.

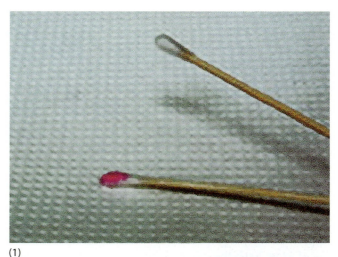
(1)

(2)

(3)

▲ **FIGURE 8-6 From blood sample to DNA "footprint"**
(1) Human biological evidence such as saliva, urine, semen, or blood is collected at the scene on cotton swabs, (2) the sample is then separated and blotted, and then (3) placed within the DNA Analyzer to determine the specific pattern or "footprint" of the sample. The electronic "footprints" are then digitally stored for comparative purposes, possibly against the DNA of a suspect, in the future. (**Courtesy Utah Department of Public Safety, Bureau of Forensic Services**)

In others, legislation has been expanded to allow for the collection of DNA specimens from all convicted offenders. This development has dramatically increased the workload of laboratories that are processing the material to establish the data banks.

In addition to individual-jurisdiction data banking, there is a national investigation support database, developed by the FBI, called the Combined DNA Index System (CODIS). CODIS is used in the national, state, and local index-system networks to link typing results from unresolved crimes with cases in multiple jurisdictions or persons convicted of offenses specified in the data-banking laws passed by the jurisdictions. By alerting investigators to similarities among unsolved crimes, CODIS can aid in apprehending perpetrators who commit a series of crimes. As of May 2007, the database contained over 4.5 million convicted-offender profiles and more than 177,000 unknown forensic profiles found at crime scenes.[36]

Today, DNA analysis is used for a variety of forensic purpose from identifying victims of mass disasters (such as 9/11 and Hurricane Katrina) to tracing a person's ancestry. Each state collects a DNA sample and fingerprints from serious offenders such as persons convicted of rape and murder, but a few states have extended this practice to all arrestees, not just those successfully prosecuted for violent crimes. California, Florida, Louisiana, Texas, and Virginia are the five states with such legislative provision, and there are others focusing more on child predators and offenders associated with crimes against children.[37]

Standards, Testing, Research, and Developments

Laboratory accreditation by the ASCLD's accreditation board in all areas of forensic science requires that quality-assurance measures be in place at the laboratory. Quality-assurance standards have been developed for DNA analysis by the FBI's DNA Advisory Board. The National Institute of Standards and Technology has tested these performance standards for the various analysis techniques discussed earlier. The National Institute of Justice supported the development of criteria for external DNA proficiency training.

The NIJ is also supporting a five-year effort to fund research on, and develop technological enhancements to, the use of DNA in the criminal justice system. Projects include DNA chip technology that will make it possible to have portable DNA analysis equipment for use at crime scenes; mass spectrometry that offers great improvements in sample processing speed and throughput; and statistical modeling that facilitates producing acceptable statistical probabilities for use in court.[38]

New developments in DNA technologies now allow forensic scientists to produce genetic profiles from a mere six cells worth of genetic material. New "high-sensitivity" labs are now able to use DNA testing to solve crimes heretofore reserved for violent crimes such as homicide, rape, and assault where significant amounts of biological evidence (e.g., blood, hair, semen, saliva) were present. The first such lab, started in 2004 in New York City, concentrates on solving routine property crimes such as burglary, auto theft, and larceny. The concept behind "high-sensitivity" labs focuses on low copy number DNA samples (or samples that have fewer than 150 cells of genetic material) that result from minutia evidence (e.g., skin cells left on a smudged fingerprint, saliva traces on a cigarette butt, or perspiration droplets left on a window). The first use of such evidence came in 1999, when low number DNA samples found on a weapon and other objects handled by a suspect helped solve a murder case being investigated by the Royal Canadian Mounted Police. Of course, the practice has become controversial, because no national standard for tests on such a small sample exists. Further, the admissibility in court of low copy number DNA analysis has not been tested. Yet, the potential for solving a wide range of crimes exists with this new technology, if not as the primary evidence against a suspect but perhaps even as a supporting part of the prosecutor's case.[39]

Familial or Kinship DNA Searches

As technology advances, so does the use of DNA. More recently, forensic investigators have begun using a practice called "familial DNA searches," or "DNA kinship searches," in investigating crimes. A familial DNA search is conducted when a DNA sample collected from a crime does not match any of the samples in the database. If this occurs, scientists can expand the search to see if the database contains any samples with similar patterns to the sample collected from the crime. Though each person's DNA is individually unique to that individual, family members will have similar DNA profiles. By expanding the search, forensic scientists are hoping that a relative to the potential suspect is in the system. The odds of finding a relative are high considering there are over three million DNA samples in U.S. state and federal databases and that a survey conducted by the U.S. Department of Justice found that 46% of jail inmates reported that they have at least one close relative who has been incarcerated.[40]

The use of familial DNA searches could have a huge impact on the justice system. If there are no known suspects for an offense, investigators will run any DNA samples collected from the scene through CODIS in hopes that the potential suspect is not in the system. Matches found this way are commonly called "cold hits." To date, there have been 30,000 cold hits using CODIS. If kinship DNA searches were used, the number of cold hits would surely increase. Forensic scientists claim that in a familial DNA search a parent/child relationship would be identified at the first lead 62% of the time, and 99% of the time the hit would be in the first 100 leads.[41]

Not everyone supports the use of familial DNA searches. Opponents believe DNA kinship searches cast suspicion on innocent family members who happen to be related to someone in the system.[42] Plus there is the concern of misuse by law enforcement officials. A familial DNA search often results in multiple hits, and forensic scientists state that it is the responsibility of the investigators to follow the leads with the highest degree of shared DNA makeup (those more likely to be a close relationship to the potential suspect). Others are concerned that the success of kinship DNA searches could lead to the creation of a universal or national database containing every citizen's DNA and fingerprints.[43]

Case Studies in Familial DNA

In 2000, Welsh police reopened the murder case of Lynette White. White had been fatally stabbed in 1988, and the case had gone unsolved for 15 years. In 2000, the police caught a break after reexamining the crime scene and finding blood spots on a skirting board that had been missed in the 1988 investigation. No exact matches were made when the DNA sample taken from the blood spots was run through the national database, but the system did find a similar DNA profile in the system. Both the sample from the crime scene and the sample in the system contained a rare form of a gene. The sample belonged to a 14-year-old boy who obviously could not be a suspect, considering that the crime took place six years before he was born. What police did have though was a lead. There was a good possibility that the offender was related to the young man. After interviewing and taking DNA samples from the boy's family, police were able to make an exact DNA match to the boy's paternal uncle, Jeffrey Gafoor, who later confessed to killing White.[44]

On the morning of August 10, 1984, Deborah Sykes was abducted on her way to work. The 25-year-old woman was raped, sodomized, and stabbed to death. Police later arrested and charged Darryl Hunt, then 19, with Sykes's murder. Hunt claimed he was innocent, but he was sentenced to life in prison. Later, in 1990 and in 1994, DNA tests from semen found on the victim's body did not match Hunt's DNA (at the time of his trial, these more reliable tests were not available). In both 1990 and 1994, law enforcement officials ignored these new findings. Eventually, further investigations of the DNA did find a close match to a man already in the system. Following this lead, police discovered that this man's brother, Willard Brown, had once attacked a woman not far from the place where Sykes had been killed. In December of 2003, when confronted with the DNA evidence, Willard confessed to murdering Sykes. That February, Darryl Hunt was released from prison after spending close to two decades incarcerated for a crime he did not commit.[45]

The Innocence Project

The Innocence Project, founded in 1992, is a nonprofit legal organization founded for the purpose of exonerating wrongfully convicted people through DNA testing. The use of DNA testing has forever changed the criminal justice system.[46] Before the use of DNA, forensic evidence relied on the comparison of hairs, particles, fibers, and blood types. As discussed in Chapter 4, blood types were determined from collected bodily fluids at a crime scene and compared with a potential suspect. Samples that were the same blood type suggested that the suspect *might be* the offender; however, conclusive statements indicating that the suspect *definitely* was the offender were not possible. As one would think, the practice of comparative blood typing is now considered outdated and has been replaced with DNA analysis. In the past five years, significant problems have arisen with the microscopic examination and comparison of hairs, fibers, and other microscopic evidence primarily because of the lack of sufficient reliability and the frequency of erroneous results.[47] The Innocence Project is especially interested in cases in which the defendant was convicted using what they consider "unreliable methods" and in cases in which the evidence was misrepresented or could have been subject to DNA analysis.

In recent years, the federal and some state governments have begun to allow incarcerated individuals who claim they are innocent to have access to DNA testing. In 2004, the federal *Justice for All Act* was created, which grants federal inmates access to DNA testing, and provides funding to similar state programs. As of July 1, 2007, 42 states have enacted legislation that permits inmates to access DNA testing.[48] There are only eight states who do not have legislation focusing on DNA retesting of evidence: Alabama, Alaska, Massachusetts, Mississippi, Oklahoma, South Carolina, South Dakota, and Wyoming.

Despite these improvements in legislative action and DNA technological access, there are still significant flaws in the process:

- Some courts will not consider newly discovered evidence *after* trial.
- Most of the new legislation fails to include adequate safeguards for the preservation of DNA evidence in the future.
- Several states do not allow individuals to appeal denied petitions for testing; therefore, the decision to retest is left to the appellate judges.
- A number of states fail to require full, fair, and prompt proceedings once a DNA testing petition has been filed, allowing the potentially innocent to languish interminably in prison.[49]

A Postconviction DNA Case

In the early morning hours of July 25, 1985, in Garland, Texas, a woman woke up to see a man standing over her bed with a knife. He then raped her and left. As he was leaving, the woman followed him to the patio door and believed she had gotten a good look at her attacker. She described her assailant as a young, white male, around 5'8", 140 pounds, blond, slim, very tan, and wearing beige pants and no shirt. The police suspected David Pope, but the victim was unable to identify him in a photographic line up. She did, however, pick him in a live lineup a month later. She also identified Pope in court as the man who raped her.

Evidence used against Pope in court included a knife found in the defendant's vehicle that resembled a knife stolen from the victim's house and a "voice print analysis" that matched Pope's voice to messages the attacker had left on the victim's answering machine in the weeks following the attack (voice print analysis is no longer used by the courts, because of reliability issues). Pope represented himself during the punishment phase of his trial and proclaimed his innocence. He stated that he had lived in the same apartment complex as the victim until the month before the attack, when he had been evicted. In the month of the attack, he had been living in his car on the apartment complex's property. He was convicted in 1986 for aggravated sexual assault and was sentenced to 45 years in prison.

In January 1999, an anonymous call to the Dallas County District Attorney's Office supported Pope's claim to be innocent. The case was reopened, and the rape kit was submitted for DNA testing. The results not only proved that Pope was innocent, but the sample matched another person already convicted and serving time for rape. Pope was granted a pardon on February 2, 2001, *after* he had served 15 years.

Exonerated from Death Row

In 2007, Curtis Edward McCarty was exonerated after spending 21 years on death row in Oklahoma. (See Figure 8-7.) He had been convicted of murdering and raping a woman in 1985. District Court Judge Twyla Mason Gray dismissed the charges after ruling that the evidence

used to convict McCarty had been tainted by the questionable testimony of former police chemist Joyce Gilchrist. In her original notes, Gilchrist stated that the hairs and other biological evidence did not match McCarty; later she changed her notes, and in two trials Gilchrist testified that McCarty could have been the killer. In both trials he was found guilty and sentenced to death. The defense requested that the hairs be retested, but subsequently the hairs were lost. A judge has said that Gilchrist either destroyed or "lost" the evidence intentionally. In recent years, DNA has also proven that another person had raped the victim, not McCarty. McCarty is the 124th person to be exonerated from death row in the United States.[50]

Automated Fingerprint Identification System (AFIS)

In the mid-1970s in San Francisco, Miriam Slamovich, a concentration camp survivor, was shot point-blank in the face. She died a month later. On the bedroom window, her killer left a full, perfect fingerprint that became the object of thousands of hours of manual fingerprint comparisons over a 10-year period. When San Francisco installed an **Automated Fingerprint Identification System (AFIS),** the latent print from the Slamovich case was the first search made, and a hit was recorded in less than 6 minutes. The killer was in custody the same day.[51]

In August 1991, two pieces of paper allegedly handled by an unknown suspect in a Jacksonville, Florida, sexual-assault case were submitted to the Florida Department of Law Enforcement regional crime lab for analysis. A number of latent prints were developed on the paper and searched in the Automated Fingerprint Identification System without success. The unidentified latent prints were entered into the AFIS Unsolved Latent Fingerprint File (ULF) so that they could be searched against incoming fingerprint cards from current arrests throughout the state. In April 1994, an individual was arrested for auto theft and released. The fingerprint card taken at the time of the arrest was submitted to the department and searched against the ULF. On May 16, 1994, as a result of the reverse search (current fingerprint cards searched against the ULF), an identification was made. The offender was eventually located in New York and extradited to Florida. As a result of the AFIS search, blood was drawn from the suspect for comparison with semen samples

◄ **FIGURE 8-7 DNA errors**
Ex-police chemist Joyce Gilchrist stated that she always based her opinion scientific findings and that she felt comfortable with her conclusions and testimony given to the court. Unfortunately, internal documents indicated otherwise. (© *The OKlahoman*) (*left*)
Curtis Edward McCarty was released after serving nearly 20 years on death row owing to the mistakes made by Joyce Gilchrist. (*right*)

obtained from the victim at the time of the offense almost three years earlier. There was a DNA match. In April 1995, the offender pled guilty to the sexual assault and was sentenced to 10 years in prison.[52]

Traditionally, fingerprints have been classified, filed, and searched according to the Henry Classification System. Technical searches of newly fingerprinted persons, conducted to determine if they have any prior criminal record, are labor-intensive but have been fairly productive. However, searches of latent fingerprints collected from crime scenes against a Henry system file have been so labor-intensive and unproductive that some jurisdictions don't even attempt them. Certainly, the larger the agency, the greater the problem.

In the early 1970s, the FBI and the National Bureau of Standards conducted feasibility research for establishing an automated fingerprint identification process. After a successful pilot study, the computers hit the market, and one of the most beneficial high-tech tools for law enforcement use in this century became a reality.[53]

AFIS allows law enforcement agencies to conduct comparisons of applicant and suspect fingerprints with literally thousands or millions of file prints in a matter of minutes. A manual search of this nature would take hundreds of hours with little hope of success. The heart of AFIS technology is the ability of the computer equipment to scan and digitize fingerprints by reading spacing and ridge patterns and translating them into the appropriate computer language coding. The computer is capable of making extremely fine distinctions among prints, lending further accuracy and reliability to the system.

The computer can map 90 or more minutia points (ridge endings, bifurcations, directions, and contours) for each finger. This number is high enough to individualize a fingerprint and distinguish it from all others. Latent prints normally do not have 90 minutia points, but matches usually can be made with as few as 15 or 20 minutia points. One agency reported a hit on 8 minutia points.

Technicians can computer-enhance fingerprints when preparing them for a search. This process enables an experienced technician to fill in missing or blurred portions of print fragments or to correct for breaks in patterns or ridges caused by burns or scars.

As noted, the computer translates patterns into mathematical computer codes. Thus, the computer is not comparing images of a suspect's prints against images of known prints; rather, it is conducting a mathematical search that can compare a subject print against file prints at a rate of up to 600 prints per second. Search time varies depending on such factors as preparation time, demographic data that are entered to limit the prints required to be searched, the size of the file, and the number of key factors, or matchers, being used to seek a match. A latent print can be searched against a file of 500,000 prints in about half an hour.

Although the accuracy of the AFIS system is 98% to 100%, this does not mean that the computer makes positive matches that frequently. In fact, the system never makes a final decision on identity. The system produces a list of possibles, called a *candidate list*. It is from this list that further determinations are made by a qualified fingerprint examiner.

The computer uses a scoring system that assigns points to each criterion used in the match. The technician sets a threshold score above which a hit is fairly well assured. The technician also sets the size of the candidate list. If any of the scores are high above the threshold, a hit may be likely. If all the scores on the candidate list are low, a hit is unlikely. Policy of the agency may dictate the placement of the threshold, thus limiting or enlarging the number of candidates. Time constraints and resources may be controlling factors in these determinations.

AFIS makes no final decisions on identity. A technician must make the final verification as to whether the system has obtained a hit. The computer assists but does not replace the fingerprint expert.

AFIS has two major duties. First is performing the functions of classifying, searching, and matching prints. Second is the storage and retrieval of fingerprint data. Data are stored on optical disks, thereby permitting side-by-side comparisons of search prints and file prints. Such comparisons are useful for verifying the data found in an AFIS search (Figure 8-8).[54]

In July 1999, law enforcement agencies began to have access to the FBI's **Integrated Automated Fingerprint Identification System (IAFIS),** a national online fingerprint and criminal-history database with identification and response capabilities. IAFIS consists of three integrated segments: AFIS, the Interstate Identification Index (III), and Identification Tasking and Networking (ITN).

Here is how IAFIS works. A local agency must have a live-scan fingerprint terminal. If it does, it can scan the prints of a person who is arrested and electronically transmit the prints and mug shots, along with personal information about the arrestee, to the state's law enforcement network for a fingerprint check. The same electronic prints and personal information are transmitted to the FBI fingerprint repository maintained by the Criminal Justice Information System (CJIS) Division in Clarksburg, West Virginia. The system was designed to support a daily traffic load of more than 62,000 fingerprint-package transmissions and hundreds of thousands of other transactions. After going through several quality-control checks, the information is run against an automated system, housing "rap sheets" on about 35 million offenders. If a match is found, it is verified by an examiner who manually compares the prints. If no match is found in the rap-sheet file, the prints are run against the FBI's AFIS system, which houses 35 million 10-print digitized files. The system can examine 3 million fingerprints per second. A potential match is manually examined to ensure accuracy. If no match is

► **FIGURE 8-8**
AFIS fingerprint comparison
This is an actual AFIS print. On the left is a file print several years old. On the right is a latent print left at the scene of a burglary. Even though a new scar is seen on the fingerprint on the right, AFIS was still able to match the prints. (Courtesy Dallas Police Department)

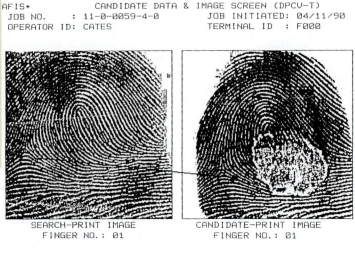

```
AFIS*              CANDIDATE DATA & IMAGE SCREEN (DPCV-T)        04/11/90 13:46
JOB NO.    : 11-0-0059-4-0         JOB INITIATED: 04/11/90            PRTY:3
OPERATOR ID: CATES                 TERMINAL ID  : F000

                                                            SEARCH-PRINT
                                                            <        >
                                                            SEX  :M
                                                            YOB/R:??/?
                                                            PAT. :RLRWR-LRLLI
                                                            REF. :     - A
                                                            QUAL.:ABBBB-BABCI
                                                            RDB-T:1
                                                            LOC. :005

                                                            CANDIDATE-PRINT
                                                            RANK :001 / 005
                                                            <01-02-00100709>
                                                            SCORE:04354
                                                            PAT. :RLRWR-LALLI
                                                            QUAL.:BBBBB-ABBBI
                                                            SEX  :M
                                                            YOB/R:51/?
                                                            RDB-T:1,6
    SEARCH-PRINT IMAGE         CANDIDATE-PRINT IMAGE        MEMO :0075-0630
    FINGER NO.: 01             FINGER NO.: 01                    1 2 3 4 5
                                                                 6 7 8 9 0
                                                            ZOOM (X2)
                                                            ZOOM (X4)
                                                              L  R
                                                              U  D
                                                            *CHARTING
                                                            ERASE
```

found in either the subject search or the fingerprint search, the record is added to the appropriate databases, an FBI identification number is assigned, and the submitting agency is notified of the search results and the assigned number.[55]

National Integrated Ballistic Information Network Program

A joint program of the Bureau of Alcohol, Tobacco, and Firearms (ATF) and the FBI, the **National Integrated**

Ballistic Information Network (NIBIN) integrates all the elements of Ceasefire and Brasscatcher (both former ATF programs) and Drugfire (an FBI program) (Figure 8-9).

Just as each fingerprint is different, so a firearm leaves unique identifiable characteristics on expended ammunition. NIBIN compares images of ballistic evidence, both projectiles and casings, obtained from crime scenes and recovered firearms. As new images are entered, the system searches the existing database for possible matches. Hits are confirmed by a firearm examiner.

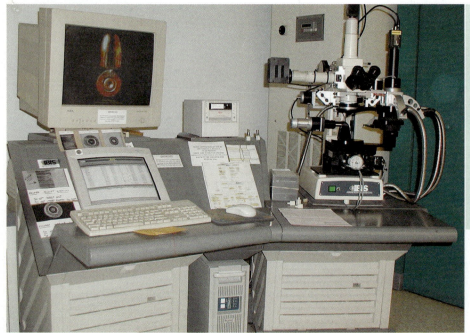

◄ **FIGURE 8-9**
NIBIN system
Just as individual fingerprints differ, each firearm leaves different, unique characteristics on expended ammunition. The National Integrated Ballistic Information System Network, developed by ATF and the FBI, compares images of ballistic evidence obtained at crime scenes to recovered firearms. Matches or "hits" are confirmed by a firearms examiner in the lab.

The system has amassed a large ballistic-image database filled with crime gun data submitted by local, state, and federal agencies throughout the country, and the intelligence information is available to all law enforcement agencies. Since the inception of the system, partner agencies have achieved over 2,200 hits.[56]

HANDLING EVIDENCE IN THE LABORATORY

Human Factors

In handling evidentiary materials, laboratory personnel—scientists and technicians alike—have always been cautious not to disturb or ruin the viability of the materials for any possible examination that would later prove to be useful. Today, because of concerns over the transmission of hepatitis and the AIDS virus, the handling of evidence is of even greater concern.

Although a few laboratories may autoclave specimens, such sterilization with heat may tend to decrease the usefulness of the specimen for analysis purposes. Most laboratories, including the FBI, are merely extra careful in handling evidence involving tissue or body fluids. The procedure followed normally is to ask the agency sending the specimen for any factual information available on the subject so that a determination can be made as to whether the evidence was obtained from a person who may have been infected. In addition, scientists and technicians are instructed to keep their work areas clean, to clean those areas between conducting examinations, and to change and clean lab coats and gloves frequently.

Instrumental Analysis

The kinds of evidence subject to laboratory examinations are many and varied. For laboratory purposes, examinations generally fall into the following categories: chemical examinations, biological examinations, physical examinations, personal identification, firearm identification, documentary examinations, and photography.

In a textbook of this nature it is not practical to present a detailed discussion of the technical intricacies of various scientific instruments. However, it is appropriate to acquaint readers with some of the capabilities of instruments used in the scientific analysis of evidence. Table 8-1 presents some of the more sophisticated equipment currently being used in full-service crime laboratories. It excludes the more obvious or technical examination methods, such as many chemical analyses, fingerprint identification, firearm identification, physical and chemical documentary examinations, photographic techniques and equipment, microscopy, and

DNA analysis; some of these methods were discussed earlier.

ATF FORENSIC SCIENCE LABORATORIES

The Bureau of Alcohol, Tobacco, and Firearms (ATF) of the U.S. Department of the Justice maintains five forensic science laboratories. The ATF National Laboratory was created by Congress in 1886. The ATF laboratories, in addition to analyzing alcohol and tobacco samples, conduct forensic examinations in support of the bureau's explosives, bombing and arson, and illegal-firearm-trafficking investigations, along with major case investigations of state and local authorities. In 2006, the ATF laboratories analyzed 8,631 new alcohol product applications, processed 3,086 forensic cases, and spent 171 days providing expert testimony in courts, 242 days at crime scenes, and 371 days training federal, state, and local investigators and examiners.[57]

The laboratories hold the distinction of being the first federal laboratory system accredited by the ASCLD.[58] The majority of the examinations conducted by the laboratories involve chemical and physical examinations of explosives, firearms, and arson evidence, as well as the document, tool-mark, and latent-fingerprint examinations associated with those investigations.

The forensic laboratories are staffed by over 130 employees, most of whom are chemists, physical scientists, document analysts, latent-print specialists, and firearm and tool-mark examiners. The remainders are evidence technicians and clerical personnel.

Evidence collected at crime scenes of suspected arsons is examined to identify accelerants, incendiaries, and incendiary-device components. Evidence collected at explosion scenes is examined to identify explosives used, blasting caps, leg wires, fuses, timing mechanisms, energy sources, containers, wires, tapes, and various other component parts used to make the bomb. The laboratory system maintains liaisons with explosive manufacturers, who provide exemplars of new explosives products on the market.

Comparative trace-evidence examinations are conducted on materials including tapes, wires, glass, metals, soil, hair, paint, fibers, ink, paper, and wood to determine whether the materials could have a common origin and thereby associate a suspect with a crime.

Questioned-document examinations are conducted to identify handwriting on firearm transaction forms. In addition, examinations are performed to identify typewriters, copy machines, and cigarette tax stamps. Attempts are also made to decipher indented and obliterated writings.

The laboratories also perform a full range of fingerprint, firearm, and tool-mark examinations in support of agency investigations.

TABLE 8-1	Instrumental Analysis in the Crime Lab	
NAME OF INSTRUMENT	PRIMARY USE	ADVANTAGES & WEAKNESSES
Light Microscopy	Stereomicroscopes, polarizing microscopes, and comparison microscopes are widely used in trace evidence analysis.	Provides search and comparison of samples under magnification.
SEM—Scanning Electron Microscope	Based on principles similar to a light microscope; however, uses a stream of electrons to search for and view minute elements or samples.	Provides a detailed 3-D black & white image of the sample viewed; expensive.
Emission Spectrograph	Identification of metals and elements (e.g., sodium, tin, iron, copper) from the light emitted when each element is burned. Hence, rapid analysis from unknown substances can be developed; detection of traces of metallic impurities in residues such as oils and glasses.	Complete analysis of an unknown substance through one operation; requires only a relatively small sample for analysis.
Mass Spectrometer	Identifies unknown samples by creating profiles of the individual compounds and molecules of a substance.	Often used in expediting DNA analysis; sample is destroyed during analysis.
Visible Spectrophotometer	Compares dyes and coloring agents in materials such as hair, cloth, paint, and glass. Records the percentages of each color in a substance or sample.	Eliminates personal error in color comparisons; requires only a relatively small sample with a rapid analysis.
Infrared Spectrophotometer	Primarily identifies and compares inorganic materials such as plastics, rubber, paint, and other chemical substances through the analysis of infrared energy passing through a substance.	Detects slight differences in the composition and molecular arrangement of minute amounts of material.
Atomic Absorption Spectrophotometer	Determines quantitative and proportional concentrations of specific elements in materials through the analysis of a vaporized sample.	Very accurate and sensitive method of determining elemental concentration; relatively economical and rapid procedure.
Gas Chromatograph	(Figure 8-10) Separates and identifies gases or liquids from complex mixtures and solutions; often used to analyze narcotics, paints, plastics, inks, and petroleum-based products such as gas, oil, explosives, and accelerants. Often used in conjunction with the mass spectrometer.	Used in a wide variety of tasks through the analysis of volatile solids, high-boiling point liquids, and gases; sample is destroyed during analysis.
X-Ray Diffraction Spectrophotometer	Identifies and compares unknown crystalline substances through the diffraction of X rays.	Requires only a small amount of sample, and the sample is not consumed in the technique.

Firearm examinations involve primarily serial-number restoration, determination of the operability of weapons, comparison of metals in sawed-off barrels, and determination of the possible common origin of silencers seized from different suspects or locations. (See Figure 8-11.) Gunshot-residue tests are conducted in shootings that involve law enforcement officers. In addition, special tests to evaluate the performance of ammunition and weapons are occasionally done.

Tool-mark examinations generally involve evidence associated with bombings and arson. This includes examination of cut wires, torn tapes, drill holes, pipe wrench marks, saw marks on wood and metal, and numerous other marks made by tools.

The bureau has four National Response Teams that respond to major bombings and arson disasters, nationally and internationally. The teams consist of highly trained investigators, forensic chemists, and explosives

◄ FIGURE 8-10
Gas chromatograph
The gas chromatograph is used to separate and identify gases and fluids from complex mixtures and solutions. In criminal investigations, it is often used to analyze organic materials such as narcotics, explosives, and paints. (Courtesy Indiana State Police)

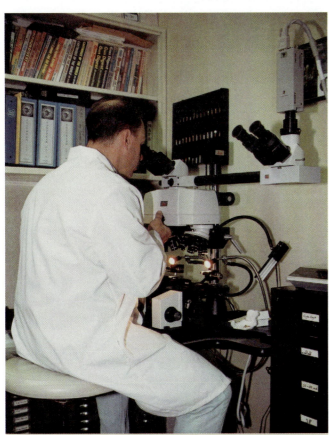

▲ FIGURE 8-11   Forensic examiner conducting firearm examination
In serious violent crimes such as armed robbery and homicide where a handgun is used, the crime lab firearms examiner often plays a major role. Frequently, he/she will be called on to examine recovered firearms in an effort to link suspects or their handguns to a particular crime.
(© AP/Wide World Photos)

technology experts. The teams respond within 24 hours, collect evidence, and complete most laboratory examinations before leaving the crime scene.[59]

THE FBI CRIME LABORATORY

The **FBI Crime Laboratory** is one of the largest and most comprehensive forensic laboratories and is the only full-service forensic laboratory. It was established in 1932. Of importance to the investigator is the fact that the facilities of the FBI laboratory are available without charge to all state, county, and municipal law enforcement agencies in the United States.[60] There are, however, some provisos concerning the submission of evidence for examination to the laboratory. The laboratory will not make examinations if any evidence in the case has been or will be subjected to the same type of technical examination by another laboratory or other experts. This policy is designed to eliminate duplication of effort and to ensure that evidence is received in its original condition, thereby allowing laboratory personnel to interpret their findings properly and ensure meaningful testimony and presentation of evidence in subsequent court cases.

To more effectively and efficiently use its current resources, the FBI laboratory has a policy not to accept cases from other crime laboratories that have the capability of conducting the requested examination. If such cases are submitted by other crime laboratories and there are no special circumstances to warrant the submissions, the cases will be returned unopened and unexamined. This policy should not be construed as lessening the FBI laboratory's continuing commitment to the scientific training of state and local crime laboratory personnel, and it does not limit the laboratory's acceptance of cases from other crime laboratories when special circumstances prevail.

Also, the FBI laboratory no longer accepts evidence from state and local law enforcement agencies regarding property crime investigations unless the cases involve personal injury or the offenses were designed to cause personal injury.

In addition to doing analysis, the FBI furnishes the experts necessary to testify in connection with the results of its examination in either state or federal courts. Again, there is no charge to local law enforcement agencies for this service.

The laboratory provides a comprehensive array of forensic services. Laboratory personnel conduct microscopic examinations of hair and fiber, fabric, tape, rope, and wool. (See Figure 8-12.) Chemical examinations are conducted on many substances, often to supplement examinations conducted by other sections. Examinations are conducted on poisons (toxicology), paint, ink, tear gas, dyes, and flash and water-soluble paper, among others.

Mineralogy examinations are conducted on soils and combinations of mineral substances such as safe insulation, concrete, plaster, mortar, glass, ore, abrasives, gems, industrial dusts, and building materials.

Firearm examiners may be asked to determine if firearms are operating properly or to conduct gunpowder shot-pattern tests. Using the same basic principles of firearm examination, the identification of telltale marks left at crime scenes by punches, hammers, axes, pliers, screwdrivers, chisels, wrenches, and other objects can be made. The explosives specialist can analyze fragments of explosives to determine their original composition and possible sources of raw materials.

The metallurgy unit is called on to restore obliterated or altered numbers on such things as firearms, sewing machines, watches, outboard motors, slot machines, automobiles, tools, and other metallic items. Tests can show whether two or more pieces of metal are related, the possible cause of metal separation, and whether production specifications for metals have been met.

Handwriting examiners agree that no two individuals write exactly alike. Even though there may be superficial resemblances in the writing of two or more persons as a result of similar training, the complexity of writing is such that individual peculiarities and characteristics appear. These characteristics can be detected by a document expert, who then can arrive at a scientific opinion.

The FBI laboratory has also developed the ability to conduct forensic examinations on chemical, biological, and nuclear hazards. In 1996, the Hazardous Materials Response Unit was established in response to the threat of terrorism involving chemical, biological, and nuclear weapons (weapons of mass destruction—WMD), and to an expanding caseload of environmental crimes. After the horrific events of September 11, 2001, and the "anthrax cases" that closely followed, the FBI Lab greatly expanded its role in determining biological, chemical, and nuclear agents that may be used by terrorists. The laboratory works closely with the Centers for Disease Control in developing standardized protocols for handling and analyzing suspected WMD materials. As mentioned earlier, the laboratory has also developed the Computer Analysis and Response Team (CART) program, capable

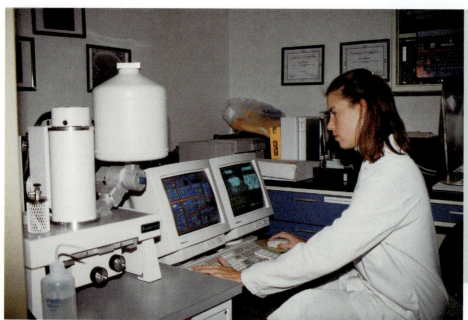

◀ **FIGURE 8-12**
Forensic examiner conducting examination with a scanning electron microscope
One of the standard instruments in today's crime labs is the electron microscope. Typically, evidence such as hair, fiber, fabric, and rope undergoes microscopic examination in the crime lab. Many criminal investigations have been solved by lab personnel, with the help of an electron microscope, matching these types of physical evidence to materials found in the possession of a suspect.
(Courtesy Indiana State Police)

of conducting examinations in which information is extracted from magnetic, optical, and similar storage media and converted into a form usable to investigators or prosecutors. The CART team also has an integral role in preventing and investigating acts of sabotage and terrorism against American infrastructure (e.g., telecommunications, computer, and transportation systems). Finally, the FBI's laboratory is leading the research and development efforts to improve and expedite DNA analysis methods and is one of the few laboratories conducting mitochondrial-DNA testing.

Reference Files

To aid examiners in their work, the FBI laboratory in 1932 established what is now one of the largest reference collections for helping solve cases. These files are of two types: standard reference files and collections, which contain known samples of items, generally of manufactured products, and reference files of questioned materials, which are composed of items actually arising from cases worked and which may form the basis for subsequent identification of individuals or their method of operation (MO). Many of these collections and reference files have been computerized to provide better and faster analyses and comparisons.

The Standard Ammunition File contains over 15,000 specimens of domestic and foreign manufacturers' samples. The Firearms Reference Collection contains over 3,500 handguns and 2,000 shoulder weapons and is used for identifying gun parts and locating serial numbers. The Reference Fired Specimen File contains test bullets and cartridge cases from weapons that have been in the laboratory.

The National Automobile Altered Numbers File is composed of selected specimens, including replica plastic impressions of altered vehicle identification numbers (VINs) found on stolen cars, trucks, and heavy equipment. The file helps investigators identify recovered stolen cars and link them with commercialized theft rings nationwide or other FBI-investigated cases. The National Vehicle Identification Number Standard File maintains standards of VIN plates from each factory of the major manufacturers of American automobiles. The file enables laboratory personnel to determine if a submitted VIN plate is authentic. In the event that bogus VIN plates are being prepared in an automobile factory, the factory as well as the particular machine used can be identified.

The Typewriter Standards File consists of original samples of typewriting from numerous styles of type made in this country as well as in foreign countries. The file permits classification of questioned typewriting on the basis of make and model. The Watermark Standards File is an index of watermarks and brands used by paper manufacturers and aids in tracing the source or origin of paper. Original samples of safety paper used for checks are the contents of the Safety Paper Standards File. These can be used to determine manufacturers. The Checkwriter Standards File is a collection of original checkwriter impressions and permits classification of questioned checkwriter impressions as to make and model. As an aid in determining the manufacturers of office copying machines (either photocopy or duplicator), the laboratory maintains the Office Copier Standards File.

The Shoe Print File contains photographs of designs used in soles and heels made by major U.S. manufacturers. The Tire Tread File, including wheelbase and tire-stance information, is now in a database against which comparisons can be made. This replaces the blueprints, drawings, and photographs of tire-tread patterns, furnished by tire manufacturers, that used to form the basis of the reference file.

The National Motor Vehicle Certificate of Title File consists of original state motor vehicle certificates of title, manufacturers' certificates of origin, and vehicle-emission stickers. This file also contains photographic copies of fraudulent titles, statements, and stickers. The National Fraudulent Check File contains over 100,000 samples of checks, writings, and other documents. More than half of all checks examined are identified with other material in this file. The Anonymous Letter File consists of photographic copies of kidnap notes and extortion and threatening letters. The Bank Robbery Note File contains photocopies of writings of known bank robbers and holdup notes. The Pornographic Materials File includes pornographic materials submitted to the laboratory; it assists in determining the production and distribution sources of the materials. The Explosive Reference Files contain technical data, known standards of explosive items, and bomb components of commercial and military explosives and improvised explosive devices or homemade bombs.

Other files maintained by the FBI are the Automotive Paint File (which can identify makes and models involved in hit-and-run cases), the Hair and Fiber File, the National Stolen Coin File, Blood Serum Files, Safe Insulation Files, and the National Stolen Art File.

PROBLEMS IN CRIME LABORATORIES

The use of DNA analysis in criminal investigations has forever changed the criminal justice system. The use of DNA not only facilitates more accurate prosecutions in current cases but also supports the reopening of old unsolved, often cold, cases, to be reexamined and potentially solved; it also helps to prove or disprove inmates claims that they are innocent. Significant legal limitations still apply to the use of DNA as part of a criminal investigation. Further, major concerns relate to the ethics and the training of the individuals who collect, process, and present DNA evidence in court. Human error is unpreventable, but negligence and the falsification of results is unacceptable and undermines the integrity of criminal justice discipline.

A number of forensic labs have fallen under investigation in recent years. For instance, in 2002, forensic lab technicians in New York City were caught "dry-labbing," or reporting results without actually performing any tests. And, in the last three years, there has been documented corruption and lack of supervision in the Houston, Texas, Police Crime Lab, resulting in the DNA section being closed for over two years.[61] Documented problems in Houston included poorly trained staff and intentional contamination of evidence. As a result, 413 cases had to be retested, because the evidence used to obtain convictions in criminal courts may have been flawed. An external investigation revealed that the serology and DNA work performed over a 12-year period (from 1980–1992) was unreliable.

Many of the problems found in crime labs can be traced to two causes: not enough funding and too close a relationship with the police. Underfunding is problematic because across the country many crime labs are backlogged with evidence that needs to be analyzed. The processing of backlogged evidence is sometimes rushed, resulting in human errors or blatant misconduct. The Massachusetts State Crime Lab reported that in mid-2007 it had more than 16,000 cases that needed to be retested and that some of the evidence was from cases as far back as the early 1980s. Even more alarming is the fact that the statute of limitations may have run out on a number of those cases. Having overly close ties to the police can potentially be a drawback because the analysis of evidence must be objective and impartial. The job of lab technicians is to analyze evidence and present the findings, not necessarily to strengthen the prosecution's case. When the line between the two functions becomes blurred, the result can be an environment conducive to misconduct.

Human and analytical errors made in these laboratories often mean the difference between freedom for the guilty and incarceration of those who are innocent. Therefore, all people concerned must understand the extent of the existing problems within local, state, and federal crime laboratories.

Lack of Training

Continuing professional development is necessary for forensic scientists to remain current and to advance to an elevated level of expertise and responsibility. They are obligated to remain up to date in their field through specific and continued education and other developmental activities.[62] Unfortunately, few universities present degrees in forensic science, and even fewer provide certification for the operation of specific analytical instruments. Most chemists, biologists, geologists, and physicists prepare themselves for careers in forensic science by training under a person who is an experienced examiner and by studying independently.[63] Few defined or organized programs exist for the profession of forensic science. There are few minimum course requirements in terms of structured courses or core curriculum, since most educational requirements are determined by individual laboratories. In fact, in the last decade the number of forensic science academic programs has declined, and the ones that do exist have such low enrollment that support from universities is limited.[64] This situation is particularly surprising given the public interest in the subject created by the myriad popular crime-scene and forensics-oriented movies and television shows (e.g., *Silence of the Lambs, CSI, The Profiler, Cold Case, Forensic Files*). This problem is further compounded by the fact that laboratory analysis and forensics require a rigorous background in the sciences (e.g., biology and chemistry) and not the social or behavioral sciences, where criminology and criminal justice students often study. As a result, many students who are interested in the wider subject matter simply do not have the technical and scientific background to enter the field. For those who are prepared properly, salary and benefits often do not match those in the scientific community, and so well-qualified individuals often choose to enter similar work in the medical or health fields.

Finally, while the formal education that scientists receive provides a foundation for learning and understanding the techniques of forensic science, for the most part, courts rely on additional training and years of experience in order to measure the actual knowledge and ability of the expert. The advancements in technology and sophisticated software used in crime laboratories across the country have created a gap between the skills of scientists and their ability to perform their tasks properly.[65] Many are not updated and trained to know how to use the new equipment appropriately, and as a result, many cases become flawed owing to the lack of training and contemporary knowledge.

Lack of Accreditation

Crime labs must identify a system for establishing its credentials as a forensic laboratory. As mentioned earlier, the primary credentialing organization is the American Society of Crime Laboratory Directors (ASCLD). Whenever a lab applies for accreditation, it has to meet certain requirements, which include the development and publication of a quality control manual, a quality assurance manual, a lab testing protocol, and a program for proficiency testing. *Quality control* refers to the way a product, such as a DNA-typing result, is measured to make certain the product meets a specific standard of quality. *Quality assurance* refers to the actions taken by the laboratory to monitor and document the quality of work being performed. A *lab testing protocol* is a technical manual that includes validation studies performed by the lab itself. Such a protocol sets forth standardized methodologies for performing routine tests in the laboratory. Lastly, *proficiency testing* monitors lab workers individually, as well as the laboratories as institutions. These tests determine whether or not lab workers are performing up to the specified standards of the institution.[66] Yet the fundamental problem with forensic science in crime labs is that, unlike clinical labs, forensic labs are unregulated by the government, allowing them to set their own standards. Forensic scientists do not have to establish competence by obtaining a license or certification. Therefore, a majority of crime labs do not seek accreditation (with the exception of New York, Texas, and Oklahoma, primarily reacting to a series of scandals within major crime labs within their states). In addition, accreditation rates are low for practicing forensic scientists, even though certification boards for all the major fields of forensics have been in existence for more than a decade.[67] According to ASCLD, of the 455 larger crime labs conducting forensic work, only 255 are accredited. Accreditation can cost a few thousand dollars for small operations and as much as $70,000 for the larger, multi-laboratory operations. This price tag does not include the more significant costs associated with implementing new training programs and the equipment needed to meet current standards.[68]

Furthermore, most forensic scientists are not independent experts. About 80% of forensic scientists in North America are affiliated with prosecution or police agencies. Indeed, most forensic scientists work in police laboratories, and many are themselves law enforcement officers, as are their superiors. This association has been known to create a sense of bias within the courtroom between forensic testimony and prosecution. Since the FBI, the police, and the crime lab have similar missions (to arrest, prosecute, and convict), the chance that forensic scientists' courtroom testimony will be unbiased by any other considerations becomes more unlikely.[69] Hence, accreditation alone does not ensure accurate, unbiased, and/or objective laboratory results. For instance in Oklahoma City, Oklahoma, a police chemist (Ms. Joyce Gilchrist, Figure 8-7) appears to have falsified evidence dating back as far as 1982. An internal police report detailed "compelling circumstantial evidence" that Ms. Gilchrist "either intentionally lost or destroyed" evidence from crime scenes. The most significant misconduct involved the case of a convicted man, sentenced to death for the murder of a police officer's teenage daughter in 1982. As a result, the Oklahoma State Bureau of Investigation and the FBI launched a review of nearly 2,000 cases—focusing first on 12 pending death row convictions and 11 cases in which death sentences had already been carried out. At least three current convictions, including the 1982 murder conviction, were reversed after DNA testing proved that the defendants were not

guilty. In overturning the convictions, the Oklahoma Court of Criminal Appeals noted that even though Ms. Gilchrist was a highly educated and well-trained technician, her testimony was "terribly misleading, if not false."[70]

DNA Contamination

DNA technology can do astonishing things. Not only can DNA be used to identify criminals with amazing accuracy when biological evidence exists, but it can also be used to clear suspects and exonerate persons who have been mistakenly accused or convicted of crimes. However, the current federal, state, and local DNA collection and analysis system needs improvement. Numerous cases have emerged revealing faulty practices of forensic crime lab experts who mishandled DNA tests causing them to become contaminated and unable to be used.

Contamination is a concern for proper preservation of evidence. As we learned in Chapter 4, DNA evidence must be collected and packaged separately in individual containers, and each piece of evidence must be segregated from other evidence.[71] Unfortunately, some forensic scientists have tainted tests with their own DNA, in addition to throwing out evidence swabs, misreading results, fingerprinting the wrong suspect, and even cross contaminating different cases.

Washington's State Patrol crime lab was investigated in 2004 after wrongly accusing and sentencing a man for committing the rape of a 10-year-old girl. The forensic scientist working on the case simply botched the test, accidentally contaminating the child's clothing with DNA from another case he had previously been working on. The investigation revealed that forensic scientists contaminated tests or made other mistakes while handling DNA evidence in at least 23 cases which involved major crimes over the previous three years in that department. They were found to have tainted tests with their own DNA in 8 of the 23 cases and made mistakes in 6 other cases by discarding important evidence and by misreading results.[72] This is not the only such incident. Similar contamination was discovered in a December 2002 audit of the Houston Police Department Crime Lab, which noted analysts' lack of training, insufficient documentation of evidence, and evidence contamination. As a result, the Harris County District Attorney's Office has reviewed over 400 cases involving DNA evidence, and the Houston PD Crime Lab has remained closed.[73]

In 1997, U.S. Department of Justice documents obtained by the National Association of Criminal Defense Lawyers identified several examples of questionable practices in the DNA Unit of the FBI laboratory. These practices included the use of plastic pipettes used to extract DNA that had been dissolved in chloroform. However, chloroform also dissolves plastic pipettes, which could have contaminated the sample. Also, examiners commonly overexposed autoradiographs so that

DNA bands appeared as football-shaped rather than as a line. This makes it difficult for an examiner to accurately locate the center of a band in order to analyze it. Some examiners would then move a band by hand for analysis, which could also have resulted in a contaminated misreading.[74]

Sentencing Mistakes and Poor Training

Josiah Sutton was tried and convicted in 1999 for rape. Although prosecutors had little to build the case on, since the victim was the only eyewitness and her recollection was faulty, they were able to get him convicted. Technicians from the Houston police crime laboratory had the rapist's DNA and told the jury that his was a solid match. They sent Sutton to prison to serve a 25-year term. After serving four years, new testing by the Houston crime laboratory showed that the DNA did not match Sutton's. He was released after spending four years of his life behind bars because of a mistake made by forensic examiners in a crime lab. The only reason his DNA was retested stemmed from a state audit and review conducted at the Houston crime laboratory. The audit found that technicians had misinterpreted data, were poorly trained, and kept poor records that did not meet specified levels of acceptance within the laboratory. They found that in most cases, they used up all available evidence, barring defense experts from refuting or verifying their results. They also discovered a leaky roof that had dripped so profusely that dozens of DNA samples of evidence had become contaminated with water.[75] Such mistakes not only harm the validity of evidence in cases, but they also cause citizens to lose confidence in law enforcement and the experts who work in the crime laboratories in their communities.

Backlog of Cases

Public crime laboratories are overwhelmed by backlogs of unanalyzed DNA samples. As a result, these labs may become ill-equipped to handle the increasing arrivals of new DNA evidence and have no space to store the samples. The problems that emerge from the backlogs result in considerable delays in the administration of criminal justice.

According to the National DNA Study Report, the number of unanalyzed DNA cases reported to state and local crime laboratories is more than 57,000. State laboratories reported approximately 37,700 cases, while local laboratories reported approximately 22,600 cases of DNA cases waiting to be analyzed. The total crime cases with possible biological evidence that is either still in the possession of local law enforcement officials or that is backlogged at forensic science laboratories was reported to be over one half million (547,700).[76] Unfortunately, the statute of limitation ends up expiring in many cases in which the evidence could have possibly been useful.

Backlogs at crime laboratories are primarily the result of growing demand and limited resources. Crime laboratory analysts often have to work overtime and on weekends to complete analysis of backlogged cases, especially when the case is considered high profile. The time that it takes to process DNA cases in crime laboratories poses significant delays in many jurisdictions. State crime laboratories take an average of 23.9 weeks to process an unnamed suspect rape kit, and local laboratories average 30.0 weeks to process such tests. The cost to test these rape kits is estimated to be $1,100 per case, not accounting for additional overhead costs.[77]

An example of crimes that could have been prevented if DNA evidence had not been backlogged deals with an incident that happened in Ohio. In 1999, two rapes occurred several months apart in nearby counties. Both of the rapes were linked through DNA. It was discovered that the perpetrator had a criminal history that included a 1994 burglary for which he was required to give a DNA sample for the DNA database. The sample was collected in 1997, and the offender was released from prison in 1999 on probation. Three months later he committed his first rape, and then several months later he raped a second time. Unfortunately, the offender's biological sample was in a backlog and remained unanalyzed until 2001, when a cold hit was made to both rapes. If there had not been a backlog of DNA evidence, the man would have been identified and arrested as a suspect in the first rape, thereby preventing the subsequent rape. The offender was also convicted in late 1999 of a home burglary and for theft of prescription drugs. These crimes would also have been prevented if the DNA match had been detected sooner.[78]

In addition to problems with backlogging, both state and local labs reported that their main concern for their DNA programs was the lack of personnel. They expressed a need for supplemental funding for additional DNA staff and to increase current salaries to avoid the loss of skilled personnel within their laboratories to other potential employers willing to pay more money. Most labs also reported that although federal funding has played an important role in assisting with backlogged DNA cases, the amount of their overall budget funded through federal sources is minimal. Only 20.5% of state crime laboratories receive 50% or more of their funding from federal sources. Local laboratories receive only 4.5% of federal funding.[79]

Furthermore, postconviction DNA testing resulting in exoneration has caused many state legislatures to impose requirements for the indefinite storage of evidence used in crime convictions, although such requirements frequently become unfunded mandates passed down to local jurisdictions. Indeed, there have been reports of large metropolitan law enforcement agencies who discarded potential DNA evidence in an attempt to create additional storage space for new evidence.[80] Therefore, evidence that could have possibly helped a victim is now gone forever and useless to future crime investigations.

Scandals and Mistakes Within the FBI Crime Lab: The Madrid Bombing Case

Another widely publicized incident relating to problems within crime labs involves the allegations made in 1995 by Frederic Whitehurst, a former FBI laboratory supervisory special agent who had worked for the lab since 1986. He alleged that over the course of several years, laboratory examiners had improperly testified outside their expertise, presented unacceptable evidence, perjured themselves, fabricated evidence, and failed to follow the appropriate procedures of the laboratory. He also said that he believed that FBI management retaliated against him for making those accusations.[81] Yet changes have been made within the FBI laboratory since Whitehurst blew the whistle on his coworkers. After intense investigation into his accusations, the FBI lab implemented a formal quality assurance plan and has since been accredited by the ASCLD.[82]

However, the most significant blunder to date in any crime lab within the United States occurred in March 2004 with the arrest of Portland, Oregon attorney, Brandon Mayfield. On March 17, 2004, the Spanish National Police provided the FBI with digital, electronically transmitted photographic images of latent fingerprints that were recovered from the plastic bag containing the detonator in the March 11 bombings in Madrid that killed 191 people and injured 2,000 others.[83] (See Figure 8-13.) The FBI Lab in Quantico, Virginia, used the Automated Fingerprint Identification System (AFIS) to search for possible matches to the fingerprints. Mayfield's fingerprints were one of 20 candidates suggested for comparison by the system.[84] At least three FBI fingerprint specialists,

including a supervisory agent with over 30 years of experience verified the identification of Mayfield as the suspect from the latent print on the plastic bag. One examiner testified that the latent print was "the left index finger of Mr. Mayfield."[85] It is not known whether the identification process was influenced by information pertaining to Mayfield's conversion to Islam or his activities as a lawyer in defending recent "terrorist" suspects prior to the match being officially declared.[86] However, what is known is that at some point in March or April, the FBI began "sneak and peak" and electronic surveillance of Mayfield under the Foreign Intelligence Surveillance Act (FISA) and the U.S. PATRIOT Act.[87] According to court documents, FBI agents began their surveillance of Mayfield two weeks after the attacks in Madrid, and, under a provision of the U.S. PATRIOT Act, they entered his home without his knowledge—but aroused suspicion by bolting the wrong lock on their way out and leaving a footprint on a rug inside the house. During a later raid based on the fingerprint identication, the FBI seized computers, modems, safe deposit boxes, assorted papers, and copies of the Quran.[88]

On May 20, the Spanish National Police reported that they had identified the latent print in question as that of a different individual . . . an Algerian national living in Spain. As the information became conflicted between the two agencies, the FBI sent agents to Spain in order to recover the original latent print. To their surprise, the print had been destroyed.

Four FBI examiners with a combined total of 93 years of experience in latent print science reexamined and reanalyzed the latent print. The examiners concurred that the latent print had multiple separations (i.e., that it was

▲ **FIGURE 8-13   The Madrid bombing case**
The FBI Laboratory error in matching the latent print (*left*) as that of Mr. Brandon Mayfield has cast doubt on the integrity of fingerprint evidence. Noting that the error print (*right*) was not rotated and cropped to match the corresponding latent print was a serious mistake that embarrassed the FBI as well as complicated the entire Madrid bombing investigation. (For more information on the technical aspects of this case, see www.onin.com.) (© AP/Wide World Photos)

divided by many lines of demarcation possibly caused by creases in the underlying material, multiple touches by one or more fingers, or both).[89] On the morning of May 24, 2004, utilizing information from this new evaluation by the four examiners, the FBI *reversed* its position on Mayfield and indicated that the print had no value for identification purposes, and Mayfield was subsequently released.

The ensuing investigation revealed that the FBI had originally sent examiners to Spain but that the investigators did not speak Spanish. Further, they never asked to see the original latent print. More problematic, if the print indeed had "no value for identification purposes," how could such a positive and previous identification to Mayfield be developed in the first place? After all, this was an international event with over 190 persons killed that focused on suspected terrorist links to al-Qaeda. It appears that the FBI violated one of the most basic rules of investigation: failing to maintain objectivity during scientific analysis and failing to compare the best evidence to samples found at the scene. Essentially, FBI fingerprint analysts drew much of their attention to Mayfield's past and relied on improper methodology to confirm the identification of a latent print to a suspect. As one expert indicated: "There were many discrepancies . . . and a competent (fingerprint) expert should have seen all the discrepancies."[90] The FBI's contention that the misidentification occurred as a result of problems with the quality of the digital image is in itself an indictment of the poor procedures followed by analysts. If the image was corrupted, then a positive identification should have never been made. Worst of all, this case has far-reaching implications concerning the scientific integrity of fingerprint identification, the acceptance of fingerprint evidence in court, and the scrutiny of crime laboratory personnel.

In a recent case, *United States* v. *Mitchell*,[91] the court concluded that latent fingerprint identification evidence, as produced by the FBI's procedures, met the requirements for admissibility established by *Daubert* v. *Merrell Dow Pharmaceuticals, Inc.* However, the FBI latent print unit's performance in Mayfield's case suggests that, notwithstanding *Mitchell's* recognition of a valid scientific basis for fingerprint identification, the potential for error in the making of an identification requires that identification testimony be rigorously tested and excluded if compliance with requirements for ensuring accuracy in its application cannot be demonstrated.[92]

Code of Ethics

The findings of forensic scientists are often the critical element in determining the guilt or innocence of an individual. The examination, which is the basis of the findings, must be conducted in accordance with the principles necessary to achieve an unfailing conclusion. Scientists must examine the subject matter as a whole and their

conclusions must be delivered under conditions that support their comprehension and use.

Different codes of ethics for forensic science have been adopted over the years. The American Society of Crime Laboratory Directors, the American Board of Criminalistics, and the Council for the Registration of Forensic Practitioners are all examples of organizations that have incorporated a specific code of ethics for forensic science.[93] An example of a code of ethics for forensic science can be found under the Preamble of the SAFS Ethics Committee, a pharmaceutical research group. It states that there is a requirement for forensic scientists to possess a comprehensible knowledge in the subject matter in which they are investigating. This requires them to have the necessary skills, background knowledge, and forensic science judgment that can be directly applicable to issues at hand. Also, it is required that scientists conduct examinations in accordance with the principles of the scientific method by using state-of-the-art methodology. In addition, it is required that scientists employ enough safeguards necessary to assure control of the quality of the examination. These safeguards include the preservation of adequate materials to allow for reexamination if necessary and ample documentation to permit a reasonable evaluation of the protocol employed and a confirmation of the accuracy of the findings. Last, it is required that forensic scientists present their comprehensive presentation, whether verbal or written, in language that is understandable to counsel for the client, the court, and the jury.[94]

These ethics codes require competence, quality, training, and integrity on the part of forensic experts and managers working in every crime laboratory across the country. Forensic experts must be competent to take on tasks that are required in the assignments they receive. They are expected to perform their tasks to the best of their abilities, conducting themselves in a trustworthy and honest manner, especially when facing obstacles that may hinder their performance.

Unfortunately, scandal has become commonplace in a realm where science and integrity must be the hallmarks of competency. For example, a publicized report in Washington revealed how a crime lab chemist was caught snorting heroin on the job for months, stealing the drug from evidence he was testing. In addition, a review of two dozen crime lab disciplinary records in the state raised questions about the professionalism of some scientists on the payroll. It was discovered that in the past five years, a lab supervisor was caught viewing pornography on his office computer, another lab manager was fired because he sexually harassed female coworkers, and a DNA analyst was found sleeping on the job.[95] Another example of a lack of ethics focuses on the issue of proficiency tests. Crime lab workers must pass one test every year in each specialty to satisfy voluntary rules set by the American Society of Crime Laboratory Directors' Laboratory Accreditation Board. For instance, a Tacoma lab forensic scientist took a routine proficiency exam in September of 1998, in which his ability to interpret footprint evidence was tested. When accreditation inspectors visited the lab a year later, they could not find any record of the exam. They discovered that the scientist's supervisor had never reviewed the test or realized that the scientist had actually failed to correctly match all the footprints with the correct shoe.[96]

Unfortunately, stories such as these have become commonplace. A number of forensic crime lab examiners have failed to conduct themselves in an ethical manner, and it has become increasingly apparent that these mistakes can lead to even more detrimental problems over time. It is also apparent that justice cannot be served fairly under such circumstances.

KEY TERMS

American Society of Crime Laboratory
    Directors (ASCLD)
Automated Fingerprint Identification
    System (AFIS)
crime laboratory
criminalistics
*Daubert v. Merrell Dow
    Pharmaceuticals, Inc.*

deoxyribonucleic acid (DNA)
familial DNA search (DNA kinship
    search)
FBI Crime Laboratory
forensic science
Frye v. United States
Integrated Automated Fingerprint
    Identification System (IAFIS)

kinship DNA searches
low copy number DNA sample
mitochondrial DNA (mtDNA)
morgue
National Integrated Ballistic
    Information Network (NIBIN)
nuclear DNA
rules of evidence

REVIEW QUESTIONS

1. Define *forensic science.*
2. What difficulties are caused by an investigator not understanding the capabilities and limitations of crime laboratories?
3. Define *criminalistics.*
4. What are the three primary purposes of digital crime labs in the United States?
5. Describe the most important resource in a crime laboratory.
6. Describe the measures of effectiveness of crime laboratories.
7. Describe the role and the importance of DNA analysis in criminal investigation.
8. Describe AFIS.

9. In light of concerns about the transmittal of hepatitis and AIDS, how are body fluids that are submitted for analysis handled in a laboratory?
10. What are the main areas of responsibility of the ATF laboratories?
11. What limitations are placed on the submission of evidence to the FBI laboratory?
12. Describe NIBIN, IAFIS, and CODIS.
13. What are the primary DNA analysis techniques that have been used since 1985?
14. Distinguish the *Frye* test from the *Daubert* test regarding the admissibility of scientific evidence.
15. What are some of the major problems confronting police crime labs?

INTERNET ACTIVITIES

1. Visit the FBI website at www.fbi.gov and search for the crime laboratory. What services are provided to law enforcement by the lab? What are the primary missions of the FBI, and how does the crime lab support those missions? What are CART and CIRG? What are the primary forensic examinations performed by the lab? Finally, what is LEO, and how is it employed in reference to sharing forensic information among law enforcement agencies?
2. Go to www.crimelynx.com and search for information about postconviction DNA cases under "Crime Policy Links." What is the most recent estimate of the number of convicted offenders who have been exonerated owing to DNA testing? Under what conditions can an offender request DNA testing? Who pays for

the testing? What occurs if the DNA tests are inconclusive? In your opinion, will the increasing popularity of postconviction DNA testing affect the nature of criminal investigations? Now go to www.innocenceproject.com and compare your information with that found on this website. Is there a difference?
3. Visit the Massachusetts State Police website at www.mass.gov/msp and explore its unique crime lab area. Click the "mock crime scene" and review the varied functions of the crime lab in analyzing pieces of evidence within the scene. Click the gas can and visit the arson-explosives unit of the lab; click the bloody rock and observe the DNA analysis unit; or click the gun in the victim's hand and explore the intricacies of the ballistics unit.

NOTES

1. Florida Bureau of Law Enforcement, "Crime Laboratory," unpublished document, p. 2.
2. Paul L. Kirk, "The Ontogeny of Criminalistics," *Journal of Criminology and Police Science,* 1963, Vol. 54, p. 238.
3. Joseph L. Peterson, Steven Mihajlovic, and Joanne L. Bedrosian, "The Capabilities, Uses, and Effects of the Nation's Criminalistics Laboratories," *Journal of Forensic Sciences,* 1985, Vol. 30, No. 1, p. 11.
4. Richard Fox and Carl L. Cunningham, *Crime Scene Search and Physical Evidence Handbook* (Washington, D.C.: U.S. Department of Justice, 1985), p. 1.
5. Statement of Kevin L. Lothridge, President, American Society of Crime Laboratory Directors, National Forensic Science Technology Center, before the House Judiciary Committee, Subcommittee on Crime, May 13, 1997.
6. Ibid.
7. www.nfstc.org/aboutus.htm (graciously supplied by NFSTC).
8. Kevin Rayburn, "U of L Teams with FBI, Other Agencies to Stop Digital Crime," *University of Louisville News,* KY, November 3, 2006, See http://php.louisville.edu/news/news.php?news+727 (September 1, 2007).
9. James W. Osterburg, *The Crime Laboratory* (Bloomington: Indiana University Press, 1968), p. 3.
10. Marc H. Caplan and Joe Holt Anderson, *Forensics: When Science Bears Witness,* National Institute of Justice (Washington, D.C.: Government Printing Office, Oct. 1984), p. 2.
11. For a discussion of working relationships between police investigators and crime laboratory personnel, see Joseph L. Peterson, *The Utilization of Criminalistics Services by the Police: An Analysis of the Physical Evidence Recovery Process,* Law Enforcement Assistance Administration, National Institute of Law Enforcement and Criminal Justice (Washington, D.C.: Government Printing Office, March 1974).
12. The President's Commission on Law Enforcement and the Administration of Justice, Task Force Report: *The Police* (Washington, D.C.: Government Printing Office, 1967), p. 90.
13. National Advisory Commission on Criminal Justice Standards and Goals, *Police* (Washington, D.C.: Government Printing Office, 1973), p. 303.
14. See Kenneth S. Field, Oliver Schroeder, Jr., Ina J. Curtis, Ellen L. Fabricant, and Beth Ann Lipskin, *Assessment of the Forensic Sciences Profession: Assessment of the Personnel of the Forensic Sciences Profession,* Vol. II, National Institute of Law Enforcement and Criminal Justice, Law Enforcement Assistance Administration, U.S. Department of Justice (Washington, D.C.: Government Printing Office, March 1977), pp. I-4–I-9.
15. National Advisory Commission, *Police,* p. 302.
16. Ibid.
17. Peterson, *Utilization of Criminalistics Services,* p. 6.
18. 293 Fed. 1013 (D.C. Cir. 1923).
19. 507 U.S. 904 (1993).
20. *United States* v. *Mitchell,* 365 F. 3d 215, (3rd Circ. 2004).
21. Office of Justice Programs and Office of Community Orientated Policing Services, National Institute of Justice, *A Resource Guide to Law Enforcement, Corrections, and Forensic Technologies* (Washington, D.C.: U.S. Department of Justice, May 2001), www.ncjrs.org, p. 53.
22. Ibid., p. 57.
23. Ibid., pp. 57–58.
24. Bureau of Justice Statistics, National Institute of Justice, "Survey of DNA Crime Laboratories, 1998" (Washington D.C.: U.S. Department of Justice, Feb. 2000), p. 1.
25. *Prosecutors in State Courts* (Washington, D.C.: U.S. Department of Justice, 1996), p. 6.
26. www.fbi.gov/kids/dna/dna.htm, July 17, 1998.
27. National Commission on the Future of DNA Evidence, National Institute of Justice, "What Every Law Enforcement Officer Should Know about DNA Evidence," pamphlet (Washington, D.C.: U.S. Department of Justice, no publication date).
28. Theresa F. Spear, "Sample Handling Considerations for Biological Evidence and DNA Extracts," California Department of Justice, California Criminalistics Institute.
29. Ibid.
30. T. Spear, "Sample Handling Considerations for Biological Evidence and DNA Extracts," and T. Spear and N. Khoshkebarr, "Analysis of Old Biological Samples: A Study on the Feasibility of Obtaining Body Fluid Identification and DNA Typing Results," California Department of Justice, California Criminalistics Institute.
31. U.S. Department of Justice, Bureau of Justice Statistics, "Survey of DNA Crime Laboratories, 2001." Updated September 2007.
32. www.fbi.gov/hq/org/dnau/htm.
33. Ibid.
34. Office of Justice Programs, *National Institute of Justice Journal* (Washington, D.C.: U.S. Department of Justice, Dec. 1997), pp. 17–19.
35. Notes from the seminar "Supporting Your Case Using DNA Evidence," Altamonte Springs, Florida, Aug. 23–24, 2001.
36. See www.fbi.gov/hq/lab/codis/clickmap.htm.
37. Ronald Bailey, "Criminal Kinship: Slouching Toward a DNA Database Nation," *Reason Magazine,* May 19, 2006. www.reason.com/news/show/116487.html.
38. Office of Justice Programs and Office of Community Orientated Policing Services, *A Resource Guide,* pp. 56–57.
39. Shaila K. Dewan, "New York Works on a Better DNA Trap to Catch Burglars," *The New York Times,* May 26, 2004, p. 1 and p. 23.
40. Frederick R. Bieber, Charles H. Brenner, and David Lazer, "Human Genetics: Finding Criminals Through DNA of Their Relatives," *Science,* Vol. 312, No. 5778 June 2, 2006, pp. 1315–1316.
41. Ibid.
42. Ibid.
43. Ronald Bailey, "Criminal Kinship."

44. Ibid.
45. Ker Than, "Family DNA Helps Cops Catch Criminals," *Live Science*, May 11, 2006 and William J. Cromie, "Catching Criminals Through Their Relatives' DNA; Finding Genetic Needles in Database Haystacks," *Harvard University Gazette*. May 11, 2006, www.news.harvard.edu/gazette/daily/2006/05/11-dna.html.
46. Cromie, "Catching Criminals."
47. The Innocence Project. http://innocenceproject.org/ September 2, 2007.
48. Ibid.
49. Ibid.
50. Ibid.
51. Scott Cooper, "Judge Releases McCarty; Rips Former Chemist," *OKC News*, May 11, 2007.
52. Thomas F. Wilson, "Automated Fingerprint Identification Systems," *Law Enforcement Technology*, Aug.–Sept. 1986, p. 17.
53. Florida Department of Law Enforcement, *Criminal Justice Information Systems Newsletter*, May 1995, p. 1.
54. Kenneth R. Moses, "A Consumer's Guide to Fingerprint Computers," *Identification News*, June 1986, p. 6.
55. Much of the material in this section is drawn from Thomas F. Wilson and Paul L. Woodward, *Automated Fingerprint Identification Systems: Technology and Policy Issues* (Washington, D.C.: U.S. Department of Justice, 1987).
56. Federal Bureau of Investigation, *CJIS* (a newsletter for the criminal justice community), 1999, vol. 3, no. 2, pp. 1–3.
57. www.atf.treas/nibin.
58. www.atf.treas.gov/labs.
59. www.atf.treas.gov/explarson.
60. www.fbi.gov/labs.
61. www.fbi.gov/lab/report/labhome.htm.
62. Roma Khanna and Steve McVicker, "Troubling" Cases Surface in Report on HPD Crime Lab" *Houston Chronicle*, July 17, 2007, and Mike Glenn, "Police DNA Lab under the Microscope," *Houston Chronicle*, July 11, 2006.
63. "Education and Training in Forensic Science: A Guide for Forensic Science Laboratories, Educational Institutions, and Students," National Institute of Justice, June 2004, p. 25.
64. Richard Saferstein, *Criminalistics: An Introduction to Forensic Science*, 6th ed. (Upper Saddle River, NJ: Prentice Hall, 1998), p. 17.
65. Randolf Jonakait, "Forensic Science: The Need for Regulation," *Harvard Journal of Law and Technology*, Spring 1999, p. 6.
66. Saferstein, *Criminalistics*, p. 243.
67. Paul Gianelli, "Crime Labs Need Improvement," *Issues in Science and Technology*, 2003, p. 2.
68. Ibid., p. 3.
69. Robert Tanner, "Crime Labs under a Microscope: Miscues Lead to Calls for Changes in Forensic Labs," *Washington Post*, July 27, 2003, p. 2.
70. John F. Kelly and Phillip K. Wearne, "Tainting Evidence" (*Denver Post Online*, 1998), p. 15.
71. "Document Says Police Chemist Falsified Evidence," *Dallas Morning News*, April 21, 2004, p. 2A.
72. Barry Fisher, *Techniques of Crime Scene Investigation*, 6th ed. (Boca Raton, FL: CRC Press, 2000), p. 15.
73. Ruth Teichroeb, "Rare Look Inside State Crime Labs Reveals Recurring DNA Test Problems," *Seattle Post Intelligencer*, July 22, 2004, p. 2.
74. "Chief Hopes Computers Restore Faith in Crime Lab," *Dallas Morning News*, p. 4A.
75. Jack King, "DOJ Aware of Problems in FBI's DNA Lab," *NADCL News Release*, p. 1–2.
76. Adam Liptak, "Houston DNA Review Clears Convicted Rapist and Ripples in Texas Could Be Vast," March 11, 2003, p. 1.
77. Nicholas P. Lovrich., Travis Pratt., Michael Gaffney, Charles Johnson, Christopher Asplen, Lisa Hurst, and Timothy Schellberg, "National Forensic DNA Study Report," February 2004, p. 3. See www.ojp.usdoj.gov/nij/pdf/dna_studyreport_final.pdf.
78. Ibid., p. 4.
79. Ibid., p. 63.
80. Ibid., p. 4.
81. Ibid., p. 17.
82. United States Department of Justice, "Background to the OIG Investigation," *FBI Labs Report*, March 1997, p. 1.
83. Ibid., p. 4.
84. Excerpted from an affidavit filed by FBI Special Agent Richard K. Werder in support of an arrest warrant for Brandon Mayfield. The warrant was signed by U.S. District Judge Robert Jones on May 6, 2004.
85. The AFIS system analyzed the print against a widely accepted 45 million fingerprint database yielding 20 possible matches.
86. Excerpted from testimony of Mr. Ken Moses, FBI Forensic Identification Services, May 19, 2004 (*U.S.* v. *Brandon Mayfield*).
87. Steven T. Wax and Christopher J. Schatz, "A Multitude of Errors: The Brandon Mayfield Case," *The Champion*, Sept./Oct. 2004. Online at the National Association of Criminal Defense Lawyers at www.nacdl.org.
88. Ibid.
89. Associated Press, "FBI Apologizes to Lawyer Held in Madrid Bombings," *MSNBC.com*, May 25, 2004.
90. Excerpted from the motion to dismiss material witness filed in U.S. District Court, Oregon on May 4, 2004.
91. Alan John Bayle, as quoted in Wax and Schatz, "A Multitude of Errors: The Brandon Mayfield Case." Note that Bayle's finding of fundamental error by the FBI analysts was consistent with the view held by the Spanish police authorities regarding the print.
92. *United States* v. *Mitchell*, 365 F.3d 215, 244-47 (3rd Circuit, 2004).
93. Excerpted from Wax and Schatz, p. 8. See also *Kumho Tire Co., Ltd.* v. *Carmichael*, 526 U.S. 137, (1999), criticizing purported expert's application of his methodology.
94. Peter Barnett, *Ethics in Forensic Science: Professional Standards for the Practice of Criminalistics* (Boca Raton, FL: CRC Press, 2001), p. 163.
95. H. Dale Nute, "An Ethical Code for Forensic Science," July 2000, pp. 2–3.
96. Teichroeb, "Oversight for Crime Lab Staff," p. 2.
97. Ibid., p. 7.

9

INJURY AND DEATH INVESTIGATIONS

▲ The investigation of deaths, whether by accidental or felonious cause, can often be aided by modern technology. For example, the underwater search for missing bodies can be facilitated by sonar tracking devices such as the one shown in this photo from Hennepin County, Minnesota, where deputies are using a side scan sonar unit to attempt to locate a body. (© AP/Wide World Photos)

The investigation of felonious injuries and criminal homicides can be the most important, yet difficult, responsibility assigned to a police investigator. First, these crimes are viewed as being among the most serious offenses committed in our society. The seriousness is reflected in all state statutes, which impose severe penalties for acts resulting in the grave bodily injury or death of a human being. Second, in the beginning stages of some homicide investigations, the inability to identify the decedent greatly complicates the investigative process and prevents it from moving forward. In all homicides, questions such as "Who were the victim's enemies?" and "Who would benefit most from the victim's death?" must be answered before any significant progress can be made in the investigation. Estimating the time of death also needs to be done early in the investigation.

Third, criminal homicides, in particular, can generate a lot of media attention and public scrutiny for the department. Pressure to solve the crime from both inside and outside the police agency creates added strain on the criminal investigator.

For these cases, in particular, investigators may need to call on the assistance of experts in the scientific and medical fields. Investigators should create working relationships with specialists such as forensic pathologists, toxicologists, entomologists, and botanists, who can all provide useful assistance to the case. In short, the severity of these crimes warrants that investigators use all available resources in their investigations.

RESPONDING TO THE SCENE

In responding to the scene of a suspected homicide or assault, fundamental rules must be followed. The officer should proceed with deliberate but not reckless speed. As the officer approaches the scene, he or she should be observant for a suspect fleeing either on foot or by vehicle. The dispatcher may have been able to obtain and relate specific details to the responding officer about the offense and suspect. If not, the officer has to rely on discriminating observations, training, and past experience. The officer should be suspicious of a vehicle being driven away from the crime scene at a high rate of speed or in an erratic manner, an individual who attempts to hide from view, or a person whose clothing indicates recent involvement in a struggle.

ARRIVING AT THE SCENE

When the investigator arrives at the scene, formal contact should be established with other official agency representatives. The investigator must identify the first respondent to ascertain if any artifacts or contamination may have been introduced to the death scene, and work with all people to ensure the scene's safety before entering the scene. In addition, the investigator must take the initiative to introduce himself or herself, identify essential personnel, and establish rapport. Before entering the scene, the investigator should identify other essential officials at the scene (e.g., fire, EMS, social or child protective services), explain his or her role in the investigation, and identify and document the identity of the first essential official(s) to the scene (the first "professional" arrival at the scene for investigative follow-up).

Determining Scene Safety

Determining scene safety for all investigative personnel is essential to the investigative process. The risk of environmental and physical injury must be eliminated before scene investigation is begun. Risks can include hostile crowds, collapsing structures, traffic, and environmental and chemical threats. To prevent injury or loss of life, the investigator must attempt to establish scene safety before entering the scene and should contact appropriate agencies for assistance with particular scene-safety issues.

Upon arrival at the scene, the investigator should assess and/or establish physical boundaries; secure his or her vehicle and park as safely as possible; use personal safety devices (physical, biochemical safety); arrange for removal of animals or secure them, if present and if possible; and obtain clearance/authorization at the scene from the individual responsible for scene safety (e.g., fire marshal, disaster coordinator).

While exercising scene safety, the investigator must protect the integrity of the scene and evidence, to the extent possible, from contamination by people, animals, and the elements. Because of potential scene hazards, the body may have to be removed before the scene investigation can continue.

Confirming or Pronouncing Death

Appropriate medically trained personnel must make a determination of death prior to the initiation of the death investigation. The confirmation or pronouncement of death determines jurisdictional responsibilities. The investigator must be certain that appropriate personnel have viewed the body and that death has been confirmed. The investigator should also identify and document the name and organizational affiliation of the individual who made the official determination of death, as well as the time of determination.

Once death has been determined and rescue/resuscitative efforts have ceased, medical and legal jurisdiction can be established.

Participating in Scene Briefing with Attending Agency Representatives

Scene investigators must recognize the varying jurisdictional and statutory responsibilities that apply to individual agency representatives (e.g., law enforcement, fire, EMT, judicial, legal). Determining each agency's responsibility at the scene is essential in planning the scope and depth of each scene investigation and the release of information to the public. Investigators must identify specific responsibilities, share appropriate preliminary information, and establish investigative goals with each agency present at the scene. When participating in the scene briefing, the investigator should locate the staging area (entry point to the scene, command post, etc.), document

the scene location (address, mile marker, building name), determine the nature and scope of the investigation by obtaining preliminary investigative results (e.g., suspicious versus nonsuspicious death), and ensure that initial accounts have been obtained from the first witness(es).

Conducting A Scene Walk-Through

Conducting a scene **walk-through** provides the investigator with an overview of the entire scene. The walk-through is the investigator's first opportunity to locate and view the body, identify valuable and/or fragile evidence, and determine the initial investigative procedures for a systematic examination and documentation of the scene and body. The investigator can also conduct a scene walk-through to establish pertinency and perimeters. Upon arrival at the scene, the investigator should reassess scene boundaries and adjust as appropriate; establish a path of entry and exit; identify visible physical and fragile evidence; document and photograph fragile evidence immediately and collect it, if appropriate; and locate and view the body. An initial scene walk-through is essential for minimizing scene disturbance and preventing the loss and/or contamination of physical and fragile evidence.

ESTABLISHING A CHAIN OF CUSTODY

Ensuring the integrity of the evidence by establishing and maintaining a **chain of custody** is vital to the investigation. This will save the investigator from subsequent allegations of tampering, theft, planting, and contamination of evidence. Before the removal of any evidence, the custodian(s) of evidence should be designated and should generate and maintain a chain of custody for all evidence collected. Throughout the investigation, those responsible for preserving the chain of custody should document the location of the scene and the time of the death investigator's arrival at the scene; determine the custodian(s) of evidence, determine which agencies are responsible for the collection of specific types of evidence, and determine evidence-collection priority; identify, secure, and preserve evidence, using proper containers, labels, and preservatives; document the collection of evidence by recording its location at the scene, time of collection, and time and location of disposition; and develop personnel lists, witness lists, and documentation of times of arrival and departure of personnel. It is essential to maintain a proper chain of custody for evidence. Through proper documentation, collection, and preservation, the integrity of the evidence can be ensured. A properly maintained chain of custody and prompt transport of the evidence will reduce the likelihood of a challenge to the integrity of the evidence.

THE MEDICO-LEGAL EXAMINATION

The **medico-legal examination** brings medical skill to bear on injury and death investigations. The medical specialist frequently called on to assist in such cases is the forensic pathologist. **Forensic pathology,** a subspecialty of pathology, is the study of how and why people die. To become a forensic pathologist, a physician first attends an approved pathology residency program and then attends three years in a strictly anatomic program or five years in a combined anatomic and clinical program. One or two additional years are devoted to studying the pathology of sudden, unexpected, natural death, as well as violent death, in an approved forensic fellowship training program (there are approximately 30 throughout the country). Most programs are centered in major cities that have a large number of deaths from various causes. The most important area of study for a forensic pathologist is death investigation, but some forensic pathology programs also include examination of the living to determine physical and sexual abuse. Physicians specializing in forensic pathology are ordinarily employed by some unit of government and are not in private practice.[1]

THE AUTOPSY

All violent and suspicious deaths require an **autopsy** to determine the time and precise cause of death.[2] The autopsy may also answer the following questions:

- What type of weapon was employed?
- If multiple wounds were inflicted, which wound was fatal?
- How long did the victim live after the injury?
- What position was the victim in at the time of the assault?
- From what direction was the force applied?
- Is there any evidence of a struggle or self-defense?
- Is there any evidence of rape or other sex-related acts?
- Was the deceased under the influence of alcohol or any type of drug?[3] (The actual analysis will be done by the toxicologist.)

Answers to all or even some of these questions increase the possibility of bringing the death investigation to a successful conclusion.

Dead body evidence checklist

The following dead body evidence checklist will assist the investigator to systematically follow all the steps necessary to be certain that no physical evidence is overlooked:

- Thoroughly photograph everything before moving or touching it

- Collect fragile evidence on the body
- Remove hair, fingernails and other trace evidence. Use toothpicks to collect evidence that might be under the fingernails if they are short. Place the items in waxed paper, bundle them, and place them in envelopes.
- Brush the head hair and the pubic region (if the body is unclothed). Hold butcher paper under the area being brushed.
- Remove trace evidence from the entire body's skin and clothing, including the face, hands, feet, legs, torso, pubic area, and neck, with Scotch tape or lint rollers. Use only frosted tape.
- Collect samples of pooled blood.
  —Use hemasticks to confirm it is actually blood.
  —Collect control samples (as close to the area as possible).
  —Use a cotton swab with one drop of distilled water on it. Place the swab in wax paper loosely, and then place it in an envelope.
- Collect exemplars from the following areas:
  —Environment (vegetation, soil, maggots, other).
  —Residence (carpet fibers, paint, misc. fibers, other).
  —Vehicle (carpet fibers, seat fibers, roll the tires, VIN number, wheel base).
  —Animals (hairs, bedding).
- Collect blood samples from the victim using the "Sexual Assault Evidence Collection Kit" blood tubes (see Chapter 10, Sex-Related Offenses, for a more detailed discussion of this topic).
- Swab the bite mark areas.
- Swab the oral cavity.
- Collect exemplar hairs.
- The victim should be fingerprinted even if there is positive proof of identification.
- If circumstances dictate, palm prints and footprints should also be obtained. They may prove useful in matching prints that are later found in the suspect's home, business, car, or other location.
- Collection of the victim's clothing.
  —If the clothing is damaged, the investigator should determine whether the damage is related to the assault or was caused by hospital or emergency personnel giving emergency treatment. When a determination is made of the cause the damage, it should be recorded in the investigation repor.[4]

ESTIMATING TIME OF DEATH

Determination of the time of death or the interval between the time of death and the time that a body is found (i.e., the *postmortem interval*) can be difficult. A forensic pathologist attempts to determine the time of death as accurately as possible, realizing, however, that such a determination is only a best estimate. Unless a death is witnessed, or a watch breaks during a traumatic incident, the exact time of death cannot be determined. The longer the time since death, the greater the chance for error in determining the postmortem interval. There are numerous individual observations that, when used together, provide the best estimate of the time of death. These include body temperature, rigor mortis, livor mortis, decompositional changes, and stomach contents. A thorough scene investigation must also be performed, and environmental conditions should be documented. The environment is the most important factor in determining the postmortem interval.[5]

Algor Mortis

After death, the body cools from its normal internal temperature of 98.6°F to the surrounding environmental temperature. Many studies have examined this decrease in body temperature, called **algor mortis,** to determine formulas that could predict its consistency. Unfortunately, because of numerous variables, body cooling is an inaccurate method of determining the postmortem interval. In general, however, evaluating a decrease in body temperature is most helpful within the first 10 hours after death. During this time, with a normal body temperature and at an ideal environmental temperature of 70° to 75°F, the body cools at approximately 1.5°F per hour.

However, the problem with using the 1.5°F-per-hour calculation is the assumption that the internal temperature is 98.6°F and the environmental temperature is 70° to 75°F. If a decedent's body temperature is higher than normal because of infection or physical exercise, the body temperature of 98.6°F cannot be used. Furthermore, the outside environment is rarely in the 70° to 75°F range. For example, a body may actually gain heat if an individual expires outdoors during the summer, when temperatures may be greater than 100°F. Conversely, if a person expires in a 25°F environment, rapid cooling takes place.

Nonetheless, if body temperature is measured at a scene, it should be taken by the attending physician on at least two separate occasions before the body is moved. A rectal or liver temperature is the most accurate measurement. The environmental temperature should also be recorded. If these relatively simple procedures are followed, a very crude estimate of the postmortem interval can be made.[6]

Rigor Mortis

After death, the muscles of the body initially become flaccid. Within 1 to 3 hours they become increasingly rigid and the joints freeze—a condition called **rigor mortis** (or postmortem rigidity or rigor) (Figure 9-1).

Rigor mortis is affected by body temperature and metabolic rate: the higher the body temperature, the more lactic acid produced and the quicker rigor occurs. For example, a person dying with pneumonia and a fever will develop rigor sooner than a person with normal body temperature. Similarly, if a person's muscles were involved in strenuous physical activity just before death, rigor develops much more quickly. The process is also retarded in cooler environmental temperatures and accelerated in warmer ones.

All muscles of the body begin to stiffen at the same time after death. However, muscle groups may appear to stiffen at different rates because of their different sizes. For example, stiffness is apparent sooner in the jaw than in the knees. Thus, an examiner must check to see if joints are movable in the jaws, arms, and legs.

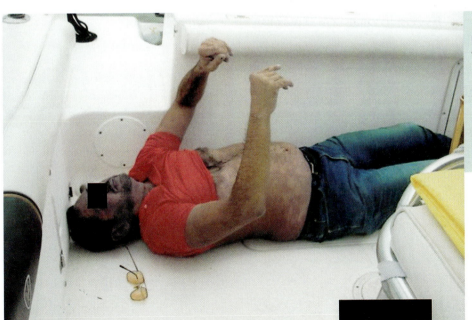

◀**FIGURE 9-1**
Rigor mortis
This individual, who died of natural causes, had been dead for approximately 10 hours. Note the arms in the upright position—the result of rigor mortis. The body will remain rigid for 24–36 hours before the muscles begin to relax.

A body is said to be in complete rigor when the jaw, elbow, and knee joints are immovable. This takes approximately 10 to 15 hours at an environmental temperature of 70° to 75°F. A body remains rigid for 24 to 36 hours before the muscles begin to relax, apparently in the same order they stiffened.

A body remains rigid until rigor passes or until a joint is physically moved and rigor is broken. Consequently, in addition to indicating an approximate time of death, body position in full rigor can indicate whether or not a body has been moved after death.[7]

Livor Mortis

Livor mortis (lividity, postmortem hypostasis) is a reddish purple coloration in dependent areas of the body due to accumulation of blood in the small vessels of the dependant areas secondary to gravity (Figure 9-2). Postmortem lividity is occasionally misinterpreted as bruising by people unfamiliar with this phenomenon.

Dependent areas resting against a firm surface will appear pale in contrast to the surrounding livor mortis, owing to compression of the vessels in this area, which prevents the accumulation of blood. Thus, areas supporting the weight of the body, for example, the shoulder blades, buttocks, and calves in individuals lying on their backs, show no livor mortis but appear as pale or blanched areas. Tight clothing, for example, such as a brassiere, corset, or belt, which compresses soft tissues, may collapse the vessels, also producing pale areas.

Livor mortis is usually evident within 30 minutes to 2 hours after death. In individuals dying a slow lingering death with terminal cardiac failure, livor mortis may actually appear antemortem (prior to death). Livor mortis develops gradually, usually reaching its maximum coloration at 8–12 hours. At about this time, it is said to become "fixed." Prior to becoming fixed, livor mortis will shift if the body is moved. Thus, if an individual

dies lying on his or her back, livor mortis develops posteriorly (i.e., on the back). If one turns the body on its face, blood will drain to the anterior surface of the body, now the dependent aspect. Livor mortis becomes "fixed" when shifting or drainage of blood no longer occurs, or when blood leaks out of the vessels into the surrounding soft tissue owing to hemolysis and breakdown of the vessels. Fixation can occur before 8–12 hours if decomposition is accelerated, or at 24–36 hours if delayed by cool temperatures. Thus, the statement that livor mortis becomes fixed at 8–12 hours is really just a vague generalization. That livor mortis is not fixed can be demonstrated by applying pressure to a dependent discolored area and noting the subsequent blanching at the point of pressure.

Although livor mortis may be confused with bruising, bruising is rarely confused with livor mortis. Application of pressure to an area of bruising will not cause blanching. An incision into an area of contusion or bruising shows diffuse hemorrhage into the soft tissue. In contrast, an incision into an area of livor mortis reveals the blood to be confined to vessels, without blood in the soft tissue. Livor mortis is extremely important for three reasons:

1. When considered with other factors, it may help estimate the time of death.
2. It may indicate that the body has been moved after death. For example, if a body was found face down with lividity on the back, this would indicate the body was moved. For this reason the exact measurements, sketches, and photographs must be made at the scene before and while the body is being recovered.
3. The actual coloration of the skin may indicate the cause of death, as in the case of carbon monoxide poisoning, certain forms of cyanide poisoning, or extreme cold, when the color of the lividity is not purplish but a cherry-red color.[8]

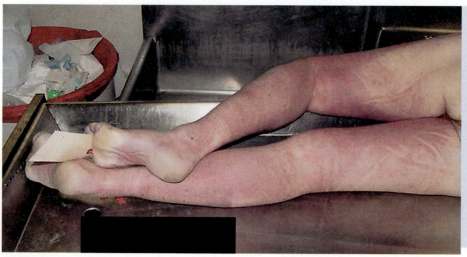

◄ FIGURE 9-2
Livor mortis
Livor mortis (lividity, postmortem hypostasis) is a reddish purple coloration in dependent areas of the body due to accumulation of blood in the small vessels of the dependent areas secondary to gravity. It is usually evident within 30 minutes to 2 hours after death, typically reaching its maximum coloration at 8 to 12 hours. Postmortem lividity is occasionally misinterpreted as bruising by people unfamiliar with this phenomenon.

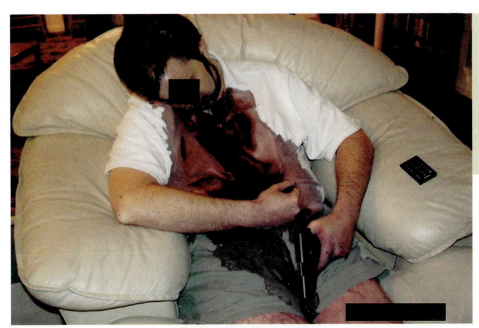

◀ FIGURE 9-3
Cadaveric spasm
Cadaveric spasm is a term used to describe the instantaneous tightening of a hand or other body part at the time of death. Note the weapon clutched tightly in the left hand of this victim of a self-inflicted gunshot wound through the head.

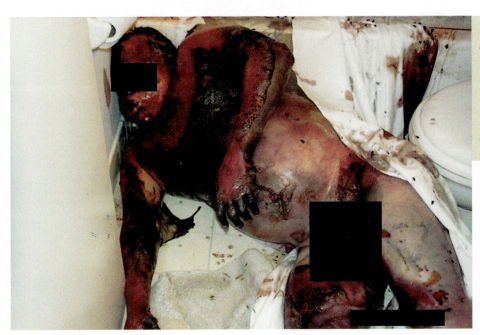

◀ **FIGURE 9-4**
Advanced stages of decomposition
This individual shown here had been dead approximately two weeks in an unheated, unventilated room. Note the extreme discoloration and swelling of the facial area as well as the abdomen.

Cadaveric Spasm

Cadaveric spasm refers to a kind of instant rigor mortis discussed earlier in this chapter. The same physiological changes occur except they occur at a more accelerated rate. Cadaveric spasm is also commonly called "a death grip." It typically involves a decedent's hand tightly clutching a weapon, usually a gun, a knife, or a razor at the moment of death.[9] (See Figure 9-3.)

Decomposition

In general, as rigor passes, skin first turns green at the abdomen. As discoloration spreads to the rest of the trunk, the body begins to swell because of bacterial methane-gas formation. The bacteria are normal inhabitants of the body. They proliferate after death, and their overgrowth is promoted in warm weather and retarded in cold weather.

The different rates and types of **decomposition** a body undergoes depend on the environment (See Figure 9-4). Bodies buried in earth, submerged in water, left in the hot sun, or placed in a cool basement appear different after the same postmortem interval. When a body is bloated, epidermal sloughing and hemoglobin degradation begin. Moreover, as bloating continues, air is forced from the skin. The increased internal pressure, caused by bacterial gas production, forces decomposed blood and body fluids out of body orifices by a process called purging. As the body undergoes skeletonization, the rate of tissue deterioration is dependent on environmental temperature. For example, a body exposed to a 100°F environmental temperature may completely decompose to a skeleton within a few weeks. In contrast, a body in a temperature of 65°F may not skeletonize for many months. In general, a body decomposing above ground for a week looks similar to a body that has been under water for two weeks or has been buried for six weeks. This generalization should serve as a reminder that an uncovered or naked body decomposes more rapidly than a covered or clothed one.

After a body is found, it is usually refrigerated until an autopsy is performed or a final disposition is made. Decomposition slows down or ceases if a body is refrigerated. When the body is exposed to room temperature, decomposition occurs rapidly. Recognition of this accelerated decomposition is particularly important if a person dies in a cold environment and is then moved to a warmer one.

Decomposition may not occur evenly throughout the body. For example, decomposition occurs more rapidly in injured areas. If a person is struck on the head and bleeding occurs only in that area, decomposition may be much more advanced on the head than on the remainder of the body. Fly larvae proliferate during summer, spring, and fall in warm, moist areas of the body such as the eyes, nose, and mouth. Larvae are attracted to injured areas, where they feed on exposed blood proteins and cause accelerated decomposition. Owing to the uneven decomposition, it is common to see skeletonization in only part of the body.[10]

FORENSIC ENTOMOLOGY

Entomology is the study of insects, and forensic entomology is the study of the insects associated with a dead body, which is used to determine the elapsed time since death. An analysis of the insects found on a homicide victim by a qualified **forensic entomologist** can also tell the investigators whether the body has been moved from one site to another, if it was disturbed after death, or the position and presence of wound sites, long after they are no longer visible as such to the naked eye. Insects can also be used in drug identification and the determination of the length of time of neglect.[11]

Insects are invariably the first witnesses to a crime, arriving within minutes or even seconds after death. There are two ways to use insects to determine time since death. The first method involves using dipteran larval development, and the second involves using insect succession over time. (See Figures 9-5 and 9-6.)

The first method is used in the first hours, days, or weeks after death and can determine the time of death

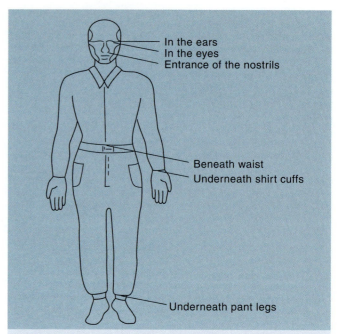

▲ **FIGURE 9-5** **Body area from which to collect insects**

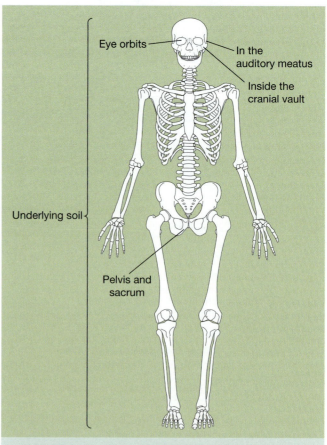

▲ **FIGURE 9-6** **Areas of skeleton most likely to harbor insects**

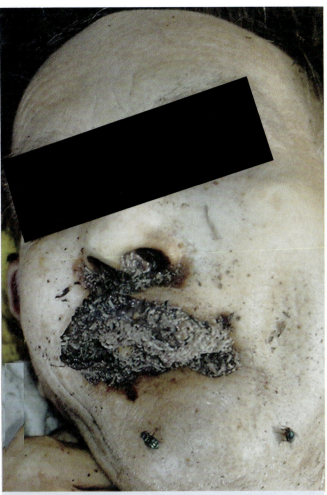

▲ FIGURE 9-7
Fly larvae
This individual had been dead for approximately four days. His body was found in the backyard by neighbors. During this period of time, temperatures had reached into the 90s. Note the fly larvae (maggots) in his eyes, nose, and mouth.

discovered allows an entomologist to determine the day or range of days in which the first insects oviposited or laid eggs on the corpse. This, in turn, leads to a day or range of days during which death occurred. For example, if the oldest insects are seven days old, then the decedent has been dead for at least seven days. This method can be used until the first adults begin to emerge, after which it is not possible to determine which generation is present. Therefore, after a single blow fly generation has been completed, the time of death is determined using the second method, that of insect succession.

The highly decomposed and maggot-infested remains of two women were found in a bushy area. Two species of blow fly were collected, and an analysis of the oldest insect stage, together with data from the local weather station, indicated that they had died more than 11 days prior to discovery. Reluctant eyewitnesses were later brought forward during the police investigation and confirmed the date of death. The eyewitnesses were also able to identify the killer. However, as the eyewitnesses had not come forward earlier, it was possible the jury might doubt their word. This became more probable when two other people came forward saying that they had seen the victims alive and well and shopping in the mall only eight days before their bodies were discovered. This conflicted with the date of death identified by the two eyewitnesses and meant that the jury would have to make a subjective decision on who was lying and who was telling the truth. However, in this case, there was also the scientific, entomological evidence which clearly indicated that the victims had died more than 11 days before discovery. This evidence refuted the testimony of the two shoppers and supported that of the two eyewitnesses. Therefore, the jury believed the earlier eyewitnesses, who were able to identify the killer. He was convicted of two counts of first-degree murder.

accurate to a day or less, or a range of days. The insects used in this method are those that arrive first on the corpse, that is, the calliphoridae or blow flies (diptera). These flies are attracted to a corpse very soon after death. They lay their eggs on the corpse, usually in a wound, if present, or in any of the natural orifices. (See Figure 9-7.) Their development follows a set, predictable cycle, and each of these developmental stages takes a set, known time. This time period is based on the availability of food and the temperature. In the case of a human corpse, food availability is not usually a limiting factor. Insects are "cold blooded," so their development is extremely temperature-dependent. Their metabolic rate increases with increased temperature, which results in a faster rate of development, so that the duration of development decreases in a linear manner with increased temperature, and vice versa.

An analysis of the oldest stage of insect on the corpse and the temperature of the region in which the body was

The second method of using insects to determine time since death is based on the fact that a human corpse, or any kind of carrion, supports a rapidly changing ecosystem. The body decomposes from the fresh state to dry bones in a matter of weeks or months depending on the geographic region. As the body decomposes, it goes through a predictable sequence of biological, chemical, and physical changes. Each of these changes is attractive to a different group of insects. Some insects, such as the blow flies, prefer to feed on the fresh body. Others prefer the remains a few days after death, while still others prefer the remains when they are dry. Some insects are not attracted to the body itself, but arrive to feed on other insects at the scene. Many species are involved at each decompositional stage, and each group of insects somewhat overlaps the ones adjacent to it. The insects that colonize a body are primarily species of flies (diptera) and beetles (coleoptera).

Therefore, with knowledge of the regional insect fauna and times of carrion colonization, the investigator can analyze the insect assemblage associated with the remains to determine a window of time in which death took place. This method is used when the decedent has been dead from a few weeks up to a year, or in some cases several years after death, with the estimated window of time broadening as time since death increases. It can also be used to indicate the season of death (e.g., early summer). A knowledge of insect succession, together with regional, seasonal, habitat, and meteorological variations, is required for this method to be successful.

The partially skeletonized remains of a man were found in a wooded area close to a freeway in early spring. A large number of empty blow fly puparia were discovered with the remains, along with several groups of insects that are commonly later colonizers, including piophilidae and fanniidae, as well as a number of beetle adults and larvae. To analyze sequential insect evidence, the entomologist must have local data for the geographical region, habitat, and season, because there can be a great deal of difference between insect arrival and tenure in one region versus another. The species of insects present in this case indicated a minimum elapsed time since death of two months. However, since the body was found in very early spring, death must have occurred earlier than this. Large numbers of empty blow fly puparia indicated the earlier presence of many blow fly larvae, which would have been present only in warm weather. This fact indicated that death must have occurred prior to the previous fall, when numerous blow flies would have colonized the remains and gone through an entire life cycle, as evidenced by the empty puparia. It would also have allowed for the later colonizers to arrive by March. The onset of cold weather would have prevented further blow fly colonization in winter, allowing some flesh to remain uneaten, which explained why the remains were only partially skeletonized. If the remains had not been discovered in early spring, blow flies from the upcoming summer would have completed the skeletonization process. Also, if the deceased had died earlier in the previous year, the body would have been entirely skeletonized before discovery. The insects, therefore, indicated that death had occurred in late summer of the previous year.

EVIDENCE FROM WOUNDS

A basic knowledge of wounds is of great assistance to officers who are responsible for injury and death investigations. It helps them reach preliminary conclusions. The five most common types of wounds encountered by police officers in injury and death investigations are firearm wounds, incised wounds, stab wounds, puncture wounds, and lacerations.

Firearm Wounds

When a bullet strikes a body, the skin is first pushed in and then perforated while in the stretched state. After the bullet has passed, the skin partially returns to its original position, and the entry opening is drawn together and is thus smaller than the diameter of the bullet. The slower the bullet speed, the smaller the entry opening. The bullet passing through the stretched skin forms a so-called contusion ring around the entrance opening as the bullet slips against the skin that is pressed inward and scrapes the external epithelial layers. (See Figure 9-8.) The skin itself, in the contusion ring, becomes conspicuous by drying after some hours. In a favorable case, rifling marks on the bullet leave such a distinct mark in the contusion ring that the number of grooves in the rifling can be counted. The combined section of the contusion ring and entrance opening corresponds to the caliber of the bullet or exceeds it slightly. When a bullet strikes the body squarely, the contusion ring is round; when a bullet strikes at an angle, the ring is oval.

Along with the contusion ring, there is another black-colored ring, the "smudge ring," which often entirely covers the contusion ring (Figure 9-8). It does not contain any powder residues or contamination from the bore of

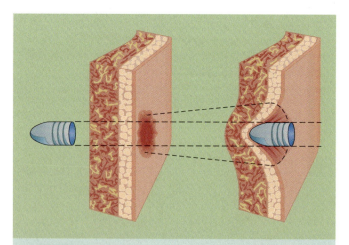

▲ **FIGURE 9-8**
A bullet penetrating the skin
The skin is pressed inward, stretched, and perforated in the stretched condition, after which it returns to its original position. The entry opening is smaller than the diameter of the bullet. Immediately around the opening is a contusion ring, because the bullet rubs against this part of the skin and scrapes the external layer of epithelial cells.
(Courtesy Nucleus Medical Art Illustration, ©2007, www.nucleusinc.com, as depicted in Vernon J. Geberth's *Practical Homicide Investigation*.)

the firearm but consists wholly of small particles originating from the surface of the bullet. The smudge ring may be absent in the case of clean-jacketed bullets or a bullet that has passed through clothing.

A bullet passing through the body forms a track that is usually straight but can also be bent at an angle in an unpredictable manner if the bullet meets or passes through a bone. Thus it is not possible to determine with certainty, from observation of the entrance and exit openings, the direction of the weapon when the shot was fired. The direction must be calculated by the pathologist from the results of the autopsy. The velocity of the bullet has a great influence on the appearance of the track: straight tracks indicate a high velocity, and bent or angular ones indicate a low velocity.

In gunshot injuries in soft parts of the body, especially in the brain, the bullet can produce a considerable explosive effect, which is greatest with unjacketed or soft-nosed bullets from large-caliber firearms. Such a bullet may split into several parts, each of which forms its own track, and thus there may be several exit wounds. When such a bullet strikes the head, large parts of the cranium can be blown away and the brain scattered around. A soft-nosed bullet that, before hitting the body, is split by striking against a hard object such as a tree branch can produce a number of irregularly shaped entrance holes.

A shot through the head is not always fatal. To be immediately fatal, the bullet must either produce a bursting effect or injure an artery of the brain or a vital brain center. A shot through the brain that is not immediately fatal does not always produce unconsciousness. Even

when the heart has been perforated by a bullet, it occasionally happens that the injured person lives for several hours, retaining some capacity of movement.

It is often difficult to distinguish the exit wound from the entrance wound, especially from a shot at long range with a metal-jacketed bullet, assuming, of course, that the bullet passes through the body intact. In a favorable case, the exit wound may have a ragged appearance with flaps directed outward. To determine the direction of the shot with certainty in such a case, an autopsy is necessary. If the bullet was damaged by its passage through the body or if there was a bursting effect, it is generally easy to determine the exit wound, which is then considerably larger than the entrance wound and shows a star-shaped, ragged character, with flaps directed outward. Note, however, that in contact shots the entrance wound may be ragged and star-shaped. A bullet that ricochets may strike with its side, or obliquely, and produce a large and characteristic entrance wound.

Close and Distant Shots

It is very important to be able to estimate the distance from which a shot was fired. In many cases this fact is the only evidence available that can distinguish between suicide, a self-defense killing, manslaughter, or murder.

In practice, a distinction is made among *contact*, *close*, and *distant* shots. A **contact bullet wound** is made when the muzzle of the weapon is pressed against the body when the shot is fired. In a close shot, the distance of the muzzle is less than about 18 inches from the body (Figures 9-9 and 9-10), whereas a distant shot is one

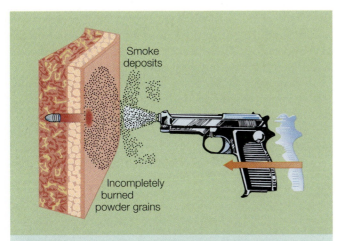

▲ **FIGURE 9-9   Firearm discharge at close range**
Close shot, short distance. The diagram shows both incompletely burned powder grains and smoke deposits in the zone of blackening. The powder grains are concentrated immediately around the entrance hole. (Courtesy Nucleus Medial Art Illustration, ©2007, www.nucleusinc.com, as depicted in Vernon J. Geberth's *Practical Homicide Investigation*.)

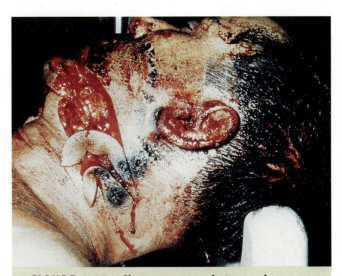

▲ **FIGURE 9-10   Close range gunshot wound**
This victim was first assaulted with a knife and then shot numerous times in the left side of the head. Note the blackened area around the bullet wound indicating direct contact or very close contact with the skin.

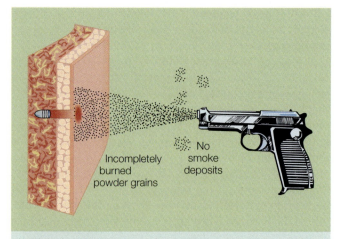

▲ FIGURE 9-11

Firearm discharged from a distance

Close shot, greater distance than in Figure 9-9. The diagram shows unburned powder grains, but no smoke deposits in the zone of blackening.

(Courtesy Nucleus Medial Art Illustration, ©2007, www.nucleusinc.com, as depicted in Vernon J. Geberth's *Practical Homicide Investigation*.)

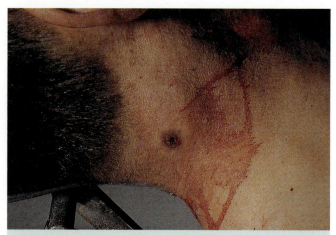

▲ FIGURE 9-12

Distant shot

When a bullet strikes a body from a distance, the skin is first pushed and then perforated while in the stretched state. After the bullet has passed, the skin partially returns to the original position, and the entry opening is drawn together and is thus smaller than the diameter of the bullet. The bullet passing into the stretched skin forms what is called a *contusion ring* around the entrance as the bullet slips against the skin that is pressed inward and scrapes the external epithelil layers.

fired at a distance greater than 18 inches[12] (Figures 9-11 and 9-12).

In the case of a contact shot against an exposed part of the body, soot, metallic particles, and powder residues are driven into the body and can be found there during the autopsy. Blackening, caused by soot and powder,

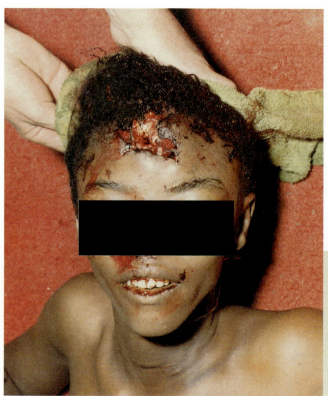

around the entry opening is often absent. A contact shot against a part of the body protected by clothing often produces a powder zone on the skin or in the clothes, and soot, powder residue, and fragments of clothing are driven into the track. In a contact discharge, the entrance wound differs considerably from an entrance wound in a close shot or a distant shot. When a contact shot is fired, the gases of the explosion are driven into the track but are forced out again and produce a bursting effect on the skin and clothes. The entrance wound is often star-shaped with flaps directed outward. (See Figure 9-13.)

A close shot produces a zone of blackening around the entrance wound of the track, either on the skin or on the clothes. Sometimes the flame from the muzzle has a singeing action around this opening, with hair and textile fibers curled up. The zone of blackening is formed of substances carried along with the explosion gases.

◄ FIGURE 9-13

Contact bullet wound

Homicidal contact bullet wound to the forehead. Note the charring of the edges and the irregularly shaped tears of the skin owing to the undermining of the scalp. This contact bullet wound was made from a .38-caliber bullet against an exposed part of the body (in this case, the head). Soot, metallic particles, and powder residue are driven into the body and can be found during the autopsy.

When a cartridge is fired, the bullet is forced through the barrel of the weapon by the explosion gases. Only a small amount of the gas passes in front of the bullet. The combustion of the powder is never complete, even with smokeless powder and still less with black powder, and the explosion gases therefore carry with them incompletely burned powder residues, the amount of which decreases as the distance increases. Thus, in a close shot, a considerable amount of incompletely burned powder residue is found on the target. In addition to carrying this residue, the gases also carry impurities from the inside of the barrel, consisting of rust (iron), oil, and particles rubbed off the bullet. Metallic residues from the percussion cap and cartridge case also occur in the gases of the explosion. If the shot is fired at a right angle to the body, the zone of blackening is practically circular; if it is fired obliquely, the zone is oval. The extent of the zone of blackening is often difficult to determine by direct observation, and it is often better to photograph it, using infrared-sensitive material, which intensifies the zone of blackening so its extent is more easily determined. The zone of blackening gives valuable information for determining the distance from which a shot was fired, which may be an important factor in deciding between murder and suicide. It is important that comparative test shots be fired with the same weapon and same type of ammunition as those used in the actual crime.

Close shots with black powder show marks of burning up to a distance of 4 to 6 inches and a distinct deposit of powder smoke up to 10 or 12 inches. Dispersed grains of powder embedded in the target may be detected even at a distance of 3 feet. In distant shots, none of the characteristics of a close shot can be detected.

Powder residues occur on the object fired at in the form of incompletely and completely burned particles. A careful microscopic examination should precede any chemical examination, as it is often possible to establish in this way the shape and color of unburned powder particles and to distinguish many kinds of powder.

Black powder, which consists of potassium nitrate, sulfur, and charcoal, is identified by the presence of potassium and nitrate in the entrance wound. Smokeless powder consists chiefly of nitrocellulose or of nitrocellulose with nitroglycerine and is identified by the presence of nitrite, which can be detected by various microreactions. The grains of smokeless powder are generally coated with graphite and occur in many forms (e.g., round or angular discs, pellets, and cylinders).[13]

High Velocity Rifle Wounds

The difference in the size of the wounds and damage done between handgun bullets and rifle bullets, especially those of a large caliber, can be considerable. For example, Figure 9-14 depicts an individual who was shot in the head one time by a police swat team member. The officer was armed with a .308 Remington 700 rifle. The subject had barricaded himself in a motel room while holding a hostage. He was shot in the head after he made the fatal mistake of slightly opening the door to the motel room and pointing his rifle in the direction of a police swat team member. The rifle the decedent was holding is depicted on the left side of his body.

Shotgun Wounds

A shotgun is a smooth-bore, shoulder-fired firearm and is typically used to fire multiple pellets, rather than a

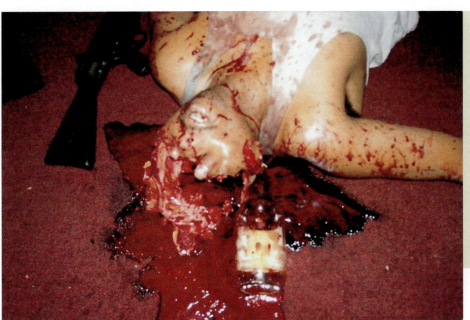

◀ **FIGURE 9-14**
High velocity rifle wound
This individual was shot in the head one time by a police swat team member. The officer was armed with a .308 Remington 700 rifle. The subject had barricaded himself in a motel room while holding a hostage. He was shot in the head after he made the fatal mistake of slightly opening the door to the motel room and pointing his rifle in the direction of a police swat team member. The rifle the decedent was holding is depicted on the left side of his body.

single slug. The most common gauges with their corresponding bore diameters are as follows:[14]

- The pellets fired range in size from 0.08 inch for a No. 9 shot to 0.33 inch for 00 Buck.
- A "wad," which may be either paper or plastic, lies between the shot pellets and the powder. Most modern shells use plastic wads.
- A shotgun shell can contain anywhere from a couple of hundred pellets to nine for 00 Buck, to one large lead slug.

Entrance Wounds From contact to 12 inches, there is a single round entrance 0.75 to 1 inch in diameter. The edge of the wound shows an abrasion ring. As the distance between muzzle and skin increases, powder tattooing appears. Powder blackening is most prominent at less than 12 inches. Powder tattooing is considerably less dense than it is in pistol wounds.

When pellets are discharged at between 3 and 6 feet of range, the single entrance wound widens to 1.5 to 2 inches in diameter and shows "scalloping" of the edges. At about 6 feet, the pellets begin to separate from the main mass of pellets. Beyond 10 to 12 feet, there is great variation in the spread of the pellets. (See Figure 9-15.)

The Wad At close ranges, the wad will be propelled into the body through the large single entrance wound. Beyond 10 to 15 feet, the wad will have separated from the pellets and will not enter. However, it may mark the body. The gauge of the shotgun and the size of the pellets can be obtained from the wad and pellets, respectively. On occasion, a plastic wad may be marked by the choke or irregularities at the end of the barrel, making ballistic comparison possible.

Range Determination Range determinations can be made later if the size of the shotgun pattern was described at autopsy and duplicated on paper. The same weapon with the same type of ammunition must be used in duplication of the pattern if accurate results are desired. Range formulas do not work.

X-ray patterns of the shot in the body are useless for range determinations, as are patterns on the body in which the shot first struck the target.

The size of the shot pattern on the body depends primarily on the choke of the gun. The type of ammunition and barrel length are secondary factors. The size of the pellet pattern is independent of the gauge of the shotgun, and an increase in gauge just increases the density of the pattern.

Exit Wounds Shotgun pellets very rarely exit except when used as instruments of suicide in the region of the head.

Firearm Residues

Detecting **firearm residues** on the hands of an individual may be of great importance in evaluating deaths caused by gunshot wounds. Detection of such residues on the hands of a deceased individual is often confirmatory evidence of a suspected suicide.[15]

One of the earliest methods of determining whether an individual discharged a weapon, the paraffin test or dermal nitrate test, was based on the detection of nitrates on the surfaces of the hands. Paraffin was employed for the removal of powder residues from the hands. Diphenylamine was the reagent used to detect the nitrates picked up by the paraffin. This test is no longer considered valid, because no distinction can be made between nitrates of gunpowder origin and those from other

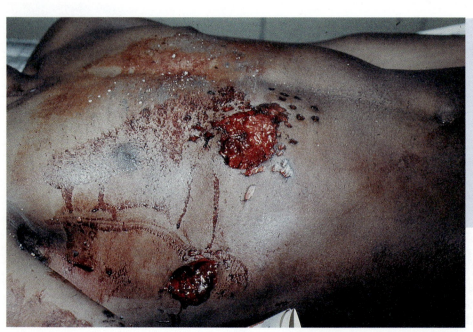

◄ **FIGURE 9-15 Close-range wound from a 12-gauge shotgun** In shotgun entrance wounds, the characteristics of the wound vary based on the distance between the muzzle and the skin. For example, from contact to 12 inches, the edge of the wound shows an abrasion ring. As the distance increases, powder tattooing appears. This photo shows that powder tattooing is considerably less dense than it is in pistol wounds.

sources, which are quite commonly encountered in day-to-day living.

Several years ago, a series of chemical spot tests for detection of metallic components of firearm discharge residues was developed. Such metallic substances originate mainly from the primer, although they can also come from the bullet or cartridge case. Spot tests were developed for the presence of antimony, barium, and lead substances found in most primers. These tests are inconclusive because they are essentially qualitative rather than quantitative.[16]

The concept of detecting metallic primer components led to more sophisticated approaches now in general use. Compounds of antimony, barium, and lead are used in modern noncorrosive primers. When a handgun is discharged, discrete particulate matter containing these elements are deposited on the thumb, forefinger, and connecting web (the back of the hand holding the weapon). The metallic compounds are removed from the hand, either with paraffin or, more commonly, with cotton swabs saturated with a dilute solution of acid. This material is then submitted for analysis.

Removal of Gunshot Residue Whatever system of analysis a pathologist uses, the procedures for removal of firearm discharge residues from the hand are the same. The solution most commonly used is of dilute acid. Four cotton swabs are used to remove the firearm discharge residues from the hands. Two swabs are used on each hand; one for the palm, the other for the "back" of the hand. The swabs of the nonfiring hand and the palm of the hand suspected of discharging the weapon act as controls. A control swab dipped in the acid also should be submitted as a blank. Cotton swabs with plastic shafts should be used. Those with wood shafts should not be used because the wood may be contaminated with metallic elements and wood also shows great variation in the concentration of such elements.

If a person has discharged a handgun, firearm discharge residues should appear only on the back of the hand that fired the weapon, not on the palm of that hand or on the other hand. Some people, because of their occupations, may have high levels of barium, antimony, or lead on their hands. Thus if the back of the hand were the only area submitted for examination, a misleadingly positive report would come back. If analysis reveals firearm discharge residues only on the palms, it strongly suggests that the individual's hands were around the weapon at the time of the discharge or were trying to ward off the weapon. However, in suicide, high levels of residue often show up on the nonfiring palm when that hand is used to steady the weapon by grasping the barrel, thus receiving the muzzle or cylinder discharge.

It must be realized that determining whether an individual fired a gun cannot be based on absolute quantities of primer residue on the hands. Rather, it is based on contrast of the levels of these compounds from right to left and from palm to back.

Incised and Stab Wounds

The **incised wound**—more commonly referred to as a "cutting wound"—is inflicted with a sharp-edged instrument such as a knife or a razor. The weapon typically employed in inflicting both incised and stab wounds is a pocketknife, although kitchen knives are also common. In comparison with shootings, fewer cutting assaults result in death, largely because the perpetrator's intention was to injure or disfigure rather than kill the victim. Cutting wounds are often found on the arms, face, and legs. Even in these "friendly" cuttings, as they are sometimes referred to, death may occur. When the victim does die from a cutting wound, it generally is found around the throat. The severity of most incised wounds is directly related to the shape and sharpness of the weapon, the part of the body being cut, and the amount of force used in striking the victim. The incised wound is typically narrow at the edges and gaping at the center, with considerable bleeding. (See Figure 9-16.) The inexperienced investigator may conclude that a gaping incised wound was inflicted by a large cutting instrument. However, a small knife with a honed blade is capable of causing very severe wounds.

Most frequently, death is caused after a stab results in severe damage to a vital organ, internal bleeding, shock, or secondary infections that develop several days after the attack. Any of these factors may itself be fatal; they

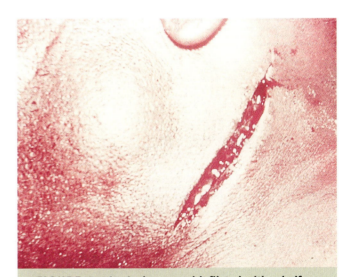

▲ **FIGURE 9-16 Incise wound inflicted with a knife**
The wound is narrow at the edge and gaping at the middle. Such wounds typically bleed a lot. Incise wounds are often inflicted with a sharp-edged instrument such as a knife or a razor. The wounds are sometimes found on the arms, face, and legs.

often occur in combination. The shape, size, and keenness of the blade all determine a wound's shape and depth, as does the manner in which the knife is thrust into and pulled out of the body. One noticeable aspect of multiple stab wounds is their different shapes when made with the same knife. The proximity of the wounds in a multiple-stabbing assault may be helpful in determining the actions of the victim prior to death. If the wounds are concentrated within a small region of the body, then there is a good possibility that the victim was immobilized at the time of the assault, that is, held down, asleep, or intoxicated. (See Figure 9-17.)

Puncture Wounds

The weapon most frequently used in assaults resulting in **puncture wounds** once was the ice pick. It is less common today. Leather punches and screwdrivers also are capable of producing puncture wounds, which are normally small and have little or no bleeding. Such wounds can be easily overlooked, particularly if they are in hairy parts of the body. Infliction of a puncture wound produces death in the same way as do stab wounds. (See Figure 9-18.)

Lacerations

When used in an assault, clubs, pipes, pistols, or other such blunt objects can produce open, irregularly shaped wounds termed **lacerations.** Such wounds bleed freely and characteristically are accompanied by bruising around the edges. There is no necessary relationship between the shape of the wound and that of the weapon employed. Occasionally, such force will be used in an

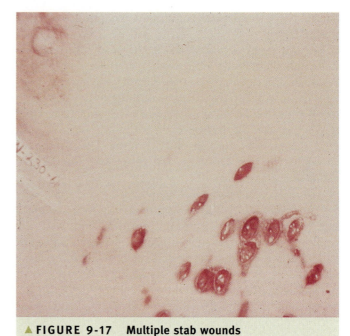

▲ **FIGURE 9-17 Multiple stab wounds**
Death from stab wounds generally results from severe damage to a vital organ, internal bleeding, shock, or secondary infection that may develop several days after the attack. The close proximity of these wounds indicates that the victim was unable to struggle to any sufficient degree. Even wounds inflicted with the same knife as depicted in this figure can be quite different in size and shape.

attack that an impression of the weapon is left on the victim's skin. Most frequently, when death results from an assault in which lacerations were inflicted, the cause is severe head injuries. Laceration wounds may be

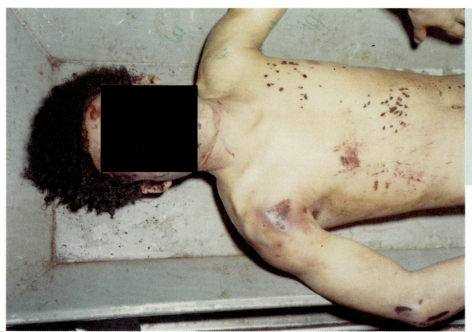

◄ **FIGURE 9-18
Puncture wound**
This victim received multiple ice-pick stab wounds. Leather punches and screwdrivers are all capable of producing puncture wounds. Because there is often little bleeding, a single wound can easily be overlooked, particularly if it is on a hairy part of the body.

inflicted accidentally, as in the case of an intoxicated person who falls and strikes his or her head against a curb or step. In some instances, circumstances may appear more suspicious:

Checking the back doors of businesses at about 9:30 P.M., an officer found the proprietor of a jewelry store dead at the open rear entrance to his store. He had sustained a large laceration on his forehead and had bled considerably. At first, it appeared that a murder had taken place during a robbery or burglary. Careful processing of the scene yielded traces of blood and one small skin fragment from the brick wall near the rear entrance.

Nothing was established as missing from the business. The medical examiner found the cause of death to be a heart attack. The head laceration contained minute traces of brick. Thus a reconstruction of events showed that as the owner was closing his business, he suffered a heart attack and convulsions, striking his head against the brick wall. The lacerations he suffered made it look as though he had suffered a fatal head wound.

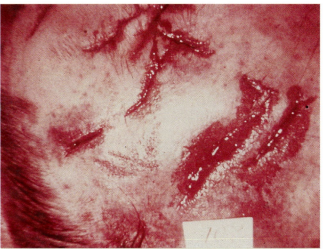

▲ **FIGURE 9-19**
Lacerations resulting from a pistol whipping
This victim was pistol whipped to death by an armed robber. This assault resulted in numerous lacerations to the head. Such wounds bleed freely and characteristically are accompanied by bruising around the edges. There is not necessarily a relationship between the shape of the wound and that of the weapon employed.

The severity, extent, and appearance of injuries due to blunt trauma depend on the amount of force delivered to the body, the amount of time over which the force is delivered, the region struck, the amount (extent) of body surface over which the force is delivered, and the nature of the weapon. If a weapon deforms and/or breaks on hitting the body, less energy is delivered to the body to produce injury, since some of the energy is used to deform and/or break the weapon. Thus, the resultant injury is less severe than would have been the case if the weapon did not deform and/or break. If the body moves with the blow, this increases the period of time over which the energy is delivered and decreases the severity of the injury.[17]

For any given amount of force, the greater the area over which it is delivered, the less severe the wound, because the force is dissipated. The size of the area affected by a blow depends on the nature of the weapon and the region of the body. For a weapon with a flat surface, such as a board, there is a diffusion of the energy and a less severe injury than that due to a narrow object—for example, a steel rod, delivered with the same amount of energy. If an object projects from the surface of the weapon, then all the force will be delivered to the end of the projection and a much more severe wound will be produced. If a blow is delivered to a rounded portion of the body, such as the top of the head (Figure 9-19), the wound will be much more severe than would be the case if the same force is delivered to a flat portion of the body, such as the back, where there will be a greater area of contact and more dispersion of force.[18]

Defense Wounds

Defense wounds are suffered by victims attempting to protect themselves from an assault, often by a knife or club. These wounds are commonly found on the palms of the hands, the fingers, and the forearms. In the most aggravated form, the defense wound may involve one or more severed fingers. (See Figure 9-20.)

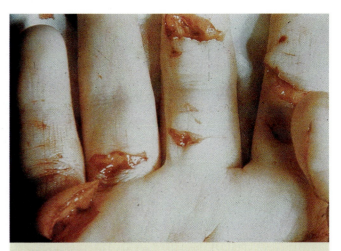

▲ **FIGURE 9-20**
Defense wounds
This victim received severe defense knife wounds on the hands while trying to stop his assailant from stabbing him to death.

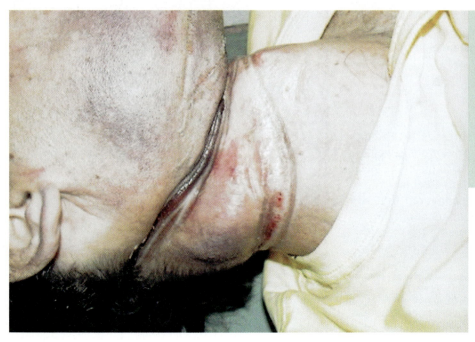

◄**FIGURE 9-21**
Ligature strangulation
The pressure on the neck is applied by a constricting band that is tightened by a force other than the body weight. Virtually all cases of ligature strangulation are homicides. The victim in this photo died as a result of strangulation by use of an electric cord.

Strangulation Wounds

Ligature Strangulation

In **ligature strangulation,** the pressure on the neck is applied by a constricting band that is tightened by a force other than the body weight. Virtually all cases of ligature strangulation are homicides. Females predominate as victims. Suicides and accidents are rare. The mechanism of death is the same as in hanging, occlusion of the vessels that supply blood and thus oxygen to the brain. Consciousness is lost in 10 to 15 seconds.[19]

Ligatures used range from electric cords (Figure 9-21), neckties, ropes, and telephone cords to sheets, hose, and undergarments. The appearance of a ligature mark on the neck is subject to considerable variation, depending on the nature of the ligature, the amount of resistance offered by the victim, and the amount of force used by the assailant. The ligature mark may be faint, barely visible, or absent in young children or incapacitated adults, especially if the ligature is soft (e.g., a towel) and removed immediately after death. If a thin ligature is used, there will be a very prominent deep mark encircling the neck. Initially, it has a yellow parchmentlike appearance that later turns dark brown.

In ligature strangulation, in contrast to hangings, the ligature mark usually encircles the neck in a horizontal plane often overlying the larynx or upper trachea. When a wire or cord is used, it usually completely encircles the neck. There may be a break in the furrow, however, usually at the back of the neck, where a hand has grasped the ligature and tightened it at that point. Aside from the ligature mark, abrasions and contusions of the skin of the neck are usually not present. They may occur, however,

if the assailant places his or her hands beneath and around the ligature and twists it, tightening it around the neck, or if the victim claws at the neck in an attempt to remove the ligature or relieve the pressure. If there is more than one loop of the ligature around the neck, there may be bruising of the skin if the ligature pinches the skin between two loops.

Manual Strangulation

Manual strangulation is produced by pressure of the hand, forearm, or other limb against the neck, compressing the internal structures of the neck. The mechanism of death is occlusion of the blood vessels that supply blood to the brain. Occlusion of the airway probably plays a minor role in causing death, if any at all.

Virtually all manual strangulations are homicides. One cannot commit suicide by manual strangulation since as soon as consciousness is lost, pressure would be released and consciousness would be regained.

In most cases of manual strangulation, the assailant uses more force than is necessary to subdue and kill the victim. Hence, marks of violence are frequently present on the skin of the neck. Usually, there are abrasions, contusions, and fingernail marks on the skin. (See Figure 9-22.)

While in most manual strangulations, there is evidence of both external and internal injury to the neck, in some cases there is no injury, either externally or internally. For example, one medical examiner reports seeing three women in a three-month period who had been manually strangled. The first woman showed absolutely no evidence either externally or internally; the second showed congestion of the face with fine petechiae of the conjunctivae and skin of the face, but no evidence of injury to the

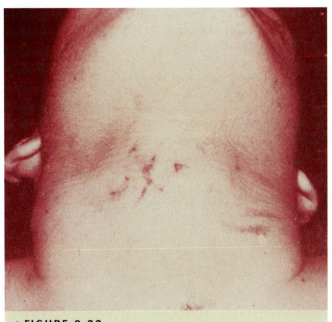

▲ FIGURE 9-22
Death by manual strangulation
This victim died as a result of manual strangulation. Note the crescent-shaped fingernail marks on the center of the throat along with bruising on the sides of the neck indicating that the assailant attacked from behind.

neck, either externally or internally; and the third victim showed the classic evidence of injury: abrasions and scratches of the skin with extensive hemorrhaging into the muscles of the neck. All three women were killed by the same individual. All three had blood alcohol levels above 0.30. The modus operandi of the perpetrator was to meet a woman in a bar, buy her liquor until she was extremely intoxicated, and then go off with her and have intercourse. He would then strangle her. At the time he strangled them, the women were unconscious due to acute alcohol intoxication, so a very minimal amount of pressure was necessary. He would place his hand over their necks and push downward, compressing the vessels of the neck. In the last case, the individual regained consciousness and struggled, with the resultant injuries. The perpetrator admitted having killed a number of other women in the same way over previous years in a number of states.

In manual strangulation, the victims are usually female. When they are male, they are often highly intoxicated. It is suggested that in all manual strangulation cases a complete toxicological screen be performed.

SUICIDE

For the investigator, a major concern in an apparent suicide case is to make certain that the death was self-induced and not the result of a homicide.

In some cases, the investigator finds overwhelming evidence to this effect at the scene. In other cases, important information about the victim's behavior before death can be obtained from relatives, friends, coworkers, and employers. **Suicide** is often committed for the following reasons:

- Ill health or considerable pain.
- Severe marital strife.
- A recent emotionally damaging experience, such as an unhappy love affair, separation, or divorce.
- Financial difficulties, including the threat of a much lower standard of living or failure to meet some significant and past-due financial commitments.
- Perceived or actual humiliation.
- Remorse over the loss of a loved one or over an act of one's own.
- Revenge, frequently for adolescents who have serious difficulties with parents or spurned lovers.[20]

These factors are far from all inclusive, but the investigator will find a significant number of suicides associated with them. Conversely, if there is an apparent suicide and thorough scrutiny fails to produce a solid motive, then the investigator's suspicion should be aroused. Thus, in all apparent suicides the possibility of a criminal homicide should never be lightly discarded.

Methods and Evidence of Suicide

Nine methods are most commonly employed in suicides: shooting, hanging, ingesting sleeping pills and other pharmaceuticals, drowning, cutting and piercing, ingesting of poisons, inhaling gases, jumping from high places, and intentionally crashing an automobile.[21]

Although all of these can be simulated in the commission of murders, there are important differences in physical evidence that distinguish suicides from murders.

Gunshot Wounds

It is sometimes difficult to determine whether a gunshot wound was self-inflicted or resulted from the actions of an assailant. However, there are certain indicators that may be helpful in reaching a conclusion. One of these is the location of the wound and the trajectory of the projectile on entering the body. The most common method of committing suicide with a firearm involves the victim's placing a handgun to the temple and firing a shot into his or her head. Frequently, there is no exit wound, and it is impossible for the investigator to determine the precise angle at which the projectile entered. This information is obtained during the autopsy, but it may be several days before this is performed. The investigator must therefore make some preliminary determination. The following case illustrates some of the points discussed thus far.

A man telephoned the police hysterically, reporting that his wife had just shot and killed herself. When the police and an ambulance arrived, the victim was dead of a bullet wound in her upper left temple. The husband was holding the gun with which he alleged his wife had shot herself. He stated that he had arrived home from work just before the incident but that neither his wife nor their three preschool-age children had been there. His wife had arrived home a short while later, and she had been drinking heavily. When he questioned her about the whereabouts of their three children, she had told him they were at his mother's home. A heated argument then followed about her neglect of their children, her drinking, and her seeing other men. According to the husband, his wife then slapped him in his face, and he slapped her back. At that point, she walked over to a nearby desk drawer, where he kept a revolver. She removed the revolver from the desk drawer, placed the barrel against her head, fired a single shot, and fell to the floor. No one else was home at the time this incident occurred.

The following set of facts was revealed by the medical examiner's autopsy report:

- The bullet entered the upper left portion of the head, traveled downward through the brain, and continued downward through the victim's body, coming to rest in her chest.
- There were no powder burns present around the gunshot wound.
- Death occurred immediately.
- If the wound had been self-inflicted, the victim would have been holding the weapon in her left hand, at least 2 feet from her head, and would have used her thumb to pull the trigger.

The relatives of both the victim and her husband provided the police with the following information:

- To their knowledge, the victim had not been despondent, nor had she ever previously attempted or discussed suicide.
- The victim and her husband had been having serious domestic difficulties because she was seeing other men, spending the house money on liquor, and not properly caring for their three young children.
- Both parties were known to have assaulted each other in domestic disputes in the past.
- The victim was right-handed.

These facts tended to indicate that the victim's death was not a suicide but a criminal homicide. An interrogation of the husband established what the facts suggested.

The husband related that he had been truthful about the events leading up to the argument but that after his wife slapped him, he had angrily knocked her to the floor, removed the revolver from the desk drawer, and gone back to his wife, who was now on her knees. Standing over her, he fired a single shot into her head. After shooting her, he became frightened and fabricated the story of his wife's suicide.

This case demonstrates the importance of two factors in the investigation of an alleged suicide. The first is the importance of the location of the wound on the body and its trajectory on entering the body. Second is the presence or absence of evidence indicating that the victim was predisposed to committing suicide.

Suicide by Use of a Shotgun

The use of a shotgun to commit suicide can result in enormous physical damage, especially if the gun is discharged into the head. (See Figure 9-23.)

Hanging

Certain misconceptions associated with suicidal hangings can lead to erroneous conclusions. The first is that the victim's neck gets broken; and second, that the feet are off the floor. Although both of these conditions may occur, they are exceptions rather than the rule. The first misconception is related to the circumstances of legal executions by hanging. In legal executions, the procedures involved in inflicting death are intended to result in the neck being broken. This is accomplished by the use of a specific type of noose and a gallows with a trap door through which the person will drop some distance before being abruptly stopped. However, in a suicidal hanging, even when the feet are suspended, the neck is rarely broken, because the fall is not long enough to cause the severe jolt necessary to break the neck. (See Figure 9-24.)

It is also common in suicidal hangings for the victim's feet or even the knees to be touching the ground. Occasionally, the victim is found in a sitting position. Finding victims in these positions often creates suspicion because it is difficult for inexperienced investigators to understand how anyone could remain in these positions while slowly choking to death. They might improperly conclude that the victim first was rendered unconscious or was killed and placed in the hanging position. It is more likely, however, that the victim did not slowly choke to death but rather first tied the rope around some supporting device and then around his or her neck. Pressure was then applied by the victim either by crouching down, if in a standing position, or leaning forward, if in a sitting position. This initial pressure painlessly cuts off the flow of blood to the brain, which results in unconsciousness. When unconsciousness does occur, the full weight of the body is then applied to the noose, whereupon all oxygen is cut off to the brain and death follows. There is very little physical pain associated with suicides of this type.

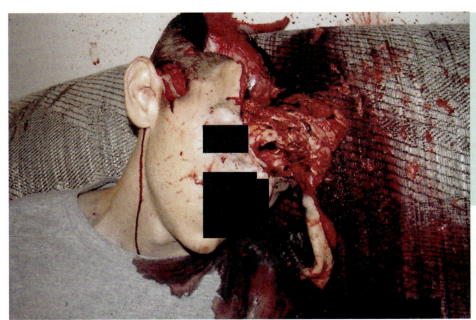

◄FIGURE 9-23
Suicide by shotgun
This individual placed a 12-gauge shotgun against his right temple and pulled the trigger. As can be noted, there are scorch marks around the entry wound near the right ear. Shotgun wounds to the head, especially those involving large-gauge shotguns generally result in enormous damage to the head.

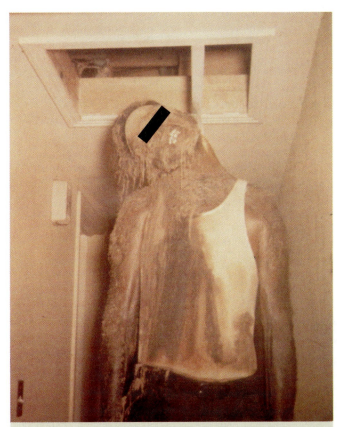

▲FIGURE 9-24
Suicidal hanging
This suicide victim has been in this hanging position for approximately three weeks. The body is in an advanced stage of decomposition; the mosslike substance on the body is dried body fluids. The victim has used a ligature-type device wrapped around a beam in the attic to suspend his body.

If one considers that many suicidal hangings occur in victims' homes, then it is logical to expect the feet not to be suspended above the floor because few household objects are strong enough to hold the weight of a fully suspended body or one that has fallen several feet from a chair or table.

Livor mortis is most pronounced in the lower portion of the arms and legs and around the face, lips, and jaw. There may be some variations in the location of the discoloration, depending on the position of the body. When death occurs in this manner, one frequently finds petechial hemorrhaging in the eyes, caused when small blood vessels in the eye bleed because blood pressure increases in response to compression around the neck. (See Figure 9-25.)

Occasionally, hangings are accidental, not suicidal. The individual may have himself in a modified hanging position while masturbating and accidentally fall, slip, and knock over the object on which he is standing, resulting in an accidental death, known as autoerotic death or sexual asphyxia; the intent is sexual rather than suicidal. In these cases, the genitals are exposed and semen may be present. (Chapter 10, "Sex-Related Offenses," provides an in-depth explanation of autoerotic death.) The presence of feces and urine is common because of the total relaxation of the bladder and bowel muscles at the time of death.

Sleeping Pills and Other Pharmaceuticals

Sleeping pills and other pharmaceuticals have for many years been a common means of committing suicide. However, some deaths resulting from the ingestion of sleeping pills or tranquilizing drugs may be accidental, not suicidal. The investigator has an obligation to determine whether the death was accidental or suicidal. Certain

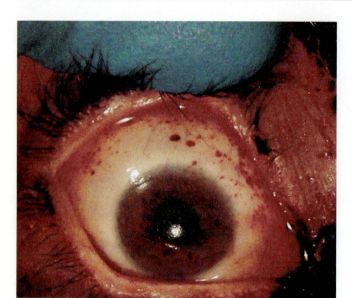

▲ FIGURE 9-25 **Petechial hemorrhaging in the eye**
The victim of a suicidal hanging. In suicidal hangings, investigators often find what is referred to as a petechial hemorrhaging in the eyes of the deceased. This is a result of the small vessels in the eye bleeding owing to an increase in blood pressure caused by the compression around the neck.

types of medication, such as barbiturates, when mixed with alcohol have a synergistic effect, which increases the potency of the drug beyond its normal strength. One should not be too quick to decide that the death is a suicide until the investigation is completed and some evidence is available to support this conclusion. In such cases, the investigator should seize as evidence any

remaining medication and its container. Frequently, the container identifies the medication, the drugstore dispensing it, and the physician prescribing it. There is always the possibility that the medication was purchased or obtained illegally, thus complicating the investigative process. As in all apparent suicides, the investigator should conduct interviews of relatives, friends, or neighbors who may be able to provide background information about the victim.

Drowning

The majority of drowning incidents are either accidental or suicidal, but some are homicidal. Three questions must be answered in apparent drowning cases before any final conclusions can be reached: Was the cause of death drowning, or was the victim first killed and then placed in the water? If the cause of death was drowning, did it take place in the water where the body was recovered, or was the victim drowned elsewhere and then placed in the water where found? Was the victim conscious when placed in the water? Answers to these questions can be obtained by external examination of the body by the investigator. External signs to indicate that the victim was alive and conscious when entering the water include:

- Objects clutched in the hand, such as grass or bottom soil commonly found in water.
- Fingernail marks on the palms of the hands.
- White, pink, or red foam extruding from the nose and open mouth. (See Figure 9-26.)
- Livor mortis most marked in the head and neck because the body settled with these parts in a dependent position.[22]

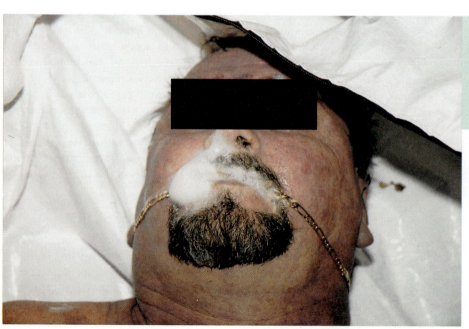

◄ **FIGURE 9-26**
Drowning victim
This individual died from an accidental drowning. Note the pink foam extruding from his nose and open mouth.

An internal examination by a physician serves to establish whether death occurred by drowning. The following may be found in drowning cases:

- The chest cavity and the lungs are distended and soggy, with fine foam in the trachea and bronchi.
- The heart is flabby, with its right side dilated and filled with dark red fluid. The blood is unclotted and usually hemolyzed owing to the absorption of the drowning fluid into the system.
- The mastoid cells of the ear have hemorrhaged.
- Air embolisms may have formed in the blood in deep-water drownings.
- There may be water in the stomach and duodenum.
- Algae and other marine particles may be found in the stomach and adhering to the sides of the air passages.

In removing the body from the water, the investigator may notice considerable damage to portions of the victim's body, especially around the head and face. This should not cause the investigator to conclude prematurely that the victim was the object of foul play. Some bodies of water contain many rocks and shells; a free-floating body that is subject to strong currents can be repeatedly slammed into and dragged across such objects, causing severe damage, especially to the forehead, knees, tops of the feet, and backs of the hands. In addition, if the water is rich with fish, crabs, and other marine life, these too can cause damage. It is not unusual for the lips, ears, and nose to be at least partially eaten away. The extent of damage from objects or marine life in the water varies; understanding what can result from their presence minimizes the possibility of premature conclusions. But the investigator must also not prematurely conclude that all damage resulted after the body was placed in the water. The medical examiner can help draw conclusions about the actual nature of wounds. (See Figure 9-27.)

Cutting and Piercing Instruments

The instruments ordinarily employed in suicides by cutting are razor blades, knives (Figure 9-28), and occasionally glass. One of the common characteristics of suicides inflicted by these instruments is the presence of hesitation marks. Hesitation marks are a series of lesser wounds inflicted by the victim in the general region of the fatal wound, often the wrists, forearms, or throat. In certain throat cuttings, it may be possible to reach a conclusion about whether the injury was self-inflicted or resulted from an assault. If a wound is self-inflicted, it tends to be deep at the point of entry and to shallow out at its terminus, which is near, or slightly past, the midline of the throat. In homicidal throat cutting, the wound appears deep from the start to the terminus. It is not unusual for a victim to inflict a series of severe cuts on different parts of the body to ensure death. The reasons vary, sometimes involving the influence of alcohol or hallucinogenic drugs.

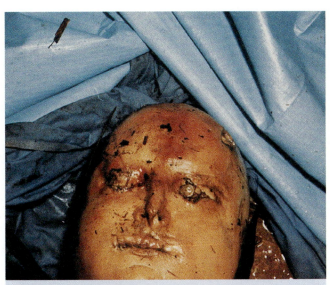

▲ **FIGURE 9-27   Decomposition and marine life damage to an immersed body**
Damage sustained by the victim in this photograph occurred while immersed in water. Note that the ears and eyelids are completely missing, and there is extensive damage to the nostrils and lips. These areas are among the first parts of the body to be attacked by marine life.

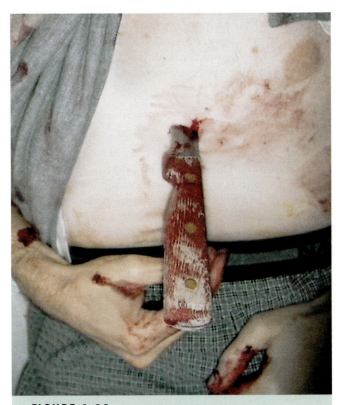

▲ **FIGURE 9-28**
Suicide by knife
This photo depicts an individual who took his life by stabbing himself in the abdomen with a knife.

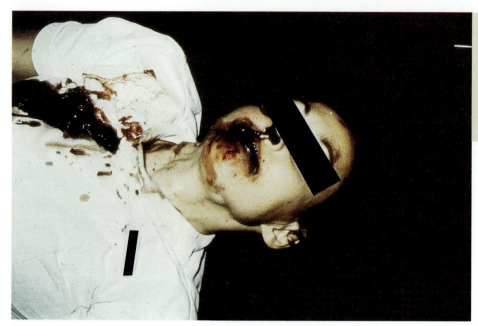

◄ FIGURE 9-29 Ingestion of a caustic drain cleaner
This victim committed suicide by ingesting a strong caustic drain cleaner. On ingestion, vomiting was induced, thereby causing severe burns to the nose, chin, and chest area.

The ingestion of drugs may have been a planned prelude to the act of self-destruction. Self-inflicted wounds can be surprisingly brutal and tend to make people disbelieve they were self-imposed. This is particularly true when mutilation of the sexual parts is involved. In one case, a 28-year-old man used a single-edged razor blade to cut off his penis. When questioned by paramedics, the man said: "It's just been eating away at me for so long and when I thought about it, I heard voices saying 'Do it, do it.' I was just angry at myself. I had it all planned out and I did it."[23]

Poisons

The ingestion of liquid **poisons** is sometimes clear from outward signs on the body. Powerful caustic lyes or acids may produce vomiting once the liquid reaches the digestive tract. There is considerable damage to lips, tongue, and mouth, and there may be blood in the vomitus, along with pieces of the esophagus and stomach. Usually, death does not occur rapidly, and victims may employ another means of suicide to stop the excruciating pain. (See Figure 9-29.)

Cases of suspected poisoning frequently pose very difficult problems to the police investigator and to the medical examiner. Many poisons produce symptoms similar to those of certain diseases, a fact that can complicate determination of whether a crime has been committed. However, if there is any reason to suspect poisoning, the investigation must proceed along the lines of a possible homicide, suicide, or accidental death until death due to natural causes is established.[24] To compound the problem, suicides and accidental deaths by poisoning are sometimes very difficult to distinguish from homicide. Alcohol, when consumed with certain medications, may result in an accidental (possibly suicidal) death by respiratory failure. An example is the combination of barbiturates and alcohol. When the alcohol level in the blood reaches about half the lethal dose, most individuals lose consciousness and thus stop breathing. But with the addition of a stimulant, such as an amphetamine, this effect may not occur, and individuals may drink a lethal dose of alcohol before they fall into a coma.

Actually, poisoning is now rarely used in homicdes because modern laboratory techniques can readily detect most poisons, thus unmasking an intended homicide. But when it is the method, a wide variety of poisons may be used. (See Table 9-1.)

Characteristics of "Ideal" Poisons

There are certain elements that characterize an "ideal" poison, including:

- Being odorless, tasteless, and colorless. This allows for the administration of the poison to the intended victim, while providing no warning signs that the victim can detect by the normal bodily senses of smell, taste, and sight.
- Being readily soluble, preferably in water. This allows for easy administration in normal foods and drinks that the victims might eat or drink.
- Having a delayed onset of action, as this allows for a time period in which the poisoner can attempt to create an alibi.
- Being undetectable, and certainly the more exotic the poison the more likely it will not be detected in more routine toxicological analyses.
- Having a low-dose lethality, which means less of the toxic material needs to be administered. It is much easier to distribute a pinch of a substance rather than a pound.

TABLE 9-1	Poisons and Associated Physical Manifestations
TYPE OF POISON	**SYMPTOM OR EVIDENCE**
Caustic poison (lye)	Characteristic burns around lips and mouth of victim
Carbon monoxide	Victim's skin takes on an abnormally bright cherry-red color
Sulfuric acid	Black vomit
Hydrochloric acid	Greenish-brown vomit
Nitric acid	Yellow vomit
Silver salts	White vomit turning black in daylight
Copper sulfate	Blue-green vomit
Phosphorus	Coffee-brown vomit with an onion or a garlic odor
Cyanide	Burnt almond odor in air, cherry-red lividity color
Ammonia, vinegar, Lysol, etc.	Characteristic odors
Arsenic, mercury, lead salts	Pronounced diarrhea
Methyl (wood) alcohol, isopropyl (rubbing) alcohol	Nausea and vomiting, unconsciousness, possibly blindness

(Source: Richard H. Fox and Carl L. Cunningham, *Crime Scene Search and Physical Evidence Handbook* [Washington, D.C.: Government Printing Office, 1985], p. 126.)

- Being easily obtained, but not traceable, so it will leave no investigative trail that would lead to the poisoner.

- Being chemically stable, which makes it easy to store without loss of potency.[25]

Role of the Crime Scene Investigator

Even though the crime scene investigators seldom can identify the chemical compound that caused the death, they should be alert to the general range of possibilities and the potentially hazardous environmental factors that may be connected with a poisoning.

Regardless of the nature of the incident—homicide, suicide, or accident—the symptoms of death by poison are the same. The field investigator should attempt to determine if the victim had any of the symptoms—vomiting, convulsions, diarrhea, paralysis, rapid or slow breathing, contracted or dilated pupils, changes in skin color, or difficulty in swallowing—just prior to death. These symptoms are general manifestations of systemic poisoning. They do not provide proof of poisoning but can be meaningful in relation to other evidence. Someone who observed the victim just before death provides the best source of information concerning his or her symptoms. If no witness is available, the investigator must rely all the more on physical evidence from the crime scene. Table 9-1 lists common poisons and their associated physical manifestations.

The investigator should collect all available information concerning the activities of the victim during the last three days of life. Information on what types of medication

were taken, when the last meal was eaten, and where it was eaten can be very important in determining the type of poison involved. Medical history may indicate that death was due to natural causes.

The **toxicologist** is concerned with the identification and recognition of poisons, with their physiological effects on humans and animals, and with their antidotes. Crime laboratories usually provide some toxicological support but vary considerably in the amount and type that they can furnish. However, full toxicological support is always available through a combination of hospital, medical examiner's, coroner's, and criminalistics laboratories. Crime laboratories can direct police to local facilities.

If the investigator suspects that poison was ingested, a diligent search should be conducted for the container. In suicides and accidental poisonings, the container frequently is close at hand. Even though a container appears empty, it should be processed for fingerprints, packaged, marked, and forwarded to the laboratory for examination. Additionally, any other object that could reasonably relate to the poisoning should be collected, such as unwashed dishes and glasses, wastebasket contents, envelopes, and medicine containers.

Gases

The gas most frequently involved in medico-legal investigations is carbon monoxide. When a death does result from this gas, it is generally accidental or suicidal. Carbon monoxide is found in automobile exhaust fumes and improperly ventilated space heaters in homes. In a death caused by auto emissions, the individual may have started the engine of the vehicle in the garage after closing the garage door or may have extended a flexible hose

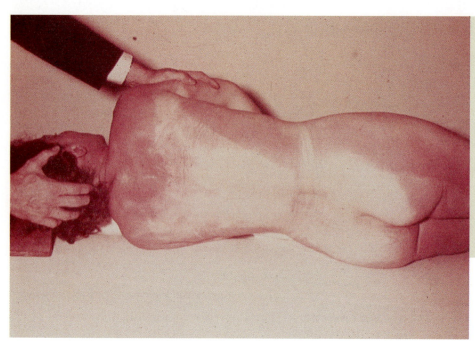

◄ **FIGURE 9-30**
Carbon monoxide death
This victim died accidentally from carbon monoxide poisoning resulting from an improperly ventilated space heater. Note the abnormally bright cherry-red color resulting from the reaction of the red blood cells to the gas and the pale area in the back region. This results because this area was resting against a firm surface and compressing the vessels in this area, which presents the accumulation of blood.

from the exhaust pipe into the vehicle and then closed the windows.

When death occurs from carbon monoxide poisoning, the victim's skin takes on an abnormally bright cherry-red color because of the reaction of the red blood cells to the gas. The red blood cells have a very high affinity for carbon monoxide molecules (approximately 250 times greater than for oxygen), absorbing them rapidly, thereby making the red blood cells incapable of absorbing oxygen and rendering them dysfunctional in the life-sustaining process. Death generally occurs when the red blood cells have reached a saturation level usually above 40%, although this varies; the level sometimes goes higher before death results if the victim is asleep, owing to the body's reduced oxygen needs. (See Figure 9-30.)

Jumping from High Places

The major question to be answered in death resulting from jumping is whether the victim voluntarily leaped or was thrown or pushed. Often, there are suicide notes, witnesses who can provide this information, or background information that indicates previous suicide attempts or a predisposition toward suicide.

The Suicide Note

Research indicates that suicide notes are not left in most suicides. One study revealed certain facts about persons who do and do not leave notes. Generally, there are no differences between the two groups in age, race, sex, employment, marital status, history of mental illness, place of suicide, reported causes or unusual circumstances preceding the act, medical care and supervision, or history of previous suicide attempts or threats. However, the note writers differed from the non-note writers in the methods used to kill themselves. The note writers used poisons, firearms, and hanging more often as a means of death than did the non-note writers.[26]

Gender Differences In Suicidal Behavior

Studies of suicide in the United States indicate that the suicide rate is higher for men than for women, whereas the attempted suicide rate is higher for women than men. Some evidence suggests that there are differences between men and women in the methods employed to commit suicide: women prefer barbiturates and poisons; if women do use a firearm, the fatal wound is frequently in the body rather than the head. It has been suggested that these methods are used because they are not disfiguring and because women are often more concerned about their appearance after death than are men. It is not uncommon for a female to leave a note to her female friends or relatives specifying in detail the clothes she wants to be buried in, along with details relating to facial cosmetics.[27]

In contrast, some males kill themselves where their bodies will not be discovered by family members, such as in the woods. These types of suicides can create investigative problems, especially if a note is not written. For example, if a passerby is tempted to steal a gun used in a suicide and valuables from a suicide victim, the police may think that the death was a murder and robbery rather than suicide.

Suicide Insurance Schemes

Sometimes individuals take their own lives and try to convey the impression that the death was accidental or even homicidal. Generally, they try to create this impression because they have invested in insurance policies that will not pay out money to the beneficiary if a death is self-inflicted. The following case illustrates such an instance:

Several years ago an Armenian man from Iran died in the Marina del Rey area of Los Angeles, California, when a bomb blew up his car. At first investigators believed that the incident might have been a terrorist killing. However, after a long investigation, they concluded that the man had killed himself in a way that looked like a terrorist attack to allow his father to collect more than $1 million from newly secured insurance policies.

Victor R. Galustian, 42, had lived in Los Angeles since 1950, when his father returned to Iran. His father had sent him money illegally from Iran for safekeeping against the day when the father would come to the United States. Galustian used the money to entertain acquaintances at lavish restaurant dinners, passing himself off as a real estate businessman or sometimes an engineer.

Because the money entered this country illegally, it is impossible to know just how much Galustian received, but investigators estimate that he spent at least $600,000 of the money his father had sent. Desperate when he learned that his father was planning to return to this country, Galustian began planning how to regain the money he had spent. He took out numerous insurance policies shortly before he died, with his father as beneficiary. All the policies had double-indemnity clauses, which double the benefits if the policyholder dies an unnatural death. The policies prohibit payoff if the policyholder commits suicide.

Early one morning, Galustian was driving his car near his apartment when a powerful explosive under his front seat went off, propelling Galustian's body 25 feet from the demolished auto and spewing debris for 600 feet. The explosion occurred after an outbreak of violence involving local Armenian and Iranian families. Authorities initially believed that the explosion, too, might be political. A few days before his death, Galustian had told a security guard in his apartment building that he had found a bomb in his car. That and other clues, including his lack of political activity in the Armenian community, convinced investigators that Galustian's death was not the result of a political attack. It took investigators several months to piece everything together, but they eventually concluded that the death was a suicide.[28]

FIRE DEATHS

Frequently, human remains are found at the scene of a fire. Properly examined, these remains may provide important data to the investigator about the facts surrounding the fire and the cause of death. Investigators should ask these questions:

- Was the decedent accidentally killed by the fire (whether or not the fire was caused by arson)?
- Was the decedent deliberately killed by the fire?
- Was the decedent already dead when the fire occurred?

To answer these questions, investigators should determine certain facts. These facts are outlined in the remainder of this section.[29]

Coordination and Cooperation

Coordination of, and cooperation between, police and fire investigators are of paramount importance in the successful investigation of any questioned fire. As with other forms of physical evidence at a fire scene, a body should never be moved until fully examined at the scene unless there is some possibility that the person is still alive or there is danger of further destruction of the body if it remains where it is. Also, because a dead human being is probably the most complex and rapidly changing type of physical evidence at a crime scene, cooperation between medical personnel (preferably forensic pathologists) and investigators is essential. This coordination should extend from the scene of the fire to the medical facility where the postmortem examination is conducted.

Degrees of Burning

Burns are medically classified into four types. The extent of burns may provide information about the proximity of the body to the point of origin of the fire, the length of time the body was exposed to the fire, and the intensity of the fire.

First-degree burns are superficial and limited to the outer layers of skin. Although the burned area is red and swollen, blisters do not form and peeling may follow. Second-degree burns involve blistering and the destruction of the upper layers of skin. They occasionally cause scarring in living victims. With third-degree burns, the entire thickness of the skin (epidermis and dermis) is destroyed. In living victims with third-degree burns, pain is usually absent as nerve endings are destroyed; scarring results, and skin grafting is usually necessary. (See Figure 9-31.) Fourth-degree burns completely destroy (char) the skin and underlying tissue.

◄**FIGURE 9-31**
Third-degree burns
This individual was driving a truck when it caught on fire. He leaped from the truck but the burn injuries he had sustained would eventually prove fatal. The area of his face, hands, and abdomen are classified as third-degree burns. The cause of his death was listed as thermal injuries.

Identification of Remains

Because fire destroys human tissue, identification of the remains may be especially difficult. Yet because identification of a decedent is a key factor in any questioned death investigation, an orderly, sequential approach must be used in the identification process. The six means that follow should be considered in sequence, from the "best" identification tools to the "worst":

- Fingerprints
- Dentition
- DNA printing
- Scars, marks, or tattoos on the exterior of the body
- Scars, marks, abnormalities, or appliances inside the body
- Identification, jewelry, and clothing on the body

Scene Considerations

As with any physical evidence, burned bodies must be sketched, measured, and photographed in place and in relation to other evidence at the scene of the fire. The actual location of the body may be crucial to the investigation. Determination as to whether the decedent was a smoker is important for establishing what caused the fire and whether he or she was alive at the time of the fire.

Examination of the External Body

The body of the deceased should be examined in detail both at the scene and again at the morgue. Significant areas for examination include those discussed next.

Signs of Trauma

Any sign of injury to the external body should be carefully noted, sketched, and photographed. The use of a five-power magnifying glass (as a minimum) is required, because fire obscures signs of injury.

Skull Fracture

Another factor that may be misconstrued is the discovery that the victim's skull is fractured. Care must be taken to determine whether the fracture is implosive or explosive. An implosive fracture may have been caused by a fall, may be evidence of a previous felonious assault or homicide, or may result from a collapsed structural member. The exact cause will be determined at autopsy and evaluated during the follow-up investigation. An explosive fracture, however, is usually a natural consequence of fire. The extreme heat may cause the fluids in and around the brain to boil and expand. The resulting steam produces pressure sufficient to cause an explosive (pressure-release) reaction. The fracture(s) that result usually follow the natural suture lines of the skull. In extreme cases, the cranium may burst, causing the expelled brain and skull matter to form a circular pattern around the head. This is more common in children than in adults: the fontanel, or membrane-covered opening between the uncompleted parietal bones, is the weakest point in a fetal or young skull. The resulting circular pattern (0 to 12 inches from the skull) is significant when compared with the type of splattering that might result from a shotgun blast or high-order explosion.[30]

Blistering and Splitting Skin

The inexperienced investigator may be somewhat apprehensive in attempting to evaluate the effects of heat and flame on the skin of the victim. The medical investigator is in the best position to render a judgment in this area.

The formation of blisters (vesicles) is part of the body's natural defense system. The exact distinction between antemortem and postmortem blistering can be made only

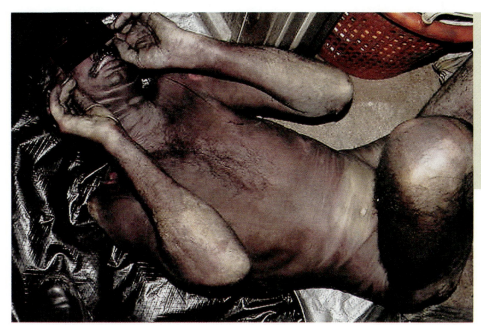

◀ **FIGURE 9-32**
Pugilistic attitude
The heat of a fire can result in the arms and legs of the body being drawn up into a posture resembling that of a boxer. That is precisely what happened to this individual who died in an accidental house fire. The cause of his death was determined to be inhalation of smoke and soot.

at autopsy. There are, however, certain signs that a medical investigator can use in developing a hypothesis. Postmortem blisters are generally limited in size and may contain only air or air mixed with a small amount of body fluid. Antemortem blisters are larger in size and contain a complex mix of body fluids. The precise determination of the fluids requires microscopic analysis. A blister surrounded by a pink or red ring can be considered to have occurred before death; the reddish ring is the result of an antemortem inflammatory reaction.

In some instances, temperatures may not have been sufficiently high to produce blistering. Likewise, if the skin is burned off or otherwise heavily damaged, blistering will not be evident.

The heat and flames of the fire also cause the skin to shrink or tighten and ultimately split. The splitting or lesions may be seen on the arms, legs, and torso. At first glance, this condition, coupled with pugilistic attitude, could be misinterpreted as indicating defense wounds.

In some cases, a seriously burned person survives the fire and is removed to a burn center. In an effort to save the person, the medical staff at the center may attempt to duplicate the natural splitting of the skin with a surgical technique known as an escharotomy. This technique is used to help foster circulation and to prevent the onset of gangrene. Should the burn victim die some time after the fire, these splits should not be misinterpreted as fire induced.[31]

Noncranial Fractures

If enough heat is applied, bones shrink, warp, and fracture. Determining whether fractures were caused by a trauma or heat requires painstaking examination.

Pugilistic Attitude

The so-called pugilistic attitude of the body is a natural result of the dehydrating effect caused by the heat from the fire and is not related to the cause or manner of death. The arms and legs will be drawn into a posture resembling that of a boxer. (See Figure 9-32.)

More often than not in **fire deaths**, a forensic pathologist who is an expert on burned bodies may have to be summoned.

Examination of the Internal Body

After the body has been closely examined, sketched, and photographed, an internal examination of it should be conducted by a forensic pathologist. Investigators should attend this procedure to get information about the facts, to correct discrepancies in data (such as measurements), and to recover evidence from the body. Significant areas for examination are as follows.

Soot, Other Debris, or Burning in the Air Passages

These findings may indicate that the decedent was breathing while the fire was burning.

Pulmonary Edema

A frothy substance in the lungs may result from irritants breathed in during a fire.

Epidural Hemorrhages

Hemorrhages above the tough membrane covering the brain (the dura mater) and under the skull may occur at the rear of the head due to heat. These hemorrhages should not be mistaken for the hemorrhages associated with blunt-force injuries.[32]

Internal Injuries

All internal injuries should be closely examined, measured, and photographed, with samples taken by the pathologist for later microscopic examination.

Foreign Objects

Any foreign objects found in the body, such as bullets, should be recovered as evidence by the investigator. Because these objects are frequently small and difficult to locate, X-ray examination of the body before internal examination is recommended.

Toxicologic Examination

The pathologist should take samples for later examination by a toxicologist. Toxicologic results may be of extreme importance to the investigation.

Alcohol

Alcohol in blood indicates whether the decedent was incapacitated at the time of the fire and thus unable to escape. A finding of high levels of alcohol raises questions for the investigator about the decedent's habits.

Other Drugs

Indications of other possibly incapacitating drugs may provide new leads. The possibility of drug interactions—barbiturates with alcohol, for example—should also be considered.

Carboxyhemoglobin

Carbon monoxide (CO) is an odorless, colorless gas present at hazardous levels in all structural fires. Carbon monoxide asphyxiation (usually above 40% saturation) is probably the most common cause of death in fires. As previously discussed, CO causes the cherry-red color of postmortem lividity (as well as that of internal organs and muscle tissue).

Presence of Other Chemicals

Chemicals given off by burning materials may indicate the accelerant of the fire, as well as offer evidence that the decedent was breathing them in at the time of the fire.

Motives In Fire Deaths

In fire deaths, the following motives should be kept in mind by investigators:

- Destruction or mutilation of the body to conceal the identity of the decedent.
- Destruction or mutilation of the body to conceal the true cause or manner of death.
- Incineration of the body with homicidal intent.
- Incineration of the body to collect on an insurance policy. For example, a decedent may have committed suicide but have an insurance policy prohibiting collection after death by suicide. Beneficiaries may burn the body to indicate accidental death by fire.
- Suicide with an accelerant.
- An attempt by a suicide victim to hide the cause of death.
- A victim trapped in a building burned by an arsonist or by accident.

SERIAL MURDER

It is believed that the term *serial murderer* was first used in the late 1970s in conjunction with the multiple murderer Theodore Robert Bundy (Figure 9-33). Before that, the most common term was *lust murder*.

For the law enforcement community, **serial murder** comprises a series of sexual attacks and resulting deaths of

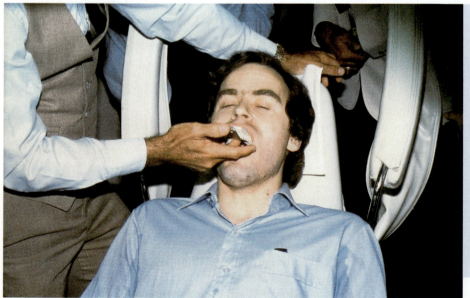

◄ **FIGURE 9-33**
Ted Bundy
This photo depicts a forensic dentist obtaining dental impressions from serial killer Theodore Robert Bundy in conjunction with the murder of two Florida State University female students. Bundy's dental impressions were compared with bite marks left on the body of one of the victims. The marks were positively identified as his. Bundy, who was suspected of killing as many as 100 women, was subsequently executed in the state of Florida. (Courtesy Sheriff Ken Katsaris, Leon County Sheriff's Office, Tallahassee, Florida)

a minimum of three or four individuals and is committed by a killer who tends to follow a distinct physical or psychological pattern. There are seven major components that may serve as flags to alert investigators to the possibility that a serial murderer is operating in their jurisdiction:

- One or more individuals (in most cases, males) commit a second murder and/or subsequent murders.
- There is generally no previous relationship between victim and attacker (if there is a relationship, it will be one that places the victim in a subjugated position relative to the killer).
- Subsequent murders occur at different times and have no apparent connection to the initial murder.
- Subsequent murders are usually committed in a different geographic location.
- The motive is not for material gain; it is for the murderer's desire to have power or dominance over his or her victims.
- Victims may have a symbolic value for the murderer, and/or they may be perceived as lacking prestige, being unable to defend themselves or alert others to their plight, or being powerless given their situation in time, place, or status within their immediate surroundings.
- Victims typically include vagrants, the homeless, prostitutes, migrant workers, homosexuals, missing children, single women (out by themselves), elderly women, college students, and hospital patients.[33]

Much of the early research on serial murder focused on the sexual component of the crime to explain the killer's motivation. Psychologists have referred to the sexual component in a number of ways, describing serial killers as those "who suffer from a deviation or perversion of the sexual impulse"[34] or who "kill because of an underlying basis of sexual conflicts."[35] "They [serial killers] usually have few normal social and sexual relationships. In fact, they often have had no experience of normal sexual intercourse."[36] Some criminologists have stated, "The serial killer is motivated by sex and sadism . . . favors immediate gratification, regardless of the consequences."[37]

Other researchers disagree, arguing that the sexual component either is overstated or is simply an instrument of the killer, not the motivating factor behind the act. For these researchers, the focus of study is on the power relationships or the issue of control. The motivation is thus the enhancement of the killer's sense of control and domination over the victims. The motivational dynamics of serial murder seem to be consistent with research on the nature of rape, which is considered to be a power and dominance crime.[38] This similarity becomes even more evident when one considers that it may take only a small increase in the fury of the rapist or the struggle of the victim to change a violent rape into a murder.

Many social science researchers have found trauma, abuse, and neglect in the childhoods of serial killers.[39]

The social and psychological deprivation consistently identified in the childhoods of serial killers would certainly indicate a strong correlation between such a childhood and serial killing. However, such childhoods can also be identified in many people who do not go on to become serial killers. Correlation does not equal causation. Indeed, if such a correlation were revealed to be the central causal factor of the serial murderer, the United States would have thousands of serial killers, given the current disturbing statistics on child abuse and neglect in this country. A terrible childhood may contribute to the serial killer's makeup, but it is apparently only one factor in the etiology of serial killing.

Research on serial murder has focused on finding similarities among murders. The victims of serial killers have largely been ignored. Serial killers seem to prey on people who are vulnerable or easy to lure and dominate, but little else is known about the victims of serial murders except that they are almost always strangers to the murderer. They appear to be selected because they happen to cross the path of the serial murderer or because their physical appearance holds some symbolic significance for the killer. Vulnerable victims may simply happen to be in the area where the killer is hunting, their appearance may trigger the selection, or the opportunity and the victim's availability in a specific location may contribute to the fatal selection.

The high-risk lifestyles of some victims (such as some cult members, released mental patients, skid-row alcoholics, and prostitutes) certainly contribute to their victimization. Serial killers seem to pick victims whom they can dominate. They do not care about their victims or have any feelings of remorse.

Serial Murder and The NCAVC

If a serial murderer confines his or her activities to a single community or a small region, local police are in a good position to see emerging patterns. But because many serial murderers cover many miles in a short period of time, the FBI has developed the **National Center for the Analysis of Violent Crime (NCAVC)**. It is designed to form a partnership among federal, state, and local law enforcement agencies in the investigation of potentially related, unsolved violent crimes. NCAVC combines law enforcement techniques, behavioral science principles, and data processing to help any law enforcement agency confronted with unusual, bizarre, particularly vicious, or repetitive crimes.

The following are the types of offenses and incidents reported to NCAVC for analysis:

- Sexually oriented murder or assault by mutilation or torture, dismemberment, violent sexual trauma, or asphyxiation.
- Spree murder (a series of indiscriminate murders or assaults, all committed within hours or days—e.g., a series of sniper murders).

- Mass murder (four or more murders in a single incident).
- Robbery murder and nonfatal robbery with extreme violence.
- Murder committed during the commission of another felony.
- Kidnapping: fatal, with injury, or for ransom.
- Murder of a hostage.
- Murder for hire, contract murder, syndicate execution.
- Murder of a law enforcement officer.
- Political or other assassination.
- Terrorist or nationalistic murder.
- Drug-related murder.
- Gang murder.
- Missing person with evidence of foul play.
- Unidentified dead body when the manner of death is classified as a homicide.[40]

NCAVC can analyze every unsolved murder in the United States, identify the existence of serial patterns, and link cases together. It then notifies the individual local agencies that have similar murders, and they in turn may establish investigative contact among themselves. NCAVC emphasizes that the primary responsibility for investigating cases lies with the state and local authorities.

NCAVC also conducts research on violent crimes and trains local officers in analytic techniques. It is located at the FBI Academy in Quantico, Virginia, where it is administered by the Behavioral Science Unit. The FBI Academy was chosen as the site because it is a national law enforcement training center with vast resources for research and many capabilities for providing investigative support.

ViCAP CRIME REPORT

When a violent crime remains unsolved for a period of time, the local law enforcement agency provides details about it on a special **Violent-Criminal Apprehension Program (ViCAP)** reporting form.[41] This form is submitted to the nearest FBI field office, which reviews and forwards it to NCAVC. Following are examples of several murder cases solved with the assistance of ViCAP.

In 1996, a suspect in a drug case in a northeastern state made an offer to the authorities—in exchange for leniency in his prosecution or at the time of his sentencing, he would give information linking his brother to a murder. He advised them his brother had killed a white male in a southeastern state with repeated strikes with a blunt object. The investigators questioned the suspect about where the crime occurred, and the suspect advised he did not know the exact location, but thought it happened near a body of water. Further, the suspect advised that his brother ran over the victim with an automobile.[42]

Investigators from the northeastern state contacted ViCAP and related the details of the case as told to them by the suspect. A crime analyst searched the ViCAP database and found a case from 1986 in a southeastern state that matched the details offered by the suspect in the drug case. The victim's cause of death was blunt force trauma, and he was run over by an automobile. Further, the murder occurred near a small lake. Authorities in the northeast with the information contacted investigators in the southeast with the open homicide case. The southeastern case was successfully closed with the identification and arrest of the offender.[43]

In 1999, a series of homicides occurred in Texas. Early in the series, the cases were presented as murders in the victims' homes. Female victims were sexually assaulted, blunt force trauma was the cause of death,[44] and items of value were stolen from the homes.[45] The murder scenes were close to railroad tracks, sometimes only a few feet away.

In May 1999, personnel from the command post in Texas called ViCAP with information about three of the murders. One of the ViCAP crime analysts remembered a case from Kentucky where railroad tracks were prominently mentioned. The analyst searched the database and quickly found the case in Kentucky where a male was killed along a pair of railroad tracks. The cause of death was blunt force trauma.[46] His male companion was sexually assaulted and left for dead. ViCAP relayed information concerning the Kentucky rape/homicide to the command post in Texas. Subsequent DNA examinations linked the Texas cases with the Kentucky case.

An itinerant freight train rider was identified as the suspect in the series of cases.[47] He was apprehended by authorities on July 13, 1999, when he surrendered at the border in El Paso, Texas. Charged with nine murders, two in Illinois, one in Kentucky, and six in Texas,[48] the subject was tried, convicted, and sentenced to death. In July 2000, he confessed to the 1997 murders of two teenagers on a railroad track near Oxford, Florida.[49] The male victim's body was found on March 23, 1997; the female victim's body was not found until July 2000, when authorities, following the killer's directions, found her skeletal remains wrapped in a blanket and jacket.[50]

While confessing to the two murders in Florida, the subject said he once killed a woman in a southeastern state, somewhere along railroad tracks. She was an old woman, hanging her wash on the line, and he killed her inside her house. He did not provide more details.

A check of the ViCAP database revealed a 1998 case from a southeastern state where an elderly woman was hanging laundry in her backyard just a few feet from a pair of railroad tracks that ran by her property. The command post in Texas and the investigator in the southeastern state were notified of the case match. When interviewed by the investigator, the subject confessed in detail and drew a diagram of the inside of the victim's house. In this case, no fingerprint or DNA evidence matched the defendant to the murder.

In 2001, a ViCAP crime analyst reviewed a state police publication that mentioned a bag of human bones found by hunters in a seaboard forest of an eastern state. The victim was a white male, about 40 to 60 years old, and between 5 feet, 7 inches and 5 feet, 9 inches in height. His cause of death was blunt force trauma to the head. Recovered with the remains was a 14-carat gold ring with engraved letters. Authorities had no leads for identification of the remains.

The ViCAP crime analyst searched the database using the physical description of the victim and made an additional search, thinking that the letters engraved in the ring might be the initials of a name. A possible match was made with a July 1998 case where three people were reported missing from a midwestern state. The report was made by a fourth member of the family, a son who waited a week before reporting his mother, father, and sibling as missing persons. Law Enforcement personnel had exhausted all investigative leads.

Authorities in the eastern and midwestern states contacted each other. In January 2001, ViCAP learned that forensic odontology had identified the bones in the bag as those of the father missing from the midwestern state. The letters in the recovered ring represented the maiden name of the missing mother and the name of the missing father.

ViCAP learned that a suspect who was identified and charged with the murder turned out to be the older son who made the report in the Midwest. The remains of his mother and sibling have not been located.[51]

The ViCAP form has been organized into the following categories:

- *Part I: Administration*
  Case administration
  Crime classification
  Date and time parameters
- *Part II: Victim information*
  Victim status
  Victim identification
  Physical description
  Scars and/or birthmarks
  Tattoos
  Outstanding physical features
  Clothing of victim
  Miscellaneous
- *Part III: Offender information*
  Offender defined
  Offender status
  Offender identification
  Physical description
  Scars and/or birthmarks
  Tattoos
  Outstanding physical features
- *Part IV: Identified-offender information*
  Offender background
  Property of others
  Offender admissions
- *Part V: Vehicle description*
  Vehicles used in the incident
  Offender's approach to the victim at time of incident
  Exact geographic location
  Location of events, body recovery site
  Site of offender's initial contact with victim
  Victim's last-known location
  Events at assault site
  Offender's writing or carving on body of victim
  Offender's writing or drawing at the scene
  Symbolic artifacts at crime scene
  Offender's communications
  Body disposition
  Restraints used on victim
  Clothing and property of victim
- *Part VI: Cause of death and/or trauma*
  Cause of death
  Bite marks on victim
  Elements of torture or unusual assault
  Sexual assault
- *Part VII: Forensic evidence*
  Weapons
  Blood
- *Part VIII: Request for profile*
- *Part IX: Other related cases*
- *Part X: Narrative summary*

COLD CASE INVESTIGATIONS

Cold case investigations tend to concentrate on two types of criminal offenses, namely murder and sexual battery. In our following discussion we will address each of these offenses separately while recognizing that very often they are intertwined and a murder may also involve a sexual battery.

Opening a Cold Case Murder Investigation

A few years ago, newspapers around the country covered the arrest of Gerald Mason for a murder that happened when Dwight D. Eisenhower was in the White House. Mason was rousted out of a comfortable life in South Carolina and charged with killing two police officers in the Los Angeles suburb of El Segundo, California, in 1957.

Police contend that on July 22 of that year, Mason kidnapped four teenagers, sexually assaulted one of them, and stole a car. Approximately 90 minutes later, Officer Milton Curtis and Officer Richard Phillips of the El Segundo Police Department saw the car run a red light. The two El Segundo officers stopped the car, and Mason shot and killed both officers. An extensive investigation turned up hundreds of tips, but the killer was never identified, and frustrated El Segundo investigators had to set it aside and move on.

The case of the El Segundo police officers' killings went cold, but a quarter century after the two officers were laid to rest, El Segundo investigators received a tip regarding this case. The lead was false, but it stirred interest in the unsolved murders, and the El Segundo Police Department decided to reexamine the evidence.[52]

Investigators from the Los Angeles County Sheriff's Department reviewed the evidence from the 1957 crime spree, and found what they believed to be the key to the case: a fingerprint. Forensic technology has changed greatly since 1957 and one of the contemporary tools that law enforcement officers have now that they did not have then was a national fingerprint database.

Using the FBI-administered national fingerprint database, investigators were able to match prints found in the stolen car to Gerald Mason. Mason's fingerprints were obtained by the FBI in 1956—a year before the murders—when he was arrested for a burglary in South Carolina. As a result, Mason, 69 at the time the case was reopened, faced trial for a crime that happened when he was 23.

While the Mason case is an extraordinary example, more and more suspects are facing prosecution for old crimes, as law enforcement agencies around the country use new technology to solve cold cases.

Introducing The Cold Case Investigation

The **cold case investigation** process involves assigning investigators to examine cases that went unsolved for various reasons, including technology that at the time was not advanced enough to analyze the evidence, witnesses that were hostile, or cases where the original investigators assigned to the case were simply overworked and could not allocate enough time to properly handle it.

No department has unlimited time, personnel, and resources, so it is important to carefully select the cases for review. Violent persons crimes are particularly well suited to cold case review. The reason for this is simple; homicides and sexual assaults tend to yield the most evidence.

Once the types of crimes to be reexamined have been determined, the parameters for selecting specific cases must be defined. This depends greatly on the agency's current caseload, however.

For example, it might be reasonable for smaller agencies to look at all unsolved sexual assaults and/or homicides over the last decade. Larger agencies, however, will have to select a limited number of cases based on several factors, including the amount and condition of the physical evidence, the whereabouts of previously identified suspects and witnesses, and the overall severity and brutality of the crime.

If a department has a crime analyst, he or she will be a great resource in helping decide which cases to reopen. A crime analyst can sort through and filter all reported crimes and provide a list of cases that meet the criteria. Departments not having a crime analyst can talk to senior investigators and other long-time personnel. Without a doubt, such personnel will remember cases that have gone unsolved for 10, 20, or even 30 years.

Time can be the enemy of some investigations, and the case may be too cold to open. A few factors determine whether a case is too old. First, is there any evidence? For example, before reopening a 50-year-old homicide or sexual assault case, it must be determined if physical evidence is still available. Second, if key witnesses, victims, and suspects have died, there is probably little point in reopening the case.

But time can also be an ally. For example, a previously hostile witness may decide the time is right to talk to the police, or a suspect might eventually make an error in judgment and talk about a crime he committed 10 years ago. Additionally, new fingerprints and DNA profiles are added to federal databases every day. A fingerprint or a DNA sample from a case that's been dormant for years can receive a hit if the offender is arrested on unrelated charges and his or her fingerprints and/or DNA are entered into the FBI databases.[53]

The Investigation

The first and possibly most time-consuming step is the review of all existing case material, including patrol reports, investigator notes, laboratory documents, photographs, crime scene diagrams, witness lists, lead sheets, and suspect information.

Examining all this old material can either be relatively easy or quite difficult, depending on the condition of the case file.

Once the file is organized and there is an understanding of the work originally completed on the case, a list of tasks to be accomplished must be made and the case strategy formulated.

Criteria for Opening Cold Case Homicides

1. Does physical evidence exist?
   DNA   yes_____ no_____
   Latent prints   yes_____ no_____
   Ballistics   yes_____ no_____
   Other   yes_____ no_____
2. Is the physical evidence still in property control or available?   yes_____ no_____
   Location_____
3. Have witnesses been identified?   yes_____ no_____
   Number of witnesses_____
   Eye witnesses_____   Other witnesses_____
   Witness availability_____
4. Have suspect(s) been identified?   yes_____ no_____
   In custody   yes_____ no_____   Status_____
   Terminally ill   yes_____ no_____   Deceased yes_____ no_____
5. Is there an opportunity for multiple clearances?   yes_____ no_____
6. Has the case been previously presented to the District Attorney's Office?
   yes_____ no_____   Arrest made yes_____ no_____
7. Clearance potential   excellent_____ good_____ poor_____
8. Should the case be submitted to review team?   yes_____ no_____
Case reviewed by _____ Date_____
Supervisor_____

Courtesy Vivian B. Lord, Ph.D., (Chair, Department of Criminal Justice, University of North Carolina at Charlotte), Implementing a Cold Case Homicide Unit—A Challenging Task. *FBI Law Enforcement Bulletin*, February, 2005 p4.

◄ **FIGURE 9-34**   Criteria for opening cold case homicides

Cold Case Checklist

To assist cold case investigators in systematically examining the criteria for opening a cold case homicide file, the Charlotte-Mecklenburg, North Carolina Police department has developed a checklist (Figure 9-34).

The Human Element

The most important components of cold case investigation are the people—victims, witnesses, suspects—and the physical evidence. Also, no matter how well organized the case file is, usually some amount of work will be needed to complete the witness list. This can be a daunting task because people move, get married, divorced, get married again, and die.

Fortunately, the Internet offers some powerful tools for investigators. Even basic searches on free websites such as www.anywho.com and www.qwestdex.com make it easy to locate people. In addition, an agency might want to consider setting up an account with www.flatrateinfo.com or other for-pay Internet search engines. These sites provide information that might not otherwise be found online. Depending on the site, one can search credit header information for most recent addresses, voter registration records, county clerk records, liens, foreclosures, marriages and divorces, and many other local, state, and national databases.

Finding people is essential to success. It is likely the original investigation left critical questions unanswered. Consequently, many cold cases are solved by conducting additional interviews.

Cold cases are often solved by gathering additional evidence from the witnesses, suspects, and victims. People can voluntarily submit or be court-ordered to submit nontestimonial evidence—fingerprints, DNA, handwriting, and so forth.

Advancement in all aspects of forensic science is the primary reason for law enforcement agencies to reopen cold cases. Thus, physical evidence is critical to a successful reinvestigation.

Using the Computer

Unsolved violent crimes are often complex, with various people recounting different events and time lines, and it can be difficult for investigators to organize and analyze these crucial aspects of the case. This is why software designed specifically for investigations can be an invaluable aid while working a cold case.

For example, a software called Analyst's Notebook 6 from i2 Inc.,[54] allows investigators to build graphical representations of complex cases that include time lines, relationship charts, and phone and financial records. This software organizes and simplifies data in such a way that it helps to see the case more clearly and make connections that might have otherwise gone unnoticed. In addition to aiding the investigative process, these graphic charts can be critical in the courtroom during prosecution. (See Figure 9-35.)

This software is being used to great effect by investigators nationwide. For example, investigators from the Gainesville (Florida) Police Department and a crime analyst from the Georgia Bureau of Investigation recently employed Analyst's Notebook 6 to solve a series of rapes in north Florida and south Georgia.

"As all criminal analysts know, the amount of data and information involved in an investigation such as this

HOMICIDE INVESTIGATION

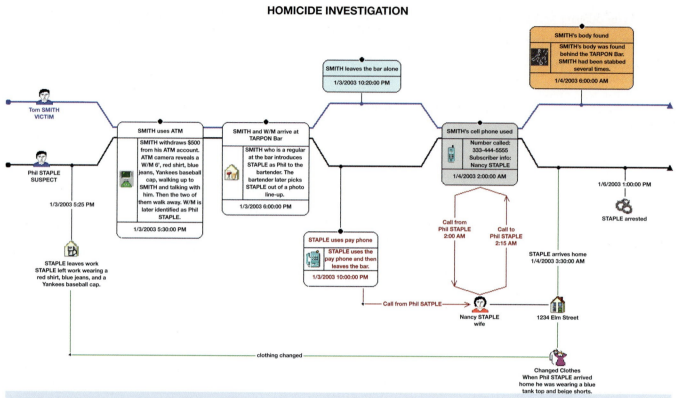

▲ **FIGURE 9-35   Homicide Investigation**

Analyst's Notebook software from i2 Inc., can create time lines and help investigators organize complex and confusing information in ways that will help them see the bigger picture regarding the crime. (Courtesy i2 Inc. Ltd)

one is enormous," says Elaine Posey, a crime analyst with the Georgia Bureau of Investigation. "Without the right analysis tools at your fingertips, investigations can take a long time and often lead down the wrong path."

Posey imported all the seemingly unrelated data from the cases into Analyst's Notebook and created a link analysis chart that showed all of the suspect's associates. She then created a time line of the suspect's movements and actions and used it to link him to 22 rape cases.

"Within two weeks of using this software, we had hardcore evidence against this suspect," Posey says. "Analyst's Notebook made my job easier, helping us catch a criminal much faster and creating a safer environment for the people of Georgia and Florida."[55]

Establishing a Cold Case Team for Sex Crimes

One law enforcement agency, the Phoenix Arizona Police Department, established a separate **cold case team** for sex crimes. An internal audit of their records revealed that 1,700 sexual assault examinations were waiting for evaluation and screening.[56] In addition, over 700 new sexual assaults were being reported each year.

Several years ago the department applied for a state grant just as some money was becoming available. After a review process, the department received the grant,

resulting in 18 months of funding for the creation of the Cold Case Crime Team.[57] A seasoned investigator, with 10 years of experience in sex crime investigation, was chosen to lead the team. It cannot be overemphasized that a complete understanding of sexual offenses, rapists, and their victims is a key component for the successful investigation of these crimes.[58]

Investigative Hurdles

Two specific hurdles of investigations and prosecutions are deceased victims and unwilling victims. A basic right of accused individuals is to face their accusers. How should this requirement be addressed when there is no victim? As with all obstacles, police departments work closely with prosecutors to develop a review process that addresses each case on an individual basis. All victims, including those long since deceased,[59] made statements at or around the time of the assault. These statements are typically given to police, medical personnel, and, on many occasions, friends. The courts have the authority to treat the statements as exceptions to the hearsay rule, and witnesses of these statements may be able to testify to them in court. Combining such statements with corroborating evidence collected at the crime scene has proven successful at dealing with the issue of deceased victims.

Many victims, however, simply do not want to pursue their case. Victims may have blocked it out and moved on, or they may just not want to relive the trauma. Ultimately, this is the victim's decision. The police department respects the decision and offers as much assistance to the victim as possible, and it does not pursue court proceedings when the victims do not want to proceed. Many times the prosecutor's office negotiates a strong plea agreement with the suspects. This practice satisfies most victims while avoiding court trauma but still holding suspects responsible for their actions.

Investigating "New" Cases

The newly created Phoenix Police Department cold case sex crime team conferred with the department's existing cold case homicide squad and adopted its successful tactics, resulting in a unique database for organizing and tracking unsolved cases. All cases were reviewed and evaluated for solvability based on a set of criteria. These criteria included the reevaluation of all evidence (still in property), initial victim interviews, and all witness interviews. Investigators also deliberated the possibility of linking cases through offenders behavior, method of operation, and signature.

Reevaluating Evidence

When reevaluating physical and biological evidence in these cases, investigators noted the evolution of DNA technology in the last five years. The cold case squad quickly learned that DNA testing used as recently as the early 2000s to test evidence was sometimes insufficient. With new and more refined methods of testing DNA, many of the reactivated cases have relinquished previously unfound evidence.

Identifying Suspects from DNA

As with all investigations, identifying the unknown suspect ranks as the first priority. After identifying the suspect, the focus shifts to locating the newly identified suspect. In many cases, a DNA hit from the **Combined DNA Index System (CODIS)** database from a cold case results in a second investigation into a suspect's current location. Not only must investigators locate and apprehend the suspect, but they must also obtain a new DNA sample to confirm the original cold hit. DNA database provide investigators with new leads in these cases, but these new leads mean starting some investigations all over again.[60]

What happens, though, when DNA matches a known suspect? Questions arise, such as "Is the suspect incarcerated?" "Is the suspect out of custody, roaming in another jurisdiction?" and "Is the suspect's exact location known?" The cold case team discovered few procedural or investigative guidelines to answer these questions. The cold case team also recognized that once a cold case hit identifies a suspect in a DNA database, the investigating agency must determine when, where, and how investiga-

tors took the original blood sample from the suspect. Chain of custody of the original blood sample can become a huge impediment for investigators. Most prosecuting attorneys concur that a second fresh sample of the suspects' blood is required. Analyzing this second sample confirms the initial database cold hit and ensures a clean chain of custody for future prosecution.

The Phoenix cold case team discovered that with multiple jurisdictions involved, legal issues addressing warrant and court orders for suspects' blood samples became substantial investigative and prosecutorial concerns. In such cases, interagency communication and cooperation became paramount. Regardless of a suspect's current location, investigators must remain aware of the local jurisdictional laws and follow them to avoid investigative errors. The key to successful prosecution is minimizing or eliminating investigative errors that may jeopardize the successful prosecution of the case.

Statute of Limitations in Sexual Battery Cases

Unlike murder, which has no statute of limitation, certain categories of sexual battery do. Thus it is advisable for investigators to contact their local prosecutor's office to be certain the case can be prosecuted if it is solved and an apprehension is made.

Alternative solutions to the Cold Case Backlog

Although many law enforcement agencies are forming cold case squads, many of them still lack the personnel to do an adequate job. Even when progress is made on a cold case, investigators often encounter difficulty in getting their physical evidence analyzed by a crime laboratory because of the backlog of current cases the laboratories are working on. In other instances, cold cases cannot be reopened because investigators are too busy working on current cases. However, efforts are being made in the private sector to address both the backlog of cold case physical evidence that cannot be analyzed in a timely fashion as well as the shortage of experienced investigative personnel.

Private Sector Crime Laboratories

One of the alternatives to dealing with publicly funded crime laboratories is to seek assistance from the private sector. Max Houck, forensic anthropologist, who worked at the FBI Laboratory in Washington D.C., has created a nonprofit Institute for Cold Case Evaluation (ICCE) through a business incubator program at the University of West Virginia where he teaches. The ICCE serve as a conduit and a repository for information identifying certified laboratories that can analyze physical evidence as well as individuals who have expertise in a broad area, including firearms, serology, pathology, entomology, and so forth.

The institute is also launching a website and information center, with a free electronic newsletter and secure chat rooms where investigators can exchange information and suggestions. ICCE hopes to handle at least 10 cases a month, and as demand grows the institute will likely add more experts, all with carefully evaluated credentials.[61,62,63]

Utilization of Criminal Justice University Students to Evaluate Cold Cases

It is not unusual for many criminal justice programs at both the community college and university levels to have numerous experienced law enforcement investigators in their classes who are pursuing associate and bachelor's degrees. This was the case at one Florida school, Saint Leo University, in Saint Leo, Florida. A senior seminar class in cold case investigations was created that dealt with 10 cold case murders that had previously been investigated by the Pasco County, Florida, Sheriff's Office, Dade City, Florida. This university class had a combination of inservice law enforcement personnel and preservice university seniors. The class provided non-law-enforcement students with an opportunity to gain real-world experience investigating actual homicides. The class was initiated in 2005 and is the first project of its kind in the United States. The program was developed and spearheaded by Professor Barry Glover, a former homicide detective captain with the Clearwater Florida Police Department (Figure 9-36). He knew from firsthand experience that the lack of personnel resources was a major contributing factor to more cold case murders not being reopened for investigation. Thus, in an effort to deal with the problem, the senior university-level seminar, with the cooperation of the Pasco County Sheriff's Offices, was created in an attempt to address several needs: namely, to develop leaders in the field of homicide investigation; to create relationships between criminal justice students and professionals from local law enforcement agencies; and more importantly, to bring closure to victim's families.

The very positive reception of the class is due in large part to the strong relationship created among faculty, students, and Sheriff Bob White of the Pasco County Sheriff's Office. The sheriff has had a long-time professional and personal relationship with Saint Leo University, which is also located in Pasco County. In addition, many of his agency's members are graduates of the Saint Leo University Criminal Justice Program.

The students were divided into teams and assigned a variety of investigative tasks aimed at developing new leads for law enforcement investigators. Graduate-level criminal justice students with law enforcement experience acted as team leaders, and law enforcement personnel offered hands-on experience in the investigation of the homicides. At the end of the course, the students presented their investigative leads to a panel of highly experienced law enforcement officials. A brainstorming session then followed, and a progress report was provided.

In its first two years, the cold case class developed many new leads and identified some likely suspects. It is fully expected that some of these cases will eventually be solved. In several cases, physical evidence that had been recovered at the crime scenes was submitted to the state's crime laboratory for analysis, and where appropriate, comparison to suspects.[64]

◀ **FIGURE 9-36 Criminal Justice University students evaluating cold cases**
Professor Barry Glover, Department of Criminal Justice, Saint Leo University, Saint Leo, Florida, is shown discussing four cold case murders with his university class. The photo on the far of left part of the figure are that an unidentified white male whose skeletal remains were found in a wooded area in Pasco County, Florida. A forensic anthropologist working with law enforcement officials did a facial reconstruction of what the individual might have looked like when he was alive. Six variations were provided to law enforcement officials. The reconstruction was done based on the victim's skull, which was recovered along with his body. The three photos below the facial reconstruction are of the victim's T-shirt found at the crime scene. Although it is not visible in the photograph, a picture of an Indian was painted on the T-shirt.

The photos of the three females to the right are of murder victims whose bodies were found dumped in a wooded area. The *modus operendi* (M.O.) indicates that two of the three murders were committed by the same person. As noted on the dates below the victims' photographs, these cases are over 30 years old.

(Photo courtesy Ashlee Castle, Department of Criminal Justice, Saint Leo University, Saint Leo, Florida)

KEY TERMS

algor mortis
autopsy
cadaveric spasm
chain of custody
cold case investigation
cold case team
Combined DNA Index Systems
   (CODIS)
contact bullet wound
decomposition
defense wound
firearm residue

fire deaths
forensic entomologist
forensic pathology
incised wound
laceration
ligature strangulation
livor mortis
manual strangulation
medico-legal examination
National Center for the Analysis of
   Violent Crime (NCAVC)

poisons
puncture wound
rigor mortis
serial murder
suicide
toxicologist
Violent Criminal Apprehension Program
   (ViCAP)
walk-through

REVIEW QUESTIONS

1. What should the investigator do when responding to a death scene?
2. What are the purposes of an autopsy?
3. What is algor mortis, and how does it help to determine the time of death?
4. Livor mortis is important for three reasons. What are they?
5. What is cadaveric spasm?
6. Briefly describe the typical entrance and exit gunshot wound.
7. Describe an incised wound, stab wound, and laceration.
8. What are defense wounds, and where are they most commonly found?
9. How is death produced by manual strangulation?
10. Which misconceptions are associated with suicidal hangings?

11. Why are poisons rarely used in homicides?
12. Discuss the differences in the suicidal behavior of men and women.
13. In regard to human remains at a fire, what three broad questions should investigators keep in mind?
14. What are the common motives in fire deaths?
15. What types of offenses and incidents are reported to the National Center for the Analysis of Violent Crime for analysis?
16. What are the first and possibly the most time-consuming steps in opening a cold case murder investigation?
17. Why is it important to reevaluate all physical and biological evidence in both cold case murder investigations and sex-related crimes?

INTERNET ACTIVITIES

1. A special forensic entomology website at www .forensicentomology.com has been created to assist in the education of crime scene technicians, homicide investigators, coroners, medical examiners, and others involved in the death investigation process. This site assists in answering these questions: What do the insects of forensic importance look like? What are the proper methods of their collection? How can communications between the police and the forensic entomologist be enhanced?

2. As the twentieth century progressed, so did technology and the scientific sophistication of toxicology. Thus, the use of poison as a weapon needed to evolve in order to remain covert and evade detection. During the century, the source, preparation, and administration of poisons was stripped away, each process becoming cleaner and more attenuated. The website www.porfolio.mvm.ed.ac.uk/ studentwebs/session2/group12/20th.htm helps address these questions: What historical changes have occurred in the use of poisons to commit homicide? Which older types of poison are still popular? What new types are being used? How have advances in technology helped make poison more detectable in the body?

NOTES

1. Jay Dix and Robert Calaluce, *Guide to Forensic Pathology* (Columbia: University of Missouri, 1998), p. 3.
2. Wisconsin Crime Laboratory, *Criminal Investigation and Physical Evidence Handbook* (Madison: Department of Justice, State of Wisconsin, 1968), p. 10.
3. John J. Horgan, *Criminal Investigation* (New York: McGraw-Hill, 1974), p. 292.
4. This information was obtained at www.crime-scene-investigator.net/deadbodyevidence.html.
5. Dix and Calaluce, *Guide to Forensic Pathology*, p. 32.
6. Ibid., pp. 35–36.
7. Ibid., pp. 33–34.
8. Francis E. Camps, ed., *Gradwohl's Legal Medicine*, 3rd ed. (Bristol: Wright and Sons, 1976), p. 83.
9. For a more detailed discussion, see Ask Dr. Baden at www.hbo.com/autopsy/baden.
10. Dix and Calaluce, *Guide to Forensic Pathology*, pp. 38–40.
11. Gail S. Anderson, Forensic Entomology, British Columbia, Canada, Simon Fraser University, School of Criminology, 2005. (This discussion was specifically developed by Dr. Anderson for this chapter. She is also a court-qualified expert and may be contacted at ganderso@sfu.ca.)
12. Vernon J. Geberth, *Practical Homicide Investigation*, CRC Boca Raton, FL, 2006, pp. 325 and 327.
13. Barry A. J. Fisher, *Techniques of Crime Scene Investigation* (New York: Elsevier, 1992), pp. 452–458. This discussion was adapted with permission from this source.
14. The information on shotgun wounds was obtained from material developed by Vincent J. M. DiMaio, M.D., Medical Examiner, Dallas County, Texas.
15. The information on firearm residue included in this chapter was developed by the Southwestern Institute of Forensic Sciences at Dallas, Texas.
16. R. C. Harrison and R. Gilroy, "Firearms Discharge Residues," *Journal of Forensic Sciences,* 1959, No. 4, pp. 184–199.
17. Dominic J. DiMaio and Vincent J. M. DiMaio, *Forensic Pathology* (New York: Elsevier, 1989), p. 87.
18. Ibid.
19. Ibid., pp. 231–243.
20. Jacques Charon, *Suicide* (New York: Scribner's, 1972), p. 56.
21. Ibid., p. 39.
22. Lemoyne Snyder, *Homicide Investigation* (Springfield, IL: Charles C. Thomas, 1973), p. 228.
23. Donna Newson, "Doctors Perform Rare Surgery," *Tampa Tribune,* July 25, 1980, pp. A1, A10.
24. Richard H. Fox and Carl L. Cunningham, *Crime Scene Search and Physical Evidence Handbook* (Washington, DC: Government Printing Office, 1973), pp. 124, 126. This discussion of poisons was taken from this source.
25. John Harris Trestrail, III, *Criminal Poisoning* (Totowa, NJ: Humana Press Inc. 2000–2001), p. 29.
26. J. Tuckman et al., "Credibility of Suicide Notes," *American Journal of Psychiatry,* June 1960, No. 65, pp. 1104–1106.
27. David Lester, *Why People Kill Themselves* (Springfield, IL: Charles C. Thomas, 1972), p. 36.
28. D. Hastings, "Long Investigation Uncovers Suicide Scheme," *Tampa Tribune-Times,* Jan. 22, 1984, p. A24.
29. Z. G. Standing Bear, *The Investigation of Questioned Deaths and Injuries—Conference Notes and Outline* (Valdosta, GA: Valdosta State College Press, 1988), pp. 78–82.
30. John J. O'Conner, *Practical Fire and Arson Investigation* (Boca Raton, FL: CRC Press, 1993), pp. 160–161.
31. Ibid.
32. Camps, *Gradwohl's Legal Medicine,* p. 358; Lester Adelson, *The Pathology of Homicide* (Springfield, IL: Charles C. Thomas, 1974), p. 610; Richard Lindenberg, "Mechanical Injuries of the Brain and Meninges," in Spitz and Fisher, *Medicolegal Investigation of Death,* pp. 447–456.
33. A. Egger, *The Killers among Us* (Upper Saddle River, NJ: Prentice Hall, 2002), pp. 4–7, 11; R. Hazlewood and J. Douglas, (1980, April). "The Lust Murderer," *FBI Law Enforcement Bulletin,* April 1980, pp. 1–5.
34. J. de River, *Crime and the Sexual Psychopath* (Springfield, IL: Charles C. Thomas, 1958), p. 99.
35. E. Revitch and L. Schlesinger, *Psychopathology of Homicide* (Springfield, IL: Charles C. Thomas, 1981); M. Reynolds, *Dead Ends* (New York: Warner Books, 1992), p. 281.
36. D. Lunde, *Murder and Madness* (Palo Alto, CA: Stanford Alumni Association, 1976), p. 53.
37. J. Levin and J. Fox, *Mass Murder* (New York: Plenum, 1985), p. 225.
38. S. Egger, *Serial Murder and the Law Enforcement Response,* unpublished dissertation, College of Criminal Justice, Sam Houston State University, Huntsville, Texas.
39. A. Ellis and J. Gullo, *Murder and Assassination* (New York: Lyle Stuart, 1971); R. Hazlewood and J. Douglas, "The Lust Murderer," *FBI Law Enforcement Bulletin,* April 1980, pp. 1–5; J. Reinhardt, *The Psychology of a Strange Killer* (Springfield, IL: Charles C. Thomas, 1962).
40. National Center for the Analysis of Violent Crime, Behavioral Science Unit, FBI Academy (Quantico, VA: 1985), p. 5.
41. VICAP Crime Analysis Report Form used by the FBI for profiling, 1999.
42. Eric W. Witzig, "The New ViCAP—More User Friendly and Used by More Agencies," *FBI Law Enforcement Bulletin,* June 2003, pp. 1–7. (These case examples were obtained from this source.)
43. Arthur Meister, ViCAP lectures at Quantico, VA, 1999–2000.
44. David McLemore, "Aliases, Trainhopping Obscure Suspect's Trail," *Dallas Morning News,* June 17, 1999, sec. A1, p. 16.
45. Pauline Arrillaga, "Town Copes after Slayings by Suspected Rail Rider," *Dallas Morning News,* June 11, 1999, sec. A., p. 29.

46. *Supra* note 12, sec. A., p. 17.
47. Michael Pearson, "Railroad Killer," *Associated Press*, June 22, 1999.
48. Mark Babineck, "Railroad Killer," *Associated Press*, July 2000.
49. "Railroad Killer," *Associated Press*, July 2000.
50. Ibid.
51. Eric W. Witzig, "The New ViCAP," *FBI Law Enforcement Bulletin*, January 16, 2003.
52. David Spraggs, "How to Open a Cold Case," *Police*, May 2003, pp. 28–30.
53. Ibid., pp. 28–29.
54. For more information, go to www.i2inc.com.
55. Spraggs, op. cit., pp. 29–30.
56. James Markey, "New Technology and Old Police Work Solve Cold Sex Crimes," *FBI Law Enforcement Bulletin*, Sept. 2003, pp. 1–5. This discussion was taken with modification from this source.
57. This grant was renewed in 2003.
58. For 2003, the federal government has earmarked additional grant funding for equipment and testing related to the backlog of DNA evidence. All agencies across the United States should apply for funding because many programs, if described correctly, are eligible for assistance.
59. These are mainly elderly victims who have passed away from causes unrelated to the rape.
60. State laws are in place as to who must provide blood samples for entry into CODIS (e.g., convicted sex offenders).
61. Vicki Smith, "Forensic scientist forms cold case consulting group," Associated Press, accessed at www.phillyburgs.com/pb-dyn/news/103-09052003-153890.htm, April 4, 2007.
62. For additional information go to Institute for Cold Case Evaluation at www.wvu.edu/icce/and West Virginia University at www.wvu.edu/forensic/index.htm.
63. The Institute for Cold Case Evaluation was created to assist law enforcement agencies with solving cold cases as well as developing management techniques to effectively control cold case backlogs. ICCE is a nonprofit 501(c)3 corporation registered in the state of West Virginia and operates within West Virginia University's Chestnut Research Park in Morgantown, West Virginia.
64. For further information about the cold case homicide seminar contact Professor Barry Glover, Department of Criminal Justice, Saint Leo University, Saint Leo, Florida, phone: (352)588-8494; fax: (352)588-8269; e-mail: barry.glover@saintleo.edu.

10

Sex-Related Offenses

▲   Jennifer W., rape victim, is consoled by her fiancé during the sentencing of Timothy Mobly in Reno, Nevada. The investigation of sex-related offenses is one of the most sensitive matters undertaken by the police and is given high priority, because these offenses involve not only physical but also psychological injury to the victim.

(© AP/Wide World Photos)

The term sex-related offenses covers a broad category of specific acts against adults, children, males, and females. **Rape** or **sexual battery** is legally defined as the crime of a person's having sexual relations with another person under the following circumstances: (1) against a person's consent, (2) while the person is unconscious, (3) while the person is under the influence of alcohol or drugs, (4) if the person is feeble-minded or insane, or (5) if the person is a child who is under the age of consent as fixed by statute. This chapter focuses primarily on sexual assaults that are typically directed toward postpubescent and adult females and discusses the considerable amount of physical evidence that is often available when sex crimes are committed.

This chapter also discusses how to best interview sexual assault victims, which can be a most delicate and challenging task for the criminal investigator. The investigator must obtain all the necessary information, yet do so with respect and concern for the victim. It is absolutely imperative that the investigator does not in any way pass judgment on the victim that results in revictimization.

Because deaf victims of sexual assault present some unique challenges to investigators who are attempting to interview them, we discuss such victims and some of the unique issues they face.

Homosexual lifestyles and homicide investigations within this community have some unique characteristics that are important for investigators to understand in order to successfully solve such cases. In this chapter, we discuss many of these characteristics.

This chapter concludes with a discussion of autoerotic death (sexual asphyxia) and the value of conducting psychological autopsies in such cases.

SEX-RELATED INVESTIGATIONS

Rape is generally considered a woman-centered issue, but growing awareness has led to a rise in reports of homosexual male rape. Keep in mind that society places greater stigma on male rape victimization. Fear, shame, and this stigmatization still prevent a large number of male victims from reporting their experience. Whether the victims are male or female, the offenders are overwhelmingly male, but it is certainly possible for a female to perpetrate rape.[1]

When police and medical examiners are confronted with a dead body, they are obviously not able to interview the deceased victim to obtain an explanation for what has occurred. Investigators must rely on their initial impression of the scene, such as the state of the victim's clothing, positioning of the body, items found, and the presence or absence of injuries related to sexual activity (e.g., bite marks, hickeys, direct genital or oral injury), in deciding whether sexual activity or attempted sexual activity was related to the cause of death. The investigator must be mindful, however, in weighing the significance of the presence of sexual evidence. Although the victim may have engaged in sexual activity with another person before death, the intercourse might not be related to the cause of death.

In the case of a homicide involving a female victim, it is a frequent and ordinary occurrence for investigators to question whether a rape has taken place. However, it is imperative that the possibility of rape is also raised when the homicide victim is male; this is especially true when a male child is involved. Currently, the U.S. Department of Justice estimates that about 1 out of every 10 rape victims over the age of 12 is male and that fully half of all underage sexual-abuse victims are male.[2] Sex is a major motivator and modifier of human behavior. Therefore, a determination of sexual activity may be of great value not only in a rape-murder case but also in natural, suicidal, or accidental deaths. Careful observation of the scene and the body may indicate a need for a rape investigation. Even if sexual intercourse does not seem to have any direct bearing on the cause of death, it may explain motives or the timing of death or simply provide a check on the veracity of a suspect or witness. The following cases illustrate these points:

A 53-year-old businessman was found dead in a motel room. There was no evidence of foul play. The bed was in slight disarray, with one of the pillows on the floor. The bed covers were bunched in an unusual position. The body on the floor was dressed in a shirt, loosened tie, trousers, underclothes, and socks. Shoes were neatly laid out next to a chair, and a jacket was on the back of a chair. Examination of the contents of the deceased's trouser pockets revealed the usual items, except for a pair of female panties. The autopsy revealed that the decedent had a massive heart attack; also, no vaginal cells were found on the penis. A logical reconstruction of the events preceding death suggested sexual foreplay with a female, in the course of which a wrestling match ensued during which the man took the woman's panties and then suffered a heart attack.

Although establishing the absence of sexual intercourse in this case did not significantly add to the medical solution of the problem, it did explain why the victim was found at a motel when he was supposedly having lunch.

A furnace repairman was found dead, slumped over the front seat of his van. There was no evidence of foul play, and the medical examiner was not called to the scene. Observation at the morgue revealed that there were peculiar parallel linear abrasions over the victim's knees, tearing of the overalls at the same region, and no underwear. His boots were reversed and loosely laced. Penile washings were positive for vaginal cells. Further investigation disclosed that he had visited a woman at 7 in the morning under the pretext of cleaning her furnace and had been stricken by a heart attack during intercourse. The woman hastily dressed him and dragged him across the back alley to his truck, not realizing that his underwear was neatly tucked under her bed.

A 15-year-old girl's body was found in a vacant lot. The absence of clothing on the lower body suggested sexual intercourse immediately before or at the time of death. Faint abrasions were present on the back of the neck, and marked hemorrhages were present in the eye. The medical examiner believed that this was a case of rape-murder. The autopsy confirmed recent sexual intercourse. The scratch on the back of the neck, however, proved to be superficial, and there were no deeper injuries. Reconstruction of the events immediately preceding death confirmed that the girl had had sexual intercourse with her boyfriend (who lived nearby), in the course of which (according to the boyfriend's testimony) the girl started making choking noises. She reported pain in her chest but said that it was going away. The boyfriend resumed intercourse. The girl started making even more violent noises. He assumed these to be related to her having an orgasm. After intercourse, he noticed the girl was motionless and unresponsive. After a few minutes, he decided she was dead and became very scared. He escaped from the scene and told investigators he had not seen his girlfriend on the night of her death.

Interview of The Rape Victim

The interview requires intimate communication between a police officer and a victim who has been physically and psychologically assaulted. As such, the investigative nature of the interview represents only one dimension of the officer's responsibility. By conducting the interview tactfully and compassionately, the officer can avoid intensifying emotional suffering. At the same time, the cooperation of the victim is gained and the investigative process is thereby made easier.

As we mentioned earlier, it is absolutely crucial that the investigator does not in any way pass judgment on the victim. The rape investigation is only the beginning of a long judicial-legal process often referred to as "the second rape" by victims and rape counselors.[3] Statements such as "She was where at what time that night?!" or "With that outfit, she was practically begging for it!" transfer blame from the perpetrator to the victim and leave the victim feeling just as helpless and abused emotionally as she was physically during the attack. There is no place for judgmental attitudes or predispositions such as these in a rape investigation.[4]

While they may at first numb themselves to the trauma and try to go on as if nothing had happened, nearly all women who have been raped experience emotional or psychological disturbance to some degree. Victims generally at some time experience fear, insecurity, anger, depression, aversion to sexual contact, and feelings of loss of control. These feelings may last for months or even years after the assault.[5]

Rape victims frequently exhibit signs of posttraumatic stress disorder (formerly referred to as the rape trauma syndrome) and, as a consequence, may experience alternating feelings of rage and helplessness. Flashbacks may leave victims overwhelmed and unable to function in mind and body.[6]

The investigator must be sensitive to the psychological state of the victim. Insensitivity can have two bad effects. First, from a practical standpoint, it might diminish the ability or the willingness of the victim to cooperate in the investigation. Second, it might cause serious psychological aftereffects. Certain steps make the interview less painful for the victim and more effective for the investigator.[7]

Interview Procedures and Investigative Questions

The attitude of the officer is extremely important and makes a lasting impression on the victim. As long as the investigator is confident that the complaint is not a false rape allegation (discussed later in this chapter) the initial interview of the victim should not be excessively long. It is frequently best to obtain only a brief account of events and a description of the perpetrator for the pickup order. Rapid placement of the pickup order is essential. Unless the circumstances of the offense make it unwise to delay the investigation, the detailed interview should be conducted the following day, when the victim has calmed down. When threats have been made against the victim, protection should be provided. The interview should be conducted in a comfortable environment with absolute privacy from everyone, including husbands, boyfriends, parents, children, friends, and anyone else personally associated with the victim. Without privacy, the victim's reluctance to discuss the details may be magnified greatly.[8]

There is some question about whether the investigator interviewing the victim should be male or female. Some argue that a female victim feels more at ease in discussing the details of the assault with another woman. Others argue that an understanding male may help the victim to overcome a possibly aversive reaction to men, especially if the victim is relatively young or sexually inexperienced. The major criterion, regardless of whether the investigator is male or female, is that the person have the ability to elicit trust and confidence from the victim, while possessing considerable investigative ability. Many police departments have moved toward male-female teams in rape investigation.[9]

In interviewing the victim, the investigator may find that the victim uses slang terms to describe the sex act or parts of the body. This may be done because the victim does not know the proper terminology. It is possible that at some point the investigator may find it necessary to use slang terms to interview the victim; however, in today's world, investigators must protect themselves from allegations of insensitivity or professional misconduct. Delicately employed proper terms can be used immediately after a victim's slang usage. This in no way demeans the victim's intellect but, rather, conveys an image of professionalism to which most victims respond positively.

When the victim has had an opportunity to compose herself, the investigator should make inquiries into the following areas.

Type and Sequence of Sexual Acts during an Assault

To determine the motivation behind a rape, it is imperative to ascertain the type and sequence of sexual acts during the assault.[10] This task may be made difficult because of the victim's reluctance to discuss certain aspects of the crime out of fear, shame, or humiliation. Often, however, investigators can overcome a victim's reluctance with a professional and empathic approach. It has been found that although interviewers are likely to ask about vaginal, oral, and anal acts, they often do not ask about kissing, fondling, use of foreign objects, digital manipulation of the vagina or anus, fetishism, voyeurism, or exhibitionism by the offender.[11] In a sample of 115 adult, teenage, and child rape victims, researchers reported vaginal sex as the most frequent act, but they also reported 18 other sexual acts. Repetition and sequence of acts are infrequently reported. Most reports state that the victim was "raped," "vaginally assaulted," or "raped repeatedly."

By analyzing the sequence of acts during the assault, the investigator may determine whether the offender was acting out a fantasy, experimenting, or committing the sexual acts to punish or degrade the victim. For example, if anal sex was followed by **fellatio** (oral sex—mouth to penis), the motivation to punish and degrade would be strongly suggested. In acting out a fantasy, the offender normally engages in kissing, fondling, or cunnilingus (oral sex—mouth to female genitals). If fellatio occurs, it generally precedes anal sex. If a rapist is experimenting sexually, he is moderately forceful and verbally profane and derogatory. Fellatio may precede or follow anal sex.[12]

Verbal Activity of Rapist

A rapist reveals a good deal about himself and the motivation behind the assault through what he says to the victim. For this reason, it is important to elicit from the victim everything the rapist said and the tone and attitude in which he said it.

A study of 115 rape victims revealed several themes in rapists' conversations, including "threats, orders, confidence lines, personal inquiries of the victim, personal revelations by the rapist, obscene names and racial epithets, inquiries about the victim's sexual 'enjoyment,' soft-sell departures, sexual put-downs, possession of women, and taking property from another male."[13]

Preciseness is important. For example, a rapist who states "I'm going to hurt you if you don't do what I say" has threatened the victim, whereas the rapist who says "Do what I say, and I won't hurt you" may be trying to reassure the victim and gain her compliance without force. A rapist who states "I want to make love to you" has used a passive and affectionate phrase and may not want to harm the victim physically. But a statement such as "I'm going to fuck you" is much more aggressive, hostile, and angry. Compliments to the victim, politeness, expressions of concern, apologies, and discussions of the offender's personal life, whether fact or fiction, indicate low self-esteem in the offender. In contrast, derogatory, profane, threatening, or abusive language suggests anger and the use of sex to punish or degrade the victim.

When analyzing a rape victim's statement, the interviewer is advised to write down an adjective that accurately describes each of the offender's statements. For example, the interviewer might record "You're a beautiful person" (complimentary); "Shut up, bitch" (hostility); "Am I hurting you?" (concern). The interviewer then has better insight into the offender's motivation and personality.

Verbal Activity of the Victim

The rapist may make the victim say certain words or phrases that enhance the rape for him. By determining what, if anything, the victim was forced to say, the interviewer learns about the rapist's motivation and about what gratifies him. For example, a rapist who demands such phrases as "I love you," "Make love to me," or "You're better than my husband" suggests the need for affection or ego-building. One who demands that the victim plead or scream suggests sadism and a need for total domination. If the victim is forced to demean herself, the offender may be motivated by anger and hostility.

Sudden Change in Rapist's Attitude during Attack

The victim should be specifically asked whether she observed any change in the attitude of the rapist during the time he was with her. She should be asked whether he became angry, contrite, physically abusive, or apologetic and whether this was a departure from his previous attitude. If the victim reports such a change, she should be asked to recall what immediately preceded the change. A sudden behavioral change may reflect weakness or fear. Factors that may cause such sudden behavioral changes include a rapist's sexual dysfunction, external disruptions (a phone ringing, noise, or a knock on the door), the victim's resistance or lack of fear, ridicule or scorn, or even completion of the rape. An attitudinal change may be signaled verbally, physically, or sexually. Because the rape is stressful for the rapist, how he reacts to stress may become important in future interrogations, and knowing what caused the change can be a valuable psychological tool for the investigator.

In attempting to determine the experience of the rapist, the investigator should ask the victim what actions the offender took to protect his identity, to remove physical or trace evidence, or to facilitate his escape. It may be possible to conclude from the offender's actions whether he is a novice or an experienced offender who may have been arrested previously for rape or similar offenses. Most rapists take some action, such as wearing a mask or telling the victim not to look at them, to protect their identity. But some go to great lengths to protect themselves from future prosecution. As in any criminal act, the more rapes a person commits, the more proficient he becomes in eluding detection. If a person is arrested because of a mistake and later repeats the crime, he is not likely to repeat the same costly mistake.

The offender's experience level can sometimes be determined from the protective actions he takes. Novice rapists are not familiar with modern medical or police technology and take minimal actions to protect their identity. Some wear a ski mask and gloves, change their voice, affect an accent, or blindfold and bind their victims. The experienced rapist's modus operandi can indicate a more than common knowledge of police and medical developments. The rapist may walk through the victim's residence or prepare an escape route prior to the sexual assault, disable the victim's telephone, order the victim to shower or douche, bring bindings or gags rather than using those available at the scene, wear surgical gloves during the assault, or take or force the victim to wash items the rapist touched or ejaculated on, such as bedding and the victim's clothing.

Theft during Rape

Almost without exception, police record the theft of items from rape victims. All too often, however, investigators fail to probe the matter unless it involves articles of value. But knowing about the items stolen may provide information about the criminal and aid in the investigative process. In some cases, the victim initially may not realize that something has been taken. For this reason, the victim should be asked to inventory items.

Missing items fall into one of three categories: evidentiary, valuables, and personal. The rapist who takes evidentiary items—those he has touched or ejaculated on—suggests prior rape experience or an arrest history. One who takes items of value may be unemployed or working at a job providing little income. The type of missing items may also provide a clue as to the age of the rapist. Younger rapists have been noted to steal items such as stereos or televisions; older rapists tend to take jewelry or items more easily concealed and transported. Personal items taken sometimes include photographs of the victim, lingerie, driver's licenses, and the like. These items have no intrinsic value but remind the rapist of the rape and the victim. A final factor to consider is whether the offender later returns the items to the victim, and if so, why. Some do so to maintain power over the victim by intimidation. Others want to convince the victim that they meant her no harm and want to convince themselves that they are not bad people.

Rapists often target their victims beforehand. A series of rapes involving victims who were either alone or in the company of small children is a strong indication that the offender had engaged in peeping or surveillance. He may have entered the residence or communicated with the victim earlier. For this reason, the investigator should determine whether the victim or her neighbors experienced any of the following before the rape:

1. Calls or notes from unidentified persons.
2. Residential or automobile break-in.
3. Prowlers or peeping toms.
4. Feelings of being watched or followed.

Frequently, rapists who target their victims have prior arrests for breaking and entering, prowling, peeping, or theft of women's clothing.

Delayed Reporting

If the victim has delayed making a complaint, the investigator should establish the reason. It may be that the victim was frightened, confused, or apprehensive. However, delays of several weeks or months reduce the likelihood of apprehending the suspect and tend to weaken the state's case should a trial be held. Nevertheless, such a complaint must be investigated in the same way as all other similar complaints, until or unless it is substantiated or considered unfounded. When a case is determined to be unfounded, that generally means either the crime was not committed or the case lacked the necessary legal elements for the specific crime. In some cases, the prosecutor will decide not to seek prosecution because of a lack of medical evidence, intoxication of the victim, a previous relationship between the victim and the suspect, or because the victim is too embarrassed or too upset to cooperate.[14]

Deaf Victims of Sexual Assault

Sexual assault victims who are deaf face unique issues not encountered by the hearing.[15] Thus it is important to distinguish their experiences as sexual assault victims from other sexual assault victims. For example, when a deaf woman reports a sexual assault, she will often encounter stereotypes about being both a sexual assault victim as well as being deaf. Also, like other rape victims she often has feelings of guilt and embarrassment because of the social stigma frequently attached to rape. These feelings can be compounded owing to the small and generally close-knit nature of the deaf community, which can contribute to a hesitancy to report a sexual assault. In addition, the closeness of the deaf community can compromise a victim's anonymity and erode privacy. Many deaf victims of sexual assault perceive a lack of support within the deaf community, particularly if the perpetrator is also deaf. Consequently, deaf victims can experience a profound sense of isolation.[16]

Another impediment to deaf victims seeking help is the lack of awareness about deafness and deaf culture among hearing people. Many view deafness from a medical perspective, focusing on hearing deficits rather than viewing deaf people as members of a linguistic and cultural community. In fact, many deaf women do not view themselves as disabled but rather as having a culture and a way of communicating not recognized by the dominant hearing culture.

Reluctance to Reach Out

Many deaf victims may be reluctant to reach out to agencies that serve sexual assault victims because most of the providers are hearing and do not have systems for effectively communicating with deaf people. For example, deaf sexual assault victims cannot count on service agencies having access to a TTY (teletypewriter), much less a staff member who knows how to operate it. Even if a social service or law enforcement agency has an interpreter, deaf victims, like hearing victims, may be reluctant to divulge intimate details to yet another stranger.

Some deaf victims of sexual assault also believe they cannot rely on interpreters to accurately represent their words and experiences. Service agencies that do not have qualified interpreters on site often use the victim's family or friends to assist in interviews, which can further inhibit a sexual assault victim's candor.

Improving Police Response

Deaf victims who were interviewed in a study conducted in Minneapolis, Minnnesota, several years ago had varied opinions on how helpful police could be after a sexual assault. Although most said they regarded law enforcement as a resource, few had actually called the police after they were victimized. Many related frustrating experiences when dealing with the police department, including 911 call-takers who could not operate a TTY machine and police officers who mislabeled a deaf person as drunk or mentally ill or who misread body language as aggressive when a deaf person was simply moving closer to lip-read.

Service providers and deaf community members agreed that law enforcement must improve its methods for communicating with the deaf community, whether they are victims, witnesses, or suspects. They also suggested that police officers need training, interpreters, and more clearly defined agency policies. For example, although this research project revealed that the Minneapolis Police department has policies for locating an interpreter, its officers know very little about how to identify if a person is deaf or how to communicate with him or her in the field.

Despite these challenges, the researchers regard the Minneapolis Police Department as a model for other jurisdictions when it comes to serving the deaf community.

WHY WOMEN DO NOT REPORT RAPE TO THE POLICE

Studies have shown that many women are reluctant to report rape to their local police. Victims do not report the crime because of:

- Lack of belief in the ability of the police to apprehend the suspect.
- Worries about unsympathetic treatment from police and discomforting procedures.
- Apprehension, a result of television programs or newspaper reports, of being further victimized by court proceedings.
- Embarrassment about publicity, however limited.
- Fear of reprisal by the rapist.[17]

Unfortunately, some complaints about the criminal justice system's treatment of rape victims are justified. In many jurisdictions, efforts are being made to correct deficiencies. Many corrections have come about through legislative changes.[18] In other instances, women's groups have worked with local police departments to educate the public, especially women, about the crime of rape and to correct much of the misinformation that may be transmitted via television programs and other news media.

The failure of victims to report rapes has serious implications, because without such information, the effectiveness of the police in protecting other women is considerably diminished. A case in point occurred a few years ago in San Francisco:

A young woman who was raped turned first to her friends for help and comfort, then sought aid from a local Women Against Rape group. No one encouraged her to make a police report; she was indecisive and did nothing. Several days later, she read a news account describing a rape similar to her own. She immediately notified the police and learned that the rapist had attacked three other women. With the additional information that she provided, the police located and arrested the rapist by the end of the day.[19]

FALSE RAPE ALLEGATIONS

During the past several years, police agencies have been more selective in assigning personnel to rape investigations. They are now more sensitive to the emotional trauma experienced by victims. However, although the vast majority of rape complaints are legitimate, investigators must remain alert to the possibility of false rape complaints.

In the rape investigation, officers have a responsibility both to the legitimate victims of rape and to men who are falsely accused of rape. There are no hard-and-fast rules to guide the investigator to the truth, but experienced investigators generally find it by carefully questioning all parties involved and scrutinizing the circumstantial and physical evidence. Investigators should conduct a complete check on the background of the victim and all suspects. If the victim is a prostitute or promiscuous, these facts should be considered in the search for the truth. But once it is evident that the legal elements for rape are present, the victim's character should be disregarded. The following case shows the importance of the victim's background in rape complaints.

An 18-year-old woman reported that she had been walking past a vacant house at night when three young men whom she knew leaped from behind some bushes and dragged her, kicking and screaming, into the house. She claimed that she resisted. While two men held her down, each took turns having sexual intercourse with her. When the last one had finished, they fled. She went to a nearby store and called the police.

The officer assigned to the case had reservations about the validity of the victim's complaint for the following reasons:

- The occupant of the house next to the vacant house said that he had heard no screams even though his house was only 20 feet away and his windows were open.
- Sand examined in the area where the men supposedly had leaped from behind the bushes. It was undisturbed, although there were a number of shoe impressions in the sandy patch leading into the house.
- The woman's clothing showed no indications of a struggle.
- The interior of the house was examined, and a large piece of cardboard was found on the floor in a back room. The woman stated that she had been forced to lie on this while the men raped her. There was a considerable amount of dirt on the floor near the cardboard, but, except for some shoe impressions, there were no tracks that would indicate that a person had been dragged through the house and to the cardboard.
- A physical examination administered at the hospital indicated the victim had recently had sexual intercourse, but there were no injuries or other traumas. As a result of additional information provided by the alleged victim the investigator

assigned to the case went to the suspects' hang-out, a pool hall. The pool hall manager reported that he knew the victim and she had voluntarily left the pool hall with the three suspects earlier in the evening.

The manager said that the girl frequently came into the pool hall to pick up men; he said he had been told by patrons she was a prostitute who took her customers to an abandoned house nearby to have sexual intercourse. The manager was asked to call the police if any of the men returned. The following day one of the young men, who had heard that the police were looking for him, voluntarily came to police headquarters. He said he and two other young men had agreed to pay the girl $1 each for her sexual services, to which she agreed. They were directed by her to a nearby abandoned house, and each had sexual intercourse with her. When they finished, they refused to pay her, and one of the men stole her brand-new shoes (which she had just purchased and was carrying in the original box) to give to his girlfriend. The victim was reinterviewed and admitted she had lied to the police because she was angry with the men for cheating her out of the money they had agreed to pay her and because they also had stolen her shoes. She was subsequently arrested and charged with making a false crime report and plead guilty. She was sentenced to 30 days in jail.

Had the victim actually been sexually assaulted, her background would have been immaterial.

Occasionally, women report that they have been raped as an attention-getting device. The following case illustrates this point.

A woman whose husband was a long-distance truck driver and frequently away from home reported to police that a house painter, who had responded to her home to apply for a painting job she had advertised in a local paper, had raped her. Because of the detailed information she gave the police, they were able to arrest the man. A lineup was conducted at police headquarters, and she positively identified the painter as the man who raped her. He was then charged with rape and bound over to the local district court. He spent three days in jail before being bonded out. Several days later the woman had second thoughts, contacted the prosecutors, and confessed that she had fabricated the rape story in order to get her husband to stay home and pay more attention to her. She was subsequently charged with and convicted of perjury.

She was sentenced to 180 days in jail and two years' probation. Further, she was ordered by the court to apologize to the man in the local newspaper and in radio advertisements. The man who was arrested lost his job and had to employ a lawyer; his children in school were confronted by other children who said "Your dad's a rapist." His wife was too embarrassed to go to town, and his 18-year-old daughter quit high school because of the way she was treated. The accused man was also fired from his primary job as a driver after being arrested. Even though he had been cleared of the charges, there was still a stigma associated with his arrest.[20]

Some inexperienced investigators are not suspicious of false allegations because of the victim's age. This complacency is an error, as the following case illustrates.

A 65-year-old great-grandmother reported that a 19-year-old neighbor had raped and robbed her in her home. The woman advised police she had invited the young man over for a cup of coffee. After a while, he told her he wanted to have sexual intercourse with her. She refused his request, whereupon he slapped her in the face and told her he would kill her great-grandson, who was asleep in a nearby bedroom, unless she had sexual intercourse with him. The woman said she agreed because of her concern for her great-grandson's safety. She went into her bedroom, disrobed, and had sexual intercourse with the man. When they were finished, he demanded she give him some money and again threatened to injure the child if she failed to comply with his wishes. She gave him money, and he left.

The police pickup order was broadcast for the man. The woman was questioned and admitted she had invited the young man to her home and had suggested they have sexual intercourse; he had agreed. When they were finished, he demanded money from her. She refused. He then slapped her in the face and he threatened her great-grandson. The woman said she became frightened and gave the man the rent money. Because she now had to explain to her husband why the rent money was gone, she made up the rape complaint. However, even though the rape complaint was unfounded, a robbery had occurred.

Although there is always the possibility that a rape accusation is false, the investigator must keep in mind the fact that, according to the FBI's *Uniform Crime Report*, in 47% of all forcible-rape cases sufficient evidence is present to make an arrest.[21] These are simply the cases in which evidence conclusively points to a particular offender. There are a large number of cases where a rape has clearly occurred, but no specific offender can be determined from the evidence. Furthermore, there are cases in which police investigators simply find no evidence that a crime has taken place. Even in these cases (which police often dismiss) there is still the possibility that in fact a rape has occurred. The following story illustrates this point.

On arriving home late one evening and before going to bed, a 30-year-old woman living alone checked all the windows and doors to be certain they were locked. After checking them, she went to bed. Shortly thereafter she was awakened by a man in her bed; he held a knife to her throat and warned her not to make any noise or attempt to resist or he would kill her. The man then proceeded to rape the woman. After raping her, he ordered her to go to the bathroom and to douche. After douching, she was instructed to flush the toilet. The suspect then fled by the front door. When the police arrived, they could find no signs of forced entry into the home. When the woman was examined at the hospital, there was no evidence of sexual intercourse or the presence of semen. The police thought the woman had fabricated the incident because of the absence of forcible entry into the home or any physical evidence of sexual intercourse. The case was classified as unfounded. Two months later the man was arrested for another rape in the same general area where this first rape had occurred. The police found in his possession a number of keys; with the cooperation of his family members, it was determined that one of the keys was for a home the family had been renting several months before. This was the same home in which the first victim had been raped. The owner of the home had failed to rekey the lock after the family moved out and the new tenant moved in. The rapist merely retained the key and used it to enter through the front door, whereupon he committed the rape.

THE VICTIM AND PHYSICAL EVIDENCE

Rape investigations usually begin when the victim either places a call to report the rape or takes herself to a hospital. The report may be filed moments after the incident occurred, or it may be days or weeks later. In either case, it is important to remember that the victim is a walking

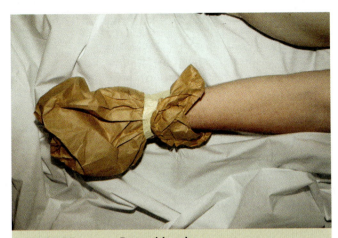

▲ **FIGURE 10-1   Bagged hands**
This victim of rape and murder had her hands bagged at the crime scene in order to avoid loss of any possible physical evidence on her hands or under her fingernails.

crime scene. Certain investigative procedures must be followed to ensure that physical evidence is not lost or accidentally destroyed.[22]

For example, when the victim is deceased and it is not practical or possible to process the victim's hands and fingernails at the crime scene it is best to bag the hands (Figure 10-1). After the body is transported to medical examiner's office the hands and fingernails can be processed for physical evidence.

Instructions to The Victim

The officer responding to a reported sexual assault should make a great effort to ensure that any evidence that may be on the victim is secure. Once evidence is destroyed, there is no getting it back. Attending to the victim's well-being is unquestionably the primary concern; if she is in immediate need of medical attention, attending to that need is the officer's first responsibility. However, a well-trained officer will tactfully find a way to meet the victim's physical and psychological needs while preserving potentially useful and incriminating evidence. For instance, the officer should encourage the victim not to shower or douche (assuming she has not already done so) and should urge her not to change clothes. These actions cause the loss of hair and body fluids such as blood or semen that could be analyzed at the crime lab and used to corroborate the victim's testimony.

The victim should also be advised not to alter the scene of the crime. Even the location of body fluids and hairs can be telling, and such routine actions as flushing the toilet may mean a loss of crucial evidence (e.g., in cases where the perpetrator used a condom and dropped it into the toilet.)[23]

Semen and Hair as Evidence

As was discussed in considerable detail in Chapter 4, "Physical Evidence," semen that contains sperm and hair that has the root attached can now be identified, through DNA typing, as coming from a specific individual. Thus, it is absolutely essential that appropriate samples of both be collected and preserved from the victim and the suspect. It should be noted that the presence of semen is not evidence that a rape occurred, nor does its absence mean that a rape did not occur. For example, because rapists sometimes experience sexual dysfunction, the examining physician may find no semen during the pelvic examination. In interviews of 133 convicted rapists, 50 (37%) admitted some sexual dysfunction. Of the rapists, 23 stated that they were unable to achieve an orgasm during the sex act; 22 experienced difficulty in achieving and sustaining an erection (impotency); and 5 experienced premature ejaculation.[24]

It must be pointed out that the terms "semen" and "sperm" are not synonymous. **Semen** is a grayish-white fluid, produced in the male reproductive organs, that is ejaculated during orgasm. In liquid form, it has a chlorinelike odor; when dried, it has a starchlike consistency. **Sperm** are the tadpolelike organisms that are contained in, and travel through, semen to fertilize the female egg. This distinction is important because the laboratory examinations and tests that are employed to search for each are quite different. Thus, if a rape was committed by a male who is sterile (having no sperm in his ejaculate), then semen but not sperm may be present. It should be noted that DNA typing is conducted on the sperm, not the semen. The physician examining the victim for sperm in the vagina therefore aspirates the vagina—removes fluids with a suction device—and microscopically examines them for sperm. The motility of sperm in the vagina is short, measured in hours rather than days; motility decreases to zero in about 3 hours. Menstruation may prolong motility to 4 hours. If large numbers of highly motile sperm are aspirated from the vagina, one may conclude that sexual intercourse had occurred 1 to 2 hours before the examination. If a few motile sperm remain, one may conclude that sexual intercourse had occurred within 3 hours of the examination. Nonmotile sperm may be found in a living female in small numbers up to 48 hours after sexual intercourse. Nonmotile sperm have been found in dead bodies for up to several hours after death.[25]

When sperm cannot be found, a second test may be employed to identify the presence of acid phosphatase. Acid phosphatase, an enzyme, is a component in the liquid portion of semen. The test should be conducted by experienced crime laboratory personnel and interpreted with care. Routine hospital laboratory techniques are not applicable to this type of examination and may be erroneously interpreted as significant. Only strong reactions should be considered evidence of semen, as mild positive reactions have been noted with vegetable matter, feces, and many other types of organic substances. Experiments have been conducted to determine the persistence of a significantly positive reaction to the acid phosphatase test over variable lengths of time following sexual intercourse. In the living, acid phosphatase may be lost from the vagina after 12 to 40 hours.

Information for The Examining Physician or Sexual Assault Nurse Examiner

The medical personnel responsible for examining the victim should be provided with all the available facts before the physical examination.

Usually, certain hospitals in a community are designated as the ones to which rape victims are taken for a physical examination. These hospitals frequently have both specially trained staffs and the necessary technical facilities. Under no circumstances should a male investigator be present in the hospital room when a female victim is being physically examined. If a male investigator believes that some physical evidence may be adhering to the victim's body, he should instruct the examining physician to collect such evidence and turn it over to him. The collection of physical evidence in this manner must conform to all guidelines for preserving the chain of custody.

Collection of The Victim's Clothing

The victim's clothing should be collected as soon as possible. If she is still wearing the clothes worn during the incident, she should undress over a clean cloth or large paper mat so that any evidence that may be dislodged from her clothes is not lost. Even if the victim was forced to disrobe before the sexual attack, it is possible that hair, semen, or fibers from the suspect's clothing have been deposited on her clothing. Each article of clothing should be placed in a separate container, properly labeled, and stored for later analysis. The victim may then be photographed before redressing to document any evidence of physical abuse.[26] Underpants should not be the only item of a victim's clothing recovered, because they often offer only limited physical evidence and are likely to be contaminated with other stains, such as vaginal secretions or urine, that interfere with the laboratory examination. Other garments, such as the dress, slip, or coat, may be of greater value in providing physical evidence. The evidence most frequently obtained from the victim's clothing is fibers from a suspect's clothing and loose pubic hairs. If the assault occurred in a wooded or grassy area, there will often be soil, seeds, weeds, and other vegetation adhering to the victim's clothing.[27]

The following actual case, which occurred before the advent of DNA typing, illustrates the importance of a careful search for physical evidence:

The partly dressed body of a 16-year-old female was discovered by two young boys traveling through a wooded area. The victim's slacks and underpants were pulled down around her ankles, and her brassiere was pulled up around her head. A check of the missing-persons file revealed that a female fitting her description had been reported missing by her parents 18 hours earlier. The body was later identified as the missing female.

The victim's body was removed from the scene in a clean white sheet and transported to a local hospital. The medical examination of the victim revealed that she had died from brain damage after being struck repeatedly with a blunt object. In addition, she had a large bruise on her right cheek, also caused by a blow from a blunt object, possibly a fist. The examination of the deceased's person and clothing yielded the following:

- Her clothing.
- Pubic-hair samples.
- Blood samples for typing.
- Grease stains on the inside of her thighs. The grease was initially deposited on the suspect's hands after he used an automobile master cylinder that had been on the floorboard of his car to batter the victim unconscious.
- A single human hair clutched in her hand, mixed with considerable dirt, leaves, twigs, and so forth.
- No semen was found either in or on her body, clothing, or in the immediate area.

Physical evidence also was obtained from the crime scene:

- Tire impressions.
- Samples of soil, leaves, weeds, and other vegetation.

A suspect who had been the last person seen with the victim and who also had an arrest record for a similar offense was taken into custody, and his vehicle was impounded. The vehicle's entire interior, including steering wheel, dashboard, door panels, seats, floor mats, and visor, was removed, as were all four wheels. These items were transported to the FBI laboratory along with all the evidence collected from the victim and the crime scene. A pair of blood-stained trousers and hair samples were obtained from the suspect. The results of the laboratory examination revealed the following:

- The victim's brassiere had several fibers caught in the hooks, which were identical to those of the terrycloth seat covers in the suspect's car.
- The grease stain on the victim's thighs was compared with the grease found under the dashboard and near the ignition switch in the suspect's vehicle and found to be identical. An examination of the ignition switch revealed that the car could be started only if someone reached under the dash and crossed the ignition wires; thus, when the suspect tried to start his car, he deposited grease from the master cylinder onto the ignition switch.
- The single hair found in the victim's hand was similar in all characteristics to that of the suspect.
- Samples collected from the victim's hair at the morgue were similar to those recovered from the floorboard of the suspect's vehicle.
- Fibers from the victim's underpants were identical to fibers recovered from the suspect's vehicle.
- A tire impression at the scene matched a tire on the suspect's vehicle.
- Debris collected from the scene matched debris recovered from the interior of the suspect's car and dirt extracted from the rims of the wheels of the suspect's car.
- Human blood was found on the steering wheel of the suspect's car, but the presence of various contaminants prevented the blood from being typed accurately.
- Because the suspect had soaked his trousers in cold water overnight, blood typing was impossible.

The suspect confessed to murdering the victim after abducting her from a teenage dance, although his confession was not needed in view of the physical evidence. As previously indicated, he identified the murder weapon as an automobile master cylinder, which he had disposed of after the crime. It was never located. He killed the victim after she had violently resisted his efforts to assault her sexually.

Examination of most hair, fiber, debris, and tire or shoe prints at the scene can narrow the field. Analysis of these materials, however, will most often yield evidence characteristic of class (discussed in considerable detail in Chapter 4, Physical Evidence), not individualized results. However, the preponderance of class-characteristic evidence, coupled with the particulars of the case, made a compelling argument against the suspect.

The Role of The Investigator In Securing the Rape Scene

It is the criminal investigator's job to collect, catalog, and store physical evidence for later analysis in the laboratory.

As soon as possible, the investigative unit should take photographs of the scene of the crime, including the specific area where the rape is believed to have occurred, the area around the rape, and the areas around the entrances, exits, and general perimeter of the facility where the rape occurred (if it occurred indoors). After this is done, various methods may be used to gather evidence for laboratory testing. Evidence recovery methods may include naked-eye searches, the use of oblique light to spot hair and fiber on the surface of furniture or other surfaces, the use of ultraviolet light to illuminate fibers, careful vacuuming of selected small areas, adhesive lifts, combing or brushing, scraping under the fingernails and certain other surfaces, the use of blue light to detect semen, and the use of lasers.[28]

Incidence of Errors In The Collection of Evidence

Physical evidence in a case is often the decisive factor in determining guilt or innocence. Developments in DNA technology over the last 20 years have added a new dimension to rape investigation. Currently, DNA analysis combined with careful hair and fiber analysis can "describe the clothes worn by the criminal, give an idea of his stature, age, hair color, or similar information," and thereby significantly limit the officers' search for a suspect.[29] With the exception of identical twins, no two persons have the same DNA structure. A good DNA sample can now be analyzed to identify with forensic and legal certainty any individual whose DNA structure is known.[30]

However, DNA testing is only as good as the investigative techniques used to gather the evidence. As items are collected, the investigator must carefully label the items and store them in such a way that they are preserved intact and uncompromised for later laboratory analysis. Current laboratory technology is accurate to such a degree that defense lawyers have little to challenge other than the chain of custody of the evidence and any possible contamination. Keeping careful records of the chain of custody of the evidence and protecting the evidence from contamination are crucial both for preserving the sample itself so that it can be analyzed and for ensuring that conclusions drawn from the analysis of the sample cannot be challenged in court.[31]

Collecting Samples for DNA Analysis from Suspects

In the past, the only acceptable method for obtaining DNA analysis from a suspect was to obtain a vial of his blood. This, however, requires that he first agree to the procedure, then sign a form, and then be transported to a local hospital to have his blood taken. This delay often resulted in the suspect changing his mind about the procedure. When this happened, a court order was the only way to obtain blood; however, there might not be sufficient probable cause for a court order to be issued and the police would be left with a suspect and no way to obtain his DNA for analysis.

This was a problem the New York City Police Department (NYPD) faced several years ago. They presented this problem to the forensic biology unit of the New York City Medical Examiner's Office which was responsible for analyzing and documenting all DNA evidence in New York City. The medical examiner's office had a simple and acceptable solution. They recommended taking a buccal swab (described below) from the suspect while in custody in lieu of obtaining blood. Several other methods (discussed in greater detail on the following page) for obtaining DNA evidence can be used by investigators to legally collect evidence against suspects that can definitely link them to particular crimes through their DNA or can exonerate those who are under suspicion.[32]

Legal Criteria

In order to obtain voluntary DNA evidence from a suspect, a signed authorization should be obtained. Suspects and others whose DNA evidence is needed in an investigation have a legal right against self-incrimination and cannot be forced to provide DNA samples for analysis. A consent form was used by the NYPD after consultation with the Manhattan District Attorney's Office for those suspects who were willing to voluntarily provide a DNA sample for analysis.

Buccal Swab

The skin cells on the inside of the mouth continually break up and fall into the saliva, which is normally swallowed or spit out. These skin cells provide a perfect opportunity for the collection of DNA. The unique genetic code that is associated with particular skin cells is exclusive to one individual and is the same genetic code that appears throughout that person's body (blood, organs, semen, hair, etc.). Items required for a buccal swab include:

- Two sterile cotton swabs in their original wrappers (medical swabs generally come in packages of two sealed in a paper wrapper).
- Paper envelope.
- Latex gloves.
- Wet paper towel.

The procedure is as follows:

- The process should be explained to the suspect to ensure that DNA is collected correctly the first time.
- Latex gloves should be worn by the investigator to prevent contamination (with his/her own DNA).
- The cotton swabs should be removed from the wrapper and given to the suspect.

- The suspect should then vigorously rub the inside of the mouth (cheek area) for 30 seconds.
- The swab should then be placed in the envelope and left open to allow the swab to dry because moisture can contaminate cells.
- When the swabs are dry, the envelope should be sealed.
- Do not lick the envelope when sealing it; instead, use a wet paper towel to moisten the glued surface of the envelope flap.
- The envelope should be signed, dated, and the time recorded. Other pertinent information such as the suspect's name and the case number, should be placed on the envelope.
- The envelope should be hand-delivered to the laboratory for testing.[33]

Surreptitious Collection of DNA from Suspects during Questioning

The simplest and easiest way to obtain DNA samples is from saliva. A discarded coffee cup, used napkin or tissue, half-eaten piece of food, or spit can all be used to obtain DNA evidence. In each of these cases, the evidence is something that was discarded by a suspect and can therefore be legally seized, provided of course that it was discarded in a public place or a facility to which the police have access. If it is discarded in a place for which the police do not have access, permission or a search warrant is required for its removal. If any questions regarding the legality of seizing items for DNA analysis arise, the local prosecutor should be consulted for guidance. If a suspect is at a police facility, the investigator can offer him a cigarette (forgetting for a moment about the no-smoking ban in the building), a cup of coffee, a soda, a sandwich, etc. The investigator must be certain not to touch the items; the suspect must be the only one who handles these items. Skin cells from the inside of the mouth fall out onto the lip and are then recoverable from cigarette butts, coffee containers, soda cans, napkins, etc. An empty clean ashtray and a wastebasket must be available to the suspect. When the object is discarded, it may be collected for analysis. The investigator must be certain to wear latex gloves while handling such objects to prevent contamination.[34]

Collecting DNA Samples from Suspects under Surveillance

In a similar manner, evidence can be collected from suspects under surveillance. Investigators have been known to spend many hours following suspects and collecting DNA samples from them when no other evidence was available. In such cases, investigators are armed with sterile cotton swabs, envelopes, and latex gloves. They follow the suspects, waiting for them to discard items that have touched their mouths or spit on the street. Investigators then seize the evidence, seal it in paper envelopes, label the envelope (as previously suggested), and hand-deliver the envelops to the laboratory for analysis. In cases where the subject is a suspect in a stranger case or a series of rapes, he is kept under constant surveillance until results are obtained. The DNA analysis may take the laboratory up to two months to complete; however, emergency procedures can be set up by the Medical Examiner's Office to expedite the process so that time can be reduced to 48 hours. This has proven especially helpful in those cases where investigative personnel were being overextended on surveillance or when there has been a threat to the public safety.

Seizing a Suspect's Clothing for DNA Evidence

Clothing may contain evidence that can be connected back to the victim. If a suspect is under arrest, his clothing can be seized as evidence, provided of course he is arrested wearing the same clothing and has not washed them. In a hospital setting, the staff can be helpful by providing medical scrubs for a suspect to wear if his clothing is seized. If a suspect is not in custody, however, and the evidence such as blood or semen is not visible, a search warrant will probably be required to seize his clothing. In either event, local prosecutors should be conferred with about the legality of seizing clothing before proceeding. It is important that items be seized in a manner that assures they will be admitted into court as evidence.[35]

Searching for DNA Evidence under Court Order: The Search Warrant

If a search warrant is obtained and evidence for DNA analysis is sought, the warrant/order should request the seizure of any item on which DNA might be found. Under some circumstances, judges may feel that this definition of possible evidence is too broad. In those cases, specific items suspected of containing the suspect's DNA should be listed on the warrant for seizure. Typical items that would appear on a search warrant include: bloodstains, bedsheets (where semen stains might exist), cigarette butts, the suspect's toothbrush (if appropriate), and the suspect's comb (if appropriate). Any additional items found that may contain DNA will require the warrant to be amended before seizure.[36] Investigators should work with their prosecutors' offices as well as magistrates to be certain they comply with the necessary legal procedures to amend a search warrant when the need to do so arises.

Sexual-Battery Examination

Most hospitals or crisis centers responsible for the collection of evidence from sex-offense victims have developed

Sexual assault victim exam kit contents

1. Collection vial—for urine.

2. Collection vial—for blood.

3. Pubic hair combings specimen envelope—used in the collection of possible foreign material in the pubic hair of the victim.

4. Head hair combings specimen envelope—used in the same way as pubic hair combings, but for hair on the head of the victim.

5. Vaginal smear slides—used in the collection of semen fluid for DNA evidence deposited by the assailant in the vagina of the victim. One slide is used for the vaginal area and the other is used for the specimen taken from the cervix of the victim.

6. Smear slides—used to collect DNA (seminal fluid) from other areas where the perpetrator's DNA may be found on the victim such as those resulting from the anal or oral penetration of victim.

7. Swabs—used in the collection of seminal fluid for DNA evidence that the perpetrator may have left on the victim (anal, oral, or other areas).

8. Vaginal swabs (4)—used to collect seminal fluid for DNA evidence of the perpetrator.

9. Cervical swabs (2)—used to collect seminal fluid from the cervix for DNA evidence of the perpetrator.

10. Saliva standard swabs—used to collect DNA evidence of the perpetrator from the victim's mouth.

11. Buccal swab—used to collect the victim's DNA.

12. Extra swabs—to collect possible semen from the perpetrator wherever it may be found on the victim.

13. Extra swabs—used to collect saliva left by the perpetrator from areas that may have been bitten, licked, or kissed.

14. Underwear specimen bag.

15. Genoprobe—used to screen for chlamydia and gonorrhea. This is taken at the time of evidence collection.

The same kit is used to collect evidence with male victims, but the differences are in the genoprobe that is used in the physical areas of the body from where the evidence is collected. Instead of vaginal swabs, penile swabs are used as well as anal or penile cultures for gonorrhea.

Source: This kit was created by the Florida Department of Law Enforcement and is provided to personnel who are responsible for gathering physical evidence from sexual assault victims. The contents depicted in this photograph were provided by Robyn Royall and Linda Brown, Sexual Assault Victim Examination Program, Pinellas Park, Florida.

◀ **FIGURE 10-2 Sexual assault victim exam kit contents**

sexual-battery examination kits (Figures 10-2 and 10-3). Such kits generally include the following components:

1. A large envelope containing all the appropriate forms and specific items needed for the collection of evidence. This envelope is also used for the storage of evidence once it is collected. It is then forwarded to the crime laboratory for analysis.

2. Sexual-assault victim examination consent form, sexual-assault victim exam summary for the patient, and the victim's confidential evaluation.

3. Blood vials used for collecting blood from the victim for blood typing; paper bag used to collect victim's panties, bra, blouse, pants, and other items; sterile Dacron-tipped applicator used in obtaining oral swabs, vaginal swabs, and anal swabs; holder for glass slide containing vaginal smears; envelope for holding oral swabs; envelope for holding possible perspiration; envelope for holding possible saliva samples; envelope for holding vaginal swabs; envelope for holding possible semen; envelope for holding anal swab; and envelope for holding fingernail scrapings.

4. Tissue paper for collecting hair samples; envelope for storage of pubic-hair pluckings; envelope for storage of pubic-hair cuttings; envelope for storage of scalp-hair cuttings; and envelope for storage of scalp-hair pluckings.

5. In cases of drug-facilitated sexual assault, rape drugs are more likely to be detected in urine than in blood. Thus a container for collecting urine specimens should be part of the sexual-battery examination kit.

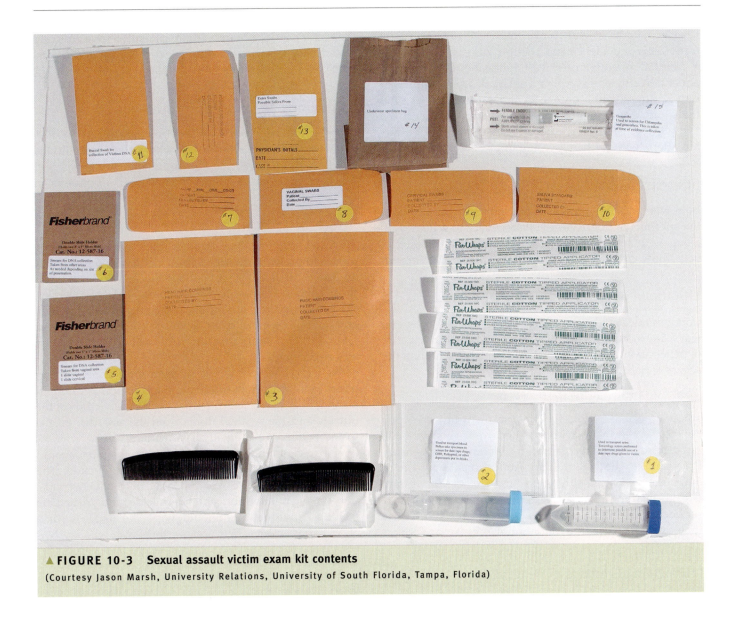

▲ FIGURE 10-3   Sexual assault victim exam kit contents
(Courtesy Jason Marsh, University Relations, University of South Florida, Tampa, Florida)

CONDOM TRACE EVIDENCE

Manufacturers produce condoms using a variety of materials, both natural and synthetic. Each manufacturer has its own formula, which may vary even among its different brands.[37] Some condoms are made from lamb membranes, and one manufacturer recently introduced a model made from polyurethane plastic. Still, latex rubber condoms have, by far, the largest share of the market, perhaps because they cost considerably less. In addition to the basic materials they use to produce condoms, manufacturers also add other substances, known as **exchangeable traces** that comprise particulates, lubricants, and spermicide.

Exchangeable Traces

Particulates

Condom manufacturers add finely powdered particulates to prevent a rolled-up latex condom from sticking

to itself. Particulates found in different brands include cornstarch, potato starch, and lycopodium (a powder found in plants), as well as amorphous silica, talc, and other minerals. In the laboratory, forensic scientists use several different techniques to characterize these particles and compare them with those obtained from other condom brands.

Lubricants

Sexual assailants prefer lubricated condoms, probably for the same reason they use petroleum jelly—that is, to help facilitate their crimes.[38] Many condom brands contain a liquid lubricant, which may be classified as either "wet" or "dry." Both types of condom lubricant have an oillike consistency, but wet lubricants are water-based and/or water-soluble, whereas dry lubricants are not. Although many different manufacturers use the same dry lubricant, the viscosity grades sometimes differ. The forensic laboratory can recover these silicone oils easily from items of evidence and possibly associate them with a condom manufacturer. Wet lubricants may contain either polyethylene glycol or a gel made from a combination of ingredients similar to those found in vaginal lubricants. Despite similarities to other products on the market, forensic examination can associate specific formulations with particular condom brands.

Spermicide

Both wet- and dry-lubricated condoms also may contain the spermicide nonoxynol-9. Its recovery and detection, along with lubricant ingredients and particulates, can help show condom use and indicate the specific brand.

The Value of Condom Trace Evidence

Condom trace evidence can assist investigators in several ways. It can help prove corpus delicti, provide evidence of penetration, produce associative evidence, and link the acts of serial rapists.

In Proving Corpus Delicti

Traces associated with condoms can help prove corpus delicti, the fact that a crime has occurred. This evidence can support the claims of either the victim or the accused. For example, the U.S. military can prosecute personnel diagnosed as HIV-positive for aggravated assault if they engage in unprotected sex, even if it is consensual. If servicemen accused of aggravated assault claim that they did in fact wear a condom but it broke or slipped off, condom trace evidence can support that claim.

In Providing Evidence of Penetration

Condom traces found inside a victim can provide evidence of penetration. In many jurisdictions, this evidence raises the charge to a higher degree of sexual assault.

In Producing Associative Evidence

Recovered condom traces may correspond to those found in a certain brand or used by a particular manufacturer. An empty packet of this particular brand found near the crime scene, especially if it bears the suspect's fingerprints, provides a strong association between the suspect and the crime. Unopened condom packages of the same brand found on the suspect, in his car, or at his residence also would help tie the suspect to the crime.

In Linking the Acts of Serial Rapists

People tend to be creatures of habit, and sexual criminals are no exception. A serial rapist likely will use the same brand of condom to commit repeated acts. Moreover, repeat offenders whose DNA profiles have been stored in a computer data bank may be likely to use a condom when committing subsequent crimes. Along with other aspects of his modus operandi, traces from

the same condom brand or manufacturer found during several different investigations can help connect a suspect to an entire series of assaults.

Guidelines For Evidence Collection

Investigators need not make any drastic changes in their usual procedures in order to include the possibility of condom trace evidence. The following guidelines will assist criminal investigators and medical examiners in collecting this valuable evidence.[39]

At the Crime Scene

First and foremost, investigators must wear powder-free gloves to protect themselves from blood-borne pathogens and to avoid leaving particulates that may be similar to those contained in some condom brands. After collecting the evidence, they should package the gloves separately and submit them with the evidence so that the forensic laboratory can verify that the gloves did not leave behind any particulates.

At the crime scene, investigators should make every effort to locate any used condom and its foil package. If a condom is recovered, the traces from the victim on the outside and the seminal fluids from the assailant on the inside will have the greatest evidentiary value.

If investigators find an empty packet, they first should try to recover any latent prints from the outside. The inside of the package will probably not contain prints, but it may contain lubricant, spermicide, and particulate residues. Investigators should wipe the inside with a clean cotton swab. The traces on this swab will serve as a standard for comparison with traces recovered from the victim and the suspect.

With the Victim

In addition to providing general information about the crime, victims may be able to supply valuable details about the condom and its wrapper. They may recall the brand itself or other important details, including the condom's color, shape, texture, odor, taste, and lubrication.

After obtaining facts about the condom, investigators should ask victims about their sexual and hygienic habits, which might account for traces not attributable to the crime. A comprehensive interview would include the following questions:

- Has the victim recently engaged in consensual sex?
- If so, was a condom used? A vaginal lubricant? What brand?
- Does the victim use any external or internal vaginal products (anti-itch medications, deodorants, douches, suppositories, etc.)?
- If so, what brands?

These questions assume an adult female victim. Investigators must modify the interview to accommodate male or child sexual-assault victims.

With the Suspect(s)

Investigators also should question the suspect about the condom. A cooperative suspect will reveal the brand, tell where he purchased it, and describe how and where he disposed of both the condom and the empty packet. An uncooperative or deceitful suspect may claim he does not know or cannot remember, or he may name a popular brand but be unable to describe the condom or the packet in detail.

Legal Considerations

When investigators know or suspect that a sexual offender used a condom, they must remember to list condoms on the warrant obtained to search the suspect's possessions. The search of a suspect's home may reveal intact condom packets, but if investigators have not listed condoms on the search warrant, they will not be able to seize this valuable evidence.

RECORD OF INJURIES

A careful record should be made of the victim's injuries and be included in the report. Photographs of the victim's injuries serve two purposes. First, if a suspect is arrested and tried for the offense, the photographs tend to corroborate the victim's account of the attack. Second, the injuries may be of an unusual nature—bite marks, scratches, or burns from cigarettes—and may provide data valuable for developing the suspect's MO. In some cases, the injuries are readily visible to the investigator. In other cases, the injuries are concealed by the victim's clothing. The examining physician can provide details of injuries not readily noticeable. Color photographs should be taken if the victim has sustained visible severe injuries. If the injuries are in a location that requires the victim to disrobe partially or completely to be photographed, then it is essential that a female nurse, female police officer, or some other female officially associated with the police department or the hospital be present. If possible, a female police photographer should photograph the victim.

DRUG-FACILITATED SEXUAL ASSAULT

The U.S. Department of Justice has estimated that over 430,000 people in this country are victimized by sexual assault each year and that three out of four victims are acquainted with their attackers. Many of the women who report being raped by an acquaintance also report unusual symptoms such as blacking out and having hazy or no memories about the attack. Sexual offenders' increasing use of **date-rape drugs,** such as Rohypnol and gamma

hydroxybutyrate, as tools of submission accounts for much of the complexity surrounding these cases.

Congress has responded to the growing use of date-rape drugs by passing the Drug-Induced Rape Prevention and Punishment Act of 1996, an amendment of the Controlled Substance Act. The law imposes a prison term of up to 20 years on anyone convicted of giving any controlled substance to another person without his or her knowledge, with the intention of committing a sexual assault. The law also requires that the U.S. Drug Enforcement Administration consider reclassifying Rohypnol and gamma hydroxybutyrate from a Schedule IV to a Schedule I controlled substance to provide for closer control, and it instructs the U.S. attorney general to create educational materials for law enforcement.

Law enforcement personnel can contribute to the successful prosecution of drug-facilitated sexual-assault cases by recognizing the symptoms of drugging, the availability and toxicology of widely used substances, and the range of delivery methods.[40]

Drugs of Choice

As already indicated, the two drugs that are most commonly used by sex offenders to facilitate their crimes are Rohypnol and gamma hydroxybutyrate.

Rohypnol

Rohypnol, also known as flunitrazepam, belongs to a class of drugs called benzodiazepines. It produces a spectrum of effects similar to those of diazepam (Valium), including skeletal muscle relaxation, sedation, and a reduction in anxiety. Of these effects, the sedative and hypnotic effects are the most important. Flunitrazepam is considered to be approximately 8 to 10 times more potent than Valium. The effect or "high" may last from 7 to 12 hours or longer after the dose. With pills or "hits" readily available for prices ranging from $2 to $5, Rohypnol is extremely sought after. Street names include "roofies," "R-2s," "roach-2s," "trip & fall," and "mind erasers."

This fast-acting drug can be ground into a powder and easily slipped into food or drink. It can take effect within 30 minutes, and symptoms may persist for up to 8 hours.[41] Symptoms of Rohypnol intoxication include sedation, dizziness, visual disturbances, memory impairment, and loss of consciousness and motor coordination.[42] These effects may be compounded, and made potentially lethal, by alcohol. It is traceable in a person's urine for only 48 to 96 hours after ingestion and in blood for only 12 hours.

The drug is easily obtained on the black market, through the Internet, and in other countries. A significant amount of Rohypnol makes its way to the United States from Mexico and Colombia. The recent notoriety of Rohypnol as a date-rape drug has prompted manufacturers to create a tablet that is more difficult to dissolve in

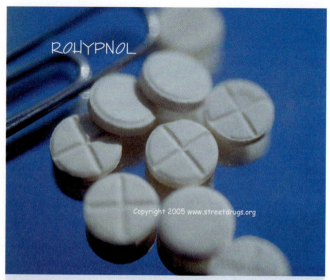

▲ FIGURE 10-4
The drug Rohypnol is commonly used by sex offenders to facilitate their crime. It produces effects such as skeletal muscle relaxation, sedation, and a reduction in anxiety. The drug can be easily slipped into food or drink and can take effect within 30 minutes. It is often found to be present in cases of date rape. (Courtesy Publisher's Group, LLC, Plymouth, MN, www.streetdrugs.org)

liquid and that will turn a drink blue. Unfortunately, the original colorless, dissolvable tablets are still widely available. (See Figure 10-4.)

Many victims of drug-induced sexual assault are targeted at parties, clubs, and bars. Members of the high school- and college-age populations are especially vulnerable to perpetrators of drug-induced sexual assault. The following case, which occurred in Prince William County, Virginia, illustrates this point.

Two 15-year-old girls were forcibly raped after unknowingly ingesting Rohypnol. During the trial, prosecutors dubbed this drug the "new stealth weapon" on the basis of its odorless and tasteless properties. Commonly known as the "date-rape drug," it dissolves rapidly when placed in a carbonated drink, making it virtually impossible for unsuspecting victims to detect. Once in the victim's system, it quickly produces physical as well as mental incapacitation. Approximately 8–10 times stronger than Valium, Rohypnol's sedative effect occurs within 30 minutes after ingestion. The main side effect is amnesia, but it also produces an intoxicated appearance, impaired judgment, impaired motor skills, drowsiness, dizziness, and confusion.

Prince William County's investigation revealed that in the late afternoon, the two young girls were taken willingly to an adult's apartment, having been reassured that they would be returned home after they saw the apartment. Once at the apartment, they were offered a soft drink. They both drank a Mountain Dew and started to feel "weird," as one victim put it, within about 30 minutes. Neither victim could remember what occurred over the next 9 hours.

The first victim woke up, disoriented, on the couch in the early morning hours. She went to the bathroom and noticed "hickeys" on her neck that had not been present the day before. She could not remember having sexual contact with anyone. She then went to look for the second victim, whom she found asleep on a pull-out bed. Once awakened, she, too, was disoriented. The second victim noticed a "hickey" on her inner thigh but did not remember engaging in any sexual contact. During the subsequent interviews, the men present in the apartment admitted having sexual intercourse with the victims but said it was consensual.

Three white tablets, marked "RH" were recovered from one of the men. These tested positive for Rohypnol. Both victims were seen by a sexual-assault nurse examiner. The internal genital findings were consistent with nonconsensual sexual assault.

After a jury trial, the defendant was found guilty of rape, distribution of a Schedule IV drug to a minor, and contributing to the delinquency of a minor. The codefendant was found guilty of contributing to the delinquency of a minor.[43]

Gamma Hydroxybutyrate

Gamma hydroxybutyrate, or **GHB** (also known as "Grievous Bodily Harm," "gamma-OH," "liquid ecstasy," "georgia home boy," and "goop"), is another central nervous system depressant that is used to perpetrate sexual assaults. It is a clear liquid, slightly thicker than water, and can easily be mixed into food or drinks. As with Rohypnol, ingestion of GHB can lead to a variety of symptoms, such as an intense feeling of relaxation, seizures, loss of consciousness, coma, and even death.[44] The effects can be felt within 10 to 20 minutes after ingestion. A coma can occur within 30 to 40 minutes. The drug is traceable in a person's blood for only 4 to 8 hours and in urine for 12 to 15 hours. (See Figure 10-5.)

It is often marketed as an antidepressant and a body-building and weight control supplement. In addition, the Internet abounds with recipes for homemade GHB. The drug's intoxicating effects have led to its increasing popularity at parties and nightclubs,[45] where in some cases it becomes the tool of sexual offenders. The following two cases illustrate this point:

▲ FIGURE 10-5   Gamma hydroxybutyrate (GHB)
This drug is a central nervous system depressant that produces a euphoric and hallucinatory state. Generally ingested orally after being mixed in a liquid, reaction to the drug is usually rapid, and an overdose results in unconsciousness that can occur within 20 minutes, and a coma within 30 to 40 minutes. GHB can be tasteless, colorless, and odorless, which makes it easy to add unobtrusively to beverages by individuals who want to intoxicate or sedate others. (Courtesy Publisher's Group, LLC, Plymouth, MN, www.streetdrugs.org)

At a party several years ago in Detroit, three men slipped GHB into a 15-year-old female's soft drink with the intention of raping her. She lapsed into a coma and died the next day. The three men were convicted of involuntary manslaughter in connection with her death.

Over a two-year period several years ago, two men had been drugging women with GHB at "raves" and night-clubs. After the Los Angeles Sheriff's Department received complaints and had sufficient evidence to obtain a search warrant, officers uncovered more than 2,000 photographs of unconscious, naked women being assaulted and in sexually explicit poses. Many of the victims were unaware they had been violated until they identified themselves in the photographs, and many of the women in the photographs have yet to be identified. The men were convicted of over 50 counts of rape and sexual assault. One of the men received a 77-year sentence; the other was sentenced to 19 years.

Males as Rape Victims

There is a tendency to think that only females are the victims of date rape or stranger rape. However, that is an incorrect assumption. For example, several years ago, a man was arrested and charged in Tampa, Florida, with raping seven men. The suspect is alleged to have given the men GHB in their drinks. According to the affidavit filed by the Drug Enforcement Administration, the suspect is accused of having purchased the date-rape drug on the Internet from Canada. Most of the victims were picked up in local bars, but in one case the victim and rapist met on an American online chat.

Other Date-Rape Drugs

Rohypnol and GHB are only two substances used to facilitate rape. A host of other depressants and benzodi-azapines can debilitate sexual-assault victims. Valium, Ambien, temazepam, Flexeril, Xanax, and Benadryl are all drugs that may be legitimately obtained but then appropriated for illicit purposes. Five teenage girls who were raped at a party went to the authorities with strong suspicions that they had been drugged. Each victim tested positive for Valium. Two men were later convicted on five counts of rape in connection with the incident.[46]

Evidence Collection and Processing

Because victims may be unaware, or may only suspect, that an assault has occurred, law enforcement personnel have the critical task of gathering as much physical evidence as they can as quickly as possible.

Investigators should be trying to look for specific types of evidence that have been present in other cases. Drug-related evidence may be found in the glasses from which the victim drank, containers used to mix drinks, and trash cans where these items were discarded. In one case, traces of GHB were found in the box of salt that was used to make margaritas. GHB is often carried in small bottles, such as eyedropper bottles, and is frequently administered in sweet drinks, such as fruit nectars and liquors, to mask its salty taste.

Recipes for making GHB have been found on an offender's computer. In several cases, rapists who use drugs to incapacitate their victims also photograph or videotape them. These pictures led to the identification of additional victims of the same offenders.[47]

Dispatchers or call takers should be trained to recognize the signs and symptoms of drug-facilitated rapes. Call takers should be prepared to handle calls in which victims are confused, incoherent, or unclear about what may have happened, and they should keep victims on the phone until an officer arrives. In addition to the standard instruction that the victim should not bathe or discard the clothes she was wearing, it is imperative to advise the victim not to urinate until she has been transported to a medical facility for an examination and there has been a proper collection of her urine. Because many drugs exit the system within hours, a urine sample should be the first order of business as soon as a sexual assault is suspected. Treating all sexual assaults as possibly drug-induced ensures consistent evidence collection of urine in every case. However, it is important to get a victim's consent before drug screening is conducted.

Many laboratories are not equipped to do proper screening for the types of drugs used in sexual assaults. For an adequate drug screen, the laboratory test should include a screen for benzodiazapines, muscle relaxants, sleep aids, antihistamines, cocaine, marijuana, ketamine, opiates, and other substances that can depress the central nervous system. However, even though a laboratory might have the capacity to test for all these substances, its tests may not be sensitive enough to detect the minute amounts that can trigger criminal prosecution. For instance, most laboratories can detect 50 to 200 nanograms of Rohypnol per milliliter of urine, but even 10 nanograms per milliliter is sufficient for the purposes of an investigation, and it is recommended that GHB should be detected as low as 1 microgram per milliliter.[48]

The Investigation

Law enforcement officers cannot rely on forensic toxicology reports alone because the drugs may already have left the victim's system by the time evidence collection is initiated. The victim may delay contacting police because of embarrassment, guilt, or lack of knowledge regarding the incident. In many cases, it may take a victim time to piece together the events that led to the blackout period. The investigator should remain objective and open-minded when interviewing the victim. A victim's inability to offer a clear and detailed account of the assault may be quite frustrating for the investigating officer, but he or she should always remember that the "not knowing" is even more frustrating and traumatic for the victim. It is quite normal for a victim of drug-induced sexual assault to have significant gaps in her memory and incomplete facts regarding the incident.

Accounts from any people at the scene of the suspected drugging can be very valuable for corroborating any unusual behavior or identifying possible suspects. These witnesses may also be useful in determining who escorted the victim from that location and what statements the suspect made about the victim. They may also provide leads to more evidence.

Inquiring about the victim's level of alcohol consumption before the incident and ascertaining the victim's typical reactions to alcohol may help clarify whether the symptoms resulted from drugging or from "normal" intoxication. Parents, roommates, or other persons residing with the victim can assist in establishing the victim's state of mind and behavior after the incident and in piecing together a time line of events.

Evidence

When the investigation reaches the point at which a search warrant can be obtained for a suspect's residence, car, or place of work, the following items should be included in the search warrant:

- Packages of Rohypnol and other drugs.
- Bubble envelopes and other types of packaging that indicate receipt of a drug shipment.
- Cooking utensils.
- Precursors and reagents.
- Prescriptions (from the United States and other countries), especially for sleeping aids, muscle relaxants, and sedatives.
- Liquor bottles, mixers, and punch bowls (in which drugs may have been mixed with liquor).
- Glasses, soda cans, bottles, and any other containers that might contain drug residue.
- Video and photo camera equipment.
- Photographs or videotapes of the victim.
- Pornographic literature.
- Internet information on Rohypnol and GHB recipes.
- Computers and computer disks.

HOMOSEXUAL LIFESTYLES AND HOMICIDE INVESTIGATION

In some but certainly not the majority of cases, the appearance, dress, and demeanor of some homosexuals fit the exaggerated *effeminate* and *butch* gestures and dress occasionally used by lesbians and gay men. These individuals are highly visible within the general population owing to these attributes. Also, some male and female homosexuals might dress as bikers and other macho types, depending on what role they assume in their sexual exploits. These lifestyles represent specific subcultures within the subculture of homosexuality.[49]

In addition, many male homosexuals engage in brief, casual sex with multiple partners, unlike lesbians, who are more likely to have a monogamous relationship. Some male homosexuals participate in what is called **cruising,** as they seek out a homosexual pick-up or partner for a brief sexual encounter.

A number of **gay bars** cater to different segments of the homosexual community. For instance, there are lesbian bars, leather bars, business suit bars, drag bars, and dancing bars. These locations provide gays and lesbians, who have a specific orientation, a place where they can be themselves. However, other establishments exist exclusively for cruising opportunities, which make multiple sexual encounters convenient and easy. Such encounters occur in back rooms and stalls, and patrons can participate in various sexual activities privately with a partner or publicly while other patrons stand around and watch. It is not uncommon for some of the more active patrons to have several sexual encounters throughout the evening. They engage in furtive eye contact, staring, smiles, suggestive bodily movements, and wearing apparel, which signal an interest in participating in a particular sexual encounter. Often they wear a particular color handkerchief in the back pocket. For example, wearing a dark blue handkerchief in the left rear pocket indicates the person prefers anal intercourse and is a giver. If it's in the right rear pocket, the person is a receiver.[50]

In fact, **straight gays**, as some homosexuals refer to themselves, speak of these extreme types of gays as "queer queers." In general, they resent these extreme types and usually avoid social contact with them, because they believe it casts all homosexuals in a bad light. However, for homicide investigators to investigate homosexual murders effectively, they must be able to break through these various subcultures in a nonthreatening and nonjudgmental manner in order to be able to effectively open up lines of communication.

Interpersonal Violence-Oriented Disputes and Assaults

Male homosexual homicides involving interpersonal violence often present patterns of injuries that can best be described as overkill. These injuries are usually directed to the throat, chest, and abdomen of the victims. It has been suggested, but not empirically proven, that the assaults to the throat takes place because of the sexual significance of the mouth and throat in male homosexual sex acts. There may also be certain **psychosexual wounds** present in homosexual and heterosexual homicides. For example, this may include the cutting of the throat, stabbing wounds to the throat and chest, attacks to the breasts of females, the slashing of the abdomen, and attacks to the genitalia. These types of injuries are indications of a sexual motive. It has been suggested that the psychological significance in an attack to the throat in male homosexual homicides manifests the destruction of this **substitute sex organ** that engulfs the penis. Anal intercourse is often thought to be the most prevalent sexual behavior between homosexual men. However, one study found that fellatio (mouth to penis oral sex) was the most common mode of sexual expression.[51]

Although most of these interpersonal violence-oriented scenarios involve male participants, there are similar cases of extreme sexual violence involving female victims engaged in a lesbian relationship. One particularly vicious case involved the brutal sexual torture and mutilation murder of a 12-year-old girl in Indiana. The victim, whose first name was Shanda, was killed because she had begun a lesbian relationship with a young girl who had previously dated another lesbian named Melinda. Melinda talked three other teenage girls into helping her kill Shanda. Shanda was taken to a remote location where she was stripped then physically and sexually assaulted. The pathologist later reported findings which indicated numerous multiple insertions had been made into the victim's anus. She was strangled, stabbed, and hit in the head with a tire iron. Her tormentors then poured gasoline on her and set her on fire while she was still alive. All four assailants were convicted and are currently serving long sentences in the Indiana Women's Prison in Indianapolis.

Interpersonal violence-oriented scenarios can also include instances in which a homosexual male solicits or is solicited by another male to engage in fellatio. Young heterosexual male subjects and others, who are described as **hustlers** (**male prostitutes**), participate in this conduct as long as the nature of the sexual activities allows them to set the "ground rules." The homosexual male (customer) is allowed to perform fellatio on the subject with the expectation that the subject will not have to reciprocate. When these ground gules are broken, homicide sometimes results. These cases usually involve the homicide of an older homosexual male involved in sexual liaisons with younger males or hustlers. The older male may attempt to carry the activities beyond performing fellatio or demand the younger male reciprocate. The younger male, who usually denies being a homosexual, suddenly has his masculinity threatened and responds with violence and viciously attacks the victim. The injuries inflicted on the victim usually indicate extreme rage and sexual violence. In any event, if presented with the death of a male in a crime scene that suggests sexual activity and in which the throat has been stabbed, cut, or slashed, the investigator should consider the possibility of a homosexually oriented interpersonal violence motivation.

Murders Involving Forced Anal Sex and/or Sodomy

Sodomy is noncoital sex—usually anal or oral sex. Homosexual homicides involving forced anal and/or oral sex are to some extent analogous to rape-homicide among the heterosexual population. These can be extremely brutal homicides, and death occurs as a result of the amount of force used to overcome the victim's resistance, or the victim is killed to prevent identification.

In prisons and institutions, many less aggressive males ("punks") and females ("bitches") are sexually dominated by macho male ("gorilla") and female ("bull") offenders. The more aggressive homosexuals (male and females) are referred as **inserters**—for example, the homosexual male who puts his penis in his partner's mouth or anus or the lesbian who performs cunnilingus on her partner (tongue to vagina). The "insertee" is the homosexual male who receives the partner's penis in his mouth or anus and the lesbian who receives her partner's tongue in her sexual parts. There is some evidence to suggest that when a belt, strap, or ligature is observed around the neck of a male victim, there is a good possibility that forced anal sodomy has occurred. This method of controlling the victim by choking off the air is sometimes employed in prisons by more aggressive male inmates in order to intimidate and sexually dominate other, weaker males.

Lust, Murders, and Other Acts of Sexual Perversion

In sadomasochistic sex, one partner is the "master," the other is the "slave." The master, who usually has a sadistic personality, obtains sexual pleasure in tying up the slave, whom he then beats or whips. The slave, who is usually a masochist, is sexually aroused from being treated this way. Often male-oriented homosexual homicides involve bizarre and sadistic methodologies such as **sado-masochism (S&M)** or **bondage and discipline (B&D)** scenarios. A male might be chained to a rack to be whipped by a master, who is dressed in a special leather suit, while the slave might wear a leather discipline mask in a display of submission. In some scenarios, in these B&D sex games, the slave is forcibly raped (anally sodomized) by the master or other dominant participant. In some cases, the slave is urinated or defecated on by others. In other male homosexual scenarios, the activities may include **urolangia** (the consumption of urine) or **coprolangia** (the consumption of human feces).

Homosexual/Heterosexual Murder/Suicide

In one rather bizarre case, a male homosexual befriended a heterosexual married couple in the hopes of eventually having a sexual relationship with the man. The nonsexual, friendly relationship with the couple had actually gone on for a number of years before the male homosexual sent the married man a sexually explicit letter indicating his romantic interest in the man (Figure 10-7, next page). He had hoped the man would respond positively to his overtures. However, the heterosexual man rejected his overtures. When this occurred, the homosexual male went to the heterosexual male's home; although it is has never been determined exactly what happened, the physical evidence indicates that the homosexual male shot the heterosexual male twice in the head and then proceeded to cut off his penis and testicles with a razor.

The homosexual male then dragged the dead man's body out to his car, put it in his car, and drove the body back to his home. Upon arrival back to his home, he removed the body from the car, dragged it inside, and laid the victim's nude body next to his bed. He then committed suicide by shooting himself in the head (Figure 10-6). The genitals were never found. The police speculated the killer may have flushed the genitals down the commode or perhaps discarded them while driving the victim's body to his home.

Fisting

Another form of sexual activity is called **fisting**. In fisting, one man inserts his lubricated fist and forearm up to the elbow into the anal cavity of another man. This voluntary sexual act can result in serious injury and death. Death sometimes results when a ruptured bowel is expelled through the anus. In such cases, investigators who arrive at the scene may be somewhat baffled at what they see. Thus, it is important for investigators to be familiar with the possible physical consequences of this sexual activity.

◀ **FIGURE 10-6 Homosexual/ heterosexual murder/suicide**
This photo depicts the crime scene where a victim (*left*) was transported after having been killed. Prior to the killing, the murderer, a homosexual, had made written romantic overtures to the man who was a heterosexual. When his written overtures were rejected, he went to the home of the man and appealed to him personally. When his overtures were rejected, he shot the man twice in the head and cut off his penis and testicles.

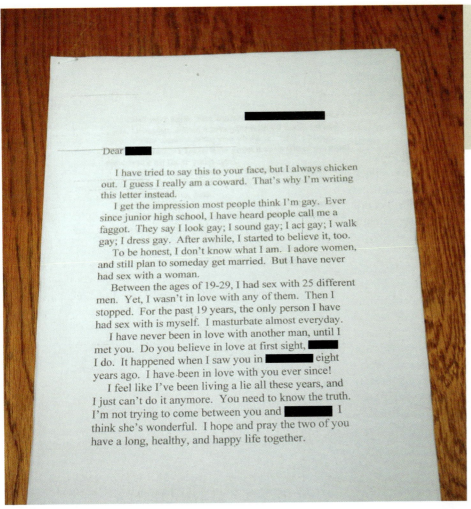

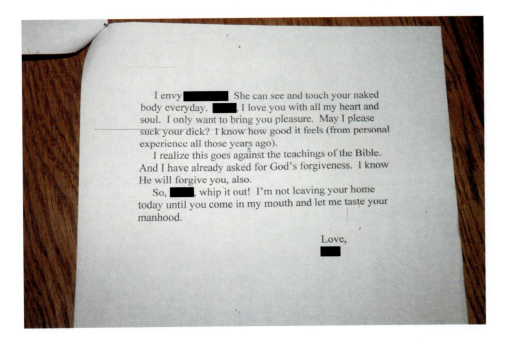

◄ FIGURE 10-7
Homosexual/heterosexual suicide-murder love letter
This letter was sent by a homosexual to a heterosexual with whom he was secretly in love. When his overtures were rejected, he murdered the victim (see Figure 10-7).

AUTOEROTIC DEATHS/SEXUAL ASPHYXIA

Autoerotic deaths/sexual asphyxia occasionally occur as a result of the masochistic activities of the deceased. Typically, this form of death involves a white male who is found partially suspended and sometimes dressed in women's clothing (Figure 10-8). In other cases the individual may be found completely nude (Figure 10-9). This type of death involves a ligature around the victim's neck, which is suspended from a fixed point usually within easy reach of the decedent. In such cases, there is no indication of suicidal intent, and the death often surprises friends, relatives, and associates. Usually the decedent has no history of mental or sexual disorder.

Individuals who regularly engage in this practice (but, obviously, do not die) report that the pressure from the ligature around their neck reduces oxygen to the brain and thereby heightens the sense of pleasure they receive from the orgasm.

Death is attributable to asphyxia. The most common method is neck compression; more exotic forms involve chest compression, airway obstruction, and oxygen exclusion with gas or chemical replacement. Neck compression is illustrated in the first case that follows, and chest compression in the second.

A 33-year-old government employee was found in a rented motel room. He was in an upright position, and his feet were resting on the floor. A T-shirt around his neck suspended him from a room divider. He was attired in a skirt, sweater, brassiere padded with socks, panties, panty hose, and high heels. In the room were two suitcases. One contained men's trousers, shirts, socks, and undergarments. The second contained a knit sweater, skirt, slip, panties, bra, panty hose, and high heels. Investigators determined that he was married, had two preschool children, had recently been promoted in his job, and was well thought of by his associates.[52]

The victim was a 40-year-old commercial airline pilot who was married and the father of two small children. On his day off, he left home, telling his wife that he was going to target practice. A fisherman discovered him a short time later, crushed against the left rear fender of his 1968 Volkswagen in a large turnaround area at the end of a secluded road. The left door was open and the motor was running. The steering wheel was tied with a rope in an extreme left-turn position and the automatic transmission was in low gear. The tire tracks indicated that the automobile had been moving in concentric circles. The body was held against the car by a heavy link chain and was totally nude except for a chain harness. The harness had a moderately tight loop around the neck and was bolted in front. The chain passed down the sternum and abdomen and around the waist to form a second loop. From the waist loop, strands of chain passed on each side of the testicles and into the gluteal fold and were secured to the waist loop in the small of the back. A 10-foot length of chain was attached from the waist loop to the rear bumper and had become wound around the rear axle five times. It is not known whether he jogged behind the car or was dragged; however, when he tired of the exercise, he approached the car intending to turn off the motor. In doing so, the chain became slack and the back tire rolled over it, causing the chain to become wound onto the rear axle. The trunk of the car contained his clothing and a zippered bag holding locks, bolts, chains, and wrenches. A lock and key were on the ground beside the body and another lock was found 20 feet from the body.[53]

Airway obstruction is illustrated in the following case:

The victim, a middle-aged male, was discovered dead in his apartment. He was totally nude and held to a pole that had been fitted into his apartment floor. Several black leather belts had been permanently affixed to the pole. These belts supported the victim from the neck, waist, and legs. Leg irons connected his ankles, handcuffs dangled from one wrist, and a gag was over his mouth. The belt around his neck was so tightly buckled that it lacerated his neck. On removal of the gag, it was found that he had placed so much paper in his mouth that he had been asphyxiated. Evidence of masturbation was also present.

The following is a case of oxygen exclusion with gas replacement:

A 50-year-old dentist was discovered dead in his office by an assistant. He was lying on his stomach, and over his face was a mask that he used to administer nitrous oxide to his patients. The mask was connected to a nitrous oxide container and was operational. His pants were unzipped, and he was thought to have been fondling himself while inhaling the gas.

◄ **FIGURE 10-8 Autoerotic death (sexual asphyxia)**
Deaths from accidental asphyxiation occasionally occur as a result of the voluntary activities of the deceased. The manner of death is described as autoerotic death or sexual asphyxia. The victim, most often a white male, is sometimes dressed in female clothing as is the case in this photograph. The individual may bind his hands behind his back in such a way so that the binding mechanism can easily be released. Unfortunately, the person sometimes waits too long to release the binding mechanism, lapses into unconsciousness, and dies.

◄ **FIGURE 10-9 Autoerotic death (sexual asphyxia)**
The victim in this photograph was found completely nude. Prior to death he was viewing pornography and very likely masturbating. Unfortunately, before he had the opportunity to reduce the pressure from the collar around his neck, he lapsed into unconsciousness and died.

Each of these cases was ruled accidental, and each occurred while the victim was involved in autoerotic activities. Although the motivation for such activity is not completely understood, asphyxia appears to be the cardinal feature of the act: "A disruption of the arterial blood supply resulting in a diminished oxygenation of the brain . . . will heighten sensations through diminished ego controls that will be subjectively perceived as giddiness, light-headedness, and exhilaration. This reinforces masturbatory sensations."[54] In autoerotic deaths, there does not appear to be a conscious intent to die, although the danger of death may well play a role. The masochistic aspect of this activity is evidenced by the elaborate **bondage** employed. Another masochistic practice associated with sexual asphyxia is the practice of infibulation, or masochism involving the genitals. The fantasies of the individuals who engage in sexual asphyxiation are heavily masochistic, involving such thoughts as one's own "penis being skewered with pins; being tied up in an initiation rite; being the leader of an imperiled group; and being raped by cowboys."[55] Evidence of the fantasy involvement may be found in the form of diaries, erotic literature, pornography, films or photographs of the individual's activities, or other such paraphernalia.

It appears that this phenomenon is quite rare among females, but the following case illustrates that it certainly does occur.[56]

This case involved a 17 year-old girl who was originally thought to have committed suicide but in fact was an autoerotic asphyxiation. Her body was found in the basement of a single-family home occupied by her family. The victim was home alone at the time of the incident. The area the victim selected was secluded from the rest of the home. There was no evidence of any break-in or entry. The victim's brother found her hanging from a wire noose, which had been affixed to a rusty metal clothes rod. There was a white towel wrapped around the victim's neck, which would have formed a padding between the wire and her neck. She was nude from the waist up and was wearing a pair of black sweat pants. A wet T-shirt was observed approximately 6 feet away and appeared to have been discarded by the deceased. A white 5-gallon bucket was observed lying on its side near the area where the deceased was found. Forensic examination of the bucket revealed latent prints, which were later identified as belonging to the right foot of the deceased, the material on the deceased's hands turned out to be rust from the metal pipe to which the wire had been affixed. (See Figure 10-10.)

(a)

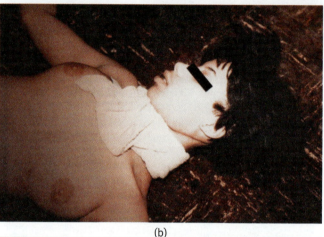

(b)

▲ **FIGURE 10-10**
Female victim of autoerotic death
(A) This victim reported as a suicide was actually an autoerotic fatality. She had been standing on a plastic bucket, which slipped out from under her feet. She was found hanging from an electrical wire fastened into a noose. (B) Close-up showing padding. The presence of the padding was a crucial factor in the analysis of this case.

The Psychological Autopsy

Occasionally the medical examiner or police investigator is confronted with a death and must determine if it is the result of autoerotic or suicidal intent. For resolving questions about the death, there is a technique employed called the **psychological autopsy**, described as follows:

Resolution of unexplai ned death has long been of concern within law enforcement agencies and for the past quarter century, an object of inquiry within the mental health specialties. The term "autopsy" is usually associated with post-mortem examination of human remains to determine the cause of death. The psychological autopsy is an analytical statement prepared by a mental health professional based upon the deceased's thoughts, feelings, and behavior.

Its specific purpose, therefore, is to form a logical understanding of death from tangible physical evidence, documented life events, and intangible, often illusive, emotional factors. To accomplish its purpose, the psychological autopsy is structured to address three questions: What was the deceased like? What occurred in his/her life that could have been stressful? For example: marital or relationship problems; business failures; problems with parents; school problems; drug or alcohol addiction etc. What were his/her reactions to those stresses? To accomplish this, structured interviews are conducted with friends, relatives, teachers and business associates of the deceased in the hope of developing psychological motivation for the death and pinpointing patterns of life-threatening behavior.[57]

KEY TERMS

autoerotic death
bondage and discipline (B&D)
coprolangia
cruising
date-rape drugs
exchangeable traces
fellatio
fisting
gamma hydroxybutyrate (GHB)

gay bar
hustlers
inserters
male prostitutes
psychological autopsy
psychological wounds
rape
Rohypnol

sado-masochism (S&M)
sexual asphyxiation
sexual battery
sex-related offenses
sodomy
straight gays
substitute sex organ
urolangia

REVIEW QUESTIONS

1. Briefly discuss the major factors that should be considered in interviewing rape victims.
2. Why is it important to understand the differences between deaf victims of sexual assault and hearing victims?
3. What are some of the major reasons that women do not report rape?
4. Why do women sometimes make false rape allegations?
5. Why is the discovery of semen, sperm, and hair valuable in rape investigations?
6. Why is the absence of semen fairly common in rape cases?
7. What items are needed to complete a buccal swab?
8. What items can be surreptitiously collected in an effort to obtain DNA from suspects during questioning?
9. What are condom exchangeable traces composed of?
10. How can condom trace evidence be of value in linking acts of serial rapists?
11. What are the effects of Rohypnol and gamma hydroxybutyrate?
12. When laboratories conduct drug screening tests in order to identify drugs that might have been used in sexual assaults, which types of drugs should they screen for?
13. In the investigation of a possible drug-facilitated sexual assault, what kinds of evidence should be collected?
14. Male homosexual homicides involving interpersonal violence often present patters of injuries that can best be described as overkill. In what ways does this overkill mainifest itself?
15. What factors should indicate to the investigator that a death may have resulted from accidental sexual asphyxiation?
16. What is a psychological autopsy?

INTERNET ACTIVITIES

1. Visit the Rape Victim Advocates Web site at www.rapevictimadvocates.org. This site provides a discussion on the phases and concerns experienced by victims of rape trauma syndrome. In addition, it presents an overview of males as rape survivors—a topic not frequently addressed.
2. According to victimization studies, more than 430,000 sexual assaults occur annually in the United States. This site, www.ncrjs.org/pdffiles1/jr000243c.pdf, answers questions about what we have learned from the victims of sexual assault. Questions include: What have victims taught us? How are victims prevented from detecting threats to their safety? How are victims inhibited from exercising self-defense? In what ways do rapists appear to present themselves as rescuers? In what ways does the victim's inability to recall what happened affect the system's response? In what ways is drugging a unique form of trauma? How does being able to forget compare with being unable to remember?

NOTES

1. Bureau of Justice Statistics, "Number of Victimizations and Victimization Rates for Persons Age 12 and Older, by Type of Crime and Gender of Victim," www.ojp.usdoj.gov/bjs/pub/pdf/cvus9901.pdf, 1999.
2. Ibid.
3. Robert Spaulding and David Bigbee, "Physical Evidence in Sexual Assault Investigations," in Robert Hazlewood and Wolbert Burgess, eds., *Practical Aspects of Rape Investigation: A Multidisciplinary Approach*, 3rd ed. (New York: CRC Press, 2001), pp. 261–277.

4. Rebecca Campbell and Sheela Raja, "Secondary Victimization of Rape Victims: Insights from Mental Health Professionals Who Treat Survivors of Violence," *Violence and Victims*, 1999, Vol. 14, No. 3.

5. Karen Carlson, Stephanie Eisenstat, and Terra Ziporyn, "Rape," *The Harvard Guide to Women's Health* (Cambridge, MA: Harvard University Press, 1996), pp. 526–527.

6. Karen Carlson, Stephanie Eisenstat, and Terra Ziporyn, "Posttraumatic Stress Disorder," in ibid., pp. 495–496.

7. *Interviewing the Rape Victim: Training Key 210* (Gaithersburg, MD: International Association of Chiefs of Police, 1974), p. 1.

8. Ibid.

9. Morton Bard and Katherine Ellison, "Crisis Intervention and Investigation of Forcible Rape," *Police Chief*, May 1974, Vol. 41, No. 5, pp. 68–74.

10. This discussion and accompanying references came from R. R. Hazelwood, "The Behavior-Oriented Interview of Rape Victims: The Key to Profiling," *FBI Law Enforcement Bulletin*, Sept. 1983, pp. 13–15.

11. L. L. Holmstrom and A. W. Burgess, "Sexual Behavior of Assailants during Rape," *Archives of Sexual Behavior*, 1980, Vol. 9, No. 5, p. 437.

12. Ibid., p. 427.

13. L. L. Holmstrom and A. W. Burgess, "Rapist's Talk: Linguistic Strategies to Control the Victim," *Deviant Behavior*, 1979, Vol. 1, p. 101.

14. C. LeGrande, "Rape and Rape Laws: Sexism in Society and Law," *California Law Review*, 1973, p. 929.

15. Lauren R. Taylor and Nicole Gasken-Laniyan, Study Revelas Unique Issues Faced by Deaf Victims of Sexual Assault, 2007, US Department of Justice: Office of Justice Programs, National Institute of Justice, pp. 24–26.

16. J. Obinna, S. Krueger, C. Osterbaan, J. M. Sandusky, and W. DeVore, *Understanding the Needs of the Victims of Sexual Assault in the Deaf Community*, final report submitted to the National Institute of Justice, Washington, D.C.: February 2006 (NCJ 212867), available at www.ncjrs.gov/pdffiles1/nij/grants/212867.pdf.

17. Queens Bench Foundation, *Rape Victimization Study* (San Francisco, 1975), pp. 81–87; E. L. Willoughby and James A. Inciardi, "Estimating the Incidence of Crime," *Police Chief*, 1975, Vol. 42, No. 8, pp. 69–70; President's Commission on Law Enforcement and the Administration of Justice, *Task Force Report: Crime and Its Impact* (Washington, D.C.: Government Printing Office, 1967), p. 80; Eugene J. Kanin, "False Rape Allegations," *Archives of Sexual Behavior*, 1994, Vol. 23, No. 1, pp. 81–90.

18. The state of Florida repealed its previous statute, Forcible Rape and Carnal Knowledge 794, replacing it with a new statute, titled Sexual Battery 794. The new law provides for various penalties for sexual battery depending on the amount of force used and the injuries sustained by the victim. In addition, the statute provides that specific instances of previous sexual activity between the victim and any person other than the defendant cannot be admitted into evidence.

19. Queens Bench Foundation, *Rape Victimization Study*, p. 86.

20. "Vicious Lies and Apologies," *St. Petersburg Times*, July 30, 1990, pp. A1, A4.

21. "Crime in the United States: 2000 Uniform Crime Reports," www.fbi.gov/ucr/cius_00/00crime3.pdf.

22. Spaulding and Bigbee, "Physical Evidence in Sexual Assault Investigations."

23. Ibid.

24. A. N. Groth and A. W. Burgess, *Rape, a Sexual Deviation*, paper presented to the American Psychological Association Meeting, Washington, D.C., Sept. 5, 1976, p. 4.

25. J. H. Davis, "Examination of Victims of Sexual Assault and Murder," material developed for a homicide seminar offered by the Florida Institute for Law Enforcement, St. Petersburg, Florida, 1965.

26. Ibid.

27. Arne Svensson and Otto Wendel, *Techniques of Crime Scene Investigation* (New York: American Elsevier, 1973).

28. William Watson, "Forensic Serology and DNA Analysis," lecture given at the University of North Texas, 2001.

29. Joe Nickell and Jolm Fischer, *Crime Science: Methods of Forensic Detection* (Lexington: University Press of Kentucky, 1999).

30. Watson, "Forensic Serology and DNA Analysis."

31. Spaulding and Bigbee, "Physical Evidence in Sexual Assault Investigations."

32. Thomas B. Carney, *Practical Investigation of Sex Crimes* (Boca Raton, FL: CRC Press, 2004) p. 55. (Reprinted with permission.)

33. Ibid., p. 55.

34. Ibid., p. 57.

35. Ibid., pp. 57–58.

36. Ibid., p. 58.

37. Robert D. Blackledge, "Condom Trace Evidence: A New Factor in Sexual Assault Investigations," *FBI Bulletin*, May 1996, pp. 12–16. This discussion was adapted from this article.

38. R. D. Blackledge and L. R. Cabiness, "Examination for Petroleum-Based Lubricants in Evidence from Rapes and Sodomies," *Journal of Forensic Sciences*, 1983, Vol. 28, pp. 451–462.

39. R. D. Blackledge, "Collection and Identification Guidelines for Traces from Latex Condoms in Sexual Assault Cases," *Crime Laboratory Digest*, 1994, Vol. 21, pp. 57–61.

40. Tamantha Chapman, "Drug-Facilitated Sexual Assault," *Police Chief*, June 2000, pp. 38–39.

41. Bureau of Justice Statistics, *Violence against Women: Estimates from the Designed Survey* (Washington, D.C.: U.S. Department of Justice, Aug. 1995).

42. Hoffman-LaRoche, Inc., "Rohypnol Fact Sheet"; Drug Enforcement Administration, "Intelligence Report (Rohypnol)," July 1995.

43. A. G. Gardiner, Jr., "Rohypnol: The New Stealth Weapon," *Police Chief*, April 1998, p. 37.

44. Drug Enforcement Administration, "Fact Sheet (GHB)," Aug. 1998; Food and Drug Administration, "Training Bulletin," Office of Criminal Investigations, San Diego, CA.

45. Executive Office of the President's Office of National Drug Control Policy, "Gamma Hydroxybutyrate (GHB) Fact Sheet," Oct. 1998.

46. Chapman, "Drug-Facilitated Sexual Assault," p. 41.

47. Nora Fitzgerald and K. Jack Reilly. *Assessing Drug Facilitated Rape.* The U.S. Department of Justice, Office of Justice Programs, National Institute of Justice. April 2000, p. 14.

48. American Prosecutors Research Institute, *The Prosecution of Rohypnol- and GHB-Related Sexual Assaults* (Alexandria, VA: April 1999).

49. Vernon J. Geberth, Practical Homicide Investigation: Tactics, Procedures, and Forensic Techniques (Boca Raton, FL) CRC Press, 2006, pp. 500–509.

50. Ibid. For a more detailed discussion regarding this topic see Table 15.1: Standard Color Codes for Homosexual handkerchiefs, p. 501.

51. R. Crooks and K. Baur, *Our Sexuality*, 4th edition, Redwood City, CA: Benjamin/Cummings, 1990, pp. 317, 324, 332–333, 340.

52. R. R. Hazelwood, *Autoerotic Deaths* (Quantico, VA: Behavioral Science Unit, FBI Academy, 1984.)

53. J. Rupp, "The Love Bug," *Journal of Forensic Science*, 1973, pp. 259–262.

54. H. L. P. Resnick, "Eroticized Repetitive Hangings: A Form of Self-Destructive Behavior," *American Journal of Psychotherapy*, January 1972, p. 10.

55. R. Litman and C. Swearingen, "Bondage and Suicide," *Archives of General Psychiatry*, July 1972, Vol. 27, p. 82.

56. Vernon J. Geberth *Practical Homicide Investigation*, 4th edition, Boca Raton, FL: CRC Press, 2006, pp. 375–377.

57. N. Hibbler, "The Psychological Autopsy," *Forensic Science Digest*, Sept. 1978, Vol. 5, pp. 42–44.

11

CRIMES AGAINST CHILDREN*

CHAPTER OBJECTIVES

1. Recognize types and patterns of burn injuries found in child abuse.

2. Define and discuss shaken-baby syndrome.

3. Explain Munchausen Syndrome by Proxy.

4. Identify types of child molesters, and explain investigative and interview techniques for cases of child molestation.

5. Define and describe human trafficking, especially as it relates to child sex trafficking.

6. Understand the relationship between child pornography and sex tourism.

7. Outline the types of child pornography.

8. Discuss the use of the computer and the Internet in child pornography.

9. Discuss additional ways that the internet is used to exploit children.

10. Be able to differentiate between sudden death syndrome and physical abuse.

11. Understand what sudden infant death syndrome (SIDS) is and its misconceptions.

12. Discuss the prevailing theories in SIDS research.

13. Understand criminal homicide as a possibility in SIDS deaths.

14. Describe the profile of the infant abductor.

15. Outline the assessments and investigative procedures used to determine whether a child has run away or has been abducted.

16. Discuss sex-offender registration and community notification laws.

17. Describe the personality traits and behaviors of individuals inclined to commit school crime.

18. Understand the role of law enforcement in school crime.

*In the first edition, Lenny Territo wrote this chapter. In later editions, Robert Taylor revised and added material, and for this edition, Bob and Jennifer Davis updated and revised this chapter.

▲ Stefan Jahn (*right*) shown entering a courtroom. Jahn was convicted of kidnapping a 12-year-old girl from the eastern German town of Eberswalde, abusing her, and then strangling her.

(© Reuters NewMedia Inc./Corbis)

Probably no other crimes are more emotionally laden than those involving children as victims. Police officers and investigators often speak of the intense emotion associated with viewing innocent children as victims of crime. Unfortunately, incidents of crime against children have increased dramatically during the past decade. Today, their prevalence seems to have reached epidemic proportions. It takes little effort to find reports of child abuse and assault in newspapers, on television, and from other media sources. As a result, increasing numbers of police departments have investigators who are assigned exclusively to the investigation of crimes against children. For this reason, this chapter focuses on issues of child abuse and assault, including some of the techniques and problems associated with investigating these crimes.

Crimes perpetrated against children occur in many forms and contexts. Children may experience abuse, for example, that results in burn injuries, yet deliberate burning often goes unrecognized. It is especially important in such cases that investigators establish good rapport with hospital workers and, particularly, emergency medical technicians, who will probably be the first persons to see the child's injuries. After discussing burn injuries, the chapter explains shaken-baby syndrome and Munchausen Syndrome by Proxy, two crimes that have recently received much media attention. Next, the chapter addresses the investigation of sexual crimes against children, such as molestation. This type of investigation is one of the saddest experiences in any officer's career, and few officers are able to complete one without some feeling of anger and remorse, particularly since in many cases these crimes are committed against children by their own parents or guardians.

Also discussed in this chapter are sex trafficking, sex tourism, and child pornography, crimes that are rapidly increasing owing to facilitation by the Internet. Other types of Internet exploitation are also covered. Next, infant abduction is defined and analyzed. In regard to older missing children, strategies are provided for use by investigators in determining whether a child has been abducted or has run away. The chapter concludes with sections on sex-offender registration and on crimes in schools, including overviews on threat assessments and on personality traits and behaviors of troubled children who commit crimes in schools.

ASSAULTS AGAINST CHILDREN

The most common cause of child deaths is physical abuse, often by their own parents. The clinical term commonly used to describe physically abused children is the **battered-child syndrome.** The possibility of abuse should be considered for any child exhibiting evidence of bone fracture, subdermal hematoma, soft-tissue swelling, or skin bruising; for any child who dies suddenly; or for any child when the degree and the type of injury are at variance with the history given regarding the occurrence of the trauma.[1]

Abuse of children takes various forms, from minor assaults to flagrant physical torture. Many times these injuries cannot or will not be explained by the parents, or the story seems inconsistent with the injuries received. For example, bruises in various stages of healing generally vary in color. Thus, one should be suspicious of an explanation of such injuries as being caused by a fall from a bike. Intentional injuries tend to occur most frequently on the face, back, ribs, buttocks, genitals, palms, or soles of the feet. Although abusers use a wide variety of instruments, the two most common are the belt and electric cord (Figure 11-1).

BURN INJURIES AND CHILD ABUSE

Although general awareness of the magnitude of child abuse is increasing, deliberate injury by burning is often unrecognized. Burn injuries make up about 10% of all child-abuse cases, and about 10% of hospital admissions of children to burn units are the result of child abuse. In comparison with accidentally burned children, abused children are significantly younger and have longer hospital stays and higher mortality rates. Child burn victims are almost always under the age of 10, with the majority under the age of 2.[2]

Children are burned for different reasons. Immersion burns may occur during toilet training, with the perpetrator immersing the child in scalding water for cleaning or as punishment (Figure 11-2). Hands may be immersed in a pot of scalding hot water as punishment for playing near the stove. A person may place a child in a hot oven as punishment or with homicidal intentions.

Inflicted burns often leave characteristic patterns of injury that fortunately cannot be concealed. Along with the history of the burn incident, these patterns are primary indicators of inflicted burns versus accidental ones. Findings in response to the following questions can raise or lower the index of suspicion, as well as help to determine whether a burn was deliberately inflicted:

- Is the explanation of what happened consistent with the injury? Are there contradictory or varying

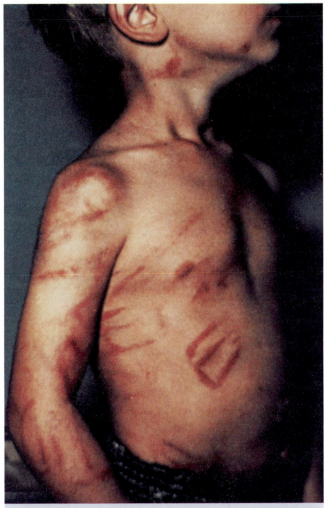

▲ FIGURE 11-1   **Boy beaten with the buckle end of a belt**
One of the most common instruments used to physically abuse children is the belt. While the leather portion of a belt can inflict significant pain, the buckle end can cause even more serious injuries to young children, as is depicted in this photo.
(Courtesy Tampa Police Department)

accounts of the method or time of the "accident" or other discrepancies in the witnesses' descriptions of what happened?
- Does the injury have a clean line of demarcation, parts within or immediately around the injured area that are not burned, a burn pattern inconsistent with the injury account, or any other typical characteristics of an inflicted burn? Are the burns located on the buttocks, the area between the child's legs, or the ankles, wrists, palms, or soles?
- Are other injuries present, such as fractures, healed burns, or bruises?
- Are the child's age and level of development compatible with the caretaker's and witnesses' account of the injury?

- Was there a delay in seeking medical attention? Less serious burns may have been treated at home.
- Does the caretaker insist there were no witnesses to the injury incident, including the caretaker?
- Do those who were present seem to be angry or resentful toward the child or each other?
- A detailed history, including previous trauma, presence of recent illnesses, immunization status, and the status of routine medical care, is critical, as is careful documentation of the scene of the injury, including photographs and drawings. To investigate a burn injury, the investigator should do the following:
  —Stay focused on the facts, and proceed slowly and methodically.
  —Ask questions, be objective, and reenact the incident.
  —Treat each case individually.

The incidence of further injury and death is so high in deliberate burn cases that it is critical for all concerned persons to be aware of the indicators of this form of child abuse.

Typologies of Burns

Children may incur various types of burn injuries. A burn may be classified by how severe, or "deep," it is or by how the injury occurred. It is essential to have an understanding of the different grades of burn severity and to recognize the cause of a burn by observing the patterns that are evident when a child's skin comes into direct contact with hot objects or liquid. An informed analysis of burn cause and severity is fundamental in ascertaining whether a child's injury is deliberate or accidental.

Medical Classification of Burn Severity

Physicians primarily categorize burns as having either partial thickness or full thickness (see Table 11-1). Only an experienced medical practitioner can determine how deeply a burn has penetrated the skin, but there are some features of partial- and full-thickness burns that can be observed immediately after the incident:

- Patches of reddened skin that blanch with fingertip pressure and then refill are shallow partial-thickness burns. Blisters usually indicate deeper partial thickness burning, especially if the blisters increase in size just after the burn occurs.
- A leathery or dry surface with a color of white, tan, brown, red, or black indicates a full-thickness burn. The child feels no pain because the nerve endings have been destroyed. Small blisters may be present but will not increase in size.

TABLE 11-1	Classification of Burns
CLASSIFICATION	**CHARACTERISTICS**
First degree	Partial-thickness burns: • Erythema (localized redness) • Sunburnlike • Not included when calculating burn size • Usually heal by themselves
Second degree	Partial-thickness burns: • Part of skin damaged • Have blisters containing clear fluid • Pink underlying tissue • Often heal by themselves
Third degree	Full-thickness burns: • Full skin destroyed • Deep red tissue underlying blister • Presence of bloody blister fluid • Muscle and bone possibly destroyed • Require professional treatment
Fourth degree	Full-thickness burns: • Penetrate deep tissue to fat, muscle, bone • Require immediate professional treatment

It is essential for investigators to develop good rapport with medical personnel, including both the hospital staff workers involved with the case and emergency medical technicians (EMTs). The EMTs, especially, can provide a wealth of information owing to the fact that they were probably the first persons to see the child's injuries. Also, an experienced social service investigator can provide valuable information regarding family history and any observed patterns of abuse.

Several factors affect the severity of a burn. A child's age plays a part in how severely the child is injured by a particular incident. For example, an adult will experience a significant injury of the skin after 1 minute of exposure to water at 127°F, 30 seconds of exposure at 130°F, and 2 seconds of exposure at 150°F. A child, however, will suffer a more severe burn in less time than an adult will, because children have thinner skin. A young child's skin will be severely harmed even more rapidly and by less heat than will an older child's skin.

Furthermore, certain parts of the body have thinner skin, including the front of the trunk, inner thighs, bottom of forearms, and inner-arm area. Thicker-skinned areas include the palms, soles, back, scalp, and back of the neck. Given the same cause, burns incurred in thinner-skin areas tend to be more severe than burns incurred in areas protected by thicker skin.

Causes of Burn Injuries

The severity of a burn is also directly influenced by the circumstances that caused the burn:

- Scald burns occur when the child comes into contact with hot liquid.
- Contact burns occur when the child encounters a hot solid object or flame.

Scald Burns

Scald burns are the most common type of burn injury to a child. They are caused by hot liquids—hot tap water, boiling water, hot drinks such as tea or coffee, and thicker liquids such as soup or grease. Scald burns may occur in the form of spill/splash injuries or as immersion burns. Most deliberate burns are scald burns caused by immersion in hot tap water (Figure 11-2).

Spill/Splash Injuries **Spill/splash injuries** occur when a hot liquid falls from a height onto the victim. The burn pattern is characterized by irregular margins and nonuniform depth. Ascertaining the area of the skin where the scalding liquid first struck the victim is the key to determining whether a burn is accidental or nonaccidental. Water travels downward and cools as it moves away from the initial contact point. When a pan of water is spilled or thrown on a person's chest, the initial contact point shows a splash pattern. The area below this point tapers down, creating what is called an "arrow-down" pattern. This pattern is more commonly seen in assaults on adults than in assaults on children.

If the child was wearing clothing at the time of injury, the pattern may be altered. This is why it is important to determine whether clothing was worn and, if possible, to retain the actual clothing. Depending on the material, the water may have been against the skin longer, which would result in a deeper injury and pattern. A fleece sleeper, for instance, will change the course of the water and hold the temperature longer in one area as opposed to a thin, cotton T-shirt.

Questions to ask in a scalding-injury investigation include the following:

- Where were the caretakers at the time of the accident?
- How many persons were home at the time?
- How tall is the child? How far can he or she reach?
- Can the child walk, and are the child's coordination and development consistent with his or her age?
- How much water was in the pan, and how much does it weigh?
- What is the height to the handle of the pan when the pan is on the stove (or counter or table)?
- Was the oven on at the time (thus making it unlikely that the child could have climbed onto the stove)?
- Does the child habitually play in the kitchen or near the stove? Does the child usually climb on the cabinets or table?
- Has the child been scolded for playing in the kitchen? For touching the stove?

It is unusual for a child to incur an accidental scald burn on his or her back, but it has happened. As in all burn investigations, factors other than location of the burn must be considered before concluding that the injury was nonaccidental. Deliberate burning by throwing a hot liquid on a child is usually done either as punishment for playing near a hot object or in anger. However, the child may have been caught in the crossfire between two fighting adults and then been accused of having spilled the liquid accidentally.

Immersion Burns When a child falls or is placed into a tub or other container of hot liquid, **immersion burns**

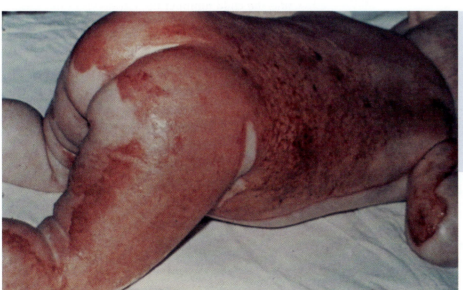

◀ **FIGURE 11-2**
Infant scalded with hot water
This infant was scalded with hot water by his mother as punishment for not responding to toilet training. Such unreasonable and absurd expectations are not uncommon for certain types of abusive parents.
(Courtesy of the Tampa Police Department)

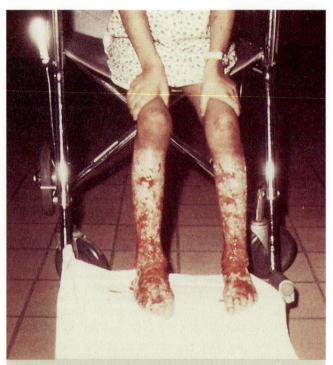

▲ **FIGURE 11-3 Immersion burn**
This child was forcibly immersed in a tub full of hot water by her mother. Note the end of the immersion line near the knees. In this case, the child's legs were placed in water hot enough to cause significant blistering. The mother who was in the process of divorcing the child's father became angry with her when she caught the child talking to the father on the phone. **(Courtesy of the Tampa Police Department)**

result (Figure 11-3). In a deliberate immersion burn, the depth of the burn is uniform. The wound borders are very distinct, sharply defined "waterlines" with little tapering of depth at the edges, and there is little evidence that the child thrashed about during the immersion, indicating that the child was held in place. Occasionally, there may be bruising in the area of the soft tissue where the child was being forcibly held.

Only children with deliberate immersion burns sustain deep burns of the buttocks and/or the area between the anus and the genitals. The motivation for this type of injury generally involves punishment for failing to toilet train or for soiling of clothing. Dirty diapers or soiled clothing may be found in the bathroom. The water in the bathtub may be deeper than what is normal for bathing an infant or child and may be so hot that the first responding adult at the scene is unable to immerse his or her own hand in it.

Several key variables must be observed in investigating immersion burns:

- *The temperature of the water:* Variables that must be taken into account include the temperature of the water heater, the ease with which it can be reset, and recent prior usage of water.

- *The time of exposure:* This is an unknown that can sometimes be estimated from the burn pattern and its depth.
- *The depth of the burn:* Several days may need to pass before the true depth of the burn can be determined.
- *The occurrence of "sparing":* There may be areas within or immediately around the burn site that were not burned.

When a child's hand is forced into hot water, the child will make a fist, thus "sparing" the palm and discounting the statement that the child reached into the pan of hot water for something. A child whose body is immersed in hot water will attempt to fold up, and there will be sparing in creases in the abdomen. Curling up the toes when the foot is forced into a hot liquid will spare part of the soles of the feet or the area between the toes. The area where the child was held by the perpetrator will also be spared. These flexing actions prevent burning within the body's creases, causing a striped configuration of burned and unburned zones, or a "zebra" pattern.

Deliberate immersion burns can often be recognized by one of the following characteristic patterns:

- *Doughnut pattern in the buttocks:* When a child falls or steps into a hot liquid, the immediate reaction is to thrash about, try to get out, and jump up and down. When a child is held in scalding hot bathwater, the buttocks are pressed against the bottom of the tub so forcibly that the water will not come into contact with the center of the buttocks, sparing this part of the buttocks and causing the burn injury to have a doughnut pattern.
- *Sparing the soles of the feet:* Another instance of sparing occurs in a child whose buttocks and feet are burned but whose soles have been spared. If a caretaker's account is that the child was left in the bathroom and told not to get into the tub, and that the caretaker then heard screaming and returned to find the child jumping up and down in the water, the absence of burns on the soles of the child's feet is evidence that the account is not true. A child cannot jump up and down in hot water without burning the bottoms of the feet.
- *Stocking- or glove-pattern burns:* Stocking and glove patterns are seen when feet or hands are held in the water. The line of demarcation is possible evidence that the injury was not accidental.
- *Waterlines:* A sharp line on the lower back, or in some cases the legs, indicates that the child was held still in the water. A child falling into the water would show splash and irregular-line patterns. The waterline on a child's torso indicates how deep the water was.

Contact Burns

Contact burns occur when a child's skin comes into contact with a flame or a hot solid object. A contact-burn injury may be caused by a curling iron, steam iron, cigarette or lighter, fireplace, stovetop burner, outdoor grill, or some other hot implement. When a hot solid object touches a child, the child's skin is "branded" with a mirror image of the object. Flame burns are a much less common cause of deliberate injury. When they do occur, they are characterized by extreme depth and are relatively well-defined as compared with accidental flame burns.

When a child accidentally touches a hot object or the object falls on the child, there is usually a lack of pattern in the burn injury, since the child quickly moves away from the object. However, even brief accidental contact, such as falling against a hot radiator or grate, can cause a second-degree-burn imprint of the pattern of the object.

Distinguishing Nonaccidental from Accidental Contact Burns Nonaccidental burns caused by a hot solid object are the most difficult to distinguish from accidental injuries. Cigarette and electric steam iron burns are the most frequent types of these injuries. Cigarette burns, especially multiple burns on the child's feet, back, or buttocks, are unlikely to have been caused by an accident; therefore, they are more suspect than individual burns in the area of the child's face and eyes, which can occur accidentally if the child walks or runs into an adult's lit cigarette held at waist height. Accidental burns are usually more shallow, irregular, and less well defined than deliberate burns.

Purposely inflicted "branding" injuries usually mirror the objects that caused the burn (such as cigarette lighters and curling irons) and are much deeper than the superficial and random burns caused by accidentally touching these objects. Most accidental injuries with hot steam or curling irons occur when the hot item is grasped or falls. These are usually second-degree injuries that are randomly placed, as might be the case when a hot electric steam iron strikes the skin in multiple places as it falls. It is important to know where the iron was—for example, was it on an ironing board or a coffee table at the child's height?

Another source of accidental burns is contact with items that have been exposed for prolonged periods to hot sun. Pavement in hot sun, which can reach a temperature of 176°F, can burn a child's bare feet; however, such burns are not likely to be deep. A child placed in a carseat that has been in a car in the sun can receive second- and even third-degree burns. Full-thickness burns have also resulted from contact with a hot seat-belt buckle.

The following key questions will help in determining whether contact burns are accidental or nonaccidental:

- Where is the burn injury, and could the child reach the area unassisted?
- Does the child normally have access to the item (such as a cigarette lighter) that caused the injury?
- How heavy is the item, and how strong is the child? For instance, is the electric steam iron a compact, travel-size one that a small child could

lift or a full-size home model that might be too heavy too lift?
- Is there any sparing that would be significant to the injury?
- How was the item heated, and how long did it take for the item to become hot enough to cause the injury?
- Is the injury clean and crisp, with the distinctive pattern of the object, or is it shallow or irregular, as from a glancing blow? Several cleanly defined injuries, especially on an older child, could indicate that the child was held motionless by a second perpetrator while the first perpetrator carefully branded the child.
- Are there multiple burns or other healed burns?
- Has the child been punished before for playing with or being too close to the hot object?

SHAKEN-BABY SYNDROME

The phrase "shaken-baby syndrome" was coined to explain instances in which severe intracranial trauma occurs in the absence of signs of external head trauma. **Shaken-baby syndrome (SBS)** is the severe intentional application of violent force (shaking), in one or more episodes, that results in intracranial injuries to the child. Physical abuse of children by shaking usually is not an isolated event. Many shaken infants show evidence of previous trauma. Frequently, the shaking has been preceded by other types of abuse.[3]

Mechanism of Injury

The mechanism of injury in SBS is thought to result from a combination of physical factors, including the proportionately large size of the adult relative to the child. Shaking by admitted assailants has produced remarkably similar injury patterns:

- The infant is held by the chest, facing the assailant, and is shaken violently back and forth.
- The shaking causes the infant's head to whip forward and backward from the chest to the back.
- The infant's chest is compressed, and the arms and legs move about with a whiplash action.
- At the completion of the assault, the infant may be limp and either not breathing or breathing shallowly.
- During the assault, the infant's head may strike a solid object.
- After the shaking, the infant may be dropped, thrown, or slammed onto a solid surface.

The last two events likely explain the many cases of blunt injury, including skull fractures, found in shaken infants. However, although blunt injury may be seen at autopsy in shaken infants, research data suggest that shaking in and of itself is often sufficient to cause serious intracranial injury or death.

Indicators and Symptoms

Crying has come under increasing scrutiny as a stimulus for abusive activity. Because shaking is generally a response to crying, a previous illness causing irritability may increase the likelihood that the infant will be shaken. The occurrence of infant abuse is a product of a delicate balance between the frequency of the stimulus of crying and the threshold for violent action by potential abusers. The effects of drugs, alcohol, and environmental conditions may trigger this interaction.

The average age of infants abused by shaking is six months. The physical alterations characteristic of SBS are uncommon in children older than one year. Many symptomatic shaken infants have seizures, are lethargic, or are in a coma. Many are resuscitated at home or en route to the hospital and arrive there in serious condition. Some children have milder changes in consciousness or a history of choking, vomiting, or poor feeding. Although gross evidence of trauma is usually absent, careful inspection may reveal sites of bruising.

Most infants in whom shaking has been documented have retinal hemorrhaging (bleeding along the back inside layer of the eyeball). Other intracranial injuries ascribed to shaking trauma are fluid between the skull and brain, tearing of brain tissue, and swelling of the brain.

Investigative Guidelines

- The use of MRI has helped detect old and new intracranial injuries and has aided recognition of subtle instances of repetitive shaking.
- Repetitive abuse has important legal and clinical implications. If abuse is repetitive, the child is at high risk for further injury unless legal action is taken. Establishing that there has been a pattern of abuse can also help in identifying potential perpetrators and may lead to increased legal penalties.
- The fact that shaken children, and possibly their siblings, often have been previously abused should dispel the notion that shaking is an isolated and somewhat "unintentional" event.
- From the perspective of the protection of the child or the criminal prosecution of the abuser, it is not as important to distinguish the precise mechanism of injury as it is to be certain that the event was nonaccidental.
- Pediatricians should not be deterred from testifying when the cause of the nonaccidental injury is not entirely clear.
- Shaking a child creates an imminent risk for an acute injury.

- Injuries that appear to be caused by shaking create a high index of suspicion of child abuse and should be followed by intensive efforts (e.g., skeletal survey, CT scan, and MRI) to identify concurrent and previous abuse of the patient and any siblings.
- If an infant's injuries are fatal, an autopsy should be performed by a forensic pathologist. Autopsies of all infants who die of causes other than known natural illness should include thorough skeletal imaging.

The Role of The Physician in Child-Abuse Cases

The problem the investigator often encounters is that the victim is either too young to explain what has occurred or too intimidated to cooperate. In injuries or deaths of young children, investigators find radiologists (physicians who specialize in the interpretation of X rays) especially helpful. It is common for abused children to be brought to the hospital emergency room by their parents or relatives, who tell hospital personnel that the child was injured in a fall or some other accident. When there is a discrepancy between the characteristics of the injury and the explanation, X rays can be useful in determining whether the injuries were accidental. X rays of the entire body reveal not only the presence of fractures and other injuries to joints and bones but also the existence of older injuries in various stages of healing.

Careful questioning of the persons bringing the child to the hospital may be sufficient to confirm the need for a complete investigation. The following facts about child abuse are helpful in such questioning:

- In many cases, only one of a number of children in the family is chosen as the target of abuse, and frequently that child was conceived or born extramaritally or premaritally.
- The marital partner tends to protect the abusive parent through denial of the facts.
- Occasionally, an abusing father also assaults his wife, but more frequently he restricts the gross abuse to a child.
- In over half the cases in which child abuse results in hospitalization, there was a preceding incident of abuse of equal severity.
- Not infrequently the battered child is taken to a different hospital after each abuse in order to conceal the recurrence of injuries.[4] However with the mandatory reporting of all suspicious child abuse injuries to the proper authorities and the computerized storage of previously reported events it has become increasingly difficult for this ploy to work.

The families of battered children range across the entire socioeconomic spectrum. The investigator cannot assume that an injured child who comes from what appears to be a "good home" is not the victim of child abuse.

In cases where medical examination is inconclusive but abuse is strongly suspected, interviewing becomes even more significant. The rule is to leave no source unexamined. To fail to do so places the abused child back into a defenseless position in which further injury or death could occur. The interviewing of baby-sitters, neighbors, teachers, and others must be conducted sensibly and sensitively. The aim is not to "get the person who did it," because there may not in fact have been an abuse incident. The primary objective is to get the information so that if there has been abuse, the child can be protected.

MUNCHAUSEN SYNDROME BY PROXY

Munchausen syndrome is a psychological disorder in which the person fabricates the symptoms of disease or injury in order to undergo medical tests, hospitalization, or even medical or surgical treatment. To command medical attention, individuals with Munchausen syndrome may intentionally injure themselves or induce illness in themselves. In cases of **Munchausen Syndrome by Proxy (MSBP),** a parent or caretaker suffering from Munchausen syndrome attempts to elicit medical attention for himself or herself by injuring or inducing illness in a child. The parent then may try to resuscitate the child or to have paramedics or hospital personnel save the child.[5] The following actual cases are examples of MSBP.

M. A., a 9-month-old boy, had been repeatedly admitted to Children's Hospital because of recurrent life-threatening apnea (cessation of breathing). At 7 weeks of age, he experienced his first apneic event, and his mother administered mouth-to-mouth ventilation. Spontaneous respiration returned, and M. A. was hospitalized, treated, and discharged with a home monitor.

During the next 9 months, M. A. experienced 10 similar events and 7 more hospitalizations. Eight of the events required mouth-to-mouth ventilation. All these episodes occurred while mother and child were alone, so only M. A.'s mother witnessed the actual events. Two episodes occurred in the hospital.

Unfortunately, despite many tests and surgical procedures, M. A.'s apnea persisted and his growth slowed. Because of his persistent apnea and failure to thrive, M. A. received home nursing care. During these home visits, several nurses observed that M. A. would refuse to eat in his mother's presence. If she left the room, however, he would eat.

In time, both medical and nursing staffs became increasingly suspicious that Mrs. A. was somehow responsible for her child's apnea. To better observe mother-child interaction, M. A. was moved to a hospital room equipped for covert audiovisual surveillance.

On the sixth day, the video clearly recorded Mrs. A. bringing on the apnea by forcing the child against her chest, which caused him to lose consciousness. M. A. became limp and experienced a falling heart rate. Mrs. A. then placed the baby back on the bed, called for help, and began mouth-to-mouth resuscitation.

The hospital immediately informed child protection services and police authorities, who reviewed the recording. Shortly thereafter, a team consisting of a physician, nurse, social worker, and police officer confronted her. At first, Mrs. A. expressed disbelief at the suggestion that she had smothered M. A., but when she was informed of the video, she made no comment. She was then arrested.

Mrs. A. was a 36-year-old occupational therapist and the mother of three boys. Late into her pregnancy with M. A., she worked in an early intervention program for developmentally delayed children. During many of M. A.'s hospitalizations, she appeared caring and concerned but emotionally distant. Clearly, Mrs. A. was the dominant parent, who made all decisions regarding medical treatment.

Mrs. A. subsequently pled guilty to felonious, third-degree assault. At the time, she stated: "The only time I ever caused M. A. to stop breathing was in the hospital." She received three years' probation, during which she was to receive psychotherapy. If she successfully completed psychotherapy, the felony charge would be reduced to a misdemeanor. She also had to live apart from her children and could visit them only in the presence of two other adults.

M. A. had no further apnea, and at 24 months of age he appeared vigorous, healthy, and normal. Eventually, the family was reunited.

C. B., a 10-month-old girl, was admitted to a hospital because of recurrent life-threatening apnea. C. B. had been born in another state and had been sexually assaulted at the age of 3 months by an acquaintance of her father. After the assault, local child protection services closely monitored the family.

At 6 months of age, C. B. experienced her first apneic episode. Her father shook her vigorously, and then administered mouth-to-mouth ventilation. She was subsequently admitted to a local hospital. After examination and treatment, she was discharged with a home monitor. During the next two months, C. B. experienced six apneic events and three hospitalizations. The family then moved to Minnesota.

During her first month in Minnesota, C. B. experienced four apneic episodes and three more hospitalizations. All required vigorous stimulations to restore spontaneous breathing. Other family members observed the child immediately after the events. However, only C. B.'s father had witnessed all the actual events. C. B. was eventually referred to Children's Hospital.

While in the hospital, C. B. had no clinical apnea or monitor alarms. Most of the time, she appeared happy and playful. However, when anyone attempted to touch her face, she became hysterical and combative. Over time, both the medical and nursing staffs began to suspect that C. B.'s parents were responsible for her apnea.

Local police and child protection services were notified, and C. B. was placed in a room with covert audiovisual surveillance. On the third day of monitoring, the video recording clearly showed C. B.'s father producing an apneic event by smothering her. Mr. B. was seen picking up the sleeping child, placing her prone on the bed, and forcing her face into the mattress. C. B. awoke and struggled to escape, wildly kicking her legs. Mr. B. continued until C. B.'s struggling stopped and she appeared limp and unconscious. Then he repositioned her on the bed and called for help. A nurse entered the room, stimulated her, and administered supplemental oxygen.

C. B.'s parents were confronted by a physician, nurse, and police officer. Mr. B. adamantly denied smothering C. B. He was subsequently arrested and removed from the hospital.

Mr. B. was a 27-year-old, unemployed, semiliterate laborer in good health. He was actively involved in C. B.'s day-to-day medical care and was clearly the dominant parent. He also became very knowledgeable about the mechanics of the various county and hospital welfare systems. Officials described him as "demanding and manipulative." During C. B.'s hospitalizations, the family lived in a hotel adjacent to the hospital with room, board, and radio pagers provided by the hospital. Throughout C. B.'s hospitalization, Mrs. B. was passive and deferred all medical decisions to her husband.

When they first arrived in Minnesota, the family had received emergency financial assistance and was closely monitored by local social service agencies. Four years earlier, Mrs. B. had allegedly been assaulted and raped. Two months prior to C. B.'s monitored episode, Mrs. B. was evaluated at a local emergency room for a "hysterical conversion reaction."

Following the incident at Children's Hospital, Mr. B. was taken to the county jail, and upon viewing the video, he admitted smothering C. B. He was charged with felonious, third-degree assault. The judge ordered a psychiatric examination. Mr. B. received a 10-month sentence in a local workhouse and 5 years' probation. Also, he was to have no contact with his daughter and no unsupervised contact with any child in the future.

J. C., a 2 1/2-year-old boy, suffered from asthma, severe pneumonia, mysterious infections, and sudden fevers. He was hospitalized 20 times during an 18-month period. Doctors were even concerned that he might have AIDS. However, they soon began to suspect that the mother may have caused the child's problems. Finally, when the boy complained to his mother's friend that his thigh was sore because "mommy gave me shots," the authorities were called.

On searching the residence, investigators seized medical charts and information and hypodermic needles. It was believed that material had also entered the boy through a catheter doctors surgically inserted in the arteries near his heart to give him constant medication.

J. C.'s mother was a 24-year-old homemaker and part-time worker in a fast-food restaurant. When the mother was 7 years old, an older sister had died of a brain tumor at Children's Hospital. During her sister's prolonged illness, J. C.'s mother, of necessity, spent long periods of time at the hospital. Although this had occurred long ago, J. C.'s mother remembered the experience vividly.

During J. C.'s many hospitalizations, the mother seemed almost obsessively involved in medical matters and hospital routines. She spent hours in the hospital library reading medical texts. She had few friends outside the hospital, and the medical and nursing staff described her as an isolated person.

J. C.'s father was a 24-year-old church janitor afflicted with many health problems, the most notable being severe insulin-dependent diabetes. During J. C.'s many hospitalizations, his father appeared distant and only marginally involved. J. C.'s 7-year-old sister was in good health and was named after her mother's deceased sister.

Since J. C. was removed from his home, he has been healthy. As in previous cases, only Mrs. C. was present when the boy became ill, and until investigators showed evidence linking her to her child's illnesses, she denied any wrongdoing. Assault charges were filed, and Mrs. C.'s case is pending.[6]

Investigative Guidelines

- Consult with all experts possible, including psychologists.
- Exhaust every possible explanation of the cause of the child's illness or death.
- Find out who had exclusive control over the child when the symptoms of the illness began or at the time of the child's death.
- Find out if there is a history of abusive conduct toward the child.

- Find out if the nature of the child's illness or injury allows medical professionals to express an opinion that the child's illness or death was neither accidental nor the result of a natural cause or disease.
- In cases of hospitalization, use covert video surveillance to monitor the suspect.
- Determine whether the caretaker had any medical training or a history of seeking medical treatment needlessly. MSBP is often a multigenerational condition.

SUDDEN INFANT DEATH SYNDROME

Although **sudden infant death syndrome (SIDS)** is a medical phenomenon, not a crime, a lack of knowledge about its elements can cause individuals involved in its investigation to erroneously conclude they have a criminal homicide.

Health professionals in the past had limited contact with SIDS families because SIDS rarely occurs outside the home. A few babies have died of SIDS while hospitalized, but the usual case involves a baby who is brought to the hospital emergency room and is pronounced dead on arrival. As a result, many physicians and nurses have had little knowledge of SIDS.[7]

What is Sudden Infant Death Syndrome?

Simply defined, SIDS (also often referred to as *crib death*) is the sudden and unexpected death of an apparently healthy infant that remains unexplained after the performance of a complete autopsy. On the average, 2 of every 1,000 infants born alive succumb to SIDS, and it is the leading cause of death among infants 1 week to 1 year of age.

In the majority of instances, the baby is apparently in good health prior to death and feeds without difficulty. Although there may be evidence of a slight cold or stuffy nose, there is usually no history of serious upper respiratory infection. In most cases, the infant is placed in a crib to sleep and is found dead several hours later.

Most SIDS deaths occur between November and March. Sudden changes in temperature may trigger SIDS. The risk of SIDS appears to be highest in crowded dwellings; in infants of young mothers; in males; in non-whites regardless of socioeconomic status; in families of lower socioeconomic status regardless of race; and in premature infants. Twins have an increased risk of SIDS, which is likely a consequence of their low birth weight and premature birth. SIDS occurs in both breast-fed and bottle-fed babies. Most victims are between the ages of 1 and 6 months, with the highest frequency of occurrence between 2 and 4 months.

Characteristics of SIDS Victims' Appearance

- Usually normal state of nutrition and hydration.
- Blood-tinged, frothy fluids around mouth and nostrils, indicative of pulmonary edema.
- Vomitus on the face.
- Diaper wet and full of stool.
- Bruiselike marks on head or body limbs (postmortem pooling or settling of blood in dependent body parts).

Autopsy Findings

- Some congestion and edema of the lungs.
- Petechial hemorrhages in thymus, heart, and lungs.
- Minor evidence of respiratory tract inflammation.

Misconceptions About SIDS

- *Aspiration, choking:* The babies do not inhale or choke on their feeding.
- *Unsuspected illness:* Particularly if the baby had a cold, the parents may feel guilty about not having taken the child to the doctor. If the baby was checked by the doctor, the parents (and the doctor) may wonder what the doctor missed. In any case, neither is at fault.
- *Freezing:* Although the body may be cold when discovered, this is a postmortem change.
- *Accidental injury, neglect, or abuse:* Law enforcement officers should not jump to the wrong conclusions because of the appearance of the infant. The results of accusations of wrongdoing have been tragic. A few innocent and grief-stricken parents have been accused of murdering their babies and put in jail. Appearances can be deceiving.

SIDS Research—Prevailing Theories

There are a number of theories about the causes of SIDS. One of the theories about the mechanism of SIDS is that it results from spontaneous, protracted apnea, or cessation of breathing. Considerable progress in understanding SIDS has been made by the SIDS Institute at the University of Maryland. In comprehensive tests of 1,000 babies, it was found that fully 10% stopped breathing for periods longer than 15 to 20 seconds or their heart rate dropped below 80 beats per minute. Detected in time, such infants are considered at risk for SIDS and are monitored with an electronic device that sets off an alarm if the child's breathing or heart rate drops below a certain level.

The most significant research supporting the apnea theory has been done by Dr. Richard Naeye of the Pennsylvania State University College of Medicine. Dr. Naeye began to look for structural changes in the infant's body during the autopsy that would indicate chronic lack of oxygen, attributable to repeated and relatively long periods of apnea.

He found the following changes in a large group of SIDS victims:

- The walls of the small arteries in the lungs were thicker than normal.
- The wall of the right ventricle of the heart was thicker than normal.
- The relative retention of brown fat around the adrenal gland was greater than normal.
- There was abnormal retention of fetal capacity for the production of red blood cells in the liver.

In a study conducted several years ago and reported in the New England Journal of Medicine, it was found that infants who usually slept in the face-down position had a significantly higher risk of SIDS than those who slept on their back.[8] Respiratory obstruction in relation to the position of infants has also been studied.[9] It was concluded that the air passage of an infant is impaired when the body is placed face down on any type of mattress or pillow. And in a 2006 study, researchers at Children's Hospital Boston and Harvard Medical School revealed that infants that die of SIDS often have abnormalities in the brainstem, particularly in those areas controlling breathing, blood pressure, temperature, and heart rate. This finding is the strongest evidence to date that suggests physiological brain differences may place some infants with an increased risk of SIDS.[10]

The Police Officer's Role

The law enforcement officer serves a key role in the SIDS case and is often the first person to encounter the shock, grief, and guilt experienced by the parents. It may be an experience such as this: The officer responds to a call, entering a house where an infant has just died. The mother is hysterical, incoherent, and unable to clarify what happened. The father is dazed yet tearless; he is confused and responding evasively. As the officer proceeds, the mother continues to sob, blaming herself. The infant is in the cradle, its head covered with a blanket. When the blanket is removed, the officer notes a small amount of blood-tinged fluid in and around the mouth and nose and bruiselike marks on the body where the blood settled after death.

Was the death a result of illness, abuse, neglect, or unexplained causes? The officer will make a preliminary assessment based on the information obtained at the scene. If the circumstances are unclear, an autopsy may establish the need for criminal investigation.

Information to be Obtained by the Police Investigator at the Scene

Obtaining answers to the following questions are of considerable value to both law enforcement officers and medical personnel in determining the cause of death.

- Age, date of birth, birth weight (if known), race, and sex.
- Who was the last person to see the infant alive (date and time)?
- Who discovered the dead infant (date and time)?
- What was the place of death (the child's crib or bed, the parent's bed, or elsewhere)?
- What was the position of the infant when found dead?
- Was the infant's original position changed (why and by whom)?
- If resuscitation was attempted, note the method employed and the name of the person who attempted the resuscitation.
- Had the infant been sick recently? Have a cold or sniffles? Any other minor illnesses?
- Was a physician consulted about the recent illness? If so, who was the physician?
- What treatment was prescribed?
- Was the child on any medication? If so, what type?
- When was the child last seen by a physician? If so, why and by whom?
- Was the infant exposed to any illnesses recently?
- Had there been any illnesses in the family recently?
- When was the time of the last feeding? What was the child fed?
- Had there been a difference in the appearance or behavior of the child within the last few days?
- Have there been any other SIDS deaths in the family?
- If someone other than the parent was caring for the child, have any other children died in his or her custody?[11]

Communication with the Parents

If nothing suspicious is found, following the investigation, the parents should be advised that the most likely cause of death was SIDS. It should then be explained to them what SIDS is. Important facts to be conveyed to them:

- SIDS can neither be predicted nor prevented—even by a physician.
- For the present, the exact mechanism of death is not known with absolute certainty.
- SIDS is not contagious.
- SIDS is not hereditary.
- SIDS occurs very quickly, without suffering, distress, or warning, and is assumed to occur while the infant is asleep.
- SIDS occurs most frequently during the first 6 months of life and virtually never beyond 10 months.
- The child usually appears healthy prior to death.
- SIDS is not caused by smothering or choking following aspiration of regurgitated or vomited food.

If the officers feel comfortable in doing so and their agencies have no objections, they may discuss the prevailing SIDS theories with the parents. However, it must be emphasized to them that these are at present theories and that no final determinations will be made until the completion of the examination by the medical examiner.[12]

Criminal Homicide as a Possibility

In spite of the findings just discussed, the police must be sensitive to the possibility of criminal homicide. Some recent studies raise the specter that in recent years there may have been cases in which children had actually been murdered but the deaths were incorrectly classified as SIDS.

Probably the most commonly missed method of homicide in infants and young children is smothering. Smothering is, after impulse homicides, the second most common type of homicide in infants. In infants, smothering is very easily accomplished. One closes off the child's nose with two fingers, at the same time pushing up on the lower jaw with the palm to occlude the airway. Other methods have involved placing a pillow or towel over the child's face, and pressing down; pushing the face down into bed clothing; or just covering the nose and mouth with one's hand. These descriptions are based on either confessions or witnessed homicides. In a few cases, attempted homicides have been videotaped.[13]

For example:

- Dr. David Southall of City General Hospital in Stoke-on-Trent, England, set up video cameras in the hospital rooms of children brought in after parents reported that the children had stopped breathing and nearly died. The cameras captured 39 instances of mothers trying to smother their babies. Fully one-third of these "near-miss-SIDS" cases, it is estimated, are actually cases of Munchausen Syndrome by Proxy. Overall, Dr. Southall concludes that 5–10% of SIDS deaths are in fact infanticides.[14]
- In an unpublished study, Dr. Thomas Truman concluded that as many as one-third of the repeated near-SIDS cases at what may be the most prestigious SIDS center in the United States may be cases of Munchausen Syndrome by Proxy. While serving a fellowship at Massachusetts General Hospital from 1993 to 1996, Truman analyzed the medical records of 155 children treated at the hospital. In 56 of these cases, the child's chart contained circumstantial evidence of possible abuse. One baby suffered repeated breathing crises at home, turning blue and limp, but only when the mother (and no one else) was present. Another one had no breathing problems during the six months he spent in a local hospital, but the day he went home alone with his mother he had a life-threatening breathing

emergency. The authorities were alerted to the possibility of the case, but no action was taken. The child died one year after being sent home.[15]

It should be noted that if death has been induced by intentional suffocation, there may be petechial hemorrhaging of the eyes and surrounding areas. (See Chapter 9, "Injury and Death Investigation," for a more detailed discussion of this condition.)

CHILD MOLESTATION

For purposes of discussion, Kenneth V. Lanning, supervisory special agent of the Federal Bureau of Investigation, divides child molesters into two categories, namely, situational and preferential.[16]

Situational Child Molesters

The **situational child molester** does not have a true sexual preference for children but engages in sex with children for varied and sometimes complex reasons. For such a child molester, sex with children may range from a once-in-a-lifetime act to a long-term pattern of behavior. The more long term the pattern is, the harder it is to distinguish from preferential molesting. The situational child molester usually has fewer numbers of different child victims. Other vulnerable individuals, such as the elderly, sick, or disabled, may also be at risk of sexual victimization by him or her. For example, the situational child molester who sexually abuses children in a daycare center might leave that job and begin to sexually abuse elderly people in a nursing home. The number of situational child molesters is larger and increasing faster than that of preferential child molesters. Members of lower socioeconomic groups tend to be overrepresented among situational child molesters. Within this category, the following four major patterns of behavior emerge: regressed, morally indiscriminate, sexually indiscriminate, and inadequate (see Table 11-2).

Morally Indiscriminate

The morally indiscriminate pattern characterizes an increasing number of child molesters. For such an individual, the sexual abuse of children is simply part of a general pattern of abuse in his life. He is a user and an abuser of people. He abuses his wife, friends, and coworkers. He lies, cheats, or steals whenever he thinks he can get away with it. His primary victim criteria are vulnerability and opportunity. He has the urge, a child is there, and so he acts. He typically uses force, lures, or manipulation to obtain his victims. He may violently or nonviolently abduct his victims. Although his victims frequently are strangers or acquaintances, they can also be his own children. The incestuous father (or mother) might be a morally indiscriminate offender. He frequently collects detective magazines or adult

TABLE 11-2	Situational Child Molesters			
	REGRESSED	**MORALLY INDISCRIMINATE**	**SEXUALLY INDISCRIMINATE**	**INADEQUATE**
Basic Characteristics	Poor coping skills	User of people	Sexual experimentation	Social misfit
Motivation	Substitution	Why not?	Boredom	Insecurity and curiosity
Victim Criteria	Availability	Vulnerability and opportunity	New and different	Nonthreatening
Method of Operation	Coercion	Lure, force, or manipulation	Involve in existing activity	Exploits size, advantage
Pornography Collection	Possible	Sadomasochistic; detective magazines	Highly likely; varied nature	Likely

(Source: Kenneth V. Lanning, *Child Molesters: A Behavioral Analysis for Law Enforcement Officers Investigating Cases of Child Sexual Exploitation*, 3rd ed. (Arlington, VA: National Center for Missing and Exploited Children, 1992), p. 10. Reprinted with permission of the National Center for Missing and Exploited Children [NCMEC]. Copyright 1986, 1987, and 1992, NCMEC. All rights reserved.)

pornography of a sadomasochistic nature. He may collect some child pornography, especially that which depicts pubescent children. Because he is an impulsive person who lacks conscience, there is an especially high risk that he will molest pubescent children.

Regressed

A regressed offender usually has low self-esteem and poor coping skills; he turns to children as a sexual substitute for the preferred peer sex partner. Precipitating stress may play a bigger role in his molesting behavior. His main victim criterion seems to be availability, which is why many of such offenders molest their own children. His principal method of operation is to coerce the child into having sex. This type of situational child molester may or may not collect child or adult pornography. If he does have child pornography, it will usually be the best kind of evidence from an investigative point of view and will often include homemade photographs or videos of the child he is molesting.

Sexually Indiscriminate

The sexually indiscriminate pattern of behavior is the most difficult to define. Although the previously described morally indiscriminate offender often is a sexual experimenter, the sexually indiscriminate individual differs in that he appears to be discriminating in his behavior except when it comes to sex. He is the "try-sexual"—willing to try anything sexual. Much of his behavior is similar to, and most often confused with, that of the preferential child molester. While he may have clearly defined sexual preferences—such as bondage or sadomasochism, he has no real sexual preference for children. His basic motivation is sexual experimentation, and he appears to have sex with children out of boredom. His main criteria for his victims are that they be new and different, and he involves children in previously existing sexual activity. Again, it is important to realize that these children may

be his own. Although much of his sexual activity with adults may not be criminal, such an individual may also provide his children to other adults as part of group sex, spouse-swapping activity, or even some bizarre ritual. Of all situational child molesters, he is by far the most likely to have multiple victims, be from a higher socioeconomic background, and collect pornography and erotica. Child pornography will be only a small portion of his potentially large and varied collection, however.

Inadequate

The inadequate pattern of behavior includes persons suffering from psychoses, eccentric personality disorders, mental retardation, and senility. In layperson's terms, the inadequate individual is the social misfit, the withdrawn, the unusual. He might be the shy teenager who has no friends of his own age or the eccentric loner who still lives with his parents. Although most loners are harmless, some can be child molesters and, in a few cases, even child killers (Figure 11-4). This offender seems to become sexually involved with children out of insecurity or curiosity. He finds children to be nonthreatening objects with whom he can explore his sexual fantasies. The child victim could be someone he knows or could be a random stranger. In some cases, the victim might be a specific "stranger" selected as a substitute for a specific adult (possibly a relative of the child) whom the offender is afraid of approaching directly. Often his sexual activity with children is the result of built-up impulses. Some of these individuals find it difficult to express anger and hostility, which then builds until it explodes—possibly against their child victims. Because of mental or emotional problems, some might take out their frustration in cruel sexual torture. The inadequate molester's victims, however, could be elderly persons as well as children—anyone who appears helpless at first sight. He might collect pornography, but it will most likely be of adults.

▲ **FIGURE 11-4**
Convicted murderer pleads for life
This photo shows Jesse Timmendequas, a convicted child
murderer, at the penalty phase of his trial. At this point in
the trial, he apologized for his actions and begged to have
his life spared. (© AP/Wide World Photos)

Preferential Child Molesters

Preferential child molesters have a definite sexual preference for children. Their sexual fantasies and erotic
imagery focus on children. They have sex with children

not because of some situational stress or insecurity but
because they are sexually attracted to and prefer children. Although they can possess a wide variety of character traits, they engage in highly predictable sexual
behavior. Their sexual behavior patterns are called sexual rituals and are frequently engaged in even when they
are counterproductive to getting away with the criminal
activity. Although preferential offenders may be fewer in
number than situational child molesters, they have the
potential to molest large numbers of victims. For many
of them, their problem is not only the nature of the sex
drive (attraction to children) but also the quantity (need
for frequent and repeated sex with children). They usually have age and gender preferences for their victims.
Members of higher socioeconomic groups tend to be
overrepresented among preferential child molesters.
More preferential child molesters seem to prefer boys
rather than girls. Within this category, at least three major
patterns of behavior emerge: seduction, introverted, and
sadistic (Table 11-3).

Seduction

The seduction pattern characterizes the offender who
engages children in sexual activity by "seducing" them—
courting them with attention, affection, and gifts. Just as
one adult courts another, the pedophile seduces children
over a period of time by gradually lowering their sexual
inhibitions. Frequently his victims arrive at the point
where they are willing to trade sex for the attention, affection, and other benefits they receive from the offender.
Many seduction offenders are simultaneously involved
with multiple victims, operating what has come to be
called a child sex ring. This may include a group of children in the same class at school, in the same scout troop,
or in the same neighborhood. The characteristic that seems
to make the seduction molester a master seducer of children is his ability to identify with them. He knows how
to talk to children—but, more importantly, he knows how
to listen to them. His adult status and authority are also
an important part of the seduction process. In addition,
he frequently selects as targets children who are victims
of emotional or physical neglect. The biggest problem for

	TABLE 11-3	Preferential Child Molester		
	SEDUCTION	**INTROVERTED**	**SADISTIC**
Common Characteristics	Sexual preference for children; child pornography or erotica	Sexual preference for children; child pornography or erotica	Sexual preference for children; child pornography or erotica
Motivation	Identification	Fear of communication	Need to inflict pain
Victim Criteria	Age and gender preferences	Strangers or very young	Age and gender preferences
Method of Operation	Seduction process	Nonverbal sexual contact	Lure or force

(Source: Kenneth V. Lanning, *Child Molesters: A Behavioral Analysis for Law Enforcement Officers Investigating Cases of Child Sexual Exploitation*,
3rd ed. (Arlington, VA: National Center for Missing and Exploited Children, 1992), p. 10. Reprinted with permission of the National Center for
Missing and Exploited Children [NCMEC]. Copyright 1986, 1987, and 1992, NCMEC. All rights reserved.)

this child molester is not how to obtain child victims but how to get them to leave after they are too old. This must be done without the disclosure of the "secret." Victim disclosure often occurs when the offender is attempting to terminate the relationship. This child molester is most likely to use threats and physical violence to avoid identification and disclosure or to prevent a victim from leaving before he is ready to "dump" the victim.

Introverted

The introverted pattern of behavior characterizes the offender who has a preference for children but lacks the interpersonal skills necessary to seduce them. Therefore, he typically engages in a minimal amount of verbal communication with his victims and usually molests strangers or very young children. He is like the old stereotype of the child molester in that he is more likely to hang around playgrounds and other areas where children congregate, watching them or engaging them in brief sexual encounters. He may expose himself to children or make obscene phone calls to them. He may use the services of a child prostitute. Unable to figure out any other way to gain access to a child, he might even marry a woman and have his own children, very likely molesting them from the time they are infants. He is similar to the inadequate situational child molester, except that he has a definite sexual preference for children and his selection of only children as victims is more predictable.

Sadistic

The sadistic pattern of behavior characterizes the offender who has a sexual preference for children but who, in order to be aroused or gratified, must inflict psychological or physical pain or suffering on the child victim. He is aroused by his victim's response to the infliction of pain or suffering. Sadistic molesters typically use lures or force to gain access to their victims. They are more likely than other preferential child molesters to abduct and even murder their victims. There have been some cases where seduction molesters have become sadistic molesters. It is not known whether the need to perform sadistic acts developed late or was always there and surfaced late for some reason. In any case, it is fortunate that sadistic child molesters do not appear to be large in number.[17]

Interviewing Molested Children

Common sense and formal research agree that children are not merely miniature adults. We know, for example, that children develop in stages during which they acquire capacities for new functions and understanding. We do not, generally speaking, read Shakespeare to 2-year-olds, nor do we expect adult commentary on political issues from them. Adults, for the most part, attempt to speak to and treat children in accordance with their capabilities. We do not ordinarily expect children to understand or function on a par with adults.[18]

When children become victims or witnesses of violence or sexual abuse, however, they are thrust into an adult system that traditionally does not differentiate between children and adults. As one attorney has said:

> Child victims of crime are specially handicapped. First, the criminal justice system distrusts them and puts special barriers in the path of prosecuting their claims to justice. Second, the criminal justice system seems indifferent to the legitimate special needs that arise from their participation.[19]

What are some of the reasons for the problems that arise when children are called to participate in criminal proceedings? The first reason is the children's immaturity with regard to physical, cognitive, and emotional development. The second reason involves unique attributes of the offense of child sexual abuse, particularly when the perpetrator is a parent, parent substitute, or other adult having a trusting or loving relationship with the child. The third reason is our limited understanding of children's capabilities as witnesses. These three factors affect children's ability to comply with the expectations of our judicial system and inform our entire discussion of interviewing molested children.

Developmental Issues

Three developmental issues are important when allegations of sexual abuse arise.[20] First is the child's developmental level relative to other children in his or her age group. Knowing this information will dictate the nature of questioning to which the child can reasonably be expected to respond. It will also help place the child's observable reactions to victimization in an appropriate context.

Second is the child's developmental level with regard to sexuality. Normal preschoolers, for example, express curiosity about the origin of babies and mild interest in physical differences between the sexes. While it is not unusual for young children to engage in self-stimulatory behavior or exhibitionism, intercourse or other adult sexual behaviors are quite rare.[21]

Third is the child's ability to respond adequately to interviews and to testify in court. Those who work with young children should be aware of the following:

- Children think in concrete terms.
- Children do not organize their thoughts logically. They often include extraneous information, and they have trouble generalizing to new situations.
- Children have limited understanding of space, distance, and time. A child may not be able to say at "what time" or in "what month" something occurred but may be able to say whether it was before or after school, what was on television, or whether there was snow on the ground.
- Children have a complex understanding of truth and lying.

- Children see the world egocentrically. Because they believe that adults are omniscient, they may expect to be understood even when they have answered questions only partially.[22]
- Children have a limited attention span.
- Children may have varying degrees of comfort with strangers.

These kinds of cognitive limitations are common among young children.

Older children tend to exhibit different, yet equally challenging, developmental patterns.[23] For example, although preadolescents have fairly sophisticated language capabilities, they may use words or phrases they do not fully understand. The emergence of sexuality and concern with sexual identities during preadolescence make these youngsters particularly vulnerable to disruption when they are sexually abused. As they enter adolescence, they tend to become very self-centered and have strong needs for privacy and secrecy. It is common for preteens and teenagers to express their feelings through the arts or physical activity or by acting out in inappropriate or socially unacceptable ways.

Some researchers have specifically explored the developmental aspects of children's understanding of the legal system.[24] Not surprisingly, they have found that older children have more accurate and complete knowledge of legal terminology (e.g., court, lawyer, jury, judge, and witness) as well as a better grasp of certain basic concepts of American justice. The researchers caution that children's understanding of the legal system is not only limited but sometimes faulty, so child witnesses may behave in ways that appear counterintuitive or inappropriate to the context.

For example, an interview with a child may begin by requesting identifying information: name, age, school, grade, home address. But young children may misinterpret these initial questions as meaning they are under suspicion or arrest.[25] Also, because they do not understand the different roles and obligations of all the people who interview them, children do not understand why they must tell their stories repeatedly to the police, social workers, doctors, prosecutors, and, ultimately, the court. While this repetition may be simply exasperating for some children, others may relive the traumatic event each time, and still others may assume the story is already known and omit important details in subsequent interviews. Some children may feel protected by the presence of the judge, but others may be intimidated by the big stranger in the dark, scary robe who yells at people in the courtroom and sits towering above the witness stand. One therapist tells of a child witness who was afraid that the judge would hit her with the gavel, which she referred to as a hammer. Children perceive the judge's power to punish and may not understand that they are not the potential object of that punishment.

To correct these problems, researchers recommend that attorneys, judges, and investigators choose their words with care when questioning child witnesses.[26] Some believe that targeted instruction for children who may serve as witnesses, possibly in the form of a "court school," would be helpful as well.[27] Many prosecutors and victim advocates take children for a tour of the courtroom and introduce them to some of the key players before their scheduled court date. Critics contend, however, that such precautions may induce unnecessary apprehension for children who ultimately are not called to testify. At a minimum, interviewers would be wise to explain thoroughly the nature and purpose of each interview or court appearance before the child is questioned.

A further problem in interviewing children who may be victims of sexual molestation centers on the delicate issue of body parts and techniques for achieving accurate communication. One of the most common methods involves the use of anatomically detailed dolls.

Anatomically Detailed Dolls

When anatomically detailed dolls (male and female dolls with all body parts, including genitals; Figure 11-5) were first introduced in the late 1970s,[28] they were widely hailed and almost universally adopted by child-serving professionals as an important advance in techniques for communicating with troubled children. Congress (in the Victims of Child Abuse Act of 1990) and eight states[29] have enacted legislation expressly permitting children to use anatomically detailed dolls as demonstrative aids when they testify in court, and many appellate courts have upheld the use of such dolls.[30] The use of dolls at trial appears limited, however: courtroom observations of child sexual-abuse trials in eight jurisdictions revealed only one use of dolls per jurisdiction over the course of a year, with one exception where dolls were used in three of the four cases observed.[31]

Yet even as the dolls' value as demonstrative aids in court has gained widespread acceptance, their use in investigative interviews to arrive at a finding, or "diagnosis," of sexual abuse that is later presented in court as expert opinion has been sharply criticized. At the core of the controversy is the extent to which anatomically detailed dolls may suggest sexual behaviors even among children with no history of abuse. Improper use of the dolls, and unsupported inferences about children's behavior with them, can imperil the search for truth.

Proponents of anatomically detailed dolls maintain that, when properly used, the dolls can facilitate and enhance interviews with children.[32] Dolls can help in the following ways:

- They can help establish rapport with the interviewer and reduce stress. Most children relate well to dolls. The dolls can have a calming effect and make the interview room appear less formal and more child-oriented.
- They can reduce vocabulary problems. Interviewers can use the dolls to learn a child's sexual vocabulary before questioning the child about the alleged abuse.

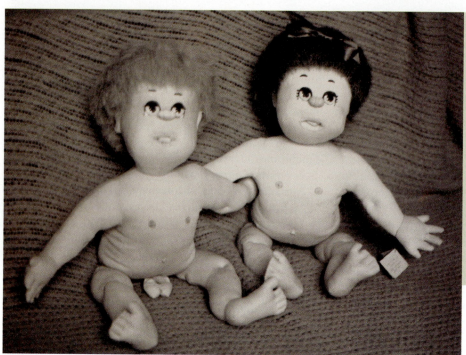

◀ **FIGURE 11-5**
Anatomically detailed dolls
Interviewing children who either have been sexually abused or have witnessed sexual abuse creates challenges for investigators. One tool that often assists investigators is the use of an anatomically detailed doll with all body parts, including genitals, present. While there is some disagreement among experts as to the overall usefulness of these dolls, many law enforcement agencies still use them.
(Courtesy Eymann Anatomically Correct Dolls, Sacramento, California)

- They allow the child to show what may be difficult or embarrassing to say. Anatomically detailed dolls can be an invaluable aid to children who are unable or unwilling to verbalize what happened to them.
- They can enhance the quality of information. Dolls may help interviewers gather information without resorting to leading or protracted questioning to overcome children's reluctance to describe sexual acts.
- They can establish competency. Interviewers can use the dolls in a general way to demonstrate the child's mental capacity and ability to communicate.

Many critics fear, however, that anatomically detailed dolls could have adverse effects, whether by provoking horror or alarm at the sight of genitalia or by eliciting apparently sexualized responses, even among children who have not been sexually abused. Even some appellate courts have raised the issue that interviewing children with anatomically detailed dolls may contaminate their memory.[33] Research offers little support for these contentions, however. For example, one study of "nonreferred" children (i.e., children with no history or current allegation of sexual abuse) found that although they did play more with undressed dolls than with dressed dolls, the children's primary activity was, in fact, dressing the dolls.[34] Others report that nonreferred children do examine the genitalia and orifices of anatomically detailed dolls but only rarely do they enact sexual behaviors.[35] It should be recognized, of course, that some proportion of nonreferred children may have experienced some form of undetected sexual abuse.

Related to this controversy is the fact that professionals in this field have yet to reach consensus on "proper" use of anatomically detailed dolls. A number of questions remain unanswered:[36]

- How "correct" in their appearance must the dolls be? Some respondents to a survey by Boat and Everson[37] revealed using Barbie dolls, Cabbage Patch dolls, and homemade stuffed dolls with varying degrees of accuracy in their representation of genitalia. Does the presence or absence of certain details influence children's behavior with the dolls? Must the dolls also be matched by age and racial features to the child and alleged perpetrator?
- When and how should the dolls be used to assist an investigation? Should the dolls be available to children at the start of the interview, or should they be introduced only after the child falters in responding to traditional questioning? Who should undress the dolls, and how should this activity be incorporated into the interview?
- How many sessions with a child are necessary before drawing conclusions about the child's behavior with the dolls?
- Should other adults be present during the interview?
- How many dolls should be available?

The answers to these questions vary with the professional orientations of the people who are asked. Clinicians' responses are more likely to reflect concerns for the children's well-being; legal professionals, on the other hand, express concern for the potential effects of certain practices when revealed in court. From the courts' perspective, it is probably least objectionable to:

- Introduce the dolls only after the child has verbally disclosed some abuse, or as a last resort to assist reluctant children.[38]
- Allow children to choose from a variety of dolls (rather than present only two to represent child and perpetrator).[39]
- Offer the child minimal or no instruction in use of the dolls.
- Incorporate information gathered from doll interviews with other data to provide a complete assessment.[40]

Similar recommendations would apply to use of other props, such as puppets or artwork.

Asking Leading Questions

Professionals who interview children who are suspected of having been sexually abused are caught in a perilous dilemma. In the words of two well-known clinicians:

In the best of all possible worlds, it would be advisable not to ask children leading questions . . . But in the best of all possible worlds, children are not sexually assaulted in secrecy, and then bribed, threatened, or intimidated not to talk about it. In the real world, where such things do happen, leading questions may sometimes be necessary.[41]

As with the anatomical dolls, leading questions are widely used as a courtroom technique to assist child witnesses,[42] but they are seriously challenged when used in investigative interviews. There is, however, a grain of truth to the argument that children can be led, coached, or even "brainwashed" by the interview process, and interviewers would be wise to reexamine their methods in light of our growing experience in the courts.

Briefly, the defense argument rests on the social psychological theory of social influence. In essence, as it applies to child sexual-abuse cases, this theory holds that children's responses to questioning are heavily influenced by the perceived authority or power of the adult interviewers. When they are praised or otherwise "rewarded" for disclosing elements of abuse, children learn what the interviewers want to hear. In other words, children answer to please adults.[43]

Furthermore, to continue this argument, the effect of social influence is magnified in child sexual-abuse cases because the children are typically interviewed repeatedly by several different adults, each of whom contributes to the child's expanding story by infusing—and reinforcing—new information. Ultimately, according to one of the leading defense experts:

In situations where a child will eventually testify, the memory will consist of a combination of recall and reconstruction influenced by all of the interrogations, conversations, and sexual abuse therapy that have occurred during the delay. The longer the delay, the greater the possibility of social influence and the more the memory may consist of reconstruction rather than recall.[44]

Challenges based on this theory have successfully undermined prosecution of several highly publicized cases, including the well-known McMartin Preschool case.

In one study, 72 children from age 5 to 7 underwent physical examinations. Half received external examinations of their genital and anal areas; the other half were examined for scoliosis (curvature of the spine). Within one month of the exam, the children were interviewed about the event using open-ended questions, anatomically detailed dolls, and specific and misleading questions. The results of this study were both illuminating and provocative. Specifically:

- The majority of children who experienced genital and anal touching did not report it, either in response to open-ended questions or when asked to demonstrate with the dolls.
- All but 5 (of 36) disclosed touching in response to specific questions (e.g., "Did the doctor touch you here?").
- Only 3 (of 36) girls who received scoliosis examinations incorrectly reported genital or anal touching; only 1 of those provided additional (incorrect) details.

In sum, based on the total number of questions asked, "When all of the chances to reveal genital/anal contact were considered, children failed to disclose it 64% of the time, whereas the chance of obtaining a false report of genital/anal touching was only 8%, even when leading questions were asked.[45]

Children's Reactions to Victimization

There are few in our society who would argue that child sexual abuse does not cause serious problems for its victims. The burgeoning research on this subject suggests that the effects of victimization on children can be far-reaching, negative, and complex. In a review of the literature, researchers found seven "clusters" of effects on children:[46]

- *Affective problems:* guilt, shame, anxiety, fear, depression, anger.
- *Physical effects:* genital injuries, pregnancy, sexually transmitted diseases, somatic complaints (e.g., headaches, stomachaches, bed-wetting, hypochondria), changes in appetite or sleep patterns.

- *Cognitive effects:* concentration problems, short attention spans.
- *Behavioral symptoms:* acting out (hostile-aggressive behaviors, antisocial behaviors, delinquency, stealing, tantrums, substance abuse), withdrawal, repetition of the abusive relationship.
- *Self-destructive behaviors:* self-mutilation, suicidal thoughts and attempts.
- *Psychopathology:* neuroses, character disorders, multiple personalities, psychotic features.
- *Sexualized behavior:* excessive masturbation, repetition of sexual acts with others, atypical sexual knowledge.

Other commonly cited effects were low self-esteem and problems with interpersonal relationships.

Many of the early studies in this area were flawed because they relied on populations of clinical samples of sexually abused children or on retrospective findings from adults who had been sexually abused as children. Neither approach allows comparisons to "normal" populations. But in one study that compared 369 sexually abused children to 318 nonabused children, a number of factors emerged to distinguish the two groups.[47] The sexually abused children were significantly more likely to demonstrate:

- Poor self-esteem
- Aggressive behaviors
- Fearfulness
- Concentration problems
- Withdrawal
- Acting out
- A need to please others

Another study compared sexually abused children to two groups of nonabused children: one from a psychiatric outpatient clinic and the other from a well-child clinic. The researchers found that the sexually abused children were more similar to the psychiatric outpatients than to the normal children.[48] Sexually abused children displayed significantly more behavior problems (particularly sexual behaviors) and fewer social competencies than did normal children.

Sexually Abused Child Syndrome

Early attempts to describe a "sexually abused child syndrome" were quickly discarded as lacking a foundation in empirical research. Today, however, some of the leading researchers and clinicians in this field are moving toward consensus on behavioral indicators of child sexual abuse. The results of a nationwide survey of professionals experienced in evaluating suspected child sexual abuse revealed high levels of agreement concerning the following factors:[49]

- The child possesses age-inappropriate sexual knowledge.
- The child engages in sexualized play.
- The child displays precocious behavior.
- The child engages in excessive masturbation.
- The child is preoccupied with his or her genitals.
- There are indications that pressure or coercion was exerted on the child.
- The child's story remains consistent over time.
- The child's report indicates an escalating progression of sexual abuse over time.
- The child describes idiosyncratic details of the abuse.
- There is physical evidence of abuse.

Note, however, that these indicators represent a broad constellation of behaviors that are frequently seen among sexually abused children as a group. Owing to the many forms sexual abuse may take and the variations in individual coping methods and personalities, every child will exhibit a different set of behaviors subsequent to abuse. Thus, a child who experienced a single abusive incident may well be consistent with his or her story over time. Conversely, a child who experienced several years of abuse by a close relative may seem to contradict his or her story over time, depending on the attitudes expressed by family members or the manner in which he or she is questioned. In other words, there is no single array of behavioral indicators that definitively identify a sexually abused child.

The Risk of False Allegations

A recent spate of highly publicized sexual-abuse allegations has caused the public to recoil and question the limits of credulity. These allegations tend to fall into two categories: alleged sexual abuse of preschool children in day-care facilities, sometimes including bizarre and ritualistic elements; and sexual abuse allegations arising in the context of divorce and custody or visitation disputes. Such cases have caused many observers to question the veracity of child-sexual-abuse reports.[50]

Researchers have attempted to determine the percentage of unsubstantiated cases that can actually be attributed to false reports. The most comprehensive of these studies analyzed all reports of suspected sexual abuse filed with the Denver Department of Social Services (DSS) several years ago. All 576 reports had been investigated by the DSS Sexual Abuse Team and designated either "founded" (53%) or "unfounded" (47%). With the assistance of DSS caseworkers, the researchers applied clinical judgments to the case files and reclassified these reports, using the following categories:

- *Founded cases:*
  Reliable accounts
  Recantations of reliable accounts
- *Unfounded cases:*
  Unsubstantiated suspicions
  Insufficient information
  Fictitious reports by adults
  Fictitious reports by children

The last two categories, "fictitious reports by adults" and "fictitious reports by children," included deliberate falsifications, misperceptions, confused interpretations of nonsexual events, and children who had been coached by adults. On reclassification by the researchers, 6% of the total cases (34 allegations) were found to be fictitious. Of those, only 8 allegations had been made by 5 children, 4 of whom had been substantiated victims of abuse in the past.[51]

In a second phase of this study, the researchers examined 21 fictitious cases that had been referred to a sexual-abuse clinic for evaluation over a 5-year period. Of these allegations, 5 had been initiated by the child and 9 by an adult; in 7 cases the researchers could not determine who had initiated the charge. Custody or visitation disputes were ongoing in 15 of these cases: in 1 child-initiated case, in 7 adult-initiated cases, and in all the "mixed" cases.[52]

Another study examined 162 consecutive sexual-abuse cases seen at a children's hospital over a 10-month period. Twenty-five of those cases involved allegations against a parent, and 7 of those (28%) involved a custody or visitation dispute. The disputed cases were less likely to be substantiated than cases without such conflict, but they were nevertheless substantiated more than half the time.[53]

Other studies have approached the relationship between custody disputes and false allegations from a different perspective, beginning with cases that are referred to clinicians for custody evaluations (rather than sexual-abuse diagnosis). These studies have found that a relatively high proportion of custody disputes involve false sexual-abuse allegations.[54] Note, however, that these studies depend on clinical populations (i.e., troublesome cases that had been referred to a specialist for evaluation or diagnosis). Findings are based on a small number of cases, and, furthermore, the decision to label a report "fictitious" is based on clinical judgment: there is no objective, definitive measure of "truth." Because of these limitations, such studies cannot generalize to a conclusion that sexual-abuse allegations associated with custody disputes are necessarily false.[55]

In fact, sexual-abuse allegations arising from divorce and custody disputes appear to be quite rare. One study that attempted to quantify this phenomenon found that in most courts, about 2–10% of all family court cases involving custody and/or visitation disputes also involved a charge of sexual abuse. As an alternative way of framing the magnitude of this problem, sexual-abuse allegations occurred in the range of approximately 2 to 15 per 1,000 divorce filings among the courts that were studied. Based on data from seven jurisdictions, 105 of 6,100 cases (or less than 2%) of custody or visitation disputes involved sexual-abuse allegations.[56]

Research also suggests that sexual abuse in day care is no more common than it is within families. Extrapolating from 270 substantiated cases in 35 states over a three-year period, researchers estimated that 500 to 550 actual cases occurred in that period, involving more than 2,500 children. On the basis of the total of 7 million children attending day-care facilities nationwide, the researchers calculated that 5.5 of every 10,000 children enrolled in day care are sexually abused. This compares to an estimated 8.9 of every 10,000 children who are sexually abused in their homes. The conclusion: The apparently large number of sexual-abuse cases reported in day care "is simply a reflection of the large number of children in day care and the relatively high risk of sexual abuse to children everywhere."[57]

Emotional Reaction to the Pedophile

Because many investigators are parents, they react strongly to the pedophile. However, for legal and pragmatic reasons, such feelings must never be translated into physical or verbal abuse. Physical abuse by police is unlawful and should result in criminal and civil charges. Verbal abuse or open expressions of revulsion minimize the possibility of obtaining the suspect's cooperation and, perhaps, of obtaining a much-needed voluntary statement. The following case illustrates this point.

A 5-year-old girl told her mother that the man next door had taken her into his home, removed her underpants, placed his penis between her legs, and rubbed her vagina with it. After putting her underpants back on, he had sent her home. The mother called the police, but when they arrived the child was very hesitant to repeat the story.

Careful handling of the interview by the officer provided enough information to justify probable cause for an arrest, although the suspect denied the offense. Supplementing the child's statements were those of neighbors who had seen the man taking the child into his house, where she had remained for about 10 minutes.

The child was taken to the hospital and given an examination. The examining physician could find no injuries, semen, or pubic hair. The victim's clothing was normal in appearance. The situation at this juncture was a shy young child who probably would not be a good witness, an absence of physical evidence, a suspect who denied the charges, and witnesses who saw the child enter the suspect's house but saw no molestation. A voluntary statement was imperative if a successful prosecution was to result.

The suspect was interrogated and at first denied the charges. But when confronted with the child's and the neighbors' statements, he admitted molesting the child in the manner she described. He said that he had been drinking heavily at the time and attributed his actions to intoxication. The suspect agreed to give a full statement under oath to the state prosecutor.

Before the suspect was sworn in, the prosecutor was advised by the investigator, outside the presence of the suspect, the facts in the case. The prosecutor requested that the suspect be brought into his office. In an angry voice, he told the suspect, "If that had been my little girl, you son of a bitch, I would have broken your god-damned neck." The prosecutor then asked the suspect if he would like to make a statement. The suspect replied, "I have nothing to say to you." Subsequently, the suspect pleaded guilty to contributing to the delinquency of a minor, a misdemeanor.

The reason for this misdemeanor rather than the felony charge was insufficient evidence. The prosecutor was not new to this job, and he had an excellent reputation. Unfortunately, what he had done was identify the victim with his own daughter, who was about the same age as the molested child.

HUMAN TRAFFICKING

Human trafficking may seem more like fodder for an episode of *Law and Order* than something that law enforcement officers would come up against on a regular basis, but the fact is that the issue has become more and more prevalent, particularly in areas with large pockets of immigrant populations. For the purposes of this chapter, we will focus on human trafficking as it relates to children, especially in the areas of sex trafficking. However, the victims of human trafficking can be women or men, girls or boys, of any age. The purposes for human trafficking can vary; recent stories in the news have highlighted individuals either taken across state lines or brought into this country for prostitution, forced labor in construction sites, strip clubs, restaurants, and even church choirs. Human trafficking victims have also been found among domestic laborers, such as live-in housekeepers or child care providers. Recent federal laws have brought increased attention to the matter, as well as raised the level of awareness among law enforcement agencies around the country. However, the practice still claims a shocking number of victims from around the world (Figure 11-7).

According to the United Nations definition, human trafficking is "the recruitment, transportation, transfer, harboring or receipt of persons, by means of the threat or use of force or other forms of coercion, of abduction, of fraud, of deception, of the abuse of power or of a position of vulnerability or of the giving or receiving of payments or benefits to achieve the consent of a person having control over another person, for the purpose of exploitation."[58] Sex trafficking would therefore involve exploitation of a sexual nature, such as forced prostitution, or forced participation in pornographic acts. The trafficking of children for such purposes is particularly

▲ **FIGURE 11-6**
Accused pedophile awaits the start of trial
Eric Franklin Rosser, who had been on the FBI's 10-most-wanted list, is shown here after his arrest. He is being prosecuted for his alleged involvement in child prostitution and pedophilia. He was arrested in Bangkok, Thailand.
(© Reuters NewMedia Inc./Corbis)

heinous, as children depend on their handlers for the basic necessities of life, like food and shelter. Those who do not perform as they are instructed to, or try to escape, risk starvation, bodily harm and even death. Even more heinous is the fact that many reports and anecdotes show evidence of infants and toddlers being brought into the country for purposes of sex trafficking.

The scope of the problem is a difficult one to measure. Human trafficking, particularly sex trafficking, is an inherently underground operation. It's further complicated by the fact that many victims are smuggled in from other countries. However, recent estimates show that between 2 and 4 million people worldwide are victims of human trafficking,[59] and of those, between 18,000 and 20,000 people per year are trafficked into the United States. Sex trafficking statistics are not available, and estimates vary wildly. However, when one considers that human trafficking is tied with the arms trade as the most profitable organized crime after drugs[60] and that the sex trade is a major source of profit for this enterprise[61] it is easy to imagine the numbers being fairly high.

Children may become involved sex trafficking in several different ways. Often, they are lured from their homes with promises of a good job or a better life in another country or state.[62] Stories of Russian girls who were lured into trafficking rings with promises of lucrative nanny or waitressing jobs are commonplace. A 2004 New York Times story tells of a Mexican girl who was told about better schools and job opportunities in order to ensnare her in a prostitution ring.[63] Parents or relatives may sell their children into sex slavery, particularly in impoverished countries. Victims of a major earthquake in Islamabad, Pakistan, were reportedly selling their children to traffickers for about 1,000 U.S. dollars out of desperation.[64] Similar stories have circulated around the international press about victims of the tsunami that struck Southern Asia in 2004. Impoverished families in India have been known to sell their daughters to traffickers in order to avoid dowry payments (large sums of money paid to a groom's family upon marriage).[65] Trafficking rings have been implicated in the kidnapping of children and young women, as well (Figure 11-7).[66]

Victims of human trafficking come from around the world but are particularly concentrated in several geographic clusters. South and Southeast Asia export the largest number of human slaves, with Thailand at the forefront of the industry. Thai sex trafficking rings generally export to Northern Europe, Japan, Malaysia and the Middle East. Many Thai exports originally hail from war-torn and impoverished areas such as Laos, Burma, and Cambodia.[67] Russia and Eastern Europe have become a major staging-ground for human traffickers in recent years, because of the financial and political instability that has plagued the area since the fall of Communism. Mexico has also become a major player in this area of organized crime, providing stop-overs for traffickers from other countries. Mexico is also becoming known for its ability to export young girls to the United States for sexual exploitation at a fraction of the cost of Asian or European trafficking rings.[68] Most trafficking victims end up in large cities, vacation and tourist areas, and near military bases. Metropolitan areas in New York, Florida, and California are major sex trafficking destinations; however, the problem is becoming concentrated in other border states, as well as smaller cities and suburbs throughout the country.[69]

Often, young women seeking a better life pay organizations thousands of dollars to smuggle them into the United States; once here, their passports are seized, and they are forced to work until they can pay off excessive fees for their transportation. This creates a bondage-debt situation, with the victims forced to prostitute for relatively small amounts of money that will essentially never add up to what they "owe."[70] The debt ploy occurs mostly with teenage girls and young women; young children are indoctrinated into a life of prostitution or pornography as a part of routine survival. Unfortunately, the demand for children has increased as many "customers" believe the younger they are, the less likely it is that they may have contracted

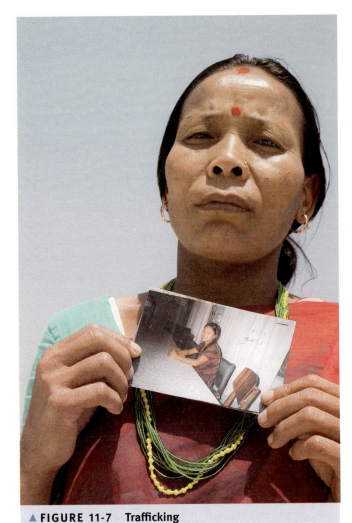

▲ **FIGURE 11-7 Trafficking**
This mother traveled from Nepal to India in search of her daughter who was trafficked into a brothel. Young girls are often promised money for their families or educational opportunities as lures into the sex trade.
(Photo by Kay Chermush for the U.S. State Department)

HIV/AIDS or other sexually transmitted diseases.[71] However, many children engaging in forced prostitution have a host of sexually transmitted diseases, including HIV, owing to their innate naiveté about protecting themselves. Children may also experience a number of urinary tract and rectal problems, as well as complications from aborted pregnancies in those able to conceive.[72]

While human trafficking is, as mentioned previously, an underground operation, the fact is that the victims are often hiding in plain sight. Children are often transported in the open to meet customers, or are held in homes on a regular residential street. In order for the customer to find victims, they must be accessible. Victims are often visible to the police as well. Very young children involved in the sex trade may be more obvious in some situations, but adolescents in sex trafficking rings are often lumped in with day-to-day vice operations, assigned to juvenile

Officers should keep in mind that calls for service that involve: prostitution or forced labor of young children; child neglect and abuse cases involving foreign immigrants; vice raids where foreign nationals are involved; and operations of strip clubs or massage parlors may involve the trafficking of young children or underage girls. In these situations, special care should be taken to observe:

- Living conditions.

- Indications of restriction of movement (locks on bedroom doors, closed-circuit video systems, etc.).

- Reports or indications of frequent moving (such as unfurnished homes, small numbers of belongings, etc.).

- Signs of abnormally dependant relationships, such as extreme submissiveness and fearful behavior around others.

- Insistence of guardians that they provide information to or act as translators between law enforcement.

- Guardians that speak English while children do not.

- A number of children from varying ethnic or geographical backgrounds under one roof.

- Isolation from the public, from schools, and from ethnic and social groups.

◄ **FIGURE 11-8**
Human trafficking checklist

courts. Most are too scared for their safety to tell officers their real situation.

Part of the dynamic in sex trafficking involves keeping an environment of fear and confusion. Often, victims are told that U.S. laws will punish them severely for being in the country illegally, so they are less likely to be honest with police if taken into custody or to contact police if they have an opportunity. Many are moved around so frequently that they have no idea what town or state they are in and therefore have no idea how to contact law enforcement.[73] Therefore, it is up to law enforcement agencies to act on behalf of the victim; many agencies are now beginning to take notice of the problem and train their officers accordingly (Figure 11-8). The U.S. Department of Health and Human Services Administration of Children and Families has released a document to help law enforcement officers to identify situations where trafficking may be involved.[74]

Special care must be taken when interviewing possible victims of sex trafficking, since the trauma experienced can be expressed in many ways. Officers must realize that cultural barriers and mistrust of the police run deep among such victims, even children. Children especially are apt to feel dependent on their captors and are likely to withdraw when removed from them. They are often reluctant to turn over information that incriminates those who have been "taking care" of them. Older children may be afraid that their families or friends will be hurt or killed, even if they themselves have been removed from the situation. Even cooperative subjects may be unable to give complete, linear accounts of their ordeal.[75] Child psychologists and experts in the trauma of sex trafficking should be consulted if possible.

Law enforcement officers that become involved in the investigation of sex trafficking rings will often be assisting in the prosecution of perpetrators on a number of state and federal charges. Locally, assault, child abuse,

and pandering charges may apply. However, sex trafficking violates a host of federal laws, including kidnapping, organized crime legislation, and several laws specific to the offense of human trafficking. As a result, partnerships and collaborations with federal entities are essential to successful prosecution. Law enforcement agencies without such federal partners should seek them out preemptively, in order to obtain resources and best practices from those with experience with the trafficking of children for sexual exploitation[76] (Figure 11-9).

The Trafficking Victims Protection Act (TVPA) of 2000 prohibits trafficking by making it illegal to recruit, entice, or obtain a person to engage in commercial sex acts, or to benefit from such activities.[77] Traffickers who exploit children are subject to more severe penalties under the law. It also specifies benefits for victims of trafficking, such as financial assistance and social services. Victims are also protected by the TVPA with eligibility for a special visa allowing them to become temporary residents of the United States. Furthermore, victims are eligible for the Witness Protection Program, if necessary. The reauthorization of the act in 2003 committed over $200 million to fight human trafficking by identifying and assisting victims, and it also included trafficking as a violation of the RICO statute, broadening the government's ability to shut down trafficking organizations. In 2005, the act was again reauthorized, this time making a special commitment to aid child victims of human trafficking. The 2005 version also required that recommendations be made for the prevention of human trafficking in postconflict areas, or in regions affected by humanitarian crises.[78] International organizations, such as the United Nations, have also become heavily involved in the prevention and research of human trafficking, especially since human trafficking now appears to be linked to the financing of terrorism (see Chapter 20).

Code enforcement officers join efforts to crack down on human trafficking

by ALEX BRANCH

FORT WORTH—The city's code enforcement officers are looking for more than illegal dumping, overgrown lots and unsafe buildings. Recognizing signs of human trafficking was recently added to their training after other law officers asked for help. "They've recruited us to be their eyes and ears on the streets," said code officer Alex Southern, a spokesman for the department. "Our officers are out in the neighborhoods every day. We see and hear a lot."

Federal, state and local authorities are trying to crack down on human trafficking in Dallas-Fort Worth, believed to be one of the fastest-growing hubs for trafficking. Human trafficking involves forcing people from other countries, other states or even other parts of the Metroplex into servitude, often to repay a debt. The work includes prostitution, housekeeping or construction. Large operations have been found in Fort Worth. In 2002, federal agents raided six bars and seven homes after officials found Honduran women being forced to work as barmaids. Authorities have busted similar operations in Dallas. In December, Fort Worth created a police anti-trafficking unit with a $600,000 grant from the Justice Department. The unit, which the grant funds for three years, is part of the North Texas Anti-Trafficking Task Force, a collaboration of law enforcement and social service agencies. The unit has several open investigations of Fort Worth-area trafficking, said Kathleen Murray, the unit's program director. But it asked code officers for help generating more leads.

"They cover a lot of ground," Murray said. "If they see any of the clues we've told them about, they'll notify us." Training consists of explaining human trafficking and describing what goes on. There were accounts of women forced to have sex with men every 15 minutes for hours a day. Half of each woman's earnings are withheld by the trafficker to pay for room and board and condoms. Victims are beaten, and food is withheld in this form of slavery, authorities said. "It is deplorable," Southern said. "After seeing the way these people are forced to live, our officers were eager to help." There are 75 code officers in the field, he said.

An example of what may raise a red flag would be a house being intermittently packed with people. Traffickers sometimes own several houses and rotate their victims. Judging from officers' reactions as police described some of the places under investigation, they will be able to help, he said. "Our people would say: 'Hey, I know exactly where that it is. It's on my beat at such-and such address,'" Southern said. "We see those places every day. We just need to know what to look for."

What is human trafficking?

- The use of force, fraud or coercion to exploit a person into involuntary servitude, debt bondage or forced labor.
- The use of force or coercion can be direct and violent, or psychological.

By the numbers

- Between 17,000 and 50,000 people are trafficked each year into the United States from other countries.
- 300,000 American youths are trafficked around the U.S. Many are runaways.
- Worldwide, 600,000 to 800,000 people are trafficked across international borders.

▲ FIGURE 11-9   Trafficking

CHILD PORNOGRAPHY

Kenneth V. Lanning, supervisory special agent of the Federal Bureau of Investigation, divides what the pedophile collects into two categories: child pornography and child erotica.[79] **Child pornography** can be behaviorally (not legally) defined as the sexually explicit reproduction of a child's image and includes sexually explicit photographs, negatives, slides, magazines, movies, videotapes, and computer disks. In essence, it is the permanent record of the sexual abuse or exploitation of an actual child. To legally be child pornography, it must be a visual depiction (not the written word) of a minor (as defined by statute) that is sexually explicit (not necessarily obscene, unless required by state law). Child pornography can be divided into two subcategories: commercial and homemade.

Child erotica is a broader and more encompassing term than child pornography. It can be defined as any material, relating to children, that serves a sexual purpose for a given individual. Some of the more common types of child erotica include toys, games, drawings, fantasy writings, diaries, souvenirs, sexual aids, manuals, letters, books about children, psychological books on pedophilia, and ordinary photographs of children. Child erotica might also be referred to as pedophile paraphernalia. Generally, possession and distribution of these items does not constitute a violation of the law.

For investigative purposes, child erotica can be divided into the categories shown next.

Published Material Relating to Children

Examples of this include books, magazines, articles, or videotapes dealing with any of these areas:

- Child development
- Sex education
- Child photography
- Sexual abuse of children
- Sexual disorders
- Pedophilia
- Man-boy love
- Personal ads
- Incest
- Child prostitution
- Missing children
- Investigative techniques
- Legal aspects
- Access to children
- Detective magazines
- "Men's" magazines
- Nudism
- Erotic novels
- Catalogs
- Brochures

Listing of foreign sex tours, guides to nude beaches, and material on sponsoring orphans or needy children provide investigators with information about access to children. Detective magazines saved by pedophiles usually contain stories about crimes against children. The "men's" magazines collected may have articles about sexual abuse of children. The use of adult pornography to lower inhibitions is discussed elsewhere in this book. Although the possession of information on missing children should be carefully investigated to determine possible involvement in abduction, most pedophiles collect this material to help rationalize their behavior as child "lovers," not abductors. Personal ads include those in "swinger" magazines, video magazines, and newspapers, and may mention "family fun," "family activity," "European material," "youth training," "unusual and bizarre,"

"better life," and so on. Erotic novels may contain stories about sex with children but without sexually explicit photographs. They may contain sketches or drawings. Materials concerning current or proposed laws dealing with sex abuse; arrested, convicted, or acquitted child molesters; or investigative techniques used by law enforcement are common.

Unpublished Material Relating to Children

Examples include items such as these:

- Personal letters
- Audiotapes
- Diaries
- Fantasy writings
- Manuscripts
- Telephone and address books
- Pedophile manuals
- Newsletters and bulletins
- Directories
- Adult pornography
- Financial records

Commercial Child Pornography

Commercial child pornography is pornography that is produced and intended for commercial sale. Because of strict federal and state laws today, there is no place in the United States where commercial "child" pornography is knowingly openly sold. In the United States, it is primarily a cottage industry run by pedophiles and child molesters. The commercial child pornography still being distributed in the United States is smuggled in from foreign countries—primarily by pedophiles. The risks are usually too high for the strictly commercial dealer. Because of their sexual and personal interests, however, pedophiles are more willing to take those risks. Their motive goes beyond just profit. Commercial child pornography is still assembled and is much more readily available in foreign countries. United States citizens, however, seem to be the main customers for this material. Some offenders collect their commercial child pornography in ways that make it appear to be homemade child pornography (e.g., by taking photographs of pictures in magazines; cutting up pictures and mounting them in photo albums, with names and descriptive information written below; or putting homemade labels on commercial videotapes). If necessary, highly experienced investigators and forensic laboratories can be of assistance in making distinctions between homemade and commercially produced child pornography.

Homemade Child Pornography

Contrary to what its name implies, homemade child pornography can be as "good" as, if not better than, the quality of any commercial pornography. The pedophile has a personal interest in the product. "Homemade" simply means it was not originally produced primarily for commercial sale. Although commercial child pornography is not openly sold anywhere in this country, homemade child pornography is continually produced, swapped, and traded in almost every community in the United States. While rarely found in "adult" bookstores, child pornography is frequently found in the homes and offices of doctors, lawyers, teachers, ministers, and other apparent pillars of the community. There is, however, a connection between commercial and homemade child pornography. Sometimes homemade child pornography is sold or winds up in commercial child pornography magazines, movies, or videos. The same pictures are reproduced and circulated again and again. With rapidly increasing frequency, more and more of both commercial and homemade child pornography is in video format. This actually increases the odds of finding child pornography in any investigation.

It is important for the law enforcement investigator to realize that most of the children in prepubescent child pornography were not abducted into sexual slavery. They were seduced into posing for these pictures or videos by a pedophile they probably know. They were never missing children. The children in child pornography are frequently smiling or have neutral expressions on their faces because they have been seduced into the activity after having had their inhibitions lowered by clever offenders. In some cases, their own parents took the pictures or made them available for others to take the pictures. Children in pubescent or technical child pornography, however, are more likely to be missing children—especially runaways—being exploited by morally indiscriminate pimps or profiteers. In contrast to adult pornography, but consistent with the gender preference of most preferential child molesters, there are more boys than girls in child pornography.

In understanding the nature of child pornography, the law enforcement officer must recognize the distinction between technical and simulated child pornography. The Child Protection Act of 1984 defines a *child* as anyone under the age of 18. Therefore, a sexually explicit photograph of a 15-, 16-, or 17-year-old girl or boy is *technical child pornography*. Technical child pornography does not look like child pornography, but it is. The production, distribution, and, in some cases, possession of this type of child pornography could and should be investigated under appropriate child pornography statutes. Technical child pornography is an exception to much of what we say about child pornography. It often is produced, distributed, and consumed by individuals who are not child molesters or pedophiles; it is openly sold around the United States; and it more often portrays females than males. Because it looks like adult pornography, it is more like adult pornography.

However, sexually explicit photographs of 18-year-old or older males or females are not legally child pornography. But if the person portrayed in such material is young looking, dressed youthfully, or made up to look young, the material could be of interest to pedophiles. This is *simulated child pornography*. Simulated child pornography looks like child pornography, but it is not. It is designed to appeal to the pedophile but it is not legally child pornography because the individuals portrayed are over 18. This illustrates the importance, and sometimes the difficulty, in proving the age of the child in the photographs or videotapes. Particularly difficult is pornography portraying underage children pretending to be overage models pretending to be underage children.

Uses of Child Pornography Collections

Although the reasons why pedophiles collect child pornography and erotica are conjecture, we can be more certain as to how this material is used. Study and police investigations have identified certain criminal uses of the material.

Child pornography and child erotica are used for the sexual arousal and gratification of pedophiles. They use child pornography the same way other people use adult pornography—to feed sexual fantasies. Some pedophiles only collect and fantasize about the material without acting out the fantasies, but in most cases the arousal and fantasy fueled by the pornography is only a prelude to actual sexual activity with children.

A second use of child pornography and erotica is to lower children's inhibitions. A child who is reluctant to engage in sexual activity with an adult or to pose for sexually explicit photos can sometimes be convinced by viewing other children having "fun" participating in the activity. Peer pressure can have a tremendous effect on children; if other children are involved, the child might be led to believe that the activity is acceptable. When the pornography is used to lower inhibitions, the children portrayed will usually *appear* to be having a good time.

Books on human sexuality, books on sex education, and sex manuals are also used to lower inhibitions. Children accept what they see in books, and many pedophiles have used sex education books to prove to children that such sexual behavior is acceptable. Adult pornography is also used, particularly with adolescent boy victims, to arouse them or to lower inhibitions.

A third major use of child pornography collections is blackmail. If a pedophile already has a relationship with a child, seducing the child into sexual activity is only part of the plan. The pedophile must also ensure that the child keeps the secret. Children are most afraid of pictures being shown to their friends. Pedophiles use many techniques to blackmail; one of them is through photographs taken of the child. If the child threatens to tell his or her parents or the authorities, the existence of sexually explicit photographs can be an effective silencer.

A fourth use of child pornography and erotica is as a medium of exchange. Some pedophiles exchange photographs of children for access to, or phone numbers of, other children. The quality and the theme of the material determine its value as an exchange medium. Rather than paying cash for access to a child, the pedophile may exchange a small part (usually duplicates) of his collection. The younger the child and the more bizarre the acts, the greater the value of the pornography.

A fifth use of the collected material is profit. Some people involved in the sale and distribution of child pornography are not pedophiles, they are profiteers. In contrast, most pedophiles seem to collect child erotica and pornography for reasons other than profit. Some pedophiles may begin nonprofit trading, which they pursue until they accumulate certain amounts or types of photographs, which are then sold to commercial dealers for reproduction in commercial child pornography magazines. Others combine their pedophiliac interest with their profit motive. Some collectors even have their own photographic reproduction equipment. Thus, the photograph of a child taken with or without parental knowledge by a neighborhood pedophile in any U.S. community can wind up in a commercial child pornography magazine with worldwide distribution.

Sex Tourism

Child pornography is closely tied to another form of child sexual exploitation—that of **sex tourism.** Sex tourism, which is also a by-product of sex trafficking, is defined by the United Nations as "tourism organized with the primary purpose of facilitating the effecting of a commercial-sexual relationship with a child."[80] Nearly half of sex tourism cases were closely connected to child pornography.[81]

Sex tourism allows pedophiles, mostly men,[82] to either arrange a trip through a travel agency that specializes in sex tours, or arrange travel themselves to an area known for child prostitution and child sex trafficking. Some of these travel agencies are virtual, or Internet based, and can be found among networks of child pornographers. Others hide behind the front of commercial travel agents. For example, Big Apple Oriental Tours, located in New York City, was discovered to have taken clients to nightclubs in Philippines, Thailand, and Cambodia, where tour guides actually negotiated fees and sexual acts on behalf of their clients.[83] However, many pedophiles simply travel to areas known for lax law enforcement and bustling child sex industries to pick and choose for themselves.

The place most associated with the child sex tourist industry is Thailand. American servicemen at military bases are seen as the root of the sex tourism industry there, because men on leave created such a demand for sex workers that young girls were swept up to meet it.[84] Today, the Thai government estimates that 10,000 children are involved in the commercial sex industry; however, nongovernmental agencies believe that the number is as high as 800,000. Growth in the demand for young boys in the area are attributed almost entirely to the sex tour industry.[85] Thailand is hardly the only destination for sex tourists, however. Other countries with abundant opportunities for child sex tourists include Mexico, India, Indonesia, Nepal, the Philippines, Cambodia, China, and Colombia[86] (Figure 11-10). What is surprising to many people is that the United States is also a popular destination for sex tourists seeking children, with Las Vegas and New Orleans serving as hot spots for affluent pedophiles.[87]

About 24–25% of the world sex tourists are American, making up the largest concentration from any one country.[88] Some travel with the singular intent of abusing children, whereas others engage in the practice opportunistically while on business trips or family vacations.[89] Regardless of the intent, American law specifically forbids the practice of sex tourism. Federal statutes under Chapter 18, sections 23 and 24 of the U.S. Code prohibit traveling across state lines or into the United States for the purpose of engaging in any illicit sexual conduct (which includes any commercial sex act with a person under 18) and furthermore prohibit an American citizen or national from engaging in illicit sexual conduct outside the United States. A violation of this law can result in a 30-year maximum sentence. The law does not require that the citizen have traveled outside the country with the intent of engaging in illicit sexual conduct in a foreign country. In 2003, the Protect Act, signed into law by President George W. Bush, reinforced these provisions.[90] The Department of Homeland Security has also developed the "Operation Predator" initiative to combat child exploitation, child pornography, and child sex tourism, with Immigrations and Customs Enforcement acting as the primary investigative agency. The US has also funded global programs that conduct major public awareness and deterrence campaigns aimed at sex tourists, including internet messages, pamphlets at international airports and public service announcements.[91]

Use of The Computer and The Internet in Child Pornography

Computers have become a pervasive part of daily life. Unfortunately, the ubiquity of the computer, and by extension the Internet, is an asset to the child pornographer (Figure 11-11). Child pornographers use personal computers to create, distribute, and catalog pornographic depictions of children and to widen their net of victimization.

Many child pornographers are compulsive record keepers, and for them the computer as a cataloging tool is electronic gold. While stable people might use computers to track a bank balance or store family vacation photos, law enforcement investigations have determined that child pornographers use computers to organize and store

GIRLS FOR SALE

By Nicholas Kristoff

Poipet, Cambodia

One thinks of slavery as an evil confined to musty sepia photographs. But there are 21st-century versions of slaves as well, girls like Srey Neth.

I met Srey Neth, a lovely, giggly wisp of a teenager, here in the wild smuggling town of Poipet in northwestern Cambodia. Girls here are bought and sold, but there is an important difference compared with the 19th century: many of these modern slaves will be dead of AIDS by their 20s.

Some 700,000 people are trafficked around the world each year, many of them just girls. They form part of what I believe will be the paramount moral challenge we will face in this century: to address the brutality that is the lot of so many women in the developing world. Yet it's an issue that gets little attention and that most American women's groups have done shamefully little to address.

Poipet, 220 miles on bouncy roads from Phnom Penh, is a dusty collection of dirt alleys lined with brothels, where teenage girls clutch at any man walking by. It has a reputation as one of the wildest places in Cambodia, an anything-goes town ruled by drugs, gangs, gambling, and prostitution.

The only way to have access to the girls is to appear to be a customer. So I put out the word that I wanted to meet young girls and stayed at the seedy $8-a-night Phnom Pich Guest House—and a woman who is a pimp soon brought Srey Neth to my room.

Srey Neth claimed to be 18 but looked several years younger. She insisted at first (through my Khmer interpreter) that she was free and not controlled by the guesthouse. But soon she told her real story: a female cousin had arranged her sale and taken her to the guesthouse. Now she was sharing a room with three other prostitutes, and they were all pimped to guests.

"I can walk around in Poipet, but only with a close relative of the owner," she said. "They keep me under close watch. They do not let me go out alone. They're afraid I would run away."

Why not try to escape at night?

"They would get me back, and something bad would happen. Maybe a beating. I heard that when a group of girls tried to escape, they locked them in the rooms and beat them up."

"What about the police?" I asked. "Couldn't you call out to the police for help?"

"The police wouldn't help me because they get bribes from the brothel owners," Srey Neth said, adding that senior police officials had come to the guesthouse for sex with her.

I asked Srey Neth how much it would cost to buy her freedom. She named an amount equivalent to $150.

"Do you really want to leave?" I asked. "Are you sure you wouldn't come back to this?"

She had been watching TV and listlessly answering my questions. Now she turned abruptly and snorted. "This is a hell," she said sharply, speaking with passion for the first time. "You think I want to do this?"

Another girl, Srey Mom, grabbed at me as I walked down the street. She wouldn't let go, tugging me toward the inner depths of her brothel—but she looked so young and pitiable that I couldn't help thinking that she really wanted me to tug her away.

So I did. I paid the owner $8 to spring her for the evening and then took her away for an interview.

The owner let Srey Mom go out unsupervised, it turned out, partly because she had been a prostitute for several years and was trusted to return—and partly because her dark complexion meant that she was of little value anyway. The brothel sold her to men for just $2.50, compared with the $10 commanded by the lighter-skinned Srey Neth.

I asked Srey Mom what her freedom would cost. Payment of about $70 in debts to her brothel owner, she said. Two girls in her brothel had been freed after they found boyfriends who paid their debts, she said, and she spoke of her longing to see her sisters and the rest of her family in her village on the other side of Cambodia.

"Do you really want to leave the brothel?" I asked.

"I love myself," she answered simply. "I do not want to let my life be destroyed by what I'm doing now."

That's when I made a firm decision I'd been toying with for some time: I would try to buy freedom for these two girls and return them to their families. I'll tell you in my column on Wednesday what happens next.

Source: *The New York Times*, January 17, 2005. The follow-up article, "Bargaining for Freedom" may be found at www.nytimes.com/2004/01/21/opinion/21KRIS.html?ex=1190088000&en=4df06d73f201c345&ei=5070.

▲ **FIGURE 11-10**

Prostitutes as slaves

Writer Nicholas Kristoff paid $203 to free Srey Mom from a Cambodian brothel. (© Naka Nathaniel/New York Times)

◀ **FIGURE 11-11**
Child pornography
Customs agent Donald Daufenbach shows off some of the computers seized in a child pornography raid. Many cyber crime investigators work in multi-agency task forces that focus on child porn and cases involving adults soliciting children for sex, so-called traveler cases.
(© AP/Wide World Photos/Douglas C. Pizac)

photographs and movies that graphically depict scenes of sexual exploitation of children.

Child pornographers can acquire additional material through instant contact with other pedophiles. Chat rooms, bulletin boards, newsgroups, instant messaging, and e-mail are just some of the means child pornographers currently use to communicate with other pedophiles. Once he has made contact with willing cohorts, a pedophile can electronically exchange photographs, movies, and other depictions of child pornography. In a matter of seconds, a child pornographer may send or receive child pornography to or from almost anywhere in the world. Web cams have even made it possible to broadcast and receive live, real-time images of child molestation and pornography.

In addition, the home computer provides tools that make it easy to store and retrieve names and addresses of accessible victims. This library of victims can be developed with great ease and efficiency by way of referral from the pedophile's perverse network of colleagues.

Also, pedophiles can use computers to directly establish a rapport with children. Adolescent boys who spend a great amount of their time online are at particularly high risk of this type of contact. Again, using chat rooms, e-mail, and instant messaging, the pedophile may pose as an adolescent to gain the trust of the child. He may then indirectly victimize the child by sharing with him or her sexually explicit information or material. He may further attempt to obtain the child's phone number or

whereabouts in order to engage in face-to-face contact and direct sexual victimization.

Desktop publishing holds unique possibilities for child pornographers. Like any other small publisher, pedophiles who use child pornography as a profit-making business can produce high-quality prints with relative ease. They can collect, record, "publish," and distribute pornographic material either as hard copy or as an electronic file. They can also create false or doctored graphic images of children in pornographic positions. The question arises, then: Are such false images punishable by law?

In the United States, Title 18, Section 2252, of the U.S. code, more commonly known as the Child Pornography Prevention Act (CPPA), deals with this aspect of child pornography and the Internet. The CPPA makes it a crime to sell, possess with intent to sell, download, or produce child pornography or any visual depiction that is intended to *represent or resemble* child pornography. This includes material "transported, by any means, including by computer, if (i) the producing of such visual depiction involves the use of a minor engaging in sexually explicit conduct; and (ii) such *visual depiction* is of such conduct."[92]

We must reiterate that there does not have to be an actual child involved in the making of such pornography in order for it to be legally punishable; there must be merely the presence of the "visual depiction" of a child. This stipulation assumes that there are harmful secondary effects associated with virtual child pornography, namely, as mentioned earlier, that pedophiles may use graphic depictions of child pornography to seduce children to join in the "fun."[93]

The movie *Traffic* contains a scene in which an underage character enacts having sex with a drug dealer. Under the CPPA, this scene would, in legal terms, be viewed as child pornography. For this reason, the Free Speech Coalition, an adult trade organization, has challenged the CPPA claiming that it is overly vague and violates First Amendment free speech rights.[94] A federal district court ruled against the Free Speech Coalition in 1997, but the 9th Circuit reversed that decision in late 2001, and the reversal was upheld by the Supreme Court in Spring 2002.[95]

Unfortunately, owing to the anonymous nature of the Internet and the sheer volume of Internet activity, transactions involving child pornography are often difficult for government agencies to track. As discussed in Chapter 16, "Computer Crime," however, some investigators are taking advantage of the anonymity of the Net by posing as minors in order to identify pedophiles. Once a pedophile has been discovered, his records of his computer activities can frequently be used as incriminating evidence. Furthermore, under strictly regulated circumstances, investigators may be able to track the Internet activity of pedophiles with the watchdog program "DCS 100."[96]

Child pornography is often found in computer files on hard drives. Whenever such a condition may exist, it is important to remember the special techniques of investigating technologically based crime and retrieving digital images as evidence. (For a more thorough discussion of digital forensics and the investigation of child pornography involving computers, refer to Chapter 16, "Computer Crime.")

Currently, 50% of Internet child pornography cases call for investigation abroad.[97] The recent upsurge in worldwide child pornography prevention and detention agencies lends credence to the notion that child pornography on the Internet cannot be tackled by one country alone but has to be dealt with globally.[98]

INTERNET CRIMES AGAINST CHILDREN

With the popularity of the Internet in homes and schools, and particularly with the advent of social networking sites such as MySpace and Facebook, child pornography is no longer the only threat to children on the internet. Cyber enticement through social sites, instant messaging, e-mail communications, and gaming connections can lure an unsuspecting child into sexual contact with a pedophile. Although only a small percentage of the nation's youth experience online solicitation for sexual purposes, the prospect is a frightening one to parents and law enforcement officers. (See Figure 11-12.)

Most of the youth exposed to online solicitations were girls between the ages of 14 and 17. Profiles of those soliciting children sexually show that they tend to be men more than 70% of the time, and about 43% of these men are over the age of 18.[99] About 75% of the time, the person soliciting the child asked to meet them in person.[100]

As a result of the nearly 30 million children[101] on the Internet today, parents, law enforcement officials, and even website managers are taking steps to ensure that online solicitations do not result in a criminal act against a child. The Internet Crimes Against Children (ICAC) Task Force Program was developed in response to these issues and provides resources to local and state law enforcement agencies to "enhance their investigative response to offenders who use the Internet, online communication systems, or other computer technology to sexually exploit children."[102] The ICAC program provides training courses, technical assistance, and presentation materials to police agencies and is tasked with organizing task forces of national, state, and local departments to tackle investigations of online exploitation. There are currently 46 such task forces throughout the nation.[103]

Websites such as MySpace have also joined in the investigation of online crimes against children. In April of 2007, the attorney generals of eight states (Connecticut, Georgia, Idaho, North Carolina, Ohio, Pennsylvania, Mississippi, and New Hampshire) drafted a letter to the popular social networking site calling on them to do more to remove pedophiles that were registered as users on the site. This followed reports of seven Connecticut girls being sexually assaulted by men they met on MySpace, and as many as 100 reports of some type of criminal activity perpetrated by adults who used the site to contact children.[104] The issue was further called into question after a *Wired News* reporter cross-indexed a number of user profiles with sex offender databases and found 744 convicted sex offenders on the site.[105] By July of 2007, MySpace announced that it had found and deleted nearly 29,000 profiles linked to sex offenders.[106]

The Internet—although providing limitless educational and entertainment possibilities to children—is clearly a means for predators to exploit children in a variety of ways. Internet crimes against children can include child pornography, communications involving sex trafficking and tourism, and even harassment among peers (discussed in Chapter 16). Although law enforcement officers can pose as children in internet chat rooms in an effort to lure sex offenders, the process is time-consuming. The best tool to protect children from Internet crime is parental education and involvement. The more a child is supervised while on the Internet, the less likely he or she is to be a victim of exploitation.[107]

NBC's popular show To Catch *a Predator* takes a vigilante approach to catching, embarrassing, and arresting men who solicit underage boys and girls in Internet chat rooms. The show, attracting up to 7 million viewers per episode, has partnered with a private watch dog group known as Perverted Justice to pose as youngsters in chat rooms. The decoys often engage in highly sexualized conversation with adults attracted to them by screen names that suggest youth and innocence. If the adult solicits an in-person meeting, the decoy gives them an address where police are stationed outside and cameramen lie in wait for the ambush. Often, the adult will come into the home, and engage in light banter with a decoy chosen because he or she looks underage. At that point, the decoy leaves the room under the pretense of getting a drink, or changing clothes. The show's host, Chris Hansen, and his cameramen descend on the hapless predator, peppering him with questions about why he would solicit a child for sex. More often than not, the adult has a number of predictable excuses at hand, including "I thought he/she was 18" or "I've never done this before". Most deny that they are there to have sex with the purported minor. Hansen will subsequently present a transcript of the graphic instant messaging chat, making for truly squirm-worthy television. Once the predator leaves the home, law enforcement descends, making an arrest or citation related to the online solicitation. The show is certainly compelling enough to watch, but critics charge that the show is ethically questionable for its vigilante techniques, blurry lines between justice and law enforcement, and issues of entrapment. This has been further strengthened after the suicide of a Texas man who was caught and taped for the show. Perhaps as a result, *Dateline* is moving away from the subject of child predators, using Hansen's trademark trapping to lure in con men and identity thieves. However, the show has certainly left its mark on national consciousness, bringing Internet-enabled exploitation to the front of the minds of parents and potential victims.

(Sources: *Dateline NBC* website: www.msnbc.msn.com/id/10912603/; B. Stelter, "To Catch a Predator Is Falling Prey to Advertisers' Sensibilities," *The New York Times*, August 27, 2007.)

▲ **FIGURE 11-12   Dateline NBC: To catch a predator**
Dateline NBC's Chris Hansen interviews a young man caught soliciting an underage girl online. (© NBC Newswire)

INFANT ABDUCTION

Infant abduction is the taking of a child less than 1 year old by a nonfamily member. Although the **FBI** (Federal Bureau of Investigation) classifies such cases as kidnappings, infant abductions occur, by definition, for reasons not typically associated with kidnappings. For the most part, infant abductions do not appear to be motivated by a desire for money, sex, revenge, or custody, which are considered traditional motives in kidnapping cases.[108]

Since 1987, an average of 14 infants have been abducted annually. These abductions had no boundaries in terms of the location or size of the hospital, or of the race, sex, or socioeconomic background of the infant.

Profile of The Abductor

The data from infant abductions indicate certain offender characteristics. Investigators can use these traits to profile and apprehend suspects.

By way of general background, infant abductors usually are women, who account for 141 of the 145 cases analyzed. Offenders whose ages were verified ranged from 14 to 48 years old, with an average age of 28. Race was determined in 142 cases: 63 offenders were white, 54 were black, and 25 were Hispanic. The typical abductor may not have a criminal record. If a criminal record does exist, it likely will consist of nonviolent offenses, such as check fraud or shoplifting. To gain further insight into infant abductors and the crimes they commit, members of the FBI's National Center for the Analysis of Violent Crime (NCAVC) interviewed 16 abductors.[109] Offenders included whites, blacks, and Hispanics and ranged in age (at the time of the abduction) from 19 to 42. They had abducted infants in 10 different states. Nine of the abductors targeted hospitals directly; 5 approached the infant's residence; and 2 chose other locations. Although none had committed a violent crime before, 4 killed the infant's mother before stealing her baby.

Five of the abductors were single, 7 were married, and 4 were either separated or divorced. Ten had no children. Although 13 offenders said they were involved in a significant relationship at the time of the abduction, many described it as "rocky," stressful, and lacking in communication.

Motivation

Although little research exists on the topic of infant abductors' motivation, the cases outlined here illustrate that the need to present their partners with a baby often drives the female offender. Ten of the women interviewed admitted they had faked pregnancy. One of them recalled crying in the parking lot of a hospital, wondering if she should tell her husband she was not pregnant. Though she knew in her heart that she should tell him the truth, she thought he would leave her if she did. She chose to remain silent. Later, she followed a mother home and stole her baby.

Another woman had feigned pregnancy successfully with her husband before they were married, but her second attempt proved unsuccessful. After her conviction for infant abduction, her husband admitted that he would not have married her had he known she was not pregnant.

Five other women claimed to have miscarried without telling their partners, although no evidence existed to confirm their pregnancies. One said she had miscarried four months into her pregnancy but had continued living the lie, rationalizing that the stress placed on her by her husband's desire to have a baby had prompted her to deceive him.

Thus, as these cases illustrate, the infant abductor frequently attempts to prevent her husband or boyfriend from deserting her or tries to win back his affection by claiming pregnancy and, later, the birth of a child.[110] She may view a baby as the only way to salvage the relationship with her partner.[111]

According to the National Center for Missing and Exploited Children (NCMEC), sometimes the infant abductor is driven by a desire to experience vicariously the birth of a child she is "unable to conceive" or carry to term.[112] She is desperate to "bask in the rapture of baby love—to feel adored and needed."[113] Just as many expectant mothers tell others the "good news," the typical infant abductor truly believes that "she is about to give birth, and she fully expects everyone to accept the reality she has attempted to create."[114]

Planning

Some of the interviewed abductors spent a great deal of time planning their crimes; others apparently acted on impulse. Their efforts ranged from a few hours to over nine months before the abduction. Eleven of the abductors interviewed gained weight prior to the abduction: one gained 61 pounds. Eleven purchased baby goods, and 12 told others they were pregnant. Then, when it came time to "deliver," the abductors employed such tactics as surveilling hospitals, monitoring birth announcements in the newspaper, following mothers home, and posing as hospital employees, baby-sitters, or social workers.

One abductor drove over 300 miles to steal an infant from an area where she had once resided. She also admitted to "checking out the security" of at least two area hospitals. While her actions appear premeditated, when asked to explain them, she responded: "I knew I was going somewhere, but I didn't know where. It was like I escaped into this little dream."

In fact, though most women planned events leading up to the abduction, many seemed to have not prepared for the act itself. They also could not, or would not, recall the mechanics of how they had carried out the abduction. One woman, who had entered a residence and murdered the mother before stealing her baby, remembered: "I had no plan of action, you know, it just was whatever happened, happened." The same woman had visited at least three hospitals, while wearing maternity clothes, prior to committing her crime.

After the abduction, 14 of the 16 offenders openly displayed the stolen infant to others. Six claimed to have given birth in an area hospital; four, out of town; and two, at home. Only three of the abductors altered the baby's appearance. According to one abductor, she cut the baby's hair to make him look younger.

The Scene of The Crime

Location

Traditionally, the hospital setting has been the primary target for infant abductions. In the analysis discussed earlier, 83 of the 145 infants were taken from within a hospital: 49 from the mother's room, 14 from the nursery, 13 from pediatric hospital rooms, and 7 from other hospital locations.

Bolder criminals try nonhospital locations. Three babies were stolen from a clinic or doctor's office; two from daycare centers. One quick-thinking abductor snatched a baby from the hospital curb. Forty brazen abductors targeted the residence of the infant or of a baby-sitter.

Time of Day

Even in these emotion-driven crimes, the perpetrators showed signs of logic. In the majority of these cases, the abductors chose to act during normal business hours: of the 145 cases, 121 occurred on a weekday, and in the 124 cases where the time of the abduction was recorded, 95 occurred between 8 A.M. and 6 P.M. The reason for this appears to be ease of movement. That is, in a hospital during normal working hours, abductors could disguise themselves as employees and slip in and out virtually undetected. Similarly, at a residence, there would be less likelihood of confronting a spouse during the workday.

Month

From January 1983 through December 1994, abductions occurred more frequently between May and October and less frequently between November and April, with the exception of December. More infant abductions occurred in December (20 total) and May (19 total) than in any other months. Historically, November has shown the lowest number of abductions (a total of 8). Although a pattern seems to exist here, it simply could be coincidence: most of the 16 abductors interviewed had feigned pregnancy; they had to "deliver" a baby 9 months later, regardless of the time of year.

Method

Whether they steal babies from a hospital or from another location, abductors usually gain access through a con or ruse, as did 101 of the 145 subjects studied. Methods vary but have included posing as hospital employees, baby-sitters, or social workers. Some abductors have asked to use the telephone to get into the victim's home.

While cons help abductors gain access, they do not always make the abduction itself easier. As a result, abductors have used force either alone or in combination with a con in 16 cases, leading to the deaths of seven mothers and one father. Of these forcible abductions, 10 occurred in the victim's home, and the abductors used guns in 11 cases.

Abductions away from the hospital pose access difficulties for the offender and may account for the need to exercise force. In these cases, the degree of force ranged from threatening or binding the mother to shooting and stabbing the parents. In one of the most gruesome cases, the abductor strangled the mother and removed her unborn child from her womb, performing a crude caesarean section with car keys. Miraculously, the infant survived. Unfortunately, the mother did not. In 25 cases, the abductor stole the infant without having direct contact with another person at the moment of abduction.

Investigative Strategies

Successful resolution of any case depends on several factors, including the efforts of law enforcement. In 135 of the 136 resolved cases, the amount of time the infants remained missing ranged from mere hours to just over 300 days. Ninety-three of the babies were recovered in two days or less. Overall, law enforcement has a 94% rate of resolution.

One of the primary investigative strategies in infant abduction cases has been using the media to activate community awareness. Friends, relatives, and/or neighbors identified the abductor after media reports in approximately 53 out of 129 cases. Anonymous phone tips resulted in the capture of 20 abductors after media exposure. Of the 16 abductors who had been arrested as a result of media exposure and subsequently interviewed by researchers; four admitted to following media reports, but none altered her plans on the basis of the coverage. In short, the media played a significant role in identifying the offenders but did not affect their actions. Accordingly, investigators probably need not fear that publicizing a case will bring harm to the infant.

The Parental Interview

It is critical that parents be interviewed separately from each other and from other family members and reporting parties. Responding officers may feel reluctant to conduct separate interviews of the parents because of their emotionally escalated state. Conversely, if the parents do not appear particularly concerned about the child's absence, the officers may not view separate interviews as necessary. While they cannot determine what a parent's "normal" reaction to a missing child would be, officers must remain objective and realize that a family member may later become a suspect if the child has been abducted. They must balance this objectivity with empathy and support if the parents are in a state of emotional crisis. Most importantly, officers must ensure that they interview parents individually, preserve potential evidence, and document each parent's demeanor and attitude throughout the interview.

During the parental interview, officers should quickly compile accurate physical characteristics of the child, such as his or her appearance, age, and clothing, and should obtain recent photographs and videotapes. Officers should attempt to include full criminal- and psychiatric-history checks of all family members who had access to the child, as well as acquire a local agency history of any prior abuse or neglect calls to the home. In separate interviews of family members, responding officers should question whether the child's absence shows a significant deviation from established patterns of behavior.[115] However, further exploration into the victimology of the missing child can answer this question.

Victimology of The Missing Child

To understand whether the child's absence is consistent with established patterns of behavior, officers first must understand the child's normal actions before the disappearance. Officers should use the following guidelines for assessing the personality of the missing child.[116]

- Develop and verify a detailed time line of the child's last known activities up to the time the child was last seen or reported missing.
- Determine habits, hobbies, interests, and favorite activities.
- Identify normal activity patterns, and determine the victim's known comfort zone. Officers should assess the child's survival skills, ability to adapt to new or strange circumstances, and intellectual maturity. Did the child frequently travel alone? Did the child have a routine where independent travel occurred on a regular basis (e.g., riding a bike to school)? What fears and phobias did the child exhibit? For example, if the child was afraid of the dark, the probability of leaving voluntarily at night is low. Similarly, if the missing child was afraid to travel without a favorite item, such as a toy or security blanket, and the item remains in the house after the disappearance, the child may not have left voluntarily.
- Note any recent changes in behavior or activity patterns and any unusual events and stressors. Officers should explore any motivations for leaving. How does the child normally deal with stressful situations? Have any recent traumatic or stressful events caused such a prompt departure? Have any abuses occurred within the residence or family? Officers also should determine whether there were any recent changes in sleeping and eating patterns that would indicate stress.
- Identify and separately interview family members, close friends, schoolmates, teachers, coworkers, and other significant individuals. The FBI's National Center for the Analysis of Violent Crime has created a general assessment form for distribution to family members and associates that can assist in police officers' efforts to understand the child's personality.[117]
- Determine any history of alcohol and other drug use. Does the child have any particular medical conditions or allergies? If so, are the child's medications for the existing conditions still in the house? The presence of medications that the child needs may indicate an involuntary departure.
- Identify and interview boyfriends and/or girlfriends; determine normal dating patterns, including sexual activity. If the missing child is a postpubescent female, are there pregnancy and abortion issues? If so, officers should consider contacting local pregnancy, health, and abortion clinics. Also, officers should familiarize themselves with department policy and legal issues concerning confidentiality if they find the missing child at such a clinic.

Obtain and review any personal writings, diaries, drawings, and schoolwork, including any entries into a personal computer or interaction with online systems or services. A critical item often overlooked in the missing-child call is the presence or absence of journals or diaries. Besides the obvious insights that diaries may provide into the child's state of mind, the presence or absence of any written communication can prove relevant. A child who consistently and regularly has expressed thoughts and feelings in writing might not depart voluntarily without leaving some form of written communication for people left behind.[118] Similarly, calendars or schedules indicating planned events may provide insight into the child's possible motivation for staying or leaving.

- Determine any history of running away, discontent with home life, or ideas of suicide. Has the child disappeared voluntarily on prior occasions? If so, officers should note the last time the child ran away and the length of time missing. Did the child go to friends, other family members, or a runaway shelter? Officers should determine what enabled the child to run away successfully or, conversely, what prevented the child from sustaining a long-term absence. What happened that prompted the child's departure in prior absences? Officers should determine whether the child exhibited any runaway tendencies (e.g., staying out all night), threats to leave, or other behaviors that violated clear directives from parents or caregivers. Officers also should determine the existence of any prior suicide attempts or gestures by the child and consider the possibility that the child has disappeared as a result of a self-inflicted injury.

These observations will assist officers in crafting the child's victimology, which will indicate whether the child had the motivation and capability of leaving voluntarily. If the victim assessment suggests that these two factors do not exist, officers must consider the possibility that an abduction has occurred.

Checklist for Law Enforcement

The following checklist describes the most important steps that law enforcement can take as the investigation begins. The order of the steps is likely to vary depending on individual circumstances.

- Issue a BOLO (Be On the Look Out) bulletin to be broadcast to local law enforcement agencies alerting them to the missing child, and send a teletype locally or regionally.
- Implement the **AMBER Plan,** which is a voluntary partnership between law enforcement and broadcasters to activate the bulletins in the most serious child abduction cases. (This plan is discussed in greater detail shortly.)

- Immediately enter the child's name into the National Crime Information Center (NCIC) registry of missing persons. There is no waiting period for entry into NCIC for children under age 18.
- Request the National Center for Missing and Exploited Children (NCMEC) fax the child's picture to law enforcement agencies throughout the country.
- Inform the **FBI's Child Abduction and Serial Murder Investigative Resource Center (CAS-MIRC)** of the case or ask for assistance if there is a chance the abduction was predatory.
- Notify the local FBI field office in case additional services and support are needed.
- Notify the state missing children's bureau and request additional services if needed.
- Secure the crime scene—for instance, the location outside a home where the child might have been abducted—and the child's bedroom. The officers who respond initially to the call must evaluate the contents and appearance of the child's room and retrieve the child's used bedding, clothing, and shoes and place them in clean bags to be used as scent articles. Also retrieve the child's toothbrush, hairbrush, and other items that might contain DNA evidence. Protect footprints in dust, mud, or snow to preserve the scent. Determine if personal items are missing, and interview the last persons known to have seen the child.
- Request tracking dogs or a helicopter equipped with an infrared or a heat-sensitive device (to detect heat emitted from the body) if needed after the residence, yard, and surrounding areas have been searched unsuccessfully.
- Advise airlines, airports, bus and taxicab companies, subways, ferries, and ports of the disappearance as necessary and distribute posters of the missing child.
- Revisit various "hot spots" or checkpoints at the same time of day and/or same day of the week following the disappearance to see if any eyewitnesses can be uncovered.
- Contact the neighborhood watch to see if anything suspicious was reported.
- Check the daily log of parking and traffic tickets and traffic stops to see if anything relates to the child's disappearance.
- Check the convicted sex offender registry to find out if a potential suspect lived or was ever stopped by the police in the area.
- Collect and review local newspapers in hopes of possible clues or leads to aid in the search. Check out local regional events and activities—such as carnivals, county fairs, festivals, sports events, and music concerts—and want ads for hired help in search of leads regarding the predator and/or any witnesses to the disappearance.

▲ **FIGURE 11-13   AMBER alert**
An AMBER alert is displayed on a highway messaging sign increasing the opportunity for a member of the public to find the missing/kidnapped child. (© AP/Wide World Photos)

- Establish a procedure for handling extortion attempts, if needed.
- Contact neighboring jurisdictions to find out if incidents of a similar nature have occurred there.[119]

The Amber Alert Plan

The AMBER Alert program is a voluntary partnership between law enforcement agencies, state transportation officials and radio, television and internet broadcasters to activate an urgent news bulletin in child abduction cases (Figure 11-13). Broadcasters use the Emergency Alert System, formerly known as the Emergency Broadcast System, to air a description of the missing child, the suspected abductor, and any vehicles involved in the abduction. The program was first introduced after the kidnap and murder of 9-year old Amber Hagerman of the Dallas-Fort Worth area and is now established in all 50 states.

How Does the AMBER Alert work?

Once law enforcement is notified of an abducted child, they must determine whether the case meets the criteria set forth in the AMBER alert plan. The national AMBER Alert Coordinator, affiliated with the US Department of Justice Office of Justice Programs, has recommended the following criteria:

- There is reasonable belief by law enforcement that an abduction has occurred.
- The law enforcement agency believes that the child is in imminent danger of serious bodily injury or death.

- There is enough descriptive information about the victim and the abduction for law enforcement to issue an AMBER alert to assist in the recovery of a child.
- The abduction is of a child 17 years old or younger.
- The child's name and other critical data elements, including the Child Abduction Flag, have been entered into the National Crime Information Center system (NCIC).

If these criteria are met, alert information is put together and faxed to radio stations designated as primary stations under EAS. These stations then send the same information to area radio, television, and cable systems where it is broadcast to millions of listeners. Radio stations interrupt programming to announce the alert, and television and cable stations run a "crawl" on the screen with a picture of the missing child.[120]

Time Factors

How long does a runaway child typically stay away from home, and how does the passage of time influence the classification of a missing-child case? The California Department of Justice's Missing/Unidentified Persons Unit has reported the following trends in runaway returns:

TIME FRAME	RUNAWAYS RETURNED
Within 7 days	50%
7–14 days	30
14–30 days	17
More than 30 days	3

These statistics indicate that the majority of runaway children cannot sustain an absence of more than two weeks from home. In general, the longer the absence, the greater the likelihood that an individual has abducted the child or that the child has fallen victim to a violent crime. If the child has a history of running away, officers should determine the length of time the child remained missing during previous absences. If the time length of the current absence grossly exceeds that of previous absences, officers should consider the current disappearance a deviation from normal behavior patterns.

Responding officers should note the amount of time that transpired between when the child was last seen and when the parents or guardian alerted authorities. While 24 hours or more may indicate apathy or neglect, this time frame also may reflect the common misconception that an individual must be missing for 24 hours before law enforcement can respond. The responding officers should construct a time line identifying the parents' activities during this interval. The time line highlights family

dynamics and clarifies the parents' potential role in the child's disappearance.[121]

SEX-OFFENDER REGISTRATION

In October 1989, 11-year-old Jacob Wetterling was abducted less than a 10-minute bike ride from his St. Joseph, Minnesota, home as he, his 10-year-old brother, and their 11-year-old friend rode home from the local video store.[122] Although law enforcement officers never found Jacob or his abductor, they did discover a number of halfway houses in their county that boarded convicted sex offenders from another county.[123]

Ten months after Jacob's disappearance, Pam Lychner, a Houston, Texas, real estate agent, entered a vacant home to prepare to show it to a prospective buyer. She was brutally assaulted by a twice-convicted felon. Her husband saved her life when he interrupted the beating.[124]

In July 1994, 7-year-old Megan Kanka went to a neighbor's home to see his new puppy. The twice-convicted sex offender—who lived across the street from Megan's Hamilton Township, New Jersey, home—raped and murdered Megan and dumped her body in a nearby park.[125]

These tragic events spurred the Wetterlings, the Lychners, and the Kankas to push for legislation that would protect the lives of others. Their efforts spawned sex-offender registration and notification laws that require that states maintain registries of sex offenders and release information about these offenders to the public.

The Laws

In 1994, Congress passed the **Jacob Wetterling Crimes against Children and Sexually Violent Offender Registration Act.**[126] The act required that states create sex-offender registries within three years or lose 10% of their funding under the Edward Byrne Memorial program.[127] Offenders who commit a criminal sexual act against a minor or commit any sexually violent offense must register for a period of 10 years from the date of their release from custody or supervision. All 50 states have sex-offender registration.[128]

The Jacob Wetterling act gave states the option of releasing information about registered sex offenders to the public but did not require that they do so. This changed in 1996 when Congress amended the act to require that states disclose information about registered sex offenders for public safety purposes. This legislation became known as **Megan's Law,** in memory of Megan Kanka.[129]

U.S. Department of Justice guidelines allow states considerable discretion in determining the extent and manner of notification when warning the public about sex offenders living in the community. At least 44 states have passed community notification laws since 1990.[130]

The Pam Lychner Sexual Offender Tracking and Identification Act of 1996[131] mandated the establishment of a national sex-offender database, which the FBI maintains.[132]

This national tracking system gives law enforcement authorities access to sex-offender registration data from all participating states. The Lychner act also requires that the FBI register, and verify the addresses of, sex offenders in states that have not met the minimum compliance standards set forth by the Jacob Wetterling act, although this may change.[133]

Registration Requirements

Although sex-offender registration requirements vary according to state laws, some common features exist in registries throughout the country. In most states, the state criminal justice agency or board (e.g., the state police or state bureau of investigation) maintains the state's registry. Sex offenders, both juveniles and adults, register at local law enforcement or corrections agencies, which then forward the information to the state's central registry. Registry information typically includes the offender's name, address, date of birth, Social Security number, and physical description, as well as fingerprints and a photograph. In addition, Iowa requires information about the sex-offense conviction that triggered the registration, and at least eight states collect samples for DNA identification.[134]

Most state laws require that offenders register only if their convictions occurred after the law's effective date, although some states, such as Minnesota, require that offenders register after they are *charged* with a sexual offense.[135] Offenders receive notice of the registration requirement from the court or registry agency. In Iowa, offenders can contest the registration requirement by filing an application for determination with the state Department of Public Safety.

Usually, offenders must register by a certain number of days after their release from custody or placement on supervision. The types of offenses requiring registration vary according to state law but must comply with the Jacob Wetterling act, which mandates registration for sex crimes against minors and for violent sex crimes. For example, in Iowa, the qualifying offenses are criminal sexual offenses against minors; sexually violent offenses; sexual exploitation; aggravated offenses, including murder, nonparental kidnapping, and false imprisonment; manslaughter; and burglary, if sexual abuse or attempted sexual abuse occurred during the commission of the crime; as well as other relevant offenses, such as indecent exposure.

The registration requirement lasts at least 10 years. Some states require lifetime registration for all or some offenses, and some states allow offenders to petition the court for a reduction.[136] Iowa law requires lifetime registration for offenders deemed "sexual predators" by the courts and for any registered offenders who are convicted of a subsequent sexual offense. In most states, it is a criminal offense to knowingly fail to register or to report subsequent changes in information, such as the registrant's name or address. In Iowa, public officials verify annually the addresses of all registrants.

Notification Features

The most basic form of notification, sometimes referred to as *passive notification,* allows citizens to access registry information at their local law enforcement agencies. In Iowa, citizens must complete a request form at their local police or sheriff's department and provide the name of the person being checked and one of three identifiers: address, date of birth, or Social Security number. If the agency finds the person's name on the registry, it can release certain information about the offender; however, federal guidelines prohibit states from releasing the identities of victims. Employers also may check potential employees. Since Iowa's law took effect in 1995, members of the public have made 14,973 requests for registry information.[137]

Several states provide a toll-free number that citizens can call to obtain information. California and New York operate 900-number services for inquiries.[138] Many states allow public access to sex-offender registry information through Internet sites maintained by criminal justice agencies. This information usually includes offenders' photographs, their biographical data, and information about their previous sex offenses.

In addition to allowing passive notification, a number of states permit government agencies to disseminate information about registered sex offenders to vulnerable individuals and organizations. Using this process, known as *active notification,* officials may choose to notify prior victims, landlords, neighbors, public and private schools, child-care facilities, religious and youth organizations, and other relevant individuals or agencies. Most officials reserve community-wide notification for only the most dangerous sex offenders. Community-wide notification usually involves using the media and public forums such as neighborhood associations and other community meetings.

States have various methods for determining which offenders qualify for active notification. In Florida and Montana, state courts determine which sex offenders pose the greatest threat to the community and target them for active notification.[139] A number of states, including Iowa, allow criminal justice officials or state registry review boards to assess the offender's level of risk, and then law enforcement officials, prosecuting attorneys, or corrections personnel typically make the notification. Louisiana requires that registered sex offenders themselves notify neighbors within one square block in the city or a 3-mile radius in rural areas.[140]

CRIME IN SCHOOLS

Sixty-five years ago, surveys of public school teachers indicated that the most pressing classroom problems were tardiness, talkative students, and gum chewing.[141] Far more serious complaints are currently heard from teachers, administrators, and students—about the presence of

◀ **FIGURE 11-14**
Students and faculty flee from school after shooting
Recently, a number of the nation's high schools have experienced situations in which students have brought guns to school and killed or wounded many people. The FBI's National Center for the Analysis of Violent Crime (NCAVC) has conducted an in-depth review of 18 school shootings. From this analysis, they have developed a threat assessment model to help prevent school violence.
(© Mark Leffingwell/AFP/Corbis)

drugs, gangs, and weapons on campus and the threat of assault, robbery, theft, vandalism, and rape.[142]

According to the popular media, such as *Time* magazine and *U.S. News and World Report,* the problems in our nation's schools may be paralyzing the system.[143] In an effort to develop a systematic procedure for threat assessment and intervention in school violence cases, the FBI's National Center for the Analysis of Violent Crime (NCAVC) conducted an in-depth review of 18 school shootings. Because of confidentiality issues, the shooting cases studied were not identified. The study analyzed the shootings from a behavioral perspective and resulted in the development of the threat assessment intervention model. The model outlines a procedure for evaluating a threat and the person making the threat so that an accurate assessment can be made of the likelihood that the threat will be carried out.

Threat Assessment

A threat is an expression of the intent to do harm or act out violently against someone or something. A threat can be spoken, written, or symbolic—for example, motioning with one's hands as though shooting at another person.

Threat assessment rests on two critical principles: (1) that all threats and all threateners are not equal and (2) that most threateners are unlikely to carry out their threats. However, all threats must be taken seriously and evaluated.

In NCAVC's experience, most threats are made anonymously or under a false name. Because threat assessment relies heavily on evaluating the threatener's background, personality, lifestyle, and resources, identifying the threatener is necessary so that an informed assessment can be made—and so that charges can be brought if the threat

is serious enough to warrant prosecution. If the threatener's identity cannot be determined, the evaluation will have to be based on the threat alone. That assessment may change if the threatener is eventually identified: a threat that was considered low risk may be rated as more serious if new information suggests the threatener is dangerous; conversely, an assessment of high risk may be scaled down if the threatener is identified and found not to have the intent, ability, means, or motive to carry out the threat (Figure 11-14).

Motivation

Threats are made for a variety of reasons. A threat may be a warning signal, a reaction to fear of punishment or some other anxiety, or a demand for attention. It may be intended to taunt; to intimidate; to assert power or control; to punish; to manipulate or coerce; to frighten; to terrorize; to compel someone to do something; to strike back for an injury, injustice, or insult; to disrupt someone's or some institution's life; to test authority, or to protect oneself. The emotions that underlie a threat can be love, hate, fear, rage, or desire for attention, revenge, excitement, or recognition.

Motivation can never be known with complete certainty, but understanding motive to the extent possible is a key element in evaluating a threat. A threat reflects the threatener's mental and emotional state at the time the threat is made, but it is important to remember that a state of mind can be temporarily but strongly influenced by alcohol or drugs or by a precipitating factor such as a romantic breakup, failing grades, or conflict with a parent. After a person has absorbed an emotional setback and calmed down, or when the effects of alcohol or drugs have worn off, his or her motivation to act on a violent threat may also diminish.

Signposts

In general, people do not switch instantly from nonviolence to violence. Nonviolent people do not "snap" or decide on the spur of the moment to meet a problem by using violence. Instead, the path toward violence is an evolutionary one, with signposts along the way. A threat is one observable behavior; another may be brooding about frustration or disappointment or fantasizing about destruction or revenge in conversations, writings, drawings, and the like.

Level of Risk

A low-level threat poses a minimal risk to the victim and public safety as in the following:

- The threat is vague and indirect.
- The information contained in the threat is inconsistent or implausible or lacks detail.
- The threat lacks realism.
- The content of the threat suggests that the threatener is unlikely to carry it out.
- A medium-level threat is one that could be carried out but may not seem entirely realistic.
- The threat is more direct and more concrete than a low-level threat is.
- The wording in the threat suggests that the threatener has given some thought to how the act will be carried out.
- There may be a general indication of a possible place and time (but the signs still fall well short of a detailed plan).
- There is no strong indication that the threatener has taken preparatory steps, although there may be some veiled reference or ambiguous or inconclusive evidence pointing to that possibility (e.g., an allusion to a book or movie that shows the planning of a violent act, or a vague, general statement about the availability of weapons).
- There may be a specific statement seeking to convey that the threat is not empty: "I'm serious!" or "I really mean this!"
- A high-level threat poses an imminent and serious danger to the safety of others.
- The threat is direct, specific, and plausible.
- The threat suggests that concrete steps have been taken toward carrying it out (e.g., statements indicating that the threatener has acquired or practiced with a weapon or has had the victim under surveillance).

Factors in Threat Assessment

Specific, plausible details are a critical factor in evaluating a threat. Details can include the identity of the victim or victims; the reason for making the threat; the means, weapon, and method by which it is to be carried out; the date, time, and place that the threatened act will occur; and concrete information about plans or preparations that have already been made.

Specific details can indicate that substantial thought, planning, and preparatory steps have already been taken, suggesting a higher risk that the threatener will follow through on the threat. Similarly, a lack of detail suggests that the threatener may not have thought through all the contingencies, has not actually taken steps to carry out the threat, and may not seriously intend violence. He or she may merely be "blowing off steam" over some frustration or be trying to frighten or intimidate a particular victim or disrupt a school's events or routine.

Details that are specific but not logical or plausible may indicate a less serious threat. For example, a high school student writes that he intends to detonate hundreds of pounds of plutonium in the school's auditorium the following day at lunchtime. The threat is detailed, stating a specific time, place, and weapon, but the details are unpersuasive. Plutonium is almost impossible to obtain, legally or on the black market. It is expensive, hard to transport, and very dangerous to handle, and a complex high-explosive detonation is required to set off a nuclear reaction. No high-school student is likely to have any plutonium at all, much less hundreds of pounds, nor would a student have the knowledge or complex equipment required to detonate it. A threat this unrealistic is obviously unlikely to be carried out.

The emotional content of a threat can be an important clue to the threatener's mental state. Emotions are conveyed by melodramatic words and unusual punctuation—"I hate you!!!!!" "You have ruined my life!!!!" "May God have mercy on your soul!!!!"—or in excited, incoherent passages that may refer to God or other religious beings or may deliver an ultimatum.

Though emotionally charged threats can tell the assessor something about the temperament of the threatener, they are not a measure of danger. They may sound frightening, but no correlation has been established between the emotional intensity in a threat and the risk that it will be carried out.

Precipitating stressors are incidents, circumstances, reactions, or situations that can trigger a threat. The precipitating event may seem insignificant and have no direct relevance to the threat, but nonetheless it becomes a catalyst. For example, a student has a fight with his mother before going to school. The argument may be a minor one over an issue that has nothing to do with school, but it sets off an emotional chain reaction that leads the student to threaten another student at school that day—possibly something he has thought about doing in the past.

The effect of a precipitating event obviously depends on predisposing factors: underlying personality traits, characteristics, and temperament that predispose an adolescent to fantasize about violence or act violently. Accordingly, information about a temporary "trigger" must be considered together with broader information about underlying factors, such as a student's vulnerability to loss and depression.

Personality Traits and Behavior

- *Leakage:* "Leakage" occurs when a student intentionally or unintentionally reveals clues to feelings, thoughts, fantasies, attitudes, or intentions that may signal an impending violent act. These clues can take the form of subtle threats, boasts, innuendos, predictions, or ultimatums. They may be spoken or conveyed in stories, diary entries, essays, poems, letters, songs, drawings, doodles, tattoos, or videos.[144] Leakage can also occur when a student tries, at times deceptively, to get unwitting friends or classmates to help with preparations for a violent act (e.g., the student asks a friend to obtain ammunition for her because she is "going hunting").
- *Low tolerance for frustration:* The student is easily psychologically bruised, insulted, angered, and hurt by real or perceived injustices done to him or her by others and has great difficulty tolerating frustration.
- *Poor coping skills:* The student has little, if any, ability to deal with frustration, criticism, disappointment, failure, rejection, or humiliation. His or her response is typically inappropriate, exaggerated, immature, or disproportionate.
- *Lack of resiliency:* The student lacks resiliency and is unable to bounce back even when some time has elapsed since a frustrating or disappointing experience, a setback, or a put-down.
- *Failed love relationship:* The student may feel rejected or humiliated after the end of a love relationship and cannot accept or come to terms with the rejection.
- *"Injustice collector":* The student nurses resentment over real or perceived injustices. No matter how much time has passed, the "injustice collector" neither forgets nor forgives the wrongs the people he or she believes are responsible. The student may keep a hit list with the names of people who have wronged him or her.
- *Signs of depression:* The student shows symptoms of depression such as lethargy, physical fatigue, a morose or dark outlook on life, a sense of malaise, and loss of interest in activities that he or she once enjoyed.
- *Narcissism:* The student is self-centered, lacks insight into others' needs and/or feelings, and blames others for failures and disappointments. The narcissistic student may embrace the role of a victim to elicit sympathy and to feel temporarily superior to others. He or she displays signs of paranoia and assumes an attitude of self-importance or grandiosity that masks feelings of unworthiness.[145] A narcissistic student may be either very

thin-skinned or very thick-skinned in responding to criticism.

- *Alienation:* The student consistently behaves as though he feels different or estranged from others. This sense of separateness reflects more than in just being a loner. It can involve feelings of isolation, sadness, loneliness, not belonging, and not fitting in.
- *Dehumanization of others:* The student consistently fails to see others as fellow humans. He or she characteristically views other people as "nonpersons" or objects to be thwarted. This attitude may appear in the student's writings and artwork, in interactions with others, or in comments during conversation.
- *Lack of empathy:* The student shows an inability to understand the feelings of others and seems unconcerned about anyone else's feelings. When others show emotion, the student may ridicule them as being weak or stupid.
- *Exaggerated sense of entitlement:* The student constantly expects special treatment and consideration and reacts negatively if he or she doesn't get that treatment.
- *Attitude of superiority:* The student has a sense of being superior and presents himself or herself as smarter, more creative, more talented, more experienced, and more worldly than others.
- *Exaggerated need for attention:* The student shows an exaggerated, even pathological, need for attention, whether positive or negative, no matter what the circumstances.
- *Externalization of blame:* The student consistently refuses to take responsibility for his or her own actions and typically faults other people, events, or situations for any failings or shortcomings. In placing blame, the student frequently seems impervious to rational argument and common sense.
- *Masking of low self-esteem:* Although the student may display an arrogant, self-glorifying attitude, his or her conduct often seems to veil underlying low self-esteem. The student avoids high visibility or involvement in school activities, and other students may consider him or her a nonentity.
- *Anger-management problems:* Rather than expressing anger in appropriate ways and circumstances, the student consistently tends to burst out in temper tantrums or melodramatic displays or to brood in sulky, seething silence. The anger may be noticeably out of proportion to the cause or may be redirected toward people who had nothing to do with the original incident. The anger may come in unpredictable and uncontrollable outbursts, and it may be accompanied by expressions of unfounded prejudice, dislike, or even hatred toward individuals or groups.
- *Intolerance:* The student often expresses racial or religious prejudice or intolerant attitudes toward

minorities or displays slogans or symbols of intolerance through such means as tattoos, jewelry, clothing, bumper stickers, or book covers.

- *Inappropriate humor:* The student's humor is consistently inappropriate. Jokes or humorous comments tend to be macabre, insulting, belittling, or mean.
- *Manipulation of others:* The student consistently attempts to con and manipulate others and win their trust so that they will rationalize any signs of his or her aberrant or threatening behavior.
- *Lack of trust:* The student is untrusting and chronically suspicious of others' motives and intentions. This lack of trust may approach a clinically paranoid state. The student may express the belief that society has no trustworthy institution or mechanism for achieving justice or resolving conflict and that if something bothersome occurs, he or she has to settle it in his or her own way.
- *Closed social group:* The student appears introverted. He or she has acquaintances rather than friends or associates only with a single small group that seems to exclude everyone else. Students who threaten or carry out violent acts are not necessarily loners in the classic sense, and the composition and qualities of peer groups can be important pieces of information in assessing the danger that a threat will be acted on.
- *Change of behavior:* The student's behavior changes dramatically. His or her academic performance may decline, or the student may show a reckless disregard for school rules, schedules, dress codes, and other regulations.
- *Rigid and opinionated outlook:* The student appears rigid, judgmental, and cynical, voices strong opinions on subjects about which he or she has little knowledge, and disregards facts, logic, and reasoning that might challenge these opinions.
- *Unusual interest in sensational violence:* The student demonstrates an unusual interest in school shootings and other heavily publicized acts of violence. He or she may declare his admiration for those who committed the acts or may criticize them for "incompetence" or failing to kill enough people. The student may explicitly express a desire to carry out a similar act in his or her own school, possibly as an act of "justice."
- *Fascination with violence-filled entertainment:* The student has an unusual fascination with movies, TV shows, computer games, music videos, or printed materials that focus intensely on themes of violence, hatred, control, power, death, and destruction. He or she may repeatedly watch one movie or read one book with violent content, perhaps involving school violence. Themes of hatred, violence, weapons, and mass destruction recur in virtually all the student's activities, hobbies, and pastimes. The student spends inordinate amounts of time playing video games with violent themes and seems more interested in the violent images than in the game itself. On the Internet, the student regularly searches for Web sites involving violence, weapons, and other disturbing subjects. There is evidence that the student has downloaded and kept material from these sites.
- *Negative role models:* The student may be drawn to negative, inappropriate role models such as Hitler, Satan, or others associated with violence and destruction.
- *Behavior relevant to carrying out a threat:* The student appears to be increasingly occupied with activities that could be related to carrying out a threat (e.g., spending unusual amounts of time practicing with firearms or visiting violent Web sites). The time spent on these activities has noticeably begun to exclude normal everyday pursuits such as doing homework, attending classes, going to work, and spending time with friends.

Classification of Threats

Types of Threats

Threats can be classified into four categories:

- A direct threat identifies a specific act against a specific target and is delivered in a straightforward, clear, and explicit manner: "I am going to place a bomb in the school's gym."
- An indirect threat tends to be vague, unclear, and ambiguous. The plan, the intended victim, the motivation, and other aspects of the threat are masked or equivocal: "If I wanted to, I could kill everyone at this school!" While violence is implied, the threat is phrased tentatively—"If I wanted to"—and suggests that a violent act *could* occur, not that it *will* occur.
- A veiled threat is one that strongly implies but does not explicitly threaten violence: "We would be better off without you around anymore." Such a statement clearly hints at a possible violent act but leaves it to the potential victim to interpret the message and give a definite meaning to the threat.
- A conditional threat warns that a violent act will happen unless certain demands or terms are met: "If you don't pay me one million dollars, I will place a bomb in the school." This type of threat is often used in extortion cases.

The Role of Law Enforcement

In the vast majority of cases, whether to involve law enforcement will hinge on the seriousness of the threat: low, medium, or high.[146]

- *Low level:* A threat that has been evaluated as low level poses little danger to public safety and in most cases would not necessitate law enforcement investigation for a possible criminal offense. (However, law enforcement agencies may be asked for information in connection with a threat of any level.) Appropriate intervention in a low-level case would involve, at a minimum, interviews with the student and his or her parents. If the threat was aimed at a specific person, that person should be asked about his or her relationship with the threatener and the circumstances that led up to the threat. The response—disciplinary action and perhaps a referral for counseling or some other form of intervention—should be determined according to school policies and the judgment of the responsible school administrators.
- *Medium level:* When a threat is rated as medium level, the response should in most cases include contacting the appropriate law enforcement agency, as well as other sources, to obtain additional information (and possibly reclassify the threat into the high or low category). A medium-level threat will sometimes, though not necessarily, warrant investigation as a possible criminal offense.
- *High level:* Almost always, if a threat is evaluated as high level, the school should immediately inform the appropriate law enforcement agency. A response plan, which should have been designed ahead of time and rehearsed by both school and law enforcement personnel, should be implemented, and law enforcement should be informed and involved in whatever subsequent actions are taken in response to the threat. A high-level threat is highly likely to result in criminal prosecution (Figure 11-15).

Investigating School Violence

Law enforcement efforts regarding school violence and crime generally center on early detection and prevention. A recent study conducted by George Mason University revealed that 69% of U.S. police chiefs support the creation of more after-school programs and educational child-care arrangements, seeing this as the most effective method of reducing juvenile crime. Among police chiefs, 30% cited prosecuting juveniles as adults and hiring more juvenile investigators as their first choices for reducing youth crime. Only 1% of the chiefs believed that installing more metal detectors and surveillance devices in schools would be the most effective method of reducing crime.[147]

When investigating threats of violence in schools, it is important to listen carefully to witnesses in order to correctly identify the level of the threat and subsequently take appropriate action. Key questions include:

- Who made the threat?
- To whom was the threat made?
- Under what circumstances was the threat made?
- Exactly what words were said?
- How often were threats made?[148]

On some occasions, undercover juvenile informants can be used by police to gain insight in a school where threats have been received or plots of violence are suspected.[149] However, this practice is usually discouraged, since it places juveniles in a very precarious and potentially dangerous position. Some jurisdictions forbid the practice; others have developed very sophisticated guidelines regulating the use of a confidential informant who is under 16 years of age.

Ascertaining who made the threat or committed the act is often the least difficult part of the investigation due to

◄ **FIGURE 11-15**
Weapon detection program
A firearm discovered in a student's locker as a result of a successful, but labor-intensive, weapon detection program at a New York City high school. Given the frequency with which handguns and other weapons have been discovered on school grounds, some school districts have gone to considerable expense to install metal detectors at entry points. In addition, security officers must be present at these sites to further review suspicious circumstances. (Courtesy of Chester A. Higgins, Jr., and the U.S. Department of Justice, Office of Justice Programs, National Institute of Justice) (© Dwayne Nelson/PhotoEdit)

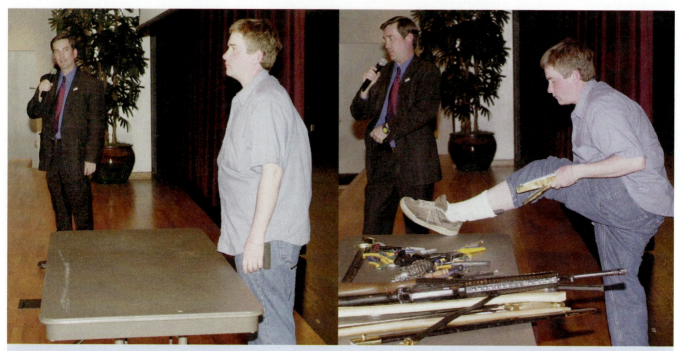

▲ **FIGURE 11-16   Schools and weapons**

Chris Dorn joins his father, national school safety expert, Michael Dorn, in a presentation of concealed weapons. Chris Dorn pulls out one of 138 weapons from grenades to a submachine gun concealed in his clothing. Easy-to-hide items, such as box cutters, are also used in most school attacks involving weapons.

(Courtesy of Fred Fox, Tampa Tribune, Tampa, FL)

the fact that juvenile perpetrators frequently use their crimes as a way of getting attention. Also, a young criminal often lacks the experience, sophistication, and self-control needed to adequately avoid detection (Figure 11-16).

Clearly, most of the police effort is on prevention, focusing on the development of programs that emphasize "team" efforts among school administrators, the police, and the community at large. When an incident does occur, specially trained teams of police intervention officers lead the investigation in an attempt to not only apprehend the suspect but also quell growing fear that might arise from recent high-profile incidents of school violence. Some departments are now using **rapid response deployment** or **quick action deployment (QUAD).** This approach focuses on training patrol officers in the principles and tactics of rapid deployment for responding to critical incidents, especially incidents of school violence. In theory, the concept has merit: immediately responding officers are able to enter buildings where life-threatening situations are in progress or where loss of victims' lives is imminent. Proponents of the concept argue that such intervention cannot wait until the SWAT team responds and therefore that police action must be taken immediately. While there is no doubt that such a condition has presented itself, the vast majority of incidents (including school shootings) are deescalated by time. It's suggested that the best approach for patrol officers responding to a critical and violent incident at a

school, especially one involving potential hostages, is to take action only when appropriate and that their primary mission is to control and contain the scene. They should let specially trained hostage negotiation and critical-incident teams handle any protracted incident of school violence. Once the scene has been secured, investigators should then treat the crime as they would any other homicide, assault, or threat.

Of course, in some instances such as the Virginia Tech University massacre on April 16, 2007, two different and separate attacks occurred.[150] Seung Hui Cho killed 32 people and wounded nearly 20 more before committing suicide, making it the deadliest school shooting in U.S. history. These types of situations are particularly difficult for responding police and investigators. The Virginia Tech incident was first reported to police as a shooting at West Ambler Johnston Hall, a coed dormitory that housed 895 students. At about 7:00 A.M. Cho shot his first victims, Emily J. Hilscher and Ryan C. Clark, in Ms. Hilsher's room. He left the scene and mailed a series of writings and video recordings to NBC News and then proceeded across campus to Norris Hall, which housed several academic programs and classrooms. Progressing to the second floor at about 10:00 A.M. (nearly three hours after the initial call to the police), Cho began shooting students at will. Local police still securing the scene of the first shooting in West Ambler Johnston Hall responded immediately, only to hear Cho fire his final suicidal shot.

▲ FIGURE 11-17   Virginia Tech massacre
Seung-Hui Cho sent this photo to NBC News on the day of the Virginia Tech massacre. He was armed with a Glock 9-mm pistol and a Walther P22 pistol. His use of hollow point ammunition made his attack much more deadly.
(© AP/Wide World Photos)

The investigation of the Norris Hall scene revealed that Cho's final shooting spree lasted nearly 9 minutes with over 300 rounds expended. Cho's choice of 9-mm hollow point ammunition had worsened the injuries and deaths (Figure 11-17).

A Virginia Tech Review Panel faulted university officials for acting too late and for prematurely concluding that the double homicide in West Ambler Johnston Hall was an isolated event and domestic in nature.[151] The lessons for responding officers to any shooting, but particularly school shootings, are not to assume that the suspects have left the scene and are finished with their homicidal terror. When responding to a shooting incident, first remember the basics of officer safety, take care to protect the lives of innocent bystanders, and expect the unexpected until the suspects are in custody.

Home Searches: For Weapons

A number of planned school shootings and bombings around the nation have been successfully averted by the use of home searches. Some years ago, officers of the Bibb County Board of Education Campus Police Department in Georgia began regularly conducting searches of students' homes for firearms, explosives, and other items. The practice has now become widely used around the nation.

Home searches are conducted when a gun or components of an explosive device are recovered from a student on campus or when investigating reports show that someone has made a threat to commit a weapons assault at a school. Home searches can be conducted with the consent of the parents in most states or with a search warrant if sufficient probable cause exists.

The Georgia Emergency Management Agency (GEMA) has shared the concept with thousands of educators and law enforcement officials from across the country in seminars, articles and training videos. This technique has been used to prevent several dozen planned school shootings and bombings.

After attending home search training, a School Resource Officer in Oklahoma conducted a home search and prevented a planned school bombing on the first day of school last year. A plot by a Georgia student to kill hundreds of his classmates was foiled with a home search. The student planned to place a bomb in a field near his school and call in a bomb threat. Local law enforcement officials found the plans and bomb-making components in the student's bedroom during a home search.

The home search should be included in every community's inventory of prevention measures. While this technique has become standard practice in many regions, there are still missed opportunities for its application.

Items to be considered when conducting a home search:

Armed Officers Home searches should be conducted only by armed law enforcement officers. In some cases, it is desirable for campus administrators or mental health staff to assist officers in the search as they may notice danger signs in a student's bedroom that could be missed by officers. Campus officials should enter the residence only when officers feel it is safe to do so.

Parental Consent In many cases, officers will be able to obtain consent from parents or guardians (in the case of K–12 students). In some cases, officers may have to agree not to pursue criminal charges for gun or drug possession in order to obtain consent. This option should first be discussed with the local prosecutor before using it. Officers should clearly advise that other offenses, such as possession of a stolen gun or evidence pertaining to an assault with the weapon, may still be prosecuted. If probable cause to obtain a search warrant does not exist, it may be more important to recover the weapon than to prosecute.

Search Warrant In other cases, a search warrant may be required. If possible, officers should be certain that the warrant specifically lists such associated items as ammunition and paperwork of the offender that may show a direct link between the offender and the weapon; how the items were illegally trafficked; and plans to commit criminal acts with the weapon(s). An effort should be made to include computer-based records in the warrant as well.

Multiple Weapons When one weapon is found, the possibility that other weapons may be present should be considered.

Avoid Publicity The use of the home search to find concealed weapons should not be publicized in order to avoid losing the element of surprise and thus providing the student with the opportunity to use alternative places of concealment in the home.

The use of the home search technique has prevented much potential bloodshed on our nation's campuses, but unfortunately, several mass school shootings have occurred when officials failed to utilize this simple technique. It is imperative that those who need to use it be familiar with the technique. It could mean the difference between life and death.[152]

KEY TERMS

AMBER Plan
battered-child syndrome
child pornography
contact burns
FBI Child Abduction and Serial Murder Investigative Resource Center (CASMIRC)
human trafficking
immersion burns
infant abduction

Jacob Wetterling Crimes against Children and Sexually Violent Offender Registration Act
Megan's Law
Munchausen Syndrome by Proxy (MSBP)
preferential child molester
rapid response deployment or quick action deployment (QUAD)
scald burns

sex tourism
shaken-baby syndrome (SBS)
situational child molester
spill/splash injuries
sudden infant death syndrome (SIDS)
threat assessment

REVIEW QUESTIONS

1. What are the two most common instruments used in child abuse?
2. What are some of the ways that intentional immersion burns are distinguished from accidental immersion burns?
3. Why was the phrase "shaken-baby syndrome" coined?
4. What is the mechanism of injuries in shaken-baby syndrome?
5. What role does the physician play in child-abuse cases?
6. What is Munchausen Syndrome by Proxy (MSBP)?
7. What are some of the major behavioral characteristics of situational and preferential child molesters?
8. Identify the three developmental issues that are important when allegations of sexual abuse arise.
9. What are some of the benefits of using an anatomically detailed doll in interviewing children?

10. How is child pornography behaviorally defined?
11. Describe the appearance of a SIDS victim.
12. What motivations are typically *not* involved in infant abduction?
13. What appears to be the major motivating factor that drives female offenders to abduct infants?
14. A parental checklist to assist police in locating a missing child should include what instructions?
15. What is the AMBER Plan?
16. What resources must a runaway child have to successfully sustain a voluntary long-term absence?
17. What are the major features of the Jacob Wetterling Crimes against Children and the Sexually Violent Offender Registration Act?
18. Threats in school violence can be classified into four categories; what are they?

INTERNET ACTIVITIES

1. The National SIDS/Infant Death Resource Center provides information services and technical assistance on sudden infant death syndrome (SIDS) and related topics. The material put out by this group and found on their website at www.sidscenter.org can answer the following questions. What is the relationship between sudden infant death syndrome and prenatal maternal smoking? Is mother/infant cosleeping a factor? What factors influence the use of home cardiorespiratory monitor for infants? Are repeated sudden unexpected and unexplained

infant deaths natural or unnatural? Does a sudden infant death syndrome gene exist?
2. For a comprehensive discussion of shaken baby syndrome, visit www.ncstl.org/education/shaken% 20%babies%20%syndrome. The site puts readers in touch with the most current medical and investigative information on SBC.
3. For more information about human trafficking, there are a host of national and international web resources. Start with www.humantrafficking.org for up-to-the-minute reports on human trafficking and

sex trafficking around the world. Then glance at http://usinfo.state.gov/gi/global_issues/human_trafficking/traffick_report.html for the latest U.S. State Department report on human trafficking. Based on that information, do you think the United States should intervene and educate governments and people of nations recently embroiled in conflict or recovering from natural disasters about the dangers presented by human trafficking?

NOTES

1. C. J. Flammang, *The Police and the Unprotected Child* (Springfield, IL: Charles C. Thomas, 1970), p. 90; Harold E. Simmons, *Protective Services for Children* (Sacramento, CA: General Welfare Publications, 1968), p. 45.
2. Phylip J. Peltier, Gary Purdue, and Jack R. Shepherd, *Burn Injuries in Child Abuse* (Washington, D.C.: U.S. Department of Justice, 1997), pp. 1–9.
3. Randell Alexander and K. Kleinmann, *Diagnostic Imaging of Child Abuse* (Washington, D.C.: U.S. Department of Justice, 1996), pp. 6–9.
4. James D. Regis, "The Battered Child," *Police Work*, April 1980, pp. 41–42.
5. Rob Parrish, *Battered Child Syndrome: Investigating Physical Abuse* (Washington, D.C.: U.S. Department of Justice, 1996), pp. 9–10.
6. Stephen J. Boros and Larry C. Brubaker, "Munchausen Syndrome by Proxy: Case Accounts," *FBI Law Enforcement Bulletin*, 1992, Vol. 61, No. 6, pp. 16–20. These case reports were taken from this article.
7. *A Resource Handbook: Sudden Infant Death Syndrome* (Tallahassee, FL: Department of Health and Rehabilitative Services, 1978), pp. 1–2. Much of the information dealing with SIDS was taken from this source.
8. Ann L. Ponsonby, Terrence Dwyer, Laura E. Gibbons, Jennifer A Cochrane, and You-gan Wang, "Factors Potentiating the Risk of Sudden Infant Death Syndrome Associated with Prone Position," *New England Journal of Medicine*, Aug. 1993, vol. 329, No. 6, p. 373. The scientists conducted the study (58 infants with SIDS and 120 control infants) and perspective cohort study (22 infants with SIDS and 233 control infants) in Tasmania. Interactions were examined and math analyses done with a multiplicative model interaction.
9. J. L. Emery and J. A. Thornton, "Affects of Obstruction to Respiration in Infants with Particular Reference to Mattresses, Pillows, and Their Coverings," *BMJ*, 1968, Vol. 3, pp. 309–313.
10. David S. Paterson, et. al., "Multiple Serotonergic Brainstem Abnormalities in Sudden Infant Death Syndrome," *Journal of American Medical Association*, Nov. 1, 2006, vol. 296; pp. 2124–2132.
11. Vincent J. DiMaio and Dominick DiMaio, *Forensic Pathology* (Boca Raton, FL: CRC Press, 2001), pp. 330–331.
12. The following are online resources for providing additional information on SIDS: First Candle, www.firstcandle.org; Interagency Panel on Sudden Infant Death Syndrome, "Guidelines for Death Scene Investigation of Sudden, Unexplained Infant Deaths," www.cdc.gov/mmwr/preview/mmwrhtml/00042657.htm; Office of Juvenile Justice and Delinquency Prevention "Recognizing When a Child's Injury or Illness is Caused by Abuse," www.ncjrs.gov/pdffiles1/ojjdp/160938.pdf; Canadian Association of Chiefs of Police "Code of Police Practice: A Guide for First-Line Officers," www.rcmp-learning.org/copp/encopp/d_infant.htm.
13. Vincent J. DiMaio and Dominick DiMaio, *Forensic Pathology* (Boca Raton, FL: CRC Press, 2001), pp. 349–350.
14. David P. Southall, "Covert Video Recording of Life-Threatening Child Abuse: Lessons for Child Protection," *Pediatrics*, Nov. 1997, Vol. 100, No. 5, pp. 735–760; Sharon Begley, "The Nursery's Littlest Victim," *Newsweek*, Sept. 22, 1997, p. 72.
15. 67. Begley, "The Nursery's Littlest Victim."
16. Kenneth V. Lanning, *Child Molesters: A Behavioral Analysis for Law Enforcement Officers Investigating Cases of Child Sexual Exploitation*, 3rd ed. (Arlington, VA: National Center for Missing and Exploited Children, 1992), pp. 6–10. This entire discussion of child molesters has been reproduced (with minor changes) with permission. No part of this may be reproduced without the express written permission of the National Center for Missing and Exploited Children, 1-800-843-5678.
17. Ibid.
18. Debra Whitcomb, *When the Victim Is a Child* (Washington, D.C.: National Institute of Justice, 1992), pp. 15–20.
19. D. Floyd, testimony before President's Task Force on Victims of Crime, Final Report, December 1982, p. 51.
20. J. Waterman, "Development Considerations," in K. MacFarlane and J. Waterman, eds., *Sexual Abuse of Young Children* (New York: Guilford Press, 1986), pp. 15–29.
21. W. M. Friedrich, J. Fischer, D. Broughton, D. Houston, and C. R. Shafran, "Normative Sexual Behavior in Children: A Contemporary Sample," *Pediatrics*, Vol. 101, No. 4, April, p. 9.
22. A. Warren-Leubecker et al., "What Do Children Know about the Legal System and When Do They Know It? First Steps Down a Less-Traveled Path in Child Witness Research," S. J. Ceci, D. F. Ross, and M. P. Toglia, eds., *Perspectives on Children's Testimony* (New York: Springer Verlag, 1989), pp. 158–183.
23. M. A. Young, "Working with Victims Who Are Children or Adolescents: Using the Lessons of Child Development with Young Trauma Victims," *NOVA Newsletter*, 1989, Vol. 13.
24. Warren-Leubecker et al., "What Do Children Know about the Legal System"; K. J. Saywitz, "Children's

Conceptions of the Legal System: 'Court Is a Place to Play Basketball,'" in Ceci et al., *Perspectives on Children's Testimony*, pp. 131–157. Also see S. P. Limber, G. B. Melton, and S. J. Rahe, "Legal Knowledge, Attitudes, and Reasoning Abilities of Witnesses," paper presented at AP-LS Division 41 Biennial Convention, Williamsburg, Virginia, March 1990.

25. R. Pynoos and S. Eth, "The Child Witness to Homicide," *Journal of Social Issues*, 1984, Vol. 40, p. 98.

26. K. J. Saywitz and C. Jaenicke, "Children's Understanding of Legal Terms: A Preliminary Report of Grade-Related Trends," paper presented at the Society for Research on Child Development Biennial Meeting, Baltimore, Maryland, April 1987.

27. Warren-Leubecker et al., "What Do Children Know about the Legal System?"

28. Whitcomb, *When the Victim Is a Child*, pp. 33–38. This discussion was adapted from this source.

29. Alabama, Connecticut, Michigan, New Jersey, New York, Pennsylvania, West Virginia, and Wyoming.

30. See, for example, *Cleveland v. State*, 490 N.R. 2nd 1140 (Ind. App. 1986); *People v. Garvie*, 148 Mich. App. 444, 384 N.W. 2d 796 (1986); *State v. Jenkins*, 326 N.W. 2d 67 (N.D. 1982).

31. E. Gray, "Children as Witnesses in Child Sexual Abuse Cases Study," Final Report submitted to the National Center on Child Abuse and Neglect under Grant No. 90-CA-1273, by the National Council of Jewish Women, New York, New York, 1990, p. 51. (Henceforth referred to as NCJW Study.)

32. K. R. Freemand and T. Estrada-Mullany, "Using Dolls to Interview Child Victims: Legal Concerns and Interview Procedures," *Research in Action*, National Institute of Justice, January/February 1988, p. 2.

33. White, pp. 472–473.

34. S. White and G. Santilli, "A Review of Clinical Practices and Research Data on Anatomical Dolls," *Journal of Interpersonal Violence*, Dec. 1988, Vol. 3, pp. 437–439.

35. L. Berliner, "Anatomical Dolls," *Journal of Interpersonal Violence*, Dec. 1988, Vol. 3, pp. 468–470; also see B. W. Boat and M. D. Everson, "Normative Data: How Non-Referred Young Children Interact with Anatomical Dolls," paper presented at the Symposium of Interviewing Children, cited in Berliner, "Anatomical Dolls," p. 469.

36. White and Santilli, "A Review of Clinical Practices," p. 431.

37. B. Boat and M. Everson, "Use of Anatomical Dolls among Professionals in Sexual Abuse Evaluations," *Child Abuse and Neglect*, 1988, Vol. 12, pp. 171–179.

38. K. MacFarlane and S. Krebs, "Techniques for Interviewing and Evidence Gathering," in MacFarlane and Waterman, *Sexual Abuse of Young Children*, pp. 74–75.

39. Ibid.

40. White and Santilli, "A Review of Clinical Practices," pp. 439–440.

41. MacFarlane and Krebs, "Techniques for Interviewing and Evidence Gathering," p. 87.

42. NCJW Study, pp. 439–440.

43. S. J. Ceci, D. Ross, and M. Toglia, "Age Differences in Suggestibility: Narrowing the Uncertainties," in S. J. Ceci, M. P. Toglia, and D. F. Ross, eds., *Children's Eyewitness Memory* (New York: Springer-Verlag, 1987), pp. 79–91.

44. H. Wakefield and R. Underwager, "Techniques for Interviewing Children in Sexual Abuse Cases," *VOCAL Perspective*, Summer 1989, pp. 7–15.

45. K. Saywitz et al., "Children's Memories of Genital Examinations: Implications for Cases of Child Sexual Assault," paper presented at the Society for Research in Child Development Meetings, Kansas City, Missouri, 1989.

46. R. Lusk and J. Waterman, "Effects of Sexual Abuse on Children," in MacFarlane and Waterman, *Sexual Abuse of Young Children*, pp. 15–29. Also see A. Browne and D. Finkelhor, "Initial and Long-Term Effects: A Review of the Research," in D. Finkelhor et al., eds., *A Sourcebook on Child Sexual Abuse* (Beverly Hills, CA: Sage, 1986), pp. 143–152.

47. J. R. Conte and J. R. Schuerman, "The Effects of Sexual Abuse on Children: A Multidimensional View," *Journal of Interpersonal Violence*, December 1987, Vol. 2, pp. 380–390.

48. W. N. Freidrich, R. L. Beilke, and A. J. Urquiza, "Children from Sexually Abusive Families: A Behavioral Comparison," *Journal of Interpersonal Violence*, Dec. 1987, Vol. 2, pp. 391–402.

49. J. Conte et al., "Evaluating Children's Report of Sexual Abuse: Results from a Survey of Professionals," unpublished manuscript, University of Chicago, undated, cited in J. E. B. Myers et al., "Expert Testimony in Child Sexual Abuse Litigation," *Nebraska Law Review*, 1989, Vol. 68, p. 75.

50. Whitcomb, *When the Victim Is a Child*, pp. 6–11.

51. D. Jones and J. McGraw, "Reliable and Fictitious Accounts of Sexual Abuse to Children," *Journal of Interpersonal Violence*, March 1987, Vol. 2, pp. 27–45.

52. Ibid.

53. J. Paradise, A. Rostain, and M. Nathanson, "Substantiation of Sexual Abuse Charges When Parents Dispute Custody or Visitation," *Pediatrics*, June 1988, Vol. 81, pp. 835–839.

54. See, for example, E. P. Benedek and D. H. Schetky, "Allegations of Sexual Abuse in Child Custody and Visitation Disputes," in D. H. Schetky and E. P. Benedek, eds., *Emerging Issues in Child Psychiatry and the Law* (New York: Brunner/Mazel, 1985), pp. 145–158; A. H. Green, "True and False Allegations of Sexual Abuse in Child Custody Disputes," *Journal of the American Academy of Child Psychiatry*, 1986, Vol. 25, pp. 449–456.

55. For an excellent summary of the drawbacks of such studies, see D. Corwin et al., "Child Sexual Abuse and Custody Disputes: No Easy Answers," *Journal of Interpersonal Violence*, March 1987, Vol. 2, pp. 91–105; also see L. Berliner, "Deciding Whether a Child Has Been Sexually Abused," in E. B. Nicholson, ed., *Sexual Abuse Allegations in Custody and Visitation Cases* (Washington, D.C.: American Bar Association, 1988), pp. 48–69.

56. N. Thoennes and J. Pearson, "Summary of Findings from the Sexual Abuse Allegations Project," in Nicholson, *Sexual Abuse Allegations,* pp. 1–21.

57. D. Finkelhor, L. M. Williams, and N. Burns, *Nursery Crimes: Sexual Abuse in Day Care* (Newbury Park, CA: Sage, 1988).

58. "Gender and Human Trafficking." United Nations Economic and Social Commission for Asia and the Pacific. www.unescap.org/esid/GAD/Issues/Trafficking/index.asp, retrieved August 19, 2007.

59. F. Miko, "Trafficking in Persons: The US and International Response." Congressional Research Service, Library of Congress (Washington D.C.: July 7, 2006), introduction.

60. J. Aita, "Efforts to Combat Human Trafficking Increasing, US Official Says." U.S. Department of State. http://usinfo.state.gov/gi/Archive/2004/Mar/05-608037.html, published March 4, 2004.

61. Donna Hughes, *The "Natasha" Trade: Transnational Sex Trafficking* (Washington, D.C.: National Institute of Justice, January 2001), pp 9-10.

62. "Sex Trafficking Fact Sheet" (fact sheet for The Campaign to Rescue and Restore Victims of Human Trafficking). U.S. Department of Health and Human Services Administration for Children and Families. www.acf.hhs.gov/trafficking/about/fact_sex.html, retrieved August 15, 2007.

63. P. Landesman, "The Girls Next Door." *The New York Times,* January 25, 2004. www.nytimes.com/2004/01/25/magazine/25SEXTRAFFIC.html?pagewanted=1&ei=5007en=43dbe6ef76e45af8ex=1390366800.

64. D. Nelson, "Earthquake orphans sold into sex trade." *The Sunday Times,* October 23, 2005. www.timesonline.co.uk/tol/news/world/article581662.ece.

65. G. Calandruccio, "A Review of Recent Research on Human Trafficking in the Middle East." International Organization for Migration: *International Migration* (Geneva, Switzerland: January 2005).Vol. 43 Issue 1-2, p. 267.

66. "Sex Trafficking Fact Sheet," ibid.

67. Factbook of Global Sexual Exploitation: Thailand: Trafficking. www.uri.edu/artsci/wms/hughes/thailand.htm.

68. P. Landesman, ibid.

69. F. Miko, "Trafficking in Persons: The US and International Response." Congressional Research Service, Library of Congress (Washington D.C.: July 7, 2006), p. 8.

70. F. Miko, "Trafficking in Persons: The US and International Response." Congressional Research Service, Library of Congress (Washington D.C.: July 7, 2006), p. 4.

71. Ibid.

72. "Common Health Issues Seen in Victims of Human Trafficking" (fact sheet for The Campaign to Rescue and Restore Victims of Human Trafficking). U.S. Department of Health and Human Services Administration for Children and Families. www.acf.hhs.gov/trafficking/campaign_kits/tool_kit_health/health_problems.html, retrieved September 4, 2007.

73. "The Crime of Human Trafficking: A Law Enforcement Guide to Identification and Investigation." International Association of Chiefs of Police. pp. 5–7. www.theiacp.org/documents/pdfs/RCD/CompleteHTGuide.pdf, retrieved August 6, 2007.

74. "Identifying the Crime of Human Trafficking" (fact sheet for The Campaign to Rescue and Restore Victims of Human Trafficking). U.S. Department of Health and Human Services Administration for Children and Families. www.acf.hhs.gov/trafficking/campaign_kits/tool_kit_law/identify_crime.html.

75. "The Crime of Human Trafficking: A Law Enforcement Guide to Identification and Investigation." International Association of Chiefs of Police. pp. 8–10. www.theiacp.org/documents/pdfs/RCD/CompleteHTGuide.pdf, retrieved August 6, 2007.

76. "The Crime of Human Trafficking: A Law Enforcement Guide to Identification and Investigation." International Association of Chiefs of Police. p.10. www.theiacp.org/documents/pdfs/RCD/CompleteHTGuide.pdf, retrieved August 6, 2007.

77. "Trafficking and Sex Tourism." U.S. Department of Justice Child Exploitation and Obscenity Section. www.usdoj.gov/criminal/ceos/trafficking.html, retrieved September 9, 2007.

78. F. Miko, "Trafficking in Persons: The US and International Response." Congressional Research Service, Library of Congress (Washington D.C.: July 7, 2006), p. 13.

79. Kenneth V. Lanning, *Child Molesters: A Behavioral Analysis for Law Enforcement Officers Investigating Cases of Child Sexual Exploitation,* 3rd ed. (Arlington, VA: National Center for Missing and Exploited Children, 1992), pp. 24–31. This entire discussion of child pornography has been reproduced (with minor changes) with permission. No part of this may be reproduced without the express written permission of the National Center for Missing and Exploited Children, 1-800-843-5678.

80. Defined as part of the United Nations General Assembly on the Promotion and Protection of the Rights of Children, September 20, 1995. Document available at www.unhchr.ch/Huridocda/Huridoca.nsf/0/97dd6479be18883f80256719005e5661?Opendocument

81. "Review of the US Department of State Office to Monitor and Combat Trafficking in Persons TIP Report 2007." *The Protection Project* (Washington, D.C.: Johns Hopkins University, June 2007), p. 28. www.theprotectionproject.org.

82. E. Klain, "Prostitution of Children and Child-Sex Tourism: An Analysis of Domestic and International Responses". (Washington, D.C.: Office of Juvenile Justice and Delinquency Programs and National Center for Missing and Exploited Children, 1999) p. 37.

83. "State Seeks to Close Dutchess and Queens Based Travel Agency." Press release from the New York State Attorney General, August 20, 2003. www.oag.state.ny.us/press/2003/aug/aug20a_03.html.

84. E. Klain, "Prostitution of Children and Child-Sex Tourism: An Analysis of Domestic and International Responses." (Washington, D.C.: Office of Juvenile Justice and Delinquency Programs and National Center for Missing and Exploited Children, 1999) p. 36.

85. E. Klain, "Prostitution of Children and Child-Sex Tourism: An Analysis of Domestic and International Responses." (Washington, D.C.: Office of Juvenile Justice and Delinquency Programs and National Center for Missing and Exploited Children, 1999) pp. 35–35.

86. F. Miko, "Trafficking in Persons: The U.S. and International Response." Congressional Research Service, Library of Congress (Washington D.C.: July 7, 2006).

87. E. Klain, "Prostitution of Children and Child-Sex Tourism: An Analysis of Domestic and International Responses." (Washington, D.C.: Office of Juvenile Justice and Delinquency Programs and National Center for Missing and Exploited Children, 1999) p. 33.

88. *The Paedo File*, End Child Prostitution, Child Pornography and Trafficking of Children for Sexual Purposes (EPCAT) Newsletter (EPCAT International: Bangkok, Thailand, April 1996), pp. 4–5.

89. E. Klain, "Prostitution of Children and Child-Sex Tourism: An Analysis of Domestic and International Responses." (Washington, D.C.: Office of Juvenile Justice and Delinquency Programs and National Center for Missing and Exploited Children, 1999) p. 37.

90. V. Silverman, "US Law Enforcement Targets Child Sex Tourism." (Washington D.C.: U.S. Department of State, December 17, 2003). http://usinfo.state.gov/gi/Archive/2003/Dec/17-227348.html

91. "The Facts About Child Sex Tourism." Fact sheet from the U.S. Department of State Office to Monitor and Combat Trafficking in Persons. August 19, 2005. www.state.gov/g/tip/rls/fs/2005/51351.htm.

92. The Child Pornography Prevention Act, U.S. Code Title 18, Section 2252: Certain Activities Relating to Material Involving the Sexual Exploitation of Minors.

93. U.S. Code, Title 18, Section 2251: Sexual Exploitation of Children.

94. In the Supreme Court of the United States, *John D. Ashcroft, Attorney General of the United States et al., Petitioners*, v. *The Free Speech Coalition et al.*, www.usdoj.gov/osg/briefs/2000/3mer/2mer/2000-0795.mer.aa.html.

95. Supreme Court of the United States, www.supremecourtus.gov/index.html.

96. Donald M. Kerr, "Internet and Data Interception Capabilities Developed by the FBI," Statement for the Record, U.S. House of Representatives, Committee on the Judiciary, Subcommittee on the Constitution, www.cdt.org/security/carnivor/000724fbi.shtml, July 24, 2000.

97. Kind Holger, "Combating Child Pornography on the Internet by the German Federal Criminal Police Office (BKA)."

98. "14 Nations Join to Bust Huge Internet Child Porn Ring," www.cnn.com/WORLD/europe/9809/02/internet.porn.02/.

99. J. Wolak et al., "Online Victimization of Youth: 5 Years Later" (Washington, D.C.: Office of Juvenile Justice and Delinquency Programs, Crimes Against Children Research Center, and National Center for Missing and Exploited Children, 2006) p. 17.

100. J. Wolak et al., "Online Victimization of Youth: 5 Years Later" (Washington, D.C.: Office of Juvenile Justice and Delinquency Programs, Crimes Against Children Research Center, and National Center for Missing and Exploited Children, 2006) p. 18.

101. V. Coleman-Wright, "For Detective, Kids' Safety Is First and Foremost." *American Police Beat*, May 2007. p. 70.

102. Information taken from Internet Crimes Against Children Task Force website. www.icactraining.org/ retrieved September 10, 2007.

103. Ibid.

104. M. Huffman, "MySpace Deletes More Sex Offenders." ConsumerAffairs.com, July 25, 2007. www.consumeraffairs.com/news04/2007/07/myspace_more.html.

105. D. Goodin, "US States Press MySpace to Give Up Sex Offender Data." *The Register*, May 14, 2007. www.theregister.co.uk/2007/05/14/myspace_offender_demand/.

106. M. Huffman, "My Space Deletes More Sex Offenders."

107. V. Coleman-Wright, "For Detective, Kids' Safety Is First and Foremost."

108. L. G. Ankrom and C. J. Lent, "Cradle Robbers: A Study of the Infant Abductor." *FBI Law Enforcement Bulletin*, Sept. 1995, pp. 12–17.

109. These interviews were conducted with funds provided by Interagency Agreement #91–MC-004, issued through the cooperation of the Office of Juvenile Justice and Delinquency Prevention.

110. P. Beachy and J. Deacon, "Preventing Neonatal Kidnapping," *Journal of GN*, 1991, Vol. 21, No. 1, pp. 11–16.

111. Ibid.

112. Ibid.

113. R. Grant, "The New Babysnatchers," *Redbook*, May 1990, p. 153.

114. Ibid., p. 152.

115. K. Hanfland, R. Keppel, and J. Weis, "Case Management for Missing Children: Homicide Investigation," Washington State Attorney General's Office, 1997.

116. Adapted from the FBI's *Child Abduction Response Plan*, Critical Incident Response Group, National Center for the Analysis of Violent Crime (Quantico, VA), pp. 15–16.

117. For more information, agencies can contact the NCAVC coordinator at their local FBI field office.

118. Interview with Supervisory Special Agent Mark Hilts, Federal Bureau of Investigation, NCAVC, Mar. 2, 1999.

119. J. Robert Flores, *When Your Child Is Missing: A Family Guide to Survival*, Department of Justice, 2002, pp. 21–22.

120. For more information about the AMBER alert, visit www.amberalert.gov.

121. Federal Bureau of Investigation, *Child Abduction Response Plan*, p. 17.

122. Alan D. Scholle, "Sex Offender Registration." *FBI Law Enforcement Bulletin*, July 2000, pp. 17–24. This discussion was adapted from this source.

123. Patte Wetterling, "The Jacob Wetterling Story," speech, in Bureau of Justice Statistics, *National Conference on Sex Offender Registries: Proceedings of a BJS/SEARCH Conference*, NCJ 168965, Office of Justice Programs, Washington, D.C., U.S. Department of Justice, April 1998, pp. 3–7.

124. Ibid., p. vii.

125. Ibid., pp. 3–7.

126. 42 U.S.C. 14071; National Criminal Justice Association, *Sex Offender Community Notification Policy Report* (Washington, D.C.: Oct. 1997), p. 5.

127. The Edward Byrne Memorial State and Local Law Enforcement Assistance Program provides grants to states to "improve the functioning of the criminal justice system, with emphasis on violent crimes and serious offenders." Available from www.ojp.usdoj .gov/BJA/html/byrnef.htm, accessed Feb. 22, 2000.

128. Scott Matson and Roxanne Lieb, *Sex Offender Registration: A Review of State Laws* (Olympia: Washington State Institute for Public Policy, July 1996), p. 5.

129. 104. P.L. 145, 100 Stat. 1345; Wetterling, "The Jacob Wetterling Story," p. 8.

130. Wetterling, ibid., p. 1.

131. 42 U.S.C 14072; Wetterling, ibid., pp. 8–9. Congress named the act after Lychner when she and her two daughters died in the TWA Flight 800 explosion off the coast of Long Island in July 1996.

132. The National Sex Offender Registry (NSOR), which became operational in 1997, initially served as a pointer system for a convicted sex offender's record in the Interstate Identification Index. The permanent registry—part of NCIC (National Crime Information Center) 2000—went online in 1999, replacing the earlier version. The NSOR flags sex offenders when agencies request authorized, fingerprint-based, criminal-history checks. Information provided by the Crimes against Children Unit, Criminal Investigative Division, FBI Headquarters, Washington, D.C., Feb. 24, 2000. 94.

133. The U.S. attorney general set October 2001 as the date by which all states should comply with DOJ standards relating to the Jacob Wetterling Act. To date, all states have developed sex-offender registries.

134. Edward Byrne Memorial, p. 1.

135. Ibid.

136. Elizabeth Rahmberg Walsh, "Megan's Laws: Sex Offender Registration and Notification Statutes and Constitutional Challenges," in *The Sex Offender*, Vol. 2 (Kingston, NJ: Civic Research Institute, 1997), p. 3.

137. Iowa Department of Public Safety, sex offender registry statistics, Apr. 28, 2000.

138. Scott Matson and Roxanne Lieb, *Sex Offender Community Notification: A Review of Laws in 32 States* (Olympia: Washington State Institute for Public Policy, July 1996), p. 3.

139. Ibid., p. 2.

140. Peter Finn, *Sex Offender Community Notification* (Research in Brief), U.S. Department of Justice, Office of Justice Programs, National Institute of Justice (Washington, D.C.: Feb. 1997), p. 3.

141. National Institute of Education, *Violent Schools—Safe Schools: The Safe School Study Report to the Congress*, Washington, D.C.: U.S. Department of Education, 1978.

142. National School Safety Center, "School Crime: Annual Statistical Snapshot," *School Safety* (Winter 1989).

143. J. Hall, "The Knife in the Book Bag," *Time* (May 22, 1993); T. Toch, T. Guest, and M. Guttman, "Violence in Schools: When Killers Come Home." *U.S. News and World Report* (Nov. 8, 1993).

144. "The School Shooter: A Threat Assessment Perspective." National Center for the Analysis of Violent Crime, FBI National Academy, Quantico, VA, 2000, pp. 2–9. (Much of this discussion on crime in school was adapted from this source.)

145. C. Malmquist, Homicidal Violence, malq001@atlas. socsci.umn.edu.

146. Op. cit., pp. 16–21.

147. Associated Press, "Police Chiefs Back After-School Programs," www.apbonline.com/cjprofessionals/behindthebadge/1991/11/01chiefs_children1101_01, Nov. 1, 1999.

148. Glenn Stutzky, "How to Battle the School Bully," an interview with *ABC News*, www.abcnews.go.com/sections/community/DailyNews/chat_bullying11298.html, Nov. 29, 2001.

149. James Blair, "The Ethics of Using Juvenile Informants: Murder in California Prompts New Bill, Raises Questions about Whether Minors Should Be Operatives," *Christian Science Monitor*,www.csmonitor.com/durable /1998/04/14 / p3s1.htm, Apr. 14, 1998.

150. "At Least 33 Dead in Virginia Rampage," *MSNBC and NBC News* April 17, 2007. See www.msnbc.msn.com/id/18134671/.

151. Commonwealth of Virginia, *Report of the Virginia Tech Review Panel*. PDF File, www.governor.virginia.gov/TempContent/techPanelReport.cfm, retrieved on August 31, 2007.

152. Michael Dorn, Senior Public Safety and Emergency Analyst—Janes Consultancy, "Home Searches: A Valuable Tool." *Campus Safety Journal*, Training Bulletins—Training Bulletin #8, 2003.

12

ROBBERY

WARNING!
Our Employees
CANNOT open this Safe.
It can only be opened by
the Armored Car Guards.

¡AVISO!
Nuestros Empleados
NO PUEDEN ABRIR
la Caja Fuerte.
Solamente Puede ser
Abierta Por los GUARDIAS
del Carro de Seguridad.

▲ In recent years, convenience store clerks, taxicab drivers, pizza delivery persons, and the like have all been targeted in armed robberies. In an attempt to forestall such robberies, many of these kinds of businesses now display "warning" signs in both English and Spanish like the one pictured below alerting would-be robbers to the fact that minimal cash is on hand or accessible.

(© Joel Gordon)

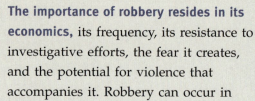

INTRODUCTION

The importance of robbery resides in its economics, its frequency, its resistance to investigative efforts, the fear it creates, and the potential for violence that accompanies it. Robbery can occur in several contexts, including visible street robberies, carjackings, home invasions, truck hijackings, bank robberies, and automatic-teller-machine (ATM) robberies. Further, taxicab drivers and convenience-store personnel in particular are easy targets for robbery because they often work alone at all hours of the day and night, with minimal or no protection from robbers, and a large part of the business they conduct is on a cash basis. Similar to their variation by place, robberies also vary in terms of the amount of time spent on their planning: Some robberies occur without any planning; others involve considerable premeditation.

Because of the face-to-face confrontation between perpetrator and victim, the potential for violence is always present in a robbery. When violence does occur, it may range from minor injury to loss of life. Due to its personal and often violent nature, robbery is one of the crimes most feared by the public, a fear that may be heightened by perceptions of police inability to deal effectively with robberies. However, witnesses are often upset and may have seen the perpetrator only briefly—factors that sometimes limit how much they can assist the investigative process. These factors, coupled with the fact that most offenders operate alone, can make robbery investigations extremely difficult. Mitigating the investigative challenge are recent identification technologies that make it possible to quickly generate and distribute a likeness of a suspect. When security cameras are present and operating, they can also be of major assistance in providing leads.

In coping with a heightened sense of fear and alarm, robbery victims often seek guidance and advice to help prevent repeat victimization. Along with arresting suspects and recovering the victim's property, investigators and their departments can serve in a crime prevention role. Providing the public with tips on what to do before, during, and after a robbery not only helps prevent robberies but also helps lessen the chance of repeat victimizations.

ELEMENTS OF THE CRIME

A **robbery** consists of the following elements: the (1) taking and (2) carrying away of (3) personal property of (4) another, with (5) the intent to deprive permanently, by (6) the use of force, fear, or threat of force.

Taking

The property taken in a robbery must be taken illegally by the robber. Someone who has the right to take such property cannot properly be convicted of robbery. This illegal taking is called **trespassory.** The property must be taken from the custody, control, or possession of the victim and, as will be seen later, from the victim's presence. This element of the crime is satisfied once the robber has possession of the property; until possession has occurred, only an attempt has taken place.

Carrying Away

Once the element of taking has been satisfied, the robber must then carry away the property. This element can be satisfied simply by showing that the accused totally removed the article from the position that it formerly occupied. It is not necessary to show that any great distance was involved in the carrying away.

Personal Property

The object of the robbery must be personal property as opposed to real estate or things attached to the land. Again, as in larceny (discussed in greater detail in Chapter 14) any tangible property and some forms of intangible property represented by tangible items, such as stocks and bonds, gas, electricity, minerals, and other such commodities, can be objects of robbery.

Another

The property taken must belong to another, not to the accused. This again relates to the first element of taking. If the taking is trespassory—illegal—then the property must be the rightful property of someone other than the robber.

The Intent to Deprive Permanently

Robbery is a crime of specific intent and requires that the prosecution establish, in court, that the defendant, at the time of taking the property by force or threat of force from the victim or the victim's presence, did, in fact, intend to deprive the victim of the use and enjoyment of that property permanently. In most cases, this fact can be concluded from the facts and the circumstances surrounding the case, but in specific-intent crime cases, juries are not permitted to assume this particular fact. Thus, the police officer's investigation must be geared to establishing this as an essential element of the crime. The fact that force or the threat of force was used to secure the property from the victim is often enough to convince a jury of the accused's intent to deprive permanently.

The Use of Force, Fear, or Threat of Force

This element of the crime requires that the force or threat of force be directed against the physical safety of the victim rather than his or her social well-being. Thus, threats to expose the victim as a homosexual or an embezzler do not satisfy this element of the crime. Proof that force was used or, at the very least, that threats were made such that the victim feared imminent bodily harm is essential for successful prosecutions of robbery cases. However, the force used to separate the victim from his or her property in robbery need not be great.

When the victim of a robbery is seriously injured, there is usually little difficulty in convincing the investigator or the jury that force was used. However, difficulties may arise in the case of a victim who claims to have been robbed under the threat of force when no actual injury occurred. In this case, the skill of the investigator in determining the facts of the case becomes crucial to successful prosecution.

There are also more subtle situations in which the investigator must know legal requirements as well as investigative techniques. The typical purse-snatching case is an illustration. Often, the force element of the crime of robbery can be satisfied only by determining whether the victim attempted to resist the force used and, if so, the extent of that resistance. It is generally accepted by courts that a woman who puts her purse next to her on the seat of a bus without keeping her hand on it or loosely holds it in her hand is not the victim of robbery if someone quickly grabs the purse and runs. In these cases, the woman has not resisted. However, if she were clutching the bag tightly and someone managed to grab it from her after even a slight struggle, sufficient force and resistance would have occurred to constitute robbery. A good rule for the investigator to follow in cases of uncertainty is that the removal of an article without more force than is absolutely necessary to remove it from its original resting place constitutes larceny. If any additional force, no matter how slight, is used, it is then robbery, provided the object is taken from the presence or person of the victim. The property does not have to be held by the victim physically or be on his or her person. It merely has to be under the victim's control. "Control" in this sense means the right or privilege to use the property as the victim sees fit. Neither is it necessary or essential that the property be visible to the victim when the crime is committed.

When force is not used but a threat to the physical well-being of the victim is indeed made, it is not necessary that the victim actually be frightened to the point of panic. It is enough that the victim is reasonably apprehensive and aware of the potential for injury.

OVERVIEW: THE OFFENSE, THE VICTIM, AND THE OFFENDER

In terms of weapons used, a firearm is used in 40% of the incidents, a knife or other cutting instrument in 8% of the cases, and "some other weapon" in another 10% of reported robberies; the remaining 42% of the incidents are **strong-armed,** meaning no weapon was used.[1] An illustration of the use of "some other weapon" is the robbery of a convenience store by a man using a hypodermic needle filled with what he claims is AIDS-contaminated blood.

Together, these data reveal that approximately 6 of every 10 robberies are armed, and the balance are strong-armed. Armed robbers often carry two or more weapons. Because of this, officers must continue to exercise great caution when approaching a suspect who has thrown a weapon down.

About one-third of all robberies result in a physical injury to the victim.[2] Females are about 10% more likely to be injured than are males, while Caucasians and African-Americans face nearly the same prospects for being injured.[3] Robbery is basically a stranger-to-stranger crime: 71% of the time the robber and the victim do not know each other.[4] About 60% of all robberies are committed by a single offender.[5] This factor tends to make robbery investigations more difficult: if the sole offender can keep his or her mouth shut, does not attract attention to himself/herself or run with other criminals, and does not get a bad break, the offender can be hard to catch. Although a small number of victims fight back in some way, in 82% of robberies it is the offender who initiates violence.[6]

The objective of the confrontation between robber and victim is to get the victim's immediate compliance. In most situations, the mere showing of a gun will accomplish this. One offender reports: "Sometimes I don't even touch them; I just point the gun right in front of their face. I don't even have to say nothing half the time. When they see that pistol, they know what time it is."[7] A victim who hesitates or is seen as uncooperative may or may not get a warning.

Other robbers are less "tolerant," and when faced with uncooperative victims, they shoot them in the leg or the foot. However, for some offenders, injuring the victim is part of the thrill, the "kick" of "pulling a job." What type of violence is used and when it is used may form part of an identifiable modus operandi. Such an MO can tie together several robberies, and the combined information from various investigations often produces significant investigative leads.

There is no question that being under the influence and committing robberies are intimately related. Victims believe that 28% of those robbing them are high on drugs and/or alcohol.[8] Some offenders use alcohol to lessen their apprehension about getting caught. Robbery is basically an intraracial crime; in one study, blacks said that they were robbed by blacks 80% of the time, and whites said that they were robbed by whites 75% of the time.[9] Nationally, among those apprehended for robbery, 90% are males, 54% are blacks, and 19% are under 25 years of age.[10]

Although no robbery is routine to victims, many cases are fairly straightforward to investigators. Some robberies, however, stand out because of unusual circumstances, as the following incidents illustrate:

A lone robber held up a bank and made off with $600. As police were chasing him, the robber crashed the stolen Chevrolet Suburban he was driving. It burst into flames, and the money burned up. Now being pursued on foot by a police officer, the robber tossed off his plaid jacket and escaped. The police found a napkin with a name and a telephone number in the jacket. With the bank's surveillance photos in hand, the police confronted the man identified on the napkin. In turn, he identified the robber as someone whom he had been letting sleep on his couch. An arrest was subsequently made in the case.[11]

Two thugs were cruising in a residential area looking for someone to rob. They spotted two men playing pool in an open garage. Blissfully unaware that the two men were off-duty police officers, the thugs approached them and placed a gun to one officer's head, and the officer began to struggle. The second officer pulled a weapon and shot both offenders.[12]

A teenage boy robbed a convenience store at knifepoint around 1:30 in the morning, taking money and merchandise and fleeing on foot. The police solved the case by following the offender's shoeprints in the freshly fallen snow straight to his home.[13]

Despite such variations, three styles of robberies—the ambush, the selective raid, and the planned operation—can be classified according to the amount of planning conducted by the perpetrators. The **ambush** involves virtually no planning and depends almost entirely on the element of surprise. A prime example is robberies in which victims are physically overpowered by sudden, crude force and in which "scores" are generally small.[14] The lack of planning does not mean, however, that there is no premeditation.

The **selective raid** is characterized by a minimal amount of casual planning. Sites are tentatively selected and very briefly cased, and possible routes of approach and flight are formulated. Scores vary from low to moderate, and several robberies may be committed in rapid succession.

The **planned operation** is characterized by larger "scores," no planned use of force, less likelihood of apprehension, and careful planning.

TYPOLOGY OF ROBBERIES

In addition to knowing the broad profile of the offense, the investigator must also be familiar with various types of robberies, such as the following.

Visible Street Robberies

Approximately 5 of every 10 robberies happen on the street.[15] In 93% of the cases, the victim is alone[16] and typically on the way to or from a leisure activity within 5 miles of his or her home,[17] such as patronizing a nightclub or restaurant:[18]

I'd watch people in bars and follow them. One time, I followed this guy and grabbed his tie and swung it down to the ground. And, uh, he hit his head, and that's when I took the money and ran.[19]

The victim is three times more likely to be confronted by a single perpetrator than by multiple perpetrators.[20] Youthful robbers are particularly likely to commit strong-armed robberies—also referred to as **muggings**—in which no weapons are involved and in which they suddenly physically attack and beat the victim, taking cash, jewelry, wallets, purses, and other valuables. Purse snatching may or may not be a robbery. If a woman is carrying a purse loosely on her open fingers and someone grabs it and runs and she then experiences fear, robbery is not an appropriate charge because the fear did not precede the taking. But if the same woman sees or hears someone running toward her and in fear clutches her purse, which is then ripped from her by the perpetrator, a robbery has occurred. If apprehended, the suspect would likely be charged with some degree of larceny, depending on the value of the object(s) being stolen. The penalty for larceny is generally much lower than that for the crime of robbery, and in many states if a firearm is used during the commission of a robbery the penalty is even more severe than for unarmed robbery.

Street robberies usually involve little or no planning by the perpetrators, who may have been waiting in one place for a potential victim to appear or walking around looking for someone to rob on the spur of the moment.

Because street robberies happen so quickly and often occur at night in areas that are not well lighted, victims often have difficulty providing anything more than a basic physical description. The description may be even more limited if the victim is injured either by a weapon or by a beating in a sudden, overpowering mugging.

Spontaneous street robbers may "graduate" to jobs that involve a certain amount of planning. For example, they may stake out ATMs or banks. In the case of ATMs, they may have decided that they are going to rob the first "soft-looking" person who is alone and driving an expensive car. In the case of banks, they may rob someone on the street whom they have watched long enough to know that the person is going to the bank to make a cash deposit or to use the night depository. Although people sometimes commit robberies for excitement or to be "one of the guys," for the most part they do it to get the money, which often goes to pay for drugs.

Use of Surveillance Cameras to Prevent Street Robberies

The use of surveillance cameras to monitor the streets to prevent robberies and other crimes is becoming increasingly common. For example the Paterson, New Jersey, Police Department makes extensive use of surveillance cameras in their city. Currently they are using 18 surveillance cameras installed in high-crime areas throughout the city. The cameras can be moved to other locations within two hours as needed. They are also monitored around the clock by a police officer (see Figure 12-1).

The monitoring officer can zoom in on a particular image as needed. These images are also recorded, so in the event something is missed officers can go back and replay the video for a closer examination. The cameras have captured several robberies in progress as well as drug transactions. The police department also reports observing drugs and weapons being discarded as police officers approach the suspects. The officers monitoring

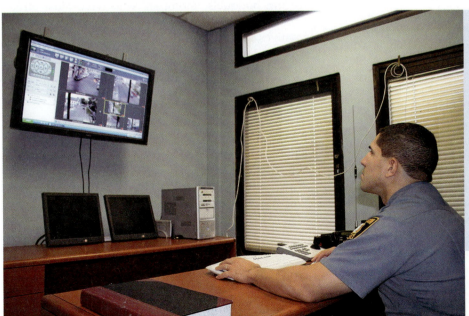

◄ FIGURE 12-1
Use of surveillance cameras to prevent robberies
A Paterson, New Jersey, police officer is monitoring simultaneously 18 high-crime areas by the use of surveillance cameras. Each camera pans on a time sequence, produces high-quality video, and also allows the monitoring officer to zoom in on a particular location. The cameras can be moved to a new location within two hours.
(Courtesy Lt. Anthony Traina, Paterson New Jersey Police Department)

the surveillance cameras can inform officers at the scene what they have observed and direct them to areas where any contraband may have been discarded. The cameras have been characterized by one high-ranking police official as having one officer walking multiple beats.[21]

Carjackings

During the 1960s, many cars were stolen as temporary transportation by youthful offenders who used them for "joyriding" and then abandoned them. In many states, the criminal statutes recognized both a felony auto theft and a misdemeanor joyriding charge. Around 1970, there was a shift to stealing cars for their parts and an increase in stealing cars for resale here and abroad, after they had been "repapered," meaning that the vehicles were given new, false identities.

In conventional auto thefts, the car is removed surreptitiously, and there is no contact between the thief and the vehicle's owner. Before 1990, if an offender used a weapon to confront an owner and steal the person's car, the crime was simply classified as a robbery. But in 1990, with the number of such incidents increasing, the term **carjacking** was coined in Detroit to describe the growing numbers of this potentially violent type of confrontation between offender and victim.[22]

One explanation for the increase in carjackings is that such crimes are the result of too much success in the antitheft-device market, including tracking devices such as Lojack, the Club, computer chips in ignition keys, and motion sensors. A second explanation is that there is a widespread supply of potential victims, no skill is required, no inside information is needed, and the need for planning is minimal.

In terms of location, 44% of carjackings occur at the victim's home or within 1 mile of the victim's home; 85% happen within 5 miles of the victim's home.[23] Often this offense is committed at gas stations, ATMs, car washes, parking decks, shopping-center parking lots, and convenience stores; at restaurant, bar, office, train station, apartment, and public transportation parking lots; and at traffic control signs and signals.[24] In 70% of the cases, at least some of the victim's property is recovered.[25]

Carjackers tend to operate in small groups of two to five perpetrators. The modus operandi used is to quickly separate the person from the car. In some instances, doing so may be as quick and violent as using a brick to shatter the driver-side window of an occupied car and manhandling the occupant out of the vehicle. Mothers with children are particularly vulnerable when confronted by offenders who threaten to harm the children if the keys to the car are not given up immediately. One method of carjacking involves accidentally bumping the victim's car from the rear; when the driver gets out to investigate, one perpetrator pulls a gun, takes control of the victim's car, and flees, followed by his or her accomplices in the "bumper car." Another tactic is to use several cars to "box in" the target vehicle

and then slow down gradually until it is stopped and the victim can be dealt with. Some carjackers target victims who drive into high-crime areas to buy drugs; some watch expensive cars in parking lots and then carjack them because they believe the victims are more likely to have jewelry and cash that can also be taken.

According to the FBI, the primary motives for carjacking are to acquire transportation away from the crime scene after robbing the driver, to get to and from another crime, such as another robbery or a drive-by shooting, to sell the car for cash, to trade it for drugs,[26] and to acquire temporary transportation. Whenever a carjacking takes place, the potential for a more serious crime exists.

Carjacking may also be a tool used by perpetrators to execute other crimes, which can lead to murder. A woman was carjacked and then forced into another car by the offenders. She was taken to a different location and raped. Later, she was forced to make several ATM withdrawals. Over the next several days, she was further abused and then executed by being slowly strangled with a coat hanger by one of the perpetrators while the others taunted her and cheered the executioner.

Home-Invasion Robberies

Home-invasion robberies (HIRs) typically target the person, rather than the residence, often selecting women and senior citizens.[27] Invaders often follow potential targets from shopping centers to their homes. They may enter the residence through an unlocked door or window, talk an unsuspecting victim into opening the door, or simply force the door open.

In some cases, the targets are "fingered," or identified, by others who pass information on to the invaders for drugs or money. Such offenders will also use deceit to gain entry into a residence. Home invaders may pose as police officers, water department employees, florists delivering bouquets, motorists who have "just struck your parked car," natural gas and electric company representatives, and "supervisors checking on your newspaper delivery service," to name just a few. The following case describes one such incident:

> **Two men** knocked on the door of a home and asked to use the telephone. After gaining entry by this ruse and casing the place, they decided the home was worth robbing. They returned that afternoon, forced their way in, severely beat the couple—who were in their late seventies—and left with valuables and the victims' pickup truck.[28]

Automatic-Teller-Machine Robberies

Automatic teller machines (ATMs) were introduced in the early 1970s, and their use has grown at a staggering rate

◄FIGURE 12-2
Automatic teller machines:
A natural target for robberies
Automatic teller machines are very popular today as a means of obtaining on-the-spot cash. At one point, robberies at these locations were so frequent that critics referred to ATMs as "magnets for crime." Placing ATMs in highly visible areas and improving surrounding lighting has led to a decrease in this form of robbery over the last few years. (© Syracuse Newspapers/David Lassman/Image Works)

since then. Today, there are approximately 12 billion ATM transactions annually.[29] At one point, robberies at these locations were so publicized that critics referred to ATMs as "magnets for crime" (Figure 12-2). However, the ATM robbery rate has dropped from 1 robbery per 1 million transactions during the 1990s to its present 1 per 3.5 million transactions.[30] A combination of factors account for this drop, including locating ATMs where customers have a high visibility of their surroundings, using landscaping of 24 inches or less in height, and keeping the ATM areas well-lit at night.[31] In addition, customers are becoming knowledgeable about self-protection measures and are adopting them. Despite such realities, public fear of being victimized at or near an ATM is substantial.

The ATM robbery victim is typically a lone woman who is using the machine between 8 P.M. and midnight.[32] To minimize the time spent with the victim and to avoid having to pressure the victim to make a withdrawal, many offenders simply wait until the transaction is completed before they pounce. Others confront the victim before the transaction, forcing her or him to make large withdrawals. Many victims report that they never saw the robber coming.

Offenders are most likely to work alone and are typically armed. They are usually about 25 years of age and tend to position themselves near an ATM, waiting for a likely victim to appear.[33] In addition to taking the cash and any valuables the victim has, offenders may carjack the victim's vehicle to flee the scene.

Taxicab Robberies

Taxicab drivers are easy targets because they work alone, are available at all times of the day and night, do business on a cash basis, and can be called or directed to locations that favor the aims of offenders. As a result, cab drivers have a higher criminal homicide victimization rate than does any other occupational group in the United States.[34] Knowing this, cabbies take precautions and a few even have miraculous escapes:

Two armed robbers sat in the backseat of a taxi. One placed a gun to the driver's head and pulled the trigger. The shooter's gun either misfired or wasn't loaded. As the gunman fiddled with his weapon, the cabbie slammed the taxi into reverse and floored it. Alarmed at being jostled around, the two robbers "bailed out," and the driver escaped unharmed.[35]

Increasingly taxicabs are having signs posted on them that clearly indicate that the driver has only a limited amount of cash available, as well as safety deposit boxes that cannot be opened by the drivers. (See Figure 12-3.)

Robberies of taxicabs frequently occur during the evening hours. Perpetrators are typically armed and have set out with the intent to do a robbery. In a common method of operation for this type of robbery, the perpetrator hails a taxi on the street or calls one to meet him or her at a particular intersection. The robber climbs inside the cab and asks to be driven to a particular location. At any point during the ride, the "fare" tells the driver to stop and then robs the driver. The robbery may take place when the cab is in a relatively secluded area or at the heart of a busy intersection where the offender can simply melt into the crowd. Calling a cab may imply that the robber does not have his or her own transportation, but sometimes the robbery occurs near a place where an accomplice is waiting with a getaway car.

▶ **FIGURE 12-3 Robbery prevention sign on taxicab**
Photo A depicts the typical location of a robbery prevention sign on a cab. Photo B provides a close-up of what the potential would-be robber would see upon approaching or entering the cab. The safety deposit box referred to in the photo is actually a heavy-gauge steel box bolted to the cab floor with a slot on top into which bills can be inserted. The box can only be opened by a key kept at the taxicab garage.

In Houston, Washington, D.C., and other cities, digital cameras have been installed in taxis, taking a picture when the doors are opened, when the meter is activated, and at unspecified intervals during the ride. Using this system, offenders are being apprehended and successfully prosecuted on the basis of the photographs taken.[36]

Convenience-Store Robberies

Although spectacular robberies, such as the $1 million robbery of a Las Vegas jewelry store by a lone gunman,[37] capture the interest of the media and public, investigators are more likely to work commercial robberies where far less is taken, such as the losses incurred by convenience stores.

Convenience stores account for about 6% of all reported robberies. These stores do a great deal of business in cash, are often open 24 hours a day, have numerous locations, typically offer little or no protection from robbers, and may have only one person on duty. Inasmuch as some of

these characteristics also apply to taxicabs, it is not surprising that convenience-store workers, like cab drivers, are among the occupational groups having the highest risk for workplace violence.[38]

A study of 1,835 convenience-store robberies showed that 59% of them happened at night, between 9 P.M. and 3 A.M., and that the offender was armed with a firearm in 63% of the cases[39] (Figure 12-4). Employees were more likely to be injured when the offender used a blunt object, as opposed to a firearm, although all worker deaths were by firearms. Among the factors that contribute to lowering the probability of employee injury are the presence of a customer in the store, the store's having previously been robbed multiple times, and the robber's getting some money as opposed to getting none.

When robbers are choosing a store to rob, the factors that are most important to them are the amount of money they can get, a good escape route, inadequate police

▶ **FIGURE 12-4 Robbery in progress**
This video photo depicts an armed robbery in progress. The robber cannot be identified because of the ski mask, but the photo still has value. If the individual continues to use the same disguise and firearms and is later arrested, these items can be linked back to this crime and other robberies. In addition, if he becomes a suspect and his home/car are searched and those items are found, once again they can link him to this and other robberies he committed. (Photo courtesy Sergeant Scott Whittington, Colorado Springs [Colorado] Police Department)

coverage, an unarmed clerk, a lone employee, no video surveillance cameras, and the absence of customers.[40]

There is some evidence that certain measures are associated with lower rates of being robbed. These include locating the cash registers in the center of the convenience store, having good visibility into the store from outside of it, installing bright parking-lot lighting, having two workers on duty, not counting money in the open, and posting signs noting that there is only a limited amount of money (e.g., $100) in the till.[41]

Truck-Hijacking Robberies

In the United States, cargo theft may be responsible for losses of $10 billion to $12 billion a year.[42] If so, the only crime category with a higher dollar loss is health-care fraud. The estimate for cargo-theft losses includes both cargo theft and truck hijacking. It is believed that hijacking accounts for a significant percentage of total cargo-theft losses, but because crime statistics on it are not kept, no one knows what the percentage really is. As cargo theft through hijacking has increasingly been recognized as a significant crime problem, there have been calls to gather statistics for it in the National Incident Based Reporting System (NIBRS). The FBI office in Long Beach, California, estimates that cargo-theft losses in that region are $1 million per day.[43] It should also be noted that truck hijacking is not a uniquely American problem. For example, in Argentina, truck hijackers are referred to as *piratas del asfalto*, which means "asphalt pirates."

The fact that accurate statistics are needed has not discouraged law enforcement agencies from making important moves to combat this crime problem. Large agencies, such as the New Jersey State Police, have created Cargo Theft and Robbery Investigative Units, while others have adopted the use of multiagency task forces and Cargo Criminal Apprehension Teams (Cargo CATs). Additionally, specialized law enforcement groups, such as the Western States Cargo Theft Association, exist to supply training and to exchange information on this subject.

Truck hijacking is committed by experienced armed robbers acting on inside information. Because transporting goods by truck generates a substantial written record, there are many points at which insiders can learn the nature of a cargo and when it will be moved. Many truck hijackings happen in or near large cities because it is easy to dispose of the goods there. If there is a seaport, the goods taken may also be quickly on their way to a foreign country within hours. The contents of some hijacked trucks are off-loaded to another truck or several smaller trucks and may be in several other states by the time the investigation is getting started. Hijackers take what is valuable, with a preference for cargoes that are easy to dispose of and hard to trace. Examples include loads of clothing and high-tech equipment components, which may each have a value of $500,000 or more.

A number of truck hijackings involve collusion on the part of the driver with those committing this specialized form of robbery. The driver may be bribed or given some portion of the cargo for his or her personal use. In a variation of this, hijackers give drugs to drivers and provide them with women and then coerce the drivers into cooperating by threatening to cut off their supply of drugs and women, to give a spouse photographs of the driver's liaisons with other women, or to expose the driver's use of drugs to employers.

Drivers of rigs may be confronted at roadblocks, or "detours," set up by hijackers. They may be forced from the road or accosted by the hijackers as they enter or leave truck rest stops. Some drivers have been tricked into stopping to help a "disabled" motorist. In more brazen moves, hijackers may invade truck parks, seize or kill security personnel, and take the trucks that they have targeted.

Bank Robbery

Although this portion of the chapter focuses primarily on bank robberies, many of the investigative and crime prevention suggestions set forth herein (some of which have already been discussed) can also be applied to large retail businesses, small convenience stores, jewelry stores, appliance stores, and so forth. This includes methods of escape, escape routes, target selection, and robbery prevention.[44]

Distinguishing Professional and Amateur Bank Robbers

Bank robberies and, for that matter, most robberies do not appear to be well-planned offenses committed by professional criminals; instead, increasing evidence suggests that many bank robberies are spontaneous and opportunistic crimes that are often acts of desperation.[45–52]

Because most bank robberies are committed by solitary, unarmed, and undisguised offenders, they can be considered the work of amateurs rather than professionals. In contrast, it is the less common armed bank robberies that more often involve multiple offenders and the use of disguises.[53–55] Distinguishing bank robberies as the work of amateur or professional robbers provides important insight about the risks or robbery in selecting crime prevention strategies most likely to be effective.

To a great extent, bank robbers can be classified as amateur or professional based on known characteristics of the robbery—the number of offenders, use of weapons and disguises, efforts to defeat security, timing of the robbery, target selection, and means of getaway (see Table 12-1).

Method of Escape

The method of escape further distinguishes amateur from professional robbers. Cars are not the sole means of escape; many offenders escape on foot or even by bicycle, at least initially. In 1978, for example, 80% of bank robbers used getaway cars,[56] whereas vehicles were observed in only one-third of robberies in the 1990s.[57–59]

	TABLE 12-1	Distinguishing Professional and Amateur Bank Robbers

	PROFESSIONAL	AMATEUR
Offenders	• Multiple offenders with division of labor • Shows evidence of planning • May be older • Prior bank robbery convictions • Travels further to rob banks	• Solitary offender • Drug or alcohol use likely • No prior bank crime • Lives near bank target
Violence	• Aggressive takeover, with loud verbal demands • Visible weapons, especially guns • Intimidation, physical or verbal threats	• Note passed to teller or simple verbal demand • Waits in line • No weapon
Defeat Security	• Uses a disguise • Disables or obscures surveillance cameras • Demands that dye packs be left out, alarms not be activated, or police not be called	
Robbery Success	• Hits multiple teller windows • Larger amounts stolen • Lower percentage of money recovered • More successful robberies • Fewer cases directly cleared • Longer time from offense to case clearance	• Single teller window victimized • Lower amounts stolen • Higher percentage of money recovered • More failed robberies • Shorter time from offense to case clearance, including more same-day arrests • Direct case clearance more likely
Robbery Timing	• Targets banks when few customers are present, such as at opening time • Targets banks early in the week	• Targets banks when numerous customers are present, such as around midday • Targets banks near closing or on Friday
Target Selection	• Previous robbery • Busy road near intersection • Multidirectional traffic • Corner locations, multiple vehicle exits	• Previous robbery • Heavy pedestrian traffic or adjacent to dense multifamily residences • Parcels without barriers • Parcels with egress obscured
Getaway	• Via car	• On foot or bicycle

(Courtesy Deborah Lamm Weisel, *Bank Robbery*, U.S. Department of Justice, Office of Community Oriented Policing Services, 2007.)

Getaway vehicles are more prevalent when there are two or more offenders: 72% of robbery teams use vehicles, which reflects some degrees of planning.[60] In contrast, 58% of solitary robbers escape on foot. Two factors discourage solitary robbers from using vehicles: without an accomplice to drive the vehicle, it must be parked and quickly accessible to the robber; further, solitary robbers typically select targets that are convenient, such as those close to their residence making a car unnecessary. In contrast, professional bank robbers appear willing to travel farther than other robbers, perhaps because there are fewer banks than other types of commercial targets or because banks tend to be clustered geographically and are open for fewer hours.[61,62]

Escape Routes in Target Selection

Because many bank robberies are the work of amateurs, it may appear that robbers randomly select targets. They do not. Instead, robbers select targets primarily based on their concern with getting away from the robbery quickly.

Although much effort to reduce bank robbery has focused on bank interiors and security measures, most bank robbers do not feel they are at risk of apprehension during the commission of the crime. Instead, robbers assume there will be easy access to cash and that the robbery will be completed quickly. Thus, robbers for the most part are relatively unconcerned about alarms and cameras, neither of which will slow their escape.

A robber's choice of target is shaped by two escape features: the type of transportation available and the ease and number of escape routes.[63–71] Because offenders prefer choices during flight, they tend to select targets that have more than one escape path.

Solitary offenders typically cannot escape in a vehicle because of the logistics of parking and retrieving a vehicle. Thus, solitary offenders typically escape on foot.

In contrast, multiple offenders typically escape in a vehicle—often stolen just prior to the robbery to reduce the likelihood that the vehicle has been reported stolen by the owner.

Bank Robbery Prevention

Following are some of the actions banks can take to reduce the likelihood of robberies and minimize their losses.

- *Limiting cash access:* Cash in banks is available at teller windows—the most frequent target of robbers—and safes. Most banks have cash management policies, such as removing cash from the teller drawers when it reaches a predetermined amount, a fairly common practice among convenience stores as well. Some banks use vacuum systems to quickly and efficiently remove cash from teller drawers.
- *Using dye packs:* Exploding **dye packs** are widely used by banks to prevent stolen money from being used. Dye packs stain both the robber and the cash, preventing use of the money and aiding in the detection of the robber. Many dye packs are supplemented by tear gas, which is triggered by an electromagnetic field near the bank exit door. When the tear gas explodes, the robber is effectively immobilized (Figure 12-5).
- *Slowing the robbery:* Because bank robbers want the crime to proceed quickly, some banks have adopted strategies that are intended to slow the pace of the robbery. A slow robbery may increase the suspect's perception of risk and will sometimes cause the robber to abandon the crime.[72,73] For example, interior obstacles such as revolving doors or customer service counters can slow the robber's escape; timed safes and withdrawal limits on cash dispensing machines can further increase the duration of the robbery.
- *Employing greeters:* Bank employees known as greeters welcome customers and reduce the anonymity of a would-be robber; this face-to-face interaction may discourage a robbery before it occurs. Greeters should be trained to be alert to suspicious behavior. They are more likely to discourage amateur robbers than professionals robbers.
- *Use of security guards:* There is disagreement regarding the effectiveness of bank security guards.[74-76] Guards are expensive, and they may also create an environment that makes customers fearful. Some research suggests that guards reduce the risk of

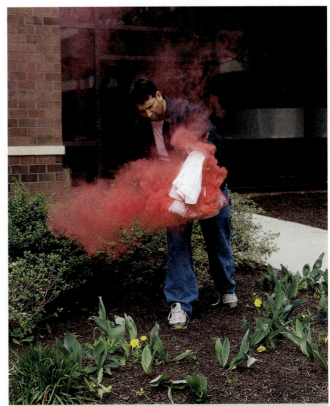

▲ **FIGURE 12-5** **Exploding dye packs**
Exploding dye packs are widely used by banks to prevent stolen money from being used. When they explode, the dye packs stain both the robber and the cash, thereby preventing use of the money and aiding in the detection of the robber. Many dye packs are supplemented by tear gas which is triggered by an electromagnetic field near the bank exit door. When the tear gas explodes, the robber will be effectively immobilized.
(Courtesy 3SI Security Systems)

bank robbery.[77-79] However, some studies also suggest that the presence of the armed guards increases the risks of violence during a robbery.[80-82]
- *Warning likely offenders:* Bank robbers tend to overestimate the amount of money they will get from a robbery, to underestimate the likelihood of arrest, and to be unaware of the sentences they face if convicted. Thus, some banks and trade associations have developed publicity campaigns designed to educate would-be offenders about the low take, high capture rate, and other perils of a career in bank robbery.[83]
- *Using tracking devices:* Some banks conceal electronic **tracking devices** with the robbery money, thus aiding police in locating offenders. Tracking devices use low-voltage transmitting microchips with transponders. However, since tracking devices are intended to increase the chance of apprehending offenders, they are not likely to prevent robberies from occurring.
- *Using bait money:* **Bait money** is cash with sequential serial numbers that are recorded by the bank.

Bank surveillance camera
A bank surveillance camera captures the image of a man who has just entered the bank for the purpose of committing a robbery. He concealed a gun inside his hat. The man had entered the bank earlier in the day to case it for a robbery. At that time he was observed by an alert bank teller who had previously seen a bank surveillance photograph of the man which had been shown to her by law enforcement officials several days before. The bank surveillance photo shown to her was of a man who had previously committed a bank robbery. She recognized the man and the police were contacted. The police then staked out the bank parking lot. The man returned several hours later, committed the robbery, exited the bank, entered his car at which time he and his companion were arrested. (Courtesy Arlington Texas Police Department)

When the money reenters circulation, police track its use in hopes of locating the suspect. Bait money is already widely used by banks.

- *Offering rewards:* Some banks actively publicize "most wanted" bank robbers, displaying their surveillance photos and offering rewards for information leading to their capture. Banks use websites, local silent witness programs, and tip lines to publicize crimes and to seek out offenders. There are also national tip organizations that coordinate information about highly mobile robbers.

- *Upgrading electronic surveillance:* Bank surveillance cameras are in widespread use: 98% of robbed banks have interior surveillance cameras. However, cameras do not appear to reduce robberies. Many bank robbers are not deterred, because they simply do not believe they will be caught. Others believe that cameras can be thwarted with a disguise or by covert behavior or that cameras can be disabled, such as with spray paint; or they simply do not think about cameras at all.[84–86] However, sometimes electronic surveillance can have unanticipated benefits. For example, one alert employee in a Texas bank noticed a man hanging around the bank lobby and thought she recognized him from a photograph she had been shown several days before by law enforcement officials. The picture of the individual, who had held up other banks, was being shown to bank employees in the general area. The individual did not stay in the bank very long, but when he left the alert bank employee contacted the police who then started to surveil the bank parking lot. Several hours later the man returned to the bank. His partner remained in the car while he walked inside the bank to commit the robbery. Once again, his image was captured by the surveillance camera, depicted in Figure 12-6. The man can be seen concealing what would turn out to be a gun in is hat. The police were not able to prevent the robbery, but once the man exited the bank and entered the getaway car, police officers were able to converge in their vehicles and to place both men under arrest. Thus, one possible strategy for bank robbery prevention could be to obtain bank surveillance photographs of individuals who committed bank robberies and show them to bank employees in the same general area in order to alert them to what the potential robbers look like. As it turned out, the individual and his partner confessed to robbing seven other banks in a half dozen nearby towns.

- *Rapidly activating alarms:* Although alarms lead to the arrest of bank robbers in only about 6% of crimes, there is evidence that prompt activation increases apprehension rates. Some bank employees do not activate alarms until after the robber has left the premises. This is so because of safety concerns about the employees and customers in case the police trapped the robber inside the bank thus creating a potential hostage situation and violence. In other cases, the delay might be due to panic or to comply with instructions made by the robber.

- *Installing bandit barriers:* The FBI recommends that banks install bullet-resistant glass **bandit barriers** between tellers and customers. Such devices are also becoming fairly common in convenience stores,

◄ **FIGURE 12-7   Bandit barriers**
Bandit barriers may discourage some bank robbers and also increase the safety of bank employees. Such devices are also becoming fairly common in convenience stores, especially those that operate 24 hours a day and are located in high-crime areas.
(Courtesy Clear Security Systems. www .clearsecuritysystems.com)

especially those that operate 24-hours a day and are in high-crime areas (Figure 12-7).[87] Although most of these are permanent installations, some bandit barriers "pop-up" when activated by tellers or when an object crosses the counter.

- *Installing access control vestibules:* Access control vestibules—also known as man-catcher vestibules or man-traps—are a specialized form of access control device. These devices can be used to scan potential customers for weapons before they access the bank interior; others are designed to be manually activated by tellers.

- *Hardening targets:* Banks have employed a wide variety of target-hardening strategies that are designed to make the bank interior appear inhospitable to would-be robbers. These include revolving doors, increased distance between entrances and teller stations, higher teller counters, queuing and other physical barriers, and single-door entrances and exits.[88–90]

- *Consider the possibility of an inside job:* When a bank robbery does occur, investigators should consider the possibility of the robber having received assistance from someone inside the bank. One interesting case occurred recently in the Atlanta, Georgia, area. A Bank of America was held up by two young women identified as the "Barbie Bandits." These two young women, who would eventually be identified as Heather Johnston and Ashley Miller, both 19, were photographed by a bank security camera and subsequently identified by people who recognized them when their pictures were shown on local television (Figure 12-8). Their arrest and the subsequent investigation led to the arrest of two additional accomplices—namely, a convicted drug dealer, Michael Darrell Chastang, 27, and a Bank of America teller, Benny Allen III, 22. The four had conspired to commit the theft and divided the money after the crime was committed.

▶ **FIGURE 12-8   Bank robbery: an inside job**
This photo depicts two young women, Ashley Miller (*left*) and Heather Johnston (*right*) both 19, dubbed by the media "the Barbie Bandits." Their images were captured on a bank surveillance camera wearing sunglasses and reportedly giggling throughout the robbery. The bank robbery occurred in the Atlanta, Georgia, area. The video camera images were broadcast on local television and the two young women were identified by viewers who knew them. As it turned out the robbery was actually an inside job in which the two women conspired with a convicted drug dealer and a bank teller who worked in the bank they robbed. (© AP/Wide World Photos)

RESPONDING TO THE SCENE

In route to the scene of a robbery call, the officer must ensure that all information available from the dispatcher has been obtained, including the answers to the following questions: What is the exact location of the offense, including the type of business? Is the offense in progress? How many suspects are involved? What type of and how many weapons were displayed? What description of the suspect is available? By what method and in what direction did the suspect flee? What is the description of the means of transportation used by the suspect?

In approaching the scene, the officer must be alert for several possibilities:

- The dispatcher may provide information on the suspects' escape, such as their direction in fleeing from the scene and whether they were on foot or in a vehicle.
- Information about the target, MO, suspects, vehicles, weapons used, and other factors in recent robberies may help the responding officer recognize the suspects if they are moving away from the scene on the street along which the officer approaches, even if the dispatcher cannot supply any specific information other than the nature of the crime.
- The fleeing suspects may, as the officer approaches them on the way to the scene, abruptly turn off, fire at the officer, or otherwise suddenly reveal themselves.

The primary tactical objectives of officers responding to a robbery call are public safety, officer protection, and tactical control of the scene. Secondary objectives include conducting the preliminary investigation, apprehending perpetrators, and recovering property. Arriving at the scene unobserved by the suspects facilitates the achievement of both primary and secondary objectives. It also allows tactical control and the element of surprise to pass from the robbers to the police. Units assigned to a robbery call should plan and coordinate the actions to be taken at the scene. Because the perpetrators may have police scanners, care should be taken with respect to radio transmissions. Arriving officers should not give away their exact positions and should refer to buildings by prearranged letter designations (e.g., "the A building").[91] They can never assume that the robber(s) have left the scene; for example, robbers have been known to hide near or at the scene, seeking to escape detection. Responding units should approach separately on streets parallel to that on which the robbery occurred or is occurring, using emergency lights but not sirens. The use of emergency lights permits more rapid progress through traffic. The reason for not using a siren is that the sound may panic suspects near or at the scene, triggering violence or hostage taking. It is believed that 9 out of 10 hostage situations that develop out of robberies occur because of a too visible first-responding officer.[92]

However, it is important to remember that most states require a police vehicle responding in an emergency mode to have both its emergency lights and siren activated. Thus, when the tactically correct decision is made to deactivate the siren, the officer's driving must be adjusted accordingly because now the motoring public no longer has the benefit of "hearing" the approaching police vehicle.

At a distance of three to five blocks from the scene in an urban area and much farther in rural settings,[93] the emergency lights should be turned off to avoid possible detection by a lookout. The police officer should begin to smoothly decelerate, thus avoiding engine noise, squealing tires, or "emergency" stops that could give away the police car's arrival.

The first officer on the scene must quickly "size up" the area to gather any possible intelligence, including location of the robbers, lookouts, and escape vehicles. The locations of the perpetrators are particularly important given the fact that such criminals may have automatic and other weapons—which they are willing to use. Actually identifying the **lookouts** may be difficult; two officers in New York,[94] for instance, were killed by a lookout disguised as a nun.[94] The officer should leave his or her car quietly and move—unobserved—to a protected position to watch, where possible, two sides (e.g., north and east) of the building. One of these sides should be the exit most likely to be used by the robbers. Moving unobserved does not necessarily imply moving quickly. Running into position may invite passersby to "rubberneck," giving away the officer's location.[95] Before moving to any position, the officer should make sure the background of that position, when viewed from the perpetrators' positions, does not silhouette him or her.[96]

The officer in the second unit should take the same precautions as the first in moving into position. The second officer's responsibility is to cover the two remaining sides (e.g., the south and the west). Both officers should keep their vehicles and portable radios at low volume to avoid being detected. The primary and backup officers should be sure that their positions in the lines of fire do not endanger each other.

It is also of particular importance when moving into their respective unobserved positions that officers not get inside of, that is, between, any possible lookouts and the robbery scene. Such a position would leave them vulnerable to fire from several sides.

Both in approaching the scene and at the scene, officers should avoid action, physical, or situational stereotyping.[97]

Action Stereotyping

Action stereotyping occurs when the officer's expectations are so set to see one thing that he or she fails to perceive the event accurately. For example, the responding officer may expect the suspect to come rushing out of the store, hop into a car, and speed away. Although this may be the case, there are also other possible behaviors:

Two robbers who confessed to over 20 "quick mart" robberies had been apprehended during a police surveillance. While being interrogated, the pair revealed that they had come close to being caught on several occasions when responding units arrived at the scene very quickly. They said they had escaped apprehension at those times by simply walking away in a normal manner. This proved to be an embarrassment for one officer who remembered the pair walking past his car. This officer said that they just appeared to be "normal" citizens and that there was nothing extraordinary about them.[98]

Physical Stereotyping

Physical stereotyping is an officer's expectations that the robber will be of a particular description. Such stereotypes may allow the suspect to escape or be fatal to officers:

An officer entered a convenience store in response to an alarm; his gun was drawn, but he started to put it away when he didn't see anything out of the ordinary. As he approached the two clerks behind the counter, the younger one yelled a warning: the other "clerk" was an armed robber whose appearance—he was 60 years old—did not fit with the officer's stereotype of a robber.[99]

Another aspect of physical stereotyping is that investigators may have difficulty believing witnesses' descriptions. For example, we expect bank robbers to be relatively young adults and vigorous. However, in northern Colorado nearly a decade ago, an 82-year-old man known as the "salt-and-pepper bandit" was arrested for a string of bank robberies; in another case, a 105-pound 70-year-old woman donned a black plastic bag as a disguise and robbed a bank, declaring, "There's a bomb here; give me the money, no bells, no sirens."[100]

Situational Stereotyping

In **situational stereotyping,** the officers' previous experience with, and knowledge of, a particular location increases their vulnerability:

A silent alarm went off at a bar; the call was dispatched and as the assigned unit drove toward the bar, the two partners joked about the inability of the owner to set the alarm properly, since he was continuously tripping it accidentally, creating frequent false alarms. The officer operating the police car parked it in front of the bar, and as the two officers began to saunter casually up to the front door of the bar, two suspects burst out with guns in hand and began shooting. Miraculously, neither officer was hit. One of the suspects was wounded and arrested at the scene; the other one escaped and was not apprehended until several weeks later.

Returning to some earlier points, although the suspects may be observed fleeing the scene or may reveal themselves in some manner to the officer assigned to respond to the call, such encounters do not take place with any regularity. In addition, deviating from the assignment to become engaged in a "pursuit," instead of proceeding directly to the call, is often unproductive. In such instances the "suspect," especially one driving an automobile, may merely be acting in a suspicious manner because he or she may have committed some minor traffic violation and is fearful that the officer is going to write a traffic citation. The officer actually assigned to the robbery call should not normally deviate from the assignment without significant reason; the officer's responsibility is to get to the scene and to get accurate, detailed information for the preliminary pickup order or BOLO as rapidly as possible. When the officer does this, more resources are then brought to bear on the offense, and the likelihood is reduced that other officers may unknowingly stop armed suspects for what they think is only a traffic violation.

If not assigned to the call as the primary or backup unit, other officers should not respond to the scene. Instead, they should patrol along a likely escape route such as entrances to expressways. They should avoid transmitting routine messages, as the primary unit will need to transmit temporary pickup orders or BOLOs concerning the offense.

If available, helicopters have the potential of being helpful in robbery investigations when a good description of the vehicle in which the robbers fled is included in the BOLO. Helicopters can cover territory rapidly. Flying at 500 feet, a helicopter provides observers accompanying the pilot with an excellent observation platform. Approximately 75% of all pursuits aided by a helicopter are successful.[101]

FOLLOW-UP ROBBERY INVESTIGATIVE PROCEDURES

To standardize the ways in which robberies are investigated, departments should have a standard operating procedure (SOP) that deals specifically with this crime. It is also extremely important that both the responding officer(s) and follow-up investigator are thoroughly familiar with this procedure. The specifics of the Robbery SOP naturally vary from jurisdiction to jurisdiction because of the sizes of communities and the number of investigative specialists that are available. However, we have attempted herein to provide a broad model from which an investigative procedure can be developed by an agency irrespective of its size or the number of investigative specialists it has.[102]

Initial Investigation

Although it may not always be possible, it is advisable to have an on-duty investigator (preferably one who works robberies) to respond to the scene of all reported robberies. If, however, a police department does not normally have investigators respond to the scenes of all robberies, then certain criteria must be set forth to determine when they should respond:

- When requested by a uniform supervisor.
- A victim or witness has been seriously injured.
- A suspect has been apprehended.
- A suspect has been identified.
- Victim(s) have been tied up or incapacitated for an extended period of time.
- Large sums of money or property have been taken.
- The robbery occurs inside a residence.
- Carjackings.
- When leads with a high solvability factor are present and will be lost by a delayed response.

Specific Responsibilities for the Robbery Investigator

- Assume responsibility for the investigation.
- Ensure that proper preliminary investigative action has been taken by Uniform personnel, and take additional steps as necessary.
- Interview victim(s) and witness(es) in detail.
- Collect physical evidence.
- Canvass the area and document the names and addresses of all persons interviewed and include a summary of their observations.
- Determine if identifiable property has been taken (serial number, bait money, etc.), and ensure that this information is entered into the National Crime Information Center (NCIC).
- Determine if a cellular phone has been taken, and identify the cellular number, subscriber, and carrier information.
- Display photographs of known offenders and suspects to the victim(s) and witness(es). Request that they respond to the Robbery Bureau to view photographic files if necessary. If identification is made: have the victim(s) and witness(es) sign and date all photographs identified. Number and initial those photographs shown with the identified photograph(s) and preserve them as evidence for court presentation by placing them in an envelope sealed with evidence tape in the case file.
- Obtain notarized identification statements from individuals who are visitors or when the investigator believes that such a statement will enhance the possibility of prosecution.
- Follow up all available leads to a proper conclusion prior to terminating the initial investigation.

- When the investigation leads to the identification of a suspect, make record checks before obtaining an arrest warrant. It must be determined that the suspect was not incarcerated at the time of the offense.
- If verification of custody or detention dates is made, make a computer printout part of the case file. In instances where confusion exists concerning the subject's confinement, verification must be obtained from the appropriate governmental agency. When received, this information will be documented in the investigator's report.
- Discuss the case with the state's prosecutor and obtain an arrest warrant(s) in a timely manner.
- When applicable, consult appropriate federal law enforcement agencies (e.g., FBI, ATF, etc.) regarding the potential for filing federal charges against the suspect(s).
- If the subject is at large, and an arrest warrant has been issued, conspicuously display all relevant information along with a photograph at key locations within police headquarters. Also distribute wanted fliers to uniform patrol officers as well as other investigators.
- Upon notification that a wanted subject has been taken into custody outside the police jurisdiction, the applicable supervisor shall evaluate the case and, if appropriate, request that Robbery Bureau personnel be utilized for the extradition. If Robbery Bureau personnel are not used, the lead investigator shall coordinate any investigative activity that is necessary immediately upon return of the subject and prior to the subject being booked into the jail.
- Review and analyze all reports prepared in the preliminary phase.
- Reinterview victim(s) and witness(es) if it appears there may be information that was not obtained owing to incomplete questioning or insufficient recall of the event. Occasionally, witnesses will remember some detail and not go to the "trouble" of looking for the police department's listing. Therefore, the investigator should leave a card with his/her name and departmental phone number.
- Return to the crime scene at exactly the same time of day that the offense was committed and attempt to locate additional witnesses; at the same time, reconduct the neighborhood check. When conducting a neighborhood check, officers must be certain to record the names of all witnesses interviewed in order to avoid any type of duplication with other investigators who may be assisting on the case. In the event that possible witnesses are not at home, this too should be recorded to be certain they are recontacted later. It is imperative that every person who was in a position to have possibly witnessed the crime be contacted and interviewed.
- Make an attempt to tie the offense to other robberies, because the combined information from several

offense reports may result in sufficient detail to identify the perpetrator.

- Review any pertinent departmental records, reports, or database.
- Seek additional information from other sources (e.g., uniformed officers, informants, other investigators, other agency investigations, or informational/ intelligence bulletins).
- Review the results of laboratory examinations.
- Determine the involvement of subject(s) in other crimes.
- Prepare the case for presentation to the Prosecutor's Office.
- Assist in the prosecution as required.

The False Robbery Report

A file check should be made of the victim's name in case the person has a history of making crime reports. For instance, certain types of businesses—such as economy gasoline stations and convenience grocery stores—may not conduct even a minimal background investigation of employees. Given the availability of cash and long periods of isolation during the night hours, an untrustworthy employee will occasionally pocket cash for personal gain and cover its absence by claiming a robbery was committed. A file check on the complaining witness may suggest such a pattern. For example, one of the authors who was a robbery investigator routinely checked the police records of robbery victims. In one instance, he found that a clerk employed at a convenience store, who regularly changed jobs, had allegedly been the victim of an armed robbery three times at three different convenience stores during an 18-month period, and in each case the suspect reportedly had the same identical physical description, said the same exact words when demanding the cash, and carried the same type of firearm. Naturally, this caused considerable suspicion, and when the victim was confronted with this string of "coincidences" he was unable to explain how it occurred and adamantly denied he was stealing the money. He was asked to take a polygraph examination to verify the authenticity of these robberies but refused. His employer was notified of the pattern of previous robberies as well as his reluctance to cooperate, and he was subsequently dismissed from his job.

The following represent two additional examples of false robbery reports.

Two teenage clerks were shot in a robbery at a Quick Mart convenience store. Despite the clerk's wounds, investigators were suspicious about the incident. Upon further questioning by the police, both "victims" admitted they made up the story about being robbed to conceal their theft of $400 and shot each other to make it look more convincing.[103]

A woman told officers that a laughing man put a gun against her 2-year-old daughter's head and robbed her at an ATM. The victim also reported that no one else was around the ATM when the incident happened at 7:52 A.M. Investigators initially thought it was highly unlikely that nobody else was at the ATM around the time of the alleged robbery. They checked the transactions at the ATM and found that a man had used the ATM just 4 minutes before the robbery and did not see anyone matching the robber's description. Moreover, the man did not immediately leave the ATM after he had finished his transaction. Based on this evidence, it was established that the woman had made up the story because she wanted some attention.[104]

THE TEAM APPROACH TO FOLLOW-UP INVESTIGATIONS

Typically, investigators are assigned to work their own individual cases, but increasingly (especially with the advent of new technology) they are utilizing a team approach. For example, the Las Vegas, Nevada, Metropolitan Robbery Section Sergeants are tasked with identifying a series of robberies caused by the same individual or individuals within a group. Once these series are identified, resources are aimed at the problem. Whereas in the past a suspect or group of suspects was able to commit over five to ten robberies before being identified by description or their modus operandi (MO), now such identification is occurring after two to four robberies. Once this is done, a team of investigators lead by a sergeant is given the task of personally identifying the suspect(s) and making the arrest. The following is an example of how this system was employed to apprehend a bandit known as *cancer man*.

At first he would rob change girls at slot machines in grocery stores (remember this is Las Vegas) but moved to more lucrative targets such as bars. He would always apologize to the victims stating he had to commit the robbery because his son had cancer. The robber was very smart and often changed his times and locations of targets to be robbed. Information was gathered that this robber would come into a bar, order a drink, and then commit the robbery. The drink was the key. Investigators discovered the bandit always ordered a Cola and Captain Morgan Rum drink. Video surveillance pictures and this information were distributed through an Internet site the police department maintains with local tavern owners. Within a week a suspect matching the description came in and ordered that drink. He did not

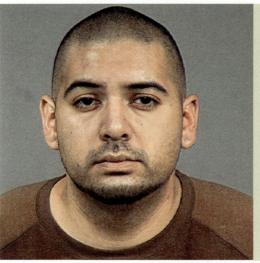

◄ **FIGURE 12-9** Facial likeness of a robbery suspect created by a forensic artist along with a police mug shot showing the resemblance The photo on the left depicts a facial reconstruction completed by Police Artist Gil Zamora, working with a robbery victim. The photo on the right depicts the police mug shot of the robbery suspect at the time he was arrested. As can be seen, the similarities are remarkable. (Photos courtesy of Police Artist Gil Zamora and Lt. Rick Martinez, San Jose, California, Police Department)

commit the robbery at that time and was likely "casing" the bar for a future robbery. Fingerprints were removed from the suspect's glass, which had been carefully handled and preserved by the bartender after the suspect finished his drink. The fingerprints taken from the glass were then compared to an automated fingerprint system that the Metropolitan Police Department maintains, and a name was acquired. After being connected to the other robberies, the suspect and accomplices were arrested the following day. A portion of some stolen money from the other robberies was recovered. Resources such as the team approach, the Internet connection with an organized tavern owners association, and an automated fingerprint system all contributed to

this arrest. After 52 occurrences from January to the beginning of May in 2004, bar robberies decreased to a total of 10 in May, June, and July of 2004. The team approach assisted in making this decrease happen.[105]

Generating a Likeness of a Suspect

The likeness of a suspect should be created and distributed as rapidly as possible. There are a number of methods available to create a likeness. One of them is through the use of a police artist (Figure 12-9). There are several software programs that can be used to generate suspect likenesses, including Sirchie's ComPhotoFit Plus Color.[106] (See Figure 12-10.)

◄ **FIGURE 12-10** Sirchie's ComPhotoFit Plus Color The composite facial reconstruction photo on the left is a computer-generated composite sketch of a robbery suspect. The photo on the right, which is remarkably similar, depicts the photo of the suspect at the time he was booked into the county jail. The facial reconstruction was made with Sirchie's ComPhotoFit Plus color. (Courtesy Laurie A. Ward, Crime Scene Administrator, and Sheriff Grady C. Judd, Jr., Polk County Sheriff's Office, Bartow, Florida)

KEY TERMS

action stereotyping

ambush

bait money

bandit barriers

carjacking

dye packs

forensic photograph analysis

hardening targets

home-invasion robbery (HIR)

mugging

physical stereotyping

planned operation

robbery

selective raid

situational stereotyping

strong-armed robbery

tracking devices

tresspassory

REVIEW QUESTIONS

1. What are the elements of the crime of robbery?
2. Give a profile of visible street robberies.
3. When is purse snatching a robbery?
4. Give three explanations for the increase in carjackings.
5. Discuss how home invaders operate.
6. What are the two occupations in which a person has the greatest danger of being the victim of a violent crime on the job?
7. How are drivers confronted in truck-hijacking robberies?
8. Discuss the characteristics that distinguish professional from amateur bank robbers.
9. Discuss the multiple techniques that can be employed in bank robbery prevention.
10. Explain action, physical, and situational stereotyping.
11. Why is it important to have a standard operating procedure for robbery investigations?
12. Why should a file check be made of the victim in a robbery case?
13. How does the team approach to follow-up investigations work in the case of robberies?

INTERNET ACTIVITIES

1. Most large police agencies in the United States have robbery investigation units. Find several such agencies in your region. What is the total number of officers assigned to these units? What are the units' functions and responsibilities? Is there information concerning the numbers of robberies that are investigated and/or cleared? Is any robbery prevention information provided? Websites such as www.officer.com provide information to both local and international police agencies.

2. Go to the website www.forensicartist.com and learn more about how forensic artists generate the likenesses of people through age composition, composite drawing, and facial reconstruction.

NOTES

1. Federal Bureau of Investigation, *Crime in the United States—1999* (Washington, D.C.: Government Printing Office, 2000), p. 28.
2. Ibid.
3. Ibid., p. 29.
4. Bureau of Justice Statistics, *Criminal Victimization in the United States—1999* (Washington, D.C.: Bureau of Justice Statistics, 2000), p. 79, table 75.
5. Ibid., p. 80.
6. Ibid., p. 27, table 27.
7. Ibid., p. 39, table 37.
8. Bureau of Justice Statistics, *Criminal Victimization in the United States*, p. 32, table 32.
9. Bureau of Justice Statistics, *Criminal Victimization in the United States*, p. 41, table 43.
10. FBI, *Crime in the United States*, p. 29.
11. Matt Nelson, "Note, Tipster Help in Search for Bank Robber," *Duluth News-Tribune* (Minnesota), Mar. 1, 2000.
12. "Two Plead Guilty in Robbery Try," *Las Vegas Review-Journal*, May 25, 2001.
13. "Deer River," *Duluth News-Tribune* (Minnesota), Feb. 21, 2001.
14. See Werner J. Einstadter, "The Social Organization of Armed Robbery," *Social Problems*, 1969, Vol. 17, No. 1, p. 76. The broad categories are those identified by Einstadter; some of the content has been extended by the authors.
15. FBI, *Crime in the United States*, p. 28.
16. Bureau of Justice Statistics, *Criminal Victimization in the United States*, p. 38, table 36.
17. Ibid., p. 68, table 64.
18. Ibid., p. 69, table 65.
19. Ira Sommers and Deborah R. Baskin, "The Violent Context of Violent Female Offending," *Journal of Research in Crime and Delinquency*, May 1993, Vol. 30, No. 2, p. 147.

20. Bureau of Justice Statistics, *Criminal Victimization in the United States,* p. 39, table 37.

21. Michael J. Feeny, "Cameras Monitor Streets for Paterson Police," *Herald News* (Passaic, County, NJ, 31307, p. B-03.

22. Tod W. Burke and Charles O'Rear, "Armed Carjacking: A Violent Problem in Need of a Solution," *Police Chief,* January 1993, Vol. 60, No. 1, p. 18.

23. Patsy Klauss, *Carjackings in the United States, 1992–1996* (Washington, D.C.: Bureau of Justice Statistics, March 1999), p. 3.

24. Ibid. On this point, also see Burke and O'Rear, "Armed Carjacking," p. 18, whose illustrations of places where people have been carjacked have been drawn on here.

25. Ibid., p. 3.

26. FBI, *An Analysis of Carjackings,* p. 3.

27. James T. Hurley, "Violent Crime Hits Home," *FBI Law Enforcement Bulletin,* June 1995, p. 10.

28. Howie Padilla, "Two Men Beat Up Couple in Their Home," *Star Tribune* (Minneapolis, MN), Sept. 6, 2001.

29. Office of Banks and Real Estate, State of Illinois, "ATM Report," www.obre.state.il.usa/agency/atm-rpt.htm, 1999, p. 1.

30. Ibid.

31. Ibid., pp. 4–5.

32. Ibid., p. 4.

33. Ibid.

34. Eric F. Sygnatur and Guy A. Toscano, "Work-Related Homicides: The Facts," *Compensation and Working Conditions,* Spring 2000, Vol. 5, No. 1, p. 4.

35. Mike Brassfield, "Taxicab Driver Survives Robbery," *St. Petersburg Times* (Florida), Aug. 11, 2001.

36. Tom Jackman and Leef Smith, "Taxi Camera Develops Its First Lead for Police," *Washington Post,* Aug. 22, 2001.

37. J. M. Kalil, "Bellagio Robber Flees with $1 Million in Jewelry," *Las Vegas Review-Journal,* July 11, 2001.

38. National Institute for Occupational Safety and Health, "Update: Risk Factors for Injury in Robberies of Convenience Stores Examined in NIOSH Study," May 1997, p. 1.

39. The information in this paragraph is drawn from H. E. Amandus et al., "Convenience Store Robberies in Selected Metropolitan Areas," *Journal of Occupational and Environmental Safety,* Vol. 39, No. 5, May 1997, pp. 442–447.

40. School of Criminal Justice, State University of New Jersey, Rutgers, "Preventing Convenience Store Robbery through Environmental Design," crimeprevention.Rutgers.edu/case_studies/cpted/cpted_cs2htm, Sept. 22, 2001, p. 1.

41. Ibid.

42. "Fighting Cargo Theft," *Transportation Topics, Trucking's Electronic Newsletter,* Sept. 8, 1999, p. 4.

43. Ibid.

44. Deborah Lamm Weisel, U.S. Department of Justice, Office of Community Oriented Policing Services, March 2007, pp. 13–49. (This discussion of bank robbery was adapted from this source.)

45. M. Gill and R. Matthews. "Robbers on Robbery: Offenders Perspectives," in *Crime and Work: Studies in Security and Crime Prevention,* ed. M. Gill Vol. 1. (Leicester, United Kingdom: Perpetuity Press, 1994).

46. M. Gill and R. Matthews. "Repeat Robbers: How are they Different?" in *Crime and Work: Increasing the Risk for Offenders,* ed. M. Gill Vol. II. (Leicester, United Kingdom: Perpetuity Press, 1998).

47. T. Gabor and A. Normandeau, "Preventing Armed Robbery Through Opportunity Reduction: A Critical Analysis," *Journal of Security Administration* 12(1) (1989): 3–18.

48. H. Leineweber and H. Buchler. "Preventing Bank Robbery: The Offense from the Robber's Perspective," *Police Research in the Federal Republic of Germany,* in eds. E. Kube and H. Storzer (Berlin: Springer-Verlag, 1991).

49. J. Haran, "The Losers Game: A Sociological Profile of 500 Armed Robbers" (Ph.D. diss., Forham University, 1982), University Microfilms.

50. T. Gabor, M. Barill, M. Chuson, D. Elie, M. LeBlanc and A. Normandeau, *Armed Robbery: Cops, Robbers, and Victims* (Springfield, Illinois: Charles C. Thomas, 1987).

51. G. Camp, "Nothing to Lose: A Study of Bank Robbery in America" (Ph.D. diss., Yale University, 1968), Ann Arbor: Michigan University Microfilms.

52. D. Johnston, "Psychological Observations of Bank Robbery," *American Journal of Psychiatry* 135:11 (1978): 1377–1379.

53. M. Borzychki "Bank Robbery in Australia," *Trends and Issues in Crime and Criminal Justice,* No. 253 (Canberra: Australian Institute of Criminology, 2003).

54. R. Matthews *Armed Robbery: Police Responses.* Crime Detection and Prevention Series, Paper 78 (London: Home Office, Police Research Group, 1996).

55. J. Verdalis and T. Cox, "A Descriptive Analysis of Bank Robberies in Dade County, Florrida, During 1994," Journal of Security Administration 21(2): 1–18.

56. Johnston, "Psychological Observations of Bank Robbery."

57. W. Saylor and M. Janus, *Bank Robberies: A Study of Bank Characteristics and Probabilities of Robbery.* Unpublished study, (Washington, D.C.: Office of Research, Federal Bureau of Prisons, 1981).

58. Verdalis and Cox, "A Descriptive Analysis of Bank Robberies in Dade County."

59. H. Buchler and H. Leineweber. "The Escape Behavior of Bank Robbers and Circular Blockade Operations by the Police," in *Police Research in the Federal Republic of Germany,* eds. E. Kube and H. Storzer (Berlin: Springer-Verlag, 1991).

60. Leineweber and Buchler, "Preventing Bank Robbery."

61. P. Van Koppen and R. Jansen, "The Time to Rob: Variations in Time and Number of Commercial Robberies," *Journal of Research in Crime and Delinquency* 36(1) (1999): 7–29.

62. P. Van Koppen and R. Jansen, "The Road to Robbery: Travel Patterns in Commercial Robberies," *British Journal of Criminology* 38(2) (1998): 230–247.

63. R. Erickson, *Armed Robbers and Their Crimes* (Seattle, Washington: Athena Research Corporation, 1996).

64. F. Desroches, *Force and Fear: Robbery in Canada* (Toronto: Nelson Canada, 1995).

65. Johnston, "Psychological Observations of Bank Robbery."

66. Gabor et al., "Armed Robbery."

67. R. Erickson and A. Stenseth "Crimes of Convenience." *Security Management* 40(10) (1996).

68. Leineweber and Buchler, "Preventing Bank Robbery."

69. E. Kube, "Preventing Bank Robbery: Lessons from Interviewing Robbers," *Journal of Security Administration* 11(2) (1988): 78–83.

70. Nugent et al., op. cit.

71. W. Tiffany and J. Ketchel, "Psychological Deterrence in Robberies of Banks and Its Application to Other Institutions," *The Role of Behavioral Science in Physical Security,* NBS Special Publication 480-38 (Washington, D.C.: U.S. National Bureau of Standards, 1978).

72. Ibid.

73. S. Morrison and I. O'Donnell, *Armed Robbery: A Study in London* (Oxford, United Kingdom: Centre for Criminological Research, 1994).

74. S. Barancik, "FBI Data on Bank Robbery Contradict Movie Myths," *American Banker* 163(232) (1998): 2.

75. Tiffany and Ketchel, "Psychological Deterrence."

76. T. Hannan, "Bank Robberies and Bank Security Precautions," *Journal of Legal Studies* 11(1) (1982): 83–92.

77. Nugent et al., op. cit.

78. Hannan, "Bank Robberies and Bank Security Precautions."

79. Saylor and Janus, *Bank Robberies.*

80. T. Baumer and M. Carrington, *The Robbery of Financial Institutions: Executive Summary* (Washington, D.C.: U.S. Department of Justice, National Institute of Justice, 1986).

81. Hannan, "Bank Robberies and Bank Security Precautions."

82. Nugent et al., op. cit.

83. Kube, "Preventing Bank Robbery."

84. Gill and Pease.

85. Vardalis and Cox, "A Descriptive Analysis."

86. J. Wise and B. Wise *Bank Interiors and Bank Robberies: A Design Approach to Environment Security* (Rolling Meadows, IL: Bank Administration Institute, 1985).

87. Barancik, "FBI Data on Bank Robbery."

88. Ibid.

89. Gill and Matthews, "Robbers on Robbery."

90. J. Archea, "The Use of Architectural Props in the Conduct of Criminal Acts," *Journal of Architectural and Planning Research* 2(4) (1985): 245–259.

91. Charles Remsberg, *The Tactical Edge: Surviving High Patrol* (Northbrook, IL: Calibre Press, 1986), p. 251.

92. Ibid.

93. Ibid., p. 248.

94. Ibid., p. 253.

95. Ibid., p. 252.

96. Ibid.

97. The distinction between these types of stereotyping is taken from Jerry W. Baker and Carl P. Florez, "Robbery Response," *Police Chief,* October 1980, Vol. 47, No. 10, pp. 46–47.

98. Ibid., p. 47.

99. Ibid.

100. Coleman Cornelius, "Police Bag Bank Heist Suspect," *Denver Post,* Dec. 4, 1998.

101. Geoffrey P. Alpert, *Helicopters in Pursuit Operations* (Washington, D.C.: National Institute of Justice, 1998), p. 3, with some additions by the authors.

102. This information was obtained from the Miami-Dade (Florida) Police Department Robbery Bureau Standard Operating Procedure, pp. 7–10 through 7–14, April 4, 2004.

103. Kevin B. O'Leary, "Robbery 'Hoax': Shootings Real," *Boston Globe,* Nov. 19, 1993, p. 1.

104. Richard Perez-Pena, "Teller Machine Robbery Was a Hoax, Police Say," *New York Times,* Feb. 19, 1994, p. A25.

105. All information referenced in this chapter to the Las Vegas Nevada Metropolitan Police Department Robbery Section was provided by Lieutenant Ted Snodgrass.

106. For more information, see the website for Sirchie's ComphotoFitPlus Color, http://sirchie.com/detail.asp?product_ID=CCID200.

Burglary

CHAPTER OBJECTIVES

1. Be familiar with the characteristics of different types of burglaries.

2. Be able to describe the characteristics of professional and amateur burglars.

3. Be knowledgeable about the steps in the burglary investigation checklist.

4. Specify actions officers responding to burglary in-progress calls should take.

5. Recognize burglary tools.

6. Identify the types of evidence to collect in safe burglary cases.

7. Explain the laws and methods associated with attacks on ATMs.

8. Profile burglaries of cars, recreational vehicles, and trailers.

9. Discuss indicators at different types of burglary scenes which may suggest juvenile subjects.

10. Briefly describe methods of reducing the risk of residential and commercial burglaries.

▲ Two burglars approached the front door of a home and knocked on the door. After determining no one was home, they went to the rear and forced an entry. They quickly removed over $100,000 in valuables and fled the scene before the police arrived. The homeowner's surveillance camera captured one of the burglars leaving through the front door carrying a signed and framed Michael Jordan basketball jersey.

(Courtesy Ft. Lauderdale, Florida, Police Department)

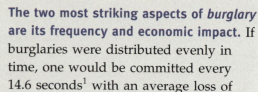

The two most striking aspects of *burglary* are its frequency and economic impact. If burglaries were distributed evenly in time, one would be committed every 14.6 seconds[1] with an average loss of $1,834.[2] Because such items as credit cards and checks may be taken in burglaries, the offense tends to spawn subsequent or secondary crimes, such as frauds and forgeries. Investigating these crimes can sometimes lead back to the identity of the burglars; to illustrate, during the breaking and entering of a convenience store, "scratch-off" lottery tickets were stolen. When the burglar attempted to cash in a few winners at another convenience store, he was videotaped by the security camera. After placing his picture in the newspaper the police quickly learned his identity, and the man was arrested. Burglaries also have the potential to turn into violent crimes, e.g., when home owners or workers return unexpectedly.

Although many homes and businesses have alarms, the alarms may be affected by improper installation, faulty equipment, or user errors. Unfamiliarity with the system or not allowing for roaming pets results in 10% to 25% of all automatic alarm calls being false ones; if all false alarms were eliminated, the result would be 35,000 officer days per year being available nationally to redirect toward genuine problems.[3] Many jurisdictions have responded to this situation by allowing one free false alarm and then charging the owner for subsequent false alarms on a flat-fee or escalating-the-charge basis for each subsequent false alarm.

Although we often think of burglaries as involving just homes and businesses, other structures may also be covered by many state burglary laws, including recreational vehicles, railroad cars, houseboats, airplanes, and automobiles.[4] Some states also have created a **coin-operated machine burglary** charge to cover vending machines outside of businesses. Unlike other types of burglaries, this offense is typically a misdemeanor; in states that lack such an offense category, the charge is for larceny, with the level of offense being determined by the value of the property stolen.

Various aspects of burglary are summarized in Table 13-1. Most burglaries are through a door rather than a window. In general, commercial establishments are attacked at the rear at night, whereas homes are mostly victimized during the day at the front door. There is some evidence that as the geographical distance between burglaries shortens, the likelihood of there being a serial offender increases; this is true, respectively, for residential and nonresidential burglaries.[5] When the same home is burglarized a second time shortly after 30 days from the initial incident, it may be by the same offender seeking to steal items left behind during the first offense; for example, something too big to take, or perhaps the first time he did not know a fence, or perhaps he came back to steal items the resident bought as replacements (e.g., televisions or video equipment) for losses in the first burglary.[6]

Commercial burglaries are also committed through other points of entry, such as skylights and chopping a hole in a roof. In certain situations, such as strip malls, burglars will break into one business and then enter the others by knocking through connecting walls. As ATMs have become more widely available, businesses such as convenience stores have been broken into by people driving vehicles as large as stolen dump trucks through the glass doors.

TABLE 13-1	Burglary Facts

Type of Premises Attacked

Residential	66.2%
Nonresidential	33.8%

Types of Attacks

Forcible Entry (e.g., used pry bar to break glass and enter)	61.0%
Unlawful Entry (e.g., through open door or window)	42.5%
Forcible Attempt	26.4%

Time of Attacks	Residential	Nonresidential	
Day	47.5%	29.9%	
Night	29.5	41.4	
Unknown	22.5	28.7	

Cases Cleared (Arrests and Exceptionally Cleared): 12.7%

Arrested Offender Demographics

Race	Gender	Age	
White 69.0%	M 86.6%	Under 15	8.7%
Black 29.2	F 13.4	Under 18	26.1
All Other 1.9		18 & over	72.6

(Source: FBI, Uniform Crime Reports -2006, issued in 2007. See www.fbi.gov/UCR/CIUS 2006, Tables 7, 15, 36, 43, and 66.)

Once inside, burglars can grab an ATM and some store goods and be gone in 2 to 7 minutes. Day burglaries of homes have a certain logic: the owners are often at work or running errands, and neighbors are used to seeing delivery people, campaign workers, and others approach front doors. So, seeing someone at a front door is not an abnormal occurrence that compels attention. Furthermore, front doors are often recessed, limiting visibility; burglary alarms are often not set; and many front doors can be quickly kicked in, facilitating the burglar's quick entry and exit.

Burglars may work alone—as illustrated by the Spiderman case discussed later in this chapter—or in organized groups or gangs. There are numerous cases of professional people becoming burglars, and burglars can be roughly categorized as professional and amateurs by their level of skill. Many juveniles and teenagers commit burglaries, including those involving cars. One study concluded that prolific burglars also shoplift, perhaps to supplement their income, to obtain goods they cannot get through their burglaries and to "lay low" when the risk of burglarizing may be perceived as too high.[7]

When police officers respond to a burglary-in-progress, officers must be alert when approaching the scene, both to protect themselves and to avoid rushing past lookouts or burglars driving calmly from the scene. At the scene, officers may have to tactically clear the building before their investigation can begin. This should never be attempted until adequate backup and specialized units, such as Canine, have arrived. During the preliminary investigation, officers have to consider the possibility of a crime staged for filing a false insurance claim; in particular, when there are fires at scenes, officers may need specialized assistance to determine if the fire is accidental or coincidental, set by the burglars to destroy evidence, or arson. In the end, a burglary is a burglary, but officers should examine each scene while being alert to all possibilities. The number of safe burglaries has lessened as we've progressed into a "cashless society," but officers still need to have a basic understanding of them to prevent the accidental destruction of evidence.

Burglars sell much of what they steal to support their lifestyle or trade the merchandise for drugs, tips from insiders about new burglary opportunities, or sex. Thus, as police try to recover stolen property, they come into contact with criminal fences and must check pawnshop records, local sales ads, swap meets, and eBay-type outlets.

THE OFFENSE AND OFFENDERS

From man's earliest times, thieves existed and committed what we recognize as burglaries. The elaborate tombs of the Egyptian pharaohs, designed to send the rulers into the next world in splendor, contained magnificent treasures. They also contained elaborate security features to protect those riches. Yet they were often plundered by thieves of that time.

The nature of burglary has stayed the same over time, but *how* it is committed constantly changes, largely as an influence of technological advances and architectural design. For example, now virtually extinct in the United States are such specialized methods of burglary as entry through coal chutes—because people in this country heat mainly with electricity, natural gas, and even solar power. As municipalities began requiring the use of fire escapes, they were appended to the outside of apartment buildings. This created a new method of burglary—the "step-over." Although people would place bars or other barriers over apartment windows by the fire escape, they would neglect to protect other windows. The step-over artist would go up a fire escape to the apartment to be hit and then step over from the fire escape to the ledge of a window that was unprotected. As interior fire escapes became more common, the opportunities to be a step-over artist gradually declined, although they certainly still exist. A slight variation on the step-over method is still in practice: parents send children as young as five years old to do the step-over and then open the apartment door from the inside to let in the parents, who plunder the premises.

In the last 20 years, a method of burglary that has gained in popularity is one in which the offenders steal a car and drive it through the front door of a gun, jewelry, or other type of store. Once inside, they quickly grab what they can, exit, get picked up by a confederate (who is often operating another just-stolen car), flee the scene, and then abandon the stolen car. This method is essentially an aggravated case of the well-known **smash-and-grab,** in which a perpetrator throws a brick or concrete block through the plate-glass window of a jewelry store, seizes what can immediately be reached, and then gets away from the scene as quickly as possible.

Some targets selected for burglaries require more than just crude force, they demand a high level of skill and daring. A former Army paratrooper who stole some $6 million in cash, jewelry, and credit cards was dubbed "Spiderman" by investigators because he specialized in burglarizing high-rise apartments—a total of 132 of them—before he was apprehended (Figure 13-1). To reach his targets, Spiderman would climb as many as 30 stories on the *outside* of the buildings—without any climbing equipment.[8] Initially, investigators had difficulty even considering this method of approaching the target because its use seemed too improbable.

▲ **FIGURE 13-1   The Spiderman burglar**
Man arrested as Spiderman gives a media interview at jail. His attorney is the man wearing the white coat, and a reporter takes notes in the background. Investigators claim that $6 million was taken during Spiderman's "career." (© AP/Wide World Photos)

Some burglaries require careful planning and coordination. For example, thieves stole merchandise from parked Susquehanna Railroad freight cars four times in three months, netting as much as $100,000. The men used 30-inch bolt cutters to force entry into the cars. Once inside, the merchandise was "selected," and walkie-talkies were then used to summon gang members driving gutted vans, which were then used to haul the loot off. To stay ahead of the police, the ring monitored a police scanner. After surveillance of the tracks failed to produce any results, officers were pulled off of that assignment, and the burglars went back to work. However, a man walking his dog at 9:30 P.M. spotted the men on top of the freight cars and alerted police, who were able to make arrests at the scene.[9]

Although some burglars prefer to work alone to maximize profits and to avoid the possibility that their partner(s) will "roll over on them" if arrested by the police on burglary or other charges, others work in gangs. These gangs vary in composition (e.g., from juveniles, to members or affiliates of organized crime, to those having ethnic or foreign ties). In one particular crime wave involving a Tennessee burglary gang, investigators were sure juveniles were involved because of the nature of the items being taken, but they were nevertheless shocked to later learn that the two members of this "gang" were both less than 13 years old. The MO was for the 12-year-old boy to boost the 10-year-old girl through a broken window, and she would then open the door and let her "partner" into the home.[10]

In Chicago in another case, a long-time burglar, with reported mob connections, operated his "crew" for 30 years. When the leader was arrested, more than $2,000,000 in jewelry and stolen property was found in his home. A member of the crew virtually signed his presence at burglaries by always taking expensive Lladro porcelain figurines and adding them to his personal collection. Part of the "formula" used so successfully by the gang for decades was that after spotting a potential victim, they would bribe a public official to run the mark's auto tag so they could immediately know where he/she lived, after which they would begin to accumulate information before making their move. The gang was also successful in identifying restaurant owners who skimmed money from their businesses and accumulated large sums of cash in home safes.[11]

In the New York City area, 52 men from Colombia operated the "Codewise Crew" burglary ring, committing 6 to 12 burglaries a day. The gang operated in groups of three members, spotting residences that looked easy and striking in the mid-afternoon when families were often not home. Lookouts would communicate with the inside man, advising him of detection threats. The men would meet at a bar in the morning and later go pull their burglaries. Ultimately, the gang's downfall occurred when some members got reckless about how they operated, leading to their arrest.[12] Another illustration of a major crime gang/group with foreign ties is Yugoslavian, Croatian, and Siberians (YACs). YACs have operated along the Eastern seaboard, specializing in burglarizing ATMs in supermarkets, which may have $100,000 in them at any time, and the safes of buildings thought to have large amounts of cash on hand, such as bars and restaurants.[13]

Although burglars are often thought to be poor and uneducated, relying on that profile may cause investigators to overlook professionals who are also burglars.

A former police officer pleaded guilty to 16 felony counts involving a string of residential and commercial burglaries he committed while on duty. Just a month before entering his plea, the 18-year law enforcement veteran was granted a disability pension after experts testified at his retirement hearing that he suffered from an obsessive-compulsive disorder that led to his pathological gambling.[14]

A church organist was arrested for committing three burglaries of churches and synagogues in which religious items of gold and silver valued at $25,000 were stolen. Following his arrest, the suspect confessed to having burglarized 500 such places, taking articles worth $2.5 million. There was little hope that any of the stolen property would ever be recovered, since it was believed to have been melted down and sold. Police were led to the suspect when a drifter was arrested for disorderly conduct. In the drifter's duffel bag, religious articles were found. He admitted having stolen them from the suspect, who had provided him with shelter for the night.[15]

Although burglars may be classified according to a number of variables, such as preferences for premises to be attacked and types of property that they will, or will not, take, the most useful classification is skill. Conceived as a continuum, the two extremes would be the amateur burglar and the professional. The largest number of burglars would be clustered toward the less-skilled end of the continuum, with progressively fewer toward the skilled end.

Professional burglars may commit only a few offenses per year, going for the bigger "scores," as in the following cases:

The FBI, working with Brazilian police officials, recovered three Norman Rockwell paintings valued at over $1 million. Nearly 25 years earlier, they were stolen from the Elayne Galleries in St. Louis Park, Minnesota. No one knows how the Rockwells ended up in Brazil. The thieves have never been caught.[16]

Space Coast Credit Union employees came to work on a Monday morning to find a hole in the roof over the vault and more than $100,000 missing. The police had responded to the alarm that went off at 12:30 and 1:30 Sunday morning, but they could not see the roof from the parking lot or the highway, nor could they find anyone with a key to the premises so that they could check inside. Several months before, a bank was successfully attacked using the same method of operation. In that case, the burglary was described as "the biggest financial loss in our city."[17]

However, professional burglars can also be quite active, committing a large number of offenses:

Members of a burglary ring were arrested for committing some 1,000 burglaries over a three-year period. They selected shops, businesses, and fast-food restaurants that would have anywhere from several thousand to $75,000 on hand. The targets included McDonald's, Pizza Hut, Burger King, and Dunkin Donuts.[18]

While many professional burglars may commit only a few offenses a year, they are of considerable interest to investigators because of the large value of cash or property taken and their intimate knowledge of sophisticated fencing systems, which are often detected, and therefore investigated, only following the apprehension of a professional. In addition to the big score, the hallmark of the professional is the thorough planning that precedes each burglary. Professionals usually refuse to place themselves in jeopardy for anything other than sizable gains and do so only after weeks or even months of painstaking study of the target selected. Knowing exactly what they want in advance, professionals do not ransack premises. Thus, if they have employed surreptitious methods of entry, articles taken may not be missed for some time. Working nationally, or at the very highest professional level, internationally, this type of burglar often operates for long periods of time without being arrested. When arrested, such burglars are usually released without being charged owing to a lack of physical evidence, coupled with their own skill in responding to the questions of investigators. When operating in elegant hotels or apartment buildings, the professional will use a businesslike appearance and manners to talk his way out of a situation. Should an occupant return unexpectedly, the burglar may pull out forged credentials identifying him as the building's security officer and say he found the door ajar and was just beginning his investigation. Or he may pretend to be drunk, ask for directions to some similarly numbered room, and stagger away acting confused.

However, if these or similar ploys fail, or if the burglar's real intent is apparent, the professional will employ violence if necessary to escape:

A well-known cardiologist was shot to death when he walked into the burglary of his home in a fashionable section of Washington, D.C. The police arrested a man who was alleged to be a "superthief" for the crimes. Upon searching the suspect's swank suburban home, the police found some $4 million worth of stolen property. It took the police 472 man-hours and 400 legal-size pages to count, tag, and describe the property. The 18-foot truck in which the seized property was transported away contained 51 large boxes and two smelters that were believed to have been used to melt down precious metals.[19]

Amateur burglars often operate on the basis of impulse or react to suddenly presented opportunities. Such burglars tend to work not only in one city but often in a relatively small segment of it. Amateurs may cruise in cars looking for businesses to victimize, prowl hotels seeking unlocked doors, or try to locate doors whose locks can be easily slipped using a credit card. While amateurs may occasionally enjoy a relatively big score, it is the absence of preplanning that sharply differentiates them from professionals. If they are narcotics addicts, amateurs must often work four or more days per week, committing several offenses each day, in order to support their habits. Even if they are not addicts, this may still be necessary to support their lifestyles. Frequently using sheer force to enter, amateurs crudely ransack businesses or residences to find anything of value. Occasionally, unlike their discerning professional counterparts, they take costume jewelry in the belief that they have found something of considerable value. When confronted by an unexpectedly returning business owner or occupant of a residence, amateurs may become immediately violent, and secondary crimes, such as murder or rape, unintended in the original intent of the offense, can occur. Finally, amateur burglars often have lengthy records and are frequently in and out of jail.

THE LAW

The crime of burglary generally consists of the following elements: (1) breaking and (2) entering (3) a dwelling house or other building (4) belonging to another, (5) with the intent to commit a crime therein. The common-law crime of burglary necessitates that the act be committed in the nighttime. This element has been deleted in a number of state statutes.

Burglary and related offenses are classified as crimes against the habitation, dwelling, or building itself; no force need be directed against a person. The breaking element may be satisfied through acts that constitute a breaking into, a breaking out of, or a breaking within. Generally, the slightest force used to remove or put aside something material that makes up a part of the building and is relied on to prevent intrusion, for example, doors or windows, constitutes breaking. This element can be satisfied whether accomplished at the hands of the perpetrator, through the use of some inanimate object like a brick, or by the participation of an innocent third party. Similarly, the element of entry is satisfied once the slightest intrusion has taken place by the perpetrator, an inanimate object, an animal, or an innocent third person.

The character of the building at which the breaking and entering takes place largely determines the type of offense committed. The most serious offense is often breaking and entering of a dwelling house, that is, a place used by another person as a residence. The nature of the dwelling itself is not determinative but, rather, the manner in which it is used. Hence, a hotel room can be considered a dwelling house.

The other major ingredient controlling the nature of the crime is the intent with which the perpetrator unlawfully breaks and enters the building. The more serious the crime intended to be committed after entry, the more serious becomes the breaking and entering itself. Thus, breaking-and-entering which is done with the intent to commit a felony carries a higher sentence in many states.

APPROACHING THE SCENE AND INITIAL ACTIONS

When responding to a burglary-in-progress call, uniformed officers should drive rapidly while avoiding excessive noise, such as the dramatic but unnecessary use of the siren. The last several blocks to the scene should be driven at lower speeds for two reasons. Doing so eliminates the possibility that the squealing tires of the police vehicle will give the perpetrators, if still on the scene, the advantage of crucial seconds of warning. Additionally, lower speeds allow opportunity for observation. A vehicle driving away from the vicinity of the scene may be seen and its description and license plate number noted as a possible investigative lead. Under such conditions, late-model, expensive cars, such as Cadillacs and Lincolns, should not be discounted. Burglars often select these, not only because of the large amounts of equipment and stolen property such cars can hold, but also because they recognize the fact that the police often act with deference to the occupants of these vehicles because of the implied social status.

When dispatched to a burglary-in-progress call, the uniformed officer working alone should attempt to coordinate his or her arrival time and position with the backup unit. This will enable the officers to secure the building immediately. One unit can arrive positioned so it can watch two sides of the building—for example, the north and east sides—while the other unit can observe the west and south sides. When a two-officer unit is dispatched to a burglary-in-progress call, the operator of the police vehicle should drop his or her partner off in a position to view two sides of the building and position the vehicle to allow observation of the remaining two sides. When working alone, if it is necessary to begin checking the exterior of the building immediately, the uniformed officer should drive around it to determine whether there is a readily observable break. If this is not possible, the officer should check rapidly, but cautiously, on foot. When a flashlight is used during hours of darkness, it should be held away from the body, as the suspect is most likely to aim at the light source if firing at the officer. If a point of entry is established, under no circumstances should an officer attempt to enter, as entering would needlessly expose him or her to extreme danger. Most burglars prefer to be unarmed because, in many states, breaking and entering while armed is a more serious offense than an unarmed breaking and entering. However, occasionally burglars are armed and willing to use their weapons to avoid apprehension:

A woman whose home overlooked the back of a shopping center saw two people break into a dress shop through the rear door. She called 911, who gave the call out as a burglary in progress, subjects on the premises. A motorcycle officer who was returning to the station at the end of his shift heard the call, which was assigned to a patrol unit, and swung by to back them up because he was close to the scene. The woman, still connected to 911, gave a running account of what happened. The motorcycle officer arrived first and pointed his motorcycle lights at the rear door. Instead of maintaining his position and waiting for assistance, he walked up to the door—fully silhouetted by his own lights. As he stood in the doorway, he was shot three times and collapsed. As the officer lay dying, one of the perpetrators stood over him and emptied his pistol into him. This death should not have occurred. It was caused because the officer used a tactically unsound procedure and because he encountered armed subjects willing to shoot it out with the police. Both subjects were arrested at the scene. Follow-up investigation revealed that they had a major incentive to use deadly force against the police—they were wanted on murder charges in two other states.

The fact that no point of entry is determined by riding or walking around the building does not mean that a forcible entry has not occurred. Whenever possible, the roof should be checked, particularly vents and skylights. Even if there is an alarm sounding, there may not be a burglary. Alarms frequently malfunction, particularly during inclement weather. However, officers must never become complacent about checking premises with a reputation for false alarms. If a breaking and entering has occurred, additional cars, if available, should be brought into the general area. Burglars often park their vehicles some blocks from the building to be attacked, and the perpetrator may not yet have had time to flee the area. "Lovers" parked in the general area should not go overlooked by the police. Burglars often use couples as lookouts or have their girlfriends remain in the car while they commit the offense. The perpetrator may have reached the car but have been unable to flee the immediate area; the use of a "just parked lovers" story may allow him to escape detection.

If a burglary has been committed and the police department has a canine unit, the uniformed officer at the scene should request its presence before entering the building. The alarm servicing company will ordinarily have a representative at the scene fairly rapidly to provide officers with access to the building. If there is no alarm, then the owner must be contacted either from information usually posted on the door or from other

Completed	Tasks
_____	Determine use of premises (e.g., residence versus commercial), point of entry and if different, point of exit. Was entry forced or unforced? What is missing?
_____	Who discovered the burglary? When? What was he/she doing when discovered? Did he/she touch or move anything? What? Why?
_____	Is the victim the complainant versus a neighbor or employee? Victim assistance? Are there independent witnesses?
_____	Is there any significant time gap between when discovered and when reported? Why?
_____	Who knows when the last time the premises was secure? When?
_____	Was any alarm set or not set? Who is responsible?
_____	What physical evidence is there? Entry tool(s) left behind? Is crime scene processing warranted under department policies/procedures?
_____	Are there exterior/interior surveillance cameras? Working? Why not? Get videos if available. Review past tapes to identify suspect casing the premises.
_____	Is there evidence the crime was staged (e.g., possible insurance fraud)?
_____	What actions did the suspect(s) take in entering, while inside, and leaving?
_____	Does the item(s) taken suggest more than one suspect and vehicle (e.g., 50" HDTV taken)?
_____	Does the scene suggest some inside knowledge of the premises (e.g., perpetrator went right to where item stolen was versus the scene being "tossed")?
_____	Were any acts of sexual deviancy committed (e.g., masturbated in victim's underwear, defecated on bed or elsewhere, or cut crotches out of victim's underwear)?
_____	Does the type of entry and articles stolen suggest juveniles are involved (e.g., change, condoms, alcohol, Nintendo games, costume jewelry taken, real jewelry left behind, only small articles taken for which a vehicle is not needed to transport)? Was school out? Were known juvenile offenders in the area absent from school?
_____	Does the method of entry and articles stolen suggest unusual skills or special knowledge (e.g., safe successfully attacked using a single method versus several different types of unsuccessful attacks, good jewelry taken, costume items left behind)?
_____	What precautions did the suspect(s) take to avoid detection? Were alarms and cameras disabled? Does the neighborhood check reveal possible lookouts? Were telephones or walkie-talkies left behind? Was phone on premises used? What number(s) was called?
_____	Have residential victims determine if checks are missing; have commercial owners determine if checks are missing from rear of business checkbook. Was checkwriter taken, or does its present position suggest its use while suspect(s) was on the premises?
_____	View evidence/enter identifiable stolen items in database.
_____	Check intelligence, field interview reports, and other databases. Check with crime analysts to determine if the MO is identifiable to an individual. Check with other investigators to see if cases they are working on may be related. Also contact other area agencies for the same reason. Read follow-on reports from lab examining evidence.
_____	Check pawnshop records (Figure 13-3).
_____	Visit flea markets and swap meets. Check newspaper for sale ads, and also eBay.
_____	Check suspect information (e.g., verify name, aliases used, criminal history, address, employment, associates). Obtain current photo, prepare photo pack, check for warrants, and issue BOLO.
_____	Check jail records and interview/interrogate suspect in custody.
_____	Schedule polygraph/Computer Voice Stress Analyzer (CVSA) examinations.
_____	Obtain arrest and search warrants as needed; file returns.
_____	Respond to information requests from District/State Attorney.

Source: Authors' experience, with some elements added from Universal Case Checklist, Assistance Chief of Police (Retired) Bill Proffitt, and Sergeant Karen Eichler, St. Petersburg, Florida, Police Department.

*This list does not distinguish between steps taken gathering information for the incident report and the follow-up.

◄ **FIGURE 13-2   Burglary investigation checklist***

sources. Before beginning the crime scene search, officers must thoroughly check the building to ensure that the burglar is not hiding on the premises. To achieve the proper degree of caution, the building check should be conducted as though it were known that the burglar was still there.

Figure 13-2 is a **burglary investigation checklist**; it makes no distinction between the tasks associated with initiating the incident report and those associated with the follow-up investigation, so that the entire scope of investigative tasks can be seen at once.

◄ FIGURE 13-3
Pawnshops: Legitimate businesses or fencing operations?
Fences are persons who knowingly purchase stolen property for a fraction of its cost and then resell it at a considerable profit. Pawnshops suffer a continuing image problem from the illegal conduct of fencing by some of its operators. Most, if not all, jurisdictions have enacted statutes and ordinances in an effort to regulate how pawnshops conduct their business.
(© Randy Faris/Corbis)

INVESTIGATIVE CONSIDERATIONS AT THE SCENE

Caution must be exercised to avoid the accidental destruction of physical evidence while attempting to make a determination of whether the burglar is still in the building. Officers should be sensitive to the possible presence of physical evidence but not act in a manner that might jeopardize the most important thing—the officer's safety. If gross physical force has been used in gaining entry, the point of attack is easily established (Figure 13-4). However, one cannot assume that it is also the point of exit. Often burglars will break into a building at a particular point and then leave by opening a door. Where gross physical force is used, the point of attack is of particular importance because examination of it may yield the types of physical evidence discussed in Chapter 4, "Physical Evidence." In combination, the determination of the points of attack and exit will suggest the avenues of approach and flight traveled by the perpetrator, which also must be explored for the possible presence of physical evidence. Officers must be particularly attentive for unusual signs that may be of investigative value. Juvenile burglars commonly commit destructive acts of vandalism (Figure 13-5). Also, age

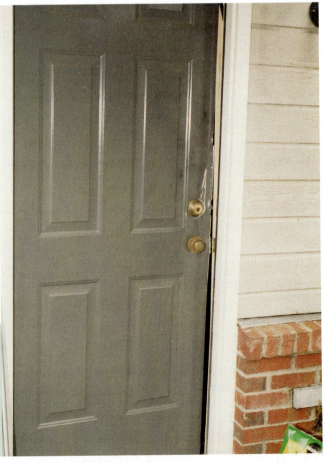

► **FIGURE 13-4   Broken front door**
The burglary of this residence was accomplished by prying the front door open. The burglar first made an unsuccessful attempt to remove the deadbolt lock. When this failed, he simply pried the door open as evidenced by the marks along the door's right edge. (Courtesy of Chief Rick Boren, Lt. Ron Griffin, and Sgt. Doug Shafer, Columbus [Georgia] Police Department)

FIGURE 13-5
"Tossed" home office
A heavily "tossed" home office. The chaotic scene suggests amateur burglars and more particularly, juvenile perpetrators who became frustrated looking for things they could easily carry away. More seasoned offenders, for example, would have methodically searched the filing cabinet at the left of the picture from top to bottom or bottom to top. The open drawer in the middle of the cabinet suggests a more random approach. (Courtesy Chief Dwayne Orrick, Cordele [Georgia] Police Department)

may be suggested from the choices of what is taken and what is left behind:

When I started hustling . . . didn't know much, like what crap be really worth and how to get bills for it . . . at first alotta stuff I just leave back . . . just grabbed things for me . . . like a nice coat or small crap you can just walk with and sell quick for cash . . . like a gun . . . main thing for me was getting some bills so I could high-cat around and get stuff . . . Nike shoes. I couldn't walk around with no stereo or TV . . . had to leave the big stuff.

The sudden removal of trophies or other prized possessions by their owner from a business or residence, followed by a burglary for the purpose of committing an arson, should raise certain questions in the investigator's mind. Further, the weight or dimensions of property taken in a burglary may suggest, if only roughly, the number of people involved in the offense. Articles or tools left behind, combined with other specifics of the crime, may be useful in the identification of an MO.

Many commercial establishments keep check imprinters on their premises. A not uncommon occurrence is for a burglar to gain entry to a commercial building, tear several checks from the company checkbook, imprint them, and cash them the next day. Thus, it is of particular importance to have the proprietor ensure that no checks

have been taken. Normally, when a burglar employs this practice the checks will be taken from the very rear of the book or from several different series in order to lessen the likelihood of detection.

Recognition of Burglary Tools

Most often, when tools used in the commission of a burglary are recovered at the scene, they are not very different from those found in many households. A partial list of **burglary tools** includes knives, screwdrivers, crowbars, tire irons, pipe wrenches, chisels, sledgehammers, hacksaws, bolt cutters, axes, and glass cutters. In the crude smash-and-grab burglary, where the display window of a jewelry store is broken and articles immediately available are taken, the "tool" may be as unsophisticated as a brick in a paper sack. However, tools left at the scene may have been subject to certain adaptations to facilitate their use in a burglary. Screwdrivers or crowbars may be carefully sharpened or shaped to increase their effectiveness in attacking doors and windows; nippers can be transformed into lock pullers if they are honed in a manner that permits firmer biting ability on exposed lock edges. Burglars will also apply masking tape in the shape of a cone to the end of a flashlight so that it emits only a very thin light beam.

Apprehension of a suspect not in the act of burglary but in possession of lock picks (Figure 13-6), specially modified tools (Figure 13-7), or standard tools that can be used in burglaries may permit a felony charge of possession of burglary tools. Some states require that a person have a

▲ FIGURE 13-6   Lock tools

An assortment of lock picks in a leather case. Such tools are commonly sold on the Internet for as little as $15 to $20 for a group of four to five picks. (Courtesy of Major Tolbert and Lt. Richard Zapal, Savannah Chatham Metropolitan Police Department)

prior conviction for burglary in order for this charge to be placed. Even where this requirement does not exist, proof of intent to commit burglary is essential for conviction.

Surreptitious Entries

Occasionally, the investigation of a burglary cannot establish a point of entry or exit. What happens in such instances is in large measure determined by the knowledge and thoroughness of the investigator, who may initiate a report indicating "entrance by unexplained means," decline to take a report owing to lack of evidence, or take a report knowing that, because to departmental policy, it will subsequently be designated "unfounded." Complaints of this nature frequently involve surreptitious entries—that is, a burglary has occurred, but there was no apparent force used. Excluding the case of closed but unlocked doors, the most common explanations are that the door was "loided," the lock was picked, or the premises were victimized by someone who has an unauthorized possession of a key.

Loiding is the act of slipping open or shimming, by using a strip of celluloid, a spring-bolt lock that does not have an antishim device. Technically, a spring bolt without an antishim device should be considered a privacy, rather than a security, device. Simply stated, **picking** is a process of manipulating a lock into an unlocked position using picks rather than a key. When picking is suspected as the means used to gain entry, the lock should be submitted to the laboratory for examination. By examining the lock, the laboratory will be able to determine whether or not the lock was picked. From the marks alone on a lock, the laboratory cannot state the type of picking device used, except in general terms. If, however, a pick is seized as evidence, it is possible to make an individual identification by comparing the marks on the lock with test marks

◀ FIGURE 13-7   Snip-ez

Battery-operated scissors modified to use as an electric lock pick. The scissors were removed, and a lock pick was mounted in their place. (Courtesy of Major Tolbert and Lt. Richard Zapal, Savannah Chatham Metropolitan Police Department)

made by the seized pick. To facilitate the reassembly of the lock after its examination by laboratory personnel, the key should also be submitted. The laboratory cannot determine whether a lock was loided, due to the lack of physical evidence associated with this technique.

Officers must be familiar with privacy and security devices, because this increases their investigative effectiveness and the credibility of their testimony, assists in the construction of MO files, generates data to support crime prevention legislation, and allows them to talk knowledgeably before community groups.

Importance of The Time Factor

An important aspect of taking burglary reports is attempting to determine when the offense took place. Typically, burglaries are reported from several hours to a number of days after they are committed. Late reporting is largely attributable to the circumstances of businesses being closed for the weekend and home owners being away for short trips or extended vacations. Summer communities, populated by people living some distance away who visit their mountain or lakefront vacation homes only intermittently, represent a large problem for the police. Such residences are particularly vulnerable to burglars, who may take all the furniture and dispose of it several months before the offense is even detected. In such instances, the estimate of the time frame in which the offense occurred will of necessity be very broad. Frequently, however, it is possible to identify a range of time during which the perpetrator attacked the premises; the range can then be correlated with other data to provide investigative leads and to include or exclude certain persons as suspects. For example, a person known to employ an MO similar to the one used in a

particular offense would be a suspect. If, however, a field interrogation report was initiated on him some distance away from the scene at about the same time that the offense occurred, his presence there would have been virtually impossible, thus excluding him as a suspect. While this example is an unusual occurrence, its essence is important. As the time range in which the offense could have taken place narrows, other information becomes more useful.

SAFE BURGLARIES

Types of Safes

Safe burglaries have been declining for decades. In part, this is due to the prevalence of cashless transactions (e.g., buyers using debit and credit cards) and target-hardening measures taken by home owners and businesses. Nonetheless, investigators need to have a basic understanding of safes and the types of evidence associated with them so evidence is not accidentally destroyed.

Many older safes are still in use, as well as numerous new ones that include such features as electronic locking bolts and entry through the use of a personal password or by swiping one of the owner's credit cards. In general, there are two broad categories of safes:

1. **Fire-resistant safes**, which historically had square or rectangular doors and were intended primarily to protect stored money and documents from being destroyed in a fire (Figure 13-8). Such safes would also provide a minimum level of burglary protection. These safes have a light metal skin with insulation between their inner and outer walls.

◄ **FIGURE 13-8   Fire resistant safe that was successfully attacked** This is a small fire safe weighing about 99 pounds; no dimension (height, width, depth) is greater than 19 inches. The burglar laid the safe on its back to get better leverage when attacking it. Note the pry marks on the bottom edge of the safe and shoe prints on the floor to the right of the safe. The hinge pins on this type of safe are unprotected and were removed during the attack. (Courtesy Chief Rick Boren and Lt. Ron Griffin, Columbus [Georgia] Police Department)

2. **Money chests or burglar resistant safes**, which historically often had round doors, were made of heavier metal and were insulated to provide fire protection. As safe construction methods continued to evolve, the use of square or rectangular doors became common on burglar-resistant safes. Burglar-resistant safes (Figure 13-9) are sometimes referred to as combination safes because they have an outer fire-resistant chamber combined with a smaller inner chamber, usually referred to as a money chest. Financial institutions use large walk-in vaults that offer substantial fire and theft protection for stored documents, provide safety deposit boxes to customers, and protect cash and other financial instruments.

There is variety in the labels that safe manufacturers give their products, including security chest, executive safe, top-opening, under counter, wall, personal, and drawer and cash management, which is used in businesses that need to track which employees used the cash drawer. Companies also often employ different terminology: one manufacturer may use "money chest" to denote small safes that are attached to the frame of houses, whereas others simply use the term "safe" to identify their line of burglar-resistant safes. Thus, when investigating a burglary where the victim says the "safe" was attacked, they may be using the term imprecisely.

Since 1913, the underwriters laboratory (UL) has tested safes and categorized them according to the level of protection they provide. These categories are commonly found on labels inside the safe. For example, a safe with a "tl-15" label means that it is resistant to attack by a burglar using common handheld and electrical tools for 15 minutes. UL also uses labels for fire-resistant capabilities. For instance, the highest level of a "type class 150" label provides fire protection to the safe's contents for up to 4 hours at 2,000° while maintaining an interior temperature of not more than 150° F. Knowledge of these labels allows investigators to have some sense of how much time a burglar spent compromising a safe.

Attack Methods for Safes

Knowledge of methods of safe attack is important because it allows the investigator to make judgments about the skill and knowledge of the perpetrator and thus narrows the focus of the investigation. The methods of safe attack include the punch, pulling, the peel, the rip, blasting, drilling, burning, manipulation, the pry, and the carry-off. Some of these methods are encountered infrequently, but they are included here because in the few instances when they are used, investigators must be prepared to respond properly. The various methods of attack are summarized in Table 13-2.

Safe-Burglary Evidence

The scenes of safe burglaries are usually rich with physical evidence. Broken parts of screwdrivers, pry bars, drill bits, and other equipment offer the possibility of making a fracture match with the remaining portion in the suspect's possession. If a drill and bit are seized from a suspect, marks on drill-bit shavings recovered at the scene can be compared to those made by the equipment

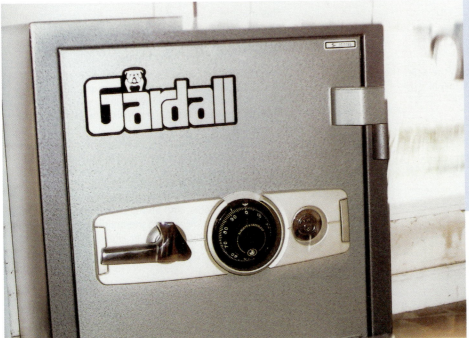

◀ **FIGURE 13-9   Gardall safe**
Fire and burglar resistant safe. Note the heavy metal phalanges protecting the hinge bolts. To facilitate use of the safe during the day when it may be necessary to open it several times, once the combination lock and handle has been used to open the safe it can be closed and opened using a key in the lock to the right of the combination dial. (Courtesy of Athens [Georgia] Lock and Key)

TABLE 13-2	Methods of Safe Attack	
METHOD	**EXECUTION**	**COMMENTS**
Punch or punching	The attacker knocks off the combination dial, either by swinging a heavy hammer down from above or by placing a cold chisel at the top center of the dial and striking its end sharply with a hammer. The attacker places a punch on the exposed head of the spindle and forcefully strikes the end of the punch. Hammering sounds are masked by deadening all to-be-struck surfaces with a piece of inner tube or cloth. The safe's locking mechanism is defeated by the force of the spindle's being driven into it.	The spindle is the axle on which the combination dial rotates the safe's tumblers or locking wheels. The punch requires little skill and little knowledge of the safe's construction. This method is most successful in attacking older fire-resistant safes; it does not work with safes that have tapered spindles because they cannot be driven into the locking mechanism, nor does it work with money chests. The principle disadvantage of this method is the amount of noise made.
Pulling, drag, or come-along	The attacker places a wheel-puller over the combination dial, flat against the safe's face, and uses the wheel-puller to extract the spindle.	Whereas the punch forces the spindle inward, this method forcibly moves it in the opposite direction. This method is rarely seen, owing to improved types of safe construction. It will work with some older fire-resistant safes but not with money chests.
Peel	The attacker makes a small hole in the safe's outer metal skin, often at the upper left-hand corner of the face of the safe. A large pry bar is then used to peel the metal skin off the face. This exposes the locking bolts and locking mechanisms, which are then compromised.	This is the common method of attack on fire-resistant safes, often after a failed attempt at punching the safe. Moderate knowledge of safe construction is required. The more skill the perpetrator has, the less damage will be done to the safe. If efforts to start the peel have failed at several locations, a less-experienced "safe cracker" is suggested. This method creates a lot of noise and physical evidence. The peel works on some fire-resistant safes but not on money chests. Inexperienced peelers will simply beat on the safe with sledgehammers until crude force creates the initial opening.
Rip or rip job	Crude physical force is used to make a hole in the safe. The hole is expanded until it is big enough to allow a hand to fit inside the safe. The attacker then reaches inside and takes whatever is in the safe.	Sometimes the "chop" is thought of as a separate method of safe attack. Technically, the chop is a rip applied to what is sometimes the weakest portion of the safe, its bottom. Often an axe is used to execute a chop. This method is very noisy and creates a large amount of physical evidence. The rip is successful with a number of fire-resistant safes but not with money chests.
Blasting or soup job	Explosives are applied to the safe. They are set off, and the safe's contents are taken.	This method, which can be effective with all types of safes, has virtually disappeared because of the stiffer state penalties associated with carrying explosives during a burglary and federal laws regulating the sale and use of explosives. If you encounter explosives, know how to protect yourself and others: Don't touch them; call the ordinance team. In the room where the explosives are located and in adjacent rooms, do not turn lights on or off, do not change settings on thermostats or equipment, open windows and doors, and do not take photographs using flash attachments. Evacuate the building; do not transmit on your radio within 300 feet or allow the use of mobile radios within 500 feet.

continued

TABLE 13-2	Methods of Safe Attack, *concluded*	
METHOD	**EXECUTION**	**COMMENTS**
Drilling	The perpetrator precisely marks off where the drilling will be done. The drill may be mounted on a jig to promote stability and accuracy when drilling to compromise the safe.	Expert knowledge of safe construction is necessary, and the perpetrator must be a skilled driller. Drilling easily defeats fire-resistant safes and is the most successful method of attacking money chests. A variant of precision drilling is using a core drill to remove a plug from the safe, usually on its sides or bottom, and then reaching in and taking the safe's contents. If a core drill is not available, the attacker may accomplish the same thing by repeatedly drilling in the same area. Diamond- and carbide-tipped bits and a high-torque drill are required.
Burning or torch job	The attacker places the oxygen and acetylene tanks near the safe and hooks up the cutting "torch." He or she precisely marks off where the cutting will be done, lights the torch, and makes the cuts.	This method is successful with fire-resistant safes and money chests, although its use on the former indicates inexperience because it is a much more advanced technique than is required to get the job done. Characteristically, an experienced cutter makes smooth, clean cuts, whereas a novice makes jagged lines that are often connected by round holes where he or she paused too long. Smaller, portable oxygen and acetylene tanks are preferred. Although cutters often wear gloves, they may roll their sleeves up to be cooler and may have unexplained burns, possibly caused by molten slag. Offenders may have committed one or more burglaries to get the equipment they need to do the job.
Combination manipulation	The combination dial is worked back and forth so that the tumblers can be heard falling into position. Using those numbers, the attacker opens the safe.	Genuine manipulation is a rarity, but it is possible on old, worn-out safes. Look for some other explanation (e.g., insider information or the combination numbers left in an obvious place). Attackers who are given the combination numbers may attempt to conceal this fact by doing damage to the safe. If the force applied would not have opened the safe, it's likely the perpetrator was given the numbers by an insider or former employee.
Pry or prying	For a fire-resistant safe, a large pry bar is used, usually on the top front edge of the safe, to separate the door from the rest of the safe. Occasionally, a logging chain attached to a hydraulic jack is used for the same purpose.	This is an amateurish method and will not compromise money chests.
Carry-off	Strictly speaking, the carry-off is not a method of attacking safes. The safe is simply removed from the premises and then attacked elsewhere using any of the preceding methods.	Often, the safe will be taken to an isolated location, such as the woods, a barn, a warehouse, or an abandoned building.

seized. Drilling is noisy, so safe crackers may make special sound-deadening boxes in which to place their drills. The materials used have the potential to be matched with the remaining material in the suspect's possession. Bolt cutters recovered from the suspect's home can be tested in the laboratory to see whether the striae made match those on chains, padlock hasps, or fences at the burglary site. Slag seized at the scene of a burning job can be analyzed for consistency with samples obtained from the suspect's car or home. At some

burglaries, opportunities to locate DNA evidence exist: offenders may have left hats with dandruff in the sweatbands; may have cut themselves accidentally when using equipment, leaving blood; may have left their saliva on water or other bottles they brought to or used at the scene; or may have used the bathroom but forgot to flush, leaving urine. They may have used company telephones to make calls, providing investigative leads, and one cannot ignore the possibility of finding latent prints and impressions. Whenever an attack on a safe has exposed the safe insulation, samples should be collected as evidence.

Depending on the circumstances, particles of insulation may be found on the perpetrators' tools, their clothing, under their fingernails, in their shoes, pants cuffs, or pockets, on the floormat of their car, or embedded in their shoes. In a number of cases, safe insulation has been found in the nail holes of shoe heels several weeks after the commission of the offense.

It is the variation among insulations that makes them valuable as class evidence. Many safes made before 1930 contain an insulation of natural cement made by burning to a powder certain claylike limestones, used without gravel or cement only as safe insulation. A number of more recently made safes use an insulation of diatomaceous earth, portland cement, and vermiculite mica—a combination used only in safe insulation. Many brands of safes contain distinctive insulation, samples of which are kept in the FBI laboratory files. It is, therefore, possible to compare insulation found on a suspect's tools or person with those in the file and name the make of safe from which it came. Some safe manufacturers use material for insulation, such as gypsum mixed with wood chips, which is not peculiar to safe insulation. In such instances, however, laboratory examination can establish consistency, or the lack thereof, between insulation samples from the scene and from the suspect.

As a final note on the value of safe insulation as evidence, establishing intent is important in charging a person with **possession of burglary tools.** Tools found with what can be conclusively established as safe insulation on them may be the basis for providing that intent.

ATM ATTACKS

Some premises are burglarized for the purpose of attacking ATMs inside buildings—for example, gas stations, convenience stores, fast-food restaurants, and bank and credit union lobbies. Stand-alone ATMs in convenience and other types of stores may not be bolted to the floor and weigh roughly 200 pounds.[20] Amounts of money in these ATMs vary based on recent servicing and use, but typical losses range in the area of a few thousand dollars.[21] The store hosting the stand-alone ATM, which is often a private venture as opposed to being one which is bank-operated, may be conventionally burglarized, and then the stand-alone ATM is physically carried off to a waiting panel truck, a truck with a lift, a pickup, or U-Haul-type trucks. These vehicles are often stolen and may have separately stolen license plates on them.

In some surveillance photos, offenders can be seen entering with a hand truck/dolly to help move the stand-alone ATM with greater ease. Several other methods of burglarizing premises and stealing stand-alone ATMs are also used. In smash and grabs, heavy trucks (such as a dump truck in one case) are driven right through the glass doors,[22] the ATM is snatched up, loaded into the vehicle, and then taken to a place, such as a wooded area, where it is opened. Insurance companies report that carry-off attacks on ATMs result in so much damage to the unit that it is a total loss.[23] From an investigator's point of view, **ATM attacks** may yield considerable forensic evidence, including tire and shoe impressions, tools and tool marks, fingerprints on dropped currency, beer cans, blood from skinned hands, and food wrappers. Some businesses no longer have stand-alone ATMs because they attract crime, the premises suffers damage that needs to be repaired, retail floor space is taken up by the ATMs, and items are also stolen.[24] To prevent the loss of business, ATM owners are making use of some new measures, including placing GPS tracking devices in the machines and using Fog Security Systems, which emit a heavy, impenetrable fog that lasts several hours and makes suspects simply bolt the premises as soon as they can.[25]

Different from stand-alones are the ATMs that are located at the drive-throughs of banks or are embedded in walls outside of banks, pharmacies, apartment buildings, or other structures. Embedded ATMs tend to be operated by banks. Attacks on these ATMs, depending on the applicable state laws and prosecutorial discretion, may be charged as a burglary or as a larceny to the amount of the property stolen. Also, some ATMs enjoy the protection of Title 18, United States Code 2113(b): "Whoever takes and carries away with the intent to steal or purloin, any property or money or other thing of value exceeding $1,000 belonging to, or in the care, custody, control, management, or possession of any bank, credit union, or any savings and loan association . . ." may be fined and/or imprisoned for up to 10 years. Thus, in some ATM cases there may be concurrent jurisdiction between the FBI and the local enforcement agency.

Embedded ATMs carry more cash than the stand-alones because they are intended for use by a much larger population. Attacks on these range from the crude to the bizarre. There have been reports of heavy trucks backing into them at high speed to jar them loose or to allow heavy chains to be attached to them.[26] After the chains are affixed, the trucks accelerate forward, ripping the ATM out. Suspects have also used acetylene torches on embedded ATMs[27] and tried blasting at them with shotguns.[28]

In addition to solving burglaries involving ATM attacks through the follow-up investigation, many arrests are made by alert officers patrolling the area, aided by the stores' use of silent alarms (which means police cars are responding to the scene without the burglars knowing it) and by neighbors and bypassers who witness unusual activity and call the police.

RESIDENTIAL BURGLARY

Earlier in this chapter, we noted that residential burglaries were primarily committed during the day, with the front door being the point of attack. Black home owners are victimized at a higher rate than is any other group.[29] The younger the head of a household is, the more likely that the residence will be burglarized.[30] As shown in Table 13-3, the losses associated with residential burglaries are not intrinsically significant. However, to many households, even relatively small losses are devastating. Moreover, when you consider the residual feelings of the victims, there is another type of loss: Victims feel as though their privacy has been violated. They often struggle psychologically afterward to regain a sense of security in their own homes.

Many burglars are amateurs in the sense that even though they may commit the crime numerous times, they often act on impulse, driven by the need for money:

> **Usually when** I get in my car and drive around I'm thinking, I don't have any money, so what is my means for money? All of a sudden I'll just take a glance and say, there it is, there's the house! . . . Then I get the feelin', that very moment that I'm moving then.[31]

Some burglars report that "legitimate" financial emergencies are the only reason they resort to breaking in:

> **Usually what** I'll do is a burglary [or a couple of them] if I have to . . . helps get me over the rough spot until I can get it straightened out. Once I get it straightened out, I just go with the flow until I hit a rough spot where I need the money again . . . The only time I would go and commit a burglary is if I needed money at that point in time. That would be strictly to pay light bill, gas bill, rent.[32]

Although such cases clearly exist, burglaries are more often committed for other reasons:

> **I might find** somebody with some good crack . . . while I'm high I say damn I want me some more of that good shit. Go knock a place off, make some more money, go buy some more dope.[33]

TABLE 13-3	Home-Burglary Victimizations by Amount of Loss

AMOUNT OF LOSS	PERCENTAGE OF BURGLARIES
No loss	1.4%
Less than $50	9.7
$50–$99	9.6
$100–$249	19.4
$250–$499	12.6
$500–$999	13.1
$1,000 or more	26.5
Not known/not available	7.7

(Source: Bureau of Justice Statistics, Criminal Victimization in the United States—2005. Washington, D.C.: U.S. Department of Justice, December 2006; Internet edition without page numbers, Table 85.)

> **I use** the burglary money for gifts for young ladies—flowers or negligee or somethin'. Some shoes . . . put them shoes on, them pumps . . . then watch 'em dance nude.[34]

> **See I go** steal money and go buy me some clothes . . . See, I like to look good. I likes to dress . . . own only one pair of blue jeans 'cause I like to dress [well].[35]

> **Burglary is excitin'** . . . it's just a thrill to going in undetected and walking out with all their shit . . . like going on a treasure hunt.[36]

From these quotes, it can be seen that burglars tend to commit their crimes for four broad reasons: (1) keeping themselves and their families fed, clothed, and sheltered; (2) keeping the party going; (3) keeping up appearances so that they can look better off financially than they are; and (4) keeping adventure in their lives.[37]

Whereas amateur burglars act on impulse, the more professional burglars are, the less likely they are to take chances. They develop information on their own or pay tipsters for it. They may simply cruise well-to-do neighborhoods looking for opportunities or follow expensive cars to their homes. Once they have identified a preliminary target, they begin a "workup," watching the house until they have become familiar with the people who live there, their daily routines, the absence or presence of alarms and dogs, views of possible attack points from other homes in the area, and the frequency of private and public police patrols.

One way of developing information on their own is simply to read the newspapers. Wedding announcements often reveal that a couple will honeymoon in another city or country and then reside in whatever community. With a little effort, burglars can often find out the couple's address and burglarize the home, stealing wedding gifts and other items, while the victimized couple are blissfully enjoying their honeymoon. Other types of announcements that might provide similar opportunities include funeral arrangements and gala charity events or parties, which many wealthy people can be expected to attend. Butlers and maids can get lists of the people attending such events. Tipsters—sometimes called "spotters," "fingermen," "noses," or "setup people"—provide another source of information that can be used in selecting homes for burglaries. For example, insiders at cruise ship operations can provide passenger lists. Medical personnel know when patients will be in their offices for appointments. Workers in various occupations such as telephone installers and flower delivery workers, enter numerous homes legitimately and have the chance to size up opportunities. Coworkers know when their bosses are going on vacation. Insurance office personnel know which homes' contents have been heavily insured and which may have special riders attached for silverware or other valuables. Armed with such information, professional burglars reduce the risk of apprehension and increase the probability of "making a nice haul."

Homes are burglarized during the day because that's when the occupants are most likely to be gone—working, attending school, or running errands. The same generally holds true with many neighbors, who might otherwise witness the attack. Burglars do not want to attract attention to themselves, but they also do not want a confrontation with an occupant. If they have learned the home's telephone number, they will call to see if anyone is there. While an answering machine encourages some burglars, it makes others leery of going ahead, fearing that someone is home and using the machine to screen the calls.

Alarms and dead-bolt locks are a deterrent to amateur burglars but not to more professional ones. Residential burglars usually do not have to carry an assortment of tools because so many targets are "soft." Often, they carry little other than workman's gloves and a large screwdriver or small pry bar (Figure 13-10). If they cannot easily effect entry at the front door, they will try to enter through the garage—which is ideal because they are out of sight—or a rear window. Most home burglars go straight to the bedroom, because that's where most people keep small valuables, such as jewelry, cash, furs, and guns. The master bathroom is also where most

▲ **FIGURE 13-10**
Pry marks on residence's front door
Pry marks left on the front door frame of a residential burglary. This is a general orientation photograph; closeup photographs of the marks with a ruler alongside them would also be taken. The positions of the pry marks would also be documented by notes and a sketch, using precise measurements. Ideally the marks would be cut from the door frame to be able to make comparisons with tools that may subsequently be found in the possession of a subject arrested for the crime. Failing that, they could be cast using Mikrosil, Silmark, or some similar putty. The drying times for putty varies, most drying in 5 to 8 minutes in normal temperatures and 12 to 15 minutes when very cold. (Courtesy of Chief Rick Boren and Sgt. Doug Shafer, Columbus [Georgia] Police Department)

people keep their prescription drugs. As their experience builds up, burglars will begin to check the "clever" places where people hide their valuables, including in freezer compartments and behind towels in linen closets. If they have an accomplice, they will call him or her to bring the vehicle into which televisions, VCRs, stereo systems, tools, and other valuables are loaded. Table 13-4 shows the seven types of property most commonly taken in burglaries.

TABLE 13-4	Property Most Frequently Taken from Homes with Reported Losses
PROPERTY	**PERCENTAGE OF CASES**
Portable electronic and photographic gear, jewelry, clothing, and other personal effects	40.8%
Household furnishings	13.5
Tools, machinery	1.4
Cash	9.9
Purse, wallet and credit cards	5.8
Bicycles and their parts	4.0
Firearms	2.4

(Bureau of Justice Statistics, Crime Victimization in the United States, 2005 Statistical Tables. Washington, D.C.: U.S. Department of Justice, December 2006, Table 84.)

CAR, RV, AND TRAILER BURGLARIES

In most states, breaking into cars, recreational vehicles (RVs), and trailers constitutes a burglary. **Car burglars** tend to be juveniles, teenagers, and young adult offenders. Many entries by these offenders are done by simply opening unlocked car doors; others involve breaking a window to reach inside and take whatever is available. Unlocked trunk releases are also pulled and items in the trunk stolen. Some street-wise suspects carry a spark plug with them, which when thrown hard easily breaks a car window. Additional "tools" include tire irons, slim jims, or other pry-bar type instruments, hammers, door lock punches, or whatever is handy, such as portable signs and rocks.

Typical items taken include visible change, wallets left in the center console and purses left on the floor board, car electronics, CDs, speed detectors, laptops, cameras, and cellular phones. Juveniles and teenagers often do more damage than is necessary in removing dashboard electronics. When valuable, but larger items, such as golf clubs, are left behind, the lack of a vehicle to transport them out of the area and/or the inability to sell them quickly also suggests youthful offenders. People on drugs of all ages commit auto breaking-and-enterings (B&Es), stealing items that they can quickly convert to cash to support their drug use. Wherever cars are parked, they can become a target. Apartment complexes, sorority and fraternity houses, and mall, mass transit, campus, and employee parking lots offer plentiful targets that allow offenders to quickly commit a larger number of car burglaries. Cars that are burglarized on railroad cars and new car sales lots tend to suggest more experienced car burglars. In most jurisdictions, car burglaries increase sharply around Christmas time, when shoppers leave many packages in plain view in their vehicles.

Modest pop-up campers may cost in the $5,000 to $10,000 range, whereas RVs can top out at $1.5 million. Burglaries at dealerships tend to focus on electronics, and often the damage to the RVs is greater than the amount of the property stolen. Many RV burglaries occur at RV storage sites and along interstate and major state highways, because those routes are typically used by travelers. Pop-ups are often attacked in state or national parks when the owners are away hiking, photographing, hunting, or fishing. High-end RVs often have safes where the owners keep valuables and sometimes surprisingly large amounts of cash. High-end RVs have also been the target of home invasion–style robberies.

In addition to apprehensions made by patrol officers viewing crimes in progress, such crimes are often foiled or solved by reviewing surveillance data, targeting repeat offenders, owners returning unexpectedly to their vehicles, perpetrators bragging about their success, juveniles displaying their goods to classmates at school, suspects stopped for traffic offenses with the stolen property in plain view in the rear seat, and the use of "bait cars" by police.

INVESTIGATING CRIMINAL FENCES AND OTHER OUTLETS FOR STOLEN PROPERTY

Criminal **fences** or receivers are persons who knowingly purchase stolen property at a fraction of its cost and then resell it at a considerable profit (but still at a "really good" price) to the consumer. Fences usually buy at 10% to 20% of an item's actual cost or may simply set a flat price for the goods—for example, $700 for a particular year, make, and model of car. How "hot" the goods are and how quickly they can be safely resold are also factors in setting the price. When confronted with someone who bought property that later turned out to be stolen, officers must determine whether the purchaser acted in good or bad faith. Among the indicators of a buyer's lack of good faith are

1. Paying a price below that of a "good bargain."
2. Purchasing from persons who are not known to them.
3. Buying from persons whom they don't know how to recontact.
4. Accepting items without a receipt.
5. Buying property that bears an obliterated identification number or from which the number has been removed.

6. Purchasing articles that have unusual property control numbers on them, such as those identifying the owner as a state agency.
7. Having a past history of receiving stolen property.

The most basic notion of a fence is that after committing a burglary or another crime (e.g., hijacking a truckload of clothing), the thief takes the merchandise (e.g., a television) to the fence and says, "How much will you give me for it?" While this approach is still used, fencing has become considerably more complicated, and there are numerous types of fences,[38] as shown by these examples:

- *Amateurs fences*, who usually do fencing intermittently, have limited resources, and may buy stolen goods for resale to friends, as gifts to girlfriends, or for their own personal use.
- *Store owners and individuals*, who often buy only the goods for which they have placed an order with the thief or only from a thief who works for them relatively full time. Such thieves may also work as freelancers or as members of gangs, some of which are ethnically based, in multistate areas.

Theft of luxury clothing items, such as leather coats and upscale designer-label clothing, is a growth industry. The property may be stolen in burglaries or some other type of crime, including "mopping," another term for shoplifting. The clothing is then sold to fences or underground boutiques. Inside one drab family residence in Queens, police uncovered over $500,000 in stolen clothes. Said one detective, "The inside of this place looks like Macy's."[39]

Pakistani owners of a convenience store also led a three-state ring of thieves. They recruited 200 professional shoplifters and illegal Pakistani immigrants with promises of a better life and plenty of money to send home. Members of this group stole over-the-counter cosmetics, computers, DVD players, jet skis, pharmaceuticals, and anything else they could get their hands on. The merchandise was taken to a warehouse where it was repackaged and sent to coconspirators in two different states and in Pakistan. Competition to "bring in the most" was intense. One thief, enraged that another thief had brought in more than he had, hired thugs to beat up the higher-performing member of the gang. Gang cohesion was also reduced when some members "skimmed" some items for themselves, reducing the "take" for the rest of them. As investigators "rolled" individual gang members, the investigation snowballed, resulting in the eventual recovery of $450,000 in cash and $1.6 million in stolen goods.[40]

- *Professionals*, who have substantial bankrolls, do business with a select clientele known by them or reliably referred to them, may work for long periods without being caught, and usually have several locations at which to store their purchases.
- *Occasional or opportunistic fences*, who normally conduct their businesses legally (e.g., as garages or **pawnshops**) but who from time to time "turn a deal."
- *Providers of illicit goods and services*, such as those who trade drugs and access to prostitutes for stolen merchandise.
- *Technology-proficient fences*, who do their business on the Internet. Some of these "fences" are the thieves themselves:

Two career thieves who may have committed as many as 100 burglaries in Massachusetts and New Hampshire sold approximately $30,000 worth of their booty on eBay. They had another $70,000 in stolen property that they also planned to sell there when police arrested them.[41]

Many fences can operate for long periods of time without being detected because they are often "invisible" until some situation creates the need for police to take a closer look at individuals and/or locations (Figure 13-11). Outlets for stolen property include swap meets, flea markets, for-sale advertisements in local newspapers, second-hand furniture stores, eBay and other Internet, outlets and overseas venues, often in third-world countries. In some instances, knowledge about fencing operations comes to the police under more unusual circumstances:

Two men approached a police sergeant with an offer of a $25,000 cash bribe in return for destroying physical evidence that tied them to a robbery. They were given some items and appeared satisfied with having bought themselves a cop. However, the officer was actually working the two men with the knowledge and support of his department and the local FBI field office. Ultimately, the two men and their associates were linked to warehouse burglaries and container thefts that totaled more than $3 million in stolen goods, and they had acted as fences for stolen laptop computers.[42]

From a policy viewpoint, the police know that the more the receiver markets can be disrupted or eliminated, the greater the likelihood that there will be some reduction in burglary and other offenses, whose profits

◄**FIGURE 13-11**
Police raid uncovers stolen bicycles and other property
A police raid on a fencing operation in an inner-city neighborhood recovered a great deal of stolen property, some of which the police are inventorying in this picture. The operators of the fence paid for stolen goods with cash, drugs, and access to prostitutes.
(Courtesy Major Tolbert and Lt. Richard Zapal, Savannah Chatham Metropolitan Police Department)

depend on the availability of these illicit markets. Plainclothes officers quietly visit swap meets, flea markets, and other likely outlets, looking for known burglars or their associates offering merchandise for trade or sale. Such locations may be good candidates for the use of facial recognition software. Articles being offered are examined for possible signs of being stolen, such as missing or newly attached serial numbers. Arrested burglary offenders are always asked, "What did you do with the stuff you took?" When squeezed between facing almost certain prison time and giving their fences up, some will barter the information for a more lenient sentence. Because drug users usually steal to support their habits, whenever they are arrested, they are going to be asked, "What can you give me?" Their answers to this question may help identify drug dealers, fences, and other types of offenders.

Once in a great while, such questioning may yield a professional, big-time fence, but more frequently this is not the case. Professional fences usually screen their customers carefully and have worked with them over a period of years. Moreover, an arrested offender knows that by giving up a big-time fence, he or she will risk getting "wacked" for talking. Thus, the more usual case is that offenders try to get away with giving up "little fish."

Once a suspected fence is detected, officers work the case, investigating to confirm or disconfirm the fencing operation. When this is accomplished, officers attempt to broaden the case and apprehend more than just the offenders in front of them. This often entails both physical and electronic surveillance to identify the places fences frequent and who their associates are. An undercover officer may then be assigned to begin frequenting these places, covertly gathering additional information and/or attempting to develop a relationship with the fence and his or her

associates. This method is also used when active burglars are targeted for arrest and surveillance is initiated. At some point, arrest and search warrants will be issued. When multiple locations and perpetrators are involved, raids executing the warrants should be conducted simultaneously to prevent offenders from slipping away.

As an industry, pawnshops suffer a continuing image problem from the illegal conduct of some operators. When the illegality was perceived as a serious problem, state statutes and local ordinances were enacted to regulate their shops' conduct, and this has reduced the number of pawnshops acting as fences. Usually these laws require that the pawnshops provide the names and addresses, and in some instances fingerprints, of persons pawning property, along with a full description of the property. In some locations, all secondhand dealers of property must provide the same type of information. In both instances, this must ordinarily be done within 24 hours of each transaction. Because of the temptations created by the high profits that can be gained by buying and selling stolen property, pawn and other second-hand dealers are closely scrutinized. State investigative agencies and many individual agencies maintain pawnshop databases to monitor secondhand merchandise transactions:

While entering information in the database, an officer working with the burglary squad noticed that a subject had sold an expensive loose diamond to a local used-jewelry store. She further noticed that the subject had also previously sold expensive jewelry to the same business. In the sale that had attracted the officer's attention, the subject had received $10,400 for the diamond. On the transaction slip from the jewelry store, it was noted that the seller lived in a nearby jurisdiction and worked as a plumber, so the officer contacted the police department there to find out if any high-priced jewelry thefts had occurred. She was not successful there, but ultimately she found a department in the area where investigators had noted a pattern in which the subject did plumbing jobs and subsequently there would be missing jewelry from the homes he had worked in. Eventually, the diamond, actually valued at $63,000, was matched with a victim's ring from which the plumber had pried it.[43]

In another case, the same officer noted that the home of one of the department's employees had been burglarized, resulting in the loss of a camera, zoom lens, and credit card. While processing transaction slips, she found a pawnshop that had taken in the camera and zoom lens, along with a diamond ring and bracelet, which had been purchased with the stolen credit card. Investigation revealed that the subject selling the articles to the pawnshop had an extensive criminal background and lived within a few blocks of the employee. On the basis of this and other evidence, he was arrested and the property recovered.[44]

Police **sting operations** are an effective means of combating fences, identifying active criminals, penetrating criminal organizations, and recovering property. In a typical sting, officers set up a legitimate-appearing "front" business in which they slowly develop a reputation as being fences. As all transactions are videotaped, a great deal of intelligence is gathered that can be used in their current investigation or in collateral ones. Alternatively, the officers may do business in a different type of setting and use a warehouse located elsewhere to store the stolen property:

An FBI agent, a cooperating witness, and participating local departments ran a fencing operation out of a Brooklyn social club. The "drop" for the merchandise was a warehouse they had rented at another location. This undercover operation resulted in the indictments of 39 individuals on charges of selling stolen property, drug trafficking, gun dealing, and loan-sharking. Over $5 million in property was recovered, including a hijacked truckload of designer gowns valued at more than $1 million.[45]

In Chapter 7, "The Follow-Up Investigation and Investigative Resources," the enhanced capabilities of NCIC 2000 were discussed. The NCIC databases are of great importance for investigators, particularly since images of stolen property have been added. This new capability enhances the opportunity to recover stolen property.

THE INVESTIGATOR'S CRIME PREVENTION ROLE

While at the scene of a burglary, investigators should tell the victims the precautions they can take to decrease the likelihood of their being "hit" again.

Reducing the Risk of Commercial Burglary

Many of the suggestions provided in the next section for preventing residential burglaries also apply to businesses. In addition, operators of businesses should be told to prevent easy access to their roofs by securing all vents and roof openings; to use security-providing locks, frames, and doors properly; to light the exterior of the building; to use, if feasible, an alarm system and surveillance camera; to use a money chest rather than a fire-resistant safe; and to set the safe in concrete in open view at a place that can be lighted at night. Completion of the office security checklist in Figure 13-14 serves two purposes: It provides the owners with useful information about how to improve their security, and it may provide important investigative leads, particularly if a surreptitious entry is involved.

Reducing the Risk of Residential Burglary

To protect their residences as well as businesses, when appropriate, occupants should do the following things when they are on vacation or otherwise away:

1. Stop delivery of mail and newspapers, or arrange for a neighbor to pick them up daily.
2. Arrange for a special watch on their premises by patrol officers.
3. Use timers to turn on lights and radios at various times to make it look like the residence is occupied.
4. Ask reliable neighbors to immediately report any suspicious activity to the police.
5. Ask a trusted neighbor to come over occasionally and change the position of drapes, blinds, and other things.
6. Put up "Beware of Dog" signs, or if they really have a dog, ask someone to take care of it in the home whenever feasible.

		Yes	No
1.	Do you restrict office keys to persons who actually need them?	☐	☐
2.	Do you keep complete, up-to-date records of the disposition of all office keys?	☐	☐
3.	Do you have adequate procedures for collecting keys from terminated employees?	☐	☐
4.	Do you restrict duplication of office keys, except for those specifically ordered by you in writing?	☐	☐
5.	Do you require that all keys be marked "Do not duplicate" to prevent legitimate locksmiths from making copies without your knowledge?	☐	☐
6.	Have you established a rule that keys must not be left unguarded on desks or cabinets, and do you enforce that rule?	☐	☐
7.	Do you require that filing-cabinet keys be removed from locks and placed in a secure location after opening cabinets in the morning?	☐	☐
8.	Do you have procedures that prevent unauthorized personnel from reporting a "lost key" and receiving a "replacement"?	☐	☐
9.	Do you have some responsible person in charge of issuing all keys?	☐	☐
10.	Are all keys systematically stored in a secured wall cabinet either of your own design or from a commercial key-control system?	☐	☐
11.	Do you keep a record showing issuance and return of every key, including the name of the person, the date, and time?	☐	☐
12.	Do you use telephone locks or access codes to prevent unauthorized calls when the office is unattended?	☐	☐
13.	Do you provide at least one lockable drawer in every secretary's desk to protect personal effects?	☐	☐
14.	Do you have at least one filing cabinet secured with an auxiliary locking bar so that you can keep business secrets under better protection?	☐	☐
15.	Do you leave a night light on?	☐	☐
16.	Do you record all equipment serial numbers and file them in a safe place to maintain correct identification in the event of theft or destruction by fire?	☐	☐
17.	Do you shred all important papers before discarding them in wastebaskets?	☐	☐
18.	Do you lock briefcases and attaché cases containing important papers in closets or lockers when not in use?	☐	☐
19.	Do you insist on identification from repair people who come to do work in your office?	☐	☐
20.	Do you deposit incoming checks and cash each day so that you do not keep large sums in the office overnight?	☐	☐
21.	Do you clear all desks of important papers every night and place them in locked fireproof safes or cabinets?	☐	☐
22.	Do you frequently change the combination of your safe to prevent anyone from memorizing it or passing it on to a confederate?	☐	☐
23.	When working alone in the office at night, do you set the front-door lock to prevent anyone else from getting in?	☐	☐
24.	Do you have the police and fire department telephone numbers posted and handy?	☐	☐
25.	Do you check to see that no one remains in hiding behind you at night if you are the last to leave the office?	☐	☐
26.	Are all windows, transoms, and ventilators properly protected?	☐	☐
27.	Do you double check to see that all windows and doors are securely locked before you leave?	☐	☐
28.	Are all doors leading to the office secured by heavy-duty, double-cylinder, dead-bolt locks?	☐	☐
29.	If your office is equipped with a burglar alarm system or protected by a guard service, do you make sure the alarm equipment is set properly each night?	☐	☐
30.	Do you have a periodic security review by a qualified security expert or locksmith?	☐	☐
31.	Are computer access codes and/or selected files password-protected on a need-to-know basis?	☐	☐
32.	Are all computer disks and tapes containing sensitive, client, or secret information maintained under controlled conditions during the day and locked securely at night?	☐	☐

◄ **FIGURE 13-12**
Sample office security checklist
(Source: Courtesy Bolen Industries, Hackensack, New Jersey, with modification)

For day-to-day security, occupants can take other actions that will help them avoid being burglary victims or, if they are victimized, will help reduce their losses:

1. Create an uninviting target: use motion-sensor lights, purchase an alarm system, use dead-bolt locks on solid doors mounted in steel frames, and place locks on windows.
2. If possible, avoid placing valuables where they can be seen through windows.
3. Cut plants low around doors and windows so that burglars can't conceal themselves while breaking in.
4. Grow thorny plants around places where someone might attempt to force an entry.
5. Don't leave ladders or tools lying around in the yard or clothes on an outside line—a thief who initially may have thought of just taking them will see the greater opportunity they create.
6. Don't tell strangers about your comings and goings.
7. Don't allow strangers to use your telephone, and don't give your correct number to anyone who claims they are calling by mistake; instead, ask the caller whom he or she was trying to reach at what number. Baby-sitters and children should be instructed to do the same thing.
8. Don't keep spare keys in the usual places—under the mat, over the door, and in flower pots. Burglars know these places.
9. Don't go out to run a quick errand without locking all doors, including garage doors.
10. Engrave valuables with special identifying numbers. Alternatively, mark them with small translucent decals that have your special identification data on them. These microdots are about the size of a speck of pepper and are virtually invisible to the naked eye.
11. Keep strong control over your keys. It may be helpful to leave them for service workers or give them to maids, but at the cost of greater risk exposure.
12. Don't leave notes on the door saying where you have gone or when you will be back.
13. Get to know your neighbors; they'll be more likely to respond faithfully to requests to "watch my place while I'm gone."
14. When new snow is on the ground, back out of your driveway and pull back in several times; do the same walking in and out of your door. This makes it harder for burglars to figure out if you are home.
15. To enhance recovery of your property if you are victimized, take pictures of valuables and record makes, models, and serial numbers of your property.

KEY TERMS

amateur burglar
ATM attacks
burglary
burglary investigation checklist
burglary tools
car burglars

coin-operated machine burglary
fences/receivers
fire resistant safe
loiding
money chest (burglary resistant safe)
pawnshop databases

picking
possession of burglary tools
professional burglar
safes
smash and grab
sting operation

REVIEW QUESTIONS

1. Describe the dimensions of the crime of burglary.
2. What is the profile of persons arrested for burglary?
3. How are professional and amateur burglars distinguished?
4. What are the elements of the crime of burglary?
5. What considerations are important in approaching the scene of a burglary?
6. How are attacks on ATMs committed?
7. The text noted that black home owners and younger people are victimized more frequently than others. What are some possible explanations for this?
8. What signs at a burglary scene may suggest juvenile perpetrators?
9. How are fire-resistant safes and money chests differentiated?
10. What special actions are required if there are explosives at a burglary scene?
11. How do burglars get their information?
12. With respect to the possible illegal receiving of stolen property, what are some indicators of the absence of good-faith purchasing?
13. Explain two investigative approaches to locating fences.
14. What measures can home owners and business operators take to lessen their chances of being burglarized?

1. The two most famous burglaries in American are usually referred to by one word, "Watergate." What were these burglaries about, and what was their ultimate importance?

2. To learn how different police agencies across the country are attacking burglary problems go to www.cops.usdoj.gov (the Community Oriented Policing Services [COPS] website), click on "Resource Information Center (RIC), and enter "burglary" in the search field.

| NOTES

1. Federal Bureau of Investigation (FBI), Crime Clock 2006, www.FBI.gov/ucr/05cius/about/crime_clock. html, September 2007.

2. FBI, Burglary, www.FBI.gov/ucr/05cius/property_ burglary.html, September 2007.

3. 3. Rana Sampson, False Burglar Alarms (Washington, D.C.: U.S. Department of Justice, 2003), p. 1. Also see Rana Sampson, False Burglar Alarms (Washington, D.C.: Off ice of Community Oriented Policing Services, February 2007).

4. See Todd Keister, Thefts of and From Cars on Residential Streets and Driveways (Washington, D.C.: Off ice of Community Oriented Policing Services, February 2007).

5. C. Bennell and N. J. Jones, "Between a ROC and a Hard Place: A Method for Linking Serial Burglaries by Modeus Operandi, Journal of Investigative Psychology and Offender Profiling, Vo. 2, No. 1, pp. 23–41, 2005.

6. Experienced investigators are familiar with these two possibilities. One limited study involving 221 total cases from San Diego and Dallas found only support for the replacement theory and even then it only explained a small number of repeat burglary victimizations. The study noted that the same items were taken in the first and second burglaries of the same residence more frequently that expected statistically, supporting the "replacement item" theory somewhat. See Ronald V. Clarke, Elizabeth Perkins and Donald J. Smith, Jr., "Explaining Repeat Residential Burglaries: An Analysis of Property Stolen," in Graham Farrell and Ken Pease, Editors Repeat Victimization Vol. 12 (Monsey, New York: Criminal Justice Press, 2001) pp. 119–132.

7. J. L. Schneider, "Prolific Burglars and the Role of Shoplifting," Security Journal, Vol. 16, No. 2, pp. 49–59, 2003.

8. Mildrade Cherfils, "Jury Convicts 'Spiderman,' " Associated Press, www.canoe.ca/TopStories/ Spiderman_dec8.html, Dec. 8, 1998.

9. Paulo Lima, staff writer, The Bergen Record Online, www.bergen.com/bse/trainrob199811281.htm, Nov. 28, 1998.

10. Anderson County (Tennessee) Sheriff's Department, "Juvenile Burglary Ring Stopped," News Release, July 1, 2003.

11. Frank Main and Annie Sweeney, "Burglary Ring's Formula Worked for Decades," Chicago Sun-Times, January 2, 2005.

12. Bryan Joiner, "Codewise Crew Burglarized Queen's Homes for Millions," Queen's Chronicle, April 29, 2004.

13. See Richard A. Ballezza, "YACs Crime Groups," FBI Law Enforcement Bulletin, Vol 67, No. 11, 1998, pp. 7–12.

14. Sandra Gonzales, "Ex-Cop Admits Burglary Charges," San Jose Mercury News, Dec. 8, 1998.

15. Marvine Howe, "Anger Mixed with Sorrow for Organist Suspected in Church Burglaries," New York Times, Jan. 6, 1992, p. B4.

16. "FBI Recovers Norman Rockwell Paintings Stolen from Twin Cities Gallery," Minneapolis Star Tribune, Dec. 13, 2001.

17. Marilyn Meyer, "Burglars Hit Titusville Bank," Florida Today.com, www.flatoday/!newsroom/ localstorya1264A.htm, Dec. 12, 2001, pp. 1–2.

18. Richard Perez-Pena, "3 Arrests Hit Burglary Ring in Manhattan," New York Times, Nov. 14, 1992, pp. 21–22.

19. "Loot Jams Va. Home of Alleged Superthief," Atlanta Constitution, Dec. 16, 1980, p. 20D.

20. Ann All, "ATM Smash/Grabs Impact Industry," ATM Marketplace.com, March 18, 2004, p.1.

21. Ibid.

22. For examples, see (no author) "Thieves Smash Store, Grab ATM," Thc BostonChannel.com, Aug. 17, 2004, p. 1.

23. All, "ATM Smash/Grabs Impact Industry," p. 1.

24. Ibid., p. 2.

25. Ibid., p. 3.

26. See, for example, (no author) KATC3, Acadiana, Louisiana, "Man Arrested While Trying to Drive Off with ATM," Dec. 10, 2004, and Ann All, "ATM News of the Weird," ATM Marketplace.com, Jan. 21, 2005, p. 1.

27. (No author), "Ozark Man Charged in Attempted ATM Machine Break-ins," Ozark Alabama News, June 9, 2002, p. 2.

28. (No author) "ATM Burglary Tried with Shotgun," BillingsGazzette.com (Montana), June 18, 2000.

29. Bureau of Justice Statistics, Criminal Victimization in the United States—2000 (Washington, D.C.: National Institute of Justice, 2002).

30. Ibid., Table 19, no page number in downloaded copy.

31. Wright and Decker, Burglars on the Job, p. 36.

32. Ibid., p. 37.

33. Ibid., p. 39.
34. Ibid., pp. 41–42.
35. Ibid., p. 43.
36. Ibid., p. 58.
37. Ibid., pp. 38, 58, with some restatement.
38. For example, see P. F. Cromwell, J. N. Olson, and D. W. Avary, "Who Buys Stolen Property? A New Look at Criminal Receiving," *Journal of Crime and Justice,* 1993, Vol. 16, No. 1, pp. 75–96.
39. Guy Trebay, "Shoplifting on a Grand Scale: Luxury Wear Stolen to Order," *New York Times,* Aug. 8, 2000, p. 8.
40. Federal Bureau of Investigation, "Operation American Dream," www.fbi.gov/majcases/dream/dream.htm, Aug. 28, 2001, p. 2.
41. Richard Zitrin, "Two Accused of Fencing Loot Online," APB News.com, www.apbnews.com/news-cetern/breakingnews/2000/06/02/burglaries0602_01.html, June 2, 2000, p. 1.
42. Alexis Muellner, "Good Cop, Bad Cop Played in Miami Cargo Theft Sting," southflorida.bcentral.com/southflorida/stores/1999/11/15/newscolumn3.html. *South Florida Business Journal,* Nov. 12, 1999, pp. 1–2.
43. Fort Lauderdale Police Department, "Investigative News," ci.ftlaud.fl.us/police/cid1200.html, Dec. 2000, p. 8.
44. Ibid., p. 6.
45. Federal Bureau of Investigation, untitled news release, www.geocities.com/pentagon/9719/129117.txt, Jan. 23, 1997, p. 2.

14

LARCENY/THEFT AND WHITE-COLLAR CRIME

CHAPTER OBJECTIVES

1. Distinguish between tangible and intangible property

2. State the difference between petit/petty and grand larceny

3. Define, from two different perspectives, white collar crime

4. Explain why so little property from larceny/thefts is recovered

5. Describe how a three-person pickpocket crew works

6. Contrast organized retail theft and organized retail crime

7. Explain methods of identity theft and the uses made of stolen identities.

8. Be familiar with credit card and check frauds.

9. Discuss different items which are counterfeited.

10. Explain different types of frauds, scams, and cons.

11. Define and describe methods of money laundering.

12. Describe security and investment frauds.

13. Identify and summarize telephone and pager scams.

14. Outline common telemarketing and postal frauds.

▲ This image taken from a surveillance videotape released by the Bedford, N.H. Police Department, Wednesday, Aug. 9, 2006, shows, according to police, an unidentified older woman, at right, stuffing items down her shirt at the Consignment Gallery, Aug. 2, 2006, in Bedford, N.H., while at left, an unidentified employee works a cash register at the store, according to police. A woman, who identified herself as the older woman, shown at right, told WMUR-TV on Wednesday that she was shopping for a bed with her daughter and grandchildren when the children began to misbehave. The woman, at right, whom the station did not identify, said her daughter (not shown here) was not stealing jewelry but rather trying to get her children to put back items they had taken.

(© AP Photo/Bedford, N.H. Police Department)

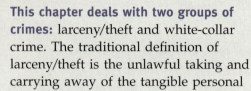

This chapter deals with two groups of crimes: larceny/theft and white-collar crime. The traditional definition of larceny/theft is the unlawful taking and carrying away of the tangible personal property of another with the intent to permanently deprive that person of his interest in the property. **Tangible personal property** means things that have both a physical existence that can be touched and intrinsic value—such as jewelry, lawn mowers, cameras, laptop computers, televisions, furniture and clothing, and collectibles such as coins and civil war uniform buttons.

In contrast, **intangible property** has value, but it is more abstract—such as stocks, bonds, checking and saving accounts, and other types of financial instruments, as well as patents and copyrights. State statutes have historically addressed the theft of intangibles through specific statutes, which supplemented the existing larceny statutes. Larceny essentially incorporates the elements of the crime of robbery, except the element of the use of force, threat, or fear is not included (see Chapter 12, "Robbery"). Additionally, although robbery is a face-to-face crime, the law does not require that the victim of a larceny be present at the time of a crime. However, the victim may be present as illustrated by purse snatching, pickpocketing, and an owner driving home from work in time to see a stranger pick up his daughter's bicycle from the lawn of his home, toss it in the back of a SUV, and drive away. Larceny/theft is often divided into **grand larceny** and **petit** *or* **petty larceny**; the former is a felony and the latter a misdemeanor. The difference between the two is the value of the property stolen, which varies by state; the dividing line between the two is often that if the value of the property stolen is $1,000 or more, it is a felony. In some states, larceny/theft statutes are divided into grades or classes of offending, such as "Class A, Class B," and so on; the gradations of offenses are usually based on the amount of loss to the victim, and the legal penalties are tied to the grade or class of the theft.

Many states have also enacted specifically titled larceny/theft statutes that reflect special aspects of their economy, such as "timber theft or fraud," or special problems, e.g., "transit fare evasion, identity theft" or "organized retail theft" to distinguish between prosecutions that are aimed at rings of professional shoplifters causing significant losses and that have more serious penalties versus those directed at the teenager who "lifts or boosts" a CD, tube of lipstick, or shirt (Figure 14-1) and is charged with "theft from retail merchants," a lesser shoplifting offense.

The term **white-collar crime** was coined in 1939 by sociologist. E. H. Sutherland. His white-collar criminals were characterized by respectability and higher social status, which they used to commit more complex offenses such as **fraud** and **embezzlement**, as opposed to street crimes. Now, almost 70 years later, the U.S. Department of Justice defines **white-collar crime** as nonviolent, illegal activities that rely on deceit, deception, concealment, manipulation, breach of trust, subterfuge, or illegal circumvention. Note that Sutherland's definition was based on the characteristics of the offender versus the present orientation of white-collar crime being the characteristics of the actions taken by the offender.[2] There is no set of laws titled "white-collar crime." It is a construct, useful for how we think about such crimes, but offenders are often charged with larceny/theft crimes, such as theft by fraud.

▲ **FIGURE 14-1   Theft from retail merchant**
Teenage shoplifter takes one last look around before concealing merchandise in her backpack. (© Index Stock Imagery)

Statistically, pickpockets are not a large problem in the United States; the crime accounts for only about one-half of 1% of all larceny/thefts, but losses are still serious to victims. Abroad, pickpockets flourish in all major cities, such as Milan, Shanghai, Paris, Berlin, and London. In foreign countries tourists lose not only their valuables but often their passports, too, which interrupts their vacations while they seek to get a replacement. The crime flourishes where people congregate at peak hours, such as transportation centers, along crowded streets, and at sporting events.

Children as young as five and six years old are trained as pickpockets in some foreign countries. There are schools in South America from which, in order to graduate, the would-be pickpocket must "lift" items from all the pockets of a mannequin dressed in a three-piece men's suit. Each pocket is guarded with a bell that cannot ring if the "student" is to pass. Pickpockets may work alone, although a "crew" of three is common: one distracts the mark (e.g., drops something, bumps him/her, or feigns a medical emergency or accident), another takes the valuables, which are immediately handed to a third accomplice, who quickly slips away. A seasoned operator can take the wristwatch off your arm without you realizing it; in Oslo, Norway brazen pickpockets even lifted the wallet of the Police of Chief. Some very skilled pickpockets morph over to shoplifting expensive jewelry because of the higher values. Investigators should exercise caution when arresting pickpockets, a small number of whom turn violent when apprehended. They should also be on-guard for assaults from previously unnoted accomplices.

Most victims had exposed valuables, such as their wallet, within the 30 minutes prior to their victimization; pickpockets study the crowd and carefully select their target. Women are more likely to be victimized then men are, and men are more likely to be pickpockets. Secondary crimes included credit card fraud and withdrawals from the victim's ATM account because the victim's personal identification number (PIN) was written down in the wallet.[1]

THE OFFENSE AND THE OFFENDER

A larceny/theft occurs every 4.8 seconds, a rate of three times that for burglary,[3] and the average loss is $855.[4] This crime bears a low clearance rate; only 17.4% are resolved by arrest or exceptional means.[5] Four out of ten larceny/thefts (42%) produce losses of $1 to $99, and roughly 75% of all such offenses involve losses of less than $299; the value of property taken exceeds $1,000 only 6.1% of the time.[6] Larceny/theft is often an opportunistic act; fishing rods and tool boxes are taken from open beds of pickup trucks parked at a Sam's Club, or a thief loitering at an airport notices that someone waiting for a flight is distracted and takes her purse, carry-on luggage, or laptop. Overwhelmingly, as seen in Table 14-1, these offenses are committed by young, white males.

Because small items of low value are often stolen and there are frequently no leads, many larceny/theft cases are simply inactivated after the incident report is taken, and they receive no investigative follow-up. This fact accounts for the reality that the recovery of property in larceny/theft is low; in only 3.7% of all such cases is at least some property recovered. However, 4.7% of the time all of the property is recovered, often from offenses with larger losses and significant leads.[7]

TABLE 14-1	Characteristics of Arrested Larceny/Theft Offenders				
AGE		**RACE**		**SEX**	
Under 15	8.7%	White	68.6%	Male	62.3%
Under 18	25.7	Black	28.9	Female	37.7
Under 21	40.4	All other	2.5		
Under 25	52.2				

(Source: *Uniform Crime in the United States*, 2006. Washington, D.C.: FBI, 2007, www.fbi.gov/ucr/cius2006. See Tables 41, 42 and 43, no page numbers.)

ELEMENTS OF THE CRIME

Although the traditional definition of larceny is still operative in some states, others have eliminated the distinction between the theft of tangibles and intangibles and created more comprehensive larceny/theft statutes to cover both types of losses. Such statutes drop the former "tangible personal property of another" and use "property of another," to cover the loss of a wide range of things, such as stocks and bonds, services—such as electricity, natural gas, television cable, high-speed Internet access, tickets to the symphony and sporting events, lawn mowers, paintings, hotel rooms and rental cars, computer software and information files, cash and jewelry. To illustrate, in some states the failure to return a rental car within 72 hours of the agreed-on time in the lease is evidence of intent to commit larceny/theft.

The person from whom the property is taken in a larceny/theft need not own it and may simply be the custodian of it. Although he/she is the victim of the crime for reporting purposes, if the property is recovered it is returned to the owner. If there is no recovery, the owner receives the fair market value from his/her insurance company.

The broader larceny/theft laws recognize that the taking may be accomplished in a variety of ways, such as:

1. **theft by trick,** such as con games and swindles;
2. **theft by receiving stolen property,** meaning knowingly receiving and disposing of property he/she should have known or knew was stolen.
3. **theft by deception,** e.g., the removal of a price sticker from one item for sale and replacing it with a less expensive sticker);[8]
4. **theft by fraud,** illustrated by the unauthorized use of another's credit card, using someone else's medical insurance card or Social Security number to get benefits, and "pump and dump" stock schemes, whereby a stock is heavily promoted—after the stock runs up in price, its promoters dump it.
5. **theft of services,** covering such things as "skipping out" on hotel, restaurant and bar bills, or illegally connecting or reconnecting an electrical meter.

In states with comprehensive larceny/theft laws, the crime of embezzlement has often disappeared because the language of the larceny/theft law usually provides a means to bring charges for that conduct, often by a crime titled **theft by conversion.** Where it remains, the elements of embezzlement are the same as the traditional larceny charge, with the addition that a person who has been entrusted with something of valuable converts it to their own purpose or use in contravention of his/her legal obligation.

SHOPLIFTING AND ORGANIZED RETAIL CRIME (ORC)

Shoplifting

Nationally, **shoplifting** produces losses of $37.4 billion annually with an average loss of $129.[9] Security experts calculate that for every $40 dollars stolen, only one dollar of merchandise is recovered. A significant problem is that there is no single profile of who shoplifts; they can be ordinary people or professional thieves.[10] Slightly more men (55%) than women (45%) shoplift, although women take higher value items, and juveniles account for roughly 33% of all cases.[11] Saturdays (18%) and Fridays (15%) account for a third of all offenses, and 60% of all cases occur between noon and 6:00 P.M.[12] There are also seasonal variations in shoplifting, with spikes in activity just before students go back to school in August, before Christmas, Easter, and when schools are letting out for summer. There are five types of shoplifters: (1) kleptomaniacs or those who have a compulsion to steal; (2) amateurs, who steal on impulse or because of peer pressure; (3) professionals, who are the least numerous but produce the largest losses; (4) drug users, who steal to support their habit, often selling what they take to criminal fences; and (5) "desperate straits" people, such as vagrants or the homeless and mothers who cannot afford items for their babies.

Retail establishments combat shoplifting by a combination of prevention strategies, such as sales staff greeting customers to make them feel singled out, posting signs about prosecuting shoplifters, placing expensive items in locked cases, putting on display only one of a pair of items, keeping aisles uncluttered to facilitate observation, roving employees and uniformed security officers, using electronic tags, and placing dummy surveillance cameras in plain sight. In recent years, "clamshell blisters" have gained popularity. This type of packaging seals of a product in a clear plastic container, which allows 360-degree visibility of the product and is difficult to open. Retailers also use a strategy of apprehension that involves the use of observable, real surveillance cameras, "spy cameras" (e.g., inside of clocks, smoke detector sprinklers, and heads of mannequins), observation ports, and the use of store security to work the floor. *Source tagging* is used widely—merchants place a small insert between the pages of a book or in a package of tools; the tag emits a narrow-band radio frequency that triggers an alarm if the item has not been scanned.

Investigators working a shoplift detail should be alert for customers in a retail establishment who (1) avoid contact with sales personnel; (2) pick up a small item and wander about the store because they may finally palm it, and leave; (3) "have their heads on swivels" to assess their opportunity to steal; (4) wear baggy clothing or coats in weather not requiring it; (5) distract sales personnel or serve as shields so their partner can take and conceal items; (6) make repeated trips to fitting rooms, sometimes to wear store merchandise out under the clothes they wear; and (7) carry large handbags or push strollers in which items can quickly be concealed.

Theft by employees includes such activities as the removal of products, supplies, merchandise, money, data, information, and intellectual property.[13] Estimates vary across studies, but roughly 50% of all shoplifting is done by employees. The annual cost of embezzlement and employee theft is between $20 and $90 billion and upward of $240 billion if thefts of intellectual property are included; it is believed that 30% to 50% of all business failures are caused by embezzlement and employee theft.[14]

Organized Retail Crime (ORC)

Shoplifting has long suffered from the misperception that it is "small-time crime." Yet, its previously noted annual losses of $37.4 billion dwarf the combined annual losses of burglary ($4 billion) and motor vehicle theft ($7.9 billion).[15] Recognition of such facts has lead to important new initiatives in combating shoplifting and other crimes against retailers. In 2006, legislation was signed creating an Organized Retail Theft Task Force at the FBI and mandating the creation of a public database on retail theft. A related database already exists, the National Retail Federation's (NRF) Retail Loss Prevention Intelligence Network (RLPIN), which was designed with the assistance of the FBI and other law enforcement agencies.

Two terms which have emerged recently are **organized retail theft (ORT)** and **organized retail crime (ORC)**. ORT refers to the problem of significant losses to retailers caused by crews or rings of often mobile professional shoplifters. ORC has emerged as a broader term and includes not only professional shoplifters but also other associated problems such as thefts from merchandise distribution centers, truck hijacking, credit card fraud, counterfeit goods, and the fences and other outlets for stolen merchandise.

As many as seven subjects, all from Puerto Rico, flew into Salt Lake City and rapidly began shoplifting at area malls. Although none of them was caught in the act of stealing, an alert security guard called the police about a suspicious rental car parked in front of a store.

The car was already a day late in being returned, and in the back seat of the car were thousands of dollars of premium merchandise that still had price and security tags on them. Documents in the car led investigators to two motels where the subjects were staying. The follow-up investigation recovered $25,000 in goods from motel rooms and another $30,000 worth in a van.

Two subjects were arrested, and as many as five others may have been involved but were not immediately apprehended. Investigators learned there were reservations in some of the names used by the subjects to fly to New York City, where they may have intended to continue their shoplifting.[16]

ORC offenders range from independent, loosely tied together crews to more organized entities, including traditional crime families to the ultra-violent transnational gangs such as Mara Salvatrucha (MS-13, Figure 14-2), which established itself in the Rampart section of Los Angeles, where many Salvadorans fled in the 1980s as their country was in the grips of a civil war. While some ORC groups may essentially specialize in crimes against retailers, others, like MS-13, have diverse interests including alien, drug, and gun smuggling. One MS-13 leader has called for gang action against volunteer border patrol groups, such as the Arizona Minutemen, because that state is often a gateway into the United States from Mexico for their activities. Some ORCs run by persons with ties to Middle Eastern countries wired "profits" to Jordan, Egypt, and Palestine, where they were allegedly used to finance terror organizations such as Hamas and Hezbollah; tracing the money once it reaches unfriendly foreign countries has proven difficult, but it seems clear that some ORC profits are used to finance terrorism.[17]

Some of the most violent organizations, MS-13 members have long worn their numerous tattoos with pride. However, continued pressure from federal, state, and local investigators has resulted in a number of indictments and convictions of the easily identifiable gang members. Consequently, some MS-13 leaders have quietly encouraged members to be less ostentatious with the tattoos.

ORC offenders are known to have paid illegal immigrants, the homeless, and drug addicts to steal items for them (e.g., $1.00 for each can of baby formula). Because some of the people in these categories might shoplift on their own, it is difficult for investigators to know exactly

◀FIGURE 14-2 Gang tattoos
(© Elmer Martinez/AFP/Getty Images)

what they are dealing with when they make some shoplifting arrests. Yet, it is important to try and find out not only from a case investigation standpoint but also because of the potential national security implications.

Some ORC operations have their own warehouses chock full of stolen goods, which are sold through controlled convenience stores and neighborhood stores, flea markets, and other outlets, as well as shipped to unsuspecting wholesalers. Some stolen goods have expiration dates ("use by" or "use before") on them, such as diabetes-testing and teeth-whitening strips, batteries, baby formula, condoms, pharmaceuticals, and food products. The public health is endangered when expiration dates on stored stolen products are altered to make them marketable. This endangerment also exists when other items, such as frozen dinners, are allowed to thaw and then are refrozen or stored at improper temperatures before being sold.

IDENTITY THEFT AND FOLLOW-ON CRIMES

Identity theft, which began to emerge as a problem in the 1990s, has been called the "crime of the new millennium."[18] The normal daily activities of consumers include purchasing tickets and merchandise online, cashing checks, using credit and debit cards, and renting videos—all of which result in information being shared. At all points where personal data is collected, processed, or stored, there are opportunities for identity theft.[19] Identity theft may be the fastest growing crime of any kind in our society. In a single year, almost 10 million Americans were victimized by this crime with combined individual costs and losses to businesses placed at nearly $50 billion.[20] The person whose

identity is stolen is one victim; the businesses that suffered losses owing to the criminal use of the stolen identity represent another group of victims. Estimates of the cost to individual victims to clear their names vary, but sources maintain that it requires as few as 24 to as much as 600 hours of effort and from $80 to $1,500 worth of lost earnings to correct credit and other related problems. Over 1,300 victims have been the subjects of criminal investigations, arrests, or wrongful convictions.[21]

Identity crimes involve two types of criminal acts: (1) identity theft and (2) the **follow-on crimes** that occur, such as credit card and check fraud.

How Identity Theft Occurs

Abundant opportunities exist for identity thieves to get the personal information of those they victimize. Among methods used to obtain data are these:

1. Stealing wallets and purses containing identification, bank, credit, membership, and other types of cards.
2. Stealing mail, which provides bank and credit statements, preapproved credit offers, Social Security numbers, and other personal data. Some thieves follow mail carriers at a distance and then steal from mailboxes that appear to have just had a large stack of mail delivered. Alternatively, they might cruise affluent neighborhoods looking for raised red flags on mailboxes and stealing outgoing correspondence.
3. Going to the post office and completing a change of address form to divert mail to another location.
4. Rummaging through the victims' trash, or the trash of businesses, to "mine" for personal data—a practice described as **dumpster diving.**
5. Fraudulently obtaining the victim's credit report by posing as a potential landlord or employer.

6. Stealing personal identification from the victim's home.

7. Opportunistically using information from lost wallets and purses.

8. Family members, relatives, roommates and acquaintances misappropriating information.

9. Stealing personal data assistants (PDAs), such as Palm Pilots, and laptops; this area may become more significant in the future, because at least one spyware virus for PDAs is known to exist.

10. Obtaining personal information by hacking into home and business computers or by such tactics as downloading spyware programs. (Identity thieves posing as a legitimate business duped an Atlanta-area company out of personal information for perhaps as many as 400,000 people nationally.[22])

11. Stealing information from employers, medical and insurance offices, student records, and other locations or bribing corrupt employees to provide the victims' personal data.

12. Scamming victims out of personal information on the Internet is done by a technique known as **phishing.**[23] Two common phishing scams are sending an e-mail to potential victims that appears to be from a legitimate source, such as eBay, AOL, Yahoo, Best Buy, Wells Fargo, a credit card company, or a bank, and asking that they update their account information data. The second method involves using an e-mail to notify victims they have won a prize, such as the Canadian or Netherlands Lottery, but need to pay a processing fee to receive it, thereby tricking the victims into completing an accompanying credit form.[24]

   There are numerous variations on these two methods. One is an e-mail promising a free credit report subject to the recipient completing a personal information form. A second method is an e-mail from the U.S. Internal Revenue Service offering an $80 credit if they will participate in an online satisfaction survey, Form IR-2007-148, which also requires the disclosure of personal information.

   Any time a possible victim reports an unsolicited e-mail contact from the IRS it is a phishing attack, because the IRS neither initiates unsolicited contacts that way nor does it ask for passwords and other related information. Other bogus forms falsely attributed to the IRS include IR-2007- ending in 49, 75, 104, 109, or 116. Victims should be directed not to open attachments associated with such e-mails and to report the attack to phishing@irs.gov. Since this mailbox was established in 2006, more than 30,000 taxpayers have reported 400 separate phishing incidents.

13. **Shoulder surfing,** or watching and listening from a nearby location as victims identify themselves and use credit cards or write checks or are punching in their long-distance calling-card numbers.[25]

14. Using technology, such as skimmers, to obtain personal data. **Skimmers** are pager-sized data collection devices that cost roughly $300. These are attached to the telephone line running between a business' legitimate card swipe and a telephone jack. During what appears to be a normal transaction, the skimmer reads and stores the data, which is retrieved later by the user. There are also portable skimmers through which waiters and clerks can run victims' cards while they are in the back of the restaurant. More difficult to detect is "skimmer bug" software that can be inserted into point-of-sale terminals. These bugs store the data read in the terminals' circuitry, and then the modem is used to send the data to the thieves' computers. Some banks have found dispensers filled with bank pamphlets attached to the side of their ATMs. What they discovered is that these thief-placed dispensers actually contain miniature cameras that record the names, debit card numbers, and codes of ATM users.[26]

15. Employing *card trappers.* One example of this involves attaching a false card slot to the front of the ATM. As legitimate users enter their codes, shoulder surfers wait nearby or use binoculars or a camera with a telephoto lens to get the accounts' access codes. Unable to retrieve their cards, customers leave the ATM, and the thieves have both the access codes and the ATM cards.[27]

16. Picking up discarded computers. From these, thieves recover sensitive files between 33% and 50% of the time.[28]

17. Sending a fraudulent letter and IRS-like form to nonresident aliens who have earned income in the United States. The form is an altered version of IRS Form W-8BEN, "Certificate of Foreign Status of Beneficial Owner for United States Tax Withholding." This form asks for many types of personal information and account numbers and passwords. United States citizens receive a similar phony IRS Form, W-9095 (Figure 14-3), the intent of which is also identity theft.

18. Calling a home and telling the person that because he or she failed to come to court as required by "the jury duty summons sent to their residence" that the judge is going to issue a bench warrant for his or her arrest. When the panicked recipient of the calls insists no such summons was sent, the "Clerk of the Court" says "perhaps there has been a mistake, let's verify some information" and gets enough personal information to commit identify theft.

19. Offering "debt consolidation" services by phone, promising the unwary that by working with the holders of their credit cards, they can immediately get up to 50% of their debt immediately forgiven, and the one remaining monthly payment "will be less than 20% of the total you are paying now; all I need to get you started right now is your credit card numbers."

Form **W–9095**
(Rev. July 2001)
Department of the Treasury
Internal Revenue Service

**Application Form For Certificate Status/
Ownership For Witholding Tax**
(Fax this Form to 1-914-470-9245)

For Official Use Only
EFIN: | ETIN:

OMB Number 1545-0991

Please check the box(es) that apply to this application:
☐ New
☐ Reapply
☐ Revised   EFIN:_____
Revision Reason: _____

☐ On-line Filing [check only if you will process income tax return information for taxpayers who are preparing their returns at home, via an On-line Internet site, or fax mail (see fax mail number below)]
☐ Fax mail number in the foreign country if applicable.

Type or print name (first, middle, last)

☐ Tax Payer Identification Number(EIN) ☐ Social Security Number(SSN)
(State as applicable)

Title ☐Mr. ☐Mrs. ☐Others   Sex: ☐Male ☐Female
U.S. Citizenship? ☐ Yes ☐ No ☐ Legal resident alien

Date of Birth: Month [   ] Day [   ] Year [   ]
Place of Birth:

Marital Status: ☐Married ☐Single ☐Divorce ☐Widowed
Spouses Name (if any):
Father's Name /
Mother's Maiden Name /
Passport No. (Indicate Place and Date of Issue / Expiration):

Country of Permanent Residence (Address in Full, Not P.O.Box):
Branch (Address in full, including Telephone numbers):

Account Name and Date it Was Opened:
PIN Number (if any)

Password or Code (if any):
Index Number (if any):

Date and Amount of last deposit
Account Officer (Full name & Rank if any)
State Other Accounts (if any):
Day Time Phone / Fax No.
Where did you work in the last 12 months?
When did each employment begin and end?
Was any part of these employments carried out in the U.S.? ☐ Yes ☐ No
Do you intend to stay in the U.S. for 6 to 12 months period? ☐ Yes ☐ No
How often do you come to the U.S. and when did you arrived last?
Are your spouse and children living in your country of residence? ☐ Yes ☐ No
Are your parents and relations living in your country of residence? ☐ Yes ☐ No

CERTIFICATION

Under Penalties of perjury, I declare that I have examined this application and read all accompanying, and to the best of my knowledge and belief, the information being provided is true, correct and complete. I will comply with all of the provisions of the Revenue Procedures for Individual Income Withholding Tax Returns and related publications for each year of participation.

SIGNATURES

Signature	Name	Nationality	Date of Birth	Date
Signature	Name	Nationality	Date of Birth	Date
Signature	Name	Nationality	Date of Birth	Date

◀ **FIGURE 14-3**
Phishing attack that uses a phony IRS FORM W-9095

The U.S. Department of Education's (USDOE) Office of Inspector General reports that some students are receiving calls from people falsely claiming that they represent USDOE and offering them scholarships or grants. This financial assistance can be immediately obtained for a $249 processing fee that the student can pay with their credit card number. The USDOE does not charge a processing fee for financial assistance.[29]

Follow-On Crimes

Once armed with enough stolen personal identification data, the process of identity theft is executed and follow-on crimes are committed by:

1. Calling credit card companies, asking them to change the address "your" bill is mailed to and quickly running up charges on accounts. The victim may be unaware of any problems for a month or more. This practice is called **account takeover.**
2. Opening up new, fraudulent, credit card accounts using the victim's name, banking information, Social Security information, and other data. The first hint of trouble for a victim may be when a card company or collection agency calls because the "account" is in serious arrears.
3. Establishing new accounts for wireless telephone service, which go unpaid.
4. Opening bank accounts on which they write worthless checks.
5. Using counterfeit checks and debit cards to drain victims' banking accounts.

6. Purchasing cars by taking out loans using the victim's name, defaulting on payments and then fleeing with what is now a stolen vehicle.

7. Using the victim's identity if involved in an automobile accident, stopped for a traffic violation, or arrested by the police. If released by the police or bonded out of jail following an arrest, they don't show up for any required court appearance and an arrest warrant is issued in the victim's name.[30]

8. Fraudulently obtaining other types of identification, including passports, drivers' licenses, and Department of Defense cards.

9. Committing mail, investment, telemarketing, and Social Security frauds.

From the preceding list, three main patterns of identity theft can be established: (1) financial identity theft, in which the thief uses the information for financial gain; (2) criminal identity theft, wherein the imposter provides someone else's name to law enforcement officers issuing a traffic citation or conducting a criminal investigation;

and (3) identity cloning, which permits the thief to establish a "new life."[31] In Chapter 7, the use of visual link analysis software was discussed and an application of it shown. Figure 14-4 demonstrates the use of this technique applied to an identity theft. In terms of main patterns of identity theft, the thief, Steven Black, is involved with two patterns: (1) financial identity theft and (2) establishing a "new life."

Investigation of Identity Theft and Follow-On Cases

From an investigatory view, the co-entwining of identity theft and follow-on crimes almost invariably means investigating multiple crimes, with a number of victims. Additionally, these crimes may be committed in many different jurisdictions, requiring careful case coordination and information sharing among the investigative agencies involved. All states and the District of Columbia have specific identity theft statutes;[32] Federal jurisdiction comes from United

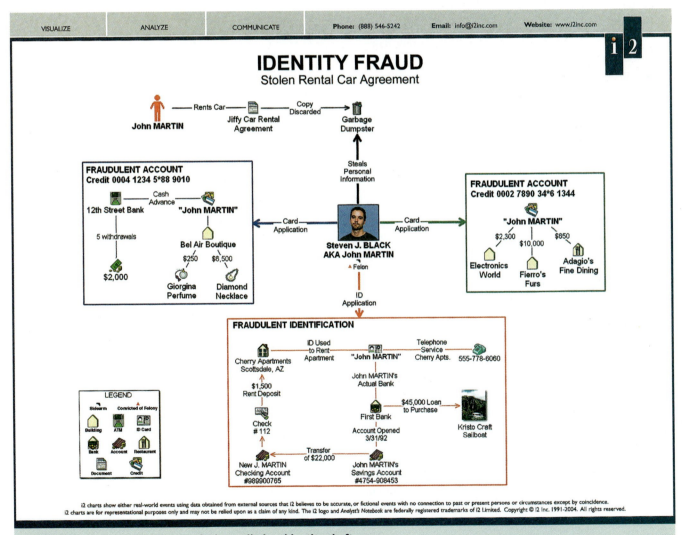

▲ **FIGURE 14-4   Visual link analysis applied to identity theft case**

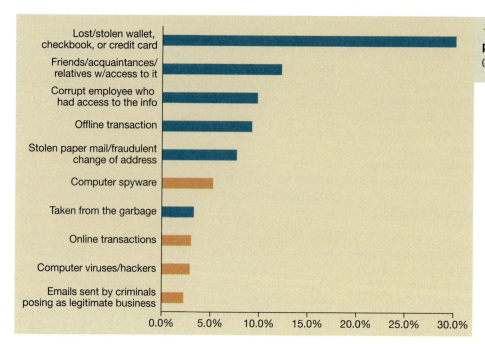

◀ FIGURE 14-5   How was victim's personal information obtained?

(© 2005 Javelin Strategy & Research)

States Code, Title 18, Section 1028, The Identity Theft and Assumption Deterrence Act of 1998. This means there is often joint jurisdiction in identity theft cases. Depending on the nature and the specifics of the case, federal agencies with whom state and local investigators may work include the FBI, the Secret Service, the Social Security Administration, the Post Office, and Homeland Security. In deciding whether there will be federal or state jurisdiction, one consideration will be the level of seriousness and extent of harm, with the most flagrant cases often becoming the responsibility of the jurisdiction with the most substantial criminal penalties.

Figure 14-5 summarizes how personal information is obtained by identity thieves. Note that the "big three," which account for more than 50% of cases, are lost/stolen wallet, checkbook, or credit card; friends/acquaintances/ relatives with access; and corrupt employees with access to the information. Unless the available information dictates otherwise, the big three may initially provide fruitful avenues for the investigation. Eighty-five percent of victims report that their first realization about the theft comes from a negative contact[33] (e.g., a credit card company soliciting payment of past due amounts) or a collection agency. This means investigators are responding to calls where victims are angry, confused, and worried about their financial futures and personal reputations. Another immediate difficulty for the investigator is that most identity thefts and the follow-up crimes come to light only one to six months after they began,[34] meaning that victims' recollections about how and when the identity theft occurred may not be very helpful and that documentary evidence is of vital importance in working the case.

Figure 14-6 is an identity theft and follow-on crimes checklist, with emphasis on the unique types of determinations which need to be made.

CREDIT CARD FRAUD

The link between identity theft and credit card fraud was established earlier in this chapter. However, there are also other types of credit card frauds. Altogether these frauds create losses of $2 billion globally according to the Federal Trade Commission. Credit card fraud is particularly prevalent in this country because Americans hold 71% of all credit cards issued worldwide.[35] Credit card fraud has become so lucrative that some organized crime rings and drug dealers have shifted their "careers" to engage in it because it is simple to execute and quickly profitable.[36] Figure 14-7 illustrates a credit card fraud which simply involves the illegal use of the victim's credit card account.

The quickest exact growing sector of credit card fraud may be the counterfeiting of credit cards; the continuing availability of new technologies has helped counterfeiters produce exact replicas of bona-fide cards, including the so-called "hidden" security features, such as holograms, used by legitimate credit card issuers.[37] One source of the necessary equipment is the Far East; another is corrupt vendors. A Canadian vendor was arrested for supplying equipment to thieves and terrorist organizations as part of a multimillion dollar credit and debit card ring.[38] In the advanced payment scheme, the accounts created by credit cards that were obtained through yet-to-be detected thefts, identity theft, or counterfeiting are overpaid by the "card holder," with a bad check. The money is then quickly withdrawn by a cash advance before the check clears the bank. There are also other scams associated with credit cards. In the advanced fee scheme, a person with poor credit pays in advance to have their record "repaired." Other variants of advanced fee schemes involve victims

Completed	Task
	How did victim become aware of identity theft?
_____	Fraudulent charges on credit card bill(s)
_____	Received bills for accounts not opened
_____	Found irregularities in credit report
_____	Contacted by creditor demanding payment
_____	Denied a loan
_____	Sued for debt victim did not incur
_____	Not receiving bills from legitimate accounts
_____	Received legal filing, such as bankruptcy
_____	Denied employment
_____	Driver's license suspended for violations not committed
_____	Incident report completed naming victim as suspect
_____	Victim advised of warrant or arrested
_____	Other (specify): _____
_____	What date did victim become aware of ID theft?
_____	When reported? Explain any gaps.
_____	When did the first fraudulent activity begin?
_____	What is the presently known chronology of fraudulent activities?
_____	Assign victim the responsibility for describing in as much detail as possible activities associated with all fraudulent activities.
_____	What is the full name, address, birth date, and other identifying information that the fraudulent activities were committed under?
_____	What documents and identifying information were stolen or compromised? If known, when?
_____	Credit card: list banks, contact information, and account numbers.
_____	ATM card: contact information and account numbers.
_____	Get voided check or checking account number, bank info, and contact information.
_____	Brokerage and/or stock account numbers: who holds accounts, contact information.
_____	Passport: obtain all relevant information, including country issuing.
_____	Driver's license or license number; state issuing.
_____	State identity card: number, state issuing.
_____	Social Security card or number, get number.
_____	Birth certificate (identify state and locality issuing), number.
_____	Resident alien green card or other documents, get all particulars.
_____	Bank and other account password/secret word, such as mother's maiden name.
_____	Other (specify).
_____	Unknown.
	To the best of the victim's knowledge, what crimes have been committed?
_____	Use of victim's actual credit cards or numbers without authorization?
_____	Opening new credit card accounts in victim's name?

Completed	Task
_____	Opening utility/phone accounts in victim's name?
_____	Unauthorized withdrawals from victim's bank accounts?
_____	Loans taken out in victim's name?
_____	Access to/withdrawals from securities/investments accounts?
_____	Obtaining government benefits in victim's name?
_____	Obtaining employment in victim's name?
_____	Obtaining medical services or insurance in victim's name?
_____	Committing crimes attributed to victim?
_____	Check fraud?
_____	Passport/Visa fraud?
_____	Other (specify).
	To assist in pinpointing when and by whom ID was stolen or compromised, determine whether in the last 6 months if:
_____	Victim carried social security daily.
_____	Kept PINs and passwords in wallet or purse.
_____	Had mail stolen. What? When? Get any reports.
_____	While away, mail kept at Post Office/collected by someone else.
_____	Traveled on business or pleasure outside of home vicinity. When? Where?
_____	Mail diverted by forwarding request to Post Office or in a way unknown to the victim.
_____	Expected new credit card which did not arrive. Get particulars. Issuer contacted by victim? Report made?
_____	Garbage was stolen or gone through.
_____	Left stamped payment bills in unlocked mailbox.
_____	Service providers (maids, delivery, electricians, etc.) in home.
_____	Placed documents with personal information in garbage without shredding—e.g., envelopes with victim's name on them, bank statements, payroll stubs.
_____	Placed pre-approved credit cards and "convenience" checks in garbage without shredding.
_____	Threw ATM and credit card receipts away without shredding.
_____	Shared PIN and password information with someone else.
_____	Home/office/car burglarized? When? Reported? If not, why?
_____	Checkbook, wallet, purse stolen.
_____	Provided personal information to service providers—e.g., blood collection agency, financial adviser, took out auto/health/life insurance. Identify, get details.
_____	Copy of credit report issued to someone claiming a legitimate business interest or using victim's name.

continued

▲ **FIGURE 14-6   Identity theft/follow-on crimes checklist**

Completed	Task	Completed	Task
_____	Victim authorized a business to obtain credit report information. Which? When?	_____	What information does the victim have about the suspects?
_____	Some personal information was available on the Net—e.g., genealogy or school reunion site.	_____	Run records checks on suspects identified by victim.
_____	Gave personal information to telephone solicitor, telemarketer, "government worker" working door-to-door, charitable organization, entered contest, or to claim prize supposedly won.	_____	Have the victim list all banks which have legitimate accounts, identify accounts which have fraudulent activities.
_____	Made legitimate purchase, but clerk was out of sight with card during transaction.	_____	Have the victim list all legitimate credit card companies and banks which have issued credit cards, identify those with fraudulent activities.
_____	A new credit card account was just opened by the victim.	_____	Have victim specify all legitimate utility company accounts, identify those with fraudulent activities.
_____	Victim's home/property was refinanced.		
_____	Victim provided information to obtain lease.	_____	Have victim identify all legitimate loans, leases, and mortgages, list those with fraudulent activities.
_____	Victim opened new utility account(s).		
_____	Victim applied for occupational or other license or permit.	_____	Have victim list all merchants with whom he/she. has a store credit account—e.g., pharmacies and department stores. List all fraudulent activities.
_____	Victim took out new loan or finished paying one.		
_____	Victim applied for government benefits.	_____	Have victim list all financial institutions where fraudulent accounts were opened.
_____	Victim was featured in local paper, industry publications, on Internet, school site.	_____	Victim should list all fraudulent documents obtained in his/her name.
_____	Online purchases were made using victim's credit card.	_____	Provide assistance to the victim by suggesting he/she contact the three major credit reporting companies, Equifax, TransUnion, and Experian, as well as financial institutions, the Department of Motor Vehicles, Social Security, and other entities. Victim should do this immediately by phone and follow up within 48 hours with letters, asking for return receipts.
_____	Released information to family member/friend.		
_____	Over the past 6 months, what purchases did the victim make from which sites, when, and for what merchandise?		
_____	Have the victim list all persons, businesses, nonprofits, or others to which he/she provided Social Security number.		
_____	Does the victim have his/her Social Security number imprinted on checks?	_____	Provide any agency ID theft Victim Assistant, packages available. This information should include web addresses, such as the one at the Federal Trade Commission, which provides detailed guidance and sample forms and letters to use. Advise victim to log and carefully file all correspondence and return receipts from the Post Office.
_____	Get a list of all places such checks were tendered.		
_____	Has victim or others written his/her Social Security and driver's license numbers on checks tendered? List all such instances.		
_____	Are identity crimes affecting the victim's business?		
_____	Whom does the victim identify as possible suspects? For what reasons?		

(Source: This information was adapted from content on an undated "Identity Theft" compact disk prepared by the Secret Service, United States Postal Inspection Service, and the International Association of Chiefs of Police.)

▲ **FIGURE 14-6** **Identity theft/follow-on crimes checklist** *continued*

paying by credit card to have a company find them new jobs, work-at-home employment (such as stuffing envelopes), scholarships, and low-cost car or other loans. These offers may appear in newspaper ads, be delivered by the postal service, or appear in the victim's e-mail inbox. Once victims have been taken in by a credit card or other type of fraud, criminals compile lists with their names to sell to other defrauders, including those who contact the victims with an offer to recover their lost assets.

CHECK FRAUD

Check fraud (Figure 14-8) is the forgery, alteration, counterfeiting, or knowing issuance of a check on an account that is closed or has insufficient funds to cover the amount for which the check is written.[39] People may innocently "bounce" a check because of nonsufficient funds owing to a math error in their checkbook or mistiming a deposit. Investigation and prosecution rarely happen because the check is made good, and the necessary fees are paid.

Others write checks they know are no good and cannot cover; people leaving one state for another may write a bad check because they think there is no consequence; and others write checks on accounts they or others have closed. **Check kiters** open accounts at several banks, knowingly, issuing a check that overdraws their account at Bank 1 and then depositing a check in that account from their Bank 2 account to cover the first worthless check. This process is repeated with ever-increasing amounts until the scheme falls apart because it cannot be continued indefinitely. An employee with the standing

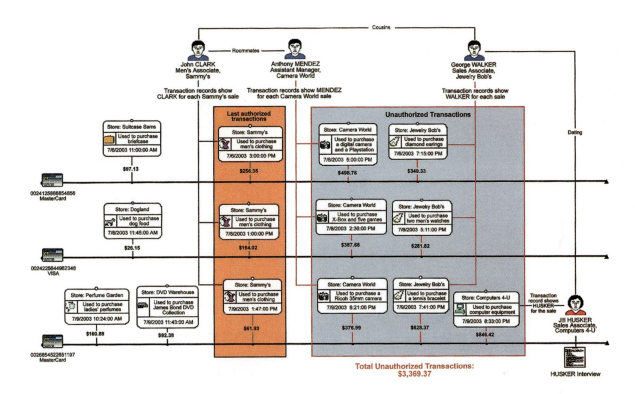

▲ **FIGURE 14-7** **Visual Link Analysis applied to credit card fraud** (© i2 Incorporated, 1991–2004. All rights reserved.)

authority to issue checks may sign unauthorized checks or forge the manager's or owner's signature. Among the signs that an employee in a position of trust such as bookkeeper or business manager may be or is committing check based crimes are these:

1. checks made payable to the business or to cash by customers are deposited in an account the employee controls;
2. replacement checks to the employee are issued when there is no need to do so, e.g., the original check was not lost;
3. payroll advances to the employee are not subtracted from the next paycheck;
4. there is no documentation explaining why checks are made payable to "Cash" or what happened to them;
5. the employee is reimbursed for unexplained expenses;
6. the employee keeps promising to show the business owner the bank statements, but it never seems to happen; and

7. vendors and suppliers are complaining about slow and late payments.

Altogether, check fraud produces losses of some $24 billion annually,[40] and in addition to the practices previously described, others involve more sophisticated techniques. In one, an individual learns that he/she has gotten a job applied for online, which offers "signing bonuses" of $2,500 or more to "new hires." The "new employer" advises the "employee" that by mistake a larger amount in the $19,000 to $50,000 range has been sent to the employee, who is instructed to keep the signing bonus but wire the remaining funds to the employer, often at a European location. Of course, the job doesn't really exist, and the check sent by "mistake" is fraudulent. Because the "new employee" deposited the check originally, it is his/her responsibility to make it good. A wrinkle on this technique is when someone shows up to buy a car or other large-ticket item with a counterfeit cashier's check from a bank or a credit union that was "made out for too much," and the unsuspecting seller not only gives the

◀**FIGURE 14-8** **NSF stamped check**
For one reason or another, 40% of all Americans are without a credit card and are totally dependent on paying bills with a written check. With an estimated 30 billion checks written annually, it is remarkable that only an estimated 1.2 million checks were not honored owing to "not sufficient funds" (NSF). NSF checks that are not made good are often sold to collection agencies for 80% or more of their face value. NSF checks are "bad checks," and the issuer may be subject to criminal charges, which may be a misdemeanor or a felony, depending on the amount for which the check was written. The amount separating these charges varies by from one state to another. (© Tony Freeman/PhotoEdit)

buyer a check for the difference but also allows the suspect to drive off with the car, which may be quickly sold, creating an additional profit for the suspect. Very good counterfeit checks can be produced by using around $10,000 to purchase a computer system and software. It is estimated that counterfeit checks account for about $1 billion in annual losses.

Checks can be altered by washing them in commonly available chemicals and then dried with little damage to the checks. This process removes ink from the check. The checks can then be scanned into a computer, many copies can quickly be printed, and the checks cashed for the amounts desired by the "payees," who are in on the scheme and may be using identification obtained through identity theft.

COUNTERFEITING

Manufacturing counterfeit United States currency (Figure 14-9) or altering genuine currency to increase its value violates Title 18, Section 471 of the United States Code and is punishable by a fine of $5,000 or 15 years imprisonment, or both; the Secret Service is the primary federal agency responsible for enforcing Section 471 crimes. Some counterfeiting activity is tied to small-time methamphetamine dealers who use counterfeit currency to buy materials for their illicit labs and other purchases; they may produce the bills or purchase them. At the other end of the spectrum are the international drug cartels. In Western Colombia, Secret Service agents and Colombian police found a counterfeit plant beneath the Andes Mountains that could produce $3 million weekly in "funny money." Colombian-manufactured counterfeit dollars represent 33% of all "bad currency" passed in

▲**FIGURE 14-9** **Counterfeiting**
Colombian police officers counting counterfeit U.S. currency seized during a raid. International drug lords also use their smuggling routes to move counterfeit currencies. Often such seizures involve the assistance of American federal enforcement agencies. (© Eduardo Munoz/Reuters/Corbis)

the United States, and the Colombian cartels are able to use the same smuggling routes and couriers for phoney bills as they do for drugs.[41] The cash-strapped North Korean government has also been tied to substantial counterfeiting of financial instruments that they attempt to pass in another country; one example of this was the unsuccessful attempt by diplomatic passport-carrying members of a North Korean trading company to pass $250,000 in phoney securities in Macao.[42]

Although we most often associate counterfeiting with currency, there is a vast range of other types of counterfeiting, including stamps, checks, bonds, and securities, as well as ski lift, sporting event, rodeo, and concert tickets. None of these are just-emerging crimes; the 1966 Beatles concert in Cleveland was plagued with this problem.

Gangs counterfeiting Universal Product Codes (UPC) have been operating a number of years. UPC codes help with inventory control and proper pricing at the point of sale where cashiers scan in the price. In particular Wal-Mart, Lowe's, and Home Depot have been hard-hit, with Wal-Mart's losses reaching $1.5 million.[43] The modus operandi was to counterfeit UPCs in large numbers at print shops or by using personal computers, enter the stores and affix these UPCs over real ones, thereby lowering the price of the item that would be scanned in at the point of sale:

A kitchen faucet worth $169 would suddenly wear a UPC code indicating the price to be $39 or a lighting fixture's price would shift from $249 to $55.[44] Later the same day at a different location for the same retailer, another person would show up—with the phoney UPC removed—and get a refund for the actual amount; doing this several times per day easily netted $1,000 to $1,500 daily. False identifications were presented at the refund counter, including English or Irish passports.[45]

FRAUDS, SCAMS, AND CONS

Charity and Disaster Frauds

There are some 70,000 charities. Unfortunately, a very small number are frauds and create two types of problems: (1) people are scammed out of their money and do not get a tax deduction, and (2) public confidence in charities is undermined, making it harder for legitimate charities to raise funds for really important causes. Sham charities are skillful at their pitches, using words that suggest good causes; included are terms such as veterans, hunger, children, and orphans. They also often use names that are similar to those of legitimate charities and religious organizations. These pitches are made in person at homes, with buckets at intersections, through the mail, and Internet solicitations. In the aftermath of the 9-11

attacks in 2001, the earthquakes in eastern Turkey in 2004, and the Tsunami of 2004 (Figure 14-10), sham charities used the tragic events to line their pockets.

Insurance Fraud

Insurance frauds can be **hard fraud** or **soft fraud**.[46] Hard fraud is when someone deliberately fakes an injury, accident, theft, arson, or other loss to illegally collect from insurance companies.

Virgil made a car collision insurance claim, stating that he had been trying to avoid a deer and crashed into a wall. The insurer deemed the car a total loss, and the claim was paid. Later, the insurance company learned that Virgil's son Brian was driving the car even though he was not covered by the policy. Both were arrested on one felony count of insurance fraud.[47]

In contrast, soft fraud, also called opportunity fraud, involves normally honest people who tell "little white lies" and collect reimbursements to which they are not entitled, as in the case when the value of the items reported stolen in burglary is overstated. Too, insurance companies have been known to scam insurers by charging them more than is warranted or declaring bankruptcy and going out of business when faced with a flood of claims they cannot pay following a natural disaster. Other types of insurance frauds are discussed next.

Health-Care Fraud

Annual health-care costs are estimated to be $2.2 trillion; the magnitude of spending is a magnet for fraud.[48] Estimates of the dollar loss attributable to fraud range from 3% to 14% of annual expenditures.[49] The most commonly affected agencies in health-care fraud are two federal programs: (1) Medicare, which provides comprehensive care for the disabled and people 65 or older, and (2) Medicaid, a provider of services for low-income people.[50]

Perhaps the most common health-care fraud scheme is billing for services never provided. This is done by making claims for services, equipment, and tests not actually rendered, by filing claims for tests on patients who had, but did not show up, for appointments or by using patient information to file entirely fictitious claims.[51] Other fraud methods used by medical providers:

1. Filing duplicate claims.
2. "Upcoding" or using billing codes for more expensive tests or longer office visits than actually occurred.
3. "Unbundling charges," which is the practice of charging separately for each component of service.

U.S. Department of Justice
Federal Bureau of Investigation

◄ **FIGURE 14-10** Tsunami disaster relief fraud alert from the FBI

For Immediate Release   **Washington D.C.**
January 5, 2005   **FBI National Press Office**

TSUNAMI DISASTER RELIEF FRAUD ALERT

Washington, D.C. - The FBI today is alerting the public to a variety of scams currently being facilitated online involving the solicitation of additional relief funds for the victims of the recent Tsunami disaster. The FBI, through the Internet Crime Complaint Center (IC3), has received reports of websites being established purportedly to assist with collection and relief efforts. Complaints submitted to the IC3 have identified several schemes that involve both unsolicited in-coming emails (SPAM), as well as reports of responses to posted email addresses, to assist for a fee, in locating loved ones who may have been a victim of the disaster. A fraudulent relief donation website has also been detected containing an imbedded Trojan exploit which can infect the user's computer with a virus if accessed.

The FBI, in conjunction with domestic with international law enforcement and industry partners, take seriously these egregious actions and are resolved to aggressively pursuing those who would attempt to victimize philanthropic individuals.

The IC3 is cautioning citizens against participating in this type of on-line correspondence. Consistent with previous guidance on incidents of Phishing/Spoofing and Identity Theft, when considering on-line options for providing funding to this relief effort consumers should consider the following:

- Do not respond to any unsolicited (SPAM) incoming emails.
- Be skeptical of individuals claiming to be surviving victims or foreign government officials asking for help in placing large sums of money in overseas bank accounts.
- To ensure that contributions to U.S. based non-profit organizations are used for intended purposes, go directly to recognized charities and aid organizations websites, as opposed to following a link to another site.
- Attempt to verify the legitimacy of non-profit organizations by utilizing various Internet based resources which may assist in confirming the existence of the organization as well as its non-profit status.
- Be leery of emails that claim to show pictures of the disaster areas in attached files, as the files may contain viruses. Only open attachments from know senders.

Several variations of this scam are currently in circulation. Anyone who has received an email referencing the above information or anyone who may have been a victim of this or a similar incident should notify the IC3 via the website. www.ic3.gov.

| [Press Releases](#) | [FBI Home Page](#) |

This produces a greater claim than if the service was properly billed as one single charge.

4. Misrepresenting the diagnosis in order to get paid for services not covered by the health plan or to charge for costly tests not actually provided.

5. Performing unnecessary tests;[52] a Massachusetts orthopedic surgeon routinely gave patients potentially harmful X rays and steroid injections they didn't need so he could falsely bill Medicaid. In less than three years, one patient was X rayed 74 times and given steroid injections on 112 occasions.[53]

6. Billing using the names of people who are deceased.

7. Charging for home health aide visits which were not made.

Others involved in health-care fraud are employers and employees. Employers may enroll employees who are actually not eligible in plans or change the dates of employment or termination to expand the dates of coverage. Members enrolled in health plans may alter the documents they submit in order to get a greater reimbursement than they are entitled to or to let someone else use their plan identification to obtain services.[54] An often overlooked effect for many types of medical fraud is that a person may end up with a false medical history, which may affect their ability to get life insurance or alter how they are subsequently treated medically.

The Food and Drug Administration (FDA) identifies another type of health-care fraud: "It is the deceptive promotion, advertising, distribution, or sale of articles represented as being effective to diagnose, prevent, cure, treat, or mitigate an illness or condition, or provide a beneficial effect on health, but has not been scientifically proven safe and effective for such purposes."[55] Products identified as such by the FDA may also cause serious health problems. Some of these products are counterfeit drugs with no therapeutic value, while others claim they can produce rapid weight loss, or cure skin cancer, Alzheimer's disease, rheumatism, hardening of the arteries, diabetes, improve virility, and eliminate gangrene and prostate problems.

Workers Compensation Fraud

The most common worker compensation fraudulent claim is when people falsely claim that they were injured on the job. They may have actually been injured while away from the job, faked the injury while working, or have an actual injury about which they report exaggerated symptoms. In New York, 18 people, including several teachers and a chiropractor, were arrested for defrauding the workers compensation system out of $550,000 because they were seen working other jobs while receiving benefits.[56] In addition to state workers compensation agencies being defrauded, cases may also involve insurance companies providing disability coverage.

Arson Fraud

Chapter 18, "Arson and Explosives," addresses arson fraud. Here, a case is offered because it illustrates the point that such frauds can go tragically wrong.

> **Helen hired two local teenagers** to "torch" her Tampa restaurant, Gram's County Kitchen, so she could collect insurance money. However, fumes from the gasoline the teenagers poured in the restaurant accidentally ignited, causing an explosion. One died and the other was permanently scarred.[57]

Automobile Fraud

One source of automobile fraud is staged accidents, which include the **swoop and squat,** the **drive down,** and the **paper accident.** In the swoop and squat, a car quickly cuts in front of a legitimate motorist, hits the brakes, and creates a rear-end collision for which repair and fake medical claims can be made. The drive down involves waving to another driver to go ahead and make a turn in the intersection or elsewhere and then driving into the car, making it appear that the struck vehicle is at fault. Paper accidents are exactly that: no accident has taken place. Collusion is required by a body shop operator, who may even provide a wrecked car for the adjuster to inspect. By only filing for the cost of repairs, which are not done, the amount paid by the insurance is not out of line and therefore not scrutinized closely. Naturally, the insured and the body shop owner split the money for the repairs. Owners who cannot make their car payments, which often involve luxury cars, arrange to have them stolen, and the insurance pays for the car. Then the car is sent to a chop shop. The owner protects his/her credit record and receives some money from the chop shop profit. To make false claims of injuries in accidents believable, the collusion of a doctor is necessary. In one very aggressive case, a chiropractor had "runners" out scouting for accidents and recruiting people to his practice, where false treatment bills were submitted to insurers and false medical records were created to submit to insurance companies.

Vendor Fraud

Virtually every unit of government and businesses are dependent on outside vendors who supply such things as office supplies, equipment, vehicles, merchandise for retail, and consulting services. Vendor fraud costs businesses more than $400 billion in losses annually. Among the fraudulent practices used by vendors are these:

1. Collusion among bidders to set bids at a higher than warranted price per unit and bidders concealing they are insolvent or have a record of defaulting on their bids.
2. Providing employees in the procurement office with cash and other types of bribes, such as trips in exchange for being the winning bidder.
3. Substituting lower-costing or counterfeit goods to fulfill the terms of a bid.
4. Consultants or contractors overstating the number of days worked or the amount of materials required to do the job.
5. Submitting bogus invoices for office supplies or other goods in the hope they will be paid.
6. Bogus Yellow Page advertising. In the minds of most people the "Yellow Pages" are legitimate ads in the local telephone directory; however, because the phrase was never copyrighted or registered others can use it. Fraudsters may offer "yellow page" advertising and either produce just a few one-page copies for the subscribers or simply abscond with the money.

In large corporations, these crimes may be investigated internally and the information turned over to the police, or the police may be invited in at an earlier stage. In units of government, the agency having jurisdiction will investigate instances of criminal fraud by bidders.

Home Improvement and Repair Frauds

Common home improvement and repair scams include unneeded roofing, gutter, plumbing, chimney, or other repairs or replacements; paving driveways with a thin surface that quickly cracks; using materials and methods that do not meet local building codes; substituting cheap paint for higher-quality paint; not replacing rotted or missing decking when roofing; charging for more expensive shingles or for more bundles of shingles than were actually used, or not replacing valley gutters and shingles in places that are hard for the owner to see; using whitewash instead of paint; and "free" home, furnace, or other inspections that turn up "serious problems." Often, the "inspector" causes the damage that needs to then be repaired. These scams are usually worked going door-to-door using high-pressure sales and scare tactics, particularly with older people. Mention may be made that they just finished a job "nearby" and have leftover materials so "I can make you a good deal." Representations will be made that "we are having a sale and I can knock 20% off of the bottom line," although the actual price is never specified. The "vendor" usually refuses to provide a written estimate or contract and evades giving information about the location of his business. Natural disasters, including tornados, hurricanes, floods, and mud slides often bring out packs of repair scammers who prey on people desperate to get their lives back in order.

These scam artists often ask for a down payment or the whole amount and are never seen again; do the work in a substandard manner or not at all; or urge the victim to make temporary repairs that are poorly done when more substantial work is needed, only worsening a problem.

The Federal Trade Commission recommends dealing only with licensed and insured contractors, checking references and consumer affairs agencies for complaints about the vendor, getting recommendations from family, friends, and coworkers who have used contractors, not doing business with door-to-door solicitors, obtaining several bids from reputable contractors, and not using homes as financing collateral because owners may end up losing them.

Internet Gambling

There are at least 1,800 Internet gambling sites (Figure 14-11); that offer the convenience of playing from your home and the potential of winning money.[58] The extent to which some of these sites are honest appears to be an open question, because so many are set up off-shore, beyond the reach of gaming regulatory agencies and American law enforcement scrutiny. Some states have enacted laws prohibiting online gambling, but enforcement is difficult. The games offered include ones commonly found in casinos, such as keno, slots, blackjack, poker, baccarat, roulette, and sports betting. Fraudulent gaming sites offer unattainable prizes, run rigged games, lure gamers to play foreign lotteries, which is illegal for citizens in this country, and misuse players' personal information.[59]

◄ **FIGURE 14-11**
Internet gambling
There are approximately 1,800 online casinos worldwide, most based in the Carribean, with revenues of $5 billion annually. Fifty percent of that amount is wagered by U.S. bettors. The American Psychological Association (APA) maintains that people who gamble online may tend to have more serious gambling addictions than do those who use other forms of gambling.

(© Park Street/PhotoEdit)

Pigeon Drop and Bank Examiners Cons

Confidence games are practiced by individuals who understand human nature, gain the mark's trust by being good listeners, and through smooth talking, set the hook, and run the scam. As many as 70% of con games may be run against the elderly, who are often very trusting. Among the most enduring con games are the pigeon drop and the bank examiner scheme.

The **pigeon drop** is run in many variations; commonly, two cons operate it. The first one strikes up a conversation with the mark on a street filled with shops or at a mall. The job of the first con is to make a "quick connection" with the mark and gain his/her confidence; they talk about the mark's family or whatever is comfortable. The second con approaches with a story of having just found an envelope filled with a lot of money and asks them if it belongs to them. When the envelope is opened, there will be some paperwork suggesting that it came from drug sales or other illegal activity. After asking the first con and the mark what should be done with the money, the mark is lead to the conclusion that all three should share it. Because there is no identification in the envelope, the money cannot be returned, and there is no real harm because the person who lost the money is dishonest. The two cons, quickly joined by the mark, talk about all the things they could do with the money. One of the cons calls his/her employer, who is an "attorney." The attorney advises that the money be put in "his firm's" trust account while a due diligence search is made to find the owner of the lost money. Additionally, the mark and the two cons are to provide a sum of money, as a show of good faith until the found money can be distributed, which will also be placed in the mythical trust account. After the mark withdraws his good faith money, the lawyer may take the group to lunch and take control of all of the money. The victim—the pigeon—has thus lost all the money he withdrew from the bank.

The **bank examiner con** often begins with a call to the mark's home in which the caller identities himself as a bank examiner who relates there is some apparent wrongdoing at the bank, and the assistance of the mark is solicited in finding out who it is. The mark is asked to withdraw some money from his/her account and then to meet the examiner at a nearby location. The bank examiner may be accompanied by "Sgt. Jones," who flashes a badge and praises the mark for his help. The bank examiner gives the mark a counterfeit cashier's check to replace the funds withdrawn but asks him or her not to deposit it for the week it takes to complete the investigation. By then, the scam has been run several times in that community, and the con men are long gone before the mark finds out that the check is bogus.[60]

Nigerian 419 and Black Money/Wash Wash Schemes

The **Nigerian advanced fee scam** begins with a potential victim getting an unsolicited fax, e-mail, or letter that purports to be from a current or former Nigerian governmental official or a relative of such. The recipient is told that a "confidential source has recommended the contact." The con takes its name from Chapter 42, Section 419, of the Laws of the Federation of Nigeria and Lagos, which deals with advanced fee frauds. Millions of U.S. dollars are available through an over-invoiced deal with the Nigerian national Petroleum Company, the recovery of unclaimed insurance money, money from a dead or defeated former government official, or other such spin. The letter writer wants the victim's help in investing in the United States and will pay handsomely for it, up to 30% of the "total." Another 10%–15% of the money will be set aside to pay for miscellaneous expenses in getting the money transferred. The victim provides personal information, including bank account numbers to facilitate the movement of funds from Nigeria to this country. The personal information is not immediately abused; later it may be sold or employed in another type of fraud. The victim is pressured into sending money to cover unanticipated costs, which continues as long as the victim sends money. The money requests to the victim are accompanied by official-looking government and bank documents with embossed seals and verification stamps, all of which are counterfeit or phoney.

"Wash wash" (Figure 14-12) is what Nigerian cons call the black money scheme, also an advanced fee scam. It may be run in conjunction with a 419 or as a stand-alone con. The con reports that the dollars he is trying to get into this country have been treated with a chemical that turned them black, disguising their true value; in order to be able to wash the $100 bills clean so they can be used, special, expensive chemicals must be bought, and the victim must pay for them. A meeting is set up outside the United States, to avoid the higher risk of arrest. The victim flies there to actually see the money that will be "cleaned and divided." The meeting is conducted in a hotel room or other location. The con has a specially treated bill that is black, and he uses the "small amount of special cleaning chemicals he has left" to demonstrate the process, and the bill is partially cleaned. This process is actually very cheap and on the order of a sleight-of-hand trick. The victim advances several thousand dollars to buy the chemicals; but then, the vial is "accidentally left in a cab or broken." So, the victim advances more money. This is repeated as many times as the victim pays up and then the fraudsters disappear, allegedly to get the chemicals themselves.[61]

MONEY LAUNDERING

Criminals want to launder money to avoid prosecution, increase their profits, avoid seizure of their accumulated wealth, evade paying taxes whenever possible, and appear legitimate.[62] In laundering cases prosecuted, 60% of the money came from embezzlement or fraud, 17% involved drug trafficking, and 7% involved racketeering or customs charges.[63] **Money laundering** is the illegal practice of filtering "dirty" money or ill-gotten gains through a series of transactions until the money is "clean," appearing to be proceeds from legal activities. The United States Criminal Code defines money laundering as the concealment of the source and/or the destination of money, which has usually been gained through illegal activities.[64] Worldwide money laundering activity is estimated to be $1 trillion each year.[65] Money launderers have access to all the speed and ease of modern electronic finance to move funds globally. Thus, substantial cooperation and information sharing among law enforcement agencies are essential to identify the sources of illegal proceeds, trace the funds to specific criminal activities, and confiscate criminals' financial assets.[66]

At the risk of oversimplifying a complex subject, money laundering involves three distinct steps: (1) **placement,** (2) **layering,** and (3) **integration** (Figure 14-13).[67]

Placement

Placement is the process of placing unlawful proceeds into legitimate financial institutions or systems. Transactions are kept to $10,000 or less to avoid triggering the requirements of the federal Bank Secrecy Act (BSA, 1970). The BSA obligates institutions to report single transactions exceeding $10,000 to the U.S. Department of Treasury's Financial Crimes Enforcement Network (FinCen). FinCen is one of the Treasury's primary agencies to establish, oversee, and implement policies to prevent and detect money laundering. It also provides intelligence and analytical support to law enforcement. With FinCen's leadership, a meeting of financial intelligence units (FIUs) was held in 1995 in Brussels. An outgrowth of this meeting was the formation of the Egmont Group, which is an international network of FIUs dedicated to information sharing and coordination.

The BSA also requires a report when one entity makes multiple deposits exceeding $10,000 in a single day. In 1996, under regulatory authority granted by the Annunzio-Wylie Money Laundering Act (1992), the U.S. Treasury adopted a rule requiring banks and other depository institutions to report to FinCen any *suspicious* activities involving $5,000 or more.

Placement is often done by **smurfing,** or making multiple deposits of cash or buying multiple bank drafts, which are checks issued by one bank against funds deposited in that bank that authorize a second bank to make payment to the entity named in the draft. One or more individuals conduct these transactions, often at multiple financial institutions. Other methods include buying money orders or travelers' checks at one institution, depositing them at another and using cash to buy chips at a casino, participating in gambling activities, and then cashing in the chips for a casino check. As a general matter, casinos withhold federal income tax at a 25% rate on winnings above $5,000. Placement has also been facilitated by bribing bank officials to ignore FinCen reporting requirements (which is increasingly difficult) by purchasing entire banks and operating them as part of a criminal enterprise and using "safe haven" **off-shore accounts** in some 60 nations that advertise "untraceable" financial

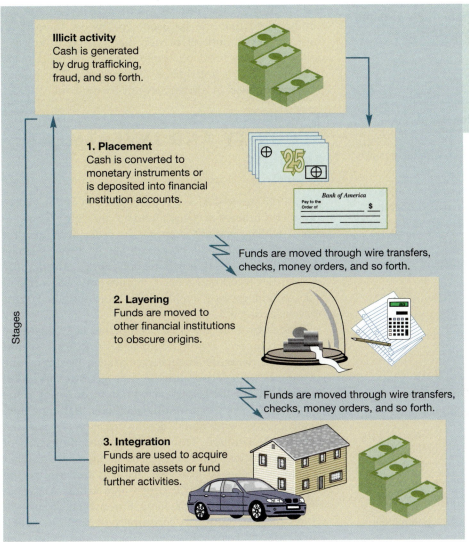

► **FIGURE 14-13**
**Money laundering: Placement,
layering, and integration**
(Source: United States General Accounting
Office, Money Laundering: Extent of Money
Laundered Through Credit Cards Is Unknown
[Washington, D.C.: 2002], p. 7)

services. These nations include the Cook Islands, Egypt, Guatemala, and Ukraine. In these jurisdictions, launderers may buy a "shelf company" that has been registered for years and open accounts into which illegal funds are deposited. Laws in the Seychelles Islands provide immunity to depositors from all outside criminal charges, even if it is known the money came from criminal acts. The only government requirement is that investors not engage in illegal activities in the Seychelles Island chain.[68]

Another method of placement is the Colombian **black market peso exchange** (BMPE).[69] Colombian drug dealers export drugs to North America and Western Europe. Sales of drugs produce vast amounts of money in the currency of the countries in which the drugs are sold. The drug cartel contacts a peso broker, who will give it pesos for the currency held in foreign countries for roughly 80 cents on the "dollar." The cartel thus has its money, and the BMPE must now pick up the money and get it placed into the banking systems of the respective countries. In the final phase, the broker advertises to Colombian importers that they have foreign funds available to buy goods from other countries. On behalf of importers, the BMPE purchases goods from foreign manufacturers whose goods are shipped to the Carribean or a South American country. These goods are then smuggled into Colombia to avoid expensive tariffs. Once the goods are sold, the broker is paid in pesos, which are then deposited into a legitimate banking system.

Money from illegal sources also still gets laundered in the traditional way. Front businesses—such as bars, restaurants, night clubs, and vending machine companies—and illicit source funds are commingled with legitimate revenue, with taxes being paid on all of it. These front businesses may be owned by criminals or be ones that they control. Indications of accounts being used for money laundering are summarized in Table 14-2.

Layering

Layering involves converting the funds placed into other assets or moving them to other financial institutions, the purpose of which is to further distance the funds from

TABLE 14-2	Indicators Associated with Accounts Used for Money Laundering

1. Smurfing.

2. Unusual underlying business plan.

3. Account holder's wealth atypical for his/her profile.

4. Unusually high rates of return for low-risk business activity.

5. Reactivation of dormant account, often with increasingly large deposits.

6. Questionable, unrealistic, or conflicting explanation of business plan or account activity; account holder has lack of knowledge about the field his/her business is in.

7. Transactions are unnecessarily complex.

8. Disbursement of funds by several checks when one would do.

9. Account holder has criminal record or suspicious associates.

10. Account holder has defensive stance when asked about account activity.

11. True beneficiary of account is deliberately concealed.

12. Last-minute changes in fund transfer instructions.

13. Account holder is discovered to use false/stolen identification.

14. Account revenue is atypical for size and nature of business.

15. Funds transferred to personal or relative's accounts.

16. Account behavior changes without explanation.

17. "Tidy" or rounded sums used to pay for commodities.

18. Business lacks normal documentation.

(Source: No author, *FIUs* [Financial Intelligence Units] in *Action: 100 Sanitized Cases*, London: Egmont Group, 2000, drawn from a 170-page document.)

their illegal source; these assets include bonds, stocks, works of art and jewelry. The money may also be wired to another institution to pay into a controlled account for non-existent goods or simply move through multiple other accounts anyplace in the world.[70]

Integration

In integration, the illegal funds that have been placed and layered are now clean and are virtually indistinguishable from wholly legal money. They are then used to buy luxury items or to invest in legitimate business ventures, real estate, or other sectors.[71] Both in the layering and integration phases some credit card accounts are used, although the actual extent is not known. In this country, the practice appears limited, but it is practiced through off-shore banks.[72] These banks offer anonymous ATM and credit cards that bear no user name, just an account number, and that can be used worldwide; there is no limit on the amount of money that can be withdrawn daily. The cards must be "preloaded" or deposits made to cover 200% of anticipated expenditures. The money not spent is held in a trust account by the bank.

SECURITY AND INVESTMENT FRAUDS

In the 1987 movie *Wall Street,* the character Gordon Gekko soothingly intones at a stockholders' meeting, "Greed is good," which seemed to become the order of the day for some individuals and corporations. In 1990, Michael Milken (Figure 14-14), the "junk bond king," plead guilty to securities fraud and related charges and paid a fine of $600 million, thereby avoiding the more serious charges of racketeering and insider trading.

Formed by a merger of two companies in 1985, energy trading company Enron (Figure 14-15) quickly soared due to the deregulated energy markets, becoming the seventh largest corporation in this country. By 2001, Enron had filed for bankruptcy, brought down by some five years of using accounting methods that concealed massive losses, leading to a downward estimate of its net value by $1.1 billion. The scandal caused thousands of employees to lose their retirement savings and resulted in massive losses to investors. Its activities lead to the conviction of some Merrill Lynch and Arthur Anderson officials, prison terms for some Enron officials, one of whom pleaded guilty to conspiracy to commit money laundering and conspiracy to commit wire fraud. The Board of Directors paid a $168 million fine to settle charges that they failed to adequately protect investors.

Securities fraud is any manipulation or deception that affects the purchase or sale of a security and usually includes the misrepresentation or omission of significant information. In general, a security is an investment instrument from which an investor expects to derive financial benefit through the efforts of others.[73] Illustrations include stocks, bonds, and other financial instruments. The two primary laws governing the securities industry and protecting investors are the Securities Act of 1933 and the Securities Exchange Act of 1934, both of which have been amended through the years.[74] In addition to these federal laws, each state has statutes and regulations pertaining to securities transactions, and the various stock and commodity exchanges also have regulatory requirements.[75]

Ponzi/Pyramid Schemes

Carlos "Charles" Ponzi formed the Security Exchange Company in Boston in 1919 and promised to double people's investments in the company within 90 days

◀ **FIGURE 14-14   Security fraud**
Michael Milken, the "junk bond king,
pleaded guilty to security fraud in
1990 but remained a wealthy man
even after paying a fine of $600
million. He is now a cancer survivor
who has funded research on
treatments for that disease.
(© Terry Ashe/Time Life Pictures/Getty
Images)

▲ **FIGURE 14-15   Corporate accounting scandal**
By early 2002, the Enron logo came to symbolize the kind of
corporate greed and scandal that would eventually surface at
major companies, including WorldCom, Adelphia, Tyco, and
Enron, and sparked wide ranging investigations by Congress,
the Justice Department, New York's State Attorney General,
and the Securities and Exchange Commission—a regulatory
agency that saw its own share of trouble.
(© James Nielsen/Getty Images)

(Figure 14-16). For early investors, this actually happened because he used the deposits of subsequent investors to pay for the money doubling of previous investors. Eventually, the scheme collapsed, because recruitment of new investors could not be sustained. Ponzi was arrested, convicted, and imprisoned for various crimes. This type of investment fraud is still practiced today and is referred to as a **Ponzi, pyramid,** or endless chain **scheme.** As with most frauds, there are numerous variations. For example, these schemes may be run as "gifting clubs" or "women empowering women" programs. Eight new participants, called *givers*, are recruited, and each "gifts" the "receiver," who is the person at the head of the pyramid, with $2,000. When the receiver has $16,000 in hand, the pyramid splits, and the eight new participants move upward in the pyramid, each hoping eventually to become the receiver; to do so requires each of them to recruit new entry-level givers. Figure 14-17 summarizes a pyramid scheme run in Alaska with entry-level participants gifting the receiver with $5,000. New participants in pyramid schemes are often required to sign confidentiality agreements requiring them not to discuss the specifics or the names of participants and attesting that they were not promised anything for participating in the program (although each is led to believe that they all will become receivers). As the following sections indicate, Ponzis can be run in many different ways.

Pump and Dump Schemes

The U.S. Securities and Exchange Commission describes **pump and dump** schemes, which are also called "hype and dump manipulation," as involving the touting of a company's

▲ **FIGURE 14-16** **Ponzi Schemes**
Carlo Ponzi (1882–1949) immigrated to the United States, where he swindled thousands of investors out of millions of dollars. He was deported to his native Italy in 1934 and at one point worked for the dictator Mussolini. In 1949, he died penniless in Brazil. The scam he developed is timeless; in 2007, Norman Hsu was charged with defrauding investors out of at least $60 million in a massive ponzi scheme and with making illegal political contributions.
© Bettmann/Corbis

stock through false and misleading statements to the market place often by using the Internet.[76] After distributing favorable, but false, information to drive up the price of the stock (the pump), the price of the stock rallies by its being bought. The pump or hype may include urging potential investors to "buy now before it is too late," suggestions that the recommendation is based on "inside" knowledge, or that an "infallible" economic model identified the stock.[77]

The pump is often done with microcap stocks, issued by the smallest companies, over half of which have capitalizations of less than $1.25 million.[78] Thus, "microcap" means companies that have micro capitalizations. Microcap stocks are traded in the over-the-counter (OTC) market, which has no listing standards. This is in sharp contrast to the great amount of information on companies whose stocks are traded on the major exchanges. Therefore,

detailed, accurate information about the company is usually not available for victims who need such data in the face of a pump hustle.

Affinity Fraud

Affinity fraud is run on groups of people who share some affinity to one another, such as religious, ethnic, and professional groups and groups whose members have a high sense of friendship and trust in one another.[79] The scammers often recruit the most respected members of the group to help promote the program, which offers "guaranteed returns." The use of such members makes it easier to recruit victims, and when it is apparent that the group has been defrauded, it may choose not to report the victimization to spare the respected member and the group embarrassment. The investment fraud can be run as a Ponzi scheme or as one of many other iterations:

> **African-American groups** were approached by a company that was portrayed as being successful and having more than $36 million in assets, when in fact it had a negative net worth of more than $27 million. The company promised to insure all investments made, and make a 30%, tax-free return. Eventually, groups were conned out of $52 million before the company was stopped; the defendant later pleaded guilty to conspiracy to commit securities fraud.[80]

Pay Phones/ATM Machine Investments

Another type of investment fraud involves coin-operated, customer-owned telephones (COCOTs) or ATMs,[81] which investors "purchase" at $5,000 to $7,000 each. They are then "leased" back to a management company for five years; the company collects rental fees from telephone companies or banks, maintains the machine, and pays the investor monthly profits. The profits promised are a 12.5%–15% annual return.[82] These offers usually come from life insurance agents or other persons not licensed to sell securities, and the investment is not properly registered. This type of investment is inherently risky, because the companies making the offers often have weak balance sheets; the realistic downside is that companies cannot provide the services promised, the phones or ATMs are never purchased, or the investment offer is actually being run as a Ponzi scheme.[83] This type of fraud became so prevalent that 26 states acting in concert took legal action on behalf of 4,500 investors who lost an estimated $76 million.[84]

One-Year Callable Certificates of Deposit

The stock market has been volatile in recent years, and many older investors have fled it looking for more stable

State of Alaska
Department of Law

Gregg D. Renkes
Attorney General
P.O. Box 110300
Juneau, Alaska 99811

Press Contact: Mark Morones

907-269-6393
FAX: 907-269-6305

NEWS RELEASE

www.law.state.ak.us

FOR IMMEDIATE RELEASE: July 1, 2004

<u>**CONSUMER ALERT**</u>: **Women's "Gifting" Club is an Illegal Pyramid Scheme**

(Juneau) - Attorney General Gregg Renkes warns Alaskans against participating in a pyramid scheme that is operating in Fairbanks and perhaps other parts of the state. The scam targets women and claims that by making a "gift" of $5000, a participant will join a gifting circle and ultimately receive $40,000 in "gifts" after new women join.

"Everyone should be aware of pyramid scams," said Renkes. "When it sounds too good to be true, that's probably the case."

Like all pyramid schemes, this gifting network is illegal because it depends on continuous investments by new participants. The initial promoters recruit investors who in turn recruit more investors. The schemes are called "pyramids" because at each level, the number of investors increases. Eventually the pool of investors dries up and the pyramid collapses, depriving the majority of participants without their initial investment, let alone any profit.

The promoters for this gifting club claim that it is legal because the investment is a "gift" that does not need to be declared to the Internal Revenue Service.

"While recruiters claim that the scheme is a way of empowering women, the recruiters in fact are exploiting participants by convincing them to invest in a scheme that is bound to fail," said Renkes.

Pyramid schemes are illegal under Alaska's Unfair Trade Practices and Consumer Protection Act. Under the Act, violators are subject to civil penalties of $5000 per violation. Participants in such schemes may also be subject to criminal prosecution.

Attorney General Renkes advises people who have participated and obtained earnings in such schemes to refund money immediately.   Victims of these or any other unfair trade practices are urged to file a consumer complaint with the Attorney General's Office. Go to www.law.state.ak.us/consumer/ for a copy of the complaint form or call 907-269-5200.

For additional information, please contact Assistant Attorney General Cynthia Drinkwater at (907) 269-5200.

###

investments, such as certificates of deposit (CDs). CDs issued by local banks insured by the Federal Deposit Insurance Corporation (FDIC) have long been a trusted investment, because they are covered for losses up to $100,000. In purchasing a CD, the buyer agrees to invest a fixed amount for a fixed time. In return, the issuing entity agrees to pay the purchaser interest at regular intervals.[85] In addition to banks, CDs are now sold by national and regional brokerage firms and independent sales people or "deposit brokers." These brokers can sometimes negotiate a higher interest rate for their customers on the promise of bringing a certain sum of money to the bank.[86]

Unscrupulous sellers of CDs often trumpet the higher rates of interest to be paid but do not explain to investors about the terms used, thus misleading them. For example,

a **one-year callable CD** has a "one-year call provision," meaning that the entity issuing the instrument can choose to call (terminate it by redeeming) a CD before its maturity date. The option to call a CD is with the bank and not with the investor. However, investors typically may not understand this language or are mislead about its meaning, thinking that after a year of earning interest they can terminate their investment and use the money any way they want. Not only can they not do so, penalties for early withdrawal may amount to 25% or more. There are numerous cases across the country of investors in their 90s being sold CDs by unscrupulous entities that do not mature for 20 to 30 years. In addition to selling people unsuitable investments, these "brokers" may not be working with an FDIC institution but acting as the agent for other investors, or the investor is not told that they own only a portion, and not all, of the CD. Moreover, some CD programs are operated as pyramid schemes, with the early investors receiving "Ponzi payments."

Promissory Notes

A **promissory note** is essentially a short-term written I.O.U. that promises to pay its holder, the investor, the fixed amount invested plus a fixed amount of interest at some specified date in the future.[87] While promissory notes can be legitimate investments, those which are mass-marketed, sold door-to-door, promoted on the Internet or through telemarketing are often scams, which amount to some $300 million annually. Most promissory notes have to be registered as securities with the Securities Exchange Commission and in the states where they are to be sold, but notes with maturities of nine months or less may be exempt from being registered. Therefore, when notes are not registered and mature in nine months or less, it is another sign that a scam may be in the offering instead of a great investment opportunity. Legitimate corporate promissory notes are not usually sold to the general public, but to sophisticated buyers who conduct a due diligence search before investing.[88]

The fraudsters recruit a sales staff with lucrative commissions ranging from 20% to 30%; frequently, life insurance agents known and trusted in the community are recruited for this role.[89] These agents do not have a license to sell securities and rely solely on the information their employer provides, which later turns out to be false or misleading.[90] Enticed by promises of a 15% or 20% return on an "insured, guaranteed, no risk investment" and dealing with someone who is familiar to them, few victims ask any tough questions.[91] The pitch may include statements that reinforce the notion that this is a no risk investment, there is substantial collateral, and the investment is insured against loss. The money raised by the promissory notes may be needed to "open oil wells that were capped years ago because they were unprofitable to operate then, but new technology now makes it profitable to bring them on line." The notes may also be associated with activities such as "bringing out new products, funding a new television show, helping a real estate company acquire prime land for development, modernizing a Mexican gold, Colombian emerald, or South African diamond mine, or financing an e-commerce venture."

The fraudsters may simply take the money and run, leaving their unwitting sales agents to face charges, or operate the investment fraud as yet another variation on a Ponzi scheme. Promissory note fraud is also run as a type of affinity fraud.

Prime Bank Notes

International defrauders invented the prime bank note investment scam, which promises extremely high yields in a relatively short period of time.[92] They claim to have special access to investments that are usually "limited to only the very wealthy." The yields promised range from 5% per month to hundreds of percent annually. Victims are told that their money will be pooled to trade in prime bank notes, prime bank guarantees, prime bank debentures, letters of credit, bank purchase orders, zero coupon bonds, or other official sounding instruments.[93] Victims believe that such instruments can be purchased for a steep discount and then quickly resold for a substantial profit. They may also be advised that the profits are so vast that the International Money Fraud or the Federal Reserve Bank requires that a certain percentage of it be spent for charitable relief in third-world countries or elsewhere, which adds respectability to the pitch. The funds are actually sent to overseas banks in Geneva, London, or elsewhere. From there, they are transferred to off-shore institutions, where they are laundered, and the victims' money disappears. As is frequently the case in many types of frauds, this one can also be operated as a Ponzi scheme. Although individual investors are frequently victims, units of government are sometimes reeled in by the scheme—for example, the city of Clovis, New Mexico, lost $3.5 million in a prime note investment fraud.

Viatical Settlements

Viatical settlements were developed during the 1980s, in part to help dying AIDS patients pay their bills; their life insurance policies were bought by investors for less than the face value of the policy, and the investors had their money returned and a profit made upon the death of the insured.[94] Later, the practice was extended to others, especially the elderly. Because some people live longer than their medical diagnosis suggests is possible, and because new treatments are constantly developed that extend the life of the insured, this is a risky venture even when operated legitimately.[95]

Viatical settlement frauds are conducted in many guises—for example:

The National Medical Funding Company placed ads in gay publications soliciting terminally ill patients to sell their life insurance policies. The company never bought the policies; instead, they used the information from applicants to fabricate phoney viatical contracts, which were then sold to Arizona investors as fully insured 12- to 16-month investments that paid 14% or more. As investors started complaining about bounced checks and payments that never arrived, the fraud was identified, with investors losing $13 million.[96]

TELEPHONE AND PAGER SCAMS

Unrelated to telemarketing fraud are three scams related to telephone billing, such as: (1) 1-900 and foreign exchange numbers, (2) the Mexican collect call scam, and (3) cramming.

1-900 and Foreign Exchange Messages

Scammers will leave a telephone message, dial a pager, or send an e-mail from someone offering to engage in phone sex, telling the recipient they have won a prize (which may end up being only a few dollars), telling them that a family member is sick, or some other bogus message. The return number may be a 1-900 (pay for service calls, some of which may be legitimate), 809 (Dominican Republic), 284 (British Virgin Islands), 876 (Jamaica), or some other three-digit code.[97] While international calls normally require a "011" prefix, calls to the just-identified countries, Canada, and some other Carribean countries do not. The recipients think they are making a domestic long-distance call, but they are actually being connected to a number outside the United States and are billed at international call rates. Return callers often have to wade through automated menus and hear "dentist office" music to keep them on the line. These scams average $35 per call or more, which appears on the victims' telephone bills. Victims' vulnerability can be greatly reduced if they determine what country the three-digit prefix designates.

Mexican Collect Call Scheme

The Mexican collect call scam originated in that country, preys upon Hispanic consumers, and is basically a reverse of the scheme just described. The telephone rings and a voice, using the correct names of family members, says this is an emergency collect call, and the caller accepts the charges only to discover a stranger is on the line talking about something entirely different.

Cramming

It is entirely legal for phone companies to bill consumers for certain types of services as part of their regular telephone bill. **Cramming** is the practice of placing unauthorized, misleading, inaccurate, or deceptive charges on the victims' telephone bills, which may be accidental but is often intentional. Categories of cramming include voicemail, long-distance service, paging, Internet access, memberships, and pornography. Worldwide, pornography is a $57 billion industry, $12 billion of which is earned in the United States; a full 25% of all search engine requests involve pornography.[98] It did not, however, become a major industry simply by providing "free pornography." One source of its revenue is cramming—for example, visitors to some porn sites read that they can "download movies for free; no credit card needed," but the next month there is a charge on their telephone bill for having done so.

TELEMARKETING AND POSTAL FRAUDS

Many of the types of frauds discussed earlier in this chapter can be run as telemarketing and postal frauds. These two mediums of communication are a means of reaching massive numbers of potential victims quickly. Table 14-3 identifies the top 10 telemarketing frauds, a number of which were discussed earlier in this chapter. Note that many of these top 10 telemarketing schemes are variations on advance fee frauds. It is estimated that consumers lose $40 billion to telemarketing annually, and one out of six consumers is cheated each year.

In the postal or mail fraud content that follows, some scams not already covered are described. Remember that these can also be run by other means, such as telemarketing. Included in postal scams are real estate, franchise scams, unsolicited merchandise, fees for normally free services, and phoney inheritance cons. The top five postal frauds are (1) free prize schemes, (2) foreign lotteries, (3) pyramids scams, (4) investment frauds, and (5) work-at-home cons.[99]

Land Fraud

Offerings to sell parcels of land arrive in the mailboxes of potential victims, describing wonderful land on which to build vacation cabins or retirement homes or even just to hold as a "prime investment." The letters and brochures are slick and the language is glowing. Potential buyers should check with other brokers in the area or see if there are complaints against the person or company making the offer. This may simply be a version of an advanced fee scheme, or the land is worth very little because it is far from utility connections or cannot be built on without enormous costs because it is on the side of a steep ridge or mountain. Once they purchase the land, victims cannot resell it for even a fraction of what they paid for it.[100]

Franchise Cons

Franchise offers arrive in the mail touting fast food or quick printing business opportunities that require a substantial investment. These offers mention brand names, such as Kinko's or McDonald's, which are familiar to people or "soon to be very big in this area of the country." Using the cover of appearing to be a legitimate business opportunity, con men drain money from victims for application and other fees and then disappear.[101]

TABLE 14-3	Top Ten Telemarketing Scams of 2006		
NUMBER	SCAM	% OF ALL COMPLAINTS	AVERAGE LOSS
1	**Fake Check Scam**; seller of something is paid with bogus check; "buyer" asks seller to wire balance back. Has many variations.	31	$3,278
2	**Prizes/Sweepstakes**; you have won a fabulous prize, but must pay claim registration or other fee.	26	$2,749
3	**Magazine Sales**; the true cost of the subscription is misrepresented; may also pretend to be publisher inquiring about renewal.	8	$77
4	**Scholarships and Grants**; mentioned earlier in chapter; false promise of financial assistance for college costs, but must pay processing or other fee in advance.	6	$236
5	**Advance Fee Loans**; even if your credit is bad you can get personal or business loans for an "upfront" fee.	6	$1.164
6	**Lottery/Lottery Clubs**; this is a variation of number 2 (above) and usually involves foreign lotteries. It is also run with the twist that you can join a lottery club and pool monies to win.	5	$3,189
7	**Credit Card Offers**; bogus offer of credit card, even if your credit is bad; issuance fee to be paid in advance.	4	$237
8	**Phishing**; e-mails and calls from a well-known source, asking to confirm personal information because of some special circumstance.	3	$387
9	**Work-at-Home Plans**; materials sold on false promise of big profits from working in home; pay for materials in advance and they never arrive or are of shoddy quality.	1	$104
10	**Travel/Vacation**; offers of free or heavily discounted travel that never materialize; may have to join club or pay other cost upfront.	1	$812

(Source: National Fraud Information Center, 2007.)

Unsolicited Merchandise

People may receive gifts in the mail they didn't request, such as key chains, return address labels, and pens. Accompanying the gift is a postcard that suggests the sender's affiliation, such as recording for the blind, scholarships for students, and after-school programs. Money may not be directly solicited by the postcard, but many people send a check, thinking of it as payment for the gift or a small donation. Recipients of unsolicited merchandise have several alternatives: (1) if unopened, they can return it to the sender, which the Post Office does for free; (2) if opened and the contents are unattractive, throw them away, and (3) if opened and the merchandise is attractive, keep it without any obligation.[102] If recipients elect either of the last two options, they may get a high-pressure call or even a visit. In both cases, they should hang up, or not talk to the visitor or allow him or her inside the home. They are under no obligation to pay for unsolicited merchandise.

Fees Charged for Normally Free Services

Many services are available for free from the government or other legitimate organizations. A mail come-on hopes that you are unaware of these services and offers to provide them for a fee. Victimization schemes include child-support collection, unclaimed income tax refunds, and filing for property tax exemptions, all of which are run as advanced fee frauds.[103]

Missing Relatives

One of the cruelest frauds is the **missing person fraud**, which plays on victims' hopes of locating a missing loved one. The con men read the newspapers and visit official police sites where there are Internet postings soliciting information about missing persons, including personal information and the circumstances surrounding the disappearance. The fraudsters send a letter in which they pose as "people recovery specialists," offer phony credentials as former FBI, CIA, or other governmental agents, tout their national and international contacts, provide false accounts of successes, including recovering people from cults, and mention their access to special databases.

Once the offer is accepted, preliminary information is gathered by telephone, an advance fee is required, a face-to-face meeting is scheduled, and the fraudsters are never heard from again. Alternatively, they may come back with some vague information, which to follow up on involves some costs that require an additional sum of money.

Phony Inheritance Schemes

Everybody fantasizes about winning the lottery or inheriting some money from a distant relative. Con men know this and fuel our fantasy with letters delivered to our mailboxes from "**estate locators**" or "**research specialists**" which purport to be efforts "to locate the heirs of a substantial sum of money." These letters are, like other mail frauds, sent out in the thousands to unwary recipients who are asked to pay $30 or more for an "estate assessment."[104] This scam may also ask for personal information as the first step in an identity theft.

KEY TERMS

account takeover	integration	pump and dump
affinity fraud	layering	shoplifting
bank examiner con	missing person fraud	shoulder surfing
black market peso exchange	money laundering	skimmers
check kiters	Nigerian advanced fee scam	smurfing
cramming	off-shore accounts	soft insurance fraud
drive down	one-year callable certificates of	swoop and squat
dumpster diving	deposit (CD)	theft by conversion
embezzlement	organized retail crime	theft by deception
estate locators and research specialists	organized retail theft	theft by fraud
follow-on crime	paper accident	theft by receiving stolen property
franchise offer	petit or petty larceny	theft of services
fraud	phishing	theft by trick
grand larceny	pigeon drop	tangible property
hard insurance fraud	placement	viatical settlement
identity theft	Ponzi/pyramid fraud	white-collar crime
intangible property	promissory note	

REVIEW QUESTIONS

1. Shoplifting is often thought of as a "small time" crime. Is this true or false?
2. Why is so little property stolen in larceny/thefts recovered?
3. How does a three-person pickpocket operation work?
4. Give two definitions of *white-collar crime.*
5. List eight ways identity thieves can get a victim's personal information.
6. What are organized retail theft and organized retail crime?
7. After identity theft is committed, follow-on crimes occur. Identify five types of follow-on crimes.
8. What is smurfing?
9. What is shoulder surfing?
10. What are upcoding and unbundling charges used for?
11. What is the most common type of worker compensation fraud?
12. How does the swoop and squat method work?
13. Describe a viatical settlement fraud.
14. Why is it difficult to know how honest Internet gambling sites are?
15. How are bank examiner and pigeon drop cons run?
16. What is money laundering, and why do criminals want to do it?
17. What are pump and dump schemes?
18. How are prime bank and promissory note frauds operated?
19. Identify and discuss two telephone/pager scams.
20. The missing person fraud is cruel. How is it run?

| INTERNET ACTIVITIES

1. Review the shoplifting statutes for three different states that are geographically dispersed. How are those laws alike or different?

2. List three Internet sites that provide detailed information about what to do if your identity is stolen, and give a brief synopsis of the information.

| NOTES

1. David Young, "Pickpockets, Their Victims and Transit Police," *FBI Law Enforcement Bulletin*, 72 (12), December 2003, pp. 1–5; no author, ShanghaiDaily .com, "Pickpockets Attack Police," September 25, 2007; no author, "Pickpockets Target Oslo Police Chief," *Tech E-Newsletter*, May 25, 2007, with restatement and additions.

2. This paragraph is restated with additions from John S. Baker, *The Sociological Origins of White Collar Crime* (Washington, D.C.: The Heritage Foundation, Oct. 4, 2004), pp. 1–2.

3. Crime Clock 2005, from Uniform Crime in the United States, 2006 (Washington, D.C.: FBI, 2007), www.fbi .gov/ucr/cius2006/about/crime_.clock.html, no page number.

4. Uniform Crime in the United States, 2006 (Washington, D.C.: FBI, 2007). www.fbi.gov/ucr/cius2006/offenses/ property_crime/larceny-theft.html.

5. Uniform Crime in the United States, 2006 (Washington, D.C.: FBI, 2007). www.fbi.gov/ucr/cius2006/ clearances/inex.html#figure, Table 25, no page number.

6. Bureau of Justice Statistics, Criminal Victimization in the United States, 2005 (Washington, D.C.: U.S. Department of Justice, December 2006), Table 85, no page number.

7. Bureau of Justice Statistics, Criminal Victimization in the United States (Washington, D.C.: U.S. Department of Justice, December, 2006), Table 86. Printed from the Internet, no page number.

8. To learn more about theft by deception, see such sources as the New Jersey Statutes Annotated (N.J.S.A.) 2C:20-4.

9. Jack L. Hayes International, Inc. 19th Annual Theft Survey (Fruitland Park, Florida: Hayes International, October 1, 2007), pp. 8 and 2. Data based on a 2006 national survey of retailers.

10. Michigan Retailers Association, "How Do I Spot Shoplifters?" Feb. 16, 2005, p. 1. http://www.retailers.com/eduandevents/ask/askshoplifters.html.

11. Ibid.

12. Ibid.

13. No author, "Embezzlement/Employee Theft" (Fairmont, WV: National White Collar Crime Center), Sept. 2002, p. 1.

14. Ibid., p. 2.

15. Uniform Crime in the United States, 2006 (Washington, D.C.: FBI, 2007), www.fbi.gov/ucr.cius2006/Offenses/ property_crime/burglary.html and www.fbi.gov/ ucr.cius2006/Offenses/property_crime/motor_ vehicle.html.

16. Pat Reavy, "Salt Lake City Police Bust Shoplifting Ring," *Deseret Morning News*, September 24, 2007, with restatement.

17. See Dean T. Olson, "Financing Terror, *FBI Law Enforcement Bulletin*, Vol. 76, No. 2, February 2007, pp. 1–5, and Mark Clayton, "Is Black-Market Baby Formula Financing Terrorism?" *The Christian Science Monitor*, June 29, 2005.

18. Sean B. Hoar, "Identity Theft: The Crime of the New Millennium," *United States Attorneys' USA Bulletin*, Vol. 49, No. 2, March 2001, p. 1.

19. Ibid., p. 1.

20. Federal Trade Commission, "Putting an End to Account-Hijacking Identity Theft," Dec. 15, 2004, p. 1.

21. United States General Accounting Office, *Identity Theft: Prevalence and Cost Appear to Be Growing* (Washington, D.C.: March 2002), p. 8.

22. Bill Husted, "Database Raid Fallout Escalates" *The Atlanta-Journal Constitution*, Feb. 17, 2005.

23. Federal Trade Commission, *Identity Crime: When Bad Things Happen to Your Good Name* (Washington, D.C.: September 2002), p. 3, with some restatement and additions.

24. See (no author) "Protect Your Identity," *PC World*, Vol. 22, No. 12, Dec. 2004, pp. 107–112.

25. Federal Trade Commission, *Identity Crime: When Bad Things Happen to Your Good Name*, pp. 2 and 9.

26. Richard Hamilton, *The Police Notebook* (Norman, OK: University of Oklahoma), Jan. 7, 2005, pp. 14–17.

27. Ibid., pp. 13–14.

28. No author, "Stop Thieves from Stealing from You," *Consumer Reports*, Oct. 3, 2003, p. 5.

29. Cindy Maggiulli, "Identity Theft Is a Risk on Campus," *The Ranger* (Amarillo College Newspaper), September 20, 2007.

30. Federal Trade Commission, *Identity Crime: When Bad Things Happen to Your Good Name*, p. 4.

31. Linda and Jay Foley, Executive Directors, Identity Theft Resource Center, "Identity Theft: The Aftermath 2003," Summer 2003, p. 5.

32. National Conference of State Legislatures, Identity Theft, 2007, see www.ncsl.org/programs/lis/privacy/idt-statures.htm.

33. Linda and Jay Foley, "Identity Theft: The Aftermath 2003," p. 4.

34. Ibid., p. 8.

35. No author, "Credit Card Fraud" (Fairmont, WV: National White Collar Crime Center), Jan. 2003, p. 2.

36. Ibid., p. 1.

37. Ibid., p. 1–2.

38. Laura Czekaj, "Card Scam Bust," *The Ottawa Sun*, July 23, 2004, p. 1.
39. No author, "Check Fraud" (Fairmont, WV: National White Collar Crime Center), Sept. 2002, p. 1.
40. Barbara Hurst, Financial Institution Fraud Statistics," BankersOnLine.com, Feb. 5, 2005, http://BankersOnLine.com/security/gurus_sec090202c.html.
41. The White House, Office of the Press Secretary, "Fact Sheet," released in Cartagena, Colombia, Aug. 30, 2000, p. 1.
42. William Bach, U.S. Department of State, "Drugs, Counterfeiting, and Arms Trade: The North Korean Connection," statement before the Senate Committee on Governmental Affairs, Subcommittee on Financial Management of the Budget and International Security, May 20, 2003, p. 2.
43. Ian Dempsky, "Theft Operation 'Staggering,' Say Police," Tennessean.com, Dec. 30, 2004, www.Tennnessean.com/local/archives/04/12/63484418.shtml.
44. Kara Platoni, "Trailers Are for Travelers," *East Bay Express* (Weekly Newspaper, Emeryville, CA), Sept. 10, 2003, p. 2.
45. Ibid.
46. No author, "Insurance Fraud," (Fairmont, WV: National White Collar Crime Center), Sept. 2002, p. 1.
47. No author, "San Jose Father, Son Arrested on Auto Fraud Charges," *Insurance Journal*, Feb. 7, 2005, www.insurancejournal.com/news/west/2005/02/07/50896.htm.
48. No author, "Health Care Fraud" (Fairmont, WV: National White Collar Crime Center), Sept. 2002, p. 2. For an overview of this subject, see Malcolm K. Sparrow, "Fraud Control in the Health Care Industry," (Washington, D.C.: National Institute of Justice), Dec. 1998.
49. No author, "Health Care Fraud," (Fairmont, WV: National White Collar Crime Center), p. 3.
50. Ibid., p. 1.
51. Ibid.
52. Ibid., pp. 1–2, and Oxford Health Plan, "Healthcare Fraud," 2005, p. 1, www.oxhp.com/main/fraud/fraud.html.
53. No author, "Insurance Fraud," (Fairmont, WV: National White Collar Crime Center), p. 3.
54. Ibid., p. 1.
55. Statement of John M. Taylor, Food and Drug Administration (no title), United States Senate's Special Committee on Aging, John B. Breaux, Chair, September 10, 2001, p. 1.
56. No author, "Big Apple Selects 10 'Rotten Apples'," *Insurance Journal*, April 5, 2004, p. 1, http://insuranceJournal.com/magazines/east/2004/04/05/fraud.
57. No author, "Insurance Fraud: The Crime You Pay For," Coalition Against Insurance Fraud, Feb. 9, 2005, p. 3.
58. No author, "Internet Gambling," (Fairmont, WV: National White Collar Crime Center), August 2003, pp. 1–3.
59. Ibid., p. 2.
60. This information was provided by Bill Flowers, United States Secret Service via e-mail on Feb. 17, 2005. Agent Flowers correctly points out that most Nigerians are hard-working and honest and that these scams do not represent them as a whole.
61. Ibid., pp. 1–3.
62. No author, "Money Laundering," (Montreal, Canada: Royal Canadian Mounted Police), January 26, 2005, p. 2.
63. Mark Motivans, Money Laundering Offenders, 1994–2001 (Washington, D.C.: Bureau of Justice Statistics), July 2003, p. 1.
64. No author, "Money Laundering," (Fairmont, WV: National White Collar Crime Center), August 2003, p. 1.
65. No author, "Economic Perspectives: The Fight Against Money Laundering" (Washington, D.C.: U.S. Department of State), Vol. 6, No. 2, May 2001.
66. Ibid., p. 1.
67. No author, "Money Laundering," (Fairmont, WV: National White Collar Crime Center), Aug. 2003, p. 1.
68. Ibid., p. 2.
69. Bonni Tischler, Assistant Commissioner U.S. Customs Service, "The Columbian Black Market Peso Exchange," Statement before the Senate Caucus on International Drug Control, June 21, 1999, and no author, "Black Market Peso Exchange," *Dictionary of Financial Scam Terms*, Jan. 26, 2005, p. 1.
70. Ibid., p. 1.
71. Ibid.
72. No author, "Money Laundering: Extent of Money Laundering Through Credit Cards is Unknown," Report to the Chairman, Permanent Subcommittee on Governmental Affairs, U.S. Senate (Washington, D.C.: United States General Accounting Office), July 2002, p. 3.
73. No author, "Securities/Investment Fraud" (Fairmont, WV: National White Collar Crime Center), June 2003, p. 1.
74. Ibid.
75. Ibid.
76. No author, "Pump and Dump Schemes," U.S. Securities and Exchange Commission, March 12, 2001, p. 1, www.sec.gov/answers/pumpdump.htm.
77. Ibid.
78. No author, "Microcap Stock: A Guide for Investors," U.S. Securities and Exchange Commission, Aug. 2004, pp. 1–2 is the source of information in this paragraph.
79. No author, "Securities/Investment Fraud" (Fairmont, WV: National White Collar Crime Center), June 2003, pp. 2–3.
80. No author, "Affinity Fraud: How to Avoid Scams that Target Groups," U.S. Securities and Exchange Commission, p. 2, www.sec.gov/investor/pubs/affinity.htm. Also see *SEC* v. *A. B. Financing and Investments, Inc.*, and Anthony Blissett, Case No. 02-23487-CIV-Ungaro-Benages (South District, Florida, Dec. 6, 2002).
81. No author, "Securities/Investment Fraud" (Fairmont, WV: National White Collar Crime Center), June 2003, p. 3.

82. No author, "Insurance-Agent Scams," *Consumer Reports,* Aug. 2004, p. 5.

83. Ibid.

84. No author, "Pennsylvania Joins 25 States in Actions Against Sellers of Payphone Schemes, Losses at Least $70 Million," news release, Pennsylvania Securities Commission, March 13, 2001, p. 1.

85. No author, "Certificates of Deposit: Tips for Savers," Federal Deposit Insurance Corporation, Feb. 12, 2005, p. 1.

86. Ibid.

87. No author, "Broken Promises: Promissory Note Fraud," U.S. Securities and Exchange Commission, Jan. 11, 2005, p. 1.

88. Ibid.

89. Ibid.

90. Ibid.

91. Ibid.

92. No author, "Common Fraud Schemes," Federal Bureau of Investigation, Feb. 12, 2005, p. 7, http://FBI.gov/majcases/fraud/fraudschemes.htm.

93. No author, "Prime Investment Schemes," (Montreal, Canada: Royal Canadian Mounted Police), Oct. 16, 2003, p. 1.

94. No author, "Insurance-Agent Scams," *Consumer Reports,* Aug. 2004, p. 4.

95. Ibid.

96. Ibid.

97. No author, "FCC Consumer Advisory: 809 Phone Scam-Beware," (Washington, D.C.: Federal Trade Commission), Oct. 6, 2003, p. 1.

98. Family Safe Media, "Pornography Statistics 2003," www.familysafemedia.com, Feb. 18, 2005.

99. United States Postal Service, "Get Rich Quick? Don't Count on It!" Press Release of Feb. 2, 2004, p. 1.

100. No author, "Consumer and Business Guide to Preventing Mail Fraud" (Washington, D.C.: U.S. Postal Service), 1999, p. 12.

101. Ibid., p. 20.

102. Ibid., p. 22.

103. Ibid., p. 16.

104. Ibid., p. 13.

15

VEHICLE THEFTS AND RELATED OFFENSES

▲ Today, many vehicles are stolen primarily to be stripped for their parts. Once stripped for parts, such vehicles are abandoned, leaving owners with expensive repair bills.

(© Joseph Sohm, ChromoSohm Inc./Corbis)

Motor vehicle theft is one of the most significant issues facing law enforcement today. In 2005, there was one motor vehicle theft every 25.5 seconds.[1]

Although the number of thefts had been dropping for about 10 years prior to 2000, it is starting to increase in the United States, and with the collapse of communism and the opening of free-market economies in eastern Europe, auto theft has become an enormous problem. This, coupled with the increase in fraudulent insurance claims and other factors, has created a real challenge for law enforcement. In addition, investigating motor vehicle thefts can be difficult, and in some cases very complex, for several reasons.

When investigating vehicle theft, officers must determine the reason for the theft. Vehicles may be stolen temporarily, for example, for use in the commission of other crimes such as robberies or drive-by shootings, after which the vehicles are abandoned. Often, the stolen vehicle is not reported as such because it is considered secondary or incidental to the robbery or drive-by shooting. Other reasons for theft can include joyriding, professional theft, and fraudulent schemes.

Professional thieves use a variety of means such as chop shops, stripping, salvage switches, and export to other countries to dispose of stolen vehicles. Once a vehicle has been chopped or stripped, trying to identify particular stolen vehicles and/or parts can be extremely difficult. However, this seemingly formidable task has been made easier in part by the creation of standardized vehicle identification number systems. Finally, investigators are often faced with situations where the perpetrators are not strangers or professional thieves but the owners themselves.

Given limited law enforcement resources, vehicle theft may not be considered a top priority. Nonetheless, investigators have many major resources and organizations at their disposal. This chapter provides an overview of several of these resources, such as the National Insurance Crime Bureau and the American Association of Motor Vehicle Administrators, as well as the information they can provide. Although motor vehicle theft is the main topic of this chapter, also addressed is the theft of other high-value items, such as heavy equipment; commercial vehicles and cargo; marine vehicles; and aircraft and avionic equipment. We also discuss prevention programs that can help minimize the theft of motor vehicles and other items.

MOTOR VEHICLE THEFT

The number of motor vehicle thefts in the United States for 2005, as reported by the FBI, was estimated at 1.2 million, with a national loss of $7.6 billion in vehicle value. Of the total thefts, 73.4% were automobiles.

Although a high percentage of stolen vehicles are later recovered, only 13.1% of the cases are cleared by law enforcement agencies.

Other statistics for 2005: The average value of vehicles stolen was $6,173; and the number of reported thefts increased by .2% from the previous year.[2] The total number of thefts has decreased 11.4% compared with1996.[3]

Preliminary estimates are that there has been a 4.7% decrease from 2005 to 2006.[4]

Note that small increases or decreases in numbers are not significant. They could be caused by changes in reporting procedures, changes in crime classifications at local levels, more or fewer agencies reporting their statistics for central processing, or a variety of other reasons. Nevertheless, motor vehicle theft remains a problem of national concern.

Miscellaneous Statistics and Notes

- It has been estimated that approximately 2% of reported thefts are of motorcycles. A substantial portion of the thefts are directed at Harley-Davidsons.
- National and international rings, particularly those in cities near ports, export vehicles to countries all over the developing world where they can be sold for three or more times the price for which they are sold in the United States.
- Since the collapse of communism in eastern Europe, the theft of motor vehicles has skyrocketed. More than 2 million vehicles are stolen annually in Europe. Many are illegally exported to developing countries, particularly in the Middle East.
- The theft of airbags and the resale of stolen salvaged airbags is becoming epidemic. One company that insures about 20% of the cars in the United States annually pays out over $10 million because of stolen airbags. Several states have enacted legislation that is largely ineffective because there is no national system in place to identify and respond to this problem. The National Insurance Crime Bureau (NICB) has been spearheading a drive to develop strategies for attacking this problem.
- Heavy-truck and tractor-trailer thefts are on the increase. The insurance industry annually pays out $18 million because of commercial-vehicle theft, excluding cargo losses. California and Florida have the highest number of tractors stolen, while California, Texas, and Florida are ranked as the top three for trailer theft.

Auto Theft—Myths

- Auto theft happens to other people, not to me.
- Auto theft is a victimless crime. Insurance companies pay the costs.
- Most of the vehicles stolen are new models, so I don't need to worry if my car is a couple of years old.
- Most stolen vehicles disappear forever, because they are either exported or cut up into pieces.
- When an auto thief is caught, punishment is severe.

Auto Theft—Facts

- It is estimated that in 20% to 30% of auto thefts, the operator has left the keys in the car.
- Everyone with comprehensive insurance pays for auto theft and fraud through increased premiums, even if he or she never has a vehicle stolen.
- 62.1% of stolen vehicles are recovered, but only 13% of the cases are cleared by arrest.
- Punishment for auto theft is not swift and sure.
- The theft of older-model cars is prevalent. For example, in 2002, 85% of the vehicles reported stolen to law enforcement were model years 1985–1996.[5]
- Everyone's tax dollars pay the cost of fighting auto theft, including the costs of components of the criminal justice system.
- Auto theft is not a victimless crime. Insurance does not pay for the victim's insurance deductible, work loss, inconvenience, emotional trauma, and time loss (estimated to average more than 40 hours that include making telephone calls; filling out police reports; purchasing a replacement vehicle; completing insurance claim forms; and dealing with licensing and registration problems, vehicle inspection, and repairs, which may take many weeks if parts have to be ordered).[6]

Types of Theft

Motor vehicle thefts generally fall into one of four categories: temporary theft, joyriding, professional theft, or fraud.

Temporary Theft

The term **temporary theft** isn't used to imply that the crime is not serious but, rather, to distinguish joyriding from something more ominous. Of growing concern are the thefts of vehicles specifically for use in the commission of other crimes such as robberies or drive-by shootings, after which the vehicles are abandoned. These thefts are on the increase and, when reported, are often recorded only as the underlying crime rather than also as a motor vehicle theft, thereby skewing the actual theft figures.

Joyriding

Joyriding is most often engaged in by teenagers—15 to 19 years old—who steal a car simply to drive it around before abandoning it. Among the reasons teenage joyriders cite for the thefts are that joyriding makes them feel important, powerful, and accepted among their peers; it's fun and exciting; they did it on a dare; it relieves boredom and gives an adrenaline rush; they don't feel like walking; they want to impress girls; to make money by stripping cars and selling the parts; to get even with parents, or to escape family problems; and it was done as part of a gang membership or initiation. Since many youngsters are not professionals, they frequently target vehicles that are easy to steal and generally lack any anti-theft devices. The large number of apprehensions in this age category may be due to the arrests of joyriders.

Nationally, in 2005, persons under 18 years of age were involved in 15.2% of the cleared motor vehicle thefts, while persons under the age of 25 accounted for 58.2% and persons under the age of 18 accounted for 25.5% of the 108,301 people arrested for motor vehicle theft. Almost 75% of the people arrested for motor vehicle theft were adults, and 82.4% of the people arrested were males. Most (62.8%) of the arrestees were white, and just under 35% were black.[7] Nevertheless, no definitive statement is offered that joyriding is the foundation crime for these arrests; in fact, many of the thefts committed by, or in support of, the activities of professional vehicle thieves are accomplished by young people.

Professional Theft

In **professional theft** (Figure 15-1), the car thief is motivated by very high profits and generally low risk. The profits to be gained are second only to those from drugs. Anyone who has ever purchased a replacement part for a car is aware that the cost of replacing all the parts of a vehicle is much higher than the original cost of the entire vehicle. The professional can often sell the parts of a stolen car for up to five times the original assembled value. Considering what the thief "paid" for the vehicle, the profit margin is substantial.

▲ **FIGURE 15-1**
Thief breaks car window
The professional car thief is motivated by high profits and relatively low risk of apprehension. These thieves use a variety of means for entering locked cars, including breaking windows to open locked doors. The professional thief can break into a car, start it, and drive away in as little as 20 seconds.
(© Premium Stock/Corbis)

However, professionals do have costs in operating their "businesses." It is not infrequent for professional thieves to employ and train youths to steal cars. Often a youth is paid a set amount, several hundred to several thousand dollars, for each theft. The amount varies depending on the make, model, and year of the vehicle. There are even "training schools" in some areas of the country where juveniles and young adults are taught how to steal cars, trucks, motorcycles, and other vehicles. The professional thief, for example, can break into a locked, high-priced car, start it, and drive it away in as little as 20 seconds.

Fraud

Although certain types of theft involve fraud perpetrated on innocent purchasers, the major category of **vehicle fraud** as described here does not actually involve the theft of vehicles by professionals or even strangers. The various types of vehicle fraud are generally committed by the owner or someone acting on behalf of the owner, with the underlying purpose of profiting at the expense of an insurance company.

The NICB estimates that anywhere from 15% to 25% of all reported vehicle thefts involve some type of fraud and that a vast majority of them involve fraudulent insurance claims. Insurance crime is an enormous problem, and its true magnitude is almost impossible to pinpoint. The associated crimes of identity theft and credit card fraud, both of which have reached epidemic proportions, make the fraud problem even more complex.

In addition, some insurance experts estimate that between 16 and 35 cents of every dollar in premiums paid by the public for motor vehicle insurance is used to pay fraudulent claims or to fight fraud. The NICB says that if the amount of insurance claim fraud and vehicle theft occurring in the United States represented a corporation, it would rank in the top 25 of the Fortune 500 and be called a growth industry. In addition, insurance fraud is on the rise because it is an easy crime to successfully commit. Insurance companies, even those with highly qualified special investigation units whose function is to investigate suspected cases of fraud, must be concerned about potential liability resulting from lawsuits if someone is wrongly accused or a claim is wrongly denied. The fact that insurance companies are believed to have a great deal of money—deep pockets—makes these companies even more susceptible to civil suits and potential liability and, in turn, even more cautious.

Fraudulent auto-theft claims are not the only type of fraud to which the insurance industry is subjected, but they account for a significant part of the overall fraud. Fully 10% of all property and casualty claims are either inflated or outright fraud. Estimates are that fraudulent insurance claim payouts are $100 billion annually. This amount fluctuates, since it is well recognized that fraud increases as the economy worsens.

▲ **FIGURE 15-2 Interior of a chop shop**
A chop shop such as the one pictured here is a place where stolen vehicles are disassembled for resale of their parts. Stolen vehicles are cut apart in as little as 8 minutes in these chop shops. Parts are then sold to repair shops or salvage yards. Sometimes the repair shop operator is in collusion with the thief or the chop shop. (Courtesy of National Insurance Crime Bureau)

Methods of Operation—The Professional

To turn a profit, professional thieves use a variety of means to dispose of stolen motor vehicles. Among the most common are chop shops, salvage switches, exportation, and cloning.

Chop Shops

Very simply, a **chop shop** is a place where stolen vehicles are disassembled for resale of their parts (Figure 15-2). The operators and employees of chop shops cut stolen motor vehicles apart with torches, power saws, and other tools, sometimes in as little as 8 or 9 minutes. They alter or dispose of the parts that are potentially traceable and sell the untraceable parts to repair shops or salvage yards. Sometimes the parts buyers are unsuspecting. Often, the salvage yard or repair shop operator is in collusion with the thief or the chop shop. In fact, a chop shop may well direct the theft of a specific type of motor vehicle in order to "fill an order" for a specific part needed by a repair shop or salvage yard.

A modification of the typical chop-shop operation is illustrated by the following:

Thieves steal a car, disassemble it carefully so that the parts are not damaged, have the remainder conveniently recovered and disposed of through a salvage sale, buy the salvage, reassemble the vehicle with all its original parts, and sell the vehicle, which has already been classed as a recovered theft and is no longer considered stolen.

Quick Strip

In a **quick strip,** a vehicle is stolen and stripped mainly for valuable accessories such as seats, stereos, car phones, and tires. These items are attractive to thieves because they normally do not contain any identifying numbers, thus making them difficult to identify and easy to dispose of.

Salvage Switch

Generally, a **salvage vehicle** is one that has been damaged or wrecked to such an extent that the cost of repairing it is beyond its fair market value. Thus, its primary value in the legitimate market comes from the sale of its undamaged parts. To the criminal, however, the value of a salvaged vehicle is far greater than its parts. The real profit is made after the criminal buys the salvage, provided it is accompanied by the certificate of title and the vehicle identification number (VIN) plate. Often the offender does not even want the vehicle and leaves it at the salvage yard from which it is purchased or disposes of it elsewhere. The thief then steals a vehicle identical to the wreck, changes the VIN plate, and sells the stolen vehicle, with a matching title, to an innocent purchaser or to a purchaser who is offered such a "good" price that no questions are asked. Through the **salvage switch,** the thief is able to disguise and dispose of stolen vehicles in the legitimate market.

Export

Vehicles manufactured in the United States are extremely popular in other countries. The sale of American-manufactured vehicles can also be highly profitable. Vehicles manufactured in other countries for sale in the United States are also stolen for export. Buyers in foreign nations often pay double the purchase price for quality cars, some of which is due to high tariffs. The NICB estimates that 13% of all vehicles stolen in the United States are illegally exported.[8] Mexico and Central and South American countries are among the most popular but certainly not the exclusive destinations for stolen U.S.-manufactured vehicles. It has been estimated that as many as 20,000 stolen or embezzled cars, trucks, buses, motorcycles, and other vehicles are transported into Mexico each year. This amounts to between 6.6% and 10% of the estimated number of stolen vehicles exported each year.

Contributing to this problem are the limited, although effective, controls exercised by Mexican customs and the few effective controls exercised by the United States over southbound traffic entering Mexico. The volume of traffic going into Mexico makes it almost impossible to inspect and investigate all vehicles. Many stolen vehicles are also taken to Canada. Some are resold, but many are exported to their final destinations. Exports account for a growing percentage of unrecovered stolen vehicles, and the problem is even greater in port cities.

With the collapse of communism and the opening of free market economies in eastern Europe, auto theft has grown to become an enormous international problem. According to Interpol, auto theft has become the second largest source of terrorist funding.[9]

Cloning

Vehicle cloning is a crime in which stolen vehicles receive the identity of nonstolen, legally owned vehicles of the same make and model. This is accomplished by counterfeiting labels, stickers, VIN plates, and titles to make the stolen car look legitimate. Illicit profits from vehicle cloning in the United States are estimated by the NICB to be in excess of $12 million each year. Many high-priced, luxury vehicles are objects of cloning.[10]

Cloning is not confined to the United States. Many offenses have occurred in Mexico, Canada, and the United Kingdom. Exportation of legitimate vehicles is also used by professional thieves to clone vehicles. Once exported, the VIN number and other counterfeit indicia appear on stolen, cloned vehicles titled and registered in one or more states. These vehicles are referred to as being "reborn." Often, multiple copies of the counterfeit indicia will appear on stolen vehicles and, unless the vehicles are thoroughly inspected by trained investigators, these stolen vehicles are almost impossible to identify as being fraudulent. Many of the stolen, cloned vehicles are then exported to such popular destinations as Eastern Europe, Russia, the Caribbean, the Dominican Republic, Central and South America, and the Far East.[11] The NICB says that cloned vehicles are also used to facilitate drug trafficking, money laundering, and for transportation to and from crime scenes by organized crime.[12]

Many of the fraudulent theft schemes described in the next section apply equally to the cloning of a vehicle.

Fraudulent Theft Schemes

Fraudulent auto-theft claim schemes fall into three major categories: false-vehicle claims, in which no vehicle exists or the vehicle is not owned by the criminal; false-theft schemes; and inflated-theft schemes.

False-Vehicle Schemes

False-vehicle schemes are particularly prevalent where insurance companies are lax or have ineffective programs to verify the existence of a vehicle before issuing an insurance policy. As a general rule, this type of fraud is planned well in advance of obtaining insurance coverage. The criminal purchases a policy that has a provision covering loss by theft. In fact, the vehicle does not exist except on paper, has already been salvaged, or does not belong to the person who buys the insurance. Most often, the vehicle insured is a recent model. Some time later (generally within three months, to hold down the cost of the insurance coverage purchase) a theft report is filed with a law enforcement agency, and a claim is made to the insurance company.

Several modifications of the salvage switch, described earlier, are illustrative of false-vehicle schemes. Once a salvaged vehicle is purchased, insurance coverage is obtained. After a short time, a theft loss claim is filed for the vehicle, which, of course, was in "excellent condition."

In some jurisdictions, a **salvage title** may be issued. This does not necessarily prevent false-theft claims on salvage, it merely channels the process in a different direction. One way the criminal avoids the problems associated with the issuance of salvage titles is by **washing,** or laundering, the title. This is done by fabricating the sale of the vehicle and transferring the title to an alleged purchaser in another state that does not issue salvage titles or does not carry forward a "brand" on the title issued by another state. The "buyer" then obtains a clean title in that state and transfers it back to the insured either directly or through several other people or businesses to make it appear to be a legitimate transaction. Then, with a clean title, the insured files a theft claim.

In another technique, the salvage buyer falsifies the necessary support documentation so that it shows the salvage vehicle as being completely rebuilt or restored and thereby obtains a "clean," or regular, title. The thief may not even bother to get a clean title; upon filing a claim for the alleged theft, he or she may simply contend that the vehicle was rebuilt or restored but was stolen before the insured could file the necessary paperwork to obtain a nonsalvage title.

In still another version of the salvage switch, the VIN plate may be attached to a rented or borrowed car of the same make and model and, along with the certificate of title, may be presented to and inspected by an agent of the company from which coverage is sought. After the policy is issued, the salvage vehicle VIN plate is removed and the vehicle is returned to the person or company from which it was borrowed or rented.

Presenting a counterfeit or stolen certificate of title or manufacturer's certificate of origin (MCO) as the basis for having a policy issued on a **"paper vehicle"** or on a stolen vehicle with a concealed identity is another technique for defrauding insurance companies through the filing of false-vehicle claims. A manufacturer's certificate of origin is the original identification document issued by a vehicle's manufacturer, somewhat like a birth certificate. It accompanies the vehicle through its delivery to a new car dealer until it is first sold to a retail purchaser, after which the MCO is surrendered to the jurisdiction issuing the first certificate of title in the name of the retail purchaser.

A variation on the counterfeit- or blank-title scheme is the altered title, whereby the criminal manages to conceal the existence of a lienholder who may have already repossessed the vehicle because of missed payments. A theft report is then filed along with the fraudulent insurance claim.

It is not uncommon to find the following scenario in a fraudulent claim on a false vehicle:

Henry Johnson owns a late-model full-size car. The vehicle is paid for and Johnson has the title in his possession. Johnson decides to sell the car. After he has it advertised for a few days, he receives a satisfactory offer from a person who pays cash and takes the car to another state to have it titled and registered. Johnson signs the title over to the buyer, who takes possession of the vehicle and drives it to his own state of residence. The next day, Johnson, claiming he can't find his car title, applies for a duplicate title in his own state. The title is issued and is branded with the word "duplicate." Although it may take several weeks to receive the duplicate title, the process may still be faster than it takes for the buyer's home state to issue a new title to the buyer and send the original of Johnson's title back to his state for official cancellation. Upon obtaining the duplicate title, Johnson files a theft claim with his insurance company and surrenders the duplicate title to the company in exchange for the theft loss payment. After learning of the scam, the insurance company goes looking for Johnson and finds that all the information he provided was false, and he has now disappeared not only with the insurance money but with the money he made from selling the vehicle. Normally, the issuance of a duplicate title will render the original or any previously issued duplicate void, but this fact was unknown to the buyer of Johnson's car or to the buyer's home state, where he applied for a title in his own name.

False-Theft Schemes

As opposed to the many different fraudulent schemes in which no vehicle exists, in a **false-theft scheme**, the vehicle does exist and is in fact owned by the person who has obtained the insurance policy. The primary reason why an owner would file a phony-theft loss is generally either to avoid liability for some conduct that resulted from the use of the vehicle or to reduce or avoid some financial loss. The specific motivation leading to the filing of the fraudulent claim may exist at the time the policy coverage is obtained or may result from circumstances that develop later.

Among the vast number of motivations—and there are as many motivations as there are false claims—for filing false-theft loss claims are the following:

- To cover or avoid personal responsibility for a hit-and-run accident. The owner reports the car stolen (before the police come to question him or her) and subsequently files an insurance claim.
- To replace an old vehicle that just doesn't look good or drive smoothly any longer.
- To replace a "lemon" that can't be sold for a decent price.

- To obtain money for another vehicle that is in need of repair or replacement.
- To avoid loss of the vehicle without receiving any financial gain, for example, through repossession caused by a default of payments or in response to a court order to transfer the title to a former spouse after a divorce.
- To end costly car payments or repair bills.
- To avoid the hassle of selling.
- To obtain a more favorable interest rate on a car loan.
- To break a restricting car lease.

As noted at the outset of this chapter, fraud may be committed by the insured acting alone or with another person or persons. When a vehicle owner conspires with others, the fraud is often referred to as an "owner give-up." Examples of both solo and give-up false-theft schemes include the following:

- The vehicle is abandoned and later reported stolen (Figure 15-3).
- The vehicle, which may have been previously damaged or had some major mechanical defects, is reported stolen. Shortly afterward, it is recovered, and the insured claims that the damage or defects were caused by the theft.
- The vehicle is sold to an out-of-state buyer, and then a duplicate certificate of title is applied for and used to file the claim—just as in the Johnson scenario, reported earlier.
- The vehicle is not stolen but is hidden prior to the theft report and prior to the claim being filed. After the loss is paid, the vehicle can be returned to use, stripped, sold, chopped for parts, taken out of state, or otherwise disposed of.
- The vehicle is dumped in water, a method of causing damage that is increasing in use. This is often referred to as car dunking or vehicle dumping. Such vehicles generally cannot be repaired economically even if recovered.
- Vehicle burying is another way that owners dispose of unwanted vehicles. Consider the following: An employee at the Charlotte/Douglas International Airport in North Carolina was charged with insurance fraud after police unearthed his car from the ground at a remote, wooded edge of the airport. After his attempts to sell the car met with no success, the insured, who worked as a landscaper at the airport, decided to use a backhoe to dig a pit and bury his car inside. He then reported the car stolen in order to collect an insurance settlement.[13]
- Vehicle arson is another form of fraud that is planned beforehand and is motivated by a desire to collect on an insurance policy either to make a profit or to solve a financial problem. Vehicle arson will be covered in more detail later.

◀**FIGURE 15-3 Vehicle abandoned in false-theft scheme**
Vehicle owners have been known to file false theft reports on their cars, often to avoid liability for some conduct associated with the vehicle or to reduce or avoid financial loss. The owner typically attempts to abandon the vehicle in a location beyond the scope of a general search conducted by the police.

(© Chinch Gryniewicz, Ecoscene/Corbis)

Inflated-Theft-Loss Schemes

As distinguished from the preceding schemes, in the **inflated-theft-loss scheme** the vehicle actually exists, actually belongs to the insured, and actually is stolen. The fraud occurs when the insured makes a false claim concerning the physical or mechanical condition of the vehicle when it was stolen; actually causes some damage or removes some parts on recovery of the vehicle but before it is inspected by the insurance company; claims there were expensive parts on or improvements made to the vehicle before it was stolen; or, if no follow-up inspection is conducted by the insurer, claims certain damage occurred that actually did not happen.

One frequently used scam has the insured enter into a conspiracy with a repair shop, after a stolen vehicle is recovered, to allege that damages were caused during the theft. The damages do not exist. The vehicle is immediately "repaired" before the insurance appraiser has the opportunity to inspect the vehicle, and the repair shop insists that the insurer accept the repair bill, possibly using a photo of a wrecked vehicle of the same make and condition as the vehicle "before repair." A spinoff of this basic scenario has the repair shop show the appraiser an actual wrecked vehicle in its possession of the same make and model as the insured's car.

The inflated-theft-loss claim also extends to vehicle contents. The claimant alleges the vehicle contained valuable clothes, cameras, golf clubs, and other "new" items of considerable value when it was stolen.

Defrauding the Owner and the Insurer

There are times when the owner is not involved in the fraud and both the owner and the insurer become victims, as illustrated in the following example:

An individual leases a vehicle from a rental company and, during the rental period, reports the vehicle stolen to both the police and the rental company. Shortly after, the renter again calls the police and reports that the vehicle was recovered, using some excuse such as his coworker took it to the store or he forgot where he parked it the night before because he had had too much to drink. Consequently, the police never enter the "stolen" report into the National Crime Information Center (NCIC). Conveniently, the renter fails to notify the rental company, which assumes that the law enforcement agency entered the theft into NCIC. The thief may have several days' or longer use of the vehicle before the victims can put the whole story together.

Some vehicles are exported by owners for the purpose of filing and collecting on fraudulent theft claims.

Another type of export fraud occurs when a vehicle owner makes multiple copies of proof-of-ownership documents to present to U.S. Customs officials and exports his or her vehicle. After the vehicle arrives at its foreign destination, the VIN plate is removed and mailed back to the owner, who steals a car of the same make and model, switches the VIN plate, and, using the additional copies of ownership documents, exports the stolen vehicle. This is another variation of cloning.

As illustrated by the preceding examples, people who engage in insurance fraud are limited only by their imaginations. They are able to change tactics as quickly as law enforcement agencies and the insurance industry devise methods for combating current fraud schemes.

THEFT OF HEAVY CONSTRUCTION EQUIPMENT

Heavy **construction equipment** (or, simply, **heavy equipment**) is commonly referred to as **off-road equipment**. The National Crime Information Center (NCIC) received more than 17,000 reports of commercial equipment thefts in 2005, with annual loss estimates as high as $1 billion. The recovery rate is only 24%. Insurance claims have been increasing at an annual 10%–20% rate for the past decade.

The national average for a used piece of construction equipment is $135,000. The states with the highest theft and recovery rates are Texas, California, and Florida[14] (Figure 15-4).

Off-road equipment is stolen for the following reasons: its high value, a demand for the equipment, low security, low risk, and high rewards.[15]

Thieves may steal on order, for stripping, or for export. One offender was caught with a notebook filled with photographs he had taken of machinery on various farms. When interrogated, he stated he had roamed the countryside obtaining the photographs in the notebook. The notebook was then used as a "sales catalog" when meeting with prospective buyers and as a means of instructing thieves working with him as to exactly what equipment from a particular location was to be taken. This arrangement made it possible for the equipment to be consigned or sold before it was even stolen, minimizing the amount

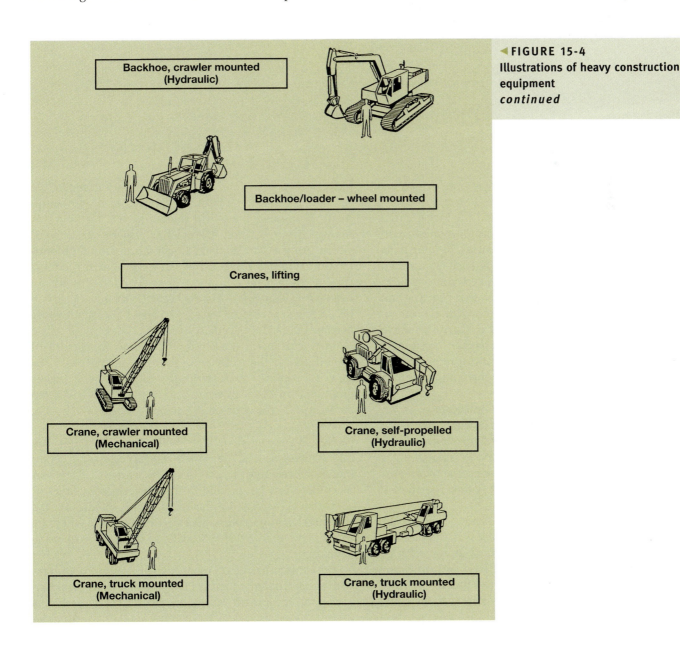

◄ FIGURE 15-4
Illustrations of heavy construction equipment
continued

Backhoe, crawler mounted (Hydraulic)

Backhoe/loader – wheel mounted

Cranes, lifting

Crane, crawler mounted (Mechanical)

Crane, self-propelled (Hydraulic)

Crane, truck mounted (Mechanical)

Crane, truck mounted (Hydraulic)

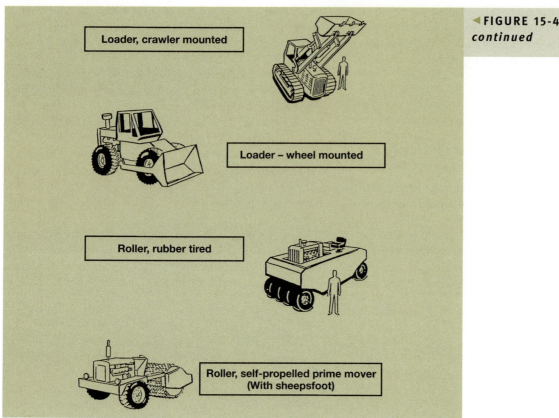

◀FIGURE 15-4
continued

of time that the equipment was in the thieves' hands and therefore their risk.

The theft of off-road equipment and the investigation of the thefts cause numerous problems for owners, manufacturers, and law enforcement agencies. Title or registration generally is not required for such equipment, and owners have traditionally resisted such requirements for several reasons. They fear that the title and registration records could be used to levy taxes on expensive items of property and that such a financial burden would have to be passed on to their consumers. Further, they believe that registration requirements would impede their ability to move the equipment rapidly and freely around the country.

Owners are also victimized by the problem of inventory control. Construction equipment is often spread over several miles of job site or over several job sites and may be left idle for days or weeks at a time in isolated areas. Thus, when the professional thief is overcome by the irresistible temptation, it is often days before the theft is noticed and reported to the police.

Another issue that compounded the construction equipment theft problem until recently was the fact that off-road equipment, unlike conventional motor vehicles, had no standard, permanently affixed identification number. Historically, each manufacturer had its own system of identification, and the numbering systems could

vary from 4 to as many as 15 alphanumeric digits. On January 1, 2000, the 237 manufacturers of heavy equipment throughout the world (including the big four U.S. manufacturers—Case, Caterpillar, Deere, and Ford) began using a standardized 17-character **product identification number (PIN)** on all new equipment models[16] (Figure 15-5). The definition of "new model" will not necessarily change by calendar year. Consequently, it will take a few years before the standardized 17-character PIN becomes uniformly applied.

In at least one instance, the PIN is now more difficult to counterfeit than has been the case in the past. The new PIN plate on Caterpillar equipment is laser-engraved on black anodized aluminum and has a bar code and a microprinted security feature—the PIN number.[17]

Heavy equipment is also easily stolen; a single key may be used to start all models produced by a particular manufacturer, and where key locks are in place, the machinery can be jumped by placing a pocket knife or screwdriver across the electrical posts on the starter. Although manufacturers offer antitheft devices, they are costly items that add substantially to the base price of the equipment.

The unfamiliarity of most law enforcement officers with the nature, identity, and terminology of construction and farm equipment is among the principal problems

◄ FIGURE 15-5 Product identification removed from stolen piece of construction equipment
The Product Identification Number (PIN) had been removed from this piece of construction equipment and, following it's recovery, an NICB special agent was able to identify the unit by other partial numbers so it could be returned to its rightful owner.
(Courtesy of National Insurance Crime Bureau)

faced by law enforcement. Few agencies have anyone with the expertise to identify specific machines or to locate and interpret identification numbers.

COMMERCIAL-VEHICLE AND CARGO THEFT

The insurance industry pays out about $18 million every year because of **commercial-vehicle theft.** It is difficult to convert this figure to the number of vehicles stolen, because commercial-vehicle theft data are incorporated into the overall motor vehicle theft statistics. Suffice it to say, the number is significant and rising. Additionally, it is further estimated that the actual number of cargo thefts is 20% more than reported.

The theft of cargo from, or in, commercial vehicles—is a rapidly growing criminal enterprise. Although not a separate crime in itself, **cargo theft,** in the United States, is estimated as accounting for as much as $25 billion in direct merchandise losses each year.[18] As an aside, cargo theft is just one aspect of a larger problem called cargo crime, which also includes smuggling, counterfeiting, and product piracy. Total direct merchandise losses from all cargo crime are estimated as approaching $50 billion per year.[19] Pre-2007, the numbers are somewhat unreliable estimates from a number of different sources. With the passage of the Patriot Act Reauthorization bill, there is now a requirement to capture cargo theft losses in the Uniform Crime Reports data collected by the FBI.[20] The products most vulnerable to cargo crime, in general, and cargo theft, in particular, are assembled computers, computer components and software, electronic products, cigarettes, and fashion apparel,[21] packaged foods, appliances, and seafood.[22]

INVESTIGATIVE TOOLS AND TECHNIQUES

Vehicle theft investigation is a fairly technical and sophisticated specialty. An effective investigator needs experience and expertise. Despite the fact that vehicle theft may not be among the offenses receiving the highest priority for the allocation of limited resources by a law enforcement agency, there are thousands of specialists in the United States and elsewhere whose expertise is available to any investigator needing assistance. Often, these resources are just a telephone call away.

In any specialized investigative field, one is not born an expert and cannot become an expert without extensive training and experience. So it is with vehicle thefts and related crimes. Individuals who possess the expertise, such as highly skilled investigators, cannot assume that uniformed officers with general policing responsibilities have any knowledge about the field beyond their limited exposure in an academy setting. Thus, if investigators are anxious for patrol officers to perform some initial investigative tasks, the investigators should offer to teach those officers how to perform the desired tasks.

Major Investigative Resources

National Insurance Crime Bureau

The **National Insurance Crime Bureau (NICB)** is not a law enforcement agency that investigates auto thefts and arrests offenders in the traditional sense. Rather, the NICB is an information-gathering and dissemination body and a law enforcement assistance agency. In this regard, its special agents do investigate professional theft rings and other auto-theft cases in conjunction with local, state, and federal law enforcement agencies.

Beginning in 1912 with the efforts of a few individuals representing different insurance companies that joined forces to disseminate information on stolen motor vehicles, the cooperation gradually spread and evolved into several independent regionalized and, later, national groups. This growth limited communication and interaction. Duplication of efforts and costs, along with the creation of considerable confusion among law enforcement officials in deciding whom to contact for information, led to the initial consolidation of all existing auto-theft information agencies and organizations into the National Automobile Theft Bureau (NATB) in 1912. In 1965, the NATB was completely nationalized and centralized.

Late in 1991, a merger took place between the NATB and the Insurance Crime Prevention Institute (ICPI), and on January 1, 1992, the National Insurance Crime Bureau was formed. The NICB now has approximately 150 investigative field agents working with another 800 fraud investigators who work for individual insurance companies.

The NICB is not a government organization. It is a not-for-profit organization operated by, funded by, affiliated with, and serving approximately 1,000 associated insurance companies nationwide. It supports engineering, research, and experiments aimed at reducing vehicle theft and fraud and is a recognized national voice for law enforcement and the insurance industry on legislative matters.

The NICB assists in the identification of vehicles and helps educate law enforcement officers in investigative techniques of vehicle identification, fraud, and theft. Online Insurance Crime Training for Law Enforcement, including material on vehicle theft fraud, can be found at www.nicbtraining.org.

In addition to the expertise of its field personnel, the computerized records developed and established by the NICB, and now maintained and administered by the Insurance Service Office, Inc. (ISO), a private company, are invaluable investigative aids. These database services include the following:

- *Insurance theft file:* More than 1,000 insurance companies report stolen vehicles. Theft records from the Canadian Automobile Theft Bureau (CATB) and most European countries are also maintained and include all types of vehicles, off-road machinery, boats, parts, and accessories. The records contain full ownership and insurance information.
- *Salvage file:* Salvage vehicle reports are received from insurance companies on vehicles for which there has been a loss settlement and the company has taken the title. These vehicles are generally sold through salvage pools or to salvage buyers.

The file contains information on both sellers and buyers of salvage.

- *Export file:* The U.S. Customs Service and others send copies of export declarations for entry into the system. The information aids in the detection of illegal exports and of fraudulent theft reports on exported vehicles in cases where a subsequent stolen vehicle report is filed.
- *NCIC mirror image and purge file:* All active and inactive theft records on vehicles and boats housed in NCIC are also contained in the mirror image file. In addition, vehicle theft records purged from NCIC since 1972 for a variety of reasons are provided to NICB on a daily basis and are entered into the system as a permanent record. The file is an important and time-saving tool for law enforcement.
- *Information-wanted file:* When a purchaser skips out on payments to a finance company that has purchased physical-damage insurance on the vehicle from one of the NICB sponsoring member companies, the information is made available to law enforcement agencies investigating the vehicle as a suspected stolen unit.
- *Inquiry file:* When a law enforcement agency makes an inquiry on a vehicle for an investigation, any subsequent information received or any inquiry on the same vehicle from another person or agency will be passed on to the original inquirer.
- *Shipping and assembly file:* This file holds the shipping and assembly records for most automobiles; light-, medium-, and heavy-duty trucks; semitrailers; motorcycles; and snowmobiles produced for sale in the United States and Canada.
- *Impound file:* An increasing number of states are now collecting and reporting impound records to NICB for entry into this file. The file helps clear many stolen records and is a valuable investigative tool.
- *VINASSIST:* This NICB program, provided to law enforcement agencies at no cost, defines, edits, evaluates, and corrects vehicle identification numbers, a process that greatly aids law enforcement in positively identifying specific recovered motor vehicles.
- *All-claims Database:* With this database, claims filed against participating member insurance companies can be compared to detect possible fraudulent claims, including auto theft–related insurance fraud.

The NICB is organized into nine geographic areas, with its headquarters in the Chicago suburb of Palos Hills, Illinois, serving as the Area 1 office. The other offices serving major metropolitan and surrounding locales are in Seattle, Los Angeles, Dallas, Tampa, Washington, D.C., New York, Columbus, and Hartford.[23]

Since 1919, the NICB or its predecessor, the NATB, has annually published the *Passenger Vehicle Identifica-*

◀ **FIGURE 15-6**
The Passenger Vehicle Identification Manual
One of the most important investigative tools used in vehicle theft cases is the Passenger Vehicle Identification Manual. Published by the National Insurance Crime Bureau, this booklet contains useful information, including: an explanation of vehicle identification numbers, the federal motor vehicle theft prevention standards, and VIN plate attachment and location.
(© Joel Gordon)

tion Manual (Figure 15-6), which contains the following information:

- Federal motor vehicle theft prevention standards.
- Explanation of vehicle identification numbers.
- VIN plate attachment and location.
- Federal safety certification labels.
- Passenger vehicle and light-duty truck VIN structure.
- Motorcycles and all-terrain vehicle VIN structure.
- General information on snowmobiles and boats.
- Vehicle shipping and assembly record information.[24]

Every five years, the NICB also publishes the *Commercial Vehicle and Off-Road Equipment Identification Manual,* which contains the following information:

- World manufacturer identification codes.
- Model year identifier.
- Truck-tractor identification.
- Commercial-trailer identification.
- Off-road equipment identification.[25]

Insurance Bureau Canada (IBC)

Known formerly as the Canadian Insurance Crime Prevention Bureau, the Insurance Bureau Canada has been functioning since 1923 but became an independent division within the Insurance Council of Canada on January 1, 1998. It is to Canada what NICB is to the United States. IBC is supported by over 90% of private-property and casualty insurers. Within the organizational structure of IBC are found the Canadian Automobile Theft Bureau (CATB) and the Canadian Police Information System, the sister organization of NCIC. IBC is headquartered in Toronto, Ontario. It has five regional offices, located in Burnaby, British Columbia; Toronto; Wesmount, Quebec; Halifax, Nova Scotia; and Calgary, Alberta.[26]

International Association of Auto Theft Investigators

Another resource available to the investigator is the International Association of Auto Theft Investigators (IAATI) and its regional affiliated chapters which are located in many parts of the world, including Europe and Australia. With a current membership of almost 3,800 representing more than 35 countries, IAATI was formed in 1952 for the purpose of formulating new methods to attack and control vehicle theft and fraud. Its members represent law enforcement agencies, state registration and titling agencies, insurance companies, car rental companies, the automobile manufacturing industry, and other interested groups. International and regional training seminars are held throughout the year. As with many such organizations, it is a great network of specialists all willing to assist any investigator who requests help.

State Organizations

Many states have organizations consisting of auto-theft investigators who meet regularly to exchange intelligence information and learn new methods of combating the problems of theft and fraud.

National Crime Information Center

Another valuable resource for the investigator is the FBI's National Crime Information Center (NCIC). Online inquiries can be made to NCIC's vehicle or license plate files to check on records for stolen vehicles, vehicles wanted in conjunction with felonies, stolen component parts, and stolen license plates. In addition, a request can be made for an off-line search, which is a tool designed to assist an investigator by providing lead information. For example, an investigator attempting to track a stolen vehicle that is known to be traveling across the country can request an off-line search to see if any stolen inquiries had been made within a specific time frame on that vehicle. A hit would identify the time and location from which the inquiry was made, thus providing a lead to locating the vehicle.

The original NCIC system held more than 40 million records in its 17 databases and processed more than 2 million transactions a day, but it was more than 30 years old. An updated, new-generation system, NCIC 2000, was implemented in July 1999. It has all the advantages of the old system plus impressive new capabilities such as: image processing, whereby mug shots, other photographs, signatures, and identifying marks can be electronically submitted; single-finger fingerprint matching, including storing and searching for right-index fingerprints; a linkage field, where multiple records concerning the same criminal or the same crime can be automatically associated; and several new databases, including the Convicted Persons on Supervised Release Database, the Convicted Sexual Offender Registry, and the SENTRY file of persons incarcerated in federal prisons. These can all be accessed through NCIC 2000.[27]

The NCIC databases can be used for many different purposes. For instance, through the linkage function, an inquiry on a gun can also identify a wanted person or a stolen car. Since vehicle information can be included in the Convicted Sexual Offender Registry, a traffic stop with an inquiry on the license plate may identify an individual as a registered sexual offender.[28]

Special Investigative Units

In the mid-1970s, Kemper Insurance Company created the first special investigative unit (SIU) for insurance companies. Its primary purpose was to investigate potentially fraudulent auto-theft claims. There are more than 800 SIU investigators employed in the insurance industry working fraud claims. Approximately 80% of the insurance companies now have SIUs. The agents and units work with and train insurance adjusters to detect oddities and "red flags" indicating potential fraud. The SIUs also work closely with law enforcement by lending assistance in investigations—providing computer information, claims histories, and statements of insureds made under oath.

AAMVANET

The **AAMVANET** computerized communication network links state and provincial agencies on matters of highway usage and highway safety. The system was initiated by and for the American Association of Motor Vehicle Administrators (AAMVA). The AAMVANET corporation, a subsidiary of AAMVA, is working with the FBI to coordinate efforts to create the **National Motor Vehicle Title Information System (NMVTIS)**. Through NMVTIS, any

inquiry will receive a complete and up-to-the-minute history of a vehicle, including whether it was reported stolen, salvaged, or exported or is otherwise incapable of being the subject of a new transfer. In addition to inquiry capability, the system will prevent the laundering of titles between states for the purpose of removing brands such as those that appear on salvage, flood-damaged, rebuilt, or unrepairable vehicles. Currently, 9 states are fully operational and online; 6 additional states are partially online; 5 more states are in online development; 9 states are providing data by batch; 2 states are developing batch data for implementation; and 21 jurisdictions have yet to join in the NMVTIS effort. Currently, 55% of the U.S. vehicle population is represented in the NMVTIS system.[29] The ultimate goal of the developers is to provide a system whereby a potential purchaser of a used vehicle will be able to inquire about the status of the vehicle before making a final commitment to purchase.

Government Agencies

In virtually all state governments, organizations or entities exist that possess information of value to investigators. Specifically, motor vehicle and driver's license offices, insurance fraud investigative units, and fire and arson investigative units may provide valuable information or assistance.

Manufacturers

Manufacturers are one of the most important resources an investigator can cultivate and turn to for assistance, particularly as it relates to the content and location of numbers on vehicles or parts. Domestic and foreign automobile manufacturers are generally most supportive of an investigator's inquiries, as are the Harley-Davidson Motorcycle Company and the John Deere, Case, and Caterpillar companies, which manufacture construction and farm equipment. This list is not meant to be exhaustive. Help will generally be given by any manufacturer when requested.

North American Export Committee

In an effort to stem the tide of stolen vehicles being exported from the country, the NICB, U.S. and Canadian Customs, Royal Canadian Mounted Police, Insurance Bureau Canada, and Miami-Dade Police Department in Florida, along with other law enforcement agencies, the insurance industry, and other interested parties, established the North American Export Committee in 1995. The committee investigates ways in which the exporting of stolen vehicles could be slowed without impeding commerce at port facilities.

Shipments of vehicles occur in two ways—some vehicles are rolled on and then rolled off a ship, and some are shipped in containers. These are quite different concepts requiring entirely different approaches. U.S. Customs is charged with the responsibility of checking the paperwork on vehicles to be exported, and the paperwork must be

◀ **FIGURE 15-7   Stolen vehicle recovered through gamma-ray scan** This stolen vehicle was located when the container in which it was found passed through a gamma ray scan at the Port of Miami. The container's manifest reported its contents as household goods.
(Courtesy of Miami-Dade Auto Theft Task Force)

received by Customs three days before a vehicle can be shipped. Only limited resources are devoted to this responsibility, however, because Customs is more concerned about property coming into the country and about commodities, other than vehicles, being exported. Customs' role has become even more limited after 9-11 being it was moved from the Treasury Department to the Department of Homeland Security and was reorganized. Customs inspectors are now part of the Bureau of Customs and Border Protection (CBP), while the law enforcement agents are part of the Bureau of Immigration and Customs Enforcement (ICE). Either Customs or local law enforcement checks the paperwork, physically examines as many of the vehicles as possible, and enters the VINs into a computer that transmits all those checked to databases with NICB, NCIC, OCRA (Mexican law enforcement database), a rental car database, and a motor vehicle liens database. Overnight, the list is run against the export, stolen, salvage, and VIN verification files of NICB and the other databases. The next morning, an exceptions report is available to the submitting agencies so that the "trouble messages" (problems) can be checked out before the vehicles are shipped. At the Port of Miami, trouble messages occur on approximately 20% of the exports. Such electronic reporting is now used at 80 ports in the United States.[30]

Containerized vehicles present a different set of problems. There are over 8 million containers exported from the United States in a year. No manifest is going to acknowledge that a container has one or more stolen vehicles. Checking a container, even if it meets a predetermined set of conditions called a profile, is hot, sweaty work—the unloading and reloading take hours—and it interferes with commerce. Stolen vehicles are usually found in the front or middle of a container, with goods packed all around them. To make enforcement more productive, an efficient, effective, and economic method of looking inside containers had to be found.

Science Applications International Corporation has developed a device that examines and photographs the contents of a container as it is passing through a gamma ray. In mid-1998, the corporation, in cooperation with the Miami-Dade County Multi-Agency Auto Theft Task Force and on behalf of the North American Export Committee, tested this equipment for a 90-day period at the Port of Miami in what is called the **Stolen Auto Recovery (STAR) System** (Figure 15-7). Before the 90 days were up, more than 7,700 containers were scanned in less than 6 seconds, each while they continued to move. A total of 630 vehicles were identified and six stolen vehicles were recovered, valued at $217,000. There were no false identifications, and the flow of commerce was not impeded. The units cost around $270,000, are very transportable, are easily installed in one day, and the gamma-ray scan preserves a video image of the contents of the container (Figure 15-8).

Because of the success of the STAR System, Florida committed to installing a total of ten systems across the state (at least three additional ports on Florida's east coast have been equipped.[31]

There are other technologies available. The use of X-ray equipment has been made safe. Portels is an X-ray system that scans from both the front and back of a container and gives an even higher definition picture than does the gamma-ray system. It is manufactured by AS&E and uses what is called "Backscatter" technology to allow X rays from both the front and rear portion of a container going through the system. The company also manufacturers a mobile system that can be mounted on a van with the equipment inside. The van can pull up to a stack of containers at a port and within seconds see sufficient contents to determine if vehicles or other items that may be contraband are inside. The equipment an "inspect" containers stacked three high.[32] VACIS is another system using X-ray technology. Customs and Border Protection has 40 of these units installed at U.S.

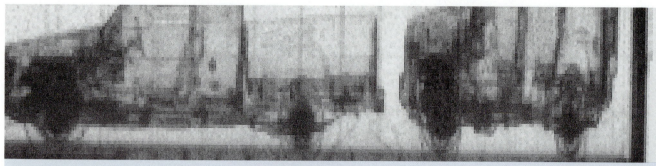

▲ **FIGURE 15-8   Gamma-ray scan showing two utility vehicles**
Advances in technology have assisted in the discovery of stolen vehicles being exported from the United States aboard ships. Science Applications International Corporation has developed a device that examines and photographs the contents of a container as it is passed through a gamma-ray scan. These units cost around $270,000, are very transportable, and are easily installed in one day's time.
(Courtesy of Miami-Dade Police Department)

ports and Canada; Mexico and Arizona have these units at border crossings.[33]

Canada has developed a task-force operation at the port in Vancouver, British Columbia, using this technology, with data transfer to the Canadian Insurance Crime Prevention Bureau. Early results were the recovery of 12 vehicles, all stolen from the province of Ontario.[34] The North American Export Committee also committed to the further development and implementation of the National Motor Vehicle Title Information System (NMVTIS).

National Equipment Register

The scope of the theft of heavy construction equipment has led manufacturers, dealers, and insurers to support the development of a national database of stolen equipment and provide the services of law enforcement specialists in the recovery of stolen equipment. The National Equipment Register (NER) facilitates the identification of lost and stolen equipment and the return of such equipment to owners and insurers and promotes due diligence in the purchase of used equipment, thereby deterring the trade in stolen equipment. The NER owner database has 7 million records, and its databases are connected to the databases of the Insurance Services Office, Inc. (ISO), the organization that provides all the computer services for the National Insurance Crime Bureau (NICB). The NER is available to law enforcement 24/7 at a toll-free telephone number for advice on where to locate product information numbers, check on the status of stolen equipment, and identify and locate owners of recovered equipment. If requested, NER can provide on-site assistance to law enforcement. The organization provides training seminars (e.g., equipment recovery) for law enforcement and theft prevention sessions for equipment owners.[35]

Indicators of Theft and Fraud

NICB publishes lists and pocket guides for law enforcement officials on the suspicious conduct of people or the status of vehicles that should cause the officer/investigator to make a closer inquiry to determine if a vehicle is stolen or if fraudulent conduct is afoot. Similarly, NER has recommendations about suspicious conduct of people or circumstances that should lead to further inquiry about possible heavy-equipment theft.

Locating and Handling Vehicles

In recent years, some investigators have gotten seriously ill while performing their jobs. Locating and handling the recovery of vehicles and parts can be very dangerous. Often, an investigator will climb or crawl around, through, and over wrecks, in a remote area of a salvage yard in order to locate or identify a vehicle part. Not only is the physical work dangerous, but, unknowingly, the investigator may be exposed to toxic waste, which can cause permanent physical damage. Gloves should be worn at all times, along with protective clothing and a mask or breathing device, when encountering the unknown. Similarly, when investigating a vehicle fire, investigators must take precautions, because toxic chemicals may be around that can cause serious long-term illness owing to exposure.

Vehicle Identification

Often the most difficult and time-consuming task facing an investigator is the identification of a recovered vehicle. Although there are a number of ways by which motor vehicles can be identified, including a description by year, make and model, or license number, these items are easily generalized or alterable. For the investigator, identification is made by numbers affixed to, or inscribed on, the vehicle.

Since 1954 American automobile manufacturers have used a **vehicle identification number (VIN)** instead of an engine number as the primary means of identification. However, before 1968, VINs, although usually inscribed on metal plates, were not uniformly located on vehicles, nor was there any standard method for attaching a **VIN plate** to a vehicle (Figure 15-9). On varying makes and models, VIN plates were affixed with screws or rivets or

Round-head "pop" rivet aluminum, stainless steel, or plastic

Used on early General Motors vehicles prior to 1965 after departure from "spot weld" method of attaching VIN plates. Still used by most foreign manufacturers.

"Rosette"-type rivet 6 petals, aluminum, or stainless steel

Used by General Motors Corp. since 1965, Chrysler Corp. since 1966, and Ford Motor Co. since 1970. There have been instances when round-head rivets were used at some assembly plants but only on very rare occasions.

"Rosette"-type rivet 5 petals, aluminum

Used by Toyota since 1985, except for the 1985 Corolla front-wheel drive, diesel, and 1989 and 1990 Cressida models, which have round aluminum rivets.

Sheet-metal screws

Screws are occasionally used to attach VIN plates on some imported vehicles.

Note: From 1974 to the present, some manufacturers have used VIN plates with both concealed and exposed rivets.

▲ **FIGURE 15-9   Attaching VIN plates**

(Source: National Insurance Crime Bureau, 2001 Passenger Vehicle Identification Manual [Palos Hills, IL: NICB, 2001], p. 46. Used with permission of NICB.)

were spot-welded on doors, doorposts, or dashes. Since 1968 VIN plates on almost all domestic and foreign cars have been attached to the left side of the dash on the instrument panel in such a fashion as to be visible through the windshield. Corvettes, prior to 1984, had the VIN

plate attached to the left-side windshield post. Tractor and semitrailer manufacturers still lack consistency in the placement of VIN plates, as do construction and farm equipment manufacturers in the placement of product identification numbers (PINs).

VIN plates still are attached by a variety of methods. Several foreign manufacturers use a round-head "pop" rivet made of aluminum, stainless steel, or some plastic material. A six-petal "rosette" rivet made of aluminum or stainless steel has been used on General Motors products since 1966, on Chrysler-manufactured vehicles since 1968, and on Ford units since 1970. Sheet-metal screws are still occasionally used on some imports (see Figure 15-9).

The use of a public VIN is designed to provide a positive, individualized means of identifying a motor vehicle. The 1981 adoption of a standardized 17-character VIN for all cars manufactured in or sold in the United States was certainly a forceful step in that direction. Previously, General Motors used a 13-digit VIN, Ford and Chrysler each used 11 characters, and imports used a host of other lengths. The standardized 17-character configuration is required of all imports manufactured for sale in the United States. The first 11 characters of the standardized VIN identify the country of origin, manufacturer, make, restraint system, model, body style, engine type, year, assembly plant, and a mathematically computed check digit that is used to verify all the other characters in the VIN. The last six characters are the sequential production number of the vehicle (Figures 15-10 and 15-11). The letters "I," "O," "Q," "U," and "Z" are not used so as to avoid confusion with similar-looking numbers.

Under the standardized 17-character system, the check digit is always the ninth character in the VIN and is calculated using the formula process illustrated on the worksheet depicted in Figure 15-12. By assigning specified numerical values to each letter and number, and then multiplying and dividing, the appropriate check digit can be determined and matched with the check digit on the VIN in question to ascertain whether there are any flaws in the construction of the VIN such as altered or transposed characters.

The tenth character of the VIN represents the year of manufacture or vehicle model year. The letter A was used to designate 1980, B for 1981, and so on. Without the letters "I," "O," "Q," "U," and "Z," the remaining 20 letters, followed by the use of numbers 1 to 9, establish a 30-year cycle before the possibility of an exactly duplicated VIN

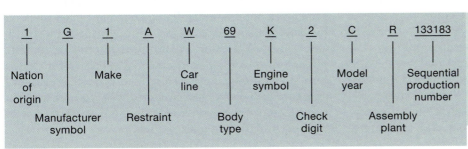

◄ **FIGURE 15-10**
Example of 17-digit VIN system

(Source: National Insurance Crime Bureau, 2001 Passenger Vehicle Identification Manual [Palos Hills, IL: NICB, 2001], p. 46. Used with permission of NICB.)

Code	Manufacturer	Code	Manufacturer
JH4	ACURA	1LN	LINCOLN
ZAR	ALFA ROMEO	SCC	LOTUS
1AM	AMERICAN MOTORS	ZAM	MASERATI
SCF	ASTON MARTIN	JM1	MAZDA
WAU	AUDI	WDB	MERCEDES BENZ
12A	AVANTI	1ME	MERCURY
ZBB	BERTONE	WF1	MERKUR
WBA	BMW	JA3	MITSUBISHI
1G4	BUICK	JN1	NISSAN
1G6	CADILLAC	1G3	OLDSMOBILE
1G1	CHEVROLET	VF3	PEUGEOT
1C3	CHRYSLER	ZFR	PININFARINA
2E3	EAGLE PREMIER	1P3	PLYMOUTH
JE3	EAGLE SUMMIT	1G2	PONTIAC
VF1	EAGLE MEDALLION	WPO	PORSCHE
SCE	DELOREAN	VF1	RENAULT
1B3	DODGE	SCA	ROLLS ROYCE
ZFF	FERRARI	YS3	SAAB
ZFA	FIAT	SAX	STERLING
1FA	FORD	JF1	SUBARU
KMH	HYUNDAI	JS3	SUZUKI
JHM	HONDA	JT2	TOYOTA
JAB	ISUZU	WVW	VOLKSWAGEN
SAJ	JAGUAR	YV1	VOLVO
1JC	JEEP		

◄**FIGURE 15-11**
World Manufacturer Identification Codes
(Courtesy of NICB, Palos Hills, Illinois)

could result from the normal manufacturing process (see Figure 15-13).

On some newer vehicles, VIN plates also have a bar code that contains all the information represented by the alphanumeric characters of the VIN (see Figure 15-14). The Federal Safety Certification Label found on the door post of most vehicles, has been required since 1970, and now includes the full VIN and bar code (see Figure 15-15).

Gray-Market Vehicles

When the U.S. dollar is strong overseas, it becomes economically feasible for individuals to purchase motor vehicles in other countries and have them shipped to the United States for sale, resale, or personal use. This effort can be profitable even though it may cost up to several thousand dollars apiece to "legalize" the vehicles for use in the United States. Since such vehicles are not manufactured for sale in this country, they are not constructed to meet U.S. emission control or safety standards, nor do they have a 17-character standardized VIN. If **gray-market vehicles** are brought into this country legally, a bond for each must be posted with U.S. Customs until such time as the appropriate modifications have been made to bring the vehicle into compliance with the U.S. Environmental Protection Agency (EPA) emission control requirements and the safety

standards promulgated by the U.S. Department of Transportation (DOT). When these steps have been accomplished and the modifications approved, the federal government will issue a replacement VIN plate that conforms with the 17-character standard.

Many vehicles are found operating on the streets and highways of this nation prior to, or without conforming to, the legal conversion requirements for gray-market vehicles. The operation of these vehicles is unlawful, and they are subject to seizure by U.S. Customs. The frequency of such seizures and the ability to ensure compliance with the EPA and DOT regulations are, of course, a direct function of the resources devoted to the programs and the priorities established. Not unlike state and local agencies, federal law enforcement programs also suffer from limited resources. In some years, gray-market imports have approached 100,000 vehicles.

The nonconforming VIN on a gray-market vehicle is sometimes nothing more than a Dymotape label stuck on the left-side dash and visible through the windshield. Often such a VIN is on a plate riveted in the appropriate place, but its construction does not satisfy the accepted format requirements. Learning the proper appearance and configuration of the accepted VIN format will aid investigators not only in identifying gray-market vehicles but also in detecting altered VINs.

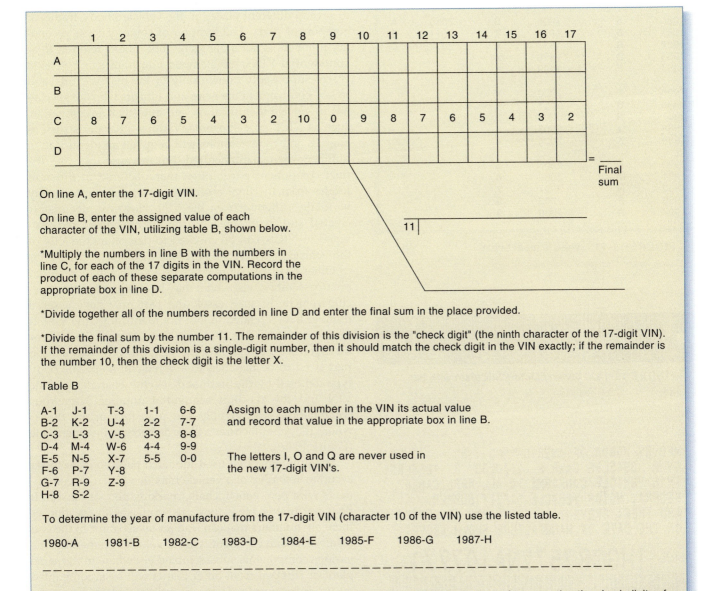

	1	2	3	4	5	6	7	8	9	10	11	12	13	14	15	16	17
A																	
B																	
C	8	7	6	5	4	3	2	10	0	9	8	7	6	5	4	3	2
D																	

= ___
Final sum

On line A, enter the 17-digit VIN.

On line B, enter the assigned value of each character of the VIN, utilizing table B, shown below.

11

*Multiply the numbers in line B with the numbers in line C, for each of the 17 digits in the VIN. Record the product of each of these separate computations in the appropriate box in line D.

*Divide together all of the numbers recorded in line D and enter the final sum in the place provided.

*Divide the final sum by the number 11. The remainder of this division is the "check digit" (the ninth character of the 17-digit VIN). If the remainder of this division is a single-digit number, then it should match the check digit in the VIN exactly; if the remainder is the number 10, then the check digit is the letter X.

Table B

A-1	J-1	T-3	1-1	6-6	Assign to each number in the VIN its actual value
B-2	K-2	U-4	2-2	7-7	and record that value in the appropriate box in line B.
C-3	L-3	V-5	3-3	8-8	
D-4	M-4	W-6	4-4	9-9	
E-5	N-5	X-7	5-5	0-0	The letters I, O and Q are never used in
F-6	P-7	Y-8			the new 17-digit VIN's.
G-7	R-9	Z-9			
H-8	S-2				

To determine the year of manufacture from the 17-digit VIN (character 10 of the VIN) use the listed table.

1980-A   1981-B   1982-C   1983-D   1984-E   1985-F   1986-G   1987-H

The decoding chart, shown above, may be photocopied to provide multiple blank work sheets for computing the check digits of the new 17-digit VIN's.

Example: 1981 Ford Mustang 1FABP12A4BR101093, final sum = 246

Check digit

$$11\overline{)246} \quad \begin{array}{r} 22 \\ \hline 246 \\ 22 \\ \hline 26 \\ 22 \\ \hline 4 \end{array}$$

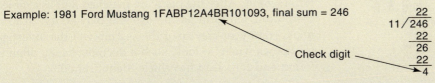

▲ **FIGURE 15-12** **Check-digit calculation formula**
(Courtesy of National Insurance Crime Bureau)

Attempts to Conceal the Identity of Vehicles

Salvage switches, cloning, defacing, or altering numbers are among the many ways of concealing the identity of a vehicle, thus making it difficult for even a trained investigator to accurately identify a vehicle.

Why is concealing a vehicle's identity so important? Simply put, if a vehicle cannot be positively identified, it cannot be proven that the vehicle was stolen, when it was stolen, or from whom it was stolen. Thus, one who is in possession of such a vehicle cannot be prosecuted as a thief. Even the most careful thief has extreme

1980	A	1995	S	2010	A
1981	B	1996	T	2011	B
1982	C	1997	V	2012	C
1983	D	1998	W		
1984	E	1999	X		
1985	F	2000	Y		
1986	G	2001	1		
1987	H	2002	2		
1988	J	2003	3		
1989	K	2004	4		
1990	L	2005	5		
1991	M	2006	6		
1992	N	2007	7		
1993	P	2008	8		
1994	R	2009	9		

▲ **FIGURE 15-13 Vehicle model year**
(Source: National Insurance Crime Bureau)

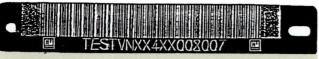

▲ **FIGURE 15-14 General Motors VIN plate with bar code**

MFD.BY HONDA OF AMERICA MFG.,INC. 2/92
GVWR 3945LBS GAWR F 2140LBS R 1885LBS
THIS VEHICLE CONFORMS TO ALL APPLICABLE
FEDERAL MOTOR VEHICLE SAFETY,BUMPER,
AND THEFT PREVENTION STANDARDS IN EFFECT
ON THE DATE OF MANUFACTURE SHOWN ABOVE:
V.I.N. 1HGCB7572NA107771
PASSENGER CAR MADE IN U.S.A.

▲ **FIGURE 15-15**
Federal Safety Certification Label with bar code
(Source: IAATI-SE newsletter, 1997.)

difficulty totally concealing the identity of a stolen vehicle.

Although it does happen, total inability to identify a vehicle is rare if the investigator doesn't hesitate to call on his or her own or others' knowledge, training, and experience. Knowing how and when to call on outside resources is important to the successful investigation. NICB special agents and other highly qualified law enforcement officers know how and where to look for clues to a vehicle's identity.

The public VIN on the dash is not the only number that identifies a specific vehicle. The VIN may be stamped in several different places on the vehicle's body, frame, or component parts. The location of some of these secondary numbers is not a big secret, but others, referred to as **confidential VINs,** are stamped into frames or bodies in places supposedly known only to the manufacturer and to law enforcement agencies and officers who are specialists in vehicle identification and auto-theft investigation, such as NICB special agents. Various other parts such as engines and transmissions will be given an identification number when manufactured, but, because they are distinct component parts, often manufactured in different locales from the final assembly plant, the numbers may be totally different from the VIN. However, documents created and maintained by the manufacturer, and provided to NICB, can be checked to determine the VIN of the vehicle in which the part was installed.

Other parts or components of a vehicle manufactured or subassembled elsewhere may be designed to fit a specific vehicle. In such cases, the part may have a serial number that is related to, but not identical to, the VIN. It may have a number that is a derivative of the VIN or that's formed from parts of the VIN, the same way a T-top may need to be matched to a vehicle of a specific body type denoted by the sixth and seventh characters of the VIN and the six-digit sequential number. Numerous combinations are possible and plausible; again, this is where the manufacturer's records become indispensable (Figure 15-16).

The numbers often used to match parts so as to foster accurate assembly of a vehicle may be written on components with pen, pencil, chalk, marking pen, or crayon. It does not matter what they are written with, as long as there are numbers that can lead an investigator to the end result of positively identifying a vehicle. Frequently, the various components subassembled elsewhere in the same plant or shipped from other plants will be accompanied by production order forms or written orders containing the VIN or a derivative number, which matches the parts for assembly. After the parts are matched and assembled, the production form has no use and may be left in some nook, cranny, or crevice of the assembly. If the investigator knows where to look, such a document may often be found and thus lead to vehicle identification.

Federal Safety Certification Label

All cars distributed in the United States since 1970 must have a **federal safety certification label.** This sticker, in addition to the required certification statements, also contains the vehicle's VIN. If the sticker is removed, it leaves behind a "footprint" that often shows the word "void." Obviously, if the correct sticker is in place and the correct public VIN shows through the windshield, the VINs should match.

The shape and size of the labels, as well as the materials from which they are constructed, vary among manufacturers. More common among domestic manufacturers is a paper label covered with a clear Mylar-type plastic.

◄ **FIGURE 15-16**
Motor number on motorcycle
The Suzuki motorcycle with the ground VIN was easily identified using the motor number (shown here).
(Courtesy of National Insurance Crime Bureau)

The label is bonded to the vehicle with a mastic compound. Construction is such that the label should be destroyed if removal is attempted. Some foreign manufacturers construct the certifying label out of thin metal and attach it with rivets. In either case, security against removal and replacement is not absolute. However, investigators are encouraged not to use the VIN on the safety certification label as absolute proof of vehicle identification. The federal safety sticker will be located on the driver's door or on the doorpost and, in recent years, also describes the vehicle and VIN on a barcode.

Federal Legislation

In an effort to reduce auto theft by easing the process of vehicle identification, Congress enacted the **Motor Vehicle Theft Law Enforcement Act** of 1984. Title I of the law requires that manufacturers place additional permanent identification numbers on up to 14 major parts of certain car lines. The car lines are selected every year for each manufacturer by the National Highway Traffic Safety Administration (NHTSA), the federal agency charged with setting the standards for the administration of the law. The car lines chosen each year for **parts marking** are those designated as high-theft lines. The parts requiring the additional identification are the major parts that are normally most sought after in a chop-shop operation and include: the engine; transmission; both front fenders; hood; both front doors; front and rear bumpers; both rear quarter panels; decklid, tailgate, or hatchback (whichever is applicable); and both rear doors (if present) (see Figure 15-17).

The numbers must either be inscribed on the designated parts or be printed on labels attached to the parts. Labels must tear into pieces if removed; if completely removed, they must leave a "footprint," which becomes visible through certain investigative techniques such as

using an ultraviolet light. The standards apply to the major parts of the designated new car lines and to replacement parts for the same car lines. The new-part labels must have the manufacturer's logo or other identifier printed on them and must use the full 17-character VIN for identification (see Figure 15-18); if, however, a VIN derivative of at least eight characters was being used to identify the engine and transmission on a particular covered line on the effective date of the law, that practice may continue. The identifier on covered replacement parts must carry the manufacturer's trade-mark, logo, or other distinguishing symbol, the letter "R" to reflect replacement, and the letters "DOT"

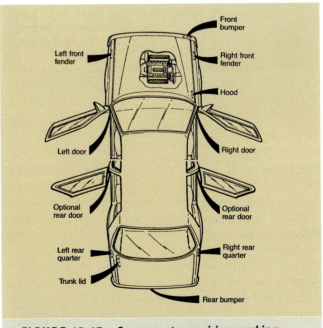

▲ **FIGURE 15-17   Components requiring marking**
(Courtesy of 3M Corporation)

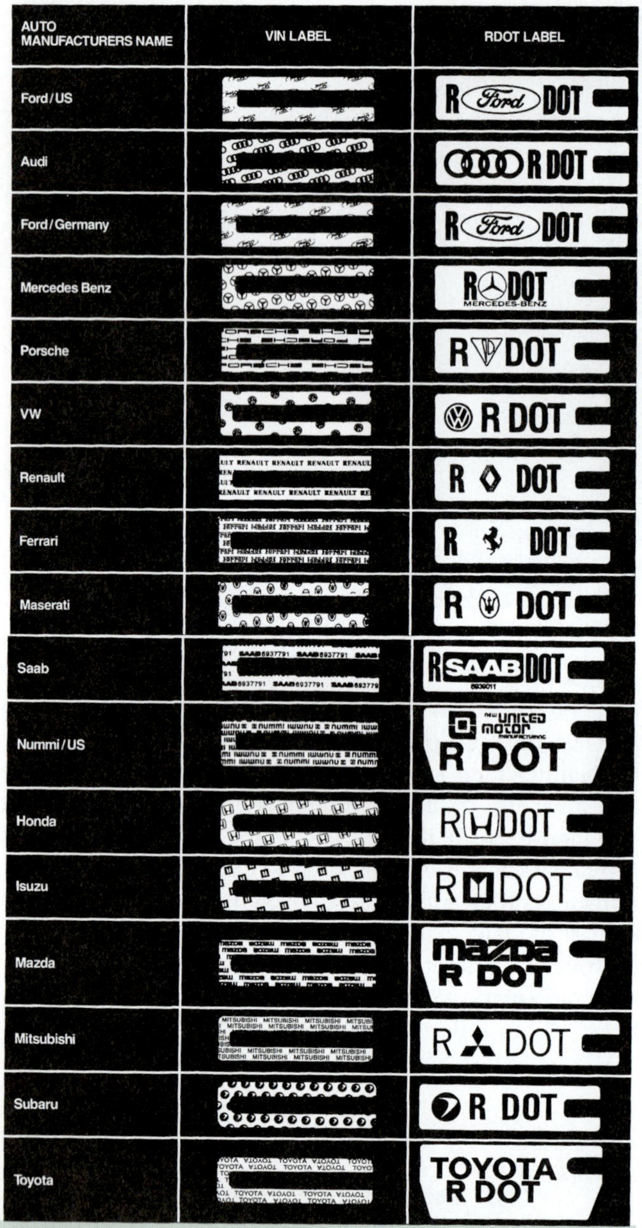

AUTO MANUFACTURERS NAME	VIN LABEL	RDOT LABEL
Ford/US		R Ford DOT
Audi		OOOO R DOT
Ford/Germany		R Ford DOT
Mercedes Benz		R ☆ DOT / MERCEDES-BENZ
Porsche		R ▽ DOT
VW		Ⓦ R DOT
Renault		R ◇ DOT
Ferrari		R 🐎 DOT
Maserati		R Ⓦ DOT
Saab		R SAAB DOT
Nummi/US		UNITED MOTOR / R DOT
Honda		R Ⓗ DOT
Isuzu		R Ⓜ DOT
Mazda		MAZDA R DOT
Mitsubishi		R ▲ DOT
Subaru		Ⓩ R DOT
Toyota		TOYOTA R DOT

▲ **FIGURE 15-18** Original- and replacement-part labels for selected manufacturers

(Courtesy of 3M Corporation)

(see Figure 15-18 again). The labels are to be affixed to the part on a surface that is not normally exposed to damage when the part is installed, adjusted, removed, or damaged in an accident. When the part is removed from the vehicle, the label or inscription must be visible without disassembling the part.

The law limits the application of the requirements to no more than 14 production car lines for any one manufacturer, and the costs to the manufacturer for compliance cannot exceed $15 per vehicle, excluding the costs of marking the engine and transmission.

There is an exemption in the law, called a "black-box" exemption, which allows NHTSA to exempt from compliance with the standards up to two car lines per year for any single manufacturer if the vehicle line is equipped by the manufacturer with a standard equipment antitheft device determined by NHTSA to be as effective in deterring and reducing vehicle theft as would be compliance with the parts-marking requirements of the theft prevention standard.

The intent underlying the passage of the law, the promulgation of standards, and the marking of original and replacement parts was to reduce auto theft by ostensibly making it more difficult for the thief to conceal the identity of major parts, by providing fewer significant parts that would be untraceable, and by making it easier for law enforcement investigators to identify stolen parts.

Having determined that the parts-marking program initiated in 1984 was effective, Congress passed the Anti-Car Theft Act of 1992, which continued and extended the program. The 1992 legislation also called for the U.S. Attorney General to conduct an initial evaluation, in 1997, of the effectiveness of the program in inhibiting chop-shop operations and deterring motor vehicle theft, with the objective of extending the parts-marking program to all lines (makes and models) by the end of 1997. The study recommended continuance of the program. The act required a long-range review of the program in 1999. In addition to evaluating whether chop-shop operations were impacted and theft had been deterred, the study was to determine whether the black-box exemptions were an effective substitute for parts marking in substantially reducing motor vehicle theft.

The act also required repair shops to check the VIN on all parts against a national file. Previously, this was the NCIC stolen-vehicle file, but the FBI, by direction of the act, established the National Stolen Parts Motor Vehicle Information System (NSPMVIS). Other provisions of the law made armed carjacking a federal crime; doubled the maximum penalty for importing, exporting, transporting, selling, or receiving a stolen vehicle; and directed U.S. Customs to spot-check vehicles and containers leaving the country.

To carry out the study mandate of the 1992 legislation, the Attorney General directed the National Institute of Justice to commission a study on the effectiveness of the parts-marking program. The report, released in 2000, concluded that the available evidence warrants application of the parts-marking standard to all motor vehicle lines. The decision was, in large measure, based on estimates and the absence of negative information. The study estimated that parts marking costs manufacturers about $5 per vehicle.[36] The study also concluded that between 33 and 158 fewer cars are stolen per 100,000 marked cars because of parts marking.[37] The research was unable to establish whether antitheft devices installed in vehicles were an effective alternative to parts marking.[38]

Manufacturers urged the Attorney General not to expand the program, but the Attorney General listened to law enforcement investigators who identified four ways that parts marking provides assistance. First, thieves often remove, alter, or obliterate the VIN plate and other numbers, but as long as one part number remains intact, the vehicle can be identified; this enables the owner to be identified and facilitates proving that the vehicle was stolen and securing an arrest. Second, auto-theft investigators in many jurisdictions have been given authority to seize parts or vehicles when markings have been removed or destroyed. Third, the absence of markings causes investigators to inquire further, and such investigations often lead to larger stolen-vehicle cases. Fourth, in jurisdictions requiring inspections of rebuilt vehicles prior to issuing a new certificate of title, a determination can be made as to whether stolen parts are being used in the rebuilding process.[39]

VIN Editing and Reconstruction

In any investigation, even when it appears that the VIN has not been altered or defaced, it is incumbent on the investigator to check the validity of the identifying numbers. Using the worksheet in Figure 15-12 will verify the correctness of the check digit only as compared with, and calculated from, the other 16 characters. A VIN edit computer program available at many law enforcement agencies and state motor vehicle regulatory offices can readily determine if the entered VIN is "good." If the VIN is invalid, computer programs can analyze the available information and at least narrow the valid possibilities of a correct VIN. Such programs replace what formerly was a long drawn-out manual process accomplished by checking manufacturers' records. VINASSIST, available from NICB, is one such program and is currently being used by over 10,000 insurers and law enforcement agencies. As noted earlier, the program edits, evaluates, and corrects vehicle identification numbers.

VIN Restoration

The restoration of manufacturers' serial numbers altered or obliterated from metal is a process that can be performed by an investigator with the proper material at hand (Figure 15-19). There is no mystery involved in number restoration as long as the investigator is willing to do the necessary preparation and has the patience to await results that are often slow in developing.

When a die is struck on metal, the molecules beneath the die are compressed, and it is on these compressed molecules that the restoration mediums are applied. The type of metal surface dictates which of the three primary methods of restoration—heat, acid, or acid and electricity—should be used. In the heat process, an oxygen-acetylene torch is used on cast iron only. An electrolytic process in which 5 to 6 volts of electricity at 2 to 3 amps are used in conjunction with a solution of hydrochloric acid is generally used on steel. For the etching of aluminum, one solution of potassium hydroxide and a second of hydrochloric acid and mercuric chloride are applied using a cotton or fiberglass swab.

Regardless of which type of surface is involved and which restoration process is used, the surface must be painstakingly prepared. All paint, oil, grease, or other foreign matter must first be removed by using any solution that will work, including paint remover and acetone (Figure 15-20). The surface is not to be scraped with a wire brush, knife, or any other tool, since one major purpose of preparation is to eliminate scratches and grind marks. Depending on how badly the surface is defaced, it may need to be polished with emery paper, a mill file, or a high-speed sanding or polishing disk to remove scratches or gouges. Polishing the surface to a mirrorlike finish is desirable. Sometimes careful preparation of the surface will make all or some of the numbers visible.

◀ **FIGURE 15-19**
Obliterating a VIN
From the appearance of the marks, the VIN was ground off with an electric grinder.
(Courtesy of National Insurance Crime Bureau)

◄ FIGURE 15-20
Vehicle Identification Number restored after use of acid on this aluminum part.
This restoration identified the vehicle, which led to the identity of the owner from whom the vehicle was stolen.
(Courtesy of National Insurance Crime Bureau)

Documenting the surface before beginning the restoration process is advisable. This can be done by photographing the area to be restored, dulling the shine with the use of fingerprint powder or carbon paper, and then taking a tape lift of the area (similar to lifting a fingerprint from a metal surface) and/or making a large-scale drawing of the area. It is always advisable to check with the manufacturer to ascertain the structure of the numbers used on a factory identification number if it is not already known. For example, the investigator should ask whether Os are rounded or squared and if 3s have rounded or flat tops. Such information can assist the investigator in determining whether visible numbers are valid.

If the heat process is to be used on cast iron, the ignited torch should be slowly moved back and forth over the area to be processed and gradually brought closer to the surface in a manner that will not crack the block. When the top of the blue cone of the flame is being moved back and forth about half an inch above the surface, the surface will soon reach a cherry-red color. When that happens, the torch should gradually be drawn away from the surface until it is about 6 inches away, all the while being slowly moved back and forth. After the surface has cooled, it should be very lightly polished with emery paper to remove the carbon deposits. The restored numbers should show up as a lighter color than the surrounding metal. If no numbers appear, either too much of the metal was removed and restoration will not produce results or the surface was not heated to a high-enough temperature, in which case the process should be repeated.

In the electrolytic process of restoring numbers on steel, two pieces of number 12 or 14 braided wire, 18 to 24 inches in length with alligator clips attached to the ends, along with a 6- or 12-volt battery, are needed. Direct current may be used if a battery is not convenient. One wire should be connected to the positive pole, with the other end grounded somewhere near the area to be restored. The other wire, connected to the negative pole, should have a swab dipped in acid solution attached to the other end; the swab should be moved one way only over the surface until any numbers are restored. The acid, speeded by the electricity, eats the surrounding metal surface until the numbers (if not totally destroyed) are revealed. In this and all acid-processing techniques, drawings or sketches should be made as individual numbers or letters are revealed because they may fade before more heavily ground characters are restored. Once the process is completed, the surface should be neutralized with water, dried, and coated with oil to prevent rust. In using any acid, good ventilation is imperative.

Good ventilation is also necessary in the acid process of restoring numbers on aluminum. Using potassium hydroxide solution and a swab, the surface area should be brushed in one direction for about 1 minute. The surface should then be dried and brushed with a solution of hydrochloric acid and mercuric chloride in the same direction for 2 minutes. The surface should be dried again. This process constitutes one application. Often, results will appear after two to four applications, but repeated applications may be made as often as necessary.[40]

Investigation of Vehicle Fires

Along with the general increase in crimes in the United States has come an increase in automobile fires. Many of the criminal fires occur when stolen vehicles have been stripped of valuable parts and the rest is burnt to destroy the evidence. However, as in other fire investigations, the investigator first must eliminate natural and accidental causes of fire.

◀ **FIGURE 15-21**
Photographing and documenting burned vehicle
A fire investigator photographs and documents the burned vehicle as part of his investigation. This process is essential in preparing for any subsequent prosecution of the arsonist. (© AP/Wide World Photos)

Before beginning the physical investigation of a vehicle fire scene, the investigator must understand that the crime scene examination includes both the vehicle and the area in which it was burned. Hence, the investigation must follow established principles by first recording the scene. Photographs should be taken immediately, before there is any disturbance of the crime scene (Figure 15-21). Measurements must be taken to establish the exact location of the vehicle in relationship to fixed objects, crossroads, houses, and so on. A description should be noted regarding the terrain, nearby roadways, and weather conditions (including prevailing wind directions).

A thorough search should be made of the area for tire-tread marks, footprints, cans, bottles, other containers, unusual residue or materials, old tires, matches, or any other item that may be related to the case. Samples should be taken of soil, which may contain evidence of flammable liquids. When found, each item should be photographed before being moved, and then it should be properly packaged and marked as evidence.

An inspection of the salvage must be completed for information on the origin and possible motive for the fire. Generally, investigators inspect the burnt automobile before contacting the owner, and the inspection is made as soon after the fire as possible. The inspection starts where the fire apparently originated. In accidental fires, this will normally be the part of the vehicle that is the most badly damaged from the intensity of the heat. Accidental fires usually spread in diminishing degrees from the point of origin according to prevailing conditions. Conditions include direction and velocity of wind and/or materials on which flames feed, such as gasoline in the tank, woodwork, or other similarly flammable parts of the vehicle. When there are significant variations

in these patterns, arson emerges as a possibility. Arson fires started with flammable materials usually show intense heat in more than one place. The investigator should carefully note the extent of the fire and its path. This information may prove valuable in the later questioning of the owner or witnesses.

The car also should be inspected for the removal of equipment such as stereo, heater, air horns, fog lights, and so forth. Notice should also be made of other irregularities such as old tires on new cars or missing spare tires.

Inspection of the Fuel System

The investigator should determine whether the cap to the gas tank was in place at the time of the fire. Sometimes gasoline to start the fire is siphoned from the tank, and the cap is carelessly left off. If the cap is blown off, it will show effects of an explosion. The drain plug in the bottom of the tank should be checked. In addition, if it was removed or loosened before the fire, there might be evidence of fresh tool marks, especially pliers marks, on it.

The gas lines should be examined for breaks between the tank and the fuel pump. Breaks should be examined for tool marks. Some arsonists disconnect the line below the tank to obtain gasoline to start the fire and fail to replace the line.

Gasoline to start the fire is sometimes obtained by disconnecting the line from the fuel pump and running the starter. If the fuel pump is melted, there should be evidence of fire on the sidepans. If the fuel pump was disconnected to allow the gasoline to run out and then be set on fire, there may be carbon deposits inside the gas line at the fuel pump.

The investigator should establish whether parts of the fuel pump are missing. If key parts of the fuel system are missing, and the owner says that the vehicle was running at the time of the fire, then there is strong reason to suspect arson. This is true regardless of whether the vehicle is equipped with a mechanical pump in a low-pressure carbureted system or an electric pump in a high-pressure fuel-injected system.

Inspection of the Electrical System

A short circuit in the electric wiring is the most common excuse offered for automobile fires. The chances of a modern automobile's burning up from a short in the wiring are negligible. Engineers have virtually eliminated this hazard. If a fire in fact did start from malfunctions in the electrical system, there generally is enough evidence to substantiate it.

The wires near where the fire started should be inspected. If the wires are not melted completely, a short can be located. A short melts the strands of wire apart and causes small beads of melted wire to form on the ends. Wires that are burned in two have sharp points. If the fire started in an electrical system, the system must be close to a flammable substance for the fire to spread. If a fire started from a short while the motor was running, the distributor points will be stuck or fused.

Inspection of the Motor, Radiator, and Parts under and near the Hood

The only possible place for an accidental fire to start at this location is around the fuel pump or carburetor and at the wiring. Any evidence of a fire on the front lower part of the motor not attributable to these parts indicates the use of flammables. If lead is melted from any lower or outside seams of the radiator, this is strong evidence of flammables. The fan belt does not usually burn in an accidental fire.

Gasoline on the motor sometimes causes the rubber cushions for the front of the motor to show evidence of fire. This evidence does not occur in accidental fires.

The radiator should also be checked. A badly burned lower right corner indicates that the gas line from the fuel pump to the carburetor was disconnected, the starter was run to pump out gasoline through the fuel pump, and then the gasoline was set on fire.

Inspection of the Body

The body of the car is usually so badly burned as to afford little evidence. However, signs of the intensity of heat sometimes point to the use of an inflammable. An excessive amount of flammable material may run through the floor of the car and burn underneath, causing oil or gasoline soot to form on the underside of the car. An examination should be made for this soot. If the hood was raised during the fire, the paint on the top panels may be blistered but not be burned off where the two panels touched. If the wind was blowing from the rear of the car to the front, the paint should be burned for almost the length of the hood. The radiator core will be burned, but there will not have been enough fire at the rear of the car to do much damage to the

gasoline tank. If the paint on the hood is burned only an inch or so from the rear toward the front, this would indicate that the wind was blowing from the front of the car toward the rear, in which case the gasoline tank may be badly damaged but the radiator will be intact.

Contact with the Owner

An investigation must be made of the car owner for evidence of intent, motive, and opportunity, and the owner must be questioned to establish his or her knowledge of the fire and to verify information. Before interviewing the owner, the investigator should learn as much as possible about him/her. This information may prove quite useful during the interview. The importance of preplanning the interview cannot be overemphasized. The more facts the investigator has available, the greater the probability of a successful clearance or later conviction.

Information should be obtained from the owner about the details of the purchase, such as date, cost, trade-in, down payment, amount of mortgage due, payments past due, name of salesperson, and so forth. The investigator should also inquire about the general condition of the car at the time of the fire and ask about defects, mileage, presence or absence of unusual equipment, and recent repairs.[41]

PREVENTION PROGRAMS

Each year, new and innovative approaches to the prevention and the detection of crime and the apprehension of offenders are developed. Some of these are related to investigative techniques, whereas others are high-tech equipment developments that are designed to reduce the vehicle theft problem or assist law enforcement officers in their efforts. Other strategies are available to reduce the incidence of fraud.

Auto Theft

Law enforcement officers and agencies in a number of jurisdictions now rely on integrated communications and computer networks of the FBI, state, and local police to identify and locate stolen vehicles. One unique system uses a small device called a micromaster, which is installed at random in a vehicle's electrical system. The micromaster is a microprocessor-controlled transceiver with its own unique code.

If a vehicle is stolen, the owner reports the theft to the local police in the usual way. The owner also tells the police that the vehicle is equipped with a micromaster. The police then announce through normal channels and the National Crime Information Center that a micromaster-equipped vehicle has been stolen. A computer then activates a transmitter that sends a signal with the stolen vehicle's own code. (The present system can manage up to 8 billion discrete micromaster codes.) The signal activates the micro-master's transceiver, and starts sending a signal identifying it as a stolen vehicle. The activation and tracking of the micromaster signal is under the control of law enforcement authorities. They have a homing device or, more recently used GPS tracking system that gives them information about the location of the car. The system also allows police officers to identify micromaster signals and determine whether the stolen car has been involved in a crime.[42] Lojack is probably the best known system in use. Some of these tracking systems rely on signal relay towers, while others use a satellite-enhanced global positioning system (GPS) method of tracking. The law enforcement vehicles are equipped with tracking computers that bring up street maps that pinpoint the location and direction of travel within a very close proximity.

Many vehicles are now being manufactured with anti-theft locks, starter disengagement systems (called *ignition kill switches*), and various other devices in an attempt to reduce the attractiveness of a particular model to the thief. Some of these are models that qualify for the black-box exemption to the labeling standards established under the guidelines of the Motor Vehicle Theft Law Enforcement Act of 1984.

In recent years, a number of private concerns have begun marketing antitheft devices that can be used effectively on older vehicles. It should be noted at the outset that no device can absolutely prevent motor vehicle theft, and one should look askance at any product or brand of product that is represented to be an absolute theft preventive.

Theft deterrent devices are of two types—passive or active. With a **passive system,** the driver does not need to do anything to activate the system, though he or she may be required to do something to deactivate the system. An **active system** requires that the operator do something every time the vehicle is driven or parked.

Audible alarm systems may be either passive or active and may be effective if anyone pays attention when an alarm is activated. Because some systems activate easily when someone passes the vehicle, a strong wind blows, or lightning strikes half a mile away, many people pay little attention, beyond a passing glance, to a vehicle with an alarm blaring. Escape from the vicinity of the noise is more important than determining if a theft is occurring. The alarms are treated more as an annoyance than as a theft deterrent.

A boot is an active device installed under a front tire that prevents the vehicle from being moved until the boot is removed. Other active devices can key lock the trans-mission or the brakes.

"Collars," which are usually constructed of steel or an alloy, deter penetration of the steering column bowl asso-ciated with the General Motors and Chrysler "Saginaw steering column." Passive collars are generally recom-mended over those that require driver interaction.

Many communities have instituted decal "alert" pro-grams that provide decals for vehicles registered with the local law enforcement agency and authorize any law enforcement officer to stop the vehicle and question the driver if the vehicle is observed on the streets during cer-tain hours (such as 2 A.M. to 6 A.M.).

A fuel shut-off device, which blocks the fuel line, may be activated by removal of the ignition key or by the throwing of a switch.

A case-hardened steering-column ignition lock that can-not be removed using a conventional slide hammer or lock puller can be effective, as can a case-hardened steel protec-tive cap that fits over the ignition lock to prevent extraction of the ignition lock cylinder. The cap fastens to a steel col-lar that fits around the steering post and over the ignition lock. The ignition key fits through a slot in the cap.

Several manufacturers install a microchip or transpon-der in the ignition key that must be electronically read when inserted into the ignition in order for the vehicle to start. Early versions of some of these systems had only a few combinations, which could easily be defeated if a thief could procure a set of masters with all the combina-tions. However, General Motors' PASS-KEY III and Ford's Passive Anti-Theft System (PATS), as well as the newer systems on many other domestic and foreign-made brands, use much more advanced and sophisticated elec-tronic systems that are deterring theft.

A steel or an alloy post, rod, or collar may attach to the steering wheel, which can be extended and locked in place. The device prevents the steering wheel from mak-ing full rotations. This type of active device can be an effective deterrent to theft if used properly, but it is inef-fective if the operator of the vehicle forgets or considers it an inconvenience to install it each time the vehicle is left unattended.

VIN etching is a process that helps identify vehicles recovered by the police after a theft has occurred. As noted earlier, thieves often attempt to conceal the identity of stolen vehicles by grinding numbers. When the VIN is permanently etched, using acid, on all the vehicle's win-dows, the identifying numbers are often over-looked by the thief or require that the thief remove all the window glass to prevent identification, a major task a thief may not be willing to undertake.

Some programs focus on the responsibilities of vehicle owners to do their part in preventing vehicle theft. The Michigan affiliate of the American Automobile Associa-tion implemented a law providing that if a car is stolen and the keys are anywhere in the passenger compart-ment, the owner, in addition to absorbing his or her insurance deductible, also absorbs an extra $500 plus 10% of the value of the vehicle. The total amount is deducted from the amount of the insurance payment made on the theft loss claim. The responsibilities of owners are also reflected in a survey initiated by the NICB that consists of scoring answers to some questions and taking neces-sary preventive actions on the basis of the total score. This is called a layered approach to theft deterrence (see Figure 15-22).

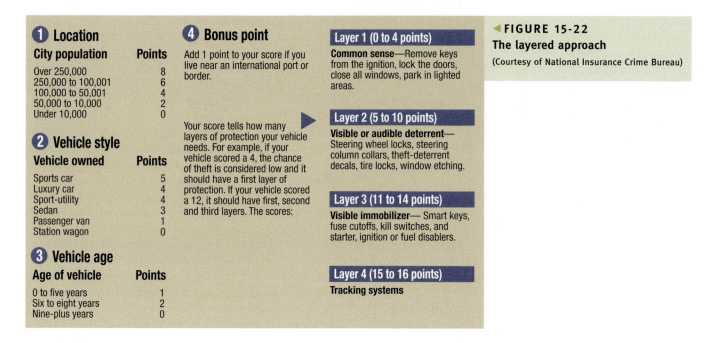

◄ FIGURE 15-22
The layered approach
(Courtesy of National Insurance Crime Bureau)

Some other prevention techniques include these:

- If a lighter receptacle is used for a radio, telephone, or radar detector, remove the item when leaving the vehicle and reinsert the lighter. Thieves look for empty receptacles.
- Always lock the vehicle and remove the keys.
- Lock valuables in the trunk. Do not leave personal identification or credit cards in the vehicle.
- Do not leave a vehicle running while unattended.
- Photocopy registration and insurance papers and carry them on your person, not in the glove compartment.
- Park in a garage or in a well-lighted, heavily traveled area.
- When parking at a curb, turn the wheels toward the curb and use the emergency brake. This makes the vehicle harder to steal.
- Do not hide spare keys in or on the vehicle.
- Write the name of the owner and the VIN in crayon under the hood and in the trunk.
- Drop business cards down window channels into door interiors. This will make later identification easier.

Theft of vehicles from new- and used-car dealers is not a new phenomenon. Sometimes the dealership knows a vehicle is missing, such as when a vehicle taken on a test drive is not returned. Other times, if an inventory is large, a vehicle may be stolen overnight and not missed for several days. Key control is an essential crime prevention practice for a dealership. Keys should be kept in a locked cabinet with only a few people having access. Keys that are out for demonstration or sales purposes must be monitored. Customers should never be allowed to test-drive a vehicle without a salesperson going along. Display lots should be well lighted, and barriers should be erected that permit

access and good observation from outside but are sufficient to deter theft at night and when the dealership is closed. Officers who are familiar with the concepts of crime prevention through environmental design should be consulted.

Car Rentals

Car rental companies are generally knowledgeable about motor vehicle theft and techniques of prevention, but an investigator would be wise to understand some basics. In daily rental, the company is handing over the keys of a car to a person no one in the company has seen before or knows anything about. The rental agreement should be completely filled out, and the picture and information on the renter's driver's license should be carefully checked to make sure it matches the description of the person to whom the vehicle is being rented.

Rental companies generally require a credit card even for a cash rental. This not only serves as a good indication that the customer is a responsible person but also helps ensure that the contract will be paid. The employee of the rental company should make sure the credit card is current and check it against the driver's license to make sure the same name is on both documents.

Theft of rental vehicles generally occurs when a vehicle is not returned after it has been rented. At least one national rental company is in the process of installing tracking systems, as described earlier, which are traceable using radio-wave or GPS systems.

Heavy Equipment

Tiny transponders that act as identification devices are now available. The device can be glued anywhere on the vehicle. Some agencies are experimenting with injecting the transponder into tires of construction equipment. If attempts are made to completely conceal or alter a stolen vehicle's identity, a receiver can accurately distinguish the vehicle from all others.

Owners of construction equipment are also encouraged to take the following actions:

- Use security devices such as ignition locks, stabilizer arm locks, and fuel shut-off valves.
- Record all product identification numbers, and participate in equipment identification programs.
- Photograph all equipment, paying particular attention to unique features such as dents, decals, and scratches, to aid in later identification.
- Leave equipment in well-lighted and fenced areas at job sites and equipment yards.
- Know the location of all construction equipment at all times.
- Keep law enforcement informed about where equipment is located and how long it will be maintained in a particular location.
- Take extra precautions on weekends. Most equipment thefts occur between 6 P.M. on Friday and 6 A.M. on Monday.
- Do not leave keys in any equipment that uses keys, and lock all machines that can be locked when not in use.
- Immediately report suspicious activity (such as a stranger taking photographs of equipment) to law enforcement officials.

Other methods of reducing or preventing theft of off-road equipment are available. Programs are available through private enterprise whereby heavy equipment can be registered, with each piece being assigned its own identification number. The equipment is "decaled" with its own number welded on at several locations. Should a law enforcement officer become suspicious, the dispatcher can call a toll-free number and remain on the line as the company calls the owner to verify the location of the equipment.

Fraud

The prevention of fraud can best be accomplished by knowing some things about both the insured and the vehicle. "Know your insured" is always sound advice for an insurance agent. Getting good identification on the person, learning why the person selected a particular agent or agency, and finding out how the insured learned of the agent or agency can all be useful in helping to determine whether the act of insuring is legitimate. Knowing about the insured vehicle is equally important in the fight against fraud.

Perhaps the most profound fraud prevention effort ever initiated is the preinsurance inspection program, particularly when photographs are required. Deceptively simple in concept and application, it is amazing that fewer than half a dozen states have even considered, much less adopted, mandatory legislation. The concept requires that before a vehicle can be insured, it must be physically inspected by a representative or an agent acting on behalf of the insurer.

A simple inspection requirement can immediately eliminate or substantially reduce two of the most prolific tactics in committing insurance fraud. First, it virtually eliminates the false-vehicle theft, which is normally based on insuring a "paper," or "phantom," car—in other words, a vehicle that does not exist—and subsequently reporting it stolen in order to file against and recover on an insurance policy. Second, a well-written preinsurance report can substantially reduce fraudulent claims about theft of expensive equipment on a vehicle or claims that damage actually present before issuance of the policy occurred when the substandard vehicle either was involved in a reported accident or was stolen.

Photographs supporting an inspection report make the program particularly effective, and color photographs are even more revealing. Photographs can show the exact condition of a vehicle at the time a policy was issued so as to dispel fraudulent damage claims filed later. It is recommended that at least two photographs be taken from diagonal corners so that one picture shows the front and one side of the vehicle and the other photo shows the rear and other side. These two photos will eliminate false damage claims, but there remains the question of proving that the photos are of the insured vehicle and not simply one of the same year, make, and model. To resolve this concern, a few of the jurisdictions having inspection programs require that a third photograph be taken of the federal motor vehicle safety certification label (often called the EPA label), which is usually found on the left door. This label contains, among other information, the vehicle identification number, which, as noted earlier, is the specific identifier for that vehicle as distinguished from all other vehicles. This reverifies the number contained in the written report, thus avoiding or explaining inadvertent omissions or the accidental transposition of numbers.

An inexpensive instant-developing camera and film can be used for the program. In 1977, New York became the first state to enact legislation mandating photographic inspection prior to the issuance of insurance policies. The program initially required that two photographs be taken from a 180-degree angle, but the law was amended in 1986 to require the third photo of the federal motor vehicle safety certification label. Massachusetts was the next state to adopt a preinsurance inspection program. Legislation followed thereafter in New Jersey and Florida, although not all these states have equally effective legislatively mandated programs. In addition to these states, two insurance companies have their own photographic inspection programs. Neither GEICO nor State Farm will insure a noninspected vehicle.

Is the program effective? Although it is difficult to measure how much crime (insurance fraud) is deterred by a photo inspection program, it has been estimated that in the state of New York, reduction in costs and in insurance fraud claims has saved well over $100 million, and these savings have been passed on to insurance buyers through premium reductions. Although insurance premiums have not actually been reduced in New York, the overall increase in premiums in that state has amounted to less than half of the national average.[43]

ODOMETER FRAUD

One of the most costly consumer frauds of modern times is **odometer fraud,** also known by various other names, including odometer tampering, rollbacks, and clocking. The National Highway Traffic Safety Administration estimates that over 3 million cars are clocked each year and that the cost of this fraud to American consumers surpasses $3 billion annually.

The most susceptible vehicles to odometer tampering are those that are relatively new with exceptionally high mileage. Of the total number of passenger cars sold in the United States each year, approximately half are sold to car rental or leasing companies or to others for business use. Each year, at least 4 million of these late-model high-mileage cars are replaced. Those that are taken off lease or are no longer used for business purposes find their way into the used-car market.

The reason for odometer rollbacks is to increase the value of used vehicles on the market. Obviously, a car with fewer miles should bring a higher price than one with high mileage. It has been conservatively estimated that on a small or intermediate-size car, the sales value increases $50 for each 1,000 miles that the odometer is set back; in larger vehicles, the value increases to around $65 per 1,000 miles the odometer reading is reduced. Thus, a late-model car that is clocked from 70,000 miles to 30,000 miles can increase its value to the seller by $2,000 to $2,600. This amounts to a nice additional profit for persons inclined to indulge in such deceitful conduct.

Besides the obvious profits to the seller of clocked vehicles, the costs to the purchaser can be even greater in the form of potential unanticipated safety problems and increased repair costs. Since cars are generally the largest purchase made by people after the cost of a home, the condition of a car and the anticipated costs for repair and maintenance figure prominently in the decision of whether to buy a particular car. But when the odometer has been clipped, mileage is not a dependable guide for estimating potential maintenance costs, since such a vehicle will be more costly to maintain and more likely to need expensive repairs. If the purchaser-owner is unable to afford the higher costs, the quality of maintenance and repairs may suffer, along with the safety and roadworthiness of the vehicle.

Because of the proliferation of this fraud, most states have created some type of investigative unit to deal with odometer tampering by accepting complaints from citizens and determining if there is any basis for enforcement action. When examining a late-model low-mileage vehicle that is suspected of being clocked, the investigator should check

for extensive wear on the brake pedal, the driver's seat, and the seals around the trunk. Does the extent of wear conform with the claimed mileage? A check should be made for service stickers on the door, on the doorpost, and under the hood. If present, a date and odometer reading may be present; missing stickers may suggest tampering. The odometer wheels should be in alignment, should not rotate freely, and should not be scratched or nicked. Any of these conditions may be indicative of a rollback and warrant further inquiry. The investigator should order a vehicle history file through the state's motor vehicle titling agency and then check with each successive owner (including individuals, dealers, and auctioneers), obtain all odometer disclosure statements, piece together an odometer history, and attempt to determine if there has been a rollback. If a rollback seems likely, the investigator should determine the possessor of the vehicle when it was clocked. Standard investigative techniques should then be applied.

Title fraud is as big a part of the odometer rollback problem as is the act of clocking. Title alteration, discarding of title reassignment forms to complicate the tracing of ownership, manufacturing of false reassignments, and title laundering are criminal acts that violators often engage in to support and cover up odometer rollbacks.

To mandate better record keeping, reduce the opportunity for odometer tampering, and assist law enforcement in the investigation of cases, Congress enacted the **Truth in Mileage Act** in 1986. This act, along with amendments made in several subsequent years, attempts to improve the paper trail of odometer readings by requiring more tightly controlled documentation and recording of odometer readings each time ownership of a vehicle changes. The law attempts to close loopholes that permit the inception of fraudulent title schemes and to reduce the incidence of title washing between jurisdictions by requiring all states to adhere to strict record-keeping criteria, thus avoiding schemes to create confusing paper trails that intentionally avoid jurisdictional boundaries of courts and law enforcement agencies.

MARINE THEFT

Marine theft is a serious problem to the boating community (Figure 15-23). It includes the theft of boats, boat trailers, outboard motors, jet skis, and all equipment associated with boating or water activities. Marine theft is a "shadow crime." It is real but difficult to define because of the lack of accurate statistical information. The main reporting mechanism, the *Uniform Crime Report* (UCR), compiled and reported annually by the Federal Bureau of Investigation, enters the theft of an outboard motor in the burglary index, the theft of a boat trailer in the vehicle file, and other related thefts in different categories. As a result, the magnitude of the marine theft problem is hidden in other crime indexes. Marine insurance theft data are similarly disjointed because there are many types

◄ **FIGURE 15-23**

Marine police on lookout
Marine theft, which includes theft of boats, trailers, and all associated equipment, is a serious problem in the boating community. In communities that have extensive waterways, local police often have a marine patrol unit that provides routine patrol and investigates theft of marine equipment.
(© Bonnie Kamin)

of policies—home owners', business, inland marine, yacht—that provide coverage for marine equipment. Nevertheless, it is estimated that nationwide losses resulting from marine theft exceed $250 million annually.

The majority of thefts occur from homes, businesses, or dry storage facilities. A boat and outboard motor on a boat trailer can be stolen in a matter of seconds by a thief who simply backs up to the trailer, hooks up, and drives away. Although locking mechanisms are available for boat trailers and may deter the amateur thief, such devices are easily overcome by the professional.

Theft by water is accomplished simply by towing the boat away with another boat or by starting the motor and driving away. Boats powered by outboard motors, under 25 horsepower, usually do not have keyed ignition switches. However, even on larger boats, a dozen master keys will start virtually any marine motor, whether outboard or inboard.

Approximately 87% of all boats stolen are under 20 feet in length. Of these, boats of 16 feet and less constitute 65% of the thefts. The National Crime Information Center reports over 27,000 boat thefts entered into the computer system. Law enforcement experts agree that most thefts are not investigated thoroughly (if at all) because of the difficulty investigators experience understanding marine equipment identification numbers and the lack of available ownership information.

Because of the absence of accurate statistical data, law enforcement is somewhat hampered in its efforts to address the problem. Consequently, there is a general lack of knowledge about marine theft and a resulting lack of commitment of resources to address the problems. In many agencies, marine theft reports are assigned to the auto theft or burglary unit and are treated as low-priority items.

Why are boats stolen? The number-one reason is profit. Marine theft is a high-profit, low-risk crime. Most often, a boat, motor, and trailer are stolen and sold as a package at a fair market value. To reduce the possibility of identification, some organized theft rings operate a chop shop, switching stolen motors, trailers, and boats or selling them separately.

There is also a lucrative market for the exportation of stolen outboard motors. In Central and South America, a used outboard motor will sell for more than a new motor in the United States. In addition, as in auto theft, insurance fraud may be involved in 25% or more of the reported marine thefts.

The increase in marine theft has often been linked by the media to drug trafficking. Experts tend to disagree. If, in fact, 87% of the boats stolen are under 20 feet in length, it is unlikely that these are being used for drug trafficking. Boats 30 feet and longer could very well be involved in drug trafficking, but such thefts constitute only 3% of the problem. Of course, larger boats are also targets for professional thieves because of their high value. On the other hand, there may be some legitimate linkage between the theft of outboard motors and the drug problem. A 300-horsepower outboard motor, which retails for over $15,000, can be sold without any ownership documents.

Most small boats are stolen not by professionals but for the personal use of the thief or, occasionally, for joyrides. This is particularly true in the theft of personal watercraft. Approximately 20% of all boat thefts involve personal watercraft stolen by juveniles for their own use. Only occasionally are boats stolen to be used as transportation in other crimes, such as burglary of a waterfront home or business.

Hull Identification

Effective November 1, 1972, the Federal Boating Safety Act of 1971 required boats to have a 12-character **hull identification number (HIN).** Before this, boat manufacturers assigned whatever numbers were needed for their own production records. The HIN was subsequently codified by federal regulation. The promotion of boating safety was the original purpose for the HIN. It enabled the U.S. Coast Guard to identify "batches" of boats produced by a manufacturer that failed to meet certain production standards. This consumer protection function soon became secondary after titling and registering authorities began using the

HIN assigned to a boat to identify ownership in much the same manner as the VIN is used for a motor vehicle.

Although manufacturers are required to affix each HIN to the outside of the boat's transom in a "permanent manner" so that any alteration or removal will be evident, in reality this is rarely enforced. Many manufacturers attach the HIN using a plastic plate pop-riveted to the transom. This can be easily removed and replaced with a false HIN. Some manufacturers of fiberglass boats place the HIN on the outer layer of the gelcoat using a "Dymo label"–type device during the molding process. However, this can easily be scraped or gouged out by a thief with a screwdriver or knife. A professional thief will replace the removed HIN with automotive body filler that often matches the color of the gelcoat. Then, by stamping a false HIN into the body filler, it appears that the HIN was affixed by the manufacturer and the alteration often goes undetected. An additional problem occurs when the Coast Guard allows a manufacturer to alter a HIN on any boat that remains in inventory by changing the production dates or model year to reflect a newer model year. Even for an experienced marine investigator, it is difficult to recognize whether a HIN was altered to cover a theft or modified by a manufacturer to reflect a newer model year.

Figure 15-24 shows the three different HIN formats approved by the Coast Guard. The straight-year and model-year formats were used from November 1, 1972, until August 1, 1984, when a new format replaced them. The only differences between the three formats are the last four characters. In the straight-year format, the last four characters reflect the calendar month and year of production. In the model-year format, the ninth character is always the letter "M" followed by the model year and a letter indicating the month of production. The new format, optional starting January 1, 1984, and mandatory as of August 1, 1984, uses the ninth and tenth characters to reflect the calendar month and year of production and the eleventh and twelfth characters to represent the model year.

The first three characters of the HIN are the manufacturer's identification code (MIC), assigned to each manufacturer by the Coast Guard. Since 1972, over 13,000 MICs have been assigned. Many codes have been reassigned after the original company went out of business. Because of this, it is very difficult even for the most experienced marine investigator to remain familiar with all the manufacturer's codes. In addition, large conglomerates such as Mercury Marine and Outboard Motor Corporation have purchased many boat manufacturers and used manufacturer's identification codes assigned to the parent corporation for multiple boat lines.

The middle five characters of the HIN are used as production numbers or serial numbers assigned by the manufacturer. Although the letters "I," "O," and "Q" cannot be used, any other letter can be used in combination with numbers. These "production" numbers can and often are repeated on a monthly basis for an entire year. Whereas the automobile VIN has a 30-year uniqueness and a check

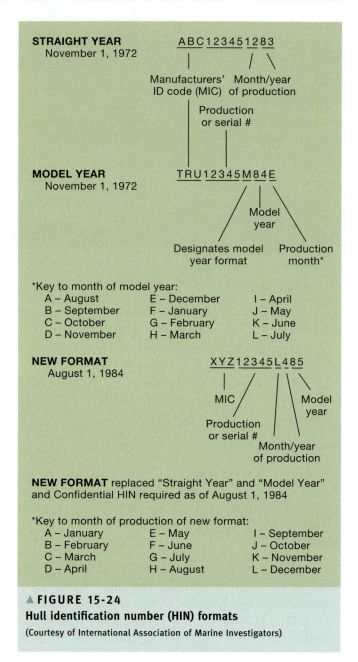

▲ **FIGURE 15-24**
Hull identification number (HIN) formats
(Courtesy of International Association of Marine Investigators)

digit to avoid unintentional or deliberate omission of numbers and intentional or unintentional transposition of numbers, the HIN does not yet have these features.

Title and Registration Issues

There are approximately 12 million pleasure boats in the United States. Roughly 160,000 of these are federally registered by the Coast Guard and are referred to as "documented." Ownership and financial disputes over **documented vessels** can be resolved in the federal courts. The remainder of the pleasure boats are registered and/or titled by each state, except Alaska, in which registration issues are regulated by the Coast Guard.

Over 30 states require that boats be titled, but only a few states require the titling of outboard motors. Even in titling states, many boats are exempted by being less than a specified length or powered by less than a specified horsepower of motor. More than half the titling programs are administered by wildlife or natural resource agencies. The remainder are operated by motor vehicle agencies.

Many jurisdictions that title boats do not have computerized ownership records or do not retain the information for more than one year. The boat registration or title files in only a few states can be accessed using the National Law Enforcement Telecommunications System (NLETS). The inability of an investigator to obtain ownership information in a timely and efficient manner makes boat theft investigation very difficult.

NCIC Boat File

As noted earlier, over 27,000 stolen boats are included in the NCIC system, under the title "Boat File." The Boat File, one of the 17 NCIC 2000 files, records information on stolen boats, boat trailers, and boat parts. Information in the file is retrievable on an online basis by entering the registration or document number, the hull identification number, or the assigned NCIC number. Unless otherwise removed or located, information in the Boat File is maintained for the balance of the year of entry, plus four years. The exception to this is records that have no boat hull identification number or other number assigned by the owner that can be used for identification purposes. These remain in the file for only 90 days after entry.

The boat theft problem may be much greater than what the NCIC statistics display. There is no mandate requiring that boat thefts be entered into NCIC and, because of the difficulty of reporting, many thefts are not entered. According to marine theft experts, new edits installed in the NCIC Boat File in late 1993 contained errors, causing valid entries to be rejected and further discouraging the entry of stolen boat information by law enforcement agencies. Another major flaw in the system is that NCIC does not enter all the Coast Guard–assigned manufacturer's identification codes and, in some cases, has assigned codes that are not those recognized by the Coast Guard.

Investigative Resources

Marine theft investigations are often complex and time-consuming. With the difficulty in obtaining ownership information, the tens of thousands of boat manufacturers, and the lack of computerized theft information, the success of an investigation is often predicated not on what the investigator knows but on whom he or she knows to contact for assistance. A major resource is the International Association of Marine Investigators. This organization has over 2,000 members who network with other law enforcement officers and agencies and insurance investigators throughout the United States, Canada, Europe, the Caribbean, and Central and South America. The organization holds an annual training seminar on marine theft issues.

Preventive Measures

There are several ways a boat owner can lessen the possibility of marine theft. For example, one individual who used to make his living by stealing boats and reselling them recommended that any boat with an electric starter should have a toggle switch that shuts off the electrical system when in the off position. The switch can be located under the dash or behind a panel. Typically, when a thief attempts to start the boat and cannot, the thief assumes that it is malfunctioning and gives up the effort to steal it.

To discourage theft, a boat owner may want to remove a vital engine part when the boat is left unattended. Trailered boats are more easily stolen than boats in the water. The best way to protect boats on trailers is to keep them out of the sight of thieves. They should be parked behind a house or behind or inside a garage where they cannot be seen from the street.

Owners should never leave boats where they will tempt a potential thief. If a boat appears difficult to steal, the thief will seek an easier victim. The owner should never leave the keys or the registration on board when the vessel is not attended. Outboard motors should be bolted through the hull and secured with clamping locks. If the owner is to be away from the place where the boat is stored for an extended period of time, the engine should be disabled or one or more wheels should be removed from the trailer.

AIRCRAFT AND AVIONICS THEFT

With approximately 225,000 general-aviation aircraft in the United States, the theft of aircraft and burglary leading to the theft of avionics are certainly not as prevalent as motor vehicle theft. Nonetheless, they are significant criminal problems that law enforcement investigators may encounter [44] (Figure 15-25).

The theft of aircraft electronic equipment, or **avionics,** can be a highly lucrative enterprise for thieves. Avionics include all the electronic radio and navigation equipment on board an aircraft—easily valued at over $10,000 in even the smallest aircraft. Many pieces of avionics look similar and can be accurately identified only by referring to the model number and/or name. Part of the difficulty encountered by many law enforcement officers is their unfamiliarity with such pieces of equipment.

There are many reasons for equipment burglaries. One of the prime reasons is the lack of security at airports and the indifference on the part of many sales outlets regarding the identification and sources of used equipment. In addition, although most avionics contain stickers and plates identifying the manufacturer, model number, part number, and even the serial number, these are often easily removed and in some cases are just stick-on labels.

Most modern avionics are designed to be easily removed from the aircraft panel to facilitate frequent

◄**FIGURE 15-25**
Stolen aircraft crashes into bank building
The theft of aircraft in the United States is a relatively rare event. However, breaking into an aircraft to steal electronic parts is relatively simple, since both door locks and ignition locks on many private planes can easily be picked. Thefts of aircraft are most likely to occur at airports that are poorly lit and unattended at night. The aircraft in the picture was stolen by a juvenile from a small airfield and ultimately crashed into a downtown bank building.
(© Chuck Sutnick/Tampa Fire Rescue/ Getty Images)

repair and maintenance of the equipment. Stolen avionics are often resold through the used-parts market or to persons who need the items and are willing to overlook the source of such reasonably priced equipment.

Much of the stolen avionics equipment is exported to other countries. Some is resold using counterfeited VIN labels and VIN plates. Other equipment is switched so that the stolen equipment is never discovered, as illustrated by the following example: A thief will identify the type of equipment desired in a specific aircraft at a specific airport. The thief or thieves will then locate the same type of equipment in another aircraft at another airport. At the time of theft, the electronic equipment will be removed from the first aircraft and placed in the second aircraft after the second aircraft's equipment has been removed. The equipment from the second aircraft is then sold on the market; normally, the owner of the second aircraft doesn't even know the equipment is missing because the same material, stolen from the first aircraft, has been installed in his or her craft. The theft of equipment from the first aircraft is reported, but it is never recovered because it is already comfortably installed in aircraft number two.

Resources

An investigator who is unfamiliar with aircraft and aircraft thefts should not hesitate to obtain assistance from those who have the necessary expertise. It is advised that before undertaking a significant investigation, an investigator should visit a local airport, contact airport management, aircraft companies, flight schools, and so forth, to learn basic information about aircraft, avionics, and the theft of both. The Aviation and Crime Prevention Institute located in Hagerstown, Maryland, is an excellent

source of assistance and support for law enforcement officers involved in the investigation of aviation theft.[45] The mission of the institute is to reduce aviation-related crime through information gathering, communication with law enforcement and the public, and education programs in theft prevention and security awareness.

Theft Techniques

The techniques thieves use to steal aircraft and burglarize aircraft for the avionics equipment are not that much different from, and most frequently parallel to, those used for stealing automobiles. Of course, if theft of the aircraft is the objective, it is unlikely that the thief will gain access by smashing a window. Indeed, smashing a window is generally not necessary. Perhaps the weakest security point of any aircraft is its locks. Most aircraft manufacturers use a limited number of key combinations, and a single key may open many aircraft of the same make. Occasionally, one manufacturer's key will open an aircraft of a different manufacturer.

Both door locks and ignition locks can easily be picked, and generally there are no antitheft devices on aircraft. Many of the more expensive aircraft don't even use ignition keys, so the only requirement for the thief is to enter the cabin.

Many of the techniques used to cover the theft of aircraft are similar to the processes used to conceal the theft of motor vehicles. The following illustrates a salvage switch involving aircraft: A thief decides on the type of aircraft desired and then purchases a total wreck of a similar aircraft from a junkyard. Rather than the certificate of title and VIN plate that come with a motor vehicle, the wrecked aircraft comes with its VIN plate and log book (a document required by the Federal Aviation Administration [FAA] that records the aircraft's history and repair record). The thief then steals (or has stolen) an aircraft of the same year, make, and model; switches the VIN plate; and installs the log book. After the thief adapts the registration markings and ensures that colors match the wrecked aircraft, the salvage switch is complete.

Thefts of aircraft are most likely to occur at airports that have poor lighting and are unattended at night, especially if they have little or no security, have no control tower, and perhaps are not even fenced.

Aircraft Identification

Aircraft have the same basic identification information as do motor vehicles. The major difference is that aircraft are regulated under a federal licensing system, whereas motor vehicles are regulated under state licensing systems. All aircraft are identified by a registration number, which is similar to a license plate number; a VIN; and make and model. The U.S. registration numbering system is part of a worldwide system under which each country has a letter and/or number code. In the United States, the code begins with the letter "N." Consequently, all U.S.-registered aircraft display an N number.

Most registered aircraft receive their N numbers when they are manufactured. It is possible for the purchaser of a used aircraft or of an aircraft currently being built to request a special N number. Such requests are processed by the FAA.

The N number is found on each side of the aircraft or on the vertical tail in large or small letter and numeral combinations. In some cases, such as on older aircraft, the N number may be displayed on the underside of one wing and the topside of the opposite wing. Helicopters have the N number displayed under the nose or undercarriage.

Most aircraft have a small plate on the instrument panel with the plane's N number on it. An investigator can look at the plate and determine whether the plate number matches the N number displayed on the exterior of the aircraft. If the plate is missing, further investigation is warranted.

Although each aircraft has a VIN, manufacturers design their own numbering systems, and the location of a VIN plate varies depending on the make. For example, on Cessna aircraft the VIN plate is found on the door-jamb; the door must be open to see the plate. The VIN plate on most single-engine and small twin-engine Beech-craft planes can be found on the right side above the wing flap; large Beechcraft planes have the VIN plate inside the main-cabin entry door frame. On Piper aircraft the VIN plate is usually found on the lower side of the tail on the aircraft's body.

As in any attempt to identify a vehicle, a vessel, or aircraft, the investigator should understand the construction process well enough to know whether and where to look for identifiers. When aircraft are built, many of the parts are subassembled elsewhere in the plant, and such subassemblies are marked with the VIN number in Magic Marker or pencil so that the aircraft can later come together at the main assembly point. If the plate is missing, the investigator should look under seats, under carpeted areas, in inspection panels, and elsewhere for ID numbers relating to the VIN.

When trying to locate a VIN plate in aircraft other than those previously mentioned, the investigator should look in some of the most common locations, such as on the doorjamb on either side of the plane, on the lower tail section on either side of the plane, on the body where the main wing is attached, near the nose wheel, or on the lower body. In other words, when in doubt, the dedicated investigator will look over the entire aircraft in an attempt to find the attached plate, which will provide make, model, and VIN information.

Theft Prevention Techniques

Following are a few examples of the theft-deterrent devices available and the actions an aircraft owner can take, some without cost, to reduce the chance of theft of the aircraft or the avionics.

- There are a number of alarm systems on the market, and some even have a pain generator, a second piercing alarm inside the cockpit that is most aggravating to the human ear.
- Ignition kills, which require entry of a security code into the control panel in the cockpit, are available. If the pilot fails to get the code right after a specific number of tries, the engine-starting circuits are disabled and, in some cases, a siren will sound.
- There should be a prearranged password known only to crew members and the airport operator. Thus, a person who calls and directs that the plane be prepared for flight must know the password in order to get the plane readied. This technique has prevented the theft of many aircraft.
- A wheel-locking device, or "boot," prevents the plane from being towed or from moving under its own power.
- More secure locks can be installed.
- Airplanes should be parked at night at airports that are well lighted, fenced, and otherwise provided with security. Window covers should be used to conceal avionics.
- Avionics equipment should be checked to ensure that it is the manufacturer-installed equipment. Each piece should then be marked with a dot, paint, engraving, or scratch, and a detailed inventory should be made and recorded.
- Propeller chains and locks are available.
- Instrument panels can be equipped with a locking bar or locking cover.

- Flight operations personnel at airports should be given a list that identifies each crew member and other persons permitted to be around the plane or to authorize service over the phone.

- Airport authorities should have a central point of contact available 24 hours a day.
- Vital aircraft records should not be kept in the aircraft.

KEY TERMS

AAMVANET
active system (theft deterrent)
avionics
cargo theft
chop shop
commercial-vehicle theft
confidential VIN
construction equipment
documented vessel
false-theft scheme
false-vehicle scheme
federal safety certification label
gray-market vehicles
heavy equipment

hull identification number (HIN)
inflated-theft-loss scheme
joyriding
marine theft
Motor Vehicle Theft Law Enforcement Act (1984)
National Insurance Crime Bureau (NICB)
National Motor Vehicle Title Information System (NMVTIS)
odometer fraud
off-road equipment
"paper vehicle"
parts marking
passive system (theft deterrent)

product identification number (PIN)
professional theft (of vehicle)
quick strip (of vehicle)
salvage switch
salvage title
salvage vehicle
Stolen Auto Recovery (STAR) System
temporary theft (of vehicle)
title fraud
Truth in Mileage Act (1986)
vehicle fraud
vehicle identification number (VIN)
VIN plate
washing (of title)

REVIEW QUESTIONS

1. Describe a chop-shop operation.
2. How does a salvage switch work?
3. Distinguish false-vehicle, false-theft, and inflated theft-loss schemes.
4. What is a "paper" vehicle?
5. How is a certificate of title "washed"?
6. What are some of the factors contributing to the theft of off-road equipment?
7. What is the National Insurance Crime Bureau, and what functions does it perform for law enforcement?
8. Why is vehicle identification the most difficult and time-consuming task faced by an investigator in an auto theft case?
9. Why do vehicles have a standardized identification numbering system?
10. What was the purpose behind passage of the Motor Vehicle Theft Law Enforcement Act of 1984?
11. Describe the three basic methods for restoring vehicle identification numbers.
12. Describe some of the principal investigative steps in determining whether a vehicle fire is an accident or arson.
13. Describe the workings and benefits of a photographic preinsurance inspection program.
14. What is odometer fraud, and why is it a significant offense?
15. Discuss the nature and seriousness of marine theft.
16. What are avionics, and why is avionics theft prevalent?

INTERNET ACTIVITIES

1. Check the web to see if your state has law enforcement and/or insurance organizations that specialize in the investigation of motor vehicle and other related thefts. What types of investigative services do they provide? Are auto theft statistics available for your state? Does the site have auto theft prevention information? If you were a criminal investigator, what other information do you think should be available on the site?

2. Learn more about the export of stolen motor vehicles and other items by logging on to the U.S. Customs site at www.customs.ustreas.gov and the North American Export Committee site at www.naexportcommittee.org. The latter website also has several related links to insurance fraud and vehicle theft prevention.

NOTES

1. Federal Bureau of Investigation, *Crime in the United States, Uniform Crime Reports, 2005* available at www.fbi.gov/ucr.
2. Ibid.
3. Ibid.
4. Ibid.
5. Thanks to Ed Sparkman, Member Relations Manager,NICB, for providing this information.
6. Citizens for Auto-Theft Responsibility, *CAR Newsletter,* Autumn 1992 (a quarterly publication of the not-for-profit public awareness and victim support organization, P.O. Box 3131, Palm Beach, FL 33480).
7. FBI, *Crime in the United States, 2005.*
8. "NICB Goes Globe Trotting to Bring Back Stolen Cars," *APB* (official publication of the International Association of Auto Theft Investigators), Nov. 1996, p. 63.
9. Speech by Lt. Greg Terp, Commander, Miami-Dade Police Department Auto Theft Task Force, Summit on Auto Theft in Florida 2002, Tampa, Florida, Sept. 16, 2002.
10. NICB, "Doing a Double Take: Vehicle Clones Are a Street-Level Problem for Insurers," *Strategic Analysis Report,* Volume 1, 2004, Oct. 10, 2004.
11. Ibid.
12. Ibid.
13. National Automobile Theft Bureau, 1990 Annual Report, p. 15.
14. Joel M McCloskey, "Heavy Equipment Theft", Strategic and Tactical Information Department, NICB, October 2006.
15. Comments by David Shillingford, President, National Equipment Register, Summit on Auto Theft in Florida 2002, Tampa, Florida, Sept. 16, 2002.
16. Gene Rutledge, "7 Character PIN for Off-Road Equipment Is Here," *APB,* July 1999, pp. 17–19.
17. "There's More than One Way to Stop a Thief," *APB,* March 2001, pp. 52, 58–59.
18. FIA International Research, "Contraband, Organized Crime, and the Threat to the Transportation and Supply Chain Function." Study conducted on behalf of the National Cargo Security Council, a coalition of public and private transportation organizations, Sept. 2001, Executive Summary, p. 1.
19. Ibid.
20. Many thanks to Special Agent Lawrence "Dave" Dempsey, NICB for this updated information.
21. FIA International Research, Op. Cit., p.1.
22. Comments by Lt. William Shiver, Florida Highway Patrol, Summit on Auto Theft in Florida 2002, Tampa, Florida, Sept. 16, 2002.
23. Thanks to Ed Staffman, Member Relations Manager, NICB, for the updated information.
24. National Insurance Crime Bureau, *2004 Passenger Vehicle Identification Manual* (Palos Hills, IL: NICB, 2004).
25. National Automobile Theft Bureau, *Commercial Vehicle and Off-Road Equipment Identification Manual,* 7th ed. (Palos Hills, IL: NATB, 2000).
26. Ibid., p. 6. And thanks to Lt. Greg Terp, Commander, Miami-Dade Auto Theft Task Force, for updated information.
27. Federal Bureau of Investigation, "The New Generation of NCIC," *CJIS: A Newsletter for the Criminal Justice Community,* Vol. 3, No. 2, 1999, pp. 5–6.
28. Ibid.
29. Bureau of Justice Assistance, "The National Motor Vehicle Title Information System (NMVTIS)", power point presentation, 2007.
30. Information provided in a conversation with Sgt. Chris Bimonte, Miami-Dade Police Department, who represents the department on the North American Export Committee.
31. Comments by Senator Bill Nelson, Florida, Summit on Auto Theft in Florida 2002, Tampa, Florida, Sept. 15, 2002.
32. Information provided by Sgt. Chris Bimonte. See also as-e.com.
33. Information provided by Sgt. Chris Bimonte.
34. Glenn Wheeler, "North American Export Committee Update," *APB,* March 2001, p. 11.
35. David Shillingford, "National Equipment Register Update," *APB,* July 2000, p. 9: current pamphlets and literature of NER; "New Resources to Fight a Heavy Problem," *Law Enforcement News,* June 30, 2002, p. 9.
36. "Attorney General Issues Report on Component Part Markings," IAATI Legal News column, *APB,* Nov. 2000, pp. 59, 61.
37. Ibid.
38. Ibid.
39. Ibid.
40. "Restoration of Altered or Obliterated Numbers," training bulletin, Alabama Department of Public Safety.
41. National Insurance Crime Bureau, *Fire Investigation Handbook* (Palos Hills, IL: NICB, 1995), pp. 31–67; National Fire Protection Association International, *NFPA 921 Guide for Fire and Explosion Investigations, 2001 Edition* (Quincy, MA: NFPA International, 2001), pp. 921–171 to 921–182.
42. This information was provided by the LoJack Corporation of Boston, Massachusetts.
43. Much of the material on this topic is drawn from Phillip J. Crapeau, "Photo Inspection Helps Deter Auto Theft," *National Underwriter,* Sept. 18, 1990.
44. Most of the material in this section is drawn from the Aviation Crime Prevention Institute, *Aviation Identification and Information Manual for Police Officers* (Frederick, MD: ACPI and the Aviation Insurance Industry, 1987), and from information supplied by Robert Collins, Aviation Crime Prevention Institute, Dec. 2001.
45. The address of the Aviation Crime Prevention Institute, Inc., is Post Office Box 30, Hagerstown, MD 21741-0030. Robert J. Collins, president of the institute, invites and welcomes inquiries and requests for assistance from law enforcement agencies and officers. Telephone numbers for the institute are 800-969-5473 and 301-791-9791. The website is www.acpi.org.

COMPUTER CRIME*

*In previous editions, Robert W. Taylor was the author of this chapter; in the eighth and ninth editions, Bob and D. Kall Loper coauthored the chapter; and for this edition, Bob once again revised and updated the material. For more information on this topic, see *Digital Crime and Digital Terrorism* by R. W. Taylor, T. J. Caeti, D. K. Loper, E. J. Fritsch, and J. Liederbach (Upper Saddle River, NJ: Pearson Prentice Hall, 2006).

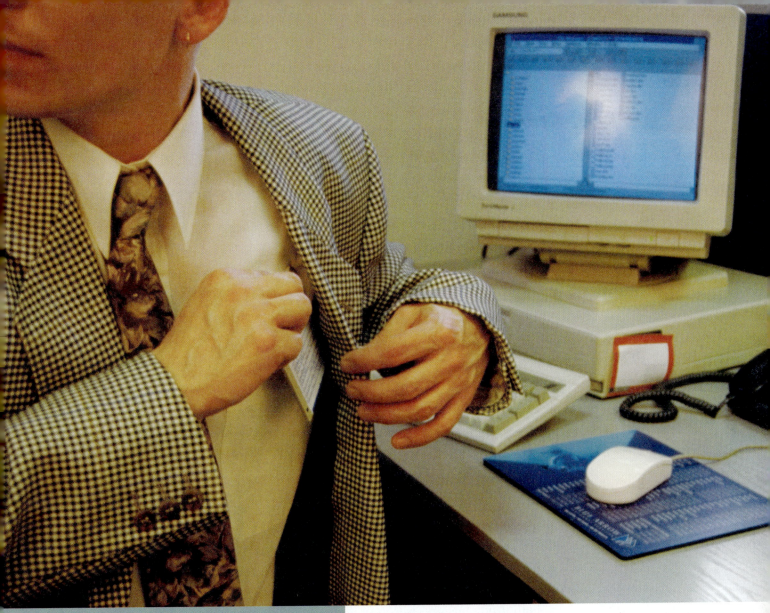

▲ Preventing the loss of critical data may be as simple as prohibiting the transfer of proprietary information, via software encryption programs and internal policies, to transportable media, such as compact discs (CDs), flash drives, and MP3 players. Here, a dishonest employee simply walks away from the business location after copying lists of external access numbers, authentication numbers, and passwords.

(© Hannah Gal/Cobis)

The first modern electronic computer was completed in 1942, and the first long-distance electronic communication on the forerunner of the Internet, a global network of computers, was sent in 1969.[1] For a few years after that monumental communication event in 1969, computers and networks were safely enclosed in major university campuses and corporate research parks. Today, however, we have restructured our "information society" to depend on computers and networks in ways that no one could have predicted at the birth of computing or later at the birth of large networks. In just a few short years, computers have become common fixtures of daily life. Students can register for or drop classes in real time from their homes by using a computer. People can withdraw money from their bank accounts at any time by using an automatic teller machine (ATM). They can get stock quotes, make flight reservations, browse reference libraries, shop at online stores, read the latest news, and make use of uncounted other resources almost instantaneously by clicking the mouse, or viewing their handheld PDAs.

Being "connected" is now less about politics and more about online access to the World Wide Web, a part of the Internet supported by service providers such as America Online (AOL) and gateways such as Google and Yahoo!, as well as many other Internet components that offer access to an amazing array of information and databases at lightning speeds.

The advance in computer and Internet technology, however, has provided new opportunities for criminal enterprise. Discoveries of computer crime committed both inside businesses, corporations, and network systems and through various means across the global network have become more prevalent each day. The purpose of this chapter is to inform the reader about many issues concerning and related to computer crime. The first section of the chapter presents information on various types of computer crime, ranging from network intrusion and data altering to the use of the computer as a facilitator for committing crimes. This chapter also addresses discovery tools and delivery vehicles for viruses and worms used to commit computer crime. Profiles of the hacker (or cracker) and the computer criminal are also discussed. Subsequent sections highlight the investigation of computer crime, including crime scene techniques and the application of digital forensic analysis. The chapter concludes with a discussion on methods of preventing computer crime.

TYPOLOGIES OF COMPUTER CRIME

The virtual explosion of the World Wide Web has dramatically increased communication between people, and the web has become a viable new conduit for business transactions. Stock quotes, flight schedules, reference libraries, online stores, the latest news, and uncounted other resources are available with a few clicks of the mouse. As is the case with many new developments, there is a dark side to this information frontier—computer abuse and computer crime.

Computer abuse includes a range of intentional acts that may not be covered by criminal laws. Any intentional act involving knowledge of computer use or technology is computer abuse if the perpetrator could have made some gain and the victim could have experienced loss.[2] By contrast, **computer crime** is any illegal act in which knowledge of computer technology is used to commit the offense. This broad term encompasses the whole domain of computer crime. It includes crimes targeting computers, crimes using computers as a means (instrumentality) to a criminal end, computers used in an otherwise legal manner that furthers a criminal end, and even crimes not involving any digital evidence, such as computer theft.[3] In most of these cases, **digital evidence,** or evidence that is held in digital storage (e.g., a computer hard drive, disk, RAID box) or transmitted through a digital communications device (e.g., modem or local area network—LAN) is present. The methodology used to recover, collect, preserve, and analyze this electronic data is called **digital forensics.** As with other evidence, the improper handling of digital evidence can destroy its court value. Digital forensics, like physical forensics (discussed in Chapters 4 and 8), seeks to develop evidence in such a way that it can not only assist an ongoing investigation, but also be used in court to prosecute the suspect or help a jury understand the complexities of a sophisticated crime.

Owing to the rapid increase in and increasingly serious nature of these offenses, several federal agencies have formed units that deal exclusively with computer crimes. These units include the FBI's National Computer Crime Squad and the U.S. Department of Justice's Computer Crime Unit. The U.S. Secret Service and the Department of Defense (as well as special units with the Army, Air Force, and Navy) also have experts responsible for computer crime investigations, as do many other federal, state, and local agencies. The first computer crime unit at the local level was developed in the early 1980s at the Maricopa County Sheriff's Office in Phoenix, Arizona. Since that time, most large police departments have special units that focus on computer-related crimes. A number of nongovernment organizations have also been developed that perform varied tasks, including investigating computer crimes, providing computer security training

and alerts, and acting as clearinghouses for both general and specific information regarding the technicalities of computer crime. These organizations are often called on as sources of experts who may be needed to assist law enforcement personnel conducting computer crime investigations. Two of the most prominent nongovernment organizations are the Computer Emergency Response Team (CERT) at Carnegie Mellon University and the Computer Security Institute (CSI), based in San Francisco, California.[4] Further, as discussed in Chapter 8, the FBI and U.S. Secret Service have also established digital crime laboratories across the nation to assist local law enforcement agencies.

As Chapter 11, "Crimes against Children," explains, even our children are not safe from exploitation and victimization on the web. A young teenage girl began visiting online with someone she believed to be a young teenage boy. She gave him her telephone number. However, the person turned out to be a 51-year-old man who made a series of obscene calls to her before he was stopped.[5] Other examples of online crimes include the interception of privileged information such as credit card numbers or passwords. Abuse of credit has reached epidemic proportions. Theft of intellectual property, ranging from stealing trade secrets to illegally reproducing copyrighted consumer materials such as music and movies, has an incalculable cost (Figure 16-1). The Recording Industry Association of America (RIAA) has estimated its losses due to music swapping through file sharing as being in the billions. Trading illicit information on the Internet has become a recurring theme in online crime. For example, a computer newsgroup, an archive of e-mail messages, dealt specifically with ways to defeat security placed on digital satellite television. Other forms of illicit information include child pornography, proprietary or privileged information leaked to websites, and illegal recordings of cellular phone calls.

Unfortunately, not all computer crimes are as restricted in their effects. "Hacktivists," politically motivated hackers, have attacked government websites, forcing them to be shut down for days until the damage could be repaired. Other online vandals have launched Denial-of-Service attacks on corporations or ISPs, shutting them down for hours or days at a time. Government studies have shown that many corporations, government agencies, and utility companies are highly vulnerable to attacks from outsiders (particularly terrorists), who in some cases may be able to seriously affect large segments of the population through a single organization's computer system. According to the National Infrastructure Protection Center (NIPC), tampering with the vital-information infrastructure could result in serious harm. On the basis of the effects of recent power failures caused by bad weather, the California power crisis in 2001, and the New York power failure in 2002, the NIPC predicts a high potential for serious national consequences from a designed attack against our nation's power and/or communication infrastructure. One of the potential sources

◀ **FIGURE 16-1**

Intellectual property theft case

Theft of intellectual property—everything from stealing trade secrets to illegally reproducing copyrighted consumer goods such as music and movies—has incalculable costs. The Recording Industry Association of America (RIAA) has estimated its losses from music-swapping networks and file sharing to be in the billions. The *Metallica* v. *Napster* lawsuit (2000) was one of the first to challenge the concept of free music swapping.

(© Graham Douglas/Corbis Sygma)

of such tampering is network intrusion conducted by terrorist organizations.

Computer Criminals

One of the more common ways to categorize computer crimes is in terms of the source of the threat: insiders or outsiders. Insider computer crimes are committed by persons who are employed by the targeted organization or have permission to be accessing its computer system. The most likely suspects in insider computer crime are programmers and system operators. Any other personnel who have inordinate amounts of autonomy, overlapping areas of responsibility, and freedom of movement within the network area are also prime suspects. No one person should ever be allowed to control all—or overlapping—aspects of information technology operations. However, the realities of finding competent network administrators often requires one good employee floating to other areas to assist less skilled employees. Within the government, computer criminals generally were found to be

young, good employees of a federal agency or a state, local, or private agency administering federal programs . . . their median age was 30. Three-quarters had spent at least some time in college. They had been with their respective agencies for an average of five years before they committed their crimes . . . Nearly three-quarters had been promoted, and two-thirds reported receiving at least an above-average performance rating. In fact, a quarter of the perpetrators told us they had received performance awards.[6]

Among the persons who should raise suspicion are employees who work late (after hours) and refuse promotions and/or transfers. Any scams they may be working on will be more lucrative than the promotions. Excess employee sick time or vacation time on the books may be another tip off. Someone committing fraud may not be able to leave the ongoing "management" of their fraudulent activities. Other suspects might be persons who show remarkable curiosity or competence toward aspects of network operations outside their job requirements. A brief overview of common management and financial data can be of tremendous assistance while investigating insider crime. Investigators should also construct a "personal demography" on suspects. This consists of three factors: (1) criminal history, (2) a list of associates, and (3) references.[7] (See Figure 16-2 for characteristics to consider when investigating possible insider computer crimes.)

Outsider computer crimes are committed by persons from outside the organization. While these individuals may sometimes have legitimate access to part of the system for specific tasks (such as surfing an organization's website), often they do not. Many of the same types of crimes, such as hardware theft and destruction of data, can be done by both insiders and outsiders.

In 1976, Donn Parker made one of the first attempts to systematically define computer crimes by the activity involved. He developed the first typology[8] of computer crime based on accounts of the crimes.[9] Parker's typology remained the state-of-the-art until Robert W. Taylor's "juvenile hacker profile" emerged in 1990.[10] David Carter modified both typologies to better suit the needs of criminologists and investigators.[11] Parker also created a new, more security-focused, typology in 1998.[12] For the purposes of this chapter, Carter's typology provides an excellent manner in which to categorize computer crimes. It is

◀ **FIGURE 16-2** **Insider crimes**

When investigating what appears to be an insider computer crime, the investigator should consider the employee factors listed here.

Opportunities
- Familiarity with operations (including cover-up capabilities).
- Occupies position of trust.
- Has close associations with suppliers and other key people.

Situational Pressures—Financial
- Has high personal debts.
- Is dealing with severe illness in family.
- Has inadequate income and/or is living beyond means.
- Dabbles in extensive stock market speculation.
- Is involved with loan sharks.
- Gambles excessively.
- Has heavy expenses incurred from extramarital involvement.
- Has undue family, peer, company, or community expectations.
- Uses alcohol and/or drugs excessively.

Situational Pressures—Revenge
- Perceives inequities (e.g., low pay or poor job assignment).
- Resents superiors.
- Is frustrated, usually with job.

Personality Traits
- Lacks personal moral honesty.
- Has no well-defined code of personal ethics.
- Is a wheeler-dealer—that is, someone who enjoys feelings of power, influence, social status, and excitement associated with rapid financial transactions involving large sums of money.
- Is neurotic, manic depressive, or emotionally unstable.
- Is arrogant or egocentric.
- Is psychopathic.
- Has low self-esteem.
- Feels personally challenged to subvert a system of controls.

(Source: R. K. Elliot and J. J. Willingham, *Management Fraud: Detection and Deterrence* [New York: Petrocelli Books, 1980:, pp. 223–226], and R. W. Taylor, T. J. Caeti, D. K. Loper, E. J. Fritsch, and J. Liederbach, *Digital Crime and Digital Terrorism* [Upper Saddle River, NJ: Pearson Prentice Hall, 2006].)

versatile enough to organize an increasing array of illegal, possibly illegal, and simply questionable actions called "computer crime."

The Computer as The Target

Crimes in which the computer is the target include the denial of expected service and the alteration of data. The computer is defined as the target when an act effectively prevents the legitimate user or owner from receiving the service or data that he or she expects. Even without malicious intent, network intruders target the computer and may cause harm to the network owner. Crimes that target the computer are the most easily understandable examples of computer crime.

Computer Manipulation Crimes

Computer manipulation crimes involve changing data or creating electronic records in a system for the specific purpose of advancing another crime, typically fraud or embezzlement. The simplest, safest, and most common form of computer crime—*data diddling*—falls within this category. In its most basic form, payroll records are changed so that a person is paid for more hours than he or she worked, or is paid at a higher rate. However, there is a great deal of variety in computer manipulation crimes.

For example, the price of a stock can be manipulated on the information superhighway. Stock shares in one little-known Canadian company, Wye Resources, Inc., were traded outside an established exchange. The value of the stock more than tripled after the company was hyped on messages posted on commercial bulletin board services and on the Internet.[13] The company reportedly owned a Zaire diamond mine where a major strike had been made. After the favorable online publicity had "pumped" up the stock's price, it was then "dumped," or sold for profit, by those in the know, and the stock collapsed.

These types of scams threaten the development of commerce on the Internet, because consumers need to

Category	% of all complaints	Average loss
1. Auctions *Goods never delivered or misrepresented*	34%	$1,331
2. General Merchandise *Sales not through auctions, goods never delivered or misrepresented*	33%	$1,197
3. Fake Check Scams *Consumers paid with phony checks for work or items sold, instructed to wire money back*	11%	$4,053
4. Nigerian Money Offers *False promises of riches if consumers pay to transfer money to their bank accounts*	7%	$3,741
5. Lotteries/Lottery Clubs *Requests for payment to claim lottery winnings or get help to win, often foreign lotteries*	4%	$1,750
6. Advance Fee Loans *False promises of business or personal loans, even if credit is bad, for a fee upfront*	3%	$1,515
7. Phishing *Emails pretending to be from a well-known source, asking to confirm personal information*	2%	no losses reported
8. Prizes/Sweepstakes *Requests for payment to claim prizes that never materialize*	1%	$2,447
9. Internet Access Services *Cost of internet access and other services misrepresented or services never provided*	1%	$920
10. Investments *Made false promises about returns on investments*	1%	$4,759

▲ **FIGURE 16-3 Common Internet scams**

The 2006 Top 10 Internet Scam Chart was developed by the National Consumers League, 1701 K. Street, NW, Suite 1200, Washington, DC. Captured on the Internet on March 22, 2008 at: http://fraud.org/stats/2006/internet.pdf

feel confident that purchases are safe and secure. The Federal Trade Commission's consumer protection laws that apply to commercial activities in media such as mail and telephone solicitation apply to online promotions as well. The FTC's prohibition on "unfair or deceptive acts or practices" extends to Internet sales and marketing thereby allowing regulators to crack down on promoters who offer phony services.[14]

Frauds on the Internet are usually based on a traditional methodology of offering goods and services that are never provided or are of very poor quality for the price paid. One of the more prolific crimes today is fraudulent goods offered via eBay. The seller never sends the offered item, or the item is broken, or it does not have the value originally placed on it. The buyer has very little recourse other than contacting eBay directly, but since the "sale" is provided between two private parties, eBay liability is minimal. Figure 16-3 outlines a number of common Internet scams. Many of these scams (Figure 16-4) fall into the broad categories of theft and fraud. Then too, new wireless technology (Figure 16-5) has broadened the opportunity for such crimes and are addressed later in the chapter.

The advance of computerization has also opened new mechanisms for fraud. For instance, the Secret Service and FBI warned Congress that a thriving new "point and click" counterfeiting scheme had been discovered that uses high-quality scanners to capture an original check, a personal computer to alter the data, and a quality laser printer to develop the counterfeit instrument.[15] Total cost for equipment used in such cases has averaged less than $5,000, providing criminals with the ability to pass phony checks that look "exactly like the originals." The Federal Reserve placed the cost of this type of check fraud to banks at more than 10 times the $59 million attributed to bank robbery.[16] More alarming than the total amount of loss is the rapid growth and expansion of this type of crime. Counterfeit check schemes are the acts not just of lone, white-collar criminals but also of well-organized gangs and groups. A significant number of the cases were committed by organized ethnic enterprises, including Nigerians, Vietnamese, Russians, Armenians, Mexicans, and Arabs. Some of these gangs were also heavily involved in the trafficking of guns and narcotics, extortion, large-scale fencing of stolen property, and the financing of terrorist groups in the Middle East.[17]

▲ **FIGURE 16-4   Computer manipulation crimes**
Computer manipulation crimes involve changing data or creating electronic records in a system for the purpose of advancing another crime, typically fraud or embezzlement. For example, electronic payroll records may be altered so that an employee is paid for more hours than he or she actually worked. Internet scams, such as the sale of merchandise that is never delivered, are another common type of fraud.
(© Phil Banko/Corbis)

▲ **FIGURE 16-5   iPhone**
Wireless access to the Internet and the web has provided unlimited opportunities for computer manipulation and data alteration crimes, challenging even the most sophisticated computer security software. (Courtesy Apple)

Even the federal government is not exempt from computer manipulation crimes. Fraudulent Internal Revenue Service tax filings cost the federal government $5 billion a year. A multimillion-dollar portion of this was due to bogus electronic tax filings. Thieves would obtain or prepare false supporting documentation to justify a refund, such as W-2s. Then they would go to a tax preparer who completed a return based on this information and filed it electronically. Within 48 hours, the IRS would confirm that the return had been accepted and that the person was eligible for a refund anticipation loan (RAL). This confirmation came in the form of a direct-deposit indicator (DDI). In effect, the IRS served as credit reference, guaranteeing that the money would actually be forthcoming. With this information, the "filer" would obtain a loan from a bank, finance company, or the tax preparer and then vanish. Subsequent to these types of cases, the IRS announced new procedures for handling electronic filings to reduce such fraud.[18]

Data Alteration or Denial

Data alteration or denial directly targets the computer by attacking the useful information stored or processed by the computer. Altered data may affect business decisions made by a company or may directly affect individuals by altering their records. In citing worst-case scenarios for data alteration, the changing of medical records often appears as an example. In a review of "shockers," author Jonathan Littman reported that a Berkeley researcher discovered a medical facility in the San Francisco Bay Area with open telephone lines to medical records.[19] An examination of medical records uncovers a great amount of personal information, but beyond the threat to privacy, alteration of those records by a single character can be fatal (in the case of blood type or a prescription). It is easy to understand why the alteration of medical data has received such attention.

Today's headlines are filled with less sinister, but expensive and damaging examples of crimes targeting computers. **Spam,** or unsolicited, mass, commercial e-mail (Figure 16-6), has exploded in the last few years. In 2001, spam accounted for 8% of all e-mail; in 2006, it accounted for approximately 40% of all e-mail (some reports ranging as high as 60%), with 12.4 billion spam e-mails sent per day.[20] As a reference, 40% of mail carried by the U.S. Postal service is commercial marketing.[21] Some studies estimate that businesses lose $10 per employee per year on spam.[22] Industrywide, 2006 is

Spam is unsolicited, unwanted advertising e-mail. It takes its name from a song in a British comedy called *Monty Python's Flying Circus*, that repeats the words "spam spam spam" with little variation. Early spam was typically sent to many Internet newsgroups, where users equated the mindless, off-topic advertising with the mindless lyrics of the song: both just keep coming.

Seedy advertising has long been popular among spammers. Advertisements for pornography, male genital enhancement, prescription sex aids, and illicit liaisons now clog the e-mail inboxes of people who would never seek such goods and services. It is common for these ads to use deceptive or salacious subject lines. Modern spam has changed to include many variations on simple advertising. *Phishing,* using an e-mail to lure computer users into revealing personal financial information, has become a popular application of spam. The Nigerian *419* scams attempt to lure people into sending money in hopes of receiving an "inheritance" or "impounded" funds, and typically start with a spam e-mail written in broken English.

The Controlling the Assault of Non-Solicited Pornography and Marketing (CAN-SPAM) Act of 2003 makes it a crime to send unsolicited, commercial e-mail messages without labeling them, including opt-out instructions, and the true physical address of the sender. Title 47 of the U.S. Code §1037: CAN-SPAM

Whoever . . .

(1) accesses a computer without authorization and transmits multiple commercial e-mail messages,
(2) uses a computer without authorization to relay or retransmit multiple commercial e-mail messages,
(3) falsifies identifying information within an e-mail message to deceive recipients as to the origin of such messages, or
(4) falsely represents oneself as the registrant of Internet addresses, e-mail addresses, or domain names and transmits multiple commercial electronic mail messages.[i]

is guilty of a crime, punishable by up to five years in prison if committed in the furtherance of a felony, continuing down to one year depending on previous offenses and the facts of the offense. For details on spam laws in your state, see www.spamlaws.com.

Spam and Free Speech
The First Amendment allows people the right to free speech, but it doesn't guarantee them the right to force others to hear their message.[ii] Previous legislation, like the Telephone Consumer Protection Act (TCPA), prevents unauthorized use of fax machines for commercial advertisement. The logic behind TCPA is that fax machines cost the receiver money. Freedom of commercial speech does not grant the right to be heard at the receiver's expense.

As the Coalition Against Unsolicited Commercial E-mail puts it:

When spammers try to hide their destructive and often illegal activities behind the First Amendment, it is helpful to remember the words of Federal Judge Stanley Sporkin in a case called *Turner Broadcasting* v. *FCC* where the plaintiffs sought to defend their activities on First Amendment grounds: "[They] have come to court not because their freedom of speech is seriously threatened but because their profits are; to dress up their complaints in First Amendment garb *demeans* the principles for which the First Amendment stands and the protections it was designed to afford."[iii]

In *Rowan* v. *U.S. Post Office*, the Court held that:

Nothing in the Constitution compels us to listen to or to view any unwanted communication, whatever its merit . . . We therefore categorically reject the argument that a vendor has the right under the Constitution or otherwise to send unwanted material into the home of another . . . We repeat, the right of a mailer stops at the outer boundary of every person's domain."

---

[i] 47 U.S.C § 1037, CAN-SPAM Act of 2003.

[ii] Coalition Against Unsolicited Commercial E-mail. "Quick FAQ," [Frequently Asked Questions], www.cauce.org/about/faq.shtml#c ensorship, retrieved Oct. 20, 2004.

[iii] Ibid.

▲ **FIGURE 16-6   SPAM**

estimated to have cost commerce in the United States $8.9 billion dollars in spam costs with another $1.4 billion dollars[23] spent on antispam products.[24] Spam has largely been a civil matter until recently. The *E-Commerce Times* reports that virus writers and spammers have begun to criminally collaborate to use other people's computers to spread spam.[25] The CAN-SPAM Act of 2003 makes it a crime punishable by imprisonment for up to five years to use deception in sending unsolicited e-mail. Both criminal elements of spam and intentional spreading of viruses are crimes targeting computers. For example, a malicious program called Mydoom surfaced in 2004.[26] Technically, Mydoom is a worm (see the sections on viruses and worms later in this chapter). A **worm** is a small program that sends itself to other computers, rather than relying on user actions, as a virus does. However, the distinction between worms and viruses is growing meaningless. The fact of the matter is that Malicious Mobile Code (MMC)[27] is growing by many means. The last few years have seen the rise of mass mailer worms. Such worms can include e-mail software to send themselves out to infect other computers. They can also exploit security flaws in existing software, such as Microsoft Outlook, to send copies to everyone in an address book. The Anna Kournikova worm lured users into clicking an attachment that they believed to be a JPEG[28] image (photograph-quality compressed digital image). The attachment was not really an image, being instead a worm engine that infected the user's system and then spread. Until recently, it was thought impossible to infect a computer by viewing an image or reading an e-mail. Highly formatted e-mail, using Hypertext Markup Language (HTML),[29] could launch scripts through disguised links, but images were generally seen as safe. In September of 2004, however, Microsoft announced a vulnerability in some of its software used to view JPEG files.[30] Indeed, all the mechanisms for system intrusion and mass mailing have attracted the attention of spammers. In 2004, a Los Angeles man who used other people's Wi-Fi networks to send thousands of unsolicited adult-themed e-mails from his car pleaded guilty to a single felony, in what prosecutors say was the first criminal conviction under the federal CAN-SPAM Act.[31]

Hacking, Cracking and Other Forms of Network Intrusion

Hacking or **cracking** is the process of gaining unauthorized entry into a computer system. For perhaps 99% of the people who do it, the hacking, or getting in, is the thrill. The remaining 1% hack for purposes ranging from pulling mild pranks to destroying or stealing data. To be able to hack, a person must get a password. People are often careless with their passwords, writing them down and leaving them in obvious places in their offices and homes, where hackers may discover them. Passwords can also be generated by using a special software program called a **hacker's dictionary.** A common hacker's tool, the dictionary generates millions of combinations of letters and numbers until it finds a combination that matches a password—and the hacker is in. The prime targets for hackers are secure sites found on the Internet.

Packet sniffers are also used in the hacking or cracking methodology. These unique programs are designed to monitor network communications and selectively keep records of sensitive information such as passwords and credit card numbers. In most computer networks, as information passes from its origin to its destination, it must pass through many computers along the way. Normally, these computers simply pass along the information, sometimes logging that it went through the system. By using a packet sniffer, it is possible not only to allow the information to pass but also to make a copy of it, undetected. Although passwords and credit card numbers are often the information of choice, other sensitive information has been gathered this way by sniffers located on government and corporate networks, online networks, and Internet service provider networks and then used in blackmail schemes.

Interestingly, proactive law enforcement programs designed to catch criminals using the Internet are, essentially, highly advanced packet sniffers. Developed as a specialized network analyzer or "sniffer" program designed to work on a personal computer via Microsoft Windows, the FBI's monitoring program, DCS 1000 (formerly Carnivore), raises the ire of many civil libertarians.[32] Essentially, DCS 1000 "sniffs" or analyzes portions of selected network packets, and copies them to a separate file for further analysis by the FBI. These packets are defined by specific filters set within the program, which conform to a court order. The filter set can be extremely fine and can comply with applications developed from Title III interception orders, pen register court orders, and trap and trace court orders. The problem, of course, is discriminating between user messages that are legal and those that are not on the Internet. This is a complex issue. DCS 1000 does not search through the contents of every message and collect those that contain certain keywords such as "bomb" or "drugs." It selects messages on the basis of criteria expressly set out in a court order, for example, messages transmitted to or from a particular account or to or from a particular user.[33] If the device is placed at some point on a network where it cannot discriminate messages as set out in the court order, it simply lets all such messages pass by unrecorded. It is precisely the issue of discriminating among all messages that provokes such strong reaction from civil libertarians. For DCS 1000 to work, it must first "read" all messages passing over the network, those from suspect accounts named in the court order *and* those from others.

Never before has the FBI had the authority or the capability to capture *all* the communications passing through a given network. This authority was certainly expanded with the passage of the USA PATRIOT Act in 2001, raising a number of issues to be discussed later in the chapter.

The primary difference between data alteration and network intrusion is the intent of the intruder. By reading or "browsing" through confidential files, the intruder actually creates a copy of the file. Thus, mere browsing may be theft, but it does not deprive the owner of the data or the use of the data. This makes the distinction between data alteration and intrusion more meaningful. It may be impossible for an investigator to determine whether data have been altered. While altered data may be used for committing fraud or for denying the expression of the owner's idea, the simple intruder might not cause actual harm. The story of Kevin Mitnick perfectly exemplifies this distinction.[34]

The prosecution of Mitnick relied on estimates of the value of software that he had downloaded but had not altered. Several major corporations placed a total value of hundreds of millions of dollars on the software Mitnick obtained. This amount was determined by using a method suggested by the FBI: the companies estimated the total development costs of the software. The amount was questioned at various stages in Mitnick's trial. Since Mitnick did not deprive the companies of the products of their research and development, it seems that the actual economic harm caused would be less than the total cost. This contention was supported by the failure of a single corporation on the list of Mitnick's victims to report the loss to the Securities and Exchange Commission (such reporting is required for losses suffered by a company that sells stocks).

However, the corporations had no way of knowing whether the data had been altered. They may have devoted significant effort to reestablishing their confidence in the data. It is also possible that Mitnick could have sold the information to rival companies. There is no evidence or even suggestion that he did so, but the initial estimate of value may have reflected this fear. Delays caused by the intrusion may have reduced the market advantage of some of the corporations affected. Thus, the calculation of actual damages is very difficult. In the three years Mitnick spent awaiting trial, the value of the Sun Microsystems operating system (Solaris) dropped from an estimated prerelease value of several million dollars to essentially zero. The delay may have had a direct financial impact, but attributing this loss to Mitnick for prosecution was virtually impossible.

When intrusion is discovered, it often leaves the owner or administrator of the affected system questioning the integrity, accuracy, and authenticity of data on the network. Although the legitimate user of the system and data is not denied access to either, there is no reasonable certainty of data's security in the system. Security measures often require the removal of web-based resources and restoration of data from, one hopes, unaffected backup copies. This is often a very timely and costly venture, since it appears that hackers are becoming much more destructive in their work (Figures 16-7 and 16-8).

Denial of Service

More direct than the subtleties of network intrusion, the denial of service leaves little room for argument about a negative effect. Although any resource may be denied to the rightful user, the most prominent example of this computer-targeting is the network **denial-of-service (DoS) attack.** For instance, the website of Yahoo! was subjected to an unprecedented attack that effectively removed the site from the Internet for three hours. Other prominent Internet sites (e.g., Barnes and Noble, CNN, ABC, the White House, and the FBI) were also attacked. The initial reaction of law enforcement, security, and even hackers was shock that a site as large as Yahoo! could be overwhelmed.[35] Subsequent investigation showed that the attacks had been aimed at choke points that funneled the majority of the site's traffic through a few routers. Although not as bad as first suspected, the attack showed that even the largest sites on the Internet were not safe.

Recent denial-of-service attacks have gone beyond targeting individual websites and have gone after the infrastructure of the Internet. In 2007, three of the 13 root servers used to control the entire Internet were targeted, putting the backbone of the Internet at risk. The servers, responsible for directing users to websites, experienced a major increase in traffic as a result of a network of infected computers bombarding them with messages. The FBI, Department of Homeland Security, and other law enforcement agencies launched a coordinated effort to shut down the attack, which was mostly rebuffed by software protections.[36] Although the root servers are generally resilient, a major attack could slow or temporarily shut down the Internet, leading to financial losses and security concerns.

Computer Vandalism

When an intruder removes valuable information from a computer system, the intruder prevents the legitimate user or owner from having access to that information. Such **computer vandalism** can result in a direct loss or represent a substantial loss of expected revenue. If the data, such as a computer program or music, were for direct sale, one could possibly estimate the value of the lost data. However, it is more likely that the disrupted data were provided to the public to generate goodwill or advertising income or for no commercial purpose. Even though a dollar value cannot be attached to the data, the owner still has a right to present the intended message and be free from disruption. Many educational organizations, such as the University of Cambridge, maintain a web presence for no apparent commercial purpose other than recruitment and advertising. On May 13, 2001, the web camera at the University of Cambridge was replaced with the calling card of a computer vandal. The vandal wanted to express nothing more important than "Ne0tz owned u!"[37] In another example of data alteration, a group named "Hacking for Girlies" defaced *The New York Times* website. The defacement caused the *Times* embarrassment and the loss of advertising revenue for its free web-based service. Although an actual dollar value of loss was not disclosed by the *Times,* the incident drew national attention and affected interstate commerce.[38] Thus, the vandalism came under the jurisdiction of the FBI. To date, no arrests have been made for either of these incidents.

The web camera at Cambridge had to be removed permanently; similarly, the *Times* web page had to be removed several times, once for an entire day, to clear the affected portions and add or repair security. In both cases, the legitimate owner was criminally deprived of the ability to express an idea through equipment and data legitimately owned for that purpose. The consequences of computer vandalism are similar to those of data alteration or denial of service; many instances of computer vandalism also include network intrusion. These offenses target the computer, and thus leave direct evidence of the crime for investigators to detect.

The Computer as an Instrumentality of The Crime

An instrumentality of crime is a device used to commit a crime (Figure 16-9). Unlike the case with crimes targeting the computer, in computer-as-instrumentality crimes the perpetrator only *uses* the computer to further

When Maurice Paynter installed his new Internet security software, he got a sobering look at modern life online.

"I realized I'm being attacked constantly," he said. "It's like I'm in a war zone."

The software, which records attempts by hackers to infiltrate the host computer, showed Paynter was being scanned for vulnerable openings 30 to 40 times a day. Scarcely a day passes now that his software doesn't detect a virus.

"It's hard to believe how bad it's gotten," he said.

According to watchers of malicious codes, hacking is becoming pandemic, a national pastime for computer enthusiasts tempted to test their skills against the establishment.

Since 1998, the number of hacking attacks and virus releases has increased sevenfold. Viruses are being produced at a rate of a dozen or more per day, with some causing tens of millions of dollars in damages and lost productivity.

To make matters worse, many hackers are employing more intentionally destructive tools and tactics, some so callous that even their fellow code crackers have denounced them as a different breed.

Shortly after September 11's terrorist attacks, some hackers exploited the catastrophe to spread a virus using what appeared to be an e-mail pleading for peace. When the message was opened, the virus loaded onto the recipient's computer and damaged files.

In what is perhaps the most disturbing new trend, hackers are infiltrating well-known news sites, including Yahoo! and the *Orange County Register,* and rewriting stories. These "subversion of information" attacks raise a host of concerns in the wake of the Sept. 11 events when news sites were a major source of information.

"There used to be a strong ethic among hackers—get in and look around, but do no harm," said William Knowles, a 32-year-old Chicago-based computer security analyst and a former "benign" hacker. "That's been lost on the younger masses."

Experts say it's changing the Internet the way crime changes a neighborhood.

People are now constantly on alert for suspicious e-mail and other applications that could potentially harbor malicious code. It's gotten so bad that several Internet service providers have been threatening to disconnect customers who don't use protective antivirus software.

Meaner Viruses

The modern hacker has a selection of tools and strategies to choose from, including viruses and worms that typically spread over networks and clog computers, and attacks, which they can launch against websites to disable them or change their contents.

Viruses and worms have typically been considered dangerous because once downloaded, say unwittingly from an e-mail attachment, they often destroy valuable files—and many still do that.

But new strains are being designed to add extra sting.

Consider the recent SirCam virus. It arrives in the form of a seemingly harmless e-mail attachment. If the attachment is opened by the recipient, the virus sends itself to every name in the victim's address book. There's nothing special about that. But SirCam doesn't stop there. Before forwarding itself on, it raids your "My Documents" folder—where people often store their most sensitive material—and randomly selects a file that it sends out with the infected e-mail. Maybe it's a boring, meaningless file; maybe it's a file that gets you fired or divorced.

"With SirCam and some of these other recent releases you see a blending of standard basic virus making with some new, more sophisticated hacking tools," said Tom Power-ledge, with security software maker Symantec.

But before a virus can do damage it has to enter a computer or a network, and hackers have taken infiltration methods to new levels as well.

Most garden-variety viruses and worms enter computers when infected e-mail is downloaded.

This usually requires some sort of a trick euphemistically known as "social engineer-ing." The Anna Kournikova virus released earlier this year (2007) as an e-mail attachment promised those who would download it a picture of the heartthrob tennis star.

But the recent Nimda virus was a different animal altogether, infecting e-mail and network servers, which regulate digital traffic, web-sites, and shared disk drives, where it automatically copied itself without the need for anyone to download it.

Nimda was so persistent, it took several major efforts on the part of network managers around the world to finally suppress it.

"Nimda was certainly alarming but not unexpected," said Chad Dougherty, an Internet security analyst at Carnegie Mellon's federally funded Software Engineering Institute. "Hackers are now using best-of-breed methods for propagating malicious code, and viruses like Nimda are the result."

Culture of Hacking

Hacking wasn't always this destructive. In fact, it started at MIT in the 1960s as a perfectly innocent pastime, aimed at tweaking higher performance out of some of the first mainframe computers to appear on college campuses. The term *hacker* was taken from a model train club at the university that amused itself by "hacking" better performance out of electronic toys.

In the 1970s, college students known as "phone phreaks" turned their fascination with technology to hacking long distance telephone networks for free calls. Apple computer founders Steve Jobs and Steve Wozniak were among hacking's early gurus.

By the 1980s, as academic and defense research computer networks began rapidly expanding into what would become the Internet, the hobby had started turning dark. Phone phreaks turned to hacking these networks, exchanging passwords and techniques on some of the first electronic message boards.

Later, the first hacking groups formed, and the movie WarGames introduced the public to hacking with a story about a teenager who nearly sparks nuclear war by meddling with defense computers.

It wasn't until 1988 that hacking publicly shook the establishment with the Morris worm.

Created by Cornell graduate student Robert Morris, Jr., the worm program spread through some 6,000 academic and defense computers, paralyzing many.

The spindly, bespectacled Morris typified the new computer nerd and showed the world what a few lines of renegade code could do. At his federal trial, covered on the front page of *The New York Times,* Morris told prosecu-tors that he never intended to crash computers, but rather only wanted to expose security flaws.

Until recently, this has been the credo of the hacker: expose weaknesses so software venders will fix them. It took exceptional skill to do this, and indeed, Morris was the son of a federal computer security expert.

But as the Internet exploded and a new generation raised on computers has taken to hacking, the hobby has degenerated into what old school hackers call "crass vandalism" perpetrated by "script kiddies."

These are typically young, suburban males, in their late teens and 20s who create often highly destructive viruses using prewritten code such as the VBS Worm Generator downloaded from the Internet. The 20-year-old hacker who released the Kournikova virus was found by police to be in possession of hundreds of viruses he had collected off the Internet.

"This is point-and-click hacking," said a San Francisco–area "white hat" hacker who calls himself Pauly Morf. "It requires no skill or understanding of network vulner-abilities. I have no respect for it or this generation."

That said, the recent spike in hacking that the script kiddies are largely responsible for has helped send a wake-up call across the Internet that should eventually make it more secure.

Despite the occasional warning of a looming digital apocalypse, many hackers and security experts alike predict more awareness, especially among home computer users, and more secure software will help keep hackers in check, at least those attracted to the cheap thrill of hurling monkey wrenches.

"Hackers have had it pretty easy lately," said Pauly Morf. "But the bar will be raised."

▲ **FIGURE 16-7 Hacker havoc**

(Source: John Yaukey, *Dallas Morning News,* Oct. 15, 2001, Section D, pp. 1–2)

Name of virus	[Alias (es)]	Date	List Reported by:
4VBS/Gedza	[. . . . .]	4 / 04	NbWW
VBS/Redlof. A-m.	[. . . . .]	10 / 02	DpFnJcKdNbSj
W32/Allaple ! ITW#1	[!21FE . . . .]	2 / 07	NbPaPn
W32/Allaple ! ITW#2	[!25C7 . . . .]	1 / 07	PaPnSj
W32/Allaple ! ITW#3	[!03B0 . . . .]	2 / 07	PaPn
W32/Areses ! ITW#1	[Scano ! FCE2 . . . .]	5 / 06	AoMt
W32/Areses ! ITW#12	[Scano ! 5709 . . . .]	6 / 06	AoMt
W32/Areses ! ITW#13	[Scano ! E7DF . . . .]	5 / 06	AoMtSr
W32/Areses ! ITW#14	[Scano ! 37C6 . . . .]	6 / 06	AoMt
W32/Areses ! ITW#15	[Scano ! 2946 . . . .]	6 / 06	AoMt
W32/Areses ! ITW#19	[Scano ! E060 . . . .]	6 / 06	AoMt
W32/Areses ! ITW#22	[Scano ! 9E42 . . . .]	6 / 06	AoMtSj
W32/Areses ! ITW#23	[Scano ! A997 . . . .]	6 / 06	AoMt
W32/Areses ! ITW#25	[Scano ! 8676 . . . .]	6 / 06	AoMt
W32/Areses ! ITW#37	[Scano ! 4B8B . . . .]	5 / 07	MtTl
W32/Areses ! ITW#41	[Scano ! 9931 . . . .]	5 / 07	MtTl
W32/Areses ! ITW#47	[Scano ! D916 . . . .]	5 / 07	FnMo
W32/Areses ! ITW#6	[Scano ! BE95 . . . .]	5 / 06	AoMt
W32/Areses ! ITW#7	[Scano ! 299C . . . .]	6 / 06	AoMt:Sj
W32/Bagle ! ITW#112	[! BF9D . . . .]	6 / 06	AoMoRsSjSrStWw
W32/Bagle ! ITW#113	[! 6FA1 . . . .]	6 / 06	AoFnRsSjSoSrStTlWw
W32/Bagle ! ITW#114	[! D6BB . . . .]	6 / 06	AoMoSjSoTlWw
W32/Bagle ! ITW#115	[! 3EF8. . . . .]	6 / 06	AoRsSrSt
W32/Bagle ! ITW#122	[! E058. . . . .]	5 / 07	FnSj
W32/Bagle ! ITW#136	[! 6AB4. . . . .]	1 / 07	SjTa
W32/Bagle ! ITW#137	[! CA93. . . . .]	12 / 06	FnMtSjSoTaT1Ww
W32/Bagle ! ITW#139	[! 770E. . . . .]	3 / 07	FnSr
W32/Bagle ! ITW#141	[! B84d. . . . .]	12 / 06	FnMtTa
W32/Bagle ! ITW#82	[! CME – 328. . . . .]	2 / 06	FnJcMoSjSoSrWw
W32/Bagle ! ITW#83	[! 442C. . . . .]	2 / 06	MtWw
W32/Bagle ! ITW#84	[Sality ! 111F. . . . .]	2 / 06	FnIsJgMtSjSo
W32/Bagle ! ITW#85	[Sality ! 7D26. . . . .]	3 / 06	FnIsMtSo
W32/Bagle ! ITW#96	[Sality ! 421F. . . . .]	3 / 06	MtSr
W32/Bagle.AA-mm	[. . . . .]	4 / 04	DpMoMtRsSj
W32/Bagle.AF-mm	[. . . . .]	7 / 04	DpMoMtSjSr
W32/Bagle.AG-mm	[. . . . .]	7 / 04	DpMoMtSjSr
W32/Bagle.AH-mm	[. . . . .]	5 / 05	MoMtRsWw

▲ **FIGURE 16-8** **Viruses in the wild**

Following is a small percentage of the 525 active, verified computer viruses as of June 2006 as listed by Wild List. Wild List employs a worldwide team of antivirus and corporate volunteers who research, verify, and compile a list of computer viruses available online at www.wildlist.org.

a criminal end; the computer and the data contained therein are not the object of the crime.

Theft

Under the common law definition of theft, a criminal actor deprives a legitimate owner of property by taking that property. As in auto theft, simply borrowing the item is still a criminal deprivation of the owner. In an electronic environment, where data are more easily copied than deleted, depriving the owner of the property is relatively rare. Donn Parker, creator of the first computer crime typology, notes that market-sensitive proprietary information, financial information, trade secrets, process technology information, human resource information, customer information, information products, transitory information, and security information can all

▲ **FIGURE 16-9**

Computers as the instrumentality of crime

In some cases, the computer is used to actually commit the crime. For example, a computer may be used to steal assets from a large number of transactions. In the round-down salami technique (this page), the computer is used to round calculated dollar amounts down to the nearest cent and then divert the remainders to a special account operated by the thief.

(Ryan McVay/Getty Images)

have value to the owner.[39] To some degree, maintaining the value of such information requires that the owner either maintain confidence in the integrity of the information or control the distribution of the information. As in the Mitnick case, depriving the owner of sole possession or depriving the owner of the right to control distribution amounts to theft by reducing the value of the information.

Other, more blatant, examples of computerized theft actually deprive the legitimate owner of a tangible asset. The **salami-slice** technique is a money crime; it is an automated means of stealing assets from a large number of transactions. In the round-down salami technique, the computer is used to round calculated dollar amounts down to the nearest cent. Normally, gains and losses from rounding even out, so neither the merchant nor the customer loses on average. By always rounding down and diverting the rounded-off amount to a special account, the criminal deprives both merchant and consumer of assets; however, the amount is often trivial, like a slice from a salami—too thin to produce a noticeable effect. Only after a number of such slices are removed, does the amount of missing salami become noticeable.

Data theft has become a major concern, owing to the incredible costs such a breach can impose on a business and an individual consumer. Nearly 85% of respondents in a survey that queried employees of 702 U.S. companies said that there had been some type of data theft from their organization.[40] Data theft includes the unauthorized access to private or personal data, such as credit card numbers, often stored in databases on corporate or government computers. Theft or loss of a computer or data storage device made up 54% of identity-theft related data breaches in 2006.[41] Hackers may also gain entry to networks, as in the 2003 attack on the University of Texas at Austin. In March of that year, a UT student named Christopher Phillips accessed the Social Security numbers and names of 37,000 current and former UT students. Although there was no further dissemination of the information, UT incurred expenses of $45,000 in an effort to warn victims of the potential for identity theft.[42] Had Phillips sold the data or used it maliciously, losses to victims could have numbered in the millions of dollars. Malicious codes such as Trojan horses or other viruses also pose a major threat to data. (A Trojan horse is a trick program that looks legitimate but that, after it's opened, does damage.) In 2006, researchers found that of the top 50 malicious code samples, two-thirds of them threatened confidential data in some way.[43]

New advances in mobile data storage devices also pose a threat to data integrity. Known as "pod slurping," data devices that are Universal Service Bus (USB) compatable, such as memory sticks, iPods, and PDAs, can be plugged into virtually any computer and used to download information that can later be sold or utilized for malicious purposes. A 60-GB iPod equipped with the right applications could be connected to a company computer by a vendor or a disgruntled employee and used to download every piece of data from a medium-sized firm in a matter of minutes.[44] Mobile storage devices may also be used to upload malicious code intended to mine data for unauthorized use.

Another type of data theft uses the hallmarks of authentic websites, such as eBay and PayPal, to trick unsuspecting consumers into providing their Social Security numbers, passwords, or account numbers to identity thieves. Known as **phishing**, this ploy often entails e-mails that appear to come from legitimate banks, retailers, or government organizations. Consumers see mail in their inbox with a subject line that reads, for example, "Account Suspended." Because such a large number of individuals use services such as eBay and PayPal, chances are that they have an account with the organization that the e-mail appears to be from. The e-mail may employ official logos cut and pasted into the body and ask the customer to click on a link that appears to direct them to the official website. However, the link actually directs the customer to a look-alike site that may then ask them to verify their account number and password. Once the information is entered into this site, the perpetrators have access to the real account and can use or sell the information for purposes of theft or fraud.

Phishing is a nearly ubiquitous occurrence for e-mail users. In June of 2006, The Anti-Phishing Working Group reported the existence of over 30,000 fake websites posing as 146 legitimate companies or organizations used to lure sensitive information from internet users.[45]

Theft of Service

Although many services available on the Internet are free, some data and services are considered proprietary. This means the users must pay to use the data or service. Using proprietary services without paying is theft. Unlike the common law definition of theft, theft in this case does not necessarily include denial of the data or service to legitimate users. Many providers invest in their ability to meet the demand for their services. For instance, in the past the Internet service provider America Online (AOL) failed to anticipate the demand for Internet access. As a result, many customers were not able to connect to AOL servers. To remedy this situation, AOL invested significant amounts of money on increasing its capacity. The amount of the increase was carefully planned to avoid spending too much. Although users had been temporarily deprived of service, this AOL incident was not theft of service. The damage from theft of service occurs when the criminal use of service forces the owner to invest in more capacity to meet the projected needs of legitimate users.

Fraud

As in the common definition of fraud, fraud using a computer exploits the trust, guaranteed by law, in a business transaction. Fraud can be perpetrated by the buyer, seller, or peer in a transaction. **Shopping cart fraud** is an example of consumer fraud against a business. After purchases are selected, the computer criminal saves a copy of the purchase page and alters the prices. Once the altered prices are in place, the criminal submits the page as normal. Some merchants do not discover the fraud until they match inventory to purchases—possibly a month or more after the merchandise is shipped.

Although basic security procedures or well-designed shopping cart programs can prevent this, many online merchants do not use either.

Other varieties of online fraud are simply hi-tech variants of the methods described in Chapter 14, "White-Collar Crime and Larceny." Old scams have found a new source of victims on the Internet. Pyramid schemes feign legitimacy with professional-looking websites and official-sounding web addresses.[46] For example, a basic pyramid scheme can claim association with a major retailer by using a trick URL, or web address.

The following URL takes a browser to Wal-Mart, the leading retailer in the United States (Figure 16-10): www.walmart.com/index.gsp?cat50&dept50&path50. The next URL, however, takes a browser to the website of whoever paid the $50 fee required to register this web address: www.walmart.com@homeshoppingforyou.com.

Without even registering a web domain name, a criminal can have URLs that provide access to his or her page from anywhere on the web. By using these URLs from a "front," the criminal can claim ignorance of where the links go. The following links can easily be altered to lead to anywhere on the Internet without changing anything in front of the "@" sign:

- www.walmart.com@192.168.23.56
- www.walmart.com@%C0%A8%17%38

Both of these URLs go to the same place. Another way to perpetrate fraud by misusing a company's name is to register a URL similar to that of the company, such as this one: www.wa1mart.com.

Although it is difficult to distinguish, the "l" in Wal-Mart is actually the numeral one, "1." Most people would not make this mistake when typing but would fail to

◄ **FIGURE 16-10 Wal-Mart**
Large retailers are often the victims of computer fraud because of their vast name recognition and international presence.
(© Najlah Feanny/Corbis SABA)

notice the difference on a link from a "front" page. Depending on which type font the browser uses, this phony URL may appear exactly like the authentic URL. The loss to Wal-Mart is obvious, as potential customers are lured to fraudulent sites.

Not all Internet fraud depends on acquiring someone else's legitimacy. The Internet is often used to spread misinformation in "pump-and-dump" schemes, as previously discussed. The scheme gets its name from unscrupulous people heavily promoting the stock of a small company that usually is suffering economic and financial problems. The stock is a thinly traded company with not many shares being actively bought and sold. The people behind this scheme intentionally "pump up" the price by providing inaccurate information. Once the stock reaches an artificially inflated high, the owners of the stock "dump" it, and the investor is left holding the relatively worthless stock.[47] In many of these cases, "freelance public relations companies" offer advice to investors or post misleading information in financial newsgroups. With more people using the Internet to avoid costly fees from traditional brokerage houses, the small investor must be especially critical of information. However, as with most fraud, basic human greed and time pressure combine to make perfect victims. Penny stocks are often used because it is easy to fake a dramatic increase. If a stock is traded at 2 cents per share, it's quite an easy jump to 4 cents or 5 cents . . . that's a 100% increase in value! One doesn't normally see such price fluctuations within a very limited time period on the New York or NASDAQ Stock Exchanges.[48]

Fraudsters can spend relatively little money to "pump" up the value. With a few well-placed, false news stories to back up the sudden jump, investors will be convinced that they are at the ground floor of a company that just received a big defense contract, bio-tech patent, or some other basis for rapid expansion. Combine this tactic with a few false news site links in an investment e-mail newsletter, and the fraudster can make huge profits. Further, those profits can be accrued in a stolen investment account or one created under a false name. The fraudster can abscond with the profits and never be seen again.

Threat and Harassment

The U.S. Department of Justice (DOJ) maintains a website that details a range of threatening behaviors conducted on the Internet. In an early case of **cyberstalking,** a Maryland man, Warren Gray, pled guilty to sending five e-mail messages that graphically threatened the lives of his victim and the victim's family. Gray had also slashed the victim's car tires and left a hatchet in the victim's office. In this case, cyberstalking coincided with real-world stalking, but the conviction under federal law stemmed from the use of "interstate wires" to transmit the threat.[49] While cyberstalking and real-world stalking

have some similarities, there are a number of differences between the two.

Major Similarities

- The majority of cases involve stalking by former intimates, although stranger stalking also occurs.
- Most victims are women; most stalkers are men.
- Stalkers are generally motivated by the desire to control their victims.

Major Differences

- In offline stalking, the perpetrator and the victim must generally be located in the same geographic area; in cyberstalking, the perpetrator may be located across the street or across the country from the victim.
- It is much easier for a cyberstalker to encourage third parties to harass and/or to threaten a victim (e.g., by posting inflammatory messages in the victim's name to bulletin boards and in chat rooms, causing readers of the messages to send threatening notes to the victim "author").
- Cyberstalking has lower barriers to harassment and threats; with technology, cyberstalkers can threaten victims more immediately and more easily than is typically possible with physical stalking.

In March 2004, the first comprehensive state law specifically addressing cyberstalking was initiated in the State of Washington. HB 2771 declared that a person is guilty of cyberstalking if he or she, with intent to harass, intimidate, torment, or embarrass any other person, makes a communication to the other person or a third party through electronic mail or the Internet:

1. Using any lewd, lascivious, indecent, or obscene words or language, or suggesting the commission of any lewd or lascivious act;
2. Anonymously or repeatedly whether or not conversation occurs; or
3. Threatening to inflict injury on the person or property of the person called or any member of his or her family or household.[50]

The law is the result of a six-year battle between Joelle Ligon of Washington and a stalker, James Murphy of South Carolina. He sent her "cruel, anonymous e-mails. He posed as her in chat rooms, solicited sex, and gave out her home and work numbers. He e-mailed her coworkers, using her name, with links to porn sites. He spread vicious lies about her."[51] As is typical in most stalking cases, Mr. Murphy knew Ms. Ligon prior to the stalking.[52] They dated from the time she was 15 until she was 22 when she moved away and later married.[53] Eight years later, harassing e-mails began, and the stalking escalated from there. Based on the personal content in the e-mail, Ms. Ligon guessed the identity of her stalker but was powerless to stop him. The effects on victims of both stalking and cyberstalking can include diagnosable stress-related disorders and life-style changes.[54] Her lengthy battle culminated in federal charges under the Federal Telecommunications Act 26 times. In July 2004, Murphy plead guilty to two counts.[55]

In another cyberstalking case, Carl Edward Johnson of Bienfait, Saskatchewan, Canada, was convicted of posting death threats against U.S. federal judges involved in the conviction of James Dalton Bell, an advocate of assassination politics. Johnson had sent the messages through "anonymous" remailers, but he was identified as the sender through technical testimony from a special agent of the U.S. Treasury's Inspector General for Tax Administration office. Convictions such as this demonstrate that the myth of the "anonymous Internet" is overly optimistic regarding its ability to protect a criminal from investigation and/or prosecution.[56]

Cyberstalking has taken on a new modus operandi in recent years, owing to the surge in popularity of social networking sites such as MySpace and Face Book. These sites let users create and maintain profiles that often contain personal information, such as where the individual works, as well as personal photographs. Although users may choose to keep their profile private, many often become virtual "friends" with individuals whom they may not know, therefore allowing them access to facts that could be used to in cyberstalking. A recent study revealed that 41% of Facebook users, when contacted, freely gave away private information such as phone numbers and e-mail addresses to complete strangers.[57] Savvy cyberstalkers can even determine a person's real life friends, family, and activities just by monitoring open comments and communications posted on a profile. MySpace also offers a calendar feature that could potentially alert stalkers to the location of their target during certain events or activities.

MySpace and similar sites have also led to the creation of a new type of harassment, known as cyber bullying. Cyber bullies utilize the blog and bulletin features of such websites to threaten, harass, or post disparaging remarks about another person. The issue has become a hot button issue in schools, where it is often punished as a violation of bullying rules.[58] However, cyber bullying can become a law enforcement issue, particularly if a student is threatened by bodily harm, or experiences bodily harm as a result of internet threats.

The use of the computer as an instrumentality of crime introduces a new realm of investigative complications, but investigators trained in the collection and use of digital evidence also have a new realm of opportunities to pursue criminals. Although the unprecedented ability of networked computers to reach individuals produces vast opportunities for criminals, it also produces huge amounts of evidence in which to prosecute criminals.

The Computer as Incidental to The Crime

The computer is incidental to crime when "a pattern or incident of criminality uses a computer simply for ease in maintaining the efficacy of criminal transactions."[59] In this category, the computer does not conduct the illegal transaction; it simply facilitates it.

Money Laundering and Criminal Enterprise

Again, as noted in Chapter 14, "White-Collar Crime and Larceny," money laundering provides criminals with the ability to spend illegally acquired money. It involves disguising financial assets so they can be used without detection of the illegal activity that produced them. Through money laundering, the criminal transforms the monetary proceeds derived from criminal activity into funds from an apparently legal source.[60] The movement of money can be greatly facilitated and, to some degree, be done anonymously by using computer systems.

Computers appeal to criminal enterprises or businesses for many of the same reasons they appeal to other businesses: they are quick, reliable, and very accurate, and they perform many business-related tasks far faster than would be the case if the tasks were done manually. Thus, computers are used to support many different types of criminal enterprises, including loan-sharking and drug rings. A number of prostitution rings have used computers to keep track of customers and payroll. In a process called **smurfing,** funds can be divided into groups that are too small to be noticed. These smaller amounts can be wired out of the country and merged together later in an offshore bank.[61] Banks and casinos are closely regulated and heavily penalized for money laundering; however, the enormous volume of financial transactions in the United States makes it difficult for regulators to identify even relatively large questionable transactions. The number of such transactions is likely to increase as more businesses and consumers begin to use electronic funds transfer services.[62]

Created in 1990, the Financial Crimes Enforcement Network (FinCEN)[63] is a part of the Department of the Treasury. It regulates and facilitates compliance with the Banking Secrecy Act of 1970 and other relevant legislation. It also acts to coordinate the effort of financial crimes investigators and regulators. Financial investigations are extremely complex and difficult to conduct. They often require investigators with many years of experience in the financial industry to understand all their intricacies. No single agency possesses a sufficiently broad or cross-jurisdictional focus and information base to track financial movements. Then, too, the sheer size, variety, and pace of change of the financial sector make such investigations even more difficult to undertake.[64] However, following the money often leads to the top of the criminal organization.

The richness of computers as sources of evidence has not been lost on investigators. The study of digital evidence has expanded beyond network intrusion. Detailed procedures and legal requirements of electronic evidence are available from a number of sources.[65]

Using the same techniques of following the money trail, investigators can map a criminal enterprise and dismantle it.

Child Pornography, Pedophilia, and Sexual Assault

Chapter 11, "Crimes against Children," details the use of the Internet for luring unsuspecting children to pedophiles and for distributing child pornography. The Internet has been the key communication medium for the sale and exchange of child pornography on both an international and a domestic basis. In September 1998, one of the largest child pornography sting operations in history occurred, resulting in the arrest of over 200 people in 21 countries.[66] Code-named "Operation Cathedral," this operation was coordinated by British police in Europe, Australia, and the United States and confiscated more than 100,000 indecent images of children. Most of the images were being traded among child pornographers over the Internet. Most of the people arrested were men; however, some were women who belonged to exclusive child pornography clubs throughout the world. One U.S.-based club, called "Wonderland," had images for sale depicting children as young as 2 years of age. The sheer size of the pornography network shocked the police as well as the general public.

In a more recent case, on January 14, 2005, Eugene Valentine, CEO of a credit card processing company named Connections USA, plead guilty to conspiracy to launder money.[67] This was only the first conviction in the investigation of an international child pornography retail business based in Belarus—where child pornography is not illegal. Their company, Regpay, is at the heart of a major international investigation called Operation Falcon. First announced on January 16, 2004, but starting in 2003, Operation Falcon included several Federal agencies such as U.S. Immigration and Customs Enforcement (ICE), U.S. Postal Inspectors, the Federal Bureau of Investigation (FBI), and the Internal Revenue Service (IRS). Agents posing as child pornography buyers acquired images from websites using credit cards and then followed the money trail created. Given the sheer volume of offenses (and offenders), agents concentrated on the offenders posing the greatest ongoing risk to children. Federal authorities first arrested subscribers with criminal records or those with occupations that involve contact with children. These included a family physician, a campus minister, a part-time teacher and church-youth coordinator, along with three sex offenders.[68]

Regpay's three principals, all Belarussians, were arrested with the cooperation of French and Spanish authorities and extradited to the United States. Investigations around the world have uncovered substantial numbers of child pornography images. Australia's Operation Auxin has netted an estimated 1 million images. The youngest child depicted was 11 months old. Many images contained sexual acts between children and between children and adults. Interviews of suspects whose e-mail addresses have been found at child pornography sites have netted a number of indictments and a cascade of new materials, some homemade. A Sydney school teacher was held without bail after he set up a camera behind a changing room mirror to capture images of children naked.[69]

The desire to create child pornography images directly stimulates a direct assaultive act. Where the act is assaulting, luring, or molesting children, the "incidental" use of a computer serves as the connection that provides motive or opportunity. Children are victimized in the creation of these images. For instance, a 10-year-old girl was molested at a slumber party by her host's father. Ronald Riva was sentenced for that act. Riva described his actions to a pedophile club via the Internet as he abused the girl. He also responded to requests from club members to conduct specific acts with the children while filming. That was for the U.S.-based club called "Wonderland."

The growing demand for fresh pornographic images has compelled pedophiles to new depths, including an act depicted in an infamous series called "baby-rape." In regard to the Wonderland investigation, New York Attorney General Dennis C. Vacco stated: "These aren't nudie pictures . . . These are graphic images of children being raped and sodomized. These are records of crimes."[70] Here we see the traffic of child pornography not only stimulating both the desire to consume more such images, showing greater levels of depravity and child victimization, but also stimulating the actual victimization of the children depicted. As a result of these cases, the United Nations called for a worldwide offensive to curb the exchange of pedophilia on the Internet, a very difficult task considering the vast number of jurisdictions and judicial systems present in the international community.[71]

Few would argue that children need to be protected from predators. It is fairly simple to set up stings for pedophiles using the Internet, and in some cases digital evidence can be linked to both motive and opportunity. Several criminal cases have introduced e-mail as evidence of the state of mind of the accused. For example, hate speech online has been used to establish a racial or sexual bias for motive. Similarly, e-mail has been used to actually trace the interaction of assailant and victim. Meetings discussed or demanded in e-mail can be used to place the assailant at the crime scene. Unlike the trafficking of pornographic images, the desire to create those images directly stimulates an act. Where the act is assaulting, luring, or molesting children, the computer often serves as the connection that provides motive or opportunity.

Crimes Associated with The Prevalence of Computers

Computer crime investigators should be aware of new targets of crime. Crimes associated with the prevalence of computers make up a subset of computer crime that relies on the relatively new computer and information industry. Targets of these crimes are mainly the industry itself but also include its customers and even people who have avoided information technology.

Intellectual-Property Violations

In an average week, adults who are online watch TV and surf the web for 10 hours, listen to radio for 5 hours, and play video games for 3.3 hours.[72] In 2004, the music industry in the United States was estimated to be worth $11.05 billion.[73] Without great fanfare or public notice, the video game industry has overtaken the film industry. Video game revenues overtook movie box-office receipts in 2001. A recent report estimates the industry to be worth $18 billion.[74] In spite of the massive sales for the electronic entertainment industry, the combined draw of the film industry, video game industry, and music industry is less than 10% of the total sales of business software. The top 500 companies producing software earned approximately $330 billion in 2004.[75] All these industries rely on the sale of information. This makes one of the fastest growing portions of the U.S. economy vulnerable to computer crime.

Intellectual-property violations are often described as **piracy.** Music piracy has recently replaced software piracy in the public mind as the leading example of this crime. Piracy involves repacking, reformatting, or in some other way distributing an unauthorized intellectual property without the pretence that it is real. The RIAA classifies counterfeit materials as unauthorized distribution of seemingly legitimate products. The most common form of piracy occurs online. Peer-to-peer file sharing networks have opened whole new avenues to intellectual property theft (Figure 16-11).

The staggering economic losses from software piracy outstrip the other intellectual property–based industries. The Business Software Alliance (BSA) is the principal software industry anti-piracy resource. The BSA estimated that in 2005, global losses due to piracy were over $30 billion.[76] This assumes that every piece of software installed on computers worldwide would have been purchased if it had not been obtained illegally. This assumption is highly questionable, but the staggering amount of piracy still makes intellectual property crimes among the most economically damaging computer crimes.

Large-scale software piracy began in Asia. The BSA reports that one person selling unauthorized copies of some 40 different popular programs in Singapore may have made several million dollars even though he charged as little as $15 for copies of programs that retailed for as much as $600.[77] Violation of U.S. copyright laws in China—particularly piracy of software, video-taped entertainment, and music—led the United States, in early 1995, to announce that it would place a 100% tariff on all products entering this country from China unless the Chinese government took action to eliminate such violations. This is one of the few incidents in history in which criminal activity actually influenced U.S. foreign policy. Unfortunately, piracy and counterfeiting of products in China (and other parts of Southeast Asia) continues to escalate.

Intellectual property disputes have also been raised with the increasing popularity of YouTube and similar sites (Figure 16-12). YouTube, a wildly popular site that hosts video sharing, boasts nearly 63 million users a month.[78] In 2007, Viacom (which owns CBS, MTV, and Comedy Central) sued the parent company of YouTube, alleging that nearly 160,000 clips of programming were posted illegally on the site. Viacom accuses YouTube of "massive, intentional copyright infringement" for posting clips from television shows and music videos. Other media companies have also issued challenges against YouTube, including the Fox network, who subpoenaed the company after leaked episodes of its hit show 24 were posted before they aired.[79] YouTube policy dictates that the site will remove clips that infringe on copyrights upon notice, but media giants complain that by the time the site removes the offending clip, millions may have already seen it. YouTube litigation, which is still moving through the courts, may prove to be a turning point where intellectual property and the Internet are concerned.

Misuse of Telephone Systems

Telephone **phreakers** are people who trick telephone systems into believing that long-distance service and airtime are being legitimately purchased. The interest of phreakers also extends to collateral areas, such as trying to break the code on magnetic subway cards for free rides and to decode the magnetic strips that are found on the back of some states' driver's licenses.[80]

In one phreaker case, a company employee figured out how to avoid the internal tracking system for long-distance charges and then sold time cheaply to friends to make telephone calls, which resulted in a $108,000 loss.[81] Cellular telephones are also subject to attack by phreakers. This is done by using one of two common fraud methods: cloning and tumbling.[82] Cellular telephones have two numbers: a mobile identification number (MIN) and an electronic serial number (ESN). Every time a call is made, the microchip in a cellular

Intellectual property: "The concept of intellectual property treats certain works and discoveries similarly to physical property. In most countries, exclusive rights policies grant certain kinds of rights to the creative output of authors and inventors, some expiring after a set period of time, and others lasting indefinitely. The term glosses over fundamental distinctions between types of exclusive rights such as copyright and patents, and encourages authors and inventors to regard these rights as natural rights."[i] The common denominator of intellectual property is that some ideas or expressions may be owned.

The Business Software Alliance (BSA), the Recording Industry Association of America (RIAA), and the Motion Picture Association of America (MPAA) are industry trade organizations for producers of intellectual property. They have familiar and benign functions. The MPAA sets movie ratings (G, PG, PG-13, R, NC-17). The RIAA certifies sales by musicians and awards Gold and Platinum records to artists. The BSA tracks sales for the software industry. They have also made the protection of their member's intellectual property rights a matter of national importance. These organizations have made news in their attempts to reduce the illegal distribution of intellectual property.

1.1 RIAA Classifications of Intellectual Property Theft for Music Recordings:[ii]

- *Counterfeit:* unauthorized duplication of not only the sounds and track listing but also of the original artwork, label, trademark, and packaging of a legitimate recording.
- *Pirate:* unauthorized duplication of sounds from one or more legitimate recordings. Sometimes advertised as "DJ" or "Dance" mixes or contain a compilation of various hits from different artists.
- *Bootleg:* unauthorized recording of a performance that has been broadcast on radio or television, or of a live concert.
- *Online Piracy:* unauthorized distribution and redistribution of a recording through the Internet or other information network technology.

1.2 Criminal Law
1.2.1 Counterfeiting

Federal copyright law 17 U.S.C. §§ 101 et seq. reserves the exclusive right to distribute a sound recording to the owner of the recording. Criminal violations usually require the intent to make a profit; penalties for such violations include up to five years in prison and fines of $250,000. Using mass-duplication

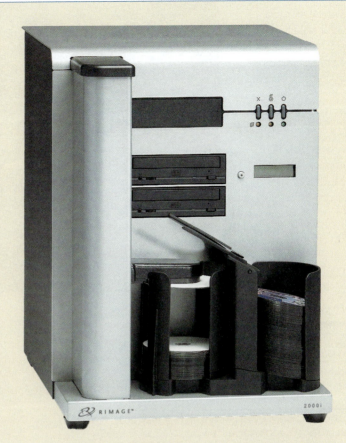

Rimage machines are legitimate tools for mass producing software and entertainment CDs. They can also be used as an instrumentality of intellectual property theft. Cases of blank CDs are commonly found near Rimage machines.

(Courtesy Rimage)

machines for CDs and DVDs called *Rimage machines,* pirates can mass-produce counterfeit software, music, and movies. Equipment used as an instrumentality of the crime can also be forfeited. Two additional laws, 18 U.S.C. § 2318 (Trafficking in Counterfeit Labels) and 18 U.S.C. § 2320 (Trademark Counterfeiting), can also draw sentences of up to 10 years and fines of up to $2 million.

1.2.2 Bootlegging

18 U.S.C. § 2319(A) prohibits unauthorized distribution, manufacture, or importation of live music performances. The law allows United States Customs to seize such items entering the country. Bootleg copies can often be purchased under the counter of local music shops, at flea markets, or from vendor's stalls. In the past, a share of the proceeds

from the sale of blank cassettes went to RIAA members. This was a compromise reached in recognition of bootlegging and illegally copying music. Today, there is no such payment from blank computer media. There have been discussions about charging extra for the sale of all blank media to help cover the costs of piracy and bootlegging.

1.2.3 Online Piracy

An early beneficiary of bootlegging, Metallica, now crusades against intellectual property rights violations. The peer-to-peer network, Napster, allowed users to trade Meticalla's music in the popular MP3 format. Since that time, the RIAA has engaged in a running battle with high-volume users on peer-to-peer networks. Criminal convictions of peer-to-peer users are rare because it often cannot be

▲ **FIGURE 16-11   Theft of intellectual property**

Commonly available equipment allows intellectual property thieves to record live or televised performances and produce a high resolution, professional-looking package to sell.

(Courtesy Deputy Chief Louis Pacheco, Raynham Police Department, Massachusetts)

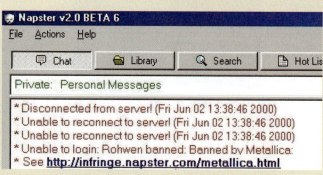

The opening shots of the peer-to-peer battles was Metallica's challenge of Napster users sharing their songs.

shown that they make a profit. The No Electronic Theft Act (NET) expanded Federal protection to include "willful reproduction and distribution of copyrighted works." It also clarified the term *financial gain* to include the receipt of other copyrighted works in return for sharing. According to the new federal law, "commercial gain" is no longer needed to regulate interstate commerce.

1.3 Technology of Intellectual Property Theft

MP3 stands for Motion Picture Expert Group Layer Three. Although the MP3 format is a popular technology in illegal distribution, it is not illegal to possess MP3s. MP3 is simply an audio compression scheme that can produce sound quality indistinguishable from a CD in much less space. Generally, 1 minute of sound takes about 1 megabyte of space. Without such a compression scheme, sharing CDs over the Internet would be much more difficult and nearly impossible for anyone without a broadband connection. To create MP3s, software called a "ripper" is used to convert the digital encoding of a CD, called Red Book or ISO 9660,[iii] to the MP3 compressed format.

A similar technology called DivX allows users to compress video. Generally, DivX allows 80–90 minutes of storage at 640 x 480 on a CD or about 650 MB (with lower resolution than a DVD, but creating a much smaller file). Once again, the DivX compression is not illegal; the theft of intellectual property is.[iv] Both DivX and MP3 rely on a codec (coder/decoder) to substitute a brief bit pattern for a longer one. The short patterns are then decoded for play. Incompatible codecs are a problem for the widespread legitimate sale of digital music.

Although peer-to-peer (P2P) networks have drawn attention, a substantial amount of intellectual property theft still occurs with blank DVDs or CDs. P2P networks allow users to connect directly to each other without using a central "node." True P2P networks function as many individual systems inefficiently sharing information. On the positive side, the lack of a central node makes it harder to control a P2P network. Napster brought P2P networks to national prominence, but it relied on central servers to coordinate file sharing. The benefit of P2P-hybrids like Napster is that the bandwidth burden of sharing large files is borne by all the users instead of the system owner. The benefit of a true P2P network, however, is that there does not have to be an owner.

[i]Wikipedia, "Intellectual Property," http://en.wikipedia.org/wiki/Intellectual_property, retrieved Oct. 29, 2004.

[ii]Recording Industry Association of America (RIAA) (2002), "Identifying Unauthorized Sound Recordings," limited distribution.

[iii]Joliet extensions and Hybrid ISO 9660 are two updates, not new data standards.

[iv]DivX is based on MPEG 4 compression. A DVD uses MPEG 2 compression.

▲ FIGURE 16-11   Theft of intellectual property *continued*

phone transmits both numbers to the local switching office for verification and billing. **Cloning** involves using a personal computer to change the microchip in one cellular phone so that it matches a legitimate MIN and ESN from numbers "hacked" from a phone company, bought from a telephone company insider, acquired from a cellular phone whose theft will not be quickly discovered, or "plucked" from the airways by a portable device—about the size of a notebook—that can be plugged into a car's lighter receptacle. The user with the cloned numbers can simply use them until service is cut off and then change the MIN and ESN and start all over again. The use of cellular phones with cloned numbers is popular with criminals, particularly those dealing in drugs, who may lease them for up to $750 per day. In a related scam, a person leases a cloned cellular phone for a day and then sells international call time cheaply to immigrants or illegal aliens. **Tumbling** requires the use of a personal computer to alter a cellular phone's microchip so that its MIN and ESN numbers change after each call, making detection more difficult. One of the newest trends in cellular-phone fraud is to use a combination

tumbler-clone, which affords the fraudulent user the untraceability of a tumbled phone with the free service of a cloned phone. There are two other types of cellular-telephone fraud: subscription fraud, in which free service is obtained through theft or forgery of subscriber information or through employee collusion; and network fraud, in which weaknesses in the cellular network's technology are exploited to defraud the cellular service provider.

Component Theft

The theft of desktop and laptop computers and other equipment has been increasing in recent years. In 1999, laptop and mobile hardware theft accounted for 10% of the total computer crime reported in the Computer Security Institute (CSI)/Federal Bureau of Investigation (FBI) annual survey. By 2006, the figure accounted for 47%. This rapid increase can be attributed partly to the increased use of mobile components, such as flash drives.[83] As discussed previously in this chapter, there is significant evidence that laptop computers and mobile hardware devices are now being stolen for the information contained on their hard drives, such as documents and passwords, rather than for the hardware itself. However, the full extent of computer theft is unknown, because many thefts go unreported and because many police departments consider theft of computer hardware as just another stolen-property crime. Organizations often don't report thefts or intrusions to law enforcement in order to prevent negative publicity.[84] Individual computer owners may not even know what they own and therefore cannot provide the police with an accurate description, let alone the serial numbers. This problem is compounded by the inability of some police officers to accurately differentiate among computer equipment and peripherals.[85]

Corporate Crime

The rapid growth of the computer industry has caused many questionable business practices to develop and eventually be accepted as a part of doing business. Examples of such practices include rebate fraud, grossly one-sided **End-User License Agreements (EULAs)**, misleading advertising, component swapping, the resale of refurbished components in "new" systems, simple fraud, and many others. Rebates are a common practice in the computer industry. The Federal Trade Commission (FTC) has become involved in actions against several companies that promised mail-in rebates but did not deliver. The first case to draw widespread attention involved the Iomega Zip Drive. With the unprecedented demand for the Zip drive (interestingly, now obsolete), the rebate fulfillment center contracted to handle the processing of rebates was overwhelmed. A large number of rebates were simply lost, and delays of a year or more were common. EULAs are contracts that specify the rights of the consumer when purchasing a license to use software.[86] Originally intended to prevent people from reselling copies of their software, EULAs have become so one-sided that they violate common tenets of contract law and consumer protection legislation. Common elements of EULAs include a stipulation that the software licensed need not function for any particular purpose, even if that function is advertised![87] Although it is legal to require a EULA, the contract's terms do not automatically supercede false-advertising legislation. There is also the assumption that an item sold is fit for use.

Component swapping and refurbishment fraud are practices that were fairly common among computer manufacturers. The Intel Inside campaign was a response by Intel, a computer processor manufacturer, to the use of chips by secondary suppliers. The Intel Inside logo assured consumers that they had a name-brand chip. In general, in the practice of **component swapping,** manufacturers use parts from the lowest-cost supplier but do not inform the customer of the change. Other than processor chips, the most infamous example of this practice was the use of computer memory from a supplier in Taiwan. The memory used tin connectors instead of the industry standard, gold. The tin quickly corroded and the memory failed. **Refurbishment fraud** is a related practice in which working components from damaged or returned computers are used in the construction of new systems or simply resold as new systems. For several years, demand for computers rose as fast as, or faster than, manufacturing capability; a devastating earthquake and fire at one of the two memory fabrication facilities in the world added pressure to manufacturers. In response, manufacturers began to reuse components. These components were sometimes defective, but, more importantly, they were not the new systems advertised.

Simple fraud and misleading advertising occur frequently in the computer industry. Simple fraud happens when a company overextends its ability to supply products but continues to take orders. A frequent result of this situation is the bankruptcy or reorganization of the company. Even during the process of bankruptcy, it is fairly common for the company to continue to take new orders. Although not rising to the level of fraud, several practices of the computer industry are considered misleading advertising by the FTC. Class-action lawsuits brought against monitor manufacturers claim that the actual dimensions of cathode ray tube (CRT) monitors are not the same as those advertised. For example, a 15-inch monitor actually measures only about 14.1 inches diagonally. While such dimensions are standardized across the industry, their use is misleading as to the actual size. Similarly, the page-per-minute (PPM) rating for printers is often based on questionable tests or simply on the theorized speed of the paper-feed mechanism.

THE TOOLS OF COMPUTER CRIME

Investigators should be aware of the tools that are unique to computer criminals. This section provides descriptions of the more common tools. In most cases, mere possession of these tools is not a crime; however, evidence of their use may be present on a suspect's system. Careful forensic analysis of such systems may produce useful leads or connect the suspect to the crime scene. Analysis of malicious code may become an important tool for prosecution of computer criminals. At the very least, familiarity with such tools can help an investigator recognize their effects. Although this section lists the major classes of exploit code, it is not a comprehensive dictionary of hacker tools; rather it attempts to explain the basic intent of families of tools, often with examples.

Discovery Tools

The first step in intruding into a system is finding the system. Most network intrusions attack targets of opportunity; this means that rather than selecting a target system, many intruders simply find a vulnerable system. Although no longer in common use, an early discovery tool called a **war dialer**[88] introduces the logic behind most modern discovery tools. A war dialer dials a sequence of numbers—for example, 555-0000 through 555-9999—to discover computers. When a person answers the phone, he or she hears silence or the squeaks of what sounds like a fax machine. The war dialer does not call back, so the incident is often dismissed. When a computer answers the phone, the war dialer notes the number and continues calling new numbers until the sequence is done. The would-be intruder is thus left with a list of phone numbers connecting to computers. Most modern discovery tools use similar techniques: they try a large number of possible connections to achieve one good connection.

A software tool called a *port scanner* can be used to probe for all computers on a given segment of the Internet. At the simplest level, a service called "ping" can be used to probe a network to see which computers are available. However, modern port scanners go beyond a mere probe. Once a target computer is discovered, the port scanner can be set to detect services available from that computer that have known vulnerabilities. When a computer is discovered to have a vulnerability, exploiting that vulnerability is as simple as entering the Internet address in another program generically called an *exploit* (see the section "Privilege Escalation Exploits" later in the chapter). The process of discovering information about a system and inferring the operating system and other security-relevant details is called *"fingerprinting" the system.*

The favorite port scanner of many intruders and network administrators alike is Fyodor's Network Mapper (NMAP).[89] NMAP uses Internet packets in novel ways to determine what computers are available on a specific network, what services (application name and version) those hosts are offering, what operating systems (and OS versions) are running, what type of security (e.g., firewalls) are in place, and dozens of other characteristics that form the backbone of the system.[90] NMAP uses several techniques to even discover hidden computers. It has a number of settings that allow a user to balance the speed, stealth, and thoroughness of the search.[91]

War driving takes its name directly from war dialing. War driving usually involves driving around town with a laptop, sometimes hooked to an external antenna, but not always. The antenna receives signals from all wireless network hubs and work stations within range, many of which are unprotected. Kismet and Airsnort are software tools that allow a user to map wireless networks and discover the security mechanisms being used. The Wired Equivalent Privacy (WEP) that shipped with most wireless cards was broken in 1995. Modern discovery tools often include mechanisms to compile enough information to break WEP automatically. For instance, Kismet is a wireless network detector, sniffer, and intrusion detection system that identifies networks by passively collecting packets and detecting standard named networks. The product also detects and decloaks hidden networks, and infers the presence of radio-silent networks via data traffic.[92]

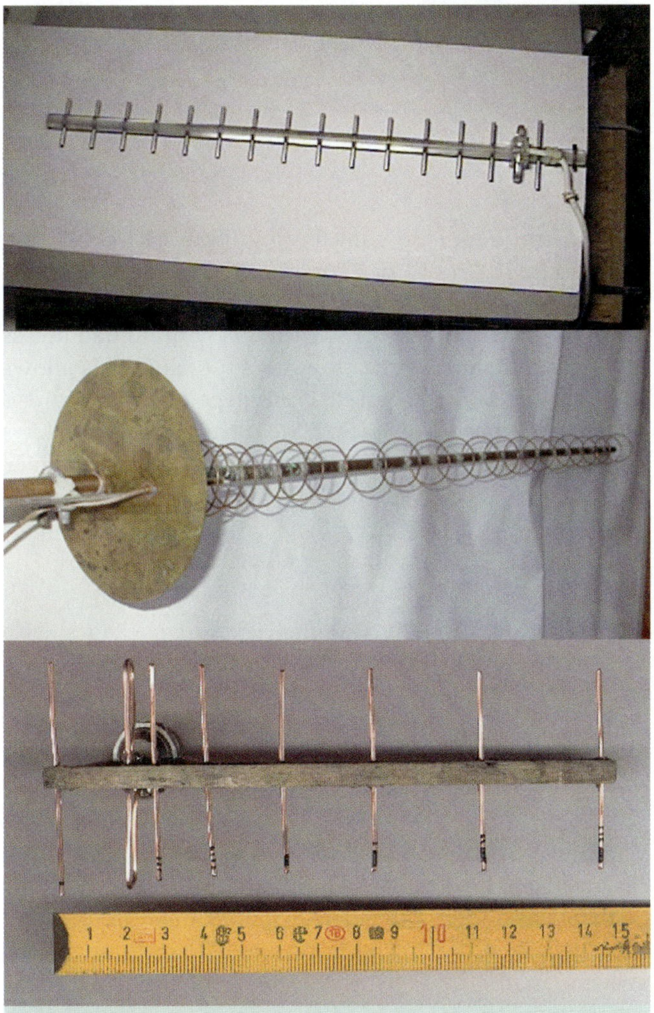

War-driving tools such as Kismet are actually a form of packet sniffer. Wireless networks usually operate employing the Institute of Electrical and Electronics Engineers (IEEE) 802.11 standard. The widely used standard for wired networks is a sister protocol called IEEE 802.3, or, more commonly, Ethernet. Kismet sniffs radio waves looking for 802.11 information, whereas packet sniffers can be used to read network traffic even if it is intended for another recipient. Traditional (wired) sniffers are typically placed on a local area network (LAN) to discover traffic being sent across the network. In truth, any computer capable of network communication can become a sniffer. There is no specific sniffing tool that stands above others, because sniffing is a basic technique for diagnosing and repairing LANs. However, sensitive information such as usernames and passwords is often transferred unencrypted, making it a target for malicious sniffers. Even when passwords are encrypted, however, they can still be broken with cryptanalysis software.

▲ **FIGURE 16-13   Directional "Yagi" antennas**
Directional "Yagi" antennas can be used to home in on radio transmitters from a great distance, in some cases miles. These antennas can be purchased or homemade; instructions for the latter are freely available on the web.

(Courtesy of Andrew Hackman, *top*)

(Photo by Kokoloko, *middle*)

Cryptanalysis Software

Cryptanalysis software is not always malicious, but it is frequently used as an intrusion aid. Bruce Schneier, author of *Applied Cryptography,* defines cryptanalysis as the art and science of accessing secured information without conventional means.[93] Functionally, cryptanalysis is about breaking **encryption,** the systematic encoding of data so that it appears to be unreadable. L0pht Heavy Industries, now merged with security company @Stake, created a cryptanalysis tool called LC5 (formerly L0phtcrack) to break Windows NT and Unix password security (Figure 16-14). Although there is no way to decrypt Windows NT or Unix passwords, LC5 exploits weaknesses in the NT password scheme with several methods to reproduce every possible password and then find matches. When a match is discovered, the L0phtcrack user has the password and eventually every other password in the system. All but the most robust passwords can be discovered in a couple of hours; many can be discovered within minutes. Most cryptanalysis uses similar methods to find passwords.

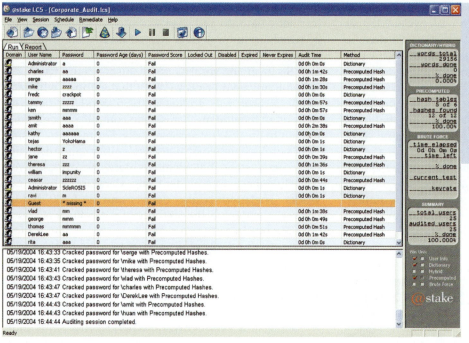

◀ **FIGURE 16-14** **Password theft**
LC5 software, formerly called "L0pht Crack," allows a user to discover all but the most robust passwords on a WindowsNT system.
(Courtesy @Stake Boston, 196 Broadway, Cambridge, MA 02139-1902)
(Source: www.@stake.com/products/lc/images/lc5–screen–lrg.gif)

There are three common attacks launched against passwords. First, a *dictionary attack* quickly searches one or more dictionaries for passwords. The default dictionary shipped with LC5 contains approximately 29,000 words, while the "big" dictionary contains approximately 235,000 words. Hacker's dictionaries provide additional word patterns to supplement the English dictionary. There are also crack dictionaries for sports, science fiction, politics, pet names, and many other fields of interest, with special vocabularies from which users might draw their passwords. Second, a *hybrid audit* checks dictionary words with one or more characters added to the beginning (prepended) or end (appended) of the word. This allows [a user] to identify weak passwords such as john01 or $bagel. Finally, a brute-force attack tries every possible combination of letters, numbers, symbols, and even commands that do not print (such as CTRL+J). This is the least efficient attack, but given enough time, it will crack every possible password.[94]

Privilege Escalation Exploits

Exploits are a generic class of programs that are written to take advantage of a security hole or back door program designed to evade normal security procedures.

Programmers often use debugging aids that provide code breaks called *back doors*. Most of the time, these breaks are removed before the software is released for general use, but sometimes their removal is overlooked or they are deliberately left in to provide easy maintenance of the program in the future. Back doors are often the victim of a specific exploit to gain access and privileges not normally available to the intruder. A common goal of intruders is to gain the privileges of the highest-level account: "root" or "superuser" in the Unix world and "administrator" in Windows environments. Once the intruder "gets root," he or she can enjoy unlimited access to virtually all areas of a computer's function. This allows the intruder to delete or alter privileged files called *logs* that may be useful in tracing the intruder. It also allows the intruder to install new software for his or her attack on the next target.

Root Kits

Root kits are specially designed exploit packages with tools that enable the intruder to maintain the level of access by installing back doors, Trojan horse programs and secret accounts, as well as altering logs and basic system services. Different root kits are available for different operating systems. There are also exploits for obtaining and maintaining administrator privileges in Windows. In the old days, once a system intruder was discovered, the system administrator had commands available to help discover the extent of the intrusion and even whether the intruder was still logged on to the system. In the Unix world, these commands are each separate programs:

- The "last" command would show you what accounts intruders were using, where they were coming from, and when they were in your system.
- The "ls"[95] command would show their files, and the "ps" command would show the sniffer, password-cracking program, and anything else being run by the intruders.

- The "netstat" command would show you the current network connections and ports on which other ports were listening for incoming connections.
- The "ifconfig" command would tell you if the Ethernet interface was in promiscuous mode (indicating it was being used by a sniffer program).[96]

Root kits often substitute modified versions of these programs to conceal the intrusion. They also include utilities with innocuous names, but nefarious intent. Such programs may allow an intruder to change time stamps on various files to prevent a system administrator from noticing illicit activities. Some root kits are self-deleting; that is, they leave no traces except for a back door to allow later reentry and reinstallation of the root kit.

Buffer Overflows

Buffer overflow refers to a family of attacks that is periodically declared to be dead owing to improved programming techniques. However, buffer overflows have been around since the earliest days of programming and probably will continue to be with us for the foreseeable future. A buffer overflow works by filling up the space allowed for a program (called a *buffer*). Any place where a program allows input is susceptible to buffer overflow. Once the buffer is filled by input data, a program that allows additional input to spill into special areas of memory used for overflow becomes vulnerable. If the overflow goes into the buffer area of a privileged program (e.g., an operating system program that has access to any command or file), the overflow can be used to execute commands with systems administrator privileges. The overflow can even be used to change the privileges of a guest account (normally very restricted) to those of a systems administrator (almost unlimited).

A recent and potentially damaging buffer overflow exploit involved the Joint Photographic Experts Group (JPEG)[97] file format. As we mentioned earlier, it was long believed that image files, since they do not execute instructions, could not be used to exploit a system. In fact, an early hoax called the "Good Times Virus" tricked users into believing that an image could harm their computers. (See Figure 16-15, for more on virus hoaxes.) However, this time it was real.[98] The program used to interpret the information in the JPEG image file is vulnerable to a buffer overflow that allows the creator of an exploit JPEG to issue commands with the real user's privileges.[99]

Attack Codes

Unlike simple intrusion aids, which may cause damage incidental to the intrusion, **attack codes,** or **malware,**[100] are malicious software intended to impair or destroy the function of another computer or network resource. These attack codes are often designed simply to harass system users or administrators. Denial-of-service attacks (p. 530), the most common manifestation of direct-attack malware, are second only to viruses/worms in terms of economic damage done by computer crime. The Computer Security Institute (CSI) and the FBI produce an annual report on economic damage done by computer crime. Denial-of-service attacks were reported to have caused an estimated $2,922,010 in damages in 2006.[101]

Denial-of-Service Attacks

AOL punters, WinNuke, Bonk, Teardrop, mail bombs, and many other software tools have been developed with the sole function of annoying users. AOL punters can be used to force an AOL subscriber off of the network. Teardrop crashes the target's computer, also removing the user from the network. Mail bombs fill a user's e-mailbox space quota and thereby deny the victim mail service. The use of any of these tools constitutes a denial-of-service attack.

Recently, a particular subclass of denial-of-service attacks has drawn attention: the distributed denial-of-service attack. Tools such as Trino and the Tribal Flood Network (TFN) have been used to deny service on a massive scale. Normally immune to simple denial-of-service attacks by virtue of their size and capacity, the largest Internet sites (e.g., Yahoo!, Barnes & Noble, and CMN) have each suffered from distributed attacks. Network-based denial-of-service attacks such as the Yahoo! attack are explained in Figures 16-16 and 16-17.

Logic Bomb Traps and Trojan Horse Programs

The attack malware mentioned above provides active attacks against a network target. Another means of attacking computers and the data structures that malware supports is called a *logic bomb*. **Logic bombs** use illegal program instructions and misuse legitimate instructions to damage data structures. *Data structure* is a broad term comprising the data, programmed uses of the data, instructions, and patterns that computers manipulate to provide requested results. Aside from damaging data structures, the primary distinction of logic bombs is that they operate at a specific time or periodically. A logic bomb may be executed on the basis of a specific date, time, or other instructions. For example, if a specific Social Security number is deleted from the salary database (meaning the employee has been fired), a logic bomb planted by that person might delete critical files. Logic bombs are highly customized traps that are most often left by a programmer or disgruntled employee. However, some "trapped" commands are available to general intruders. A malicious intruder may leave such a trapped command so that when a new user logs on or issues a common command, it will damage the system software.

Like logic bombs, altered software is written for a specific purpose, usually on a particular system. Theft-

SEND THIS TO ALL OF YOUR FRIENDS; DO NOT DELETE THIS MESSAGE; IMPORTANT ALERT. These are but a few of the opening lines of many e-mails commonly received daily via the Internet. Most of these messages are relatively harmless; however, some have a more sinister purpose. Some people think that many of the scams and hoaxes are new, when in reality they are classically old schemes being perpetuated in a new format: cyberspace. To most, these are harmless annoyances that quickly find their way into the cyber trash bin. The undeniable cost is lost productivity and time spent sifting through the increasing volume of junk e-mails typically referred to as SPAM. There is a growing body of information on the Internet concerning SPAM and e-mail hoaxes. In general, e-mails can be grouped into five general categories: SPAM, chain-mail, hoaxes, virus hoaxes, and fraud.

SPAM

Spam is the generic term (also called un-solicited commercial e-mail [UCE] and junk e-mail) for any e-mail that is sent to a large group of people typically as an advertisement or other solicitation. If your e-mail address falls into the hands of a "spammer," you will undoubtedly receive ever-increasing un-solicited advertisements. Most SPAM is easily deleted and is simply just annoying. There are several websites with detailed information on SPAM, federal legislation, and other problems with e-mails of this kind.

- http://spam.abuse.net/
- www.cauce.org/

Chain-Mail

This is simply traditional chain letters that have found a new medium. If you believe in good or bad luck, you can forward these to your friends. They are increasing because forwarding them is relatively easy using e-mail.

Hoaxes

There are almost too many hoaxes to document. Some of the more popular ones involve people spending $250 for a cookie recipe, people having their kidneys removed while they sleep, and people receiving cash awards and gift certificates by forwarding e-mail. There is no way for a company to track who you send e-mail to and they are not giving away free computers, vacations, or cash. Check out such hoaxes at these websites:

- Information on medical hoaxes: www.quackwatch.com
- Department of Energy's website for debunking myths and legends: http://ciac.llnl.gov/ciac/CIACWelcome.html
- Offers current information about hoaxes being propagated on the Internet: http://urbanlegends.about.com/culture/urbanlegends/library/blhoax.htm
- Websites dedicated to urban legends: www.nonprofit.net/hoax/hoax.html www.snopes.com

Virus Hoaxes

"We are spending much more time debunking hoaxes than handling real virus incidents." —Statement from the U.S. Dept. of Energy Computer Incident Advisory Capability (CIAC)

One hoax concerned a virus that was "infecting all digital cellular phones"; people shouldn't answer any phone calls that caller-ID couldn't track, or they would get the virus. In short, numerous hoaxes concern viruses. In fact, there is more worry about viruses than is necessary. Web resources include

- Symantec's website for virus hoaxes: www.symantec.com/avcenter/hoax.html.
- McAfee's Virus Hoax Center: http://www.mcafeeb2b.com/asp_set/anti_virus/library/hoaxes.asp.
- F-secure Corporation website: www.datafellows.com/virus-info/hoax/

Fraud

These are the most dangerous e-mails you will receive. Do yourself a favor and don't give out your credit card, send money, or involve yourself in any of these schemes. Age-old pyramid schemes involving cash, stocks, or even golf balls never work and are in fact illegal. Reputable charities and organizations do not solicit contributions or sell merchandise via e-mail.

The Federal Trade Commission (www.ftc.gov) has recently identified the 12 scams that are most likely to arrive in consumers' e-mail boxes. The "dirty dozen":

- Business opportunities
- Bulk e-mail
- Chain letters
- Work-at-home schemes
- Health and diet scams
- Effortless income
- Free goods
- Investment opportunities
- Cable descrambler kits
- Guaranteed loans or credit, on easy terms
- Credit repair
- Vacation prize promotions

Information on frauds and scams can be found at www.scambusters.org.

Tips for Survival

There is no surefire, 100% accurate way that can determine whether or not an e-mail is a hoax or not. Virtually any chain e-mail you receive (i.e., any message forwarded multiple times) is more likely to be false than true. Be skeptical. You can easily check the websites listed earlier for information on these Internet hoaxes. Any time the message tells you to forward this to everyone you know, it is probably a hoax and should be placed where it belongs: in your e-mail trash.

▲ **FIGURE 16-15** **E-mail hoaxes**

through-accrual, or salami-slice attacks use altered software to "shave" small amounts from legitimate transactions. This function has to be built into the legitimate software performing the transaction. U.S. Sentencing Guidelines[102] allow for additional penalties for the abuse of a position of trust or the use of a special skill in the commission of an offense. Either the status as a trusted programmer/system administrator or the special skill of computer programming make the user of such customized software subject to a two-level sentencing enhancement.

Trojan horse programs masquerade as legitimate programs. Technically, any program that is altered or designed to provide an unwanted or malicious function while appearing to provide a routine or benign function is called a Trojan horse. This leaves a number of interpretations open for most commercial software with unadvertised functions or functions that may harm the user—such as copyright

◄ FIGURE 16-16
Denial-of-service attack software creates problems
Recently, a particular subclass of denial-of-service attacks, known as the distributed denial-of-service attack, has drawn attention. Normally immune to simple denial-of-service attacks by virtue of their size and capacity, the largest Internet sites such as Yahoo! and CMN have suffered from recent distributed attacks.

verification mechanisms. Like the Trojan Horse of antiquity, a Trojan horse program appears to have a benign purpose, but it conceals an attack. One classic example of altered software is the Trojan Horse program Login.C, written by Len Rose, a.k.a., Terminus of the Legion of Doom. Login.C could be compiled and then run on a system to replace the legitimate login program. In addition to this function, it logged (i.e., recorded) usernames and passwords.[103]

Keystroke loggers are another form of trap that can be placed on a computer to discover anything the user types. They bypass the need to break encryption on passwords because they record every key pressed by the victim. Law enforcement officers can obtain a warrant to install a keystroke logger on a suspect's computer, but such warrants are rare and similar to the controversial "sneak and peek" warrants. A keystroke logger, in its simplest form is simply a rewritten version of the system process that acknowledges input from the keyboard; thus, it is a Trojan horse program.

Viruses and Worms

Attack malware, as described earlier, requires a user to intervene or operate the software. Another variety of malware is autonomous; that is, it does not require intervention by the user. A computer **virus** is a malicious program that is secretly inserted into normal software or into the computer's active memory. The effects of such programs, which are relatively small, range from annoying messages to more serious problems such as interference with the computer's normal operating procedures, extended run times, or deletion of data. The

2006 Annual CSI/FBI Computer Crime and Security Survey has estimated the damage done by viruses to account for 65% of the total damage caused by computer crime. From 1997 to 1999, the actual damage and the percentage of total damage from viruses declined steadily. However, the new generation of viruses, such as Love Letter and Melissa, brought the virus damage from a low of 4% of the total computer crime damage in 1999 to recent highs.[104]

A virus is not a complete program; like its namesake, the computer virus is not active without a host. A computer virus attaches to a host by inserting instructions within the other program (i.e., infecting it). Thus, whenever the host program runs, the virus runs. A virus has two distinct components: propagation and payload.[105] The propagation component allows the virus to spread. Common mechanisms include attaching to an executable program (e.g., MS Word), a system file (e.g., run32.dll), or a document with macros or scripts activated (e.g., My Document.doc). New variants can embed themselves in the scripts commonly found in web pages and HTML-based e-mail. The virus payload can carry an attack code or an intrusion code. It can issue commands to download Trojan horse programs from the web and install them in place of existing software. Fortunately, in many cases the payload is a trivial message: a symbolic "Gotcha!"

In the past, the most common methods of spreading viruses were by sharing infected floppy disks and by opening an infected file from the Internet. Today, antivirus software has become extremely adept at catching known viruses. Modern viruses rely on stealth and

Crimes targeting computers include the denial of expected service. Denial-of-service attacks (DoS) have been around for many years. One extremely simple example is a chat group tantrum. When a user wants to deny others the ability to keep up with the chat, he or she can simply create a rapid series of single letter posts. A minor variation uses the paste feature to paste in an expletive. By pressing CTRL   v (the hot key for paste) and ENTER, the delinquent user can fill the screen with "F*CK!! YOU!!" and completely disrupt ongoing conversations. The constantly repeated phrase forces useful messages off the screen rapidly. Most chat clients or instant messaging systems have an "ignore user" feature; this allows users to filter out an offensive user and continue their conversations. With a few more details, this basic process can be applied to a network denial-of-service attack.

DoS attacks can be implemented anywhere resources are scarce; even worse, many security techniques can be altered to deny service to those implementing the new security! For example, to prevent malicious users from simply guessing someone's password through repeated tries, many systems began to "lock out" users who failed too many login attempts. Similarly, to prevent automated guessing (called a brute-force attack on the password), system administrators began adding an extended wait period between login attempts. Although these systems deter guessing passwords, they also allow a malicious user to "lock out" a legitimate user.

There are relatively few ways to implement a DoS attack: use other people's resources; artificially create impossible situations; and rapidly use up scarce resources.

Use Other People's Resources
In the year 2000, a particular subclass of DoS attacks, known as the distributed denial-of-service attack (DDoS), drew attention. Normally immune to simple denial-of-service attacks by virtue of their size and capacity, the largest Internet sites, such as Yahoo! and CMN, have suffered from recent distributed attacks.[i]

The Internet was designed with several features that help network designers and administrators find problems. When misused, these features can provide an avenue for attackers to disable a single computer or even a whole portion of the network. One such feature is Internet control message protocol (ICMP). The most common function of ICMP is the "ping." Like a submarine's sonar, a ping packet will be reflected from an active computer. This lets the sender know that the other computer is on the network and that it is possible to establish a connection.

ICMP Flood Attack—Smurfing: With this method, the attacker sends multiple pings to the broadcast address of an intermediate network: a staging network. The broadcast address passes the ping to every computer on the staging network. The ping tells the staging network to reply to the target computer instead of the sending computer. The target is overwhelmed by responses from every computer on the staging network.[ii]

Creating Impossible Situations
A buffer overflow attack allows a malicious user to run information over the expected limit. By carefully selecting what information to insert, a malicious user can cause the vulnerable computer to execute any instructions. In fact, the buffer overflow is a very common method to start an intrusion. The buffer overflow goes far beyond the potential for denial of service, but it demonstrates the fact that malicious users can intentionally create situations that the programmers could not

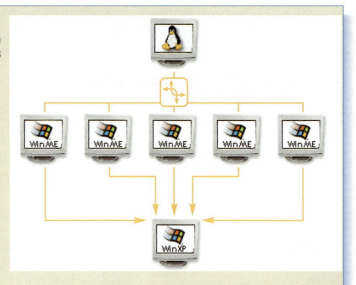

Smurf attacks use a stream of packets that follow one after another to the target.

foresee or did not believe would happen. A network denial-of-service attack uses a similar principle. It forces more information in than is expected. This either overwrites useful information in memory or causes the computer to become unstable.

Malformed-Packet Attack—Ping of Death or Teardrop: The Ping of Death uses a packet that exceeds the maximum size allowed by Internet protocol (IP); this is a supposedly impossible situation. (To transfer information, the Internet breaks large transmissions into packets and reassembles them on arrival.) Vulnerable systems receiving this large packet may freeze, crash, or reboot. Teardrop exploits the way packets are reassembled upon arrival. By forging packets that overlap, when they are reassembled, Teardrop causes another impossible situation. An analogy is cutting a pie into eight slices, having each person carry his or her own slice to the table, and then trying to place 11 slices back on the pie plate. Upon receiving this impossible packet, systems vulnerable to the Teardrop attack may freeze, crash, or reboot.

Rapidly Using Up Scarce Resources
In June of 2004, a distributed denial-of-service attack targeted a weak spot in the Internet's infrastructure. The Domain Name System (DNS) servers, run by Akamai for major clients such as Google, Microsoft, Apple, and Yahoo! were disabled or delayed during the two hours of the attack. Many users were aware of a slow down, and some received messages saying a connection could not be established.[iii] DNS server vulnerability is not new. In 1998, a widely publicized statement by Mudge, a member of a hacker group called LOpht Heavy Industries,[iv] claimed that hackers could take down the Internet in 30 minutes.[v] The DNS system translates familiar web addresses, such as www.yahoo.com, to the numerical Internet addresses needed to route information on the Internet. Denial of the DNS system through poisoning[vi] or simple request flooding can have dramatic effects. Another way to use up a scarce resource is the SYN-flood attack. It exhausts a small pool of memory reserved for incoming connection requests.

▲ **FIGURE 16-17   Denial-of-service attacks**
(Courtesy of Tory Caeti, Ph.D., Police Executive Research Forum, Washington, D.C.)

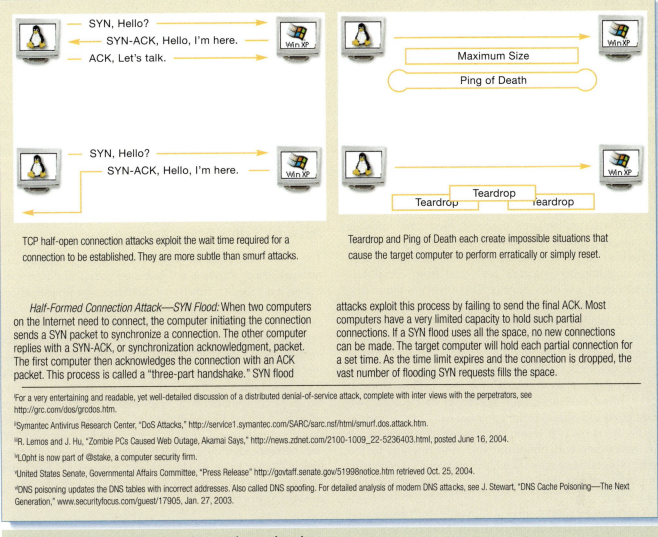

TCP half-open connection attacks exploit the wait time required for a connection to be established. They are more subtle than smurf attacks.

Teardrop and Ping of Death each create impossible situations that cause the target computer to perform erratically or simply reset.

Half-Formed Connection Attack—SYN Flood: When two computers on the Internet need to connect, the computer initiating the connection sends a SYN packet to synchronize a connection. The other computer replies with a SYN-ACK, or synchronization acknowledgment, packet. The first computer then acknowledges the connection with an ACK packet. This process is called a "three-part handshake." SYN flood attacks exploit this process by failing to send the final ACK. Most computers have a very limited capacity to hold such partial connections. If a SYN flood uses all the space, no new connections can be made. The target computer will hold each partial connection for a set time. As the time limit expires and the connection is dropped, the vast number of flooding SYN requests fills the space.

[i] For a very entertaining and readable, yet well-detailed discussion of a distributed denial-of-service attack, complete with inter views with the perpetrators, see http://grc.com/dos/grcdos.htm.

[ii] Symantec Antivirus Research Center, "DoS Attacks," http://service1.symantec.com/SARC/sarc.nsf/html/smurf.dos.attack.htm.

[iii] R. Lemos and J. Hu, "Zombie PCs Caused Web Outage, Akamai Says," http://news.zdnet.com/2100-1009_22-5236403.html, posted June 16, 2004.

[iv] LOpht is now part of @stake, a computer security firm.

[v] United States Senate, Governmental Affairs Committee, "Press Release" http://govtaff.senate.gov/51998notice.htm retrieved Oct. 25, 2004.

[vi] DNS poisoning updates the DNS tables with incorrect addresses. Also called DNS spoofing. For detailed analysis of modern DNS attacks, see J. Stewart, "DNS Cache Poisoning—The Next Generation," www.securityfocus.com/guest/17905, Jan. 27, 2003.

▲ **FIGURE 16-17 Denial-of-service attacks** *continued*

speed. Stealth viruses hide themselves by intercepting requests to view the area where the virus is hiding. Early stealth viruses on floppy disks reported the virus area as unusable. Polymorphic viruses, meanwhile, attempt to change their own codes too fast for antivirus vendors to provide updates. Some polymorphic viruses actually encrypt or compress themselves to hide telltale signs of viruslike code. Another variation on speed is rapid deployment. This strategy is most commonly used by worms.

The primary distinction between viruses and worms is that a **worm** does not rely on infecting a host program. This allows worms to be programmed to act faster. Worms such as Code Red attempt to spread rapidly, before antivirus software can be updated. The rapid-deployment variation has produced aggressive new strains that can spread through large portions of the Internet in a matter of hours. For example, the Melissa worm achieved most of its fame for destruction by spreading rapidly through e-mail. The worm had run its course before the antivirus industry was able to respond. New heuristic virus detection technology no longer attempts to match viruses or worms to known samples; rather, it attempts to detect viruslike actions. The next-generation viruses may find a way to adapt to this promising but imperfect technology.

RESPONDING TO COMPUTER CRIME

Computer crime investigation requires the investigator to take standard investigative skills and apply them to digital evidence. Trainers have often said that it is easier to teach a cop how to find and analyze digital evidence than to teach a network administrator how to put a case together. There is undeniably a learning curve to computer crime investigations, but once an investigator understands the nature of digital evidence and a few new investigative techniques, computer crimes can be discovered, investigated, and prosecuted. Further, as digital devices become more and more common in our society, it will become necessary for any investigator to learn the basics of digital evidence.

Crime Scene Investigative Techniques

Frequently, computer crime evidence is seized by the execution of a search warrant.[106] This warrant should include information about the computer, data storage devices (including internal and external hard drives), floppy disks, tape backups, modems, programs, software manuals, user notes, hardcopy output, and any peripherals that may be of concern to investigators, such as scanners. Removing non-investigative personnel from computers and terminals is a high priority. This prevents tampering or destruction of electronic evidence—intentional or unintentional. While a local network administrator may assist the efforts, only investigators should execute commands. In some cases, under the Electronic Communications Privacy Act (ECPA), the owner of a multiuser computer may not consent to a search of a user's files. Consult legal counsel if a multiuser system is to be searched. Another consideration is the potential use of the information to be seized. If there is a reasonable expectation that the owner will distribute such information to the public, special First Amendment protections reserved for publishers might apply, including protection of web pages.[107]

A computer expert—either an investigator specializing in this field, a state or district attorney assigned to a computer crime prosecutorial division, or a civilian with the necessary expertise—should be consulted for assistance in specifying what is to be searched for by the warrant and also in seizing it. The computer and related equipment and material should not be touched or moved until thoroughly documented by photography or videotaping. In particular, the screen needs to be photographed immediately in order to secure the information on it. More than one criminal case has been won because an investigating officer noticed incriminating evidence on the screen and photographed it before the screen changed. It is also important that all connections and wires be photographed and portrayed. The keyboard should not be used in a premature attempt to locate evidence. After the system has been photographed, the first step is to unplug the computer; do not use the on/off switch. All wiring connections should be tagged with notes indicating where they were connected. If there is a modem, disconnect it by unplugging the connecting cable from the wall jack. The serial numbers for all equipment should be recorded. All computer evidence should be stored in an area free from dust, heat, dampness, and magnetic fields, and chain of custody should be maintained per agency policy.[108]

Once the containers (i.e., the physical devices holding digital data) have been secured, the investigator must attempt to locate evidence which ties a specific subject to a specific act that violates a specific law. The elements of the crime must be proven and matched to the suspect. The vast majority of cases involving digital evidence would not require technical knowledge beyond the basic use of an application or device except for the fact that the investigator must be able to prove that the evidence is unaltered. The tools and skills for this are covered in forensic analysis (see the following). Otherwise, locating the evidence is just a matter of checking the most likely locations for evidence of a particular offense.

Network Crime Scene Techniques

The distinction between single scene, multiple scene, and network crime scenes is not based on technical differences; rather, it is based on functional differences for investigation. A single-scene crime involves only a single computer—for example, possession of child pornography or use of a computer to further a criminal enterprise. The techniques for investigating a single-scene crime are detailed in the previous section. A multiple-scene crime involves more than one computer with the possibility of an intervening network. Personal computers on a local area network (LAN) can often be handled like multiple single-scene seizures. Additional complications include noting network connections and network identities for each machine. Storage volumes, logical storage units, can be spread across several machines on the network but may be represented as a single unit to network users (Figure 16-18).

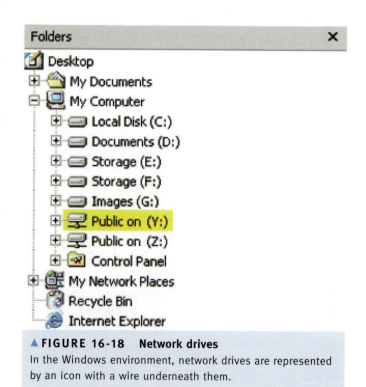

▲ FIGURE 16-18 Network drives
In the Windows environment, network drives are represented by an icon with a wire underneath them.

Network crime scenes could involve the Internet and any LAN or wide area network (WAN) that makes extensive use of dedicated servers, network or multiple-user operating systems (Unix, Windows 2003 Pro, Vista, etc.), or switching equipment. The skill set required to investigate this type of scene may challenge even a veteran investigator's ability. Although there are numerous technical distinctions between different network architectures, investigators are not charged with maintaining these systems or understanding the full complexities of them. An investigator needs to know how to reconstruct a transaction through the network and identify any potential sources of network trace evidence: latent signs of the transaction being reconstructed.

The primary distinction of interest to an investigator is between Internet and Intranet. An intranet is a wide area network that uses **TCP/IP** (Transfer Control Protocol/Internet Protocol). The key difference to an investigator is that an Intranet is often administered by one authority; thus, it may be possible to get to a system administrator or system administration team and get definitive answers. Seeking technical assistance involves identifying the network administrator. This can usually be accomplished by looking up the domain registrant on a service such as "whois" (see "The Tools of Computer Crime Investigation" section later in this chapter). The Internet is a network of networks owned and maintained by various private, corporate, and governmental interests. The only feature truly common to all these various component systems is the use of a common addressing and transfer protocol suite—TCP/IP. Seeking technical assistance involves identifying the Internet service providers (ISPs) involved. Steps taken to preserve Internet evidence must be quick. Routine logs are often quickly purged owing to the huge volume of Internet traffic. If the network can be traced to a corporation, the corporate Information Technology (IT) department may be of further assistance.

PROBLEMS RESPONDING TO COMPUTER CRIME

In addition to all of the common problems in all investigations, computer crime investigations introduce a few novel ones.

Jurisdictional Differences

The widespread nature of computer networks often places the location of evidence and crime scenes in different jurisdictions. Coordinating an investigation with investigators in another jurisdiction can be difficult. Local or even state investigators cannot always be assured of cooperation from the owners of network resources in other states. Sometimes even finding a contact in the other jurisdiction can be difficult. Although part of this can be accounted for by simple lack of concern on the part of the remote contact or witness, there are different laws and procedures in other jurisdictions. For example, some states require both parties in a telephone conversation consent to monitoring. Other states, called one-party consent states, permit law enforcement officers to monitor phone conversations if one party consents. Federal law allows for one-party consent, but if one party resides in a two-party consent state, there may be a reasonable expectation of privacy even if the other party consents to monitoring; thus, evidence obtained may be inadmissible.

Victim Reluctance to Report Crimes

Many victim organizations do not report computer crimes. In many cases, fear of loss of public confidence keeps incidents quiet. With insider crimes or intrusions, extortion, fear of reprisal, or the release of secrets prevents corporations from reporting. Fear of law enforcement intervention and confiscation of information technology assets also reduce reporting rates. Seizing a business's critical IT assets could easily do more harm to that business than the worst denial-of-service attack. Even brief downtime can cost the business substantial amounts. The seizure of evidence can also be a significant deterrent to businesses reporting computer crime. One of the first and most prominent challenges to seizure of electronic evidence came in the case of Steve Jackson Games.[109] A system administrator, Loyd Blankenship, at the Game company was implicated in the distribution of a proprietary document stolen from Bell South (now called SBC) by a hacker. Blankenship was a member of the hacker group Legion of Doom (LOD).[110] He received and distributed an online newsletter called Phrack[111] from his home electronic bulletin board (BBS).[112] With a warrant, the Secret Service seized the entire computer system of Steve Jackson Games based on the supposition that Blankenship could delete evidence from the system. What the Secret Service failed to consider was the economic impact to Steve Jackson Games. The warrant was executed on March 1, 1990. The majority of the seized materials were not returned until late June, 1990. The company's new game release was delayed, and the BBS it maintained for customer relations, play testing, and to generate general enthusiasm for its products was simply unavailable. Customers' confidential e-mail was seized. The financial records of the company were also on the seized computers.

The Privacy Protection Act[113] protects the confidential contents of electronic communication.[114] Further, the Supreme Court has established that interference with First Amendment activities—especially publishing— requires the strictest scrutiny.[115] As a publisher of games and books (not video games as often reported), Steve Jackson Games and the users of their bulletin board

Civilian training costs a premium because the skills obtained are very marketable. Such certification may speed the departure of officers for civilian employment, however. In September of 2004, the CISSP (Certified Information Systems Security Professional) review course and exam cost over $4,000 for a live course from the SANS (SysAdmin, Audit, Network, Security) Institute.[i] Such training offers an infusion of skills and the most recent developments into the law enforcement skill base. However, not all skills taught are targeted to law enforcement purposes. The typical audience for CISSP training is a Computer Security Specialist.

CISSP Knowledge Domains
Each domain requires the CISSP recipient to be knowledgeable about a critical aspect of computer security.
- *Access Control Systems and Methodology:* the ability to restrict computer or network resources to those authorized to use them.

- *Telecommunications, Network, and Internet Security:* the ability to predict, prevent, and mitigate threats from a networked environment.
- *Security Management Practices:* the policies that guide the overall security strategy. These must recognize the legitimate needs of the organization and allow for the useful function of Information Technology (IT) resources.
- *Applications and Systems Development:* these support the business of the organization and allow growth in vital IT areas.
- *Cryptography:* this is a fundamental group of technologies that can help assure the authenticity, integrity, and confidentiality of information.
- *Security Architecture and Models:* network design and controlling points of access are planned with the general operations of the network in mind.
- *Operations Security:* security planning and architecture must be constantly tested and

audited to assure that plans are being implemented as intended and not being altered unilaterally by members of the organization.
- *Business Continuity Planning:* disaster recovery is still an essential part of IT assurance. Fires, floods, power failures, and so on can all affect IT operations. CISSPs are trained to mitigate, reduce, and prevent such damage.
- *Law, Investigation, and Ethics:* knowing how far to go with an internal investigation is just as important as the ability to perform it. In addition to criminal liability for tampering with evidence, a CISSP must know when further investigation will violate employee or client rights.
- *Physical Security:* physical access to computer and network resources can completely circumvent an information security strategy. Keeping IT resources physically secure is vital to overall security.

[i]SANS Institute, www.sans.org.

▲ **FIGURE 16-19   CISSP**

system were illegally deprived of communication, expression, and commerce. Steve Jackson Games was eventually awarded tens of thousands of dollars in damages, but only after a long and expensive court battle and some breathless months wherein the company might have simply closed. With this history in mind, one can easily understand the mistrust of law enforcement's intentions.

Staffing and Resources

There is a constant demand from the private sector to hire skilled officers at wages far above law enforcement pay. The expected career length for a computer crime specialist in the FBI is only about three years.[116] This is because after about three years, when an investigator is fully seasoned, the private sector can offer salaries that can triple the investigator's salary. The turnover is so rapid that even training replacements can be difficult. Once an officer is hired away, he or she rarely has time to train a replacement. Even if an investigator doesn't want to leave law enforcement, there is often no path for advancement—in rank or pay—that will allow him or her to stay in that specialty.

Related to the issue of high staff turnover is the often cited "technical knowledge gap" between officers and computer offenders.[117] In a field that constantly changes, officers are left with few opportunities for the most recent technical training. The training used by private industry is often very expensive, because the skills attained are very marketable (Figure 16-19).

DEVELOPING COMPUTER CRIME INVESTIGATORS

In this age of international terrorism and heightened awareness of our information infrastructure's vulnerability,[118] the problems of developing competent computer crime investigators have become acute. The national security aspect of computer crime and cyber-terrorism has prodded the Federal government into helping address some of these issues. Significant strides have been made to reorganize the Federal response to computer crime. In many cases, historic turf battles have been smoothed over, although the situation is by no means perfect. Federal agencies have all extended a hand to state and municipal agencies as we finally seem to have realized the gravity of this threat. Several of the following responses stem directly from a revitalized federal response to computer crime.

Education and Training

One response is to prepare technically skilled applicants. The National Security Agency and the Department of Defense have combined efforts to create the Information Assurance Scholarship Program (IASP). IASP is described as a domestic service ROTC, trading scholarship money for degrees in information-assurance-related fields for years of national service. A simultaneous program certifies "Centers of Academic Excellence" in an attempt to add information assurance programs to college curricula.

The next part of the strategy is to train inservice officers and supervisors. The idea is not to make every officer a computer crime investigator; however, a basic familiarity with digital evidence will prevent unintentional destruction of evidence or the complete omission of it from the investigation strategy. This training attempts to make officers aware of the basic steps to preserve evidence at a crime scene. It also teaches them when to seek assistance from a supervisor or an investigator. Further training objectives attempt to make noncomputer-crime investigators aware of potential evidence in electronic devices. It also tells them how to obtain assistance in analyzing such devices. These days, it is a virtual certainty that there will at least be a cellular phone at almost ever crime scene.

Although the CISSP may be inappropriate for law enforcement on a widespread basis, there is a place for specialized training in the civilian sector. A number of private and public organizations provide training and assistance in the investigation of computer crime. The following are three important groups:

- The National White Collar Crime Center (NW3C), Computer Crime Section, in Richmond, Virginia, has established the National Cybercrime Training Partnership linking numerous private corporations to the training and development of police agencies on a regional basis. Several important national conferences and summits have been sponsored by the NW3C group.[119]
- The International Association of Computer Investigative Specialists (IACIS) is a volunteer nonprofit corporation composed of law enforcement professionals throughout the world who are dedicated to training police personnel in the investigation of computer crime. IACIS is the only body to "certify," through advanced training, digital forensic examiners in the recovery of evidence from computer systems.[120]
- The High Technology Crime Investigation Association (HTCIA) is a law enforcement–based, nonprofit organization that has chapters across the United States and in several other countries. The chapters allow local investigators to collaborate, network, and assist one another on various computer crime cases. Many chapters also provide excellent training, and the parent organization sponsors an annual national conference for a similar purpose.[121]

Task Forces

There are several different models for the task force concept. Their common feature is organized cooperation across agency boundaries and sometimes across jurisdictional boundaries for a specific purpose. They often have a co-location in one of the member agencies.

Contributions to the task force depend on the agency. Larger agencies often contribute full-time members and administrators, while smaller agencies may contribute days of an employee's time or simply a portion of the funding. The benefits of task forces include:

- Coordination of efforts in adjacent jurisdictions that reduce interjurisdictional issues. The presence of a superior jurisdiction officer in the task force (e.g., state or federal) may allow easier cross-jurisdictional efforts.
- Information sharing can be something as simple as determining whom to call at eBay to investigate fraud or how to find an expert on a particular computer system. Criminal intelligence and accumulated wisdom about local criminals can also be shared.
- Sharing rare or expensive items with a task force can fully equip a forensic lab when individual members could not. By reducing redundancy in equipment purchases, members can acquire less commonly used tools or additional training.
- Increased training efficiency can be achieved by grouping officers. By gathering officers from various agencies, training opportunities product vendor presentations, academic presentations, and even presentations from experienced field officers can be shared without duplicating costs or wasting time with excessive travel.
- Partnerships with private industry in some task forces give immediate access to vast technical skill bases, open communication, and promote trust with industry partners.
- Sometimes, simply having an open dialog with the private sector can help coordinate efforts between law enforcement, prosecutors, and private industry. Informal avenues of information may increase both public and private organizations' willingness to share and to report crime.

Many departments are frightened by the term *task force*. They assume it means that they will lose valuable employees to another bureaucracy with separate goals. They also fear the loss of discretion of the funds contributed to the task force. Although these fears are well founded, they are not necessary ingredients of a task force. The following three models of electronic crimes task forces demonstrate that there are many ways to form a task force that meets the needs of member agencies.

- The Sacramento Valley Hi-Tech Crimes Task Force[122] combines state, county, and local agencies in the Sacramento, CA area. These agencies came together to share information and resources. They also coordinate training to help fight attrition of experienced officers to the private sector. Officers in the task force collaborate on operations and difficult cases. Some member agencies do not have trained/trainable investigators to spare and simply contribute money. These member agencies can call on the expertise of the task force if they encounter digital evidence.

- The FBI sponsors and funds regional computer forensic labs (RCFLs). The FBI maintains administrative control although member agencies and often supplies supervisory personnel. Regional agencies and departments contribute officers to the RCFL and in return get access to enhanced training and first-rate facilities. "In FY 2006, the NTRCFL processed over 50 terabytes of digital evidence in 500 cases. This is an average of about 50 cases per examiner. Each case varies widely, but the average digital evidence per case was 69.5 gigabytes."[123] RCFL staff take computer crime cases from all over the region and offer training through the RCFL facilities. The labs even contribute to the field through research and development. The Dallas, Texas lab has been working to develop software and procedures for consent searches of computer hard drives. The product, Image Scan, is freely available to law enforcement agencies who have attended the free training.

- On October 26, 2001, President Bush signed into law H.R. 3162, the Uniting and Strengthening America by Providing Appropriate Tools Required to Intercept and Obstruct Terrorism (USA PATRIOT) Act of 2001. In drafting this particular legislation, Congress recognized the Secret Service philosophy that our success resides in the ability to bring academia, law enforcement, and private industry together to combat crime in the information age. As a result, the U.S. Secret Service was mandated by this Act to establish a nationwide network of electronic crimes task forces based on the New York model that encompasses this philosophy.[124] Unlike the FBI model, no contribution of personnel is required. Many companies recognize the benefit to their bottom line from well-funded and well-trained local law enforcement. Some companies provide expertise through employees assigned to task forces or as stand-by, subject-matter experts. Linkages with universities provide technical expertise to task force members. Each of the regional task forces is expected to develop its own niche based on locally available assets and talents. This is largely driven by local corporations and universities.

As an example, the North Texas Electronic Crimes Task Force (NTEC) is composed of private sector professionals from the "telecommunications corridor" in Dallas, along with myriad state, local, and federal law enforcement

and prosecutorial agencies headed by the U.S. Secret Service. The group also includes professors from local universities that have focused programs in information security, privacy law, electrical engineering, and computer technology. The task force has been highly successful in sponsoring quarterly training meetings and developing informal contacts between these three critical sectors: law enforcement/prosecutorial agencies, academia, and private corporations. The combined knowledge and skill of such a group has provided a powerful force in combating computer crime in the entire area. Indeed, the task force was instrumental in several local cases, as well as in providing key resources in a major international case within its first year of operation.

Voluntary Associations

When the resources are not available to start a task force, officers may join organizations such as the High Technology Crime Investigation Association (HTCIA) and the American Society for Industrial Security (ASIS).[125] These organizations provide individual officers with an opportunity to expand their skills and develop contacts in neighboring jurisdictions. Private associations offer most of the same advantages as task forces, but on a less frequent and more informal basis.

The benefits include the following:

- Coordination
- Training
- Information sharing
- Resource sharing
- Public/Private partnerships

TOOLS FOR COMPUTER CRIME INVESTIGATION

For the most part, computer crime investigators work in an arena often foreign to most other criminal investigators. They deal with the seizure of digital rather than physical evidence. They also routinely use an arsenal of court orders and search instruments that most officers rarely learn in the police academy, much less use as a standard part of their job.

Search Instruments

Four primary laws affect computer crime searches:

- Wire Tap (18 U.S.C. §§ 2510-22)
- Pen Register/Trap and Trace Statute (Pen/Trace, 18 U.S.C. §§ 1321-27)

- Electronic Communications Privacy Act "ECPA" (18 U.S.C. §§ 2701-11)
- USA PATRIOT Act of 2001 (Pub. L. No. 107-56)

Although it is more complex, this body of search law provides investigators with legal opportunities to leverage lesser information into new avenues of investigation. This series of laws places different burdens on law enforcement to obtain a variety of search instruments. The range of protection for information is based on Constitutional protections (i.e., Fourth Amendment) and case law from over 200 years.

The Court has continually interpreted the technologies that have shaped our communication. One of the first questions posed was how does the Fourth Amendment pertain to letters. In 1877, the Court ruled that the contents of a letter were protected as if they were part of the home; protections extending to persons and papers applied to the mail.[126] The court also decided that postcards have no such protection because they are not sealed, like letters. The transmittal information found on the outside of an envelope must be viewed by the government to deliver the mail. Anything within plain sight of that information was also within the scope of the government's view. This began a fundamental distinction in search law. Content of communication deserves more protection because of the reasonable expectation of privacy held by the person communicating.[127] Transmittal information (Figure 16-20) is addressing information

Electronic search and seizure can be very complicated. The information discussed here presents broad ideas, not specific legal advice. A more comprehensive summary of this body of law can be found at www.cybercrime.gov/s&smanual2002.htm. The following figure presents a list of legal instruments, orders, and warrants available to investigators. The column on the right presents the "showing" that must be made for an investigator to obtain the search instrument. Generally, any order listed above any other in the list (thus, meeting a higher procedural burden) allows access to the information with less procedural protection. For example, an ECPA Search Warrant would allow access to anything that an ECPA §2703 Order allows access to.

Instrument	Procedural Burden	Target of Search
Title III interception order	Probable cause standard with explicit minimization and reporting.	The content of telephonic communication.
F.R.C.P. Rule 41 search warrant—authorizing the search of physical premises and physical items or ECPA search warrant—authorizing search of "in-transit" data held by an ECS for less than 180 days	Probable cause standard.	Physical objects including data containers. This includes access to electronic communication considered to be "in transit."
ECPA §2703(d) order or ECPA §2703(d) order with notice	Specific and articulable facts showing reasonable grounds to believe that the records are relevant and material to an ongoing criminal investigation.	Basic subscriber information, records or logs pertaining to a subscriber, or contents of stored records (e.g., electronic communications over 180 days old).
"Pen register" and "trap-and-trace device" order	Relevant to a criminal investigation.	Transmittal information (i.e., telephone numbers dialed from, or calling in to, a number).
Subpoena with notice, ECPA §2703(b)(1)(B)	Filed with the court.	Electronic communications that have been received and stored or have been "in transit for more than 180 days."
Subpoena with delayed notice, ECPA §2705	Notice may be delayed in successive 90-day periods "upon the written certification of a supervisory official that there is reason to believe that notification of the existence of the subpoena may have an adverse result."	Electronic communications that have been received and stored or have been "in transit for more than 180 days."
Preservation Letter or Civil Subpoena	A preservation letter simply requires a request from a law enforcement officer made to the authority holding potential evidence. Evidence must be retained for 90 days (renewable) on receipt of a preservation letter that sufficiently identifies the information sought.	Evidence may not be deleted, but it may be illegal to turn it over to law enforcement without further search instruments being served—even if the public service provider wishes to voluntarily disclose the information.[i] However, exceptions exist.[ii]

[i] *Electronic Communications Privacy Act* 18 U.S.C. §§2703-11.

[ii] National Security Exceptions: USA PATRIOT Act §505, Immediate Danger to a Person Exception: USA PATRIOT Act §212, Inadvertently Discovered Exception: ECPA §2702(b)(6)(A), Child Protection and Sexual Predator Punishment Act of 1998, 42 U.S.C. §13032, mandates the disclosure: ECPA §2702(b)(6)(B).

▲ **FIGURE 16-20** **Search and seizure of digital evidence** needed to deliver the message content. By definition, transmittal information must be shared with the carrier; thus, it has no reasonable expectation of privacy.[128]

Wire Tap, Pen Register, and Trap and Trace

A wire tap order allows an investigator to listen in on the conversation of a suspect. Wire taps are also called Title III orders, because the law was passed as part of the Omnibus Crime Control and Safe Streets Act of 1968. A Pen Register order allows an investigator to receive a list of phone numbers dialed from a suspect's phone. It is not a "search" to use a pen register at the phone company to determine what numbers were dialed in a private home; thus, the procedural burden to obtain a Pen Register order is less than a search warrant. This makes pen register orders valuable assets to an investigator seeking to establish probable cause for a search warrant. Pen registers were originally shaped like pens and connected to the phone company's equipment. Today, the function is handled by software in the computer-based telephone switching equipment, but the function is still referred to by the old device name. A Trap and Trace order allows an investigator to receive a list of phone numbers dialing into a suspect's phone. Old, mechanical switching equipment used a lock, called a *trap*, to hold connections in place. Technicians could then trace the routing of the call back to the source—trap and trace.[129]

With the advent of the telephone, the government (both the Court and Congress) were challenged with applying Fourth Amendment protections to this new medium. The content of the telephone call actually receives more protection than does the content of a letter. The original reasoning was that people didn't understand telephone technology and could not take reasonable precautions to protect their own privacy. Transmittal information (i.e., the telephone number) required to route a call, is not protected any more than the address on a letter. Thus, wire taps[130] and Pen/Trace orders[131] follow the content transmittal distinction.

Electronic Communications

With the advent of computer network communication, Congress again attempted to balance personal rights and law enforcement necessity. Since at the time most network communication was carried over telephone lines, many asserted that a full wire tap was necessary to intercept electronic communication. Others asserted that the computer store and forward[132] method of communication meant that data traveling through wires was "in transit" and deserved the full protection of Title III's wire tap provisions. The ECPA[133] attempted to resolve the problem of defining communication by establishing a new distinction: in-transit versus electronic storage. Information in-transit deserved a higher degree of protection

than stored data—mirroring Title III's provisions. Stored data deserved less protection but still retained more protection than did transmittal information. The additional complication of the store-and-forward model was resolved with the standard of 180 days. After 180 days, information can no longer be considered in transit. If accessed or read before 180 days, it is also considered to be stored.

Computer networks also brought another question about the traditional content versus transmittal distinction. An encapsulating protocol receives data from another source and performs its required duties without modifying the data; rather, it wraps it in new commands and sends it on its way. The entire message can be encapsulated by several protocols and broken into smaller pieces without regard to anything except the operating requirements of the current network protocol at work. It doesn't distinguish between the original content of the added instructions from the last protocol. Despite this technical distinction in encapsulating protocols, only human-readable content is protected. Encapsulated protocol headers are still transmittal information.

The USA PATRIOT Act

The PATRIOT Act is a vast and complex change to civil liberties in the United States. The debate surrounding the PATRIOT Act has been confused because many of its provisions are very expansive. In some cases, it has continued the rationalizing process of dealing with electronic communication and modern realities. In others, it has eroded the protections of personal liberty in order to ferret out potential terrorists. Balancing the need for domestic security with the individual privacy rights of citizens is at the core of the debate about the PATRIOT Act. From a computer crime perspective, the act rationalizes the collection of voice-mail as evidence. Previously, it was unclear if voice-mail required a wire tap or a simple search warrant. In some cases, the contents of an answering machine cassette were ruled inadmissible even when seized with a valid search warrant in spite of the precedent set for stored and forwarded messages in the ECPA. While maintaining the established distinction between content and routing information, the PATRIOT Act also permits the seizure of voice-mail messages older than 180 days with an ECPA §2703 Order. It also permits the seizure of voice-mail messages less than 180 days old with a search warrant.[134] The act has greatly pushed the borders of what is content (and hence can be used as evidence) and what is available to law enforcement at a much lower burden than the requirements for a search warrant.[135]

Preservation Letter

With almost no procedural burden on an investigator, he or she may send a preservation letter to the custodian of potential evidence. In practice, this is often a public Internet service provider (ISP). The ECPA generally forbids public providers of Internet service (e.g., AOL, AT&T, Sprint) to voluntarily divulge their customer's information. However, the ECPA also provides investigators with a tool to be sure that the information is not lost or destroyed when legal procedures are dealt with. A provider of wire or electronic communication services or a remote computing service, on the request of a governmental entity, shall take all necessary steps to preserve records and other evidence in its possession pending the issuance of a court order or other process.[136]

Records referred to in paragraph (1) shall be retained for a period of 90 days, which shall be extended for an additional 90-day period upon a renewed request by the governmental entity.[137]

Network Tools

It is also possible to use common system administration tools to trace Internet messages to their source.[138] These basic tools are freely available or found on the World Wide Web. They can assist investigators trying to tie a network address to a real-world address. Be aware that the business office of a service provider may be in a different state than the service user being sought. However, logs and business records available for subpoena may provide very real benefits to an investigation. Another benefit is that even small-scale providers can be reached through the Internet from remote locations.

Name Service Lookup (nslookup) This network utility program allows a user to enter a host name and find its unique Internet Address (IP). A reverse lookup is available to convert an IP to its human-readable equivalent. NSLookup relies on the Domain Name Resolution protocol (DNS), which allows users to enter meaningful words instead of IP addresses to identify a computer. Thus, an investigator seeking the IP address for "www.foo.com" would use a database of domain names and matching IPs maintained by ICANN (the Internet Corporation for Assigned Names and Numbers) or its subset databases hosted throughout the Internet. Nslookup is the service used to access that database. It is the same database used by any web application, like a browser, that allows a user to type in a human readable address—such as www.foo.com. The service is available at www.internic.net.

Whois The Internet Protocol address is a unique address assigned to every computer on the Internet. The IP is usually reported in the decimal-dot notation. This is four elements of 0–255 separated by dots, for example: 192.168.0.0. IPs are often dynamically (temporarily) assigned to computers when they start up. Such dynamic addresses are part of the basic subscriber information defined in the USA PATRIOT Act and so are relatively easy to obtain with the proper search instrument. Many

hosts on the Internet, especially servers, use static IPs, which do not change.

The American Registry for Internet Numbers (ARIN) maintains the IPs assigned in North and South America. International investigations may require the use of the European and African authority (RIPE) or the Asian authority (APNIC). By submitting an IP address, the business contact address for the owner may be found. This information is often the second step (after the nslookup) in finding the company or person responsible for a user's Internet service. The ARIN database is easily accessed through their web page at www.arin.net/whois.

The traditional "whois" allows a user to search for the owner of a domain name (i.e., everything between "www" and ".com/.edu/.gov/etc." in a web address or everything between "@" and ".com/.edu/.gov/etc." in an e-mail address). The owner of the domain name and the business contact address will be returned. The service can be accessed through www.betterwhois.com/.

DIGITAL FORENSICS

Digital forensics is the science of acquiring, preserving, retrieving, and presenting data that have been processed electronically and stored on computer media.[139] As a forensic discipline, nothing since DNA technology has had such a large potential effect on specific types of investigations and prosecution as has digital forensic analysis. It is important to note that the examination of computer media for evidence is not limited to computer crimes but is relevant to the investigation of almost any traditional fraud as well as a variety of common crimes. Thus, special care must be given to the recovery of electronic data to ensure the accuracy and integrity of this metaphysical evidence.[140]

Electronic information is stored in physical media. Stored information can be accessed and analyzed for investigative purposes. That process of analysis and presentation in court is digital forensics. Accessing and understanding storage media and devices help an investigator to present evidence more clearly to a jury. Maintaining the integrity of the source is the most important task of the examiner. Without sufficient, scientific assurance that the information is valid, the courts will not find the evidence credible.

Acquisition of Data

The process described in the section Crime Scene Investigative Techniques is the preferred method to bring data to the forensic lab. Seizing the hard drive and removing it from the suspect's system allows an analyst to use a specially prepared "lab bench computer" to perform the analysis with a negligible chance of altering the data.

Acquisition, at the very least, requires obtaining active files and making them available for analysis. By imaging the data under the controlled conditions of a forensic lab, one can more easily verify the evidence's integrity. It is also possible to acquire latent data.

Other acceptable techniques exist to avoid altering the original, many of which are used in the analysis of "live" or running systems. For example, analysis can be performed against a hard drive with a write-blocker installed (see the "Write-Blocker" section later in this chapter). The analysis runs from a host computer system. Another technique uses a true read-only mount of the file system (often not possible in Windows) with analysis proceeding from a drive mounted for read-write operations.

Authentication of Data

Using a mathematical process called **hashing,** a forensic analyst can verify that not one single "bit" of evidence has been altered from the time the first hash was calculated. A hash is like an electronic fingerprint of the file. It is derived from the data in such a way that it is functionally impossible to find another meaningful file that will produce the same output. A fingerprint is far smaller than the person it represents but can still uniquely identify the person. Similarly, the hash value is much smaller than the file it was created from, but it is still able to uniquely identify it. Hashes are reported in hexadecimal: a number system using 16 as the base instead of 10. Thus, hashes contain a series of letters and numbers that can be any combination of 0–9 and A–F. For example, a sample hash is "E58D 78A0 3C14 C844 2FCA 9192 8F6D BDB9." The odds of any two different files having the same hash are $1:3.4028 \times 10^{38}$—in other words, functionally impossible. There are several hash algorithms available, each producing results in the same form, but through different methods that yield different values. The hash just shown is the product of the MD5 (Message Digest 5) hash algorithm. MD5 and a more recent algorithm called SHA (Secure HAsh) are the two most commonly used hashes in digital forensics.

Imaging of the Evidence Drive

The best current practice in storage forensics is to create an exact copy or "image" of the seized drive believed to contain evidence. An image is an exact copy of a hard drive. However, this copy is not like logical copies made with the operating system's copy command in that it includes all the latent data as well as active files.

Active files are simply the familiar files that we see on computers. They are word processing documents, pictures, web pages, saved video games, and any other file to which the user has regular access. Latent data includes all the data on a storage device that is not accessible through the operating system. There are several forms of latent data:

- Unallocated space
- File slack
- Protected files
- Virtual memory

Unallocated space is simply unused storage space. If a file was previously saved to that same space, much or all of it may remain until a new file is saved there. File slack is a byproduct of the way hard drives save files. To reduce resources devoted to keeping track of files on the disk, hard drives save files in complete blocks called sectors. To speed file saves, the operating system groups these sectors together in clusters. File slack is contained in unused sectors at the end of a cluster. Since a cluster is simply a group of contiguous sectors, a file that doesn't fill an entire cluster leaves file slack space in unused sectors.

The file depicted in Figure 16-21 is 2,304 bytes. Each of the first four sectors contains 512 bytes ($512 \times 4 = 2,048$), but the file cannot fill a fifth ($2,304 - 2,048 = 256$). Since hard drives write in sectors, Windows must "pad" the remaining space with information from somewhere. Main memory (Random Access Memory, or RAM) can quickly provide data to fill the extra space. Since this space contains the contents of RAM, it is called *RAM slack*. The remaining space in the cluster is called *file slack*.

Protected files are not usually accessible to casual users. The operating system (e.g., Windows) reserves access to some files that it needs to run. These are considered to be latent data, because they cannot be accessed while the system is running. They can, however, be accessed if the system is booted from external media (e.g., CD, DVD, and so on). Most protected files yield nothing of interest.[141] Some however, literally contain the keys to the kingdom with encryption keys and password caches.

Virtual memory (VM) is a technique that allows a computer to use hard drive space as a form of super-slow

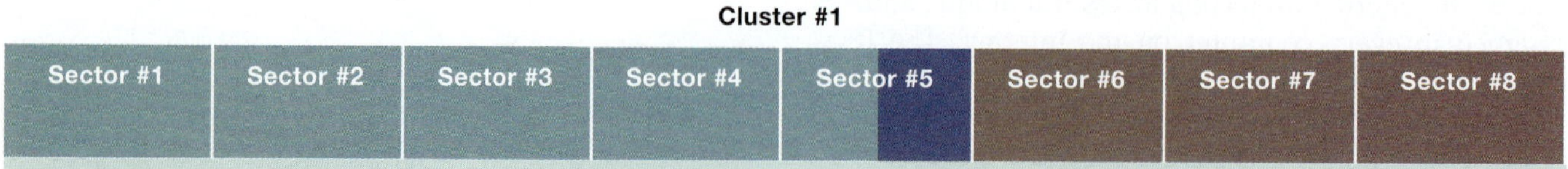

Cluster #1

Sector #1	Sector #2	Sector #3	Sector #4	Sector #5	Sector #6	Sector #7	Sector #8

▲ **FIGURE 16-21   Slack types**
Slack types have 4,096 bytes per cluster and 512 bytes per sector. Thus, there are 8 sectors per cluster (4,096 [H11004] 512 [H11005] 8). The file contained in this cluster (in green) is only 2,304 bytes. The remaining space is RAM slack (blue) and file slack (brown).

RAM. Although it is not efficient, it allows a system with insufficient memory to complete tasks and not crash when main memory runs out. The file created is called the "swap file" in Windows and a "paging file" in Unix. Accessing VM and RAM slack are two ways to read the contents of system memory. Active memory may hold lists of network connections or indicate the way a computer was being used at the time.

Wiping the Analysis Drive

The analyst must be able to assure the court that no evidence from other cases has contaminated the current analysis. For example, analysis on a child pornography case may lead to loading pornographic images from the image of a suspect's drive. If this material is not thoroughly wiped, it may be detected in a later analysis of another suspect's drive in a fraud case. To avoid having to explain this in court, it is best to establish a procedure that wipes both data and the slack space between data. By wiping the analysis drive before restoring the image, the analyst will be able to refute any claim that the drive was contaminated. Most common implementations of a wiping program meet the standards of Department of Defense Directive 5220.22—the DoD wipe.[142]

Restoring the Image to an Analysis Drive

To perform forensic analysis of the data, it must be loaded onto a clean target drive or folder. When the image is loaded, it should be authenticated to verify that it is a true copy of the original. Although small-scale, 4.7 GB or less, analysis can be performed from a DVD or other write-once media, larger volumes of data can be practically handled only from a hard drive. Consider even a relatively small evidence drive at 20 GB. If completely full, it would take five DVDs to hold the contents. Each step of an analysis protocol must be performed five times with the operator switching disks as needed. In addition to raw size, an internal hard drive has a much faster data transfer rate than do any of the current removable media. Consider that, in order to search a hard drive for one key word, the entire contents of that hard drive must be read and brought into the computer's memory. Even a marginal speed advantage makes the restoration procedure necessary.

Understanding the scale of data handled in digital forensics is difficult (see Table 16-1). In one of the defining cases in data storage, Kevin Mitnick (discussed earlier in the chapter), possessed 9 GB of data when arrested. Prosecutors and the court refused to allow Mitnick access to a computer to view the evidence against him because of fears that he could cause damage or seek revenge.[143] Astronomical figures about the amount of paper needed to print that amount of potential evidence was used to justify not releasing it to Mitnick. To print all the evidence would have required a stack of paper 1,440 feet high.

TABLE 16-1	Paper Volume and Storage		
TERM	VALUE	VALUE IN BYTES	VOLUME IN PAGES
bit	1	1/8 byte	about 1/2 page
byte	8 bits	1 byte	about 1/2 page
kilobyte (KB)	1,024 bytes	2^{10} bytes	about 1/2 page
megabyte (MB)	1,024 KB	2^{20} bytes	about 500 pages
gigabyte (GB)	1,024 MB	2^{30} bytes	160-foot stack of paper

Digital Analysis

Analysis is *never* performed directly on the evidence drive. Analyses are performed on the image or a copy of the image. This is because forensic analysis can change the underlying data structures if performed on an active drive, thus contaminating the evidentiary value of the material originally seized on the storage drive or device. Almost any action taken on a computer, even the simple act of starting it, alters potential evidence and gives the defense an avenue to attack the credibility of the analysis.

By following established procedures and protocol for evidence handling, an analyst can assure the court that the contents of the evidence drive were not altered by the analysis itself. The analyst produces a report summarizing these activities to present the facts to the jury, but also to allow experts for the defense to verify that the procedures used did not contaminate the evidence.

The product of the analysis is not evidence. It is an index to the location of evidence on the seized disk. It is a summary of evidence. An analyst's report is not the "smoking gun." When presented in court, an analyst's report simply helps the jury understand how the suspect interacted with the evidence and how and where that evidence was located. An analyst is often called upon to explain the tools and procedures used to locate the evidence. Thus, a working knowledge and certification with tools used is vital.

The Tools of Digital Forensics

In the last ten years, the size of an adequate home-use hard drive has increased from approximately 100 megabytes (MB) to approximately 120 gigabytes (GB). This represents an increase of over 1,000 times the volume of data on a standard home use computer. As can be seen in Table 16-1, 1 megabyte is equivalent to about one ream (500 sheets) of printed product, depending on the level of interpretation given to the file. To put this volume in perspective, if the entire binary content of a hard drive was printed out, it would produce a stack of paper 19,200 feet—approximately 4 miles—high. Without adequate tools to assist investigators, we would simply be unable to search for evidence in a meaningful, legal, and complete way. All electronic evidence, whether acquired from a seized hard drive or a live electronic communication (i.e., "off the wire") is simply a pattern of binary information. At the most fundamental level, it is a series of locations that are either "on" or "off." These patterns can be read by computer operating systems. Thus, the investigator can rapidly peruse the entire contents of a hard drive but risk missing key *inculpatory* (i.e., tending to establish guilt) or *exculpatory* (i.e., tending to establish innocence) evidence.

Although a wide variety of tools are necessary to conduct scientifically valid forensic analysis,[144] this section focuses on the base items of the trade: forensic analysis packages. Live network forensics—often called *post mortem analysis* or *intrusion analysis*—requires a separate set of tools and skills. Most law enforcement–oriented investigators will not attempt this form of forensic analysis.[145] Forensic packages, however, each have unique strengths that set them apart from the others. These strengths are used next to illustrate the basic requirements of a forensic package.

Forensic Packages

A good forensics package must cover each of the basic forensic functions described in the preceding section: authenticate, image, wipe, restore, and analyze. A police department or agency seeking a single-user license for a forensic package can expect to pay about $1,200–$2,000. Additional features can be purchased at additional expense, but a beginning computer crime investigator or forensic analyst will find most required features in the package. A survey of the following items should help the computer crime investigator or digital forensics examiner select the most appropriate package.

Comprehensiveness A forensic package must be versatile enough to recognize the common, binary encoding schemes as well as the commonly used proprietary data storage formats. For example, text is often stored in American Standard Code of Information Interchange (ASCII) or a compatible format, but other schemes are also available. Different binary encoding is used for different purposes. Images, for instance, are often stored in the JPEG format.[146] However, numerous other formats can be used to store images (e.g., GIF, Portable Network Graphics—PNG, Bitmap—BMP, and so on). Forensic packages must be able to interpret these reasonably "open" standards but must also be able to interpret proprietary standards such as Adobe's native file format for Photoshop. There are also numerous proprietary data formats. For example, Microsoft Outlook uses a proprietary database (called a DBX file) to store all its e-mail. Without a third-party utility program, an analyst would have to install Microsoft Outlook to read seized e-mail. However, modern forensic packages have plug-ins that can decode proprietary file formats. Although freeware utilities are available to read Outlook DBX files, exporting data to separate utilities can be cumbersome and is prone to creating errors. Further, broad search protocols do not work unless the search software is aware of various encoding schemes.[147]

Usability Given the volume of data that must be analyzed, usability features are not simple luxuries, they are necessities. The following features serve as examples of the many ways that forensic packages add usability. Usability features include ways to reduce data transfer between programs. For example, early forensic packages did not have a mechanism to conveniently identify images or transfer text to word processors. Modern packages often allow output to only a single open format, such as HTML, the text-based format used in web pages. Other common features include customizable interfaces offering easy access to the most commonly used features. Customizable report templates allow investigators to enter information directly into a department's report format, thereby reducing the chances of inadvertent transcription errors. Another usability feature is the ability to customize search items in standard list. For example, in an identity theft investigation, an investigator could load a list of several hundred items commonly found. "Social Security number," "Soc. Sec.," "SS#," and "SSN" each represent a separate search, but if the entire list is loaded, each item can be searched in one pass through the data, saving enormous amounts of time. It also allows the investigator to establish a standard search.

Accuracy Fundamentally, forensic software is a feature-rich search mechanism that must be able to identify all evidence matching the search parameters set by the analyst. False negatives and/or missing data are simply unacceptable. To increase accuracy, forensic software attempts additional verification of the file type reported to the analyst. The software uses elements hidden within the file to verify that a filename's three-letter extension accurately identifies the type of file being analyzed. Thus, attempts are often made to obscure the contents of contraband files by changing the three-letter extension at the end of the filename. Searches are based on this identification, not by simply trusting in the three-letter extension. Ultimately, accuracy is assessed through cross-validation with other search techniques and by testing software against known, standard files to see if all instances of the test data are found.

Reliability In research, reliability is defined as the ability to produce the same outcome, given the same input and other significant conditions. Although a computer can be instructed to perform the same task the same way over and over again, not all software produces the same results every time. Variables in the computer's memory or depletion of system resources (e.g., memory space) can influence the outcome of a process unless the software is written to avoid this. Like accuracy, reliability must be tested with independent means. An analyst must be absolutely certain that a process run in the lab can be reproduced by defense experts or in the courtroom itself.[148]

Verifiable Validity In research, validity is defined as an outcome that reflects the intent of the research. In other words, when you seek to measure a concept, did you actually measure that concept or something else? A related question would be "did you measure the whole concept or just a part of it?" The assessment of a forensic package's accuracy and reliability assure that the process of producing a report of the evidence is done as the analyst intends. The validity of an analysis is much more complex, but implicitly includes accuracy and reliability. The validity of digital evidence depends on the analyst's ability to find meaningful connections between data and human intent or action. A forensic package cannot guarantee the validity of an analysis. It can, however, be demonstrated through repetition in a wide range of conditions to perform as intended by the analyst. Andy Rosen, creator of the SMART forensic package said: "A scalpel is only a scalpel in the hands of a surgeon. In a butcher's hands, it's just a wicked sharp knife." Validity doesn't lie within the forensic package; it lies within the analyst's ability to achieve his or her intent with the package.

Ultimately, it is still up to the analysts to determine which evidence will be presented to the prosecutor to achieve the goal of the investigation (i.e., a conviction). It then rests on the prosecutor to "make the case." A forensic package can assist this endeavor by establishing a record of reliable, accurate, and valid analyses among many users and thereby gain acceptance in many courts. Andy Rosen also addressed this fact: "Tools are not validated in courts. Tools are validated by testing them over and over and over again and that validation is accepted by courts."[149]

Write-Blocker

A *write-blocker* is a device used to prevent unintentional destruction or alteration of evidence on a hard drive (Figure 16-22). This device is necessary because any analysis must be shown to discover unaltered evidence. Kruse and Heiser cite a statement from the Federal Law Enforcement Training Center (FLETC) that 400 files are altered in the start-up process of a Windows 9*x* machine and 500 files are altered in the start-up process of a Windows NT machine.[150] It is possible to use a Linux-based forensic suite such as SMART without a write-blocker. Unix-based systems can "mount" (i.e., open) a storage device without altering it. Windows, however, does not allow a hard drive to open in a true read-only state. Generally, the use of a write-blocker is fairly straightforward. The hard drive is installed to the write-blocker, which is installed to the analysis computer.

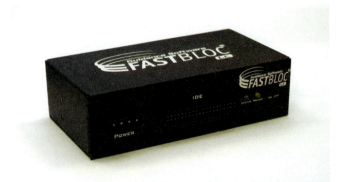

▲ **FIGURE 16-22 Fastbloc**
A write-blocker, such as Fastbloc, blocks Windows attempts to alter the data on a hard disk at startup. Seized hard drives can be connected to the write-blocker and then analyzed.
(Courtesy of Intelligent Computer Solutions, Inc.)

Data Interfaces

A wide range of methods are used to move data from one device to another. Five years ago, one of the key problems in digital forensics was accessing data in an incompatible device. The competing Small Computer Systems Interface (SCSI, pronounced "skuzzy") and Integrated Drive Electronics (IDE) families of standards made forensic analysis of nonstandard devices like a scavenger hunt, seeking adapters and compatible systems (Figure 16-23). Today, data interfaces still present a wide variety of adapters and options. The most common are still SCSI and IDE, however. Newcomers include related protocols under the name of Universal Serial Bus (USB) and IEEE 1394 (Firewire).

The latest crisis in data interfaces is the myriad proprietary cabling and connections used by small devices: PDAs, cell phones, MP3 players, and so on. The ability to analyze these devices depends on the ability to connect them to an analysis machine. Paraben Software has taken the lead in this area. Not only do they offer the software necessary to connect to these devices, they offer the cabling as well. Paraben produces the only collection of interface cables for small devices. Of course, such cables may be available if they can be seized with a computer. Unfortunately, many users do not even know that their phone can talk to their computer; hence, they do not typically own the interface cables.

Digital evidence is probably present at the vast majority of crime scenes. As both the public and criminals become more familiar with, and reliant on, electronic devices, that evidence will play an increasingly important role in human communication and interaction, and in court. For instance, the argument serving as the motive for a school assault may have occurred online, via text messages, at a time when both the victim and the assailant were in class and separated by several hundred yards; the evidence leading to a missing child may be found in online chats; and the

◀**FIGURE 16-23**
Scavenger hunt?
A wide variety of adapters can confuse even experienced investigators.

(© Lawrence Lawry/Getty Images)

evidence compelling a conviction for cyberstalking may reside in the suspect's hard drive and PDA.

Computer crime is often complex and involves an understanding of the computer and telecommunications environment. However, even as we see a generation of criminals who communicate as freely over electronic networks as they speak in person, we are also seeing a generation of officers and investigators who have been raised with the same technology. Today, it is possible that many of our officers have never known a time without a computer in their own homes. In spite of this increasingly computer-literate force, explicit training is still needed in the tools and techniques of computer crime investigations. Finally, a rigorous science is required to develop this infant science we call digital forensics. A methodology for evaluating and comparing tools may be a first step.

KEY TERMS

attack code
buffer overflows
cloning
component swapping
computer abuse
computer crime
computer manipulation crime
computer vandalism
cryptanalysis software
cyberstalking
denial-of-service (DoS) attack
digital evidence
digital forensics
encryption

End-User License Agreements (EULAs)
exploits
hacker's dictionary
hacking or cracking
hashing
logic bomb
malware
packet sniffers
phishing
phreakers
piracy
refurbishment fraud

root kits
salami slice
shopping cart fraud
smurfing
spam
TCP/IP
Trojan horse
tumbling
virus
war dialing
war driving
worm

REVIEW QUESTIONS

1. What are computer abuse and computer crime?
2. What is a computer manipulation crime? Describe some common Internet scams.
3. Define the activity of hacking or cracking.

4. What are the differences between real-world stalking and cyberstalking?
5. How do cloning and tumbling work?

6. Identify and describe the major types of exploits discussed in the chapter.

7. What is attack malware? Discuss the concept of attack malware in terms of logic-bomb traps and Trojan horse programs.

8. What are some of the problems investigators face when responding to computer crimes?

9. What are some of the advantages of forming task forces to investigate computer crime?

10. Discuss the four primary laws affecting computer crime searches.

11. What is digital forensics? What are some of the primary steps in conducting this process on a computer?

12. On what features can digital forensic packages be evaluated?

| INTERNET ACTIVITIES

1. Check out the U.S. Department of Justice's website on cyber crime at www.cybercrime.gov. This website provides policies, cases, press releases, and articles about intellectual property, the USA PATRIOT Act, privacy, and Internet and computer crimes.

2. Search several Internet media sites for information on computer crime in your area. What types of computer crimes have been reported on within the last few years? Have arrests and/or convictions been made in these crimes? What estimates have been given on the cost of these crimes? Who investigated the crimes? What were the outcomes of the investigations?

| NOTES

1. B. M. Leiner, V. G. Cerf, D. D. Clark, R. E. Kahn, L. Kleinrock, D. C. Lynch, J. Postel, L. G. Roberts, and S. Wolff, "A Brief History of the Internet. Version 3.31," Feb. 1, 2001, www.isoc.org/internet-history/brief.html and A. R. Burks and A. W. Burks, *The First Electronic Computer: The Atanasoff Story* (Ann Arbor, MI: University of Michigan Press, 1988).

2. Donn Parker, *Computer Crime: Criminal Justice Resource Manual* (Washington, D.C.: National Institute of Justice, 1989).

3. Catherine H. Conley and J. Thomas McEwen, "Computer Crime," *NIJ Reports,* January–February 1990, No. 218, p. 3.

4. CERT and CSI have extensive online services that provide detailed information on most computer crime units within federal, state, and local agencies. For more information, see www.cert.org and www.gocsi.org.

5. B. Sullivan, "Have You Seen This Geek?" zdnet.com/zdnn/stories/news/0,4586,2771692,00.html, June 8, 2001.

6. R. P. Kusserow, "An Inside Look at Federal Computer Crime," *Security Management*, p. 75 (May, 1986).

7. Ibid.

8. A criminal typology is a tool for categorizing crime by type; similar crimes are grouped together. See Julian B. Roebuck, *Criminal Typology* (Springfield, IL: Charles C. Thomas, 1967).

9. Donn Parker, *Crime by Computer* (New York: Scribner, 1976).

10. See Robert W. Taylor, "Hackers, Phone Phreakers, and Virus Makers," paper presented at the Second Annual Conference on Computer Viruses, London, England, June 1990. This paper was developed into the chapter entitled "Computer Crime" in earlier editions of this book. See Charles R. Swanson, Neil C. Chamelin, and Leonard Territo, *Criminal Investigation,* 5th, 6th, and 7th ed. (New York: McGraw-Hill, 1992, 1996, and 2000).

11. David Carter, "Computer Crime Categories," *FBI Law Enforcement Bulletin,* 1995, Vol. 64, No. 21.

12. Donn Parker, *Fighting Computer Crime: A New Framework for Protecting Information* (New York: Wiley, 1998).

13. Robert W. Taylor and Deanne Carp, "Policing the Internet: Legal Issues on the Information Super-Highway," in J. Walker, ed., *Legal Issues in Policing* (Upper Saddle River, NJ: Prentice Hall, 2002).

14. Federal Trade Commission. "Dot Com Disclosures." www.ftc.gov/bcp/conline/pubs/buspubs/dotcom/.

15. "Congress Warned of New Fraud: Computers Simplify, Reduce Cost of Check Counterfeiting," *Dallas Morning News,* May 2, 1997, p. 5A.

16. Ibid.

17. Ibid.

18. Aaron Nathans, "IRS Moves to Block 'Rapid Refund' Scam Artists," *Los Angeles Times,* Oct. 27, 1994, p. A24.

19. J. Littman, "Hacker Shocker: Project Reveals Breaches Galore," www5.zdnet.com/zdnet.com/zdnn/content/zdnn/0918/zdn0010.html, retrieved Sept. 18, 1997.

20. Evet, D. , "Spam Statistics 2006," http://spam-filter-review.toptenreviews.com/spamstatistics.html retrieved August 13, 2007.

21. J. Krim, "Spam's Cost to Business Escalates: Bulk E-Mail Threatens Communication Arteries," www.washingtonpost.com/ac2/wp-dyn/A17754-2003Mar12 retrieved Oct. 20, 2004.

22. HelpMeSoft. "NUCEM for Corporations," www.helpmesoft.com/product/corporation1.html.

23. Evet, D., "Spam Statistics 2006," http://spam-filter-review.toptenreviews.com/spamstatistics.html retrieved August 13, 2007.

24. M. Wagner, "Spam Costs $11.9 Billion; Users Favor Legal Ban," www.internetweek.com/story/showArticle.jhtml?articleID=6000048, retrieved Oct. 20, 2004.

25. E-Commerce Times "In Cyberspace, a Dark Alliance," www.ecommercetimes.com/story/In-Cyberspace-A-Dark-Alliance-37164.html, retrieved Oct. 20, 2004.

26. Known alternately as W32Mydoom, Q@mm by Symantec, W32/Mydoom.s@MM by McAfee, W32/MyDoom-S by Sophos, Win32.Mydoom.S by Computer Associates, and WORM_RATOS.A by Trend Micro. Each antivirus vendor "names" the virus/worm according to characteristics or information found on the MMC.

27. R.A. Grimes, *Malicious Mobile Code: Virus Protections for Windows* (Sebastopol, CA: O'Reilly Pub., 2001).

28. Joint Photographic Experts Group (JPEG). For more on the JPEG graphic compression standard see www.jpeg.org/committee.html.

29. HTML is the primary "language" used to create web pages. In effect, viewing an HTML e-mail is like viewing a web page—with all the risks present.

30. L. Seltzer, "Microsoft Graphics Bug Threatens Systems," www.eweek.com/print_article/0,1761,a=135314,00.asp posted Sept. 14, 2004.

31. K. Poulsen, "Warspammer guilty under new federal law," www.securityfocus.com/news/9606, posted Sept. 29, 2004.

32. See B. Steinhardt, "The Fourth Amendment and Carnivore," Statement for the Record before the U.S. House of Representatives, Committee on the Judiciary, Washington, D.C., July 24, 2000; D. M. Kerr, "Internet and Data Interception Capabilities Developed by the FBI," Statement for the Record before the U.S. House of Representatives, Committee on the Judiciary, Washington, D.C., July 24, 2000; and P. K. Craine, "Search Warrants in Cyberspace: The Fourth Amendment Meets the Twenty-First Century" www.smu.edu/csr/sum96a2.htm, 1996.

33. Ibid.

34. A. Eunjung Cha and J. Schwartz, "Hackers Disrupt Yahoo Web Site," www.washingtonpost.comwp-dyn/business/A23174-2000Feb7.html, retrieved Feb. 14, 2000.

35. See www.takedown.com/bio/mitnick.html.

36. Goodwin, B. "FBI Opens Probe Into Massive Denial of Service Attack," www.computerweekly.com/Articles/2007/02/08/221692/fbi-opens-probe-into-massive-denial-of-service-attack.htm, retrieved August 12, 2007.

37. Attrition.org, "Video Cam: University of Cambridge" (defaced web page), www.attrition.org/mirror/attrition/2001/05/13/video.cbcu.cam.ac.uk/, retrieved Aug. 30, 2001.

38. Reuters, "Hacking Closes N.Y. Times Site," www.news.com/News/Item/0,4,26301.00.html, retrieved Sept. 13, 1998.

39. Parker, *Fighting Computer Crime.*

40. Poneman, L. "The Business Impact of Data Breach," www.scottandscottllp.com/resources/data_breach.pdf, retrieved August 8, 2007.

41. "Latest Symantec Security Report Sheds Light on Data Theft," www.symantec.com/enterprise/library/article.jsp?aid=data_theft_report, retrieved August 8, 2007.

42. Press release from United States Department of Justice "University of Texas Student Charged With Hacking," www.utexas.edu/datatheft/usao-11-03-2004.pdf, retrieved August 8, 2007.

43. "Latest Symantec Security Report Sheds Light on Data Theft," www.symantec.com/enterprise/library/article.jsp?aid=data_theft_report, retrieved August 8, 2007.

44. Sturgeon, W. "Beware the Pod Slurping Employee," http://software.silicon.com/security/0,39024655,39156481,00.htm, retrieved August 8, 2007.

45. "Phishing Activity Trends Report for June 2007," www.antiphishing.org/reports/apwg_report_june_2007.pdf, retrieved August 9, 2007.

46. *Pyramid schemes* are multilevel marketing arrangements in which higher-level members make money by finding new distributors and charging for initial stock rather than taking a portion of actual sales.

47. T.F. di Stefano, "Beware the Pump and Dump Scheme," www.ecommercetimes.com/story/36358.html, posted Sep. 03, 2004.

48. Ibid.

49. Janet Reno, *1999 Report on CyberStalking: A New Challenge for Law Enforcement and Industry,*www.cybercrime.gov/cyberstalking.htm, retrieved Aug. 30, 2001.

50. Washington House Bill 2771 of 2004, www.leg.wa.gov/pub/billinfo/2003-04/House/2750-2774/2771_dig_02192004.txt retrieved 21 Oct., 2004. Signed into law March 2004.

51. V. Ho, "Cyberstalker enters guilty plea: Satisfaction and relief for victim whose ordeal led to new state law," http://seattlepi.nwsource.com/local/184213_cyberstalk30.html, posted July 30, 2004.

52. Stalking Resource Center, "Stalking Fact Sheet," www.ncvc.org/src, posted June 2004.

53. Associated Press, "Man Pleads Innocent to Internet Stalking—Charge First in the Nation under 1997 Federal Law," www.kingcountyjournal.com/sited/story/html/162111, posted Apr 24, 2004.

54. For more on cyberstalking, see www.haltabuse.org, www.cyber-stalking.net, and www.cyberangels.org/stalking/response.html.

55. V. Ho, "Cyberstalker Enters Guilty Plea: Satisfaction and Relief for Victim Whose Ordeal Led to New State Law," http://seattlepi.nwsource.com/local/184213_cyberstalk30.html, posted July 30, 2004.

56. D. Kall Loper, "A Case Study in the Forensics of Computer Crime: E-Mail Spoofing," *Journal of Security Administration 2001,* Vol. 24.

57. "Social Networking Users Happy to Reveal All to Potential ID Thieves," www.govtech.com/gt/132108?topic=117671, posted April 22, 2007.

58. "Students to be punished for MySpace postings," www.wlky.com/news/13897653/detail.html, posted August 15, 2007.

59. David L. Carter and Andrea J. Bannister, "Computer Crime: A Forecast of Emerging Trends," paper presented at the Academy of Criminal Justice Sciences Annual Meeting, New Orleans, Louisiana, March 2000.

60. Financial Crimes Enforcement Network (FinCEN), "About FinCEN:FAQs," www.fincen.gov/af_overview.html, retrieved Oct. 21, 2004.

61. B. Zagaris and S. D. McDonald, "Money Laundering, Financial Fraud and Technology: The Perils of an Instant Economy," *George Washington Journal of International Law and Economics,* 1992, Vol. 26, Num. 1, pp. 61–90.

62. S. Walther, "Forfeiture and Money Laundering Laws in the United States: Basic Features and Some Critical Comments from the European Perspective," *Crime, Law, and Social Change,* Vol. 21, No. 1, pp. 1–13, (1994).

63. See www.fincen.gov.

64. FinCEN ibid.

65. See E. Casey, *Digital Evidence and Computer Crime: Forensic Science, Computers and the Internet,* 2nd ed., (San Diego, CA: Academic Press, 2004). See also W. G. Kruse and J. G. Heiser, *Computer Forensics: Incident Response Essentials* (New York, NY: Addison Wesley, 2002).

66. Jill Sergeant, "Police Raid Global Internet Child Porn Club," *Reuters,* Sept. 2, 1998.

67. Associated Press, "Credit Card Firm at Center of Child Porn Ring," www.cnn.com/2004/LAW/01/15/child.porn.arrests.ap, posted Jan. 15, 2004.

68. R. Jones, "FBI Makes Initial Arrests in International Porn Ring," www.cwfa.org/printerfriendly.asp?id=5126&department=legal&categoryid=pornography, posted Jan. 21, 2004.

69. J. Silvester, A. Petrie, and B. Nicholson, "Suicides as Child Porn Probe Widens," www.theage.com.au/articles/2004/10/01/1096527938187.html?from=storylhs, posted Oct. 2, 2004.

70. D. L. Vial, M. J. Fine, and R. Gebeloff, "Molesters Forming Network of Abuse," *Bergen Record,* Dec. 3, 1997; retrieved from www.bergen.com/news/childporn199712030.htm, Aug. 30, 2001.

71. Sergeant, "Police Raid Global Internet Child Porn Club."

72. J.M. Pethokoukis, "Screen wars," *U.S. News,* Vol. 133, Iss. 23, p. 38, Dec. 16, 2002.

73. *Financial Times,* "Music Industry Sales Decline Slows in U.S.," www.macnn.com/news/23727, Mar. 5, 2004. The Recording Industry Association of America (RIAA) estimates that the worldwide sales for the music industry are about $40 billion. RIAA,

"Press Room: Research and Data," www.riaa.com/news/marketingdata/default.asp, retrieved Oct. 29, 2004.

74. M. Walker, "G260 Video Games: The Dominant Form of Electronic Entertainment," Dec. 2001, www.buscom.com/commu/G260.html.

75. J. P. Desmond, "2004 Software 500: Growth Came in Segments," www.softwaremag.com/L.cfm?Doc=2004-09/2004-09software-500, Oct. 2004.

76. International Data Corporation, *Worldwide Software Piracy Study* (Washington, D.C.: Business Software Alliance, May 2006).

77. "Stalking Asian Software Pirates," *Technology Review,* Vol. 95, No. 2, p. 15.

78. Press release from comScore Data, " comScore Data Confirms Reports of 100 Million Worldwide Daily Video Streams from YouTube.com in July 2006." www.comscore.com/press/release.asp?press=1023, posted October 11, 2006.

79. Borache, Ann, "Viacom Sues Google over YouTube Clips." *ZDNet News,* March 17, 2006. http://news.zdnet.com/2100-9588_22-6166668.html.

80. Jennifer Steinhauer, "Phreakers Take a Swipe at Turnstiles and Nynex," *The New York Times,* Aug. 15, 1994, p. B3.

81. Conly and McEwen, "Computer Crime."

82. The information on cellular phones is taken from William G. Flanagan and Brigid McMenamin, "Why Cybercrooks Love Cellular," *Forbes,* Dec. 21, 1992, Vol. 150, No. 14, p. 189.

83. Gorden, L., et al, "2006 CSI/FBI Computer Crime and Security Survey ," Computer Security Institute Publications, 2006.

84. Ibid.

85. Social Security Administration, Office of the Inspector General, "Annual Audit Plan Fiscal Year 2001," www.ssa.gov/oig/adopbepdf/audit%20work%20plan.pdf, retrieved Aug. 30, 2001.

86. Software licenses grant the purchaser limited rights to use the compiled version but not to reverse-engineer or sell copies. Thus, the purchaser does not buy the software; he or she buys only the right to *use* the software.

87. Most programs are written in a computer language such as C or C11. The original program or source code is readable by human beings. A special program called a *compiler* reduces the human-readable program to a set of computer instructions called the *compiled code.* Very few people can comprehend compiled code.

88. War dialers take their name from the 1983 movie *WarGames.* The lead character, played by Matthew Broderick, used a program to dial numbers until he found a computer to "play" or intrude to alter or delete data.

89. Fyodor, "Nmap Network Security Man Page," www.insecure.org/nmap/nmap_manpage.html, retrieved Aug. 30, 2001.

90. Insecure.org, "Nmap—Free Security Scanner for Network Exploration & Security Audits," www.insecure.org/nmap/, retrieved Nov. 11, 2004.

91. Fyodor, "Nmap Network Security Scanner Man Page," www.insecure.org/nmap/data/nmap_manpage.html, retrieved Nov. 11, 2004.

92. Dragorn, "Kismet Readme," www.kismetwireless.net/documentation.shtml, retrieved Nov. 9, 2004.

93. Bruce Schneier, *Applied Cryptography: Protocols, Algorithms, and Source Code in C* (New York: Wiley, 1996).

94. From @ Stake, "LC5 Frequently Asked Questions FAQ," www.atstake.com/products/lc/faq.html, retrieved Nov. 9, 2004.

95. Ls is similar to "dir" in DOS or the Windows command prompt.

96. D. Dittrich, "'Root Kits' and Hiding Files/Directories/Processes after a Break-In," http://staff.washington.edu/dittrich/misc/faqs/rootkits.faq, University of Washington, posted May 1, 2002.

97. Joint Photographic Experts Group (JPEG). For more on the JPEG standard, see www.jpeg.org/committee.html.

98. L. Seltzer, "Microsoft Graphics Bug Threatens Systems," www.eweek.com/article2/0,1759,1645808,00.asp, posted Sep. 14, 2004.

99. For technical details see Security Focus, "TA04-260A: Microsoft Windows JPEG Component Buffer Overflow," www.securityfocus.com/advisories/7211, posted Sept. 16, 2004.

100. Malware is malicious software.

101. Gorden, L., et al, "2006 CSI/FBI Computer Crime and Security Survey ," Computer Security Institute Publications, 2006.

102. 2002 Federal Sentencing Guidelines. Chapter Three—Part B—Role in the Offense. §3B1.3. Abuse of Position of Trust or Use of Special Skill, www.ussc.gov/2002guid/3b1_3.htm.

103. B. Kehoe, "Computer Underground Digest Compilation of LEN ROSE Events." Archived at www.netsys.com/library/len-prosecution.txt, retrieved Nov. 11, 2004.

104. Gordon, L., et al, ibid.

105. R. A. Grimes, *Malicious Mobile Code: Virus Protection for Windows* (Sebastopol, CA: O'Reilly Publishing, 2001).

106. This information on the search and seizure of computer crime evidence is drawn from "Crime Scene Computer Factsheet" (Washington, D.C.: National Institute of Justice), p. 1. For additional information on this subject, see U.S. Department of Justice, Office of Justice Programs, *Electronic Crime Scene Investigation: A Guide for First Responders* (Washington, D.C.: NCRJS, July 2001).

107. U.S. Department of Justice, ibid.

108. This information has been drawn from "Best Practices for Computer Forensics" (Scientific Working Group on Digital Evidence, July 2006).

109. *Steve Jackson Games* v. *United States Secret Service*, 36 F. 3d 457 (5th Cir. 1994) and *Steve Jackson Games* v. *United States Secret Service*, 816 F.Supp. 432 (W.D.Tex, 1993).

110. The name, Legion of Doom (LOD), was not designed to intimidate. It was the name of the cartoon adversaries of the Super Friends. The founder of LOD used the alias, Lex Luthor, the archrival of Superman.

111. "Phrack" combines "phreaks," as in phone phreaks and "hack." In the late 1980s, phone phreaks and hackers were joining forces to explore, invade, and master new computer-based telephone switching equipment. See R. W. Taylor, D. K. Loper, T. C. Caeti, E. Fritch, and J. Leiderbach, *Digital Crime Digital Terrorism* (New York, NY: Prentice Hall, 2005) for more details.

112. For a detailed and highly readable account of this first major computer crime investigation, see B. Sterling, *The Hacker Crackdown: Law and Disorder on the Electronic Frontier* (New York, NY: Bantam Books, 1992).

113. *Privacy Protection Act*, 42 U.S.C. §§2000aa et seq.

114. See also *Electronic Communications Privacy Act (ECPA)*, 18 U.S.C. §§2701-11.

115. *Zurcher* v. *Stanford Daily*, 436 U.S. 547 (1978).

116. R. Garcia, Special Agent in Charge, Houston FBI, personal communication, 2002.

117. L. E. Coutorie, "The Future of High-Technology Crime: A Parallel Delphi Study." *Journal of Criminal Justice*, Vol. 23, num. 1, pp. 13–27 (1995).

118. S. Ozeren and D. K. Loper, *Cyberterrorism* (working title). Unpublished manuscript.

119. For more information on this organization, visit www.nw3c.org.

120. For more information on this organization, visit www.cops.org.

121. For more information on this organization, visit www.htcia.org.

122. See www.sachitechcops.org/index.html.

123. The Dallas Regional Computer Forensics Lab, www.ntrcfl.org/.

124. United States Secret Service Electronic Crimes Task Forces, www.ectaskforce.org/Regional_Locations.htm.

125. American Society for Industrial Security (ASIS), www.asisonline.org/.

126. *Ex Parte Jackson*, 96 U.S. 727 (1877).

127. *Katz* v. *United States*, 389 U.S. 347 (1967).

128. *Smith* v. *Maryland*, 442 U.S. 735 (1979).

129. Watch old detective movies and listen for them to tell the victim to keep the suspect on the line so they can trace the call. This is the process that takes time.

130. 18 U.S.C. §§2510-22.

131. 18 U.S.C. §§1321-27.

132. Store and forward networks use transitions between servers where communications may wait for periods ranging from milliseconds to months. This is unlike the instantaneous communication of telephones.

133. 18 U.S.C. §§2701-11.

134. USA PATRIOT §209.

135. D. K. Loper, "Forgetting the Wisdom of the Past: The USA PATRIOT Act," submitted for publication (2004).

136. ECPA18 U.S.C. 2703(f)(1).

137. ECPA18 U.S.C. 2703(f)(2).

138. D. K. Loper, "A Case Study in the Forensics of Computer Crime: E-mail Address Spoofing," *Journal of Security Administration,* Vol. 24 num. 2, pp. 45–68 (2001).

139. Michael G. Noblett, Mark M. Pollitt, and Lawrence A. Presley, "Recovering and Examining Computer Forensic Evidence," *Forensic Science Communications* (Washington, D.C.: FBI, Oct. 2000).

140. Ibid.

141. In cases involving system intrusion, evidence of root kits can often be found in protected files. Some Trojans can be protected system files, too.

142. National Industrial Security Program Operating Manual (NISPOM), www.dtic.mil/whs/directives/corres/pdf/d522022_9272004/d522022p.pdf retrieved Nov. 15, 2004.

143. The underlying issue was that one GB of the data was encrypted and the prosecution did not want to release the data because they could not read it. Mitnick refused to supply a decryption key based on his Fifth Amendment privilege against self incrimination.

144. A. Rosen, CEO of ASR Data, from D. K. Loper, "Elite Interviews with Digital Forensic Software Makers" (working title), unpublished manuscript, University of North Texas.

145. For more on intrusion post mortem analysis, see the Center for Education and Research in Information Assurance and Security (CERIAS), Purdue University www.cerias.purdue.edu/. See also Computer Emergency Response Team/Coordination Center (CERT/CC), Carnegie Mellon University, www.cert.org/.

146. Joint Photographic Experts Group (JPEG). For more on the JPEG standard, see www.jpeg.org/committee.html.

147. R. W. Taylor, D. K. Loper, T. C. Caeti, E. Fritch, and J. Leiderbach, *Digital Crime Digital Terrorism* (Englewood Cliffs, NJ: Prentice Hall, 2005).

148. Demonstrations in the courtroom are risky and should be avoided if possible. Potential dramatic impact is almost never worth the very real possibility of unreliable results due to configuration errors. The careful setup of a forensic analysis performed in a laboratory is unusual in a courtroom. Do biochemists analyze DNA in the courtroom?

149. A. Rosen, CEO of ASR Data, from D. K. Loper, "Elite Interviews with Digital Forensic Software Makers" (working title), unpublished manuscript, University of North Texas.

150. W. G. Kruse and J. G. Heiser, *Computer Forensics: Incident Response Essentials* (San Francisco, CA: Addison-Wesley, 2002).

17

Agricultural, Wildlife, and Environmental Crimes

No Dumping $500 Fine City Ordinance 66-286

▲ In addition to the loss of life and destruction caused by Hurricane Katrina, one of its lingering consequences has been the spontaneous development of unpermitted dump sites for millions of tons of debris along the Gulf Coast.

(Courtesy Louisiana Department of Environmental Quality)

Conventional wisdom says that crime is fundamentally a big-city problem. However, the cost of rural and agricultural crimes is estimated at $5 billion annually.[1] Roughly, one in five farms is located in Metropolitan Statistical Areas (MSAs), which leads to an overstatement of urban crime and an understatement of agricultural/rural crime.[2] There are also many connections between agricultural/rural crime and our cities. The composition of farm labor has changed, with many workers now living in urban areas. Some of them return at night to steal from their employers or they tip off criminals as to where they can make valuable scores. Thieves run out interstate highways to raid softer targets and return to their cities to dispose of their loot with local fences. Stolen farm machinery passes through big city ports as it is sent abroad for sale, often to South America; as few as 12 hours may pass between the time the machinery is stolen and the ship sails. Wheeled tanks of **anhydrous ammonia,** a nitrogen fertilizer, are being stolen from farms and used in the production of methamphetamine, which is sold in urbanized areas, as is marijuana grown in national forests and other public and private lands. Livestock investigation is unfamiliar territory for many investigators, who may not recognize various aspects of livestock identification, breeds, scars, marks, tattoos, and brands. Some poached game ends up on the menus of city restaurants. Theft of, and vandalism to, archaeological resources (Figure 17-1) reduces our enjoyment of national parks and forests and the heritage we leave subsequent generations. Historically, many horses rustled in this country were sold to slaughter houses, and the meat products were shipped abroad from urban ports for human consumption, often in Europe and Asia. By early 2007, a patchwork of state legislation and court rulings had eliminated domestic processing of horses for human consumption, although the exportation of horses to Canada and Mexico for that purpose remains a loophole.

Environmental crimes, such as those involving the illegal treatment, storage, transportation, and disposal of hazardous waste, are often out of the spotlight but nonetheless are of crucial importance. Not only are these crimes a significant threat to public health, they also affect outdoor recreation and wildlife. The purpose of this chapter is to call attention to the nature and extent of crimes against agriculture, wildlife, and the environment and to provide information regarding their investigation.

DIMENSIONS OF AGRICULTURAL, WILDLIFE, AND ENVIRONMENTAL CRIMES

Ranchers, farmers, and others living in rural places are often the victims of thefts, including thefts of livestock, tack, pesticides, tractors, dirt bikes, all-terrain vehicles, drip lines, stock trailers, plants and timber, tools, hay, grains and citrus, irrigation pipes, and sprinkler heads. Some variation in what is stolen is accounted for by fluctuations in the economy. For example, when freezes kill oranges and grapefruit or droughts kill avocados, prices rise on the remainders, because there are fewer of them, and thieves looking for an easy buck steal them.[3] Annual losses owing to avocado theft amount to $12 to $15 million.[4] Lone "**night pickers**" may opportunistically steal from orchards and groves after dark, farm hands may throw a few sacks in the trunk of their cars to "supplement their wages," or entire crops may be picked clean in a single night by a well-organized ring. One grower reported that a tour bus stopped so people could pick fruit from his trees.

Copper theft has been in vogue for several years, because the price for scrap copper surged to approximately $4 per pound owing to a building boom on Asia; rural thieves, often methamphetamine users, stripped farm pumps, plaques from graveyards, and wires from phone lines and gutted air conditioners and catalytic converters from cars for a quick buck.[5] In Kern County, California there were 213 copper thefts in a single year; in addition to lost time and damaged crops, each water pump replaced cost a farmer from $3,000 to $10,000.[6] A van quickly loaded with stolen grapes creates a loss of $3,000 or more to a vineyard;[7] a grower loaded two trucks with 88,000 pounds of almonds valued at $260,000, which

were stolen by "nutnappers" the night before the nuts were to be driven to market.[8] In Florida, state and county parks are being plundered of palmetto berries, which are offered by herbal companies for baldness and enlarged prostates. The thieves, often illegal immigrants from Mexico and Guatemala, are organized; they are dropped off by a truck and picked up later in the day.[9] The "pickers" are paid a dollar a pound for the berries and may be able to collect up to 150 pound a day.[10]

Reported losses due to livestock theft are $19.7 million annually;[11] this crime is believed to be at least 50% underreported, so losses may actually be in the $40 to $50 million range. Horse rustling may amount to 40,000 to 55,000 head annually. Beef and calf production is a $35.7 billion industry, yet there are no definitive numbers of heads of cattle stolen each year.[12] Special Rangers for the Southwestern Cattle Raisers Association recovered over 3,716 head of cattle, 144 horses, 18 saddles, and 10 trailers, altogether valued at $4.8 million, in a single year.[13] There are also less common thefts associated with livestock. In Maryland, burglars entered an out building and took $75,000 worth of bull semen that had previously been collected from about 50 bulls and kept frozen in individual 5-inch straws with the name of the bull on them.[14] A barn was burglarized in California to take $30,000 worth of the genetically engineered rBST hormone in filled syringes, which is used to increase milk production in dairy cows; investigators believed the syringes would be sold on the black market to unscrupulous dairy farmers.[15]

Private and public lands are being invaded by stealthy fossil hunters, who are also described as **bone rustlers** (Figure 17-2). Depending on the type, a complete dinosaur skeleton may command $500,000 or more. In South Dakota, thieves dug up the graveyard of rhinoceros-like mammals called *titanotheres* and made off with 18 skulls, each worth $5,000.[16] In one national forest, park rangers marked fossils

▲ **FIGURE 17-2**

Bone rustlers (fossil thieves)

Bangkok, Thailand: a police officer inspects 78 fossils from a dinosaur that were seized following a police sting operation on a ring that stole and then illegally sold the fossils.

(© Pornchai Kittiwongsakul/Getty Images)

at several different sites with chemicals invisible to the unassisted eye. By inventorying these areas over a six-week period, they learned that 32,000 pounds of fossils had been stolen. One of the most successful fossil-poaching investigations was a joint local, state, and federal effort dubbed "Operation Rockfish," named after a fossil common in southwest Wyoming. A Lincoln County Sheriff's Department pilot noticed new holes in the ground in and around Fossil Butte National Monument. First suspecting that toxic chemicals were being dumped, he invited several federal agents to fly with him. On-the-ground investigation revealed that fossils were being stolen and sold both in the open and on black markets, some for prices in excess of $10,000. Nationally, Operation Rockfish resulted in the recovery of $7 million worth of stolen fossils. Although petrified wood can be obtained legally from some sources, it is being stolen from federal lands to make countertops and furniture, because of its great beauty.[17]

Our national and state lands are also victimized by plant poachers, whose targets vary as market conditions shift. Several years ago matsutake mushrooms, which grow in the northwest, reached $30 per pound; by 2007, prices had fallen to $3 to $5 per pound, reducing much of the incentive for wholesale poaching of them. Although ginseng roots are cultivated, it is the wild variety growing in hardwood forests that commands substantial prices. The roots are used in Asian medicine and also sold domestically with reputed good effect on reducing cholesterol and blood sugar levels, enhancing memory, and fighting colds and other conditions. Kentucky gathers more wild ginseng than any other state, a crop worth $8 million; about 50% of it is poached.[18] The prices paid pickers in good years may reach $365 to $800 per pound; it is sold to overseas brokers for as much as $2,000 per pound.[19] The theft of saguaro cacti for landscaping purposes in the southwest is episodically a problem (Figure 17-3), as is the occasional

◀ **FIGURE 17-3** **Saguaro cacti**

The theft of saguaro cacti from national lands in the West is a continuing problem. Saguaros grow very slowly; after 10 years they may be only 4 to 6 inches tall. They reach maturity in about 150 years and may live another 50 years beyond that, reaching a height of about 45 feet. Consequently, saguaro thefts amount to stealing part of our national heritage. (© Jo MacDonald/Corbis)

◀ FIGURE 17-4
The ocotillo plant
Like the saguaros, these plants are prized for landscaping and thrive in loose to stony soil in open areas that are well-drained. They occur naturally in the southwest and Mexico in desert areas below 5,000 feet. Their blood-red blooms appear in March and April. Ocotillos ordinarily grow to 15 or 20 feet in height with a corresponding width of roughly 10 to 15 feet.
(© David Muench/Corbis)

theft of quaking aspen trees from the western mountains; but recently the red-flowered ocotillo plant has been in greater favor with thieves, because many more can be stolen with less risk of detection. Depending on their size, ocotillo plants retail for $150 to $5,000 (Figure 17-4).[20]

TIMBER THEFT

Forest economists believe that thieves are stealing trees worth $1 billion annually and that 1 in every 10 trees is cut down illegally.[21] Large areas don't have to be cut down to create serious losses (Figure 17-5). In Pennsylvania, a prime black cherry tree, valued for making furniture, can bring $6,000.[22] Curly maple trees in Washington are being poached to make guitars and other musical instruments because of its beautiful swirl grain.[23] On a larger scale, two Wyoming men were charged with stealing 8,439 trees valued at $100,000 from Medicine Bow National Forest; the clear cutting operation could result in fines of $500,000.[24] Unlike thieves who must sell what they steal to fences for pennies on the dollars, thieves involved in **timber theft** get full value. In some urban areas, particularly along parkways and expressways in the month

◀ FIGURE 17-5
Illegal cutting of trees
A Federal Bureau of Land Management Ranger discovered that 17 old-growth juniper trees had been illegally cut and removed from the Badlands Wilderness Study Area (WSA) in Oregon. Such trees grow so slowly that they are considered a nonrenewable resource: a juniper tree with a 3-feet diameter takes 1,000 years to reach that size. The juniper stumps with the yellow evidence cone at the right were part of the multiple crime scenes involved with the thefts.
(Courtesy of Federal Bureau of Land Management)

► **FIGURE 17-6**
Timber theft crime scene
A Mason County Deputy Sheriff examines the work of maple tree thieves. In their haste to turn their contraband into cash, tree thieves may abandon tools and other important physical evidence.
(© Mark Hrarrrison/Seattle Times)

leading up to the Christmas holiday, Christmas-type trees "disappear" as motorists cut them down and cart the trees home to decorate. To combat such thefts, some cities chemical-coat trees that are likely targets, causing them to smell "awful." Another coating has an unnoticeable odor until it starts to heat up, and then it "smells worse than cat urine."

Investigations into the illegal cutting of timber involve a full range of investigative techniques (Figure 17-6). Examination of crime scenes continues to result in the discovery of evidence of paint transfers and tool marks on wood debris left behind by suspects. These marks and paint transfers result from the use of axes, wedges, and splitting mauls and serve to tie a suspect to a crime. Examination of tool marks on wood is based on established principles: it is possible to identify a suspect tool with the mark it leaves on a surface. In several cases, containers left at the scene of a timber theft have been processed and fingerprints developed. These fingerprints have been useful in identifying and placing suspects at the scene. In addition, casts of both shoe and tire impressions that were later identified as belonging to particular suspects and vehicles have been found at some crime scenes.[25] Increasingly, DNA is proving important as key evidence in many of the types of crimes discussed in this chapter, including plant and tree thefts, livestock rustling, and fish and wildlife poaching.

Although the crime scene examinations at the site of timber thefts are important, they are supplemented by the long process of interviewing potential witnesses to the crime, conducting investigations to develop witnesses, and checking possible outlets where forest products might be processed or sold. To conduct investigations concerning timber sales, law enforcement officers must become familiar with the variety of terms and techniques pertaining to a timber sale, from its inception to the eventual purchase.

THEFT OF AGRICHEMICALS

Agrichemical is a broad term whose meaning encompasses a variety of products used on farms, including pesticides, fertilizers, and herbicides. As a rule of thumb, fertilizers are not a target of theft because of their bulk and relatively low cost. In contrast, pesticides and herbicides can be costly; even a truckload may be worth thousands of dollars. The exact type of agrichemical taken varies by geographic region, depending on what the predominant crop is. Currently, anhydrous ammonia, mentioned earlier in this chapter, is the agrichemical of choice for thieves. Agrichemical theft from farmers may have crested around 2000, owing to operators buying in only the quantities they could immediately use and employing more stringent security measures when they are even briefly stored.

Because the theft of agrichemicals may take the form of any of several different criminally chargeable acts, it would be possible for investigators in different parts of the same agency to be working on various activities by the same ring without knowing it. For example, the hijacking of a truck might be worked on by robbery investigators, the burglary of a dealership by the property section or burglary investigators, while personnel assigned to the ranch and grove unit might be working on the theft of pesticides from a local farmer. Although one ring might not exhibit a wide range of criminally chargeable behaviors, they may be sufficiently different to cause the fragmentation of investigative information.

To be effective in the investigation of agrichemical thefts, the investigator must become familiar with the legal supply channels and the principal agrichemicals that are used in his or her region. In particular, it is important to know that the same basic chemical or formulation may be sold by several different manufacturers under different product names. For example, atrazine is manufactured and sold by Ciba-Geigy as AAtrex for use as a corn herbicide. Imagine the difficulty created for an investigation if a victim reports the theft of "50 gallons of atrazine," and the information is entered into police records that way—but the victim was using "atrazine" as a synonym for "AAtrex."

Finally, a few farmers steal agrichemicals or buy them at "bargain prices" from thieves. Once they are used, the manufacturers' containers are burned, and detection of criminal receiving of stolen property is difficult. One method of identifying farmers who are possible illegal receivers of agrichemicals is to determine whose purchasing patterns through legal supply channels are inconsistent with their crop needs.

LIVESTOCK AND TACK THEFT

It is ironic that we can land people on the moon and safely return them, but the old crime of rustling remains a problem (Figure 17-7). Although new and often sophisticated methods of rustling are now used, the object of attack—livestock—remains the same, as do the motivations: profit and food.

Livestock refers to cattle, horses, sheep, goats, hogs, mules, jackasses, and other such species. **Tack** refers to saddles, bridles, harnesses, and related equipment. Certain generalizations can be made with respect to livestock and tack thefts:

- Most livestock thefts are committed by persons who have been or are currently employed in some aspect of a livestock business. One significant exception to this broad observation is that in economically hard times, rural areas adjacent to urban centers experience more thefts; thus the physical evidence suggests that the motivation was food rather than profit. Such so-called **freezer crimes** typically involve only one or a few head of cattle, and when they are butchered at the scene, it is often in a manner that reflects only a crude understanding of the process.[26]
- It is common for livestock to be stolen, transported, and disposed of before the theft is discovered. Whereas the theft of horses may be discovered in a day to two weeks, theft of range cattle may go undetected for months.
- Except for small roadside slaughters committed as freezer crimes, livestock is stolen to be sold for economic gain. The excellent interstate systems that cross the country lend themselves—like the famous trails of frontier days—to transporting the stolen livestock rapidly for sale in states other than the one in which the crime took place.
- Because horse owners are typically very attached to their animals, such thefts are often very emotional situations.
- Horse thieves also tend to be tack thieves.

Many law enforcement agencies, particularly sheriffs' departments, have created specialized investigative units or designated a particular individual as the agency's specialist in such matters.[27] Regardless of whether the investigator works as part of a specialized unit or as the sole specialist, he/she must have or develop an expertise in the various aspects of livestock identification, including breeds, markings, blemishes, scars, marks, tattoos, and

◀ **FIGURE 17-7**
Stolen horses
Acting on a tip that rustlers in remote Nevada were driving wild horses from land belonging to the Pyramid Lake Paiute tribe, investigators located a hidden corral and released them back into the wild.
(© AP/Wide World Photos)

brands. In short, to be effective, the investigator must be able to speak "livestock."

The heaviest burden in livestock investigation often falls on the uniformed officer who takes the original offense report; this is true because such officers may have no knowledge, or only a rudimentary knowledge, of livestock and the applicable special laws.[28] Police agencies can help compensate for this by adopting forms similar to those shown in Figures 17-8 and 17-9 and by providing training in their use. When such forms are not used, a good guide to follow is that an animal is property and can be described like any other type of property, although the language may be unfamiliar to the investigator. In such situations, the frank acknowledgment of a lack of

familiarity or expertise can elicit a systematic and detailed description from the owner. Subsequent to the taking of the original offense report, the progress of an investigation often hinges on the mutual assistance, cooperation, and free exchange of information given by ranchers, feedlot operators, stock auctions, farmers, sale yards, livestock associations, and other entities.

Cattle Rustling

The majority of cattle-rustling thefts are committed by one or two people who take the animal for their own use.[29] The usual method of operation is to drive to an isolated area, locate an animal, shoot it, and either butcher

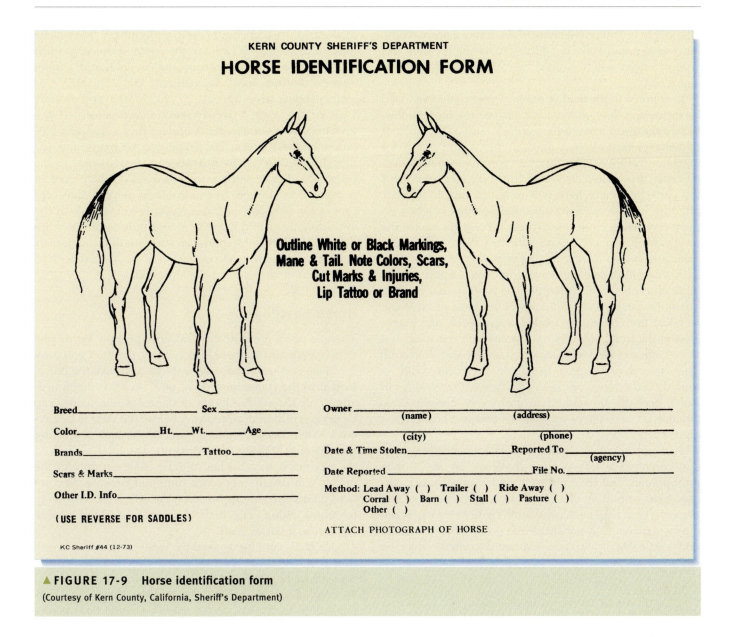

KERN COUNTY SHERIFF'S DEPARTMENT
HORSE IDENTIFICATION FORM

Outline White or Black Markings,
Mane & Tail. Note Colors, Scars,
Cut Marks & Injuries,
Lip Tattoo or Brand

Breed_____ Sex _____

Color_____Ht.___Wt._____Age_____

Brands_____ Tattoo_____

Scars & Marks_____

Other I.D. Info_____

(USE REVERSE FOR SADDLES)

KC Sheriff #44 (12-73)

Owner _____
   (name)   (address)
_____
   (city)   (phone)
Date & Time Stolen_____ Reported To _____
                                         (agency)
Date Reported _____ File No._____

Method: Lead Away ( ) Trailer ( ) Ride Away ( )
   Corral ( )   Barn ( )   Stall ( )   Pasture ( )
   Other ( )

ATTACH PHOTOGRAPH OF HORSE

▲ **FIGURE 17-9 Horse identification form**
(Courtesy of Kern County, California, Sheriff's Department)

it there or load the carcass into a vehicle and butcher it at home. Butchering the animal at the scene means the thieves must spend more time there, but it avoids the problem of having to dispose of unused remains later. At times, the thieves shoot the animal and then drive to a place where they can watch to see if anyone comes to investigate. If no one comes, they return to butcher the animal. As these incidents often occur at night, they can see the headlights of approaching vehicles for some distance, giving them ample time to depart from the area. Freezer-crime rustlers are difficult to apprehend, because they must be caught when they are committing the act or while they are transporting the carcass or meat. Surveillance methods that work well in urban areas are usually difficult to execute in rural areas. Given this, rural surveillance success depends on:

- The topography of the area
- The availability of cover for concealment

- The number and position of access roads
- The size of the area containing the cattle

One method for successful surveillances is for investigators to select an area that is attractive to thieves and well suited for surveillance.[30] Ranchers should be requested to move cattle into the area selected by the investigator. The rancher must not allow employees or other persons to learn that an operation is being set up. If other people are involved in moving the cattle to the area selected, they should be given a fictitious but plausible reason for the move—for example, a change of pasture is needed, a tally must be taken, there is going to be a veterinary inspection, or brands must be checked.

Vehicles coming out of isolated areas should routinely be visually inspected for signs of blood on the rear bumper or trunk areas.[31] Because rustlers are invariably armed with some type of firearm, extreme caution must be used when approaching suspicious vehicles. Panicky suspects, who might not otherwise think of assaulting a peace officer, may do so impulsively. In addition to having firearms, this type of rustler will also often be carrying butcher knives and ropes.

In contrast to the modest equipment usually employed by the freezer thief, professional rustlers use more sophisticated means to commit their crimes, such as light planes or helicopters, to spot vulnerable herds and watch for patrolling officers. The thieves coordinate their movements with walkie-talkies, and "dirt-bike cowboys" herd the cattle to where they will be killed and butchered, often by the use of chain saws. Refrigerated trucks with meat-processing equipment inside quickly transform the rough-butchered cattle into salable products.[32] Professionals may also have a full array of forged documents, such as a bill of sale and counterfeit U.S. Department of Agriculture inspection stamps. The professional rustling operation can be very profitable. Thirty head of cattle can be taken from the range, loaded onto a truck, and butchered in the truck; the waste is dumped off the road, and the 60 sides of beef are illegally stamped and delivered. The dressed or hanging weight in the meat cooler is roughly 300 pounds per side. This means that 60 sides of stolen beef can be sold to an unwary or unscrupulous butcher for a profit of roughly $15,000 to $17,000 for a night's work.

As a general matter, peace officers have a right to stop any conveyance transporting livestock on any public thoroughfare and the right to impound any animal, carcass, hide, or portion of a carcass in the possession of any person whom they have reasonable cause to believe is not the legal owner or is not entitled to possession.[33] To transport cattle legally, certain written documents may be required, such as:

- Bill of sale
- Certificate of consignment
- Brand inspector's certificate
- Shipping or transportation permit[34]

Because these provisions vary by state, it is essential that every investigator know:

- What documentation is required for lawful transportation (e.g., a "horse-hauling permit")
- What the investigator's precise authority is in such matters
- How to handle violations of law[35]

Equipped with such knowledge, the investigator is better prepared to deal with issues related to transportation violation or a possible theft. Although the applicable state law may permit the officer to impound livestock or meat, there are several less drastic alternatives. Under unusual conditions or when only slight suspicion exists, investigators may elect to get a full description and identifying information of the driver and the rig and its contents. Other information essential for a useful follow-up inquiry is the origin and destination

of the trip. If suspicion is more pronounced, specialists may be requested to come to the scene of the stop. Such specialists may come from the investigator's own agency, another local department, the state police or state investigative agency, or the Marks and Brands Unit of the state's department of agriculture. If the investigator is sufficiently confident that a shipping violation or theft exists, the arrest can be made and the load impounded. Live animals can be delivered to the nearest feedlot or sales yard, and meat can be placed in refrigeration storage. Such situations require that officers in the field have a basic working knowledge of the applicable laws and exercise sound judgment. They are not required to be experts in such matters, and their general investigative experience is a substantial asset in making an evaluation of the situation.

Horse Rustling

There is not a great deal of variation in how horse rustlers operate. If the horse is in a corral, the thief will park a vehicle and trailer nearby, walk up and take the horse, load it in the trailer, and drive off.[36] As such thefts usually occur during the hours of darkness, the rustler can be several hundred miles away before the theft is discovered. When horses are in a pasture, the task of stealing them is only slightly more difficult. The thief walks into the pasture with a bucket of grain. One or more of the horses will usually approach him, and because they are herd animals, if one approaches, the others are also likely to follow along. The theft then proceeds in the same fashion as a corral theft.

One tactic commonly used by horse rustlers is to knock down the corral or pasture fence after loading up the trailer with horses and chase any remaining horses down the road. The owner will think that the horses have gotten out on their own, and it may be several days before he or she realizes that some horses have been stolen. Thus, even if there is no clear evidence of a theft, the investigator should not assume that the horse has strayed off. As a minimum action, a lost report should be initiated. If the horse is later discovered to have been stolen, the incident can be reclassified.

Tack Theft

As mentioned earlier, tack is equipment that is used with horses; the most common items are saddles, bridles, and horse blankets.[37] Of all stolen tack, approximately 80% is saddles—which often have base prices in excess of $2,000. Unfortunately, tack is not always marked for identification, making tracing a very difficult proposition. A specialized reporting form (Figure 17-10) is a very useful investigative aid. Some owners have injected microchips, which are about the size of a grain of uncooked rice, in their saddles to facilitate recovery if they are stolen.

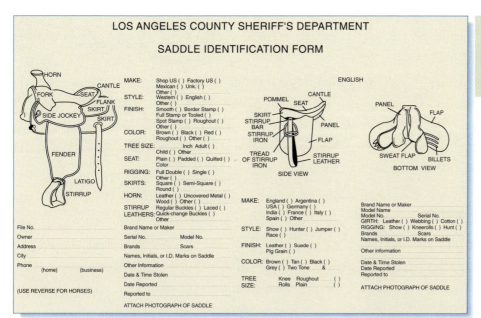

LIVESTOCK IDENTIFICATION

The purpose of **livestock identification** is to establish that a particular animal is the property of a specific owner. Methods of livestock identification continue to change. In times long past, some ranchers would supplement their brands with wattles. They were formed by pinching skin on the animals' neck or jaw, and cutting most, but not all of it off; the hanging portion was the wattle. In more recent years, ear cropping has largely fallen away, because it is expensive to do and not easy to read by the uninitiated. In the wake of the 9/11 attacks, concern about terrorists deploying pathogens to attack livestock and crops has been a driving force in the formation of the U.S. Department of Agriculture's National Animal Identification System (**NAIS**), the framework for which was announced in 2004.

Presently, NAIS participation is voluntary from a federal perspective. Under NAIS, all agricultural animals would receive a 15-digit Animal Identification Number (AIN), which ultimately could track them from cradle to grave. The national security and public health interest is compelling; every time an animal is sold, its AIN and owner information become part of a database that could quickly and accurately pinpoint where disease outbreaks occur, whether triggered by terrorists or nature, such as mad cow disease. Although program guidelines are unfolding, AINs could be by established by bar-coded ear tags or microchips implanted under the skin.

In general, people are more willing to use a wider range of identification methods on cattle than they are on their horses. Cattle are commonly branded and there are a lot of brands: over 26,000 different ones in Utah alone, some of which date back to 1847.[38] **Brands** are combinations of numbers, letters, marks, and shapes that establish a unique

identification and must be registered with the state before they can be used. The state agencies approving a brand application are often located with the department of agriculture and have a name such as "Brands and Inspections." In some states, brands must be in a specific location on the animal, whereas in others there is some flexibility. As shown in Figure 17-11, there are three ways to read brands. Treated as a separate category are picture brands, which simply mean what they represent (Figure 17-12).

There are five major methods of marking horses and cattle for identification, all of which are discussed in the sections that follow.[39]

1. **Hot-Iron** Hot-iron branding is a method of identification that has been used in this country for nearly 400 years. It is simple to use; an "iron" is heated in a fire and then the end bearing the brand is impressed on the upper hip of the animal, producing a permanent, hair-free shape in the hide that duplicates the face of the branding iron.

2. **Tattoos** When used on horses, the tattoo is applied to the inside of the top lip; on cattle, the inside of the ear is tattooed near the mid-vein. Tattoos should always be placed in the right or left ear for a herd or in both ears.

3. **Freeze Brands** Freeze branding super cools the iron using liquid nitrogen or dry ice and alcohol. When applied to a hide, it kills cells that produce hair pigments, and so white hair grows back. On light-color cattle, white hair cannot be easily seen. When branding such cattle, the iron should be applied longer, which leaves a permanent hairless brand.

4. **Ear Tags** Plastic ear tags can be bought prenumbered or blank so the rancher can use his or her own numbering system. Different colors and sizes of tags are available, and they can be read at a distance. The

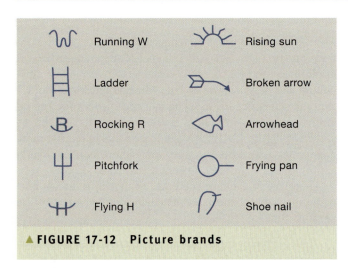

Top to Bottom		Left to Right		Outside to Inside	
H̅	Bar H	A+	A cross	Ⓚ	Circle K
2/X	2 bar X	/X	Slash X	◇P	Diamond P
DC	D hanging C	++	Double cross	☐M	Box M
Yꓑ	Y lazy P	◇/K	Diamond slash K	△S	Triangle S
◈	Rafter diamond	m(E	Lazy E, quarter circle E	⊛	Double circle, lazy K

⌶ Running W	Running W	Rising sun	Rising sun
目	Ladder	Broken arrow	Broken arrow
℞	Rocking R	Arrowhead	Arrowhead
ⴜ	Pitchfork	Frying pan	Frying pan
ⵞ	Flying H	Shoe nail	Shoe nail

▲ FIGURE 17-12   Picture brands

tags are placed through the ear of cattle at a point between the ear's second and third cartilage rib, to prevent them from being easily ripped out. But because they can be pulled out, many experts recommend that a second method of identification be used. A non-electronic ear tag is the means selected by most ranchers and farmers to identify cattle.

5. **Electronic** A microchip equipped with an antenna has Radio Frequency Identification (RFID) capabilities.[40] These chips may be injected, worn as part of ear tags, or embedded in neck collars. The information on the microchip can be read using a handheld PDA-type device or wand. If RFID-enabled ear tags are properly placed on cattle, they can be read with great accuracy as cattle move through properly positioned gates with readers.

DNA profiles of expensive horses and bulls are common as a theft deterrent, required by some breed associations and mandated by some insurance companies to prevent insurance scams (for example, a less-expensive horse is killed, and a claim is made for an expensive horse, which is sold, creating an additional source of "profit"). DNA can easily be obtained from animals by means of nasal swabs or mane or tail hair with the root attached.

PHYSICAL EVIDENCE

The processing of a crime scene where an agriculture-related theft has occurred is in many respects no different from the processing of any other crime scene. For example, when cattle rustling occurs, the perpetrators frequently cut the barbed wire or locks securing a grazing area. The cut wire and lock will have tool marks left on them from the cutting tool. In addition, if the suspect's clothing came into contact with any of the barbed wire at the scene, pieces of fiber may be found adhering to the barbs. Shoe or tire impressions found at the crime scene may later be linked to a specific suspect and vehicle. Soil samples collected at the crime scene may also prove to be valuable, linking evidence to a suspect with similar soil on his or her shoes or clothes or on the vehicle used to transport the cattle. DNA evidence is also playing an increasing role in livestock theft cases.

CRIME PREVENTION METHODS

Information about how to prevent rural and agricultural crimes can be obtained from a variety of sources, including sheriff's departments, county police, state investigative agencies, state departments of agriculture, county extension agents, and various associations. Although some techniques developed in urban areas can be readily applied to the farm, others would create costs disproportionate to the benefits that could reasonably be expected to accrue to the rancher or farmer. Consequently, the technology in this area is sometimes familiar, sometimes takes advantage of unique aspects of the rural environment, and is continuously in the process of changing and developing. The suggestions that follow are organized around the object of attack. In general, they are specialized and can be supplemented as necessary with more conventional strategies, such as the use of case-hardened padlocks.

Farm Equipment Theft

- Participate in identification programs and keep photos of equipment.
- Do not leave unattended equipment in remote fields for hours at a time or overnight. If it is necessary to do so for some reason, disable the engine by taking a vital part, and use logging chains to secure other equipment. Even if such precautions are taken, equipment in remote areas should be hidden from view from roadways.
- Equipment is best protected, in descending order of preference, by positioning it as follows: secured in a locked building near the main house or an inhabited house; secured in a gated area that is kept locked and is close to the main or an inhabited house; secured in one or more ways and not visible from commonly traveled roads.
- Immediately report all suspicious activity, such as strangers taking photographs of equipment, to local enforcement officials.

Timber Theft

- Post the property.
- Document its condition with date-stamped photographs.
- Check periodically to determine if any timber has been cut.
- Promptly report all losses.
- Take aerial photos of land.

Agrichemical Theft

- End users, whenever feasible, should buy only in quantities that they can readily use.
- If quantity purchases cannot be avoided, they should be stored in a locked, lighted building very close to the main house or an inhabited house. If available, place a few geese or guinea hens inside as watch animals.
- Rural dealers should employ security personnel during the months when they have large inventories.
- Be suspicious of people offering unusually good buys on agrichemicals; the absence of a market helps deter thefts.

Livestock and Tack Theft

- All livestock should be marked for identification; maximum deterrence is obtained when marks are readily visible.[41]
- A regular tally or count should be taken.
- Do not follow a set routine, such as going to the movies every Friday night, which would give a thief an advantage.
- Enter into cooperative arrangements with trusted neighbors to help watch one another's places.
- Avoid leaving animals in remote pastures or on faraway ranges whenever practical.
- Mark tack and keep it in a room that lends itself to security measures.
- Do not use "set guns" or "booby traps." They are often illegal and frequently injure innocent people or animals; surviving thieves have won damage suits because of the injuries that resulted.
- Keep photographic records of livestock and tack.

WILDLIFE CRIMES

Wildlife officers require many of the same types of knowledge and skills as do other peace officers, including knowledge of the laws of arrest, search, and seizure and skills such as interviewing people, crime scene processing, and interrogating suspects. In addition, wildlife investigators need to know specialized laws pertaining to their field and to be able to recognize the species and gender of wildlife. They also must be able to master unusual skills, such as interpreting tracks and being able to follow a trail (Figure 17-13). Because many poaching incidents come to light only long after the event, when the remains of the animal are discovered, wildlife officers must be familiar with methods of cold case investigation. Such discoveries may come months later when the snow melts to reveal the remains of game or predatory animals dig up remains that were buried by poachers to conceal their crime.

The U.S. Fish and Wildlife National Forensics Laboratory in Ashland, Oregon, is a premier source of assistance for wildlife investigators, as is the Wildlife Forensic DNA Laboratory at Trent University in Canada. In cases of poaching, DNA profiles can tie together the remains of a deer found at the location where it was field-dressed, dried bloodstains collected from the back of a pickup, and meat packages found in the poacher's freezer.[42] This creates scientific evidence that is very strong to overcome in court.

Because wildlife investigators often patrol alone in the wild, they encounter individuals and small groups of people who may be difficult or even deadly to deal with, including survivalists, fugitives, radical environmentalists, paramilitary units, drug smugglers, and persons engaged in illegal activities on public lands, such as growing marijuana and operating clandestine drug labs.

▲ FIGURE 17-13
Evidence of deer poaching
In the course of a major poaching investigation, wildlife investigators seized these boots, whose soles had been carved to resemble cattle hooves. By using them, the poacher tried to lay down a false trail and mislead investigators.
(Texas Parks & Wildlife Department © 2005, photo by Earl Nottingham)

Major Threats to Wildlife

There are a number of major threats to our wildlife. Urban sprawl destroys animal habitats, as does the accidental or illegal release of chemicals, land erosion, and oil spills. Wildlife **poaching** is also a major threat, and it is defined as the illegal taking or possession of game, fish, and other wildlife. Because poaching is a secretive crime committed in the wild, it is believed that wildlife investigators find only 1% to 5% of all poached animals.[43]

Poaching makes it more difficult to reestablish game populations, as some states are trying to do with elk and bighorn sheep, threatens endangered species, reduces our enjoyment of being out of doors, and hampers the development of tourism. We don't know what poaching and the illegal trade in animals and animal parts costs annually, but it is believed to be in the billions of dollars annually worldwide.

Poachers and Poaching

Poachers can be categorized into two types: **situational poachers** and **professional poachers.** Most poachers are situational, some being motivated by opportunity and others by circumstance. A driver sees an elk on the road, frozen by the car's headlights. Impulsively, or after short deliberation, he opportunistically shoots the elk out of season. Some situational poachers kill to feed their families because of economic hardship. A few opportunistic poachers kill simply for the thrill of it (Figure 17-14).[44] Although fewer in numbers, professional poachers take much more game than do situational poachers, because they kill for profit.

There is almost a fixation on possessing world-class trophies (Figure 17-15).[45] The dark side of this fixation

◄ FIGURE 17-14   Wolf killed
Faced with this scene, a wildlife investigator is quickly led to two competing theories: this is a thrill kill, or a rancher shot the wolf to stop predatory attacks on his or her herd. A detailed examination of the scene, knowledge of local events and people, and the follow-up investigation established this as a thrill kill. Although unusual, claims are made that an animal was killed in self defense; this usually involves grizzly bears. If reported promptly, the examination of the scene, particularly with an eye toward the proximity of the person and the bear, is one key to making a determination.
(Photo Courtesy New Mexico Department of Game and Fish)

results in very organized poaching and often involves unlicensed guides taking trophy seekers into areas closed for hunting, hunting out of season on public lands or on private lands for a fee, or using illegal hunting methods. Over a three-year period in Canada, rich "hunters," many of who were millionaires, rode in a helicopter until a moose was spotted. The chopper would touch down and a hunter would disembark. Once airborne again, the pilot would force the moose to run back toward the waiting hunter.[46] The use of aircraft for such purposes is periodically uncovered; nearly 20 years ago an Alaskan admitted that all 37 Boone and Crockett Club's record book grizzlies that he had helped hunters bag were illegally herded to them using an airplane.[47]

Some of the impetus to poach comes from the fact that there are only a very limited number of big game tags available each year, which are usually distributed by a statewide lottery. For hunting bighorn sheep in New Mexico during 2006/2007, only 12 out of 7,382 hunters received tags through the lottery. Moreover, in Montana, a hunter who gets a bighorn sheep tag has to wait seven years before becoming eligible for the lottery again. In New Mexico, two bighorn sheep tags a year are auctioned off to help manage that population. One of them alone brought in $177,500; the reason for the price is simple: most animals taken are Boone and Crockett record book class, and one year the biggest Rocky Mountain bighorn sheep taken in North America was in that state.[48]

There is a substantial Asian market for body parts from poached wild black and grizzly bears. Across the United States and Canada, the mutilated carcasses of bears are found with their gall bladders cut out and their paws chopped off. The gall bladders are thought to have special curative powers in traditional oriental medicine, and a single one may be sold for as much as $3,400 in South Korea, making it by weight more valuable than narcotics.[49] The sale of wild bear bladders is illegal in China, and there are domestic bear "bile milking" farms. However, because wild bear products are thought to be more potent, a lucrative black market flourishes for those willing to pay top dollar. Wild bear paw soup is a great delicacy, and a single bowl costs as much as $1,000.[50] At the end of their bile-producing days, farmed bears in China are slaughtered, but the soup from their paws is much less expensive.[51]

Investigations

Wildlife officers generally spend only about 20% of their time engaged in law enforcement activities (Figure 17-16). The balance is teaching hunting, boating, and snowmobile safety courses to the public, staffing exhibits at fairs or other functions, participating in disaster/emergency preparedness training, and conducting surveys and censuses.

Information

Information is an essential commodity in combating poachers. With it, more investigative successes are experienced. In some states, 80% of all poacher arrests come from leads from citizens. To assist wildlife officers in getting information, a number of states have established special programs such as Citizens Against Poachers (CAP) and Turn in a Poacher (TIP).

Uniformed Patrol

Uniformed wildlife officers patrol in boats and cars to see if game is being taken out of season or by illegal means They visit various sites to observe, to check licenses, and to examine the daily take. As a supplement to patrolling by car, airplanes can be used during the day to locate

◄**FIGURE 17-16**
Poaching investigation
A Nevada Department of Wildlife game warden photographs a boot impression in the snow; note the ruler laid beside the impression to establish the scale. The boot impressions were thought to be made by "hunters" poaching chukars, a medium-sized game bird in the pheasant family.
(© Brad Horn/The New York Times/Redux)

hunters, trappers, and camps in remote areas. At night, aircraft can also be useful in pinpointing places where it appears that artificial light is being used by poachers to take game, a tactic known as **jacklighting.** In both day and night uses of aircraft, the pilot or spotter relays information to ground units so that they can take appropriate action. In some instances, aircraft keep poachers from leaving an area under surveillance and direct wildlife officers in cars to intercept the poachers.

Intensive Hunting Patrols

Wildlife officers also employ intensive hunting patrols, especially during the opening weekends for various types of game such as pheasant, wild turkey, waterfowl, grouse, and deer. Intensive patrols tend to be concentrated in

areas of high public use, especially those with a history of excessive violations.

Vehicle Check Stops

Vehicle check stops are strategically set up on carefully selected roads to check vehicles for bag limits, unplugged shotguns, and licenses and to determine whether necessary special stamps (e.g., duck hunting) have been acquired.

Fishing Patrols

Fishing patrols (Figure 17-17) check to see that no protected or endangered fish, eels, crabs, lobsters, or other aquatic life forms are being taken, that takable aquatic species are taken only by legal means during the proper

◄**FIGURE 17-17**
Fishing violation arrest
(California Department of Fish and Game photo by Debra Hamilton)

seasons and times of day, that legal limits are being respected, and that the proper licenses have been obtained. Wildlife investigators are also vigilant in ferreting out the taking of sport and game fish by commercial fishing methods, such as through the use of seines and trotlines.

Resident License Verification

Despite the availability of a variety of databases, some out-of-state hunters attempt to pass themselves off as residents, primarily for two reasons: (1) the allocation of tags for residents for bears, antelope, elk and other species requiring tags is greater than for nonresidents, and (2) they can save a great deal of money: in Idaho in 2008, a combined hunting and fishing license and an elk tag cost a resident $66.75 versus $472.25 for the nonresident. It is a matter of false economy; the chances of "getting away with it" are low, detection appears to be fairly high, and penalties are stiff.

Covert Investigations

Covert investigations vary in their complexity. At the simplest, a wildlife officer who could not approach an area without being plainly visible for some distance may dress as a trout fisher and work his way along a stream watching for violations. Wildlife investigators also employ sophisticated sting operations. In Texas, some ranchers learned that their well-managed trophy deer herds were targets for poachers (Figure 17-18). The ranchers normally charge from $2,500 to more than $10,000 for the right to hunt their property legally. Undercover investigators agreed to take poachers out at night or to hunt from roads on the ranches. They received as little as $125 and a bag of marijuana from one "client." The sting operation netted dozens of arrests and broke the back of poaching for a number of ranchers.

ENVIRONMENTAL CRIME

This planet—which our children have to live in—suffers from what the inhabitants do to it. Rainforests are being chopped down for their timber. The entry of raw (untreated) sewage into water systems threatens fish populations. Worldwide, smokestack industries pour carbon dioxide into the air, polluting it and counteracting our efforts to combat the greenhouse effect and rising temperatures. Nuclear accidents render portions of countries uninhabitable. Swamps and marshes are disappearing at an alarming rate, along with their rich ecosystems. And toxins are dumped illegally. In fact, Native American tribal lands in this country regard illegal dumping as one of the major problems facing them; the Torres-Martinez Reservation outside Los Angeles identified 26 illegal dump sites across its 24,000 acres (Figure 17-19).

Although not all these events constitute environmental crimes, they do suggest that our planet is in distress. Therefore, it is incumbent on us to enforce environmental laws.

The Legal and Enforcement Framework

There are roughly 18 major federal environmental laws that form the basis for Environmental Protection Agency (EPA) programs. These laws deal with a number of issues, including chemical safety and site security, clean air and water, oil pollution, toxic-substance control, emergency planning, and environmental cleanup. Many states have substantially similar laws on some of these issues, and a number of local jurisdictions have enacted their own laws to combat environmental crimes. From this maze of laws, three patterns of enforcement emerge, regarding:

- Acts over which only the federal government has jurisdiction
- Acts for which there is concurrent federal and state jurisdiction
- Acts for which there is unique state and/or local jurisdiction

Individuals and businesses may be subject to criminal and civil fines for violating laws and consent decrees. Other sanctions that can be applied include the revocation of licenses and permits and the imposition of freezes on eligibility to receive federal grants.

▲ **FIGURE 17-18 Organized poaching ring**
Texas investigators arrest members of a highly organized poaching ring which operated at night. The group was apprehended on a private hunting preserve which specialized in having trophy deer to hunt for a substantial fee. The poachers' equipment included weapons with silencers, night-vision goggles, and GPS systems.
(Texas Parks & Wildlife Department © 2005, photo by Earl Nottingham)

◄ FIGURE 17-19   Dump Site
An illegal dumping site on the Torres-Martinez Indian Reservation in California. It caught fire periodically and burned to such an extent that it became a health problem for residents of a nearby trailer park and curtailed the outside activities of 5,600 students in surrounding elementary, middle, and high schools.
(Courtesy of the Environmental Protection Agency)

The federal Resource Conservation and Recovery Act (RCRA) of 1976 and its subsequent amendments give the Environmental Protection Agency authority over hazardous waste from "its cradle to its grave." **Hazardous waste** may be solids, liquids, sledges, or byproducts of manufacturing processes. They may also be commercial products such as battery acid and household cleaning supplies. A waste is hazardous if it has one or more of the following characteristics (Figure 17-20):

- *Ignitability:* Wastes that can create fires, those that can readily catch fire, and friction-sensitive substances (e.g., paints, degreasers, linseed oil, and gasoline)
- *Corrosivity:* Wastes that are acidic and those capable of corroding metal objects such as drums and tanks (e.g., cleaning fluids, battery acids, and rust removers)

- *Reactivity:* Substances that are unstable under normal conditions and that can create explosions and/or toxic fumes, gases, and vapors when mixed with water (e.g., sulphur-bearing wastes and cyanides)
- *Toxicity:* Substances that are harmful or fatal when ingested or absorbed and that, when improperly disposed of on land, may eventually pollute groundwater (e.g., mercury, certain pesticides, and lead)

Provisions of State RCRA Laws

Many states have enacted laws that are very similar to the federal RCRA. Among the common provisions of these laws are these:

- Identification and listing of hazardous wastes
- Establishment of permit and license systems regarding various types of hazardous waste, including their treatment, storage, and disposal (T/S/D)
- A manifest or shipping-paper system that tracks hazardous waste from "its cradle to its grave"
- Identification of the responsibilities of the generators and the transporters of hazardous waste
- Requirements for hazardous-waste management facilities, such as proof of financial reliability
- Designation of enforcement authority and criminal penalties

In a typical case, hazardous-waste crime charges are brought against one or more individuals and/or corporations involved in any combination of the three major components of the waste cycle:

- *Generating:* Among the companies engaging in activities that involve hazardous waste are chemical

| Ignitability | Corrosivity | Reactivity | Toxicity |

▲ FIGURE 17-20   Characteristics of hazardous waste
(Courtesy Environmental Protection Agency)

companies, which produce it as a byproduct of their legal activity; furniture and wood manufacturing companies working with various solvents and ignitable wastes, which must periodically be disposed of; and vehicle maintenance operations, which involve lead-acid batteries, solvents, and heavy metal and inorganic wastes.

- *Transportation:* This component involves the hauling away of hazardous waste from industrial sites. False manifests may be prepared to make the loads look less harmful, thereby allowing for inexpensive disposal of the waste. Tankers in poor condition may leak hazardous waste as they are driven along highways, and illegal disposal of hazardous waste also occurs when tankers deliberately discharge the waste in small amounts onto the road.
- *Treatment, storage, and disposal:* **T/S/D crimes** are committed by companies that treat hazardous waste without a permit or treat it inadequately, store it without a permit to do so, improperly identify the nature of the waste or store it under inadequate conditions discharge it into sewers, simply abandon it, mix it with regular waste for cheaper disposal, or store incompatible chemicals or amounts of chemicals beyond their permitted level (Figure 17-21).

Hazardous-waste generators vary in the level of regulatory requirements that they are required to meet (Table 17-1). Regardless of generator status, all generators must comply with basic RCRA requirements, including the use of manifests to track waste shipments. Conditionally exempt small-quantity generators must obtain an EPA permit once they generate more than 100 kilograms of hazardous waste per month. In all cases, waste must be properly stored and labeled. The EPA's *universal waste* list identifies items thrown out in large numbers, including batteries, some lamps, obsolete pesticides, and thermostats. The T/S/D requirements for universal waste are less stringent and do not count against a generator's status.

The most frequent violators of hazardous-waste regulations and laws are the small to midsize generating firms. Companies in this group violate hazardous-waste laws to maintain their profitability by avoiding the cost of legal disposal. However, large companies (or their employees) that have violated state RCRAs or various federal environmental laws include such well-known businesses as Texaco, Ocean Spray Cranberries, Fleischmann's, Ashland Oil, B. F. Goodrich, and Kaiser Steel.

Investigators must be alert to the fact that traditional crimes are also involved in acts that constitute environmental crimes. Examples of these include falsification of records and forgery—typically involving manifests and T/S/D records—and bribery of public officials, such as regulation inspectors and landfill operators, who accept money to certify that the hazardous waste was properly disposed of when it actually ends up being illegally dumped or abandoned.

Investigative Methods

Patrolling officers should be alert for signs that indicate the possibility or presence of **illegal dumping of hazardous waste.** Some of these signs are similar to the signs of a mass chemical attacks, but in illegal-dumping cases the scale is smaller. Among the signs to watch for:

- Suspicious discharges into waterways
- Discolored and dying vegetation that is unusual for the season
- An unusual number of dead animals, fish, and/or birds

◄**FIGURE 17-21**

Storage of hazardous waste under inadequate conditions

Properly identified hazardous waste improperly stored in deteriorated drums. The federal government and many states have enacted laws to protect against hazardous waste violations that threaten both people and the environment. Treatment, storage, and disposal (T/S/D) violations are committed by companies that fail to follow specific guidelines, including those that identify proper conditions for storage of hazardous materials. (Courtesy of Illinois Environmental Protection Agency)

| TABLE 17-1   EPA Hazardous-Waste Generator Status |

GENERATOR CATEGORY	MONTHLY GENERATION RATE	MAXIMUM QUANTITY ACCUMULATION LIMIT	MAXIMUM TIME ACCUMULATION LIMIT
Conditionally exempt small-quantity generator (CESQG)	Less than 100 kg	1,000 kg	None
Small-quantity generator (SQG)	100 to 1,000 kg	6,000 kg	180 days
Large-quantity generator (LQG)	More than 1,000 kg	No storage limit	90 days

(Source: Environmental Protection Agency)

- Unusual and persistent odors
- Odors that are accompanied by uncomfortable sensations (e.g., burning) affecting skin, eyes, and respiratory system
- New activity by trucks at closed businesses or abandoned buildings or on secondary roads
- Tankers visiting waterways in which they might illegally dump their cargoes

Officers should approach suspected hazardous-waste spills and toxic-waste sites with the wind at their backs and from the highest ground reasonably available. They should use binoculars to assess the scene in a standoff mode and notify their communications center as quickly as possible.

Leads on illegal hazardous-waste sites may be offered by disgruntled or former employees, occasionally by a current employee (who may have reservations about doing so because of the possibility of losing his or her job should the employer shut down), by home owners in the area of such sites, and by local pilots, boaters and fishers, competitors, building inspectors, and others. As in other types of investigation, the most immediate concerns are determining the reliability and the motive of the person bringing the information forward and assessing the public safety and health risks.

Surveillance is an excellent tool for gathering information, because it can establish illegal practices and the persons involved with them. Night photography equipment is essential, and thermal imaging and nightscopes are very useful in investigating "midnight dumping." Satellite and aerial photographs (Figure 17-22) of known hazardous-waste dumping areas can assist in locating the

◀ FIGURE 17-22
Aerial photograph surveillance
Aerial photograph of a New Hampshire business that cleaned out used toxic-waste barrels and recycled them, and crushed and disposed of drums that were unsalvageable. In the cleaning process, chemicals were washed into local groundwater and recreational lakes nearby, creating serious pollution problems. This photograph was important in refuting the defendant's claim in a sworn deposition that, as of a certain date, there were only 300 to 400 barrels on site. Analysts counted more than 3,000 barrels.
(Courtesy of Illinois Environmental Protection Agency)

◀ **FIGURE 17-23**
An unusual hazard
An investigator from the Illinois Environmental Protection Agency uses a blade of grass to point at an artillery projectile found at a closed military instillation. (Courtesy of Illinois Environmental Protection Agency)

sites of additional illegal dumps and are useful in determining whether generators and disposal facilities are exceeding their legal or permit capacities.

For most environmental crimes, it is necessary to form a team to conduct the investigation. Access to an attorney or inclusion of one on the team is a must because of multiple, complex laws, consent decrees, and regulatory guidance. An attorney can be helpful in drafting or reviewing requests for search warrants, arrest warrants, and other legal documents. The team should also include people whose skills match the needs of the investigation, such as backhoe operators or hydrologists. Because of the dangers associated with hazardous-waste sites, investigators must wear PPE to protect themselves. Even when properly equipped, unusual or unanticipated hazards are occasionally encountered (Figure 17-23). Specialized investigators from federal and state agencies are often available to assist with complex investigations. The EPA's National Enforcement Investigations Center (NEIC) has multidisciplinary teams for conducting investigations, has one of the leading forensic environmental chemistry laboratories, and has an extensive library, all of which are available to federal, state, and local agencies.

KEY TERMS

agrichemical	illegal dumping of hazardous waste	poaching
anhydrous ammonia	jacklighting	professional poachers
bone rustlers	livestock	situational poachers
brands	livestock identification	tack
copper theft	NAIS	timber theft
freezer crimes	night picker	T/S/D crimes
hazardous waste		

REVIEW QUESTIONS

1. In what ways are cities and agricultural crime linked?

2. Some variation in what is stolen from farms and ranches is caused by fluctuations in the economy. Theft of copper and anhydrous ammonia is a relatively recent trend. Why is this happening, and how does this reflect fluctuations in the economy?

3. If you were going to make a public presentation on the subject of timber theft, what major points would you make?

4. Compare how horse and cattle rustlers operate. What differences and similarities are there?

5. What are four concerns with respect to conducting stakeouts in rural areas?

6. What is NAIS?

7. There are five major methods of marking horses and cattle for identification. If you used your horse casually, just for recreational enjoyment, which method would you use to identify your horse? Why?

8. In our national parks and other federal lands, there are at least 29 species whose existence is threatened by poaching. What are the other major threats to wildlife?

9. Hypothetically, what kinds of physical evidence might be available where cattle have been rustled?

10. A friend of yours has just bought 20, mostly timbered, acres, on which is a small house in which she will live. She is concerned about "tree rustlers." What crime prevention suggestions do you have for her to protect her property?

11. What is the difference between situational and professional poachers? If you found a poacher in dire need who had just killed a deer to feed his family, would you "cut him some slack?" What if it was a close relative?

12. Elaborate on this statement: "Some of the impetus for poaching bighorn sheep comes from the fact there are only a very limited number of permits/tags available each year."

13. Why is information an "essential commodity" in investigating poaching?

14. Can you identify and describe the four characteristics of hazardous waste?

15. What are the three major components of the waste cycle?

16. What are three examples of T/S/D crimes?

17. What are six signs of illegal dumping of waste?

INTERNET ACTIVITIES

1. Do any sheriff's offices in your state have an agricultural or rural crime unit? What services do they provide?

2. What are some examples of livestock and crop theft in your state?

3. What species of wildlife are being poached in your state?

4. What types of environmental crimes are committed in your state? How serious are they? Who investigates them?

NOTES

1. Charles Swanson and Leonard Territo, "Agricultural Crime: Its Extent, Prevention and Control," *FBI Law Enforcement Bulletin,* 1980, Vol. 49, No. 5, p. 10. We originally estimated $3 billion annually. The figure in the text is based on the assumption of less than a 3% annual increase in losses over the past 27 years.

2. For an extension of this and related propositions, see Charles Swanson, "Rural and Agricultural Crime," *Journal of Criminal Justice,* 1981, Vol. 9, No. 1, pp. 19–27.

3. Patricia Leigh Brown, "Someone Is Stealing Avocados," *The New York Times,* Jan. 26, 2004.

4. E-mail, Laurie Hill to Charles Swanson, California Avocado Commission, October 2, 2007.

5. Jennifer Steinhauer, "Unusual Culprits Cripple Farms in California," *The New York Times,* July 31, 2007.

6. Ibid.

7. Christine Souza, "Vineyard Thieves Target Grapes, Harvest Supplies," California Farm Bureau Federation, September 19, 2007, p. 2.

8. Jesse McKinley, "Authorities Work to Crack Nut Crime Ring," *The New York Times,* October 2006.

9. Catherine E. Shoicet, "Thieves Strip Park's Palms," *St. Petersburg Times,* September 21, 2007.

10. Ibid.

11. FBI, Crime in the United States, 2006 (Washington, D.C.: FBI, 2007), Table 24. No page number in the Internet version of this document, www.fbi.gov/ucr/cius2006/data.table_24.html.

12. U.S. Department of Agriculture, Economic Research Service, U.S. Beef and Cattle Industry 2002–2005: Background Statistics and Information, p. 1. www.ers.usda.gov/news/BSECoverage.htm. For 2005, the National Agricultural Statistics Service (NASS) reported 190,000 cattle and calves lost to predation: 9.4% were attacks by mountain lions or bobcats, 12.9% involved dogs, 32.4% were killed by coyotes, and 45.3% "other or unknown predators." In contrast, that same year NASS accounted for only 21,000 head lost due to thefts, which seems very low; that same year Wyoming authorities reported 3,700 heads of cattle lost due to theft for just that state. That would mean Wyoming, one of the smaller cattle-producing states, had 17.6% of all cattle stolen, or nearly one in five.

13. Brian Brus, "Rustling Resurgence," *The Journal Record* (Oklahoma City), August 6, 2007.

14. Nelson Hernandez, "$75,000 in Bull Semen Stolen from Frederick Farm," *The Washington Post,* November 3, 2005.

15. Garance Burke and Olivia Munoz, "Hormone Theft Worries Rural Police, *Redding* (California) *Record,* February 23, 2007.

16. Mike Toner, "Brazen Fossil Hunters Are Cleaning Out U.S. Dinosaur Heritage," *Atlanta Journal Constitution,* Aug. 23, 2001.

17. William L. Hamilton, "Jurassic Bark," *The New York Times,* December 1, 2005, and No author, "Petrified

Wood Stolen on Federal Land," The Associated Press State and Local Wire, January 29, 2007.

18. Joe Corcoran, "High-Tech Measures Thwart Ginseng Poachers," Voice of America News, April 12, 2006, p. 1

19. Ibid., p. 2 with additions.

20. Janet Heimlich, "Thorny Problem," Texas Parks and Wildlife Magazine, June 2003, p.1.

21. No author, "Thieves Steal Hundreds of Millions of Dollars Worth of Trees," USA Today, May 18, 2003.

22. Chuck Hayes, "Pennsylvania: Stop Theft! Timber Theft Growing Concern in Allegheny National Forest," Times Observer (Warren, Pennsylvania), July 14, 2006.

23. Warren Cornwall, "Maples Falling Victim to Backwoods Thieves," The Seattle Times, May 17, 2007.

24. No author, "Two Charged with Timber Theft from Medicine Bow National Forest," Associated Press, February 12, 2004.

25. David Windsor, "Timber Theft: A Solvable Crime," Indiana Woodland Steward, Spring 2001, vol. 10, no. 1, pp. 1–3, www.fnr.purdue.edu/inwood/past%20issues/timberth.htm.

26. These points are drawn from Sgt. William Bacon, Livestock Theft Investigation, Los Angeles County Sheriff's Department, undated, p. 2, with modifications made by the authors.

27. Ibid., which is the source for the information in this paragraph.

28. Ibid.

29. Some of the information in this paragraph is drawn from ibid., pp. 5–6.

30. Ibid., p. 5.

31. Ibid.

32. E. N. Smith, "Modern Rustlers Steal Livestock via the Highway," Seattle Times Com, June 7, 1998, p. 1.

33. Ibid., p. 1.

34. Ibid., p. 12.

35. Ibid.

36. Bacon, Livestock Theft Investigation, p. 16, from which this paragraph was obtained with restatement.

37. Ibid., p. 24.

38. See Utah Livestock Brand Book, Utah Department of Agriculture, 2006.

39. These methods are identified in virtually all discussions of this topic. In preparing this edition we reviewed and drew a limited amount of restated content from Michael Neary, Methods of Livestock Identification, Purdue University Cooperative Extension, December 2002.

40. On this subject see No author, A Sampling of Thoughts and Opinions on Electronic Identification. The University of Tennessee, Center for Profitable Agriculture, 2004. In a small survey of farmers and ranchers it was found that among those who used a method of identification, 14.2% employed tattoos, 5.4% used brands, 77.4% used plastic ear tags, 1.8% relied on RFID devices, and 1.2% used other methods.

41. Several of these points were taken from Bacon, Livestock Theft Investigation, p. 17.

42. There are a number of articles on the use of DNA in wildlife investigations; as an illustration, see No author, "Wildlife Officers Use DNA Evidence to Solve Cold Case," US States News, August 21, 2006.

43. Randal C. Archibold, "Poachers in West Hunt Big Antlers to Feed Big Egos," The New York Times, December 9, 2006.

44. For example, see No author, "Thrill Killings Adding to Boost in Poaching of Nevada's Big Game," The Associated Press State and Local Wire, November 29, 2006.

45. Archibold, "Poachers in West Hunt Big Antlers to Feed Big Egos."

46. Ingrid Peritz, "Rich Hunters Used Copter to Stalk Terrified Moose," The Globe and Mail, Canada, December 7, 2006.

47. "Poachers Enlisted to Save Big Game," The New York Times, Dec. 26, 1990, p. A28.

48. Press Release, New Mexico Department of Game and Fish, March 16, 2005.

49. Wency Leung, "Asia's Bile Trade Takes Its Toll of Canadian Bears," South China Morning Post, August 26, 2007.

50. Ibid.

51. Press release, The Humane Society of the United States, "Congress Aims to End the Black Market Trade in Bear Parts," July 18, 2007; see www.hsus.org/press_and_publications/press_releases.

18

ARSON AND EXPLOSIVES INVESTIGATIONS

▲ Police use a dog to check a suspicious vehicle for explosives. Many federal and local law enforcement agencies now use dogs specifically trained to assist in locating illegal explosive materials.

(© Reuters NewMedia Inc./Corbis)

CHAPTER OUTLINE

The crime of arson has increased dramatically in recent years. It is estimated that more than 1,000 lives are lost each year owing to arson fires. Another 10,000 injuries are sustained each year as a result of arson fires. Conservative estimates show that approximately $2 billion in property damage is caused each year by arsonists, but this $2 billion is only the tip of the iceberg when it comes to the total amount of money lost annually as a result of arson. The cost of fire services increases that figure by at least an extra $10 billion. Untold thousands of jobs are also lost when factories are burned for profit. Likewise, thousands of homes are lost each year, forcing home owners and tenants to relocate and often incur higher house and rent payments.[1]

Arson is an inherently difficult crime to detect and prosecute, in part because the motivations for and methods of committing arson vary widely. Some arsonists may be troubled juveniles who start fires with matches or cigarettes; others are professional arsonists, who frequently use timing devices and accelerants. Arson investigation also falls between police responsibility and fire department responsibility, an area that is too often not effectively covered. Both the police and the fire services can legitimately claim authority in arson cases, but each also may rationalize that the responsibility belongs to the other. Unfortunately, in most jurisdictions, neither is prepared to devote the resources needed to achieve identification, arrest, and conviction rates commensurate with other crimes. Arson investigators need more cooperation and better training. Administrative officials need to help, but in order to help they need to give the problem a greater share of their attention. Probably the most urgent step in controlling arson rates is for top fire and police officials and local, state, and national governments to recognize the magnitude of the problem and then provide the necessary resources to combat it.[2]

In the second half of this chapter, we discuss explosive investigations, which are in many respects quite different from arson investigations. We also describe how to respond to bomb threats, search for concealed explosives, handle suspicious packages and letters, and reading the bomber's signature.

PRELIMINARY INVESTIGATION

Arson investigations entail several exceptions to fire-service training. For example, the fire service has taught firefighters that fire loss is less and public relations are better if they clean premises of debris, water, and so forth. However, if arson is suspected, firefighters should not disarrange the premises, especially at the point of origin.

Moving debris, even window glass, may destroy valuable physical evidence.[3]

In nearly all cases, there is little additional loss if the area encompassing the point of origin is not cleaned out, because this area is usually the most heavily damaged by the fire, with little salvage possible. Often, it is necessary during overhauling to move large quantities of acoustical tile, plasterboard, canned goods, cartons, and other items. If this material is beyond salvage, it is natural to throw it into the worst-burned area of the building. But this is probably the area the investigator will want to examine carefully, and such discards will have to be moved again. In the confusion, the fire's cause is likely to remain in doubt.

One effective way to determine fire causes is to determine the point of origin. For instance, a point of origin in the middle of a bare concrete basement floor typically eliminates defective heating appliances or wiring. Points of origin sometimes are established by reconstructing furniture and walls, and replacing loose boards and doors. Neighbors and occupants can help describe how things were before the fire. The direction of heat flow then can be followed by checks for the deepest charring, indications of highest temperature, and the duration of heat. Temperatures are indicated by the condition of metal, glass, wood, plastics, and other materials. Because heat rises, a general rule is to look for the lowest point of deep char as the point of origin. This rule, however, has many exceptions.

After the area of origin has been established, the investigator should check for the level of origin by examining the bottoms of shelves, ledges, moldings, and furniture and all sides of the legs, arms, and framework of reconstructed furniture. The investigator also should clean the floor carefully at the point of origin, examining and moving all objects to one side. After this is done, the floor or rugs should be swept as clean as possible for examination of burn patterns. (See Figure 18-1.)

The floor and lower areas of the room produce the most clues to the cause of the fire, because they are the living area. Most equipment and contents are near floor level, actions of occupants are conducted near floor level, and most materials drop there during a fire.

WHERE AND HOW DID THE FIRE START?

Once the fire is out, the primary task is to begin examining what is left of the building for physical evidence that may indicate how the fire began.

The point of origin can be a clue to possible arson. For example, if two or more distinct points of origin are found, two or more separate fires probably were deliberately set. Also, if the fires started in the middle of a large room or in a closet, then the index of suspicion should go up sharply.[4]

Two Factors Needed to Cause A Fire

During the investigation, it should be borne in mind that a fire always has two causes: a source of heat and material ignited.

In checking for the fire cause at the point of origin, it is usually an advantage to use the **layer-checking technique.** Before any material is moved or shoveled out, the investigator should make notes and carefully examine the strata while working through to the floor. These layers often contain wood ash, plaster, melted aluminum, window glass, charred drapery fabric, and charred newspapers. They may give a picture of the sequence of burning. If, for example,

◀ **FIGURE 18-1**

Arson investigators at work
A team of arson investigators search the scene of a suspected arson. Arson investigators receive hours of specialized training to effectively conduct this type of investigation. They must be careful not to destroy potential evidence while sifting through soot and debris.
(Courtesy of Thomas Evans, Pinellas County, Florida, Sheriff's Office)

charred newspapers were found beneath charred drapery fabric, this could indicate a set fire, particularly if papers would not usually be in the area or if they were of different types of dates. Aluminum and similar alloys melt fairly early in a fire (at about 1,150°F), often splash or run over other material near floor level, solidify, and protect the material from further damage. Draperies and heavy curtains may burn free and drop on flammable liquid, preventing it from being completely consumed, especially if the liquid is heavy or less volatile.[5]

Accidental Fires

Once the point of origin has been discovered, the next step is to determine how the fire started. Even though arson may be suspected, the investigator must first investigate and rule out all possible accidental or natural causes. Many courts have held that this elimination of accidental causes is a firm basis for an arson charge. Also, if the investigator is put on the witness stand, it is likely that a question will be raised about the possibility of accidental causes. A failure to eliminate accidental causes could substantially weaken the prosecution's case.

Some of the more common accidental or natural causes of fire fall into the following categories:

- *The electric system:* Fuses in which pennies have been inserted; broken or rotted insulation; overloaded circuits; defective switches; and improperly installed wiring.
- *Electrical appliances and equipment:* Defective electrical units with short circuits; overheated irons; and light bulbs covered by paper shades.
- *Gas:* Leaks in gas pipes; defective stoves and heating units.
- *Heating units:* Overheated stoves or steam pipes; clothing being dried too close to fireplaces or open flames; faulty chimneys; explosions from kerosene stoves; and overturned space heaters.
- *Sunlight:* The concentration of sun rays on bubbles in glasses, windowpanes, or convex shaving mirrors placed near combustible materials such as paper or rags.
- *Matches:* Children playing with matches, especially in enclosed areas such as closets or utility rooms.
- *Smoking:* The careless disposal of cigars, cigarettes, pipe ashes, and other lighted devices into trash cans in the home; individuals who fall asleep while smoking in bed or in a chair.

Indications of cigarettes in furniture or mattresses are heavy charring of the unit and the floor; a char pattern on furniture frames, heaviest on the inside; heavy staining and blackening of mirrors and window glass in the area, indicating a long, slow fire; a burning time of from 1 to 4 hours; collapsing of part or all of the core springs. Lying flat on a padded surface, cigarettes usually char a small hole and burn out. If the cigarette is partially covered at the sides or bottom, a fire usually results in an hour or so. Cigarettes ignite foam rubber padding to about the same degree as other padding. With foam rubber padding, fire occurs a little faster, because smoldering rubber reaches an ignition temperature faster and burns with greater intensity.[6]

Spontaneous Heating and Ignition

There are a few fundamental causes of spontaneous heating, but the conditions under which these factors may operate are numerous. Nearly all organic materials and many metals are subject to oxidation, fermentation, or both and, therefore, have some potential for spontaneous heating.

Spontaneous heating is produced in three major ways: chemical action, fermentation, and oxidation (the most common way). For example, chemical-action heating occurs when unslaked lime and water or sodium and water are combined. Fermentation heating is caused by bacterial action. Here, moisture is a prime factor. The most dangerous materials are those subject to combinations, such as fermentation and oxidation with drying. Fresh sawdust over 10 feet deep is subject to fermentation heating but rarely reaches ignition temperature. In oxidation heating, rapid oxidation must take place in the presence of a good insulating factor and an oxygen supply. Oxidation takes place in oils containing carbon, hydrogen, and oxygen. This combination is mostly found in vegetable and fish oils and, to some extent, in animal oils.

The susceptibility to spontaneous heating is usually determined by drying time. Unadulterated hydrocarbons, such as mineral and petroleum oils, are not considered subject to spontaneous ignition.

Spontaneous ignition is rare in residences and small businesses. It is considerably accelerated by external heat such as sunshine, steampipes, hot air ducts, and friction from wind or vibration. Spontaneous ignition is rather mysterious, because of many unknowns. Therefore, it is often used as a catch-all explanation.

The usual time required to produce spontaneous ignition by oxidation or fermentation runs from several hours to several days or months. This form of ignition is characterized by internal charring of a mass of combustibles, and some of the remains of this material usually are found at the point of origin (if the firefighters have been careful and especially if fog was used), because it normally takes a considerable mass—several inches of fairly dense material—to create the factors necessary for spontaneous heating. Sometimes when material of the appropriate type is suspected and found to be deeply charred all the way through, investigators must satisfy themselves that external heat was not responsible. When not heated internally, sacks of meals, flour, and the like usually survive fire with only an inch or two of charring on the exposed surface.

Dust and polishing mops have often been accused of causing spontaneous ignition and probably have in some rare cases. Most fires originating near a mop in a closet or on a back porch are caused by a child playing with matches.[7] It is debatable whether the average mop would have enough bulk to provide the necessary insulation to raise the temperature to the ignition point, although with favorable conditions—such as a large mop, saturated with fast-drying oils, pressed in a corner with other brooms, and receiving outside heat from a steampipe or the sun's rays through a window—ignition could occur. During the several hours required for the material to ignite, it gives off very acrid odors. Linseed and similar oils are especially odorous. People in the area during that time usually would be aware of these odors.

BURN INDICATORS

Burn indicators are the effects of heat or partial burning that indicate a fire's rate of development, points of origin, temperature, duration, and time of occurrence, as well as the presence of flammable liquids. Interpretation of burn indicators is a principal means for determining the causes of fires, especially arson. Some of the burn indicators used are the following.[8]

Alligatoring

Alligatoring is the checking of charred wood, which gives the wood the appearance of alligator skin. Large, rolling blisters indicate rapid, intense heat; small, flat alligatoring indicates low heat. (See Figure 18-2.)

Depth of Char

Analysis of the depth of char is most reliable for evaluating fire spread, rather than for establishing specific burn times or intensity of heat from adjacent burning materials. By measuring the relative depth and extent of charring, the investigator may be able to determine which portions of a material or construction were exposed the longest to a heat source. The relative depth of char from point to point is the key to appropriate use of **charring**—locating the places where the damage was most severe owing to exposure, ventilation, or fuel placement. The investigator may then deduce the direction of fire spread, with decreasing char depths being farther away from the heat source. (See Figure 18-3.)

Depth of char is often used to estimate the duration of a fire. The rate of charring of wood varies widely depending on such variables as:

- Rate and duration of heating
- Ventilation effects
- Surface area-to-mass ratio
- Direction, orientation, and size of wood grain
- Species of wood (pine, oak, fir, etc.)
- Moisture content
- Nature of surface coating[9]

▲ **FIGURE 18-2 Unusual burn patterns and alligatoring**
Unusual burn patterns on wood floors should be closely examined. Flooring that was saturated with flammable liquid, like this, has deeply pronounced char. Burning between floorboards indicates that flammable liquid seeped down into the cracks. The area beneath the floor should also be examined for evidence of burning, and a sample of the burned floor should be sent to a laboratory for analysis. Also note the checked pattern on the burnt wood. Investigators should carefully examine burned wood in order to determine the heat intensity of the fire. Large, rolling blisters indicate rapid,

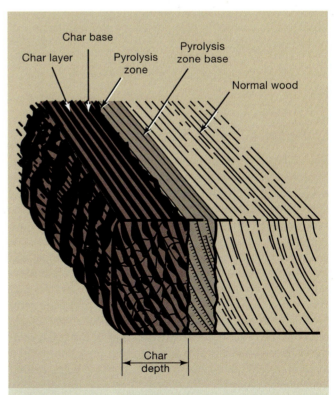

▲ **FIGURE 18-3 Line of demarcation in a wood section**
(Source: Factory Mutual Engineering Corporation, Norwood, Massachusetts. Reprinted with permission.)

Breaking of Glass

If a pane of glass is mounted in a frame that protects the edges of the glass from the radiated heat of a fire, a temperature difference occurs between the unprotected portion of the glass and the protected edge. Researchers estimate that a temperature difference of about 158°F (70°C) between the center of the pane of glass and the protected edge can cause cracks that start at the edge of the glass. The cracks appear as smooth, undulating lines that can spread and join together. Depending on the degree of cracking, the glass may or may not collapse from its frame. If a pane of glass has no edge protection from the radiated heat or fire, the glass breaks at a higher temperature difference. Research findings suggest that fewer cracks are formed and the pane is more likely to stay whole.

Glass that has received an impact will have a characteristic "cobweb" pattern: numerous cracks in straight lines. The glass may have been broken before, after, or during the fire.

If flame suddenly contacts one side of a glass pane while the unexposed side is relatively cool, a stress can develop between the two faces and the glass can fracture between the faces. *Crazing* is a term used in the fire investigation community to describe a complicated pattern of short cracks in glass arising from this condition. These cracks may be straight or crescent-shaped and may or may not extend through the thickness of the glass. While crazing is still a theory and has not yet been confirmed, research has established that it can be created by the rapid cooling of glass brought on by the application of water spray in a hot environment. Occasionally with small-size panes, differential expansion between the exposed and the unexposed faces may result in the pane's popping out of its frame.[10]

Collapsed Furniture Springs

The collapse of furniture springs may provide the investigator with various clues concerning the direction, duration, or intensity of the fire. However, the collapse of the springs cannot be used to indicate exposure to a specific type of heat source or ignition, such as smoldering ignition or the presence of an ignitable liquid. The results of laboratory testing indicate that the annealed springs, and the associated loss of tension (tensile strength), are a function of the application of heat. The tests revealed that short-term heating at high temperatures and long-term heating at moderate temperatures over 750°F (400°C) can result in the loss of tensile strength and in the collapse of the springs. The tests also revealed that the presence of a load or weight on the springs while they are being heated increases the loss of tension.

By analyzing furniture springs, the investigator can compare the differences between the springs and other areas of the mattress, cushion, frame, and so forth. Comparative analysis of the springs can assist the investigator in developing hypotheses concerning the relative exposure of various items or areas to a particular heat source. For example, if the springs at one end of a cushion or mattress have lost their tension and those at the other end have not, then hypotheses may be developed. The hypotheses should take into consideration other circumstances, effects (such as ventilation), and evidence at the scene concerning the duration or intensity of the fire, the area of origin, direction of heat travel, and the relative proximity of the heat. Areas characterized by the loss of tensile strength may indicate greater relative exposure to heat than do areas without the loss of strength.

Other circumstances and effects to consider are the loss of mass and material; the depth of char in a wood frame; and color changes, possibly indicating intensity, in metal frames. Comparative analysis should also include consideration of the covering material of the springs. The absence of material may indicate a portion closer to the source of heat, while the presence of material may indicate an area more remote from the heat source. The investigator should also consider the condition of the springs before the fire.[11]

Spalling is the breakdown in the surface tensile strength of concrete, masonry, or brick that occurs when exposure to high temperatures and rates of heating produces mechanical forces within the material. These forces are believed to result from one or more of these factors:

- Moisture present in uncured or "green" concrete
- Differential expansion between reinforcing rods or steel mesh and the surrounding concrete
- Differential expansion between the concrete mix and the aggregate (this is most common with silicon aggregates)
- Differential expansion between the fine-grained surface or finished layers and the coarser-grained interior layers
- Differential expansion between the fire-exposed surface and the interior of the slab

Spalling of concrete or masonry surfaces may be caused by heat, freezing chemicals, or abrasion. It may be induced more readily in poorly formulated or finished surfaces. Spalling is characterized by distinct lines of striation and the loss of surface material, resulting in cracking, breaking, and chipping or in the formation of craters on the surface. Spalled areas may appear lighter in color than adjacent areas. This lightening can be caused by the exposure of clean subsurface material. Also, adjacent areas may tend to be sooted.

Spalling of concrete, masonry, brick, or painted surfaces (such as plaster) has often been linked to unusually high temperatures caused by burning accelerants.

While spalling can result from high rates of heat release or a rapid change in temperature, an accelerant need not be involved. The primary mechanism of spalling is the expansion or contraction of the surface while the rest of the mass expands or contracts at a different rate. Another

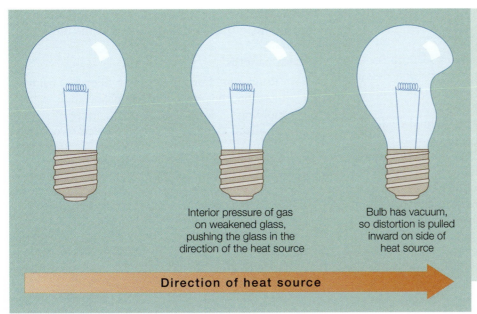

Interior pressure of gas on weakened glass, pushing the glass in the direction of the heat source

Bulb has vacuum, so distortion is pulled inward on side of heat source

Direction of heat source

◀ **FIGURE 18-4**
Distorted light bulbs
Heat can affect the glass of a light bulb, and the investigator can examine the distortion of a light bulb to determine the direction of the heat source. Bulbs over 25 watts expand toward the heat, and bulbs that are 25 watts or less pull inward on the side of the heat. The bulbs in this figure demonstrate this phenomenon. The bulb in the middle is greater than 25 watts, and the bulb on the right is less than 25 watts.
(Courtesy of National Fire Protection Association, Inc., Quincy, MA)

factor in the spalling of concrete is the loading and stress in the material at the time of the fire. Since high-stress or high-load areas may not be related to the fire, spalling of concrete on the underside of ceilings or beams may not be directly positioned over the origin of the fire.[12]

Distorted Light Bulbs

Heat can also have an effect on the glass of a light bulb. The investigator can examine the distortion of a light bulb, for instance, to determine the direction of head impingement. Bulbs over 25 watts expand toward the heat, and bulbs that are 25 watts or less pull inward on the side of the heat. The bulbs in Figure 18-4 demonstrate this phenomenon. The bulb in the middle is greater than 25 watts, and the bulb on the right is less than 25 watts.[13]

Temperature Determination

If the investigator knows the approximate melting temperature of a material, an estimate can be made of the temperature to which the melted material was subjected. This knowledge may be of help in evaluating the intensity and duration of the heating, the extent of heat movement, or the relative rates of heat release from fuels.

When using such generic materials as glass, plastics, and white pot metals for making temperature determinations, the investigator must be aware of the wide variety of melting temperatures for these materials.

The best approach is to take a sample of the material and have its melting temperature ascertained by a competent laboratory, materials scientist, or metallurgist. Wood and gasoline burn at essentially the same flame temperature. The turbulent diffusion flame temperatures of all hydrocarbon fuels (plastics and ignitable liquids)

and cellulosic fuels are approximately the same, although the fuels release heat at different rates.

The temperature achieved by an item at a given location within a structure or fire area depends on how much the item is heated. The amount of heating depends on the temperature and velocity of the airflow, the geometry and physical properties of the heated item, its proximity to the source of heat, and the amount of heat energy present. Burning metals and highly exothermic chemical reactions can produce temperatures significantly higher than those created by hydrocarbon- or cellulosic-fueled fires.

Identifiable temperatures achieved in structural fires rarely remain above 1,900°F (1,040°C) for long periods of time. These temperatures are sometimes called **effective fire temperatures,** because they reflect physical effects that can be defined by specific temperature ranges. The investigator can use the analysis of the melting and fusion of materials to assist in establishing whether higher-than-expected heat energy was present.[14]

FIRE SETTING AND RELATED MECHANISMS

It is the duty of an arson investigator to search the debris of a suspicious fire, particularly around the point of origin, to gather evidence pointing to the mechanism used by the fire setter in the arson effort.[15]

An arsonist may use the simplest of methods, a match and some paper, or elaborate mechanical or chemical methods. An **incendiary mechanism** may be mechanical or chemical, and consists of an ignition device, possibly a timing device, one or more "plants" to feed or accelerate the initial flame, and, frequently, "trailers" to spread the fire about the building or from plant to plant.

Ignition Devices

Matches

Only juvenile arsonists and **pyromaniacs** seem to favor striking matches. Other fire setters want some delay, so they adapt the ordinary match to some timing mechanism.

Several matches may be affixed to a lighted cigarette with a rubber band or tape, the heads of the matches set about halfway down the cigarette from its glowing end. In some cases, matches are laid alongside a cigarette. Books of paper matches are also popular. Because cigarettes will continue to burn when laid on their sides, they are effective ignition devices; the slow-burning cigarette allows the fire setter a few minutes to get away from the scene before the fire makes any headway.

Gasoline and Other Accelerants

Gasoline and other **accelerants** ("boosters" that speed the progress of a fire) are very popular with many different types of arsonists. (See Figure 18-5.) The investigator should remember that gasoline and many types of liquid accelerants burn at about 3,000°F as opposed to ordinary combustibles, which burn at 1,600°F. If, for example, the investigator observes a metal door melted in a pile, gasoline was probably used as an accelerant because steel generally reaches its melting point at 3,000°F.

Telltale Signs of Accelerants

- A distinct burn/damage pattern
- Witness observations (smelling gasoline, etc.)
- Explosion
- Burns to the hands, face, legs, or hair of a suspect/witness
- Unnatural fire spread (downward, very fast, etc.)
- Flames appear suddenly in an entire room followed by heavy black smoke
- Bright yellow/orange flames with black smoke
- Flames seen burning directly from the floor
- Intense localized rusting/warping (especially to the undersides and lower portions) of metal appliances and metal objects within the suspected liquid burn-pattern area
- Light, moderate, and heavy floor burn patterns in puddle or trailer shapes corresponding to the original shape of the accelerant pool on tight or nonporous floors (burn patterns vary with the type of accelerant, surface texture, and ventilation)
- Gapping of wood or vinyl floor seams within the pour burn pattern that may be caused by a liquid accelerant burning inside the seam
- Rainbow-colored sheen on the surface of suppression water over the pour area
- Even height of smoke and heat patterns in the room of origin
- Accelerant containers in or near the scene

- Increased burn damage pattern at the bottom of furniture, boxes, etc., on the floor in the burn pattern
- Burn patterns
  - "Rundown" burn patterns on floor just below loose floorboards, board seams, or edge moldings
  - Localized staining on the underside of carpet padding
  - Pool-shaped, mottled, black-and-brown staining on a concrete floor with a tendency for the mottled portion to repel water—area may retain odor of accelerant
- Fire damage with no identifiable point of origin
- Wall burn patterns running from the floor seam upward, or appearing in corners
- Burned-out flooring beneath heavy appliances or furniture, which would usually protect the floor
- Localized "clean burn" areas on a wall, appliance, or similar vertical surfaces above the floor pattern where intense heat burned away soot deposits
- Sharp line of char demarcation in a cross section of wood stud or a sharp line of calcination (color change) in plaster or drywall—indicates rapid (rather than smoldering) heat buildup
- Window glass that has melted down like "ribbon candy" and has a clean interior face (little or no soot) on the side with the accelerant
- Spring annealing in furniture/bedding—sometimes results from liquid accelerant being poured on, or adjacent to, furniture
- "Inverted cone" burn/scald patterns on vertical surfaces with the pour pattern[16]

Chemicals

Various chemical combustions have been used to set fires. Saboteurs have used such means for years. Units that provide for an acid to be released on some combination of chemicals are favorite devices, with the acid releasing itself by eating its way through the cork or even the metal of its container. The time lag from setting to ignition can be estimated with some certainty by an arsonist with a little knowledge of chemistry.

Various rubber receptacles—such as hot water bottles, ice bags, or contraceptives—have been used for a phosphorus and water ignition device. A pinhole is made in the rubber container, allowing the water to seep out. Once it drains below the level of the phosphorus, ignition takes place. As this chemical ignites upon contact with air, a time lag is secured by controlling the amount of water and the size of the hole in the container.

Even the ordinary fire setter sometimes uses a chemical that ignites on contact with water. The device is activated by rain. Holes in a roof or a connection to the building's gutter system have been used to trigger such devices. Another device is used to divert the sewage line

▲ **FIGURE 18-5   Gasoline used as an accelerant**
These photographs depict in sequential order an incendiary device involving a plastic milk jug, a birthday candle, and gasoline. The cap of the milk jug was drilled to the proper size to hold the candle. As the candle burned it eventually fell into the gasoline and ignited the vapors at the level of the hole. The burning vapors then expanded which in turn intensified the fire. The delay time for the device was approximately 20 to 25 minutes. These photographs depict a test that was done prior to the upcoming trial of a person who allegedly used the device in the interior of a car, supporting investigators' suspicions that the car had been intentionally burned. (Courtesy of Dave Crosbie, Burnsville, MN, Fire Department)

in a building. It is set up at night to trigger the next morning when the toilet is flushed for the first time.

Most chemical ignition units leave some residue, have a distinctive odor, or both. Debris must be analyzed at a laboratory if it is suspected that chemicals have been used as ignition devices. Fortunately, most arsonists do not know enough to use chemical ignition or timing devices, and the machinery and tools necessary for the construction of some of these devices are not always readily available. The devices usually are fairly simple. Most complex devices, in contrast, are used only in a time of war by enemy agents.

Gas

Although not commonly encountered, the combination of gas and the pilot light on the kitchen stoves of many residences is always a possibility. Illuminating gas rises to the ceiling, being lighter than air, and then slowly moves to floor level as it continues to escape. When it reaches a combustion buildup, it is close to the pilot-light level. An explosion, usually followed by fire, takes place. A candle placed in a room adjoining the kitchen has also been used as a means of ignition. Therefore, arson investigators must remember that although such explosions usually follow suicide attempts or accidents, arsonists may use an ordinary gas range as a tool.

In such cases, investigators should get help from an engineer at the local public utility. The time lag between the initial release of the gas and the explosion can be estimated from the size of the room involved, the number of openings, the type of gas, and related data. For example, a kitchen 10 by 15 feet with a ceiling 9 feet high equals a total volume of 1,350 cubic feet. When 71 cubic feet of gas are introduced into the room, the lowest limit of explosive range will have been reached. In a well-ventilated room, it is almost impossible to build up to this limit, but an arsonist seals off the room so that the gas builds up. In a fairly well-sealed room, a single burner left open on a kitchen gas stove will deliver enough gas to explode in about 5 hours. The oven jets will build up the same volume in 2 hours; an oven plus four burners, 30 minutes to 1 hour.

The widespread use of gas as an arson tool has been thwarted because of its smell. Neighbors usually detect the smell, call the police or the fire department, or break in themselves, ruining a carefully planned arson attempt.

Electrical Systems

Any wiring system, including doorbell and telephone circuits, can be used as a fire-setting tool. Ignition devices hooked to the wiring systems of buildings have been used throughout the country by arsonists. The time can be established by a study of the habits of those using the premises. Possibly a security guard switches on the light every hour while inspecting the various portions of the building, or employees turn on the lights at opening time, and so on.

Although a doorbell system can be used to trigger an ignition device, the bell may be rung by some chance visitor and the plans of the fire setter thwarted. Telephone timing devices have the same fault. A wrong number or an unexpected call can start the fire, possibly days ahead of schedule.

Electrical appliances have also been used to set fires. An open heater is placed close to a flimsy set of curtains, and an apparently accidental fire results. An electrical circuit is deliberately overloaded with several appliances until it heats up. Sometimes an accelerant such as kerosene is dropped into a switch box. In a few cases, a length of normal wiring is removed and lighter wire substituted so that it overheats and, without blowing the fuses, serves as an ignition device.

Investigators generally discover physical traces of electrical ignition devices after a fire.

Mechanical Devices

Alarm clocks were once a favored weapon of arsonists. With a simple alarm clock, some wire, and a small battery, a fire setter was "in business." But a search of the fire debris usually sent the arsonist to prison. Some arsonists used the lead hammer in the clock to break a glass tube that fed flammable matter to a fixed flame. This action pushed one container of chemicals into another, closing an electrical circuit. Some arsonists attached matches to the hammer, where they were pressed against an abrasive surface to ignite flammable material. The clock was activated by setting the alarm for a certain time. The weights in a grandfather's clock have been used in a similar manner.

Some mechanical devices are childish, some are worthy of a master craftsperson, and others are truly fiendish. Unfortunately for many of these ingenious incendiaries, their machines do not burn and can later be used in their prosecution.

Plants

A **plant** is the material placed around the ignition device to feed the flame. Newspapers, wood shavings, rags, clothing, curtains, blankets, and cotton waste are some plants. Newspapers are the most frequently used; cotton waste is used extensively in factory or industrial fires.

Accelerants are also usually part of the plant. Kerosene and gasoline are favored accelerants; alcohol, lighter fluid, paint thinners, and other solvents are also popular. However, any flammable fluid or compound may be used to accelerate the blaze.

Trailers

Trailers are used to spread the fire. A trailer is ignited by the blaze from the plant. It carries the fire to other parts of a room or building. Usually a trailer ends in a second plant, another pile of papers, or excelsior sprinkled with gasoline, kerosene, or some other booster. From the primary plant, the fire setter may lay four trailers to four secondary plants. Four separate fires thus result from one ignition device.

Rope or toilet paper soaked in alcohol or similar fluid, motion picture film, dynamite fuses, gunpowder, and other such substances have been used as trailers. Sometimes rags or newspapers are soaked in a fire accelerant and twisted into rope. Some arsonists use a liquid fire accelerant such as kerosene as a trailer by pouring a liberal quantity on the floor in a desired path.

Missing Items

Sometimes items that are missing from the fire scene can prove valuable. For example, does it appear that many of the building's contents, especially furniture, clothing, or valuable items, were removed prior to the fire? Were house pets removed? Moving a pet to a kennel or the home of friends just before a fire should raise the suspicions of the investigator.

ARSON FOR PROFIT

Understanding the motive of the arsonist is extremely important if the investigation is to be successful. There are several common motivations among arsonists for setting fires. The motive behind committing arson for profit is economic gain, whether it be the enormous gain derived from inflating insurance coverage beyond the building's value or the limited economic gain derived from cutting one's losses before oncoming financial disaster.[17]

To decide where and how to begin the investigation, the investigator needs to determine whether the arson in question was due primarily to financial stress, to a fraud scheme (without much stress), or to a combination of some stress and the profitability of fraud.

Financial Stress as The Primary Cause

The home owner or business owner who decides to arrange an arson fraud may do so out of submission to financial stress. In general, two primary factors influence the insured person's decision to commit arson fraud: (1) the desire for financial relief, and (2) greed—the desire for easily obtained financial assistance. One way to conceive of an arson-fraud scheme is to view it as the result of the interplay between these two factors. Experience in cases where owners have been caught in arson-fraud schemes indicates that the more extreme and immediately pressing the financial stress, the more desperate the insured becomes. Certainly, the number of insureds who are not persuaded to commit arson—no matter how severe their financial stress—is great, and the swelling bankruptcy court dockets reflect the prevailing honesty of most citizens. However, a rapidly developing situation of financial stress can place the insured in a position where he or she desperately examines all kinds of options both legal and illegal.

Perhaps we can understand the arson-fraud motive of a home owner who has just been fired or who faces mortgage foreclosure and burns a home or business. It is important to conduct a search for evidence for those forms of stress. The investigator is likely to find a great deal about such matters in court papers associated with divorces, foreclosures, bankruptcies, and liens. Although it is not fully accepted as a rule of thumb, the more severe the financial stress of an insured, the more likely the person is to either personally set the fire or to involve a minimum number of people—usually a professional arsonist—in the crime.

Investigators often view real estate arson schemes as purely the result of the fraudulent motives of the owners.

Actually, the motives for committing real estate arson split between those that are pure scams (discussed later) and those that result from the owner's or landlord's deteriorating financial position. Financial stress in the latter instance can result from any number of factors: strong net migration out of the neighborhood, a long and expensive backlog of code violation citations and fines, or a steady deterioration in the quality of the housing—sometimes by design of the landlords. Whatever the specific reasons, housing that no longer produces net income for the owner or landlord can help place the person (and perhaps the coinvestors) in a financially precarious position. The clues to determining whether the financial condition of a building or a real estate corporation would make arson-fraud attractive lie in the financial records of investment, income, and tax depreciation.

Short-Term Business Problem

The businessperson on the brink of insolvency faces financial stress that is more severe than the one who faces a short-term problem, such as a slack period in a seasonal business or an unforeseen problem of cash flow. Because of the regularity with which insurance settlements occur (when claims are not denied), the businessperson who selects arson can be fairly sure of having much of the money or all of it in hand within a short period of time. One reason to suspect that a short-term business problem, rather than a more serious one, led to the arson is the absence of creditors threatening to force the owner into bankruptcy, and thus the absence of a bankruptcy filing. An examination of the business's books enables the investigator (or accountant) to infer better whether the cash-flow problem was the likely motive for arson.

Desire to Relocate or Remodel Arsons do occur in businesses that are subject to quickly shifting consumer tastes, and this type of arson-fraud scheme may be motivated by the desire of the owner to secure enough money to remodel or move. In this way, the insured feels able to keep up with changing tastes or to move to a more fashionable location with better market potential. Examples of businesses vulnerable to these trends are beauty salons, "theme" restaurants, and furniture stores. Frequently, such owners arrange for the arson because they realize that shifting tastes have caught them unprepared. However, an owner may also sense the onset of a new trend in its early stages and try to avoid financial distress and arrange for the arson to occur early enough to remodel or move by using the insurance proceeds. In cases where an inventory no longer sells because of shifting tastes, a variety of internal business and supplier records can help establish whether this was the motive. In this type of arson for profit, as in many other types, the actual discomfort of financial distress may not be the motive as much as the perception that the insured will soon be in such distress—unless he or she acts immediately.

Buildup of Slow-Moving Inventory A short-term cash-flow problem can be caused by an unusually large buildup of slow-moving inventory. Although the inventory problem may not appear to the investigator to be a logical motive for the arson, this issue may be easier to understand if the investigator becomes familiar with what are normal or abnormal levels of inventory for a particular type of business, for certain periods of the year. If an inventory problem led to the arson, it is likely that the insured has filed a full and possibly even inflated claim to recoup the value of the allegedly destroyed inventory. For this reason, such documentation may point toward the motive but in itself be insufficient to establish the motive. The investigator should look also for multiple points of fire origin and the attempt to destroy all inventory.

Outmoded Technology Several years ago, two of the largest arson-for-profit cases prosecuted in this country involved companies that failed to keep pace with the technological progress of their competitors. The arson frauds involving the Sponge Rubber Products Company and the Artistic Wire Products Company originated partly because the technologies for making the respective products had changed to more efficient, profitable forms. For whatever reasons, the owners had not kept pace. Where an industrial concern may be destroyed because of these technological problems, tell-tale signs of arson for profit are usually present. First, professional arsonists, even good ones, can rarely destroy a large industrial facility simply by burning it. Incendiary devices, sometimes involving explosives, may be required. Remnants and residues of these can often point to a "professional" arson job. Second, books and business records of the companies often reveal financial stress in ways such as corporate debt reorganizations as well as documented searches for new capital or drastic changes in marketing strategies prior to the arson. Third, since an owner involved in an industrial arson may claim that a labor-management grievance led to it, investigators should search for documentation on formally filed labor grievances, both with the local union and with state and federal regulatory bodies, in order to confirm or deny the validity of such a claim.

Satisfaction of a Legal or Illegal Debt

The businessperson or home owner whose property is destroyed by fire does not always broadcast clear signals of financial stress. One reason for this is that the source of the stress may not be apparent. It may not show up in the books of a business or in other indicators such as divorce or bankruptcy records. For example, if the owner incurred an illegal loan-sharking debt that the lender has called in, the tremendous pressure and threats of violence can make an incendiary fire an acceptable risk to the business owner. On many occasions, the owner either sets the fire or arranges for it to be set. In others, however, the loan shark sets it or has it set, knowing that the businessperson has

fire and perhaps other (e.g., business interruption) insurance in force.

Evidence of an illegal debt will be difficult to locate if the investigator follows only the "paper trail" from the insured to his or her business and personal records of transactions. If arson to satisfy an illegal debt is suspected, it is important for the investigator to seek out information on the owner's actions that led to the indebtedness—for example, a recent gambling junket, heavy betting during the sports season, or borrowing from a loan shark for a highly speculative venture that initially appeared to have enormous profit potential but later failed to meet expectations. When the trail leads to an illegal debt involving the insured but his or her denial of any involvement is convincing, the investigator should examine the possibility that the loan shark arranged the fire without the insured's knowledge or consent.

Purely Fraud Schemes as the Primary Motive

Many types of arson occur because of the actual or anticipated problem of financial stress; others result from schemes where there was not, and probably would not be, any financial problem. These types of arson-fraud schemes result from the planning and plotting of professional fraud schemers and their associates. Their objective is to defraud insurance companies, as well as banks and even creditors, of as much money as possible. Some of the common types of frauds encountered by investigators follow.

Redevelopment In cases where a defined tract has been designated for receipt of federal redevelopment funds, owners and investors may stand to make more money if existing buildings on the tract are razed at no cost to themselves. Arson is a convenient vehicle, for although it may not destroy the building, the city or redevelopment authority will usually raze the remains at no cost to the owner, especially if the building is a safety hazard. Investigators who study tracts designated for redevelopment can often plot which blocks and even which buildings may burn as a result of redevelopment fraud schemes. Owners who decide to arrange this type of arson realize that if the building is only partly damaged, the adjusted insurance settlement may pay for repairs (which they do not want) but not for rebuilding. Therefore, in the interest of ensuring maximum destruction, professional arsonists are likely to be called on for their expertise.

Building Rehabilitation In order to improve the condition of old or run-down dwellings, a variety of federal and state loan and loan insurance programs are available for housing rehabilitation. Certain unscrupulous owners, contractors, and others who know the "rehab" business realize that they stand to reap huge profits by obtaining funds to make repairs and then claiming that fire destroyed the rehabilitated unit. In most cases, the claimed repairs were not made, or they were only partially completed, or they were done with inferior (cheaper) materials. Therefore, in addition to reaping a profit from that portion of the loan that was not used to buy materials and pay laborers, this type of arsonist often files insurance claims for the full amount of the allegedly completed work. In addition to arson and insurance fraud, such persons commit a variety of frauds against the federal or state government that provides the rehabilitation program assistance. Financial records should indicate the cost of the work actually done.

Real Estate Schemes In many core urban areas, the most common form of arson for profit involves the destruction of dilapidated multifamily housing. Because such housing is usually in an advanced state of disrepair, there may be little if any financial stress facing the owners. This is so because either the owner recouped the investment through depreciation of the building and through rent gouging or the owner recently purchased the building for a small fraction of the amount for which it was insured. The typical MO involves an owner purchasing the housing for a small cash-down payment, often accompanied by a large, unconventional mortgage. The owner then sells the building to another speculator (usually an associate) for an inflated amount, again with little money down and a large mortgage. Often the building is insured not only for the inflated, artificial value of the second sale but for the replacement value of the building, which is even greater. Then the building burns, the policyholder is almost routinely paid, and the speculating schemers split the proceeds according to a preset formula.

To reap the maximum profit from this type of scheme, the speculators often involve one or more kinds of specialists:

- Several arsonists, so that one arsonist will not know all the plans or be easily recognized because of repeated trips to the neighborhood
- A public insurance adjuster to help inflate the claim on the building
- A realtor who scouts around for "bargain" properties to buy
- An insurance agent who may be corrupted and who is helpful in insuring buildings far beyond what normal, reasonable underwriting standards would permit

This type of real estate–arson scheme is very lucrative, and its perpetrators realize that the greater the number of buildings burned, the greater the profits. Soon, another speculator, perhaps in league with a contractor or realtor, sees how "well" the first speculator is doing, and out of greed the latter begins the same type of arson scheme, creating a chain reaction. The idea spreads to still other speculators, and shortly an entire city can find itself in the midst of a real estate arson-for-profit epidemic.

Planned Bankruptcy Although this variation of arson for profit is not encountered often, its incidence does seem to be growing. In a typical bankruptcy fraud, the owner establishes a business and buys quantities of goods on credit. The owner pays the first few creditors quickly and in cash in order to increase the volume of merchandise he or she can then buy on credit. The inventory is then sold, often surreptitiously through another company or to a fence, and then the business declares bankruptcy. Often the creditors are left with large numbers of unpaid bills. One way to satisfy them is by paying them off with insurance proceeds obtained after a "mysterious" fire in the business. Additional money is generated from such a fraud scheme because the owner represents in the fire insurance claim that substantial amounts of inventory were destroyed, when in fact merchandise was purposely moved out before the fire. Occasionally, a cheaper grade of merchandise is substituted in its place. Because the creditors are paid, their incentive to complain or report the probable fraud is reduced. Because the destroyed records of such inventory are hard to reconstruct, it is difficult to determine exactly what was destroyed in the fire, and hence its value. Also, since bankruptcy-fraud fires always seem to destroy the office and files where the books are kept, it is difficult for the investigator to reconstruct the flow of money into and out of the business, as well as the flow of merchandise.

Arson Generated by Third Parties

This is another broad category of arson for profit, where the beneficiary of the fire is not the owner-insured but a third party who arranges for the fire out of some economic motive. Because the insured is really the major victim here, rather than the culprit, the investigator must determine whether a third-party arson for profit did occur in order to avoid targeting the wrong individual. The following are some examples of major forms of third-party arson.

Elimination of Business Competition

This type of scheme is motivated by someone who seeks to create a business monopoly or at least to maintain a competitive edge. Businesses most prone to this type of arson are those that stand to suffer from too great a concentration of similar businesses in a limited geographic area. Examples include restaurants, taverns, and sex-oriented establishments (e.g., topless bars, adult bookstores, and massage parlors), which need to generate a large volume of business in order to make a profit. Increased competition can pose an economic problem to similar businesses in a limited area, which can cause some or all of them a degree of financial distress. Consequently, the financial records of a burned business may indicate the existence of financial problems that could lead the investigator to the mistaken assumption that the owner arranged the fire in order to obtain relief from that condition. Actually, in this example, a competitor is more likely to set the arson in order to improve his or her business situation.

The following case illustrates the type of arson in this category.

A brand-new nightclub had recently been opened in fairly close proximity to an older nightclub. The new nightclub was highly successful and started to draw business away from the old nightclub. Two employees of the old nightclub thought they would take matters into their own hands and "torch" the new nightclub one night after it closed, in hopes that this would help get back some of the old club's customers. Sometime during the early morning hours these two individuals broke into the new nightclub and set out eight 2½-gallon cans of gasoline at strategic locations throughout the business. Three 12-inch pipe bombs were then inserted into three of the cans of gasoline. The fuses were lit, and the individuals quickly fled the business and drove away. Unbeknown to the would-be arsonists, the gasoline-soaked black powder could not be ignited. Thus, when the fuse finally made contact with the black powder, nothing happened. The following morning, when the business was reopened, the unexploded devices and cans of gasoline were found. (See Figures 18-6 and 18-7.)

▲ **FIGURE 18-7**
Internal view of pipe bomb found at nightclub
This photograph depicts the pipe bomb that was used in conjunction with the can of gasoline in Figure 18-6. Pipe bombs have been a favorite device of arsonists for years, owing to the inexpensive costs of the materials used to construct them. International and domestic terrorists have also used pipe bombs in their efforts. (Courtesy of Michael M. Gonzalez, Chief of Fire Investigations, Tampa Fire Department, Tampa, Florida)

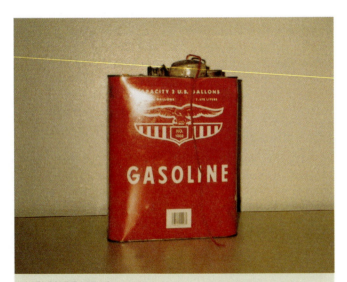

▲ **FIGURE 18-6**
Pipe bomb and gasoline found at nightclub
A pipe bomb intended to be used in conjunction with a can of gasoline. A hole was cut out of the top of the gasoline can between the handle and the lid to allow the bomb to be inserted into the can. The pipe bomb was immersed into the can. It was at this point that the gasoline saturated the inner workings and got the gunpowder wet, therefore making it impossible to ignite. (Courtesy of Michael M. Gonzalez, Chief of Fire Investigations, Tampa Fire Department, Tampa, Florida)

During the initial investigation, it was suspected that at least one of the possible motives for this attempted arson was to eliminate competition with the older nightclub. Thus, the investigators focused their efforts on the owners and employees associated with the older nightclub. Several days after the attempted arson, an investigative inquiry was made at the nightclub and it was determined that two employees had recently left town and were working in a companion business of the old club 260 miles away. Not surprisingly, the sudden departure of these individuals caused them to emerge as major suspects. Their fingerprints, which were on file, were compared with fingerprints found on the gasoline cans, and a positive fingerprint identification was made of both suspects. Unfortunately, the suspects had assumed that any fingerprints they left on the cans would be destroyed once the cans were ignited, so they failed to take any precautions to ensure their fingerprints were not left on the cans. They were subsequently arrested and convicted of attempted arson. An interesting sidelight to this was the presence of a handwritten number on one of the pipes. After checking with several local hardware stores in the general area of both businesses, the investigators determined that the number was actually the price of the pipe and had been handwritten on it by one of the hardware store employees (Figure 18-8). The employee who had written the number

on the pipe was not able to make an identification of the individuals who had purchased it, but the possibility of an identification had to be considered by investigators.

Although this was not considered to be an organized crime–related arson attempt, the same category of arson is fairly common when an organized-crime figure maintains a financial interest in this type of business and either seeks a monopoly or offers to hire out his or her services to create the monopoly for a client or associates in that business. In either case, it is important to involve investigators who are familiar with organized-crime intelligence gathering and investigation when elimination of business competition is suspected as a motive for arson.

Extraction of Extortion Payments

The identity of the criminal who drives out competitors by burning them out may not be known to the victim. However, offenders who demand extortion payments to let someone remain in business will necessarily identify themselves (if only through their collectors) in order to effect timely payment. In this motive pattern, the arson may be a warning signal to a businessperson to "pay up or else," or it may be a signal to similar businesstypes to either pay or wind up like the burned-out victim. This pattern is similar to that found in the elimination of business competition, in that an organized-crime figure or someone who wants to appear to victims as such a figure (e.g., a juvenile gang leader) is often behind this type of scheme. Investigators who suspect this motive should examine the possibility of extortion payments being demanded of similar businesses in the locality.

Labor-Management Grievances

Arsons in business establishments may be the result of an unresolved labor-management grievance for which the perpetrator felt there was insufficient redress or resolution. Investigators should be careful to distinguish whether this type of arson is part of a more regularized pattern of violent activity in the industry or whether it could have resulted from a lone disgruntled employee. It is important to approach the possibility of this motive pattern carefully, because it can occur in an industry that is feeling the effects of an economic downturn, and thus the management logically may be reluctant to accede to labor demands because of their cost. Therefore, the financial records of the business, as well as of the entire industry, may signal financial stress. In reality, the arson may have been caused by an employee unsympathetic to that economic condition. Investigators who suspect this motive pattern should examine the history of labor-management grievances in the business by reviewing records of complaints filed with state and federal labor regulatory agencies.

OTHER MOTIVES FOR ARSON

Revenge-Motivated Arson

Revenge-motivated fires are set in retaliation for some injustice, real or imagined, perceived by the offender. Often revenge is an element of other motives. Concept of mixed motives is discussed later in the chapter. The primary motive of revenge can be divided into four subgroups.

Personal Revenge

The subgroup with a personal revenge motive, as the name implies, uses fire to strike at an individual owing to a personal grievance. This one-on-one retaliation may be a one-time occurrence and not the product of a serial arsonist. Triggering such retaliation may be an argument, a fight, a personal affront, or any of an infinite array of events perceived by the offender to warrant retaliation. Favorite targets include the victim's vehicle, home, or property possessions.

Societal Retaliation

Perhaps the most dangerous of the revenge-motivated arsonists is the one who feels he/she has been betrayed by society in general. This type of person generally suffers from a life-long feeling of inadequacy, loneliness, persecution, and/or abuse and strikes out in revenge against a society perceived to have wronged him or her. Such a person may suffer from a congenital condition affecting appearance or health. The targets are random and fire-setting behavior often escalates. All known cases involve serial arsonists.

Institutional Retaliation

Arsonists with retaliation against institutions in mind focus on such institutions as government, education, military service(s), medicine, religion, or any other entity reflecting and representing the establishment. Often these arsonists are serial arsonists, striking repeatedly at these institution(s). The offender, in such cases, uses fire to settle grievances with the institution and to intimidate those associated with it. Buildings housing the institutions are the most frequently selected targets.

Group Retaliation

Targets for group retaliation may be religious, racial, fraternal (such as gangs or fraternal orders), or other groups. The offender tends to feel anger toward the group or members of the group collectively, rather than anger at a specific individual within the group. The target may be the group's headquarters, church, or meeting place, or symbolic targets such as emblems or logos, regardless of what they are attached to. Arsonists motivated by group retaliation sometimes become serial offenders.[18]

DETECTION AND RECOVERY OF FIRE-ACCELERANT RESIDUES

Because flammable liquids flow to the lowest level, heat travels from this level up, and the charring on the bottom of the furniture, ledges, and shelves will be as deep as, or deeper than, the charring on the top.[19]

After a fire has been extinguished, the floor should be carefully cleaned. Many signs may be found there, such as charred, inkblot-like outlines of flammable liquids. A rug that appears charred all over may, when dried out and swept with a stiff broom, show a distinct pattern of the flammable liquid. This pattern occurs because the liquid is absorbed into the nap of the rug and burns more heavily. Flammable liquid usually soaks into the joints of wooden flooring, and as a result the joints will be heavily burned.

The baseboards and sills should be checked, because flammable liquid often runs under and chars them on the bottom. Corners of the rooms should also be checked, because few floors are perfectly level, and flammable liquid often runs into and burns out the corners. In most common household fires, the corners at floor level are least damaged. The depth of charring in the floor and ceiling should be compared. If the floor is charred as much as or more than the ceiling, this indicates a flammable material directly at floor level. In the average fire, the floor temperature is only about one-third that of the ceiling.

When gasoline or similar material is suspected to have been thrown on porches or buildings without basements, especially those with single constructed flooring, the soil beneath the burned area should be checked. The investigator should dig 1 or 2 inches into the earth and smell for the odor of flammable liquids. A vapor tester is better for this purpose, because flammables such as alcohol have little or no odor in cold, wet earth.

If recovered material is suspected of containing flammable liquids, it should be sealed in an uncoated metal paint can, not in plastic bags or plastic containers. Uncoated metal paint cans can be purchased at almost any hardware store. Plastic should never be used because it gives off hydrocarbons that contaminate the material. The container should be tightly sealed to minimize evaporation or contamination. Evidence tape should be used to ensure integrity of the chain of evidence. The container may also be marked for identification purposes with permanent ink. Before they can be analyzed, accelerant residues must first be separated from the ashes, wood, carpeting, or other material in which they are found. This extraction is usually accomplished by simple, steam, or vacuum distillation. These are listed in increasing order of efficiency, particularly for petroleum products, and increasing complexity of apparatus. Steam distillation and vacuum distillation are capable of extracting 65 percent of any gasoline from debris; for fuel oil, the efficiencies are 30% and 90%, respectively.[20]

SCIENTIFIC METHODS IN ARSON INVESTIGATION

The presence of flammable liquids may establish arson and sometimes link a suspect to the fire.[21] The objection is sometimes raised that identifiable amounts of liquid fire accelerants rarely survive a fire, and efforts to detect them would be largely wasted. But arson investigators often find accelerant residues, and accelerants can survive fires. One expert, for example, performed the following experiment: He poured 2½ gallons of kerosene over furniture and rugs in one room of a wooden building, and 1 gallon of gasoline over straw in another room, and then he left a trail of gasoline as a fuse. The building was allowed to burn freely and completely. He was able to extract identifiable amounts (more than 1 milliliter) of both kerosene and gasoline from the debris.[22]

The areas most likely to contain residues of liquid fire accelerants—floors, carpets, and soil—are likely to have the lowest temperatures during the fire and may have insufficient oxygen to support the complete combustion of the accelerant. Porous or cracked floors may allow accelerants to seep through to underlying earth. Numerous instances have been recounted of the excellent retention properties of soil for flammable liquid.[23] Another place where accelerants may be discovered is on the clothes and shoes of a suspect.

Because each method of accelerant detection (including the human nose) has a threshold of sensitivity, another question that arises is the vapor concentration that is produced by accelerant residues. Some idea of the order of magnitude can be obtained from the experiment of two experts. They burned small (2-milliliter) samples of various accelerants for 30 seconds and then measured vapor concentrations ranging upward from 60 parts vapor per million of air—within the range of detection of currently available portable detectors and generally, but not always, well above readings produced by hydrocarbons from such things as burnt wood and burnt mattresses.[24]

Another way of looking at the potential vapor concentration is to consider the following hypothetical case: Suppose that a gallon of gasoline is used to accelerate a fire in a 15-by-15-by-8-feet room and that 1% (39 milliliters) survives the fire in cracks in the floor. (The residue would consist of higher boiling-point components, such as naphthalene.) The subsequent evaporation of 1 milliliter (3%) of the residue would produce an average vapor concentration of 2.7 parts per million throughout the entire room. Such a concentration can be detected with available equipment. Ventilation of the room, of course, dissipates the vapor and generally causes the vapor concentration to be highest at the points where the residues are located, a situation that can be used to advantage in locating evidence samples to be preserved for laboratory analysis.

Detection of Fire Accelerants

Several types of portable equipment are available to the arson investigator for detecting residues of flammable liquids at fire scenes. Some of these use chemical color tests, catalytic combustion, flame ionization, gas liquid chromatographs, and infrared spectrophotometers and ultraviolet fluorescence. The sensitivities, limitations, advantages, and disadvantages of each of these are discussed next.

Olfactory Detection

The sensitivity of the human nose to gasoline vapor is about 1 part per 10 million. Gasoline is a complex mixture of chemical compounds, the proportions of which vary with the source of the crude oil and the type of process used in its manufacture. Benzene and other aromatic hydrocarbons, for example, may constitute from 0.1% to 40% of the mixture. Although no conclusive data on the

sensitivity of the nose to gasoline are available, the sensitivity of the nose to benzene vapor is 0.015 parts per million. Assuming that 15% (or more) of gasoline vapor consists of aromatic hydrocarbons to which the nose is as sensitive as it is to benzene, then the sensitivity to gasoline is 1 part in 10 million (or greater). Thus, the nose is as sensitive as any of the currently available detecting equipment. But there are flammable liquids to which the nose is not sensitive. Another problem is the tendency of the nose to lose its sensitivity to an odor after prolonged or intense exposure to it. Further, the odor of fire accelerants may be masked by another strong odor, such as that of burnt debris. In fact, in one case an arsonist attempted to camouflage gasoline by mixing it with vanilla.[25] Finally, it may be impractical or impossible to search with the nose for accelerant odors along floors or in recessed areas.[26]

Increasingly, agencies are using specially trained canines for the detection of accelerants. They have proved to be quite effective. On occasion such dogs are even brought to the scene of the arson while the fire is occurring in the hopes that the dogs will be able to detect accelerants on individuals who may have set the fire and are in the crowd watching it.

Chemical Color Test Detectors

Chemical color tests may be used to detect both liquid accelerant residues and their vapors. Certain dyes indicate the presence of hydrocarbons by turning red. Dyes are less sensitive and less specific to flammable liquids than other available methods. Dyes also may interfere with laboratory identification of the accelerant. Hydrocarbon vapors can be detected by pumping a suspected sample through a glass container of reagent that changes color in the presence of hydrocarbons. The reported sensitivity of this method is on the order of 1 part per 1,000. Again, the method is less sensitive and less specific (reacting to hydrocarbons that are not fire accelerants) than others available. Its main advantages are low cost and simplicity.[27]

Catalytic Combustion Detector

The most common flammable vapor detector operates on the catalytic combustion principle and is popularly known as a sniffer, combustible-gas indicator, explosimeter, or vapor detector. A **catalytic combustion detector** is portable, moderate in cost, and fairly simple to operate. Vapor samples are pumped over a heated, platinum-plated coil of wire that causes any combustible gas present to oxidize. The heat from the oxidation raises the electrical resistance of the coil, and this change in resistance is measured electronically. A sensitivity (to hexane vapor) on the order of a few parts per million can be achieved with this method. Because oxygen is required for the operation of the detector, its sensitivity is reduced in oxygen-deficient areas, but these are unlikely to occur in arson investigations. (An internal source of oxygen could be fitted to a detector if required.) Another problem is the gradual loss of sensitivity when this type of detector is exposed to gasoline containing lead. Lead deposits form on the platinum catalyst and interfere with its operation.[28]

Flame Ionization Detector

In the **flame ionization detector,** the sample gas is mixed with hydrogen, and the mixture is burned. Ionized molecules are produced in the flame in proportion to the amount of combustible organic gases in the sample. (Pure hydrogen, air, and water vapor produce little ionization.) The degree of ionization is then measured by electrometer. The sensitivity of this method (to methane) is on the order of 1 part in 10 million. It is thus more sensitive but more complex and expensive than the catalytic combustion method.

Gas Liquid Chromatograph

The portable **gas liquid chromatograph (GLC)** adapted for field use (sometimes called the *arson chromatograph*) is one of the most common detectors in arson investigations. The sample gas is first separated into components on the basis of the speed with which they travel through a tube filled with packing material. The amounts of each component are then measured by either a catalytic combustion or flame ionization detector. The sensitivity ranges from a few hundredths of a part per million to a few parts per million, depending on the type of detector used. The main advantage is specificity because of the preliminary separation process. The main disadvantages are its size, weight, and cost. Also, the time required for the analysis of each sample is about 12 hours, a disadvantage in some situations. In addition, there is a setup time of about 1 hour. The operation of the gas chromatograph requires a certain amount of technical training.

Infrared Spectrophotometer

Infrared spectrophotometers can achieve high specificity to flammable liquids and high sensitivity (on the order of hundredths of a part per million). Infrared light of varying wavelengths is directed through the sample, and the amount of light passing through is plotted on a pen recorder. The recording is compared with those of known compounds to determine the identity of the sample. Because the chemical bonds in a compound determine how it absorbs infrared radiation, these recordings (called spectrograms) are unique for different compounds. However, evidence mixed with impurities must be purified before it can be successfully identified. In particular, since water vapor absorbs infrared light, it interferes with the identification of flammable vapors. This is a disadvantage in arson investigation, where water is commonly present. A final disadvantage is the high cost of this type of detector.

Ultraviolet Fluorescence

Ultraviolet fluorescence consists of illuminating the darkened fire scene with an ultraviolet lamp. Certain substances, including constituents of gasoline and its residue, absorb the ultraviolet light and release it as visible light. They appear to glow against the darkened background. The color of the glow is affected by exposure to heat, and so the method also can be used to locate the point of origin of a fire. The only equipment required is an ultraviolet lamp and a portable power supply. The sensitivity of the method appears comparable to that of other methods of detection. The main disadvantage of the method is that it requires extensive testing, particularly to identify fire accelerants to which it does not respond.[29]

INTERVIEWS

To establish possible motives and develop suspects, the arson investigator must interview people who might know about the fire and how it started. The following kinds of people may provide information.[30]

Possible Witnesses

Prospective witnesses include tenants, businesspeople, and customers from the burnt building or surrounding buildings, as well as passersby such as bus drivers, taxi drivers, delivery people, sanitation workers collecting garbage, police patrols, and people waiting for buses and taxis.

Questions to Ask

Did you observe the fire? At what time did you first observe the fire? In what part of the building did you observe the fire? What called your attention to the building? Did you see any people entering or leaving the building before the fire? Did you recognize them? Can you describe them? Did you observe any vehicles in the area of the fire? Can you describe them? Can you describe the smoke and the color of the flame? How quickly did the fire spread? Was the building burning in more than one place? Did you detect any unusual odors? Did you observe anything else?

Firefighters at the Scene

Firefighters can be an invaluable source of information to arson investigators because of their technical knowledge and what they observe at a fire.

Questions to Ask

What time was the alarm received? What time did you arrive at the scene of the fire? Was your route to the scene blocked? What was the extent of burning when you arrived? Were doors and windows locked? Were the entrances or passageways blocked? What kind of fire was it? What was the spread speed of the fire? In what area(s) did the fire start? How near was the fire to the roof? Was there evidence of the use of an accelerant? Was any evidence of arson recovered? Did the building have a fire alarm system? Was it operating? Was there any evidence of tampering with the alarm system? Did the building have a sprinkler system? Did it operate? Was there any evidence of tampering with the sprinkler system? Was there anyone present in the building when you arrived? Who was the person in the building? Did that person say anything to you? Were there any people present at the scene when you arrived? Who were they? Did you observe any vehicles at or leaving the scene when you arrived? Can you describe them? Were there contents in the building? Was there evidence that contents had been removed? Was the owner present? Did the owner make a statement? What did the owner say? What is the fire history of the building? What is the fire history of the area?

Insurance Personnel

The profit in many arson-for-profit cases is an insurance payment. Three people may be interviewed to determine if the profit centers around an insurance claim: the insurance agent or broker, the insurance adjuster, and the insurance investigator.

There may be restrictions on the amount of information insurance personnel can turn over without a subpoena, but the investigator should be able to determine enough to indicate whether a subpoena or search warrant would prove fruitful.

Questions to Ask the Agent or Broker

Who is the insured? Is there more than one person insured? Is the insured the beneficiary? What type of policy was issued? What is the amount of the policy? When was it issued? When does it expire? What is the premium? Are payments up-to-date? Have there been any increases in the amount of coverage? What amount? When did the increase take effect? What was the reason for the increase? Are there any special provisions in the policy (e.g., interruption of business or rental income)? What are they, and when did they take effect? Does the insured have any other policies? Were there previous losses at the location of the fire? Were there losses at other locations owned by the insured?

Questions to Ask the Insurance Claims Adjuster

Did you take a sworn statement from the insured? Did the insured submit documents regarding proof of loss, value of contents, bills of lading, value of building, and the like? Did you inspect the fire scene? Did you inspect the fire scene with a public insurance adjuster? Did you and the public adjuster agree on the cost of the loss? Have you dealt with this public adjuster before? Has he or she represented this owner before? Has the insured had any other losses with this company? (If so, get details.)

Questions to Ask the Insurance Investigator

Were you able to determine the cause of the fire? Did you collect any evidence? Who analyzed the evidence? What were the results of the analysis? Was the cause of the fire inconsistent with the state of the building as known through an underwriting examination? Have you investigated past fires at the location? Have you investigated past fires involving the insured? What were the results of the investigations? Have you had prior investigations involving the public adjuster? Have you had prior investigations involving buildings handled by the same insurance agent or broker? What were the results of these investigations? Does this fire fit into a pattern of fires of recent origin in this area? What are the similarities? What are the differences? Have you taken any statements in connection with this burning? Whose statements did you take? What do they reveal?

Property Insurance Loss Register

The insurance industry maintains a modern computerized data bank, the **Property Insurance Loss Register (PILR),** to keep track of fire, burglary, and theft claims. PILR is a listing of everyone who has an insurable interest in fire claims and a listing of *only* the insureds in burglary and theft claims. Thus, PILR is one of the most effective routes for determining a repeated pattern of claim activity on the part of individuals and organized rings. Most insurance companies are members of PILR and routinely submit data, listing insureds and claim details, to the registry after fire and burglary losses. The information is immediately entered into the PILR data bank; should the name of an insured (or of a person with an insurable interest, in the case of fire losses) have been entered before, a "hit" will be reported to the insurance company that submitted the entry. Hits can vary widely in significance, as shown by the following examples:

- *Probably insignificant:* A major landlord or mortgagee experienced a minor fire at another location 12 months prior to the immediate loss.
- *Inconclusive:* A home owner experienced a $4,000 burglary loss 18 months prior to the immediate fire loss.
- *Suspicious:* A business owner made two expensive burglary loss claims against two other insurers during the 12 months preceding the immediate, very suspicious fire loss under investigation. (Why is the owner having such bad luck, and why is he or she changing insurance companies so frequently?)
- *Highly suspicious:* A home owner or tenant experienced two expensive and suspicious fire losses at previous addresses during the 24 months prior to the immediate loss.
- *Probably incriminating:* An insured has made claims against two different insurers for the same immediate loss under investigation. There can be legitimate circumstances in which double claims are made; for example, the building and some of its contents may be insured by one carrier, while special inventory or equipment is insured by another.[31]

The insurance company that has made an entry is notified only when a hit occurs. Thus, the lack of a PILR response in the claim file may indicate either that there was no hit or that no entry was made. When obtaining the claim file, the investigator should ask the claims adjuster whether PILR entries were submitted and, if so, which individuals were listed on the entries. If no PILR entries were made or if the names of some of the possible suspects with an insurable interest were not included, the National Insurance Crime Bureau (NICB) can request PILR data if it is a party to the investigation.[32] If previous fire, burglary, or theft losses are reported by PILR, it then becomes possible to compare the claimed losses to see whether the same furnishings, inventory, or equipment were already reported lost, stolen, or destroyed. Likewise, PILR's records can be a means of constructing the "big picture" for an arson-for-profit conspiracy. By running the names of every possible suspect in one suspicious fire through PILR and/or the NICB's database, a dozen or more interrelated claims may be uncovered and used to develop evidence against the entire ring. In some states, model arson laws may allow the investigator to easily obtain the claim files for the previous losses from the insurance companies involved. In instances where such laws do not apply or where suspicious prior burglary claims are not covered by the laws, the NICB may be able to secure copies of the previous claims when it is a party to the investigation.[33]

Other Witnesses Concerning Finances of The Insured

A number of other people may have information on the finances of the owner, including business associates, creditors, and competitors. This information may indicate how the owner stood to profit from the burning.

Questions to Ask

How long have you known the owner/insured? What is the nature of your relationship with the owner/insured? Do you have any information on the financial position of the business? Is the owner/insured competitive with similar businesses? Have there been recent technological advances that would threaten the owner/insured's competitive position? Has there been a recent increase in competition that would affect the owner's/insured's position? Have changes in the economy affected the owner/insured's position? Has the owner/insured had recent difficulty in paying creditors? Has the owner/insured's amount of debt increased recently? Has the owner/insured lost key employees lately? Has the location where the owner/insured does business changed for the worse recently? Has the owner/insured increased the mortgage or taken out a second or third mortgage? Has the owner/insured had difficulty making mortgage payments? Do you have any other information about the owner's/insured's financial position?

News Media Personnel

This category includes both the print and electronic media. Individuals affiliated with these groups may have noticed something of value to the investigator or perhaps have video footage of the fire and fire scene. For example, if the arsonist remained in the area after the fire and mingled with spectators, his or her presence may be captured on video and prove quite valuable in an investigation.

The Medical Examiner

The autopsy should reveal whether any victim found dead in the fire was dead or alive before the fire started and what the cause of death was. It is not uncommon for a person to be murdered and the scene made to appear as if the person had been killed by fire. (See Chapter 9, "Injury and Death Investigations," for a detailed discussion of fire deaths.)

Interviewing a Suspect

The following questions are based on the assumption that the person to be interviewed is involved in arson for profit, that the investigator has enough evidence to make an arrest or to convince the subject that he or she is liable to arrest and that the subject is more valuable to the investigation in a cooperative role than as a defendant.

Questions to Ask the Suspect

What method was used to accomplish the arson? Specify whether what was used was an incendiary device, gasoline or another inflammable fluid, or some other means. If an incendiary device was used, be specific as to the type of device. Where did you obtain the incendiary device? If it was improvised, who made it? How much did it cost? Who paid for the incendiary device? Was it paid for by cash or check? If gasoline or another flammable fluid was used, where was it obtained? How much was obtained and used? Were any special techniques used in setting the fire (or causing an explosion) to avoid detection?

Questions to Ask the Torch, Specifically

Are you willing to cooperate in this investigation? How many other people are involved in the arson-for-profit scheme? How are they involved? What role does each person play in the scheme? Explain (in detail) how the scheme works. How did you first become involved in the scheme? How did you meet the other participants? Where did you meet the other participants? Are you still in contact with the other participants? How often do you see them? Where do you see them? What do you talk about when you meet with them? Would you be able to record your conversations with them? Are you willing to record your conversations with them? Would you be willing to introduce an undercover investigator into the group?

Could you introduce an undercover investigator into the group without the other participants' becoming suspicious? How far in advance of an arson are you told about it? What role do you play in connection with the arson (torch, driver, fence, and so forth)? Are you willing to swear to an affidavit for a search warrant? Are you willing to testify before a grand jury? Are you willing to testify at trial? Do you have information on other arson-for-profit schemes?

Interviewing the Target and the Owner

The target of the investigation may be an owner, a landlord, a fire broker, or the like. The interview should take place after obtaining the background information on the fire and after interviewing the individuals previously listed.

Questions to Ask the Target

Tell me in your own words what you know about this fire. When did you first hear of the arson? Who told you? Where were you, and what were you doing before, during, and after the arson? Who was with you? Do you know who committed the arson? Do you have any knowledge of any previous fire at the building? Do you have any knowledge of any previous incidents of any kind and at any location owned or rented by the owner/occupant of the building? Do you know of any recent changes in insurance coverage? Do you know the owner of the arson property? Describe your relationship to the owner. Do you have any financial interest in the burned property?

Questions to Ask the Owner

Tell me in your own words what you know about this fire. How long have you owned the burned property? What was the purchase price? What was the total amount of the mortgage? Who is your insurance company? Agent? Broker? Public adjuster? How much insurance do you carry? Is there more than one policy on this property? On its contents? On rental or business interruption? Have you increased your insurance coverage on the property in the past year? If so, why and at whose suggestion? Have you ever received an insurance cancellation notice on this property? Where were you at the time of the fire? When did you first hear of the arson? Who told you? When were you last in the building? Was the building secured? If so, in what manner? Who else has access to, or keys, to the building? Who was the last person to leave the building? Do you have any knowledge that the sprinkler system or burglar alarm system was on and working? Indicate the name and address of all lienholders. What is the amount of each lien? What was the value of the inventory on hand immediately before the fire? Can you provide documentation for this value? Was any inventory removed from the premises before the fire? If yes, by whom and for what purposes? Where did it go, and why was it removed? Was any inventory removed from the premises after the fire? If yes, by whom and for what purpose? List the inventory removed and its value. Did you set the fire or cause it to be set? Do you know who set it?

Interviewing a Potential Informant Who is Not a Suspect

Before interviewing a potential informant who is not a suspect, investigative efforts should be made to determine if the informant has any police record and, if so, if it could have any bearing on the reliability of the information provided. For example, if a potential informant was previously convicted of arson and perjury, then the investigator should be cautious about acting on that person's information.

Questions to Ask a Potential Informant

How are you currently supporting yourself? Do you have any pending prosecutions against you? Where? What are you charged with? Do you have any information about arson for profit in this city, county, state? How did you acquire this information? Do you know anyone engaged in arson for profit? What roles does that person play in the scheme? How do you know this? What is your relationship with this person or persons—loan shark, bookmaker, fence, other? Where does this person live, frequent? Who are his or her associates? Do you know them? Are they part of the scheme? Have you been asked to involve yourself in the scheme? In what way? Have any of these people talked freely to you about their activities? Have they talked in your presence? What was said? Can you engage them in conversation about past arsons? Future arsons? Would they be suspicious of you? Could you wear a concealed recorder during conversation? Could you introduce an undercover officer into the group? Would you be willing to testify before a grand jury? Would you be willing to testify at trial? Would you be willing to swear to an affidavit for a search warrant? What do you expect in return for your help?

THE ARSON SUSPECT

In some arson investigations, a single prime suspect may emerge and investigative efforts will be focused accordingly. However, in most cases, a number of suspects emerge, and merely establishing that one or more of them had a motive to set the fire is not proof enough for an arrest and conviction. The investigator must also determine which of the suspects had the opportunity and the means to commit the crime. This determination must be related to the background, personal characteristics, past activities, and financial status of each of the suspects. For example, 10 people may have had a chance to set the fire, but only 4 or 5 may have had a motive, and of this number, perhaps only 1 or 2 would risk an arson conviction for the expected profit or satisfaction.

In probing an arson fire, seldom does direct evidence link a suspect with a fire. Because arsonists tend to take elaborate precautions not to be seen near the fire, they are seldom caught in the act. It may be best for the investigator to concentrate on gathering circumstantial evidence and some provable facts from which valid conclusions can be drawn. For example, let us assume that a warehouse fire was ignited by a timing device—a slow-burning candle attached to some flammable material triggered 2 hours before the fire actually started. The owner, who is also a prime suspect, is identified but can prove his whereabouts at the time of the fire. However, he cannot prove where he was 2 hours before the fire. In addition, the structure was locked when the fire department arrived to fight the fire, and the owner is the only one with a set of keys. The owner also took a large insurance policy out on the warehouse a short time ago.

Although far more evidence would likely be needed to arrest and convict the owner, there is sufficient justification for focusing a considerable amount of the investigation in his direction. If some other evidence is found to link him more directly to the fire (say, candles and flammable material found in the trunk of his car), then the circumstantial evidence becomes significant.

PHOTOGRAPHING THE ARSON SCENE

Still Photography

Photographing a fire scene can be a challenge. Adverse conditions—poor lighting, time constraints, inconvenient angles, and so forth—necessitate the use of camera equipment that is reliable and quick because there rarely is time to adjust the focus on every shot or arrange perfect lighting. Therefore, the ideal still camera is one that is fully automatic, such as a 35-millimeter camera with a good-grade film. This type of camera (which is still the one used primarily to capture crime scene images) is more than adequate for taking interior as well as exterior photos. The adjustable setting on a 35-millimeter camera allows close-up photos at approximately 3 feet. In cases where the crime scene photographer wants more detail, photos can be enlarged.

High-end digital cameras for professional use can also be used. The advantages of digital cameras are that the images can be immediately viewed, printed, and if necessary quickly transmitted and disseminated. Polaroid cameras can also be used. They are simple to operate; however, enlargements or duplicates may take some time to get.

The photo session should take at least as long as the physical examination; however, it is not necessary to photograph every step. The investigator should follow the same path in photographing the structure as is followed in the physical examination—the path of the burn trail from the least to the greatest amount of damage. The photos are as important as the written report because they show what happened rather than merely telling what happened.

Ideally, the investigator should be concerned with photographing things and areas that show, in detail, what happened. For example, if there are severely darkened ventilation patterns out of a window or a door, the investigator should photograph them. The investigator should also photograph burn patterns at lower levels and those that show distinct lines of demarcation, melted or stained glass, areas where explosions occurred, broken locks, and areas where the electric service enters the building. If the investigator does not know what happened, detailed photos will help in assessing what took place.

In some cases, it is necessary to compile a panoramic view. This can be accomplished with a composite of several photos that are taped together to create a much larger overview. The area of the fire's origin should be photographed twice, first before the rubble is disturbed and then after the debris has been removed. Severe burn patterns should be documented, especially patterns that show how the fire burned. Burn patterns at the base of doors and underneath door moldings are a strong indication that flammable liquids were used. This is because a fire spreading of its own accord burns upward, not downward.

If clocks are present, the investigator should always photograph the faces of the clocks showing the times they stopped. Fires often cause interruptions in electricity, which means electrical clocks will usually stop within 10 minutes to an hour after the time the fire started. Knowing when the fire started is crucial to the case.

Videotape

Another form of visual documentation is videotaping, discussed in Chapter 3, "Investigators, the Investigative Process, and the Crime Scene." Although the average fire investigation does not require videotaping, it should be done if the investigator reasonably believes that the case will involve litigation.[34]

EXPLOSIVES INVESTIGATION

Under the fire and explosion investigation definition, an **explosion** is a physical reaction characterized by the presence of four major elements: high-pressure gas; confinement or restriction of the pressure; rapid production or release of that pressure; and change or damage to the confining (restricting) structure, container, or vessel that is caused by the pressure release. Although an explosion is almost always accompanied by the production of a loud noise, the noise itself is not an essential element of an explosion.[35] The generation and violent escape of gases are the primary criteria of an explosion.

Types of Explosions

There are two major types of explosions: mechanical and chemical. These types are differentiated by the source or mechanism by which the explosive pressures are produced.

Mechanical Explosions

In **mechanical explosions,** the high-pressure gas is produced by purely physical reactions. None of the reactions involves changes in the basic chemical nature of the substances. The most commonly used example of a mechanical explosion is the bursting of a steam boiler. The source of overpressure is the steam created by heating and vaporizing water. When the pressure of the steam can no longer be confined by the boiler, the vessel fails and an explosion results.

Chemical Explosions

In **chemical explosions,** the generation of high-pressure gas is the result of reactions in which the fundamental chemical nature of the fuel is changed. The most common chemical explosions are those caused by the burning of combustible hydrocarbon fuels such as natural gas, liquified petroleum gas, gasoline, kerosene, and lubricating oils.

An example of a chemical explosion is the one that destroyed the Alfred P. Murah Federal Building in Oklahoma City several years ago. In this case, the convicted and subsequently executed bomber, Timothy McVeigh, loaded a van with 4,000 pounds of ammonium nitrate (commonly used as a fertilizer) that had been soaked in fuel oil and detonated with high explosives. The destructive force of such a device is enormous. The explosion killed 167 people.[36] (See Figure 18-9.)

Investigating the Explosion Scene

The objectives of the explosion scene investigation are no different from those for a regular fire investigation: to determine the origin, identify the fuel and ignition sources, determine the cause, and establish the responsibility for the incident. A systematic approach to the scene examination is just as important in an explosion investigation as in a fire investigation—or even more so—because explosion scenes are often larger and more disturbed than fire scenes. Without a preplanned, systematic approach, explosion investigations become more difficult or even impossible to conduct effectively.[37]

The first duty of the investigator is to secure the scene of the explosion. First responders to the explosion should establish and maintain physical control of the structure and surrounding areas. Unauthorized persons should be prevented from entering the scene or touching blast debris remote from the scene itself because the critical evidence from an explosion (whether accidental or criminal) may be very small and may be easily disturbed or

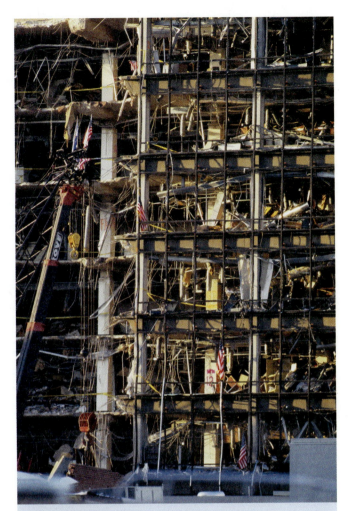

▲ **FIGURE 18-9**
Damage resulting from a chemical explosion
The effects of a chemical explosion that destroyed the Alfred P. Murah Federal Building in Oklahoma City. The destructive force of this chemical explosion killed 167 people. Timothy McVeigh was eventually convicted and executed for committing the crime. (© Ralf-Finn Hestoft/Corbis)

moved by people passing through. Evidence is also easily picked up on shoes and tracked out. Properly securing the scene also tends to prevent additional injuries to unauthorized and/or curious persons who may attempt to enter an unsafe area. As a general rule, the outer perimeter of the incident scene should be established at one and a half times the distance of the farthest piece of debris found. Significant pieces of blast debris can be propelled great distances or into nearby buildings or vehicles, and these areas should be included in the scene perimeter. If additional pieces of debris are found, the scene perimeter should be widened.

The investigator should establish a scene pattern. Investigation team members should search the scene from the outer perimeter inward toward the area of greatest damage. The final determination of the location of the explosion's epicenter should be made only after all the scene has been examined. The search pattern itself may be spiral, strip/line, grid, zone/quadrant, or pie/wheel. (See Chapter 3, "Investigators, the Investigative Process, and the Crime Scene," for a detailed description of these patterns.) Often the particular circumstances of the scene dictate the nature of the pattern. In any case, the assigned areas of the search pattern should overlap so that no evidence is at the edge of any search area.

It is often useful to search areas more than once. When this is done, a different searcher should be used on each search to help ensure that evidence is not overlooked. The number of actual searchers will depend on the physical size and complexity of the scene. The investigator in charge should keep in mind, however, that too many searchers can often be as counterproductive as too few. Searchers should be briefed as to the proper procedures for identifying, logging, photographing, marking, and mapping the location of evidence. The location of evidence may be marked with chalk marks, spray paint, flags, stakes, or other marking means. After being photographed, the evidence may be tagged, moved, and secured.

Structures that have suffered explosions are often more structurally damaged than those burned in a fire. The possibility that a floor, wall, ceiling, roof, or entire building will collapse is much greater and should always be considered. Explosion scenes that involve bombings or explosives have added dangers. Investigators should be on the lookout for additional devices and undetonated explosives. The modus operandi (MO) of some bomber-arsonists includes using secondary explosive devices specifically targeted for the law enforcement or fire service personnel who will be responding to the bombing incident.

Locating and Identifying Articles of Evidence

Investigators should locate, identify, note, log, photograph, and map any of the many and varied articles of physical evidence. Because of the propelling nature of explosions, the investigator should keep in mind that significant pieces of evidence may be found in a wide variety of locations, including outside the exploded structure, embedded in the walls or other structural members of the exploded structure, in nearby vegetation, inside adjacent structures or vehicles, or embedded in adjacent structures. In the case of bombing incidents or incidents involving the explosion of tanks, appliances, or equipment, significant pieces of evidence debris may have pierced the bodies of victims or be contained in their clothing.

The clothing of anyone injured in an explosion should be obtained for examination and possible analysis. The investigator should ensure that photographs are taken of the injuries and that any material removed from a victim during medical treatment or surgery is preserved. This is true whether the person survives or not. Investigators

should note the condition and position of any damaged and displaced structural components, such as walls, ceilings, floors, roofs, foundations, support columns, doors, windows, sidewalks, driveways, and patios. Investigators should also note the condition and position of any damaged and displaced building contents, such as furnishings, appliances, heating or cooking equipment, manufacturing equipment, victim's clothing, and personal effects. Investigators should note the condition and position of any damaged and displaced utility equipment, such as fuel gas meters and regulators, fuel gas piping and tanks, electrical boxes and meters, electrical conduits and conductors, heating-oil tanks, parts of explosive devices, or fuel vessels.

Investigators should identify, diagram, photograph, and note pieces of debris that indicate the direction and relative force of the explosion. They should keep in mind that the force necessary to shatter a wall is more than that necessary to merely dislodge or displace it and that the force necessary to shatter a window is less than that necessary to displace a wall but more than that necessary to blow out a window intact. The greater the force, the farther pieces of debris will be thrown from the epicenter.

Investigators should log, diagram, and photograph varying missile distances and directions of travel for similar debris, such as window glass. Larger, more massive missiles should be measured and weighed for comparison of the forces necessary to propel them. The distance as well as the direction of significant pieces of evidence from the apparent epicenter of the explosion may be critical. The location of all significant pieces should be completely documented on the explosion scene diagram, along with notes as to both distance and direction. This enables investigators to reconstruct the trajectories of various components.

Collecting Evidence at the Explosion Scene

After locating and identifying articles of evidence, the investigator begins the collection process. The collection of evidence at the explosion scene is a form of scene documentation that involves among other things the correct selection and use of containers in which to hold the evidence materials. The containers should be selected according to the type of evidence recovered and should afford sufficient protection to the materials that would permit their collection, storage, transport to the laboratory for examination, and subsequent use in any legal proceedings. Various containers depicted in this chapter can be used to contain evidence from bombing crime scenes.[38]

The containers are available in various sizes, depending on the size of the specimen and number of items of evidence to be placed in it. The items of evidence are collected and logged in depending on where they have been found at the scene—essentially, from which grid or

▲ **FIGURE 18-10 Collecting evidence at the bomb scene**
Evidence collection containers include, among others, (a) antistatic polyethylene bags, (b) biohazard bags, (c) metal cans, (d) paper bags, and (e) Ziplock polyethylene bags. (Copyright © 2006 From *Practical Bomb Scene Investigation* by James T. Thurman. Reproduced by permission of Taylor and Francis, a division of Informa plc.)

designated collection area. In the grid collection method, (discussed in much greater detail in Chapter 3, "Investigators, The Investigative Process, and the Crime Scene"), all similar items of evidence from one grid can be placed into one container. However, this does depend on the quantity of materials in that grid and the type of laboratory examination to be requested on those items. Consider the container guides for collection of evidence materials in Figures 18-10 and 18-11. For instance, in one grid the search team finds evidence that will not have to undergo residue analysis. This evidence can be placed in

a polyethylene Ziplock bag. In yet another grid, pipe fragments, logically ones containing the explosive main charge, are present, along with pieces of miscellaneous debris. Because the pipe fragments would require residue analysis, they would be placed in a metal can or a nylon bag and the other materials in a polyethylene Ziplock bag. The use of a nylon bag, can, or glass container for materials requiring residue analysis is necessary to retain the volatile residues and prevent them from permeating through the container. Regular polyethylene or paper bags are not suitable for volatile compounds. The properly

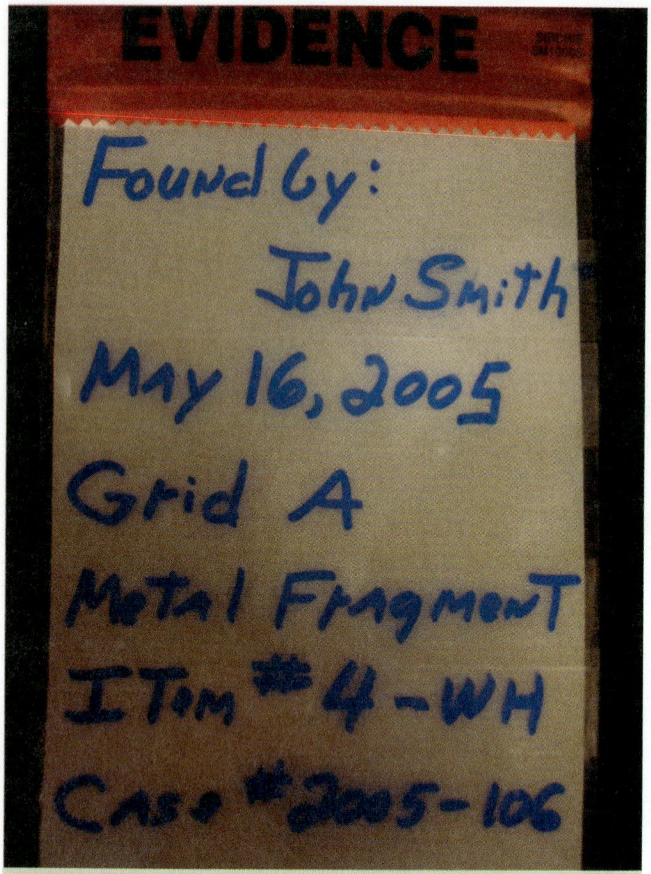

▲ **FIGURE 18-11** **Marking evidence containers**
Evidence containers, regardless or their type, should include
the name of the person finding the evidence, date and location
where found, a short description of the evidence, case number,
and the evidence log item number. The container should be
sealed with tamperproof evidence tape. (Copyright © 2006 From
Practical Bomb Scene Investigation by James T. Thurman. Reproduced by
permission of Taylor and Francis, a division of Informa plc.)

must be appropriately marked for its identification and
accountability. This is effected by placing the following
minimum details on the evidence container.

- The name of the person finding the evidence
- Date
- Location where found
- A short description of the evidence
- Item number
- Case number and the evidence log number

Other data, such as the specific street or area address,
case number, time found, etc., may be included, depending on the departmental policy. These data should be
marked with a permanent marker and then covered with
transparent tape to prevent its inadvertent removal. If
nylon bags are used, most of which do not have a Ziplock
closing feature, they must be heat-sealed to retain the
residue vapors. Other containers, polyethylene and paper
bags, cans, and glass should be closed and sealed with
tamperproof evidence tape (this tape gives a visible indication when it is removed or altered). Evidence too large
for a normal container, depending on the type, can be
wrapped with plastic or paper or placed into a clean
wooden box constructed for this specific purpose. Evidence accountability marking can be effected with the use
of an evidence tag or label attached to the item or the
container.

Depending on departmental policy and the complexity of the scene, the procedures for the collection and
inventory by the evidence custodian vary. One method
is to place the marked evidence containers on the
ground or floor within the grid in which they were
found; the evidence custodian then walks through the
scene, places the evidence item number on each container with his or her initials, enters the item number
and the descriptive data into the evidence log, and then
collects the container. Or the evidence searcher who
found and placed the evidence into the container takes
the evidence and the evidence containers to the evidence custodian for entry into the evidence log, as the
evidence is collected from each grid or a number of
grids. In both methods, the custodian places the item
number on the container with his or her initials and
enters that number and descriptive data into a log. Preference may be given to the first procedure, in which the
custodian, finder, and person placing the evidence into
the container are the same individual. This assists in
any legal proceedings, because only one person enters
all the evidence into the court record, rather than all
evidence searchers entering what they individually
found. This streamlines the proceedings.

The plotting of each item of evidence on the diagram
is not required during the explosion scene investigations. However, should the team leader want selected
items of evidence plotted, the plotting should be completed before the evidence is removed from the location

heat-sealed nylon bag, such as that used for narcotics evidence, provides an adequate barrier to retain residues of
most volatile explosives. Metal cans and glass containers
can be used if nylon bags are not available. It should be
noted that when using nylon to contain sharp objects, the
sharp edges should be padded to prevent the material
from puncturing the bag.[39]

As a general rule, individual items of evidence from
the same grid are placed in separate containers. The use
of separate containers places a great burden on the evidence custodian by having to account for and secure the
many unnecessary containers. However, more than one
container may be used if there is a large quantity of evidence received or for the reasons stated previously
regarding the residue analysis.

Following the placement of evidence into a suitable
container by a member of the search team, the container

where it was found. Therefore, during the evidence identification and collection stages, coordination must be effected between the team leader (who directs what items he or she wants plotted on the diagram and photographed) and the sketcher, photographer, and the evidence searchers or finders. Additionally, at this time the team leader may want to direct the sketcher to indicate, without identifying specific items of evidence with regard to their item numbers, the types of evidence in some or all of the search areas or grid zones. Again, this is not a specific item description but a generic designation of evidence that when reviewed on the diagram can provide a relative direction and extent of the type and quantity of evidence or debris spread in specific areas of the scene. This is sometimes referred to as the "fan" effect: evidence emerging from the epicenter in a narrow arc and extending out into the scene in an ever-widening arc, or fan. The photographer may also document this fan effect.

If a bomb has been used, depending on the type of bomb components recovered, known standards or samples of materials (organic or indigenous to the scene) may be collected and inventoried. These materials include electrical components, switches and wiring, papers, boxes, and metal components from a vehicle or structure. These materials are collected from the scene when the bomb component fragments and paraphernalia may be similar to materials present in the target area at the time of the explosion. Also known as elimination or comparison samples, they are very useful in laboratory examinations by providing a "standard" of the materials at the scene and are used for comparison with the recovered evidence that usually contains not only bomb components but also materials from the scene. By identifying those items as having been present when the bomb exploded one can exclude them as bomb components. As an example, in an explosion in a vehicle in which various types of electrical wires were identified and recovered during the scene investigation, the investigation team also collected a number of the electrical wires from the vehicle wiring harness and submitted them to the laboratory as "known samples." During the laboratory examinations of the debris, a comparison was conducted between the known wires from the vehicle and the recovered wires. This examination resulted in an association between some of the recovered and known wires, effectively eliminating the possibility of those wires having been a part of the bomb. The remaining wires were ultimately identified as being part of the electrical fusing system of the bomb. The laboratory examiners' job would have been more difficult without the known and comparison standards.

Analyzing the Fuel Source

Once the origin, or epicenter, of the explosion has been identified, the investigator should determine what type of fuel was employed. This is done by comparing the nature and type of damage to the known available fuels at the scene.

The available fuel sources must be considered and eliminated until one fuel is identified as meeting all the physical damage criteria. For example, if the epicenter of the explosion is identified as a 6-feet crater of pulverized concrete in the center of the floor, escaping natural gas can be eliminated as the fuel. Chemical analysis of debris, soot, soil, or air samples can be helpful in identifying the fuel. For explosives or liquid fuels, gas chromatography, mass spectrography, or other chemical tests of properly collected samples may be able to identify their presence. (See Chapter 8, "The Crime Lab and Crime Scene Reconstruction," for a detailed discussion of instrumental analysis.)

Air samples taken in the vicinity of the area of origin can be used in identifying gases or the vapors of liquid fuels. For example, commercial "natural gas" is a mixture of methane, ethane, propane, nitrogen, and butane. The presence of ethane in an air sample may show that commercial natural gas was there rather than naturally occurring "swamp," "marsh," or "sewer" gas, which are all-methane.

Once a fuel is identified, the investigator should determine its source. For example, if the fuel is identified as a lighter-than-air gas and the structure is serviced by natural gas, the investigator should locate the source of gas that will most likely be at or below the epicenter, possibly a leaking service line or malfunctioning gas appliance. All gas piping—including that from the street mains or LP-gas storage tanks, up to and through the service regulator and meter, to and including all appliances—should be examined and leak-tested if possible.

Odorant verification should be part of any explosion investigation involving, or potentially involving, flammable gas, especially if there are indicators that no signs of leaking gas were detected by people present. Its presence should be verified.

BOMB THREATS

Bomb threats are numerous and occur for a number of reasons. Since relatively few reported threats actually result in the finding of a bomb or explosive device, law enforcement officers may consider following the procedures discussed next.

Responding to Threats

Telephone Call

There are generally several explanations for why someone would telephone to report that a bomb is about to go off in a particular location. First, the person may have definite knowledge or may believe that an explosive device has been, or will be, placed and may want to minimize the potential personal injury or property damage. Second, the caller may want to create an atmosphere of fear and/or panic, which will, in turn, possibly result in the disruption of normal activities.[40]

When a telephone bomb threat is made, the caller should be kept on the line as long as possible. The call should be taped or monitored on an extension telephone whenever possible. The person answering the call should determine the following:

- The time the call was received
- The sex and age of the caller (on the basis of the caller's voice)
- Voice characteristics of the caller (such as accent, calm, stutter, giggling, stressed, disguised, slow, deep, nasal, sincere, crying, loud, angry, lisp, squeaky, slurred, broken, rapid, excited, normal)
- Background noises

In addition, the person answering the call should ask questions designed to elicit:

- The location of the bomb
- The caller's reason for placing the bomb
- When the bomb is going to explode
- What the bomb looks like
- What kind of bomb it is
- What will cause it to explode
- Whether the caller placed the bomb

Evacuation

The decision to evacuate the premises should be made by the responsible party at the scene. If the responsible party decides to evacuate, law enforcement officers generally recommend that the evacuation be completed, including all searchers, at least 15 minutes prior to the time designated by the suspect as the blast time and remain in effect for at least 15 minutes after the designated time. The officers should assist with the evacuation and crowd control if requested. If officers have reason to believe that an extreme emergency exists, they should take whatever action is necessary to save lives, including an order to evacuate the building.

Industrial Plants, Shopping Centers, and the Like

When a bomb threat is reported at an industrial plant, office building, shopping center, or apartment complex, the assigned officer should contact the owner or manager of the scene and advise the responsible party that search procedures, evacuations, and so forth, are the responsibility of the building owner or person in charge. The law enforcement officer responding should request any specific equipment necessary (fire, utility, etc.). Employees of the business should be briefed on what to look for (e.g., unusual or out-of-place items) and

cautioned that suspicious items should not be touched if located.

Private Homes and Small Businesses

If it is necessary to search a private home or small business and there are no responsible persons present to do a search, officers should conduct the search themselves. Canine teams and/or bomb detail personnel may be contacted for assistance.

Police and Public Safety Buildings

If a bomb threat is received against a police or public safety building by a civilian employee, the employee should refer the threats to a sworn officer and the chief of police should be notified. Usually, the chief will make arrangements to have a systematic search done of the facility. If a possible explosive device is located, the bomb detail should be notified and will then take charge.[41] (See Figure 18-12.)

Search of Abandoned Vehicles

It is apparent from events in the United States, Europe, and the Middle East that vehicles are especially popular for use as explosive devices of mass destruction. If an abandoned vehicle is located in the vicinity of any government building, investigators should use a bomb-sniffing dog to check it out before efforts are made to move it. (See Figure 18-13.)

Searching for Concealed Explosives

Search procedures should always stress measures for protecting life and property. To help detect anything suspicious or out of the ordinary, search procedures should include interviews with persons familiar with the buildings or structures to be searched. Such people include maintenance or security personnel, janitorial staff, and personnel in charge of specific areas. It is important to eliminate some areas in order to focus attention on others that are potentially more dangerous.[42] Search personnel must be cautioned not to move, jar, or touch any suspicious object.

In general, the following search techniques should be employed to ensure an orderly and systematic search: The suspected area should be cordoned off on all sides (by at least 300 feet, if possible). In multistory buildings, at least the floors directly above and below the suspected area should be evacuated. The doors and windows should be left open. All electrical equipment should be disconnected. However, the building's main power source should not be shut down. Entry and exit to the building should be controlled by management with police assistance. Traffic should be directed away from the scene. Radio and cellular-phone transmissions

◀FIGURE 18-12
Bomb squad officers
Officer in a bomb suit preparing to respond to a bomb threat call. In searching a bomb threat site, searchers look for items that are foreign or out of place. If a suspicious object is located, all search operations should be suspended within a radius of 300 feet. The suspicious object should be observed but not touched until a trained bomb technician arrives and takes charge. (Courtesy of Jack H. Adkins, Bomb Squad Commander, Big Bend Bomb Disposal Team, Tallahassee, Florida)

◀FIGURE 18-13
Bomb-sniffing dog
Bomb-sniffing dog checking out an abandoned vehicle with a police handler. If an abandoned vehicle is located in the vicinity of any government building, bring a bomb-sniffing dog in to check it out before efforts are made to move it, if at all possible. (© Mannie Garcia/AFP/Getty Images)

are prohibited in the area of a possible explosive device, that is, within 1,000 feet of a suspected area. Search team members should be selected from volunteer personnel who are most familiar with the building or area to be searched. Areas accessible to the general public should be searched first, unless there is reason to suspect some other location. Searchers should look for items that are foreign or out of place. The search area should be divided equally among search team personnel. A recommended technique is to stand still with eyes closed and listen for the sound of a mechanical timer. An attempt should be made to locate and determine the source of all noise. The search sweep should be systematic, left to right, ground to waist level, waist

to eye level, and eye level to the highest level that can be searched. Each area should be marked and controlled upon completion of the search to avoid duplication and later contamination. Whenever a suspicious object is located, all search operations should be suspended within a radius of 300 feet. The object should be left untouched until the bomb technician determines that it is safe.

What Not To Do

- Do not ignore bomb threats.
- Do not touch suspected explosives.
- Do not touch suspected bombs.

- Do not move suspected bombs.
- Do not move things if you do not know what they are.
- Do not open things if you do not know what they are.
- Do not place items in water.
- Do not shake any items.
- Do not turn, or turn on, any suspicious objects.
- Do not cut any wires.
- Do not pull any wires.
- Do not cut any strings.
- Do not pull any fuses.
- Do not stamp out fuses.
- Do not undo any glued packages.
- Do not pass metallic tools near any suspected bomb.
- Do not move any switches.
- Do not release any hooks.
- Do not smoke near suspected bombs.
- Do not carry the bomb outside.
- Do not place suspected items near heat.
- Do not place any items near vital equipment.
- Do not use insulating materials (bomb blankets or sandbags) unless you know how the bomb works.
- Do not move the bomb away from people. Instead, move the people away from the bomb.
- Do not get near bombs.
- Do not transmit on radios. Turn beepers and all other transmitters off.[43]

Potential Concealment Areas For Bombs

Buildings and Structures

- Elevator wells and shafts, including nooks, closets, false panels, walk areas, motors, cables, etc.
- All ceiling areas
- Rest rooms
- Access doors
- Crawl spaces in rest rooms and areas used as access to plumbing fixtures
- Electrical fixtures
- Utility and other closet areas
- Spaces under stairwells
- Boiler (furnace) rooms
- Flammable storage areas
- Main switches and valves
- Indoor trash receptacles and covered ashtrays
- Storage areas, including record-storage areas
- Mailrooms
- Ceiling lights with easily removable panels
- Firehose racks and fire extinguishers
- Basements
- Areas around windows hidden by drapes or shades
- Inside desks
- Inside storage cabinets and containers
- Under tables and chairs

Auditoriums and Theaters

- Under each seat and into cut seat cushions
- Stage areas
- Microphones, cameras, and radios
- Speaker platforms
- Crawlways
- Tunnels
- Trapdoors
- Dressing rooms
- Rest rooms
- Storage areas
- Ceilings
- Props
- Hanging decorations
- Lighting fixtures
- Sound systems
- Air-conditioning systems
- Roofs
- Heating systems
- Projection booths
- Offices and personal articles

Outside Areas

- Street drainage systems
- Manholes in streets and sidewalks
- Trash receptacles
- Garbage cans
- Dumpsters
- Incinerators
- Mailboxes
- Parked cars, trucks, carts, and outside storage areas[44]

SUSPICIOUS PACKAGES AND LETTERS

Note that items do not have to be delivered by a carrier. Most bombers set and deliver the bombs themselves. The following are precautions that should be followed when encountering a suspicious package or letter:

- If delivered by carrier, inspect for lumps, bulges, or protrusions, without applying pressure.
- If delivered by carrier, do a balance-check to determine if package is lopsided or heavy-sided.
- If there is a handwritten address or label from a company, check to see if the company exists and if it sent the package or letter.[45]

Any of the following characteristics could denote a suspicious package or letter:

- Packages wrapped in string, as modern packaging materials have eliminated the need for twine or string

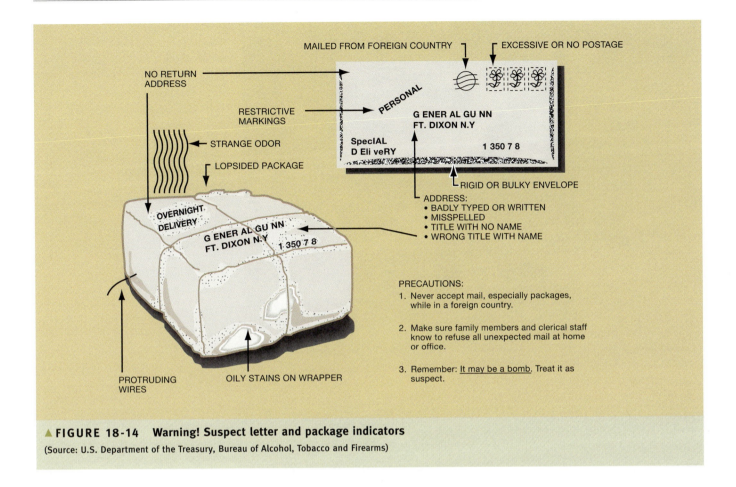

▲ **FIGURE 18-14   Warning! Suspect letter and package indicators**
(Source: U.S. Department of the Treasury, Bureau of Alcohol, Tobacco and Firearms)

- Excess postage on small packages or letters, which indicates that the object was not weighed at a post office
- Any foreign writing, address, or postage
- Handwritten notes, such as "To Be Opened in the Privacy of . . . ," "Confidential," "Your Lucky Day Is Here," and "Prize Enclosed"
- Improper spelling of common names, places, or titles
- Generic or incorrect titles
- Leaks, stains, or protruding wires, string, tape, etc.
- Hand delivery or a "drop-off for a friend"
- No return address or a nonsensical return address
- Delivery before or after a phone call from an unknown person asking if the item was received[46] (Figure 18-14).

Use of Robotic Devices in Moving and Destroying Dangerous Objects

Because handling suspicious packages can be quite dangerous to law enforcement personnel, they have increasingly resorted to the use of robots to move and destroy such objects. The two photos shown depict dual-purpose robots. The first photo shows a robot designed to move potentially dangerous objects; the second depicts a robot engineered to detonate a suspicious object. (See Figures 18-15 and 18-16.)

Bomb Threat Standoff

Law enforcement officers should be aware of what the bomb-threat standoff distances are in order to maximize the safety for both uninvolved citizens as well as themselves. Figure 18-17 provides a detailed description of these distances along with other relevant information.

READING THE BOMBER'S SIGNATURE

Probably one of the earliest identified serial bomb builders in the United States was George Metesky, the "mad bomber" of New York City. Metesky terrorized New York City for 16 years with more than 30 pipe bombs between November 16, 1940, and his arrest in December, 1956. Not only did Metesky build devices that were similar to one another, but he also often included a threatening letter to

◄**FIGURE 18-15**
Robot for moving potentially dangerous objects
This photograph depicts a MAX BR-100 intrepid configured with arm turntable that allows 90° movement of the arm assembly. It permits law enforcement personnel to safely remove a potentially dangerous device while minimizing danger to themselves and others who might be in the area. (Courtesy of HDE Robotics Group, Inc., Fort Worth, Texas)

◄**FIGURE 18-16**
Robot configured with a shotgun that is fired remotely
MAX TR 2000 Enhanced Technical Robot System configured with a Benelli 90 shotgun that is fired remotely. This device can be used to detonate a suspicious object or remove it from its existing location to a safer area. (Courtesy of HDE Robotics Group, Inc., Fort Worth, Texas)

the local power company, Consolidated Edison, within the bomb. He also sent letters to various businesses, including Consolidated Edison and the police, signed with the initials "FP," which were later identified after his arrest as an acronym for "Fair Play." Metesky's case is strikingly similar to that of the most recent serial bomber in the United States, Unabomber Ted Kaczynski, who used the initials "FC," later identified as "Freedom Club," in his bombs.[47] (See Figure 18-18.)

Serial bombers are associated with the term **bombers' signature**, which refers to an identifiable pattern or characteristic of using essentially the same or similar bomb construction components and construction, fabrication, and design techniques for multiple bombs. In other words, forensic examinations can establish a specific pattern of the use of materials and, in concert with the selection of targets, establish a direct link between different bombings, similar to being able to

Terrorist Bomb Threat Stand-Off

THREAT	THREAT DESCRIPTION	EXPLOSIVES CAPACITY[1] (TNT EQUIVALENT)	BUILDING EVACUATION DISTANCE[2]	OUTDOOR EVACUATION DISTANCE[3]
	PIPE BOMB	5 LBS/ 2.3 KG	70 FT/ 21 M	850 FT/ 259 M
	BRIEFCASE/ SUITCASE BOMB	50 LBS/ 23 KG	150 FT/ 46 M	1,850 FT/ 564 M
	COMPACT SEDAN	500 LBS/ 227 KG	320 FT/ 98 M	1,500 FT/ 457 M
	SEDAN	1,000 LBS/ 454 KG	400 FT/ 122 M	1,750 FT/ 534 M
	PASSENGER/ CARGO VAN	4,000 LBS/ 1,814 KG	640 FT/ 195 M	2,750 FT/ 838 M
	SMALL MOVING VAN/DELIVERY TRUCK	10,000 LBS/ 4,536 KG	860 FT/ 263 M	3,750 FT/ 1,143 M

This card supersedes any previous undated versions 11/99

THREAT	THREAT DESCRIPTION	EXPLOSIVES CAPACITY[1] (TNT EQUIVALENT)	BUILDING EVACUATION DISTANCE[2]	OUTDOOR EVACUATION DISTANCE[3]
	MOVING VAN/ WATER TRUCK	30,000 LBS/ 13,608 KG	1,240 FT/ 375M	6,500 FT/ 1,982 M
	SEMI-TRAILER	60,000 LBS/ 27,216 KG	1,570 FT/ 475 M	7,000 FT/ 2,134 M

All personnel must either seek shelter inside a building (with some risk) away from windows and exterior walls, or move beyond the Outdoor Evacuation Distance.

Preferred area (beyond this line) for evacuation of people in buildings and mandatory for people outdoors.

All personnel must evacuate (both inside of buildings and out).

Building Evacuation Distance

Outdoor Evacuation Distance

Threat

[1] Based on maximum volume or weight of explosive (TNT equivalent) that could reasonably fit in a suitcase or vehicle.
[2] Governed by the ability of an unstrengthened building to withstand severe damage or collapse.
[3] Governed by the greater of fragment throw distance or glass breakage/ falling glass hazard distance. Note that pipe and briefcase bombs assume cased charges which throw fragments farther than vehicle bombs.

◄ FIGURE 18-17
Terrorist bomb threat standoff
These two cards depict the terrorist bomb standoff distances that can be used as a guide for law enforcement personnel. (Courtesy of U.S. Government Bookstore, 2007)

associate handwriting with specific components found in the possession of a subject with components used in one or more bombs. In other cases in which a device has been previously linked to a specific person, then that device can be associated with similar or other identical devices. It is far easier to establish that multiple devices were constructed with similar materials and construction techniques by unknown persons or groups rather than by an individual. When investigators establish a single source or person, the results of the intercomparison examinations usually reveal singularly specific materials or construction techniques that preclude participation of others in the building process.

Understanding and recognizing the bombers' signature are significant to the post-blast investigation. There are two primary ways of establishing or recognizing the bombers' signature: first, by the field investigator who sees a similarity between several bombings, and, second, by association of bombings through forensic examinations. By associating two or more incidents, investigators can focus by looking at the totality of information derived from all the incidents, rather from each one individually. Essentially, by combining the investigative data investigators may notice a pattern that can help identify a subject, which would not have been possible by looking at the investigative leads from the incidents separately. One aspect of field investigation data can supplement another lead from a related investigation to form a whole picture, rather than both remaining pieces of an unconnected puzzle.

Similarities between Bombings

Whenever the field investigator believes that there is an association between multiple incidents and that possibly a bombers' signature exists, this belief should be communicated to the laboratory. This is even more important if the incidents are spread over a period of time, because it is entirely possible that the same laboratory examiner who received the first submission, say, from bombing #1, may

◄ FIGURE 18-18   The bomber's signature
Ted Kaczynski (The Unabomber) was responsible for 16 mailed and package bombs that killed three people and injured 23 between 1978 and 1995 in attacks around the county. Federal investigators knew some types of wires used in the bombs were out of production. He always used stamps long past their due dates and scraped the labels off batteries to erase their serial numbers. Some of the bomb components had markings indicating they had been taken apart and reassembled repeatedly. He marked some components with numbers, so when he disassembled and reassembled the bombs he would not make any errors. He is presently serving a life sentence in a federal prison after having been convicted for his crimes. (© AP/Wide World Photos)

not be the same examiner who receives the evidence from incident #2. Also, the evidence from multiple bombings may have been provided to different laboratories. It is possible, however remotely, that forensic laboratories may not associate similar devices if the possibility of association is not drawn to their attention by the field investigator. However, laboratories do have searchable databases in place that should preclude this oversight from occurring.

Association of Bombings through Forensic Examination

The second way in which multiple incidents may be associated with one another is through forensic examination of devices. Most explosions, unless they are large or unless the targets are considered significant by the media, are usually not reported on a national or worldwide basis. As such, it may not be possible for investigators from different parts of the country to know what types of devices may have been used hundreds or even thousands of miles away. Therefore, within federal laboratories, when multiple devices are received in the laboratory from different parts of the country, possibly spanning weeks, months, or longer, an association of componentry and fabrication techniques may be effected through forensic examinations. It is noted that in this age of instant communication and sharing of information by investigators and bomb technicians, the likelihood of incidents and bomb-building technology not being known from one part of the United States to another is also remote. Additionally, as a direct result of this sharing of bomb construction data between state and municipal laboratories, associations between multiple devices may be made in laboratories other than the large federal laboratories.

It is possible to conclude that a person (or persons) made multiple devices with just one point of comparison, but this is rare indeed, just as it is sometimes possible to make a latent fingerprint identification with only one, exceptionally specific point of identification. In most cases, the associations between devices/bombings are effected with multiple points of identification. How many are needed? It is impossible to provide an answer, because every bombing series is different from another. However, the more components used and the more specific the fabrication techniques used, the better the association.

KEY TERMS

accelerant	explosion	Property Insurance Loss
alligatoring	flame ionization detector	Register (PILR)
bomber's signature	gas liquid chromatograph (GLC)	pyromaniacs
burn indicators	incendiary mechanism	spalling
catalytic combustion detector	infrared spectrophotometer	spontaneous heating
charring	layer-checking technique	spontaneous ignition
chemical explosions	mechanical explosions	trailer
effective fire temperatures	plant	ultraviolet fluorescence

REVIEW QUESTIONS

1. If arson is suspected, why should firefighters not alter the premises, such as by mopping up or over-hauling the scene of the fire, especially at the point of origin?
2. What two factors are needed to cause a fire?
3. What is the layer-checking technique, and how can it assist in determining the cause and the origin of a fire?
4. What are some of the more common causes of accidental or natural fires?
5. What types of burn indications can be examined by the arson investigator to assist in determining whether a fire is accidental or incendiary in nature?
6. What are some of the most commonly used ignition and timing devices in the commission of arsons?
7. Why can items missing from the fire scene be as valuable as things remaining at the scene?
8. What are some of the most common motives for arson?
9. Why should uncoated metal paint cans (or similar containers), not plastic bags or containers, be used for the storage of material suspected of containing flammable liquids?
10. What are some of the advantages and disadvantages of olfactory detection in determining

the presence of fire accelerants at the scene of a fire?
11. What types of individuals might be able to provide information relevant to the fire?
12. What is the purpose of the National Insurance Crime Bureau?
13. What are the two basic types of explosions? Briefly describe each.
14. What are the principal objectives of an explosion scene investigation?
15. What is the first duty of the investigator at the scene of an explosion?
16. What criteria should be employed in order to make a determination as to the types of containers that should be used for storage of evidence at the bomb scene?
17. What are the minimum details that should be placed on an evidence container?
18. Once the origin, or epicenter, of the explosion has been identified, the investigator should determine what type of fuel has been employed. How is this typically done?
19. In general, certain techniques should be employed to ensure an orderly and systematic search for explosive devices. What are they?
20. What does the term "bomber signature" mean?

INTERNET ACTIVITIES

1. The Bureau of Alcohol, Tobacco and Firearms provides updates and statistics concerning arson and explosion incidents. Go to the bureau's website at www.atf.treas.gov. Search the site for information on fire and explosion incidents for your state. The website also has information about arson and explosion training for police officers. What topics are covered in the training curriculum?
2. Many large police agencies and/or states have investigative units specializing in arson and bomb

detection. Check several municipal and state police agencies in your region by using websites such as www.officer.com and www.leolinks.com. What are the functions and the responsibilities of these units? Under what conditions do they respond (arson investigation, bomb threats, etc.)? Are any statistics provided concerning the number of cases they have responded to and/or investigated?

NOTES

1. This information was obtained from "Stop Arson Now," a brochure published by the Florida Advisory Committee on Arson Prevention.
2. K. D. Moll, *Arson, Vandalism, and Violence: Law Enforcement Problems Affecting Fire Departments* (Washington, D.C.: Government Printing Office, 1977), pp. 20–21.
3. C. W. Stickney, "Recognizing Where Arson Exists," *Fireman Magazine*, September–December 1960, p. 3.
4. *Touched Off by Human Hands*, 1979. This booklet was originally published by the Illinois Advisory Committee on Arson Prevention in cooperation with the Illinois Chapter of the International Association of Arson Investigation and was reprinted for distribution

by the State Farm Fire and Casualty Company, Bloomington, Illinois. Much of the information in this section was taken from this source, pp. 7–11.

5. Stickney, "Recognizing Where Arson Exists," p. 4.

6. Ibid., p. 8.

7. Ibid.

8. C. W. Stickney, "Recognizing Where Arson Exists," *Fire and Arson Investigator,* October–December 1970; W. A. Derr, "Wildland Fire Investigation: Information from Objects," paper presented at the 18th Annual Fire and Arson Investigators Seminar, Palm Springs, California, June 14–18, 1971.

9. National Fire Protection Association, *921 Guide for Fire and Explosion Investigations* (Quincy, MA: NFPA, 2001), pp. 921–27, 921–28.

10. Ibid., p. 921–33.

11. Ibid., p. 921–33.

12. Ibid., p. 921–29.

13. *User's Manual for NFPA 921—Guide for Fire and Explosion Investigation* 2nd edition, (Quincy, MA) National Fire Protection Association, Inc. 2005, p. 46.

14. Ibid., pp. 921–30.

15. B. P. Battle and P. B. Weston, *Arson: A Handbook of Detection and Investigation* (New York: Arco, 1972), pp. 19–28. Much of the information in this section was taken with permission from this source.

16. Joseph Toscano. *"Motive, Means & Opportunity: A Guide to Fire Investigation,"* American Re-Insurance Company, Princeton, N.J., 1996, pp. 87–88.

17. C. L. Karchmer, M. E. Walsh, and J. Greenfield, *Enforcement Manual: Approaches for Combating Arson for Profit Schemes* (Washington, D.C.: U.S. Department of Justice, 1981), pp. 15–31. This discussion was adapted from this source.

18. Joseph Toscano. *"Motive, Means & Opportunity: A Guide to Arson Investigation,"* American Re-Insurance Company, 1996, Princeton, N.J., pp. 10–23. Much of this discussion of other motives for arson was obtained with permission from this source.

19. Stickney, "Recognizing Where Arson Exists," 1960, pp. 11–12.

20. B. B. Caldwell, "The Examination of Exhibits in Suspected Arson Cases," *Royal Canadian Mounted Police Quarterly,* 1957, Vol. 22, pp. 103–108.

21. J. F. Bordeau, Q. Y. Kwan, W. E. Faragker, and G. C. Senault, *Arson and Arson Investigation* (Washington, D.C.: Government Printing Office, 1974), pp. 77–83. Much of the information in this section was taken from this source.

22. J. D. Nicol, "Recovery of Flammable Liquids from a Burned Structure," *Fire Engineering,* 1961, Vol. 114, p. 550.

23. D. Q. Burd, "Detection of Traces of Combustible Fluids in Arson Cases," *Journal of Criminal Law, Criminology, and Police Science,* 1960, Vol. 51, pp. 263–264; P. Rajeswaran and P. L. Kirk, "Identification of Gasoline, Waves, Greases, and Asphalts by Evaporation Chromatography," *Microchemical Journal,* 1962, Vol. 6, pp. 21–29.

24. R. Milliard and C. Thomas, "The Combustible Gas Detector (Souffer), an Evaluation," *Fire and Arson Investigator,* January–March 1976, pp. 48–50.

25. D. M. Lucas, "The Identification of Petroleum Products in Forensic Science by Gas Chromatography," *Journal of Forensic Sciences,* 1960, Vol. 5, No. 2, pp. 236–243.

26. P. L. Kirk, *Fire Investigation* (New York: Wiley, 1969), pp. 43–44; E. C. Crocker and L. B. Sjostrom, "Odor Detection and Thresholds," *Chemical Engineering News,* 1949, Vol. 27, pp. 1922–1931; and H. Zwaardemaber, "Camera Inoorata," *Perfumery and Essential Oil Record,* 1921, Vol. 12, pp. 243–244.

27. P. L. Kirk, *Crime Investigation, Physical Evidence, and the Police Laboratory* (New York: Interscience, 1966), p. 717; H. P. Wonderling, "Arsonists—Their Methods and the Evidence," *International Association of Arson Investigators Newsletter,* October–December 1953, reprinted in *Selected Articles for Fire and Arson Investigators,* International Association of Arson Investigators, 1975; K. Ol'Khosvsbaya, "Colormetric Determination of Hydrocarbons, Gasoline, Kerosene and White Spent in the Air of Industrial Installations," *Gigiena Truda i Professional'nye Zabolevaniza,* 1971, Vol. 15, No. 11, pp. 57–58.

28. J. W. Girth, A. Jones, and T. A. Jones, "The Principle of Detection of Flammable Atmospheres by Catalytic Devices," *Combustion and Flame,* 1973, Vol. 21, pp. 303–312.

29. C. M. Lane, "Ultra-Violet Light . . . Gem or Junk," *Fire and Arson Investigator,* Dec. 1975, Vol. 26, No. 2, pp. 40–42.

30. C. L. Karchmer, M. E. Walsh, and J. Greenfield, *Enforcement Manual: Approaches for Combating Arson for Profit Schemes* (Washington, D.C.: U.S. Department of Justice, 1981), pp. 249–252.

31. National Insurance Crime Bureau, *Fire Investigation Handbook* (Palos Hills, IL: NICB, 1995), pp. 24, 25.

32. The purpose of the National Insurance Crime Bureau is to investigate questionable insurance claims and cooperate with public law enforcement agencies in securing the prosecution of insurance criminals.

33. National Insurance Crime Bureau, *Fire Investigation Handbook,* p. 26.

34. John Barracato, *Burning: A Guide to Fire Investigation* (Stamford, CT: Aetna Casualty and Surety, 1986), pp. 14–16.

35. National Fire Protection Association, *Guide for Fire and Explosion Investigations,* pp. 921-94–921-100.

36. George Buck, *Preparing for Terrorism* (Albany, NY: Delmar, 1998), pp. xi–xii.

37. National Fire Protection Association, *Guide for Fire and Explosion Investigations,* 1992, pp. 921-103–921-107.

38. T. James T. Thurman *Practical Bomb Scene Investigation* (Boca Raton, FL) CRC 2006, pp. 251–259.

39. Detail packaging instructions for different types of evidence can be found in the FBI Laboratory Division Publication, *Handbook for Forensic Services,* as revised in 2003.

40. *Public Safety News,* Dec. 1996, No. 34.
41. City of Phoenix Police Department, "Operations Order D-5, Explosives and Bomb Threat 495," p. 3.
42. Honolulu Police Department, "Procedure: Bomb Threat," Nov. 18, 1996.
43. Lesson plan prepared by the New Orleans Police Department, "Bombs and Hazardous Devices," Oct. 21, 1996, p. 8.
44. Ibid., p. 11. *Note:* Law enforcement and fire personnel should use the information in this chapter only within the framework of their training and departmental guidelines and policies.
45. This checklist was provided by the U.S. Department of the Treasury, Bureau of Alcohol, Tobacco, and Firearms, 1999.
46. Ibid.
47. James T. Thurman, Practical Bomb Scene Investigation (Boca Raton, FL) CRC 2006, pp. 391–392. This information was obtained from this source with permission.

19

RECOGNITION, CONTROL, AND INVESTIGATION OF DRUG ABUSE

▲   Colombian drug kingpin Ochoa. The illegal drug industry
is truly international in nature. The United States must often
rely on foreign governments to assist in locating and
apprehending drug fugitives.

(© Reuters NewMedia Inc./Corbis)

Currently, every major police department in the United States has assigned—with ample justification—a top priority to the control of drug abuse and related offenses. Most of the departments have narcotics or drug units that specialize in the identification, arrest, and prosecution of drug traffickers, ranging from low-level street dealers to leaders of organized-crime syndicates. As a result, most police agencies have allocated significant resources for narcotics officers, undercover agents, drug surveillance and recovery equipment, and agreements with drug informants. The illegal importation, manufacture, sale, and use of drugs, however, have increased more rapidly than the resources for combating them.

Explanations for the phenomenal growth of drug abuse abound in the literature on this subject. Many cite variables associated with socioeconomic and political conditions. Others suggest that the inability of some individuals to deal with personal stress and emotional problems has led to the increase in drug abuse. Regardless of the contributing factors, police must deal with the violation itself, not the motivations and human conditions that produce it.

This chapter focuses on the categories of drugs that are most commonly encountered by law enforcement officers in their enforcement activities: opium-derived drugs, synthetic narcotics, stimulants, depressants, and hallucinogens. The procedures involved in narcotics investigations are also addressed. Most of the techniques used in investigating dangerous drug and narcotics cases are the same as those used in investigating other cases. The identification of the source of the drug and the risk factors in apprehending a drug suspect, however, make investigations of these cases unique.

Another aspect of drug and narcotics cases that makes the investigation process atypical is the use of drug informants. Drug informants can provide valuable information on various types of drug activity, but compared with informants used in other investigations, they are perhaps the most difficult to manage. Drug informants have different motivations for helping the police, such as fear of punishment for criminal acts, revenge against their enemies, money, repentance, or altruism. Regardless of the motivation, informants who have entered into agreements with police agencies should initially be screened carefully and then, subsequently, be monitored. The chapter concludes with discussions on clandestine laboratories, search warrants, evidence handling, and gangs and drugs.

DRUGS AND SCHEDULING

Officers and agents charged with investigation and interdiction of illegal drug activities are responsible for a vast array of information in order to properly carry out their duties. Although many facts about drugs never change, synthetic drugs provide opportunities for new formulations, higher potency, and more difficult identification by law enforcement. Further complicating the jobs of drug investigators is the fact that the flow of illegal drugs is constantly changing and adapting in response to law enforcement practices, socioeconomic circumstances, market conditions, and availability of product. Therefore, those involved in drug interdiction must stay on top of current information regarding source countries and the types of drugs that may be encountered in the field by law enforcement officers. Frequent updates are available from federal agencies, such as the National Drug Intelligence Center, which publishes drug identification guides with updated photographs and new information.[1] Before undertaking any drug investigation, investigators should also familiarize themselves with the street slang. Commonly used terms often change over time and are different in different parts of the country. Up-to-date information about drug trafficking trends and common or emerging drugs is essential to the credibility of those working with informants or undercover. This type of information also helps law enforcement agencies target and prioritize investigations.

Title II of the Comprehensive Drug Abuse Prevention and Control Act of 1970, also known as the Controlled Substances Act (CSA), consolidated a number of laws related to the manufacture and sale of drugs. **Narcotics,** stimulants, depressants, hallucinogens, steroids, and chemicals that could be used in the illicit production of those drugs were classified by Federal Law as belonging to one of five schedules (Figure 19-1).

OPIATES

Several drugs are derived from the opium poppy (Papaver somniferum). Known as **opiates,** they include opium, morphine, heroin, codeine, and other drugs less well known.

Schedule I

a. The drug or other substance has a high potential for abuse.

b. The drug or other substance has no currently accepted medical use in treatment in the United States.

c. There is a lack of accepted safety for use of the drug or other substance under medical supervision.

Examples: Heroin, LSD, marijuana.

Schedule II

a. The drug or other substance has a high potential for abuse.

b. The drug or other substance has a currently accepted medical use in treatment in the United States or a currently accepted medical use with severe restrictions.

c. Abuse of the drug or other substances may lead to severe psychological or physical dependence.

Examples: Morphine, cocaine, methadone.

Schedule III

a. The drug or other substance has a potential for abuse less than the drugs or other substances in schedules I and II.

b. The drug or other substance has a currently accepted medical use in treatment in the United States.

c. Abuse of the drug or other substance may lead to moderate or low physical dependence or high psychological dependence.

Examples: Anabolic steroids, ketamine, OxyContin.

Schedule IV

a. The drug or other substance has a low potential for abuse relative to the drugs or other substances in schedule III.

b. The drug or other substance has a currently accepted medical use in treatment in the United States.

c. Abuse of the drug or other substance may lead to limited physical dependence or psychological dependence relative to the drugs or other substances in schedule III.

Examples: Valium, Xanax.

Schedule V

a. The drug or other substance has a low potential for abuse relative to the drugs or other substances in schedule IV.

b. The drug or other substance has a currently accepted medical use in treatment in the United States.

c. Abuse of the drug or other substance may lead to limited physical dependence or psychological dependence relative to the drugs or other substances in schedule IV.

Example: Cough medicine with codeine, such as Robitussin AC.

◄ **FIGURE 19-1**

Federal schedule of controlled substance

21 United States Code, Section 812

Opium

One of the first drugs of abuse was **opium.** Its pleasurable effects were known to many ancient civilizations, including the Egyptians, as early as 1500 B.C.E. During the Renaissance in Europe, opium was employed in the treatment of hysteria, making it one of the early therapeutic agents in treating mental disorders.

In the seventeenth century, opium smoking spread throughout China, and opium dependence was recognized as a problem. Opium eating was known in the United States and England during the Revolutionary War. Opium was later used by eighteenth-century doctors to treat venereal disease, cancer, gallstones, and diarrhea and to relieve pain at childbirth.

Opium comes from the poppy plant, whose pod is carefully cut to allow a milky white fluid to ooze onto the surface of the pod. Thereafter, it air-dries into tan beads. It is then carefully scraped by hand and allowed to further air-dry, after which it turns a blackish brown color. Raw opium has a pungent odor and may be smoked, making the user appear sleepy and relaxed. Prolonged use creates both physical and psychological dependence. Raw opium is the source of morphine, heroin, and codeine. (See Figure 19-2.)

Morphine

Morphine is obtained from raw opium; 10 pounds of raw opium yield 1 pound of morphine. A German named Sertner first isolated the substance in 1804 and a few years later named it "morphine" after the Greek god of sleep, Morpheus. The drug was later used in medicine in 1825 as a painkiller and is still used as such today. It is important to understand that morphine is the most effective pain reliever known to man.[2]

The use of morphine increased considerably with the invention of the hypodermic syringe by an Englishman around 1843. The syringe was introduced to this country about 1853 and was used extensively for wounded Union troops during the American Civil War. Some developed physical and psychological dependence, because doctors did not clearly understand the addictive nature of opiates until around 1870.

Morphine appears in tablet, capsule, and liquid forms, has no distinguishing color and provides the medical standards by which other narcotics are evaluated. It is usually administered by injection. The drug creates both physical and psychological dependence in the user, who feels euphoric and seems sleepy or relaxed. The pupils of the eyes may constrict.[3]

Heroin (Diacetylmorphine)

Heroin was developed in England in 1874, but it evoked little interest until about 1890, when it was found to be

▲ **FIGURE 19-2**
Traditional method of gathering opium
Historically, one of the first drugs to be abused was opium. Opium comes from the poppy plant. The poppy pod is cut to allow the milky, white fluid to come to the surface of the pod. After it is dried, it is hand scraped and allowed to be further air-dried after which it turns a blackish brown color.
(© AP/Wide World Photos)
(Source: Drug Enforcement Administration, *The Mexican Heroin Trade*, 2000, www.usdoj.gov/dea/pubs/intel/20014/20014.html)

considerably stronger than morphine. Commercial production of heroin was begun in 1898 in Germany by the Bayer Company. Heroin was advertised as a cure for morphine dependence, but it was soon learned that heroin dependence was even more difficult to cure.

Heroin is an odorless, crystalline, white powder. It is usually sold in glassine paper packets, aluminum foil, or capsules. The darker the color, the more impurities it contains. Being about four to five times stronger than morphine, heroin is the principal drug of addiction among the opium derivatives. It is generally injected.

By the time the heroin reaches the addict, it often has been diluted considerably. Heroin reaching this country is perhaps 20% to 80% pure. Deaths from overdoses are not uncommon and ordinarily occur because a dose was more pure than that to which the addict's body was accustomed. Addicts may also have a fatal allergic reaction to the drug or some substance used to "cut," or reduce, the purity level of the drug, such as powdered milk, sugar, or quinine. Such incidents have routinely been documented at emergency rooms, since hundreds of juveniles and young adults from around the country have been admitted for heroin overdoses and allergic reactions to the "cut" placed in snorted heroin, known as **chiva.**[4] Spanish for heroin (goat), chiva hit the streets across America in the late 1990s, originating primarily from

Colombia. It has a very high concentration level made from clandestine laboratories that normally process cocaine. In addition, the powders are cut with various substances, from ground-up metal, crushed wood, sand, and cyanide to strong nasal constrictors and/or stimulants such as ephedrine and caffeine. Allergic reactions to the "cut substances" have been attributed to hundreds of deaths, as well as to the exceptionally strong concentration of heroin causing accidental overdose. The numbers continue to rise as chiva use escalates along with a spike in smoking black tar heroin (Figure 19-3) derived from chiva processing.[5] The fatal overdose is not always accidental. On occasion, addicts suspected of being police informers have been given "hot shots"—pure heroin—to eliminate them.

In addition to facing the perils of the law, withdrawal, and other aspects of addiction, the drug addict also faces the serious health problems associated with dirty needles. Many suffer STDs (sexually transmitted diseases) and hepatitis B. These are transmitted diseases, so people sharing needles with other drug abusers run the risk of injecting themselves with traces of blood from a disease carrier and thus becoming infected. Drug users who administer their drugs through intravenous injections and share their needles with others face the additional danger of contracting the human immunodeficiency virus (HIV) and subsequently acquired immune deficiency syndrome (AIDS).[6]

Colombia has become a major source of heroin production; the Drug Enforcement Administration (DEA) estimates that as much as 5% of the heroin in the United States comes from Colombia. Although this percentage may not seem high in comparison to the amount of heroin imported from other countries, it should be noted that the rate of importation has grown enormously since the early 1990s.

Seizures of Colombian heroin by the DEA indicate that it is 80% to 99% pure. It is usually a light brown or tan powder. The poppies are being grown in the mountains of the Cauca Province around Popayan. It is anticipated that within the next several years Colombia will become an even more important source of heroin in the United States, because existing organized crime cartels in Colombia have well-established routes developed from years of cocaine smuggling. The high-purity concentration of new heroin derivatives (chiva and black tar) from Colombia is a significant factor in recent heroin overdoses.[7]

Further, with the war in Iraq and the revolutionary change in governments in Afghanistan, significant exportation of heroin from the historical "Golden Crescent" area (Iran, Pakistan, and Afghanistan) is also expected to rise. For years under the Taliban rule in Afghanistan, opium poppy growing and production were severely limited. The offense was punishable by death, often accompanied by the confiscation of private property and land.

▲ **FIGURE 19-3 Powder and black tar heroin**
On the street, heroin is most commonly observed in the powder form, ranging in color from dark brown to white, depending on cultivation location and the level of impurities in the sample. Black tar heroin is named for its characteristic dark color and sticky touch. It is often snorted, smoked, or ingested rather than taken through intravenous injection. Smugglers often transport heroin in concentrated amounts that are "stepped-on" or diluted before individual sales.
(© Uwe Schmid/Corbis) (Source: Drug Enforcement Administration, *The Mexican Heroin Trade*, 2000, www.usdoj.gov/dea/pubs/intel/20014/20014.html)

The rule was often ruthlessly enforced by the Taliban government. Since the U.S. invasion into Afghanistan (in 2002) forcing the ouster of the Taliban government, opium poppy cultivation is again thriving.[8] Unfortunately, continued unrest and revolution are often ripe conditions for drug, gun, and human smuggling. These have been particularly interesting subjects with a strong financial nexus to terrorism. In Chapter 20 (Terrorism), we discuss the financing of terrorism from such sources.

Heroin Cheese

In the past few years the Dallas, Texas, Police Department has raised the alarm about a new and dangerous combination of drugs being used in the city Dallas. Called **heroin cheese**, it is a combination of heroin, approximately 8% (sometimes black heroin), and a large quantity of crushed Tylenol-PM® tablets. Teens have named the drug *cheese* because of its yellowish color (it is really tannish in color). It generally comes in powder form and is administered by snorting through the nose through a tube much in the same way that cocaine is often used (discussed later in this chapter). It costs approximately $2 per dose.

The physical symptoms include:

- bloodshot eyes
- runny/bloody nose
- unexplainable cough
- sleeping a lot
- changes in behavior
- disorientation
- lethargy
- hunger
- severe headaches
- chills
- abdominal pain
- muscle pain and anxiety so severe the user may return to using the drug regularly within one to three days

An increasing number of teenage deaths have been confirmed as a result of an overdose from cheese. Most of the victims who died because of an overdose died in their sleep after a night of partying and were discovered by family members.[9]

Codeine

The alkaloid **codeine** is found in raw opium in concentrations from 0.7% to 2.5%. It was first isolated in 1832 as an impurity in a batch of morphine. Compared to morphine, codeine produces less analgesia, sedation, and respiratory depression. It is widely distributed in products of two general types. Codeine to relieve moderate pain may consist of tablets or be combined with other products such as aspirin; liquid codeine preparations for the relief of coughs (antitussives) include Robitussin AC, Cheracol, and terpin hydrate with codeine. Codeine is also manufactured in injectable form for pain relief.

OxyContin

Another powerful narcotic that is presently sold legally is **OxyContin.** This drug, which is usually prescribed for cancer patients, has pushed aside marijuana, cocaine, and other narcotics as the drug of choice for addicts and teenage abusers. The active ingredient in OxyContin is a morphinelike substance called oxycodone, which is also found in the prescription drugs Percodan and Tylox. But unlike those drugs, which need to be taken in repeated dosages, OxyContin is a time-released formulation that is effective for up to 12 hours. Experts say, however, that addicts can achieve an intensely pure high by crushing the pills and snorting or injecting them. A telltale piece of paraphernalia among adolescent users is a pill crusher, sold by drugstores to help elderly people swallow their medication.[10]

With the abuse of OxyContin on the rise, police in at least three states are reporting a record number of pharmacies being broken into. The homes of people with legitimate OxyContin prescriptions are being robbed, and home invasions are targeting the pills. These patients are often tracked down by relatives who know what is inside their medicine cabinets or by neighbors who hear them talk about their prescriptions. Illegal users are even accosting drugstore customers in parking lots on the hunch that they might be carrying this sought-after drug.[11]

In an effort to deal with this growing problem, drug manufacturers have come up with blueprints for a "smart pill" that would make it more difficult to abuse the drug. The new painkiller is designed to destroy its own narcotic ingredients if crushed into powder for snorting or injecting—the typical manner in which OxyContin is abused to achieve a quick heroinlike nod. (See Figure 19-4.)

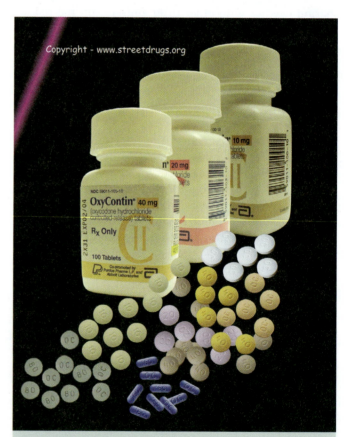

▲ **FIGURE 19-4 OxyContin**
OxyContin is a powerful narcotic that is sold legally. This drug is usually prescribed for cancer patients. There is some evidence that it is more popular among addicts and teenagers than is marijuana and cocaine. Addicts can achieve an intensely pure high by crushing the pills and snorting or injecting them. OxyContin is often the target sought in pharmacy burglaries. (© 2005 www.streetdrugs.org) (Source: Publishers Group, Street Drugs: Drug Identification Guide [Plymouth, MN] 2003)

Other Opium Derivatives

Other opium derivatives abused and stolen from pharmacies, hospitals, and physicians are Dilaudid, Papaverine, and Pantopon.

SYNTHETIC NARCOTICS

Synthetic narcotics, though chemically related to the opium alkaloids, are produced entirely within the laboratory. A continuing search for a drug that kills pain but does not create tolerance and dependence has yet to yield a drug that is not susceptible to abuse.

Meperidine (Demerol)

The commercial name for **meperidine** is Demerol, and it was the first synthetic narcotic. Next to morphine, it is probably the most widely used drug for the relief of intense pain. It is available in pure form and in combination products. The drug is administered by mouth or by injection; the latter is the more common method of abuse.[12]

Methadone

Methadone is known by the commercial names Dolophine Hydrochloride and Methadone HCl Diskets. A heroin-dependent person can be treated with doses of methadone as a replacement for heroin. Methadone is manufactured in a solid form and administered orally. It's considered a "maintenance drug" and is used to maintain a heroin addict at a stable level of opiate use, protecting the addict from the incidental dangers of heroin use.

The beneficial properties of methadone are that it is longer acting than most opiates and addicts do not build up tolerance as fast as with heroin. Also, oral administration is less potentially hazardous than injection, since it significantly reduces the addict's risk for diseases such as hepatitis B, hepatitis C, and AIDS. As a rule of thumb, it takes about three weeks on methadone before a heroin addict completes the withdrawal stage and moves to the maintenance stage. However, it must be noted that the simultaneous use of methadone and heroin do not totally negate the physiological effect of the heroin on the user.

There is considerable controversy over the adoption of methadone maintenance programs. Critics argue that drug dependence is not cured. Proponents argue that it presents a cheaper way of supporting drug dependence and gets abusers out of crime and back to a conventional life. Proponents recognize that the programs need to include appropriate psychiatric help for overcoming the psychological dependence.[13]

STIMULANTS

Drugs falling into the **stimulants** group directly stimulate the central nervous system, producing excitation, alertness, wakefulness, and, in some cases, a temporary rise in blood pressure and respiration rate. The major stimulants abused are cocaine, amphetamines, phenmetrazine, and methylphenidate. The effects of an overdose are agitation, an increase in body temperature, hallucinations, convulsions, and possibly death. The withdrawal symptoms are apathy, long periods of sleep, irritability, depression, and disorientation.[14]

Cocaine

Cocaine is a naturally occurring stimulant that is extracted from the leaves of the coca plant (Erythroxylon coca). The leaves of this western South American shrub have been chewed by Colombian, Bolivian, and Peruvian Indians since antiquity for religious, medicinal, and other reasons. Allegedly, the chewing of coca leaves has enabled the Indians to work in high altitudes and on inadequate diets. The chewing of the coca leaf, which continues to the present day, should not be confused with the use of the extracted drug, cocaine. Coca leaves contain only about ½% to 1% cocaine; the cocaine contained within them is released more slowly, and the route of administration (oral) is different from that in most cocaine use.[15] (See Figure 19-5.)

Because reports of native coca use generated considerable interest in Europe, efforts were made in the nineteenth century to isolate the purified psychoactive ingredient in coca leaves. When success was achieved in the 1880s, cocaine's potential value as a tonic, its general stimulant properties, its possible value for specific ailments, and its local anesthetic properties were explored. Its use as an anesthetic was particularly important because it could be used in eye surgery, for which no previous drug had been suitable. Cocaine also constricted blood vessels and limited bleeding in an anesthetized area. This property made it valuable for surgery of the nose and throat, areas that are richly supplied with blood. Although many of cocaine's uses as a therapeutic drug have been abandoned, it continues to be used as a local anesthetic.[16]

Illicit cocaine is sold as a white, translucent, crystalline powder, frequently adulterated to about half its volume. The most common adulterants are sugars (especially lactose and glucose) and local anesthetics (Lidocaine, Procaine, and Tetracaine) similar in appearance and taste to cocaine. Amphetamines, other drugs with stimulant properties, are also used. Given the high cost of cocaine, the temptation to adulterate at each level of sale is great. The combination of high price and the exotic properties attributed to it have contributed to cocaine's street reputation as the status drug.

▲ FIGURE 19-5   Cocaine powder and leaves
Leaves from the coca plant grown in South America are harvested and dried. The leaves are crumbled and mixed with high distillant chemicals that extract the cocaine from the plant material. The liquid chemicals are then evaporated causing the cocaine alkaloid to form into chunks or rocks. Cocaine is usually shipped in pressed kilo (2.2-pound) bricks of highly concentrated material. (© 2005 www.streedrugs.org) (Source: Publishers Group, Street Drugs: Drug Identification Guide (Plymouth, MN), 2003)

Cocaine is most commonly inhaled, or snorted, through the nose. It is deposited on the mucous linings of the nose, from which it is readily absorbed into the bloodstream. Repeated use often results in irritation to the nostrils and nasal mucous membranes. Symptoms may resemble those of a common cold—that is, congestion or a runny nose. Users therefore often resort to cold remedies, such as nasal sprays, to relieve their chronic nasal congestion. They may be unable to breathe comfortably without habitually using a spray.

A less common route of administration for cocaine is intravenous injection. The solution injected may be cocaine or a combination of heroin and cocaine. This route of administration carries the dangers of any intravenous use. Furthermore, intravenous injection introduces unknown quantities of cocaine or cocaine and heroin directly and suddenly into the bloodstream, leaving body organs wholly unprotected from the toxic effects of the drug. Cocaine deaths from intravenous injection are more numerous than from snorting, despite the greater prevalence of the latter method.

Freebasing

The practice of freebasing cocaine involves the dissolving of cocaine in a base solution, usually distilled water and calcium carbonate or lactose. The mixture is then shaken so that cocaine is dissolved completely. Several drops of ether are then added, and the mixture is shaken again. The cocaine is attracted to the ether, while the other additives are attracted to the base solution.

The ether-cocaine solution separates from the base (like oil and water), with the ether rising to the surface. An eyedropper is commonly used to suction off the ether-cocaine solution, which is then placed on an evaporating dish or crucible and allowed to evaporate naturally. This process can be accelerated by the use of a flame; however, this practice is extremely dangerous since the ether is highly flammable.

The cocaine crystals are then scraped off the dish with a metal spatula, placed in a glass pipe or bong (water pipe), and smoked. The resultant high is alleged to be greater than that from simple snorting, although users remark that injection of the drug provides a more intense high than does freebasing.

The pleasant effects of freebasing begin to decrease in duration as usage increases, and users display changes in moods and irritability if a high cannot be maintained. As freebasing usage becomes chronic, a person can experience the same symptoms as a chronic nonfreebasing abuser of cocaine.

Crack or Rock Cocaine

A relatively inexpensive form of cocaine called **crack** or **rock cocaine** has grown tremendously in popularity among cocaine users. (See Figure 19-6.) The drug is made by mixing ordinary cocaine with baking soda and water and then heating the solution in a pot. The material,

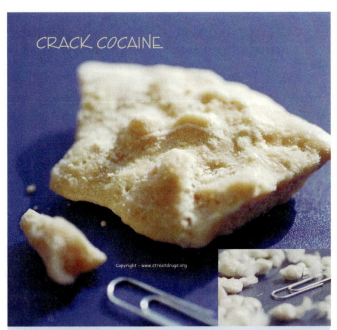

▲ FIGURE 19-6

Crack or rock cocaine

Crack, the smokable form of cocaine, provides an immediate "rush." This form of cocaine is relatively inexpensive and very popular among cocaine users. The drug is made primarily by mixing ordinary baking powder and water and then heating the solution in a pot. The resulting crack rocks are purer and more concentrated than regular cocaine.

(© 2005 www.streedrugs.org)

(Source: Publishers Group, Street Drugs: Drug Identification Guide (Plymouth, MN), 2003)

which is somewhat purer and more concentrated than regular cocaine, is dried and broken into tiny chunks that dealers sell as crack rocks. These little pellets are usually smoked in glass pipes and are frequently sold in tiny plastic vials. Rock cocaine is 5 to 10 times more potent than powdered cocaine; the high lasts about 5 minutes and leaves the user wanting more. According to mental health specialists, crack users are more likely to show serious psychiatric consequences, including intense paranoia, extreme depression, and often suicidal and even violent behavior. Part of the attraction to the dealer is the enormous profit that can be made by the sale of crack. For example, in Los Angeles an ounce of cocaine can sell for $1,000 to $1,500. Since each ounce contains 28 grams and each gram can produce up to six rocks selling for $25 each, the dealer can realize a profit of around $2,700.

Amphetamines

Amphetamine, dextroamphetamine, and methamphetamine are so closely related chemically that they can be differentiated from one another only in the laboratory. These compounds resemble the natural body hormones

of epinephrine and norepinephrine. As a result of this similarity, they can act directly, by mimicking the natural hormones in their effects on nerve endings, and/or indirectly, by causing increased release of the natural hormones. In either case, the **amphetamines** stimulate certain areas of the nervous system that control blood pressure, heart rate, and respiratory and metabolic rates, all of which are increased. Appetite is markedly decreased, and the senses are hyperalert. The body is in a general state of stress, as if it were extremely threatened or expecting a violent fight. This group of drugs artificially intensifies and prolongs such stimulation, keeping the body in a state of tension for prolonged periods of time.[17] Many different classes of people employ amphetamines in abusive quantities, including middle-aged businesspeople, housewives, students, athletes, and truck drivers. Government studies indicate that young people are the greatest abusers. Drivers take them to stay awake on long trips; students take them while cramming for exams; and athletes take them for extra energy and stamina.[18] When the drug is prescribed, the dose frequently ranges between 2.5 and 15 milligrams per day. Abusers have been known to inject as much as 1,000 milligrams every 2 or 3 hours. Medical use of amphetamines is now limited to control of narcolepsy, appetite control, and control of hyperactivity in children.

Phenmetrazine (Preludin), Methylphenidate (Ritalin), and Pemoline (CYLERT)

Phenmetrazine is related chemically to the amphetamines, and its abuse produces similar effects. Like phenmetrazine, methylphenidate (Ritalin) is related chemically to amphetamines. It is prescribed for treatment of mild depression in adults and attention deficit disorder in children. Pemoline, like amphetamines, is a stimulant. These stimulants were developed and approved for marketing as a drug to be used in the treatment of hyperactive children.

Crystallized Methamphetamine

Crystallized methamphetamine, better known as *crystal meth* and *speed* during the 1960s and 1970s, was originally taken as pills or injected.

Currently, the drug is most typically either injected or smoked using a glass pipe similar to those employed by crack cocaine users. Crystal meth first appeared in Hawaii, possibly via Korea, but has spread throughout the United States and has become particularly problematic in rural areas of Texas, Oklahoma, Missouri, Kansas, and Arkansas owing to the ease of manufacturing and the inherent availability of anhydrous ammonia from agricultural fertilizer.[19] The other ingredients for the drug, such as lithium (found in batteries), ether (found in antifreeze), and pseudoephedrine (found in cold medicine), are also easy to obtain, and the manufacture of the drug is fairly straightforward. Guides to the manufacture of the drug can be found on the Internet and manufacturers can set

▲ **FIGURE 19-7 Ice**

Made from powdered methamphetamine, "ice" is often observed as a crystalline substance. Users usually smoke "ice," resulting in an intense high for as long as 12–14 hours. (© 2005 www.streedrugs.org)

(Source: Publishers Group, Street Drugs: Drug Identification Guide (Plymouth, MN), 2003)

up shop in motel rooms, abandoned houses or trailers, and even cars.[20]

Crystal meth, also known as *ice* or *glass*, owes its special appeal to several factors (See Figure 19-7.):

- A puff of crack cocaine buoys its user for approximately 20 minutes, but the high from smoking ice endures for 12 to 24 hours. It does, however, share crack's addictive properties, and it produces similar bouts of severe depression and paranoia as well as convulsions.
- Ice can be manufactured in clandestine speed labs, whereas cocaine must be extracted from the leaf of the coca plant, refined, and imported by smugglers at considerable risk.
- Because it is odorless, ice can be smoked in public virtually without detection.

In its solid form, the drug resembles rock candy or a chip of ice. When lighted in a glass pipe, the crystals turn to liquid and produce a potent vapor that enters the bloodstream directly through the lungs. Ice reverts to its solid state when it cools, thus becoming reusable and highly transportable.[21] One gram of crystal meth is enough for 15 to 20 hits, making it extremely cost effective to many users.

Crystal meth or "ice" production has several obvious hallmarks, owing to the fact that many of the ingredients can be found in discount stores. Large purchases

of items containing ingredients required for crystal meth production, such as cough medicine and batteries, may indicate illicit activity. Furthermore, the use of anhydrous ammonia in the production of crystal meth produces a noxious odor that is noticeable by neighbors and visitors. Clandestine meth labs and special considerations for officers going into such labs are discussed later in the chapter.

Strawberry Quick Meth

Reports of candy-flavored methamphetamine are emerging around the nation, stirring concern among police and abuse prevention experts that drug dealers are marketing a new drug to younger people. According to intelligence gathered by the Drug Enforcement Administration (DEA) agents from informants, local police, and drug counselors, the flavored crystals have shown up in California, Idaho, Kansas, Minnesota, Missouri, Nevada, New Mexico, Texas, and Washington. The DEA has concluded that drug traffickers are trying to lure in new customers, no matter what their age, by making the meth seem less dangerous. Normally methamphetamine is a white or brownish, bitter-tasting crystalline powder that dissolves in water and that, as already indicated, is usually smoked or snorted. The new version looks like the "Pop Rocks" candy that sizzles in the mouth. Among the new flavors are Strawberry Quick, chocolate, cola, and other soda flavors. (See Figure 19-8.) One DEA agent reported a red amphetamine that had been marketed as a powered form of an energy drink. **Strawberry Quick meth** is reportedly popular among new users who snort it because the flavoring can cut down on the taste. Teenagers who have been taught meth is bad may see this flavored version as less

▲ **FIGURE 19-8**
Strawberry-Colored Crystal methamphetamine
Crystals of methamphetamine, colored with a strawberry-flavored children's drink mix, are a prime example of the new line of drugs.
(© FILE/ The Associated Press)

harmful. Law enforcement officials have concluded that Strawberry Quick is definitely designed for the younger crowd. As methamphetamine's popularity has waned, drug dealers have found it necessary to create new ways to market it.

Strawberry Quick came to prominence in January 2007 after the Nevada Department of Public Safety issued a bulletin describing the type of meth discovered in their state. It certainly has spread to other states.[22]

Ya-Ba or Nazi Speed

Ya Ba, also know as *Nazi Speed*, is a highly pure methamphetamine pill originating from Southeast Asia. The brightly colored pills are candylike and often flavored (e.g., cherry-red, grape-purple, white-vanilla) apparently to make them more appealing to young people. As could be predicted, ya-ba pills are fast becoming a favorite drug at all night rave parties, since their high is much stronger and longer lasting than that of other club drugs such as ecstacy and gamma hydroxy butrate (GHB), a drug commonly used in the crime of date rape. (see Chapter 10, "Sex-Related Offenses," for a more detailed discussion.) Users generally take a pill orally or place it in foil, heat it, and inhale the smoke. The high commonly lasts up to 10 hours.[23]

Methcathinone

Methcathinone, called *cat* or *goob*, is a psychomotor stimulant with a chemical structure similar to methamphetamine.[24] Originally patented in Germany in 1928 and later used in the Soviet Union in the late 1930s and 1940s for the treatment of depression, methcathinone was all but unknown in the United States until 1957, when an American pharmaceutical firm received a patent for it and began animal studies to determine its potential as an appetite suppressant.

Because initial testing revealed that methcathinone was approximately one and a half times as potent as methamphetamine, clinical trials were never initiated and testing was discontinued. The formula for methcathinone languished in the archives of the pharmaceutical firm until 1989, when it was rediscovered and "liberated" by a college intern working for the firm. He shared the formula, and in 1990 a close friend set up a clandestine laboratory on the campus of Northern Michigan University (NMU) and attempted to develop a market for cat.

Although cat use did not take hold among the students at NMU, it rapidly found acceptance among the local population of Michigan's upper peninsula (UP). The relative ease with which cat is manufactured made it readily available, and its use and abuse rapidly spread throughout the UP and northern Wisconsin.

Methcathinone first came to the attention of law enforcement in the winter of 1990, when the Michigan State Police in the UP purchased a sample of what was purported to be a "new" drug more powerful than crack. The substance was analyzed to be methcathinone, closely related to, but more powerful than, methamphetamine. In January 1991, the Michigan State Police seized the first clandestine methcathinone lab ever discovered in the United States, in a college dormitory room in Marquette, Michigan. Six months later, the DEA raided another methcathinone lab in Ann Arbor, Michigan. However, much to the surprise of law enforcement authorities, methcathinone was not a controlled substance under either Michigan state law or federal statute.

On May 1, 1992, under the DEA's emergency scheduling authority, methcathinone was placed in Schedule 1 of the Controlled Substances Act. After a scientific and medical evaluation, this classification was made permanent on October 7, 1993.

The effects of methcathinone on the human body are very similar to those of methamphetamine. Cat is reported by users to induce feelings of omnipotence and euphoria, marked by increased energy. Other reported effects include relief from fatigue, increased self-assurance, acute alertness, hyperactivity, talkativeness, a sense of invincibility, confidence, and increased sexual stimulation.

Cat is usually a white or off-white powdered substance, very similar in appearance to methamphetamine. It is usually sold in gram quantities for $75 to $100 and snorted in lines ranging from $1/10$ to $1/4$ of a gram. Because cat is usually sold in pure form, it reportedly can produce an immediate "rush," with a high that lasts 4 to 6 hours or more. There is typically a delay of 1 to 2 hours between dosages.

Users rapidly develop a tolerance for cat, requiring them to use larger amounts more frequently. Because cat destroys the sinus membranes, causing chronic nosebleeds and sinusitis, users may eventually resort to intravenous injection or oral ingestion.

Chronic cat use is characterized by binging. Addicts often go for days without sleep—eating very little, if at all—until they finally collapse. The onset of the "crash" occurs 4 to 6 hours after the last instance of use. Users often sleep for several days before beginning the cycle again.

Undesirable side effects reported by users include loss of appetite, weight loss, dehydration, stomachaches, profuse sweating, temporary blindness, deterioration of the nasal membranes, dry mouth, and an increased heart rate. Other side effects include anxiety, nervousness, depression, and hallucinations. The most consistently reported side effect—one with a serious implication for law enforcement officers—is extreme paranoia. In one case, a cat abuser killed himself when he thought he was about to be arrested.

Symptoms of methcathinone intoxication can include profuse sweating, sweaty palms, increased heart rate, restlessness, increased body temperature, and uncontrollable shaking. Officers encountering suspected cat users should be particularly aware of withdrawal symptoms, which include irritability and argumentativeness. Other withdrawal symptoms include convulsions, hallucinations, and severe depression.

Khat

Not to be confused with the previously described methcathinone (street name *cat*), **khat** (pronounced "cot") is a leafy import from a large flowering shrub that grows in northeast Africa and the Southern Arabia peninsula. The active ingredients in khat are cathinone and cathine. Fresh khat leaves are a glossy brown color and contain an ingredient chemically similar to amphetamine. The cathinone in khat begins to degrade 48 hours after the plant has been cut. Thus, khat has to be refrigerated and kept moist or frozen to retain its potency for a longer period. Drying the leaves too fast causes the active ingredient (cathinone) to dissipate.[25] (See Figure 19-9.)

The plant has been cultivated for centuries and is in widespread use today, primarily in Yemen, Somalia, and parts of Ethiopia and the Middle East. References to khat first appeared in the United States as American soldiers encountered rebels in Somalia, high on the drug during combat encounters. Ingestion of the drug does not impair motor skills, but rather creates a mild, amphetamine-like euphoria that heightens the senses, self-esteem, and aggressiveness. The drug is also known as *Abyssinian Tea*, *African Tea*, and *African Salad*.

While khat is legal in countries such as the United Kingdom and Canada, it was recently classified as a Schedule I drug carrying penalties similar to heroin and cocaine in the United States. Khat is often transported into the U.S. from Europe, Canada, and North Africa wrapped in plastic bags or, as mentioned, in banana leaves to retain moistness. It is commonly sold by word of mouth, or in ethnic specialty shops in cities such as Boston, Dallas, Houston, Los Angeles, Detroit, Buffalo, Philadelphia, Washington, D.C., and New York.[26]

DEPRESSANTS (SEDATIVES)

Depressants, or **sedatives,** depress the central nervous system and are prescribed in small doses to reduce both restlessness and emotional tension and to induce sleep. The drugs most frequently abused are **barbiturates,** glutethimide, methaqualone, and meprobamate. Chronic use produces slurring of speech, staggering, loss of balance and falling, faulty judgment, quick temper, and quarrelsomeness. Overdoses, particularly in conjunction with alcohol, result in unconsciousness and death unless proper medical treatment is administered. Therapeutic doses cause minimal amounts of psychological dependence, while chronic excessive doses result in both physical and psychological dependence. Abrupt withdrawal, particularly from barbiturates, can produce convulsions and death. Barbiturates are frequently nicknamed after the color of the capsule or tablet or the name of the manufacturer. The barbiturates most frequently abused are secobarbital and amobarbital.[27] These are among the short- and intermediate-acting barbiturates. The onset time is from 15 to 40 minutes, and the effects last for up to 6 hours.

◀ **FIGURE 19-9 Khat**
In the United States, khat use is most prevalent among immigrants from Somalia, Ethiopia, and Yemen. The drug is usually smuggled while wrapped in wet newspapers or banana leaves in order to keep the leaves moist, since khat's chemical composition begins to deteriorate quickly when the leaves are dried too fast.
(© Simon Maina/Getty Images)
(Source: U.S. Department of Justice, National Drug Intelligence Center)

Glutethimide (Doriden)

When introduced in 1954, glutethimide was wrongly believed to be a nonaddictive barbiturate substitute. The sedative effects of glutethimide begin about 30 minutes after oral administration and last 4 to 8 hours. Because the effects of this drug last for a long time, it is exceptionally difficult to reverse overdoses, and many result in death.

Glutethimide used with 16-milligram codeine tablets is one of the most popular pill combinations on the black market today. This combination gives a heroinlike effect and is known as *dors and 4s* or *Ds and Cs.* It is commonly taken by oral ingestion.

Methaqualone

Methaqualone was at one time very popular in the United States but has since been significantly reduced in the market. The drug was widely abused because it was mistakenly thought to be safe and nonaddictive and to have aphrodisiac qualities. Methaqualone caused many cases of serious poisoning. When administered orally, large doses produce a coma that may be accompanied by thrashing or convulsions. It was marketed in the United States under various names, including Quaalude, Parest, Optimil, Somnafac, and Soper. Most methaqualones found on the street today are counterfeit and usually test as diazepam (Valium).

SPEEDBALLING

Speedballing is a slang term that refers to the simultaneous ingestion, usually through injection, of heroin (a depressant) and cocaine (a stimulant). The cocaine provides the user with a tremendous euphoric "rush," after which a drowsy or depressing sensation arises. An overdose of either drug can cause convulsions and death. Death by overdose using this type of drug mix was reportedly instrumental in the demise of several well-known rock musicians and celebrities, including Jimmy Hendrix, Janis Joplin, John Belushi, and River Phoenix.

HALLUCINOGENS

Hallucinogenic drugs, natural or synthetic, distort the perception of objective reality. In large doses, they cause hallucinations. Most of these drugs are processed in clandestine laboratories and have yet to be proved medically valuable. The effects experienced after taking hallucinogens are not solely related to the drug. They are modified by the mood, mental attitude, and environment of the user. The unpredictability of their effects is the greatest danger to the user. Users may develop psychological dependence but not physical dependence, so far as is known. The most commonly abused hallucinogens are PCP (phencyclidine), LSD 25 (lysergic acid diethylamide), mescaline (peyote), psilocybin, and psilocyn.

Phencyclidine (PCP)

Phencyclidine, commonly called **PCP,** in its pharmaceutically pure form is a solid white powder. Because the hydrochloride salt readily dissolves in water, and as a street drug is often adulterated or misrepresented as other drugs, its appearance is highly variable. It is sold in powder form and in tablets, both in many colors. Often it is placed on parsley or on other leaf mixtures to be smoked as cigarettes (joints).[28]

When misrepresented, PCP is commonly sold as THC (the main psychoactive ingredient in marijuana, which is rarely available on the street). But phencyclidine has also been sold as cannabinol (another marijuana constituent), mescaline, psilocybin, LSD, and even amphetamine or cocaine. Because of the variability in street names and appearance, and because PCP is sometimes found in combination with barbiturates, heroin, cocaine, amphetamine, methaqualone, LSD, and mescaline, users may be mistaken about its true identity. The mixture of marijuana and PCP has been thought to be common, but it has rarely been reported by street-drug analysis laboratories.

Significantly adding to the risk of using PCP, especially when it is taken orally, is the wide variability in purity of the street drug. Even when PCP is not misrepresented, the percentage of PCP has been found to be quite variable. Depending on how carefully PCP is synthesized, it may contain impurities, including potassium cyanide. Generally, samples represented as "crystal" or "angel dust" tend to be purer than those sold under other names or misrepresented as different drugs.

In addition to phencyclidine, over 30 chemical analogues, some of which are capable of producing similar psychic effects, can also be synthesized and may appear on the street. Thus the problems of identifying and tracking the use of PCP and related drugs is unusually difficult.

Phencyclidine is used legally in veterinary medicine to immobilize large animals. Although it was originally developed as an anesthetic for humans, it was later abandoned because it produced psychological disturbances and agitation in some patients. PCP made its first illicit appearance in the United States in 1965 on the West Coast. At that time it rapidly developed a bad street reputation and had only limited popularity.

Because of its great variation in appearance, PCP is difficult to identify by sight. It is found in powder and tablet forms; on parsley, mint, oregano, or other leafy material; as a liquid; and in 1-gram "rock" crystals. When PCP is sold as a granular powder ("angel dust"), it may consist of 50% to 100% phencyclidine. Sold under other names and in other guises, the purity varies from 10% to 30%; leafy mixtures contain still smaller amounts of the drug.

PCP is most commonly smoked or snorted. By smoking a leafy mixture on which the drug has been sprinkled, users can better regulate the dose. Because of the longer period before the drug takes effect and the greater purity, overdoses are probably worse when the drug has been taken orally.

The effects of PCP include feeling weightless, smaller, out of touch with the immediate environment, and dying or being already dead. Common signs of PCP use include flushing of the skin, profuse sweating, involuntary eye movements, muscular incoordination, double vision, dizziness, nausea, and vomiting. Police officers have reported that individuals under the influence of PCP can be extremely violent and almost superhumanly strong.

Methylenedioxy Methamphetamine (MDMA or Ecstasy)

Methylenedioxy methamphetamine, commonly known as **MDMA** or **ecstasy,** is a bitter white powder. It enjoys a high popularity among ravers and has now become a very common drug of abuse in the nightclub and party scene. The drug's popularity has grown at an alarming rate. Although it is difficult to say exactly how many people are experimenting with it, law enforcement officials consider ecstasy to be one of the most troubling illicit drugs because of its widespread use. (See Figure 19-10.)

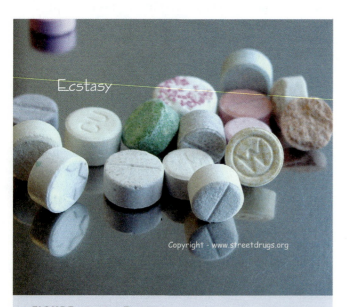

▲ **FIGURE 19-10 Ecstasy**
Ecstasy pills come in a variety of colors with unique markings, including shamrocks, stars, letters, and skull/crossbones, depending on where the drug was manufactured. The use of ecstasy is very popular in the nightclub and party scene. This drug has become increasingly popular among juveniles and is commonly used as a recreational drug at raves. (© 2005 www.streedrugs.org) (Source: Publishers Group, Street Drugs: Drug Identification Guide (Plymouth, MN), 2003)

Many ecstasy users are drawn to the drug by its ability to reduce inhibitions, promote euphoria, produce light hallucinations, and suppress the need to eat or sleep. One pill's effects can last as long as 6 hours, but users build up a tolerance. An overdose can cause an accelerated heart rate, high blood pressure, aching muscle cramps, and panic attacks. According to many experts, ecstasy is psychologically addictive and can result in paranoia and psychosis.

The drug is manufactured to a large extent in laboratories in Belgium and the Netherlands. It can be created for as little as 50 cents, sold in the country of origin, and then smuggled into the United States, where it is sold for as much as $40 a pill. For the most part, Israeli organized-crime syndicates have been implicated as the main source of the drug's distribution in the United States. This so-called club drug has become increasingly popular among juveniles and is commonly used as a recreational drug at raves.[29]

Lysergic Acid Diethylamide (LSD 25)

Lysergic acid diethylamide, or **LSD,** is a semisynthetic compound produced from lysergic acid, a natural substance found in ergot fungus, a disease that affects rye and wheat. An average dose of 30 to 50 micrograms—about the size of a pinpoint—will take the user on a "trip" lasting 10 to 12 hours. Drops of the solution are taken on a lump of sugar or on blotted paper. Along with experiencing mental changes, the user may have dilated pupils, a lowered body temperature, nausea, goose bumps, profuse perspiration, increased blood sugar levels, and a rapid heart rate. Subsequent flashbacks are not uncommon.

Before 1972, there was no way to detect LSD in the body chemically. However, scientists at Collaborative Research, Inc., in Waltham, Massachusetts, developed a means for detecting it in small amounts in human blood and urine and for measuring the amount present. This discovery made it possible to study the distribution of LSD in the bodies of animals to determine the residual effect of the drug.[30] The DEA reports that LSD is making a comeback with juvenile circles and is also used frequently at raves.[31]

Mescaline (Peyote)

The primary active ingredient of the peyote cactus is the hallucinogen **mescaline,** which is derived from the buttons of the plant. Mescaline has been used by the Indians of Central America and the southwestern United States for centuries in religious rites. Generally ground into a powder, it is taken orally. A dose of 350 to 500 milligrams of mescaline produces illusions and hallucinations for 5 to 12 hours. Like LSD, mescaline is not likely to produce physical dependence but may produce psychological dependence.

▲ **FIGURE 19-11   Psilocybin**
Another popular drug among adolescent youth is psilocybin. The mushrooms are eaten, causing hallucinations, disorientation, impaired coordination, and confusion on the part of the user. Mushrooms covered in chocolate, as observed in this photo set, look like candy and are often found at raves. (© 2005 www.streedrugs.org) (Source: Publishers Group, Street Drugs: Drug Identification Guide (Plymouth, MN), 2003)

Psilocybin and Psilocyn

Psilocybin and **psilocyn** are obtained from mushrooms generally grown in Mexico. Like mescaline, they have historically been used in Indian rites. They are taken orally, or placed in tea, and their effect is similar to mescaline's, except that a smaller dose—4 to 8 milligrams—produces effects for about 6 hours. Psilocybin has also become a popular drug on the party scene and at raves. (See Figure 19-11.)

Foxy and 5-MeO-AMT

Foxy became a controlled substance via emergency scheduling by the Drug Enforcement Agency in the spring of 2003. This Schedule I hallucinogen is a synthetic compound with chemical properties similar to those of psilocybin and psilocin. The drug is found in powder form, which is then often used to fill capsules or create tablets. The tablets may be imprinted with graphics. Most often, the drug appears at clubs and raves and is used primarily by teenagers and young adults. Effects begin to manifest in the user within about 30 minutes, and they include visual and auditory hallucinations, extreme talkativeness, and decreased inhibitions. These effects peak between 1 and 2 hours after administration and can last from 3 to 6 hours.[32]

More commonly called *AMT, alpha,* or *alpha-O,* 5-MeO-AMT shares many similarities with Foxy. Both have similar chemical properties, induce hallucinogenic effects, and are generally used within the club or rave scenes. Additionally, the powdered AMT may be dissolved in water and distributed onto blotter paper, sugar cubes, or candy. AMT is longer-lasting than Foxy, often producing hallucinations for up to 18 hours.[33]

Ketamine

Ketamine hydrochloride is a synthetic drug that was developed in the mid-1960s and is an anesthetic agent that has legitimate uses, mostly in veterinary medicine. Ketamine was used extensively in the Vietnam War because it is fast-acting and has a relatively short duration, making it a drug of choice for "battlefield medicine." However, it soon became obvious that many humans who were anesthetized with ketamine often became agitated and suffered hallucinations when they awoke. It has since been replaced as an anesthetic for humans by other, more efficient agents with fewer side effects.

Ironically, the side effects that made ketamine unpopular and unsafe as a legitimate medical drug have spawned its use in the illegitimate market. On the street, ketamine is called *Vitamin K, Special K,* or *K.* It has also been closely associated with the all-night rave party phenomenon. Ketamine causes hallucinations, excitement, and delirium similar to the drugs phencyclidine (PCP) and LSD; however, the effects are not as pronounced or as long in duration. Hallucinations caused by ketamine may last only an hour or two, but the intoxication-like effects of the drug may be noticeable for several hours. Because ketamine is an anesthetic, it may temporarily mask the feeling of pain. Users of ketamine can injure themselves and not know it.

Because ketamine is so difficult to produce, it is not manufactured in clandestine laboratories. Most of the ketamine abused today comes from stolen veterinary stock and is known by brand names such as Ketalar and Ketaset. The legitimate drug is usually supplied in vials of liquid, although it can be in the form of white powder or pills.

In liquid form, ketamine may be injected into a large muscle. This route allows for a slower absorption and longer duration than the intravenous route. In powder form, ketamine is usually snorted in the same manner as cocaine. Both powder and liquid can be sprayed or sprinkled on vegetable matter and smoked or mixed with a drink. While it is not known if a person can become physically dependent on ketamine, tolerance and psychological dependence are distinct possibilities with frequent use.

The average street dose of ketamine ranges from 0.2 to 0.5 gram. The size and weight of the abuser, the desired effects, and the presence of other drugs in the abuser's system determine the ultimate effect. A vial of liquid ketamine is equivalent to approximately 1 gram of powder and sells for $100 to $200. A 0.2-gram dose of powder, or a *bump,* commonly sells for $20. Ketamine may be packaged for sale in small plastic bags, aluminum foil, paper folds, or gelatin capsules.[34] Obviously, an abuser must also possess hypodermic syringes and needles to administer the drug by injection. (See Figure 19-12.)

CANNABIS

Marijuana

Although classified as a mild hallucinogen, the Schedule I substance **cannabis** is often considered separately owing to its wide availability and popularity. Drugs obtained from the cannabis plant include **marijuana** and hashish. Marijuana is found in the flowering tops and leaves of the cannabis-sativa (also known as *hemp*) plant. The leaves of the plant always grow in odd numbers. The plant thrives in mild climates around the world, but the principal sources of import into the United States are Colombia, Mexico, and Jamaica. Its most common nicknames are *pot, reefer, grass, weed, Maryjane,* and *a joint.* Marijuana is made by crushing or chopping the dried leaves and flowers of the plant into small pieces. The cleaned or manicured leaves are then rolled into a cigarette and smoked, smoked in some other fashion, or mixed with food and eaten. The principal psychoactive substance is thought to be delta-9-tetrahydrocannabinol (THC), a chemical found nowhere else in nature. Most marijuana is found to have less than 5% THC, but improvements in horticulture and chemistry in the cultivation process have led to much more concentrated varieties. Hybrid varieties, such as those found in the potent sinsemilla strain of the plant, and plants grown in carefully controlled indoor operations may yield up to 20% THC.[35] (See Figure 19-13.)

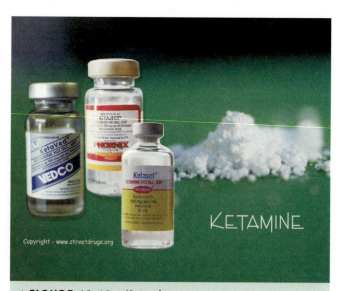

▲ **FIGURE 19-12   Ketamine**
Ketamine hydrochloride is a synthetic drug developed in the mid-1960s as an anesthetic agent. Two of the street names used for this drug are Vitamin K and Special K. Ketamine causes hallucinations, excitement, and delirium similar to LSD or PCP. Because it is an anesthetic, it may temporarily mask pain—so much so that users can even injure themselves and not be aware of it.
(© 2005 www.streetdrugs.org)
(Source: Publishers Group, Street Drugs: Drug Identification Guide (Plymouth, MN), 2003)

▲ **FIGURE 19-13   Manicured marijuana and seeds**
Note the smaller size of a marijuana cigarette compared to a regular cigarette on the left. The cleaned or manicured leaves of the marijuana plant are used to fill these "cigarettes." Low doses of the smoked drug tend to produce initial restfulness and a sense of well-being. Other effects include an alteration of sensory perceptions, including an illusory expansion of time and space. (Courtesy of the Drug Enforcement Administration)

Although the effects of the drug vary among users, in many cases low dosages of marijuana produce an initial restfulness and well-being, followed by a dreamy, carefree state of relaxation and food cravings. Larger dosages can result in altered perceptions, impaired memory, and rapid changes of emotion. Effects of the drug are usually felt almost immediately by the user and may last several hours.

As of this writing, the Supreme Court was considering whether users who have doctor's approval and were permitted by state law to use homegrown marijuana to mitigate side effects from chemotherapy or symptoms of AIDS, cancer, glaucoma, and other medical conditions could be prosecuted by federal agents.[36] Currently, marijuana is not permitted for medical use, and those prescribing the drug are not protected from federal prosecution. However, the debate as to the medicinal uses of marijuana is ongoing. Perhaps the main reason for the unwillingness of the federal government to legalize marijuana for medicinal use is the drug's reputation as a "gateway" drug. The gateway theory states that the use of marijuana causes an eventual graduation by users to harder drugs such as cocaine and heroin. However, this idea is controversial. Several studies have recently disproved this association, but marijuana remains a Schedule I drug at this time.[37]

Marijuana Grow Houses

Marijuana grow houses are normal houses in residential areas that are converted for the purposes of growing marijuana. Large houses are often used because they provide greater capacity for growing marijuana, but such operations may be found in any home, in any neighborhood.

To make a house suitable for cultivating marijuana, significant changes are made to the home's structure. High-intensity lighting is needed to grow the plants (which is costly), so many home grow operations bypass the electricity illegally, putting the neighborhood at risk of fire and electrocution. Combined with construction to provide water and ventilation for the grow operation, the house becomes uninhabitable for future residents. Unless major repairs are made, the house is ruined, and the property value of other houses in the area is lowered.

Marijuana grow houses often have links to criminal elements and organized crime. Individuals associated with grow operations have been found to carry weapons and may be considered dangerous. Also, there is a risk of increased violence and residual crime in neighborhoods associated with illegal activity. Marijuana grow houses are not only a police concern; they are also a public safety Issue.[38]

What are the Dangers?

There are many dangers associated with marijuana grow houses and problems that can result from having one in a neighborhood. These include:

- *Poisonous fumes:* Noxious fumes from the growing operation can build up inside the house or be vented outside (which affect the neighboring homes).
- *Fires:* Electricity is bypassed, by being diverted from neighboring homes. This increases the chance of fires starting owing to the amateurish rewiring jobs.
- *Electrocution:* People inexperienced with rewiring electrical systems may electrocute themselves, or people exposed to the wiring may be electrocuted.
- *Violence:* To protect distribution and production of marijuana, those involved in a growing operation may be armed, and have been known to carry out assaults or homicides.
- *Increased crime:* Marijuana from home grow operations are sold to children and other members of the community. The money raised from these sales is used to fund organized crime.
- *Booby traps:* Traps may be set by growers to protect their product from unauthorized persons entering the home or property. These traps can be life threatening and expose emergency responders (and others entering the property) to hazardous conditions.
- *Environmental damage:* Chemicals used in the grow operation are improperly disposed of by being drained into the ground and water system.
- *Hazard to children:* Children in the neighborhood are exposed to the dangers mentioned above, and may be sold marijuana. Police have found children living in or brought by their parents to the grow houses, exposing them to these hazards.[39]

What are the Signs of a Marijuana Home Grow Operation?

There are a number of factors that may indicate the presence of a marijuana home grow operation. These include:

- Residents rarely appear to be at home and may be in the house only for brief periods of time (such as a few hours) before leaving. Despite this, radios or televisions may be left on all night, making it sound as if someone were there.
- Visitors behave strangely or visit at odd hours.
- Entry into the home is often made through the garage or side/back entrance, to conceal activities.
- Windows are boarded or covered up, preventing light from entering the house and concealing activities inside. Bright lights may be seen escaping from the windows, and the windows may have a layer of condensation on them. Even though the windows are always closed, air conditioners never run.

- Equipment used in the growing operation (such as large fans, lights, plastic plant containers, and other items) is carried into the home.
- Sounds of construction or electrical humming from equipment may be heard.
- Exterior appearance of the property is untidy. There is little outside maintenance done (unshoveled snow, uncut grass, etc.), and garbage bags containing used soil and plant material may be discarded in areas surrounding the house. Mail delivered to the house may be left unchecked, so that flyers and junk mail pile up in the mailbox.
- Warning signs are posted in windows or around the outside the house. These may warn people to "Beware of the Dog" or that "Guard Dogs" are on the property.

Cash Value

The amount of money that marijuana grow houses generate is well into the billions. For example, recently the Riverside County California Sheriff's Department conducted raids on nine houses and found a total of 14,000 plants with an estimated value of $60 to $80 million.[40] Thus, this clearly is a very lucrative criminal enterprise. (See Figure 19-14).

Hashish

A drug-rich resinous secretion from the flowers of the cannabis plant, **hashish** is processed by drying to produce a drug several times as potent as marijuana. The resin from the flowers is richer in cannabinols than the leaves and tops, and THC content is from 5% to 12%. (The leaves range from 0.27% to 4% in THC content.) Hashish is most commonly smoked in a small "hash pipe."

Hashish Oil

The Middle East is the main source of hashish entering the United States. Liquid hashish, or **hashish oil,** is produced by concentrating THC. The liquid hashish so far discovered has varied between 20% and 65% THC. There is reason to suspect that methods are now being employed to make an even more powerful concentrate. The purity of the final product depends on the sophistication of the apparatus used.

Like other forms of the drug, liquid hashish can be used several ways. Because of its extraordinary potency, one drop of the material can produce a high. A drop may be placed on a regular cigarette, used in cooking, added to wine, and even smeared on bread. When smoked, a small drop of hashish oil is smeared inside the glass bowl of a special pipe with a flattened side. The user exhales deeply, tilts the bowl, and holds the flame from a match under the oil. In one inhalation, the smoker draws slowly on the pipe as the oil begins to bubble, continuing as it chars and burns.

There are many ways to produce hashish oil, but most clandestine operations use a basket filled with ground or chopped marijuana suspended inside a larger container, at the bottom of which is contained a solvent, such as alcohol, hexane, chloroform, or petroleum ether. Copper tubing or similar material is arranged at the top, and cold water circulates through it. The solvent is

◄**FIGURE 19-14 Cash value**
Riverside County California Sheriff's deputies clear out a house that was used for growing marijuana in a home in Eastvale; the plants were estimated to be worth one million dollars.
(© Thomas Cordova/Inland Valley Daily Bulletin)

heated, the vapors rise to the top, they condense, and then they fall into the basket of marijuana. As the solvent seeps through the plant materials, the THC and other soluble chemicals are dissolved, and the solution drops back to the bottom of the container. Continued heating causes the process to recur. The solution becomes increasingly stronger until the plant material is exhausted of its THC.

Drug Paraphernalia

Under federal law, *drug paraphernalia* refers to "any equipment, product, or material of any kind which is primarily intended or designed for use in manufacturing, compounding, converting, concealing, producing, processing, preparing, injecting, ingesting, inhaling, or otherwise introducing into the human body a controlled substance." This equipment can include roach clips, glass and ceramic pipes, water pipes, bongs, miniature spoons, and hypodermic needles. Since 1990, it has been illegal for anyone to sell, transport, or import/export drug paraphernalia, and those violating this federal law can be sentenced to up to 3 years in prison.[41]

Drug paraphernalia are readily available in retail establishments and from Internet sites, often tailored with trendy designs or references to popular music acts that appeal directly to young consumers. In an attempt to skirt federal law, paraphernalia are usually sold with disclaimers that indicate they are to be only used with tobacco products. However, the law states that there is no requirement to prove that a merchant has to have direct knowledge that the products are being used for illegal purposes.

Recently, targeting the supply of drug paraphernalia has become an increasingly popular initiative among federal and state agencies. Taking the position that purchasers of paraphernalia are generally involved in the abuse, production, or distribution of illegal drugs, and are therefore a valuable target in drug investigations, there has been a renewed focus on paraphernalia. Recently, law enforcement agencies in 11 states seized nearly 130 metric tons of paraphernalia, shut down several websites, and arrested 55 people during the Operation Pipedreams initiative.[42] Similar initiatives are ongoing nationally to target manufacturers and distributors of paraphernalia.

INHALANTS

A common misconception about inhalant *sniffing, snorting, bagging* (fumes inhaled from a plastic bag), or *huffing* (inhalant-soaked rags placed in the mouth) is that it is a childish fad similar to youthful experiments with cigarettes. But inhalant abuse is deadly serious and one of the most dangerous of "experimental behaviors." Sniffing volatile solvents, which includes most inhalants, can cause severe damage to the brain and nervous system. By starving the body of oxygen or forcing the heart to beat more rapidly and erratically, inhalants can kill adolescent sniffers.

Inhalant abuse came to public attention in the early 1950s when the news media reported that young people who were seeking a cheap high were sniffing glue. The term *glue sniffing* is still widely used, often to include inhalation of a broad range of common products besides glue. Although different in makeup, nearly all abused inhalants produce effects similar to anesthetics, which act to slow down the body's functions. When inhaled via the nose or mouth in sufficient concentrations, inhalants can cause intoxicating effects that can last a few minutes or several hours if taken repeatedly. Similar to alcohol, users initially may feel slightly stimulated; with successive inhalations, they may feel less inhibited and less in control; in severe cases, the user loses consciousness. Sniffing highly concentrated amounts of the chemicals in solvents or aerosol sprays can directly induce heart failure and death. This is especially common from the abuse of fluorocarbon and butane-type gases. High concentrations of inhalants also cause death from suffocation by displacing oxygen in the lungs, and in the central nervous system causing breathing to cease.

MAJOR COUNTRIES OF ORIGIN AND TRAFFICKING PATTERNS

The history of drug abuse in the United States is intertwined with trends and patterns of not only use but also illicit traffic. As world affairs change, so do the patterns of drug use and trafficking. For instance, after World War II and up through the early 1960s, most heroin entering the United States originated from the Middle East was refined in either Italy or Marseilles, France, and imported by major American Mafia and La Cosa Nostra organizations through major east coast cities such as New York and Philadelphia (e.g., *The French Connection*). However, with American involvement in Southeast Asia (Vietnam, Cambodia, and Laos) from 1965 on into the 1970s, heroin trafficking patterns significantly changed, utilizing new source countries and organizations. The 1980s witnessed an explosion of cocaine onto the American continent giving rise to the crack epidemic of the 1990s. Today, heroin and cocaine trafficking patterns have again changed, with sophisticated criminal organizations and cartels working more closely together. In addition, clandestine methamphetamine labs have become a major domestic problem giving rise to new criminal elements and raising environmental safety issues for local police officers. With the war in Iraq and leadership changes in historically important opium-growing countries such as Afghanistan, expected

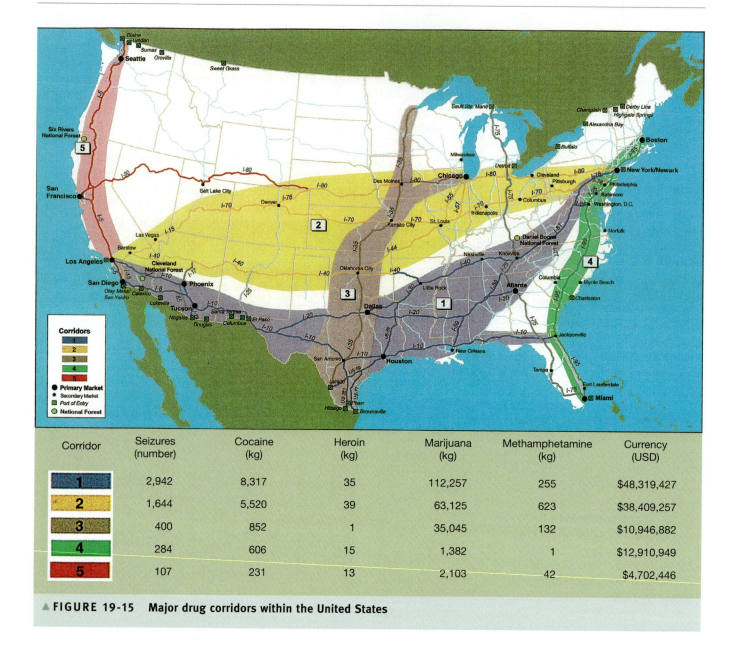

Corridor	Seizures (number)	Cocaine (kg)	Heroin (kg)	Marijuana (kg)	Methamphetamine (kg)	Currency (USD)
1	2,942	8,317	35	112,257	255	$48,319,427
2	1,644	5,520	39	63,125	623	$38,409,257
3	400	852	1	35,045	132	$10,946,882
4	284	606	15	1,382	1	$12,910,949
5	107	231	13	2,103	42	$4,702,446

▲ **FIGURE 19-15** **Major drug corridors within the United States**

increases in heroin and marijuana production may once again characterize changes in trafficking patterns. (See Figures 19-15 and 19-16.)

The following geographical areas provide a summary of today's existing trafficking patterns:

Mexico

Mexico has the distinction of being not only a major source of heroin, methamphetamine, and cocaine, but also as the major pathway for drugs from South America into the United States. The country has almost 2,000 miles of border shared with the United States, most of which is unsecured, making transport of drugs from Mexico a challenge to United States law enforcement at all levels. Furthermore, United States Customs officials are able to inspect only about 2% of commercial shipments from foreign countries, including Mexico.[43]

Mexico produces the majority of the marijuana consumed in the United States. The drug is smuggled into the United States via ports of entry located along the border and is generally dispersed throughout the country in private and commercial vehicles along major interstates and highways, particularly to large markets, such as Chicago, Los Angeles, New York, Miami, and Dallas.[44]

Mexico is also the principal source of foreign-produced methamphetamine in the United States. Because the United States has enacted measures to control many of the ingredients found in methamphetamine, Mexican labs have taken advantage of the lack of regulation on such items within their own country, as well as the ease of importing chemicals such as pseudoephedrine from Canada and the Middle East.[45] As a result, methamphetamine labs in Mexico have increased their capacity to export to the Southwestern United States in the past

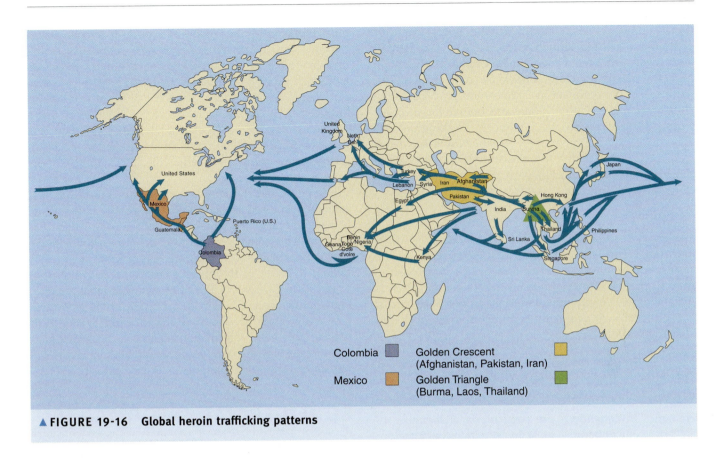

▲ **FIGURE 19-16   Global heroin trafficking patterns**

decade. Most methamphetamine trafficked from Mexico enters the United States via pedestrian couriers and both private and commercial vehicles, particularly through points of entry in Arizona, Texas, and California.[46]

Mexico also exports nearly 7 tons of heroin a year into the United States. Black tar heroin, a powerful yet inexpensive variety of the opiate, is made exclusively in Mexico.[47] The drug is smuggled into the United States mostly via pedestrian couriers and commercial and private vehicles. The most common points of entry are in Texas, particularly at Laredo and El Paso, and California at San Ysidro.[48]

Colombia

The country of Colombia, located in South America, has a political and environmental climate perfectly suited for the production and distribution of cocaine, heroin, and marijuana. Fertile valleys, which are generally removed from populated areas, are ideal for cultivation of opium poppies, marijuana plants, and coca leaves. Colombia also imports the coca plant, from Peru (the world's main source of the plant) and Bolivia for manufacture. Government corruption and political unrest in the country has created an atmosphere where clandestine cocaine production facilities can operate without fear of government intervention. These labs, in turn, are able to manufacture more cocaine than any other country in the world.[49] The drug is then generally delivered to Mexican traffickers for delivery into the United States through Texas, California, Arizona, and New Mexico. After the drug reaches the

United States, it is transported to either Mexican or Colombian trafficking groups for distribution into markets such as Baltimore, Boston, Detroit, Newark, and Phoenix. Marijuana and heroin are transported similarly, often through complex maritime shipments to Mexico. Heroin may be shipped directly into the United States by couriers aboard commercial airline flights.[50]

The Golden Crescent

The Golden Crescent is the moniker adopted for three countries in Southwest Asia: Afghanistan, Pakistan, and Iran. Currently, these countries contribute between 5% and 20% of the heroin imported to United States markets.[51] Afghanistan is also the world's leading cultivator of the opium poppy, especially since political turmoil in the region has made opium one of the few profitable crops in the region. Most of the crops, along with those from Pakistan and Iran, are exported into Turkey, where traffickers then use couriers to bring the drugs into the United States via commercial airlines. Most of these smuggled shipments are bound for New York and Chicago, where they are either sold locally or transported to other markets.[52] Pakistan and Afghanistan are also the largest producers of hashish.

The Golden Triangle

Burma, Laos, and Thailand make up the area referred to as the Golden Triangle, known mainly for heroin and marijuana production (see Figure 19-16). Thailand is also a major producer of methamphetamine. Drugs from this area are transported to the United States by Thai nationals, as well as Nigerian and Chinese traffickers. The main modes of transport include couriers on commercial flights, mail, and by concealment in cargo containers. Most of the shipments to the United States are bound for the East Coast, particularly to the Baltimore, Washington DC, New York, and Chicago areas. Another route for drugs from the Golden Triangle into the United States is through the U.S./Canadian border, particularly at Detroit and Buffalo, New York.[53]

Europe

Western Europe remains the biggest producer of MDMA, or ecstasy. The DEA estimated that nearly 80% of the ecstasy coming into the United States came from Western Europe, particularly Belgium and the Netherlands.[54] This drug is often directly transported by couriers into major U.S. airports such as JFK International in New York and Los Angeles International.

DRUG INVESTIGATIONS

Narcotics investigations are particularly challenging to law enforcement because most investigations begin before a crime actually occurs. The goal of any narcotics investigation, then, is to establish that there is probable cause that an individual or group is breaking the law by using, manufacturing, or selling drugs. Once probable cause has been established by methods such as surveillance, informant use or undercover work, search warrants may be granted and arrests can be made.

Gathering Information

Drug investigations must rely heavily on information from outside sources in order to develop a case. In fact, initiating a drug case depends on how well investigators can locate and identify leads that will strengthen their case against an identified target. Sources of information relevant to drug investigation targets can include telephone complaints, confidential informants, patrol officers, private sector sources, outside agencies, and internal police records.

Anonymous Tips

Anonymous tips can come from people with varying motives: relatives or neighbors may be concerned about a loved one's health or about their own safety if drug manufacture or other such activity is taking place near their home; the exgirlfriend or boyfriend of a drug dealer may turn them in for the sake of revenge; or a disgruntled customer may anonymously tip off police if he or she feels cheated by a dealer.

Telephone calls to law enforcement agencies are the most common form of anonymous tip. Because anonymous tipsters generally prefer to remain anonymous, great care

must be taken by those who answer such phone calls to capture as much relevant information as possible. Narcotics investigators should train telephone operators to consistently ask specific information that will help to prioritize complaints. Narcotics complaints are different from others in that there is often no obvious victim or evidence that a drug crime has happened after it has been committed. It is therefore important that those taking telephone reports of a drug crime ascertain whether the information is more than hearsay.[55] When taking a telephone complaint about a drug crime, one should note whether the complainant has actually witnessed the crime that he or she is reporting. One should also note whether or not the complainant has personally been involved in a narcotics transaction with the person he or she is registering the complaint against and is willing to assist in the investigation or talk to police or prosecutors if necessary. If a complainant is merely reporting what he or she heard from a third party, the report will take a lower priority than one from a caller who reports specific, first-hand information relating to drug manufacture or sale. However, any information that might corroborate an existing investigation should be a priority.

CONFIDENTIAL INFORMANTS

Although legitimate telephone or walk-in complaints from the public are valuable to drug investigators, they are relatively rare. Narcotics investigators have to rely heavily on the use of confidential informants, who generally know dealers, manufacturers, and users personally. Confidential informants are useful because they are able to gather information not usually available to law enforcement officers through their personal knowledge and familiarity with narcotics offenders. They are often able to gain first-hand and up-to-the-minute information about drug crimes that can be the basis of warrants for searches and arrests if properly corroborated by the investigator.[56] However, the ability of informants to gather such information often means that they are criminals themselves, making their motivations suspect and the management of such informants difficult. The career of a narcotics investigator often depends on how well he or she is able to recruit, develop, and manage informants. As a result, it is crucial that investigators understand motivations and types of informants.

Informants: Motivations and Types

Like most people, informants need motivation to produce. The more motivated they are, the more likely they are to apply themselves to the task at hand and remain committed to achieving success. Therefore, by identifying an informant's true motives, an investigator greatly enhances the potential success of an investigation. Initially, informants commonly voice a specific motive for providing assistance. However, as a case proceeds and a relationship with an investigator develops, other reasons may surface. Some of the more common motivational factors encountered by drug enforcement investigators are fear, revenge, money, repentance, and altruism.[57]

The most frequently encountered motivational factor may be the confidential informant's (CI's) fear of punishment for criminal acts. Severe criminal penalties tend to increase the number of persons wanting to cooperate with drug enforcement authorities. Informants may also fear their criminal associates. Individuals wrongly accused by drug dealers of being informants may then become informants for self-preservation, money, or both.

Informants frequently cooperate with the government to seek revenge against their enemies. Jealousy may also prompt their acts of vengeance.

Some individuals provide information or services for money. These money-motivated informants, known as *mercenaries*, are usually the most willing to follow the directions of their handlers. Mercenaries frequently possess other motives as well.

Repentance can be a motivating factor. Informants often claim they cooperate in order to repent for past crimes. However, this is seldom their only motive for cooperating.

Some individuals are motivated by a sense of altruism. People with professional obligations or feelings of responsibility frequently provide information to the police. Examples of altruistic informants include airline ticket agents and private mail-service carriers.

Problem Informants

Some informants have personalities that make them difficult, if not impossible, to manage. These individuals may also have questionable motives for offering their services to a law enforcement agency. Investigators who misjudge the true motives of informants experience tremendous control problems, which can create safety issues and place department resources and personnel in jeopardy. Therefore, investigators should avoid recruiting certain types of individuals, if possible.

Egotistical Informants

Egotistical informants, who are encountered frequently, may not have received positive reinforcement from their parents or schoolmates when growing up. Consequently, they seek positive feedback from their handlers as their primary reward. Investigators who provide this positive reinforcement motivate egotistical informants to continue supplying information. Unfortunately, these informants are often the hardest to handle, because their egos prevent them from relinquishing control of the investigation entirely to their handlers.

Informants with "James Bond Syndrome"

Some persons see their roles as informants as a way to have their lives imitate art. While working as informants, they imagine themselves in a police or spy drama. Sometimes they even attempt to orchestrate events to parallel a scene from a movie or novel. Frequently hard to handle, these informants often exaggerate their knowledge of criminal activity to enhance the likelihood of their becoming informants.

Wannabe Informants

Wannabe informants are people who, for whatever reason, failed to qualify for a law enforcement position and now seek to become involved in law enforcement as informants. Because they lack criminal associates, these individuals usually cannot provide specific information about drug dealing. Therefore, they do not make good informants.

Perversely Motivated Informants

The most dangerous and disruptive informants in drug law enforcement are perversely motivated CIs. They offer their services in order to identify undercover agents; learn the department's methods, targets, and intelligence; or eliminate their own competition in drug sales. Sometimes criminal organizations instruct these individuals to infiltrate departments and learn whatever they can to assist the traffickers. These individuals may even provide genuine information about specific events as a decoy to divert resources from more significant trafficking activity.

Therefore, investigators must question all walk-in and call-in informants (i.e., individuals who volunteer their services without prompting), because they may be, or have the potential to be, perversely motivated. After completing a thorough background investigation of CIs, investigators must constantly guard against providing more information than informants furnish in return. Furthermore, investigators should not discuss specific details of methods and techniques used during drug investigations with informants.

Restricted-Use Informants

In addition to problem informants certain other informants, by virtue of their criminal background or other status, pose special management challenges to both investigators and supervisors.[58] Department managers should carefully scrutinize these individuals before using them as CIs. Examples include juveniles, individuals on probation or parole, individuals currently or formerly addicted to drugs, felons with multiple convictions, and individuals known to be unreliable.

Investigators should not use these individuals as informants until a supervisor approves them. In fact, because these informants require special scrutiny, only senior investigators should handle them. Furthermore, investigators must constantly reevaluate the motives of these individuals.

Department Policy

Agencies should not leave the management of drug informants exclusively to investigators. Formulating a written policy ensures consistency in the use and management of CIs and serves as a guide for inexperienced investigators.[59]

The policy should indicate which investigators may maintain informants, as well as who will supervise these CIs. In addition, the policy should clearly establish that informants are assets of the department, not of individual investigators. In this regard, management should both authorize and encourage investigators to share informants. Also, checks and balances must be in place to ensure that the policy is followed.

Policy concerning the management of confidential informants should establish procedures in several areas. These include creating and documenting informant files, debriefing and interacting with informants, and determining methods and amounts of payments for services rendered.

The Informant File

Investigators should formally establish files for CIs who regularly furnish information, as well as for those who expect compensation for information they supply. Informant files document investigators' interactions with CIs. In fact, investigators should not use any source that cannot be documented.

Although investigators should document their contacts with CIs, not everyone in the department needs to know an informant's identity or have access to informant files. Access should be on a need-to-know basis, including only the investigators and their supervisors who deal directly with the informant.

To further protect informants' identities, investigators should use code numbers in lieu of informants' names in investigative reports. Informants should keep the same number throughout their working relationships with the department.

The informant file should include information pertaining to the CI's vital statistics, such as physical description, work and home addresses, vehicles driven, contact telephone numbers, next of kin, and so forth. National Crime Information Center searches, performed before the informant is used and then systematically thereafter, ensure that the informant has no outstanding warrants. These records should be kept in the informant's file, along with the CI's photograph, fingerprints, and FBI and state "rap" sheets.

Establishing an informant file sends a not-so-subtle message to CIs that investigators document every encounter and verify all information that CIs supply. Such documentation may also deter a perversely motivated informant. In addition, informant files enhance the credibility of the department in the eyes of the court and the public, who view CIs as inherently unreliable and who may believe that the agency fabricated information. Therefore, every time an informant provides information concerning an actual or a potential criminal matter, the agency should include a written report detailing this information in the CI's file. The original report should remain in that file, and a copy should be maintained in the case file.

The department must also document what steps it takes to corroborate information provided by a CI. This is especially important when informants act unilaterally. As a matter of policy, all CI information should be verified regardless of the CI's past reliability.

Informant Debriefings

Each time investigators initiate investigations on the basis of information received from a CI, the designated handler should interview and debrief the CI in order to ascertain the informant's motive(s) and to advise the informant of the department's rules. For example, informants should know that they carry no official status with the department, that the department will not tolerate their breaking the law or entrapping suspects, and that the department cannot guarantee that they will not be called as witnesses in court.

At the end of the interview, the investigator should put this information in writing in an "informant agreement." This agreement should be signed by the informant, witnessed by the handler, and placed in the informant's file. Investigators should debrief their informants on a regular basis—for example, every 30, 60, or 90 days—to keep them active or, if necessary, to terminate their association with the department because of lack of productivity.

Investigator-Informant Contact Procedures

The department must establish investigator-informant contact procedures and train employees in their use. For example, the handler should meet with the informant in private, if possible, but always in the presence of another investigator. In fact, the department should either strongly discourage or prohibit investigators from contacting informants alone, especially if the officer plans to pay the informant. Meeting with or paying a drug informant alone leaves the officer and the department vulnerable to allegations of wrongdoing.

Although informant handlers often develop special working relationships with their informants, department policies should preclude contact with informants outside the scope of official business. Investigators must keep their relationships with CIs strictly professional. This is particularly important when the informant and the investigator are not of the same sex. Policies should also expressly prohibit such contact as socializing with informants and/or their families, becoming romantically involved with informants, conducting nonpolice business with them, and accepting gifts or gratuities from them.[60]

To ensure adherence to department policy, supervisors should review informant files regularly. In addition, they need to attend debriefings periodically to oversee the entire informant management process.

Finally, departmet administrators must establish procedures for investigating alleged policy violations by investigators or informants. Thorough investigations of this type maintain the integrity of the department by dispelling any notion that the department does not enforce its own policies.

Informant Payments

Payments to CIs can be divided into two distinct categories—awards and rewards. Awards take a monetary form. They are based on a percentage of the net value of assets seized during a drug investigation as a result of information provided by a CI. Advising the informant of the exact amount of the percentage at the beginning of the case provides incentive for the CI to seek out hidden assets that might otherwise go undetected. However, because payments based on seized assets are not universally accepted in the courts, the investigator should consult the case prosecutor before promising a specific amount to the informant.

Rewards, however, do not represent a percentage of the value of the seized assets. Amounts are usually determined by the type and the quantity of drugs seized, the quality of the case produced, the number of defendants indicted, the amount of time and effort the CI exerted, and the danger faced by the CI during the course of the investigation. Unlike awards, rewards come directly from an agency's budget.

While an informant might receive money as a reward, many informants cooperate with law enforcement agencies to receive a reduced sentence for a pending criminal matter. Regardless of the form of compensation, the department's policy must address the circumstances under which an informant qualifies for an award and/or reward, who can authorize such payments, and the conditions under which payments will be granted.

Although many informants receive substantial awards when they locate the assets of drug dealers, agency budgets may limit the dollar amount of rewards paid to informants. For this reason, investigators should exercise caution when explaining the payment policy to informants. They should avoid mentioning a specific dollar amount that the informant will receive. Otherwise, the informant may try to hold the department to that amount, regardless of future budgetary constraints.

In addition to providing awards and rewards, departments can reimburse informants for expenses incurred during an investigation. In fact, the department may want to reimburse the CI with small amounts of money beyond actual expenses as added incentives to continue working.

It is highly recommended that informants be paid only in the presence of witnesses, with the final payment being made after all court proceedings have been completed to help ensure the informant's presence at the trial. Once a payment is made, a record documenting the date, exact amount, and payer must be included in the CI file in anticipation of future court inquiries.

Other Sources for Information

Patrol officers are a valuable asset to narcotics investigators, and every effort should be made by investigators to foster a good relationship with them. Patrol officers have inherent advantages over investigators because they already have a routine presence in neighborhoods where drug activity takes place, allowing them to collect specific information without arousing suspicion. Furthermore, patrol officers are familiar with the layout of neighborhoods and, on occasion, specific houses or buildings, making them invaluable in planning surveillance or raids.[61] Patrol officers may also have unofficial informants who may be parlayed into formal informants for narcotics investigators. Because of the additional resources that they offer, developing relationships with patrol officers is a sound strategy in drug investigations.

Information from Private Sector Sources

The private sector can provide a wealth of information valuable to drug cases about suspects and their behavior. Drug offenders tend to come into contact with a predictable group of private sector businesses, such as travel agents, car rental employees, hotel clerks, retail clerks, and pharmacists, who may volunteer information to investigators.[62] Travel agents can show investigators patterns of travel that may outline trafficking destinations. Retail clerks may be able to tell officers about customers who repeatedly purchase large quantities of the materials found in crystal meth. Realtors are often able to obtain floor plans for homes they have sold, aiding in the planning of raids or searches.

Telephone/cellular phone providers and Internet service providers are also valuable tools to investigators. Internet service providers can pull and track e-mails that may be pertinent to investigations. This generally requires a court order. Lists of telephone calls made from a phone must also be obtained via subpoena. This information is one of the most important tools available to a narcotics investigator as it allows them to track communications between drug offenders, leading to identification of other involved parties or triangulation of hiding places, clandestine labs, and the like.[63]

Outside Agencies

Outside agencies can also offer a wealth of information about a suspect in a narcotics investigation. Outside police agencies, such as the Drug Enforcement Administration (DEA), the Federal Bureau of Investigation (FBI), the Internal Revenue Service (IRS), Immigration and Customs Enforcement (ICE), and others, may have useful information or resources to offer investigators. For example, the IRS may be investigating a suspect on money laundering charges and could provide information pertinent to that suspect's drug activities. Investigators should keep in mind, however, that not all outside law enforcement agencies are forthcoming with information that they have obtained about a suspect. Often, developing relationships with agents in organizations that an investigator has frequent contact with is a good way to obtain information that would not normally be shared with other agencies. Many agencies use shared databases where information about ongoing cases, upcoming busts, and suspects is available at the click of a mouse. Police agencies may subscribe to such databases or may obtain access by way of task forces or other forms of interagency cooperation.

Internal Records

One of the best sources of information for investigations is the drug unit's own police department. Investigators should look for the following types of information when searching for intelligence on a suspect, criminal organization, or geographical area: police intelligence reports organized by suspect name, address, or type of criminal activity; incident reports that contain records of previous offenses; National Crime Information Center (NCIC) records, which contain in-depth information on a person's criminal history; field interview cards filled out routinely by patrol officers investigating criminal activity; traffic citations, which are helpful in obtaining physical descriptions and other identifiers; fingerprint files; arrest records; and warrant files, which include detailed information about a suspect or a physical location.[64]

Surveillance

Surveillance, defined as the "surreptitious observation of persons, places, objects, or conveyances for the purpose of determining criminal involvement,"[65] is an excellent tool used by narcotics investigators to gather information about a suspect. Surveillance is required to corroborate intelligence from informants, confirm criminal activity, obtain probable cause and to gather intelligence about a suspect's routines and behaviors that may be of use in planning apprehension.

Surveillance is an expensive and very time-consuming activity. It requires the efforts of multiple officers at a time, including a supervisor. Equipment required for surveillance, such as binoculars, cameras with telephoto lenses, communication systems, and night-vision devices is costly. Furthermore, officers may spend long periods of time trying to achieve the objectives of any surveillance operation. Anywhere from a few hours to a couple of weeks may be spent watching a subject, depending on the complexity of an investigation.

Before any type of surveillance begins, officers should have already gathered basic information about a suspect. Physical descriptions of the suspect and his or her vehicle are crucial, as well as descriptions of associates. The suspect's home and business address should be ascertained, in addition to the addresses of locations he or she frequents.

Once this basic information has been determined, investigators should scout out the locations where surveillance will take place. Investigators should map out

the area, finding the best places from which to conduct surveillance. It is also a good idea to become familiar with the layout of the area, noting street names and traffic conditions to ensure maximum mobility. Officers should also determine what types of vehicles are more likely to go unnoticed in the area, and how they should dress so that they don't look suspicious or out of place while conducting surveillance.

Electronic Surveillance

Electronic surveillance is often used to supplement mobile and stationary surveillance and is also very useful as supporting evidence in court cases. However, electronic surveillance is also subject to a number of legal considerations because of its intrusive nature. Officers should familiarize themselves with case law relevant to electronic surveillance and always consult with prosecutors before utilizing these types of surveillance.

The most prominent method of electronic surveillance is wiretapping, using third-party eavesdropping devices placed on telephone lines to capture conversations. As often as wiretaps are seen as investigative tools on fictional law enforcement television shows, they are actually used as a last resort in many cases. They are very expensive and time-intensive. Furthermore, they are quite complex, legally speaking. In *Katz v. United States*, 389 U.S. 347 (1967), the United States Supreme Court held that wiretaps create an intrusion into a person's reasonable expectation of privacy and therefore constitute a "search and seizure" as defined by the Fourth Amendment to the Constitution of the United States. As a result, wiretaps require probable cause and a warrant to authorize the intrusion. However, they are a very useful tool in many complex investigations.

When an officer is a party to a conversation with a suspect, generally in cases in which undercover officers are being utilized, he or she can record the conversation without violating the suspect's reasonable expectation of privacy. Recording telephone conversations between an officer and a suspect is allowable then, as is use of a concealed microphone.

Pen registers are another means of telephone surveillance. These tools actually decode the dialed impulses on phone lines in order to record all numbers dialed from that phone. They record the date and time of all phone calls made and are effective tools when the suspect routinely uses his or her phone to conduct drug transactions. However, the information gained is of little value unless investigators invest time into following up information obtained by the pen registers.

Video and Photo Surveillance

Known as *visual surveillance*, the use of both still and video cameras to corroborate audio surveillance and officer observation is important to drug investigations and their prosecution. When using still photography, investigators can use 35-mm or small digital cameras to document criminal

◄ **FIGURE 19-17   Undercover officer making an immediate narcotics arrest on the street**
"Buy/Bust" operations are commonly used by the police to control drug traffic. Most often, they yield low amounts of drugs and cash but are designed to have an immediate impact on the visible trade in a specific area or neighborhood.
(© Steve Starr/Corbis)

activity. Although basic camera setups are sufficient, attachments such as telephoto lenses and night-vision equipment can enhance photographs. Date and time stamps on cameras may also be helpful for purposes of corroboration.

Video cameras provide a more complete document of surveillance activity than photographs do and can also be fitted with night-vision or infrared equipment for nighttime surveillance.[66]

Trash

Searching through discarded trash is another supplement to surveillance. Often, suspects may discard documents or materials that are helpful to investigators trying to establish probable cause. For example, crystal meth manufacturers often discard telltale signs that they are operating a meth lab, such as large quantities of empty blister packs that contained pseudoephedrine pills or battery packages. Investigators should take care to remain surreptitious when retrieving and going through a suspect's trash. *Trashing,* as it is sometimes called, does not require a warrant because there is no expectation of privacy with discarded trash that is essentially in plain view for all to see.

Undercover Operations

Often portrayed by popular television and movies, undercover drug operations are actually used quite sparingly by law enforcement. These operations are very dangerous and can take a large toll on the personal lives of undercover officers. However, they are quite useful in identifying participants in drug conspiracies, whether they involve manufacturers, distributors, or users. Undercover officers can often predict which participants may be cooperative with law enforcement and are able to identify

evidence for prosecution of drug crimes. They are often privy to locations of drugs or other evidence and usually know the locations of drug proceeds as well. The undercover officer is also very useful in determining the time and place appropriate for search and seizures and arrests.[67] (See Figure 19-17.)

The officers selected for undercover work ultimately determine the success of the operation. They should be intelligent, reliable, confident, resourceful, and have good judgment and excellent communication skills. They should also have a solid knowledge base of the types(s) of drug they are investigating. Training is essential to the success of the undercover officer. Experienced undercover officers should always be the first choice for assignments, unless a less-experienced officer has a special skill required in the investigation that other officers do not (such as Spanish-language proficiency).[68]

Undercover operations may be as simple as a one-off purchase from a dealer or as in-depth as posing as someone who possesses a special skill needed by a drug trafficker, such as a truck driver or a pilot. The amount of preparation and back story needed will vary depending on the complexity of the operations. Smaller operations are the norm in drug investigations, and minimizing the contact between undercover officers and suspects is ideal, because the longer a suspect and officer have contact, the more likely it is that the officer will be discovered. Long-term undercover operations are expensive and dangerous, and generally are not used by local law enforcement entities.

Buying drugs from a suspect is the best means of gathering evidence about a drug operation. When an undercover officer develops a relationship with a suspect, he or she will generally have many opportunities to purchase drugs as evidence. Officers should have some type of monitored surveillance, such as a hidden microphone, ongoing throughout the transaction, allowing for corroboration as well as officer safety. This is a situation unique to drug investigations, because the officer is actually participating in the commission of a crime. This is lawful, provided that it can be shown that the suspect would have committed the act with or without the presence of the officer.[69] **Drug buy operations** by undercover officers generally fall under one of four categories.

Buy-Walk

These types of buys are usually made as part of an ongoing investigation whereby investigators attempt to make cases against distributors by working up the ladder to the source or merely attempting to gain the confidence of the seller. In buy-walk cases, the undercover officer purchases drugs from the suspect but does not initiate an arrest after completion of the deal. The officer often makes multiple buys from the suspect. This method fosters a business relationship with the suspect and generates a number of investigative leads. Once the suspect feels comfortable with the officer, the officer may get an opportunity to identify places of residence and observe other associates.[70] Small, multiple purchases may be chemically analyzed for purity and for signatures that can be traced back to distributors. Furthermore, with each drug purchase, larger quantities may be negotiated in order to pinpoint the source of the drugs. One successful technique is to work up to requesting a quantity that the dealer is incapable of providing without traveling to his or her supplier and then conducting vehicle surveillance to identify the supplier.[71]

Buy-Bust

In the buy-bust, the undercover officer completes a drug buy, resulting in the immediate arrest of the seller. These operations generally take place only with small amounts of drugs or cash and are considered very dangerous to the undercover officer, owing to the proximity between the officer and the suspect when the arrest commences. Undercover officers should not be physically involved with the arrest and should in fact back away from the situation as much as possible once they have completed the transaction. This method is generally used in small cases, where conspiracies are not involved.[72]

Buy(Flash)/Bust

This is the most commonly used technique in undercover drug enforcement operations. The "flash" is a large quantity of money that an undercover officer shows to a suspect without actually giving it to them. It serves as a guarantee that the undercover officer can pay for a large quantity of drugs upon delivery. This operation is very dangerous; undercover officers have been murdered for the flash money, which can range from $5,000 to $100,000. Following is a list of considerations essential to ensuring safe management of the buy(flash)/bust:[73]

1. Whenever possible, isolate the suspects and get them on neutral ground to do the transaction.
2. Do not allow the suspects to isolate the undercover officer. The best way to avoid this is by staying on neutral ground. The undercover officer should dictate the time and the place to the suspects.
3. Flash the money in an open location, isolating suspects from one another if possible. Do not flash the money twice in the same location.
4. Minimize the vulnerability of the undercover officer during the bust.
5. The undercover officer should always be armed.

Flash busts are very effective, but must be carefully managed to ensure the safety and the integrity of the investigation. Informants should never be allowed to handle flash rolls, and if possible, two undercover officers should be used in these types of transactions. If one officer handles the money, he or she can leave as soon as the flash is completed, increasing the safety of both officers.[74] Flash busts require extensive training and a consistent policy on the part of police departments, and should only be attempted by experienced undercover officers.

Reverse Operations

The final type of undercover operation is the reverse operation. Reverse undercover operations are those in which the officer acts as the seller of the drug, in an effort to obtain probable cause against drug buyers. This type of operation is more controversial than the buy/busts previously discussed, because of the element of entrapment bound to be brought up in defense claims. Investigators must take care to show other evidence that the buyer was predetermined to commit the crime, with or without the presence of the officer.[75]

Undercover operations are far more complex than a few pages in a textbook can convey. Entire books have been written about the factors involved in such operations, and undercover officers receive careful and in-depth training to help them prepare for all levels of undercover work. Undercover work in narcotics investigation is a valuable tool but requires immense operational planning to be successful and safe.

Informant Purchases

A tool similar to undercover purchases of drugs involves confidential informants obtaining drugs via a controlled purchase. This usually occurs when use of an undercover officer would be impractical. If a peddler will sell only to an informant, and not to an undercover officer, the informant must be searched before the sale to make sure that he or she has no narcotics already on his or her person. Officers should ensure that the informant have no money on him, except official funds with recorded serial numbers for the purchase. The informant should be wired with a hidden microphone in order to corroborate the transactions. Surveillance teams should monitor the informant constantly throughout the transaction, and the informant should go to a designated location immediately after the transaction in order to be searched. At that time, evidence should be recovered from the informant, and he or she should be thoroughly debriefed. Evidence obtained through "informant buys" is admissible in court, but the testimony of the informant may be required.

Drug Canines

Drug dogs are extremely useful to narcotics investigations; a positive alert by a canine can provide probable cause to further search a suspect. Dogs have a keen sense of odor, with nearly 30 times more olfactory cells than humans. When properly trained, canines can be used in a variety of settings to detect the presence of drugs. Drug dogs are usually used to provide passive alerts that drugs are present. This means that the dog either sits or uses some other signal (such as a bark) when the odor of drugs is detected. Canines can be used in vehicle examinations, freight examinations, consensual encounters between suspects and officers in homes, airports, businesses, bus stations, and storage facilities. Canines may also be used in limited person examinations.[76]

The Supreme Court ruled in *U.S.* v. *Place*, 462 US 696 (1983), that use of a drug canine to sniff property is not considered a search. However, use of a drug dog to sniff a person is less clear legally. Many courts have ruled that using canines to sniff a person for presence of drug odors requires reasonable suspicion and that random and suspicionless dog sniffs are not reasonable.[77]

Drug dogs differ from track-and-bite canines, which are taught to be aggressive upon apprehension of a subject. Drug dogs must never use aggression toward a suspect. Canines are a very expensive undertaking for a police department. They must be carefully trained, and a handler must be selected and trained. The training of a drug dog is ongoing and is critical to the admissibility to the any evidence obtained through its use. (See Figure 19-18.)

Field Testing

A variety of field testing kits are available to law enforcement to give valuable clues about the identity of substances. Field tests can test for the presence of specific substances, including marijuana, cocaine, amphetamine, and heroin. Investigator kits usually include vials of chemicals in small pouches. When small samples of a substance are put into the pouch and then the chemicals in the vials are released, the mixture will produce certain colors. Those colors indicate the presence of controlled substances.[78]

Field tests are easy to perform. They are, however, only presumptive because they may produce false positives. Any drug that will be used as evidence must be positively identified by a qualified chemist. Additionally, a negative test does not preclude the possibility that another similar drug may be present.[79]

▲ FIGURE 19-18   Drug dog in action
Canines provide an invaluable service to police officers in detecting the presence of drugs in clandestine places. They are often used during search warrant executions as well as during routine checks of international flights to detect smuggled drugs and paraphernalia.
(© Dale C. Spartas/Corbis)
(Source: www.dogswithjobs.com/about_dogs/about.htm)

High-Intensity Drug Trafficking Area (HIDTA) Programs

HIDTA programs are an invaluable resource to narcotics investigations. HIDTA programs were created by the Anti-Drug Abuse Act of 1988 and provide federal assistance to better coordinate and enhance counterdrug law enforcement efforts of local, state, and federal agencies in areas where major drug activity occurs. Currently, there are 28 HIDTAs in the nation, including Puerto Rico and the U.S. Virgin Islands (see Figure 19-19). HIDTAs are joint efforts of regional, local, and federal agencies, whose leaders work together to assess regional drug threats, to design strategies to combat those threats, and to develop initiatives to implement the strategies. Regional strategies include building multiagency task forces. HIDTA legislation also provides for investigative support centers in designated areas that create a communications infrastructure that can facilitate information-sharing between agencies.[80]

◀ FIGURE 19-19
High intensity drug trafficking area—HIDTA task force locations

The High Intensity Drug Trafficking Area (HIDTA) program enhances and coordinates drug control efforts among local, state, and federal law enforcement agencies. The program provides agencies with coordination, equipment, technology, and additional resources to combat drug trafficking and its harmful consequences in critical regions of the United States.

For example, the Washington/Baltimore area HIDTA offers software for participating agencies that provides case management functions and also notifies agencies if another agency is collecting information on the same suspect. They also grant access to a number of databases that allow investigators to access law enforcement records and financial information.[81] The North Texas HIDTA analyzes information from participating departments, and identifies major drug trafficking organizations, including patterns and trends of these organizations. The North Texas HIDTA's Investigative Support Center prepared 644 intelligence profiles and conducted over 10,000 database searches in 2002. That same year, the North Texas HIDTA seized 23 pounds of methamphetamine in the course of one investigation in the Dallas area, and indicted 24 participants in a crack-cocaine distribution ring in Denton, TX.[82]

HIDTAs are just one example of a task force in action. Each jurisdiction may have its own drug task forces, involving a variety of law enforcement or outside agencies, which are valuable to narcotics investigations. Investigators should take full advantage of these resources, when available.

SEARCHES, SEIZURES, AND WARRANTS

Drug investigations are useless without evidence. Therefore, it is vitally important that an investigator be knowledgeable of the latest legal guidelines that govern the search for, and seizure of, evidence. Case law in the United States provides literally thousands of decisions that affect how officers may handle searches and seizures. There are some major principles, however, that every narcotics investigator should be familiar with in order to present a legally sound case against drug criminals. Things that are commonly searched for and seized in drug crimes include the drugs themselves or other contraband; instrumentalities of a crime, meaning those items that are not necessarily illegal on their own but that are used to carry out a crime; fruits of a crime, such as things bought with drug proceeds; and mere evidence of a crime.

Probable Cause

The general requirements for searches and seizures of evidence or persons are a search warrant or recognized exception to the warrant requirement (to be discussed later) and probable cause. Probable cause to search and seize exists when "facts and circumstances in a given situation are sufficient to warrant a person of reasonable caution to believe that seizable objects are located at the place to be searched."[83] Generally, a single fact cannot establish probable cause. It is usually several facts and circumstances taken together that do. Probable cause may also be established by hearsay, which is typically the case with informants. This information may be used as long it can be shown that the totality of the circumstances surrounding the information suggests that it is reliable. Information should be verifiable, and corroborating information is helpful in establishing probable cause.[84]

Search Warrants

The search warrant is one of the most valuable tools available to a narcotics investigator. The warrant authorizes searches of homes, businesses, and automobiles of subjects and generally results in the arrest of multiple suspects, expediting the investigation and its closure.[85]

Searches require search warrants, or a recognized exception to a warrant in order to be legal. There are four requirements for the valid issuance of a search warrant. The first is that a neutral and impartial magistrate authorizes the warrant. The second requirement is that probable cause exists to search the place described in the warrant. Third, the warrant must be precise in describing both the places and persons to be searched and the items to be seized. Fourth, the warrant requires a supporting oath or affirmation by the requesting officer. Narcotics officers requesting a warrant should follow additional guidelines when requesting warrants, since so much of the information provided to law enforcement officers comes from confidential informants.

Past Reliability of The Confidential Informant

The past reliability of the confidential informant is of considerable importance, especially when the effort to determine probable cause to obtain a search warrant is based exclusively on such information. One should consider the length of time the applicant has known the informant and the number of occasions on which reliable information was supplied. For example, how many times before did the confidential informant's information result in the seizure of contraband or paraphernalia on persons, on premises, or in vehicles, and how many of these offenses resulted in a conviction? To confirm that the confidential informant has been reliable, the officer should be prepared to cite specific instances of reliable information. Other considerations are the informant's familiarity with the type of offense involved in the affidavit and familiarity with paraphernalia used in connection with the offense.

Information Supplied by The Informant

Information to be considered in this area includes the date, time, and place of the meeting between police and the informant; the substance and content of the information; and the date, time, and place that the information was obtained.

The law enforcement officer should try to elicit from the informant as many facts as possible that can be corroborated—for example, the telephone number and address of the suspect's residence, a physical description of the suspect, the occupation of the suspect, vehicles owned or operated by the suspect, a description of the vehicle and the tag number, and the time at which the suspect may be observed at the premises or within the described vehicle.

Corroboration of The Information Supplied

All efforts should be made to corroborate information supplied by a confidential informant. In some instances, corroboration is a simple check of the accuracy of portions of the information, such as the suspect's address, associates, vehicle, hangouts, patterns of behavior, and criminal record. When information is corroborated, careful records should be kept, including the date, time, and method of corroboration. Some jurisdictions have found it useful to attach a mug shot of the suspect along with a photograph, diagram, or sketch of the property, vehicle, store, or other place to be searched.

There are also requirements for the valid execution of a search warrant. The first is that time limits set out in the warrant or by statute are observed. This requirement ensures that probable cause remains until the warrant is executed. Next, time-of-day limits should be observed. This means that officers should serve warrants at a reasonable hour, mostly because of safety and privacy concerns. Officers must knock and announce their presence before gaining entry to a home or business, unless an exigency exists. Another requirement states that police can not go beyond the terms spelled out in the search warrant. Finally, officers must leave an inventory of items seized with both the suspect and the judge who issued the search warrant.

The Exclusionary Rule

This rule states that courts will exclude any evidence that is obtained in violation of the Fourth Amendment's provisions against unreasonable searches and seizures, no matter how pertinent it is to the case at hand. This includes *Fruit of the Poisoned Tree* items. This means that evidence recovered from constitutionally sound methods may be excluded if the initial action was proven to be illegal. For example, an officer may legally search a person incident to their arrest. However, if that initial arrest is later determined to be illegal, the items recovered during the post-arrest search may be thrown out.[86] There are exceptions to the exclusionary rule, however. The first is the *Good Faith Exception*. This states that if officers act in reasonable reliance on a search warrant, that is issued by a neutral magistrate but is ultimately found to be invalid, the evidence may still be used.[87] The second is the *doctrine of inevitable discovery*. This doctrine holds that evidence that would have been discovered with or without the illegal search or seizure is allowed into court.[88] The computer errors exception allows evidence to be admitted even though the search or seizure was based on an erroneous piece of information.[89]

Warrantless Searches

There are cases where warrants are not necessary, although these are each fairly narrowly defined by the courts. The first is the consent search. These types of searches are permissible without a warrant and without probable cause as long as consent has been voluntarily given by a person who has authority to give consent and that the scope of the search doesn't exceed the consent given. Narcotics officers should keep in mind that the scope of a consent search must be consistent with the nature of the consent given and that the consenter can place limitations on the search.

Vehicle searches are also exempt from the warrant requirement. This is a boon to narcotics officers, because many drug traffickers conceal drugs within their vehicles. The logic behind allowing warrantless searches of vehicles is that there is a reduced expectation of privacy in vehicles because they are mobile and used in public areas, their interiors are visible to the outside, and because vehicles are highly regulated by the government.

Vehicles also create an exigency in that they are inherently moveable. In other words, by the time a narcotics officer is able to write an affidavit and obtain a warrant, the vehicle may be gone. As a result, a narcotics officer may stop a car based on reasonable suspicion and then search that vehicle, including all passenger areas, containers, and the trunk when they have probable cause to believe evidence or contraband is contained.[90]

Vehicles that have been lawfully impounded may also be searched without a warrant, but the search may not be a pretense for further investigation. Searches of impounded vehicles are allowed for the safety of officers and the impounding agency, and as a result must take place within agency guidelines and procedures.

Open-field searches are another type of search that can take place without a warrant. The Supreme Court has held that open fields outside the curtilage surrounding buildings or homes are not constitutionally protected and are therefore allowable without a search warrant. There is no reasonable expectation of privacy in an open field.[91] This particular exception is useful to narcotics officers who might encounter marijuana fields in their investigations.

Another situation in which a search warrant is not required is an exigent situation known as the evanescent evidence exception. In this case, evidence is likely to disappear in the time it would take to get a warrant. In drug cases, this could involve drugs that may be flushed down the toilet in the time needed to secure a warrant. The evanescent evidence exception requires a rough approximation of probable cause and the evidence must be seized in a reasonable manner. Officers may also search without a warrant if there is a threat of a subject escaping in the time it would take to get a warrant, or if there is danger to a person's life.[92]

Plain-view searches may also be conducted without a warrant. Officers may confiscate evidence that they find in plain sight, which is a useful tool to narcotics officers. Often, drug paraphernalia that may be useful evidence are left in plain view. The Supreme Court has ruled that "objects falling in the plain view of an officer who has a right to be in the position to have that view are subject to seizure and may be used as evidence."[93] However, officers may not move other objects to gain a better view of evidence otherwise hidden from view, and the objects cannot be in a position where officers would have to dislodge or move it to examine it closely.

Stop-and-frisk searches are another example of the warrantless search. These are conducted in the interest of officer safety and/or crime prevention. To stop a suspect, the officer must have articulable facts and reasonable suspicion that criminal activity is afoot. For further procession to a frisk, which is essentially a pat-down of a suspect's outer clothing, there must be reasonable facts to suggest that the individual is presently armed and dangerous.[94] If the officer happens to come across drug paraphernalia during the frisk, that evidence would be admissible in court.

Finally, searches incident to arrest are allowable without a search warrant. In these cases, officers are allowed to search the area under the immediate control of the suspect, which is essentially their armspan.[95] In an automobile, this includes the entire passenger compartment of the vehicle, including the glove box if it is unlocked.[96] (See Figure 19-20.) If the arrest occurs in the suspect's home, then the officers are allowed to make a protective search of the home to look for additional suspects. Plain view doctrine would apply in such a case.[97]

◄ **FIGURE 19-20 Officer searching vehicle for drugs** Once the contraband has been detected by the dogs, an officer will thoroughly and painstakingly search the car. (© AP/Wide World Photos)

Search Procedures

Once a search begins, narcotics officers should survey the entire site and make a determination as to the best way to conduct the search, keeping the legal aspects of searches in mind. The leader of the search should establish a work station where paperwork can be filled out and evidence collected.

Searches should be careful, thorough, systematic, and within the limitations of the search warrant. Most drug searches permit the opening of packages, checking the insides of light fixtures, and looking in ceiling panels and other potential hiding places. Other places that should be checked are attics and crawl spaces; furnace ducts; plumbing access panels; furniture (including mattresses and boxsprings); dresser drawers; kitchen appliances; food containers; children's furniture and toys; and personal property such as cameras, storage sheds, garages, and other outbuildings. Each room should be subject to two separate searches by different individuals to ensure that all areas are covered. Drug criminals are extremely good at hiding money and drugs, making searching for drugs a skill that requires quite a bit of patience and experience.[98]

The following items are generally related to drug crimes and should be listed in the warrant and included in the search:[99]

1. Drugs, in any quantity
2. Cash, which should be checked against money lists for buy money from undercover and controlled buys
3. Drug packaging and processing materials, such as plastic baggies, balloons, and so on
4. Drug paraphernalia
5. Weapons
6. Paperwork, which can include address books with drug contacts, personal correspondence, notes, telephone bills, and other records of possible drug transactions
7. Financial records
8. Computers
9. Keys—a key to a target location may prove a suspect's direct connection to it
10. Surveillance equipment
11. Other items specifically relevant to the investigation at hand

Searches should be well documented, with photographs taken of evidence in its original place and with narratives detailing where evidence was found and who found it. The suspect and the warrant judge, as noted earlier, should receive a detailed inventory of anything removed from the location as evidence.

Evidence Handling

Aside from the burglaries, larcenies, and other crimes committed because of narcotics, additional related problems sprout from the drug-culture vine. Some of these growths entwine the individual police officer and the overall police function. One offshoot, the handling and securing of narcotics and dangerous drugs after they are collected and seized, has emerged as an area of growing concern to police administrators for a number of reasons (Figure 19-21).

Once seized by the police, narcotic and dangerous-drug evidence requires protection so that it may be preserved in its original state until it is brought before a court or destroyed through a legal process. It is during this period that the greatest demands are placed on personnel of the law enforcement agency concerned. Narcotic and dangerous-drug evidence must be protected against not only loss and outside threats of incursion but, unfortunately, sometimes from internal theft as well.

Although relatively uncommon, there have been occasions when narcotic and dangerous-drug evidence has disappeared from a "secure" area under the control and

◄ **FIGURE 19-21 Drug seizures**

Large seizures of drugs pose special problems and considerations for testing the concentration and holding of evidence for trial. In most cases, samples of the large seizure are tested, and only a small portion of the drugs are actually kept as evidence. Most courts allow a sample of the drugs to be admitted as evidence along with officer/agent testimony linking the sample with the confiscated seizure. The remaining drugs are then destroyed after testing.

◄FIGURE 19-22
Money and Drugs
During sophisticated investigations involving large-scale operations, it is not uncommon to seize huge caches of cash. Literally, millions of dollars are bartered each year in the drug trade, making for high-stake risks and potentially dangerous situations.
(© AP/Wide World Photos)
(Source: www.ccn.com/US/9805/18/money. laundering/cash.jpg)

within the confines of a police agency. The following methods for handling drug evidence will go far in addressing this concern and minimizing its occurrence.[100]

There are two recognized methods for introducing narcotic and dangerous-drug evidence into the processing sequence immediately after it is seized and marked. Neither method omits any of the processing steps; the difference is found in the manner in which the sequential steps are arranged.

The first method (the laboratory-first method) requires that all seized evidence (after it is field tested, marked, photographed, weighed, and initially inventoried) be transported immediately to the laboratory for analysis. Drop boxes are provided in the laboratory for the deposit of evidence during periods when the facility is not operational. All seized narcotic and dangerous-drug evidence is taken directly to a room in the vicinity of the laboratory. This room, known as an inventory room or a display room, is specially equipped for inventorying narcotic and dangerous-drug evidence and is not used for any other purpose. Weighing scales, cameras, film holders, lighting equipment, evidence seals, evidence containers, appropriate forms, desks, typewriters, tables or counters, and necessary administrative supplies are maintained in the room. When not in use, the room is locked, and the keys (two) are retained in a secure location (normally, one key is kept in the laboratory and the other is controlled by the watch supervisor or desk officer). To achieve even greater control over inventory rooms, departments that have a high volume of narcotic evidence are employing more sophisticated entry-control systems, including "entry" or "swipe" cards on a system that records the cardholder's identity and time of entry and departure. Video cameras may also be used to record all behavior in the inventory room.

After seizure of the evidence and while en route to police headquarters, the seizing officer requests a witnessing officer of supervisory grade (at least one grade above that held by the seizing officer) and a member of the laboratory staff (technician on duty) or a technician from the mobile laboratory unit, if available, to meet with him or her at the narcotic and dangerous-drug inventory room. When the supervisory official arrives at the inventory room, the seizing officer displays the material seized (the witnessing officer does not handle any of the evidence). After the evidence package has been marked and displayed in the manner best suited for a photographic inventory, the laboratory technician photographs the evidence (the photographer does not handle any of the evidence). When photographs of the evidence have been taken, the evidence is weighed and inventoried under the direct supervision of the supervisory officer. Appropriate forms are then completed and witnessed, and the evidence is sealed in containers or envelopes provided for that purpose.

After these steps have been accomplished, in company with the witnessing officer and the laboratory technician, the seizing officer carries the evidence to the laboratory drop box and deposits it therein. If the drop box cannot accommodate the evidence package, the laboratory evidence-room custodian or an alternate is requested to come to the laboratory, assume custody of the evidence, and store it in the laboratory evidence room. If the evidence is taken to the laboratory during normal operational hours, the drop box is not used; the evidence is turned over directly to the laboratory evidence custodian or alternate.

On completion of the analytical process by the laboratory, the evidence is delivered to the narcotic and dangerous-drug evidence room in the property room. Here, the evidence custodian assumes control of the evidence and provides for its preservation and subsequent processing as required.

In the second method (the evidence-room-first method), seized narcotic and dangerous-drug evidence, after being field tested, marked, photographed, weighed, and inventoried, is sealed in an appropriate container and deposited in a drop box or delivered directly to the evidence room in the property room. There are variations to the procedure; in some cases, certain intermediate steps (photographing the evidence, for example) are omitted or the initial processing (weighing, photographing, and inventorying) may be accomplished in the property room or evidence room. The single difference between the two methods is that in one the evidence is analyzed before it is stored, whereas in the other the evidence is taken directly to the narcotic and dangerous-drug evidence room (or to an adjunct depository), receipted, and then removed to the laboratory for analysis.

Of the two methods used for introducing narcotic and dangerous-drug evidence into the processing sequence, the laboratory-first procedure is preferred and should be followed whenever possible. The main advantage of this method is that it reduces actual handling of the evidence and decreases the number of custody transfer points. By first delivering the evidence to the laboratory, the evidence must undergo only one journey to the narcotic and dangerous-drug evidence room—that is, after analysis, rather than before and after. Consequently, the exposure of the evidence to various loss hazards is reduced and its security is enhanced.

It must be recognized, however, that establishment of the laboratory-first method depends on the existence of certain features that are not available to many law enforcement agencies. The laboratory-first method requires that a mobile laboratory unit or laboratory technician be on call for around-the-clock operation. Second, this method requires an easily accessible laboratory—preferably located in the same building housing the headquarters of the police agency itself.

Pharmaceutical Diversions

The diversion of pharmaceutical drugs is considered an increasing problem within the drug enforcement community, especially with the popularity of narcotic drugs such as OxyContin. Health-care professionals are sometimes involved with the distribution of controlled substances from hospitals, clinics, pharmacies, and doctor's offices. In fact, the DEA has estimated that around 13,000 practicing physicians or pharmacists may be involved in the illegal diversion of drugs.[101] Investigation of these types of activities are difficult because doctors and other health professionals are usually seen as highly educated, productive members of society. Diversions are also easy to cover up. Careful records regarding controlled substances are required to be kept by doctors and pharmacists, but suspicious fires, break-ins, and robberies may act as covers for drug shortages or the destruction of records. Furthermore, many investigators are unfamiliar with the problem of diversion and how to deal with it.

Doctors and Diversion

There are generally four types of doctors who divert drugs. The first is the dishonest physician, who profits from the illegal sale of controlled substances. The second is the impaired doctor, who diverts drugs for his or her own use and addiction. The third type is the dated doctor. The dated doctor has been in practice for a number of years and may be willing to hand out drugs to anyone who appears to have a legitimate reason. These doctors are generally unwilling to conform to new rules and regulations about prescription drugs. Finally, there's the gullible physician who falls victim to scams by patients regarding prescription drugs. Gullible physicians are not considered criminals.[102]

Among the most common indications that a physician may be unlawfully diverting drugs are these:

- A physician places excessively frequent orders for narcotics.
- A physician picks up and pays for filled narcotics prescriptions from a pharmacy.
- A physician places an emergency call for a narcotic medication to a pharmacy and requests delivery. The deliverer is met by the physician and given a prescription for the drugs. In some instances, no patient exists, or if one does exist, the narcotics are retained by the physician, and other medication is substituted.
- A narcotics prescription is issued to a patient by a physician with instructions to have it filled and to return with the drug for administration. Substitute medication is then given to the patient.
- In narcotics records, a physician uses fictitious or deceased people's names and addresses.
- The physician frequently requests that a prescription for an alleged patient be taken to the pharmacy by a nurse, a receptionist, or a member of the family and be returned to the doctor personally.
- While other physicians are in the operating room or making hospital rounds, the addict-physician searches their vehicles or medical bags for narcotics.
- A physician obtains a key to the narcotics locker in a hospital and has a duplicate made.
- A physician may place an order for a patient in a hospital; when the drug is prepared by a nurse, the doctor takes it over and either uses a substitute syringe containing a placebo or administers only a small portion of the drug.

Nurses and Diversion

Nurses tend to be more likely to divert drugs for their own personal use than to divert drugs for resale. Investigators may choose to deal with personal diversions far differently than they would diversions that are destined for resale.

CLANDESTINE DRUG LABORATORIES

Clandestine drug laboratories throughout the United States produce a variety of illegal drugs for sale and distribution. The processes used in production of these drugs range in their degree of sophistication from primitive to advanced. By the same token, those who operate such laboratories may range in expertise from the novice experimenter to the professional chemist. These factors alone can have a serious impact on the safety of the general public and on police and fire department personnel who may deal with these laboratories in enforcement and emergency situations.[103]

Raids conducted on clandestine drug laboratories are inherently dangerous, irrespective of the dangers associated with taking suspects into custody. The degree of danger is based largely on the types of chemicals that are typically used and the chemical processes employed. These dangers may be heightened by the operator's lack of expertise and experience and by the physical limitations and restrictions of the facility being used, as well as by weather conditions and other factors. Such dangers cannot be overemphasized. Major accidents resulting in loss of life have occurred during raids conducted on such facilities by those who are untrained, inexperienced, or careless in the dismantling, handling, transportation, storage, or disposal of the involved chemicals.

Normally, direct physical involvement with drug laboratories takes place during the execution of a search warrant on a suspect property. Under these circumstances, there is generally enough information to forewarn police officers about the nature of the operations and the types of chemicals that are most likely involved. Adequate safety precautions can thus be developed and employed. However, police officers may inadvertently encounter a laboratory operation while conducting other enforcement or investigatory operations. In such instances, unless there is imminent danger of loss of life, police officers and civilians alike should be restricted from entering laboratory premises. Clandestine laboratories typically employ processes using chemicals that are toxic, corrosive, caustic, and flammable. The laboratory environment may pose explosive toxic or carcinogenic risks that should be dealt with only by specially trained and equipped personnel.

Identifying Laboratory Operations

Clandestine laboratory operations are typically identified in one of four ways. In some instances, fire departments responding to the scene of a fire or explosion find evidence of laboratory operations. Positive determinations, however, depend on the ability of emergency service personnel to recognize the type of substances and equipment typically used in such operations. It is important, therefore, that these personnel be trained in identification of clandestine lab operations. Since fire departments should be close at hand during police raids of drug laboratories, responsible personnel from both agencies should develop a working relationship in dealing with problems that arise from these types of operations.

Evidence of drug laboratory operations may also be generated through informants. Laboratory operators who are attempting to establish operations in a new community often need to determine sources for the purchase of specific chemicals. Plans for development of a lab and related involvement of suppliers or distributors frequently are revealed by confidential informants and intelligence gathered from arrestees.

The community at large may also provide valuable tips on laboratory operations on the basis of observations of unusual activities or circumstances. Many drug labs operate in urban or suburban residential communities where citizens who are alerted to the common signs of laboratory operations can provide valuable information to the police. These indicators include:

- A residence where one or more individuals visit but where no one lives. Laboratory operators are generally cautious about the risks of fire, explosion, or contamination and attempt to limit their exposure and risk.
- Residences or other buildings that have sealed doors and windows, although they are not abandoned facilities.
- The presence of ventilating fans that operate irrespective of weather conditions.
- A strong ammonia or related odor.
- An unfurnished "residence."
- A "resident" who frequently goes outside for a cigarette or to get some air.

Although these circumstances do not prove the existence of an illegal drug manufacturing operation, several of these factors together may be suggestive enough to warrant establishment of low-profile police surveillance.

Meth Labs

One of the fastest-growing types of clandestine laboratories is the methamphetamine lab. **Meth labs** have been around since the 1960s, when they were organized and operated by outlaw motorcycle gangs. To stop the spread of "clan labs," chemicals such as ether and ephedrine were restricted by the Chemical Diversion and Trafficking Act of 1988. Rogue chemical companies that sold to clan-lab precursors were prosecuted and put out of business by the DEA and other local, state, and federal law enforcement agencies.[104]

In the late 1980s and early 1990s, the biker manufacturers began to be edged out of the market by new and very violent methamphetamine manufacturers—the Mexican national methamphetamine organizations. Today, they dominate the meth manufacturing market. Their industrial-size labs are producing methamphetamine in mass quantities for distribution across the United States. This is evidenced by recent DEA operations that resulted in methamphetamine arrests in California, Texas, and North Carolina.

With the restriction of methamphetamine manufacturing chemicals, lab seizures started to decline in the late 1980s. Since then, however, the trend has been reversed with a vengeance, and lab seizures have started to skyrocket. One of the reasons for this increase is the Internet. Now all a methamphetamine manufacturer has to do is turn on his or her computer, point and click to find a recipe, and point and click again to find the chemicals. If the "meth cook" has any questions during the manufacturing process, he or she can simply visit one of the methamphetamine-manufacturing chat pages. These small "tweeker"-type labs are capable of making anywhere from ounce to pound quantities of methamphetamine. Size does not matter when it comes to clan labs; these small labs are just as dangerous for law enforcement officers as are the biker and Mexican national labs.

Meth labs can be broken down into six different styles:

- Biker or traditional
- Mexican national
- Cold-cook
- Pressure cooker
- Hydrogenation
- Tweeker

Chemicals used to manufacture methamphetamine are easily obtainable, even with chemical restrictions. Laboratory equipment used to manufacture methamphetamine runs the full spectrum from the scientific to the yard-sale purchase. Heating mantles, condensers, vacuum pumps, buchner funnels, and 22-liter reaction vessels are regularly seized at clandestine labs. Not wanting to attract attention of law enforcement, clandestine laboratory equipment manufacturers are turning to other types of clan-lab equipment. They now use pressure cookers, hot plates, mason jars, sun tea dispensers, nalgene containers, homemade compressed-gas cylinders, Pyrex bowls, sports bottles, microwave ovens, and other such material.[105]

Lab Seizure and Forfeiture

Laboratory operators may be arrested under a wide variety of circumstances, only the most typical of which are discussed here. Most laboratory operations are closed as the result of police raids following intensive investigative work.

On occasion, police officers will inadvertently discover a clandestine lab operation while responding to other public safety situations. It is essential that officers take only those steps necessary to protect their lives and the lives of bystanders and that they make arrests only if entry into the laboratory is not required. Normally, if the officer's presence has not been detected, this involves relaying information to supervisory personnel and/or other appropriate personnel in the department who have received specialized training in handling clandestine laboratories.

Once the scene is secure, it may be possible to interview neighbors in order to determine information on occupancy. Officers should make note of all vehicles parked in the immediate area of the laboratory.

Another means of interdiction involves the civil forfeiture of illicit chemicals and drug-manufacturing paraphernalia. This procedure, which pertains to individual laboratory operators as well as chemical suppliers, allows federal agents to seize anything used or intended to be used to illegally manufacture, deliver, or import drugs. Most states have similar prohibitions, and officers should be familiar with the provisions and limitations of these laws. Use of the forfeiture statutes may be a reasonable alternative to attempts to establish a criminal case, particularly where staffing constraints limit surveillance and other operations, when suspects' discovery of surveillance may necessitate terminating the investigation, or when it is feared that the laboratory operation is preparing to relocate quickly. Often the circumstances that justify a civil seizure will lead thereafter to successful prosecution under criminal statutes relating to conspiracy or the attempt to manufacture controlled substances.

When making a decision concerning civil seizure of illegal drugs and manufacturing materials, officers should contact their local prosecuting attorney for advice. Evidence not sufficient to support criminal prosecution may be adequate for a civil seizure. Normally, successful seizure requires that officers demonstrate the suspect's probable intent to manufacture a controlled substance. This can be accomplished by reference to the type and combination of chemicals and paraphernalia on hand, furtive activity, use of subterfuge, or other questionable practices.

Those who supply materials to clandestine laboratories with knowledge of their use are also subject to civil and criminal penalties under various federal and state laws. Chemical companies or supply houses may knowingly sell chemicals to laboratory operators without reporting the sales to the police, disguise sales records, assist buyers in using the chemicals, or otherwise assist in the preparation or merchandising process. It is normally possible to apply seizure and forfeiture actions to such merchants if investigation can establish any factor that shows the suppliers' "guilty knowledge" of the illegal uses of their merchandise.

An undercover purchase of chemicals from suspected suppliers is the most typical means of developing criminal cases against them. In addition, chemicals seized at drug laboratories may display manufacturers' labels, including lot numbers, and equipment may have manufacturers' plates and serial numbers that can be used to trace their sales or transfers.

Under proper circumstances, therefore, civil seizure may be an acceptable, if not preferred, approach to termination of illegal drug-manufacturing operations. Additionally, once such actions are taken, perpetrators will often cooperate with the police and provide intelligence that assists in additional enforcement operations.

Conducting A Laboratory Raid

Conducting a raid on an occupied laboratory requires careful planning. Normally, a planning meeting involves the police tactical unit, bomb squad, hazardous-material or chemical-waste disposal personnel, a chemist, and fire department representatives—all of whom are specially trained. The nature of the operation from initial entry to dismantling should be reviewed with particular attention to the types of chemicals most likely being used, the nature of the suspects involved, and contingency plans for emergency services should a fire, explosion, or toxic reaction take place.

The initial entry team should be outfitted with Nomex clothing, body armor, and goggles. Nomex provides short-term protection from fire, and goggles protect one's eyes from airborne fumes and thrown chemicals. The tactical unit is responsible only for securing the suspects and exiting the laboratory as quickly as possible and with the minimum amount of force.

To avoid unduly restricted movements, the tactical team should wear the minimum amount of protective clothing necessary. It is important, therefore, that the team's exposure to the laboratory environment be extremely limited. The team should make a mental note of the laboratory environment and report its findings to the assessment team members who follow. Laboratory operators, in anticipation of possible raids, sometimes booby-trap the facility in order to destroy evidence. The ability to recognize traps and other potential hazards depends on the training and experience of team members, a factor that underscores the importance of special training for such operations. After leaving the facility, the tactical team should undergo decontamination.

After the site is secured, the assessment team is free to enter. Team members should wear Nomex clothing covered with disposable protective suits, as well as chemical-resistant gloves and boots covered with disposable gloves and boots. All seams of the suits should be taped with nonporous adhesive tape, and each team member should be equipped with a self-contained breathing apparatus. The team should also be outfitted with two air-monitoring devices—a combustible-gas indicator and indicator tubes.

The combustible-gas indicator is an essential air-monitoring device that tests for oxygen levels, airborne gas particle levels, and the combustibility of the environment. The indicator tubes test for the presence and quantity of specific types of chemical vapors. A pump is used to force air through the individual tubes.

Assessment team members test the lab environment at several locations and make notes of instrument readings. They should also make a diagram of the interior, noting any dangers or problems that may be encountered. When their work is completed, the assessment team should leave the facility, decontaminate, and give their report to the dismantling team.

The dismantling team should wear the same type of protective clothing as the assessment team. (See Figure 19-23.) Even though dangerous substances may not have been found, there is always the possibility of spills and damage during dismantling, which could create a hazardous situation. A chemist trained in laboratory dismantling should be on hand to take samples of chemicals and of products being manufactured so that informed judgments can be made on safety in packaging, transportation, storage, disposal, and handling of evidence samples.

Crime scene personnel, under the close supervision of the dismantling team supervisor, should conduct standard crime scene processing procedures, including taking photographs and searching for latent fingerprints. Videotaping of laboratory operations is also helpful for evidentiary purposes and for court presentation.

The chemist can direct the proper packaging of chemical substances. Care must always be taken that only compatible chemicals are packaged together. Typically, chemicals are placed in drums filled with vermiculite or a similar absorbent, nonflammable substance. A waste disposal company approved by the Environmental Protection Agency (EPA) can be of great value in the packaging process.

Chemicals that are not being used in court because of potential hazards, together with contaminated clothing and equipment, must be packaged, transported, and stored or disposed of according to EPA guidelines.

CONSPIRACY INVESTIGATIONS

A **conspiracy** is defined as two or more people entering into an agreement to violate the law with a commission of one or more overt acts in furtherance of the agreement. Drug investigators undertake conspiracy cases when they desire to get the leaders of a drug organization who may not handle drug transactions and would otherwise be too insulated from the day-to-day operations by associates operating further down the chain of command. The law of conspiracy makes it possible for each conspirator to be held accountable for the actions of anyone else involved.[106]

◀ **FIGURE 19-23**
Meth-lab raids and assessment
The methamphetamine cooking process is extremely dangerous owing to fumes and the volatility of ingredients. After the site is secured, the assessment team (shown in the photo) enters the lab. Team members should wear Nomex clothing covered with disposable suits, as well as chemical-resistant gloves and boots covered with disposable gloves and boots. Each team member should be equipped with a self-contained breathing apparatus. Finally, the team should have two air-monitoring devices.
(© AP/Wide World Photos)
(Courtesy of Detective David Street, Riverside County, California, Sheriff's Department)

There are three main types of conspiracies. The first is the *chain conspiracy.* In a chain conspiracy, the investigator must show that a group of conspirators are all working toward a common goal, depending on one another to further the success of the scheme. Each participant must be aware that their success depends on each member of the conspiracy.

In the more complex *wheel conspiracy,* there is a central or primary conspirator called the *hub.* The hub makes an agreement with other conspirators, referred to as *spokes.* Each spoke is aware of everyone else's role in the scheme. All are bound together by the *rim,* which is a common agreement, tying each person to the conspiracy.

Finally, the *enterprise conspiracy* is defined by federal statutes. In this type of conspiracy, the enterprise may have a number of different criminal activities going on. These activities are called *racketeering* and include such things as drug violations, loan-sharking, mail fraud, bribery, counterfeiting, and obstruction of justice. The members of an enterprise do not have to be aware of one another's roles, and investigators have to show only that members have agreed to participate in the enterprise. Enterprise conspiracies in narcotics investigations must obviously include drug violations, as well as one other activity defined under racketeering.[107]

GANGS AND DRUGS

Street gangs, outlaw motorcycle gangs, and prison gangs are the main distributors of drugs in the United States. Currently, there are about 31,000 gangs and 850,000 active gang members in the country.[108] Gangs present numerous problems for narcotics investigators, because they are difficult to infiltrate. Their use of violence makes confidential informants scarce, and undercover operations are exceptionally risky to the officer.

Street gangs are located throughout the county in cities of various sizes and characteristics. Large, well-organized gangs are the most likely to be involved with drug trafficking, because their networks allow for the manufacture, sale, transportation, and distribution of drugs throughout the nation. These gangs are mostly involved with drugs such as cocaine, heroin, and marijuana. Violence is employed regularly within these gangs in an effort to control and expand distribution activities.

Outlaw motorcycle gangs are smaller than street gangs but are highly organized. The three main outlaw motorcycle gangs are the Hell's Angels Motorcycle Club, the Bandidos, and the Outlaws Motorcycle Club. The primary drugs associated with outlaw motorcycle gangs are methamphetamine, marijuana, and cocaine. Like street gangs, outlaw motorcycle gangs have been known to use violence to further distribution activities.

Prison gangs are much smaller than street or outlaw motorcycle gangs and are aligned along racial or ethnic lines. The most prominent prison gangs include the Aryan Nation, Mexican Mafia, and Nuestra Familia. These gangs consist of a select group of inmates who are organized into a hierarchy and operate within prisons and on the streets to distribute cocaine, marijuana, methamphetamine, and heroin. These gangs are notoriously difficult to infiltrate and are considered extremely violent and dangerous.[109]

KEY TERMS

amphetamines
barbiturates
cannabis
chiva
clandestine drug laboratories
cocaine
codeine
conspiracy
crack (rock) cocaine
crystallized methamphetamine
depressants (sedatives)
drug buy operations
hallucinogenic drugs
hashish
hashish oil
heroin (diacetylmorphine)

heroin cheese
HIDTA
ketamine
khat
lysergic acid diethylamide (LSD)
marijuana
marijuana grow houses
meperidine (Demerol)
mescaline
meth labs
methadone
methaqualone
methcathinone
methylenedioxy methamphetamine
 (MDMA) or ecstasy
morphine

narcotics
opiates
opium
OxyContin
phencyclidine (PCP)
psilocybin and psilocin
speedballing
stimulants
Strawberry Quick meth
surveillance
synthetic narcotics

REVIEW QUESTIONS

1. What major drugs of abuse are derived from opium?
2. What role does the drug methadone play in treating heroin addicts?
3. What are the acute and chronic effects of cocaine use?
4. What is freebasing?
5. According to the Drug Enforcement Administration, what are drug traffickers attempting to accomplish by introducing Strawberry Quick meth onto the market?
6. What is methcathinone?
7. Why is the drug OxyContin so attractive to drug addicts?
8. What is speedballing?
9. What are some of the known side effects of PCP?
10. What are the signs of a Marijuana Grow House Operation?
11. What are the major exceptions to searching without a search warrant?
12. How are clandestine drug laboratory operations typically identified?
13. Which major factors should be considered when attempting to secure a search warrant solely on the basis of information supplied by a confidential informant?
14. What is a HIDTA?
15. Define a conspiracy, and give examples of conspiracy cases.
16. What are the two recognized methods for introducing narcotics and dangerous drugs into the processing sequence immediately after they are seized and marked?

INTERNET ACTIVITIES

1. The U.S. Drug Enforcement Agency website, www.dea.gov, provides a variety of statistics and information on drug trafficking use in various countries around the world. For the most recent drug trafficking intelligence, log on to the website and click "Law Enforcement—Intelligence Reports." Find the most recent reports about Colombia. See how enforcement efforts and policy changes have affected the drug cartels in that country.

2. Find out about the changes in abused drugs commonly found on the party scene or at all-night raves. Visit the National Drug Intelligence Center at their website, www.usdoj.ndic, and browse the site for information pertaining to "club drugs" and teenagers. What new drugs are becoming popular among America's youth? How pervasive is inhalant abuse? What are the so-called club drugs?

NOTES

1. The National Drug Intelligence Center (NDIC), established in 1993, is a component of the U.S. Department of Justice. The General Counterdrug Intelligence Plan, implemented in February 2000, designated NDIC as the nation's principal center for strategic domestic counterdrug intelligence. As such, the NDIC produces national, regional, and state drug threat assessments, various drug information bulletins, and a series of pamphlets providing detailed information on specific drugs. The NDIC is a very valuable resource for local and state police officers engaged in drug enforcement in this country, and hence, much of the description, usage, and abuse of drugs in this chapter is supported and grounded within the NDIC publications. See www.usdoj.gov/ndic.

2. Gregory Lee, *Global Drug Enforcement: Practical Investigative Techniques* (Boca Raton, FL: CRC Press, 2004), p. 19.

3. Several references and books have been developed to categorize individual drugs of abuse and articulate their specific impact on the physical body over the last 50 years. One of the first of these references was the landmark text by Samuel F. Levine, *Narcotics and Drug Abuse* (Cincinnati, OH: The W. H. Anderson Company, 1973). For additional references, see Erich Goode, *Drugs in American Society*, 5th ed. (New York: McGraw-Hill, 2000); James Inciardi and Karen McElrath's, *The American Drug Scene*, 4th ed. (Los Angeles, CA: Roxbury Press, 2004); and Oakley Ray and Charles Ksir, *Drugs, Society, and Human Behavior*, 9th ed. (New York: McGraw-Hill, 2002).

4. David Holthouse, "The Chiva Game," (Denver, CO: Westworld, Oct. 7, 2004).

5. Jane C. Maxwell, *Drug Abuse Trends* (Austin, TX: Texas Commission on Drug and Alcohol Abuse, June 1998).

6. Clyde B. McCoy and James A. Inciardi, *Sex, Drugs and the Continuing Spread of AIDS* (Los Angeles, CA: Roxbury Press, 1995).

7. David Holthouse, "The Chiva Game."

8. Ibid.

9. For a more detailed discussion of heroin cheese, see http://msnbc.msn.com/id/18792099/print/1/displaymode/1098/, http://abcnews.go.com/print?id=1898386, and www.usdoj.gov/dea/programs/forensicsci/microgram/mg0506/mg0506.html.

10. "Prescription Cancer Drug Is a Narcotic of Choice," *Law Enforcement News*, Feb. 14, 2001, p. 5.

11. Timothy Roche, "Potent Perils of a Miracle Drug," *Time*, Jan. 8, 2001.

12. Oakley Ray and Charles Ksir, *Drugs, Society, and Human Behavior.*

13. The controversy surrounding methadone treatment continues to be a hot topic in the drug research literature. See Charles E. Faupel, *Shooting Dope: Career Patterns in Hard-Core Heroin Users* (Gainesville, FL: University of Florida Press, 1991); James A. Inciardi, Frank M. Tims, and Bennet W. Fletcher, *Innovative Approaches in the Treatment of Drug Abuse: Program Models and Strategies* (Westport, CT: Greenwood Press, 1993); and *About Methadone*, 2nd ed. (Washington, DC: Drug Policy Alliance, 2004).

14. Oakley Ray and Charles Ksir, *Drugs, Society, and Human Behavior.*

15. Robert C. Petersen, "Cocaine: An Overview," in *Drug Enforcement* (Washington, D.C.: Government Printing Office, 1977), pp. 9–12.

16. Oakley Ray and Charles Ksir, *Drugs, Society, and Human Behavior.*

17. Ibid.

18. National Drug Intelligence Center, "Amphetamines—Fast Facts" (Washington, D.C.: U.S. Department of Justice, 2004). See www.usdoj.gov/ndic.

19. "Hawaii's Problems with 'Ice,'" *Police*, Oct. 1989, p. 14.

20. Patrik Jonsson, "Appalachia's New Cottage Industry: Meth." *Christian Science Monitor*, March 21, 2003.

21. Adapted and excerpted from "The Menace of Ice," *Time*, Sept. 18, 1989, p. 28.

22. For a more detailed discussion of Strawberry Quick meth, see Donna Leiwand, *USA Today*, "DEA: Flavored Meth Use on the Rise," accessed at http://usatoday.printthis.clickability.com/pt/cpt?action=cpt&title-DEQ%3A+Flavored+meth; "Strawberry Meth: Email Fliers Warn of a New, Candy-Flavored Form of Methamphetamine Targeted at Young People Called Strawberry Meth or Strawberry Quick Meth" accessed at http://urbanlegends.about.com/library/bl_strawberry_meth.htm: "Candy-Flavored Meth Targets New Users," MY 2, 2007, accessed at http://cbsnews.com/stories/2007/05/02/health/printable2752266.shtml.

23. Donna Leinwand, "10 Held in Smuggling of 'Nazi Speed,' " *USA Today*, Aug. 21, 2002, p. 1-A.

24. James McGiveny, ""Made in America": The New and Potent Methcathinone," *Police Chief*, April 1994, pp. 20–21 (this discussion was adapted with permission from this source). Methcathinone is also known as 2-methylamino-1-phenylpropan-1-one, n-methcathinone, monomethylproprion, and ephedrone; street names include *go, goob, sniff, crank, star, wonder star, bathtub speed, gaggers, wildcat,* and *cat*.

25. Todd Bensman, "Ancient Use, New Import," *Dallas Morning News*, June 27, 2002, p. A-21 and A-28. Also, see National Drug Intelligence Center, "Khat—Fast Facts" (Washington, D.C.: U.S. Department of Justice, 2004). See www.usdoj.gov/ndic.

26. Ibid.

27. National Drug Intelligence Center, "Barbiturates—Fast Facts" (Washington D.C.: U.S. Department of Justice, 2004). See www.usdoj.gov/ndic.

28. Robert C. Petersen and Richard C. Stillman, "Phencyclidine Abuse," in *Drug Enforcement* (Washington, D.C.: Government Printing Office, 1978), pp. 19–20. See National Drug Intelligence Center, "PCP—Fast Facts" (Washington, D.C.: U.S. Department of Justice, 2004). See www.usdoj.gov/ndic.

29. Raymond Hernandez, in "New Drug Battles, Use of Ecstasy among Young Soars," *The New York Times* on the Web, Aug. 2, 2000.

30. "Way Found to Detect LSD in Humans," *Tampa Tribune*, Sept. 8, 1972.

31. National Drug Intelligence Center, "LSD—Fast Facts" (Washington, D.C.: U.S. Department of Justice, 2004). See www.usdoj.gov/ndic.

32. National Drug Intelligence Center, "Foxy—Fast Facts" (Washington, D.C.: U.S. Department of Justice, 2004). See www.usdoj.gov/ndic.

33. National Drug Intelligence Center, "5-MeO-AMT—Fast Facts" (Washington, D.C.: U.S. Department of Justice, 2004). See www.usdoj.gov/ndic.

34. National Drug Intelligence Center, "Ketamine—Fast Facts" (Washington, D.C.: U.S. Department of Justice, 2004). See www.usdoj.gov/ndic.

35. Gregory Lee, *Global Drug Enforcement: Practical Investigative Techniques*, p. 43.

36. "Supreme Court Weighs Marijuana as Medicine," *CNN.com*, Nov. 29, 2004. Available at www.cnn.com/2004/LAW/11/29/scotus.medical.marijuana.ap/index.html.

37. Drug Policy Research Center. "Research Brief: Using Marijuana May Not Raise the Risk of Doing Harder Drugs" (Santa Monica, CA: RAND Corporation, 2002). Available at www.rand.org/publications/RB/RB6010/.

38. "Marijuana Home Grow Operation," Crime Prevention and Information, Niagara Regional Police Service, cited at website: http://nrps.com/community/marijuana.asp.

39. Ibid., pp. 2–3.

40. Wes Woods II. "Authorities seize 14,000 plants worth $60 million to $80 million," *Inland Valley Daily Bulletin*, California, 2007.

41. See U.S. Code Title 21, Section 863.

42. National Drug Intelligence Center. "Drug Paraphernalia Prosecution: Stopping Criminal Facilitators of Drug Use," Information Brief. (Washington, D.C.: U.S. Department of Justice, July 2003).

43. Gregory Lee, *Global Drug Enforcement: Practical Investigative Techniques*, p. 11.

44. National Drug Intelligence Center. "National Drug Threat Assessment 2004: Domestic Drug Flows" (Washington, D.C.: U.S. Department of Justice, May 2004).

45. Gregory Lee, *Global Drug Enforcement: Practical Investigative Techniques*, p. 12.

46. National Drug Intelligence Center, "National Drug Threat Assessment 2004: Domestic Drug Flows."

47. National Narcotics Intelligence Consumers Committee, "The NNICC Report 1995: The Supply of Illicit Drugs to the United States" (Washington, D.C.: U.S. Government Printing Office, 1996).

48. National Drug Intelligence Center, "National Drug Threat Assessment 2004: Domestic Drug Flows."

49. Gregory Lee, *Global Drug Enforcement: Practical Investigative Techniques*, p. 7.

50. National Drug Intelligence Center, "National Drug Threat Assessment 2004: Domestic Drug Flows."

51. Gregory Lee, *Global Drug Enforcement: Practical Investigative Techniques*, p. 14.

52. National Drug Intelligence Center, "National Drug Threat Assessment 2004: Domestic Drug Flows."

53. Ibid.

54. Jason Burke, "Europe Supplies World's Ecstasy," *The Observer*, Sept. 1, 2002. Available at www.guardian.co.uk/drugs/Story/0%2C2763%2C784304%2C00.html.

55. Paul Mahoney, *Narcotics Investigative Techniques* (Springfield, IL: Thomas Books, 1992), p. 5.

56. *New York v. Belton*, 452 US 454 (1981).

57. Gregory D. Lee, "Drug Informants, Motives, and Management," *FBI Law Enforcement Bulletin*, Sept. 1993, pp. 10–15. This information was obtained with some modifications from this article.

58. Drug Enforcement Administration, *Agent's Manual*, Appendix B: "Domestic Operations Guideline, 2004."

59. Several police agencies have general orders, special guidelines, and/or policies relating to investigator-informant relationships. Such guidelines include specific direction on confidential informant management and control. Topics that should be addressed in these types of policies include (1) procedures to establish a person as a CI; (2) documenting contacts with the CI; (3) debriefing the CI; (4) restricting the use of the CI and protecting the identity of the CI; (5) designation of an informant control officer or supervisor; (6) documentation and registration of the CI; (7) documentation of payment to the CI and receipts; (8) developing control unit records on the CI; (9) using the CI in controlled purchases; and (10) using the CI in a search warrant affidavit. In addition, many departments require officers to attend special training on the management and control of confidential informants previous to their assignment in a narcotics or drug unit.

60. *DEA Integrity Assurance Notes*, 2004.

61. Paul Mahoney, *Narcotics Investigative Techniques*, p. 17.

62. Michael Lyman, *Practical Drug Enforcement*, pp. 10–13.

63. Gregory Lee, *Global Drug Enforcement: Practical Investigative Techniques*, pp. 92–93. Paul Mahoney, *Narcotics Investigative Techniques*, pp. 92–93.

64. Michael Lyman, *Practical Drug Enforcement*, pp. 6–7.

65. Ibid., p. 113.

66. Ibid., p. 127.

67. Gregory Lee, *Global Drug Enforcement: Practical Investigative Techniques*, p. 116.

68. Ibid., p. 123.

69. Michael Lyman, *Practical Drug Enforcement*, p. 31.

70. Ibid., p. 34.

71. Gregory Lee, *Global Drug Enforcement: Practical Investigative Techniques*, p. 147.

72. Paul Mahoney, *Narcotics Investigative Techniques*, pp. 309–310.

73. Ibid., p. 311.

74. Michael Lyman, *Practical Drug Enforcement*, pp. 156–159.

75. Paul Mahoney, *Narcotics Investigative Techniques*, pp. 312–314.

76. Steffen, George and Samuel Candelaria. *Drug Interdiction: Partnerships, Legal Principles, and Investigative Methods for Law Enforcement.* (Boca Raton, FL: CRC Press, 2003), pp. 73–84.

77. *B.C. v. Plumas Unified School District,* 192 F.3d 1260 (1999).

78. Gregory Lee, *Global Drug Enforcement: Practical Investigative Techniques,* pp. 164–165.

79. Drug Enforcement Administration, "Field Testing for Controlled Substances" (Washington, D.C.: National Training Institute, U.S. Department of Justice, 2000), pp. 1–6.

80. Office of National Drug Control Policy, "The High Intensity Drug Trafficking Area Program: An Overview." Available at www.whitehousedrugpolicy.gov/hidta/frames_overview.html.

81. Washington/Baltimore HIDTA website. Available at www.hidta.org.

82. Office of National Drug Control Policy, "North Texas HIDTA." Available at www.whitehousedrugpolicy.gov/hidta/frames_ntex.html.

83. Charles Whitebread and Christopher Slobogin, *Criminal Procedure: An Analysis of Cases and Concepts* (New York: Foundation Press, 2000), p. 150.

84. *Illinois v. Gates,* 462 US 213 (1983).

85. Michael Lyman, *Practical Drug Enforcement,* p. 138.

86. Whitebread and Slobogin, *Criminal Procedure: An Analysis of Cases and Concepts,* p. 37.

87. *U.S. v. Leon,* 468 US 897 (1984).

88. Nix v. *Williams,* 467 US 431 (1984).

89. *Arizona v. Evans,* 514 US 1 (1995).

90. California v. *Acevado,* 500 US 565 (1991).

91. *Oliver v. U.S.,* 466 US 170 (1984).

92. Gregory Lee, *Global Drug Enforcement: Practical* Investigative *Techniques,* p. 148.

93. *Harris v. United States,* 390 US 234 (1968).

94. Terry v. *Ohio,* 392 US 1 (1968).

95. *Chimel v. California,* 395 US 752 (1969).

96. New York v. Belton, 452 US 454 (1981).

97. Maryland v. *Buie,* 494 US 395 (1990).

98. Paul Mahoney, *Narcotics Investigative Techniques,* p. 206.

99. Ibid., pp. 206–209.

100. There are a number of different techniques and methods for securing drug evidence. These two methods have been adapted from Gregory D. Lee, *Global Drug Enforcement: Practical Investigative Techniques,* p. 12.

101. Michael Lyman, *Practical Drug Enforcement,* p. 227.

102. Ibid.

103. Reprinted from Training Key 388, *Clandestine Laboratories* by L. Ray Brett. Copyright held by the International Association of Chiefs of Police, Inc., 1110 North Glebe Road. Suite 200, Arlington, VA 22201, U.S.A. Further reproduction without the express written permission from IACP is strictly prohibited.

104. Michael Cashman, "Meth Labs: Toxic Timebombs," *Police Chief,* Feb. 1998, p. 44.

105. Ibid., pp. 44–45.

106. Michael Lyman, *Practical Drug Enforcement,* p. 45.

107. Ibid., pp. 45-46.

108. National Drug Intelligence Center, "Gangs and Drugs in the United States," *Drugs and Crime* (Washington, D.C.: U.S. Department of Justice, July 2003).

20

TERRORISM

▲   America's invasion of Iraq has escalated violence aimed at destroying the United States. Terrorist incidents in Southeast Asia as well as in the Middle East have generated great concern for police officers in this country tasked with preventing another attack on our homeland.

(© AP/Wide World Photos)

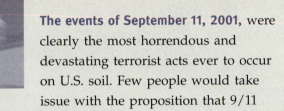

The events of September 11, 2001, were clearly the most horrendous and devastating terrorist acts ever to occur on U.S. soil. Few people would take issue with the proposition that 9/11 forever changed the lives of all Americans. The events of that day evoked a sense of national outrage, caused profound losses, and created a sense of vulnerability.

This chapter discusses various aspects of terrorism and their relation to the work of a criminal investigator. The chapter opens with an overview of international terrorism and the international groups that have committed terrorist acts against the United States and its allies. There is specific focus on Middle Eastern groups, since they pose perhaps the greatest threat against America. Such acts of terrorism are not a recent phenomenon. Although the significant terrorist events listed in this chapter occurred within the last few decades, they are only part of a long-standing pattern of worldwide violence. The chapter then turns to an examination of domestic terrorism and its perpetrators, including right-wing and left-wing domestic groups. Some of the most publicized events of the past decade, such as the Branch Davidian incident in Waco, Texas, and the Oklahoma City bombing in 1995, are associated with right-wing terrorism. The next section addresses the financing of terrorism, with a focus on drug, arms, and human smuggling, credit card and charities fraud, and theft. This is followed by a discussion of several U.S. national agencies charged with the task of gathering information on terrorism, terrorism prevention and investigation, and counterterrorism.

Although federal agencies are clearly important in assessing the threat of future terrorist acts, the role of criminal investigators at both the state and the local law enforcement levels should not be underestimated. The remainder of the chapter outlines the ways that criminal investigators can assist in the fight against terrorism. Confronting terrorism is not an occasional or a seasonal venture; it is an ongoing responsibility. Now, more than ever, criminal investigators must be prepared to encounter and handle terrorist-incident crime scenes.

The world and the United States are not strangers to terrorism. The first U.S. plane hijacking occurred in 1961, when Puerto Rican Antuilo Ortiz, armed with a gun, diverted a National Airlines flight to Cuba, where he was given asylum.[1] A rebel faction in Guatemala assassinated U.S. Ambassador John Mein in 1968 after forcing his car from the road. Black September terrorists struck in Munich at the Olympics in 1972 and the following year killed U.S. Ambassador Cleo Noel in the Sudan. The Baader-Meinhof group and the Popular Front for the Liberation of Palestine (PFLP) seized a French airliner in 1976 and flew the 258 passengers to Uganda, precipitating the Entebbe hostage crisis. In 1979, the Italian Prime Minister was kidnapped and killed by Red Brigade members; the U.S. Embassy in Tehran was seized by Iranian radicals; and Mecca's Grand Mosque was taken over by 200 Islamic terrorists who took hundreds of pilgrims hostage, an incident that left in 250 people dead and 600 wounded. Today, our newspapers highlight the almost daily occurrences of suicide bombers in Israel, new plots of violence against airliners in London, and the gruesome beheadings of innocent civilians by the Shiite al-Mahdi Army in Iraq.

Even a partial accounting of terrorist activities over the past two decades indicates a continuing pattern of such violence worldwide. Across the United States, people are wondering if the September 11, 2001, attacks were harbingers of the future or anomalies. They were not anomalies: the United States is opposed by international and domestic terrorist groups, and the likelihood of further incidents is quite real. Together, globally and locally, police have to be smarter and work harder using better tools to eliminate, disrupt, minimize, and investigate terrorist attacks.

INTERNATIONAL TERRORISM

"**International terrorism** involves violent acts or acts dangerous to human life that are the violation of the criminal laws of the United States or any state, or that would be a criminal act if committed within the jurisdiction of the United States or any state. Acts of international terrorism are intended to intimidate a civilian population, influence the policy of a government, or affect the conduct of a government. These acts transcend national boundaries in terms of the means by which they are accomplished, the persons they intend to intimidate, or the locale in which perpetrators operate."[2] The FBI further defines terrorism as the unlawful use of force or violence against persons or property to intimidate or coerce a government, the civilian population, or any segment thereof, in furtherance of political or social objectives. It is impossible to discuss all of the groups around the world now labeled "terrorist"; however, it is important to give a brief description of those groups that pose the most significant threat to the United States. Many originate from the Middle East, where anti-American tensions have recently escalated, primarily because of the wars in Afghanistan and Iraq. For that reason, this discussion focuses on groups stemming from that area.

Radical Islam

Radical Islam has long been a component of terrorist activity throughout the world (Figure 20-1). Groups with ties to radical Islamic beliefs have been at the forefront of the news since the late 1970s, when the Islamic revolution in Iran reached its peak and led to the capture of the U.S. embassy in Tehran. Terrorist organizations that lay claim to radical Islamic beliefs, whether from the Sunni tradition (making up over 92% of the Islamic world) or the Shi'ite

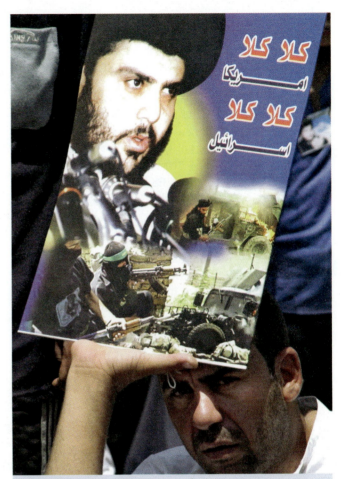

▲ **FIGURE 20-1   Radical Islam**
The Mahdi Army is a militia force created by Iraqi Shiite cleric Muqtada al-Sadr in 2003. It rose to international prominence in April 2004 when it began the first major armed confrontation against the US-led forces in Iraq. Since that time is has been actively engaged in using IEDs (Improvised Explosive Devises or roadside bombs) against U.S. forces as well as malicious beheadings of Iraqi police officers and civilians.
(© AP/Wide World Photos)

tradition (centered primarily in Iran), have garnered widespread press attention over the past 30 years, particularly since al-Qaeda claimed responsibility for the September 11, 2001 attacks.

Radical Islamic groups are generally characterized by a belief that is not shared by mainstream Muslims: violence is a means to an end. These radical groups believe that Western culture poses an imminent threat to the sanctity of the Muslim religion, corrupting morals and threatening to overtake the Muslim way of life. Western interventions in Israeli/Palestinian affairs and in Iraq have served as prime examples of western "colonialization" in the minds of Muslim terrorist groups, further fueling their resolve to take action against the United States and its allies.[3]

Some factions that help compose three major radical and fundamentalist movements within Islam pose a direct threat to the interests of the West, and specifically to the United States. They are discussed next.

The Wahhabi Movement

An Islamic orientation owing much of its basic ideology to the writings of Abd al-Wahhab (1703–1792),[4] who espoused a very conservative form of Sunni Islam. His teachings are commonly referred to as "salafi," which fundamentally means adhering to the ways of the earliest Islamic generations. The basic concept of the **Wahhabi movement** is that the teachings of Islam were corrupted after the time of the Prophet Muhammad. Much like the early Christian Inquisition during the twelfth and thirteenth centuries, the Wahhabis dealt harshly with those non-observant of their Muslim traditions. Thus, the early Wahhabi focus was internal, on other nominally devout Muslims. The Wahhabi tradition today is centered in Saudi Arabia, with followers primarily on the Arabian Peninsula, including Qatar and Yemen. It is a conservative, closed-society tradition that is intolerant of nonbelievers. Some believe this stance encourages violence against the West.

Many practitioners of Wahhabism prefer to be called *muwahhidun* (unifiers of Islamic practice) or *salafists*. There is no single approach to salafism, which in part accounts for the variety of orientations associated with it, such as: (1) the *shumuliyas*, who believe that religion, politics, and government are inseparable; (2) the *wasatiyyans*, who are reformers/moderates but not necessarily anti-Western and entertain ideas about how to simultaneously accommodate some Western values with those of Islam; and (3) the Islamic revivalists/fundamentalists, which includes the Muslim Brotherhood and radical Jihadist Salafism.

The Muslim Brotherhood

The **Muslim Brotherhood** movement was formed in 1928 as an Egyptian youth organization and grew into a political party by 1939, influenced by the writings of Hasan al-Banna (1906–1949) and Sayyid Qutb (1906–1966) in Egypt.[5] Building on the tenets of Wahhabism, al-Banna believed that the Islamic faith is not just a religion, but an all-encompassing way of living and governing. As such, its focus included not only a rejection of the secularization of Islam but a renunciation of Western colonialization and the modern views and values that often accompanied it throughout the Middle East. The Muslim Brotherhood supports the use of violence to return the entire Middle East to its original and purest form of Islam under the rule of the Shari'a, the first books of the Holy Koran. The term *Jihad* is interpreted as an obligation for all Muslims to engage in a "holy war" against the West.

The Muslim Brotherhood has a past history of attempted and successful assassinations of Arabic leaders, including Egyptian President Anwar-al-Sadat (1918–1981), who was seen as too moderate following his 1979 signing of peace accords with Israel. Some of its members helped found al-Qaeda, have been elected to parliamentary seats throughout the Middle East, and have established banks, including one in the Bahamas in 1988 that helped finance terror activities worldwide. Brotherhood members have fought with al-Qaeda in Afghanistan against the Russians and in support of radical Muslims in Kashmir, Chechnya, and Iraq.

Jihadist Salafism

This is the radical branch of **Salafism,** whose ideology rocketed during the 1980s and 1990s as a direct result of the Soviet-Afghan War (1980–1989). It embraces a strict, literal interpretation of Islam combined with an emphasis on jihad as a holy war against all western influences in the Middle East (Figure 20-2). This is the ideology of the al-Qaeda and Jemaah Islamiah terrorist groups. More interestingly, it is the newly adopted perspective of new radical groups sympathizing with al-Qaeda and fighting U.S. troops in Iraq and Afghanistan, such as Abu Musab al-Zarqawi's Tawhid and Jihad group.

Radical Islamic groups and their history, goals, leaders, tactics, and operational methods were for the most part unknown to state and local investigators prior to 9/11. However, the new imperative is to master such knowledge. Sun Tzu, who lived around 400 B.C.E., observed that "if you are to win a war, you must know your enemy."[6] Of necessity then, the first part of this chapter deals with who terrorist enemies are, their history, what they want, what they've done, and why they are a threat to us. Using this overview, the subsequent portions of the chapter dealing with responses to terrorism and its investigation assume greater meaning. Although there are several Islamic terrorist organizations that are active, the following groups pose the most significant, dangerous, and continued threat to U.S. interests.

Al-Qaeda

Al-Qaeda ("the base") is easily the most recognized and feared of all radical Muslim terror groups. The group has its basis in the mujahedin, or "holy warriors," who fought against the Russians when they invaded Afghanistan in 1979. During the 1970s, Afghanistan's leaders were dependent on the Soviet Union for economic and political support. As a result, Islamic movements in Afghanistan were suppressed in favor of Soviet Marxism. When the procommunist government faltered in the late 1970s, Russia invaded in a doomed attempt to prop it up.[7] The invasion caused Afghanistan's tribal and religious leaders to abandon their infighting and band together to resist the Russians. The U.S. government, eager to undermine the Soviet Union's power, offered assistance in the form of funding and personnel. The result was a jihad against the Soviet Union, fought

◄ **FIGURE 20-2   Jihad**
For nearly 1.3 billion people, Islam is a religion of discipline and peace. However, radical elements within Wahhabism and Jihadist Salafism promote violence and jihad (holy war) against the United States, modernization, and the West in general.
(© AP/Wide World Photos)

by a coalition consisting of Afghans, Central Intelligence Agency operatives, and scores of young Arab men, drawn from places such as Saudi Arabia, who were eager to fight for Islam.[8]

One such Saudi citizen was Osama bin Laden (Figure 20-3), who came from a wealthy family and who had studied civil engineering prior to arriving in Afghanistan. He set up the organization known as "the base," or al-Qaeda, in order to track the movements of fighters and money coming into the Afghan resistance. The United States and Saudi Arabia both applauded the efforts of bin Laden, whose efficiency and strategic knowledge led Afghan fighters toward victory. Soviet troops withdrew from Afghanistan in 1989, and bin Laden returned, victorious and a hero, to Saudi Arabia, where he rejoined his family.[9] Bin Laden quickly came into disfavor with the Saudi Arabian government as a result of his vocal opposition to the Saudi alliance with the United States during the first Gulf War. He fled Saudi Arabia and returned briefly to Afghanistan in 1991, finally settling in Sudan in 1992, a country that welcomed his arrival.[10] It was there that bin Laden stepped up his sponsorship of training camps for fundamental Islamic young men, particularly those who subscribed to Jihadist Salafism.[11] Because of these and other activities, the Saudis revoked his citizenship in 1994, and his family, at least publicly, disowned him.

Following the 1993 World Trade Center bombings, American interest in bin Laden escalated, although he denied involvement in the attack. The United States was also interested in his training camps in Sudan, believing that graduates from bin Laden's schools were responsible for attacks on U.S. forces in Somalia and Riyadh. Sudan, acting under pressure from the United States and Egypt, finally expelled him in 1996.[12]

Bin Laden again returned to Afghanistan, where the Taliban, a strict Muslim faction, had united Afghanistan under their harsh rule. The Taliban offered sanctuary to bin Laden and benefited greatly from his wealth. In return, bin Laden and his al-Qaeda organization were protected and allowed to recruit hundreds of followers in his pursuit of jihad against the United States.

The goals of the jihad were to drive U.S. forces out of the Arab peninsula, overthrow the pro-Western Saudi government, thereby liberating the holy sites Mecca and Medina, and support radical Islamic groups throughout the world. By the late 1990s, al-Qaeda's training camps were turning out hundreds of "graduates" annually.[13]

In 1998, al-Qaeda made its first strike against the United States. A suicide bomber drove a truck into the U.S. embassy compound in Nairobi, Kenya, killing 216 people and injuring over 4,500. Eight minutes later, another truck bomb detonated in Dar as Salaam, Tanzania, killing 11 and injuring over 100. The United States reacted by launching cruise missiles on the training sites in Afghanistan, attempting to kill bin Laden. As a result of the embassy bombings, bin Laden made his way onto the list of America's most wanted men.[14] He was also indicted for the attacks, along with 17 other al-Qaeda members.

The October 12, 2000, bombing of the *U.S.S. Cole* has also been attributed to al-Qaeda. Although bin Laden never formally took responsibility for the suicide attack, which killed 17 U.S. Navy personnel, the key suspect in the case told Yemini authorities that he and the suicide bombers were acting under the directions of Osama bin Laden.[15]

On September 11, 2001, planes hijacked by al-Qaeda cells crashed into the Twin Towers in New York City and the Pentegon. Aboard another hijacked flight,

▲ **FIGURE 20-3 Osama bin Laden**
Instrumental in several attacks against the United States, including the events of September 11, 2001, Osama bin Laden (leader of the al-Qaeda terrorist group) remains at large as the "most wanted person" in the world, with a bounty of $50 million on his head. (© AP/Wide World Photos)

FBI TEN MOST WANTED FUGITIVE

MURDER OF U.S. NATIONALS OUTSIDE THE UNITED STATES;
CONSPIRACY TO MURDER U.S. NATIONALS OUTSIDE THE UNITED STATES;
ATTACK ON A FEDERAL FACILITY RESULTING IN DEATH

USAMA BIN LADEN

Date of Photograph Unknown

Aliases: Usama Bin Muhammad Bin Ladin, Shaykh Usama Bin Ladin, the Prince, the Emir, Abu Abdallah, Mujahid Shaykh, Hajj, the Director

DESCRIPTION

Date of Birth:	1957	Hair:	Brown
Place of Birth:	Saudi Arabia	Eyes:	Brown
Height:	6' 4" to 6' 6"	Complexion:	Olive
Weight:	Approximately 160 pounds	Sex:	Male
Build:	Thin	Nationality:	Saudi Arabian
Occupation(s):	Unknown		
Remarks:	He is the leader of a terrorist organization known as Al-Qaeda "The Base." He walks with a cane.		

CAUTION

USAMA BIN LADEN IS WANTED IN CONNECTION WITH THE AUGUST 7, 1998, BOMBINGS OF THE UNITED STATES EMBASSIES IN DAR ES SALAAM, TANZANIA AND NAIROBI, KENYA. THESE ATTACKS KILLED OVER 200 PEOPLE.

CONSIDERED ARMED AND EXTREMELY DANGEROUS

IF YOU HAVE ANY INFORMATION CONCERNING THIS PERSON, PLEASE CONTACT YOUR LOCAL FBI OFFICE OR THE NEAREST U.S. EMBASSY OR CONSULATE.

REWARD

The United States Government is offering a reward of up to $5 million for information leading directly to the apprehension or conviction of Usama Bin Laden.

www.fbi.gov

May 1999

---

passengers unsuccessfully fought to retake the plane to prevent its use in another attack, resulting in its crash in rural Pennsylvania and the loss of everyone aboard. The United States promptly declared war against the terrorist groups responsible and went after bin Laden and his supporters in Afghanistan.

The subsequent wars in Afghanistan and Iraq have resulted in the killing or capture of hundreds of al-Qaeda fighters and operatives. Hundreds of documents linking al-Qaeda to the September 11 attacks have been found, and other documents suggest future plans to attack U.S. interests. By December of 2001, the Taliban rule in Afghanistan had been toppled. However, bin Laden and many of his closest cohorts within al-Qaeda were still at large.

Six years after the September 11 attacks, Osama bin Laden remains a wanted man. Many had presumed that bin Laden was either dead from U.S. bombing raids early in the Afghan offensive or hiding in the rough tribal areas between Afghanistan and Pakistan. In either event, the

core leadership of al-Qaeda had been destroyed and a new face, that of bin-Laden's top lieutenant and personal cleric, Dr. Ayman al-Zawarahi, was now on top of the dismantled organization.[16] America had become familiar with this new leader, and the myriad of video tapes that derided the American "invasion" into Iraq for the past three years. In January 2006, an unmanned Predator drone guided by the CIA hit a house in the village of Damadola, in northwest Pakistan in an a attempt to kill al-Zawarahi. The missile destroyed the house and killed a dozen people, but al-Zawarahi was not among them. Although much of the leadership of al-Qaeda has been taken out in air strikes and special forces missions, the top of the organizational pyramid has proven elusive. On September 7, 2007, speaking in a soft but firm voice, Osama bin Laden surprisingly reappeared after a three-year absence (October 2004) in a new, half-hour video tape that intelligence sources confirmed as being authentic and made recently. Bin-Laden apparently had survived the Afghan and Iraqi offensives and is not dead, and, more importantly, appears to still be the active leader of al-Qaeda. Most likely hiding in the conservative Muslim areas of the war-torn border areas between Afghanistan and Pakistan, bin Laden has secured a safe haven to potentially rebuild al-Qaeda's inner circle and train a new generation of radical Islamic terrorists to strike at the Middle East, North African, Europe, and of course, the United States. From hide-outs in Pakistan, intelligence reports indicate that the now newly formed central core of al-Qaeda has organized into cells with separate missions, such as fund-raising or logistics, and composed of over 200 hard-core loyalists to bin Laden.[17] This new al-Qaeda leadership has already been suspected of orchestrating dozens of success-ful attacks, such as the bombings of the British consulate and HSBC Bank in Istanbul in 2003 and the London tran-sit system in 2005. The leadership has also been respon-sible for a number of plots in the past several years, including plans to blow up transatlantic flights from Brit-ain in August 2006 and the JFK Airport in 2007.[18]

Al-Qaeda likely has new operatives within the United States and has also been linked to numerous other terror-ist organizations throughout the Middle East and Asia, such as Hizbollah, Al-Jihad, Harakat ul-Mujahidin, the Islamic Movement of Uzbekistan, HAMAS, the Chech-ens, and Jamaah Islamiayah. It is due partly to its wide reach that al-Qaeda remains powerful. Despite the fact that its power center has been disrupted in the past and hidden, al-Qaeda communicates regularly with the Arab world through the media. As in the September 2007 bin Laden tape, al-Qaeda continues to condemn U.S. involve-ment in Muslim affairs and urges jihad and violent ter-rorist attacks against the United States and its allies. The basis of their threat to the United States is in their ideol-ogy, past actions, continuing intent, and capability, and their financial resources help to make such plans reality.

Jemaah Islamiyah

Jemaah Islamiyah (JI) began when two radical Indone-sian clerics named Abdullah Sungkar and Abu Bakar Ba'asyir (Figure 20-4) established a pirate (unauthorized) radio station in 1960, which advocated Shari'a, strict Muslim law. Subsequently, they opened an Islamic school, which taught a hard-line version of Salafi Wahhabism. Increasingly in conflict with their government, both men were arrested in 1978, and sentenced to four years impris-onment. In 1984, there was a massacre of Muslim protes-tors, and both men were drawn into a campaign against the Indonesian government. Their involvement in several bombings against the government led to arrest warrants, and the two men fled to Malaysia.

In Malaysia, the pair developed a large following of other refugee Indonesians. Two prominent radical Islam-ics, both of whom had been mujahidins in Afghanistan, became part of JI's leadership. The first of these, Riduan Isamuddin (a.k.a., Hambali), taught recruits bomb-making and combat.[19] The other, Abu Jibril, helped JI

▲ **FIGURE 20-4** **Abu Bakar Ba'asyir**
The leader of Jemaah Islamiya has been implicated in the nightclub bombing in Bali, Indonesia, which killed 202 people.
(© AP/Wide World Photos)

establish numerous cells and supervised the training of all al-Qaeda operatives in Southeast Asia. Together, this core group of four men preached jihad and the establish-ment of an Islamic republic across Malaysia, Indonesia, southern Thailand, and the southern Philippines.[20] One prominent tactic of JI is to have recruits marry local women to gain the support of their wives' communities; this permitted JI to set up cells in the target countries from the mid to late 1990s.[21]

These cells operated fairly independently of one another and with some rough differences. The largest, in Malaysia, established "front" companies to channel funds and weapons, and arranged for the training of recruits by al-Qaeda.[22] The smallest, in the Philippines, was respon-sible primarily for the procurement of weapons and explosives. Though the Singapore cell was also small, it was there that the JI began to plot its largest attacks against U.S. and Western interests in order to further their goal of establishing a Muslim state. The Indonesian cell became the center for foreign funding of JI, and contin-ued the tradition of establishing training camps for new recruits.[23]

The cells established throughout Southeast Asia did little but increase their membership until after the collapse of the Indonesian dictatorship in 1998. At that time, most of the senior leadership relocated to Indonesia and began actively planning terrorist attacks for the first time. In 2000, a series of bombings were carried out in Indonesia.[24] These attacks were aimed at Christian churches who had voiced support for Christian paramilitary groups then organizing around Indonesia's islands. Hambali was the primary planner in these attacks, which called for 30 bombs to detonate, killing thousands and sparking a religious civil war in the country. The attacks did not achieve the cells' goals, because only 18 of the bombs actually detonated, killing only 5 people.[25] Hambali also masterminded several bombings in Manila that resulted in 22 deaths.

There were also plans for large-scale attacks against the United States in Singapore. JI and al-Qaeda had procured mass amounts of explosives and ammunition with the help of the Lebanese group Hizbollah in order to attack U.S. ships in Singaporean waters, as well as the U.S., British, and Israeli embassies, and several American companies based there. However, in December of 2001, crackdowns on terrorist groups spurred by the September 11, 2001, attacks led to the arrest of several key figures in the Singapore attacks. The attack was aborted, and plans shifted to attack Israeli and U.S. embassies in the Philippines. These plans were also foiled by arrests of key JI members in mid-2002.[26]

The efforts of JI were subdued, temporarily. Hambali was angered that so many of his prime associates in the Filipino and Singapore cells had been arrested, and looked to lash out. He began to shift his focus from large-scale attacks on symbolic Western interests to smaller strikes against places frequented by Western tourists, such as bars and nightclubs. This planning culminated in the 2002 bombing of a nightclub in Bali, a small Indonesian island popular with U.S., British, and Australian tourists. Two hundred and two people died in the attacks, which devastated the Indonesian tourist economy.[27]

The Indonesian government immediately sought the arrest of the responsible parties. Ba'asyir was arrested only a week after the attacks, and four additional suspects were apprehended in the following months. By January of 2003, JI was blamed for the attack, and Hambali became the focus of the investigation.[28] He was arrested in August of 2003[29] and is reportedly being held and interrogated in a foreign country for intelligence leads. In September of 2003, Ba'asyir received a four-year sentence for attempting to subvert the Indonesian government but was acquitted of involvement with JI.[30]

The arrests of key leaders did not destroy JI, nor did it curtail its operations. On August 5, 2003, a bomb ripped through the Marriott hotel in Jakarta, Indonesia, killing 13 people. Suspicion immediately fell on JI and a group associated with it. Indonesian officials are further questioning Hambali about the transfer of a large amount of money to a Manila group linked with JI just before the bombing.[31] It appears that the networks established by JI throughout Southeast Asia have resulted in a strong backbone of radical Islamic terrorists who are willing to carry on JI's fight, with or without its original leaders. JI's dangerousness to the United States and its allies is due to its al-Qaeda–trained operatives, its strong network, good resources, and its ability to strike at "soft" targets, such as resorts and clubs that Westerners visit and foreign businesses located throughout Southeast Asia. With its links to other terrorist organizations and their resources, it has the potential for wider-reaching and more complex scenarios. For instance, in August, 2007, the Caliphate Conference of Hizb ut-Tahrir (HuT) was held in Jakarta, Indonesia, bringing together the global leadership of radical Islam from more than 20 countries. Speakers reemphasized the establishment of a pan-Islamic state with strict Muslim governance to the over 100,000 supporters attending the conference. Abu Baker Ba'asyir, recently released from jail after serving a short sentence in June 2006, addressed the conference as well. In his speech, Ba'asyir called for a radical Islamic network (presumably through the existing JI group) in Southeast Asia to establish a pan-Islamic state in the region. Intelligence reports indicate that Ba'asyir now aspires to political leadership in Indonesia and is nurturing his ambition as a potential candidate in the 2009 Indonesian presidential elections.[32] The HuT conference provided him with a unique forum to build support for his potential candidacy and, more importantly, a venue in which to reemphasize radical Islamic values to students attending the myriad of **madrasas** (Islamic boarding schools) that fuel JI membership throughout Southeast Asia. Quite interesting, much of the HuT conference also focused on Malaysia and its role as an Islamic state. The southern districts of Thailand bordering Malaysia have been rocked by radical Islamic terrorism and violence for the past three years, and activities increased after the conference. The Hizb-ut-Tahrir is clearly an organization that is deeply rooted in radical Islam ideologically and is propagating itself as the venue for global Islamic movements.[33]

Hizbollah

Hizbollah, or "the Party of God," was founded in 1982 in reaction to the Israeli invasion of Lebanon. This invasion was generally precipitated by continuing Palestinian military action from Lebanon in Northern Israel and more particularly by the unsuccessful assassination attempt on the life of Israel's Ambassador to the United Kingdom by the Abu Nidal organization. During the invasion, Israel battled Palestinian Liberation Organization (PLO), Syrian, and Muslim Lebanese forces, driving halfway across Lebanon to Beruit.

The roots of Hizbollah go back to the late 1970s, when hundreds of Shi'ite clerics and students were forced to leave Iraq and settle in Lebanon. These exiles recruited young militants and formed the Committee Supportive of the Islamic Revolution, which identified closely with the Shi'ite Muslim government in Iran. The group was also loosely associated with a Lebanese Shi'ite militia, known as Amal,[34] led by Nabih Berri.

The 1982 invasion of Lebanon by Israel damaged or destroyed more than 80% of the villages in southern Lebanon with 19,000 Lebanese killed and another 32,000 injured. The invasion caused a mass exodus from the southern areas of Lebanon, owing mostly to the total destruction of Lebanese agriculture by the Israelis. The exiles flooded into northern Lebanon, settling into refugee camps that were also occupied by displaced Palestinians. These refugee camps quickly became a hotbed of discontent against Israel and Western Zionist sympathizers, such as the United States. Militant groups such as Amal organized a Lebanese resistance front to fight the Israelis, but it wasn't until Iran sent 1,500 troops to the aid of the Lebanese fighters that the development of Hizbollah truly began. The Iranian fighters further fostered the desire among the Lebanese Shi'ites to model their government after Iran's, where Muslim clerics and disciples of the Ayatollah Khomeni ruled. The Shi'ites wanted the same for Lebanon.[35]

The final stage of Hizbollah's development occurred when a schism arose within Amal. Nabih Berrie (the leader of Amal) had begun to participate in a committee whose head was pro-Israeli. Others within Amal felt this was a manipulation conceived of by Americans who wished to water down Lebanese militancy. They also considered it a betrayal of Islam. As a result, the more radical Islam faction of Amal broke free and joined the smaller radical groups and the Iranian forces to establish the *Committee of Nine,* Hizbollah's first decision-making council. Hizbollah eventually absorbed all the smaller Shi'ite resistance groups, becoming a powerful force against the Israeli occupation.[36] Guerrilla attacks were conducted against the Israelis, which included the use of car bombs, sniper attacks, and suicide bombers.

Hizbollah's terrorist activity began to escalate. On April 18, 1983, a suicide bomber drove into the U.S. embassy in Beirut, Lebanon, killing 63 people, including the top-level American intelligence officials in Lebanon at the time.[37] On October 23, 1983, another suicide bomber drove at least 6 tons of dynamite into a U.S. Marine command center located at Beirut's International Airport, killing 241 Marine and Navy personnel (Figure 20-5). Twenty seconds later, another blast erupted at the barracks of a French military contingent. Fifty-eight French soldiers died in the attack. Hizbollah claimed responsibility for both attacks, claiming them to be retaliation for French and U.S. support of Christian governmental factions in the Lebanese civil war.[38]

U.S. troops were ordered out of Lebanon in early 1984 by President Ronald Reagan, a move that did not lead to a drop in the violence. Malcom Kerr, President of the American University of Beirut (AUB), was assassinated on January 18, 1984; another American embassy bombing occurred on September 20, 1984, which killed 14 people;

▲ **FIGURE 20-5 Sayyad Hassan Nasrallah**
The head of Hizbollah in Lebanon; aside from involvement in the 1983 suicide bomber attack on the Marine barracks in Beirut which killed 241 Marines, Hizbollah is very active in the financing of various terrorist operations through trafficking of drugs, arms, and human beings.
(© AP/Wide World Photos)

and kidnappings of Westerners by Hizbollah escalated. The rising toll of the dead and missing led the United States to stage a complete withdrawal from Lebanon, leaving only six diplomats in the country by November of 1984.[39]

Again, retreat by the U.S. did not mean an end to terrorist attacks against U.S. and Western interests. In 1985, TWA flight 847 was hijacked by Hizbollah affiliates, resulting in the death of one American on board. Hizbollah also claimed responsibility for the kidnappings of 18 American and British journalists and church officials, three of whom were killed, including Beirut Central Intelligence Agency (CIA) Station Chief William Buckley, who was held 19 days and then executed. In 1992, the Israeli embassy in Buenos Aires, Argentina, was bombed, killing 29 people. Although Hizbollah never directly claimed responsibility, they did release a surveillance tape of the embassy that overtly implied their responsibility. In 1994, a Jewish community center in Buenos Aires was bombed, killing 95 people. Hizbollah was also responsible for this act.[40]

In 2000, faced with mounting casualties, Israel ordered a complete retreat from Lebanon after nearly 18 years of occupation. This act served to legitimize Hizbollah not only in the Shi'ite community but also the Arab world at large. No other Arab group had been able to successfully drive Israel from occupied lands. Palestinians waging the current Intifada (or uprising) cite Hizbollah as a major inspiration in their battles. Futhermore, Hizbollah holds 12 seats in the Lebanese parliament and has built an extensive educational and social aid network within the Lebanese Shi'ite community.[41]

Although the 1994 Jewish community center attack in Buenos Aires is the last terrorist act directly linked to Hizbollah, the organization remains a risk to the United States and Israeli interests. Attacks against Israeli troops have continued in the Sheeba area, which Israel claims is a part of Syria and therefore not subject to withdrawal. Hizbollah forces claim that Sheeba is part of Lebanon and has continued to launch missile attacks against Israeli forces.[42]

Hizbollah has also established cells throughout the world in an effort to recruit members, raise money, and network with other similar organizations. Cells were discovered in the United States in July of 2000, primarily working to raise funds for the organization. Nearly $283,000 in money and assets was seized from 18 people in North Carolina.[43] Hizbollah was also accused of using its networks to smuggle a boatload of arms to the Palestinian authority in January of 2002 and of recruiting Singaporeans for a failed attack on U.S. and Israeli ships in the waters off of Singapore.

Although initially dismissed because of the religious differences between the groups, evidence has been found linking Hizbollah to al-Qaeda. Leaders of both groups apparently met several times in the 1990s, and there is some evidence that the groups have been coordinating logistics and training for specific operations.[44] Investigators of a 2002 bombing of an Israeli-owned hotel in Mombasa that killed 16 people have found clues that point to such a collaboration. Materials and techniques used in the attack, formally blamed on al-Qaeda, are the same as those used by the Hizbollah suicide bombers in the attacks on the U.S. Marine barracks and embassy in the 1980s. Furthermore, the only claim of responsibility for the attack was made on Hizbollah radio. Also, missiles found after an attempt to shoot down an Israeli charter jet by al-Qaeda were identified as SAM-7s, used almost exclusively by Hizbollah fighters against Israeli targets.[45]

More recent intelligence also indicates that Hizbollah provided aid to al-Qaeda operatives fleeing Afghanistan at the end of 2001. Between 80 and 100 al-Qaeda fighters were given fake passports by Hizbollah, allowing their safe passage into Saudi Arabia and Yemen. Some 10 to 20 senior al-Qaeda commanders are believed to have settled within Lebanon since 2001, as well.[46] As a result, Hizbollah remains a designated foreign terror organization, classified as having a high activity level by the U.S. State Department. During his 2002 State of the Union address, President George W. Bush singled the organization out as a target of the U.S. War on Terror.[47]

In 2004, Hizbollah won nearly a quarter of the parliamentary seats in the Lebanese government and was largely responsible for starting the Second Lebanon War in July 2006 by firing rockets into northern border towns of Israel and capturing several IDF soldiers. The incident became an international topic of debate as over a thousand civilians were killed in the ensuing bombing and ground invasion by Israel. The war ended after a short,

but deadly 34 days, rendering Lebanon's infrastructure in chaos and parts of southern Lebanon uninhabitable because of unexploded cluster bombs. Hizbollah and Nasrallah emerged as "victors" against the Israeli forces and boasted that their armed forces were now much stronger than before, and much better armed with missiles supplied by Iran. Over a million people attended Nasrallah's speech in Beirut in late August 2006 declaring "victory" over the Zionist state. Today, Hizbollah is a viable and effective terrorist organization world wide. It has a strong following with an impressive intelligence gathering force supplemented and trained by Iran's Ministry of Intelligence Service (MOIS). Agents associated with Hizbollah have been observed in Latin America and across Europe. Although their primary target is the destruction of Israel, Hizbollah continues to be a partner with other Middle East groups in funding major drug and arms trafficking operations.[48]

Palestinian Terrorist Groups

The current conflict between the Israelis and the Palestinians is a decades-old dispute regarding land rights that grows increasingly complex by the day. The issues arose with the creation of Israel in 1948, which eventually resulted in the loss of the Palestinian state and the displacement of the Palestinian people. This conflict is worsened owing to the two fundamentally different ideologies of both sides and a general unwillingness of both to compromise. The most dangerous manifestation of this conflict comes in the form of terrorist groups that are often willing to go to any length to draw attention to their cause. Palestinian terrorist groups, whether secular or grounded in Islamic fundamentalism, are known throughout the world for their extreme tactics (including suicide bombing) used against the Israelis and their supporters. These organizations focus their attacks on civilian and political targets within Israel, often in reaction to Israeli aggression upon Palestinians.

The Popular Front for the Liberation of Palestine (PFLP)

The PFLP is a Christian-led Marxist-Leninist group founded in 1967 by George Habash as a direct response to the Six-Day War of 1967. George Habash, code-named "al-Hakim," or the doctor, is a Christian Palestinian doctor. The PFLP essentially established the concept of skyjacking an airplane, back in the late 1960s. Their motivation was relatively benign: to make the world aware of the plight of the Palestinian people. Killing passengers and using skyjacked planes as weapons (e.g., the attacks on September 11, 2001) were *not* PFLP tactics. However, PFLP did conduct other violent attacks aimed directly at Israel.

The Abu-Nidal Organization (ANO)

This organization was formed by Sabri al-Banna, code-named Abu Nidal (meaning father of the "Holy Struggle"). The group formed after it split from the Palestinian Liberation Organization as a result of perceived moderation on the part of Yassir Arafat in 1972. Al-Banna was strictly antimoderation and adhered strongly to the doctrine that Israel must be destroyed at any cost, branding Arafat, the PLO, and the rest of the al-Fatah as traitors. Al-Banna continued to launch international terrorist operations against Israeli interests and even struck at pro-Arafat groups and moderate Arab countries in his list of targets. The Abu Nidal organization has been financially backed by Syria, Libya, Iraq, and Iran.[49]

The Abu Nidal Organization has attacked more foreign and Arab interests than any other Palestinian terrorist organization to date, and at one point was considered the most dangerous group in the world, having been accused of killing or wounding nearly 1,000 people in 20 different countries. Over the past 30 years, ANO attempted or carried out assassinations of Arab government officials and high-ranking PLO officers. This is one of the few Palestinian groups to have actually claimed an attack within the United States, having conducted a robbery in St. Louis, Missouri, in the mid-1980s. In August 2002, Sabri al-Banna's body was found in an Iraqi apartment with multiple gunshot wounds. Reports state that he committed suicide, but intelligence sources believe he was killed by Iraqis so Saddam Hussein could have access to the Abu Nidal Organizational network, which is still active, yet diminished, throughout the world.

The Palestinian Islamic Resistance Movement (HAMAS)

HAMAS, a radical fundamentalist organization, came to prominence as the foremost opponent of the Oslo peace accords following the first major Palestinian Intifada in the 1990s (Figure 20-6). The primary modus operandi of HAMAS is **suicide bombings** against civilian targets.

HAMAS has been directly responsible for over 90% of the suicide bombings against Israel. The bombings have been notoriously ruthless, often aimed at inflicting the most civilian damage possible. For example, on March 27, 2002, in the Israeli resort of Netanya, a bomber blew himself up at a hotel, killing 28 Israelis who were celebrating Passover. This attack remains one of the most deadly HAMAS actions to date.[50]

Deconstructing the Suicide Bomber For most Americans, trying to understand the motivation behind suicide bombing is very difficult. In our culture, such actions are often labeled unpredictable, irrational, and fanatical. However, a careful analysis of the phenomenon shows that suicide bombings are not spontaneous outbursts of emotion but rather calculated, strategic moves by a specific group for a specific purpose. Indeed, suicide bombers are actually trained in the actions. They undergo a relatively long period of indoctrination filled with group pressure, pep talks, organizational support, and personal commitment. Quite interestingly, suicide is strictly forbidden in the Holy Quran; however, when deemed by a religious edict to protect the Kingdom of Islam, suicide bombing serves as a means to an end. Some argue that the huge difference in might between Israel and the Palestinian people militarily gives legitimacy to the act, while others suggest that people who have little political power in the present or no hope for the future engage in the ultimate desperate measure.[51]

Under the religious and ideological leadership of radical Islamic cleric, Sheikh Ahmed Yassin, people who engage in suicide bombing became a *shahid*, or martyr fulfilling a religious command. Most suicide bombers in Israel fit a specific profile: young men between 18 and

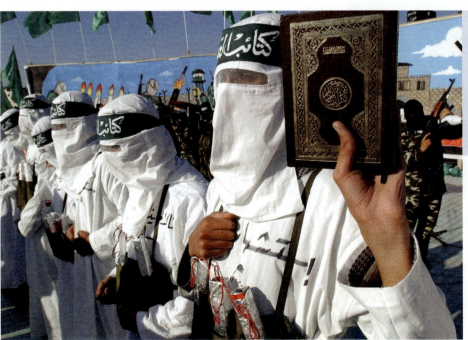

◄FIGURE 20-6 HAMAS
This group is responsible for over 90% of the suicide bombings in Israel, with most bombs being relatively crude homemade devices aimed at killing a relatively small number of people.
(© AP/Wide World Photos)

24 years old, born in relative poverty with little or no education and with no real understanding of the outside world or of the geopolitical issues surrounding the Middle East. For the most part, the shahid is a victim of some personal tragedy or event from the Israeli occupation in West Bank or Gaza. This person seeks honor, praise, and financial reward for his family after the action has been completed, as well as the personal religious rewards of seeing the face of Allah and the temporal love and servitude of 72 dark-eyed virgins in heaven. Most suicide bombers in Israel kill themselves and two other individuals. They often walk less than two miles from their home before engaging in their deadly action. For the most part, their "weapon" is crude: TNT or dynamite wrapped with iron nuts and bolts, or metal ball bearings worn in a vest or around their waist (Figure 20-7). In a crowded café or on a bus, or in a shopping center, suicide bombers wreck havoc on their unsuspecting victims. However, on March 22, 2004, Yassin was killed by the Israeli Moussad returning from prayer services at a West Bank mosque. The radical leader was gone, and the number of suicide bombings in Israel dramatically decreased.

U.S. intelligence officials have consistently warned that HAMAS may strike U.S. interests or American gathering places in Israel and throughout the Middle East. The report does not rule out attacks on American soil. The FBI has long suspected there are HAMAS sympathizers among Islamic extremists in the United States. Federal and local law enforcement officers are closely tracking

▲ **FIGURE 20-7 Shahid**
Suicide bomber wearing a satchel-style bomb of TNT wrapped with metal ball bearings and ignited by a simple finger push device. The bomber wears a jacket or coat over the deadly cargo upon entering a crowded café or night spot.

thefts of explosives (like those used in HAMAS backpack bombs) and unusual sales of fertilizer, chemicals, and fuel that could be used to make a truck bomb.[52]

HAMAS is clearly one of the most interesting groups in the Middle East. Although it has been responsible for the vast majority of suicide bombings and radical violence in Israel (particularly under the leadership of Yassin), it enjoys a favorable opinion among the Palestinian people. HAMAS has consistently tried to focus on helping the people within the occupied territories of the West Bank and Gaza, collecting million of dollars in aid and rebuilding schools, mosques, and hospitals. In fact, in 2006 it was elected the governing body for the Palestinian territories of the West Bank and Gaza in Israel. Essentially, HAMAS is the government of the Palestinian Authority, and although they have recently denounced violence and suicide bombings, their motives and intentions still focus on the destruction of Israel.

Other Active International Groups

Aum Supreme Truth

Also known as *Aum Shinri-kyo*, the group gained infamy for releasing sarin nerve agent in the Tokyo subway system, killing 12 people and injuring up to 6,000. Established in 1987, the Aum aimed to take over Japan, and then the world. It adopted a view that the United States would initiate Armageddon by starting World War III with Japan. Control changed hands in 2000, and under Fumihiro Joyu, the Aum changed its name to Aleph and now claims to reject the teachings of its founder. Membership is 1,500 to 2,000.

Basque Fatherland and Liberty

Known by its Basque initials, ETA, the group was founded in 1959 with the aim of establishing an independent, Marxist Basque homeland in the border area between Spain and France. The group has killed more than 800 people and targets primarily Spanish officials. It finances activities through kidnapping, robbery, and extortion. Estimated membership is in the hundreds.

Kach and Kahane Chai

Israeli terrorists whose goal is to restore the biblical state of Israel. Radical Israeli American Rabbi Meir Kahane founded Kach. Kahane Chai, or "Kahane Lives," was founded by Binyamin Kahand following his father's assassination in New York in 1990. Both were declared terrorist groups by Israel in March 1994. The younger Kahane and his wife were murdered in a drive-by shooting in Israel on December 31, 2000. The Kahanes' groups protest against the Israeli government and harass and threaten Palestinians in Hebron and the West Bank. They receive support from sympathizers in the United States and Europe; their numbers are unknown.

Kurdistan Workers' Party

Founded in 1974 as a Marxist-Leninist insurgent group, the Kurdistan Workers' Party (PKK) is primarily composed of Turkish Kurds bent on forming an independent Kurdish state in southeastern Turkey. Turkish authorities captured Chairman Abdullah Ocalan in 1999, tried him, and sentenced him to death. Shortly thereafter, Ocalan announced a "peace initiative" in August 1999, ordering members to refrain from violence and to withdraw from Turkey. Members supported the initiative and publicly claim to use only political means to achieve the new goal of improving the rights of Kurds. There are 4,000 to 5,000 supporters, most in northern Iraq, and thousands of sympathizers in Turkey and Europe. Syria, Iraq, and Iran have harbored party members and offered limited funds. Turkey reports that over 30,000 people have died at the hands of PKK terrorists over the last decade. As of early 2005, Ocalan had not been executed and is reportedly imprisoned on Imrali Island in a special facility.

Liberation Tigers of Tamil Eelam

Founded in 1976, Liberation Tigers is the most powerful Tamil group in Sri Lanka. Its aim is to establish an independent Tamil state. It began attacks on the Sri Lankan government in 1983 and relies on a guerrilla strategy that includes terrorism. One group, the Black Tigers, carries out suicide bombings and assassinations. The Tigers have some 8,000 to 10,000 combatants in Sri Lanka and control most of the northern and eastern coastal areas of Sri Lanka.

National Liberation Army

Based in Colombia, this Marxist insurgent group formed in 1965 and is currently in a dialogue with the Colombian government. The group's 3,000 to 6,000 armed combatants engage in kidnapping, hijackings, bombings, extortion, and guerrilla war. Its strength lies mostly in rural and mountainous areas of north, northeast, and southwest Colombia.

Revolutionary Armed Forces of Colombia

The *Fuerzas Armadas Revolucionarias de Colombia* (FARC), established in 1964 by the Colombian Communist Party, is Colombia's oldest, largest, most capable, and best-equipped Marxist insurgency (Figure 20-8). It operates with impunity in many areas of the country. It engages in bombings, murder, kidnapping, extortion, hijacking, and guerrilla and conventional war against Colombian political, military, and economic targets. The majority of Colombia's 3,000 annual kidnappings are FARC operations. There are 9,000 to 12,000 armed members and an unknown number of supporters, mostly in rural areas. Cuba provides some medical care and political consultation.

▲ FIGURE 20-8
Revolutionary Armed Forces of Colombia
FARC is one of the most successful Marxist organizations in the world, having derived significant income from the lucrative cocaine trade in Colombia. Interestingly, many of the "soldiers" of FARC are female, and the average age is only 19.
(© AP/Wide World Photos)

Revolutionary Organization 17 November

A Greek radical leftist group established in 1975, it is named for the 1973 student uprising that protested Greece's military regime. It is not only against its government but also the United States, Turkey, and the European Union. It wants Greece out of the EU and NATO, and the Turkish military out of Cyprus. It's responsible for killing various U.S. officials and Greek public figures; its most recent victim, in June of 2000, was the British defense attaché.

Turkish Revolutionary People's Liberation Party/Front

Also called Dev Sol, this Marxist group formed in 1978 is virulently anti-American and anti-NATO. It finances activities through robbery and extortion. The Turks crippled Dev Sol in a series of attacks. Their size is unknown.

Sendero Luminoso

The "Shining Path" terror group of Peru, Sendero Luminoso is based on founder Abimael Guzman's belief in militant Maoist doctrine. Some 30,000 persons have died since Shining Path took up arms in 1980. Its stated goal is to replace Peruvian institutions with a communist peasant revolutionary regime. Peruvian counterterrorist operations, arrests, and desertions in recent years have reduced membership to an estimated 100 to 200 armed militants.

The preceding groups have much closer ties than was thought previously, as revealed by international financial investigations that "follow the money trail" and by records originating in Afghanistan and Iraq.[53]

DOMESTIC TERRORISM

As defined by the FBI, **domestic terrorism** is the unlawful use, or threatened use, of violence by a group or an individual based and operating entirely within the United States or its territories, without foreign direction, committed against persons or property to intimidate or coerce a government, the civilian population, or any segment thereof, in furtherance of political or social objectives.[54] Its perpetrators can be divided into two groups: right-wing terrorists and left-wing terrorists.

Right-Wing Terrorists

Domestic **right-wing terrorist** groups often adhere to the principles of racial supremacy and embrace antigovernment, antiregulatory beliefs.[55] They may also cling to anti-abortion and survivalist views and the need for paramilitary training in "militias." In general, right-wing militias believe that inevitably there will be a "showdown" with the federal government, so they stockpile weapons and food. In contrast, patriot groups tend to be more focused on the overthrow and destruction of the federal government. There has been some movement toward "leaderless resistance," which is enacted by small groups autonomously. The Montana Freemen illustrate the antiregulatory attitude of some right-wing groups. They refused to register their cars or pay income taxes, filed liens on government property, established their own court system, announced rewards for the arrest of government officials, and forged financial documents such as money orders. A 960-acre farm was declared sovereign territory and named "Justus Township." The 21 armed freemen surrendered after being under siege from authorities for roughly 90 days in 1996.[56]

More traditional right-wing groups have included the Ku Klux Klan and the Neo-Nazi Party. Although these anti-Semitic and hate-oriented groups have continued to plague American society, they have been relatively quiet over the last five years, primarily owing to the success of

civil litigation against specific groups brought about by the Southern Poverty Law Center, the focused attention given by law enforcement to such groups, and the natural death of several leaders within the movement.[57]

Christian Identity Theology

The **Christian Identity (CI) theology** is built around the central idea that the Jews of today are actually of demonic lineage and set on the destruction of the white, Aryan race (Figure 20-9). Their "two-seed" theory explains this in the following manner. The first seed is derived from an unholy sexual union between Eve and Satan, producing Cain and making him part of the devil's family. CI

▲ **FIGURE 20-9 CI**
Richard G. Butler was an instrumental leader in the Christian Identity movement, having led the Church of Christ's Christians and the Aryan Nation, two white supremacist, anti-Semitic organizations for over three decades in Hayden Lake, Idaho. In October 2000, he lost his 20-acre compound as the result of an innovative civil suit brought against him by the Southern Poverty Law Center in Birmingham, Alabama. Butler died in 2004.

(© Jerome Pollos/Getty Images)

believes this is the real source of original sin. The second seed is Abel, the son of Adam and Eve, who is in God's family. Adam was not the first man, just the first white man. Preceding him were the pre-Adamites, who were created from mud (people of color) and fashioned in the image of animals, meaning that they are less than human and without souls. After Cain killed his brother Abel, he had sexual unions with pre-Adamites, producing "spawn-of-the-devil" Jews. (The CI believes that today Jews are orchestrating a conspiracy, by controlling the U.S. government and financial institutions, to take over the world and destroy the "chosen" white race.) Adam and Eve's son, Seth, who was also part of the family of God, later continued Abel's creation of the pure Adamic (white) race.

Other ideas on the origins of the "pre-Adamite" (i.e., nonwhite individuals) also flourish. One argues that the "beasts of the field" in Genesis were actually the non-white races. These "beasts of the field" were in place to act as laborers for Adam's race (white people). A different approach is offered by the Reverend Richard Butler (Hayden Lake, Idaho): a pre-creation battle in space-ships took place between Satan and God. When Satan lost and fell to earth, the aliens in his fleet, who came from other planets in the galaxy, also fell. Therefore, the nonwhite races are really aliens, and the white race was placed on earth to fight them in a continuation of that great cosmic battle.

Other beliefs central to Christian Identity include the idea that the "millennial kingdom" will come into existence only after the battle between the Aryan people and the forces of Satan (the Jews and nonwhites) is won. The Aryan people must cleanse the earth of all others in order to allow for the millennium. An important point of the millennial beliefs is that they do not support the idea of rapture, the faithful being raised up all at once by Christ.[58] They believe the faithful have to be present to fight the final battle of good and evil, called the *tribulation*. Followers believe that the only laws that should be followed are biblical laws.

Another idea, *posse comitatus*, is central to CI thinking. Originally, it referred to the power of the county sheriff to summon men to help arrest criminals and restore the peace—essentially an empowerment of citizens. In modern times, it also denotes the inability of the federal government to use the armed forces to assist civilian law enforcement without Presidential authorization. During the 1980s, however, Posse Comitatus became the name of an organization that helped spread the CI movement. It maintained that citizens are not obliged to yield to authority or agents above the local level because homosexuals, communists, Jews, and people of color had taken over the federal government, making it the Zionist Occupational Government (ZOG).

In CI, the institutions of the federal government are compared to the evil forces in the book of Revelations. As such, the federal government is seen as a puppet of the forces of Satan and thus must be destroyed. The U.S. government is often equated to the seven-headed dragon, with the ATF, FBI, IRS, EPA, and other agencies as the heads that feed the beast. The World Bank and the United Nations are seen as supposedly trying to impose a New World Order on Aryan people.[59] Thus, white Aryans must be ready to fight the demonic foes in a natural race war that will evolve from the urban ghettos and end in the Rocky Mountains.

At the national level, examples of Christian Identity include right-wing hate groups such as the Church of Christ's Christians, the Aryan Nation, the World Church of the Creator (WCOTC), and the National Alliance.[60] They often express their views via the Internet, through "white-power" music, and in publications. Some white-supremacist groups have toned down the openness of their racial opinions in order to appeal to a broader audience.[61]

The incidents with the Weaver family at Ruby Ridge, Idaho, and the Branch Davidians in Waco, Texas, were catalysts for the militia and Christian patriot groups.[62] There was a subsequent upswing in right-wing terrorist incidents afterward, the most destructive being the Oklahoma City bombing in 1995, for which Timothy McVeigh and Terry Nichols were later convicted; both men harbored antigovernment views and may have had some indirect ties to a militia.[63] Other specific acts of violence have also been attributed to the right. Members of the Order were convicted for murders and armed robbery in the late 1980s, and Posse Comitatus leader Gordon Kahl killed three law enforcement officers in the 1970s. More recent attacks include the 1999 shootings at the North Valley Jewish Community Center by Buford Furrow in Los Angeles, and the beating deaths of gay men by the Phineus Priesthood in several northwestern cities in the late 1990s. As more attention is being focused on international terrorist groups, home-grown right-wing entities are beginning to rise. Mark Potok, from the Southern Poverty Law Center identified over 751 domestic hate groups in 2004, a 6% increase over the previous year.[64] Since 9/11, several right-wing incidents have been documented, including the arrest of a man in Tennessee with ties to the KKK who attempted to acquire chemical weapons and explosives to blow up federal buildings, and the arrest of several white supremacists in Texas who had stockpiled boxes of explosives, sodium cyanide, nine machine guns, and over 100,000 rounds of ammunition.[65]

Left-Wing Terrorists

Left-wing terrorists generally profess a revolutionary socialist doctrine and view themselves as protectors of the people against the "dehumanizing effects" of capitalism and imperialism.[66] They advocate revolution as the means of transforming society; from the 1960s to the 1980s, leftists were the most serious domestic terrorist

▲ **FIGURE 20-10 Left-wing extremists**
Black Bloc groups often demonstrate while prepared for encounters with the police by wearing gas masks and latex protective suits. The Anarchist A is a common symbol associated with left-wing groups. (© Tom Uhlman/Getty Images)

threat.[67] Their demise as a threat was brought about by law enforcement efforts and the fall of communism in Eastern Europe, which deprived them of ideological support.[68]

The traditional left-wing extremist was replaced in the 1990s by a right-wing opposite as the most dangerous domestic terrorist, but subgroups of the left have developed that are potentially just as dangerous as the right and arguably more economically destructive.[69] A resurgence of anarchist groups, including those associated with Anarchist International, have dramatically increased since September 11, 2001. Most of these groups are relatively small and confine their activities to "rallies" against what they see as incursions of the government into the individual rights of people. Several "Black Bloc" (Figure 20-10) rallies in protest of the USA PATRIOT Act and the increased security associated with terrorism prevention have been held. However, unlike the anarchist groups of the 1960s (e.g., the Weather Underground and the Symbionese Liberation Army), there have been few violent acts attributed to these newly formed groups.

Today's extreme-left movements are best represented by modern ecoterrorists.[70] The FBI defines **ecoterrorism** as the use, or threatened use, of violence of a criminal nature against innocent victims or property by an environmentally oriented, national group for environmental-political reasons, or aimed at an audience beyond the target, which is often chosen for its symbolic nature.[71]

Although these groups are considered left-wing extremists, they are most often referred to as "special interest or single-issue extremists."[72] Special-interest extremists are seen as different from traditional right- and left-wing extremists because they are not trying to

effect a more widespread political change, but instead seek to resolve specific issues. These issues include animal rights and environmentalism on the left, and pro-life, anti-gay, and anti-genetic on the right.[73] In attempting to understand these groups, it is important not to be clouded by the political rhetoric of the left or the right, since these groups typically step outside discourse and attempt to change one aspect of the social or political arena through terrorism.[74]

Many special-interest groups try to claim that they are not terrorist groups because they do not harm any animal, human or non human by their actions. Because of this, they often enjoy a sympathetic welcome from many liberal affluent Americans unaware of the true actions of these groups. Although in the United States to date, no murders have been directly attributed to environmental activists, they have used intimidation tactics on those they see as enemies and have caused millions of dollars in damage. The FBI estimates that the Animal Liberation Front (ALF) and the Earth Liberation Front (ELF) have committed more than 600 criminal acts in the United States since 1996, resulting in damages that exceed $43 million.[75] Unfortunately, other single-issue groups like those associated with the anti-abortion movement have been very violent, having been responsible for the murder of numerous doctors and nurses who perform such operations.

Contrary to the claims of their partisans that ecogroups of this sort are not terrorists because they have not killed or injured any living being, thus making their acts mere vandalism and not terrorism, their use of arson and pipe bombs challenges such claims. A great part of the intent of these groups, too, is to influence policy by intimidation and coercion.[76]

◄ **FIGURE 20-11**
Picture of Vail fire and map of arson incidents
Since 1987, over $70 million in damage has been attributed to special-interest terrorists ALF and ELF owing to arson, primarily in the western states, including the 2000 arson of the Vail Ski Resort shown here.

(© AP/Wide World Photos)

Special-Interest Groups: ELF and ALF

The Animal Liberation Front (ALF), established in Great Britain in the mid-1970s, is a loosely organized movement committed to ending the "abuse and exploitation of animals." The American branch of ALF began its operations in the late 1970s. Similar to the right-wing's leaderless resistance orientation, individuals become members of ALF by simply engaging in direct action against those who utilize animals for research or economic gain. *Direct action* is generally defined by the group as criminal activity, which is aimed at causing economic loss or destroying company operations. ALF activists have engaged in a steadily growing campaign of illegal activity against fur companies, mink farms, restaurants, and animal research centers.[77]

In 1980, Tucson resident Dave Foreman created Earth First! and began a campaign of civil disobedience and monkey-wrenching (vandalism) at construction sites and logging locations. One tactic involved driving nails into trees, which broke chain saws and foiled logging operations but that also injured innocent workers.[78] In 1992, when some members wanted to mainstream Earth First! and back away from violence, others broke away to continue their illegal tactics; these splinter groups eventually founded the Earth Liberation Front (ELF). ELF has since been responsible for numerous ecoterrorism attacks in this country. One of the more infamous examples of these was the $12 million in damages that occurred when they set fire to a Vail, Colorado, ski lodge in 1998.[79] (See Figure 20-11.)

In 2004, several cases highlighted the continuing ecoterrorism of ELF and ALF. In Utah, a man sprayed "ELF" at a lumber yard where he set a fire that resulted in some $1.5 million in damages. Seven people associated with ALF were arrested for allegedly setting fire to the cars of Huntington Sciences Lab employees', vandalizing shareholders' homes, and threatening families.[80] The company was targeted because they used animals for product testing.

In January 2006, after nine years of investigation, the FBI indicted 11 people in connection with a five-year wave of arson and sabotage claimed by the ELF and ALF groups. The indictment named 17 separate attacks conducted by the ecoterrorists, which occurred from 1996 to 2001, resulting in no deaths but an estimated $23 million in damage, including the Vail, Colorado, ski resort arson.[81] Clearly, members within each group collaborated on specific actions and crimes. The arrests and ensuing conspiracy cases have made a dramatic dent in the leadership and activity of both organizations. Arson and vandalism cases attributed to both groups have dramatically declined, and although their websites and blogs continue to expound on the righteousness of their actions, most certainly, from an operational standpoint, both ELF and ALF have been dealt a significant setback.

FINANCING TERRORIST ORGANIZATIONS

After 9/11, U.S. agencies shifted gears, from identifying and thwarting individual terrorists/cells to adopting a broader strategy that includes targeting the financial operations and networks supporting terrorism.

In response to this new focus, steps were taken to strengthen America's ability to combat the flow of funds into terrorist organizations. In late 2001, President Bush issued Executive Order 13224 on Terrorist Financing.[82] It authorized the seizure of assets that belong to terrorist or terrorist supporters and dovetailed with the Anti-Terrorism and Effective Death Penalty Act of 1996, which established penalties for people who finance terrorism.[83] Later in 2001, the USA PATRIOT Act was enacted, which strengthened U.S. measures to prevent, detect, and prosecute terrorist financing and money laundering.

New Laws and Legal Tools

In the United States, a number of initiatives were created to help combat the financing of terrorism. These include the Foreign Terrorist Asset Tracking Center (FTAT), which brings together members of the Treasury Department, FBI, and CIA to identify terrorist financial infrastructures and focus on eliminating the ability of terrorists to obtain funds through the international financial system. Operation Green Quest is an initiative out of the Treasury Department aimed at denying terrorist groups access to the international financial system and is the investigative arm of FTAT and FinCen. The Financial Review Group (FRG) was originally formed to analyze the terrorist financing as it related to the 9/11 attacks. It now works to investigate all financial and fundraising activities related to terrorism.[84]

On the international front, the United Nations passed UN Resolution 1373, which imposed binding measures on all member states to help prevent terrorism worldwide including the suppression of the financing of terrorism. The United Nations also created the Counter-terrorism Committee (CTC) to monitor, assist, and promote the implementation of this resolution.[85] In 2001, the task of creating standards in the fight against terrorism was added to the mission of the FTAT.[86]

Drug Smuggling

Although the illegal drug trade has been around for centuries, recently much attention has been given to the link between the illegal drug trade and terrorism. The term **narco-terrorism** has been used to define this linkage. Some estimates are that terrorist organizations in as many as 30 different countries finance a significant portion of their operations through the use of profits obtained trading in the drug market. Many of the increases came about at the end of the Cold War, which was accompanied by a decline in state-sponsored terrorism. New countries, many of which belonged to the former Soviet Union, were grappling with conflicts both from inside and outside influences. This provided the opportunity for many criminal organizations, particularly those from Central Asia to take advantage of these unstable conditions and become more active in illegal activities such as drug trafficking.[87] Terrorist groups known to be involved with drug trafficking include al-Qaeda, Hizbollah, HAMAS, Sendero Luminoso, the PPK, and the Basque group, ETA.[88]

In Colombia, the current government finds itself in a long-standing struggle with the pro-communist group the Revolutionary Armed Forces of Colombia (Fuerzas Armadas Revolucionarias de Colombia, or FARC). This terrorist organization seeks to replace the current government with a leftist, anti-American regime. It is one of the largest and best-equipped insurgent organizations in the world, controlling large portions of Colombia and producing much of the cocaine that is distributed around the world. These drugs allow the FARC to generate large sums of money so they can purchase arms and other commodities to support their cause. It is estimated that as much as $400 to $600 million a year is generated through drug trafficking.[89] In 2002, the United States indicted several members of FARC, which marked the first time that members of a terrorist organization had been charged with engaging in illegal drug trafficking.[90]

Al-Qaeda obtained much of its initial financial support through the illegal opium trade in Taliban-controlled Afghanistan. This was an example of a state-sponsored narcotic operation openly supporting a known terrorist organization. The U.S.-led invasion of Afghanistan and the subsequent dismantling of the Taliban as the ruling party forced groups such as al-Qaeda to seek other funding sources. Often, the groups simply changed tactics from an open environment to a more clandestine operation similar to those in Colombia. Lately, however, because of the international focus on Iraq, reports have surfaced that the opium trade is returning to higher levels across Afghanistan. A recently released UN report stated that over a half-million people were involved in the illegal trafficking of drugs in Afghanistan, generating more than $25 billion annually.[91] Last year (2006), the government offered Afghan farmers $500 per acre to destroy their fields, but drug processors and traffickers are believed to have given farmers $6,400 per acre in profits for growing poppies. More than 225,000 acres are believed to have been cultivated in 2006. Further, U.N. figures in September 2007 reveal that Afghanistan's poppy production has risen 15% since 2006. The higher yields brought world production to a record high of 7,286 tons (in 2006), 43% more than in 2005.[92] This emphasizes the difficulty in eradicating something that, to a particular region, is its primary cash crop. In addition, the desire to obtain profits from such crops usually invigorates terrorist organizations to try and gain a foothold in the country.

According to the Drug Enforcement Administration (DEA), there are three critical elements to attacking narco-terrorism: law enforcement efforts, intelligence gathering, and international cooperation.[93] Rarely do terrorist organizations operate within one specific country. Instead, they tend to be more global in their boundaries, particularly when it comes to fundraising. Attacking the problem of terrorist use of the drug market to fund their operations requires international cooperation. Law enforcement across the globe must work together to eliminate the petty territorial wars of the past. Even within the United States there is an attempt to dismantle many of the obstacles that had plagued previous efforts at cooperation. The most notable is the creation of the Department of Homeland Security (DHS), which was the biggest governmental reorganization since the creation of the Department of Defense.

In April of 2004, the Congressional Research Services (CRS) office issued a report to the U.S. Congress outlining the links between illicit drugs and the terrorist threat. The findings indicated that the international drug market contributes to terrorist risk through at least five mechanisms:

- Supplying cash for terrorist operations;
- Creating chaos in countries where drugs are produced and through which they pass, or in which they are sold at retail and consumed—chaos sometimes deliberately cultivated by drug traffickers—which may provide an environment conducive to terrorist activity;

- Generating corruption in law enforcement, military, and other governmental and civil-society institutions in ways that either build public support for terrorist-linked groups or weakens the capacity of the society to combat terrorist organizations and actions;
- Providing services also useful for terrorist actions and movements of terrorist personnel and material, and supporting a common infrastructure, such as smuggling capabilities, illicit arms acquisition, money laundering, and the production of false identification or other documents, capable of servicing both drug-trafficking and terrorist purposes; and
- Competing for law enforcement and intelligence attention.[94]

There are several cases within the United States that highlight drug smuggling as a major method of operation for Middle Eastern terrorist groups operating within the United States. For instance, Operation Mountain Express (see Figure 20-12) culminated in 2002 with the arrest of over 136 persons and the seizure of 36 tons of pseudo-ephedrine, 179 pounds of methamphetamine, $4.5 million in cash, 8 real-estate properties, and 160 vehicles. The operation was conducted over a year and focused on two very large Middle Eastern drug trafficking groups: the Jaffar organizations out of Detroit, Michigan, and the Yassoui organization in Chicago, Illinois. This sophisticated, multinational trafficking operation was primarily involved in the smuggling of pseudoephedrine (the precursor to methamphetamine) from Canada through Michigan to several West Coast labs operated by Mexican cartels. Much of the organization, resources, and profits

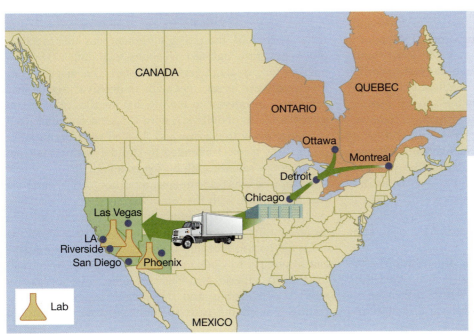

◄ FIGURE 20-12
Operation Mountain Express
Culminating in the arrest of over 136 people linked to Hizbollah in 2002, Operation Mountain Express involved the smuggling of methamphetamine from Canada to cities in the southwest United States.

from this operation were directly linked to various Middle Eastern terrorist groups, primarily Hizbollah.

In 2002 and 2003, several Middle Eastern subjects were arrested for attempting to sell 600 kilos of heroin and 5 tons of hashish to fund the purchase of four Stinger anti-aircraft missiles for al-Qaeda. The negotiations with undercover officers for this deal transpired in San Diego, Hong Kong, and other cities in Southeast Asia. And finally, Operation White Terror culminated in 2004–2005 with the arrest of four people (two in Houston, Texas, and two in San Jose, Costa Rica) associated with FARC in Colombia. The individuals attempted to trade $19 million (nearly 17 tons) in cocaine and cash for five containers of "Warsaw Pact" weapons stored in Cuba. The arms cache consisted of 9,000 AK-47 assault rifles, over 1,000 grenade launchers and over 300,000 grenades, hundreds of shoulder-fired SAM-7 missiles, and over 50 million rounds of ammunition.

In 2006 and 2007, several cases have revealed Islamic extremists embedded in the United States, posing as Hispanic nationals and partnering with violent Mexican drug gangs to finance terrorist networks throughout the Middle East. Several of the cases centered on Laredo, Texas, on the southern border with Mexico. According to the DEA, Middle Eastern terrorists have crossed the border and adopted Hispanic surnames. The long-standing drug cartels in northern Mexico, along the U.S. border from Tijuana to Juarez to Nuevo Laredo, have developed highly sophisticated smuggling and money-laundering networks now accessible to Islamic terrorists (jihadis).[95] According to the Department of Homeland Security, U.S. Border Patrol agents apprehended 1.1 million people along the Mexican border in 2005. In 2007, in response to increasing violence along the U.S-Mexican border reaching an all-time high, the Border Patrol established "Operation Community Shield," a two-week law enforcement round-up of illegal aliens focused on Laredo, Texas. Of the 2,388 gang members arrested, nearly a thousand belonged to the notorious MS-13 gang (from El Salvador), whereas others were classified as non-Mexican immigrants from the Middle East. Although the vast majority of illegal immigrants on the border continue to be Mexicans and Central Americans lured by the hope of a better life, the fear that Middle East terrorists could infiltrate the United States is real. Teamed with active drug and gang cartels on the border, foreign terrorists may well have an easier access to America versus entering the country through international airports on valid passports, as did every one of the September 11th hijackers.

Arms Smuggling

One of the main goals of a terrorist organization is to inflict would-be victims with paralyzing fear. Often this can be done with only the implied threat of the use of force. However, to maintain a level of fear and to demonstrate their capabilities, inevitably violence is used as an object lesson. This can be done by kidnappings, bombings, and the torture and/or execution of prisoners, hostages, and anyone who is, or may be, a threat. To do these things, terrorists must buy, capture, or trade for weapons. Thus, there is a lively illicit international market for conventional weapons as well as a desire for sophisticated arms, such as stinger missiles. In addition to being buyers of weapons on the international market, terrorist groups may use their knowledge of drug or other types of smuggling routes to sell arms to anyone with the requisite cash. Trades of weapons for commodities, such as drugs that can profitably be sold, are also part of the arms smuggling landscape. The collapse of the Soviet Union late in the twentieth century created an influx of weapons into the market.[96] The former Soviet republics are in need of funds, and the terrorist organizations desire weapons. The result is that terrorist groups across the globe are increasingly better equipped with more dangerous weapon systems, often purchased with drug trafficking profits.

In 2000, FARC bought some 10,000 rifles using a timber export business as a cover. Most of the weapons were Russian-made Kalashnikov (AK-47) and AKM rifles and were flown to Central America by a Russian transport plane. Once on site, the weapons were dropped by parachute into the dense jungle that serves as the operating area for FARC. The operation was foiled by the Peruvian government. Later, it was determined that the weapons were purchased with profits obtained from FARC's extensive drug-dealing network.[97] In yet another case in 2004, agents of the Immigration and Customs Enforcement (ICE) agency arrested a Colombian for attempting to purchase over $4 million worth of weapons for FARC. A portion of the payment was to be paid with 15,000 kilos of cocaine, again solidifying the connection between terrorist organizations and the drug trade.[98]

The arms smuggling network is not limited to Latin America. In 2004, the U.S. government was able to stop a plot to purchase high-tech weapons, including 200 Stinger missiles for private buyers in Pakistan. The suspects, residents of New Jersey, met with undercover agents and expressed an interest in buying 200 missiles at a cost of several millions of dollars. A third U.S. citizen was arrested in connection with the case and charged with money laundering. The suspect intended to launder the profits from the weapons sale through his job as a Wall Street trader.[99] According to court documents, a portion of the purchase was to be made with the use of heroin.[100]

As governments around the world began to give more scrutiny to financial institutions, groups such as al-Qaeda had to look for alternate ways to move financial resources. Al-Qaeda purchased diamonds with cash from both Liberia and Sierra Leone, creating easily moved, convertible, and untraceable assets. The two countries used the cash to purchase weapons and to support its security forces. Estimates of the value of diamonds purchased are generally $19 million. These transactions occurred in 2000, and the 9/11 attacks happened the following year.

Human Smuggling and Prostitution

The illegal trafficking of humans is growing at an alarming pace and has become a serious problem in the United States and throughout the world. Each year, an estimated 600,000–800,000 men, women, and children are trafficked against their will across international borders, 14,500–17,500 of whom are trafficked into the United States. Victims of trafficking are recruited, transported, or sold into all forms of forced labor and servitude, including prostitution, sweatshops, domestic labor, farming, and child armies. Approximately 80% of trafficking victims are female, and 70% of those female victims are trafficked for the commercial sex industry. It is estimated that the annual illegal immigrant business is worth between $12 and $30 billion annually.[101] These sorts of proceeds should make it no surprise to find that terrorist organizations are using this activity to help fund their operations.

Hizbollah has been tied to human trafficking in Lebanon and other parts of the Middle East. However, the area of the world that is experiencing the greatest trouble with human trafficking is in Southeast Asia.[102] Human traffickers and smugglers make high profits while risking relatively short prison sentences compared to drug dealers. The undocumented immigrants usually reimburse the price of the passage after their arrival. Unable to pay off their debt, many start working for organized groups in low-skilled jobs, the sex industry, and in criminal endeavors. Terrorist organizations have gotten involved in the smuggling as well as in the exploitation of illegals. Many undocumented workers in Asia have relied on human smugglers to illegally enter their final destinations. A majority of these illegal immigrants are now women and children, who often fall into the hands of people-traffickers. Thousands of women and children from China, Laos, Cambodia, and Myanmar work as prostitutes in Thailand, Japan, and the United States. Vietnamese girls are also trafficked to Cambodia to supply the sex trade and to China and Taiwan for marriage. More disturbing are the myriad child sex shops and child pornography locations throughout Southeast Asia (e.g., the Svey Pak-Kilo 11 district in Cambodia, Pat Pong in Bangkok, Thailand, and Manila in the Philippines) and the new phenomenon of **child sex tourism** catering to U.S. and European men. Customers make dates via the Internet, and arrangements are made for men traveling to Southeast Asia to visit child sex brothels. As a result, the U.S. Congress passed new legislation to specifically address these issues: The Victims of Trafficking and Violence Protection Act (TVPA) of 2000. The act establishes new definitions of the crime and defines *severe human* trafficking as:

- Sex trafficking in which a commercial sex act is induced by force, fraud, or coercion, or in which the person induced to perform such act has not attained 8 years of age; or
- The recruitment, harboring, transportation, provision, or obtaining of a person for the labor or services, through the use of force, fraud, or coercion for the purpose of subjection to involuntary servitude, peonage, debt bondage, or slavery.[103]

Further, the PROTECT ACT, enacted in 2003, allows law enforcement officers to prosecute Americans who travel abroad and sexually abuse children, without having to prove prior intent to commit an illicit crime (e.g., rape, sodomy). The law also strengthens the punishment of child sex tourists with a focus on protecting children from sexual predators worldwide.[104]

Credit Card Fraud and Theft

The problem of identity theft and follow-on crimes such as credit, credit card, and ATM frauds were covered in Chapter 14, "White-Collar Crime and Larceny."

In 2004, the French government announced that it had detected ten suspected Islamic militants who were stealing more than $100,000 a month from ATM-accessed accounts in several European countries. Shoulder surfing and other techniques (described in Chapter 14) were being used to acquire the information needed to execute these crimes. Although no exact figure is available on the amount of money terrorists acquire each year through such frauds, law enforcement has found significant direct links between terrorist missions and credit fraud.

When the 9/11 hijackers entered America, many did so with false identification or engaged in credit card fraud. In the failed plot to blow up Los Angeles International Airport, two of the three Algerian terrorists admitted they engaged in credit card fraud and used those proceeds to finance their operation. A fourth accomplice was caught in London in possession of a credit card duplicating machine, laminating equipment, and several cards from a local department store. A few weeks after 9/11, authorities in Spain arrested several individuals who were members of a suspected Algerian Islamic terrorist group. They explained that they used credit fraud to support their mission, which involved shipping computers to Algeria and propaganda equipment to others in Chechnya.[105]

In Chicago, a joint terrorism task force secured indictments against two businesses that allegedly used credit fraud to defraud about $1.7 million from banks and credit card companies. These individuals were suspected of having ties to Hizbollah, the Iranian-backed Lebanese terror group.[106] Also, during testimony to a Senate subcommittee on technology, terrorism and government information, a former Secret Service agent gave testimony concerning two Middle Eastern groups who had known affiliations to Islamic terrorist organizations (Hizbollah and al-Qaeda). These two groups had allegedly bilked financial institutions out of $21 million.[107]

Another major funding source for many terrorist organizations has been the illicit sale of cigarettes and other commodities. Traffickers can make as much as $60 per carton sold illegally. Although not yet reaching the scope of the drug trade, the risks and penalties are far lighter. This is making the illicit cigarette trade a new method of choice for financing terrorist operations. Federal investigators have uncovered traffickers who are providing material support to Hizbollah, as well as having ties to al-Qaeda, HAMAS, and the PKK, among others. Many terrorist organizations are working in concert with traditional organized crime groups to establish supply routes and business contacts. Many states are reporting losses in their state taxes from cigarettes in excess of $1.4 million, demonstrating the significant amount of proceeds that can be generated from the illegal sale of cigarettes.[108]

Charities Fraud and Linkages

During the past 20 years alone, several groups (including HAMAS, Hizbollah, the Palestinian Islamic Jihad, and al-Qaeda) have used a variety of charities, educational thinktanks and religious studies programs to raise tens of millions of dollars. In a 1996 report, the CIA claimed that there were more than 50 Islamic nongovernmental organizations operating within the United States, and of these "approximately one third support terrorist groups or employ individuals suspected of terrorist connections."[109] Some of those identified since 9/11 as having connections to terrorist organizations include the Benevolence International Foundation (BIF), the Muslim World League, the Qatar Charitable Society, the Holy Land Foundation (HLF), and the International Islamic Organization. These groups have used some funds for charitable purposes but have also diverted million of dollars to terrorist activities.

BIF and its companion, Illinois-based charity, the Global Relief Foundation (GRF), have been publicly accused of providing financial support to al-Qaeda and other international terrorist organizations. The BIF had offices in ten countries and raised millions of dollars in the United States for humanitarian aid but funneled a portion of other proceeds directly to terrorist groups. The GRF operated in 25 countries and also raised millions of dollars, sending a large percentage of it to Islamic extremists with significant links to terrorist groups. The FBI was conducting an investigation into both groups prior to 9/11 but was stymied by a lack of coordination and an unwillingness to assign the necessary resources. However, after the 2001 attacks, the government aggressively moved to seize the assets of both groups on terrorism-related charges, effectively shutting them down.[110]

The Al Haramin Islamic Foundation (HIF) was widely known as the "United Way" of Saudi Arabia. It was established in the early 1990s and exists to promote Wahhabi Islam by funding the construction of mosques, religious education, and humanitarian projects. Although considered to be a private organization, it has been supported by the government of Saudi Arabia both publicly and privately since its inception. Since 1996, the U.S. government has been gathering information on HIF leading to the belief that certain parts of the group were funneling funds to terrorist organizations. The U.S. requested assistance from the Saudi government but failed to receive any meaningful cooperation. Following 9/11, there were increased efforts to obtain information about those connected with HIF. Several well-publicized meetings took place ending in a commitment from the Saudi government to cooperate in the investigation. However, real help failed to occur until a bombing in Riyadh, Saudi Arabia, killed many westerners and Saudi Arabians. Since then, the Saudi government has taken significant steps to curtail the flow of funds to terrorists. It remains to be seen if the Saudi government is willing to make the difficult political and religious decisions necessary to significantly affect the flow of funds to terrorists from their kingdom.[111]

The Holy Land Foundation (HLF) was originally founded to assist Palestinians affected by the intifada, the Palestinian uprising against the Israeli occupation of Gaza and the West Bank. Headquartered in Texas, HLF had been under investigation for several years. However, as with the HIF, only limited measures were taken against the group until 9/11. Using new legislation, law enforcement developed a case against HLF and accused them of sending approximately $12.4 million dollars to HAMAS.[112] HLF has since had its assets seized and its leaders indicted on charges of providing assistance to a known terrorist organization. In addition, the head of the HLF was linked to the INFOCOM Corporation, which was subsequently charged with supplying computers and computer parts to Libya and Syria, both of which are designated state sponsors of terrorism.[113]

Another front has recently opened up against these "charities" in the form of civil judgments. A federal appeals court ruled in 2002 that the U.S. antiterror law permitted suits to be brought against the organizations that have been identified as supplying funds to terrorist organizations. In 2004, the first major case was won against the HLF, granting the family of a terrorist victim $156,000,000 in damages. According to the ruling, not only the organization but also contributors can now be held liable. This was a major part of the 2007 case in Dallas, Texas, against the HLF, proving that donors as well as the suspect knew that donations would be used to fund terrorist activities. However, in a controversial mistrial the government did not appear to prove their case, and all five defendants were free, ending a 14-year, multimillion-dollar Department of Justice investigation

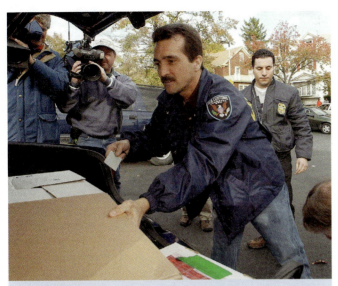

▲ **FIGURE 20-13   Terrorists records**
Information about al-Qaeda and its allies being unloaded by FBI personnel. The boxes contain videotapes, maps, notebooks, and other documentary sources seized by military, intelligence, and law enforcement personnel in Afghanistan and brought to the United States for closer investigation. The proof for investigators in linking specific terrorist organizations to charities, foundations, and state sponsorship are often found in financial records, an often time-consuming and tedious investigative process that may yield an important conviction. (© AFP/Getty Images)

into the one of the largest Muslim charities in the United States.[114] The complexity of such a case often lies in providing financial records that prove knowledge and association with a terrorist group (Figure 20-13) as well as understanding charitable giving in Islamic cultures.

One of the five pillars of Islamic faith is known as *zakat*, or charitable giving. It is much broader in its reach into Islamic society than giving is in Western cultures. It can also function as a form of income tax, educational assistance, foreign aid, and political influence. The Western idea of the separation of civic duty and religious duty does not exist in many Islamic cultures. Thus, charitable organizations take advantage of the Islamic sense of religious and duty to raise significant amounts of money.[115] Another unique aspect of the Islamic faith that played a role in the difficulty of tracking expenses was the use of the system known as *hawala*. This system is based on individual trust, family relationships, and regional affiliation. It is an integral part of the economies of many countries in the Middle East and Southeast Asia. It is a method that has been used for centuries to transfer funds from one person or place to another without the issue of federal banking or monetary reporting systems.[116] Since hawala is based largely on trust, there is an absence of the traditional paper trail used in most forensic financial investigations (Figure 20-14). The difficulty for law enforcement is to promote regulation of the hawalas in order to prevent their abuse by terrorist organizations without harming the financial centers of the populations they serve. One approach being tried in the UAE is to require that hawalas be licensed and regulated.[117] It is not known how many hawalas operate within the United States, but many believe that they have existed in America since the 1980s. Based on a 1994 law, hawalas were supposed to register with the government, but no enforcement activity was ever created. Following 9/11, Congress quickly passed the USA PATRIOT Act, part of which requires that hawalas operating within the U.S. register with the Treasury department and report any suspicious activities.[118] Failure to comply with this law gives law enforcement a justification for investigation. This is similar to the tactic that resulted in the 1930 indictment and conviction of Chicago gangster Al Capone for tax evasion.[119]

- Spiral notebooks, scraps of paper, or diaries listing information for numerous financial transactions, which generally include the date, payer name, amount received, exchange rate, and payment method or remittance code
- An unusually high number of phone lines at a residence or business; short incoming calls and lengthy overseas calls
- Fax transmittal logs/receipts, which may contain name of sender, beneficiary, or a code
- Wire transfer receipts/documents
- Phone records/documents; multiple calling cards
- Multiple financial ledgers (one for legitimate transfers, one for criminal activity, and one possibly for settling accounts)
- Bank account information, particularly multiple accounts, under same name
- Multiple forms of identification (false ID for the subject and for several other individuals)
- Third-party checks
- Evidence of other fraud activity

◄ **FIGURE 20-14**
Checklist of items common in an illegal hawala operation

(Adapted from Dean T. Olson, "Financing Terror," *FBI Bulletin*, Volume 76, Number 2, February 2007)

NATIONAL COUNTERTERRORISM INTELLIGENCE STRUCTURES

The National Infrastructures Protection Center (NIPC) is responsible for protecting and investigating unlawful acts against U.S. computer and information technologies and unlawful acts, both physical and electronic, that threaten or target critical U.S. infrastructures.[120] NIPC manages computer intrusion technologies, coordinates specialized training related to its spheres of interest, and supports national security authorities when unlawful attacks go beyond crimes and become foreign-sponsored events. Founded in 1998, NIPC is housed by the FBI. In addition to protecting national security information, NIPC is engaged in preventing and investigating **cyber-terrorism,** the use of electronic tools to disrupt or shut down critical components of our infrastructure, including energy, transportation, and government operations. For example, massive thefts of credit card numbers and other such acts could do serious harm to the public's confidence in using e-commerce transactions.[121]

The U.S. PATRIOT Act of 2001 provides law enforcement with new, broadened electronic surveillance authority; using DCS 1000, an Internet surveillance program formerly designated as "Carnivore," the FBI can intercept e-mail messages. Other methods of communication that the PATRIOT Act allows surveillance of include digital pagers, wireless telephones, fax machines, and videoconferencing. Terrorists, child molesters, pornographers, drug traffickers, spies, money launderers, hostile governments, hackers, and nations waging information warfare against the United States all use these means of comunication.[122]

The Departments of Justice, Defense, Energy, and Health and Human Services, the Environmental Protection Agency, and the Federal Emergency Management Agency form the National Domestic Preparedness Office (NDPO). Established in 1998, it is responsible for assisting state and local authorities with the planning, equipment, and training (including health and medical support), needed to respond to weapons of mass destruction attacks.

The FBI Counterterrorism Center has steadily expanded since its creation in 1996. It operates on three fronts: international terrorism operations both within the United States and abroad, domestic terrorism operations, and counterterrorism measures at home and abroad.[123] The center is staffed by 18 participating agencies, including the Department of State, the Central Intelligence Agency, and the Secret Service.

Other Criminal Activities Linked to Terrorist Groups

In addition to the major types of terrorist financing already mentioned, there are many smaller operations that raise funds. Some of these include selling baby formula on the black market for a significant markup, coupon scamming involving hundreds of stores,[124] and counterfeit goods including cheap copycat designer clothes, purses, and CDs.[125] Interpol has issued a report indicating strong links between terrorist organizations and intellectual property crime.[126] Even the music industry has its own dark side with the racist genre of "hatecore" music that is producing millions of dollars in profits, most of which goes to the neo-Nazi movement in Germany.[127] Each of these actions may not garner the attention that more high-profile actions like drug or weapons smuggling do, but each represents a part of the financial portfolio of many terrorist organizations.

The creation of the Department of Homeland Security represents one of the largest federal reorganizations since the modern Defense Department was developed in 1947. The 170,000-employee department absorbed the U.S. Coast Guard; the Immigration and Naturalization Service; the Customs Department; the Secret Service; much of the Bureau of Alcohol, Tobacco, and Firearms; the Federal Emergency Management Agency; the Border Patrol; and a host of other enforcement agencies.

Created in 2001 as an immediate response to the 9/11 attacks, the Department of Homeland Security (DHS) was established by President Bush to develop and coordinate the implementation of a comprehensive national strategy within the federal executive branch needed to prevent, respond to, and recover from terrorist acts within the United States. (See Figure 20-15.) The DHS thus absorbed the U.S. Coast Guard; the Immigration and Naturalization Service; the Customs Department; the Secret Service; much of the Bureau of Alcohol, Tobacco, and Firearms; the Federal Emergency Management Agency; the Border Patrol; and a host of other enforcement agencies.

Among its responsibilities are facilitating the exchange of information across agencies, reviewing and assessing the adequacy of federal plans relating to terrorism, and increasing, as necessary, vaccine and other pharmaceutical stockpiles. The Department of Homeland Security also plays a significant role in intelligence gathering and analysis. The development of Homeland Security Operation Centers across the United States places significant emphasis on information and intelligence analysis.

Investigation of Terrorist Activities

The role for local and state officers in combating terrorism has greatly expanded since 9/11. Terrorists may be operating alone, or in concert with sophisticated narcotics cartels, insurgent organizations in foreign countries, or state sponsors. In any event, they are often involved in criminal activity directly affecting state and local officers. Analysis of terrorist operations has revealed a pattern of

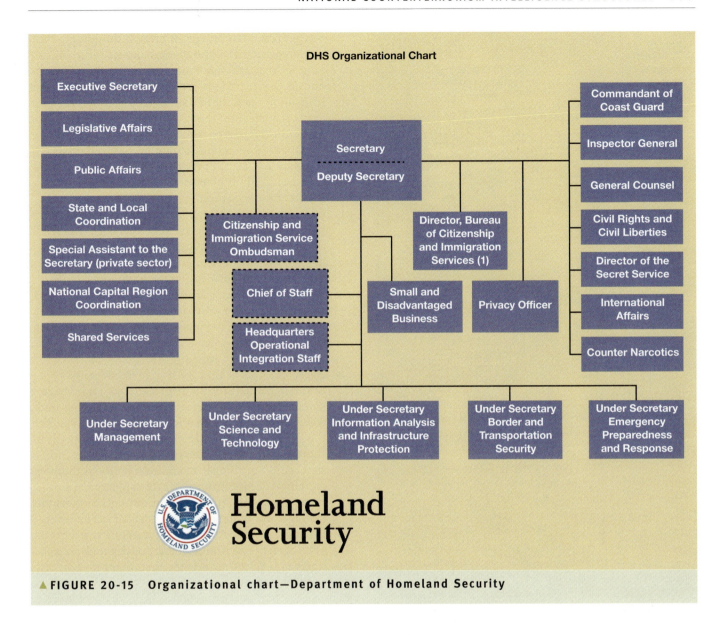

▲ FIGURE 20-15 Organizational chart—Department of Homeland Security

activity—actions that typically precede major incidents. These *pre-incident indicators* have become a primary subject of training for law enforcement officers. Coupled with knowledge of group ideology and stated goals, pre-incident indicators provide insight concerning group behavior and plans. They provide a framework to monitor and analyze group activities and to assess potential threats against the United States. (See Figure 20-16.) The Institute for Intergovernmental Research (IIR), sponsored by the Bureau of Justice Assistance, has been actively training law enforcement officers in this area for the past ten years. The SLATT (State and Local Anti-Terrorism Training) Program provides free terrorist investigation and intelligence-related training for street officers as well as officers assigned to narcotics, organized crime, and terrorism task forces.

While the role of state and local agencies in combating domestic and international terrorism is rapidly evolving, there are several steps that police agencies and their officers can take immediately to thwart attacks:

- *Participate in joint terrorism task forces.* Joint terrorism task forces (JTTFs) are responsible for gathering and acting on intelligence related to international and domestic terrorism, conducting investigations related to planned terrorist acts, preventing such acts, and investigating terrorist acts in their geographic areas of responsibility. Consisting of representatives of federal agencies and state and local enforcement officers, JTTFs are directly supervised by the FBI. Nationally, there are 27 JTTFs; the first one was established in 1980 in New York City.[128] That city's JTTF was instrumental in preventing two bombings by Shaykh Rahmain in 1993 and the attempted bombing of the New York City subway system in 1997.[129]

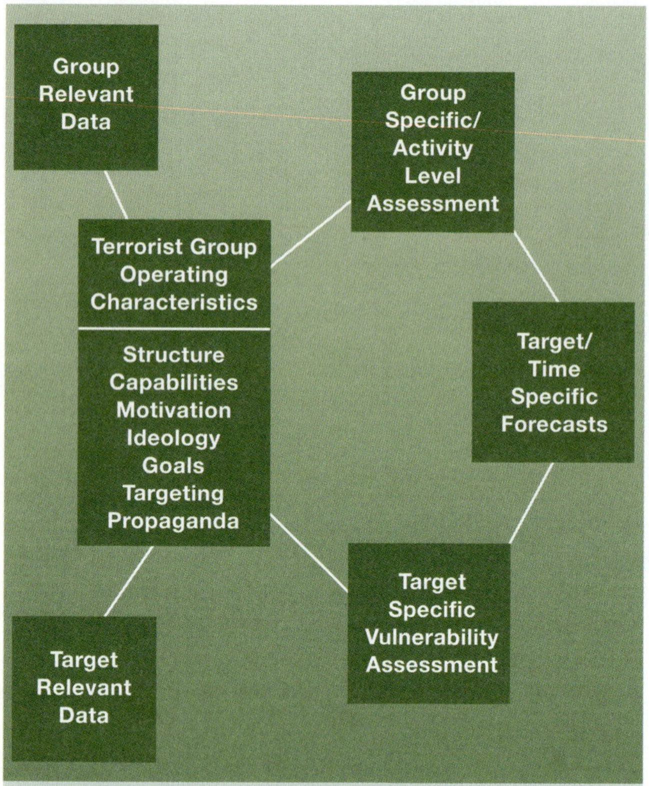

▲ **FIGURE 20-16   The Threat Assessment Model**
Incidents do not occur in a vacuum. They are planned, organized, and executed by individuals acting alone or in groups. The nature of the group often determines the nature of the incident, its target(s), the level of force and violence used, the number of people involved, and the behavior of the suspects before, during, and after the operation.
(Source: Terrorist Pre-Incident Indicators, BJA State and Local Anti-Terrorism Training—SLATT Program, Institute for Intergovernmental Research, Tallahassee, Florida)

recognized components of critical thinking: (1) possessing the knowledge and skills to be able to look at "data" and see it in a new light, and (2) having the personal and mental discipline to use the "new light" as a guide. Things are not always what they seem at first glance. For instance, the person running out of a bank where a robbery is in progress may be the robber, or she may not be. Occasionally, police officers have shot innocent civilians fleeing from the crime.

- *Be alert for reconnaissance operations.* The execution of an attack is predated by reconnaissance, often involving multiple efforts, although not necessarily by the same person. While some of these efforts are carried out in stealth at night, many occur during normal business hours. Operatives may rent rooms that give them a view of the target and recruit insiders to provide them with drawings or copies of plans. They may also take legitimate jobs that allow them to have access to the sites (e.g., driving a delivery truck).

- *Apply and Update Your Knowledge Base.* Just as terrorist groups study our precautions and design countermeasures to defeat them, investigators must continually update there knowledge and skills. The "shelf life" of knowledge is growing increasingly shorter as the pace of change quickens. Thus, to stay on top of things, it requires continual training, ongoing learning from other investigators, a program of personal development through professional reading, and memberships in specialized investigative associations. Additionally, absolute mastery of your agency's critical incident policies and procedures is required, and is the final word on how to conduct yourself.

USP3—U.S. Private-Public Partnership and TrapWire

USP3 is a not-for-profit corporation started just after 9/11. Its goal is to provide a trusted sharing environment for intelligence and information between public law enforcement and the private sector. Specifically, USP3 is partnered with the FBI to provide an electronic phone-book of federal agents and law enforcement officials with private security professional from most of the Fortune 500 companies in America. USP3 boasts over 40,000 names in an electronic format than can be searched geographically by the end-user. It is linked via an open portal to other law enforcement networks such as RISS (Regional Information Sharing System) and LEO (Law Enforcement Online) and has the ability to send up to 5,000 simultaneous e-mails to its membership. The website utilizes high level mapping software (see www. globalincidentmap.com) to maintain a current and historic log of events for users).

- *Be aware of suspicious activity and keep a log.* Some terrorist events have been prevented by individual, astute officers recognizing that "something was wrong," as in the case with Ahmed Ressam (Figure 20-17). It is easy to forget details, especially if they seem only a little suspicious and probably inconsequential. To combat this possibility, keep a separate log of suspicious activities.[130] Using the disparate entries, it may be possible for you or others to "connect the dots" and foil an attack or some criminal activity. Do not just make records of events; apply critical thinking to them.

- *Use critical thinking.* Critical thinking involves rigorously challenging your own views and those of others. "Challenging" does not mean being verbally confrontational at every encounter; rather, it means reasonably assessing the basis of assumptions and beliefs. There are two generally

Born May 19, 1967, in Algeria, Ahmed Ressam grew up as an ordinary young man, attending school and helping his father in the family business. He fished in the Mediterranean Sea, frequented local discotheques, and wanted to attend college. By all appearances, he was a typical young man.

In 1998, Ressam attended a basic training camp in Afghanistan sponsored by al-Qaeda. It consisted of four months of intensive training, concentrating on the use of firearms; physical exercise; basic concepts in intelligence gathering and warfare; targeting; and surveillance, as well as bomb-making, a subject to which Ressam was particularly drawn. The true identities of his classmates were hidden by code names and false identities, although they were from all parts of Asia, Europe, and the Middle East.

After graduating from the camp, Ressam went to a "Kurdish camp" in northern Iraq, where he sharpened his terrorist skills and was formally indoctrinated into radical Islam. His final training came several months later at a camp known as Durenta, located in Afghanistan. Ressam was further schooled on various bomb compounds, bomb mechanisms, target selection, and placement of explosives for maximum damage.

Upon graduation, Ressam was given $12,000, a large sum by Middle Eastern standards, and sent to Montreal to develop a plan for a specific target within the United States. He lived a modest life in Montreal, remaining in constant contact with a known Arab cell operating there.

From Montreal, he flew to Vancouver, British Columbia, and rented a small, one-bedroom apartment. Authorities believe Ahmed made relatively large quantities of nitroglycerin in his apartment. This conclusion is based on a large chemical burn on his leg noted at the time of his arrest, which was similar to burns found on his apartment furniture.

Ressam's plan targeted Los Angeles International Airport (LAX) on the eve of the millennium (January 1, 2000). He would explode a large suitcase bomb in one of the terminals. Fortunately, on December 12, 1999, an observant and cautious U.S. Customs Inspector in Port Angeles, Washington, noticed something odd about the slightly built, dark-complected, profusely sweating Middle Eastern businessman attempting to cross into the United States from Canada. Further investigation revealed contraband material and explosives, which led to Ressam's arrest. On March 13, 2001, Ahmed Ressam was convicted of nine counts of conspiracy to commit international terrorism and sentenced to 130 years in a federal penitentiary.

For additional information regarding Ahmed Ressam, view the 2001 Frontline video, Trail of a Terrorist and visit www.pbs.org/wgbh/pages/frontline/shows/trail on the web.

▲ **FIGURE 20-17   Profile of a terrorist: The journey of Ahmed Ressam**

Although USP3 is an important and ambitious endeavor designed to further the relationship between public law enforcement and private security, the valuable potential for USP3 may well lie within the application software partnered within the project. *TrapWire* is a unique, predictive software system that attempts to detect patterns of pre-attack, terrorist events.[131] TrapWire performs real-time analysis of potential threats and dramatically enhances situational awareness. It may well be one of the only programs that attempts to provide real-time analysis of potential threats focused on disrupting and preventing a terrorist incident versus mitigating an incident after the fact. The software program uses advanced algorithms based on the assumption that terrorists are most vulnerable to detection and disruption (and hence prevention) when they are *planning* their attacks.

An analysis of past terrorist attacks (both domestically and internationally) reveals significant planning by the terrorist group. Indeed, members of the group often visit the scene ("case") on multiple occasions and even rehearse the event before it actually occurs. It is at this point that terrorists are most vulnerable! For instance, counterintelligence information and analysis reveal that organized groups and terrorists plan their attacks very well. This includes multiple visits to the scene (up to 20 times involving 3-person teams) before the incident. During these visits to the scene, the terrorists make notes

FEDERAL BUREAU OF INVESTIGATION

TERRORISM QUICK REFERENCE CARD

First responding officers should be aware of suspicious factors that may indicate a possible terrorist threat. These factors should be considered collectively in assessing a possible threat. This quick reference guide is intended to provide practical information for line officers but may not encompass every threat or circumstance. State and local law enforcement may contact their local FBI field office or resident agency for additional assistance.

Suspicious Factors to Consider

1) Possible Suicide Bomber Indicators—A.L.E.R.T.
  A. **A**lone and nervous
  B. **L**oose and/or bulky clothing (may not fit weather conditions)
  C. **E**xposed wires (possibly through sleeve)
  D. **R**igid mid-section (explosive device or may be carrying a rifle)
  E. **T**ightened hands (may hold detonation device)

2) Passport History
  A. Recent travel overseas to countries that sponsor terrorism
  B. Multiple passports with different countries/names (caution: suspect may have dual citizenship)
  C. Altered passport numbers or photo substitutions; pages have been removed

3) Other Identification—Suspicious Characteristics
  A. No current or fixed address; fraudulent/altered Social Security cards, visas, licenses, etc.; multiple IDs with names spelled differently
  B. International driver's ID:
    1. There are no international or UN *drivers' licenses*—they are called *permits*.
    2. Official international *drivers' permits* are valid for one year from entry into the U.S., they are paper-gray in color, not laminated, and are valid only for foreign nationals to operate in the U.S.

4) Employment/School/Training
  A. No obvious signs of employment
  B. Possess student visa but no English proficiency
  C. An indication of military-type training in weapons or self-defense

5) Unusual Items in Vehicles/Residences
  A. Training manuals; flight, scuba, explosive, military, or extremist literature
  B. Blueprints (subject may have no affiliation to architecture)
  C. Photographs/diagrams of specific high-profile targets or infrastructures; to include entrances/exits of buildings, bridges, power/water plants, routes, security cameras, subway/sewer, and underground systems

  D. Photos/pictures of known terrorists
  E. Numerous prepaid calling cards and/or cell phones
  F. Global Positioning Satellite (GPS) unit
  G. Multiple hotel receipts
  H. Financial records indicating overseas wire transfers
  I. Rental vehicles (cash transactions on receipts; living locally but renting)

6) Potential Props
  A. Baby stroller or shopping cart
  B. Suspicious bag/backpack, golf bag
  C. Bulky vest or belt

7) Hotel/Motel Visits
  A. Unusual requests, such as:
    1. Refusal of maid service
    2. Asking for a specific view of bridges, airports, military/government installations (for observation purposes)
    3. Electronic surveillance equipment in room
  B. Suspicious or unusual items left behind
  C. Use of lobby or other pay phone instead of room phone

8) Recruitment Techniques
  CAUTION: The following factors, which may constitute activity protected by the United States Constitution, should be considered only in the context of other suspicious activity and not be the sole basis of law enforcement action.
  A. Public demonstrations and rallies
  B. Information about new groups forming
  C. Posters, fliers, and underground publications

9) Thefts, Purchases, or Discovery of:
  A. Weapons/explosive materials
  B. Camera/surveillance equipment
  C. Vehicles (to include rentals—fraudulent name; or failure to return vehicle)
  D. Radios: short-wave, two-way, and scanners
  E. Identity documents (State IDs, passports, etc.)
  F. Unauthorized uniforms

▲ **FIGURE 20-18 Terrorism quick reference card**

on the behaviors of law enforcement officers and private security guards, photograph the location of surveillance cameras, sketch the presence of targets (such as fuel depots at an airport), assess maximum casualty and damage potentials, and map escape routes. TrapWire systematically captures suspicious events at a location or multiple locations in a given geographic area (e.g.,

airport, oil refinery, bank) over a specific period of time and stores them in a structured and networked database. The heart of the system is a unique, rules-based engine that not only detects patterns of behavior and anomalies indicative of pre-attack surveillance activity by terrorists but also issues a threat warning in sufficient time to prevent the attack. (See Figures 20-19 and 20-20.)

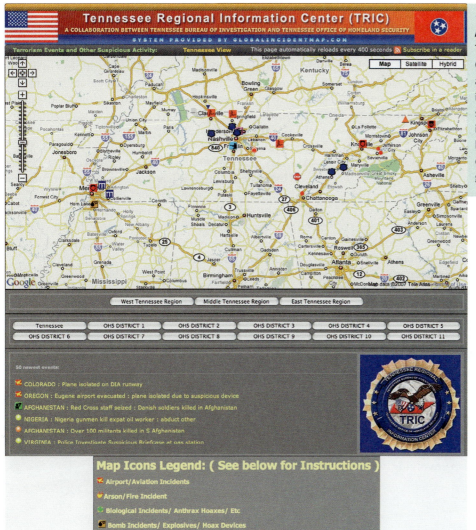

Antiterrorism software
The Tennessee Regional Information Center (TRIC) displays terrorist events and other suspicious activity via interactive web-based mapping software (photo A). For more information, view the TRIC website at http://tnfusion.globalincidentmap.com/home.php or see www.globalincidentmap.com.

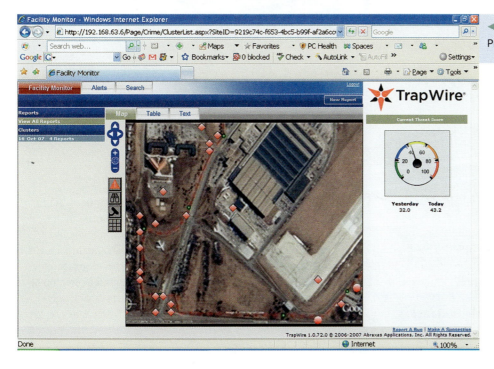

◄ FIGURE 20-20   Trapwire
Pre-attack detection of terrorist events

TERRORIST CRIME SCENES

It is beyond the scope of this section to cover crime scene safety issues for every type of terrorist attack, particularly those that might include WMDs (weapons of mass destruction). Therefore, the section focuses on two areas of major concern: limited biological attacks and chemical attacks that produce mass casualties. Nuclear and radiological weapons are not discussed in depth, because the use of these types of weapons would have a catastrophic national impact and fall squarely within the realm of national security and defense, not the police.[132]

In the past, suspicious letters and packages might have contained explosives (see Chapter 18, "Arson and Explosives"). Today, they might also contain lethal biological agents (Figure 20-21). Fire departments have extensive training, appropriate equipment, and experience in handling hazardous-material (HAZMAT) situations. Because of this, they, along with public health officials and other specialists, play major roles in processing biological and chemical threats and attack sites. In addition, the FBI has developed a number of Hazardous Materials Response Teams (HMRTs), which are situated in sensitive locations around the country. HMRTs are composed of special agents uniquely trained and equipped to collect evidence in hazardous environments. They are a crucially important part of the FBI's responsibility to investigate acts of terrorism involving weapons of mass destruction.[133]

Inappropriate or Unusual Labeling
- Excessive postage
- Misspelled common words
- Strange or no return address
- Handwritten or poorly typed address
- Incorrect title or a title with no name
- No specific person as addressee
- Restrictions (e.g., "personal," "confidential," or "Do not X-ray")
- Postmark from a city that does not match the return address

Appearance
- Powdery substance, felt or seen, on the letter or package
- Oily stains, discoloration, or odors
- Lopsided or uneven
- Excessive packaging material (e.g., masking tape or string)

Other Suspicious Signs
- Excessive weight
- Ticking sound
- Protruding wires or aluminum foil

(Source: Centers for Disease Control, "Updated Information about How to Recognize and Handle a Suspicious Package or Envelope." www.bt.cdc/documents/app/anthrax/10312001/han50.asp, Oct. 31, 2001)

▲ **FIGURE 20-21 Suspicious-mail indicators**

Limited Biological Attacks: Anthrax

Biological agents include both living microorganisms and the toxins produced by organisms. Their effect on humans ranges from various degrees of illness to death. Compared with chemical agents, biological agents are generally slower-acting. Among the biological agents that could be used in a terrorist attack are smallpox, anthrax, plague, botulism, tularemia, hemorrhagic fevers, and Q fever.

Anthrax (Figure 20-22) is an acute infectious disease caused by a bacterium;[134] it has a one- to six-day incubation period, although in some unusual cases incubation may take as long as eight weeks. In nonwarfare situations, it most commonly occurs in hoofed animals, but it can also infect humans. There are three types of anthrax, each with its own means of transmission.

In *cutaneous anthrax*, a cut or abrasion in the skin allows the anthrax bacterium to enter the body. This type

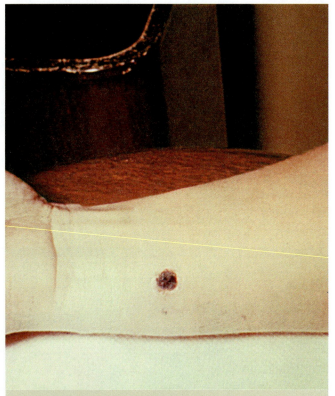

▲ **FIGURE 20-22**
Cutaneous anthrax on victim's arm
Note the darker spot, which is an area of dying flesh. Anthrax is an acute infectious disease caused by a bacterium. It is one of the biological agents that terrorists could use in an attack against the United States. In cutaneous anthrax, a cut or abrasion in the skin allows the anthrax bacterium to enter the body. Death is rare with appropriate antibiotic treatment.
(Courtesy of the U.S. Public Health Service)
(© CDC/Phil/Corbis)

of anthrax develops fairly rapidly: the incubation period can be one to seven days but is usually two to five days. There is no latent period for its development. Starting as a raised itchy patch resembling the site of an insect bit, it progresses into a red-brown bump that becomes filled with fluid and may be accompanied by local swelling. This ruptures the skin, creating a painless ulcer 1 to 3 centimeters wide. At the center, a black area emerges, caused by dying flesh. The affliction may be accompanied by fever and sweating. The affected skin dries and falls off in one to two weeks, often leaving no scar.[135] Cutaneous anthrax can spread via the substantially clear fluid that oozes from the rupture site. Death is rare with appropriate antibiotic treatment, and even without it there is an 80% to 95% recovery rate.[136]

Intestinal anthrax is contracted by eating anthrax-contaminated meat that has been insufficiently cooked; it produces an acute inflammation of the intestines. Initial symptoms are nausea, vomiting (including vomiting of blood), fever, abdominal pain, and severe, bloody diarrhea. The incubation period is one to seven days.[137] The mortality rate is estimated to be 25% to 75%;[138] the latter figure may indicate a lack of timely diagnosis and treatment.

Inhalation anthrax enters the body through the respiratory system; its usual incubation period is one to six days, but there have been a few latent cases that did not reveal themselves until six weeks after exposure. During the first one to three days after exposure, the physical symptoms are similar to those of a cold or flu; thus they are not very specific. They may include a sore throat, fever, fatigue, muscle aches, mild chest discomfort, and a dry, hacking cough. A period of brief improvement may follow, lasting from several hours to days. Then the symptoms return and quickly advance to severe respiratory distress, shock, and, typically, death. Death usually results within 24 to 36 hours of the onset of respiratory distress. Therefore, it is important to begin antibiotic treatment early. The effectiveness of treatment started after the onset of significant symptoms is limited,[139] and mortality rates at this stage are estimated to be 90% to 100%.

Inhalation anthrax is extremely unlikely to occur through person-to-person contact, so communicability is not a concern. The disease is spread by a deliberate act. Large amounts of high-quality, weapon-grade inhalation anthrax delivered in an aerosol form could produce horrific mass casualties. The Centers for Disease Control (CDC) recommends getting annual flu shots to facilitate early differential diagnosis because flu presents many of the same symptoms as does inhalation anthrax. There is a vaccination for the anthrax virus, but it is not yet available to the general public.

Biological Scene with No Overt Dissemination: Unopened Suspicious Letters and Packages

In the past, workers have died from handling unopened mail containing inhalation anthrax, so new precautions

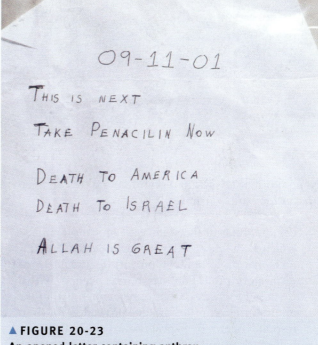

▲ **FIGURE 20-23**

An opened letter containing anthrax

One of the ways terrorists or others can disseminate anthrax is through the use of the mail system. Following 9/11, numerous letters containing inhalation anthrax were found throughout the United States. One such letter was sent to NBC News Anchor Tom Brokaw. Following these discoveries, postal workers and others were given additional training on how to spot suspicious mail. Unfortunately, some individuals died as a result of their contact with mail containing inhalation anthrax.

(© AP/Wide World Photos)

(Courtesy of the Federal Bureau of Investigation)

have been implemented to reduce the potential for receiving anthrax-tainted mail through the U.S. Post Office and other major carriers. For instance, guidelines have been issued to help spot suspicious mail, postal workers are being trained to identify such mail (Figure 20-23), and many post offices are using electronic beams to kill biological bacteria such as anthrax. However, even at a **biological scene with no overt dissemination**—such as one in which suspicious mail is unopened, the situation is well controlled, and there

◀FIGURE 20-24 PPE
Officers use personal protection equipment with special sensing devices to make sure the air is free from potentially harmful chemical or biological agents before entering a building.
(© Alex Wong/Getty Images)
(Source: North Carolina State Bureau of Investigation)

is no known dissemination of a biological agent—precautions are warranted:

1. If individuals at the scene are not symptomatic—which is the most likely scenario—extensive PPE (personal protection equipment) (Figure 20-24) and respiratory protection may not be needed.[140] The Centers for Disease Control recommends that the minimum level of respiratory protection for first responders at a biological-hazard site is the use of a half-mask or full-face-piece air-purifying respirator with particulate filters from N95 to P100.[141] Disposable hooded coveralls, shoe covers, and gloves are also warranted.[142] Currently, this equipment is not routinely carried in police cars. Therefore, wait for support specialists, such as a HAZMAT or public health team, if they are needed.

2. Control the scene and assess the threat (e.g., is it credible?). If the threat is credible, let other responding officers know what the situation is; the 911 dispatch center will notify the appropriate federal, state, and local agencies, which, in turn, will determine whether they accept the threat as credible. Direct people to leave the room, and close windows and doors. Have all people from the room in which the suspicious mail was discovered stay together in a room some distance away or, preferably, outside the building.

3. Allow only qualified emergency personnel to enter the scene.

4. You and other responders should not smell, shake, or handle the mail (except as necessary when seizing it as evidence).

5. The person handling the evidence should triple-bag the suspicious mail in heavy plastic evidence pouches; limit handling of it to an absolute minimum, and do not drop the mail. When sealing the pouches, avoid creating a puff of air that could spread pathogens. This is most likely to happen if the pouches are sealed too vigorously or if they are noticeably larger than the size actually needed.[143]

6. Mark "Biohazard" on each evidence pouch. Place the evidence in a rigid, leak-proof container, seal the container, and mark it "Biohazard." Repeat this process two more times. The evidence should then be taken by police courier to the appropriate public health laboratory.

7. Get the names of and locator information for everyone who was in the room, anyone who came into the room, and the primary handler of the mail. Determine how the mail traveled through the organization before it reached the point at which it was discovered. Consider the possibility of additional contaminated mail.

8. Do not conduct your preliminary investigation in or near the room where the suspicious mail was found.

9. Have the organization's health and safety officer advise persons who have been exposed to the biological threat about the precautions they should take and any follow-up health measures they should pursue.

10. Do not allow site decontamination to take place until the crime scene is released.

11. Inspect the ventilation system to see if it was tampered with, since other attack modes and agents could also be in operation.

12. Follow standard procedures for discarding disposable PPE items and for decontamination.

Biological Scene with Limited Dissemination: Opened and Easily Bagged Letters and Packages

A somewhat higher level of personal protection equipment (PPE) is required at a **biological scene with limited dissemination**—such as one in which dissemination occurs only through an opened letter or package—even if the situation is still fairly contained:

1. A full-face-piece respirator, giving facial coverage roughly from the hairline to the chin, with a P100 filter or air-purifying respirator (PAPR) with a high-efficiency particulate air (HEPA) filter and appropriate PPE are needed for safety.[144] Disposable hooded coveralls, shoe covers, and gloves are sufficient for this situation.[145]
2. Control the scene and assess the threat; communicate the facts to other responders. If the threat is credible, close windows and doors; direct people to leave the room immediately without taking anything with them or touching anything.
3. Ask the organization's health and safety officer to attend to the people who have been exposed and to consider turning off the ventilation system.
4. Proceed with your investigation along the lines outlined in the previous list.

Chemical Attacks: Mass Casualties

Chemical attacks may be accomplished with V agents, mustard gas, sarin, soman, and tabun. With some **chemical agents,** incapacitation of victims occurs in only 1 to 10 minutes. We have no experience dealing with mass casualties from a chemical-agent attack. Depending on the size of the jurisdiction, the nature of the chemical agent, the method of dispersal, the timeliness of any warning that might be given, weather conditions, and other factors, casualties could number in the hundreds of thousands or even higher. Atropine autoinjectors are available to the military, emergency first responders, and civilians for use as an antidote for most nerve gases. They should not be used on children, who require a pediatric dose. Within the context of what we presently understand, the actions discussed next are appropriate if a chemical attack occurs and produces mass casualties.

Initial Response to the Scenes

There may or may not be a warning before the attack; you must be on the alert for signs of danger when you patrol or are assigned to the scene of a possible chemical threat or to a **chemical attack scene.** If assigned to such a site, always approach with the wind at your back and from the high ground.[146] To achieve these favorable conditions, you may find it necessary to drive across open areas; remember, you are not restricted to driving on roads. Watch for the following signs of chemical attacks:

1. Lack of insects.
2. Birds falling from the sky, dying animals acting in an unusual manner, and dead animals.
3. Discoloration and withering of some types of grass, plants, shrubs, and trees. (These signs may become evident a few minutes to several days after the attack. The discoloration may be light or dark.)
4. Unexplained casualties, multiple victims, or victims with confused behavior, nausea, headaches, severe twitching, burning, or runny eyes, nose, or mouth, extremely small pupils, labored breathing, reddened or blistered skin, loss of bladder or bowel control, convulsions, or cardiac arrest.
5. Unusual liquid droplets with an oily film. (Liquids may be any of several colors—e.g., clear, amber, or dark.)
6. Unexplained odors such as the smell from bitter almonds, freshly mown grass or hay, onions, sulfur, geraniums, garlic, mothballs, fruit, or fish. (Nerve gas has no odor.)
7. Vapor, mist, thin fog, or low clouds unrelated to the weather.
8. Unusual metal debris or unusual equipment such as abandoned sprayers and unexplained munitions.[147]

Protection Measures

1. The most important thing you can do is resist the urge to rush in and help. First protect yourself; put on the highest level-PPE you have, including respiratory protection, immediately. Control the scene and assess the threat. The greatest contribution you can make is keeping others advised of conditions. You must be prepared to operate in somewhat of a standoff mode. Use binoculars, if you have them, to assess the scene.
2. In the absence of appropriate PPE, turn off your car's air conditioner and ventilation system, make sure windows are completely shut, and work from inside the car. It is crucial that you protect your respiratory system. Even placing a cloth or your sleeve over your mouth is beneficial.
3. Inform other responders about the dangerous conditions, as well as the direction in which suspicious plumes and clouds are moving, the color and odor of such plumes and clouds, the scene condition, and the numbers, symptoms, and conditions of casualties.[148] Identifying the chemical agent or giving others sufficient information to do so is a high priority.
4. You will not be alone long; an integrated team will soon be there to help. Standing plans will immediately go into effect, and key federal agencies such as the Environmental Protection Agency (EPA), the Department of Defense (DoD), the Federal Emergency Management Agency (FEMA), and

the Centers for Disease Control (CDC) will handle tasks appropriate to their responsibilities regarding terrorist attacks. The FBI is designated as the lead federal agency for such incidents. At the same time, state and local terrorist plans, which are coordinated with the federal efforts, will go into effect. Fairly quickly, additional officers, public health officials, the fire department, and rescue and medical personnel will be arriving to help control the scene and to consider decontamination, triage, treatment, and transportation of living casualties.

5. Deny entry to the area to all but emergency responders.
6. Identify a staging area for responders.
7. Direct survivors to a single area; assure them that help is on its way.
8. Be alert to the possibility of secondary devices being present—e.g., command-detonated car bombs to kill rescuers. Watch for suspicious people.

After emergency responders arrive at the chemical attack scene, these better-equipped and trained specialists will enter and work the "hot zone." Your responsibilities then will be to help maintain the scene perimeter and to write the incident/offense report. When you are relieved from duty at the scene, follow your agency's post-incident decontamination procedures.

Ideally, contingency planning, disaster preparedness drills, and the rapid arrival of an incident commander will relieve officers from the responsibility of making some of the decisions discussed earlier. If traffic or other conditions delay or prevent their arrival, officers must make the best decisions they can based on their training and experience, the available resources, and the situation.

TERRORISM AND THE FUTURE

In addition to the dangers already discussed, other types of terrorist acts are possible, including agroterrorism, threats to water supplies, and the use of high-energy radio frequency (HERF) and electromagnetic pulse (EMP) weapons. **Agroterrorism** is the deliberate and malicious use of biological agents as weapons against the agricultural and food supply industries.[149] HERF weapons direct a high-energy radio signal at particular targets, such as computers and networks. They are essentially Denial-of-Service weapons (see Chapter 16). EMP bombs can destroy electromagnetic systems over a wide area when detonated.[150] Then, too, there is the possibility of a nuclear device or a much less sophisticated **dirty bomb** that renders an isolated area inhabitable for a period of time. Such dirty bombs involve combining nuclear waste from medical X rays or commercial, low-level nuclear material with high explosives, sending the radioactive material into the nearby environment.

Confronting terrorism is not an occasional or seasonal venture; it is an ongoing responsibility. With the help of allies, the United States has the capacity to significantly disrupt terrorist groups and their finances and operations. Information systems must be improved and the products shared; genuine teamwork across numerous agencies will ensure such progress. The United States must have the political will to be decisively and continuously engaged, and the public must help sustain the effort and provide information. The greatest untapped resource in the fight against terrorism is local public safety officers: they are an army of eyes and ears on the nation's streets, and the first line in preventing the next terrorist attack.

In assessing future trends in terrorism, Hoffman, a leading terrorism researcher at the RAND Corporation, has offered several suggestions relating to the understanding of terrorism in the future.[151] According to him, the fundamental nature and character of terrorism has changed since 9/11. It has become increasingly difficult to categorize individual terrorists and terrorist groups. The traditional way of understanding terrorism and looking at terrorism based on organizational definitions and attributes in most cases is no longer relevant. Increasingly, lone individuals with no connections or formal ties to established or identifiable terrorist organizations are rising up to engage in mass violence. These individuals are often inspired or motivated by some larger political movement that they are not actually part of, instead drawing spiritual and/or emotional sustenance and support from them. The Unabomber (Theodore Kaczynski), Timothy McVeigh, Eric Rudolph, the Washington D.C. snipers (John Muhammad and John Lee Malvo), and Virginia Tech shooter Seung-Hui Cho all demonstrated the power to inculcate fear and terrorize a target society through relatively modest levels of violence. This is not to take lightly those terrorist organizations that have conducted significant events in the past. The multiyear planning periods and sophistication of attacks exhibited by al-Qaeda, Jemaah Islamiyah, and Hizbollah suggest that the potential for a future event is highly likely. Accordingly, some monumental new operation may have been set in motion well before 9/11 that is now slowly and inexorably unfolding. Indeed, because of the destruction of the Taliban in Afghanistan, the continued conflict in Iraq, and because of what al-Qaeda sees as America's global "war on Islam," the movement's sense of commitment and purpose against the United States may well be greater than ever. Indeed, the challenges facing American law enforcement at all levels may be unprecedented in the future.

KEY TERMS

agroterroism
al-Qaeda
anthrax
biological agents
biological scene with limited
   dissemination
biological scene with no overt
   dissemination
chemical agents
chemical attack scene

child sex tourism
Christian Identity (CI) theology
dirty bomb
domestic terrorism
ecoterrorism
HAMAS
hawala
Hizbollah
international terrorism
Jemaah Islamiyah (JI)

jihad
left-wing terrorists
madrasas
Muslim Brotherhood
narco-terrorism
right-wing terrorists
Salafism and Jihadist Salafist
suicide bomber
Wahhabi movement

REVIEW QUESTIONS

1. How does the FBI define *terrorism*?
2. What are the three major radical or fundamental movements within Islam?
3. How did Osama bin Laden vault to power in Afghanistan? Name some of the important terrorist incidents that al-Qaeda has conducted in the last decade.
4. What does *Hizbollah* mean?
5. What types of events are associated with the Palestinian group known as HAMAS?
6. Explain the Christian Identity movement in America. How does this movement relate to right-wing terrorism?

7. What is ecoterrorism? Name two important special-interest groups associated with ecoterrorism that are active in the United States.
8. Assess the threats from domestic and foreign terrorists.
9. Discuss how terrorist organizations are financed. Give examples.
10. List several steps that every police agency and/or officer can do to help prevent terrorism.
11. What is anthrax and how does it relate to terrorism?
12. List some of the signs that a chemical attack may have taken place. How can officers protect themselves from such attacks?

INTERNET ACTIVITIES

1. Since September 11, 2001, several police departments and law enforcement institutes throughout the country have begun to offer training for police personnel on preparing for, investigating, and responding to terrorist crime incidents. Search the web for information on this training. What types of training are available? What topic areas do they cover? Do you think the training would be helpful to a criminal investigator? Why or why not? Is there any specific type of training that you think should be provided but is not available?

2. Visit the home page for the Department of Homeland Security at www.dhs.gov/index.shtm and determine what the National Threat Level is. Click on "Information Sharing and Analysis" and read about the Homeland Security Information Network and the Homeland Security Advisory System. As a side note, click "Careers" and learn about the myriad job opportunities existing within the Department of Homeland Security.

NOTES

1. Office of the Historian, *Significant Terrorist Incidents, 1961–2001* (Washington, D.C.: U.S. Department of State, 2002), 10 pp. The information in this paragraph was extracted, with restatement, from this source.
2. Phillip W. Thomas (Special Agent in Charge, Memphis Division, Federal Bureau of Investigation), "Statement for the Record before the House Committee on Government Reform, Subcommittee on Government Efficiency, Financial Management, and Intergovernmental Relations," Mar. 1, 2002, p. 1.

3. The role of religion as a motivator or causation of terrorism has been argued by several scholars, with a recent focus on radical Islam and terrorism. See David C. Rapport, "Fear and Trembling: Terrorism in Three Religious Traditions," *American Political Science Review,* vol. 78, no. 3 (September 1984); Walter Laqueur, *The Age of Terrorism* (Boston: Little, Brown, Inc., 1987); Mark Juergensmeyer, "Terror Mandated by God," *Terrorism and Political Violence,* vol. 9, no. 2 (Summer 1997); Mark Juergensmeyer, *Terror in the Mind of God: The Global Rise of Religious Terrorism*

(Berkeley and Los Angeles: University of California Press, 2000); Bruce Weitzman, *Religious Radicalism in the Greater Middle East.* Volume 4 (New York: Frank Cass Publications, 1997) p. 10; Jonathon R. White, "Political Eschatology: A Theology of Antigovernment Extremism," *American Behavioral Scientist,* 44, pp. 937–956 and *Terrorism: An Introduction,* 3rd ed. (Belmont, CA: Wadsworth Thomson Learning, 2003) pp. 46–61; Bruce Hoffman, "Holy Terror: The Implications of Terrorism Motivated by a Religious Imperative," *Studies in Conflict and Terrorism,* volume 18, pp. 271–284; John Murphy, *The Sword of Islam* (Amherst, MA: Prometheus Books, 2002); Lawrence Davidson, *Islamic Fundamentalism* (Westport, CT: Greenwood Press, 1998); and John Esposito, *Islam and the Straight Path* (New York: Oxford University Press, 1991).

4. Lansine Kaba, *The Wahhabiyya* (Evanston, IL: Northwestern University Press, 1974 and Lawrence Davidson, *Islamic Fundamentalism* (Westport, CT: Greenwood Press, 1998).

5. Henry Munson, *Islam and Revolution in the Middle East* (New Haven, CT: Yale University Press, 1989) and Ziyad Abu Amr, *Islamic Fundamentalism in the West Bank and Gaza* (Indianapolis, IN: Indiana University Press, 1994). In addition, Sayyid Qutb wrote over a hundred books mainly focusing on social justice and Islam. One of his central themes is the Islamic concept of *tawhid* (the singularity of God and, therefore, of the universe). See Sayyid Qutb, *Milestones* (Beirut, Lebanon: The Holy Quoran Publishing House, 1980).

6. Sun Tsu, *The Art of War,* translated by Lionel Gates (London: British Museum, 1910).

7. Malis Ruthven, *A Fury for God* (London: Hanover Books, 2002), pp. 170–171.

8. John Esposito, *Unholy War: Terror in the Name of Islam* (New York: Oxford University Press, 2002), pp. 9–11.

9. Ibid.

10. Congressional Research Service, "Terrorism: Near Eastern Groups and State Sponsors, 2002" (Washington, D.C.: Library of Congress, 2002), p. 16.

11. Esposito, pp. 13–14.

12. Ibid., pp. 18–21.

13. Dilip Hiro, *War Without End* (London: Routledge, 2002), pp. 267–274.

14. ABC News report, Jan. 8, 2001, "Orders from Osama," http://abcnews.go.com/sections/world/DailyNews/yemen010108.html.

15. Zachary Abuza, *Militant Islam in Southeast Asia: A Crucible of Terror* (London: Rienner Publishers, 2003), pp. 127–128.

16. Tom Lasseter and Jonathan S. Landay, "Conditions Ripe for bin-Laden's Survival." *Dallas Morning News,* September 9, 2007.

17. Fred Burton and Scott Steward, "Terrorism Intelligence Report- Al-Qaeda and the Strategic Threat to the U.S. Homeland, (Austin, TX: Stratford, July 25, 2007.

18. Craig Whitlock, "Al-Qaeda Is Rebuilt, Re-Stored and Renewed," *Washington Post,* September 10, 2007.

19. Ibid.

20. Ibid., pp. 128–132.

21. Ibid., pp. 133–136.

22. Ibid., pp. 140–141.

23. Council on Foreign Relations, "Terrorism Q and A: Jemaah Islamayiah," www.terrorismanswers.com/groups/jemaah_print.html.

24. Abuza, p.153.

25. Ibid., pp. 155–164.

26. Ibid., pp. 164–166.

27. BBC News report, Oct., 9, 2003. "Timeline: Bali Bomb Trials," http://news.bbc.co.uk/2/hi/asia-pacific/3126241.stm.

28. BBC News report, Aug. 15, 2003. "Hambali: Asia's bin Laden," http://news.bbc.co.uk/2/hi/asia-pacific/2346225.stm.

29. BBC News report. Sept. 2, 2003. "Profile: Abu Bakar Ba'asyir," http://news.bbc.co.uk/2/hi/asia-pacific/2339693.stm.

30. BBC News report. Aug. 19, 2003. "Jakarta Bombing Suspects Named," http://news.bbc.co.uk/1/hi/world/asia-pacific/3162457.stm.

31. Amal Saad-Ghorayeb, *Hizbu'llah: Politics, Religion* (London: Pluto Press, 2002) pp. 1–11.

32. Pankaj Jha and Alok Mukhopadhyay, "Hizb-ut-Tahrir's Jakarta Conference," Institute for Defense Studies and Analysis. *Strategic Comments,* August 18, 2007.

33. Ibid.

34. Ibid., pp. 12–14.

35. Ibid., pp. 15.

36. Robin Wright, *Sacred Rage: The Wrath of Militant Islam* (New York: Simon and Schuster, 2001), p. 16.

37. Ibid., pp. 73–76.

38. Ibid., pp. 102–106.

39. Congressional Research Service, 2002, p. 6.

40. Council on Foreign Relations, "Terrorism Q and A: Hezbollah," www.terrorismanswers.com/groups/hezbollah_print.html.

41. BBC News report, Feb. 16, 2001, "Israeli Killed in Hizbollah Attack," http://news.bbc.co.uk/1/hi/world/middle_east/1173682.stm.

42. Congressional Research Service, 2002, p. 7.

43. Council on Foreign Relations, "Terrorism Q and A: Hezbollah."

44. Associated Press report, Dec. 8, 2002, "Mombasa Bombing Reveals Possible al-Qaeda-Hizbollah Link," www.lebanonwire.com/0212/02120805TGR.asp.

45. Ibid.

46. Council on Foreign Relations, "Terrorism Q and A: Hezbollah."

47. International Policy Institute for Counter-Terrorism, "Terrorist Organizations: The Abu Nidal Organization," www.ict.org.il/.

48. The Daily Star–Lebanon, (September 12, 2007) see www.dailystar.com.lb/July_War06.asp.

49. BBC Online, "Israel's History of Bomb Blasts."

50. United Press International, "Report: HAMAS Attacks Possible in the U.S.," March 16, 2003.

51. See Bruce Hoffman, "The Logic of Suicide Terrorism," *Atlantic Monthly,* June 2003 and The Palestinian Report, "An Interview with Eyad Sarraj," *Media Monitors Network,* 2001.

52. Dennis M. Lormel, (Chief, Financial Crimes Investigations, FBI), "Statement for the Record before the House Committee on Financial Services, Subcommittee on Oversight and Investigations," Feb. 12, 2002, p. 9.

53. Dale L. Watson (Executive Assistant Director, Counterterrorism and Counter intelligence, FBI), "Statement for the Record on the Terrorist Threat Confronting the United States, before the Senate Select Committee on Intelligence," Feb. 6, 2002, p. 3.

54. Ibid.

55. Federal Bureau of Investigation, *Terrorism in the United States* (Washington, D.C.: FBI, 1996), p. 7.

56. Several important and relatively recent developments have helped to reduce the impact of right-wing, Christian Identity theology in the United States. First, the natural deaths of prominent leaders in the movement, including William Pierce, author of the *Turner Diaries* and a leader in the National Alliance and American Nazi Party, and the Reverend Richard Butler, pastor of the Church of Christ's Christians of Hayden Lake, Idaho, who died on September 8, 2004. In addition, several civil suits have been successfully litigated by Mr. Morris Dees and the Southern Poverty Law Center against the Christian Identity movement and the Ku Klux Klan.

57. Michael Barkum, *Religion and the Racist Right: The Origins of the Christian Identity Movement* (Chapel Hill, NC: The University of North Carolina Press, 1997).

58. Philip Lamy, *Millennium Rage* (New York: Plenum Press, 1996).

59. Watson, "Statement for the Record."

60. Ibid.

61. Federal Bureau of Investigation, *Terrorism in the United States* (Washington, D.C.: FBI, 1999), p. 30.

62. Ibid.

63. Larry Copeland, "Domestic Terrorism: New Trouble at Home," *USA Today,* Nov. 14, 2004.

64. Ibid.

65. Watson, "Statement for the Record," p. 4.

66. Ibid.

67. Ibid.

68. James F. Jarboe (Feb. 12, 2002) (Domestic Terrorism Section Chief, Federal Bureau of Investigation) "The Threat of Ecoterrorism," speech before the House of Resources Committee, Subcommittee on Forests and Forest Health.

69. Ibid.

70. Louis J. Freeh (Director, FBI) "Threat of Terrorism to the United States," speech before the U.S. Senate, Committees on Appropriations, Armed Services, and Select Committee on Intelligence (May 10, 2001).

71. Brent L. Smith, *Terrorism in America: Pipe Bombs and Pipe Dreams* (Albany, New York: State University of New York Press, 1994), p.125.

72. Louis J. Freeh, *Threat of Terrorism to the United States.*

73. Brent L. Smith, *Terrorism in America: Pipe Bombs and Pipe Dreams.*

74. James F. Jarboe, "The Threat of Ecoterrorism."

75. Center for the Defense of Free Enterprise (CDFE), "Ecoterrorism," www.cdfe.org/ecoterror.hml.

76. James F. Jarboe, "The Threat of Ecoterrorism."

77. Off-Road.com, "A Short History of Ecoterrorism," www.off-road.com/land/ecoterrorism_history.html, viewed July 2003.

78. James F. Jarboe, "The Threat of Ecoterrorism."

79. Off-Road.com, "A Short History of Ecoterrorism."

80. Larry Copeland, "Domestic Terrorism: New Trouble at Home," p. 3.

81. See Blaine Harden, "11 Indicted in Eco-Terrorism Case," *Washington Post* (January 13, 2006) and U.S. Department of Homeland Security, Office of Intelligence and Analysis, *Domestic Extremism Digest,* March 2006.

82. Center for Arms Control and Non-Proliferation, "Financial Actions Against Terrorists," www.armscontrolcenter.org/terrorism/issues/Financing.html.

83. United States Mission to the United Nations, statement by James Shinn, Special Adviser to the U.S. Mission to the United States, on Agenda Item 160, Measures to Eliminate International Terrorism, in the sixth Committee of the Fifty-Seventh Session of the United Nations General Assembly, October 2, 2002. USUN Press release #142-2 (02) October 3, 2002, www.un.int/usa/02_142-2.htm.

84. Financial Action Task Force on Money Laundering, "FATF Cracks Down on Terrorist Financing," Oct. 31, 2001, www1.oecd.org/fatf/pdf/PR-20011031_en.pdf.

85. Canadian Foundation for Drug Policy, "The Scope of the Problem: The Value of Illegal Drugs for Terrorist and Criminal Organizations, 2001," www.cfdp.ca/eoterror.htm.

86. U.S. Drug Enforcement Administration, Drug Intelligence Brief, "Drugs and Terrorism; A New Perspective," p. 4.

87. Canadian Foundation for Drug Policy, "The Scope of the Problem: The Value of Illegal Drugs for Terrorist and Criminal Organizations."

88. U.S. Drug Enforcement Administration, Drug Intelligence Brief, "Drugs and Terrorism; A New Perspective," p. 5.

89. Ibid.

90. Ibid.

91. United Nations Office of Drugs and Crime, *The 2007 World Drug Report* (New York: UN Publications, 2007).

92. Jerry Seper, "Afghanistan Leads Again in Heroin Production," *The Washington Times,* Aug. 12, 2003, http://www.washingtontimes.com/functions/print.php?StoryID=20030811-100220-8928r.

93. U.S. Drug Enforcement Administration, Drug Intelligence Brief, "Drugs and Terrorism; A New Perspective," p. 5.

94. Mark A. R. Kleiman, "Illicit Drugs and the Terrorist Threat: Causal Links and Implication for Domestic Drug Control Policy," Congressional Research Service, April 2004, pp. 1–2.

95. See "Thugs, Drugs and Coyotes on the U.S.-Mexican Border" (Austin, TX: Stratfor Reports), March 14, 2006 and Sara A. Carter, "Terrorists Teaming with Drug Cartels," *Washington Times,* August 8, 2007.

96. International Policy Institute for Counter-Terrorism, "Peru Breaks Up FARC Arms Smuggling Ring," Press release, Aug. 2000. www.ict.org.il/spotlight/det.cfm?id=474.

97. Eric Green, "U.S. Arrests Colombian for Trying to Buy Arms from Terrorist Groups," Embassy of the United States to Japan, http://japan.usembassy.gov/e/p/tp-20040406-10.html.

98. Terry Frieden. "Federal Agents Charge Four with Arms Smuggling," CNN.com, June 15, 2001, http://archives.cnn.com/2001/LAW/06/15/arms.smuggling/.

99. Jon Burstein, "Former Boca Jewelers Might Be Crucial to Arms Smuggling Case," *The South Florida Sun-Sentinel*, Aug. 7, 2001, http://billstclair.com/911timeline/2002/sunsentine1080701.html.

100. Ibid.

101. Center for the Study of Democracy—Public Policy Institute for Bulgaria, "Trafficking of Human Beings," www.csd.bg/publications/book10/2.4pdf.

102. Franic T. Miko, "Trafficking in Women and Children: The U.S. and International Response," Congressional Research Service, March 26, 2004, p. 2.

103. Victims of Trafficking and Violence Protection Act of 2000, Publication L. No 106-386, Div. A. 114 Statutes 1464, enacted October 28, 2000. Division A of this law is referred to as The Trafficking Victims Protect Act of 2000 (TVPA). Amended in December 2003.

104. The Prosecutorial Remedies and Other Tools to end the Exploitation of Children Today Act of 2003 (the PROTECT Act) was signed into law in April 2003. It further established the development of interagency task forces to monitor and combat human trafficking within the United States.

105. From Internet discussion forum: Discussion42, "Terrorist Using ATMs and Fake Credit Cards for Financing," Dec. 11, 2004. www.secularislam.org/discussion42/_disc42/000001fd.htm.

106. "Fraud, ID Theft Finance Terror," *Chicago Tribune*, Nov. 4, 2001, www.chicagotribune.com/news/specials/chi-011104identity,0,5867496,print.story?.

107. FBI Terror Task Force Probed Credit Card Fraud Case, *The Detroit News*, May 27, 2004, www.detnews.com/2004/metro/0405/27/metro-165657.htm.

108. William Billingslea, "Illicit Cigarette Trafficking and the Funding of Terrorism," *The Police Chief*, Feb. 2004.

109. United States Action, remarks by President Bush in his announcements on the financial aspect of terrorism.

110. National Commission on Terrorist Attacks upon the United States, "Monograph on Terrorist Financing," p. 87–113.

111. Ibid., pp. 114–130.

112. U.S. Immigration and Customs Enforcement—news release, "Holy Land Foundation, Leaders Accused of Providing Material Support to HAMAS Terrorist Organization," July 27, 2004, www.ice.gov/graphics/news/newsreleases/articles/072704hamas.htm.

113. U.S. Department of State, Office of International Information Programs, "U.S. Government Indicts 7 for Helping Finance Terrorist," Dec. 19, 2002, http://usinfo.org/wf-archive/2002/021219/epf405.htm.

114. See Monty Sagi, "Landmark 156 Million Dollar Judgment Against Islamic Charities," *International Policy Institute for Counter Terrorism*, December. 9, 2004, www.ict.org.il/spotlight/det.cfm?id=1027; Jason Trahan and Michael Grabell, "Judge Declares Mistrial in Holy Land Foundation Case," *Dallas Morning News*, October 22, 2007; and Jason Trahan, "Should Holy Land Case be Retried?" *Dallas Morning News*, October 27, 2007.

115. *The 9/11 Commission Report: Final Report of the National Commission on Terrorist Attacks Upon the United States* (New York: W.W. Norton & Company, 2004), p. 372.

116. Ibid., p. 172.

117. U.S. Department of State, Office of International Information Programs, Embassy of the United States of America, Jakarta, Indonesia. "Tracking Informal Terrorist Financing Next Task of U.S.-led Coalition," speech by Kenneth W. Dam Deputy Secretary of the Treasury delivered to the Council on Foreign Relations New York, New York on June 8, 2002, June 11, 2002, p. 4, www.usembassyjakarta.org/terrorism/coalition2.html.

118. Kathleen Day, "Hawalah Cash Outlets Investigated as Source for Terror Funds," *Washington Post*, Nov. 7, 2001. Obtained through the Internet site for United States action, Jan. 12, 2005, www.unitedstatesaction.com/islam-money-changing.htm.

119. Sina Lehmkuhler, "Countering Terrorist Financing: We Need a Long-Term Prioritizing Strategy," April 2003, p. 8, www.homelandsecurity.org/journal/articles/Lehmkuhler.html.

120. National Infrastructure Protection Center, www.nipc.gov, Mar. 12, 2001, p. 1.

121. Watson, "Statement for the Record," pp. 7–8.

122. Donald M. Kerr (Assistant Director, Laboratory Division, Federal Bureau of Investigation), "Statement for the Record on Carnivore Diagnostic Tool" before the Senate Committee on the Judiciary, pp. 1–12, Sept. 6, 2000.

123. Ibid., p. 8.

124. United States Action, remarks by President Bush in his announcement on the financial aspect of terrorism.

125. Kathleen Millar, "Financing Terror: Profits from Counterfeit Goods Pay for Attacks," *U.S. Customs Today*, Nov. 2002, www.customs.ustreas.gov/xp/CustomsToday/2002/November/interpol.xml.

126. Text of public testimony by Ronald K. Noble, Secretary General of Interpol on the links between intellectual property crime and terrorist financing, July 16, 2003, www.interpol.com/Public/ICPO/speeches/SG20030716.asp?HM=1.

127. United States Action. U.S. NEO-Nazi Group: National Alliance, Jan. 12, 2005, www.unitedstatesaction.com/national-alliance-nazi.htm, p.1.

128. Federal Bureau of Investigation, *Terrorism in the United States*, 1999, p. 44.

129. Watson, "Statement for the Record," p. 11.

130. International Association of Chiefs of Police, *Leading from the Front: Law Enforcement's Role in Combating Terrorism* (Alexandria, VA: IACP, 2001), p. 7.

131. This material was adapted from a white paper with permission from John J. Reis, President, Abraxas Applications, entitled "TrapWire General Description" (Reston, VA: Abraxis Applications, 2007). For more information, see www.trapwire.com.

132. For an important discussion of WMDs regarding the police, refer to Daniel R. Symonds, "A Guide to Selected Weapons of Mass Destruction," *Police Chief,* March 2003, pp. 19–29.

133. Christopher Rigopoulos, "The FBI Philadelphia Division's Hazardous Materials Response Team," *Police Chief,* March 2003, p. 20.

134. The singular of "bacteria."

135. Thomas V. Inglesby et. al., "Anthrax as a Biological Weapon," *Journal of the American Medical Association,* Vol. 281, 1999, p. 7.

136. U.S. Department of Defense, "Information Paper: Anthrax as a Biological Warfare Agent," www.defenselink.mil/other_info/agent.html, June 1998, p. 2.

137. Centers for Disease Control, "Use of Anthrax Vaccine in the United States," *Morbidity and Mortality Report,* Dec. 15, 2000 (Vol. 49, No. RR-15), p. 3.

138. Centers for Disease Control, "Anthrax," www.cdc.gov/ncidod/dbmd/diseaseinfo/anthrax_t.htm, last reviewed Oct. 30, 2001, p. 1.

139. Ibid.

140. National Domestic Preparedness Office, "On-Scene Commanders Guide for Responding to Biological and Chemical Threats" (Washington, D.C.: Nov. 1, 1999), p. 19.

141. Centers for Disease Control, "Interim Guidelines for Firefighters and Other First Responders for the Selection and Use of Protective Clothing and Respirators," www.bt.cdc.gov/docuementsapp/anthrax/protective/10242001.asp, Oct. 14, 2001, p. 2.

142. Ibid.

143. Ibid., p. 3.

144. Ibid.

145. Ibid., p. 4.

146. National Domestic Preparedness Office, "On-Scene Commanders," p. 4, with minor additions by the authors.

147. Ibid., pp. 9–10.

148. Ibid., p. 10.

149. Steve Cain, *Agroterrorism: A Purdue Extension Backgrounder* (West Lafayette, IN: Purdue University 2001), p. 1.

150. Federal Bureau of Investigation, *Terrorism in the United States,* 1999, p. 240.

151. Some of this final material was excerpted from Bruce Hoffman's, "Al-Qaeda, Trends in Terrorism, and Future Potentialities: An Assessment," a paper presented at the RAND Center for Middle East Public Policy and Geneva Center for Security Policy 3rd Annual conference, "The Middle East after Afghanistan and Iraq," Geneva, Switzerland, May 5, 2003, pp. 16–17.

21

THE TRIAL PROCESS AND THE INVESTIGATOR AS A WITNESS

▲ The investigation, arrest, and subsequent prosecution of organized crime figures are quite interesting to many Americans. Local and federal investigators work closely with the prosecutors' office to ensure their cases will meet the highest standards of the legal system.

(© Stephen Frischling/AP/Wide World Photos)

At some point during the investigation of a crime, the investigator will decide to invoke the processes of the judicial system. If preparing for and taking a case to court were not the goal or, at least, one of the goals of a criminal investigation, there would be little point to investigating. That goal, however, may not always mesh with reality. Sometimes, despite the high level of investigative work done by the law enforcement agency, cases may not be prosecutable. First, even if a case is investigated as thoroughly as possible, many investigators at some time throughout their careers will be faced with the fact that the suspect simply cannot be identified. Second, if there is a suspect, investigators may not have enough evidence to arrest and later convict the perpetrator. Third, there may be situations in which legal requirements, such as probable cause, Miranda rights, and evidence-collection rules, are violated. Finally, because of certain rules of evidence or evidentiary privileges, some information garnered in an investigation may not be admissible. In short, investigators should always be aware of potential factors that may prevent or impede the prosecution of a criminal case.

The time at which the judicial system becomes involved during the course of an investigation is not uniform. The decision to begin involving the judicial system may come at the conclusion of the investigation, or it may occur at some earlier point. That decision will be based on a variety of factors, including identification of a suspect, collection of essential evidence and information for the case, and cooperation of witnesses and victims. Regardless of when the decision is made, the first step is bringing the accused before the court. How, when, where, and why this is done is called evaluating the case. This chapter discusses the trial process, including the order in which a trial is conducted and the elements of a criminal trial. This is followed by the rules of evidence, evidentiary privileges, and the investigator as a witness.

EVALUATING A CASE

The decisions investigators must make involve a great deal of discretion. Investigators must consider what may be termed risk factors. As suggested by Figure 21-1, the fact that probable cause exists does not require that the arrest be made at the moment, nor does it mean that the investigation is complete. Certain disadvantages may result from a premature arrest, even one that is valid. In Figure 21-1, B1 through B7 represent the alternative times when arrest may take place between the establishment of **probable cause** and the existence of certainty requiring arrest as a prerequisite to prosecution.

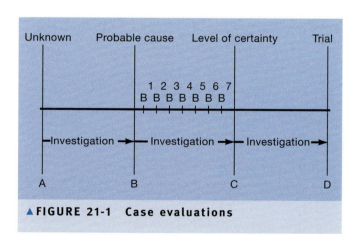

▲ FIGURE 21-1   Case evaluations

(The spacing and numbering are arbitrary and are intended for graphic purposes only.)

One prime consideration is whether the suspect is likely to flee if allowed to remain free. If there is a high risk of this, the investigator should make an arrest as soon as probable cause can be established and complete the investigation while the suspect is in custody. In evaluating the likelihood of flight, the investigator will consider such factors as the nature and seriousness of the offense, whether the suspect is a transient or an established member of the community, the suspect's occupation and income, and whether the suspect has a family to support.

Another risk that must be considered by the investigator deals with the potential danger posed to others if the suspect is allowed to remain free. Again, the nature of the offense along with any past criminal record or history of the suspect must be carefully evaluated. If the case under investigation involves a violent crime or one that tends to reveal violent propensities on the part of the suspect, early arrest is most probably the wisest course of action.

The investigator should also consider the hardships imposed on the suspect by early incarceration. Is the suspect gainfully employed? Is the suspect supporting a family or dependent children as a single parent? Does the suspect suffer from a serious illness or unique malady that will cause serious medical or psychological concerns for the jail staff and other inmates, thus making early arrest a less desirable choice? Although this is often overlooked, it is one additional portion of the investigator's responsibility in evaluating the case.

THE TRIAL PROCESS

Some law enforcement officers and criminal investigators are not fully aware of the order in which a trial is conducted, because time often prohibits them from attending a complete trial from beginning to end. Also, witnesses are often sequestered from the courtroom before and after giving testimony and are instructed not to discuss the case with anyone other than the attorneys representing the prosecution or defense. This very common practice is used to minimize the possibility that a witness's testimony might be affected by other witnesses' testimony.

Jury Selection

The courtroom process begins with the selection and swearing in of a jury. Jury selection is more of an art than a science, although there may be jury selection "experts" who would disagree. Jury selection can last a few hours or a few weeks, depending on the selection process and the nature of the case. The more serious the case, the longer the selection process normally lasts, as can be

seen in some of the more notorious and publicized cases such as the O. J. Simpson trial and the Scott Peterson trial. No matter how much time and effort are expended on jury selection, one still can't predict how a jury will decide a case. The jury panel from whom the jurors in the trial will eventually be picked is called a **venire.** Some general questions are asked of each prospective juror concerning his or her occupation, spouse's occupation, information about any children, hobbies, any potential conflicts with the date(s) of the trial, physical infirmities that might interfere with the prospective juror's ability to see, hear, sit, or understand what will happen during the trial, an inquiry as to whether any prospective juror has been convicted of a crime, and whether each person could follow the law as the judge will give it to them (Figure 21-2).

Following the general questions, the prosecutor and the defense attorney get to ask questions to determine attitudes of prospective jurors on any number of topics. What they cannot do, however, is to talk about the facts of the case to be tried. They may say that the defendant is charged with murder and, if the jurisdiction has the death penalty, ask if any of the prospective jurors would be unable to vote for the death penalty should that decision be presented to them. Although both the prosecutor and the defense attorney say they are trying to pick a fair and impartial jury, each side, of course is trying to pick jurors they believe will support their side of the case.

Once the questioning is done, the judge meets with the attorneys to pick the trial jury. Each side may challenge for cause any prospective juror it believes has demonstrated an obvious bias for or against one side of the case, an obvious lack of understanding or indifference to what the jury selection process is about, or what the trial process will involve. A language barrier may also occasionally be a basis for a **challenge for cause.** There is no limit on the number of challenges for cause but the judge is the ultimate source for deciding whether to excuse a prospective juror for cause. Each side then has a specific number of **peremptory challenges.** These are challenges that may be used for any reason as long as the reason is race and gender neutral and is not a pretext for racial or gender motivation. Again, the judge has the final authority whether to allow the challenge.

Once the final jury is selected, which frequently includes one or more alternates in case something happens to one of the jurors during the trial, the jury is sworn to try the case fairly, listen to all the testimony and consider all evidence, along with the instructions on the law to be given by the judge, before making a decision. The swearing of the jury is an important point in the process because, in many jurisdictions, this is the point when jeopardy attaches. This means that, if the prosecution decides it cannot proceed for some reason, such as a defect in the formal charging document that needs to be corrected, the defense can claim that any such change

◀ **FIGURE 21-2**
An attorney questioning potential jurors
Members of the jury panel or venire are being questioned by one of the attorneys to determine their fitness (as that term is interpreted by each side) to serve on a criminal case jury. Only a portion of the whole jury panel is shown in this photo.
(© Billy E. Barnes/PhotoEdit)

◀ **FIGURE 21-3**
Attorney giving an opening statement before a jury
A prosecutor attempts to tell the jury what he intends to present to convince the jury that a crime was committed and that the defendant committed the offense. However, in an opening statement by a defense attorney, the emphasis is usually that no crime was committed or that the defendant did not commit the offense.
(© John Neubauer/PhotoEdit)

creates double jeopardy for the defendant and, if the prosecution is unable to proceed, the defendant is freed and cannot be retried for the same offense.

The Trial

The trial starts with an opening statement by the prosecutor and the defense attorney (Figure 21-3). These statements acquaint the jury with the allegations in the case. The prosecutor tells the jury how he or she will attempt to prove that a crime was committed and that it was committed by the defendant. The defense tells how it will attempt to convince the jury that either no crime

was committed or the crime was not committed by this defendant.

Then the prosecution presents its case, calling witnesses and introducing evidence to establish that a crime was committed and that it was committed by the defendant. While the prosecution is presenting its case, the questioning of witnesses it calls to testify on behalf of the prosecution is called **direct examination.** When the same witness is questioned by the defense attorney, the process is called **cross-examination.** In most jurisdictions, the scope of cross-examination is limited to matters brought up during direct examination. If on cross-examination the defense attorney manages to confuse a point raised on

◄ **FIGURE 21-4**
A judge instructs a jury
The jury is considered the finder of fact in a trial. The jury is not expected to know the law. At the conclusion of all the evidence and after closing arguments by both the prosecution and defense, the judge has the responsibility of instructing the jury on the procedures it must follow in making a decision and the law that is applicable to the case. When the jury retires to begin deliberations, it is equipped with the law, the procedures, and the facts as they heard and saw from the evidence and testimony.
(© Michael Newman/PhotoEdit)

direct examination, the prosecutor has the opportunity to conduct a **redirect examination** after the defense attorney has completed cross-examination, and likewise the defense later has an opportunity to conduct a **re-cross-examination** of each witness.

When the prosecution finishes introducing all its evidence and presenting all its witnesses, the defense attorney usually moves to dismiss the charge on the grounds that the state failed to prove that a crime was committed or that the defendant committed it. This is a normal procedural response to the state's case by the defense attorney. If, in fact, the judge is convinced that the prosecution did substantially fail to establish that a crime was committed or that the defendant is guilty, charges are dismissed and the trial ends. But if the judge feels that the jury could reasonably decide that the defendant is guilty after hearing the defense case, the motion is denied, and the defense attorney is permitted to present the case for the defendant.

The presentation of the defense case follows the same pattern as that for the state. Evidence is introduced at the appropriate time, and witnesses are called. Witnesses called by the defense are directly examined by the defense attorney and cross-examined by the prosecutor. The procedures for redirect and re-cross-examination are applicable. Note that a defendant is not required to testify, and this failure may not be mentioned or commented on by the prosecutor. The burden to prove the defendant's guilt beyond a reasonable doubt is on the prosecution. The defendant is never required to prove his or her innocence.

After the defense rests its case, the prosecution has an opportunity for **rebuttal.** New evidence may be presented, or witnesses may be reexamined to clarify earlier testimony. If the prosecutor uses the opportunity to present rebuttal evidence, then the defense is given equal opportunity to rebut this, through the process called **surrebuttal.**

After the introduction of all evidence by both sides, both attorneys may make a closing argument. They summarize for the jury the evidence they have presented. The prosecutor attempts to show the jury that sufficient evidence has been presented to indicate that the defendant is guilty of the particular crime charged, and that it should find guilt. The defense attorney attempts to persuade the jury that the prosecution has failed to prove its case against the defendant and that the jury should acquit.

Once closing statements are completed, the judge has the responsibility of instructing the jury on the law applicable to the case and of advising the jury of its responsibilities: to weigh the testimony of witnesses and the evidence presented (Figure 21-4). The judge also tells the jury the various decisions it may reach in terms of guilt or innocence and the elements of the crimes—including lesser offenses—of which they may find the defendant guilty. The judge advises the jurors of the degree to which they must be convinced of guilt or acquit the defendant.

THE RULES OF EVIDENCE

Every law enforcement officer must have a working knowledge of the rules of evidence. This requirement is particularly true for the criminal investigator, on whose shoulders falls the responsibility of collecting and preserving evidence that will be useful to presenting the prosecution's case in court. Therefore, the investigator must be able to distinguish between factual material that is admissible in court and that which is worthless as evidence.

The language and terminology used in the field of law are quite different from those that most of us are accustomed to using. In the rules of evidence, many terms have specific meanings that investigators must know and understand. Many of these are set forth in this chapter.

Evidence Defined

Evidence can be defined as anything that tends logically to prove or disprove a fact at issue in a judicial case or controversy. Simply put, anything that might have the slightest bearing on the outcome of a case can be broadly classified as evidence, provided it has a logical tendency to relate to the outcome of the case. In a criminal case, if the matter has a bearing on the guilt or innocence of the defendant, it is evidence. The word "anything" should be emphasized because, in its broadest sense, anything can be evidence.

The First Rule of Evidence

The rules of evidence are designed primarily to keep a jury from hearing or seeing improper evidence, and the first rule of evidence is designed to set parameters on the preceding definition of evidence. Because evidence can be anything that has a bearing on the outcome of the case, the first rule of evidence provides that anything is admissible as evidence unless there is some rule that prohibits its admissibility. Thus, this first rule provides that all the other rules of evidence may limit the things that a jury is entitled to hear, see, and decide on. From this, it can be surmised that most of the rules are stated in negative form.

Proof

Many people confuse proof with evidence. They are separate but related elements of the judicial process. As noted, evidence consists of individual facts submitted to the jury for its consideration. **Proof** may be defined as the combination of all those facts—of all the evidence—in determining the guilt or innocence of a person accused of a crime. Thus, in referring to Figure 21-5 one can see that the entire pie might constitute proof of guilt, while slices of the pie are matters of evidence.

Testimony

Although testimony and evidence often are considered to be interchangeable, they are distinct. **Testimony** is simply evidence given in oral form. It consists of spoken facts of which witnesses have knowledge. Even though the gun found at the scene, fingerprints, and tire treads are evidence, they require testimony to explain their significance to the case. In Figure 21-5, it is apparent that all six segments of the pie constitute evidence. But only segments 2, 3, and 5 are testimonial evidence.

Admissibility

Admissibility is the essence of the rules of evidence. The rules of admissibility protect the trier of fact, generally a

▲ **FIGURE 21-5** **The relation of evidence and proof**

jury, from hearing improper evidence that may be unreliable or untrustworthy and that may prejudice the case unjustifiably against the defendant. The majority of the rules of evidence deal with what is admissible. Questions of admissibility are decided by the judge, and these decisions are made outside of the hearing of the jury.

Relevance

One of the rules governing the admissibility of evidence requires that the evidence be relevant. The evidence must have a bearing on the issues in the case being tried. The relevance of a particular piece of evidence can easily be determined by the answer to this question: "Does this piece of evidence have probative value?" Alternatively stated, "Will it aid in proving or disproving a particular point that the jury should consider in determining the guilt or innocence of the defendant?" If it cannot throw some light on the case, it is irrelevant.

Materiality

Admissibility is also governed by the test of materiality. Even assuming that a particular piece of evidence is relevant, if it is such an insignificant and unimportant point that its admissibility will not affect the outcome of the case, it may be inadmissible. Thus, materiality deals with the importance of the item of evidence in question.

Competence of Evidence

The test of competence of evidence relates to evidence's legal significance to the case. Because of certain statutory requirements or other rules of evidence, a particular item of evidence may not be admissible. For example, there is a rule of evidence to the effect that the defendant's character cannot be attacked by the prosecution unless and until the defendant tries to show that he or she is of good character. Hence, unless the defendant did proceed in this direction, any attempt by the prosecution to introduce evidence of the defendant's character would be inadmissible on the grounds of incompetence.

The competence of physical evidence must also be established as a condition of admissibility. This is done through a process known as laying a foundation. For instance, the admissibility of an electronically recorded conversation would have to be prefaced by testimony about the date, time, place, and circumstances under which the recording was made; the satisfaction of legal requirements in the making of the recording; proper identification of the voices on the tape; assertions about the functioning of the recorder and tape at the time of the recording; and assurances about the absence of editing or modification of the tape.

Competence of Witnesses

Regardless of their knowledge of the facts of a case, certain individuals are not permitted by law to testify for or against a defendant in a criminal case. For example, the rules of evidence generally prohibit people who have been declared legally insane from testifying in a criminal case. A child "of tender years" may or may not be declared a competent witness. A person intoxicated by alcohol or drugs at the time of testifying will not be permitted to relate his or her knowledge in court. In some circumstances, a witness may be competent to testify regarding particular aspects but be held incompetent to testify regarding other matters. One spouse may be competent to testify for or against the other spouse on certain matters but not others. This aspect of the competence of a witness is discussed in greater detail later in the chapter.

Weight of Evidence

Once evidence has been admitted into the trial, it must be weighed by the jury. The object of the attorney for either side in a case is to persuade the jury to believe his or her side's view of the facts at issue and the responsibility of the defendant. The jury must then weigh all the evidence and determine which is the more believable. Guilt or innocence is then determined. **Weight** then deals with the elements of persuasion and believability. Within certain guidelines, discussed next, the jury is free to give whatever weight it desires to the evidence presented to it. In essence, the entire judicial system in the United States is directed toward persuading the jury to weigh one side more favorably than the other.

Presumptions

Among the guidelines that the jury is required to follow in weighing and applying evidence are those regarding presumptions. There are two types of presumptions: conclusive and rebuttable. A conclusive presumption is one that the jury must follow without alternatives. For example, when the prosecution creates a reasonable belief in guilt, and the defense does not contradict any of the prosecution's case, the jury must follow a conclusive presumption that guilt has been established and must find the defendant guilty. A rebuttable presumption requires that a specific conclusion be drawn unless that conclusion has been dispelled or rebutted by evidence presented to the jury for its consideration. The presumption that one is innocent until proven guilty is an example of a rebuttable presumption. Another presumption of this type is that all persons are presumed sane at the time they commit criminal acts. This presumption can be rebutted by the introduction of evidence to the contrary indicating insanity.

Inferences

An inference is similar to a presumption but differs in that the jury has more latitude in accepting or rejecting an inference. Thus an inference is a permissible deduction that the jury may make. An inference is a natural conclusion arrived at by deduction, in logical sequence, from given facts. For example, if fact A—the gun found at the scene of the crime belongs to the defendant—and fact B—testimony by a witness placing the defendant near the scene just before the shots were fired—are both known facts, this is not conclusive proof that the defendant committed the crime. However, on the basis of these known facts, the jury may logically infer that the defendant did in fact commit the crime. But it is equally free to reject that inference if it feels that the evidence is not sufficient for that conclusion.

Burden of Proof

In each criminal case, the prosecution has the responsibility of affirmatively proving the allegations on which it has based its accusation. This is known as the **burden of proof.** The burden of proof rest on the prosecution and never shifts to the defense. The defendant is never required to prove innocence. Innocence is presumed. The state must prove guilt. Assuming that both the prosecution and the defense present evidence in the trial in support of their theories of the case, the prosecution must establish proof beyond, and to the exclusion of, every reasonable doubt. The jurors must be convinced that the prosecution has proved the defendant guilty beyond any doubt to which they can attach a reason. Often only the defendant knows positively whether he or she is guilty or innocent. Because juries are composed

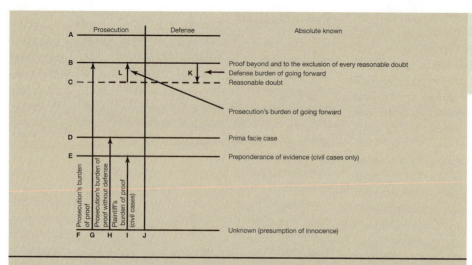

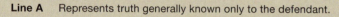

�pFIGURE 21-6

Relations among burden of proof, burden of going forward, and preponderance of evidence

Line A Represents truth generally known only to the defendant.

Line B Level of proof needed to convict. Area between lines A and B represents human doubt but not reasonable doubt.

Line C Can be anywhere below line B and represents reasonable doubt.

Line D Represents prima facie case (level of proof needed to convict if no defense is offered).

Line E Level of proof needed for decision in civil case.

Line F Starting point–presumption of innocence.

Arrow G Represents prosecution's burden of proof.

Arrow H Represents prosecution's burden of proof necessary to convict if no defense is offered.

Arrow I Plaintiff's burden of proof in civil cases.

Line J Represents the continuum between unknown and absolute known.

Arrow K Defense burden of going forward with evidence to create a reasonable doubt (line C).

Arrow L Prosecution's burden of going forward with evidence to overcome reasonable doubt created by defense, thereby elevating level of proof (pushing line C up to overlie line B).

of human beings, they are subject to some doubt in every case and must rely on testimony and physical evidence in reaching their decision. However, if the prosecution so thoroughly convinces the jurors of the defendant's guilt that they cannot give a reasonable explanation of why they doubt that guilt, then the burden of proof has been satisfied beyond, and to the exclusion of, every reasonable doubt. The word "reasonable" is included to separate human fallibility from the alleged in fallibility of machines.

There is one exception to the requirement that the state prove its case beyond reasonable doubt. When the prosecution shows sufficient facts to indicate that the defendant more likely did commit the crime than did not, it has a prima facie case. The prosecution has satisfied its burden of proof if it presents a prima facie case, provided

that there is no contradiction by the defense. Figure 21-6 illustrates these relationships.

Burden of Going Forward

The requirements concerning burden of proof do not mean that a defendant has no responsibility for convincing the jury of his or her innocence. The defense carries a **burden of going forward** with evidence. That responsibility is a great deal less than the burden of proof carried by the prosecution. The burden of going forward with evidence is placed on the defense so that it will present evidence that creates a reasonable doubt of guilt. In other words, the defense need present only enough evidence to overcome the prosecution's contentions and create a reasonable doubt of guilt in the minds of the jurors.

When a unanimous decision by the jury is necessary to find the defendant guilty, the burden is even lighter, for the defense need create that reasonable doubt in the mind of only one juror to avoid a verdict of guilty.

This explanation sounds as though every benefit is being given to the defendant, and it is. The very essence of our entire criminal justice system is to place the heaviest responsibility on the accuser—the prosecution.

The prosecution also has the burden of going forward with evidence. If the prosecution presents a prima facie case that is contradicted by evidence presented on behalf of the defendant, the state must then erase the reasonable doubt by presenting evidence that contradicts that offered by the defense.

Preponderance of Evidence

In a civil case, the party allegedly wronged is called the **plaintiff.** The plaintiff may be an individual, a group, a business, or a representative of some other private concern. The plaintiff in a civil action is not required to prove allegations beyond and to the exclusion of every reasonable doubt. All that is required is a **preponderance of evidence**—that is, that the evidence the plaintiff presents be considered weightier by the jury than the contrary evidence presented by the defendant. Thus, if the civil jury believes that the plaintiff's story offers a higher probability of being true than does the defendant's contention, the plaintiff will win the case. But the defendant wins if the jury gives greater credibility to the defense. In nonlegal terms, if evidence had to be weighed on a 100-point scale of probability, 50% plus a feather believability would win.

Order of Proof

Court procedures generally require that the prosecuting attorney prove the existence of the corpus delicti at trial before attempting to show the guilt of the defendant. The **corpus delicti** is the combination of all the elements of the crime. It is, of course, only logical that the prosecution be required to show that a crime has been committed before it can begin proving the defendant's guilt. Trial judges rarely exercise their discretionary power to allow evidence to be submitted to prove a point out of order. The judge has the prerogative of allowing the introduction of evidence to establish the guilt of the defendant prior to the prosecution's showing the existence of all the elements of the crime. However, this is done only on rare occasions, when to maintain the order of proof might be a major inconvenience to a particular witness. Permission is given only on the condition that the prosecution guarantee it will later establish the corpus delicti. If the guarantee is made and the prosecution later cannot show the corpus delicti, grounds exist for a mistrial or a directed verdict of acquittal.

Judicial Notice

The doctrine of judicial notice is an evidentiary shortcut. Judicial notice is designed to speed up the trial and eliminate the necessity of formally proving the truth of a particular matter when that truth is not in dispute. **Judicial notice,** then, is proof without evidence and may be taken in three situations:

1. Judicial notice may be taken of matters of common knowledge that are uniformly settled and about which there is no dispute. If the fact is known to most reasonably informed people in the community where the trial is being held, judicial notice may be taken of that fact. For example, the fact that a particular intersection, located in a city where an accident occurred, is a business district might well be a matter of common knowledge of which judicial notice could be taken if the trial is held in that city. Since most reasonably informed people in a community would know that a particular intersection was a business area, the court would accept that as a given fact without requiring formal proof.

2. Judicial notice may be taken of laws. A state court, for example, is required to take judicial notice of the state statutes of the jurisdiction in which the court operates; a municipal court takes judicial notice of municipal ordinances.

3. Judicial notice may be taken of matters that may be ascertained as true by referring to common authoritative sources such as books or official agencies. Included in this category are scientific facts, medical facts, historical facts, and meanings of words, phrases, and abbreviations. Examples would include the official time of sunset on a particular date by reference to a weather bureau; the fact that the abbreviation "M.D." following a name stands for "medical doctor"; the fact that the hair and blood types of human beings differ from those of animals; and the fact that no two individuals have identical fingerprints or DNA. The exception for DNA is that DNA is identical between identical twins.

Judicial notice must be distinguished from judicial knowledge. The latter refers to knowledge possessed by a judge. The fact that the judge may know a fact is not material in applying the doctrine of judicial notice. Personal knowledge may not be substituted for common knowledge in the community or for facts capable of being ascertained.

Judicial notice may be taken only on a collateral or minor point of fact in a case. Judicial notice may never be used to prove a fact that the jury is required to decide in determining the proper charge and verdict. For example, in the case of a defendant on trial for stealing a car, the court may not take judicial notice of the value of the

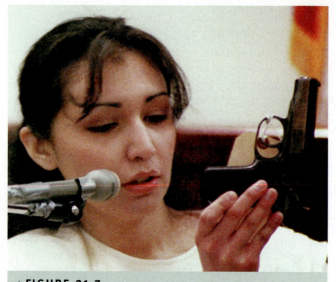

▲ **FIGURE 21-7**
Witness examining a gun during trial
This weapon is a piece of real evidence or physical evidence involved in the offense being tried. Here, an investigator examines the weapon closely to be able to positively state that it was the weapon found at the scene.
(© AP/Wide World Photos)

car if that value will determine the seriousness of the charge against the defendant. Even if it is a matter of common knowledge that a brand new Cadillac El Dorado is worth more than $100, judicial notice may not be taken, because the value is an important element that the prosecution must prove to ensure the propriety of the charge placed against the defendant.

Types of Evidence

There are many ways of classifying evidence. Not all authorities agree on the classifications, but the differences are immaterial as long as the principles are understood. Five types of evidence are defined next.

Direct Evidence

Direct evidence usually is the testimony of witnesses that ties the defendant directly to the commission of the crime, such as the testimony of an eyewitness who can positively state that the defendant committed the crime. It is based on the firsthand knowledge of the witness regarding the guilt of the defendant.

Real Evidence

Sometimes referred to as *physical evidence, real evidence* is connected with the commission of the crime and can be produced in court. Items of physical evidence found at a crime scene, such as a weapon used to commit a homicide (Figure 21-7), a crowbar used to pry open a window, and fingerprints, all constitute real evidence that can be observed by the jury.

Demonstrative Evidence

Demonstrative, or *illustrative*, *evidence* is not identical to real evidence even though the items introduced are tangible (Figure 21-8). It consists of maps, diagrams, sketches, photographs, tape recordings, videotapes, X rays, and visual tests and demonstrations produced to assist witnesses in explaining their testimony. When testimony

◄ **FIGURE 21-8**
The introduction of demonstrative evidence at trial
Demonstrative evidence is sometimes referred to as *illustrative evidence.* Demonstrative evidence consists of visual tests and demonstrations such as pictures produced to assist the witness with the testimony.
(© Bob Daemmrich/The Image Works)

alone would be inadequate to describe a victim or crime scene, photographs taken by police officers are used to help the jury understand the conditions that existed.

The use of demonstrative evidence is governed by complex and highly restrictive rules to ensure that the jury is not prejudiced against the defendant.

Circumstantial Evidence

It is a myth that one cannot be convicted of a crime based solely on circumstantial evidence. The broad definition of circumstantial evidence encompasses all evidence other than direct evidence, provided that it logically connects the defendant to the crime. Circumstantial evidence is sometimes referred to as *indirect evidence* for this reason. Circumstantial evidence is used in a criminal case by inferring from a series of known facts the existence of an unknown fact. In other words, by the process of deductive reasoning, inferences are logically drawn from a series of known facts, and a conclusion is reached. For example, the fact that the defendant's fingerprints are detected on a weapon found at the scene of a homicide does not necessarily mean that the defendant committed the crime. The fingerprints tie the defendant to the gun, and finding the gun at the scene of the crime may be a circumstance relating the gun to the commission of the crime. Likewise, testimony that the defendant was seen near the scene of the crime shortly after its commission does not necessarily constitute guilt; but again, it may lead the jury to infer guilt.

It is possible that an accumulation of circumstantial evidence may be nothing more than a series of unfortunate coincidences for which the defendant may have a logical and truthful explanation. How much circumstantial evidence is required for a jury to convict someone of a crime varies from case to case and depends largely on the composition of the jury.

Circumstantial evidence can be considered analogous to links in a chain. Each link might be an unfortunate coincidence, but the greater the number of links, the more a jury is likely to infer guilt by joining the links into a chain of overwhelming circumstantial evidence.

Opinion Evidence

Witnesses ordinarily are not permitted to give their opinions or draw conclusions on matters about which they are testifying. Their function is to present the facts about which they have firsthand knowledge. It is within the province of the jury to determine the truthfulness of those facts and to draw whatever conclusions it believes are necessary. However, there are a few exceptions to that general rule. Everything a human being perceives through the senses is generally expressed in the form of a conclusion. It is difficult, if not impossible, to describe something perceived as an absolute fact without expressing it in the form of a conclusion. The only things on which a nonexpert may give opinion evidence are matters of description in which fact and opinion are so interwoven that they cannot be separated without losing most of their probative value. Matters of description in which a nonexpert may give an opinion include color, size, shape, speed, mental condition, identity, race, and language.

An expert is someone with special skills or knowledge not ordinarily possessed by others. The skills or knowledge may be acquired through experience, study, observation, or education. To be an **expert witness,** one need not necessarily have a formal education. The expert witness is permitted to interpret facts and give opinions about their significance; the lay witness may present only facts that are a matter of firsthand knowledge. The expert witness is called on to assist the jurors in understanding facts that they are ordinarily not sufficiently trained to understand, such as the results of medical examinations, chemical analyses, ballistics reports, and findings from questioned documents. Results of DNA analysis, for example, would certainly require the supporting testimony of an expert witness.

The Hearsay Rule

Most people have heard a story from several different sources and recognized how different the versions sound. Whether these alterations are caused by poor memory or deliberate attempts to spice up the truth is immaterial in a legal context. The fact that stories tend to be changed when they are repeated makes their reliability and truthfulness questionable. For this reason, the hearsay rule was created. **Hearsay** is derived from "heard say." Testimony in court that repeats what others were heard to say means testifying to a second version of what actually happened. The witness has no personal knowledge of the facts in question. Thus, the truth of the testimony depends on the truthfulness and the competence of the person from whom the information was heard rather than of the person testifying. For these reasons, the hearsay rule is perhaps one of the most important yet most confusing rules of evidence.

Inaccuracy, unreliability, and untrustworthiness are only some of the reasons why hearsay evidence is excluded. The inability of the judge and jury to observe the demeanor or conduct of the person who actually has firsthand knowledge of the information is another.

Other reasons for generally excluding hearsay rely on protections guaranteed in the Constitution. The Sixth Amendment guarantees a defendant the right to be confronted by the witnesses against him or her and the right to cross-examine those witnesses. Because the person with firsthand knowledge is not present in court, that person cannot be confronted or cross-examined by the defendant.

Hearsay is a version of the truth repeated in court by one who does not know whether the assertion is true. People may assert things lightly and casually out of court without being overly concerned about the truth; but they would likely be more careful about speaking truthfully in court, when an individual's life or liberty may be at stake and when they are testifying under oath.

The hearsay rule also excludes written statements by people not in the courtroom to testify. Because the writer's personal knowledge is in his or her head, writing that knowledge makes it secondhand information.

If the out-of-court assertion is being offered as evidence not to prove the truth of a matter but only to show that it was said, it is not hearsay and thus may be admissible. This is one of the rare occasions in which the hearsay rule would not be applicable. For example, a homicide victim may have made threats against the defendant. These threats can be repeated in court to show the defendant's state of mind when he or she killed the victim and to support a claim of self-defense. The truth or falsity of the threats is not the issue.

A second exception deals with reputation. The reputation of a defendant or a witness in a trial may be questionable. A third party may testify about what he or she has heard concerning another's reputation. Because an individual's reputation is representative not of actual character but, rather, of what other people think of that person, the truth of the reputation is immaterial. But the fact that such a reputation exists is admissible. For example, if the defendant presents evidence in a trial for assault that he or she is a calm individual, a witness may testify to having heard that the defendant is extremely short-tempered.

In these situations, evidence is offered only to show that the statements were made, not that they are true. Because the witness has personal knowledge, it is not hearsay, and because the statements are not offered for the truth of their contents, they are admissible.

The hearsay rule is based on the recognition that human beings have weaknesses and that the testimony of human witnesses provides the majority of evidence presented to juries in modern trials. Because we will continue to rely on the testimony of human beings as the principal source of information for trying cases, the law must continue to impose standards to ensure the most accurate and reliable testimony possible. Unequivocal application of the hearsay rule to all situations does, however, present certain injustices in our modern judicial system. For this reason, a number of specific exceptions to the hearsay rule have developed.

Exceptions to The Hearsay Rule

The sheer number of exceptions often creates doubt about whether the hearsay rule has any merit. Among the many reasons for the existence of the hearsay rule, two stand out as the most critical: the unreliability and the untrustworthiness of declarations repeated under oath in court. Until March 8, 2004, the exceptions to the rule could be justified only if these two major drawbacks could be overcome. If the circumstances surrounding the hearsay evidence could ensure a high degree of trustworthiness and reliability, that evidence was admissible as an exception to the rule in order to minimize any injustice. Each exception had to meet many tests to satisfy the criteria of reliability and trust-worthiness before it was admissible. Supreme Court decisions eliminated concern over the constitutional issues by holding that the exceptions did not violate the Sixth Amendment guarantees of confrontation and cross-examination,[1] and did not violate the due process guarantees of the Fourteenth Amendment.

In the 2004 case of *Crawford* v. *Washington*,[2] the U.S. Supreme Court decided that some hearsay evidence, that which contains "testimonial" statements, is inadmissible in a criminal prosecution if the original declarant who made the out-of-court statement is unavailable to testify unless the defendant had the opportunity to confront and cross-examine the witness in an earlier proceeding. Thus, with one decision, the Court unraveled many years of judicial precedents that justified many of the exceptions on the basis of trustworthiness and reliability. The Court, in overturning its prior decisions that found the exceptions did not violate those constitutional principles, is now saying that the constitution does require confrontation and the opportunity for cross-examination if the hearsay evidence is a testimonial statement.

The question of what qualifies as a testimonial statement, was not answered by the Court when it said

> We leave for another day any effort to spell out a comprehensive definition of "testimonial." Whatever else the term covers, it applies at a minimum to prior testimony at a preliminary hearing, before a grand jury, or at a former trial; and to police interrogations. These are the modern practices with closest kinship to the abuses at which the Confrontation Clause was directed.[3]

Although it appears that the general consensus is that if it is conceivable an out-of-court statement might later be used in court against the defendant, it is testimonial and the *Crawford* decision does apply, but as of this writing, in the three and one half years since the *Crawford* decision, over 2500 federal and state cases have been decided interpreting the application of the decision to differing factual scenarios and many of the decisions conflict with one another. As is typical for U.S. Supreme Court decisions, time and many court decisions, including more from the high court, will result in a clearer picture of the requirements for adhering to this change of philosophy.

Some hearsay exceptions apply in both civil and criminal cases; others apply only to civil or criminal cases. The following paragraphs discuss several exceptions applicable in criminal cases. In each case, note is made of whether the *Crawford* decision is potentially involved. It should be noted that examples of applications of *Crawford* to specific fact situations will serve no purpose at this point because of many different interpretations of *Crawford*'s applicability in the thousands of cases in state and federal courts.

Confessions

A **confession** is an acknowledgment by a person accused of a crime that he or she is guilty of that crime. To constitute a confession, the admission of guilt must apply to all the elements of the crime and exclude any reasonable doubt about the possibility of innocence. Confessions are generally of two types. A judicial confession is an in-court confession made before a judge. A judicial confession can also take the form of a guilty plea. Judicial confessions do not fall within the hearsay rule, because they are in-court assertions of the truth of the matter asserted by the person directly involved.

Confessions made out of court fall within the hearsay rule. For such confessions to be admissible, they must meet the tests of admissibility and overcome the assumptions of unreliability and untrustworthiness.

The admissibility of a confession usually raises questions about constitutionality. First, it must be shown that the confession satisfies constitutional requirements of voluntariness. A confession that is obtained involuntarily certainly would not be admissible under modern law. Second, courts admit confessions as an exception to the hearsay rule on the theory that it is highly unlikely that a person will say something against his or her own interest unless it is true. Therefore, a confession tends to establish the reliability and trustworthiness of the truth of the matter asserted. People do not often deliberately make statements that jeopardize their own life or liberty unless those statements are true. Based on this assumption, the major objections to admitting confessions, as hearsay, are overcome. (See the discussion in Chapter 5, "Documenting the Interview and Interrogation.")

Since a confession is made by the defendant, confrontation and cross-examination are not an issue, and the *Crawford* decision is not applicable.

Admissions

One who makes an **admission** does not acknowledge all the facts surrounding the crime necessary to constitute guilt but does admit to certain facts or circumstances from which guilt may be inferred by the jury. For example, without confessing to the crime, an accused may admit having been at or near the scene of the crime at the time it occurred, having a motive to commit the crime against the victim, possessing the gun used in the crime, having foot impressions that match those found outside the window of the victim's house, and leaving town the day after the crime was committed. These admissions may be introduced in the trial by a witness who overheard the accused make these statements or in the form of a written document or electronic recording repeating these statements. They may be introduced for basically the same reasons as confessions are admissible. The contents of the admissions are certainly against the interest and welfare of the defendant and, like confessions, must have been made voluntarily to be admissible. If these factors exist, it is unlikely that a defendant would make such admissions unless they were true. Therefore, the courts allow the admissions on the basis that the principal objections to the hearsay rule—unreliability and untrustworthiness—have been overcome. Here again, the *Crawford* decision is not applicable for the same reasons that it does not apply to confessions.

Spontaneous and Excited Utterances

Human nature is such that speaking the truth is an instinctive reaction. Therefore, if one makes a spontaneous or excited utterance after something startling or unusual has happened, the utterance may be admissible as an exception to the hearsay rule when testified to by one who heard it made. It may be offered to prove the truth of the matter asserted. The spontaneity of the utterance and its declaration under startling and unusual circumstances lend credence to its reliability and trustworthiness. To illustrate, a 5-year-old girl, observing a playmate struck at a railroad crossing, was heard by a passerby to scream, "The engine runned over Billy!" The passerby was permitted to testify in court about what he had heard the girl say. If the little girl is available and qualified, she can be cross-examined as to what she said. Since a third person is testifying to what the girl said, it is most likely that the girl is unavailable for an acceptable reason. This is one of those instances when the applicability of *Crawford* has resulted in conflicting decisions.

It is under this exception that electronic recordings of 911 emergency calls are sought to be introduced. The impact of *Crawford* on the admissibility of 911 recordings have been extremely varied, even within a single jurisdiction and are evaluated on such things as the length of time after the occurrence before the 911 call was made. Was it the first call made? Where was the call made from? Was there a questionable underlying purpose of the call? In other words, courts look to all the circumstances to determine if they think the caller had prosecution in mind when the call was made. If so, it could be considered "testimonial" and be excluded under *Crawford*.

Dying Declarations

A declaration concerning the facts and circumstances of the fatal injury made by the victim of a homicide who is about to die, expects to die, and does not hope to recover is admissible as an exception to the hearsay rule. The theory is that a person about to die has no reason to lie. Statements admissible under this exception must concern the injury inflicted to the declarant and are admissible only in the trial of the person charged with the declarant's death.

Former Testimony

Written or oral testimony in a hearing or trial falls within the hearsay rule if that testimony is sought to be introduced in a later judicial proceeding. For example, if a witness testifies against the defendant in a preliminary hearing to determine probable cause to hold the defendant for trial, the court record is not admissible in the later trial unless it meets the tests of the former-testimony exception to the hearsay rule. Because the testimony was given in a court under oath, it is presumed reliable and trustworthy and is admissible provided the two judicial proceedings involve the same defendant, who is charged with committing the same act, under the same circumstances. In addition, the witness who originally testified at the former hearing must be unavailable for testimony before the transcript of the hearing is admissible, and, to show that constitutional requirements have been satisfied, it must be proved that the defendant had the right to cross-examine the witness in the former hearing or trial. As the Supreme Court pointed out, this is one of the specific instances when the *Crawford* decision is applicable. The requirement that the defendant must have had the opportunity to cross-examine the declarant is long standing to satisfy the reliability element of this exception to the hearsay rule.

Evidentiary Privileges

Defendants and other witnesses have a right to have certain matters of communication barred from disclosure in court—for example, confidential communications between husband and wife, confidential communications between attorney and client, and grand jury proceedings that are confidential requirements of law are barred.

The **evidentiary privileges** may vary from state to state. Some are universally recognized as necessary and have existed since the early days of common law. Others exist only if the state legislature has created the privilege by statute. Some of the more common evidentiary privileges fall into four basic categories. The first might be called professional privileges and includes those that exist between attorney and client, physician and patient, priest and penitent, and journalist and informant. Government communications and information, state secrets, and matters of diplomacy are classified as political privileges. The third category is social privileges and includes confidential communications between husband and wife or between a guidance counselor and a child. Finally, judicial privileges include grand jury proceedings, communications among jurors deliberating a verdict, and the privilege against self-incrimination guaranteed by the Fifth Amendment.

All these privileges can be waived by the person against whom the evidence is to be used or who would suffer from its disclosure. Thus, an attorney cannot disclose evidence of a confidential communication between attorney and client unless so directed by the client. Likewise, a spouse cannot testify against a mate without the latter's express permission, unless the spouse is the victim of the mate's crime.

Although only confidential communications are excluded by the privilege, it is the relationship, not the communication, that is privileged. The theory underlying evidentiary privileges creates a balance between the disclosure of truth and the welfare of society. The assumption is that the public benefits more by protecting these relationships than it does by requiring disclosure of the truth to seek to convict one defendant.

WITNESSES

Until a few hundred years ago, witnesses appeared at a trial voluntarily. There were no legal means to compel attendance. With the advent of the rules of evidence, procedures had to be established for requiring the presence of people who possessed knowledge of the facts of the case. The **subpoena** is used for this purpose. It is a written order commanding the person named to appear in court at a specified date and time to testify, under oath, before a judicial tribunal, to facts within the witness's personal knowledge that are pertinent to the case. A *subpoena duces tecum* commands the individual to bring certain records or documents in his or her possession. Refusal to obey, subjects the individual to punishment for contempt. Likewise, refusal to testify or answer specific questions may be grounds for contempt unless valid grounds exist, such as the self-incrimination protections guaranteed in the Constitution. People who possess firsthand knowledge have a duty, not a right, to appear in court.

In early common law, defendants had no right to call witnesses on their behalf. Therefore, the prosecution was required to call all witnesses having knowledge of facts, regardless of which side those facts favored. Today, the defense has an equal right to compel the attendance of witnesses. Hence, the state may use only those witnesses it chooses. Witnesses may also be called by the judge, but this power is rarely exercised.

Once in court, the witness's competence to testify must be ascertained. Competence of witnesses was discussed earlier in this chapter. If the witness is not insane, intoxicated, or excluded for other reasons, and if the testimony will not fall within any of the evidentiary privileges, he or she will be presumed competent to testify, though this must first be asserted by taking an oath or affirmation.

In common law, taking an **oath** was a process by which individuals swore to tell the truth on the basis of their sacred belief in a supreme being. Today, of course, the oath is still a recognized means of establishing a witness's competence, but it is no longer the only method. The affirmation is also used for people who refuse, for personal reasons, to take the oath. Because they are otherwise competent to testify, some guarantee that they will tell the truth is necessary. A witness may be declared competent if he or she understands and undertakes the obligation of an oath. This obligation is to tell the truth with a realization of the penalties for perjury. As long as the witness understands and undertakes the obligation, even without swearing to a supreme being, the witness is considered competent to testify. This process is called **affirmation.**

A declaration of a witness's competence in no way guarantees the credibility of the testimony. Credibility deals with believability, which, like the weight of any other evidence, is determined by the jury. Attitude, personality, appearance, hygiene, and general demeanor all affect a witness's credibility, along with the substance of the testimony.

The Investigator as A Witness

The success or failure of a criminal investigation is often ultimately measured in terms of the quality and effectiveness of an officer's presentation of evidence to a court and jury. Because one aim of the entire process of criminal investigation is to bring about the apprehension and prosecution of violators of the criminal laws, the presentation of the case in court must be of paramount concern to the investigator from the moment of arrival at the crime scene. Inability to understand and appreciate this crucial role in the judicial process not only adversely affects the investigator's performance as a witness but also reflects on the investigator's overall professional effectiveness.

Every law enforcement witness, whether a uniformed officer or criminal investigator, must become skilled at testifying on the witness stand. Preparation should include a knowledge of the rules of evidence so that the officer not only can perform in the field more effectively but also can have a better understanding of courtroom procedures and the functions of the prosecution and the defense. To prepare a case adequately, the investigator must understand the rules of admissibility and the relevance of evidence collected. The best witnesses are those who have an understanding and appreciation of their role in the courtroom and their relationship to other participants in the judicial process.

The Role of the Law Enforcement Witness

The function of any witness in the courtroom, including the investigator, is to present firsthand knowledge of facts to the jury for its consideration. The investigator must inform the jury of the matters investigated in the case and present this information so that the jury understands the sequence of events and their significance. But the investigator may not offer personal conclusions.

To understand his or her role in the courtroom completely, the witness must also understand the functions of the other participants in the criminal process. Specifically,

the witness must understand the functions of the judge and the jury in relation to the role of a witness.

As mentioned earlier, the function of any witness is to present facts from firsthand knowledge. The jury's function is to weigh the facts presented by witnesses from both prosecution and defense and to interpret these facts, giving appropriate weight and credibility to the evidence and to the witnesses for the purpose of reaching a decision regarding the guilt or innocence of the defendant. The responsibility of the judge is twofold. The judge functions as a referee to ensure compliance with the rules of evidence and interprets the law as applicable to the facts of a case.

Credibility

A law enforcement officer is not entitled to any more credibility in the courtroom than is any other witness. The officer has an equal responsibility, through presentation, appearance, demeanor, and the substance of testimony, to persuade the jury to believe the facts being related.

The issue of credibility is of special concern to the law enforcement witness. Few people from the general population ever view a criminal offense or act as witnesses in court. It is likely that the trauma of such an event would be so vivid for them that remembering it would not be difficult. However, police officers regularly deal with criminal cases and investigate some with striking similarities. Thus, for officers, the frequency and similarities of, and the time lag between, investigations and court appearances may create difficulties in the presentation of testimony.

A related area that may affect the credibility of the law enforcement witness stems from public expectations and perceptions of the law enforcement role. Many citizens expect nothing less than perfection from law enforcement officers in both the performance of their duties and their presentation of testimony in court. They often lose sight of the fact that law enforcement officers are subject to human frailties. An officer's credibility may suffer if his or her recall is less than perfect.

Another issue in the investigator's credibility relates to the perceptions of the jurors. Some individuals regard as suspect any statements made by police officers. The predisposition of jurors with this attitude may be reinforced by defense attorneys who, on cross-examination, seek to discredit the testimony of the officer on the basis of his or her occupation.

The law enforcement witness can overcome all these barriers by preparing meticulously for testimony and by giving straightforward, unemotional responses (Figure 21-9).

Characteristics of a Good Witness: Preparation, Preparation, and Preparation

The successful testimony of the investigator is based on adequate preparation of the case, familiarity with the

◄ FIGURE 21-9
An officer on the witness stand
In the American criminal justice system, cases that ultimately result in trials are relatively few. However, for those that do go to trial, the courtroom testimony by investigators can be very important. The success or failure of a criminal investigation may ultimately be measured in terms of the quality and the effectiveness of an officer's presentation of evidence to the court and jury. Every police witness, whether a uniformed officer or criminal investigator, must become skilled at testifying on the stand.
(© Spencer Grant/PhotoEdit)
(Courtesy of the Los Angeles County Sheriff's Department)

rules of evidence and with how juries think and react, knowledge of trial processes, and maintenance of proper appearance and conduct at all times.

Preparation for testimony, as has already been indicated, is of extreme importance and cannot be overemphasized. For the law enforcement witness, the first step in preparation is to ensure that a complete investigation was conducted, that all leads were followed and all avenues explored. It must be remembered that the prime responsibility of the investigator is not to convict but to ascertain the facts objectively. The investigator must also prepare complete and accurate notes on information obtained and evidence gathered. Before appearing in court, the investigator must review all notes, reports, electronic recordings, and physical evidence; on the stand, he or she must recall events in as much detail as possible with minimal referral to notes. In addition to reviewing notes, it is critical that the investigator thoroughly review all written reports, all evidence, and any deposition that may have been given prior to trial to ensure that his or her memory is complete and accurate.

Many prosecution offices have sworn law enforcement investigators. How these investigators function in criminal investigation cases depends on their authority, the role of the prosecutor during the investigation and the working relationships with the officers and investigators from the initiating agency. In some jurisdictions, once the case is referred for prosecution, the prosecutor's investigators take over and assist in getting the case ready for trial. In other jurisdictions, the prosecutor's investigators are there to assist the local agency investigators or assist in doing some follow-up investigation asked for by the prosecuting attorney as he or she prepares for trial. The working relationship between the investigators from the local agency and the prosecutor's office may take a completely different form from those described, and some communities may not have investigators employed full time but rather have an investigator hired for specific case.

The investigator should review the case with prosecuting officials so that they will know the testimony the investigator can offer and the evidence available. This review also gives the investigator a chance to learn the nature of the questions that might be asked on direct examination. Admittedly investigators rarely can spend much time with the prosecutor before a trial. The demands on prosecutors' time and the caseloads that most prosecutors carry make in-depth preparation with each witness a virtual impossibility. This is also true because of the caseloads and time demands on the investigator. But even a short time spent in preparation is valuable. It is true that the more serious the case, the more time investigators and uniformed officers will spend with the prosecutor. It is not uncommon for investigators to spend less than an hour with the prosecutor before trial in many less serious cases but, a lot can be accomplished during that time.

Understanding the Jury

The jury's task is unique. In theory, it is constrained in what it may consider by rules of evidence and other procedural requirements. In practice, juries are composed of human beings who are subject to influences other than those that might appear in written rules and regulations. The study of jury psychology is fascinating, because it points out the flexibility and the fallibility of the human mind and, in turn, the absurdity of some of the procedural requirements imposed on the jury. The good law enforcement witness, at the very least, understands and appreciates the fact that juries do not make their determination of guilt or innocence solely on the substance of testimony and evidence offered. The appearance and demeanor of the defendant, attorneys, and witnesses; the manner in which witnesses make their presentations and answer questions; the professionalism displayed by law enforcement officers while in the courtroom; and the way in which witnesses respond to cross-examination all bear on the reactions of individual jurors. A good witness is conscious of these factors at all times.

Appearance and Demeanor

Law enforcement authorities disagree as to whether officers should wear uniforms or civilian clothes to court. Some believe that a law enforcement officer should always wear a uniform when testifying in court for immediate identification by the jurors. Others contend that civilian clothing is proper dress because the uniform presents an authoritarian appearance that may be offensive to the jury. A third group takes the view that the officer should wear the type of dress—that is, uniform or civilian clothes—worn at the time of the arrest. Often this decision is largely a matter of departmental policy.

In any event, dress should be clean and neat. If civilian clothes are worn, a degree of formality is appropriate. Conservative clothes are less likely to offend members of the jury than are wild, flashy outfits, even though neat. Identifying items such as jewelry representing a specific occupation or association membership should be avoided. Lapel pins from specific civic clubs or tie tacks with emblems of handcuffs or service revolvers should not be worn. Although these are extremely small points, one can never predict who might be offended. Additionally, all the fundamentals pertaining to personal hygiene should be scrupulously observed.

Law enforcement witnesses should be conscious of their demeanor from the time they arrive at the courthouse. Prior to trial or during recesses, jurors may be standing around the courthouse. If an officer makes a bad impression through his or her appearance or actions, this may be remembered by a juror when the officer takes the stand and may adversely affect the credibility of the officer in that juror's mind. Consequently, any actions that could be offensive to jurors are to be avoided. The law enforcement officer should avoid talking to the prosecutor, court clerks, or judges and should refrain from acting overly friendly to anyone involved in the trial. Although there is nothing inherently wrong with idle talk or friendliness, jurors may perceive it as collusion.

Taking the Witness Stand

From the moment the law enforcement witness enters the courtroom, people are forming opinions. The officer should walk naturally when approaching the witness stand, not look at or speak to the prosecutor, and not frown at the defendant. If the jury sees these expressions,

it interprets them as signs of partiality. The law enforcement witness should stand erect while being sworn in and, when permitted to be seated, should sit erect, facing the jury. The investigator should not continually cross his or her legs or fidget uncomfortably. Hands should be kept comfortably in the lap or on the arms of the chair.

Nervousness is natural for anyone who appears as a witness. Usually it disappears with experience. However, if the law enforcement witness is properly prepared and answers all questions accurately and truthfully to the best of his or her knowledge, nervousness is minimized.

Eye contact and speaking voice are extremely important. Many authorities contend that the witness should maintain eye contact with the jury while answering questions rather than watching the prosecutor or defense attorney. But this skill must be developed. It is difficult for most people to look at the jury when responding to a question from an attorney who may be standing on the opposite side of the courtroom. If the jury cannot hear or understand what the witness is saying, the testimony is worthless. Witnesses should speak loudly enough for people in the back of the courtroom to hear clearly and understand what they are saying. Then they can be sure that the jury, the attorneys, and the judge also can hear them.

Answering Questions

The ability to answer questions under direct and cross-examination is usually developed through experience. The law enforcement witness must answer without emotion or partiality. Sarcasm, witty remarks, or an attitude of "I'm out to get the defendant" must be avoided at all times. The good law enforcement witness must be positive and firm in answering all questions and should readily admit not knowing an answer if this is the case. The witness who constructs an answer to avoid embarrassment jeopardizes the case for the prosecution. Even the slightest fabrication of testimony is perjury and is likely to be discovered on cross-examination. It should be remembered that to err is human. It is not impossible for law enforcement witnesses to make mistakes in their testimony. Although it is slightly embarrassing, the witness should not hesitate to admit having made a mistake. This acknowledgment should be accompanied by an explanation. Even if the mistake is not discovered until after testimony is complete, the witness should immediately advise the prosecutor of the mistake so that the prosecutor will have the opportunity to correct it before the conclusion of the trial.

The requirement of being positive and firm in responding to questions also means that the witness must avoid the use of such expressions as "I think," "I believe," or "as I recall." It is difficult to avoid using expressions such as these because they are part of everyday usage of the English language, but in court they can raise questions as to the definitiveness of the officer's testimony and can be a factor in the degree of credibility given to the testimony by the jury.

There are two basic methods by which witnesses are examined. The narrative technique allows the witness to tell the facts in his or her own words as they are known to be, in response to a question such as, "Now tell us what you found at 1234 Elm Street." This technique is used if the examiner knows the witness well and has confidence that the witness will relate only relevant, unobjectionable matters. The advantage of the narrative technique is that it permits the witness to relate details chronologically and make them clearer to the jury. The obvious disadvantage is that an inexperienced witness may ramble, give objectionable or irrelevant testimony, or expose the jury to tainted evidence, potentially causing a mistrial. Hence, prosecutors use this technique sparingly.

Usually attorneys use the question-and-answer technique for examining witnesses. They ask a single, pointed question and receive an answer to it. When the question-and-answer technique is used, the law enforcement witness should hesitate momentarily before answering. This allows time for the opposing attorney to raise any objections. It also gives the witness an opportunity to digest the question to make sure it has been clearly understood. If not, the witness should ask that the question be repeated as many times as necessary. If the question does not make any sense after several repetitions, the witness may ask that the question be phrased in different terms. The witness should not volunteer information.

Courtesy and respect are important qualities of an effective witness. The judge should always be addressed as "Your Honor." The witness's language should be intelligible and understandable to the jury. Police witnesses should deliberately avoid the use of slang and words unique to the police service, for these may not be understood by the jury. Profanity should not be used in the courtroom unless the witness is repeating a direct quote. If such is the case, the officer should not hesitate in repeating the exact words used during the investigation.

Occasionally a yes or no answer may be demanded of a witness, particularly on cross-examination. Sometimes such an answer is not an appropriate response to the question. If this occasion arises, the witness should not be pressured into an inaccurate response for the sake of brevity. The witness is always permitted to qualify answers and should persist in this right, if necessary asking the judge for permission to qualify the answer. But if the question can be accurately answered with a simple yes or no, the witness should respond accordingly.

Cross-Examination

The purpose of cross-examination is to ensure that testimony given under direct examination has been accurate and truthful. Through cross-examination the attorney attempts to impeach witnesses called by the opposing side. **Impeachment** is the process of discrediting or contradicting the testimony of the witness to show that the witness is unworthy of belief. It is designed to weaken or destroy the effect of the testimony presented under direct examination and thus to destroy the credibility of the witness in the eyes of the jury. Cross-examination tests the reliability of the witness by attempting to detect whether testimony was intentionally slanted or whether an error or misstatement was made.

The five basic methods for attacking the credibility of a witness are these:

1. Showing that the witness's previous statements, personal conduct, or conduct of the investigation is inconsistent with the witness's testimony in court.
2. Showing that the witness is biased or prejudiced for or against the state or the defendant because of a close relationship, personal interest in the outcome of the case, hostility toward the opposing party, or similar biases.
3. Attacking the character of the witness—revealing prior criminal convictions or other irrefutable characteristics that would render testimony unworthy of belief.
4. Showing the witness's incapacity to observe, recollect, or recount owing to mental weakness, a physical defect, influence of drugs or alcohol, or the like.
5. Showing that the witness is in error, that the facts are otherwise than as testified.

Cross-examination tactics used by attorneys vary widely, but they fall into two basic categories. Browbeating or belligerent cross-examination is designed to put the witness under pressure to provoke an unprofessional reaction. The attorney may ask a series of questions rapidly in an attempt to confuse the witness and force inconsistent responses. The attorney may try to reverse the witness's words or may continually repeat the same questions in an attempt to elicit inconsistent or conflicting answers.

The cross-examiner who assumes a friendly, condescending role attempts to lull the witness into a false sense of security to bring about less caution in listening to and answering questions. Once the witness's guard is down, the cross-examiner often resorts to leading questions. Leading questions suggest the answer desired. Although leading questions are not permitted in direct examination, they are permitted in cross-examination.

Another danger that should be avoided in cross-examination involves questions regarding whether the officer has talked with anyone about the case. Law enforcement witnesses often have the impression that this kind of question is designed to attack their integrity by attempting to show that they discussed the details of the case with the press or others in an attempt to create prejudice toward the defendant. In fact, discussing the case with the prosecutor before the trial is perfectly permissible. If the officer answers no to the question and this later turns out to be false, his or her credibility suffers. Likewise, if the witness responds no to the question, "Did the prosecutor tell you how to testify?" the answer is only partly complete. Obviously, the prosecutor generally has instructed the witness to testify to firsthand knowledge of facts and to tell the truth. But the question is designed in such a manner as to imply that an affirmative response means the prosecutor told the witness exactly how to answer each question. The best way of handling this type of situation is to respond, "Yes, I talked with the prosecutor about the case. The prosecutor advised me to relate the facts about which I had firsthand knowledge."

Use of Notes and Reports on the Stand

It is permissible for witnesses to use notes and reports to help refresh their memory while testifying; the human mind can retain only so much information. The witness is not and cannot be expected to remember minute details such as dates and numbers that are of lesser importance than the major facts of the case. However, the witness should constantly be aware of the proper use of notes and reports and the ramifications of their use.

There are two reasons why a witness may refer to notes and reports. The first is a need to remember a particular fact in question. In this case, the officer does remember the case and is permitted to use the notes and reports to help recall minor details. This use of notes and reports is perfectly permissible. However, if the officer's references to the notes and reports are necessitated by an inability to remember anything about the events preceding the trial, the consequences of referring to notes and reports are entirely different.

In the rules of evidence, using notes and reports simply to refresh the memory is referred to as *past recollection refreshed*. As indicated, this is permissible but should be used with restraint, because it may indicate a lack of pretrial preparation. When notes or reports are used by a law enforcement officer in direct examination, the defense attorney has an absolute right to examine those notes and reports and test the witness's memory before allowing the witness to continue testifying under direct examination. This is done to ensure that the witness is, in fact, testifying from memory.

In the event that the witness cannot remember the facts of the case but uses the notes or reports as the sole basis of testimony without any independent recall, the term applied is *past recollection recorded*. In this instance the oral testimony of the law enforcement officer becomes worthless, as the knowledge is entirely based on the notes or reports. Should this occur, the prosecutor most likely will, at the insistence of the defense attorney, dismiss the officer as a witness and introduce the notes or reports as evidence in the trial. If the notes are meaningless to everybody but the law enforcement officer who took them and the report contains inaccuracies, the entire substance of the knowledge will be excluded from evidence.

For the various reasons just described, it is highly recommended that officers use loose-leaf notebooks during their investigations. In this way, materials not relevant to the particular case at hand can be removed before the trial and only the notes that are pertinent will be brought into the courtroom. If this is not done, the defense attorney may question the officer on any irrelevant part of the contents of the notebook and perhaps, by embarrassment, decrease the officer's credibility with the jury.

Leaving the Witness Stand

How witnesses leave the witness stand is just as important as how they enter, because the eyes of the jury follow them. It is improper for the witness to rise and leave the witness stand on completion of cross-examination. The prosecutor may conduct a redirect examination, or the defense attorney may think of a last-minute question. During this time, the witness should be careful not to be caught off guard. A common tactic in cross-examination is to ask a last-minute question while the witness is preparing to leave the stand, in hopes of catching the witness in an error after the pressure of testifying seems over. The witness should wait to be excused by the judge and should leave the courtroom without smiling, speaking, or glaring at anyone.

| KEY TERMS |

admissibility	evidence	probable cause
admission	evidentiary privileges	proof
affirmation	expert witness	rebuttal
burden of going forward	hearsay	re-cross-examination
burden of proof	impeachment	redirect examination
challenge for cause	judicial notice	subpoena
confession	oath	surrebuttal
corpus delicti	peremptory challenge	testimony
cross-examination	plantiff	venire
direct examination	preponderance of evidence	weight (of evidence)

REVIEW QUESTIONS

1. During an ongoing criminal investigation, what factors must the criminal investigator consider in deciding whether to make an arrest and when to make it?
2. Why must a criminal investigator know the rules of evidence?
3. Define the following concepts:
   (a) evidence
   (b) proof
   (c) testimony
   (d) admissibility
   (e) relevancy
   (f) materiality
   (g) competency of evidence
   (h) competency of witnesses
   (i) weight
4. Distinguish between *burden of proof* and *burden of going forward with evidence*.
5. What is the purpose of judicial notice?
6. Describe the manner in which circumstantial evidence is used in a criminal prosecution.
7. Why does the opinion rule of evidence exist?
8. What is the hearsay rule, and why does it exist?
9. What is the philosophy under which exceptions to the hearsay rule have evolved?
10. For what proposition does the U.S. Supreme Court case of *Crawford* v. *Washington* stand?
11. Describe the philosophy underlying the existence of evidentiary privileges.
12. What is the role of the investigator as a witness?
13. What factors affect the credibility of the investigator as a witness?
14. What are the characteristics of a good witness?
15. How important are a witness's appearance and demeanor to credibility?
16. What is the function of cross-examination?
17. When and how may a witness use notes and reports on the witness stand?

INTERNET ACTIVITIES

1. Find out what investigative methods may or may not be protected from disclosure in court by going to the FBI's Law Enforcement Bulletin website at www.fbi.gov/publications/leb/leb.htm. Find the article entitled "The Qualified Privilege to Protect Sensitive Investigative Techniques from Disclosure" in the May 2000 issue. Under what conditions have courts recognized privilege for investigative techniques?
2. Search your state statutes for information on privileged communications. Legal research websites such as www.megalaw.com and www.Findlaw.com are good places to start. What types of communication are privileged in your state?

NOTES

1. *Ohio* v. *Roberts*, 488 U.S. 56 (1982).
2. 124 S.Ct. 1354 (2004).
3. Crawford, 124 S.Ct. 1354, at 1374.

A

A Child Is Missing (ACIM) This program, started in 1997, was created to assist law enforcement officers in locating missing children, as well as disabled and mentally challenged individuals, and elderly persons, such as those suffering from Alzheimers.

AAMVANET Maintained by the American Association of Motor Vehicle Administrators, this computerized network allows U.S. and Canadian agencies to share information about driver's licenses and motor vehicle matters.

accelerant In fire starting, any flammable fluid or compound that speeds the progress of a fire. Also called a *booster.*

account takeover A follow-on crime to identity theft. In this scenario, the possessor of your identity changes where your bill is being mailed to and quickly runs up charges before you are aware of the problem.

action stereotyping Occurs when an officer expects an event to unfold in a particular way; it can result in the officer's failure to see the event the way it actually occurred.

active system A type of vehicle antitheft device which requires that the driver do something to activate and deactivate the system every time the vehicle is parked or driven.

administrative log A written record of the actions taken by the crime scene coordinator, including assignments and release of the scene.

admissibility A legal criterion used to determine whether an item of evidence can be presented in court; requires that the evidence have relevance, materiality, and competence.

admission A person's acknowledgment of certain facts or circumstances that tend to incriminate him or her with respect to a crime but are not complete enough to constitute a confession.

advance-fee scheme These are operated in a bewildering variety of ways; goods, services, or a portion of a fortune are promised contingent upon the person being contacted paying an advanced or "up-front" fee. The essence of these is always (1) you pay before receiving anything, and (2) you never receive anything, unless it is a smaller amount designed to "hook" you into coming up with a really large advanced fee.

affidavit A sworn, written statement of the information known to an officer that serves as the basis for the issuance of an arrest warrant or a search warrant.

affinity fraud These include many different types of frauds perpetrated upon groups such as church members who know and trust each other, and have an affinity for one another. Often, a person of high status in the group, such as its pastor, president, or a member of the governing board will be recruited and will unknowingly help further the scheme by endorsing it.

affirmation The process in which a witness acknowledges that he or she understands and undertakes the obligation of an oath (i.e., to tell the truth with a realization of the penalties for perjury); a means of establishing a witness's competence.

agrichemical Any of various chemical products used on farms; includes pesticides, fertilizers, and herbicides.

agroterroism The use of biological agents as weapons against the agricultural and food supply industries.

algor mortis The decrease in body temperature that occurs after death.

alligatoring The checking of charred wood, which gives it the appearance of alligator skin.

alternative light systems (ALSs) Portable lasers and handheld ultraviolet lighting used to locate physical evidence at the crime scene; particularly helpful in locating trace evidence.

amateur burglar Burglars who operate on the basis of impulse or opportunity, with no planning. Often use sheer force to enter, ransacking the premises for anything of value. May become violent if detected and commit secondary crimes (e.g., murder, rape).

Amber Plan A voluntary partnership between law enforcement agencies and broadcasters to activate an urgent news bulletin in the most serious child abduction cases.

American Society of Crime Laboratory Directors (ASCLD) An international society devoted to maintaining the highest standards of practice at crime laboratories; conducts an accreditation program for laboratories and education programs for lab personnel.

Americans with Disabilities Act (ADA) A federal law which establishes the workplace rights of those with perceived or actual disabilities.

amido black A dye that is sensitive to blood and thus is used in developing fingerprints contaminated with blood.

amphetamines Stimulants that increase blood pressure as well as heart, respiratory, and metabolic rates; produces decreased appetite, hyperalert senses, and a general state of stress that lasts a prolonged period.

anger-excitation rape-murder This crime is designed to inflict pain and terror on the victim for the gratification of the perpetrator. The prolonged torture of the victim energizes the killer's fantasies and temporarily satisfies a lust for domination and control.

anger-retaliatory rape-murder This type of planned murder involves overkill. It is an anger-venting act that expresses symbolic revenge on a female victim.

anthrax An acute infectious disease with three forms (cutaneous, intestinal, and inhalation), which differ in the means of their transmission, symptoms, and lethality; also, a biological agent.

anthropometry Developed by Alphonse Bertillon in the late 19th century, the study and comparison of body measurements as a means of criminal identification.

archaeological looting The illegal, unscientific removal of archaeological resources from public, tribal, or private land.

arrest The process of taking a person into legal custody to answer a criminal charge.

arrest warrant A judicial order commanding that a particular person be arrested and brought before a court to answer a criminal charge.

assignment sheets Written reports completed by persons assigned tasks at a crime scene that document what they have done and found.

associative evidence Bidirectional evidence that connects the perpetrator to the scene or victim, or connects the scene or victim to the perpetrator.

ATM attacks The seizure and removal of ATMs from their rightful location to another place where they can be broken into, or the attempted or successful act of breaking into them where they are located. Applicable state statutes vary, so such attacks may be charged as a larceny or a burglary depending on the location of the crime.

attack code A malicious software program intended to impair or destroy the functioning of a computer or a network resource.

autoerotic death Death from accidental asphyxiation as a result of masochistic activities of the deceased. Also called *sexual asphyxia.*

Automated Fingerprint Identification System (AFIS) A computerized system, maintained by the FBI, that stores and compares millions of fingerprints and is used to find matches for identification purposes.

autopsy The medical examination of a body to determine the time, and cause, of death; required in all cases of violent or suspicious death.

avionics The electronic equipment (e.g., radio, navigation) on an aircraft.

B

bank examiner con A tried-and-true trick to separate unwary people from their money. The scam usually unfolds this way: A con identifying themselves as a bank examiner or police officer approaches a person with a tale about how someone is embezzling money at the bank and help is needed to identify that person. The victim is asked to withdraw money from their account and then meet the bank examiner who gives them a "cashier's check" for the money withdrawn. The victim is told not to deposit the check for a week in order that the investigation not be compromised. This action is repeated with other victims during the week and then the cons disappear along with the money they collected, leaving the victims holding worthless "cashier" checks.

barbiturates Short-, intermediate-, and long-lasting depressants (e.g., secobarbital, amobarbital) that when stopped abruptly can cause convulsions and death; nicknamed after the capsule or pill color, or the manufacturer's name.

basic yellow 40 Used after superglue fuming, a dye that causes latent prints to fluoresce under alternative lighting.

battered-child syndrome The clinical term for the mental difficulties sustained by a physically abused child.

behavioral evidence analysis (BEA) A deductive and evidence-based method of criminal profiling.

be-on-the-lookout (BOLO) Part of the preliminary investigation, a notification broadcast to officers that contains detailed information on suspects and their vehicles.

Bertillon, Alphonse Recognized worldwide as the father of personal identification; he developed anthropometry.

Biggers-Brathwaite Factors Test A test that balances the reliability of eyewitness identification (as determined by five factors specified by the Supreme Court) with the corrupting effect of any suggestive procedures; enables a highly reliable identification to be used in court even if something jeopardized the fairness of the identification procedure.

biological agents Certain microorganisms and toxins produced by organisms (e.g., smallpox, anthrax, plague, botulism) that cause human illness or death and could be used as terrorist weapons; typically slower acting than chemical agents.

black market peso exchange (BMPE) A sophisticated method of money laundering which is typically operated to convert drug or other illicitly gained money into funds which appear to be from legitimate sources.

bobbies A colloquial term used in reference to British police constables; derived by the public from the first name of Sir Robert Peel, whose efforts led to the creation of the first metropolitan police force in London.

body language Gestures, demeanor, facial expressions, and other nonverbal signals that convey, usually involuntarily, a person's attitudes, impressions, truthfulness, and so on.

bone rustlers Unauthorized fossil hunters, who loot public and private lands.

bore The diameter of a gun barrel's interior between its opposing high sides (the lands).

Bow Street Runners Established by Henry Fielding in 1748, a group of volunteer, nonuniformed home owners who helped catch thieves in London by rushing to crime scenes and beginning investigations, thus acting as the first modern detective force. By 1785, some were paid government detectives.

brands On livestock, registered combinations of numbers, letters, marks, and shapes that establish unique identifications.

buccal swab Sterile cotton swabs used to obtain saliva from the mouth of a suspect for DNA analysis.

burden of going forward In a criminal trial, the responsibility of the defense to present enough evidence to create a reasonable doubt of guilt in the jurors' minds; an optional burden, as the defense is not required to present any evidence.

burden of proof In a criminal trial, the requirement that the prosecution establish the defendant's guilt beyond, and to the exclusion of, every reasonable doubt.

burglary The crime of breaking and entering a house or other building belonging to another with the intent to commit a crime therein.

burglary checklist A police-generated written list of investigative steps which begin with the arrival of the first officer at the scene through prosecution.

burglary tools Tools used in the commission of a burglary; often are ordinary household tools, but may be modified for increased effectiveness in breaking and entering.

burn indicators Any effects of heat or partial burning that indicate a fire's rate of development, points of origin, temperature, duration, and time of occurrence and the presence of flammable liquids.

C

cadaveric spasm The instantaneous tightening of an extremity or other part of the body at the time of death. Also called *death grip.*

caliber The diameter of a bullet; somewhat larger than the bore of the weapon from which the bullet is fired.

car, recreational vehicle, and trailer burglaries The act of breaking and entering such places to commit an unlawful act therein. These acts may, depending on the state and fact situation, be chargeable as a burglary or as a larceny. Their inclusion in the burglary chapter is predicated by the fact that regardless of what charge is actually made, the techniques used to gain entry and the investigation of these acts is kindred to burglaries generally.

cargo theft The theft of items from or in commercial motor vehicles.

carjacking The crime of taking a motor vehicle from the motorist or passenger, or from his or her immediate presence, by use of force, fear, or threat of force, with the intent to temporarily or permanently deprive the owner of its use.

catalytic combustion detector A portable device that oxidizes any combustible gases in a sample; used to detect residues of flammable-liquid accelerants at fire scenes. Also called *sniffer, combustible-gas indicator, explosimeter,* and *vapor detector.*

chain of custody The witnessed, unbroken, written chronological record of everyone who had an item of evidence, and when each person had it; also accounts for any changes in the evidence.

charging The act of formally asserting that a particular person is to be prosecuted for a crime.

charring The scorching of materials by fire; used to deduce the direction of fire spread by comparing relative depths of char throughout the scene.

check kiters People who open accounts at several banks and then knowingly write a bad check on their account at bank 1 and then cover it with a bad check written on their account at bank 2 and so on. Eventually the scheme falls apart because the sums keep getting larger and larger and cannot be maintained indefinitely.

chemical agents Rapidly acting substances (e.g., mustard gas, sarin, V agents) that produce a variety of incapacitating symptoms or death; as weapons, can cause mass casualties and devastation.

chemical explosions Explosions in which a high-pressure gas is produced by reactions that involve changes in the basic chemical nature of the fuel; commonly caused by the burning of hydrocarbon fuels (e.g., natural gas, gasoline, lubricating oils).

child pornography The sexually explicit visual depiction of a minor (as defined by statute); includes photographs, negatives, slides, magazines, movies, videotapes, and computerized images.

chop shop An illegal operation at which stolen cars are disassembled and their traceable parts altered or disposed of so that untraceable parts can be sold to repair shops, salvage yards, and indiscriminate buyers.

Christian Identity theology A right-wing philosophy expressing the superiority of the white Aryan race over the forces of Satan (people of color and Jews). Central to the CI belief is a distortion of the Bible supporting the creation of "pre-Adamites," or people of color, the sexual union of Eve and Satan in the Garden of Eden giving rise to the Jewish race, and the future physical battle of Armageddon between Aryan people and the forces of Satan (Jews and non-whites).

clandestine drug laboratories Illicit operations that produce a variety of illegal drugs for sale and distribution; due to the chemicals, processes used, and workers' inexperience, police and firefighters, as well as the public, can face severe danger on location.

class characteristics Characteristics of physical evidence that are common to a group of objects or persons.

cleared by arrest The classification assigned to an offense when the suspect has been arrested and there is sufficient evidence to file a formal charge.

cloning (1) The creation of a second legitimate vehicle by counterfeiting or duplicating identification numbers and ownership documents.

cloning (2) The illegal programming of cellular phones by overwriting their access codes with the codes of legitimate cellular customers; done through a personal computer or cloning "black box."

cocaine A natural stimulant extracted from the leaves of the coca plant; illegally sold as a white, translucent, crystalline powder, which is often adulterated.

codeine An opiate in tablet, liquid, and injectable forms that produces less analgesia, sedation, and respiratory depression than morphine.

CODIS *See* **Combined DNA Index System.**

cognitive interview technique An interviewing approach in which a witness is asked to recall events and details in different ways as a means of fostering the witness's recollections.

cold case investigation Assigning detectives to examine cases that went unsolved, which includes using new advanced technology that was unavailable before to analyze old evidence, and re-interviewing witnesses who were previously hostile. In some cases, the original detectives assigned the case were simply overworked and could not allocate enough time to properly work it.

Combined DNA Index System (CODIS) Developed by the FBI, a database of convicted-offender and known- and unknown-subject DNA profiles that is used to find matches and to link unsolved crimes in multiple jurisdictions.

commercial-vehicle theft The theft of vehicle tractor units and trailers.

competency (of a witness) A witness's qualification for testifying in court, which depends on circumstances that affect the person's legal ability to function as a sworn witness (e.g., age, mental state).

component swapping A fraudulent practice in which manufacturers (e.g., of computers) use parts from the lowest-cost supplier but do not inform consumers that the parts are nonstandard.

computer abuse Any intentional act involving knowledge of computer use or technology in which the perpetrator could have made a gain and the victim could have experienced a loss; includes acts that may not be covered by criminal laws.

computer crime Any illegal act in which knowledge of computer technology is used to commit the offense.

computer manipulation crime Any act that involves changing data or creating records in an electronic system for the purpose of facilitating another crime, typically fraud or embezzlement.

computer vandalism The unauthorized removal of valuable information from a computer system, thereby preventing the legitimate user or owner from having access to that information.

Computer Voice Stress Analyzer (CVSA) A method of lie detection originally developed in 1988 by the National Institute for Truth Verification (NITV). By 2004, some 1,400 agencies were using it instead of the polygraph. The CVSA notes microvariations in the audible and non-audible portions of speech to identify deception. The CVSA is presently the first significant challenge to the dominance of the polygraph in 85 years.

concentric fracture lines Lines that roughly circle the point of impact in a glass window.

confabulation In hypnosis, the subject's fabrication of recollections to fill in gaps in his or her actual memory.

confession The acknowledgment by a person accused of a crime that he or she is guilty of that crime and committed every element of the offense; must exclude any reasonable doubt about the possibility of innocence.

confidential VIN A duplicate vehicle identification number stamped into a vehicle's frame or body in a place known only to the manufacturer and law enforcement specialists in vehicle identification and auto theft investigation.

contact burns Burns on the skin caused by contact with flames or hot solid objects (e.g., irons, cigarettes).

contaminated/visible prints Prints created when fingers contaminated with blood, face powder, or a similar material touch a clean surface.

corpus delicti evidence Evidence that substantiates elements whose commission or omission must be demonstrated to have occurred in order to prove a case.

crack or rock cocaine *See* rock cocaine.

cramming The intentional process of placing unauthorized, misleading, inaccurate or deceptive charges on the victims' telephone bills. While telephone companies may legally place such charges on your bill on behalf of other companies, it is also a method by which scams can also be run by those other companies.

credibility (of a witness) That quality of a witness that renders his or her testimony worthy of belief; established in terms of presence, consciousness, and attentiveness during interviews.

credit repair scam A type of advanced fee scam in which people with bad or poor credit are promised their records can be cleansed of negative entries. New credit cards may also be promised as part of the scam.

crime The commission of any act that is prohibited, or the omission of any act that is required by the penal code of an organized political state.

crime analysis The use of systematic analytical methods to acquire timely and pertinent information on crime patterns and trend correlations; subdivided into administrative, strategic, and tactical analysis.

crime laboratory A scientific organization that analyzes material collected from crime scenes and suspects to help determine whether a crime was committed and, if so, how, when, and by whom it was committed.

crime scene The location at which a crime was committed.

crime scene control The procedure of limiting and documenting access to the crime scene to ensure that physical evidence is not accidentally or deliberate altered or removed. The procedure begins with the arrival of the first officer at the scene and continues until the scene is released from police control.

crime scene entry log sheet A written chronological record of all persons who enter and leave the crime scene and the times they do so, along with their reason for entering.

crime scene release The end of crime scene processing and the return of the premises or area to the owner or another responsible person; determined by the scene coordinator.

crime scene search patterns Used to locate physical evidence at a crime scene; there are five patterns: spiral, strip/line, grid, zone/quadrant, and pie/wheel.

criminal enterprise homicide A murder committed for material gain.

criminalistics The application of scientific disciplines, such as geology, physics, chemistry, biology, and mathematics, to criminal investigation and the study of physical evidence.

crimogens (1) An individually known offender who is responsible for a large number of crimes; (2) one victim who reports a large number of crimes.

cross-contamination In a trial, the questioning of a witness who was initially called by the opposing party.

cross-examination In a trial, the questioning of a witness who was initially called by the opposing party.

cryptanalysis software Software used to intrusively access secured information by breaking down encryption.

crystal violet A dye used to develop latent prints on the adhesive side of almost any kind of tape.

crystallized methamphetamine A long-acting stimulant originally in pill or injectable form (*crystal meth, speed*) but now in a smokable, odorless version (*ice*); in solid form, resembles an ice chip but liquifies when lighted.

cyberstalking The crime of harassing or threatening victims by means of electronic technologies (e.g., through e-mail and Internet chat rooms or news groups).

cyberterrorism The use of electronic tools to disrupt or shut down critical infrastructure components, such as energy, transportation, and government operations.

D

dactylography The study and comparison of fingerprints as a means of criminal identification; first used systematically for that purpose in England in 1900, but a means of identification since the first century.

date-rape drugs Drugs that facilitate rape by debilitating the victim; they include Rohypnol, GHB, and many depressants and benzodiazapines.

Daubert v. Merrell Dow Pharmaceuticals, Inc. A 1993 case in which the Supreme Court held that the admissibility of an expert's testimony or a scientific technique's results depends on a preliminary assessment, made by the trial judge, of the principles and methodology involved.

decoys A police officer who is disguised to resemble the type of victims who are being targeted for robbery. This is especially true for street robberies.

deductive reasoning The thought process that moves from general premises to specific details—for example, a hypothesis about the crime is developed and then tested against the factual situation to arrive at a conclusion.

defense wounds Wounds suffered by victims while attempting to protect themselves from an assault; often inflicted by a knife or club.

delay-in-arraignment rule Based on a 1943 Supreme Court decision, the principle that the failure to take a prisoner before a committing magistrate without unnecessary delay will render his or her confession inadmissible even if it was freely obtained.

dental identification The identification of an individual on the basis of dental records (or, sometimes, "smiling" photographs); performed by a forensic dentist, who compares before-death records with after-death findings to see if there is a match.

dental stone The preferred material for casting tire, footwear, and foot impressions; stronger and faster setting than plaster of paris and provides more detailed impressions.

deoxyribonucleic acid (DNA) A nucleic acid consisting of the molecules that carry the body's genetic material and establish each person as separate and distinct.

depressants or sedatives Drugs that depress the central nervous system, reducing tension and inducing sleep; can cause, in chronic use, loss of balance, faulty judgment, quick temper, and in overdose, unconsciousness and death.

detention A temporary and limited interference with a person's freedom for investigative purposes. Also called *investigative detention, street stop,* and *field interrogation.*

DFO (diazafluren-9-one) A very effective chemical for developing latent prints on paper; produces red prints that may be visible to the naked eye and that fluoresce under most laser and alternative lighting.

digital forensic analysis The process of acquiring, preserving, analyzing, and presenting evidentiary electronic data relevant to an investigation or prosecution.

direct examination In a trial, the questioning of a witness by the party that calls the witness to testify.

disposition (of incident report) After approval of an incident report, the determination of how the case will be handled (i.e., unfounded, inactivated, retained for investigation by officers, referred to plainclothes investigators); usually made by the supervisor of the officer who wrote the report.

document Anything on which a mark is made for the purpose of transmitting a message.

documented vessel A boat that is registered by the U.S. Coast Guard.

domestic terrorism The use or threatened use of violence against persons or property by a group (or an individual) whose operations are entirely within the victims' nation, without foreign direction, and are done to further political or social objectives.

Drug Enforcement Administration (DEA) Created in 1973, this federal agency is responsible for enforcing laws on illicit drugs and fighting international drug traffic; also trains state and local police in investigative work regarding illegal drugs, surveillance, and use of informants.

due process Fairness.

due process clause The title of clauses appearing in both the Fifth and Fourteenth amendments to the Constitution of the United States.

dumpster diving Going through people's trash for the purpose of finding sufficient sensitive information to commit identity theft.

E

EDTA A preservative used to prevent coagulation.

effective fire temperatures In structural fires, identifiable temperatures which reflect physical effects that can be defined by specific temperature ranges.

embezzlement The misappropriation or misapplication of money or property entrusted to one's care, custody, or control.

emotional approach An interrogation technique in which the interrogator appeals to the suspect's sense of honor, morals, family pride, religion, and so on; works better with women and first-time offenders.

encryption A means of data security in which the data are scrambled into nonsense for storage or transmission and then unscrambled, as needed, by legitimate users.

Enderby cases Two rape-murder cases in England that involved the first use of DNA typing, in 1987, in a criminal case. DNA samples recovered from both victims led to the release of an innocent man and the subsequent arrest and conviction of the killer.

estate locators and research specialists These cons approach people by mail, purporting to be looking for heirs to a substantial fortune. In order to determine their eligibility, victims are asked to pay an "estate assessment fee" up-front, another variation on an advanced-fee scheme. This scam may also be operated as part of an identity theft operation.

evidence Anything that tends logically to prove or disprove a fact at issue in a judicial case or controversy.

evidence recovery log A chronological record of each item of evidence, listing who collected it, where and when it was collected, who witnessed the collection, and whether it was documented by photos or diagrams.

evidential intelligence Factual, precise information that can be presented in court.

evidentiary privileges Certain matters of communication that defendants and other witnesses can rightfully have barred from disclosure in court; classified as professional, political, social, and judicial.

exceptionally cleared The classification assigned to an offense when a factor external to the investigation results in no charge being filed against a known suspect (e.g., the death of the suspect).

exchangeable traces Particulates, lubricants, and spermicide added to condoms by manufacturers; can help identify particular brands and indicate condom use.

excusable homicide The killing of a person in which the slayer is to some degree at fault but the degree of fault is not enough to constitute a criminal homicide.

exigent circumstances An exception to the requirement that law enforcement officers have a search warrant; occurs when there is a compelling need for official action and there is no time to get a warrant.

expert witness A person who is called to testify in court because of his or her special skills or knowledge; permitted to interpret facts and give opinions about their significance to facilitate jurors' understanding of complex or technical matters.

exploits Software programs written to take advantage of security holes or "back doors" and thereby provide the user with illegal access to computer files.

explosion A physical reaction characterized by the presence of high-pressure gas, confinement of the pressure, rapid release of the pressure, and change or damage to the confining structure, container, or vessel as a result of the pressure release.

eyewitness identification The identification of someone or something involved in a crime by a witness who perceives the person or thing through one or more senses.

F

facial identification systems Manual kits or computer programs for preparing a likeness of a suspect; creates a composite from individual facial features.

facial recognition software Any of various computer programs that compare video images of persons' faces (taken by cameras at arenas, airports, hotels, and so on) with mug shots of known offenders for the purpose of identifying and apprehending wanted persons.

false-theft scheme An insurance fraud in which the owner of a vehicle reports it stolen but has actually hidden or disposed of it.

false-vehicle scheme An insurance fraud in which a person insures a vehicle that: does not exist; has already been salvaged; or belongs to someone else and later reports the vehicle stolen.

farm equipment Motorized equipment used on farms and on lawns; usually does not require a title or registration. Also called *off-road equipment.*

FBI Child Abduction and Serial Murder Investigative Center (CASMIRC) Provides investigative support through coordination and providing federal resources, training and application of multidisciplinary expertise, and to assist federal, state, and local authorities in matters involving child abductions, mysterious disappearances of children, child homicide, and serial murders across the country.

FBI Crime Laboratory A comprehensive forensic laboratory that conducts a broad range of scientific analyses of evidence and provides experts to testify in relation to analysis results; offers its services without charge to state and local law enforcement agencies.

federal safety certification label The sticker certifying a vehicle's safety, including its VIN; usually located on the driver's door or doorpost.

felonious assaults An assault committed for the purpose of inflicting severe bodily harm or death; usually involves use of a deadly weapon.

felonious homicides Killings that are treated and punished as crimes; includes murder and manslaughter.

felony A serious violation of the criminal code; punishable by imprisonment for one or more years or by death.

fences/receivers Individuals & businesses which knowingly buy, sell, or dispose of stolen merchandise, vehicles, financial instruments, and other things of value.

field interview/information report A form on which a patrolling officer notes details about a person or vehicle that seems suspicious but is not connected with any particular offense.

field notes The shorthand written record made by a police officer from the time he or she arrives at a crime scene until the assignment is completed.

Fielding, Henry Chief Magistrate of Bow Street in London beginning in 1748. In 1750, he formed a group of volunteer, non-uniformed homeowners, who hurried to the scene of crimes to investigate them. These "Bow Street Runners" were the first modern detective unit. In 1752, he created *The Covent Garden Journal,* which circulated the descriptions of wanted persons.

Fielding, John The brother of Henry Fielding. Following Henry's death in 1754, John carried on his work for 25 years, making Bow Street a clearing house for crime information.

Financial Crimes Enforcement Network (FinCen) Part of the Department of the Treasury, an agency responsible for investigating major financial crimes (e.g., money laundering); provides assistance to law enforcement agencies.

fingerprint classification A system used to categorize fingerprints on the basis of their ridge characteristics.

fingerprint patterns Patterns formed by the ridge detail of fingerprints; primarily loops, whorls, and arches.

fingerprints Replicas of the friction ridges (on palms, fingers, toes, and soles of the feet) that touched the surfaces on which the prints are found.

flame ionization detector A device that produces ionized molecules in proportion to the amount of combustible organic gases in a sample; used to detect residues of accelerants at fire scenes.

fluorescent powders Powders, dusted on areas being examined, that chemically enhance latent prints viewed under UV, laser, or alternative light illumination.

follow-up investigation The process of gathering information after the generation of the incident report and until the case is ready for prosecution; undertaken for cases receiving a supervisory disposition for further investigation.

footwear impressions Impressions that result when footwear, feet, or tires tread on a moldable surface such as earth, clay, or snow.

footwear prints Prints that result when footwear, feet, or tires contaminated with foreign matter such as mud, grease, or blood are placed on a smooth, firm surface (e.g., a floor, a chair, paper). Also called *residue prints.*

forensic entomology The study of insects associated with a dead body in order to determine the elapsed time since death.

forensic odontology A specialty that relates dental evidence to investigation.

forensic pathology The study, by physicians, of how and why people die; can also include examination of the living to determine physical or sexual abuse.

forensic photograph analysis The comparison of photos from a security surveillance camera with file pictures of suspects to identify a perpetrator or acquire information about him or her.

forensic science The examination, evaluation, and explanation of physical evidence in terms of law.

fracture match The alignment of the edges of two items of evidence, thereby showing that both items were previously joined together.

franchise fraud Scam in which people are conned into believing they are purchasing a legitimate franchise, such as a copy shop, convenience store, fast food restaurant, or other business.

free inspection fraud Most often, this type of fraud is associated with home repair or improvement scams, although it is also operated using automobiles. A person appears at your home promising a free inspection of your heating and cooling system, gutters, chimney, roof shingles, or your entire home. Serious defects are found and scare tactics are used to maneuver victims into correcting the situation "right away." Any actual damage is caused by the inspector, who may ask for an advance fee to buy materials or who offers a great deal because they have "just finished a job nearby and have some materials left over." Any work actually done is shoddy, uses inferior materials, and does not meet local building codes.

free-and-voluntary rule Based on a number of Supreme Court decisions since 1936, the principle that the exertion of any kind of coercion, physical or psychological, on a suspect to obtain a confession will render the confession inadmissible.

freehand forgery Written in the forger's normal handwriting, with no attempt to mimic the style of the genuine signature.

freezer crimes Thefts of livestock (usually only one or a few animals) in which the motivation is food rather than profit.

Frye v. United States A 1923 federal case which established that the results of a scientific technique would be admissible only if the technique had gained general acceptance in its field. (Per *Daubert,* this was superceded by the federal rules of evidence.)

G

Galton, Francis Galton published, in 1892, the first definitive book on dactylography, *Finger Prints,* which presented statistical proof of their uniqueness and many principles of identification by fingerprints. Charles Darwin's cousin.

gamma hydroxybutyrate (GHB) A central nervous system depressant used to perpetrate sexual attacks; mixed into a victim's food or drink, can induce relaxation or unconsciousness, leaving the victim unaware of the attack; can also cause seizures or death.

gas liquid chromatograph (GLC) A portable device that separates a sample gas into measurable components; used to detect residues of accelerants at fire scenes.

geographic profiling An investigative strategy in which the locations of a series of crimes (or, sometimes, the scenes of a single crime) are used to determine the most probable area of the offender's residence.

Girard, Stephen Bequeathed $33,190 to Philadelphia to develop a competent police force. In 1833, the city passed an ordinance creating America's first paid daytime police department.

Goddard, Calvin A U.S. World War I veteran and physician, he is widely considered to be most responsible for raising firearms identification to a science and for perfecting the bullet-comparison microscope.

Goddard, Henry One of the last Bow Street Runners, who in 1835 made the first successful identification of a murderer by studying a bullet recovered from a murder victim. In the case, a bullet mold with a noticeable defect was found at the suspect's home; this defect corresponded to a defect found on the recovered bullet.

gray-market vehicles Vehicles purchased abroad and shipped to the United States; may require modifications to meet U.S. emission control and safety standards.

grooves In a firearm's rifled bore, the low cuts that separate the higher lands.

Gross, Hans Austrian prosecutor who wrote the first major book on the application of science to investigation in 1893.

group cause homicide Involves two or more people with a common ideology, who sanction an act committed by one or more of the group's members that results in another person's death.

H

hacker's dictionary A software program that provides unauthorized access to computer systems by generating millions of alphanumeric combinations until it finds one that matches a password.

hacking or cracking The process of gaining unauthorized entry into a computer system.

hallucinogenic drugs Natural or synthetic drugs that distort perception of objective reality and, in large doses, cause hallucinations; can lead to unpredictable effects based on user and environment.

hard and soft insurance frauds Hard fraud is when a person fakes an injury, loss, accident, theft, arson, or other loss to illegally collect from an insurance company. Soft frauds are when people tell "little white lies" to increase the amount of an actual loss for which they will be compensated by their insurer.

hashish A natural hallucinogen, derived from resinous secretions of the cannabis plant, that is more potent than marijuana; sold in soft lumps and usually smoked in a small hash pipe.

hashish oil An extremely potent hallucinogen, derived by distilling THC from marijuana, that produces a high from a single drop; smoked in a cigarette or glass-bowled pipe, or ingested in food or wine.

hazardous wastes Solid, liquid, sludge, and manufacturing by-product wastes that are ignitable, corrosive, reactive, and/or toxic; may pose a serious threat to human health and the environment if improperly managed.

hearsay Testimony by a witness that repeats something which he or she heard someone say out of court and which the witness has no personal factual knowledge of; inadmissible in court.

heavy equipment Heavy construction equipment; usually does not require a title or registration. Also called *off-road equipment*.

Hemident A reagent used in preliminary or presumptive field tests to check for the presence of blood.

Henry system Devised by Edward Henry, the fingerprint classification system that facilitated the use of fingerprints in criminal identification; adopted in England in 1900 and today used in almost every country.

hepatitis B (HBV) and hepatitis C (HCV) Viruses present in blood (and, for HBV, other bodily fluids) that attack the liver and can lead to death; a health hazard at scenes where bodily fluids are exposed.

heroin (diacetylmorphine) An opiate that is much stronger than morphine and often causes death due to its purity or diluents; an odorless, crystalline white powder, which is usually sold diluted and is injected.

home-invasion robbery (HIR) A crime in which one or more offenders deliberately enter a home to commit robbery; characterized by gangs who target individuals rather than residences and use violence to terrify and control their victims.

homicide The killing of a human being by another human being; can be felonious or nonfelonious.

hot spots A location where various crimes are committed on a regular basis, usually by different offenders. Also called a *hot dot*.

hull identification number (HIN) Identification number assigned to boats.

human immunodeficiency virus (HIV) The blood-borne pathogen, also present in other bodily fluids, that can progress into AIDS, which reduces the body's defenses against diseases and leaves victims vulnerable to infections from which they die; a health hazard at scenes where bodily fluids are exposed.

hypercompliance In hypnosis, the situation in which the desire to please the hypnotist or others leads the subject to provide information that does not reflect his or her actual memories.

hypersuggestibility In hypnosis, the subject's heightened degree of suggestibility, which creates the possibility of the hypnotist's influencing the subject, intentionally or inadvertently, to give false information.

hypnosis A state of heightened awareness in which subconscious memories may surface that can be of help to an investigation.

I

identity theft The assumption of another person's identity for use in fraudulent transactions that result in a loss to the victim; accomplished by acquiring personal information about the victim (e.g., date of birth, address, credit card numbers).

immersion burns Burns on the skin that occur when part or all of the body falls into, or is placed into, a tub or other container of hot liquid.

impeachment In a trial, the process of discrediting or contradicting the testimony of a witness to show that he or she is unworthy of belief.

incendiary mechanism A fire-starting mechanism that consists of an ignition device, possibly a timing device, one or more plants to accelerate the flame, and, often, trailers to spread the fire; can be mechanical or chemical.

incest Broadly, any sexual abuse of a minor by an adult who is perceived by the minor to be a family member; also, under some statutes, sexual activity between closely related adults.

incident report The first written investigative record of a crime, usually compiled by the uniformed officer assigned to the call, who conducts the preliminary investigation.

incised and stab wounds Wounds inflicted with a sharpedged instrument such as a knife or razor; typically narrow at the ends and gaping at the center, with considerable bleeding. Also called *cutting wounds.*

in-custody interrogation The legal condition under which the *Miranda* warnings are required, although case decisions vary on the definitions of "custody" and "interrogation."

indicative intelligence Information pertaining to emerging and new criminal developments; may include fragmentary or unsubstantiated information, as well as hard facts.

individual characteristics Characteristics of physical evidence that can be identified as coming from a particular person or source.

inductive reasoning The thought process that moves from specific details to a general view; e.g., the facts of a case are used to arrive at a logical explanation of the crime.

infant abduction The taking of a child less than one year of age by a nonfamily member; classified by the FBI as kidnapping, although the motive is usually to possess the child rather than to use the child as a means for something else (e.g., money, sex, revenge).

inflated-theft-loss scheme An insurance fraud in which the owner of a stolen vehicle reports a greater financial loss—based on alleged current value, damage, or stolen parts—than is the case.

infrared spectrophotometer A device that identifies samples by recording the amount of infrared light that passes through them; used to detect residues of flammable-liquid accelerants at fire scenes.

Integrated Automated Fingerprint Identification System (IAFIS) Maintained by the FBI, a national online fingerprint and criminal-history database with identification and response capabilities; may be accessed by local law enforcement agencies.

intelligence/analytical cycle A five-part process designed to produce usable information for the client.

international terrorism The use or threatened use of violence against persons or property by a group (or an individual) whose operations transcend national boundaries and are done to further political or social objectives.

interrogation A conversation between an investigator and a suspect that is designed to match acquired information to the suspect and secure a confession.

interrogatory questions Who? What? Where? When? How? And Why?

interviewing The process of obtaining information from people who have knowledge that might be helpful in a criminal investigation.

investigative psychology A criminal-profiling approach based on interpersonal coherence, significance of time and place,

criminal characteristics, and the offender's criminal career and forensic awareness.

investigator An official who gathers, documents, and evaluates evidence and information in the investigation of a crime.

iodine A dye used in developing latent prints on porous (particularly paper) and nonporous surfaces; one of the oldest and most proven means of locating prints.

J

Jacob Wetterling Crimes against Children and Sexually Violent Offender Registration Act A 1994 federal act requiring that states create and maintain registries of sex offenders. See also **Megan's law.**

jail booking report A document containing complete personal information about a suspect, including a photograph, fingerprints, and a list of the suspect's personal property at the time of booking.

joyriding The theft and use of a motor vehicle solely to drive it, after which it is abandoned; usually committed by teenagers.

judicial notice An evidentiary shortcut whereby the necessity of formally proving the truth of a particular matter is eliminated when that truth is not in dispute.

justifiable homicide The necessary killing of a person in the performance of a legal duty or the exercise of a legal right when the slayer is not at fault.

K

ketamine A synthetic hallucinogen that produces hallucinations, excitement, and delirium of less intensity and shorter duration than the effects of PCP and LSD; sold as liquids, tablets, or white powder, and injected, smoked, or ingested in a drink.

kinesics The relationship between body language (limb movements, facial expressions, and so on) and the communication of feelings and attitudes.

Kirk, Paul A biochemist, educator, and criminalist; wrote *Criminal Investigation* in 1953; helped to develop the careers of many criminalists.

known samples (1) Standard or reference samples from known or verifiable sources; (2) control or blank samples from known sources believed to be uncontaminated by the crime; (3) elimination samples from sources who had lawful access to the crime scene.

L

lacerations Wounds inflicted by blunt objects such as clubs, pipes, and pistols; typically open and irregularly shaped, bruised around the edges, and bleeding freely.

lands The high sides in a firearm's rifled bore.

laser illumination A method of developing latent prints in which lasers are used to illuminate a crime scene, causing otherwise-undetectable fingerprints to fluoresce when viewed through a special lens.

latent/invisible prints Fingerprints created when friction ridges deposit body perspiration and oil on surfaces they touch; typically invisible to the naked eye.

Lattes, Leone Made a key discovery in forensic serology in 1915, which permits blood typing from a dried blood stain.

Law Enforcement Online (LEO) Maintained by the FBI, an intranet system through which enforcement officers can communicate, obtain critical information, and participate in educational programs and focused dialogs.

layer-checking technique In arson investigation, the process of examining the strata of debris, working through to the floor; may indicate the sequence of burning.

left-wing terrorists Terrorists who usually profess a revolutionary socialist doctrine and view themselves as protecting the people against capitalism and imperialism.

LEO *See* **Law Enforcement Online.**

letter of transmittal In the context of criminal investigation, it is the letter which accompanies physical evidence to the crime laboratory; its elements include the identity and locator information of the submitting individual, the case facts, examinations requested, and other related information.

lifted-prints log A written record of lifted-prints evidence that contains the same type of information as that listed in the evidence recovery log.

lifters Various materials and devices used to "lift" evidence, especially fingerprints and footwear prints, from a surface and preserve it; include flap, electrostatic, rubber-gelatin, and clear-tape lifters.

ligature strangulation Pressure on the neck applied by a constricting band that is tightened by a force other than body weight; causes death by occluding the blood vessels that supply oxygen to the brain.

lineup A procedure in which a number of similar-looking persons, including the suspect, are shown simultaneously or sequentially to a witness who may be able to identify one of them as the perpetrator; can also be conducted with photos.

link analysis he process of charting or depicting temporal and other data gathered during a criminal investigation to uncover and help interpret relationships and patterns in the data.

livestock Farm and ranch animals raised for profit.

livor mortis Soon after death, a purplish color that appears under the skin on the portions of the body that are closest to the ground; caused by settling of the blood.

Locard, Edmond Researcher interested in microscopic evidence; all crime sense today comes under the presumption of Locard's Principle—that there is something to be found.

logic bomb A computer program that uses illegitimate instructions or misuses legitimate instructions to damage data structures; operates at a specific time, periodically, or according to other instructions.

loiding The act of slipping or shimming, by means of a celluloid strip or credit card, a spring-bolt lock that does not have an antishim device.

lookout Accomplices of a robber who watch for police and may provide armed backup for the offender.

lysergic acid diethylamide (LSD) A semisynthetic hallucinogen that produces mental changes lasting up to 12 hours; taken as drops on a sugar lump or blotted paper, was popular in the 1960s and is now making a comeback among juveniles.

M

macroscopic scene The "large view" of a crime scene, including things such as locations, the victim's body, cars, and buildings.

manslaughter A criminal homicide that is committed under circumstances not severe enough to constitute murder but that cannot be classified as justifiable or excusable.

marijuana A natural hallucinogen, derived from certain hemp plants, that produces a dreamy, carefree state and an alteration of sensory perceptions; in the form of crushed dried leaves and flowers, it is smoked or eaten in food.

marine theft The theft of boats, boat trailers, outboard motors, jet skis, and all equipment associated with boating or water activities.

mechanical explosions Explosions in which a high-pressure gas is produced by purely physical reactions; commonly caused by steam (e.g., the bursting of a steam boiler).

media statement Information released to the news media; must not prejudice the suspect's right to a fair and impartial trial.

Megan's law An amendment to the Jacob Wetterling act, legislation requiring that states disclose information about registered sex offenders to the public.

meperidine (Demerol) A synthetic narcotic that in illicit use is usually injected but can be taken orally; the first synthetic opiate.

mescaline A natural hallucinogen, derived from the peyote cactus, that produces hallucinations for up to 12 hours; ground into a powder and taken orally.

meth labs Illegal laboratories that manufacture methamphetamine; range from industrial-size organizations to oneperson tweeker labs, with prevalence skyrocketing due to the availability of "recipes" and chemicals via the Internet.

methadone A synthetic narcotic used to maintain a heroin addict at a stable level of opiate use during and after withdrawal from heroin; administered orally, thus reducing dangers from injection.

methaqualone A strong depressant that can cause poisoning and convulsive comas; removed from the legal U.S. market; street versions are usually counterfeit.

methcathinone A psychomotor stimulant chemically similar to methamphetamine but more potent, often producing extreme paranoia; usually a white or off-white powder that is sold pure and snorted. Also called *cat* and *goob.*

methylenedioxy methamphetamine (MDMA) or **ecstasy** A hallucinogen that produces reduced inhibitions, euphoria, light hallucinations and can result in paranoia and psychosis; sold as a white powder, with usage increasing alarmingly.

Metropolitan Police Act (1829) An act of Parliament that created the London Metropolitan Police, the first centralized, professional police force in Britain, which soon became the international model of professional policing.

microscopic scene A crime scene viewed in terms of specific objects and pieces of evidence associated with the crime, such as knives, guns, hairs, fibers, and biological fluids.

minutiae The characteristics of friction ridges on palms, fingers, toes, and soles of the feet.

Miranda v. Arizona The 1966 case in which the Supreme Court established that law enforcement officers must advise a person of his or her constitutional rights before beginning an in-custody interrogation.

mirror To match a person's words, actions, and mannerisms in order to eliminate communication barriers, foster trust, and create the flow of desired information.

misdemeanor A violation of the criminal code that is less serious than a felony; often punishable by imprisonment for no more than one year and/or a fine of no more than $500.

missing person frauds A particularly cruel type of advancedfee scam. Cons gather information on missing persons and then contact relatives explaining how they might be able to find the person for an up-front fee.

mitochondrial DNA (mtDNA) DNA found in the mitochondria of a cell; inherited only from the mother, it thus serves as an identity marker for maternal relatives.

mobile data terminal (MDT) An electronic system in a police car that provides features such as secure communication with 911, and among police units, direct access to national and local databases, and computer functions (e.g., e-mail, Internet access, computing, word processing).

money laundering The process of making illegally obtained money seem legitimate by filtering it through a business and falsifying the business's accounts and invoices.

morgue A crime lab that determines cause of death; when the cause is questionable or is other than a known disease, conducts analyses that produce investigative information.

morphine An opiate in tablet, capsule, and liquid form (but usually injected) that produces euphoria, drowsiness, and relaxation; provides the medical standards by which other narcotics are evaluated.

Motor Vehicle Theft Law Enforcement Act (1984) Federal legislation requiring that manufacturers place permanent identification numbers on major parts of certain car lines.

mugging See **strong-armed robbery.**

Mulberry Street Morning Parade Instituted by Chief Detective Thomas Byrnes in New York City in the late 1800s, an innovative approach to criminal identification in which all new arrestees were marched each morning before detectives so that the detectives could make notes and later recognize the criminals.

Munchausen syndrome by proxy (MSBP) A psychological disorder in which a parent or caretaker attempts to elicit medical attention for himself or herself by injuring or inducing illness in a child.

N

narrative style In incident reports, the officer's written chronological account of events at the crime scene from the time he or she arrived until the assignment was completed.

National Center for the Analysis of Violent Crime (NCAVC) Operated by the FBI, an organization that provides investigative and operational assistance to agencies dealing with violent crimes; consists of the BEA, CASMIRC, and VICAP.

National Crime Information Center (NCIC) The FBI's online system of extensive databases on criminals and crime; available to federal, state, and local agencies.

National Incident-Based Reporting System (NIBRS) An FBI program for crime reporting that features a detailed report format documenting far more data than does a basic incident report; involves voluntary participation, but made mandatory by some states.

National Institute-Based Reporting System The FBI's *Uniform Crime Reporting System (UCR)* began in 1929 and its focus is on reporting the types and numbers of crimes.

National Integrated Ballistic Information Network Program (NIBIN) A joint program of the ATF and the FBI, a computerized database of crime gun information that stores images of ballistic evidence (projectiles and casings), against which new images are compared for identification.

National Motor Vehicle Title Information System (NMVTIS) Under development; a computerized database that will include complete histories of vehicles in all states and will prevent title laundering between states.

NCAVC See **National Center for the Analysis of Violent Crime.**

NCIC See **National Crime Information Center.**

neighborhood canvas A systematic approach to interviewing residents, merchants, and others who were in the immediate vicinity of a crime and may have useful information.

neuro-linguistic programming (NLP) An approach used in interviewing and interrogating that emphasizes establishing rapport, through mirroring, as a means of improving communication and thus obtaining useful information.

NIBRS See **National Institute-Based Reporting System.**

ninhydrin A chemical used in developing latent prints on paper and cardboard; produces purplish prints, making it unsuitable for use with money.

NMVTIS See **National Motor Vehicle Title Information System.**

nuclear DNA DNA found in the nucleus of a cell; inherited from both the mother and the father.

O

oath A formal attestation in which a witness swears to tell the truth on the basis of his or her belief in a supreme being and acknowledges a realization of the penalties for perjury; a means of establishing a witness's competence.

odometer fraud The crime of rolling back a vehicle's odometer so that it shows a lower mileage than is the case, and obtaining or altering paperwork to support the fraud. Also called *odometer tampering, rollback,* and *clocking.*

off-road equipment Heavy construction equipment and farm equipment.

off-shore accounts Accounts in so-called safe-haven foreign banks, often operated by small island-nations which promise untraceable financial services.

one-year callable certificates of deposit Unscrupulous sellers tout these certificates of deposit (CDs) (which trumpet high rates of interest), but mislead or do not explain to investors about the actual terms of the investment.

opiates Drugs derived from the opium poppy (e.g., opium, morphine, heroin, codeine).

opium An opiate in the form of blackish-brown, pungentsmelling beads of dried fluid, which are smoked; produces drowsiness and relaxation and is the source of morphine, heroin, and codeine.

organized/disorganized offender patterns A criminalprofiling approach in which offenders are categorized as organized or disorganized on the basis of personal and crime scene characteristics. Mixed organized-disorganized crimes reflect aspects of both patterns.

Osborn, Albert In 1910, wrote *Questioned Documents,* still considered one of the definitive works on document examinations.

OxyContin A powerful narcotic consisting of oxycodone, a morphinelike drug, in a time-release formulation that, when crushed and snorted or injected, produces an intense heroin-like high; the latest drug of choice among addicts and teenage abusers.

P

packet sniffers Computer programs designed to monitor network communications and selectively record sensitive information (e.g., passwords, credit card numbers); used by hackers and, with a court order, by the FBI.

palo verde seedpod case A 1992 murder case in Phoenix, Arizona in which DNA analysis of plant evidence was used for the first time in criminal proceedings to help secure a conviction.

"paper vehicle" A vehicle that does not exist but is insured on the basis of a counterfeit title or manufacturer's certificate of origin so that it can later be reported stolen.

paralanguage Characteristics of speech—such as volume, pitch, tone, and tempo—that communicate, often unconsciously, meanings and attitudes of the speaker that may not be evident in the words themselves.

parts marking The process, mandated by law, of attaching VIN labels to the major parts of vehicles in high-theft lines.

passive system (theft deterrent) A type of vehicle antitheft device which activates automatically but may require that the driver do something to deactivate the system.

Peel, Robert *See* **bobbies.**

peremptory challenge The limited number of race and gender-neutral challenges each side has in a criminal case to excuse a juror for any other reason.

personal cause homicide Homicide motivated by a personal cause, which ensues from interpersonal aggression. The slayer and the victim(s) may not be known to each other.

personal protection equipment (PPE) Equipment and clothing designed to protect individuals at high-risk crime scenes from injury and infection.

phencyclidine (PCP) A hallucinogen in powder (angel dust), tablet, liquid, leafy mixture, and rock-crystal forms that produces unpleasant effects and can cause extreme violence and strength; as a street drug, often adulterated and misrepresented, yet usage is increasing notably.

phishing E-mails or letters soliciting personal and account information with which the collector can commit identity fraud or sell the information to someone who will commit that crime.

photographic log A written record listing the photographs taken at a crime scene and detailing who took them, where and when they were taken, and under what conditions.

photographing The primary means of documenting a crime scene.

phreakers People who misuse telephone systems through a variety of fraudulent methods that make it seem as if long-distance service and airtime are being legitimately purchased.

physical stereotyping Occurs when an officer expects that the robber will fit a preconceived description; can result in the escape of a suspect or harm to the officer.

pigeon drop con Another old, but effective scam in which one con strikes up a conversation with someone on the street. Another con approaches them with a bag of money, which is from some illicit source, which he/she just found. After talking about what they could do with the money, one of the cons calls his/her boss, an "attorney" who meets them. The attorney says they will be able to keep the money after they do a reasonable search for the owner, but that "good faith money" must be put up. After the mark puts up his/her money, the cons disappear with it.

PIN *See* **product information number.**

Pinkerton, Allan Formed the Pinkertons in 1850 along with Edward Rucker; the only consistently competent detectives in the United States for over 50 years.

placement, layering, and integration The three main phases of laundering money from illicit sources so it can take on the appearance of legitimate income.

plaintiff In a civil case, the party that was allegedly wronged and that files the lawsuit.

planned operation A robbery that involves careful planning and no planned use of force; has less likelihood of apprehension and generates a large score.

plant In arson, the material placed around the ignition device to feed the flame.

plastic prints Prints created when fingers touch moldable material, such as newly painted surfaces, the gum on stamps, putty, and the sticky side of adhesive tape.

poaching The illegal taking or possessing of game, fish, and other wildlife.

"police spies" In early nineteenth-century England, a derogatory term used in reference to plainclothes detectives; coined by persons who feared that the use of such officers would reduce civil liberties.

polygraph A mechanical device that records physiological changes that occur in a person while he or she is being questioned, with deviations from normal readings indicating deception; can be used only with subject's voluntary consent. Also called a lie detector.

Ponzi/pyramid fraud Basically this involves recruiting people who are promised great returns on their money. The early investors are paid with the money from later investors. The scheme always collapses because the recruitment of investors cannot be sustained and the cons will ultimately steal the funds for their personal use.

Popay, Sergeant Dismissed from London's Metropolitan Police in 1833 for infiltrating a radical group and advocating the use of violence after he acquired a leadership position. Today, we would call Popay's call for violence entrapment.

positive match In DNA analysis, an identical match of a suspect's DNA with that found on evidence at the crime scene.

power-assertive rape-murder A series of acts in which the rape is planned but the murder is an unplanned response of increasing aggression to ensure control of the victim. The acts within the rape assault are characterized by forceful aggression and intimidation.

power-reassurance rape A planned single rape attack followed by an unplanned overkill of the victim. Motivated by an idealized seduction and consequent fantasy, the killer focuses on acting out a fantasy and seeks verbal reassurance of his sexual adequacy.

preferential child molester A person who molests children because he or she has a definite sexual preference for children.

preliminary investigation The process undertaken by the first officer (usually a patrol officer) to arrive at the scene of a crime; includes assessment, emergency care, scene control, a BOLO, scene determination, incident report, and, sometimes, evidence procedures.

preponderance of evidence The burden of proof in civil cases; requires only that the evidence presented by one side be seen by the jury as more believable than the evidence presented by the opposing side.

primary scene The location at which the initial offense was committed.

probable cause A condition in which an officer has suspicion about an individual and knowledge of facts and circumstances that would lead a reasonable person to believe that a crime has been, is being, or is about to be, committed.

procedural criminal law That branch of criminal law that defines what can and cannot be done with, or to, people.

product identification number (PIN) PIN stands for product identification number.

professional theft (of vehicle) The theft of a vehicle to fill a specific order or to resell the parts.

promissory notes Essentially short term I.O.U.s which promise to pay its holder, the investor, the fixed amount invested, plus a fixed interest at some future specified date. While these may be operated legally, many such investments are simply frauds and the money disappears.

proof The combination of all the evidence in determining the guilt or innocence of a person accused of a crime.

Property Insurance Loss Register (PILR) An insurance industry database that lists the insureds in burglary and theft claims and everyone with an insurable interest in fire claims; detects repeated patterns of claim activity.

proximity The amount of space between the participants in a conversation—neither too close, which causes discomfort, nor too far apart, which causes a loss of connectivity.

psilocybin and psilocin Natural hallucinogens, derived from certain mushrooms, that produce hallucinations for about 6 hours; taken orally.

psychological autopsy An analysis of a decedent's thoughts, feelings, and behavior, conducted through interviews with persons who knew him or her, to determine whether a death was an accident or suicide.

pump and dump A scheme where glowing, but false, information about a stock is widely distributed, often through the Internet, and the rapid buying of it "pumps" the price of the stock up. Once pumped, the fraudsters "dump" the stock for a quick profit.

puncture wounds Wounds inflicted with piercing instruments such as leather punches, screwdrivers, and ice picks; typically small, with little or no bleeding.

pyromaniacs Arsonists who lack conscious motivation for their fire setting.

Q

quick strip (of vehicle) The process of removing from a stolen vehicle valuable parts (e.g., seats, stereos, tires) that have no identifying numbers and thus can be easily sold.

R

radial fracture lines Lines that move away from the point of impact in a glass window.

rape or sexual battery The crime of having sexual relations with a person against her or his will; with a person who is unconscious or under the influence of alcohol; or with someone who is insane, feeble-minded, or under the age of consent.

rape-murder Murder that results from or is an integral part of the rape of the victim; either an unplanned response (of increasing aggression or panic over sense of failure) or a planned act (of revenge or sadism).

rapid response deployment or quick action deployment (QUAD) An intervention approach in which patrol officers are trained in the principles and tactics of rapid deployment for critical incidents so that responding officers can take action immediately rather than wait for a SWAT team.

rapport In interviews and interrogations, the harmonious relationship with the witness or suspect that must be established by the investigator to foster trust and meaningful communication.

rebuttal In a trial, the optional process in which the prosecution, after the defense has closed its case, presents new evidence or calls or recalls a witness; it occurs at the discretion of the prosecution.

re-cross-examination In a trial, the requestioning of a witness initially called by the opposing party.

redirect examination In a trial, the requestioning of a witness by the party that called the witness.

reflected ultraviolet imaging system (RUVIS) Lighting and imaging system in which ultraviolet light applied to undetected fingerprints is "bounced" back, highly intensifying the prints.

refurbishment fraud A practice in which working components from damaged or returned items (e.g., a computer) are used in the construction of new items or are resold as new items.

revenge-motivated arson Fires set in retaliation for some injustice, real or imagined, that is perceived by the offender.

rhodamine 6G An excellent fluorescing chemical for enhancing developed latent prints and revealing others; used on metal, glass, plastic, wood, and other nonabsorbent surfaces.

rifling The lands and grooves in the rifled bore of a firearm.

right-wing terrorists Terrorists who usually espouse racial supremacy and antigovernment or antiregulatory beliefs; they often hold antiabortion and survivalist views and call for paramilitary training in "militias."

robbery The crime of taking and carrying away the personal property of another by means of force, fear, or threat of force, with the intent to permanently deprive the owner of its use.

rogues' gallery Instituted by the New York City Police Department in 1857, a display in which photographs of known offenders were arranged by criminal specialty and height for detectives to study so that they might recognize criminals on the street.

Rohypnol A benzodiazapine used to perpetrate sexual attacks; mixed into a victim's food or drink, can induce sedation, memory impairment, or unconsciousness, leaving the victim unaware of the attack. Also called *flunitrazepam*.

root kits Exploit packages that enable computer-system intruders to maintain the highest level of access by installing back doors and secret accounts and altering logs and basic system services.

rough sketch A drawing made at the crime scene; not drawn to scale, but indicates accurate dimensions and distances.

rules of evidence Federal evidentiary rules which state that scientific, technical, or other specialized knowledge is admissible if it will help the trier of fact understand the evidence or determine a fact at issue.

S

safes Locked receptacles for protecting valuables; classified as fire-resistant safes (offering protection from fire but minimum security) or money chests (providing security and reasonably good protection from fire).

salami slice A computerized-theft technique in which dollar amounts are automatically rounded down and the difference is diverted to the perpetrator's special account.

salvage switch A method of disguising a stolen vehicle whereby the title and VIN plate of a salvage vehicle are transferred to an identical stolen vehicle, which can then be sold in the legitimate market.

salvage title The title issued to an insurance company after it has paid a total-loss claim; remains with the vehicle until it is destroyed.

salvage vehicle A vehicle that has been damaged to such an extent that the cost of repairing it is more than its fair market value.

scald burns Burns on the skin caused by contact with hot liquids, either through spills/splashes or immersion; most common type of burn injury to children.

Scotland Yard The original headquarters of the London Metropolitan Police, so-called because the building formerly housed Scottish royalty. Since 1890, the headquarters have been located elsewhere, but have been still known as New Scotland Yard.

search The process of looking for evidence of a crime.

search and seizure The process of looking for evidence of a crime and taking that evidence into the custody of a law enforcement agency.

search warrant Written authorization by a judge allowing law enforcement officers to look for specified items of evidence of a crime in a specified place.

secondary scenes The locations of all events subsequent to, and connected with, the event at the primary scene.

selective raid A robbery that involves a minimal amount of casual planning and may be repeated several times in rapid succession.

semen A grayish-white fluid produced in the male reproductive organs and ejaculated during orgasm; has a chlorinelike odor and dries to a starchlike consistency.

series A crime characteristic in which crimes of the same type are committed over a short period of time, usually by the same offender.

sex offenses Crimes related to sexual activity; classified as serious (e.g., rape), nuisance (e.g., voyeurism, exhibitionism), and mutual consent (e.g., adultery, prostitution).

sexual homicide In sexual homicide, a sexual element (activity) is the basis, or the sequence of, acts leading to the death.

shaken-baby syndrome (SBS) Severe intracranial trauma caused by the deliberate application of violent force (shaking) to a child.

Shoeprint Image Capture and Retrieval System (SICAR) Computer software that classifies, archives, and identifies shoeprints.

shopping cart fraud A computer crime in which the offender selects purchases at an online store, saves a copy of the purchase page and lowers the prices, and then submits the altered page and continues the checkout process.

shoulder surfing When identity thieves stay close enough to people using their credit cards, pins, telephone calling cards, and writing checks that they can gather sensitive identity information.

situational child molester A person who molests children because the opportunity exists to do so or because of his or her inadequacy, regressed personality, or desire for experimentation; does not have a sexual preference for children.

situational stereotyping Occurs when an officer's knowledge and experience with a location creates the expectation that the present situation will be the same as past situations; increases the officer's vulnerability.

sketching The process of drawing a crime scene using rudimentary methods; sketches made can be "rough" or "smooth."

skimmers Data collection devices through which credit cards are passed. When used illegally, they are employed to obtain the credit card numbers used by customers so credit card and/or identity theft can be committed.

small-particle reagent (SPR) A chemical used in developing latent prints on objects that have been immersed in water, dew- or rain-soaked cars, surfaces covered with a residue such as ocean salt, waxed materials, plastics, tile, and glass.

smooth bore A bore without rifling; characteristic of most shotguns.

smooth sketch A finished sketch of the crime scene, often drawn to scale using information contained in the rough sketch.

smurfing A method associated with money laundering. Multiple deposits of cash are made at different accounts in different banks or bank drafts are bought; the transactions are kept under $10,000 to avoid the bank rendering a required report of the transaction to federal authorities.

snow print wax An aerosol wax sprayed on footwear impressions in snow to tint the highlights so that the impressions can be photographed before being cast.

solvability factors Used to screen and evaluate the information in an offense/incident report to determine if there is sufficient information to warrant a follow-up investigation. Such factors include whether suspects are named, the existence of significant physical evidence, the use or display of deadly weapons, and similarities to recently reported crimes.

spalling The breakdown in the surface tensile strength of concrete, masonry, or brick that occurs when exposure to high temperatures and rates of heating produces mechanical forces within the material.

speedballing The simultaneous ingestion of heroin (a depressant) and cocaine (a stimulant); produces a euphoric rush followed by a drowsy or depressing effect. Can cause convulsions and death.

sperm Tadpolelike organisms that are contained in, and travel through, semen to fertilize the female egg.

spill/splash injuries Burns on the skin that occur when a hot liquid falls from a height and splashes onto the body.

spontaneous heating An increase in temperature that results from a natural process; caused by chemical action, fermentation, or oxidation.

spontaneous ignition The catching afire of materials subjected to spontaneous heating; usually requires several hours to several months of oxidation or fermentation.

sprees A crime characteristic in which crimes of the same type are committed at almost the same time by the same offender.

STAR *See* Stolen Auto Recovery System.

stimulants Drugs that directly stimulate the central nervous system, producing excitation, alertness, wakefulness, and, sometimes, a temporary increase in blood pressure and respiration rate; in overdose, can cause hallucinations, convulsions, and death.

sting operations In combating fences, this is a tactic in which undercover officers pose as fences in a "front" business to gain information. Such operations have proven to be an effective means of identifying criminals, penetrating criminal organizations, and recovering property.

Stolen Auto Recovery System (STAR) A method of examining and photographing the contents of shipping containers, by means of gamma rays, while they are entering a port or being loaded onto a vessel; used to identify stolen vehicles being shipped abroad.

stop and frisk A limited pat down of the outer clothing of a person encountered by a law enforcement officer when the person is acting suspiciously, and the officer, concerned about safety, seeks to determine if the person has a weapon.

strategic intelligence Information gathered and analyzed over time that usually confirms new or recently discovered patterns of criminal activity.

striae Tiny furrows made by the action of a tool on an object's surface (e.g., marks left on a door's hinge from an attempt to force the door open with a pry bar).

strong-armed robbery A robbery in which the perpetrator attacks and beats the victim but no weapons are involved.

subpoena A written order commanding a particular person to appear in court at a specified date and time to testify as a witness.

substantive criminal law That branch of criminal law dealing with the elements that describe and define a crime.

sudden infant death syndrome (SIDS) The sudden and unexpected death of an apparently healthy infant, usually during sleep, the cause of which has yet to be determined.

superglue fuming The process of heating cyanoacrylate in a high-humidity chamber so that the condensing of the resultant fumes develops any latent prints.

surrebuttal In a trial, the process in which the defense, after a rebuttal by the prosecution, presents new evidence or calls or recalls a witness; permitted only if the prosecution conducts a rebuttal.

surreptitious entries Burglaries in which no apparent force is used and thus a point of entry or exit cannot be established; may indicate loiding, picking, an unlocked door, a perpetrator with authorized access, or an occupant-staged crime.

surveillance The secretive and continuous observation of persons, places, and things to obtain information concerning the activities and identity of individuals.

swoop and squat One of several varieties of auto fraud. In this version, a person suddenly swoops in front of the car you are driving and hits his/her breaks, causing you to rear-end them. The person then claims medical injuries were caused by you and your insurer usually pays the "victim."

synthetic narcotics Narcotics that are chemically related to opiates but that are produced entirely within laboratories; primarily used as painkillers.

T

tack The equipment used with horses (e.g., saddles, bridles, horse blankets).

tactical intelligence Information that implies immediate action and can lead to arrests or the collection of additional information; may be derived from surveillance, informants, and intelligence analysis.

telephone record analysis time-event charting An intelligence technique in which telephone records are compiled and analyzed to obtain information on the relationships between the subscriber and the numbers called.

testimony A witness's oral presentation of facts about which he or she has knowledge.

threat assessment The process of determining the risk level posed by a threat and whether law enforcement should be called in and a criminal prosecution pursued; includes evaluation of the threatener.

title fraud For motor vehicles, any act that involves altering, laundering, or counterfeiting a title or title reassignment form; often engaged in to support and cover up odometer rollbacks.

T-men Agents of the Bureau of Internal Revenue (which enforced Prohibition), so-called because the bureau was part of the Department of the Treasury.

tool mark Any impression, cut, gouge, or abrasion made when a tool comes into contact with another object.

totality of the circumstances In determining the applicability of the *Miranda* warnings, an approach that takes all the circumstances into consideration, rather than imposing a strict interpretation based on formal procedures.

trace evidence Evidence that is extremely small or microscopic in size or is present only in limited amounts.

trace evidence vacuum A vacuum which gathers small (even microscopic) evidence at the crime scene. Examples of evidence gathered by it include hairs and fibers.

traced forgery Created by tracing over a genuine signature, commonly found on fraudulent (questioned) documents such as contracts, checks, and monetary instruments.

tracing evidence Evidence that helps identify and locate the suspect.

traditional powders The basic powders, available in a number of colors, that have been used for decades for developing latent fingerprints.

trailer In arson, any substance used to spread the fire from the plant to other parts of a room or building.

trends A general tendency in the occurrence of crime across a large geographic area over an extended period of time.

Trojan horse Any computer program that is altered or designed to perform an unwanted or malicious function while appearing to perform a routine or benign function.

Truth in Mileage Act (1986) Federal legislation that requires more tightly controlled documentation and recording of odometer readings each time ownership of a vehicle changes.

T/S/D crimes Any illegal acts involving the treatment, storage, and disposal of hazardous wastes.

tuberculosis A chronic bacterial infection, spread by air, that usually infects the lungs and can lead to death if untreated; a health hazard for anyone in contact with high-risk individuals such as drug addicts and homeless persons.

tumbling The illegal altering of a cellular phone's microchip so that its access codes change after each call, making it difficult to trace the fraudulent user; done through a personal computer.

U

ultraviolet fluorescence A technique in which a darkened fire scene is illuminated with an ultraviolet lamp so that certain substances glow; used to detect residues of accelerants and to locate the point of a fire's origin.

unbundling A medical fraud technique in which each component of service is separated and billed separately, creating a higher charge than if properly billed as a single category of service.

unknown or questioned samples (1) Recovered crime scene samples whose sources are in question; (2) questioned evidence that may have been transferred to an offender during the commission of a crime and may have been taken away by him or her; (3) questioned evidence recovered at multiple crime scenes that associates a particular tool, weapon, or person with each scene.

upcoding A type of medical fraud in which patients and insurers are billed for longer office visits than occurred, or are billed for more expensive tests which were never done.

V

vehicle canvass A systematic approach to documenting every vehicle in the immediate vicinity of a crime as a means of locating the suspect's vehicle.

vehicle fraud Any fraudulent activity involving motor vehicles; includes theft of vehicles, fraud perpetrated on purchasers of vehicles, and fraud committed by owners (or persons acting on their behalf) against insurance companies.

vehicle identification number (VIN) The 17-character identification number assigned to every car manufactured or sold in the United States.

venire The large panel of potential jurors from which a trial jury will be picked.

viatical settlements Though some viatical settlements are operated legally, many are scams. An example of a viatical settlement is when people's life insurance policies are bought for less than face value. The seller thus has access to cash and the buyer makes a profit on the difference between the face value of the policy and the amount paid to the insured.

VIN *See* **vehicle identification number.**

violation In some states, this is a minor transgression of the law, often punishable by a fine of no more than $250 (e.g., littering).

Violent Criminal Apprehension Program (VICAP) FBI unit whose mission is to facilitate cooperation, communication, and coordination between law enforcement agencies and to provide support in their efforts to investigate, identify, track, apprehend, and prosecute violent serial offenders.

virus A malicious program that is secretly inserted into normal software or a computer's active memory and runs when the host runs; causes effects ranging from annoying messages and deletion of data to interference with the computer's operation.

Vollmer, August Often thought of as an administrator, Vollmer's other contributions are towering: he helped John Larson develop the first workable polygraph in 1921 and established in Los Angeles in 1923 America's first full forensic laboratory.

Vucetich, Juan Worked on the use of fingerprints in Argentina. In 1894, he published his own book on the subject, *Dactiloscopia Comparada.*

W

washing (of title) The process of fabricating a vehicle's sale to a purchaser in a jurisdiction that does not issue salvage titles or carry title brands forward, thereby obtaining a clean title on the vehicle.

weight (of evidence) The amount of believability a jury gives to the testimony of a witness or the presentation of an item of evidence.

West case A 1903 incident in which two criminals with the same name, identical appearances, and nearly identical measurements were distinguished only by fingerprints, thus significantly advancing the use of fingerprints for identification in the United States.

white-collar crime Any illegal act committed by concealment or guile, rather than physical means, to obtain money or property, avoid payment or loss of money or property, or obtain business or personal advantage. While these may be operated legally, many such investments are simply frauds and the money disappears.

witness A person who has firsthand knowledge regarding a crime or who has expert information regarding some aspect of the crime.

worm A malicious program that attacks a computer system directly, rather than infecting a host program; spreads rapidly through the Internet or e-mail.

Entries with the letter *f* are for figures.
Entries with the letter *t* are for tables.